The Gospel
According to St. Matthew

The Gospel
According to St. Matthew

The Greek Text with Introduction,
Notes, and Indices

Alan Hugh McNeile

Baker Book House

Grand Rapids, Michigan

Reprinted 1980 by
Baker Book House Company
from the edition issued in 1915 by
Macmillan and Co.

ISBN: 0-8010-6099-0

PHOTOLITHOPRINTED BY CUSHING - MALLOY, INC.
ANN ARBOR, MICHIGAN, UNITED STATES OF AMERICA

VIRI REVERENDO

HENRICO BARCLAY SWETE, S.T.P.R.

HUNC LIBELLUM

EO AUCTORE INCEPTUM

DEDICO

PREFACE

The Christ of history is known to us from the Gospels; the Christ of experience is known to us from the Gospels and from all the subsequent history of the Christian Church to the present moment, including for each individual the spiritual experience of his own soul. To say that the evangelists exhibited a 'tendency' in allowing their spiritual experience to reveal itself in their narratives is to assume that we are able to determine what the 'bare facts' were without it. But this we cannot do. If we penetrate to Q, or any other early stratum of Gospel literature, a radiance not of this world still emanates from the person of Jesus; and it is begging the question to assert that the evangelists 'put the radiance in.' So far as we can see, the bare facts shone from the first with their own inherent light; and all that the writers of sources or of Gospels could do was to shew to the best of their power, in their several ways, in human language, how the light appeared to each of them. διαφόρους γὰρ ἔχει ὁ Λόγος μορφάς, φαινόμενος ἑκάστῳ ὡς συμφέρει τῷ βλέποντι, καὶ μηδενὶ ὑπὲρ ὃ χωρεῖ ὁ βλέπων φανερούμενος. It is in this conviction, increasingly confirmed by fresh study, that the present commentary has been written.

It is hoped that many readers will be gratified by the brevity of the Introduction. Many things might have been included in it which more properly belong to general Introductions to the New Testament, to monographs on particular points, or to works on Christian theology. The volume might, further, have been enlarged, without corresponding advantage, by a fuller citation of authorities in the notes, especially the principal modern commentaries. What I owe to the writings and the friendship of English scholars I need not try to formulate. But my indebtedness to German scholars I gladly acknowledge. I am often unable to accept their solutions; but their microscopic detection of problems to be solved supplies a large part of the material for study. I much regret that I had not the advantage of seeing more than Part I. of the *Vocabulary of the Greek Testament* by Professors Moulton and Milligan, and that two other much-looked-for works were not available, Professor Stanton's *The Gospels as Historical Documents*, vol. iii., and Mr. I. Abrahams' *Notes on the Synoptic Gospels*. The latter is occasionally referred to by anticipation on the strength of references given in Mr. Montefiore's Commentary, to which it is to form an additional volume.

I am very grateful to Professor Burkitt for several valuable suggestions, and to Mr. Abrahams for allowing me to consult him freely on matters Rabbinic. I should also like to thank Messrs. R. & R. Clark's readers and workmen for their care and accuracy.

A. H. M^cNEILE.

CAMBRIDGE,
    Easter 1915.

CONTENTS

ADDITIONAL NOTES (*continued*)—

INTRODUCTION

THE literature on the Gospels is endless, because the subject is endless. A modern commentator has better cause than Jerome for saying, 'Primum enim difficile est omnes legere qui in evangelia scripserunt; deinde multo difficilius adhibito iudicio quae optima sunt excerpere.' Archdeacon Allen gives a catalogue of qualifications required by a commentator on the First Gospel, terrifying enough to anyone who aimed at ideal completeness, but on the other hand encouraging as shewing from how many angles it can be approached. The present volume makes little attempt to deal in close detail with the intricacies of the synoptic problem. It holds (1) that the compilers of the First and Third Gospels used the Second almost in its present form; (2) that they also used different recensions of a written Greek source cited as Q, which consisted mainly of Sayings of Jesus, many, perhaps all, of them provided with a narrative framework; (3) that the compiler of our Gospel, for convenience named 'Matthew,' also used material from other sources: *e.g.* part of the Sermon on the Mount, and many sayings peculiar to his work, the Genealogy and the Birth narratives, some narratives about S. Peter and about Pilate; also a Greek writing, translated from an Aramaic original, containing passages from the Old Testament (*testimonia*), probably with brief explanations of their fulfilment in Christ's life, drawn from a Hebrew text not identical with the Masoretic. There is no clear evidence that S. Matthew ever translated independently from the Hebrew. Apart from *testimonia* he normally employed the LXX.

Nor are textual matters handled with any fulness. Textual criticism is like an ordnance survey; most readers need a map in which the broad features are not obscured by multiplication of detail. Westcott and Hort's text has been adopted throughout, and the Apparatus deals only with the variants to which reference is made in the notes. Nor again has space been occupied with such lists as are provided by Sir J. Hawkins (*Horae Synopticae*) and Archdeacon Allen (Commentary, Introd.) of S. Matthew's characteristic expressions, grammatical peculiarities, his stylistic treatment of the Second Gospel, and the like. The more striking points are mentioned in the notes.

The literary problems are important mainly in their bearing on the historical. It is the study of the latter to which, together with the necessary exegesis of the text, this volume is primarily directed.

§ 1. *The Earthly Career of Jesus.*

It may be useful at the outset to indicate the attitude adopted in the commentary with regard to some of the more important problems.

1. *The Events* of the Lord's life are arranged by S. Matthew for the most part on the basis of the Second Gospel. For the principal departures from the Marcan order see the notes on viii. 18 and ix. 18. His scheme is as follows:—

(*a*) Chs. i., ii. Genealogy, Birth, and Infancy of Jesus.

(*b*) Chs. iii.–iv. 16. Preparation for the Ministry.

(*c*) Chs. iv. 17–xiii. 58. Work in Galilee.

(*d*) Chs. xiv.–xvi. 12. Hostility. Retirement from Galilee (see Add. n. after xvi. 12).

(*e*) Chs. xvi. 13–xviii. 35. Instruction of the disciples.

(*f*) Chs. xix.–xxv. Journey to the South, and work in Judaea.

(*g*) xxvi.–xxviii. The last days.

The scheme in the Second Gospel, except (*a*), and in the Third, is broadly the same. But in the latter, (*d*) and (*e*) are represented only by Lk. ix. 7–50, while a large mass of non-Marcan material (Lk. ix. 51–xviii. 14) is placed after (*e*), as though occurring on the southward journey.

The Gospels are not biographies; it is impossible to write a 'Life of Christ.' The events cover probably less than two years, and their true sequence cannot be traced. They are, as H. J. Holtzmann says, 'little pictures in wooden frames.' But, broadly speaking, they are hung in such a way as to suggest a trust-worthy outline of the Lord's movements during the few strenuous months of His public life. He was for a time the Hero of the populace; but the opposition of the authorities became so acute that He retired, concentrating His energies during the remainder of the time on the teaching of the disciples; and then went deliberately to His death.

2. *The Chronology* is as yet an unsolved problem. It is inaccurate to say that the Fourth Gospel relates a three years' ministry. It speaks of three Passovers (Jo. ii. 23, vi. 4, xi. 55), *i.e.* a period of just over two years. The synoptists record only the last Passover. But since the plucking of the ears of corn during the second stay at Capharnaum (Mk. ii. 23, Mt., Lk.) must have occurred near harvest time, not many weeks after a Passover, and a reference to the following spring is probably to be seen in the 'green grass' of Mk. vi. 39, where the parallel in Jo. vi. 4 speaks of a Passover, nearly two years seem to be required for the Ministry. The growth of the fame of Jesus must have taken some time in a country of peasants, who would seldom travel far from their homes; the mission of the Twelve must have been of some duration; and this was followed by a considerable period of retirement (see on xv. 29) before the movement to Jerusalem. There are also indications of activity in Judaea before the last fatal visit (see on iv. 23, v. 23 f., viii. 1, and notes before v. 1 and xv. 1). At the first of the Passovers in the Fourth Gospel the writer places the cleansing of the temple, which the synoptists relate at the end of the Ministry (see Add. n. after xxi. 13). But even if the Johannine

narrative be left out of account, the events up to the feeding of
the multitude must have occupied the greater part of a year, and
the events from that point till the Crucifixion another year.
The synoptic Ministry is thus hardly shorter than the Johannine.
The date which Professor Lake claims for the life of Jesus, A.D. 6,
the date of the census, to 36, is discussed in the Add. n. after
xiv. 12. If thirty years was the length of the Life, and the
Ministry lasted two, S. Luke's expression 'about thirty years
old' (Lk. iii. 23) must be interpreted as 'twenty-eight years
old' (cf. Lk. ix. 28 'about eight days,' Mt., Mk. 'after six days').

3. *The Miraculous Element.*—In the narrative of the *Virgin
birth* the central fact is framed in material which, both in the
First and in the Third Gospel, doubtless contains an imaginative
or midrashic (not mythological) element. This was a not unnatural effect of the marvellous nature of the fact. But for the
record of the fact itself, it is maintained in the Add. n., p. 10–13,
that no adequate explanation has yet been offered other than its
occurrence in history; it can be traced to no earlier literary
origin.

S. Matthew's account of the *events after the Resurrection,*
though he again introduces a legendary element, is probably
based not only on the fragment of Mk. xvi. which survives, but
also on the lost ending. Some details in the synoptic narratives
are frankly irreconcilable; but the Galilean accounts in the
first two Gospels do not completely exclude the possibility of
appearances in Jerusalem, and conversely the Lucan narrative,
though it deliberately omits the return of the disciples to
Galilee, does not completely exclude the possibility of it.
See Add. n. pp. 438, 439. The fact of the Lord's Resurrection
is independent of these difficulties.

The Miracles of Jesus may for convenience be divided into
two groups : those of which we are beginning to think that
we understand something in the light of modern medical and
psychological study, and those which we do not understand at
all. In the first group are the miracles of healing and of

intuition and foreknowledge, and in the second such actions as the feeding of the multitude, the walking on the water, and the stilling of the storm.   The former are usually understood to-day to have been due to the powers of a wonderful personality, the power of suggestion (the mental condition of the patient being in many cases rendered favourable by faith), the power of thought-transference, and the like.   But if this be granted, the rejection of the miracles of the latter class involves the assumption that we know the limits of the power of personality.   Of such limits we are wholly ignorant.   The authority of 'spirit' over 'matter' is a fact which is daily becoming more clearly recognized, but its boundaries—if it has boundaries—are far beyond our ken.   Much less can we be confident as to the limits of authority of a Personality avowedly unique.   Even for those who cannot accept what is involved in the word 'Incarnation' it is becoming increasingly rash to commit themselves to a denial of the Gospel miracles.   Rationalizing 'explanations' may be occasionally possible; but many students still venture to say 'miraculous and *therefore* legendary.'   The possibility of legend cannot of course be denied.   It is possible in a given case, perhaps probable in one or two cases, that a saying of Jesus, or an 'ordinary' event, may have been transformed into a miracle in the course of tradition.   Each case must be examined on its merits, in the light of literary and other evidence, as well as with a consciousness of our ignorance.   But the total impression which the life and person of Jesus produced was one in which records of miracles were entirely in place.   The total impression could not have been produced without them.   It is open to anyone to refuse to say more than this; but to say less is impossible.   See Hardy, *The Religious Instinct*, 110–36.

4. *The Sayings of Jesus* are for the most part arranged by S. Matthew in five discourses, and are thus given the aspect of authoritative orations.   That Jesus delivered extended discourses cannot be doubted; like the prophets of old He spoke wherever He could find an audience, and in particular, like the Rabbis of His day

He preached in the synagogues.   But literary reasons forbid us
from thinking that the Matthean discourses represent those which
He actually uttered (see Add. n. after ch. vii., and the notes preceding
x. 5, xiii., xviii., xxiii.).   Hence the *sequence* and *emphasis* of
thought are in many cases due to editorial arrangement, and not
infrequently a sequence is undiscernible.   Further, it is obvious
that in no single saying can we claim with certainty to possess
more than an approximation to His actual words.   He spoke
in Aramaic; possibly sometimes in Greek; but as a Galilean
addressing Galileans it cannot have been His normal habit.   For
a brief period, oral Aramaic tradition must have preserved in
fluctuating forms the disciples' recollections.   Then came the
representing of them to Greek ears by preaching and conversation,
and in translated collections.   Lastly, the evangelists edited those
which came under their hands, each with a view to embodying
the impression of Jesus which had reached him, and emphasizing
the aspects which appealed to him.   To deny, however, the value
of the sayings as we have them, because they are not a 'phono-
graphic' reproduction of His words, is to deny the value of the
impression which the writers severally received, and their fitness
for their work.   The Jewish reverence for the laws in the
Pentateuch as divinely dictated, and infallible, produced disastrous
results; and Christian doctrine and practice would probably never
have been a living growth had the early Church felt bound by
a *verbatim* report of the Lord's teaching.   See some useful remarks
by Emmet, *Nineteenth Century*, Jan. 1914, 141–7.

§ 2. *S. Matthew's Purpose in Writing.*

Jesus said, 'From their fruits ye shall know them.'   Contemporaries know a man immediately through his words, actions,
looks, influence; later generations through the impressions of him
produced, partly by the lasting results of his influence, and partly
by traditional reports about him.   In the case of Jesus Christ the
results were, and are still, seen in the life of the Christian Church.

The traditional reports reached the evangelists in the form of various writings and survivals of unwritten narratives. The result of their work is that we possess four records of an impression. But the vaster the subject, the wider is the room for differences in the impression produced. Absence of differences would have indicated a smallness of personality in Jesus, small enough for tradition to have grasped it in its entirety and formed a clear-cut portrait of it. The four portraits are those of the same Person, but in each is seen a dominant aspect. In two of them the Lord's wonderful birth, and in all four His actions and His resurrection, are on the same plane as His wonderful words, character, and personality—the plane of the Incarnation. But the special impression which S. Matthew embodies is that of royalty: Jesus is the Messiah. This is taught in the genealogy through the royal line, the worship offered by the Magians to Him that was ' born King of the Jews,' the authoritative ' fulfilment ' of the Law in the Sermon on the Mount, the drastic denunciations of the ' tradition of the elders,' the reiterated use of the title ' Son of David,' the veiled intimations of His own destined Messiahship, Peter's confession, the superiority of Jesus to the Law and the Prophets manifested in the vision of the Transfiguration, His repudiation of the claims of the earthly monarch asserted in connexion with the didrachm, His predictions of future regal glory and His claim to be Judge at the last day, the entry into Jerusalem, the cleansing of the temple, the words about David's son and Lord, the claim before Pilate to be ' King of the Jews,' the same truth expressed unconsciously in the soldiers' mockery and in the *titulus* on the Cross, the final claim to the possession of all authority in heaven and on earth, together with the Old Testament quotations which found their fulfilment in Him, and other details and turns of expression by which S. Matthew alone in several narratives adds touches of purple and gold. And if Jesus is the Messiah, the national privileges—the privileges of those who thought themselves 'the sons of the Kingdom'—had passed into the possession of His followers, the ' few chosen ' who constitute His *ecclesia*.

It is the evangelist's 'aim to justify this transition by shewing from the life of Jesus how it was not the claim of a heretical sect who misread the Bible by the light of their own presumptuousness, but the realization of a divine purpose and the verification of divine prophecies in the sphere of history' (Moffatt, *LNT.* 244). He 'is unconsciously self-portrayed in xiii. 52' (*id.* 255): he is like a scribe instructed in the Kingdom of Heaven, like to a householder who bringeth forth from his treasure things new and old. This combination of new and old has led to the theories that the Jewish or particularistic elements were due to a Judaistic recension of the Logia, and that the universalist, 'catholic' elements, with some of the less historical portions of narrative, were the work of a later editor, or editors, more friendly to Gentiles. Or that the original author was opposed to Judaism, and the editor was a Jewish Christian with catholic tendencies. But such theories, which attempt to analyze the gospel into self-consistent strata, disregard the important fact that in the Lord's own teaching two elements appear, the Jewish, and something far wider and deeper (see next section). His transformation, His spiritualizing of eschatological and other Jewish conceptions, constantly leads to *formal* inconsistencies which in His own mind were not inconsistencies. And the evangelist, writing half a century after His death, presents the same two elements, but not with the same complete balance. The Jewish aspect of the teaching of Jesus, His attitude to the Law, and His eschatological language, are preserved and emphasized. The supra-Judaic, the spiritual and therefore universal aspect, tends to become Jewish-Christian or anti-Judaic. Jesus fused new and old in a higher synthesis, S. Matthew places them side by side. But when this has been said, it is impossible to overestimate the value of what has been called his 'archaeological interest,' since it resulted not in a description of Jesus with His thoughts and characteristics sifted and annotated, but in a living portrait thrown upon the canvas with a complexity that defies analysis, the more *alive* for not being meticulously 'accurate.'

§ 3. *The Teaching of Jesus.*

The Lord's teaching is closely bound up with the expressions 'the Kingdom of Heaven (*or* God)' and 'the Son of Man.' But the meaning which He attached to each must be arrived at by a study of His teaching as a whole in its relation to Jewish thought.

In the Heb. and Gk. O.T. 'the Kingdom of Heaven' is never found; 'the Kingdom of God' only in Wisd. x. 10, σοφία . . . ἔδειξεν αὐτῷ (*sc.* Jacob) βασιλείαν θεοῦ, which is ambiguous, but probably means that Jacob in his vision at Bethel was shewn 'the place where God reigns, Heaven, at the top of the ladder.' This has no bearing on the meaning in the N.T. 'The Kingdom of God' occurs four times in Mt. (xii. 28, xix. 24, xxi. 31, 43), fifteen in Mk., thirty-two in Lk. 'The Kingdom of Heaven' occurs only in Mt. thirty-two times. 'The Kingdom,' without further definition, Mt. iv. 23, viii. 12, ix. 35, xiii. 19, 38, xxiv. 14, Lk. xii. 32. Other expressions are: 'Thy Kingdom': of God, Mt. vi. 10 = Lk. xi. 2; of Jesus, xx. 21, Lk. xxiii. 42. 'My K.': Lk. xxii. 30 (cf. 29). 'His K.': of God, vi. 33; of the Messiah, xiii. 41, xvi. 28, Lk. i. 33. 'The K. of their (My) Father': xiii. 43, xxvi. 29. 'The coming K. of our father David': Mk. xi. 10.

The passages in which 'the Son of Man'[1] occurs fall into three groups :—

(1) Mt. (with Mk., Lk.) xxiv. 30 b, xxvi. 64 ; (with Lk.) xxiv. 27, 37, 44; (alone) x. 23, xvi. 28, xix. 28, xxiv. 30 a, 39, xxv. 31; Lk. (alone) xi. 30, xii. 8, xvii. 22, 30, xviii. 8, xxi. 36.

(2) Mt. (with Mk., Lk.) xvi. 13, xvii. 22, xx. 18, xxvi. 24 a; (with Mk.) xvii. 9, 12, xxvi. 24 b, 45; (alone) xxvi. 2 ; Lk. (alone) xix. 10, xxiv. 7.

(3) (*a*) Mt. (with Mk., Lk.) ix. 6, xii. 8 ; (with Lk.) xii. 32.

    (*b*) Mt. (alone) xii. 40, xiii. 37, 41 ; Lk. (alone) xxii. 48; see on Mt. xxvi. 50.

    (*c*) Mt. (with Lk. ; = Q) viii. 20, xi. 19.

---

[1] The philology of the expression, constantly discussed in recent years, is fully treated by Driver, *HDB.* iv. 579–83.

Groups (1) and (2) are dealt with below. In group (3) in the (a) passages it is shewn in the notes that 'the Son of Man' probably represents an expression which originally meant 'man-kind,' 'men.' The (b) passages are on independent grounds of very doubtful genuineness. There remain the (c) passages, which alone in group (3) can be assigned with safety to Q. There is little doubt that they are based on genuine sayings, but in the face of the overwhelming evidence that Jesus elsewhere used the title 'the Son of Man' only with an eschatological reference, it is extremely probable that in these two cases, in which it seems to be a mere substitute for the first personal pronoun, the compiler of Q was mistaken in ascribing the use of it to Him.

In O.T. times the nation of Israel thought of God as the Owner and Master of His people and of their land. Whether human kings were reigning or not, Yahweh was the real king. When foreign enemies were approaching, the prophets declared that God was sending them to punish His people, and they hoped for the time when Israel, purified by punishment, would be established in their land, vindicated and victorious, with a succession of ideal kings reigning as the representatives of Yahweh, who would be acknowledged as the real king for ever. In spite of the usurpation of Israel by enemies, 'the kingdom is Yahweh's' (Ps. xxii. 28), and this ideal would become actual. Prophet after prophet hoped that this condition of bliss would arrive immediately after the next threatening punishment was over. But it always receded before their gaze. And the time came when Israel's troubles were felt to be so acute, the foreign yoke was so firmly fixed upon their necks, that the divine sovereignty, it was thought, could not be established by ordinary means; no ordinary human king could restore the national fortunes. So the expectation arose in many minds that God would establish His sovereignty, which also meant the sovereignty of Israel, by a supernatural act of power. His own Being was far removed from men in transcendent majesty ; but He would send a super-human Agent, who would destroy their enemies and become the ideal king, the representative of the supreme king, God. As to the exact nature of this super-human Agent, and his methods, the popular ideas were vague and various. In some minds, indeed, the hopes of an earthly conqueror were not yet dead. But in any case the glorious result would be the actualizing of the sovereignty of God. Meanwhile His sovereignty, even though foreign rulers were reigning, must be recognized by the pious, by obedience to the Mosaic law, fenced with scrupulous care by the scribal traditions. Hence the later Rabbinic expressions, 'to take upon oneself the Kingdom of Heaven' (B. Berach. 10 b), 'the yoke of the K. of Heaven' (Berach. ii. 5, Gamaliel), 'to refuse the K. of Heaven' (*id.*).

Then appeared John the Baptist. He declared, like his contemporaries, that the divine sovereignty would be established, but he went further and said that it would be established in the near future—a stirring echo of ancient prophecy. But also, like the ancient prophets, he warned his nation that the coming of the divine sovereignty would not be for bliss but for punishment. God would purge the nation of sinners; therefore 'Repent ye!'

And directly afterwards came Jesus of Nazareth. Like the Baptist, He called men to repent. And, like many in His day, He expected the divine sovereignty to be established suddenly, as a catastrophic event, in describing which He appears to have made considerable use of current phraseology. Like them also He expected that a super-human Agent would be sent to bring it about, whom He is reported to have referred to frequently as 'the Son of Man.' With this specifically Jewish meaning the expression occurs eighteen times; see the first group of passages above. Once more, like the Baptist, He expected the great event to take place in the immediate future. But His teaching was, nevertheless, unique. He made use of Jewish thought but transformed it from four points of view.

1. He taught that the ideal community over whom God would reign by His Agent was to consist of those whose characters were in accordance with the moral principles that He laid down.

Though the sovereignty of God was to be established transcendentally, it was in its nature immanent and spiritual; and the spiritual life of men was complementary to it. Those only were destined, and fitted, to enjoy this who hungered for it now, and shewed the fruits of repentance and love to God now. His expectations and aims were utterly remote from anything political. 'My Kingdom is not of this world' truly expresses His attitude. Of all the many forms of Jewish Messianic hopes, few were wholly free from the thought that the advent of the Kingdom would involve the subduing or the annihilation of the enemies of Israel, either in this world—in Palestine—or in another world, when Heaven and earth had passed away. For Jesus, the present usurper of the sovereignty was not Caesar, but the devil. He penetrated beneath earthly hopes and ideas to spiritual principles. The polity of the redeemed Israel will be a polity of righteous souls. Hence to enter into the Kingdom could be described by the terms 'to enter into, or get, or inherit, *life*.' It was a reward, a possession stored up in readiness for the poor in spirit, for those who were persecuted for righteousness' sake. It must be sought like a pearl, obtained by any sacrifice like a treasure. The righteousness that would secure entrance into it was not obedience to the Mosaic law, much less to scribal tradition, but to the eternal principles which 'fulfilled' them. And this involved a complete renunciation of everything that bound men to this world. To save his Self, a man must lose it. Since character, therefore, was what mattered, human society was being prepared for the great day by a secret growth, like the growth of corn in the earth or leaven in dough. The great day was at hand, it would come within the lifetime of that generation, when God would reign over righteous men, and such alone, by His Agent, who would come from Him. But none knew when He would come; His Parousia would be as sudden as lightning, as a thief in the night, as a bridegroom returning with his bride from the wedding. A true preparation, therefore, included a vigilant watchfulness. When He came there would be found a mixture of bad and good in Israel, many called but few chosen. To describe the exclusion of the bad, Jesus mostly employed current eschatological metaphors —fire, outer darkness, the shut door, torment, and the like. And conversely the enjoyment of the Kingdom by those who were worthy of it He pictured as a banquet. The important fact is that Jesus revealed a new conception of the character which made men worthy of it. This character He enjoined by commands which embody fundamental principles. The particular form in which some of them were cast was determined by the thought of the immediacy of the Kingdom. They do not cover all possible situations for all time (see *e.g.* note on v. 32). Since the coming of the Kingdom has proved to be an age-long process which began at Pentecost, the principles must be applied by Christians in such a way as to meet the growing complexity of life.

This being His conception of the Kingdom, it is not a matter of great moment whether He described it as the 'Kingdom of God' or the 'Kingdom of Heaven.' It is quite possible that He used both terms. In the former He expressed simply the truth that God would reign; in the latter, that God who now reigned in Heaven would reign also on earth, ὡς ἐν οὐρανῷ καὶ ἐπὶ γῆς. Cf. Orig. Fragm. in Jo. iii. 5 (Brooke ii. 251): λεκτέον Ματθαῖον μὲν ἀπὸ τῶν βασιλευομένων, ἢ τῶν τόπων ἐν οἷς εἰσὶν οὗτοι, τὸν δὲ Ἰωάννην καὶ Λουκᾶν ἀπὸ τοῦ βασιλεύοντος θεοῦ ὠνομακέναι. 'Heaven' was, indeed, a Jewish periphrasis for the divine Name (see Dalman, *Words*, 206 ff.), and the evangelist may possibly have been influenced by the usage. But it cannot have been his only reason for introducing the word, since He never, except in this expression, substitutes it where the Second or Third evangelist has 'God.' By his almost invariable use of it in this expression he emphasizes the contrast between Heaven and earth, while they in some cases probably avoided the Jewish term for their Gentile readers. The plur. οὐρανῶν probably has no special force. In the LXX. the sing. occurs some 550 times, the plur. only 45, of which 25 are in the Psalms. In Mk. and Lk. the sing. predominates, in Mt. the plur.; his 'archaeological' turn of mind led him to preserve the plur. of the Heb. and Aram. in which the sing. does not exist.

2. The eternal principles of righteousness taught by Jesus were summed up negatively in self-abnegation, positively in love to God the Father and to men.   But in teaching self-abnegation for the sake of gaining the Kingdom of Heaven, Jesus introduced an element that was utterly new.   Men must deny themselves for *Him*, and cast the devotion of their whole heart and life on *Him*.   He stood in a unique relation to God, and therefore to men.   See x. 32 f., 37–39 (Lk.), xvi. 24–27 (Mk. Lk.).   This relationship to God was that of a Son to a Father.   See xi. 27 (Lk.), xxi. 37 (Mk. Lk.), xxiv. 36 (Mk.).   Being God's Son, He was able, as none other, to reveal the Father's will in teaching the principles of righteousness.   The personal claims of Jesus are unique in history.

3. The full consciousness of Sonship seems to have come to Him at His baptism.   But it led Him to something further.   As to any stages or development through which His consciousness passed, we have no certain knowledge.   But if it could be said of Him that He 'advanced in wisdom' (Lk. ii. 52), and 'learned obedience from the things that He suffered' (Heb. v. 8), He may also have learned during the brief period of His ministry more of the Father's purposes for Him.   He was conscious of a divine mission : He was 'sent,' x. 40 (Mk. Lk.), xxi. 37 (Mk. Lk.), xv. 24; Lk. iv. 43 (Mk. 'I came forth'), x. 16.   But if He was the divinely sent Agent for revealing the will of God, obedience to which fitted men for the Kingdom, He was the divinely appointed means for saving the lost sheep of the house of Israel. And no other Agent would do it; He was conscious of His own uniqueness.   All the aspirations and predictions in the O.T. which had personified the ideal Israel, and its ideal prophets and kings, had led men in more recent times to centre their hopes upon an Individual.   He, then, was that Individual.   In Himself Israel was to receive the age-long promises of God.   All that He had inherited of Jewish eschatological ideas took a new shape

and colour.   Not only was the advent of the divine sovereignty imminent, but He, a *Man*, was to be the Agent of it.   And this found expression when He spoke of Himself, after Peter's confession, as 'the Son of Man,' *i.e.* the fulfilment of 'one like unto a son of man (a human being)' spoken of in Dan. vii. 13, who received glory and dominion.   It was not a mere title, equivalent to 'Messiah,' but a title in which the word 'Man' played a real part; it was a Messiah who was now human.   His use of it as a title of *office* was always proleptic; because He was the Son of God He would one day appear as the Son of Man; but it always included, when applied to Himself, a reference to His present human life.

4. But though a few accepted His teaching of the divine principles of righteousness, the many were still unrepentant. More seed fell into bad ground than into good.   Preaching proved unable to win them.   But if He sacrificed His own unique life, the Father would accept it as an atonement, an equivalent, for the many.   It may be that He realized at an early date in His ministry the possibility that He must die a violent death (ix. 15, Mk., Lk.), without perceiving at first all that His death would mean.   At any rate it was late in His ministry that He began clearly to predict His death (xvi. 21, Mk., Lk.), and to apply to Himself the title 'the Son of Man' in connexion with the thought of suffering and subsequent glory. See the second group of passages above.   But whether early or late, the two thoughts coalesced in His mind that by His death He would be a 'ransom for many' (xx. 28, Mk.; cf. Mk. xiv. 24), and that also by His death He would return to the Father, to come very soon as His Agent to establish the divine sovereignty over His ransomed people.

These four threads of His teaching are too closely interwoven in the texture of the Gospels for any one of them to be eliminated by a theory of interpolation.   He either taught them all, in which case He really gave expression to a 'Messianic consciousness,' or He taught none of them, and our knowledge of His teaching is *nil*. Unnecessary difficulty has often been felt in the fact that the Parousia of the Messiah did not take place, and has not yet taken place, as a catastrophic event as He pictured it. He Himself balanced His Jewish language by non-Jewish conceptions. But the pictorial language must be frankly accepted as Jewish. His human intellect, like all other human intellects before and since, was compelled—not consciously but inevitably —to employ symbolism in order to express the transcendental; and He employed that of His age and country, the language of prophets and apocalyptists of centuries past. (See the classical exposition of this by Tyrrell, *Christianity at the Crossroads*, chs. x., xii.) The divine translation of it in history must be seen, as the evangelists recognized, in the Christian Church, which was, in fact, born in a sudden outburst within the generation then living, and which, in its ideal, is a polity of redeemed souls living in righteousness, over whom God reigns on earth in the Person of Jesus the Messiah.

§ 4. *The Date of the Gospel.*

A *terminus a quo* is afforded by the fact that our evangelist used the Second Gospel practically in its present form. The latter must probably be placed shortly before the fall of Jerusalem in A.D. 70; many, however, prefer a date shortly after it. The relation between the First Gospel and the Third affords no evidence; they appear to be quite independent, and neither shews distinct signs of priority. The *terminus ad quem* is disputed, since opinions differ as to the patristic parallels to the Gospel. There are similarities in Clement Rom. (A.D. 94– 96); see notes on v. 7, vi. 14, vii. 1, 2, xi. 29, xiii. 3, xviii. 6. But they are not necessarily quotations. Sayings of Jesus, especially some which now stand in the Sermon on the Mount, were collected and employed in writing for teaching purposes before the Gospels were compiled. If Clement knew such a collection, the same may have been true of the writer of Ep. James (cf. Jam. i. 5, ii. 8, iii. 12, iv. 3, v. 3, 9, 12), Polycarp

(see notes on v. 3, 7, vi. 13, 14, vii. 1, 2), and the writer of the
Two Ways (*Did.* i.–vi.; see Stanton, *Gosp. Hist. Doc.* i. 70). The
latter part of the *Didache* (vii.–xvi.) almost certainly quotes our
Gospel, which would give *c.* 100 as a *term. ad quem* if the two
parts were of the same date; but this is doubtful. Ignatius (A.D.
110–115) seems to be the first fixed point. Most of his parallels
are not decisive (see notes on ii. 1, vii. 20, x. 16 b, xv. 13, xix. 12);
they might be drawn from earlier traditions or collections. But
in *Smyrn.* i. the reference to Mt. iii. 15 is unmistakable. The
Shepherd of Hermas (? 110–125) is clearly acquainted with all
four Gospels; he adapts, and sometimes weaves together, passages
from them in such a way as to suggest a knowledge of them.
The Epistle of 'Barnabas' has been assigned to dates varying
from 70 to 132. The writer seems to quote our Gospel as Scripture:
iv. 14, προσέχωμεν μήποτε, ὡς γέγραπται, πολλοὶ κλητοί, ὀλίγοι
δὲ ἐκλεκτοὶ εὑρεθῶμεν (Mt. xxii. 14). But even this is denied
by J. Weiss (*Der Barn. Brief*, 108–12), who explains some of
the parallels as derived from other sources, and rejects some as
interpolations. External evidence, therefore, cannot fix the date
more nearly than A.D. 70–115.

Internal evidence is hardly more helpful; xxii. 7 clearly
presupposes the fall of Jerusalem. The expressions ἕως ἄρτι
(xi. 12), ἕως τῆς σήμερον (xxvii. 8), μέχρι τῆς σήμερον ἡμέρας
(xxviii. 15) suggest no more than some lapse of time since the
days of Jesus. But a few indications point to a comparatively
late date. Church government is alluded to (xvi. 19, xviii. 18),
and excommunication (xviii. 17). The apostles, as the foundation of the Church, are so highly reverenced that their faults
are often minimized or concealed (see note on viii. 26). False
Christian prophets had appeared (vii. 15, 22); cf. *Did.* xi.–xiii.
Additions which are certainly apocryphal had begun to be made.
And the writer, though he had not abandoned the expectation,
still found in the 2nd century, that the Parousia of Christ was
near, and freely recorded the Lord's predictions to that effect,
was yet able to look forward to a period during which the

evangelization of 'all nations' (*sc.* of the known world) would be carried on (xxviii. 19 f.).   These facts, which are in keeping with the impression produced by the Gospel as a whole, forbid a date earlier than *c.* A.D. 80, but do not require one later than 100.

§ 5. *The Author*

The First Gospel breathes, as a whole, a Palestinian atmosphere, and the traditions which the evangelist employed, apart from Mk. and Q, were Palestinian.   And yet he apparently had no knowledge, or at least made no independent use, of the Hebrew Old Testament.   He seems to have lived at some place in Syria where the Christians were not in close touch with Jerusalem, and where the traditions which reached him were of very varying value, ranging from those which bear the unmistakable stamp of genuineness to stories of a purely legendary character, which must have grown up outside the range of the control which apostles or other eyewitnesses would have exercised.   His archaeological bent of mind made him collect freely from all quarters with very little critical sifting.   He was certainly not Matthew the apostle.   Apart from the characteristics just mentioned, one who could write with the paramount authority of an eyewitness would not have been content to base his work on that of a secondary authority.   It clearly exhibits reflexion, not recollection ; it is a portrait of a Person rather than a chronicle of events.   Moreover an early tradition had it that S. Matthew wrote in 'Hebrew,' i.e. Aramaic, a tradition which led to a confusion between the canonical Gospel and other evangelic records written in 'Hebrew.'   But our Gospel is not a translation.   Though Hebraic to the core, it is quite clearly a Greek composition.   If it were a translation, its close dependence on the Second Gospel would involve the extreme improbability that the latter was translated into Aramaic, that our author employed the Aramaic translation, which was afterwards retranslated into Greek in the present Second Gospel, and that all

the close verbal similarities between that and our First Gospel
in Greek were accidental, while the original Greek of the Second
Gospel, as well as its Aramaic translation, disappeared.

The earliest trace of the tradition that S. Matthew wrote in
'Hebrew' is the much discussed statement of Papias (see below).
If the later patristic statements were based on this, the writers
understood that by τὰ λόγια Papias meant a Gospel. Other
suggestions have been made. τὰ λόγια is thought to denote a
collection of passages in the O.T. which were considered 'Messianic'
as being fulfilled in the life of Christ. If so, ἡρμήνευσε cannot
mean 'translated,' since the LXX. translation was available for all,
but 'interpreted'; i.e. each person explained on his own account
the way in which the passages were fulfilled. Or τὰ λόγια was
a writing which contained the Messianic passages, together with
a narrative pointing out their fulfilment in each case; this was
composed in Aramaic, and each person 'translated' it according
to his ability. Against both these conjectures is the consideration
that, although the object of our Gospel is to present a portrait of
Jesus as the King, the Messianic passages, as such, form so small
a part of it that it is difficult to account for the transference of
the name Matthew from the *Logia* to the Gospel. If any trust
is to be placed in the words of Papias, the usual explanation is
the most probable, that the apostle Matthew compiled in Aramaic
a collection of Sayings of Jesus with narratives stating the
occasions on which they were uttered. In the first generation
of Christians the events were for the most part well known,
especially the events of the Passion, and there was no necessity
for one of the Twelve to commit them to writing. What was of
real importance was to record the authoritative teaching of the
Master, which had been heard by few. After this had been
delivered for a short time orally, the multiplication and dispersion
of believers necessitated the crystallizing of it in written form.
An apostle was a suitable person for this important task, so that
the tradition of the Lord's teaching was inseparably connected
with his name. The document, which on this hypothesis may

be called the *Logia*, was soon translated by various hands, and
these Greek recensions were quickly enlarged and altered. Some
of them were probably known to the author of Ep. James, to
Clement, Ignatius, and others (see p. xxvi. f.), and two of them,
now generally cited by the common symbol Q, were employed by
the authors of the First and Third Gospels, and another was
possibly known to S. Mark. Our evangelist, for whom the
Lord's authoritative teaching (which he largely arranges in five
orations, a second Torah corresponding with the five books of the
Law) formed a leading element in his portraiture of the King,
attached to his work the name Matthew. This, with its greater
fullness, and the exalted portrait which it presents, gave it a
wider popularity in early days than was accorded to the others.
It was scarcely a case of mere pseudonymity. The tradition
of the Lord's teaching, at every stage in its growth, would be
connected with the name Matthew, and the author in all good
faith would describe his work as the Christian message ' as
Matthew delivered it,' κατὰ Ματθαῖον.

The following are the chief patristic passages bearing on the
authorship and composition of the First Gospel. A useful collection of passages dealing with the Canon of the New Testament
may be seen in Kirchhofer, *Quellensammlung zur Geschichte des
neutestamentlichen Canons bis auf Hieronymus*; Engl. Trans.,
Charteris, *Canonicity*. For passages referring to non-canonical
Hebrew Gospels see Preuschen, *Antilegomena*, pp. 3–10.

Papias (Eus. *H.E.* iii. 39): Ματθαῖος μὲν οὖν Ἑβραΐδι
διαλέκτῳ τὰ λόγια συνεγράψατο. ἡρμήνευσε δ' αὐτά, ὡς ἦν
δυνατός, ἕκαστος.

Irenaeus III. i. 1 (Eus. *H.E.* v. 8): ὁ μὲν δὴ Ματθαῖος ἐν
τοῖς Ἑβραίοις τῇ ἰδίᾳ αὐτῶν διαλέκτῳ καὶ γραφὴν ἐξήνεγκεν
εὐαγγελίου, τοῦ Πέτρου καὶ τοῦ Παύλου ἐν Ῥώμῃ εὐαγγελιζο-
μένων. καὶ θεμελιούντων τὴν ἐκκλησίαν. μετὰ δὲ τὴν τούτων
ἔξοδον, Μάρκος κτλ.

Origen, *Comm. in Joh.* T. i. 6 : Ματθαῖος μὲν γὰρ τοῖς προσδοκῶσι τὸν ἐξ Ἀβραὰμ καὶ Δαβὶδ Ἑβραίοις. γράφων· Βίβλος, φησί, γενέσεως Ἰησοῦ Χριστοῦ, υἱοῦ Δαβίδ, υἱοῦ Ἀβραάμ. *id.* T. vi. 32 : ἔχοντες τοίνυν τὰς ὁμοίας λέξεις τῶν τεσσάρων, φέρε κατὰ τὸ δυνατὸν ἴδωμεν ἰδίᾳ τὸν νοῦν ἑκάστης καὶ τὰς διαφοράς, ἀρξάμενοι ἀπὸ τοῦ Ματθαίου, ὃς καὶ παραδέδοται πρῶτος τῶν λοιπῶν τοῖς Ἑβραίοις ἐκδεδωκέναι τὸ ᾿εὐαγγέλιον, τοῖς ἐκ περιτομῆς πιστεύουσιν.

Eusebius, *H.E.* iii. 24 : ὅμως δ᾽ οὖν ἐξ ἁπάντων τῶν τοῦ Κυρίου διατριβῶν ὑπομνήματα Ματθαῖος ἡμῖν καὶ Ἰωάννης μόνοι καταλελοίπασιν, οὓς καὶ ἐπάναγκες ἐπὶ τὴν γραφὴν ἐλθεῖν κατέχει λόγος. Ματθαῖος μὲν γὰρ πρότερον Ἑβραίοις κηρύξας, ὡς ἤμελλεν καὶ ἐφ᾽ ἑτέρους ἰέναι πατρίῳ γλώττῃ γραφῇ παραδοὺς τὸ κατ᾽ αὐτὸν εὐαγγέλιον, τὸ λεῖπον τῇ αὐτοῦ παρουσίᾳ τούτοις ἀφ᾽ ὧν ἐστέλλετο διὰ τῆς γραφῆς ἀπεπλήρου. *id.* v. 10 : ὧν εἷς γενόμενος καὶ ὁ Πάνταινος καὶ εἰς Ἰνδοὺς ἐλθεῖν λέγεται· ἔνθα λόγος εὑρεῖν αὐτὸν προφθάσαν τὴν αὐτοῦ παρουσίαν τὸ κατὰ Ματθαῖον εὐαγγέλιον παρά τισιν αὐτόθι τὸν Χριστὸν ἐπεγνωκόσιν. οἷς Βαρθολομαῖον τῶν ἀποστόλων ἕνα κηρύξαι, αὐτοῖς τε Ἑβραίων γράμμασι τὴν τοῦ Ματθαίου καταλεῖψαι γραφήν, ἣν καὶ σώζεσθαι εἰς τὸν δηλούμενον χρόνον.

Cyril Jerus. *Catech.* xiv. : Ματθαῖος ὁ γράψας τὸ εὐαγγέλιον Ἑβραΐδι γλώσσῃ τοῦτο ἔγραψεν.

Epiphanius, *Haer.* II. i. 51 : καὶ οὗτος μὲν οὖν ὁ Ματθαῖος ἑβραϊκοῖς γράμμασι γράφει τὸ εὐαγγέλιον καὶ κηρύττει, καὶ ἄρχεται οὐκ ἀπ᾽ ἀρχῆς ἀλλὰ διηγεῖται μὲν τὴν γενεαλογίαν ἀπὸ τοῦ Ἀβραάμ.

Jerome, *De Vir. Illustr.* iii. : Matthaeus, qui et Levi, ex publicano apostolus, primus in Judaea propter eos qui ex circumcisione crediderant evangelium Christi hebraicis literis verbisque composuit, quod quis postea in Graecum transtulerit non satis certum est. Porro ipsum hebraicum habetur usque hodie, etc. (Preuschen, p. 4).

Prol. in Matt. : Matthaeus primus evangelium in Judaea hebraeo sermone edidit.

Praef. in Quat. Ev.: De novo nunc loquor testamento quod graecum esse non dubium est, excepto apostolo Matthaeo, qui primus in Judaea evangelium Christi hebraicis literis edidit.

Ad Hedib.: Mihi videtur evangelistam Matthaeum qui evangelium hebraico sermone conscripsit, etc.

Comm. in Jesai. vi. 9 : Matthaeus autem et Joannes quorum alter hebraeo, alter graeco sermone evangelia texuerunt, testimonia de hebraico proferunt.

Comm. in Oseam, xi. 2 : Cui nos brevitur respondebimus : primum Matthaeum evangelium hebraeis literis edidisse, quod non poterant legere nisi qui ex Hebraeis erant.

OLD TESTAMENT QUOTATIONS AND ALLUSIONS

(Quotations are cited in thick type)

1. Ascribed to Jesus

O.T.		Mt.	O.T.	Mt.
Gen.	i. 27, v. 2	xix. 4	2 Kings iv. 42	xiv. 16
	ii. 24	xix. 5	Job xlii. 2	xix. 26
	vii. 7	xxiv. 38	Ps. vi. 9	vii. 23
	xviii. 14	xix. 26	viii. 3	xxi. 16
Exod.	iii. 6	xxii. 32	xxi. [xxii.] 1	xxvii. 46
	xx. 12	xv. 4, xix. 19	xxiii.[xxiv.]3,4	v. 8
	xx. 13 [14]	v. 27, xix. 18	xxxvi. [xxxvii.]	
	xx. 15 [13]	v. 21, xix. 18	11	v. 5
	xx.14[15], 16	xix. 18	xl. [xli.] 10	xxvi. 23
	xxi. 16 [17]	xv. 4	xli. [xlii.] 6	xxvi. 38
	xxi. 24	v. 38	xlvii. [xlviii.] 3	v. 35
	xxiv. 8	xxvi. 28	lxi. [lxii.] 13	xvi. 27
Lev.	xiv. 2	viii. 4	lxviii. [lxix.] 22	xxvii. 34, 48
	xix. 18	v. 43, xxii. 39	cvi. [cvii.] 3	viii. 11
	xxiv. 20	v. 38	cix. [cx.] 1	xxii. 44, xxvi. 64
Num.	xxx. 3 [2]	v. 33	cxi. [cxii.] 10	viii. 12
Deut.	v. 16	xv. 4, xix. 19	cxvii. [cxviii.]	
	v. 17 [18]	v. 27, xix. 18	22, 23	xxi. 42
	v. 18 [17]	v. 21, xix. 18	cxvii. [cxviii.] 26	xxiii. 39
	v. 19, 20	xix. 18	Prov. xxiv. 12	xvi. 27
	vi. 5	xxii. 37	Isa. v. 1, 2	xxi. 33
	vi. 13	iv. 10	vi. 9, 10	xiii. 14, 15
	vi. 16	iv. 7	ix. 1, 2 [viii. 23	
	viii. 3	iv. 4	ix. 1]	iv. 15, 16
	xiii. 1 [2]	xxiv. 24	xiii. 10	xxiv. 29
	xviii. 13	v. 48	xiv. 13, 15	xi. 23
	xviii. 15	xvii. 5	xix. 2	xxiv. 7
	xix. 15	xviii. 16	xxvi. 20	vi. 6
	xix. 21	v. 38	xxvii. 13	xxiv. 31
	xxiii. 21 [22]	v. 33	xxix. 13	xv. 8, 9
	xxiv. 1	v. 31	xxxiv. 4	xxiv. 29
	xxx. 4	xxiv. 31	xlix. 24, 25	xii. 29
	xxxii. 5	xvii. 17	lvi. 7	xxi. 13
1 Sam. xxi. 6		xii. 4	lxi. 1, 2	v. 3, 4, xi. 5
1 Kings x. 1		xii. 42	lxvi. 1	v. 34, 35

O.T.	Mt.	O.T.	Mt.
Jer. vi. 16 [Heb.]	xi. 29	Dan. xii. 2	xxv. 46
vii. 11	xxi. 13	xii. 3	xiii. 43
xii. 7	xxiii. 38	xii. 11	xxiv. 15
xiv. 14	vii. 22, 23	Hos. vi. 6	ix. 13, xii. 7
xxi. 8	vii. 13, 14	Jon. ii. 1 [i. 17]	xii. 40
xxxiv. 12		Zeph. i. 3 [Heb.]	xiii. 41
[xxvii. 15]	vii. 22	Mic. vii. 6	x. 21, 35, 36
Dan. ii. 28	xxiv. 6	Zach. ii. 6 [10]	xxiv. 31
iv. 18 [21]	xiii. 32	viii. 6 [LXX.]	xix. 26
vii. 13	xxiv. 30, xxvi. 64	**xiii. 7**	**xxvi. 31**
ix. 27	xxiv. 15	xiv. 5	xxv. 31
xi. 41 [LXX.]	xxiv. 10	Mal. **iii. 1**	**xi. 10**
xii. 1	xxiv. 21	iv. 5 [iii. 24]	xi. 15, xvii. 11

2. MADE BY THE EVANGELIST, OR ASCRIBED BY HIM TO SPEAKERS OTHER THAN JESUS

(The latter are marked with an asterisk.)

O.T.	Mt.	O.T.	Mt.
Gen. iv. 24	xviii. 21	Ps. cxvii. [cxviii.] 25, 26	*xxi. 9, 15
xxxviii. 8	*xxii. 24	Isa. **vii. 14**	**i. 23**
Exod. iv. 19	ii. 20	**xl. 3**	**iii. 3**
Num. xxvii. 17	ix. 36	xlii. 1	*iii. 17
Deut. xxv. 5	*xxii. 24	**xlii. 1-4**	**xii. 18-21**
2 Kings i. 8	iii. 4	l. 6	xxvi. 67
Ps. ii. 7	*iii. 17	**liii. 4**	**viii. 17**
xxi. [xxii.] 7	xxvii. 39	**lxii. 11**	**xxi. 5**
xxi. [xxii.] 8	*xxvii. 43	Hos. **xi. 1**	**ii. 15**
lxxvii. [lxxviii.] 2	xiii. 35	Mic. **v. 2 [1]**	*ii. 6
xc. [xci.] 11, 12	*iv. 6	Zach. **ix. 9**	**xxi. 5**
cviii. [cix.] 25	*xxvii. 39	xi. 12	xxvi. 16
		xi. 13	**xxvii. 9, 10**

SOME ABBREVIATIONS EMPLOYED IN
THE NOTES

AJTh. American Journal of Theology.
Allen. W. C. Allen, *St. Matthew* (International Critical Commentary).
BDB. Brown, Driver, and Briggs, *Hebrew and English Lexicon of the O.T.*
Beng. J. A. Bengel, *Gnomon Novi Testamenti.*
Blass. Fr. Blass, *Grammar of N.T. Greek* (transl. H. St. J. Thackeray).
CIG. Corpus Inscriptionum Graecarum.
Dalman, *Gr.* G. Dalman, *Grammatik d. jüdisch-palästinischen Aramäisch.*
DCA. Dictionary of Christian Antiquities (ed. Smith and Cheetham).
DCG. Dictionary of Christ and the Gospels (ed. Hastings).
Deissm. *B.St.* G. A. Deissmann, *Bible Studies* (transl. Grieve).
ExpT. Expository Times.
HDB. Hastings' Dictionary of the Bible.
JBL. Journal of Biblical Literature.
JQR. Jewish Quarterly Review.
JSL. Journal of Semitic Languages.
JThS. Journal of Theological Studies.
KAT[3]. E. Schrader, *Die Keilinscriften u. das Alte Testament* (3rd ed. Zimmern and Winckler).
𝕃. Latin Versions.
L. & S. Liddell and Scott, *A Greek-English Lexicon.*
M.-M. *Vocab.* Moulton and Milligan, *Vocabulary of the Greek Testament.*
Moffatt, *LNT.* Moffatt, *An Introduction to the Literature of the New Testament.*
Moulton i. J. H. Moulton, *A Grammar of N.T. Greek* (vol. i. Prolegomena).
NH. New (late) Hebrew.
Ox. Pap. *Oxyrinchus Papyri* (ed. Grenfell and Hunt).
Oxf. Stud. *Oxford Studies in the Synoptic Problem* (ed. Sanday).
PEFQ. Palestine Exploration Fund, Quarterly Statement.
RWB. Realwörterbuch.
𝕊. Syriac Versions.
Schürer, *HJP.* E. Schürer, *The Jewish People in the time of Christ* (2nd ed. transl. Macpherson).
Smith, G. A., *H.G.* Smith, Geo. Adam, *Historical Geography of the Holy Land.*
Swete. H. B. Swete, *The Gospel according to St. Mark.*
Thackeray, *Gr.O.T.* H. St. J. Thackeray, *Grammar of the O.T. in Greek*, vol. i.
ThLZ. Theologische Literaturzeitung.
TR. Textus Receptus.
ThStKr. Theologische Studien und Kritiken.
ZNW. Zeitschrift f. die neutestamentliche Wissenschaft.
ZWTh. Zeitschrift f. wissenschaftliche Theologie.

*In evangelicis sermonibus semper literae
iunctus est spiritus, et quidquid primo frigere
videtur aspectu si tetigeris calet.*

HIERON. in Matth.

ΚΑΤΑ ΜΑΘΘΑΙΟΝ

ΒΙΒΛΟΣ γενέσεως Ἰησοῦ Χριστοῦ υἱοῦ Δαυεὶδ υἱοῦ Ἀβραάμ. 1   I.

Ἀβραὰμ ἐγέννησεν τὸν Ἰσαάκ,   2

i. 1–17. The Genealogy of Jesus.

1. βίβλος κτλ.] Since the superscription is formed on the analogy of Gen. ii. 4 a, v. 1 (αὕτη ἡ βίβλος γενέσεως, cf. vi. 9, x. 1, xi. 10, 27), which are followed by narrative as well as genealogy, Mt. may have intended it to introduce the whole account in chs. i., ii. But more probably it refers only to the genealogy, since the narrative is introduced in i. 18 by a fresh heading, in which γένεσις has a somewhat different force. David and Abraham were the primary names, 'quia ad hos tantum est facta de Christo repromissio' (Jer.); cf. Lk. i. 69 f., 73. On υἱὸς Δαυείδ see ix. 27. The Davidic descent of Jesus is asserted in Ac. ii. 30 ff., xiii. 23, Rom. i. 3, 2 Tim. ii. 8, Apoc. xxii. 16 (cf. v. 5); and see Heb. vii. 14. Cf. the account of the grandsons of Judas, the Lord's brother, in Hegesippus, ap. Eus. H.E. iii. 20. Lk. (iii. 38) goes back to 'Adam son of God,' Jo. (i. 1) to 'In the beginning.'

2–12. The names are compiled from the LXX. of 1 Ch. i.–iii., agreeing in some cases with cod. A when it differs from other MSS., and in some with the Lucianic recension.

2–6 a. Ἀβραάμ κτλ.] Abraham was the name divinely given when the national privileges began in the covenant of circumcision (Gen. xvii.). Of Judah it was foretold (Gen. xlix. 10) that sovereignty would be the inalienable prerogative of the tribe. καὶ τ. ἀδελφοὺς αὐτοῦ summarizes the names of Judah's brethren given in 1 Chr. ii. 1 f., intimating that out of several possible ancestors of the royal line Judah was chosen. Judah's twin sons Perez and Zerah were the result of Tamar's sin (Gen. xxxviii.). Jewish tradition traced the royal line to Perez (Ruth iv. 12, 18 ff.), and 'son of Perez' is a Rabb. expression for the Messiah. On ἐκ τῆς Θάμαρ and ἐκ τῆς Ῥαχάβ see Add. n. Mt. assumes, what is not stated in the O.T., that the mother of Boaz was the harlot who received the spies. The LXX. form is Ῥαάβ (cf. Jam. ii. 25, Heb. xi. 31). On ἐκ τῆς Ῥούθ see Add. n. Ruth was a Moabitess, against whose nation oracles were uttered by Am., Jer., Ezek., and Zeph., and in Deut. xxiii. 3 (cf. Neh. xiii. 1) a Moabite, coupled with a bastard and an Ammonite, is

1

Ἰσαὰκ δὲ ἐγέννησεν τὸν Ἰακώβ,
Ἰακὼβ δὲ ἐγέννησεν τὸν Ἰούδαν καὶ τοὺς ἀδελφοὺς αὐτοῦ,
3 Ἰούδας δὲ ἐγέννησεν τὸν Φαρὲς καὶ τὸν Ζαρὰ ἐκ τῆς Θάμαρ,
Φαρὲς δὲ ἐγέννησεν τὸν Ἐσρώμ,
Ἐσρὼμ δὲ ἐγέννησεν τὸν Ἀράμ,
4 Ἀρὰμ δὲ ἐγέννησεν τὸν Ἀμιναδάβ,
Ἀμιναδὰβ δὲ ἐγέννησεν τὸν Ναασσών,
Ναασσὼν δὲ ἐγέννησεν τὸν Σαλμών,
5 Σαλμὼν δὲ ἐγέννησεν τὸν Βοὲς ἐκ τῆς Ῥαχάβ,
Βοὲς δὲ ἐγέννησεν τὸν Ἰωβὴδ ἐκ τῆς Ῥούθ,
Ἰωβὴδ δὲ ἐγέννησεν τὸν Ἰεσσαί,
6 Ἰεσσαὶ δὲ ἐγέννησεν τὸν Δαυεὶδ τὸν βασιλέα.

Δαυεὶδ δὲ ἐγέννησεν τὸν Σολομῶνα ἐκ τῆς τοῦ Οὐρίου,
7 Σολομὼν δὲ ἐγέννησεν τὸν Ῥοβοάμ,
Ῥοβοὰμ δὲ ἐγέννησεν τὸν Ἀβιά,
Ἀβιὰ δὲ ἐγέννησεν τὸν Ἀσάφ,

forbidden to enter the congregation 'till the tenth generation,' i.e. for ever. The art. before Δαυείδ is strictly incorrect when τὸν βασιλέα is added; the addition emphasizes the fact that the genealogy is royal. The same addition in Ruth iv. 22 (A) may have been derived from Mt.; see, however, Jos. Ant. v. ix. 4.
6 b–11. Δαυεὶδ δέ κτλ.] Σολομῶνα (LXX. Σαλωμών, indecl.) is the form in the best uncc. In the Gospp. and Josephus the nom. is always Σολομών. Some MSS. (the best in Ac.) decline it -ῶντα, -ῶντος. Lk.'s genealogy passes through Nathan, son of David. A Jewish tradition recognized a double line; cf. Targ. Zach. xii. 12: 'The descendants of king Solomon of the house of David mourn . . . and the descendants of the prophet Nathan, son of David.' ἐκ τῆς Οὐρίου (see Add. n.) is added from Mt.'s knowledge of 2 Sam. xi. f. ; in 1 Chr. iii. 5 she is not called the wife of Uriah, but Bathshua (Βαρσάβεε), daughter of Ammiel. Ἀσάφ, at one time the prevailing spelling

in the LXX., was mostly corrected to the Heb. form Ἀσά under the influence of Origen's Hexapla (Burkitt, Ev. da Meph. ii. 203). If Ὀζείαν (v. 8) = Ὀχοζείαν (Ahaziah, 2 Chr. xxii. 1), a mistake made in 1 Chr. iii. 11, the names Joash, Amaziah, and Uzziah, given in 1 Chr., are here omitted. Uzziah is generally Ὀζείας in the LXX., and Mt. apparently took advantage of the confusion of names, and omitted three generations in order to adhere to the number 14. καὶ τ. ἀδελφοὺς αὐτοῦ (v. 11) seems to mark the fact that after the Exile there existed more than one Davidic family, any of which might have inherited the monarchy. The words are a summary, similar to that in v. 2, of the sons of Josiah and Jehoiakim named in 1 Ch. iii. 15 f. But the latter is here omitted. It is not likely that Ἰεχονίαν is for Jehoahaz, as in 1 Esd. i. 32 (1 Chr. omits Jehoahaz) ; or for Ἰωακείμ (Jehoiakim); the names in vv. 11, 12 must both mean Jehoiachin. He had, indeed, no brothers, but Zedekiah might be

Ἀσὰφ δὲ ἐγέννησεν τὸν Ἰωσαφάτ,   8
Ἰωσαφὰτ δὲ ἐγέννησεν τὸν Ἰωράμ,
Ἰωρὰμ δὲ ἐγέννησεν τὸν Ὀζείαν,
Ὀζείας δὲ ἐγέννησεν τὸν Ἰωαθάμ,   9
Ἰωαθὰμ δὲ ἐγέννησεν τὸν Ἄχας,
Ἄχας δὲ ἐγέννησεν τὸν Ἐζεκίαν,
Ἐζεκίας δὲ ἐγέννησεν τὸν Μανασσῆ,   10
Μανασσῆς δὲ ἐγέννησεν τὸν Ἀμώς,
Ἀμὼς δὲ ἐγέννησεν τὸν Ἰωσείαν,
Ἰωσείας δὲ ἐγέννησεν τὸν Ἰεχονίαν καὶ τοὺς ἀδελφοὺς 11
αὐτοῦ ἐπὶ τῆς μετοικεσίας Βαβυλῶνος.

Μετὰ δὲ τὴν μετοικεσίαν Βαβυλῶνος Ἰεχονίας ἐγέν- 12
νησεν τὸν Σαλαθιήλ,
Σαλαθιὴλ δὲ ἐγέννησεν τὸν Ζοροβάβελ,
Ζοροβάβελ δὲ ἐγέννησεν τὸν Ἀβιούδ,   13
Ἀβιοὺδ δὲ ἐγέννησεν τὸν Ἐλιακείμ,
Ἐλιακεὶμ δὲ ἐγέννησεν τὸν Ἀζώρ,
Ἀζὼρ δὲ ἐγέννησεν τὸν Σαδώκ,   14
Σαδὼκ δὲ ἐγέννησεν τὸν Ἀχείμ,
Ἀχεὶμ δὲ ἐγέννησεν τὸν Ἐλιούδ,
Ἐλιοὺδ δὲ ἐγέννησεν τὸν Ἐλεάζαρ,   15
Ἐλεάζαρ δὲ ἐγέννησεν τὸν Ματθάν,
Ματθὰν δὲ ἐγέννησεν τὸν Ἰακώβ,

mistakenly considered as such. In
1 Chr. Ἰωακείμ and Ἰεχονίας are
each followed by Σεδεκίας, and Mt.'s
statement (repeated by Clem. *Strom.*
i. 121) seems to be a confused product
of the two verses. μετοικεσία (Vulg.
transmigratio) is a late word ; LXX.
more frequently has αἰχμαλωσία, in
Jerem. mostly ἀποικία. For the gen.
Βαβυλῶνος cf. Jo. vii. 35, 1 Pet. i. 1.
12–15. μετὰ δέ κτλ.] One generation in this section is missing. This
cannot have been due to the confusion
in *v.* 11, since the second period is
clearly intended to close with the
loss of the royal power. In 1 Chr.
iii. 17 Ἀσίρ occurs as a name between

Jeconiah and Salathiel. The Heb.
אָסִּר should probably be read הָאָסִיר
' the captive ' ; and Mt. may have had
a Gk. text of Chron. which did not
treat אסר as a proper name. But if
he wrote Ἰεχ. ἐγέννησεν τὸν Ἀσίρ,
Ἀσὶρ δὲ ἐγέννησεν τὸν Σαλαθ., a
scribe's eye may have passed from
the first verb to the second. After
Zerubbabel the LXX. continues with
the descendants of Hananiah his
brother ; Mt.'s names are traditional
(cf. Judith viii. 1). All are Heb. in
form, and all occur in the O.T. except
Ἀχειμ (cf. Ἀκούμ 1 Chr. ix. 17) and
Ἐλιούδ. Ἀβιούδ (cf. 1 Chr. viii. 3)
is probably the Ἰωδά of Lk. iii. 26.

16 Ἰακὼβ δὲ ἐγέννησεν τὸν Ἰωσὴφ τὸν ἄνδρα Μαρίας, ἐξ
ἧς ἐγεννήθη Ἰησοῦς ὁ λεγόμενος Χριστός.

16. Ἰακὼβ δέ κτλ.] The nature
of the genealogy shows that ἐγέννησεν throughout denotes legal, not
necessarily physical, descent. Not
till the Lord's mother is reached
is the formula altered, and ἐγεννήθη
denotes physical birth. τὸν ἄνδρα
Μαρίας is written from the same
point of view ; Joseph acknowledged

his betrothed as his lawful wife.
But to some Christians this was
naturally of less importance than the
miracle ; hence an early alteration
was made in the text, from which
sprang a variety of readings. See
below, and Heer's table in Bar-
denhewer's *Bibl. Stud.*, 1910, 1–
226.

Additional Note on i. 16.

(a) ...Ἰωσὴφ τὸν ἄνδρα Μαρίας, ἐξ ἧς ἐγεννήθη Ἰησοῦς ὁ λεγόμενος
Χριστός uncc minu^{pler} (om. Ἰησοῦς 1. 64. om. ὁ λεγόμενος 64) 𝔏 vg 𝔖 pesh.
hcl aeth Tert (*De Carne Chr.* xx.).

(b) ...Ἰωσὴφ ᾧ μνηστευθεῖσα παρθένος Μαριὰμ ἐγέννησε Ἰησοῦν τὸν
λεγόμενον Χριστόν 346–556–826–828 (' Ferrar group ').

This is also implied by the various forms of the O.L. :

...Josef· cui desponsata· virgo· Maria genuit Jesum Christum *k*

...Joseph cui desponsata· virgo Maria peperit Christum Jesum *d* (D *vacat*).

...Joseph cui desponsata virgo Maria genuit Jesum qui dicitur [vocatur *g*]
Christus· *a g*

...Joseph cui desponsata erat virgo Maria· virgo autem Maria genuit
Jesum...*b*

...Joseph cui desponsata virgo Maria; Maria autem genuit Jesum...*c*

and by the text underlying the arm (see J. A. Robinson, *Euthaliana* 82) :

...Joseph, the husband of Mary, to whom having been betrothed Mary
the virgin from whom was born Jesus who was named Christ.

(c) ...Joseph. Joseph to whom was betrothed Mary the virgin, begat
Jesus called the Messiah. 𝔖 sin.

(d) ...Joseph, him to whom was betrothed Mary the virgin, she who
bare Jesus the Messiah. 𝔖 cur.

(e) ...Joseph the husband of Mary, him from whom was born Jesus...
Pal. lect (Lewis, B and C).

The last of these (e) is really (a) ; a scribe carelessly wrote ܗܡܒܠܘ (' him
from whom ') for ܗܡܒܠܗ (' her from whom ').

(d) probably does not represent a Gk. reading ; it is an attempt to
rewrite (c).

(c) when translated into Gk. runs quite differently from the sentences
in the rest of the genealogy. Burkitt (*Ev. da Meph.* ii. 263) points out
that 'the practice of the writer is to interpose no words between the
name and the verb ἐγέννησεν, so that the clause ᾧ μνηστ. παρθ. M.
ought to follow the first mention of Joseph, not the second.'   (b) and (c)
appear to be derived from a common 'Western' corruption of (a), arising
from a desire to avoid 'the husband of Mary.'   (a) is clearly the last

Πᾶσαι οὖν αἱ γενεαὶ ἀπὸ 'Αβραὰμ ἕως Δαυεὶδ γενεαὶ 17
δεκατέσσαρες, καὶ ἀπὸ Δαυεὶδ ἕως τῆς μετοικεσίας Βαβυ-

step in a statement of the *legal* descent of the Messiah from David
and Abraham ; and the mention of Mary, together with that of Tamar,
Rahab, and the wife of Uriah, has a special purpose. But if (*b*) is based
on an original reading ...'Ιωσήφ· 'Ιωσήφ δὲ ἐγέννησεν τὸν 'Ιησοῦν τὸν
λεγόμενον Χριστόν (of which no other trace remains), not only is the
insertion of 'to whom was betrothed Mary the virgin,' pointless as a
doctrinal safeguard, but the genealogy itself becomes an enigma. If it was
once a separate document (without the women's names), constructed in
circles that believed in the Virgin birth, it is extraordinary that they
should so have worded it as to give an easy handle to opponents. If
they were ignorant of the Virgin birth, it is in the last degree improbable, apart from the fact that Lk. knew another genealogy, that
they should have constructed it at all.

That orthodox persons could make unorthodox slips is shown by (*e*),
and also by the Arabic Diat. (Vat. MS., Ciasca's A), '...Joseph, who
from her begat Jesus the Messiah.' Burkitt shows it to be probable that
'who from her begat' is a blundering translation of the Pesh. 'from whom
(הדמא) was born.' In the *Dialogue of Timothy and Aquila* (*a*) is quoted
three times, twice very loosely (in one case ᾧ μνηστευθεῖσα Μαρία being
substituted for τὸν ἄνδρα Μαρίας), and once accurately. In the last case,
the Jew, arguing with the Christian, extracts from the words the meaning,
which they can, in fact, bear apart from their context, 'Joseph begat
Jesus that is called Christ...it says he begat [him] from Mary.'

Additional Note on the Genealogy.

The genealogy is artificially arranged in three groups of 14 generations,
which would be convenient for the memory in oral use. Box (*Interpreter*,
Jan. 1906, and *ZNW.*, 1905, 80) suggests that it was 'invested with the
character of a sort of numerical acrostic on the name David,' the numerical
value of the letters in דוד being $4 + 6 + 4 = 14$. This is unexampled in
the N.T., except perhaps in the 'number of the beast' (Apoc. xiii. 18), but
analogous to the Rabbinic aids to memory, and suitable in a piece of popular
instruction.

Women's names would not normally occur in a Jewish genealogy.
But Mt. seems to have wished to disarm criticism by showing that irregular
unions were divinely countenanced in the Messiah's legal ancestry : Ruth,
though a Moabitess, was a humble and virtuous woman ; Rahab, though
a harlot, was saved by her good action, and a Christian writer declared
her 'justified' (Jam. ii. 25 ; cf. Heb. xi. 31); Tamar and Bathsheba were
adulteresses, but the former was pronounced 'more righteous' than
Judah (Gen. xxxviii. 26), and the latter afterwards bore a son who
was 'beloved of Yah' (2 Sam. xii. 25). And Mt. triumphantly closes the
genealogy with 'Joseph the husband of Mary,' declaring that Mary was,
after all, his legally acknowledged wife. How this was is shown in
vv. 18–25.

λῶνος γενεαὶ δεκατέσσαρες, καὶ ἀπὸ τῆς μετοικεσίας Βαβυλῶνος ἕως τοῦ χριστοῦ γενεαὶ δεκατέσσαρες.

18 ΤΟΥ ΔΕ [ΙΗΣΟΤ] ΧΡΙΣΤΟΥ ἡ γένεσις οὕτως ἦν. Μνη-

18 Ιησου Χριστου] ℵCE al minn 𝕾 pesh.pal.diat^Eph me sah arm ; om Ιησου
71 𝕷 omn [incl. d, vac. D] 𝕾 sin.cur ; Χριστου Ιησου B

On the relation between the genealogies in Mt. and Lk. see *HDB*. ii.
137–41, and Plummer, *St. Luke*. Three explanations have been offered :
(1) Julius Africanus in his letter to Aristides (Eus. *H.E.* i. 7) suggested
a levirate marriage of either Jacob or Heli, Joseph's father according
to Mt. and Lk. respectively. They were brothers, and Joseph, the son
of one of them by his brother's widow, was reckoned as the son of the
deceased. Thus the two genealogies are those of Jacob and Heli. But
even if this were possible, the same would have to be assumed in the
case of Salathiel's father, who is Jechonias in Mt. but Neri in Lk. ;
and yet again in that of Eleazar (Mt.) and Levi (Lk.), if Matthan and
Matthat are identified. The explanation is altogether improbable. (2)
Annius of Viterbo (*c.* A.D. 1490) assumed that the genealogy in Lk. is
that of Mary, not of Joseph. This is still held by some. ὡς ἐνομίζετο
Ἰωσήφ is thought to be a gloss, and τοῦ Ἡλεί is explained as 'the grand-
son (or descendant) of Heli,' who was the father (or a forefather) of Mary.
(3) Lord A. C. Harvey's suggestion (*Genealogies of our Lord*, and art.
'Genealogy of Jesus Christ' in Smith's *DB.*²) is the only possible one, that
Lk. provides a pedigree of actual descent, while Mt. gives the throne-
succession. Mt.'s whole object was to show, in the face of current calumnies,
that the Messiah's genealogy was divinely ordered, and legally correct.

18–25. THE BIRTH OF THE
MESSIAH.

18. τοῦ δὲ Χριστοῦ κτλ.] The
whole course of the royal line formed
the βίβλος γενέσεως of the Messiah :
His actual γένεσις is now related,
substantiating the statement in *v.* 16.
Westcott and Hort (*App.* 7) differed
as to the reading, but 𝕾 sin has
since been added to the evidence, and
the omission of Ἰησοῦ is almost certainly right. τοῦ δὲ Ἰησοῦ Χριστοῦ
is grammatically abnormal, and must
have arisen under the influence of
vv. 1 and 16. If it were correct,
the only explanation would be that
Mt. refers to these verses : 'and the
birth of this "Jesus Christ" was
on this wise.' For οὕτως as pred.

cf. xix. 10, xxvi. 54, Rom. iv. 18
(LXX.).

μνηστευθείσης κτλ.] The Jewish
laws of marriage, though in many
respects analogous to the Roman,
differed widely from them as regards
betrothal. Later Roman law knew
of betrothal much in the English
·sense of the word. But in Jewish
law not only an actual betrothal
(קִדּוּשִׁים or אֵרוּסִים), but the mere
possibility that one party believed
him- or herself to be betrothed to the
other, constituted an affinity which
prevented the marriage of their
relatives within the forbidden degrees
(*Kidd.* iii. 10 f.) ; and a betrothed
girl was a widow if her *fiancé* died
(*Kethub.* i. 2), and this whether the

στευθείσης τῆς μητρὸς αὐτοῦ Μαρίας τῷ Ἰωσήφ, πρὶν ἢ
συνελθεῖν αὐτοὺς εὑρέθη ἐν γαστρὶ ἔχουσα ἐκ πνεύματος
ἁγίου. Ἰωσὴφ δὲ ὁ ἀνὴρ αὐτῆς, δίκαιος ὢν καὶ μὴ θέ- 19
λων αὐτὴν δειγματίσαι, ἐβουλήθη λάθρᾳ ἀπολῦσαι αὐτήν.

19 δειγματισαι] א^{a vel b}BZ 1 ; παραδειγματισαι א* ^{et c}CE al minn

man had 'taken' her to his house
or not. After betrothal, therefore,
but before marriage, the man was
legally 'husband' (cf. Gen. xxix. 21,
Dt. xxii. 23 f.); hence an informal
cancelling of betrothal was impossible : the man must give to the
woman a writ (gêṭ), and pay a fine
(see Merx, *Ev. Mat.* 9–12). The
formalities necessary for the due
deliverance of the gêṭ to the woman
are laid down in Mishn. *Giṭṭin.* On
the graecized form Μαρία and the
indecl. Μαριάμ, used in the LXX. and
Targg. for the Miriam of the M.T.,
see WH. *App.* 156. Another graecized form is Μαριάμ(μ)η, employed
frequently by Josephus.

πρὶν ἢ συνελθεῖν κτλ.] After the
gen. absol. a new subject should follow;
see Blass, § 74. 5, and on πρὶν ἢ *id.*
§ 69. 7. Like *convenio* (𝕷) and
coeo, the verb denotes the consummation of the marriage ; there is no
evidence of its use for the marriage
ceremony in which the bride was
brought to the bridegroom. Πνεύματος ἁγίου could grammatically
denote the personal Holy Spirit, the
articles being omitted owing to the
preposition (Blass, § 46. 7) ; but
the narrative breathes the air of the
O.T., and πνεῦμα should probably
be understood in its O.T. sense, as
'the power of God in active exercise,'
though the Church has doubtless
been right in identifying this with
the Third Person of the H. Trinity.
'Holy Spirit' occurs in the O.T. in
Ps. li. 11, Is. lxiii. 10 only, while the
advance of theology in Christianity

led to its use in the N.T. more than
80 times. See art. 'Holy Spirit'
in *HDB.* ii. 405, and Swete, *The H.
Sp. in the N.T.* 27–31.

19. Ἰωσὴφ δέ κτλ.] On ὁ ἀνὴρ
αὐτῆς see *v.* 18. δίκαιος is used of
Zacharias and Elizabeth (Lk. i. 6),
and Symeon (Lk. ii. 25) ; the former
passage shews what it connoted to
the Jewish mind—conscientiousness
in the observance of the law. See
Sanday-Headlam, *Romans,* 29. καὶ
μὴ θέλων, 'and yet not willing.'
As a good Jew he would have shewn
his zeal if he had branded her with
public disgrace. For the καί cf. vi.
26 (Blass, § 77. 6). The converse
meaning is possible, 'and *therefore*
not willing,' δίκαιος being understood of general moral uprightness
which would include benevolence ;
e.g. 𝕾 sin.cur 'because he was [an]
upright [man] was not willing' ; so
Hil. *al.* But the former is more in
accordance with the spirit of the
time. A divorce was not a matter
which would come into court ; it
was a private arrangement (λάθρᾳ)
which involved only the presence of
two witnesses that he had given her
the gêṭ. But he might have brought
her into publicity for her supposed
crime. δειγματίσαι is not 'put her
to shame' (Vg. *traducere*), but merely
'proclaim,' 'publish' : *divulgare* (*k*),
'would not pupplische her' (Wycl.).
It is a rare word, occurring in Col.
ii. 15, *Asc. Is.* ii. 3, Amh. Pap. I.
i. 8. 21, *Acta Pauli et Petri,* 33.
δειγματισμός occurs on the Rosetta
Stone. The stronger meaning appears

20 Ταῦτα δὲ αὐτοῦ ἐνθυμηθέντος ἰδοὺ ἄγγελος Κυρίου κατ᾽ ὄναρ
ἐφάνη αὐτῷ λέγων Ἰωσὴφ υἱὸς Δαυείδ, μὴ φοβηθῇς παρα-
λαβεῖν Μαρίαν τὴν γυναῖκά σου, τὸ γὰρ ἐν αὐτῇ γεννη-
21 θὲν ἐκ πνεύματός ἐστιν ἁγίου· τέξεται δὲ υἱὸν καὶ καλέσεις τὸ ὄνομα αὐτοῦ Ἰησοῦν, αὐτὸς γὰρ σώσει τὸν λαὸν

to attach to the *v.l.* παραδειγματίσαι :
cf. Heb. vi. 6. δειγματίσαι μὲν γάρ
ἐστι τὸ ἁπλῶς ἀπολῦσαι, παραδειγματίσαι δὲ τὸ ἐπὶ κακῷ φανερῶσαι
(Petr. Laod.) ; and see Eus. *Steph.*
221 (quoted by Tisch.). ἀπολῦσαι,
of divorce, is rare and unclassical ;
cf. v. 31, xix. 3, 7 ff. = Mk. x. 2, 4,
11, Lk. xvi. 18 ; in the LXX. 1 Esd.
ix. 36 only (elsewhere always ἐξαπο-
στέλλειν = שָׁלַח).

20. ταῦτα δὲ αὐτοῦ κτλ.] 'These
thoughts having passed through his
mind' ; a short but tragic struggle
between his legal conscience and his
love. ἐνθυμεῖσθαι, freq. in the LXX.,
recurs in the N.T. in ix. 4 only ;
διενθυμ. Ac. x. 19. ἰδού is Hebraic,
derived from the LXX., Mt. 34, Mk. 9,
Lk. 30 ; καὶ ἰδού Mt. 28, Lk. 26, never
in Mk. ἄγγελος Κυρίου : always
without an article in the N.T, except
when referring to an angel already
mentioned (cf. *v.* 24). In the O.T. the
מַלְאַךְ יְהוָה denotes Yahweh Himself
in a temporary theophany or activity
on earth ; but the personification of
His activities led, after the Exile, to
the thought of them as individual
angelic beings. Joseph, like Abraham
(Gen. xxii. 11 f.), was divinely hindered
from injuring, in obedience to his
conscience, one in whom all the
families of the earth should bless
themselves. κατ᾽ ὄναρ for the class.
ὄναρ : ii. 12 f., 19, 22, xxvii. 19 only ;
Photius condemns it as βάρβαρον
παντελῶς.

Ἰωσὴφ υἱὸς Δαυείδ κτλ.] The
form of address summarizes the
thought of the genealogy. On the
nom. for the voc. see Blass, § 33. 4.

On μή with the aor. subj., 39 times
in Mt., always in sayings of Jesus,
except here and iii. 9, see Moulton
i. 124. On γυναῖκα (avoided in
Ｓcur 'thy betrothed') see note on
μνηστευθείσης, *v.* 18. τὸ γεννηθέν
is 'that which hath been engendered,'
not *natum fuerit* (k). In the earlier
message to Mary (Lk. i. 35) the
present tense is used : so Ｓ sin.cur
here ; cf. *Protev.* 14 τὸ γὰρ ἐν αὐτῇ ὄν.

21. τέξεται δὲ υἱόν κτλ.] The
wording of the narrative has been
coloured by that of the quotation
in *v.* 23. On the addition 'to thee'
in Ｓ sin.cur see Burkitt (*Ev. daMeph.*
ii. 261 f.), 'a mere stylistic addition to
the Syriac...it never had a place in
the Greek text.' αὐτός is perhaps
emphatic : 'it is He who will save,
etc.' The Messiah will bring about
the redemption (cf. Lk. i. 68, xxiv. 21)
ascribed in the O.T. to God (Ps.
cxxix. [cxxx.] 8) ; see Dalman, *Words,*
297. λαός (עַם) is the privileged
people of God, as distinct from ἔθνη
(גּוֹיִם) : the Christian 'laity' now
possess their privileges ; see Hort,
1 Peter, 128 a. σώσει involves a
play on the Heb. יוֹשִׁיעַ ('shall save')
and יֵשׁוּעַ ('Jesus') ; since such a play
is not possible in Aramaic, a Hebrew
original must underlie the verse. The
angel's words may have been in the
form of Heb. poetry, taken from a
collection current in Palestinian
circles. If so, a point of contact is
afforded with Lk.'s narrative, of
which Hebraic poetry forms so
marked a feature. The popular
expectations of 'salvation' from sin
were based on the O.T., and were

αὐτοῦ ἀπὸ τῶν ἁμαρτιῶν αὐτῶν. Τοῦτο δὲ ὅλον γέγονεν 22
ἵνα πληρωθῇ τὸ ῥηθὲν ὑπὸ Κυρίου διὰ τοῦ προφήτου
λέγοντος

Ἰδοὺ Ἡ παρθένος ἐν γαστρὶ ἕξει καὶ τέξεται υἱόν,   23
καὶ καλέσουσιν τὸ ὄνομα αὐτοῦ Ἐμμανουήλ·

mainly concerned with salvation from
the punishment of sins ; 'righteousness' (= vindication) would be the
result, rather than the cause, of
national redemption. But Christian
thought finds in the words, as the
evangelists doubtless did, a promise
of individual forgiveness for all sinners; cf. Ṣcur, 'he shall save alive
the world from its sins' (see Burkitt,
op. cit. 257).

22. τοῦτο δὲ ὅλον κτλ.] The
perf. γέγονεν (cf. xxi. 4, xxvi. 56,
Heb. vii. 14) denotes that the event
stands recorded in the abiding
Christian tradition ; cf. similar per-
fects with reference to O.T. records,
Heb. vii. 6, 9, 11, viii. 5. ἵνα (and
ὅπως ii. 23, viii. 17, xiii. 35) in
this and similar formulas is not
equivalent to ὥστε : in the early
Church it was a leading conception,
particularly marked in the 1st and
4th Gospels (cf. ii. 15, 23, iv. 14–17,
viii. 17, xii. 17–21, xiii. 35, xxi. 4
f., Jo. xii. 38 f., xiii. 18, xix. 24,
28, 36 f. ; see *Camb. Bibl. Essays*,
221), that the events of Christ's life
were divinely ordered for the express
purpose of fulfilling the O.T. An
exact parallel is not found in Jewish
writings, but somewhat similar
formulas occur : לקיים מה שנאמר 'to
fulfil that which is said'; או נתקיים
'then was fulfilled' (cf. Mt. ii. 17,
xxvii. 9); see Bacher, *Exeg. Term.* i.
171. Cf. 1 Kings ii. 27, viii. 15,
24, Jer. xliv. 25. τὸ ῥηθέν κτλ.
and similar expressions are confined
to Mt. ii. 15, 17, 23, iii. 3, iv. 14,
viii. 17, xii. 17, xiii. 35, xxi. 4,

xxii. 31, xxiv. 15, xxvii. 9. The
words were spoken by Yahweh
(Κυρίου without the article is a
quasi proper name); the prophet
was only His instrument. For διά
(= בְּיַד) cf. Jos. xx. 2 ; Lk. (i. 70 ; Ac.
i. 16 *al.*) prefers διὰ στόματος = בְּפִי
(2 Chr. xxxvi. 22 only).

23. ἰδοὺ ἡ παρθένος κτλ.] The
quotation is from Is. vii. 14 : ἰδοὺ ἡ
παρθένος ἐν γαστρὶ λήμψεται (B; ἕξει
אAQ) καὶ τέξεται υἱόν, καὶ καλέσεις
κτλ. For the last verb there are
variants : καλέσεις (BA) = קָרָאתְ; so
Aq., Sym., Theod. *ap.* Eus. and Jer. ;
καλέσει (א) = M.T. קָרָאת ; καλέσουσιν (apparently Γ, probably derived
from Mt.) is a periphrasis, *more Aram.*,
for the passive κληθήσεται, and
suggests that the passage was current
in Mt.'s time in an Aramaic translation from the Heb., and formed
part of a collection of *testimonia*.
παρθένος was understood by Mt. in
the sense of 'virgin'; and Iren. (*ap.*
Eus. *H.E.* v. 8) blamed the daring
of Theodotion and Aquila who rendered Isaiah's word עַלְמָה by νεᾶνις.
But, as Jerome (*in loc.* Is.) admits,
'porro ALMA apud eos verbum am-
biguum est'; the Heb. word does
not necessarily denote 'virgin'; see
BDB. s.v., and cf. the cognate עֶלֶם
'young man,' and עֲלָמִים 'youth.' It
could be applied to any young woman,
and approaches נַעֲרָה ('girl') in meaning, rather than בְּתוּלָה ('virgin').
Similarly παρθένος, while it is the
normal rendering of בְּתוּלָה, also represents נַעֲרָה in Gen. xxiv. 14, 16, 55,
xxxiv. 3 *bis* (in the latter case of

24 ὅ ἐστιν μεθερμηνευόμενον Μεθ᾽ ἡμῶν ὁ θεός. Ἐγερθεὶς δὲ
ὁ Ἰωσὴφ ἀπὸ τοῦ ὕπνου ἐποίησεν ὡς προσέταξεν αὐτῷ
ὁ ἄγγελος Κυρίου καὶ παρέλαβεν τὴν γυναῖκα αὐτοῦ·
25 καὶ οὐκ ἐγίνωσκεν αὐτὴν ἕως οὗ ἔτεκεν υἱόν· καὶ ἐκάλεσεν
τὸ ὄνομα αὐτοῦ Ἰησοῦν.

25 ουκ εγινωσκεν αυτην εως ου] om 𝕃 k 𝕾 sin ; 'lived purely with her until'
𝕾 cur.diat^Eph

one who had lost her virginity).
It occurs only twice for עַלְמָה (Gen.
xxiv. 43, Is. *l.c.*), which is further
rendered by νεᾶνις (Ex. ii. 8, Ps.
lxvii. [lxviii.] 26, Cant. i. 3, vi. 7 [8])
and νεότης (Prov. xxiv. 54 [xxx. 19]).
Whatever, therefore, may have been
Isaiah's thought—and it has yet
to be proved that, under Babylonian
or other foreign influence, he expected
the birth of a Redeemer-King from a
virgin (so Burney, *JThS.* x. 580–4, but
see Gray, *Expos.*, Apr. 1911, 289 ff.)
—the LXX. translation did not necessarily use παρθένος in the sense of
'virgin,' although the *substitution* of
νεᾶνις by Aq., Sym., Theod. was an
anti-Christian protest. On the use
made of the passage in early contro-
versies with Jews see Justin, *Dial.* 43,
67 f., 71, 77. Earlier than Justin no
writer except Mt. cites it in connexion
with the birth of Christ. See Add.
n. For μεθερμηνευόμενον, found as
early as the Prologue of B. Sira, cf.
Mk. v. 41, xv. 22, 34.

25. καὶ οὐκ κτλ.] The words
between καί and ἔτεκεν are omitted in
𝕃 k 𝕾 sin, and their omission seems to
be supported by 𝕾 cur.diat (see Appar.).
It is not unlikely that they are a
gloss, added to safeguard the sentence
from misunderstanding. Mt., having

already related the fact of the Virgin
birth, 'was only concerned at this
point to assert that Joseph publicly
accepted Mary as his lawful wife,
and publicly acknowledged her son
as lawfully born in wedlock' (Burkitt,
Ev. da Meph. ii. 261). As they
stand the words reiterate the miracle.
But they do not necessarily assert
the perpetual virginity of the mother.
In the N.T. a negative followed by
ἕως οὗ (*e.g.* xvii. 9), ἕως (*e.g.* xxiv. 39),
or ἕως ὅτου (Jo. ix. 18) always implies
that the negatived action did, or
will, take place after the point of
time indicated by the particle ;
contrast, however, Gen. viii. 7, cited
by Chrys. 'Non sequitur ut postea
convenerint' (Jer.) is true whether
υἱόν be read or τὸν υἱ. αὐτῆς τὸν
πρωτότοκον (probably from Lk.),
since 'first-born' no more involves
'later-born' than 'son' involves
'daughter' (Lightft. *Galat.* Diss. II).
But doubtless, like πρὶν ἢ συνελθεῖν,
the words are concerned only with
the fact of virginity at the time.
The subject of ἐκάλεσεν is probably
Joseph (so 𝕾 sin) in accordance with
καλέσεις (*v.* 21): contrast Lk. i. 31.
By naming the Child, Joseph publicly
acknowledged Him a lawfully born
member of his family.

Additional Note on the Virgin Birth.

1. If the event is historical, the narrative was not due to Isaiah's
words. Mt. adduces them only as a corroborative illustration, as words
which were divinely intended to be fulfilled in the event. The name

Immanuel was to him the kernel of Christianity. But his use of it may be understood in two ways, according as 'God with us' describes the *nature* of the Child, or His *work*. (*a*) In the former case it follows that Mt. believed the Holy Spirit to have inspired the prophet to utter words which were to find fulfilment in the two natures of Jesus Christ. The Child *is* God with us. (*b*) In the latter case Mt.'s object was apologetic rather than dogmatic. He wanted to shew—and this is the more probable explanation of his words—that there was nothing new or extravagant in the thought of a miraculous birth. A birth from a παρθένος only fulfilled Isaiah's prophecy concerning Immanuel, whose appearance would mark the moment when Israel could say 'God (is) with us' to release us from foreign invasion, to save us from the result of our sins (cf. Ps. xlvi. 7–11).

2. Some who cannot accept the narrative as historical have thought that Isaiah's words in their Greek form *gave rise to* the belief in the Virgin Birth (Harnack, *Hist. of Dogma*, i. 100). But it is astonishing that though the Christianity of the N.T. is based upon the belief in the Incarnation, the O.T. passage which, according to this theory, is the foundation of the whole, is nowhere even remotely alluded to, apart from Mt. i. 23. Others hold that though Isaiah's words were not the origin of the belief, the convictions of Christians as to the uniqueness, the purity, and the holiness of Jesus may have taken their rise from the O.T. ; that they read such passages as Ps. ii. 7 ('Thou art my son'), Ps. lxxii. (the glorious rule of the king's son), Is. xi. 2 (the inspiration of the Davidic king), xlii. 1 (of the Servant of Yahweh), lxi. 1 (of the Messianic Prophet), and transformed them into the Christian faith in one who was God's Son, and who, by the action of the divine spirit, became Immanuel (Lobstein, *The Virgin Birth of Christ*, p. 96). Harnack (*Date of the Acts*, 142–149) suggests two factors which contributed to the belief ; (*a*) Christians held that Christ was the Son of God, by the action of the Holy Spirit, in the Resurrection (Rom. i. 4), but that His Sonship was then carried further back, to the divine voice at the Transfiguration (Mk. ix. 7), then to the divine voice at the Baptism (Mk. i. 11), and finally to the Birth ; (*b*) with this thought of divine Sonship by the action of the Holy Spirit was coupled Isaiah's prediction. But even if the Sonship was carried back, in this way, to the Birth or the Conception, Isaiah's prediction must still, on this theory, be regarded as an essential factor in the production of a belief in the *Virgin* Birth, and it remains astonishing, as said above, that no N.T. writer except Mt. should have alluded to it.

3. Several writers have held that the origin of the belief was not Jewish, but *pagan* (*e.g.* Schmiedel, *Enc. Bibl.*, art. 'Mary,' Usener, *ib.*, art. 'Nativity,' Pfleiderer, *Das Urchristentum,* and *Early Christian Conceptions of Christ*, Soltau, *The Birth of Jesus Christ*). Pagan myths of goddess mothers whose sons were divine redeemers are easy to collect. But, as these writers admit, the belief produced from such myths could not have taken its rise in Palestinian Jewish circles. The adaptation of pagan ideas must have been the work of Gentile Christians, and their incorporation into the Christian tradition must have taken

place at a late date. But such a theory is confronted with the difficulty that the narratives of the Nativity are intensely Jewish; the language is Hebraic, and the atmosphere Palestinian. If the portions which deal with the Virgin Birth are Gentile insertions into an earlier Jewish story, they should present distinctively Greek features; but they do not: they are as Hebraic as the surrounding context (see Bp. Chase, *Camb. Theol. Essays*, 411–414). This is true not only of Mt.'s account but also of Lk. i. 34, 35, which many hold to be an interpolation.

A modification of the theory ascribes to the narrative a composite origin. It is held that pagan mythology had moulded the ideas of certain Jewish circles, and that from these ideas, 'which had become, so to speak, "international," but may in the last resort be traced to Babylonia,' Jewish Christians obtained, with many alterations of detail, 'a poetic and popular symbol of a primary religious truth—of the truth that inestimable blessings, which, for us, have their fountain-head in the Crucified, do indeed come from above (Jo. viii. 23), and not from below, are not humanly introduced, but have their origin in God' (Cheyne, *Bible Problems*, 95 f.). If the theory is true, it is remarkable that the humble and unlearned Jewish Christians treated the international myth with a bold freedom found in no other community. The goddess is not, as in all the mythologies, a heavenly being, and the son a god or an emperor, but both are lowly and obscure country folk. And Dr. Cheyne admits that 'the stress laid on the virginity (in the ordinary sense of the word) is peculiar to the evangelist.' Moreover, there is not the faintest trace of the alleged pre-Christian Jewish phase of the belief, intermediate between the pagan and the Christian. Apoc. xii., to which the same writer refers, is of a totally different character, and even if it contains pagan elements there is no evidence that it passed through a non-Christian Jewish phase before it reached its present form. Finally, it is improbable that Palestinian Jewish Christians would be unaware that the international myth was of pagan origin, and that, if aware of it, they would have embraced and adapted it.

4. Supporters of the pagan origin of the belief can at least produce pagan parallels. But those who hold that the Virgin Birth of the Messiah was a purely Jewish expectation can produce no parallels at all. Harnack can say only that it seems to him probable. It is irrelevant, for example, to point to a section of the Ebionites, which 'did not deny that the Lord was born of a virgin and the Holy Spirit' (Eus. *H.E.* iii. 27). Gunkel (*Zum religionsgesch. Verständnis d. N.T.* 68 f.), recognizing the Jewish character of Mt.'s narrative, holds that mythological ideas could not have made their way into Jewish Christianity 'if Judaism itself had not previously possessed these or analogous ideas.' But this is only a deduction from the phenomena of Mt.'s narrative. In the large amount of Jewish pre-Christian material that we possess, there is not a trace of the belief. Badham (*Academy*, June 8, 1905), indeed, attempts to find it in late, in some cases very late, Rabbinic literature. But he admits that the references are 'slight and disappointing.' Some are no longer extant; and he makes no attempt to determine whether any are due to Christian influence.

Τοῦ δὲ Ἰησοῦ γεννηθέντος ἐν Βηθλεὲμ τῆς Ἰουδαίας 1 II.

5. We are thus led to the conclusion that no non-Christian source, written or oral, has been found which satisfactorily accounts for the phenomena of the Gospel narratives. It is impossible to determine how early the event of the Virgin Birth was known to Christians. From the nature of the case it would not be common knowledge at first. It did not form part of the Marcan tradition, or it lay outside S. Mark's plan in writing for Roman readers, as it lay outside the plan of the compiler of Q. It is often said that Mt.'s account must have been derived from Joseph, and Lk.'s from the Lord's mother; this, however, cannot be considered proved, and must not be pressed, although they were obviously the ultimate authority for the fact. But at least the written narrative was current within the lifetime of members of the family who were in a position to know the facts, and could have contradicted false statements. S. Paul's silence—if he was silent—on the subject, need not involve ignorance, as it certainly does not in the case of the fourth evangelist. 'God sent forth His Son born of a woman' (Gal. iv. 4) may be ambiguous; but the teaching of vv. 1–7 about 'adoption'— the granting of a new kind of sonship — can be better understood if it presupposes the Virgin Birth. And the belief, if not necessary to, is entirely congruous with, the apostle's attitude towards Christ as the 'new Man,' the 'second Adam,' i.e. the Founder and Source of a new and spiritual race. It is this congruity with the whole body of Christian belief, with the Incarnation, the Atonement, the Sacraments, which turns the scale for those who will not assert that miracles do not happen, much less that a miracle, avowedly unique, did not happen, but whom the literary evidence leaves in suspense.

ii. 1–12. The Visit of the Magians.

1. τοῦ δὲ Ἰησοῦ κτλ.] There was a Bethlehem in Galilee, 7 m. NW. of Nazareth (Jos. xix. 15; cf. Neubauer, Géogr. du Talm. 191); but Palestinian readers could not be in doubt as to which Bethlehem was the birthplace of the Son of David. Mt. probably employed the conventional form of the name. For the topographical genitive τ. Ἰουδαίας cf. Ναζαρὲθ τ. Γαλιλαίας (xxi. 11, Mk. i. 9), Κανὰ τ. Γ. (Jo. ii. 1, 11, iv. 46). The name appears in the O.T. as Bethlehem of Judah (Jud. xvii. 7 ff., xix. 1 f., 18, Ruth i. 1 f.), which (as Jer. suggests) probably stood here (see v. 5); Ἰουδαία represents יְהוּדָה in 1 Regn. xxvii. 6, 10, Is. i. 1. Bethlehem, the modern Beit-laḥm,

5 m. S. of Jerusalem (Jos. Ant. VII. xii. 4), was the home of David, and the scene of the story of Ruth his ancestress. The Lord's family, therefore, according to Lk. ii. 3 f., considered it their true home, and went thither for the enrolment. 'In the days of Herod': the only date explicitly specified by any N.T. writer except Lk. Herod the Great became governor of Galilee in 47 B.C., and was given the title 'King of Judaea' by Antony and Octavius in 40; he began to build the temple in 20, and died in 4 B.C. See however Add. n. after xiv. 12.

ἰδοὺ μάγοι κτλ.] On ἰδού see i. 20. If Herodotus (i. 101) is to be trusted, the Magians were originally a Median tribe, but became a priestly caste among the Persians (i. 132), as

ἐν ἡμέραις Ἡρῴδου τοῦ βασιλέως, ἰδοὺ μάγοι ἀπὸ ἀνα-
2 τολῶν παρεγένοντο εἰς Ἱεροσόλυμα λέγοντες   Ποῦ ἐστὶν

the Chaldeans in Babylon (Dan. i. 4
etc. ; see Driver, p. 12–16). The
word acquired later the more general
sense of 'magician' (Ac. xiii. 6, 8 ;
cf. viii. 9, 11) : it stands for 'asshāph,
'charmer' (Dan. ii. 2, 10 etc. LXX.
Theod.), 'ōbh, 'necromancer' (1 Regn.
xxviii. 3, 9 Aq.), ḥartummim, 'magi-
cians' (Gen. xli. 24 Sym.).   Mt.
appears to use it with the specific
force of 'astrologer.'   Its derivation
is still uncertain (see *KAT*.[2] 417 ff.,
[3]590. In Persian inscriptions of the
age of Darius *māgŭš* is found, and it
occurs in Jewish literature and in
Syriac as מְגוּשָׁא). Many of the fathers
understood it to have a sinister force,
and drew out the thought that magic
was overthrown by the advent of
Christ (cf. Ign. *Eph.* 19, Justin, *Dial.*
78, Tert. *De Idol.* 78, Orig. *c. Cels.* i.
60, Hil. *in Mat.* 1), and this idea
prevailed in mediaeval writings ; but
there is not a hint of it in the
narrative. ἀπὸ ἀνατολῶν is to be
connected with μάγοι, not with
παρεγένοντο : cf. iv. 25, Jo. xi. 1.
'The East' might designate Arabia
(Gen. x. 30), as Just. Tert. concluded
from the nature of the gifts, or
Babylonia the home of astrology
(Orig., Jer., Aug.), or Persia (Clem. Al.,
Chrys.). But attempts to determine
the country intended are guesses.
That the Magians are represented as
Gentiles can be gathered from their
use of the term 'the Jews,' which was
probably not employed at the time
except by foreigners ; the Mishna
speaks only of 'Israelites.'   Such
passages as Is. lx. 3, Apoc. xxi. 24
gave rise to the tradition that they
were kings, and the triple gift that
they were three in number.   For
apocryphal accretions to the story
see 'Magi,' in *HDB.* and *DCG.*   The

Gk. form Ἱεροσόλυμα, neut. plur.
except in *v.* 3 and perhaps iii. 5, is
invariable in Mt.[11] (except xxiii. 37),
Mk., Jo., and Josephus.   The Heb.
form Ἱερουσαλήμ is used in xxiii.
37, usually in Lk., who strives to preserve a biblical style, S. Paul (except
Gal. i. 17 f., ii. 1), and Heb. xii. 22,
Apoc. iii. 12, xxi. 2, 10.   In a translation from a Semitic original the Gk.
form would be employed deliberately,
and Mt. adheres to it.   Where the
forms alternate, as in Ac., some explain that the Heb. form expresses
special solemnity.   See Harnack,
Apostelgeschichte, 72 ff., and somewhat
differently Ramsay, *Expos.* VII. iii.
109 ff., 414 ff. Against this Schütz,
ZNW., 1910, 169 ff.

2. ποῦ ἐστίν κτλ.] On 'king of
the Jews' see xxvii. 11.   Assyr. and
Babyl. records contain omens as to
the fortunes of Aḥarrû (the West
land, Phoenicia and Palestine), drawn
from astronomical phenomena ; see
Allen, *ad loc.,* who also refers to
the constellation from which, on the
birthnight of Alexander, Magians
foretold that the destroyer of Asia
was born (Cic. *De Divin.* i. 47).   In
JThS., 1902, 524 Moulton refers to
the Magian belief that a star could
be the *fravashi,* the counterpart
or 'angel' (cf. Mt. xviii. 10) of a
great man.   Throughout the civilized
world ideas of a 'Messianic' kind
were in the air.   The birth of the
Roman Empire was diffusing law and
order, and hence peace and wealth
(Jos. *Ant.* XVI. ii. 3, iv. 3) ; Virgil
(*Ecl.* iv.) shews what a Roman expected from Augustus ; and see the
inscriptions in his honour, quoted
by Soltau (*Birth of J. Chr.* 68–
72).   Similar expectations afterwards
centred upon the Flavian family ;

ὁ τεχθεὶς βασιλεὺς τῶν Ἰουδαίων; εἴδομεν γὰρ αὐτοῦ τὸν
ἀστέρα ἐν τῇ ἀνατολῇ καὶ ἤλθομεν προσκυνῆσαι αὐτῷ.
Ἀκούσας δὲ ὁ βασιλεὺς Ἡρῴδης ἐταράχθη καὶ πᾶσα 3
Ἰεροσόλυμα μετ᾽ αὐτοῦ, καὶ συναγαγὼν πάντας τοὺς ἀρχι- 4
ερεῖς καὶ γραμματεῖς τοῦ λαοῦ ἐπυνθάνετο παρ᾽ αὐτῶν

3 πασα] om D

Jos. B.J. VI. v. 4, Tac. Hist. v. 13,
Suet. Vesp. 4. It is not impossible,
therefore, that eastern astrologers,
perhaps proselytes, or influenced by
Jews, should travel to the place
where they expected the birth of the
world's king. See Bousset, Rel. d.
Jud. 212 f. With the Magians' intention to worship Jesus cf. Seneca's
account (Ep. 58) of Magians in Athens
who brought sacrifices to Plato after
his death.

ἐν τῇ ἀνατολῇ] 'At its rising,'
possibly a technical expression describing the moment when the phenomenon first became visible. It can
hardly have the same meaning as the
preceding ἀνατολῶν, plur. without
article. The appearance of a bright
star, noted by astrologers though no
other record survived, affords no
evidence of the date. See Moulton,
op. cit.

3. ἀκούσας δέ κτλ.] The public
excitement leads to nothing, and is
not again referred to in the narrative.
Possibly καὶ πᾶσα Ἰερ. μετ᾽ αὐτοῦ
is a scribal insertion, since elsewhere
in Mt.[10] Ἰεροσόλυμα is probably
always a neut. plur. (see on v. 1).
Hence D omits πᾶσα. For the sing.
cf. Tob. xiv. 4, Jos. Ant. I. x. 2.

4. καὶ συναγαγών κτλ.] From the
time of Herod till the fall of Jerusalem
there were, according to Josephus,
28 high priests, appointed either
by the Herodian princes or by the
Romans ; Herod himself appointed
no less than seven. They were
chosen, for the most part, from a
few aristocratic families. The title

'high priests' (Vg. principes sacer-
dotum) was applied to all those who
were ἐκ γένους ἀρχιερατικοῦ (Ac.
iv. 6). The particular high priest at
this time, according to the ordinary
chronology of the life of Jesus, was
either Matthias son of Theophilus
or Joasar son of Boethos (Jos. Ant.
XVII. iv. 2, vi. 4). See Schürer,
HJP. II. i. 195–206. The sacerdotal
nobility at first formed the governing
body of the Jewish Church (τοῦ λαοῦ).
But when the power of the Pharisees
grew, the priestly party felt compelled to admit Pharisaic doctors,
the 'Scribes' (see v. 20 note), into
the assembly. And the Sanhedrin
also included 'Elders' (cf. xvi. 21
note, xxi. 23, xxvi. 3, 47, 57, xxvii.
1, 3, 12, 20, 41), but in several
passages (as here) Mt. does not mention
them. In xxvi. 59 he speaks of 'the
high priests and the whole Sanhedrin.'
See Schürer, op. cit. 174–8.

ἐπυνθάνετο παρ᾽ αὐτῶν κτλ.] The
summoning of the whole Sanhedrin
for this purpose is open to grave
doubt. Not only is Herod said to
have begun his reign with a massacre
of its members (Jos. Ant. XIV. ix. 4),
—he certainly reduced its importance and influence to a minimum—
but he could easily ask the question
privately of a single Scribe. The
narrative emphasizes the zeal of the
foreigners who sought the Messiah,
in contrast with the indifference of
the official rulers. γεννᾶται is the
prophetic present, the writer giving
the orat. recta of Herod's words (Blass,
§ 56. 8 f.).

5 ποῦ ὁ χριστὸς γεννᾶται. οἱ δὲ εἶπαν αὐτῷ Ἐν Βηθλεὲμ
τῆς Ἰουδαίας· οὕτως γὰρ γέγραπται διὰ τοῦ προφήτου

6   Καὶ ϲΎ, Βηθλεέμ ΓΗ̂ Ἰογ́Δα,
ογ́ΔαμΩ̂ϲ ἐλαχίϲτη εἶ ἐΝ τοῖϲ ἡΓεμόϲιΝ Ἰογ́Δα·
ἐκ ϲογ́ Γὰρ ἐξελεγ́ϲεται ἡΓογ́μεΝοϲ,
ὅϲτιϲ ποιμαΝεῖ τὸΝ λαόΝ μογ τὸΝ Ἰϲραήλ.

7 Τότε Ἡρῴδης λάθρᾳ καλέσας τοὺς μάγους ἠκρίβωσεν παρ'

5. ἐν Βηθλεέμ κτλ.] The Jewish
belief that Bethlehem was to be the
Messiah's birthplace is referred to
in Jo. vii. 42 on the authority of
'Scripture.' Cf. Targ. Mic. v. 1:
'out of thee shall come forth before
me the Messiah.' Targ. Jon. Gen.
xxxv. 21 explains the 'tower of
Eder' near Ephrath as the place
where the Messiah would be revealed.
Rabbinic passages express the same
expectation: Jer. *Berak.* 5 a, Midr.
Lam. i. 16. Ἰουδαίας was perhaps
originally read Ἰούδα (so Jer.), in
accordance with the following quotation; see *v.* 1.

6. καὶ σύ κτλ.] The quotation is
from Mic. v. [2] 1; it differs both from
Heb. and LXX., and was probably
taken from a collection of *testimonia.*
LXX. has καὶ σύ, Βηθλεέμ οἶκος
Ἐφράθα, ὀλιγοστὸς εἶ τοῦ εἶναι ἐν
χιλιάσιν Ἰούδα· ἐκ σοῦ μοι ἐξελεύ-
σεται τοῦ εἶναι εἰς ἄρχοντα τοῦ
Ἰσραήλ. Except for the insertion
of οἶκος (from a repetition of the בית
in 'Bethlehem') and εἰς, this follows
the M.T. Mt.'s γῆ Ἰούδα is loosely co-
ordinated with Βηθλεέμ, so that the
expression is equivalent to 'Bethlehem
[of] Judah' (so 𝕷*k*). On γῆ see ix.
26. οὐδαμῶς ἐλαχίστη εἶ is a paraphrase of the original, emphasizing
the honour which Bethlehem was to
receive; ἐλαχίστη means 'least in
honour.' ἐν τοῖς ἡγεμόσιν = בְּאַלְפֵי
for the M.T. בְּאַלְפֵי ('thousands,' i.e.
clans), the clans being personified in

their rulers. γάρ is inserted in consequence of the paraphrase 'thou art
by no means the least'; in the original
the second clause is sharply contrasted
with the first, without a connecting
particle. לִי (μοι) was probably absent
from the text of Micah, from which the
passage was drawn. The passage was
understood to mean that the Messiah
was to be *born* at Bethlehem; but
the prophet probably meant that,
wherever he might be born, he would
'come out of Bethlehem,' i.e. out of
the stock of David, since David was
born there.

ἡγούμενος, ὅστις ποιμανεῖ κτλ.]
The thought of Mic. v. 3 ('he shall
stand and feed (LXX. ποιμανεῖ) in the
strength of Yahweh') is combined
with 2 Regn. v. 2: 'thou shalt feed
my people Israel, and thou shalt be
for a ruler (ἡγούμενον) over Israel.'
Cf. 2 Regn. vii. 7, Jer. xxiii. 2: and
see Ps. ii. 9 (LXX.), quoted in Apoc.
ii. 27, xii. 5, xix. 15. ἡγούμενος is
inserted (probably from Mt.) in Mic.
v. 1 cod. A. ὅστις draws attention
to the ruler as a type rather than
an individual (Moulton i. 92); cf.
vii. 15, 24, 26, xiii. 52, xx. 1, xxi.
33, xxii. 2, xxv. 1.

7. τότε Ἡρῴδης κτλ.] All the
details of Herod's action raise difficulties. No report of the private
interview was likely to reach the
Church either from Herod or the
Magians. τότε is characteristic of
Mt. as a particle which carries the

αὐτῶν τὸν χρόνον τοῦ φαινομένου ἀστέρος, καὶ πέμψας 8
αὐτοὺς εἰς Βηθλεὲμ εἶπεν Πορευθέντες ἐξετάσατε ἀκριβῶς περὶ τοῦ παιδίου· ἐπὰν δὲ εὕρητε ἀπαγγείλατέ μοι,
ὅπως κἀγὼ ἐλθὼν προσκυνήσω αὐτῷ. οἱ δὲ ἀκούσαντες 9
τοῦ βασιλέως ἐπορεύθησαν, καὶ ἰδοὺ ὁ ἀστὴρ ὃν εἶδον ἐν
τῇ ἀνατολῇ προῆγεν αὐτούς, ἕως ἐλθὼν ἐστάθη ἐπάνω οὗ
ἦν τὸ παιδίον. ἰδόντες δὲ τὸν ἀστέρα ἐχάρησαν χαρὰν με- 10
γάλην σφόδρα. καὶ ἐλθόντες εἰς τὴν οἰκίαν εἶδον τὸ παιδίον 1.1
μετὰ Μαρίας τῆς μητρὸς αὐτοῦ, καὶ πεσόντες προσεκύνη-

9 ου ην το παιδιον] του παιδιου D 𝔏 b c g¹ k q

reader to the next event in the narrative, often with no strict historical sequence. Mt. so uses it 61 times. It is virtually equivalent to the Heb. 'waw consecutive,' which does not occur in Aram. It is strikingly illustrated by the use of אידין and בידין in the Aram. portions of Dan. and Ezra. See the writer's note in *JThS.*, 1910, 127 f. ἀκριβοῦν (= ἐξετάζειν ἀκριβῶς, v. 8) recurs in the N.T. in v. 16 only ; cf. Philo, *De Mund. Op.* xxv. μετὰ πάσης ἐξετάσεως ἀκριβοῦντες.

8. καὶ πέμψας κτλ.] The partc. is synchronous with εἶπεν (see Blass, § 74. 3). Their inquiries were to be 'concerning' the Child, not His whereabouts but any information that they could report. ἐπάν, only Lk. xi. 22, 34.

9. καὶ ἰδού κτλ.] Since he told them to what town they were to go, the reappearance of the star, though an omen of success, was no longer needed for guidance. Patr. writers emphasize its miraculous nature ; cf. Ign. *Eph.* 19, Protev. Jac. 21. The *v.l.* in D seems intended to avoid the awkwardness of ἐπάνω οὗ. Protev. Jac. has ἐπάνω τοῦ σπηλαίου ἐπὶ τῆς κεφαλῆς τοῦ παιδίου : see next note.

11. καὶ ἐλθόντες κτλ.] Lk. speaks of an inn, with a stable attached. According to an early tradition the Birth was in a cave ; Just. *Tryph.* 78 'in a cave near the village,' Protev. Jac. *l.c.*, Orig. *c. Cels.* i. 51. It can hardly have arisen from a desire to add local colouring, for rock stables were not common. It may have been due to Is. xxxiii. 16. But if it was a fact, and if the narrative had an Aram. basis, εἰς τὴν οἰκίαν may have originated in ביתא, 'inside,' 'within' (cf. 2 Regn. v. 9, 3 Regn. vii. 13 [25]), in which case Mt. may have written in v. 9 ἐπάνω τοῦ σπηλαίου οὗ, which a scribe altered to ἐπ. οὗ, because 'cave' and 'house' seemed to be mutually exclusive. On the aor. προσεκύνησαν see Blass, § 57. 4. For θησαυροί for that in which they were carried cf. Deut. xxviii. 12. All the gifts were products of Arabia, but gold was found also in Babylonia and elsewhere. Herod. (iii. 107) wrongly states that frankincense, myrrh, and some other spices, were procurable only in Arabia. But many considered Persian frankincense the best (Strabo xvi. iv. 25), and it was also found in India and Syria (*Bibl. RWB.* 'Weihrauch'). Symbolic meanings of the gifts were widely adopted ; e.g. Juvencus, *Ev.* i. 249 f., 'Tus, aurum, murram, regique, hominique, deoque'; and cf. Caswall's hymn, *A. and M.* 76, based on Prudent. *Cathemerinon* xii. 70 ff.

σαν αὐτῷ, καὶ ἀνοίξαντες τοὺς θησαυροὺς αὐτῶν προσήνεγ-
12 καν αὐτῷ δῶρα, χρυσὸν καὶ λίβανον καὶ σμύρναν. καὶ χρηματισθέντες κατ᾽ ὄναρ μὴ ἀνακάμψαι πρὸς Ἡρῴδην δι᾽
13 ἄλλης ὁδοῦ ἀνεχώρησαν εἰς τὴν χώραν αὐτῶν. Ἀναχωρησάντων δὲ αὐτῶν ἰδοὺ ἄγγελος Κυρίου φαίνεται κατ᾽
ὄναρ τῷ Ἰωσὴφ λέγων Ἐγερθεὶς παράλαβε τὸ παιδίον
καὶ τὴν μητέρα αὐτοῦ καὶ φεῦγε εἰς Αἴγυπτον, καὶ ἴσθι
ἐκεῖ ἕως ἂν εἴπω σοι· μέλλει γὰρ Ἡρῴδης ζητεῖν τὸ παι-
14 δίον τοῦ ἀπολέσαι αὐτό. ὁ δὲ ἐγερθεὶς παρέλαβε τὸ
παιδίον καὶ τὴν μητέρα αὐτοῦ νυκτὸς καὶ ἀνεχώρησεν εἰς
15 Αἴγυπτον, καὶ ἦν ἐκεῖ ἕως τῆς τελευτῆς Ἡρῴδου· ἵνα

12. καὶ χρηματισθέντες κτλ.] Vg.
responso accepto. In class. Gk. the
verb denotes ' to do business, manage
public affairs,' hence 'to advise, or
consult, on public affairs.' In later
Gk. it gained the force of 'to give
an authoritative answer,' as by an
oracle : Jos. *Ant.* v. i. 14, Fay. Pap.
137 (1st cent. A.D.); or more generally
'to give a divine command or warning' : Lk. ii. 26, Jer. xxxii. 16 [xxv.
30], Job xl. 3 [8]. The pass. of
the person warned is rare : Lk. ii.
26 (D), Ac. x. 22, Heb. viii. 5, xi. 7,
Jos. *Ant.* III. viii. 8, Ox. Pap. 886
(3rd cent. A.D.). A further meaning
of the active occurs in Ac. xi. 26.
In Protev. Jac. xxi. 4, Chrys. *ad loc.*,
Orig. *c. Cels.* i. 60 the warning is
ascribed to an angel, as in Joseph's
case. ἀναχωρεῖν, virtually 'escape'(see
M.-M. *Vocab. s.v.*), is frequent in Mt.
(¹⁰ Mk. ¹ Jo. ¹ Ac. ²). For διά cf. vii. 13.

13-15. THE FLIGHT INTO EGYPT.
13. ἀναχωρησάντων δέ κτλ.] In
spite of the wonder of His birth, the
human Infant must be rescued not
by miracle but by flight ; see Orig.
c. Cels. i. 66. The angel does not
explain why Herod should seek to
kill the Child. ἐγερθείς is redundant,
as in i. 24.
14. ὁ δὲ ἐγερθείς κτλ.] The
nearest route to Egypt would be by

unfrequented paths to the coast plain
(cf. *Gosp. Ps.-Mat.* xvii. 2 'per viam
eremi'), and then by the high road ;
see Jos. *BJ.* IV. xi. 5. τελευτή is
not found elsewhere in the N.T. In
apocryphal traditions the stay in
Egypt lasted variously from one to
seven years (Resch, *Das Kindheits-
cvang.* p. 167).

15. ἵνα πληρωθῇ κτλ.] On the
formula see i. 22. The quotation is
from Hos. xi. 1. Heb. וּמִמִּצְרַיִם קָרָאתִי
לִבְנִי 'And from Egypt I called to
my son' (or perhaps ' called my son ').
LXX. καὶ ἐξ Αἰγύπτου μετεκάλεσα
(A -έσατο) τὰ τέκνα αὐτοῦ (= לְבָנָיו).
Targ. 'and from Egypt [*sc.* until now]
have I called them sons' ; and Sym.,
Theod., Pesh. interpret similarly.
But Aq. differs from Mt. only in
using ἀπό for ἐξ. Mt. employed a
translation which he found in a collection of *testimonia*. The origin of
the quotation was unknown to early
Christians who were acquainted only
with the LXX. A scribe actually adds
a note in א referring to the book of
Numbers, i.e. to Num. xxiv. 8. The
prophet referred only to an event in
Israel's history : Mt. finds in the wording a point of comparison with the
Messiah, in that God's 'Son' was in
each case 'called from Egypt.' The
narrative of the flight seems mainly

πληρωθῇ τὸ ῥηθὲν ὑπὸ Κυρίου διὰ τοῦ προφήτου λέγοντος
Ἐξ Αἰγύπτου ἐκάλεσα τὸν γίόν μογ.   Τότε Ἡρῴδης 16
ἰδὼν ὅτι ἐνεπαίχθη ὑπὸ τῶν μάγων ἐθυμώθη λίαν, καὶ ἀπο-
στείλας ἀνεῖλεν πάντας τοὺς παῖδας τοὺς ἐν Βηθλεὲμ καὶ
ἐν πᾶσι τοῖς ὁρίοις αὐτῆς ἀπὸ διετοῦς καὶ κατωτέρω, κατὰ
τὸν χρόνον ὃν ἠκρίβωσεν παρὰ τῶν μάγων.   Τότε ἐπληρώθη 17
τὸ ῥηθὲν διὰ Ἰερεμίου τοῦ προφήτου λέγοντος

intended to lead up to the quotation.

There was a Jewish tradition,
known to Origen (c. Cels. i. 38), that
Jesus, after growing up in obscurity,
served in Egypt as a labourer, and
practised miraculous arts, on the
strength of which, when he returned
to Palestine, he gave himself out to
be a God (cf. Just. Apol. i. 30). An
earlier form of it is traced to R.
Eliezer b. Hyrcanus (80–120 A.D.),
that the son of Stada (i.e. Jesus)
'brought with him magic arts out
of Egypt in an incision [i.e. by
tattooing the formulae] on his body'
(Shabb. 104 b). See Laible, J. Chr.
in the Talm., ed. Streane, 46 – 9.
This attempt to ascribe the Lord's
miracles to Satanic agency seems to
be independent of Mt., and may have
been known to him, so that one
object of his account may have been
to combat it.

16–19. THE MASSACRE OF THE
INFANTS.

16. τότε Ἡρῴδης κτλ.] For
ἐνεπαίχθη 'was deluded' (Vg. illusus
esset) cf. Jer. x. 15. Elsewhere in
the N.T. it is used only of the
'mocking' at the Lord's passion.
θυμοῦσθαι, very frequent in the LXX.,
occurs only here in the N.T. ἀπὸ
διετοῦς κτλ. : cf. 1 Ch. xxvii. 23,
ἀπὸ εἰκοσαετοῦς καὶ κάτω, Ex. xxx.
14, Num. i. 3. If the Magians
saw the star at the time of the
conception, they might arrive at

Jerusalem shortly after the birth of
Jesus, which is the impression produced by vv. 1 f. But Mt. may
have supposed that Herod would
think it safer to conclude that the
star appeared at the Child's birth.
But it would be in keeping with his
character to vent his anger upon as
many persons as possible. The
killing of 20 or 30 children—and
there would hardly be more in
Bethlehem — would be nothing to
one who massacred on a large scale
(see Jos. Ant. XVI. xi. 7, XVII. ii. 4,
vi. 4, 5). The mot of Augustus
that it was better to be Herod's sow
(ὗς) than his son (υἱός), is quoted
by Macrob. (Sat. II. iv. 11), who
erroneously speaks of the emperor
as having heard that Herod's son was
among the children whom he had
commanded to be killed in Syria
under two years old. The murder
of the children, but the failure to
kill Israel's Saviour, recalls the story
of Pharaoh, Ex. i. 15–ii. 10. See
Add. n.

17. τότε ἐπληρώθη κτλ.] This
formula (see on i. 22) instead of ἵνα
(ὅπως) πληρώθῃ, is employed only
here and in xxvii. 9, both referring
to Jeremiah the prophet of sorrow.
The attempts of Herod and of Judas
to compass the Lord's death fulfilled
O.T. language, but Mt. possibly
altered the expression because he
shrank from ascribing them to a
divine purpose.

18   Φωνὴ ἐν ῾Ραμὰ Ηκούσθη,
         κλαυθμὸς καὶ ὀδυρμὸς πολύς·
         ῾Ραχὴλ κλαίουσα τὰ τέκνα αὐτῆς,
         καὶ οὐκ ἤθελεν παρακληθῆναι ὅτι οὐκ εἰσίν.

19 Τελευτήσαντος δὲ τοῦ ῾Ηρῴδου ἰδοὺ ἄγγελος Κυρίου φαί-
20 νεται κατ᾿ ὄναρ τῷ ᾿Ιωσὴφ ἐν Αἰγύπτῳ λέγων ᾿Εγερθεὶς
παράλαβε τὸ παιδίον καὶ τὴν μητέρα αὐτοῦ καὶ πορεύου
εἰς γῆν ᾿Ισραήλ, τεθνήκασιν γὰρ οἱ ζητοῦντες τὴν ψυχὴν
21 τοῦ παιδίου. ὁ δὲ ἐγερθεὶς παρέλαβε τὸ παιδίον καὶ τὴν
22 μητέρα αὐτοῦ καὶ εἰσῆλθεν εἰς γῆν ᾿Ισραήλ. ἀκούσας δὲ
ὅτι ᾿Αρχέλαος βασιλεύει τῆς ᾿Ιουδαίας ἀντὶ τοῦ πατρὸς

22 της 1°] אB 1 13 33 124 127 ; pr επι uncc.caet [ut freq. in LXX] minn.pl

18. φωνὴ ἐν ῾Ραμά κτλ.] The
quotation is from Jer. xxxviii. [xxxi.]
15. It differs widely from the LXX. :
φωνὴ ἐν ῾Ραμὰ ἠκούσθη θρήνου
καὶ κλαυθμοῦ καὶ ὀδυρμοῦ· ῾Ραχὴλ
ἀποκλαιομένη οὐκ ἤθελεν παύσασθαι
ἐπὶ τοῖς υἱοῖς αὐτῆς, ὅτι οὐκ εἰσίν.
The chief variant in LXX. MSS. is
τῇ ὑψηλῇ (א* A) for ῾Ραμά ; cf. Jer.
(in Mat.) : ' vox in excelso audita est,
id est longe lateque dispersa.' Mt.,
or the collection of testimonia which
he employed, follows the Heb. fairly
closely : ὀδυρμὸς πολύς is a paraphrase of בְּכִי תַמְרוּרִים (' weepings of
bitterness '), the second καί has no
equivalent in the M.T., and the second
עַל בָּנֶיהָ is omitted.
    Jeremiah sees in imagination the
exiles being led out of Jerusalem,
and on their way passing Ramah (cf.
Jer. xl. 1), 5 m. north of the city, at
the northern border of Benjamin.
Near it was Rachel's tomb (1 Sam.
x. 2) ; and she is pictured as weeping
over her sons as they go by. But in
Gen. xxxv. 19, xlviii. 7 the tomb is
said to be near Ephrath, and the
words ' which is Bethlehem ' are
added. Either this was an incorrect
gloss, or there were two traditions as
to the site of the tomb. Mt., knowing this gloss or tradition, was able

to quote Jeremiah's words to illustrate
his narrative. Since the 4th cent.
A.D. a traditional site of the tomb
has been shewn (HDB. iv. 193 a).

19-23. THE SETTLEMENT AT
NAZARETH.

19-21. τελευτήσαντος δέ κτλ.]
These verses are a repetition, mutatis
mutandis, of vv. 13, 14 a. γῇ ᾿Ισραήλ
is a general expression for Palestine
as contrasted with a foreign country ;
cf. Ab. Zara i. 8. Since Herod alone
sought the Child's life, the plur.
τεθνήκασιν οἱ ζητοῦντες does not
refer to the Sanhedrin (Jer.) ; the
language has been coloured by the
story of Moses' life (Ex. iv. 19). See
Add. n. θνήσκειν does not occur
elsewhere in Mt. For ζητεῖν τὴν
ψυχήν (= בִּקֵּשׁ אֶת נֶפֶשׁ) cf. Rom. xi.
3 (LXX.).

22. ἀκούσας δέ κτλ.] On reaching Palestinian territory, Joseph
heard that Archelaus had succeeded
his father. Herod bequeathed to
him Judaea, Samaria, and Idumaea,
giving him the title of ' king ' ;
Antipas received Galilee and Peraea
with the title of tetrarch, and Philip,
with the same title, Gaulonitis,
Trachonitis, and Paneas (Jos. Ant.
XVII. viii. 1, BJ. I. xxxiii. 7).

αὐτοῦ Ἡρῴδου ἐφοβήθη ἐκεῖ ἀπελθεῖν· χρηματισθεὶς δὲ
κατ᾽ ὄναρ ἀνεχώρησεν εἰς τὰ μέρη τῆς Γαλιλαίας, καὶ 23
ἐλθὼν κατῴκησεν εἰς πόλιν λεγομένην Ναζαρέτ, ὅπως πλη-

Augustus soon afterwards refused Archelaus the title of 'king,' till he should have won it by good behaviour (*Ant.* XVII. xi. 4); but at the moment the situation could be correctly represented by βασιλεύει. (On the pres. tense see Blass, § 56. 9, and on the gen. τῆς Ἰουδαίας *id.* § 36. 8.) Archelaus might well be feared merely as being his father's son. He soon shewed his character by the ruthless massacre that he committed directly after his accession (*Ant.* XVII. ix. 3; cf. *BJ.* II. vi. 2). The placing of the narrative at the time of Herod's death raises difficulties in connexion with the chronology, and must perhaps be rejected as inaccurate. See Add. n. after xiv. 12. On ἐκεῖ for ἐκεῖσε (cf. xvii. 20) see Blass, § 25. 2. χρηματισθεὶς δέ κτλ. is modelled on *v.* 12.

23. καὶ ἐλθών κτλ.] ἐλθών is redundant, and κατῴκησεν, implying motion, correctly takes εἰς, as in iv. 13; cf. Thuc. ii. 102, κατοικισθεὶς εἰς τοὺς περὶ Οἰνιάδας τόπους. Nazareth, the modern *en Nāṣira*, had no importance for Israel's life apart from the Gospel history (cf. Jo. i. 46), and is not mentioned in the O.T., Josephus, or the Talmud. It lay on the slope of a hill (Lk. iv. 29), commanding a wide view, in a luxuriant district, a day's journey from the Mediterranean, and from Capharnaum and Tiberias, and three from Jerusalem (G. A. Smith, *HG.* p. 432 ff.). Its scenery must have done much to give the Child Jesus, as He grew, the love of Nature which He afterwards shewed in His teaching. And its seclusion kept it free from the narrow ecclesiasticism and other influences of the capital.

The name is always spelt Ναζαρέθ in Mt. and Lk. (except Mt. iv. 13, Lk. iv. 16 Ναζαρά), Ναζαρέτ in Mk. i. 9, Jo. i. 45 f. (Tisch. *Prol.* p. 120); —ράθ and —ράτ occur in some MSS. (WH. *App.* Notes on Orthogr. 160), τὰ Νάζαρα in Orig. (*in Joh.*), Africanus (*ap.* Eus. *H.E.* I. vii. 14), and Eus. (*Dem.* VII. ii. 46, 50). Its derivation is unknown; the *Onomasticon* gives various guesses connected with the roots נצר and נזר; Dalm. (*Gramm.* p. 119) suggests the Aram. נָצְרָה, נָצְרַת (= Heb. נֹצֶרֶת), 'a watch-tower,' in reference to the position of the city on a hill. But the transliteration of צ by the Gk. Z is very rare and doubtful; see Burkitt, *Syr. Forms of N.T. Proper Names,* 28 ff.

ὅπως πληρωθῇ κτλ.] On the formula see i. 22. Since the words Ναζωραῖος κληθήσεται do not occur in the O.T. as we have it, the plur. προφητῶν is usually explained as referring to the general teaching which may be gathered from Scripture (so Jer.). For Ναζωραῖος (xxvi. 71, Jo.[3] Ac.[7]) Mk.[4] Lk.[2] have the latinized form Ναζαρηνός, from Ναζαρά (cf. Μαγδαληνή from Μάγδαλα); ട always Naz^a̦rāyā' for both forms. ὁ Ναζωραῖος may be equivalent to ὁ ἀπὸ Ναζαρέθ (xxi. 11, Jo. i. 45, Ac. x. 38), as Mt. clearly intends here. But some derive both forms from the name of a district rather than a town, connecting them with Nesar, *i.e.* Gennesaret, 'the vale *or* garden of Nesar'—the termination perhaps shewing a confusion with Nazaret. Mt.'s reference to the O.T. is sometimes improbably explained as giving a play on *nēzer* 'a shoot' in Is. xi. 1 (where the Targ. refers it to the Messiah); cf. *ẓemaḥ* 'a shoot'

ρωθῇ τὸ ῥηθὲν διὰ τῶν προφητῶν ὅτι Ναζωραῖος κληθήσεται.

in the 'Messianic' passages Is. iv. 2, Jer. xxiii. 5, xxxiii. 15; cf. Zech. iii. 8. So most recently Abbott, *The Fourfold Gospel*, Append. I. Possibly, as Allen suggests, ὅτι N. κληθήσεται is a gloss, and the sentence, ending at προφητῶν (cf. xxvi. 56), referred only to the settlement of Jesus in Galilee; the O.T. reference might thus be to the passage of Isaiah which Mt. quotes later in iv. 14 ff. If the copyist thought that Ναζωραῖος was derived

from נָזִיר, 'Nazirite,' his gloss may refer to Jud. xiii. 7, 'a Nazirite of God shall the child be,' which might be represented by 'shall be called' in an Aram. paraphrase (see on Mt. v. 9); προφητῶν might then be a reference to the second division of the Heb. canon, in which *Judges* is one of the 'Former Prophets.' Resch (*Texte u. Unt.*, 1893, 4 and 1896, 7) boldly reads τοῦ προφητοῦ, and conjectures a reference to the apocr. Book of Jeremiah (see on xxvii. 9).

Additional Notes on Chap. ii.

The narrative of the Magians is rich in spiritual significance. It affords a type of the early history of Christianity: the Son of God was revealed 'to the Jew first, and also to the Gentile'—to the mother and Joseph first, and also to the foreign astrologers. This, as Zahn says, is heard again throughout the gospel, viii. 10–12, xii. 18–21, xv. 24–28, xxiv. 14, xxviii. 19. He was revealed to the humble and ignorant first, and then to the honourable and learned; cf. 1 Cor. i. 26. To the poor first, and then to the rich; to the West first, and then to the East. It also has other lessons: He was revealed to the astrologers by a method suited to their habits and understanding. And their object in coming to Jesus was not personal advantage, but solely to give Him homage.

The origin of the narratives is disputed. 1. The story of the star is thought to be derived from Num. xxiv. 17, where the Targ.[onk] has 'a king shall arise out of Jacob.' Patristic references to Baalam's 'star' are frequent: *e.g.* Just. *Dial.* 106, Iren. II. ix. 3, Orig. *Cels.* i. 59 f., Eus. *Dem.* IX. i. 1–10, Jer. *in Mat.* Hence the tradition that the Magians were descendants of Balaam (Theoph. *al.*). But the star which pointed out the Messiah's birthplace could hardly have been derived from a star which would be the Messiah Himself. If it had been, Mt. would doubtless have quoted the passage. And such passages as Is. xlix. 7, lx. 3–6, 10, Ps. lxviii. 29, lxxii. 10 f., which speak of the homage of the Gentiles, may have occurred to the evangelist, but could not form the basis of his detailed narrative. Nestle and Holtzmann refer to Num. xxiii. 7, ἐξ ὀρέων ἀπ' ἀνατολῶν, which is not very convincing, though a late legend makes the Magians observe the star from a mountain; see *ZNW.*, 1907, 73.

2. Others would find for the story a pagan source. Astronomical portents were often thought to herald the birth of heroes and kings; see Suet. *Aug.* 94. The visit of the Magians is held to be a transformation of

the account in Dio Cass. lxiii. 7, Pliny, *Nat. Hist.* xxx. 6, Suet. *Nero* xiii.,
of the visit of Tiridates the Parthian king with his Magians to Nero
in A.D. 66. See Conybeare in *Guardian,* Apr. 29, 1903, on the apocryphal
Syriac fragment published by Wright in *JSL.* Apr. Oct. 1866. It is only
necessary to read the passages from Dio Cassius and Pliny (quoted by
Soltau, *The Birth of J. Chr.*) to see what an effort of imagination is
required to suppose that so complete a transformation took place in
Palestinian circles. Usener (*Enc. Bibl.* art. 'Nativity') goes so far as
to illustrate the flight into Egypt by the flight of the Olympian gods
to that country when attacked by the giant Tryphon! Cheyne, Pfleiderer
and others think, as in the case of the Virgin Birth, that the story was
derived from pre-Christian international myths. But this is beset by
the same difficulties as those noticed on p. 11 f. No theory is probable
which assigns a pagan origin to narratives which are Jewish to the
core. 3. A much more probable explanation is that of Zahn (*Comm.
Mat.*) who sees throughout chs. i., ii. an analogy between the history of
Israel and that of Christ. The genealogy is a sketch of the history,
leading to its culmination. Christ, like Israel, was God's Son (Dt. xxxii.
18). And Mt.'s quotations from the O.T. all shew the same purpose.
Loisy (*Les Év. Synopt.* i. 370) takes a similar line. The narratives, according to this theory, are a Christian midrash. The same is suggested in
another form by Box (*Interpreter,* Jan. 1906 and *ZNW.,* 1905), *i.e.* that they
are a midrash on the story of Moses. In *Ex. Rabb.* it is related that
Pharaoh's astrologers perceived that the mother of Israel's future Redeemer
was with child, and that he was destined to suffer punishment through water.
Not knowing whether he was to be an Israelite or an Egyptian, Pharaoh
commanded all children to be drowned. Though not itself earlier than the
8th cent. A.D., this embodies older material. It is alluded to in B. Sanh.
101 b, and in its main features was known to Josephus (*Ant.* II. ix. 2).
On this basis Box holds that Mt.'s story was written to shew 'that the
prophecy of Dt. xviii. 15 was fulfilled in the birth of Jesus, in whom the
narrator saw a second and a greater Moses.' And it was further influenced
by the desire to suggest the homage of the heathen world in accordance with
O.T. prophecy. It is not in itself impossible that Magians came to
Jerusalem because of an astronomical phenomenon. That is perhaps a
historical fact. But the impression of the chapter as a whole is that of
a narrative which reflects the story both of Moses and of Israel, and was
written in Jewish-Christian circles in which the use of 'midrashim'
was common, and their purpose well understood.

If this is the true explanation, the wide divergences between the
narratives of Mt. and Lk. do not call for harmonization. 1. Mt. shews
no knowledge that the Lord's mother and Joseph were already living at
Nazareth at the time of the Conception (see Lk. i. 26, ii. 4); he speaks
of the settlement there as something new, decided upon by Joseph in
accordance with divine warning after the return from Egypt. His chief
purpose seems to be to shew that the settlement at Nazareth, as well as
the return from Egypt, fulfilled O.T. prophecy. 2. Lk. shews no knowledge of the flight into Egypt; ii. 39 distinctly implies that the return to
Nazareth followed immediately upon the rite of purification in Jerusalem;

III. 1   ΕΝ ΔΕ ΤΑΙΣ ΗΜΕΡΑΙΣ ἐκείναις παραγίνεται Ἰωάνης ὁ
2 βαπτιστὴς κηρύσσων ἐν τῇ ἐρήμῳ τῆς Ἰουδαίας λέγων Μετα-

1 δε] אBC 1 33 al. pl 𝔏 vet.nonn.vg. 𝔖 cur.pesh.pal^B; om DE al 𝔏 b ff¹
g¹ k q 𝔖 sin.pal ^{AC}   2 λεγων] אB 𝔏 g² q me sah aeth; pr και CDE al minn 𝔏
vet.pler.vg 𝔖 omn

and that the Holy Family returned thither for no other reason than that
Nazareth was their home. The complete independence, however, of their
narratives favours the truth of their common tradition that Jesus was
born in Bethlehem.

iii.-iv. 6. PREPARATION FOR THE
MINISTRY.

iii. 1–12. (Mk. i. 1–8, Lk. iii. 1–
17; cf. Jo. i. 6–31.) THE MINISTRY
OF JOHN THE BAPTIST.

1. ἐν δὲ ταῖς κτλ.] The reader
is assumed by Mt. to know the period
to which the events belong; cf. Mk.
i. 9, viii. 1, etc., Exod. ii. 11, Jud.
xviii. 1, 4 Regn. xx. 1. Mt. similarly
refers to more confined periods with
καιρός (xi. 25, xii. 1, xiv. 1) and ὥρα
(xviii. 1, xxvi. 55), without a connecting δέ, which should perhaps be
omitted here. Lk. gives the date as
the 15th year of Tiberius, and names
contemporary rulers; see Add. n.
after xiv. 12.

παραγίνεται κτλ.] The historic
present (Mk. ἐγένετο, Lk. ἦλθεν) is a
feature of chs. iii., iv.; cf. vv. 13, 15,
iv. 5, 8, 10, 11. Mt. usually substitutes an aorist, except in the case
of λέγει, -ουσιν (Allen, pp. xx., lx.,
Oxf. Stud. 333 f.).

ὁ βαπτιστής] cf. Jos. Ant. XVIII.
v. 2, Ἰωάνου τοῦ ἐπικαλουμένου
βαπτιστοῦ. Mk. has ὁ βαπτίζων,
and in vi. 14. He is introduced
as a person well known to the readers,
appearing on the stage of history as
suddenly as his counterpart Elijah.
Lk. has prepared for his appearance
by an account of his birth, but, in
the O.T. manner, gives his father's
name; cf. the first verse of Is., Jer.,

Hos., Joel, Jonah, Zeph., Zach. 'The
wilderness of Judaea' (cf. Ps. lxii.
[lxiii.] title (א)) is the region which
slopes down from the highlands of
Judaea to the Dead Sea, but could
include the whole of the Jordan
valley (the mod. Ghôr) on both sides
of the river, so far as it belonged to
Judaea at the time. For the limits
of Judaea see Jos. BJ. III. iii. 5, G. A.
Smith, Hist. Geogr. ch. xiii. Mk.
has simply ἐν τῇ ἐρήμῳ, an echo of
Is. xl. 3, which Mt. afterwards quotes;
John could not strictly be said to
baptize in the wilderness, where there
was no water. Lk. more accurately
distinguishes ἐν τῇ ἐρήμῳ, where the
word of God came to John, from
πᾶσαν τὴν περίχωρον τοῦ Ἰορδάνου,
to which he came preaching; cf. also
Lk. iv. 1. His activity must have
extended beyond Judaea into Peraea,
since he came into conflict with
Herod Antipas, to whom the latter
belonged, and Lk.'s expression perhaps implies this; see on xiv. 3.
This would agree with Jo. x. 40,
where it is placed on the E. of
Jordan; two unknown spots are
named: Bethany (i. 28, v.l. Betha-
bara) and Aenon near Salim (iii. 23).
ἔρημος, like מִדְבָּר, is not necessarily
a sandy waste, but a tract suitable
for pasturage.

2. μετανοεῖτε κτλ.] The preaching of the Baptist, as of the Lord
(iv. 17), is summed up, by Mt. alone,

νοεῖτε, ἤγγικεν γὰρ ἡ βασιλεία τῶν οὐρανῶν.   Οὗτος γάρ 3
ἐστιν ὁ ῥηθεὶς διὰ Ἠσαίου τοῦ προφήτου λέγοντος

ΦωΝΗ ΒοῶΝτος ἐΝ τῇ ἐρΉμῳ
'ΕτοιμΆ́ςατε τΗΝ ὁδὸΝ ΚγρίΟγ,
εγθείας ποιεῖτε τὰς τρίβογς αγτΟγ.

Αὐτὸς δὲ ὁ Ἰωάνης εἶχεν τὸ ἔνδυμα αὐτοῦ ἀπὸ τριχῶν 4

in a sentence. μετανοεῖν (frequent
in the LXX. for נִחַם) is not merely
penitential sorrow (Vulg. *poenitentiam
agere*) but a change of *nous*. 'In
graeco sono poenitentiae nomen non
ex delicti confessione, sed ex animi
demutatione compositum est' (Tert.
c. Marc. ii. 24). That was now the
one necessity, in view of the near
advent of the Kingdom. Jewish
teachers were divided as to whether
repentance was necessary for the
coming of the Kingdom (Volz, *Jüd.
Esch.* 112 f., Lightfoot, *Hor. Heb. ad
loc.*), but according to Mt. the Baptist
has no doubt about it, not as a means
of bringing the Kingdom, but as a
preparation for it. He is imbued
with the desire for moral righteousness which marked the Heb. prophets.
But his thoughts are not only ethical
but eschatological. It is true that in
Mk. and Lk. he is said only to proclaim
'a repentance-baptism for remission
of sins,' and Mt. may have avoided
εἰς ἄφεσιν ἁμαρτίας in view of the
Lord's submission to the rite (see
on *v.* 14). But whether or not the
expression 'Kingdom of Heaven,'
like the account of his preaching
which is absent from Mk., was derived
from Q (so Streeter, *JThS.*, July
1913), John takes from the prophets,
in Lk. (*vv.* 7–9) as well as in Mt.,
not only their ethical, but also their
eschatological teaching, which was
the starting-point of the current
expectations found in the apocalypses.
And his baptism had an eschatological
meaning, as a preparation by which

men could 'flee from the wrath to
come.' Echoes of his words are
sometimes heard from the Lord's
lips; cf. *v.* 7 with xii. 34, xxiii. 33;
v. 8 (κάρπος) with vii. 16–20; *v.* 9
('sons of Abraham') with Jo. viii.
37–41; *v.* 10 with vii. 19; *v.* 12
with xiii. 30. But while both proclaimed the near advent of the Kingdom, with the one it was a warning,
with the other chiefly an εὐαγγέλιον
(see on iv. 17).

3. οὗτος γάρ κτλ.] He preached
repentance, *for* that was necessary in
one who was to fulfil the prophet's
words. The masc. ὁ ῥηθείς is unique
in the N.T., but the formula is
analogous to that in i. 22. The
quotation is from Is. xl. 3. (In Mk.,
whose Introduction is still a disputed
problem, it is preceded by words
from Mal. iii. 1, used in another
connexion in Mt. xi. 10 = Lk. vii. 27.
Mk. places together the only O.T.
passages in which פַּנֵּה דֶּרֶךְ occurs;
see *Camb. Bibl. Essays* 179.) αὐτοῦ
is substituted for τοῦ θεοῦ ἡμῶν,
since Κυρίου is made to refer not
to God the Father but to Christ;
otherwise it agrees with the LXX.,
which loses the parallelism of the
M.T. in which 'in the wilderness' is
connected with 'prepare,' and 'in
the desert' is added after 'make
straight.' The prophet refers to
the return of Israel from exile,
accompanied by their God. The
evangelists use the words but not
the sense.

4. αὐτὸς δέ κτλ.] 'The afore-

καμήλου καὶ ζώνην δερματίνην περὶ τὴν ὀσφὺν αὐτοῦ, ἡ δὲ
5 τροφὴ ἦν αὐτοῦ ἀκρίδες καὶ μέλι ἄγριον. Τότε ἐξεπορεύετο
πρὸς αὐτὸν Ἱεροσόλυμα καὶ πᾶσα ἡ Ἰουδαία καὶ πᾶσα ἡ
6 περίχωρος τοῦ Ἰορδάνου, καὶ ἐβαπτίζοντο ἐν τῷ Ἰορδάνῃ
ποταμῷ ὑπ᾽ αὐτοῦ ἐξομολογούμενοι τὰς ἁμαρτίας αὐτῶν.
7 Ἰδὼν δὲ πολλοὺς τῶν Φαρισαίων καὶ Σαδδουκαίων ἐρχο-

mentioned John'; cf. xii. 45 (D),
αὐτοῦ τοῦ ἀνθρώπου, Mk. v. 16 (D),
vi. 17, 18 (D), 22 ; see Moulton i.
91, who gives examples from papyri
of the 1st and 2nd cent. A.D.
Wellhausen (*Einl. in d. drei ersten
Evang.* 27) refers it to the Aram.
idiom. Mt. transposes Mk.'s order,
in describing the person of the
Baptist before his success. The
description (absent from Lk.) of his
person, ascetic and prophetic, is thus
made to carry on the thought of the
prophecy 'a voice of one crying in
the desert.' τὸ ἔνδυμα αὐτοῦ : the
garment was probably not made of
camel's skin (as D in Mk. i. 6 δέρρην
καμήλου, and Chrys.), but of rough
sackcloth woven from camel's hair.
The conjecture τρυχῶν ('tatters,'
'rags') is unnecessary. The description is partly taken from that of
Elijah's clothing (2 Kings i. 8). ἡ
στολὴ αὐτοῦ τοὺς Ἰουδαίους μᾶλλον
ἐφείλκετο τὸν μέγαν Ἠλίαν ἐν αὐτῷ
βλέποντας (Chrys.). Mt.'s ἡ δὲ τροφὴ
αὐτοῦ avoids Mk.'s loose construction
καὶ ἔσθων. For further notes on
the passage see Swete. The gloss
which he quotes from the Ebion.
gospel may have been suggested by
the similarity of ἀκρίς to ἐγκρίς (a
'cake').

5, 6. τότε ἐξεπορεύετο κτλ.] The
city and districts are personified, as
in Mk., πᾶσα ἡ περίχ. τ. Ἰορδ. being
added : Lk. mentions this alone, and
says that John came to the region,
not the region to John (see *Oxf. Stud.*
p. 7). On Ἱεροσόλυμα see ii. 1. Mt.
and Lk. must have derived πᾶσα ἡ

περίχ. τ. Ἰορδ. either from a non-
Marcan source or from a recension
of Mk. different from that which
we possess. For further notes see
Swete. To his references for ἐξομ.
τὰς ἁμαρτίας may be added Jos. *Ant.*
VIII. iv. 6 ; cf. *BJ.* v. x. 5.

7–10. (Lk. iii. 7–8.) A specimen
of the Baptist's preaching, not found
in Mk., probably derived from Q.
Lk. (*vv.* 10–14) extends the account,
from a different recension of Q,
or from another source, relating the
response of the poor and despised to
the call ; or Mt. may have omitted
it in order to confine himself to the
thought of judgment.

7. ἰδὼν δὲ πολλούς κτλ.] Only
in xvi. 1 do Pharisees and Sadducees,
as here, take common action. Here
a strong attraction, there a strong
repulsion, made them for the moment forget their differences. On
the Sadducees see Add. n. after xxii.
33. Lk., who sometimes minimizes
anti-Pharisaic controversy (see *Oxf.
Stud.* p. 70), says only that the
Baptist spoke τοῖς ἐκπορευομένοις
ὄχλοις who have not been previously
mentioned. But it is less likely that
he addressed the people indiscriminately as γεννήματα ἐχιδνῶν than
that he singled out their religious
leaders. The presence of the people
would add force to the rebuke. And
Lk. perhaps implies in vii. 30 that
his source mentioned Pharisees in
connexion with John's baptism.
Whether αὐτοῦ is added after
βάπτισμα or not, ἐρχομένους κτλ.
need not mean that they came (as

μένους ἐπὶ τὸ βάπτισμα εἶπεν αὐτοῖς Γεννήματα ἐχιδνῶν,
τίς ὑπέδειξεν ὑμῖν φυγεῖν ἀπὸ τῆς μελλούσης ὀργῆς; ποιή- 8
σατε οὖν καρπὸν ἄξιον τῆς μετανοίας· καὶ μὴ δόξητε λέγειν 9

7 βαπτισμα] ℵ*B sah ;   add αυτου ℵᵇCDE al minn 𝔏 omn 𝔖 sin.cur.hcl. ; 'to
be baptized' 𝔖 pesh.pal

𝔖 pesh) for the purpose of being
baptized (contrast v. 13); they came
with the populace, drawn by the
general excitement, to the scene of
the rite. Other passages (xxi. 25,
32, Lk. vii. 30) shew that they
refused to repent, while the masses
counted John as a prophet. εἶπεν
describes a single rebuke (i.e. to the
Pharisees and Sadducees); ἔλεγεν
(Lk.) a summary of what he was
in the habit of saying to the people.
γεννήματα ἐχιδνῶν κτλ.] Vg.
progenies viperarum (so xii. 34 ; but
xxiii. 33, Lk. iii. 7, genimina vip.).
Only Mt. (ll.c.) relates that Jesus used
the same expression; see on v. 2.
It is probably only an equivalent
for ἐχιδναί: cf. ἔκγονα ἀσπίδων Is.
xi. 8, xiv. 29, xxx. 6, in each case
a single Heb. word (ZNW., 1913,
267 f.). See class. parallels in Aesch.
Cho. 249, Soph. Ant. 531, Trach.
1099. Though the question τίς
ὑπέδειξεν κτλ. is ironical, the Baptist
does not despair of their repentance,
as v. 8 shews. ἡ μέλλουσα ὀργή
(cf. 1 Thes. i. 10) is a reference to
the day of judgment upon sinners
which the prophets had foretold (Is.
xiii. 9, Zeph. i. 15, ii. 2 f., Mal.
iii. 2, iv. 1, 5); but John's hearers,
like their forefathers, thought that
the divine wrath could be destined
only for the heathen; or if (as
several apocalyptic writers had recognized) sinners in Israel would
also be included, they at least were
among the pious few who would be
saved. The words perhaps suggest
the fleeing of snakes from a field
when the harvest begins. On the

various Jewish conceptions of the
coming wrath see Volz, Jüd. Esch.
268–282.

8. ποιήσατε οὖν κτλ.] By re-
sorting to me you have apparently
taken the first step in the way of
escape; go on then (οὖν) and make
it good. This fruit can be produced
instantaneously (aor. ποιήσατε); ἀρκεῖ
θελῆσαι, καὶ τὸ δένδρον εὐθέως
ἐβλάστησεν (Chrys.). ποιεῖν καρπόν
occurs in Arist. Plant. i. 4, ii. 10 ;
but καρπός used metaphorically as
the result of character is purely
biblical : xxi. 43, Is. x. 12, Jer. xvii.
10 etc., Jam. iii. 18, Gal. v. 22,
Phil. i. 11 ; and the illustrations in
Mt. vii. 16–20 are virtually metaphors. A possible rendering is
'worthy fruit (consisting) of repentance'; 'dignum fructum poenitentiae'
(Hil.) : 'worthi fruytis of penaunce'
(Wycl. and the Commination Service);
but the fruit is not the change of
heart, but the acts which result from
it. Cf. Ac. xxvi. 20, where both are
spoken of. 'Repentance and good
works are a shield against punishment' (Aboth iv. 15 ; cf. 24, with
Taylor's notes).

9. καὶ μὴ δόξητε κτλ.] 'Do not
imagine [that you have a right] to
say.' Cf. Aphr. 'be not boastful and
saying,' Vg. ne velitis. The expression is difficult; 𝔖 sin.cur omit
δόξητε. Lk. has μὴ ἄρξησθε : if this
stood in his recension of Q, it may
represent the Aram. תשׁרון (Dalman,
Words, 27 f., Moulton i. 15), and
δόξητε may be a stylistic alteration ;
but since ἄρχεσθαι is frequent in Lk.,
it may have been his alteration of

ἐν ἑαυτοῖς Πατέρα ἔχομεν τὸν Ἀβραάμ, λέγω γὰρ ὑμῖν
ὅτι δύναται ὁ θεὸς ἐκ τῶν λίθων τούτων ἐγεῖραι τέκνα τῷ
10 Ἀβραάμ. ἤδη δὲ ἡ ἀξίνη πρὸς τὴν ῥίζαν τῶν δένδρων
κεῖται· πᾶν οὖν δένδρον μὴ ποιοῦν καρπὸν καλὸν ἐκκόπτεται
11 καὶ εἰς πῦρ βάλλεται. ἐγὼ μὲν ὑμᾶς βαπτίζω ἐν ὕδατι εἰς

the difficult word. On μή with the
aor. subj. see i. 20. To be a son of
Abraham (cf. Jo. viii. 33, 53, Jam. ii.
21, 2 Cor. xi. 22) was thought to be
a pledge of safety : the 'merits of the
Fathers,' and of Abraham in particular, were so great as to be available
for all Israelites. See Schechter,
Some Aspects of Rabb. Theology, ch. xii.,
Edersheim, *LT.*² i. 271.

ἐκ τῶν λίθων κτλ.] He pointed
to the stones as he spoke, and perhaps
played upon the words אבניא 'stones'
and בניא 'sons' (see xxi. 15 note).
ἐγεῖραι (cf. ἀναστήσει σπέρμα, xxii.
24) probably represents the Aram. קים
(Heb. הקים); it could be used of
erecting a structure made of stones
(Jo. ii. 19 f., 1 Esd. v. 43, Sir. xlix.
13), so that Abraham's children
would form a 'house,' and of producing and establishing men before the
eyes of the world (xi. 11, xxiv. 11,
24, Ac. xiii. 22; cf. Rom. ix. 17;
frequent in LXX.). It is unnecessary
to see a reference to the Gentiles;
God could, if He wished, produce
Jews out of stones (so Chrys.), *i.e.* true
sons of Abraham, who could enter
into the privileges of the coming
Kingdom. Mythological parallels
are suggested by Jeremias, *Bab. im
N.T.* 80, Köhler, *ZNW.* ix. 77 ff.

10. ἤδη δέ κτλ.] But the doom
is imminent; your repentance, therefore, must be immediate. Lk. has
ἤδη δὲ καί, his favourite expression
of emphasis. For the metaphor cf.
Is. x. 34, Jer. xlvi. [xxii.] 22. The
prophetic presents ἐκκόπτεται and
βάλλεται continue to mark the
imminence of the doom; for the

thought of each cf. Lk. xiii. 7, 9,
Jo. xv. 6. Fire as a metaphor for the
final punishment was frequent in
Jewish Apocalypse; see *s.v.* 'Gehenna'
in *HDB.* and in Charles, *Eschat.*
(Index), and 'Feuer' in Volz, *Jüd. Esch.*
(Index). In the Gospels it is found
mostly in Mt.: *v.* 12 (Lk. iii. 9, 17),
v. 22, vii. 19, xiii. 40, 42, 50, xviii.
8 f. (Mk. ix. 43, 48 ff.), xxv. 41. To
be 'cast into the fire' is a favourite
expression in *Enoch.* An echo of the
Baptist's words is heard on the lips
of Jesus in vii. 19; see on *v.* 2 above.

11, 12. (Mk. i. 7 f., Lk. iii. 15–17,
Jo. i. 26 f.; cf. Ac. xiii. 25.) A
second feature in the Baptist's teaching: the heralding of a Coming One.
Lk. relates that John's reason for so
preaching was the growth of an idea
among the people that he might be
the Messiah, a natural symptom of
the popular excitement. Mt. and Lk.
are dependent both upon Mk. and Q:
οὗ τὸ πτύον κτλ. has no parallel in
Mk., and the subject to which οὗ
refers must have been mentioned in
Q; the order of the clauses in Mt.,
Lk. is also due to Q.

11. ἐγὼ μὲν ὑμᾶς κτλ.] In Mt.
the words 'I am baptizing you,' etc.,
are attached unsuitably to the rebuke
to the religious leaders: in Mk.
(καὶ ἐκήρυσσεν ἔλεγεν) and Lk.
(ἀπεκρίνατο λέγων πᾶσιν ὁ Ἰωάνης)
they are given separately as addressed
to the people. Mk.'s parallel clause
(without μέν) follows the reference to
the sandals; his aor. ἐβάπτισα, if it
is not merely an Aramaism, makes
the Baptist look back upon his work
as a completed whole. Parallelism

μετάνοιαν· ὁ δὲ ὀπίσω μου ἐρχόμενος ἰσχυρότερός μου
ἐστίν, οὗ οὐκ εἰμὶ ἱκανὸς τὰ ὑποδήματα βαστάσαι· αὐτὸς
ὑμᾶς βαπτίσει ἐν πνεύματι ἁγίῳ καὶ πυρί· οὗ τὸ πτύον 12
ἐν τῇ χειρὶ αὐτοῦ, καὶ διακαθαριεῖ τὴν ἅλωνα αὐτοῦ, καὶ

seems to require an expression contrasted with εἰς μετάνοιαν. The latter
may be a gloss, added in view of
vv. 2, 8.

ὁ δὲ ὀπίσω μου κτλ.] Mk.
ἔρχεται ὁ ἰσχ. μου ὀπίσω μου. Lk.
omits ὀπίσω μου; but see Ac. xiii.
25. The vagueness of the description
of 'the Coming One' reflects the condition of Messianic expectations at
the time (see Add. n.), but John was
certain that He would be mightier
than himself in His person and origin,
in the instruments at His command,
and the effects that they would produce. For ἱκανός cf. viii. 8 (Lk.);
the synonym ἄξιος is used in Jo.,
Ac. ll.c. Mk.: κύψας λῦσαι τὸν
ἱμάντα τῶν ὑποδημάτων αὐτοῦ,
followed by Lk., but omitting the
redundant κύψας. If Mt. is not a
mere shortening of Mk., βαστάσαι
and λῦσαι may both represent the
Aram. שׁרא, which denotes either
'carry' or 'carry away.' βαστάζειν
with the latter meaning occurs in
Fay. Pap. 122, and BU. 46, 157,
388; and cf. Jos. xii. 6, xx. 15. On
the two servile acts, possibly suggested by the baptismal rite, see
Swete, and Kidd. 22 b (quoted by
Lightfoot, Hor. Heb. ad loc.).

αὐτὸς ὑμᾶς βαπτίσει κτλ.] The
effusion of the Spirit as a mark of the
Messianic age is foretold in Is. xliv.
3, Ez. xxxvi. 26 f., xxxvii. 9 f., 14,
xxxix. 29, Joel ii. 28 f., but baptism
in the Spirit is a new expression : life
in the coming age is in the sphere of
the Spirit, and must be entered, so
to speak, by immersion. But Spirit
and Fire are coupled with one preposition as a double baptism. Mk.,

who did not possess the eschatological
warning in vv. 7–10, lacks also καὶ
πυρί here. For Jewish parallels to
'baptism by fire' see Abrahams,
Notes on Syn. Gospp. 3, Edersheim,
LT.² i. 273 n., and for a metaphorical
use of 'baptize' cf. Mk. x. 38 f., Lk.
xii. 50. Fire will purify that which
can stand it (Mal. iii. 2 f.; cf. Is.
iv. 4), but will burn away all that is
unworthy (Mal. iv. 1, Mk. ix. 49,
1 Cor. iii. 13–15); see v. 10 n. A
reference to the fiery tongues at Pentecost (Cyr. Jerus., al.) is impossible.
On ἐν πνεύματι ἁγ. see Blass, § 46. 7.

12. οὗ τὸ πτύον κτλ.] πτύον is
the pala (Cato, R.R. vi. 45, 151,
Tert. Praescr. iii.), the wooden
winnowing shovel, with which the
corn, threshed by oxen, was thrown
up into the wind ; Vg. ventilabrum.
It is already 'in his hand,' ready to
be used immediately. The threshing-
floor, i.e. its contents, is cleansed by
removing the chaff from the corn ;
cf. Alciphr. Ep. iii. 26, ἄρτι μοι τὴν
ἅλω διακαθήραντι καὶ τὸ πτύον
ἀποτιθεμένῳ κτλ. To the Baptist
the floor must have meant Palestine,
the scene of the final judgment. The
corn is His (αὐτοῦ Mt. ; not Lk.),
but the chaff is not. In xiii. 41,
xxiv. 31 the gathering of the good and
the burning of the bad are assigned to
the angels. ἄχυρον (more frequently
plural) was a common article of
fuel. It is a general term, covering
chaff, straw, and stubble ; cf. the
striking parallel in Ber. R. 83 (quoted
by Edersheim, LT.² i. 273 n.) ; and
see Nidda 31 a 'like a man who
winnows in the threshing-floor, and
takes the food, but lets the refuse

συνάξει τὸν σῖτον αὐτοῦ εἰς τὴν ἀποθήκην, τὸ δὲ ἄχυρον
13 κατακαύσει πυρὶ ἀσβέστῳ.   Τότε παραγίνεται ὁ Ἰησοῦς
ἀπὸ τῆς Γαλιλαίας ἐπὶ τὸν Ἰορδάνην πρὸς τὸν Ἰωάνην
14 τοῦ βαπτισθῆναι ὑπ᾽ αὐτοῦ.   ὁ δὲ διεκώλυεν αὐτὸν λέγων

remain.' For the word cf. Ex. v. 7, 10 ff., Is. xvii. 13, Jer. xxiii. 28, Dan. ii. 35 (LXX.). For its use in papyri see M.-M. *Vocab. s.v.* οὗ τ. πτ. αὐτοῦ imitates the Semitic use of the relative : cf. x. 11 (D), xviii. 20 (D), Mk. i. 7, vii. 25 *al.* πῦρ ἄσβεστον is fire so fierce that nothing can quench it before it has done its work ; cf. Eus. *H.E.* vi. 41 : two martyrs ἀσβέστῳ πυρὶ κατεκάησαν. The expression, however, implies nothing as to the duration of the punishment, to which Jewish thought assigned no limit ; cf. xviii. 8, where αἰώνιον is substituted for Mk.'s ἄσβεστον. The adj., frequent in Homer, was revived in later Gk. ; it occurs as a variant in Job xx. 26 (A). An echo of the Baptist's words is ascribed in xiii. 30 to Jesus (see *v.* 2 note), the thought of which is akin to Is. lxvi. 24 (= Mk. ix. 48), 4 Regn. xxii. 17, Is. i. 31, Jer. vii. 20. Lk. here adds (*v.* 18) what appears to be an editorial note, pointing out that only specimens of the Baptist's exhortations and good tidings have been given ; and he completes his account of him by referring to his imprisonment (*vv.* 19 f.) ; see on iv. 12 below.

13–17. (Mk. i. 9–11, Lk. iii. 21 f.; cf. Jo. i. 32–34.) THE BAPTISM OF JESUS.

Mt. is influenced by Mk. ; but the Baptism must have been related also in Q, from which Mt. and Lk. drew their accounts of the Temptation, since it is there presupposed. Perhaps it stood in Q in a form similar to Lk.'s, in which the Baptism is

mentioned incidentally, the stress being laid on the descent of the Spirit and the Voice. This would account for Lk.'s omission to state that Jesus came from Galilee ; he introduces Him quite suddenly into the narrative, for the first time since the visit to the Temple in childhood.

13. τότε παραγίνεται κτλ.] Mt.'s characteristic τότε brings the incident loosely into relation with the Baptist's work ; it means little more than 'the next event to be related is—' (see on ii. 7). Neither Mk. nor Lk. is more precise. On the historic present (Mk. ἦλθεν) see *v.* 1. Mk. has ἀπὸ Ναζαρὲτ τῆς Γαλ., mentioning Nazareth for the first time, which Mt. omits, having already related the settlement there (ii. 23). τοῦ βαπτισθῆναι for ἐβαπτίσθη (Mk.) emphasizes the purpose in the act ; cf. πειρασθῆναι (iv. 1) for καὶ ἦν . . πειραζόμενος (Mk.).

14. ὁ δὲ διεκώλυεν κτλ.] For the conative imperf., 'he tried to prevent him,' cf. Lk. i. 59 (ἐκάλουν), Ac. vii. 26 (συνήλλασσεν). The meaning is not 'It were more fitting for Thee to administer the rite to me,' but 'I have need of Thy baptism with Spirit and fire, and comest Thou to my water-baptism ?' This and the following verse, which imply that the Baptist knew Jesus to be the Messiah, are confined to Mt. The question would naturally arise how it was that He who was born 'of the Holy Spirit' (i. 20) could need baptism from the preacher of repentance (see *v.* 2 note). The evangelist saw a profound significance in the event.

Ἐγὼ χρείαν ἔχω ὑπὸ σοῦ βαπτισθῆναι, καὶ σὺ ἔρχῃ πρός
με; ἀποκριθεὶς δὲ ὁ Ἰησοῦς εἶπεν αὐτῷ Ἄφες ἄρτι, οὕτω 15
γὰρ πρέπον ἐστὶν ἡμῖν πληρῶσαι πᾶσαν δικαιοσύνην. τότε
ἀφίησιν αὐτόν. βαπτισθεὶς δὲ ὁ Ἰησοῦς εὐθὺς ἀνέβη ἀπὸ 16
τοῦ ὕδατος· καὶ ἰδοὺ ἠνεῴχθησαν οἱ οὐρανοί, καὶ εἶδεν

16 ανεωχθησαν] אB Ϸ sin.cur sah ; add αυτω אᵇCDE al minn 𝕷 omn Ϸ
pesh.hcl.pal

15. ἄφες ἄρτι κτλ.] Permit [me]
just now ; the time is coming when
it shall be known that my baptism
is the greater. Chrys. compares Jo.
xiii. 7. By ἡμῖν the Lord associates
Himself with the Jewish people, for
whom repentance was necessary ; and
submission to baptism, the symbol of
it, was completely to bring about
(πληρῶσαι) the condition result-
ing from the performance of πᾶν
δικαίωμα : cf. Ps. cxviii. [cxix.] 172,
Prov. viii. 20 b (A). The Lord's
action was an instance of the
principle ὤφειλεν κατὰ πάντα τοῖς
ἀδελφοῖς ὁμοιωθῆναι (Heb. ii. 17).
μετὰ τῶν δούλων ὁ δεσπότης, μετὰ
τῶν ὑπευθύνων ὁ κριτὴς ἔρχεται
βαπτισθησόμενος (Chrys.). And see
the fine passage in Ambr. (on Lk. iv.
6). The ring of spiritual truth can
be contrasted with the false note
struck in the Naz. Gosp. (Jer. adv.
Pelag. iii. 2) : 'ecce mater Domini et
fratres eius dicebant ei, Ioannes
baptista baptizat in remissionem
peccatorum ; eamus et baptizemur ab
eo. Dixit autem eis, Quid peccavi
ut vadam et baptizer ab eo? nisi
forte hoc ipsum quod dixi ignorantia
est.' Cf. Praedic. Pauli (Ps.-Cyp.
De rebapt. xvii.) : 'ad accipiendum
Joannis baptisma paene invitum a
matre sua compulsum.' Ign. (Smyrn.
i.) says that Jesus was baptized by
John ἵνα πληρώθῃ πᾶσα δικαιοσύνη
ὑπ' αὐτοῦ, the earliest certain allusion
to this gospel. ἄρτι is characteristic
of Mt. (⁷ Mk.⁰, Lk.⁰). On the historic
present ἀφίησιν see v. 1.

16. βαπτισθεὶς δέ κτλ.] ἀπὸ τοῦ
ὕδατος, if the preposition can be
pressed, describes the return of Jesus
up the bank of the river (cf. Lk. iv.
1), Mk.'s ἐκ pictures His emergence
out of the water. Lk. says that the
Lord's baptism took place 'when all
the people had been baptized' (see
Plummer), and that the vision
occurred 'while He was praying.'
Theoph., al. refer to the Manichean
statement that Jesus left His body
in the Jordan, and received another
body κατὰ φαντασίαν.
καὶ ἰδού κτλ.] Mt.'s account is
based upon Mk.'s, but appears to be
influenced by the O.T.: ἠνεῴχθησαν
(for Mk.'s vivid σχιζομένους) recalls
Ez. i. 1. The addition of αὐτῷ (see
Appar.) only emphasizes the fact that
the vision was seen by Jesus ; Mk. :
εἶδεν σχιζ. τ. οὐρανούς. 'Aperiuntur
autem coeli non reseratione ele-
mentorum sed spiritualibus oculis'
(Jer.). εἶδεν πνεῦμα θεοῦ does not
suggest that anyone but Himself saw
it. John probably went into the
water with Jesus (cf. Ac. viii. 38);
but he can hardly be the subject of
ἀναβαίνων and εἶδεν in Mk. (so
Spitta). Mt. prefers πνεῦμα θεοῦ
(cf. xii. 28), an O.T. expression,
to τὸ πν. τὸ ἅγιον (Lk.), which
would be the more usual in the
mouth of a Jew of the period.
But both are probably nearer to the
original Aram. than τὸ πνεῦμα (Mk.),
since רוח alone could mean only
'demon' or 'wind' (Dalman, Words,
203).

πνεῦμα θεοῦ καταβαῖνον ὡσεὶ περιστερὰν ἐρχόμενον ἐπ'
17 αὐτόν· καὶ ἰδοὺ φωνὴ ἐκ τῶν οὐρανῶν λέγουσα Οὗτός
ἐστιν ὁ υἱός μου ὁ ἀγαπητός, ἐν ᾧ εὐδόκησα.

17 ουτος εστιν] συ ει D 𝕷 a 𝔖 sin.cur.pal Iren^oxyr Aug

καταβαῖνον κτλ.] The two participles describe two stages in the
descent. ὡσεὶ περιστεράν is not 'as
a dove comes down' (*i.e.* with a gentle
descent), but, as Lk. interprets it,
σωματικῷ εἴδει ὡς περιστ. Cf. Lk.
x. 18, Ac. x. 11, where, as here, the
phenomenon is a subjective experience, a θεωρία νοητή (see Orig. fragm.
on Jo. i. 32, Brooke ii. 236 ff.). ἐπί
(Mt., Lk.) for εἰς (Mk.) may have
been due to Is. xlii. 1 (ἔδωκα τὸ
πνεῦμά μου ἐπ' αὐτόν), the first
part of which Mt. cites in the following verse. The Ebion. Gosp. (*ap.*
Epiph. *Haer.* xxx. 3) has ἐν εἴδει περιστερᾶς κατελθούσης καὶ εἰσελθούσης
εἰς αὐτόν. In Lk. D 𝕷 pler. vg.
also read εἰς. If this means 'into,'
the subjective nature of the spiritual
vision is further emphasized. Spitta
strangely argues from it that the
mention of the dove was a later
insertion. Jer. seizes the significance
of the event : 'mysterium Trinitatis
in baptismate demonstratur.'

17. καὶ ἰδοὺ φωνή κτλ.] A
Voice was heard at the Transfiguration (xvii. 5), by S. Peter (Ac. x. 13,
15), and S. Paul (Ac. ix. 4) ; cf. Jo.
xii. 28. The later Talmudic *bath ḳôl*
(*e.g. Berak.* 3 a) was analogous, but
the conceptions attaching to it were
sometimes so frivolous and even
profane, that the more intelligent
rabbis condemned it as a super-
stition (Edersheim, *LT.*² i. 285 f.). ἐκ
τ. οὐρανῶν (so Mk. ; Lk. ἐξ οὐρανοῦ)
meant to a Jew 'from the place
where God dwells' ; here it is
virtually, though not actually, a
periphrasis for God ; cf. Dan. iv. 28

[Engl. 31] (Dalman, *Words*, 218).
See Mt. v. 12, 34.
οὗτός ἐστιν κτλ.] Mk., Lk. σὺ εἶ
. . . ἐν σοί. In Mt., in the ordinary
text, the words are assimilated to
those at the Transfiguration, where
all the synn. have οὗτος (xvii. 5, Mk.
ix. 7, Lk. ix. 35). σὺ εἶ ὁ υἱός μου
is taken from Ps. ii. 7 (υἱός μου εἶ
σύ LXX.), and the remainder from Is.
xlii. 1 (which the Targ. interprets of
the Messiah). The juxtaposition of
the two quotations was rendered
easier by the fact that παῖς in Is.
(Heb. עֶבֶד) could be understood as
meaning 'child' (Dalman, *Words*,
276–80). The force of the second
quotation is heightened by the fact
that the next words in Isaiah are 'I
have put my Spirit upon him.'
The titles, therefore, 'My Son'—'the
Beloved,' in the two quotations are
distinct. (𝔖 sin.cur Ephr. separate
them by 'and' ; see Burkitt, *Ev. da
Meph.* ii. 116.) Sonship and Messiahship are not necessarily identical conceptions (see Dalman, *Words*, 268–73):
the former was taught to the disciples
(xi. 27) before the latter (xvi. 16 f.),
and Jesus Himself perhaps arrived at
the certainty of the former before He
realized that it involved the latter.
The divergent traditions as to the
second clause (see Add. note) suggest
the possibility that the words of the
Voice were originally limited to 'Thou
art My Son'(Bacon,*AJTh.*, 1905, 451–
73). To say, however (as Bacon does),
that Messiahship could not have been
present to the Lord's thoughts at this
time, is to go beyond our knowledge.
ὁ ἀγαπητός κτλ.] Heb. בְּחִירִי, LXX.

ὁ ἐκλεκτός μου. Cf. Lk. ix. 35, μου ὁ ἐκλελεγμένος. 'The Beloved' and 'the Elect' were interchangeable terms at the time when Mt. and Lk. were written. The former sometimes stands in the LXX. for יָחִיד (*i.e.* μονογενής): Gen. xxii. 2, 12, 16, Jud. xi. 34 (A), Am. viii. 10, Jer. vi. 26. υἱὸν ἀγαπητόν is used of the only son of the owner of the vineyard (Mk. xii. 6, Lk. xx. 13). ὁ ἠγαπημένος is a title of the Messiah in Eph. i. 6, *Ep. Barn.* iii. 6, iv. 3, 8,

Ign. *Smyrn.* (salutation), *Act. Thecl.* 1, Clem. *Paed.* I. vi. 25, and ἀγαπητός is frequent in *Asc. Is.* (see Charles on i. 4). See further J. A. Robinson, *Ephes.* 229–33, and Swete, *St. Mark ad loc.* The aor. εὐδόκησα (so xvii. 5) represents the Heb. perf. רָצְתָה נַפְשִׁי; LXX. προσεδέξατο αὐτὸν ἡ ψυχή μου, Mt. xii. 18 ὃν εὐδόκησεν ἡ ψ. μου, 2 Pet. i. 17 εἰς ὃν ἐγὼ εὐδόκησα. The passage was thus current in the Church in various forms.

Additional Notes on Chap. iii.

1. John's Baptism.

John's choice of baptism as the rite with which he so closely identified himself that he was known as 'the Baptist' was doubtless due partly to the fact that purificatory rites were already known to the Jews. In accordance with the Law, Levitical pollutions of various kinds must be washed away with water (cf. Lev. xi., xiii., xiv., xv., Num. xix.). And if a Jew was frequently compelled to bathe for the sake of ceremonial purity, a Gentile, on becoming a proselyte, would be in even greater need of it, because he had lived his entire life in a state of pollution. 'Judaeus quotidie lavat quia quotidie inquinatur' (Tert. *de Bapt.* xv.); 'omnibus licet membris lavet quotidie Israel, nunquam tamen mundus est' (*de Orat.* xiv.). It may therefore be taken for granted that the Gentile would be obliged to undergo the purifying bath (טְבִילָה). That it involved complete immersion is shewn by Abrahams against Rogers (see *JThS.* Apr., July, 1911, April, 1912). It has often been pointed out that we possess no written evidence before the Christian era that Gentiles were so bathed. Josephus and Philo do not mention it, but perhaps because they never had occasion to do so. But a reference prior to A.D. 70 occurs in *Tosephta Pesach.* vii. 13 (Zuckermandel 167) = *Jer. Pesach.* viii., cited by Abrahams, *Notes on the Syn. Gospp.* no. 3: R. Eleazar b. Jacob, who was well known as 'one of the most trustworthy reporters of Temple events and rites' says 'Soldiers were guards of the gates in Jerusalem; they were baptized and ate their Paschal lambs in the evening.' The Mishna treats the baptism of proselytes as an established and authoritative custom. In *Pesach.* viii. 8 (= *Eduyoth* v. 2) the question is discussed whether a proselyte who had been circumcised on the 14th of Nisan could, on the same day, wash, and in the evening partake of the Passover, or whether his Gentile pollution was such that he was unclean for seven days, 'like one who comes from a grave,' according to Num. xix. Two writings, both of the 2nd cent., speak of baptism, without mention of circumcision: Arrian (*Diss. Epict.* ii. 9): 'when we see someone acting in contradiction to his beliefs, we are wont to say "He is not a Jew, but is only pretending to be one." But when he adopts the manner of life required of one who has been baptized and chosen [into religious fellowship], then he is both called a Jew and is one in reality.' In the *Sib. Oracl.* (iv. 164), probably of Jewish origin, it is insisted that proselytes must be baptized as an outward token of their conversion. To these may be added the Eth. version of Mt. xxiii. 15 : 'ye compass sea and land to baptize one proselyte.' The Talmud lays down three requirements for proselytes—circumcision, baptism, and a sacrifice, the last two being incumbent upon women (see *Kerith.* 81 a, *Jeb.* 46 a). And this rule must date from a time before the destruction of the Temple, because after it sacrifices necessarily ceased. (See Schürer, *HJP.* II. ii. 319 ff., Edersheim, *LT.*² i. 745 ff., Lightfoot, *Hor. Heb.* on Mt. iii. 6.) Further, it is probable that the Lord's words in Mk. x. 38 would have been unintelligible if baptism had not been a recognized symbol of the entry into a new manner of life. And S. Paul (1 Cor. x. 2) appears to be referring to current Jewish usage. On the other hand John's baptism was not a form of admission into any religious body. It does not appear that those whom he baptized became thereby his disciples. The 'disciples of John' (Mk. ii. 18, vi. 29), like the 'disciples of the Pharisees,' were those who reverenced and personally accompanied him. There is no evidence that their number was large. The 'disciples' of Ac. xix. 1 were probably adherents of the Christian Church, who had received a 'baptism of repentance,' possibly, though not necessarily, by John himself, but not baptism into the name of Jesus. John's baptism, nevertheless, was novel and unique, in that it did not (as Josephus implies, *Ant.* XVIII. v. 2) cleanse from ceremonial impurity, but was an outward and visible sign of a change of heart, and was therefore 'from heaven,' not 'from men' (xxi. 25); hence it could be applied even to those who scrupulously avoided ceremonial impurity. In Rabb. theology a permanent change of heart was not considered possible (see Abrahams, *op. cit.*). But while it meant more than Jewish, it meant less than Christian, baptism, since it was neither a 'means' nor a 'pledge' of 'an inward and spiritual grace.' 'Baptismum Johannis coeptum non cessavit, sed additum est ei quod deerit' (Ps.-Aug. *Quaest.*).

2. *The Coming One.*

It is clear from xi. 10, 14 that the Lord declared John to be the true fulfilment of the Jewish expectation based upon the prophecy in Mal. iv. that Elijah should prepare the way of the Lord (cf. Sir. xlviii. 10); and in xvii. 12 He taught the disciples the same truth. The description of John's person (iii. 4) recalls that of the great prophet. But he never himself claimed to be Elijah (cf. Jo. i. 21), and the people never thought of him as such, though some of them are said to have wondered whether he were the Messiah (Lk. iii. 15). 'He that cometh after me' (Mt. iii. 11) must be compared with 'Art thou he that cometh?' (xi. 3). This is usually held to denote the Messiah, though it is agreed that 'the Coming One' was not a recognized title. But in the conversation with the people after the departure of the Baptist's messengers, Jesus said (xi. 14) he [John] is Elijah who is destined to come (ὁ μέλλων ἔρχεσθαι). The Baptist's question might, therefore, mean 'Art thou Elijah who is to come?' It was a popular expectation that Elijah's advent would usher in the Last Day (cf. xvi. 14, xvii. 10 f., xxvii. 47); and nothing could add greater emphasis to John's prediction of the imminence of the divine kingdom than to declare that Elijah would come immediately after him. This is a leading feature in Schweitzer's *Von Reimarus zu Wrede* (Engl. *The Quest of the Historical Jesus*). But, though attractive, it presents difficulties. The Baptist's descriptions of the future action of him who should come after him ('He shall baptize you etc.,' *vv.* 11 b, 12) did not correspond with the popular expectations of Elijah. They are coloured by Mal. iii. 2 'he is like a refiner's fire,' and Joel ii. 28 [Heb. iii. 1] 'I will pour out my Spirit upon all flesh.' The former passage refers to the preceding words : 'The Lord whom ye seek shall suddenly come to His temple, and [*or* even] the messenger [angel] of the covenant etc.' The 'messenger,' it is true, is the same as that in *v.* 1 : 'Behold I send my messenger, and he shall prepare the way before me,' a passage which is applied (Mk. i. 2, Lk. i. 76, Mt. xi. 10 = Lk. xii. 27) to the Baptist, whom Jesus identified with Elijah. But in Mal. Elijah is not mentioned till iv. 5 [Heb. iii. 23], and the 'messenger' is to be understood as a manifestation of Yahweh Himself, or an undefined heavenly person sent by Him. Joel describes the outpouring of the spirit in the future ideal age ; but of Elijah, who was to precede the dawn of that age, it could not be said 'he shall baptize you with holy spirit and fire,' nor could the land be described as '*his* threshing-floor,' nor the judicial actions mentioned in *v.* 12 be assigned to him. It is safer, therefore, to refrain from deciding the exact nature of the Baptist's expectations. In all probability they were not exact. The Apocalyptic conceptions of a Messiah were various and vague ; much confusion existed as to the Messiah himself and his fore-runners ; there were numerous Messianic figures, some of them forerunners of Yahweh Himself (Volz, *Jüd. Esch.* 196 f.). In Jo. vi. 14 (*e.g.*) Jesus is thought to be ὁ προφήτης ὁ ἐρχόμενος εἰς τὸν κόσμον, in i. 25 ὁ προφήτης is distinguished from Elijah, and in vii. 40 f. from the Messiah ; and cf. Mt. xvi. 14. It is only possible to say that John looked forward to an undefined, but divinely sent, Personality. See Bacon, *Expos.*, July 1904, p. 1–18.

3. *The Baptism of Jesus.*

It is difficult to escape from H. Holtzmann's contention (*Die Synopt.* 198) that a public proclamation of the Messiahship of Jesus at the outset of His career makes the whole course of His ministry unintelligible. Chrys. does not satisfactorily answer his own question καὶ πῶς οὐκ ἐπίστευσαν τούτων γινομένων ; Had a crowd of people seen the open heavens and the dove, and heard the voice, the report must have spread rapidly over the whole district. But xvi. 13–17, 20, and many other indications, shew that the Lord's Messiahship was an unknown truth. If He and the Baptist were alone (see Plummer, *St. Luke,* 98) the difficulty is not lessened : John would have told his disciples, and the report would have spread almost as quickly. Moreover, if John did not receive such a sign from heaven, it is easier to understand how he could ask the question recorded in Mt. xi. 3. There is nothing in Mk. or Lk. to suggest that the vision or the voice was vouchsafed to anyone but Jesus ; and the same is true of Mt. (apart from *vv.* 14 f. ; see note) if, as is quite possible, σὺ εἶ was the original reading (see Appar. and Burkitt, *Ev. da Meph.* ii. 267), and οὗτός ἐστιν merely a scribal assimilation to xvii. 5.   The fourth evangelist alone, in an idealized narrative, ascribes to the Baptist, as the result of the vision, the conviction that Jesus was 'he that baptizeth with the holy Spirit' (Jo. i. 33), 'the Son of God' (*v.* 34), 'the Lamb of God' (*vv.* 29, 36).

The vision and the voice, then, were a real subjective experience. The sight of the opened heavens was not unnatural to one in a state of spiritual exaltation (cf. Ez. i. 1, Ac. vii. 56).   The voice was an expression —as in the case of many other mystics—of the deepest convictions of His soul.   He was doubtless, as Lk. states, praying ; and it would be natural, at such a moment, to pray for an outpouring of the divine Spirit ; and some train of thought, *e.g.* a meditation on Ps. xci. 4—a psalm which soon afterwards rose to His mind (iv. 6)—or on the Spirit of God brooding, fluttering, over the waters, might well lead to the visualizing of the Spirit's action in the form of a descending dove.

As regards the meaning of the event in relation to His life work, it is arbitrary to understand 'Thou art My Son' to mean 'Thou art My Son *from this moment.*'   The Virgin Birth and the Baptism are not, as Holtzmann thinks, mutually exclusive.   The voice did not make Him either Son or Messiah ; but it came to Him as a final and convincing mystical expression of (probably) many previous ponderings, and was the impelling force which sent Him out to His public ministry.   From Him alone must the disciples have derived the account of the wonderful moment.

The variations of the narrative in early literature are interesting.   They are collected into a continuous passage in the Ebionite Gospel (Epiph. *Haer.* xxx. 13): 'And a voice came (ἐγένετο) from heaven saying "Thou art the beloved Son (ὁ υἱὸς ὁ ἀγαπητός), in thee (ἐν σοί) I am well pleased " ; and again "I have to-day begotten thee."   And straightway there shone round the place a great light.   Seeing which (it says) John saith to Him "Who art thou Lord ? "   And again a voice from heaven unto Him, "This is my Son the Beloved, in whom (ἐφ' ὅν) I am well pleased."   And then (it says) John fell before Him and said, "I pray thee Lord, do thou baptize me."   But He forbade him saying "Suffer it (ἄφες), because thus it is fitting that all things should be fulfilled."'   The last two sentences 'And then John fell before Him, etc.' are peculiar to the Eb. Gospel, but the other two variations—(*a*) the light and (*b*) the words 'I have to-day begotten thee,'— had a wide currency. (See Taylor in *JThS.*, July 1906, 560 ff.)

(*a*) Justin, *Tryph.* 88 : 'when Jesus had gone down to (ἐπί) the water, then (καί) a fire was kindled in Jordan.'   Justin, however, implies that this was not written by the Apostles.   𝔏 a g¹ : 'et cum baptizaretur (+ Jesus g¹) lumen ingens circumfulsit (magnum fulgebat g¹) de aqua, ita ut timerent omnes qui advenerunt (congregati erant g¹).'   Six other references are given by Resch (*Agrapha*², p. 224); see also Burkitt (*Ev. da Meph.* ii. 114 f.).   Resch suggests that the light was due to assimilation to the story of the Transfiguration.   Perhaps other traditions also contributed.   John's question 'Who art thou Lord ?', and the light, recall S. Paul's conversion (Ac. ix. 3 ff.).

Τότε ὁ 'Ιησοῦς ἀνήχθη εἰς τὴν ἔρημον ὑπὸ τοῦ πνεύ- 1 IV.

(b) The reading, in Lc. iii. 22, of D 𝕷 a b c ff² 1 υἱός μου εἶ σύ, ἐγὼ σήμερον γεγέννηκά σε is found in a large number of patristic passages (Resch 223). The words of Ps. ii. 7 lent themselves to the view of the Ebionites that the man Jesus became the Messiah at the Baptism. Epiph. (xxx. 14) says of them βούλονται τὸν μὲν 'Ιησοῦν ὄντως εἶναι ἄνθρωπον . . . Χριστὸν δὲ αὐτῷ γεγεννῆσθαι τὸν ἐν εἴδει περιστερᾶς καταβεβηκότα. The Nazarene Gospel (according to Jer. on Is. xi. 2) goes further : 'factum est autem cum ascendisset dominus de aqua, descendit fons omnis spiritus sancti et requievit super eum et dixit illi, Fili mi, in omnibus prophetis exspectabam te ut venires et requiescerem in te. Tu es enim requies mea ; tu es filius meus primogenitus, qui regnas in sempiternum.' This forms a link between Ebionism and Jewish Gnosticism.

---

iv. 1–11. (Mt. i. 12 f., Lk. iv. 1– 13.) THE TEMPTATION.

The influence of Mk. is probably to be seen in vv. 1, 2, 11, but the narrative as a whole is from Q. It would not be out of place in a collection of sayings, since the substance of it, as that of the Baptism, must have been derived from the lips of Jesus Himself ; cf. Gosp. Heb., where He relates the event in the first person. Some see in Mk. either a fragmentary reminiscence, or a deliberate abbreviation, of Q (Oxf. Stud. 168) ; but 'in the primitive Christian world even Q had no monopoly of such traditions' (Moffatt, LNT.² 221).

The three temptations arise from the Lord's consciousness of His divine Sonship. Lk. follows a geographical sequence, the only change of locality, from the desert to Jerusalem, occurring last. Mt. arranges a psychological climax : the first temptation is to doubt the truth of the revelation just received, the second to test it, and the third to snatch prematurely at the Messiahship which it involves. In actual fact, however, it is probable that the Lord was frequently assailed in all three ways during His period of trial (see on v. 2), and perhaps throughout His life. Studies of the spiritual significance of the temptations will be found in Du Bose, The Gospel in the Gospels, 35–41, Bp. H. J. C. Knight, The Temptations of our Lord, King, The Ethics of Jesus, 91 ff.

1. τότε ὁ 'Ιησοῦς κτλ.] Mk. καὶ εὐθύς. Lk., with no note of time, πλήρης πνεύματος ἁγίου ὑπέστρεψεν ἀπὸ τοῦ 'Ιορδάνου, which Spitta (Synopt. Grundschrift) explains as the beginning of a return to Galilee, which was prevented because Jesus was first led into the wilderness ; after the temptations He returned (Lk. iv. 14) as He had intended. ἀνήχθη (Mk. ἐκβάλλει) εἰς τ. ἔρ. describes a single act, Lk. ἤγετο ἐν τῇ ἐρήμῳ a wandering about during the 40 days. ἀναγαγών in Lk. v. 5 is different ; see on v. 8 below. The impelling force was the divine Spirit ('Holy Spirit,' 𝕾 sin.cur) which had just descended upon Him. πειρασθῆναι (for πειραζόμενος Mk., Lk.) points out a divine purpose in the event, not the wish of Jesus to court temptation, as Jer. 'voluntate pugnandi.' τοῦ διαβόλου (so Lk.) : Mk. τ. Σατανᾶ. Apart from this narrative διάβολος recurs in the synn. in xiii. 39, xxv. 41, Lk. viii.

2 ματος, πειρασθῆναι ὑπὸ τοῦ διαβόλου. καὶ νηστεύσας
ἡμέρας τεσσεράκοντα καὶ νύκτας τεσσεράκοντα ὕστερον ἐπεί-
3 νασεν. Καὶ προσελθὼν ὁ πειράζων εἶπεν αὐτῷ Εἰ υἱὸς εἶ

12 only. In the LXX. it stands for
הַשָּׂטָן. Mt. has [ὁ] Σατανᾶς in sayings of Jesus : v. 10, xii. 26, xvi. 23.

2. καὶ νηστεύσας κτλ.] The
temptations were probably continuous from the beginning of the
period (as suggested by Mk. i. 13
ἦν . . . πειραζόμενος), the intensity
of spiritual struggle causing oblivion
to the claims of the body ; cf. Clem.
Hom. xi. 35, xix. 2, Orig. in Luc.
29. If so, they were not successive
isolated events, but instances of the
struggles which frequently assailed
the Lord during the period. Mt.
places the three at the end of the
fast ; this is probably from Q, since
Lk. does the same ; but the latter
nevertheless adopts Mk.'s frequenta-
tive πειραζόμενος. It is not impossible that the 'forty days (and
forty nights' Mt. only) are an
assimilation to the stories of Moses
(Ex. xxiv. 18) and Elijah (1 Kings
xix. 8), and to the 40 years in the
desert where the Israelites hungered
(Dt. viii. 2 f.) and were fed with
'angels' food' (Ps. lxxviii. 24 f., Wisd.
xvi. 20) ; see Ambr. in Luc. iv. 15.
ὕστερον in the synn. is confined to
Mt.(7), except Lk. xx. 32 (= Mt.),
'Mk.' xvi. 14 ; Mk. prefers ἔσχατον.
Both occur adverbially in the LXX.
(= אַחַר). On the form ἐπείνασεν see
Blass, § 16. 1. Mt., Lk. omit Mk.'s
καὶ ἦν μετὰ τῶν θηρίων : cf. Test.
Naph. viii. ὁ διάβολος φεύξεται
ἀφ' ὑμῶν, καὶ τὰ θήρια φοβη-
θήσονται ὑμᾶς, καὶ οἱ ἄγγελοι
ἀνθέξονται ὑμᾶς.

3. καὶ προσελθὼν κτλ.] προσ-
έρχεσθαι is a characteristic word,
occurring more than 50 times in
Mt. For ὁ πειράζων (Lk. ὁ

διάβολος) cf. 1 Thes. iii. 5, and the
Logion in Clem. Hom. iii. 55 : τοῖς
δὲ οἰομένοις ὅτι ὁ θεὸς πειράζει,
ὡς αἱ γραφαὶ λέγουσιν, ἔφη· ὁ
πονηρός ἐστιν ὁ πειράζων. The
participle describes him as belonging
to a class ; cf. xiv. 21, xvii. 24,
Mk. i. 4 (ὁ βαπτίζων). The personal
spirit of evil, and other details of the
narrative, belong to 'the traditional
machinery of Judaism' of which the
Lord (from whom the account must
have been derived) makes use ; see
Sanday, Life of Chr. in Rec. Research,
27 ff.

εἰ υἱὸς εἶ κτλ.] Hunger was the
instrument of the temptation, but
the mere satisfaction of hunger could
not have been wrong, nor, in the
estimation of the evangelists, the performance of a miracle for His own
advantage, for that He is recorded
to have done elsewhere (xvii. 27,
Lk. iv. 30). The temptation lay in
the 'If,' i.e. in doubt as to the truth
of His Sonship, the realization of
which He had just experienced ;
He might test the truth of it, by
ascertaining whether He had the
power to work a miracle. The precise nature of the miracle was of
secondary importance, and was
suggested by the stones which lay
around. By treating it as the
primary point, patristic and other
writers have obscured the true
significance. υἱός as a predicate is
without the article (Blass, § 46. 4).
For ἵνα γένωνται (cf. xx. 21)
equivalent to an inf. see id. § 69. 2,
3. Lk. has τῷ λίθῳ τούτῳ : this is
more graphic, but may be due to
the sing. ἄρτῳ in the next verse ;
Mt. however is fond of plurals. If

τοῦ θεοῦ, εἰπὸν ἵνα οἱ λίθοι οὗτοι ἄρτοι γένωνται. ὁ δὲ 4
ἀποκριθεὶς εἶπεν Γέγραπται Οὐκ ἐπ᾽ ἄρτῳ μόνῳ ζήϲεται ὁ
ἄνθρωπος, ἀλλ᾽ ἐπὶ παντὶ ῥήματι ἐκπορεγομένῳ Διὰ ϲτόματοϲ
θεογ. Τότε παραλαμβάνει αὐτὸν ὁ διάβολος εἰς τὴν ἁγίαν 5
πόλιν, καὶ ἔστησεν αὐτὸν ἐπὶ τὸ πτερύγιον τοῦ ἱεροῦ, καὶ 6

God could change stones into sons
of Abraham (iii. 9), the Son of God
could change them into loaves.

4. γέγραπται κτλ.] The reply,
as in vv. 7, 10, was an utterance
addressed to His own heart. The
quotation is from Dt. viii. 3, agreeing
with the LXX. (AF, Luc.; B τῷ ἐκπορ.).
In Lk. it extends only to ὁ ἄνθρωπος,
but that was enough to suggest the
whole passage, the remainder of
which Mt. supplies. The suggested
miracle was a spurious test of Sonship; the real test was perfect human
obedience (cf. Jo. iv. 34). It stands
written (γέγραπται) in Deut. that
Israel was led through the desert
40 years in hunger and hardship,
that they might have an opportunity
of exhibiting this mark of sonship;
but where they failed, the Son of
God, who was also, like Israel,
ὁ ἄνθρωπος, must succeed. 'Ipsa
responsio Salvatoris hominem fuisse
indicat qui tentatus est' (Jer.).

5. τότε παραλαμβάνει κτλ.] τότε
does not decide the order of the
temptations; see iii. 13 note.
παραλαμβάνειν is frequent in Mt.;
Lk. ἤγαγεν, a verb which Mt. uses
only in x. 18, xxi. 2, 7 and (intrans.)
xxvi. 46. On the historic pres. see
iii. 1. In the last two temptations
in Mt. the devil takes Jesus from
place to place. But Spitta suggests
that in Lk. it is the Spirit that
'leads' Him, and that ὁ διάβολος
has been omitted in v. 9 after εἶπεν
αὐτῷ (cf. vv. 3, 6) in conformity
with Mt. 'The holy city' is Mt.'s
equivalent for 'Jerusalem' (Lk.; so
Gosp. Naz., cf. Resch, Agrapha, p.

250 ff.); see xxvii. 53, Apoc. xi. 2,
xxi. 2, 10, xxii. 19, Is. lii. 1, Neh.
xi. 1, 18, Tob. xiii. 9 (A), Dan. iii.
28, ix. 24 (Theod.). Philo has ἱερό-
πολις, Joseph. ἱερὰ πόλις. The expression was rare among the later
Jews, probably owing to their banish-
ment from the city by the Romans
who named it Aelia Capitolina. With
the Jewish Christians it was common,
and from them passed to the Arabs,
who still call it el-Kuds.

πτερύγιον] A diminutive used in
popular speech (Blass, § 27.4); fasti-
gium (k), pinnaculum (Vg.). Various
suggestions are the top (1) of Solomon's
Porch, (2) of the Royal Porch, on the
S. of the temple court, which commanded a dizzy abyss (Jos. Ant. xv. xi.
5), (3) of the temple proper; 'sum-
mum templi' (Hil.). Nestle refers to
Dan. ix. 27 (LXX. τὸ ἱερόν), but the text
is certainly corrupt (see Bevan). The
force of 'wing'—something reaching
out sideways — must probably be
maintained. In the LXX. it stands
for כָּנָף, even in an applied meaning
such as the end of a flowing garment
(Num. xv. 38, 1 Regn. xv. 27), and
for סַנְפִּיר, the 'fin' of a fish (Lev. xi.
9 ff., Dt. xiv. 9 f.). In later Heb.
כָּנָף is used for the ends of a yoke
(Kel. 14) and the extremity of a
lung (Hol. 45 a). Ṣ cur, Ephr. render
it 'horn,' i.e. 'corner.' It was probably a projecting turret or buttress.
τὸ ἱερόν was a wide term covering
the complex of buildings on the
whole temple area, which occupied
a space of 1 × 2 stadia, and was
surrounded by a high wall, περίβολος
τοῦ παντὸς ἱεροῦ (Jos. BJ. v. v. 1);

λέγει αὐτῷ Εἰ υἱὸς εἶ τοῦ θεοῦ, βάλε σεαυτὸν κάτω·
γέγραπται γὰρ ὅτι

Τοῖς ἀγγέλοις ἀυτοῦ ἐντελεῖται περὶ σοῦ
καὶ ἐπὶ χειρῶν ἀροῦσίν σε,
μή ποτε προσκόψῃς πρὸς λίθον τὸν πόδα σου.

7 ἔφη αὐτῷ ὁ Ἰησοῦς Πάλιν γέγραπται Οὐκ ἐκπειράσεις Κύριον
8 τὸν θεόν σου. Πάλιν παραλαμβάνει αὐτὸν ὁ διάβολος εἰς

but here it is perhaps used in the narrower sense of ναός, the temple proper. Hegesippus (*ap.* Eus. *HE.* II. xxiii. 11) relates that James the Lord's brother was placed ἐπὶ τὸ πτερύγιον τοῦ ναοῦ.

6. εἰ υἱὸς εἶ κτλ.] See *v.* 3 note. To cast Himself down without injury would be another spurious test of Sonship; at the same time it would be a spurious proof of it to the amazed onlookers, such as Simon Magus is said to have attempted (see *Enc. Bibl.* 4544, 4621 f.). The impulse in this case was the more alluring, since it involved not a selfish satisfaction of the needs of the body, but a self-abandonment of the body. Streeter's explanation (*Foundations,* p. 101) that the Lord was tempted to anticipate His descent as Son of Man on the clouds of heaven, is far-fetched.

γέγραπται γὰρ κτλ.] The subtlety of an internal struggle is vividly depicted; the Lord's very familiarity with scripture adds to the force of the temptation. The quotation is from Ps. xc. [xci.] 11, 12. The opening ὅτι, which WH. print as *recitativum,* is probably part of the quotation, since it is not used in *vv.* 4, 7, 10. The passage agrees with the LXX., except for the omission of τοῦ διαφυλάξαι σε ἐν [πάσαις] ταῖς ὁδοῖς σου. (The καί before ἐπὶ χειρῶν is inserted in LXX. ℵ*, but omitted in ℵ^{c.a} B.) Lk. continues the

quotation as far as τοῦ διαφυλάξαι σε, the remaining words being hardly suitable to the occasion. He omits the καί, introducing the second half with καὶ ὅτι, as a separate quotation.

7. πάλιν γέγραπται κτλ.] πάλιν, not to be taken with ἔφη αὐτῷ ὁ Ἰ., introduces another quotation (cf. Jo. xii. 39, Heb. i. 5, ii. 13, iv. 5), parrying the insidious reminder of the words from the Psalter, and confirming the former passage from Deut. Lk. has εἴρηται for γέγραπται, apparently for the sake of variety. The quotation is from Dt. vi. 16 (LXX.), a passage which is alluded to in Ps. lxxvii. [lxxviii.] 18, 1 Cor. x. 9. Elsewhere in bibl. Gk. the compound ἐκπειράζειν occurs only in Dt. viii. 2, 16, Lk. x. 25. The words of scripture are, as in *v.* 4, addressed by the Lord to Himself, and the spirit of the reply is the same: what was wrong for God's 'son' Israel is wrong for God's Son Jesus.

8. πάλιν παραλαμβάνει κτλ.] In their accounts of this temptation Mt. and Lk. coincide in hardly a single word, except in the quotation. If they drew them from Q, it must have been from different recensions. Both writers shew characteristic features of style. On παραλαμβάνει see *v.* 3. Lk., with no mention of the mountain, has simply ἀναγαγών, describing an exaltation into a state of spiritual vision; cf. Ez. iii. 12, 14, xi. 1, 24, Herm. *Vis.* I. i. 3. If this

ὄρος ὑψηλὸν λίαν, καὶ δείκνυσιν αὐτῷ πάσας τὰς βασιλείας
τοῦ κόσμου καὶ τὴν δόξαν αὐτῶν, καὶ εἶπεν αὐτῷ Ταῦτά 9
σοι πάντα δώσω ἐὰν πεσὼν προσκυνήσῃς μοι. τότε λέγει 10
αὐτῷ ὁ Ἰησοῦς Ὕπαγε, Σατανᾶ· γέγραπται γάρ Κύριον

10 ὑπαγε] אBC* al 1 al.pler 𝕃 f k vg 𝕊 pesh.pal me sah ; add οπισω μου
C²DE al 𝕃 vet.pler 𝕊 cur.hcl* arm aeth [οπ. σου 𝕊 sin.diat^Eph]

was the original account, Mt. may
have added the mention of the
mountain under O.T. influence ; see
Dt. xxxiv. 1–3, Ez. xl. 2. δείκνυσιν
describes a vivid mental suggestion ;
cf. Apoc. iv. 1, xvii. 1, xxii. 6, 8 ;
in Jer. xxiv. 1, Zech. i. 20 [ii. 3],
iii. 1 and freq., it represents הִרְאָה :
the devil plays the part of an *angelus
interpres*. For τοῦ κόσμου Lk. has
τῆς οἰκουμένης, which he frequently
employs ; and he adds ἐν στιγμῇ
χρόνου—the vision of the whole
panorama was instantaneous. He
also transfers the words τὴν δόξαν
αὐτῶν (see n. on next *v.*) to the
devil's offer, producing an ungram-
matical sentence, since αὐτῶν has no
antecedent ; he seems to have felt
that the δόξα of the kingdoms, *i.e.*
every element of human wealth and
splendour, and of natural beauty,
could not, even in a mental vision,
be apparent to the eye.

The 'high mountain' perhaps gave
rise to the words ascribed to Jesus in
the *Gosp. Heb.* (*ap.* Orig. *in Joan.* t.
ii. 6): ἔνθα αὐτὸς ὁ σωτήρ φησιν·
ἄρτι ἔλαβέ με ἡ μήτηρ μου τὸ
ἅγιον πνεῦμα ἐν μιᾷ τῶν τριχῶν
μου [probably from Ez. viii. 3 ; cf.
Bel 36], καὶ ἀνήνεγκέ με εἰς τὸ ὄρος
τὸ μέγα Θαβώρ. Parts of this are
found also in Orig. (*Hom.* on Jer. xv.
4), Gosp. Heb. *ap.* Jer. (on Mic. vii.
7), and Gosp. Naz. (*ap.* Jer. on Is. xl.
9 ff. and Ez. xvi. 13). But some
patristic writers took Tabor to be the
mountain of the Transfiguration ; see
Swete on Mk. ix. 2. Zahn's sugges-

tion that Tabor is a corruption of
טוב רם 'exceeding high' is more
ingenious than probable.

9. ταῦτά σοι πάντα κτλ.] The
words imply a thought which the
Lord shared with His contemporaries,
that the world was at present under
the authority of Satan ; Lk.'s expanded form expresses it more clearly.
It was to be the Messiah's work to
restore the spiritual sovereignty to
God to whom it belonged, and
to consummate it, in God's time and
in God's way. The temptation was
threefold : to gain a temporal, not a
spiritual, dominion ; to gain it at
once ; and to gain it by an act of
homage to the ruler of this world,
which would make the self-constituted
Messiah the vice-regent of the devil
and not of God.

10. ὕπαγε, Σατανᾶ] ὑπάγειν (class.
'to go, or withdraw, slowly') occurs
in the LXX., transitively 'to cause to
go' (Ex. xiv. 21), intransitively =
πορεύεσθαι, only as a variant (א) in
Jer. xliii. [xxxvi.] 19, Tob. viii. 21,
x. 12 f., xii. 5, 4 Mac. iv. 13, but is
frequent in the Gospels. The reading ὕπαγε ὀπίσω μου is due to
harmonization with xvi. 23 ; Orig.
and Jer. expressly reject it. It may
point to an original זל אל אחורך, lit.
ὕπαγε εἰς τὸ ὀπίσω σου: the addition
of the pronoun is an Aram. idiom
occurring in 𝕊 sin here and xxiv.
18, Lk. ix. 62, Jo. xviii. 6, xx. 14
(𝕊 sin is lacking in xvi. 23), but the
meaning is simply ὕπ. ὀπίσω or
ὕπαγε. Lk., who places this tempta-

11 τὸν θεόν coy προcκγνήceιc καὶ αγτῷ μόνῳ λατρεγ́ceιc. Τότε
ἀφίησιν αὐτὸν ὁ διάβολος, καὶ ἰδοὺ ἄγγελοι προσῆλθον καὶ
διηκόνουν αὐτῷ.

12   Ἀκούσας δὲ ὅτι Ἰωάνης παρεδόθη ἀνεχώρησεν εἰς τὴν

tion second in order, omits the command of dismissal. If this is the
true order, Mt. may have taken the
command from xvi. 23 ; but there is
no reason for supposing that the
whole incident has been derived from
the later occasion. Σατανᾶς, apart
from the vocative, always has the
article (= הַשָּׂטָן) in the N.T., except
in Mk. iii. 23, Lk. xxii. 3. The
graecized form is not found in the
LXX. till Sir. xxi. 27 [30]. σατάν
is a substantive ('an adversary') in
3 Regn. xi. 14, 23 (A), and in Aq.
Numb. xxii. 22, Aq. Sym. Theod.
1 Regn. xxix. 4. For the personal
evil spirit Aq. uses it in Job i. 6,
and Aq. Sym. Theod. in Zech. iii. 1 ;
cf. Enoch, xl. 7, with Charles' note.
The LXX. render it by ἐπίβουλος,
ἀντικείμενος or, more frequently, (ὁ)
διάβολος.

γέγραπται γάρ κτλ.] For the
third time the Lord quotes from
Deut. (vi. 13) ; but προσκυνήσεις, in
answer to the προσκυνήσῃς of the
tempter, is substituted for the LXX.
φοβηθήσῃ (producing the class. construction of the verb with the acc.,
although in v. 9, and elsewhere in
Mt., it takes the dat.), and μόνῳ is
added for emphasis. Both variations
occur in LXX. (A), and μόνῳ in the
Luc. text, probably by assimilation to
Mt. As before, the Lord addresses
the quotation to Himself, attacking
the central point of the temptation
—submission to the ruler of this
world.

11. τότε ἀφίησιν κτλ.] On the
historic present see iii. 1. Lk. relates
that the devil departed when he had
exhausted all his shafts (συντελέσας

πάντα πειρασμόν), but adds ἄχρι
καιροῦ, which is abundantly borne
out by the subsequent records of the
Lord's life ; cf. Lk. xxii. 28. Elsewhere Satan is representing as tempt-
ing Him only through the agency of
men, διὰ τῶν οἰκείων αὐτῷ ὀργάνων
(Chrys.). The angelic ministry is
derived from Mk. (Lk. does not record it), and his imperf. διηκόνουν.
Both the food and the angelic help,
which He had refused (vv. 4, 7) when
they involved sin, were now given
to Him as victor. Angels were sent
forth to minister to the Heir (cf.
Heb. i. 14).

iv. 12–xviii. THE GALILEAN
MINISTRY.

12–16. (Mk. i. 14, 21 a, Lk. iv.
14 a, 31.) RETURN TO GALILEE AND
SETTLEMENT AT CAPHARNAUM.

Mt. gives a general introduction
to the Ministry, anticipating the
arrival at Capharnaum in order to
shew that the Lord's place of abode
fulfilled O.T. prophecy. It is difficult
to harmonize the Johannine with
the synoptic narratives : the events
of Jo. i. 19–28 appear to take place
during the days of the Temptation ;
i. 29–iii. 36 (which includes a journey
of Jesus to Galilee with His mother,
brethren, and disciples, and a return
to Jerusalem) has no parallel in the
synn. ; possibly iv. 3, 43 is intended
to coincide with the present Galilean
journey. The synoptic accounts do
not definitely exclude the possibility
of unrecorded journeys.

12. ἀκούσας κτλ.] The Baptist's
imprisonment is here the reason
for the Lord's departure to Galilee ;

Γαλιλαίαν. καὶ καταλιπὼν τὴν Ναζαρὰ ἐλθὼν κατῴκησεν 13
εἰς Καφαρναοὺμ τὴν παραθαλασσίαν ἐν ὁρίοις Ζαβουλὼν
καὶ Νεφθαλείμ· ἵνα πληρωθῇ τὸ ῥηθὲν διὰ Ἡσαίου τοῦ 14
προφήτου λέγοντος

Mk. (μετὰ τὸ παραδοθῆναι τ. Ἰωάν.) gives it merely as a date. The incidental reference to it shews that it was well known to the readers; see also xi. 2. Not till xiv. 3–12 are the details narrated. Mt., Mk. do not indicate the time that has elapsed since the Temptation. But Lk., who appends to his account of John's preaching a reference to his imprisonment (iii. 19 f.), here omits the date, and by ὑπέστρεψεν ἐν τῇ δυνάμει τοῦ πνεύματος seems to imply that the return was immediate, and therefore that Jesus started His work before John was arrested. This is more probable, for it is unlikely that Jesus would go into the tetrarchy of Antipas immediately after he had shown his hostility to the preacher of repentance. The Marcan tradition may have been influenced by the thought that the forerunner's work must be completed before the Messiah appears. Cf. Jerome, quoted by Swete.

13. καὶ καταλιπών κτλ.] The arrival at N. is not recorded. If Q was the source of the (? vernacular) form Nazara (see ii. 23) here and in Lk. iv. 16 where alone it recurs, Q possibly placed at this point a visit on which Lk. iv. 16–30 is based (see Mt. xiii. 54–58), and Mt. shews a reminiscence of it. On ἐλθ. κατῴκ. εἰς see ii. 23. The arrival at Capharnaum is mentioned here because the next incident, the call of Simon and others, is by the sea. This gives the opportunity of introducing the O.T. quotation. In Mk. Capharnaum is not named till after that incident. Καφαρναούμ

is probably either *Khân Minyeh* or *Tell Ḥûm*. Sanday inclined to the former (*Sacr. Sites,* 36 ff.), but afterwards adopted the latter (*JThS.* Oct. 1903, and *DCG.* 'Capernaum'). *Tell Ḥûm* lies on the NW. shore of the Lake of Galilee, close to its northernmost point; *Khân Minyeh* is 2½ m. SW. of it. The spelling Καπερναούμ is not older than the 5th cent. A.D. (WH. *Notes,* 160). In Jos. *Vita* 72 the form Κεφαρνωκόν (? Καφαρνωμόν) occurs. See Sanday (*ll.c.*) and Swete on Mk. i. 21. In Jo. ii. 12 it is related that the mother and brethren of Jesus went to Capharnaum; He made it ἡ ἰδία πόλις (Mt. ix. 1)—διὰ τὸ πολλάκις ἐκεῖσε ἐπιδημεῖν (Victor)—and seems to have occupied a house there (see on ix. 10, 28, xvii. 24). But Nazareth was still His πατρίς (xiii. 54), where His sisters, who were probably married, continued to live (*v.* 56).

τὴν παραθαλασσίαν κτλ.] Mt.'s readers would be well acquainted with the site of the town, but he inserts the details in view of the following quotation. The adj. refers to the Mediterranean in 1 Mac. xi. 8 *al.,* and to the Red Sea in 2 Chr. viii. 17; but the Galilean lake, λίμνη in Lk. (v. 1 f., viii. 22 f., 33), is always θάλασσα in Mt., Mk. (see on *v.* 18). ὁρίοις denotes one 'territory' (cf. ii. 16, viii. 34 *al.,* Ex. vii. 27, x. 14 = בְּגֻל) consisting of the districts formerly occupied by the tribes. For the form Νεφθαλείμ see Hatch-Redp. *Suppl.* 120. D has the Aram. -λείν; cf. Ps. lxvii. [lxviii.] 28 Rᵃ.

14. ἵνα πληρωθῇ κτλ.] On the formula see i. 22.

15   ΓΗ ΖαΒογλὼν καὶ ΓΗ Νεφθαλείμ,
       ὁδὸν θαλάσσης, πέραν τοῦ Ἰορδάνογ,
       Γαλιλαία τῶν ἐθνῶν,
16   ὁ λαὸς ὁ καθήμενος ἐν σκοτία
       φῶς εἶδεν μέγα,
       καὶ τοῖς καθημένοις ἐν χώρᾳ καὶ σκιᾷ θανάτογ
       φῶς ἀνέτειλεν αὐτοῖς.

17   ΑΠΟ ΤΟΤΕ ἤρξατο ὁ Ἰησοῦς κηρύσσειν καὶ λέγειν
       Μετανοεῖτε, ἤγγικεν γὰρ ἡ βασιλεία τῶν οὐρανῶν.

17 μετανοειτε et γαρ om 𝕷 k 𝕾 sin.cur

15. γῇ Ζαβουλών κτλ.] The
quotation is from Is. ix. 1, 2 [Heb.
viii. 23, ix. 1]. With the exception
of a phrase in *v.* 16 it is independent
of the LXX., and was probably drawn
from a collection of *testimonia.* The
opening clauses of the Heb. ('At the
first time He degraded the land of
Zeb. and the land of Naph., but at
the latter He made (them) honourable') are omitted, but the two
geographical expressions are taken
from them and thrown into the
nominative. On γῇ see ix. 26.
ὁδὸν θαλάσσης (absent from the
LXX., but found in Theod. ; so Aq.
ὁδ. τῆς θαλ., Sym. ὁδ. τὴν κατὰ
θάλασσαν) stands for דֶּרֶךְ הַיָּם, 'towards the sea' (*i.e.* westward), which
describes the westward extent of N.
Israel invaded by Assyria, as distinct
from the parts on the E. of Jordan.
Mt. applies it to the district round
Capharnaum (τὴν παραθαλασσίαν).
For the adv. acc. ὁδόν (cf. πέραν) see
Num. xiv. 25, xxi. 4, Dt. i. 40.
πέραν τοῦ Ἰορδάνου (cf. *v.* 25, xix. 1,
Mk. iii. 8, Jo. i. 28, iii. 26, x. 40) is
employed in Rabb. writings for the
district E. of the Jordan and the
lake, also known as ἡ Περαία,
Περαῖος, Περαίτης (Jos. *BJ.* III. iii.
3, IV. vii. 3, 6) ; see Schürer, *HJP.*
II. i. 2 f., 113. Γαλιλαία τῶν ἐθνῶν
= גְּלִיל הַגּוֹיִם; cf. 1 Mac. v. 15, Γαλ.
ἀλλοφύλων. Elsewhere the name

is simply הַגָּלִיל, 'The Circle.' Its
origin, and the extent of the district
in O.T. times, are alike uncertain ;
but it corresponded roughly with
Asher, Naphtali, Zebulun, and
Issachar. Jos. (*BJ.* III. iii. 1 ; cf.
Vita 37) gives the boundaries of
Upper and Lower Galilee in his day.
16. ὁ λαός κτλ.] ὁ καθήμενος
(Heb. הַהֹלְכִים, LXX. ὁ πορευόμενος) is
perhaps assimilated to the following
τοῖς καθημένοις, which rightly
renders יֹשְׁבֵי (LXX. οἱ κατοικοῦντες).
The first καί is absent from Heb.
and LXX. ἐν χώρᾳ καὶ σκιᾷ θανάτου
is the only point of correspondence
with the LXX., where the phrase,
without the καί, occurs as a bald
rendering of בְּאֶרֶץ צַלְמָוֶת. Lk. (i. 79),
who adapts the sentence, used, like
Mt., a text which contained καθημένοις. The prophet depicts the
change which the Deliverer will
work in N. Palestine ; formerly it
was despoiled and ruined by Assyria,
but the new era will dawn upon it
with a flood of light. To Mt. the
words have a splendid application ;
the same district lay in spiritual
darkness and death, and the new era
dawned when Christ went thither.

17–25. (Mk. i. 14 b–20.) WORK
IN GALILEE. CALL OF FOUR DIS-
CIPLES.

17. ἀπὸ τότε κτλ.] Mt. uses

Περιπατῶν δὲ παρὰ τὴν θάλασσαν τῆς Γαλιλαίας εἶδεν 18
δύο ἀδελφούς, Σίμωνα τὸν λεγόμενον Πέτρον καὶ Ἀνδρέαν
τὸν ἀδελφὸν αὐτοῦ, βάλλοντας ἀμφίβληστρον εἰς τὴν θάλασσαν, ἦσαν γὰρ ἁλεεῖς· καὶ λέγει αὐτοῖς Δεῦτε ὀπίσω 19

ἀπὸ τότε again in xvi. 21 (elsewhere
it occurs only in xxvi. 16), thus
dividing into two main parts the
teaching of Jesus: in the first it
consisted mainly of public preaching
about the imminence of the Kingdom ; in the second, of private
instructions to the disciples about
His own sufferings, the necessary
prelude to His advent to inaugurate
the Kingdom.   The verse is an
abbreviation of Mk. i. 14 b, 15 a (Mk.'s
'believe in the Gospel' is probably
due to later editing ; see on xvi. 25,
xix. 29).   In Mt. ἤρξατο is never
quite superfluous, as sometimes (see
on xiii. 54) in Mk., Lk. ; it either
describes the beginning of a continuous action or marks a fresh start or
phase in the narrative ; xi. 7, 20,
xii. 1, xvi. 21 f., xxvi. 22, 37, 74.

μετανοεῖτε κτλ.]   Identical with
the preaching of the Baptist ; see iii.
2 note. If, however, μετανοεῖτε and
γάρ are to be omitted (see Appar.), Mt.
summarizes only the glad announcement that the Kingdom was at
hand, i.e. 'the good tidings of the
Kingdom' (v. 23), and a sign of its
nearness was the healing of the sick
(vv. 23 f.), which shewed that the
powers of evil were being undermined.   The immediate result was
the enlisting of followers.   In sending out the Twelve (x. 7) the Lord
delivered to them the same happy
message, and the performance of the
same signs.   On the causes which
led to the simultaneous appearance
of the Baptist and Jesus with the
same message see J. Weiss, Die Pred.
Jesu v. Reiche Gottes, 66–8.   By
relating the arrival at Capharnaum

in v. 13, Mt. makes the preaching of
Jesus to begin there.   But in Lk.
His preaching is famous in Galilee
directly He returns thither, a specimen of it being given at Nazareth
(iv. 16–30), before Capharnaum is
visited (v. 31).

18–22.   The section is derived
from Mk. with a few alterations of
language. Lk. (v. 10 f.) preserves a
different tradition of the call of
Simon, James, and John (Andrew is
not mentioned), which he places a
little later than Mt. and Mk., and in
which the words to Simon 'from
henceforth thou shalt catch men'
gain force from the miraculous haul
of fish which precedes it (see n. before
v. 1).

18. περιπατῶν δέ κτλ.]   Mt. avoids
Mk.'s repeated preposition παράγων
παρά, a construction which seems to
be unique.   'Sea of Galilee' (so Mk.)
recurs only in xv. 29 (= Mk. vii.
31); elsewhere Mt., Mk. write simply
'the sea.' Cf. Jo. vi. 1 τῆς θαλ. τῆς
Γ. τῆς Τιβεριάδος, but in xxi. 1 τῆς
θαλ. τῆς Τιβεριάδος.   Lk. always
speaks of the 'lake' (λίμνη) ; once
(v. 1) ἡ λίμνη Γεννησαρέτ. 'Sea' is
derived from the O.T. in which the
lake is called the 'sea of Kinnereth'
(Num. xxxiv. 11, Jos. xiii. 27).

Mt. introduces to the reader 'two
brothers,' and (v. 21) 'other two
brothers,' while Mk. names the four
as though they were already well
known.   On the form Σίμων see x.
2. For βάλλοντας ἀμφίβληστρον
(Mk. ἀμφιβάλλοντας) cf. Hab. i. 17.
The explanatory addition ἦσαν γὰρ
ἁλεεῖς is copied direct from Mk.

19. δεῦτε ὀπίσω μου κτλ.]   Cf.

20 μου, καὶ ποιήσω ὑμᾶς ἁλεεῖς ἀνθρώπων. οἱ δὲ εὐθέως
21 ἀφέντες τὰ δίκτυα ἠκολούθησαν αὐτῷ. Καὶ προβὰς ἐκεῖθεν
εἶδεν ἄλλους δύο ἀδελφούς, Ἰάκωβον τὸν τοῦ Ζεβεδαίου καὶ
Ἰωάνην τὸν ἀδελφὸν αὐτοῦ, ἐν τῷ πλοίῳ μετὰ Ζεβεδαίου
τοῦ πατρὸς αὐτῶν καταρτίζοντας τὰ δίκτυα αὐτῶν, καὶ
22 ἐκάλεσεν αὐτούς. οἱ δὲ εὐθέως ἀφέντες τὸ πλοῖον καὶ τὸν

4 Regn. vi. 19. ποιήσω points to a future period; before they could become preachers they had much to learn, and were not sent out till eight others had been called and trained (x. 1). For ποιεῖν of 'appointing' to an office cf. Mk. iii. 14, Ac. ii. 36, Heb. iii. 2 (see Westcott), Apoc. v. 10, 1 Regn. xii. 6 (ὁ ποιήσας τὸν Μωυσῆν καὶ τὸν Ἀαρών). For the metaphor ἁλεεῖς ἀνθρώπων cf. Jer. xvi. 16, Diog. Laert. ii. 67 ἄνθρωπον ἁλιεύσω. Lk. has ἀπὸ τοῦ νῦν ἀνθρώπους ἔσῃ ζωγρῶν (cf. 2 Tim. ii. 26).

20. οἱ δὲ εὐθέως κτλ.] Lk. v. 3 and Jo. i. 40 ff. suggest, what is in any case probable, that the prompt response of Simon and Andrew was due to previous intimacy with the Lord. The same may have been the case with the other pair of brothers.

21. καὶ προβάς κτλ.] The second pair of brothers was not far off (Mk. ὀλίγον). The Gk. form Ἰάκωβος (Jacobus) is used in the N.T. for the apostles of that name and the Lord's brother; the Heb. form Ἰακώβ (Jacob, יַעֲקֹב) for the legal 'grandfather' of Jesus (Mt. i. 15 f.), and (as always in the LXX.) for the patriarch. The name Ζεβεδαῖος appears as Ζαβαδαίας (1 Esd. ix. 35), Ζαβδαῖος (ib. 21), and Ζαβδειά (2 Esd. viii. 8, x. 20) = זְבַדְיָה or an abbrev. זַבְדִּי. The Gk. form Ἰωάνης (WH. Notes, 159), invariable in the N.T., is not found in the LXX., except 2 Chr. xxviii. 12 (B vid.), and 1 Mac. ii. 1 f. (Ἰωάννης); elsewhere Ἰωανάν (= יוֹחָנָן, יְהוֹחָנָן), Ἰωανάς, Ἰωνά[ν].

καταρτίζειν is to make ἄρτιος, 'fitted or equipped,' for a duty or function (cf. Lk. vi. 40, 2 Tim. iii. 17), either by 'making, constructing,' or by 'mending, correcting,' or generally by 'providing.' In the LXX. it occurs only in Pss. and 2 Esd. (except Ex. xv. 17). Vg. here reficientes retia sua, but in Mk. componentes retia (Wicl. 'makynge nettis'). The brothers were making the nets ready for use: the verb need not be defined more closely. Elsewhere in the N.T. (except Heb. x. 5, xi. 3) it is always metaphorical.

22. οἱ δὲ εὐθέως κτλ.] Mt. transfers Mk.'s εὐθύς from ἐκάλεσεν αὐτούς, where (as often in Mk.) it is otiose, to the action of the brothers, emphasizing the promptness of their obedience. He also emphasizes their sacrifice: they left their means of livelihood (τὸ πλοῖον) and their family ties (κ. τ. πατέρα αὐτ.); Mk. τὸν πατ. αὐτ. Ζ. ἐν τ. πλοίῳ. Lk. simply πάντα. The simplicity of the wording only enhances the abandonment required by the call of Christ; cf. ix. 9, x. 37, xix. 27. Mk.'s μετὰ τῶν μισθωτῶν is omitted perhaps for brevity.

23-25. The verses are a résumé of the Lord's work in Galilee, similar to those given later in Mk. i. 39, Lk. iv. 44. διδάσκων καὶ κηρύσσων sums up chs. v.–vii., and θεραπεύων viii. 1–17. After the account of the second stay at Capharnaum (ix. 1–34), the résumé is again inserted (v. 35) as an introduction to the similar work to which the disciples were sent out.

πατέρα αὐτῶν ἠκολούθησαν αὐτῷ.   Καὶ περιῆγεν ἐν 23
ὅλῃ τῇ Γαλιλαίᾳ, διδάσκων ἐν ταῖς συναγωγαῖς αὐτῶν καὶ
κηρύσσων τὸ εὐαγγέλιον τῆς βασιλείας καὶ θεραπεύων
πᾶσαν νόσον καὶ πᾶσαν μαλακίαν ἐν τῷ λαῷ.   καὶ ἀπῆλθεν 24

23. καὶ περιῆγεν κτλ.] For
Galilee (Mt., Mk.) Lk. has εἰς τὰς
συναγωγὰς⁻ τῆς Ἰουδαίας, an independent tradition of great value;
see n. before v. 1. Mt. expands
Mk.'s κηρύσσων εἰς τὰς συναγωγὰς
αὐτῶν. Teaching (moral truths),
Proclaiming (the good tidings of the
kingdom), and Healing (which was a
sign of the nearness of the kingdom)
sum up the Lord's work; cf. ix. 35,
xi. 1. On αὐτῶν see vii. 29.

Perhaps τὸ εὐαγγ. τ. βασιλείας is
derived from Mk.'s τὸ εὐαγγ. τοῦ
θεοῦ (i. 14), which Mt. omitted at iv.
17. βασιλείας is an obj. gen., 'the
good tidings consisting of the announcement that the Kingdom was
near.' εὐαγγέλιον in Hom. means
'reward for good tidings'; so in
Attic Gk. in the plur. (cf. 2 Regn.
iv. 10). With the meaning 'good
tidings' it occurs as early as the
inscription to Augustus at Priene
(B.C. 9), and in Luc. and Plut. This
meaning may have been carried over
from Gk. to the Aram. בְּשׂוּרְתָא (see
Wellh. Einleitung, 109). In the
N.T. it occurs in ix. 35, xxiv. 14,
xxvi. 13, Mk.⁸, Ac.³, 1 Pet.¹, Apoc.¹,
and freq. in the Paul. Epp. The
LXX. has the fem. εὐαγγελία = בְּשׂרָה
(2 Regn. xviii. 20, 27, 4 Regn. vii. 9).
On the vb. -λίζεσθαι, see xi. 5.
For ἡ βασιλεία, with no further
definition, see viii. 12 note.

καὶ θεραπεύων κτλ.] μαλακία of
physical ailment is confined to late
Gk.; cf. Dt. vii. 15 (πᾶσαν μαλακίαν·
καὶ πάσας νόσους), xxviii. 61, Test.
Joseph 17, Herm. Vis. III. xi. 2, xii. 3.
In the N.T. it recurs only in x. 1
(where the expression θεραπεύειν . . .

μαλακίαν is repeated), and ix. 35
(where the whole verse is repeated
almost verbatim, and followed, as here
(v. 1), by ἰδὼν δὲ τοὺς ὄχλους). Mt.
is inclined to punctuate his narrative
with recurring formulas. See the
healing in viii. 16 f., followed by
ἰδὼν δὲ ὁ Ἰησοῦς ὄχλον, and xv.
30 f., followed by σπλαγχνίζομαι ἐπὶ
τὸν ὄχλον. The present passage is
alluded to in a Christian amulet of
the 6th cent. (Milligan, Gk. Pap.
no. 55). ἐν τῷ λαῷ: to a Jewish
writer this meant Israel; 'the laity,'
then as in the Christian church,
meant the whole privileged body (cf.
ii. 4, xxi. 23, 26 (note), xxvi. 3, 5,
47, xxvii. 1, 25, 64). When the
Lord preached elsewhere than in the
synagogues, Gentiles no doubt heard
Him—a fact which is not sufficiently
recognized; but He was 'not sent
but unto the lost sheep of the house
of Israel' (xv. 24; cf. x. 6), and the
healing of Gentiles was a rare exception (viii. 5–13, xv. 21–28). For
other general statements of healing
see viii. 16, ix. 35, xii. 15, xiv. 14,
xv. 30, xix. 2, xxi. 14.

24. καὶ ἀπῆλθεν ἡ ἀκοή κτλ.]
This anticipates the results of a considerable period of work; hence,
possibly, the omission of the sentence
in ℵ sin. The whole of (Gentile)
Syria is contrasted with the λαός in
'the whole of Galilee.' Syria, therefore, seems to denote not the whole
Roman province, which included
Palestine, but that part to the N.
and NE. for which Jews of Palestine
employed the name (Ac. xv. 23, 41,
Gal. i. 21; cf. Jos. BJ. VII. iii. 3,
Ab. Zar. i. 8). The words are perhaps

ἡ ἀκοὴ αὐτοῦ εἰς ὅλην τὴν Συρίαν· καὶ προσήνεγκαν αὐτῷ
πάντας τοὺς κακῶς ἔχοντας ποικίλαις νόσοις καὶ βασάνοις
συνεχομένους, δαιμονιζομένους καὶ σεληνιαζομένους καὶ παρα-
25 λυτικούς, καὶ ἐθεράπευσεν αὐτούς. καὶ ἠκολούθησαν αὐτῷ
ὄχλοι πολλοὶ ἀπὸ τῆς Γαλιλαίας καὶ Δεκαπόλεως καὶ
Ἱεροσολύμων καὶ Ἰουδαίας καὶ πέραν τοῦ Ἰορδάνου.

based on Mk. i. 28, 'Syria' being
Mt.'s equivalent for τὴν περίχωρον
τῆς Γαλιλαίας. The passage forms
the basis of the legend of Abgar the
toparch of Edessa (Eus. *HE.* i. 13).
ἀκοή *c. obj. gen.* occurs in the N.T.
only here (= Mk. i. 28) and xiv. 1.

καὶ προσήνεγκαν κτλ.] The impers. vb. is used, *more Aram.*, instead
of a passive (cf. viii. 16, ix. 2, 32, xii.
22). βάσανος of disease is rare ; cf.
1 Mac. ix. 56 ; and the verb, Mt. viii.
6, 1 Regn. v. 3. συνεχομένους: 'in
the grip of' (Vg. *comprehensos*) ; cf.
Lk. iv. 38, Ac. xxviii. 8. With ποικ.
νόσοις κ. βασ. it is a nearer definition of κακῶς ἔχοντας, followed
by three particular instances in a
descending scale of violence — demoniac, moon-struck, paralytic. For
σεληνιάζεσθαι cf. xvii. 15 ; σεληνιό-
βλητος and -ιασμός occur in late Gk.
For παραλυτικούς (so Mk. ; not class.
or LXX.) Lk. prefers παραλελυμένους ;
cf. 1 Mac. ix. 55, 3 Mac. ii. 22.

25. ἀπὸ τῆς Γαλιλαίας κτλ.] The
single article does duty for all the
names ; cf. Lk. v. 17, Ac. ii. 9. The
'Decapolis' denoted certain Hellenistic towns, perhaps originally ten
in number. Subjected by Alex.
Jannaeus, and liberated by Pompey,
they formed a confederacy which was
afterwards joined by other towns.
Ten names are given by Pliny (*Hist.
Nat.* v. xviii. 74), including the N.T.
names Damascus, Gadara, and Gerasa,
all of them on the E. of Jordan
except Scythopolis (= Bethshan). See
Schürer, *HJP.* II. i. 94–6. On Ἱεροσόλυμα see ii. 1.

v.–vii. THE SERMON ON THE
MOUNT.

Mt. places this in the forefront of
the Lord's teaching, influenced by
Mk.'s statement (i. 21), which he
reached at this point, that He was
teaching in the synagogue at Capharnaum. At the close of the sermon
(vii. 29) he adopts Mk.'s next verse.
But its position in Lk. (ch. vi.) is
probably nearer the true one. There
has been time for the 'disciples' (Lk.
ὄχλος πολὺς μαθητῶν αὐτοῦ) to become a body of adherents distinct
from the ὄχλοι; and the 'mountain'
seems to be due to Mk. iii. 13, where
Jesus calls the Twelve on a mountain,
which, in Lk., immediately precedes
the sermon.

Spitta's treatment (*Die synopt.
Grundschrift*) of Lk. v., vi. is noteworthy. Apart from his theory that
Mt. and Mk. were dependent upon
an original form of Lk., he makes it
probable that Lk. had access to a
source or sources from which is derived a consistent narrative. In Lk.
iv. 43 Jesus, in Galilee, says that He
must preach 'to the other cities also';
and in the next verse He preaches in
Judaea. The haul of fish, after which
three disciples follow Him (v. 1–11),
is in Galilee. But in *v.* 12 Jesus
heals a leper 'in one of the cities,'
which is probably a direct continuation of iv. 43 f. ; and the command
to shew himself to the priests also suggests Judaea. Lk. v. 1–11 is therefore
an insertion which breaks the order
of events. The events of v. 12–vi.
20 are as follows : the paralytic, the

Ἰδὼν δὲ τοὺς ὄχλους ἀνέβη εἰς τὸ ὄρος· καὶ καθίσαντος 1 V.
αὐτοῦ προσῆλθαν αὐτῷ οἱ μαθηταὶ αὐτοῦ· καὶ ἀνοίξας τὸ 2
στόμα αὐτοῦ ἐδίδασκεν αὐτοὺς λέγων
   μακάριοι οἱ πτωχοὶ τῷ πνεύματι, ὅτι αὐτῶν ἐστιν ἡ 3
   βασιλεία τῶν οὐρανῶν.

call of Levi and the discussion on
fasting, the disciples in the cornfield,
the withered hand ; after these conflicts with the religious authorities,
Jesus, needing retirement and prayer
in preparation for the next stage in
His work, spent a night praying on
a mountain ; next day He called the
Twelve to be apostles. On descending
from the mountain He was met by
a crowd from Judaea and Jerusalem,
and also from the coast of Tyre and
Sidon (no Galileans being mentioned),
and He healed their sick ; and then
delivered the sermon on the plain,
in which the Beatitudes were addressed to the disciples before He
turned to address the crowds. In
all this series, the ascent of the mountain and the descent to the plain are
the only geographical notices since
the mention of Judaea in iv. 44
(apart from v. 1–11). The religious
leaders, with whom Jesus is in conflict, are more naturally to be found
in Judaea than in Galilee ; and the
whole series of events seems to take
place in Judaea. The people who
came from the coast (τῆς παραλίου)
of Tyre and Sidon would reach the
Plain of Sharon by sea. And that
was the locality of the sermon.

On the sermon as a whole, and the
relation between Mt. and Lk., see the
Add. n. after ch. vii. Heinrici, *Beiträge*, iii., gives suggestive instances
of similarities of language, but differences of thought, between it and
classical writers.

v. 1. *ἰδὼν δέ κτλ.*] See on iv. 23.
Since in Mt. and Mk. the Lord is in
Galilee, τὸ ὄρος is the high ground

which rose W. of the lake. Like
the Mosaic law, the righteousness
which ‘fulfils’ it is taught from a
mountain. Some would harmonize
this with Lk.’s τόπος πεδινός by
explaining the latter as a flat place
on the mountain side ; but in Lk.
the sick are carried thither, and it is
very improbable that they would be
carried up any portion of the mountain.

καὶ καθίσαντος κτλ.] He sat to
deliver a formal discourse ; cf. xiii.
2, xxiv. 3, xxvi. 55, Lk. iv. 20, v.
3, Ez. viii. 1. Iren. *ad Flor.* (*ap.*
Eus. *HE.* v. 20) : ὥστε με δύνασθαι
εἰπεῖν καὶ τὸν τόπον ἐν ᾧ καθεζό-
μενος διελέγετο ὁ μακάριος Πολύ-
καρπος.

2. *καὶ ἀνοίξας κτλ.*] A marked
instance of Semitic redundancy ; see
Ac. x. 34, Job iii. 1, xxxii. 20, Dan.
x. 16 ; and cf. ‘he lifted up his eyes’
(Gen. xxii. 4, 13), ‘his feet’ (Gen.
xxix. 1). The imperf. ἐδίδασκεν is
an Aramaism.

3–12. (Lk. vi. 20–23.) THE BEATI-
TUDES.

As they stand they are nine in
number. It is arbitrary to make
them a second Decalogue by reckoning *v.* 12 as a separate one. More
probably there should be eight : the
change in *v.* 11 from μακάριοι οἱ to
μακ. ἐστε suggests either that *vv.*
10–12 are one Beatitude (Hil., Ambr.,
Jer.), or, as is more likely, that *v.*
11 f. did not originally stand in this
position (see note).

3. *μακάριοι οἱ πτωχοί κτλ.*]
‘Parens quaedam generatioque virtu-

4 μακάριοι οἱ πενθοῦντες, ὅτι αὐτοὶ παρακληθήσονται.

tum' (Ambr.). μακάριος in the LXX. represents אַשְׁרֵי (e.g. Ps. i. 1), which, like the Aram. טוּב, is interjectional, 'Oh, the happiness of—!' The connecting verb is, therefore, not needed, though it is found in xi. 6, Lk. xii. 38, Jam. i. 25. The adj. (not used in Mk., but occurring in Q, cf. xi. 6, xiii. 16, xxiv. 46) connotes, in Heb. thought, happy and successful prosperity, and never represents בָּרוּךְ, which is always rendered by εὐλογητός, -μένος. Lk. has simply μακ. οἱ πτωχοί, which is probably the original wording, but Mt. rightly seizes the thought which underlies it. πτωχός represents עָנִי (Aram. עַנְיָא), which does not mean 'lacking wealth' (רָשׁ, אֶבְיוֹן), or 'humble' (עָנָו), but describes the pious in Israel, for the most part literally poor, whom the worldly rich despised and persecuted. It is frequent in the Psalter. See HDB. art. 'Poor.' Those whom the Lord addressed, who were despised by the recognized pious of His day, were really pious, not outwardly and conventionally, but 'in their spirit.' Cf. the allusion to this saying in Jam. ii. 5, where τοὺς πτωχοὺς τῷ κόσμῳ are further defined as πλουσίους ἐν πίστει, and Ep. Polyc. ii. 3, μακάριοι οἱ πτωχοὶ καὶ οἱ διωκόμενοι ἕνεκεν δικαιοσύνης, ὅτι αὐτῶν ἐστιν ἡ βασιλεία τοῦ θεοῦ. The addition τ. πνεύματι, therefore, points to the sphere in which the πτωχεία is to be found; cf. τῇ καρδίᾳ, v. 8, τῷ πνεύματι, Ps. xxxiii. [xxxiv.] 19, 1 Cor. vii. 34. The interpretation, 'those who spiritually make themselves poor,' i.e. detach themselves from earthly things (Clem. Qu.Div.S. 16–20, Bp. Gore, The Serm. on the Mt. 23–26; cf. 1 Cor. vii. 29–31), is less in keeping with Jewish language and thought. With the thought of

the verse cf. Arist. Eth. Nic. VIII. v. 2 where μακάριος is contrasted with ἐνδεής. See Heinrici, Beiträge, iii. 17 f.

ὅτι αὐτῶν κτλ.] Lk. has the 2nd pers. throughout his four Beatitudes, and Woes, making οἱ πτωχοί etc. vocatives. Cf. xi. 18 (λέγουσιν) with Lk. vii. 33 (λέγετε). Perhaps the original form was 'How happy it is for the poor [in spirit] that (Aram. דְּ) theirs, etc.' So ܣ sin.cur; see Burkitt, Ev. da Meph. i. on Lk. vi. 20. The tense of ἐστιν must not be pressed: it is timeless, and in Aram. the connecting verb would not be used. As a potential right, the kingdom is theirs now and always: as an actual possession it is still future, as is shewn by the verbs in vv. 4–9, which describe various aspects of its bliss. κληρονόμος ἕτοιμος οὐρανοῦ βασιλείας (Clem. Al.)..

4. μακ. οἱ πενθοῦντες] Lk. μακ. οἱ κλαίοντες νῦν, ὅτι γελάσετε. His insertion of νῦν here and in his next verse shews that the verbs are strictly future. Mt.'s form recalls Is. lxi. 2: παρακαλέσαι πάντας τοὺς πενθοῦντας. Both πενθεῖν and κλαίειν are quite general, and cannot be confined to penitence for sin (as Clem. Al., Chrys., Ambr., Hil.). πενθεῖν is most frequent in the LXX. for mourning for the dead, and for the sorrows and sins of others. μακάριοι οἱ πενθοῦντες περὶ τῆς τῶν ἀπίστων ἀπωλείας (Didasc. v. 15). Both κλαίειν and νῦν are freq. in Lk.: κλαίειν, Lk.[11], Mt. ii. 18 (LXX.), xxvi. 75; νῦν, Lk.[13], Ac.[24], Mt.[4]; and γελᾶν occurs only in Lk., here and v. 25.

ὅτι αὐτοί κτλ.] As the poor in spirit are, in one aspect, mourners, so their share in the kingdom will be παράκλησις. Compare Mk. xv. 43 with Lk. ii. 25. 'Comforter' (מְנַחֵם) is a name of the Messiah, and

μακάριοι οἱ πραεῖς, ὅτι αὐτοὶ κληρονομήσογοι τὴν γῆν.   5
μακάριοι οἱ πεινῶντες καὶ διψῶντες τὴν δικαιοσύνην, ὅτι 6
αὐτοὶ χορτασθήσονται.

'to see consolation' (נֶחָמָה) is a frequent expression in Rabb. writings (Volz, *Jüd. Esch.* 305).

5. μακ. οἱ πραεῖς] The poor in spirit are pious in God's sight, and mourners because of the sorrows in the world; πραεῖς expresses their attitude towards God and men. The words are based on Ps. xxxvi. [xxxvii.] 11 : οἱ δὲ πραεῖς κληρονομήσουσιν γῆν.   πραΰς = עָנָו (Aram. עַנְוְותָן); in the N.T. only in xi. 29, xxi. 5, 1 Pet. iii. 4. The subst. πραΰτης is commoner.

ὅτι αὐτοί κτλ.] The metaphor of inheritance (see Westcott, *Hebr.* 167 ff.) was primarily derived from the occupation of Canaan by the Israelites who had been oppressed in Egypt (Dt. i. 8, etc.). The Psalmist (*l.c.*) uses it of ultimate prosperity in this life, and triumph over the wicked, which are described in the remainder of the Psalm. Here the words supply another aspect of the possession of the kingdom. Cf. xix. 29, xxv. 34, 1 Cor. vi. 9 f., xv. 50, Gal. v. 21, Heb. i. 14, Jam. ii. 5, 1 Pet. i. 4 (with Hort's note). The meek will be συγκληρονόμοι (Rom. viii. 17) with the κληρονόμος (Mt. xxi. 38). The thought of inheritance is also found in Apocal. writings; *e.g.* Enoch v. 7 (τὴν γῆν κληρονομεῖν), *Pss. Sol.* xiv. 6 (ζωήν κλ.). For other passages see Volz, *Jüd. Esch.* 306.

Vv. 4, 5 are transposed in D 33, 𝔏 vet. vg. 𝖲 cur. diat^Eph Aphr. Clem. Orig. Greg. Nyss. Vict. Hil. Ambr. Jer. Aug. Lk. gives no help, since he omits the πραεῖς, and places the κλαίοντες after the πεινῶντες. The order in the text is probably due to the occurrence of πτωχοί and

πενθοῦντες together in Is. lxi. 1, 2 (and cf. *v.* 7 τὴν γῆν ἐκ δευτέρας κληρονομήσουσιν). But the evidence for transposition is strong, and it is favoured by the striking contrast between τῶν οὐρανῶν and τὴν γῆν, and the effect produced by the juxta-position of עֲנָיִים and עֲנָוִים. There are not sufficient reasons for considering *v.* 5 a gloss (Wellh., Bacon), though its absence, with that of either *v.* 10 or *vv.* 11 f. (see note), would give the complete number of seven Beatitudes.

6. μακ. οἱ πεινῶντες κτλ.] Another aspect of the πτωχοί. Lk. has simply μακ. οἱ πεινῶντες νῦν, expressing their actual earthly condition; Mt.'s added words bring out its spiritual side (as ἐν πνεύματι, *v.* 3); cf. Bar. ii. 18 ἡ ψυχὴ ἡ πεινῶσα. Mt. alone records that Jesus used the word δικαιοσύνη (iii. 15, v. 10, 20, vi. 1, 33, xxi. 32). But the words κ. διψῶντες τ. δικαιοσύνην are possibly a gloss : πεινᾶν with acc. is unique, though a few late instances of διψᾶν with acc. occur, and χορτασθῆναι denotes the satisfaction of hunger, not of thirst (xiv. 20, xv. 37, Lk. xv. 16, xvi. 21, Phil. iv. 12; Ps. cvi. [cvii.] 9. For its metaphorical use cf. Ps. xvi. [xvii.] 15, Tob. xii. 9 ℵ). 'Righteousness' is probably not intended to mean 'moral goodness' (as λίμος ἀρετῆς Philo, *De Septen.* vi.), which can be a present reality and is assumed in the 'poor in spirit,' but (as in vi. 33) the longed for blessing in the coming kingdom (τῆς δικ. ; contrast *v.* 10 where the art. is absent) which consists of 'vindication'; God will declare the true character of the

7 μακάριοι οἱ ἐλεήμονες, ὅτι αὐτοὶ ἐλεηθήσονται.

8 μακάριοι οἱ καθαροὶ τῇ καρδίᾳ, ὅτι αὐτοὶ τὸν θεὸν ὄψονται.

9 μακάριοι οἱ εἰρηνοποιοί, ὅτι αὐτοὶ υἱοὶ θεοῦ κληθήσονται.

righteous, to the confusion of their enemies (see J. Weiss, *Die Pred. Jesu v. Reiche Gottes*, 76 and Excursus II.). Cf. *Test. Levi* xiii. 5 which combines both meanings : ποιήσατε δικαιοσύνην ἐπὶ τῆς γῆς, ἵνα εὕρητε ἐν τοῖς οὐρανοῖς. S. Paul, who realized the present reality of the divine kingdom, taught, in consequence, the present reality of the divine gift of righteousness.

7. μακ. οἱ ἐλεήμονες] A special aspect of the poor in spirit. They are like the High Priest Himself (Heb. ii. 17, the only N.T. passage in which the adj. recurs). In the LXX. it is used frequently of God (= חָנוּן) ; of men, only in Ps. cxi. [cxii.] 4 (the whole Ps. is a beatitude on the 'righteous' man) and Prov.[3] Righteousness and Mercy were closely connected in the best Heb. thought. They are correlative in the character of God (Ps. xxxv. [xxxvi.] 11, lxxxiv. [lxxxv.] 11), and of good men (Ps. l.c.) ; and צְדָקָה is sometimes actually rendered by ἐλεημοσύνη and ἔλεος (see vi. 1 note). 'Non miserebitur sapiens, sed succurrit' (Seneca).

ὅτι αὐτ. ἐλεηθήσονται] As in the case of 'Righteousness,' those who practise Mercy shall, in the coming kingdom, receive it. Cf. Prov. xvii. 5 (ὁ δὲ ἐπισπλαγχνιζό-μενος ἐλεηθήσεται). And the converse : Jam. ii. 13 ; cf. Mt. xviii. 33 ff. The saying ἐλεᾶτε ἵνα ἐλεηθῆτε is ascribed to Jesus in Clem. Rom. xiii. 2, *Ep. Polyc.* ii. 3, Clem. Al. *Strom.* ii. 91.

8. μακ. οἱ καθαροὶ τῇ καρδίᾳ] The dat. has the same force as τῷ πνεύματι (v. 3) ; it implies a contrast between real and ceremonial purity

(cf. 1 Pet. iii. 21). The words recall Ps. li. 12, lxxiii. 1 (בָּרֵי לֵבָב), but their source is probably Ps. xxiii. [xxiv.] 3 f. : He who can ascend into the hill of Yahweh, and stand in His holy place [so that he can see Him] is the ἀθῷος χερσὶν καὶ καθαρὸς τῇ καρδίᾳ (cf. Jam. iv. 8). To possess the kingdom will be to see God. That is a final and future reward, but it can be progressively realized now in proportion to man's purity of heart. Heb. xii. 14 combines the substance of this and the next Beatitude. See the contrast in 1 Jo. iii. 2 ; 'there the Beatific vision produces the change into the same image : here the incipient God-likeness is rewarded by the Beatific vision' (J. H. Moulton). οὐκ ἀδύνατος τῆς καρδίας καθαρότης ...· οὐ τὸ γνῶναί τι περὶ θεοῦ μακάριον ὁ Κύριος εἶναί φησιν, ἀλλὰ τὸ ἐν ἑαυτῷ σχεῖν τὸν θεόν ... οὐκοῦν ὁ ἑαυτὸν βλέπων ἐν ἑαυτῷ τὸ ποθούμενον βλέπει (Greg. Nyss.). See also the passages in Philo quoted by Allen.

9. μακ. οἱ εἰρηνοποιοί] The adj. is rare (Xen., Pollux, Plut.) ; the verb occurs in Col. i. 20, Prov. x. 10, Is. xxvii. 5 (Aq., al.), and εἰρήνην ποιεῖν in Jam. iii. 18, Eph. ii. 15, Is. l.c. Cf. *Secr. Enoch* lii. 11, 'Blessed is he who establishes peace and love'; *Peah* i. 1, 'To produce peace between a man and his neighbour is reckoned among the things which bring forth good fruit in this life and benefit in the life to come.'

ὅτι αὐτοί κτλ.] God is the *auctor pacis et amator* ; and in the coming age one of the blessings of the Kingdom will be the manifesta-

μακάριοι οἱ δεδιωγμένοι ἕνεκεν δικαιοσύνης, ὅτι αὐτῶν 10
ἐστὶν ἡ βασιλεία τῶν οὐρανῶν.

μακάριοί ἐστε ὅταν ὀνειδίσωσιν ὑμᾶς καὶ διώξωσιν καὶ 11
εἴπωσιν πᾶν πονηρὸν καθ᾽ ὑμῶν ψευδόμενοι ἕνεκεν

11 ονειδισωσιν . . . διωξωσιν] tr D 33 𝕷 h k 𝕾 cur me aeth Cyp | ψευδομενοι]
om D 𝕷 b c g¹ h k m 𝕾 sin | καθ᾽ υμων] post ειπωσιν D 𝕷 h k m 𝕾 omn Tert Lcif

tion of peace-makers as His sons,
because they share His nature. The
perfect peace-maker is the Son of
God (Eph. ii. 14 f.). κληθήσονται is
virtually ἔσονται (cf. v. 19, xxi. 13
[with Lk. xix. 46], Lk. i. 32, 35).
The name reveals, and is identical
with, the nature. This, and the
thought that 'sons' are those who
share their father's nature, are
thoroughly Hebraic (cf. v. 45, xxiii.
31, Jo. viii. 39, 41 f., 1 Cor. iv. 15 f.,
Apoc. xxi. 7). But the words con-
trovert the Jewish belief that Israel,
and even all individual Israelites,
were sons of God (see Dalman,
Words, 184–9). For the thought
of divine sonship in connexion with
the coming age cf. Lk. xx. 36, Sib.
iii. 702, Enoch lxii. 11, Pss. Sol.
xvii. 30.

10. μακ. οἱ δεδιωγμένοι κτλ.] The
perf. participle does not materially
differ from a present; an Aram.
participle which it represents would
be timeless. Thus Polycarp (Phil. ii. 3)
could ascribe to the Lord the words
μακ. οἱ πτωχοὶ καὶ οἱ διωκόμενοι
ἕνεκεν δικ., ὅτι αὐτῶν ἐστιν ἡ βασ.
τοῦ θεοῦ. In v. 6 'righteousness'
(τὴν δικ.) is a future object for which
men hunger; here (without the art.)
it is a quality for which they are
persecuted. ἕνεκεν δικ. is an addition
by Mt. of the same type as τῷ
πνεύματι and τῇ καρδίᾳ (vv. 3, 8):
δεδιωγμένοι by itself implies religious
persecution, but Mt. states it explicitly. The 'persecuted' are the
'poor' of v. 3, and their μακαρισμός
is the same; the 'golden chain'

(Chrys.) of the Beatitudes is thus
linked into a circle which contains
them all. Cf. Polyc. (quoted above).

11. μακάριοί ἐστε κτλ.] This
and the foll. verse are an expansion
of v. 10; the persecution is described
in detail, and the 2nd pers. is substituted for the 3rd. This can
hardly, therefore, be their true
position, although they stood here
in Q. It is less probable that v. 10,
as some think, was constructed out of
these verses. The order διώξ., ὀνειδ.
in D may be correct, but it is probably a harmonization with Lk.
who places ὀνειδ. last of his three
verbs. Lk. adds οἱ ἄνθρωποι: Mt.
preserves the Aram. impersonal verb.
For εἴπωσιν . . . καθ᾽ ὑμῶν Lk.
has ἐκβάλωσιν τὸ ὄνομα ὑμῶν ὡς
πονηρόν: but ἐκβάλλειν can represent the Aram. אפס 'to bring
out' (sc. words from the mouth), i.e.
'to utter'; cf. Is. xlii. 3 (הוציא =
ἐκβάλλειν Mt. xii. 20), Num. xiii.
32, xiv. 36 f. (LXX. ἐξήνεγκαν and
κατείπαντες). The Aram. underlying Mt. and Lk. can perhaps be
represented by εἴπωσιν [or ἐκ-
βάλωσιν] ὄνομα πονηρὸν καθ᾽ ὑμῶν
(Wellh.). The falseness of the evil
speaking is clearly implied without
ψευδόμενοι, which is probably a
gloss. The evidence for placing καθ᾽
ὑμῶν to follow εἴπωσιν is strong;
the insertion of ψευδ. may have
drawn it to its present position, producing the meaning 'lying against
you.' ἕνεκεν ἐμοῦ (Lk. ἕν. τοῦ υἱοῦ
τοῦ ἀνθρωποῦ cannot be genuine)
introduces a thought different from

12 ἐμοῦ· χαίρετε καὶ ἀγαλλιᾶσθε, ὅτι ὁ μισθὸς ὑμῶν πολὺς ἐν τοῖς οὐρανοῖς· οὕτως γὰρ ἐδίωξαν τοὺς προφήτας τοὺς πρὸ ὑμῶν.

that in *v.* 10 (ἔν. δικαιοσύνης); see x. 18 (note), xxiv. 9.

12. χαίρετε κτλ.] Lk. χάρητε ἐν ἐκείνῃ τῇ ἡμέρᾳ, *i.e.* in the day of persecution. The joy is to be, not in spite of, but because of persecution. For the late ἀγαλλιᾶσθε Lk. has the class. σκιρτήσατε (cf. Lk. i. 41, 44), and for ὅτι his favourite ἰδοὺ γάρ (⁶, Mt.°, Mk.°). On ὁ μισθός see Add. note. ἐν τοῖς οὐρανοῖς does not locate the bliss of the coming age; it means 'with God' (see Dalman, *Words,* 206–8); cf. vi. 1, 20, Mk. x. 21, Targ. Jer. II. on Num. xxiii. 33: 'Happy are ye, O ye righteous; what a good reward is prepared for you with your Father which is in heaven for the world to come.' *Pss. Sol.* ix. 9: ὁ ποιῶν δικαιοσύνην

ἐπὶ τῆς γῆς θησαυρίζει ζωὴν ἑαυτῷ παρὰ κυρίῳ.

οὕτως γάρ κτλ.] Lk. κατὰ τὰ αὐτὰ γὰρ ἐποίουν. For the impers. ἐδίωξαν (cf. *v.* 11) Lk. adds a subject, οἱ πατέρες αὐτῶν. So here, b c k [*fratres*] Cyp^codd, and ['your fathers'] 𐎐 cur, while 𐎐 sin substitutes it for τοὺς πρὸ ὑμῶν. These variants arise partly from the fact that in Latin (*qui fuerunt ante vos*) and Aram. (דקרמיכון) τοὺς πρὸ ὑμῶν can be taken as the subject. Wellh. suggests that οἱ πατέρες αὐτῶν stands for דקרמיהון, which differs only in a single letter. It may, however, merely be derived from Lk. xi. 47 f. (Harnack). τοὺς πρὸ ὑμῶν need not imply that the disciples are reckoned as prophets (Chrys.); see x. 41 note.

Additional Note on *v. 12.*

Ideas concerning Reward form a marked feature of the Lord's teaching.

(*a*) Many passages reflect, at least on the surface, the current opinions of His day. He speaks of reward as a treasure heaped up like capital, or waiting to be enjoyed (v. 12, vi. 4, 6, 18, 20, xix. 21). The relation between God and men is that of employer or master and labourers or slaves (xx. 1–16, xxiv. 45–51, xxv. 14–30). The religious leaders of the time forfeit their heavenly reward because they have snatched a reward already by hypocrisy and ostentation (v. 46, vi. 1 f., 5, 16). The reward is sometimes a strict equivalent for something done (v. 7, vi. 14, x. 32, 41 f., xxv. 29), or a compensation for loss or self-sacrifice (x. 39, Lk. xiv. 8–11); it is also graduated according to the success with which a duty is performed (v. 19 ἐλάχιστος, xviii. 1–4, xix. 30, Mk. ix. 41, Lk. xix. 17, 19); and punishment is similarly graduated (x. 15, xi. 22, 24, Lk. xii. 47 f.). These were the ordinary Jewish ideas, in which reward was payment, graduated and *quantitative,* though protests were occasionally heard; *e.g.* Antigonus of Socho said 'Be not as slaves that minister to the master in order to receive a recompense' (*Aboth* i. 3; see Taylor).

(*b*) But on the other hand the Lord introduced new elements, which transformed the idea. Reward is purely *qualitative,* and is identical for all (xx. 1–16, xxv. 21, 23). See Swete on Apoc. xxii. 12. It is the Kingdom of Heaven, with all that that involves (v. 3–10). It is given

Ὑμεῖς ἐστὲ τὸ ἅλας τῆς γῆς· ἐὰν δὲ τὸ ἅλας μωρανθῇ, ἐν 13
τίνι ἁλισθήσεται; εἰς οὐδὲν ἰσχύει ἔτι εἰ μὴ βληθὲν ἔξω

to those for whom it has been prepared (xx. 23, xxv. 34). And since
the opportunities for good actions are themselves a divine gift (xxv.
14 f.), service is a mere duty which cannot merit reward (Lk. xvii. 9 f.).
Reward therefore becomes free, undeserved grace, and is pictured as great
out of all proportion to the service rendered (xix. 29, xxiv. 47, xxv. 21,
23, Lk. vi. 38, xii. 37). This teaching really eliminates the idea of reward
altogether, though Jesus frequently employs the popular language when He
points out the sort of actions, and spirit, that God demands. See Holtzmann, *NTTheol.* i. 192–7 (²258 ff.), and the literature cited there.

13–16. SALT AND LIGHT.

13. ὑμεῖς ἐστέ κτλ.] The first
clause is peculiar to Mt. and its
source is unknown ; the second
(preceded by καλὸν τὸ ἅλας) occurs
in Mk. ix. 49 as part of a catena
of sayings about salt ; the second
(preceded by καλὸν οὖν τὸ ἅλας) and
third occur in Lk. xiv. 34, probably
from Q, of which Mk.'s saying is possibly a reminiscence.

Salt has no beneficial effect upon
soil ; salty land is unfruitful (Dt.
xxix. 23, Ps. cvii. 34) ; 'sal, ut
arbitror, terrae nullum est' (Hil.).
The metaphor, therefore, is confined
to ἅλας, and ἡ γῆ is 'the world of
men,' being thus synonymous with
κόσμος in *v.* 14 (cf. x. 34, Apoc.
xiii. 12, Gen. xviii. 25). Iren. (I.
vi. 1) has τὸ ἅλας καὶ τὸ φῶς τοῦ
κόσμου. The two sayings probably
belong to different occasions. Bischoff
(*Jesu u. d. Rabb.* 21) suggests that
the original Aram. contained a word-
play, תבלא דתבל. Salt, ἀρχὴ πάσης
χρείας εἰς ζωὴν ἀνθρώπου (Sir. xxxix.
31 [26]), seasons food (Job vi. 6,
Col. iv. 6), and prevents corruption
(Lev. ii. 13, Ez. xliii. 24) : human
life would be both insipid and
corrupt but for the presence of good
men. They will not only be rewarded in the future (*vv.* 3–12) but
are advantageous to the world now.
ἅλας is a late form for the class. ἅλς.

ἐὰν δὲ τὸ ἅλας κτλ.] *Infatuatum
fuerit* (k); *evanuerit* (vg.). Mk. ἄναλον
γένηται. μωρός is the opposite of
σοφός, which is probably from the
same root as *sapere, sapiens, sapor* ;
it thus represents both *insipiens* and
'insipid.' For the verb cf. Rom. i.
22, 1 Cor. i. 20. ἁλισθήσεται :
Mk. ἀρτύσετε, Lk. ἀρτυθήσεται.
These parallels forbid ἡ γῆ to be
understood as the subject of the
verb (*in quo sallietur terra* k).
The Lord may have been using
a current proverb ; Joshua ben
Hananya (*c.* 80–120 A.D.) when asked
'Salt when it becomes stale wherewith shall one salt it ?' replied
'Does salt become stale ?' (*Bekor.*
8 b). The fact that it does not
('natura salis semper eadem est, nec
immutari unquam potest' Hil.) causes
no difficulty : salt may be so adulter-
ated that its taste is lessened. Where
salt and other commodities were
highly taxed (cf. Jos. *Ant.* XIII. ii.
3), the poor must sometimes have
bought salt without savour. Pliny
(*Hist. Nat.* xxxi. 82) speaks of
springs yielding 'salem inertem nec
candidum.'

εἰς οὐδὲν ἰσχύει κτλ.] For the
construction cf. Jer. xxxi. [xlviii.]
14 (εἰς), Sir. l. 29 (πρός). Lk.
εὔθετόν ἐστιν, a class. word (elsewhere only Lk. ix. 62 ; ἀνεύθετος,
Ac. xxvii. 12) ; and for εἰς οὐδέν he

14 καταπατεῖσθαι ὑπὸ τῶν ἀνθρώπων. ὑμεῖς ἐστὲ τὸ φῶς
τοῦ κόσμου. οὐ δύναται πόλις κρυβῆναι ἐπάνω ὄρους κει-
15 μένη· οὐδὲ καίουσιν λύχνον καὶ τιθέασιν αὐτὸν ὑπὸ τὸν
μόδιον ἀλλ᾽ ἐπὶ τὴν λυχνίαν, καὶ λάμπει πᾶσιν τοῖς ἐν τῇ

has οὔτε εἰς γῆν οὔτε εἰς κοπρίαν.
The thought occurs, with a different
metaphor, in Lk. xi. 34 f. 'Si
doctor erraverit, a quo alio doctore
emendabitur?' (Jer.). The words
find an illustration in Judas Iscariot.
See also Heb. vi. 4-8, x. 26-29.

14-16. Four distinct sayings are
here combined (14 a, 14 b, 15, 16),
of which all except the third are
peculiar to Mt.

14 a. τὸ φῶς τοῦ κόσμου] οὐ
λέγει δὲ ὑμεῖς ἐστὲ φῶτα, ἀλλὰ
φῶς, ἅμα σῶμα ὄντες Χριστοῦ ὃς
φῶς ἐστι τοῦ κόσμου (Petr. Laod.).
Cf. Phil. ii. 15. Ye are to the
world of men morally and spiritually
(φῶς νοητόν Chrys.) what light is
to them physically. 'Nihil esse
corporibus utilius sale et sole' (Pliny,
Hist. Nat. xxxi. 102). Spiritually 'sal
terrae' may stand for the influence
of character, 'lux mundi' for that of
teaching. The Jews claimed to be
φῶς τῶν ἐν σκότει (Rom. ii. 19);
cf. Test. Levi xiv. 3: 'Ye are the
lights of Israel'; Gen. Rab. 2, 'Let
there be light,—that is the works of
the righteous'; and see Lightft. Hor.
Heb. on Jo. viii. 12. The claim is
also made by the Christian missionary
(Ac. xiii. 47 = Is. xlix. 6). On the
status of Christians in the world see
Ep. Diogn. vi.

14 b. οὐ δύναται πόλις κτλ.] The
conspicuousness of an elevated character is the slight point of contact
with the preceding saying. Cf. Logia
Jesu 7, πόλις ᾠκοδομημένη ἐπ᾽ ἄκρον
ὄρους ὑψηλοῦ καὶ ἐστηριγμένη οὔτε
πεσεῖν δύναται οὔτε κρυβῆναι. Aug.
uses the words of the Civitas, 'fun-
data super insignem magnamque

justitiam.' Possibly a neighbouring
town illustrated the words when
they were spoken.

15. οὐδὲ καίουσιν κτλ.] It is
assumed to be impossible that a disciple, as such, can hide his light; the
ideal is that of Rom. vi. 2, 1 Jo. iii. 9.
Cf. Mk. iv. 21, Lk. viii. 16, xi. 33.
Mt. shews little or no trace of Mk.,
but Lk., in both passages, has affinities
both with Mk. and Mt. The saying
must have stood in Q (Oxf. Stud. p.
171 f.), but not in the Sermon. The
impers. plurals καίουσιν, τιθέασιν,
and the καί, point to an Aram.
original: 'a lamp is not lit and
then placed (i.e. only to be placed)
etc.' Lk. in both passages supplies
a subject, οὐδεὶς λύχνον ἅψας (the
verb, in this sense, being confined
to Lk., Ac.). Mk.: μήτι ἔρχεται ὁ
λύχνος. καίειν and ἅπτειν represent
the same original (𝔖 vet.pesh have
the same verb ܢܚܡ). For μόδιον Lk.
has σκεῦος in viii. 16 but μόδιον in
xi. 33; like Mk. (ἢ ὑπὸ τὴν κλίνην)
he adds ἢ ὑποκάτω κλίνης and εἰς
κρυπτήν. The modius was a dry
measure containing 16 sextarii, i.e.
about a peck; 𝔖 sin.pesh render it
ܣܐܬܐ = 'seah,' σάτον (cf. xiii. 33
= Lk. xiii. 21), about 1½ peck. A
'bushel' (E.V.) is about three seahs.
The article with μόδιον and λυχνίαν
is either generic or, less probably,
represents the Aram. emphatic termination.

ἀλλ᾽ ἐπὶ τὴν λυχνίαν κτλ.] The
'lampstand' (class. λυχνίον) is the
metal stand which supported the
earthenware lamp. Like the tabernacle (Ex. xxv. 31 [30] ff., Heb. ix.
2) the home lit by the lamp is a

οἰκίᾳ. οὕτως λαμψάτω τὸ φῶς ὑμῶν ἔμπροσθεν τῶν ἀνθρώ- 16
πων, ὅπως ἴδωσιν ὑμῶν τὰ καλὰ ἔργα καὶ δοξάσωσιν τὸν
πατέρα ὑμῶν τὸν ἐν τοῖς οὐρανοῖς.

Μὴ νομίσητε ὅτι ἦλθον καταλῦσαι τὸν νόμον ἢ τοὺς 17

type of the heavenly temple (Apoc.
i. 12 f., 20, ii. 1, xxi. 23). For καὶ
λάμπει κτλ. Lk. in both passages
has ἵνα οἱ εἰσπορευόμενοι βλέπωσιν
τὸ φῶς [τὸ φῶς βλ.], perhaps pressing
the simile to include the mission
preaching which brought men into
the Church (Harnack). On the
consecutive καί see Blass, § 77. 6.

16. οὕτως λαμψάτω κτλ.] This
saying passes from the ideal to the
actual; it is only too possible for
disciples to hide their light. οὕτως
does not look backwards to v. 15
(which was probably spoken on a
different occasion), but forwards to
ὅπως. The Hebraic ἔμπροσθεν (Aram.
קדם) takes the place of the dat. πᾶσιν.
The light is not now the influence of
preaching but of deeds—a Tatpredigt,
as conspicuous as possible in such a
way that (οὕτως ὅπως) men may
glorify, not the worker but, Him
who is the Source of the light (cf.
ix. 8). 1 Pet. ii. 12 seems to be a
reminiscence of the words. On the
other hand the deeds may be conspicuous in such a way that the
worker and not God is glorified (vi.
1, xxiii. 5 ff.). καλόν describes a
work as it is seen by others (xxvi.
10, Jo. x. 32 f., Heb. x. 24, Past.
Epp.⁸), ἀγαθόν in its intrinsic character, i.e. as seen by God (Rom. ii. 7,
xiii. 3, 2 Cor. ix. 8, Eph. ii. 10, Col.
i. 10, 2 Thes. ii. 17, Past. Epp.⁶).

τὸν ἐν τοῖς οὐρανοῖς] This expression is attached to 'my, our,
your Father' 20 times in Mt., once
in Mk. (xi. 25), and not in Lk. (see,
however, xi. 13). The appellation
'the Father which is in heaven' is
not found in the O.T., but appears

in Rabb. writings from the end of
the 1st cent. A.D. Earlier written
evidence is wanting, but since Jews
would be unlikely to adopt the
expression from Christians, it was
probably current at least when Mt.
was written; and Jesus may have
employed it occasionally. The
Fatherhood of God in the O.T.
largely stands for His relation to
His people as a whole, and is derived
from the early conception of a chief
as 'father' of his tribe. In late
Jewish writings His fatherly relation
to individuals begins to be understood; but in the Lord's teaching
it is central and paramount. See
further, vi. 9 note.

17-48, vi. 1-18. REAL AND LEGAL
RIGHTEOUSNESS: (a) The Law not
annulled but transcended (vv. 17-20).
(b) Application of this principle to
the teaching of the Scribes (vv. 21-
48), (c) to the life of the Pharisees
(vi. 1-18). The 'good works' just
spoken of must not, like the scribal
Tradition, consist in obedience to
the letter of the Law; without
annulling it they are to transcend
it by giving expression to the deepest
principles involved in love to God
and to man. Lk. preserves only the
sayings which treat of love to man.

17-20. THE LAW NOT ANNULLED
BUT TRANSCENDED.

17. μὴ νομίσητε κτλ.] Cf. x. 34;
also ix. 13, xx. 28. Enough time
had elapsed since the beginning of
the Ministry for the Lord's words
and actions to give the impression
that He came to destroy. For καταλῦσαι (= λύειν v. 19) cf. Ac. v.
38, Rom. xiv. 20, 2 Mac. ii. 22,

18 προφήτας· οὐκ ἦλθον καταλῦσαι ἀλλὰ πληρῶσαι· ἀμὴν
γὰρ λέγω ὑμῖν, ἕως ἂν παρέλθῃ ὁ οὐρανὸς καὶ ἡ γῆ, ἰῶτα

Jos. *Ant.* xx. iv. 2. ἀκυροῦν (xv.
6) has much the same force, and
S. Paul's favourite καταργεῖν. The
disjunctive ἤ in a negative sentence
takes the place of καί (cf. *v.* 18, Jo.
viii. 14, Blass, § 77. 11): 'the Law
and the Prophets' (so 𐤔 sin.cur, Aphr.)
comprise the Jewish Bible, the em-
bodiment of God's moral requirements (vii. 12, xi. 13, xxii. 40, Lk.
xvi. 16, Ac. xiii. 15, xxiv. 14, xxviii.
23, Rom. iii. 21); similarly 'Moses
and the Prophets' (Lk. xvi. 29, 31,
xxiv. 27, Jo. i. 45). To annul them
would be to annul the social and
religious order of Jewish life. In
the following verses, however, Jesus
speaks only of the Law; He was
never charged with annulling the
moral teaching of the prophets; ἤ
τοὺς προφήτας, therefore, may be a
later addition (see on vii. 12, xxii. 40),
reflecting the thought expressed in
Mt.'s frequent formula ἵνα πληρωθῇ.
But πληρῶσαι cannot (as in Hil.,
Chrys., *al.*) bear two different meanings as applied to the Law and to
the Prophets. Nor does it mean
'to accomplish,' in the sense of
obeying; it must refer, like καταλῦσαι, to the *teaching* for which
Christ 'came.' (For ἐλθεῖν in the
sense of a life mission cf. ix. 13, x.
34 f., xi. 18 f., xx. 28, xxi. 32, and
see xxvi. 24 note.) He came to *fill*
the Law, to reveal the full depth of
meaning that it was intended to hold
(cf. Rom. xiii. 8, Gal. v. 14, and the
instructive use of the verb in Lk.
xxii. 16). 'Although the moral law
is external, yet under the Gospel
it loses its form of external law,
and becomes an internal principle of
life' (Liddon). See Hort, *Jud. Chr.*
14 ff. Iren. uses a variety of equivalents: *adimplere* (so Vulg.), *implere*,

extendere, dilatare, augmentare; and
Tert.: *ampliare, adjectionem super-
struere*. Marcion omitted the words
(Tert. *c. Marc.* iv. 7); and his followers
declared that Jesus said οὐκ ἦλθον
πληρῶσαι τὸν νόμον ἀλλὰ καταλῦσαι (*Dial. Adamant.* ed. Bakhuyzen
88, Isid. *Ep.* i. 371); cf. the addition
to Lk. xxiii. 2 in some lat. MSS.:
'et solventem legem [nostram] et
prophetas.' Harnack, *Sitz. Akad.
Wiss. Berlin*, 1912, 184 ff., shews the
uses made of the verse in the early
Church. It is referred to in *Shabb.*
116 b (Edersheim *LT.* i. 537).

18, 19. These verses do not seem
to be in their right context, for (1)
the thought of πληρῶσαι is continued
not here but in *v.* 20, (2) *v.* 18 finds
a parallel in *v.* 20. Possibly *v.* 19 is
a later gloss (see note).

18. ἀμὴν γὰρ λέγω ὑμῖν] Mt.³¹,
Mk.¹³, Lk.⁶ Lk. (ix. 27, xii. 44
[D ἀμήν], xxi. 3) substitutes ἀληθῶς.
Jo.²⁵ has ἀμὴν ἀμὴν λέγω ὑμῖν [σοι].
In xii. 31, xxvi. 29 Mt. omits ἀμήν
where Mk. preserves it. No one but
the Lord is recorded to have used
the expression; it was a personal
peculiarity which the Christian
tradition preserved. It is not an
oath, but (like אָמְנָה 2 Kings xix. 17
(ἐν ἀληθείᾳ), Job xix. 4, xxxvi. 4 (ἐπ'
ἀληθείας)) adds force or solemnity to
an utterance. Jer. thinks of it as
equivalent to 'Thus saith the Lord'
in the O.T. prophets. ναί (xi. 9, 26,
Lk. vii. 26, xi. 51) has a similar
force; cf. ναί, ἀμήν (Apoc. i. 7).
הימנותא 'in truth' is used in the
Talm. (*Sanh.* 20 c). This is different
from its use in the Heb. of 1 Kings
i. 36, Jer. xi. 5, xxxiv. [xxviii.] 6
(LXX. γένοιτο), and its liturgical use
among Jews and Christians.

ἕως ἂν παρέλθῃ κτλ.] *i.e.* 'for

ἐν ᾗ μία κερέα οὐ μὴ παρέλθῃ ἀπὸ τοῦ νόμου ἕως ἂν
πάντα γένηται. ὃς ἐὰν οὖν λύσῃ μίαν τῶν ἐντολῶν τού- 19

ever' (= εἰς τὸν αἰῶνα), the existence
of heaven and earth constituting the
present age. For the perpetuity of
the Law see Jewish parallels quoted
by Allen (p. 45), and Jos. *Ant.* III.
viii. 10. τὰ πρὸ οὐρανοῦ καὶ γῆς
παρερχόμενα ἐσήμανεν μὴ ὄντα τοῦ
ὄντως νόμου (*Clem. Hom.* iii. 51).
See Mt. xxiv. 35 note.

ἰῶτα ἕν κτλ.] Lk. (xvi. 17) has
μία κερέα alone. For Greek readers
Mt. represented the Heb. *Yōd* by the
corresponding Gk. letter. The Engl.
'jot' was originally spelt 'iote' in
the A.V.; 'iott' (Tynd.) ; *iota* (Vulg.).
'Tittle,' originally 'title' in the A.V.,
and in previous Engl. versions, is
the Lat. *titulus*, which in late usage
meant the stroke above an abbreviated word, and hence any small
stroke or mark. The meaning of
κερέα or κεραία ('horn') is doubtful.
It is usually explained as the small
apex (Vulg.) or projection which
distinguishes certain pairs of Heb.
letters (the Rabb. קוֹץ, 'thorn' or
'spike'). But to erase one of these
may make an enormous difference in
the sense, not a small one as the
words imply. In *Vay. R.* 19 the
guilt of altering one of them is
pronounced to be so great that if
it were done the world would be
destroyed. Moreover in the early
Heb. script, and sometimes in the
square characters, the *Yōd* was
practically indistinguishable from the
Vāv, which was not a very small
letter (Lidzbarski, *Handb. d. nordsem.
Epigr.* 191). The smallness, therefore, of the alteration in the Law
is perhaps connected not with the
size of the letter *Yōd*, but with
the fact that in many words it can
be dispensed with ;—'not even a
Yōd, which is only demanded by

correctness of spelling, shall pass
away.' And κερέα is treated similarly,
if (as Burkitt conjectures) it can
mean the 'hook (letter),' *i.e. Vāv*,
which is as frequently dispensed with
as *Yōd*. But Lk.'s omission of ἰῶτα
ἕν suggests a further conjecture. If
in an early Aram. document, in
which *Yōd* and *Vāv* were indistinguishable, the words were written
as 'one ׳,' different translations might
represent them by ἰῶτα ἕν and μία
κερέα, the latter being used in Lk.,
the former in Mt. ; ἢ μία κερέα may
then have been a later harmonizing
addition in Mt. On οὐ μή in the
N.T. see Moulton, i. 190–2.

ἕως ἂν πάντα γένηται] Not in
Lk. In this position the clause is
obscure, but seems to repeat the
thought of 'till heaven and earth
have passed away.' It is probably
a gloss, due to the similar expression
in xxiv. 34 f. (Mk. xiii. 30 f., Lk.
xxi. 32 f.) which refers to the portents just described as ushering in
the Last Day. See *ZNW.* v. 253 ff.

19. ὃς ἐὰν οὖν κτλ.] On the
vernacular ἐάν for ἂν see Moulton, i.
24 f. The Jews recognized that
some of the 613 commandments in
the Law were of less importance than
others ; they sometimes distinguished
them as 'heavy' and 'light.' See
instances in Wetstein (*ad loc.*). They
also recognized that the Kingdom of
Heaven would not bring equality
to its members (xi. 11, xviii. 1–4 ;
cf. v. 12 note). See Dalman, *Words,*
113 f. ἐλάχιστος in both clauses
may be elative, 'very small' (Blass,
§ 11. 3), but in the second it is contrasted with μέγας ; under the influence of Aram., which has no adj.
forms of comparison, the three Gk.
forms could be employed almost inter-

των τῶν ἐλαχίστων καὶ διδάξῃ οὕτως τοὺς ἀνθρώπους,
ἐλάχιστος κληθήσεται ἐν τῇ βασιλείᾳ τῶν οὐρανῶν· ὃς
δ᾽ ἂν ποιήσῃ καὶ διδάξῃ, οὗτος μέγας κληθήσεται ἐν τῇ
20 βασιλείᾳ τῶν οὐρανῶν. λέγω γὰρ ὑμῖν ὅτι ἐὰν μὴ
περισσεύσῃ ὑμῶν ἡ δικαιοσύνη πλεῖον τῶν γραμματέων
καὶ Φαρισαίων, οὐ μὴ εἰσέλθητε εἰς τὴν βασιλείαν τῶν
21 οὐρανῶν. Ἠκούσατε ὅτι ἐρρέθη τοῖς ἀρχαίοις ΟΥ

changeably to express either positive
or superlative (cf. xi. 11, xviii. 1,
xxii. 36, xxiii. 11). On κληθήσεται
= ἔσται see v. 9. The verse (which
is absent from Lk.) is drawn, if
genuine, from another context, but is
possibly a gloss since no 'commandments' have been mentioned to which
τ. ἐντολῶν τούτων can refer; the use
of λύσῃ after καταλῦσαι (v. 18) is
also noticeable. But it is unnecessary
to see in it an anti-Pauline polemic.

20. λέγω γὰρ ὑμῖν κτλ.] The
γάρ forms a logical sequence with
πληρῶσαι (v. 17), not with vv. 18,
19. Something more is needed than
the ἐθελοπερισσοθρησκεία (Epiph.)
of the Scribes and Pharisees. περισσεύσῃ . . . πλεῖον: 'is more abundant
than'; cf. 1 Thes. iv. 11, Phil. i. 9.
For the brachylogy τ. γραμματέων
(= τῆς τ. γρ.) cf. Jo. v. 36. For
εἰσέρχεσθαι of attaining to final bliss
see vii. 13, 21, xviii. 3, 8 f., xix.
17, 23 f., xxiii. 14, xxv. 21, 23.

The *Scribes* (who were not all Pharisees, Mk. ii. 16, Ac. xxiii. 9) were a
comparatively small body of men who
(1) expounded the Law, (2) developed
it, (3) administered it as assessors in
courts of justice. The *Pharisees* were
the whole body of orthodox pietists
who lived the 'separated' life (Schürer,
HJP. ii. i. § 25, ii. § 26, and Swete
on Mk. i. 22). The teaching of the
Scribes is now dealt with in vv. 21-
48, the life of the Pharisees in
vi. 1-18 (cf. xxiii. 14-33). The high
moral character and teaching of many
of the Rabbis of later days cannot

be taken to prove the excellence of
Rabbinism as a whole in the time of
Jesus. Allowing for some bias on
Mt.'s part, there is enough evidence
in the synn. to shew that there were
serious grounds for the Lord's rebukes.
See also the polemic against them in
the *Fragm. of a Zadokite Work* (Charles,
Introd. p. xi.). That Rabbinism had
its good elements is seen in Mk. xii.
32-34; and after the discipline of
trouble in the upheaval of Jewish
life under Vespasian and Titus, these
elements revealed themselves in many
a remarkable life of true piety. See
Burkitt, *Gosp. Hist.* 169-173.

21-48. SPECIMENS OF LAWS WHICH
CHRIST 'FULFILLED.' Vv. 39 f., 42,
44, 48 find parallels in Lk. vi. 29 f.,
27 f., 32-36.

21, 22. *Thou shalt not murder.*

21. ἠκούσατε κτλ.] Cf. Jo. xii.
34. 'In the past (and up till now)
you always heard'; an aor. of indefinite time-reference (Moulton, i.
140). The Lord contrasts the oral
teaching of the Rabbis with His own.
The mass of the people in Galilee
could not read; they learnt the
Scriptures by hearing them read and
explained in the synagogues. ἐρρέθη
= נאמר, frequent in Rabb. writings
as a formula of bibl. quotation
(Bacher, *Exeg. Term.* i. 6). τοῖς
ἀρχαίοις, 'to men in the past' (not
'*by*,' as A.V., but no earlier E.V.);
this is not confined to the Israelites
of the time of Moses, but is as
general as possible, in contrast with

φονεγceιc· ὃς δ᾽ ἂν φονεύσῃ, ἔνοχος ἔσται τῇ κρίσει.
Ἐγὼ δὲ λέγω ὑμῖν ὅτι πᾶς ὁ ὀργιζόμενος τῷ ἀδελφῷ αὐτοῦ 22
ἔνοχος ἔσται τῇ κρίσει· ὃς δ᾽ ἂν εἴπῃ τῷ ἀδελφῷ αὐτοῦ

22 αυτου ¹°] אBΔ² 48 198 𝔏 m vg aeth ; add εικη DE al minn.pler 𝔏 vet 𝕾 omn
me arm Cyp Lcif | ρακα] א⁻B al minn.pler 𝔏 fᵇk ; ραχα א*D 𝔏 vet.pler.vg

ὑμῖν. It perhaps represents דקדמין,
or the shorter Palest. דקומין, 'those
who were before' (cf. τοὺς πρὸ ὑμῶν,
v. 12).

οὐ φονεύσεις κτλ.] The prohibition is from Ex. xx. 15 [13], Dt. v.
18 [17]; the remainder of the verse
represents the 'tradition of the elders,'
which would arise from such passages
as Ex. xxi. 12, Num. xxxv. 16–33.
ἔνοχος (cf. ἐνεχόμενος, Gal. v. 1) is
equiv. to the Rabb. חיב. Except in
its literal meaning 'held fast by'
(Heb. ii. 15; cf. Sir. Prol.) it is
always used forensically: 'liable to'
consequences (as here; cf. Ox. Pap. ii.
275, ἔνοχ. ἔστω τοῖς ἴσοις ἐπιτείμοις,
Ach. Tat. viii. 10, δυσὶ θανάτοις
ἔνοχ.); so with gen. (xxvi. 66, Gen.
xxvi. 11); 'guilty of' a crime, c. gen.
or dat. (Mk. iii. 29, Dt. xix. 10,
2 Mac. xiii. 6); 'guilty of' [violating]
a law or other object (1 Cor. xi. 27,
Jam. ii. 10). τῇ κρίσει is 'legal
proceedings,' a mild term for the
punishment of murder, chosen in
order to lead up to, and throw into
relief, the contrast in v. 22 (Wellh.).

22. ἐγὼ δὲ λέγω ὑμῖν] τίς γὰρ
προφητῶν οὕτω ποτὲ ἐφθέγξατο; τίς
δικαίων; τίς πατριαρχῶν; ἀλλὰ
Τάδε λέγει κύριος (Chrys.).

πᾶς ὁ ὀργιζόμενος κτλ.] The overt
act of murder does not exhaust the
meaning of the commandment. ἀδελφός (vv. 23 f., vii. 3 ff., xviii. 15, 21),
like ὁ πλησίον (Lk. x. 27, 29), would
to Jewish ears mean only a fellow-
Jew; but for a real 'fulfilling' of
the Law it must embrace every human
being. εἰκῇ is supported by strong
textual evidence, but intrinsically it

is more probable that the Lord did
not say it; the sharp antithesis
between act and feeling, with no
qualifying addition, is in keeping
with many of His utterances (see v.
32 note). Orig. (on Eph. iv. 21)
notices both readings, but rejects
εἰκῇ; so Basil and Jer., probably
following him; and it is said to have
been omitted in the Naz. Gosp. (Texte
u. Unt., 1911, pp. 22, 39). ἔνοχος
ἔστ. τ. κρίσει must have a meaning
analogous to that in v. 21; anger,
like murder, is a crime. Orig.ˡᵃᵗ.
(on Jos. ix. 3) represents the words
by 'homicida est'; and 1 Jo. iii. 15
is perhaps an interpretation of them.
But since no civil court can take
cognisance of angry thoughts or
feelings ('cogitationis poenam nemo
patitur'), ἡ κρίσις here means judgment at God's hands. Cf. Jer. Baba
K. v. 2, 'absolved from the judgment
of men, but guilty in the judgment of
Heaven.'

ὃς δ᾽ ἂν εἴπῃ κτλ.] The Lord
passes from feelings to words. ῥακά
is probably the Aram. ריקא (abbrev.
form ריק), 'empty'; cf. Jam. ii. 20.
A plur. רקייא, without the diphthong,
is cited by Dalman (Gr. 138 n.).
On the v.l. ῥαχά see id. 304 n.
As an expression of contempt it is
not infrequent in Jewish writings
(see reff. in Lightfoot, Hor. Heb., and
Allen (ad loc.)). Aug., indeed, was
told by a Jew that it had no meaning,
but was an angry interjection; and
Chrys. explains it as a haughty mode
of addressing an inferior (cf. Engl.
'Sirrah'); but both can be rejected.
It is here treated as expressive of

Ῥακά, ἔνοχος ἔσται τῷ συνεδρίῳ· ὃς δ' ἂν εἴπῃ Μωρέ, 23 ἔνοχος ἔσται εἰς τὴν γέενναν τοῦ πυρός. ἐὰν οὖν προσφέρῃς τὸ δῶρόν σου ἐπὶ τὸ θυσιαστήριον κἀκεῖ μνησθῇς

abuse so gross or libellous as to be actionable. τῷ συνεδρίῳ: hebraized as סנהדרין. Probably not the supreme court at Jerusalem, but the local court of discipline (Jos. *Ant.* IV. viii. 14 ; cf. Mt. x. 17 = Mk. xiii. 9), which met in the synagogue (see Hatch, *Organization*, 58) ; ﬡ vet.pesh render ܟܢܘܫܬܐ (= συναγωγή). In *Sanh.* i. 6 an inferior Sanhedrin (ס״ קְטַנָּה) is mentioned, consisting of thirteen persons ; such a court, in every town with a population above 120 [or 230], was competent to deal even with capital charges (*id.* 4). See Schürer, *HJP.* II. i. 153 f. ; and for an account of the word συνέδριον, *id.* 169 f. ; it was not a *governing* body, but a court of judgment.

ὃς δ' ἂν εἴπῃ Μωρέ] 'Fool' ; 𝕃 *fatue* (cf. *v.* 13 note). The Gk. word was adopted in the Midrashim (Neubauer, *Stud. Oxon.*, 1885, p. 55, Levy, *NHebWörterb.*), and may have passed into Aram. by the time of Jesus. It hardly differs in meaning from ῥακά, and was probably intended to be its equivalent (see below). It occurs in the Gospels only in Mt.[7] Before εἰς τὴν γέενναν the words τοῦ βληθῆναι must be understood (cf. *vv.* 29 f., xviii. 9).

For τ. γέενναν τ. πυρός cf. xviii. 9. 'Gehenna' (גֵּי הִנֹּם, 'the valley of Hinnom') was a ravine on the W. of Jerusalem, the supposed site of the fire-worship of Molech introduced by Ahaz, and later the place where the offal of the city was burnt ; hence it became a symbol of the place of future punishment. See further Swete on Mk. ix. 43, and Volz, *Jüd. Esch.* 288–292 ; and on the form of the word, Dalman, *Gr.* 146. For fire

as a symbol of final punishment see iii. 10 note.

The verse has been variously explained. It is usual to see in it an ascending scale of wickedness, with a corresponding scale of punishment, *i.e.* angry feelings are punishable by the local court (κρίσις), *raka* by the supreme court (συνέδριον), and *more* by God (γέεννα). But the above notes shew that this is improbable ; others, equally improbable, are mentioned by Allen. The best yet offered is that of Peters (*JBL.*, 1892, 131 f.) and Bacon (*Serm. on the Mt.*), *i.e.* that both *v.* 21 and the *raka* sentence (*v.* 22 b) contain the current Jewish teaching, to each of which Jesus opposes His own teaching in *v.* 22 a and the *more* sentence (*v.* 22 c) respectively. The Rabbis say that murder is liable to judgment, but I say that anger, its equivalent, is liable to (divine) judgment. And (the Rabbis say that) abusive language such as *raka* is punishable by the local court, but I say that abusive language such as *more*, its equivalent, is punishable by the fire of Gehenna.

23–26. *Two illustrations of the above principle* (*v.* 23 f. ; *v.* 25 f. = Lk. xii. 58 f.).

23. ἐὰν οὖν προσφέρῃς κτλ.] The lay worshipper brought his gift, whether an animal or otherwise, to the inner court of the temple, in which the altar stood. Into this he might enter only 'when it was necessary for the purpose of laying on of hands, or for slaughtering, or waving' (Schürer, *HJP.* II. i. 284). ἔχει τι κατὰ σοῦ: cf. Apoc. ii. 4, 14, 20. It is implied that the offerer has been in the wrong ; con-

ὅτι ὁ ἀδελφός σου ἔχει τι κατὰ σοῦ, ἄφες ἐκεῖ τὸ δῶρόν 24
σου ἔμπροσθεν τοῦ θυσιαστηρίου, καὶ ὕπαγε πρῶτον διαλλάγηθι τῷ ἀδελφῷ σου, καὶ τότε ἐλθὼν πρόσφερε τὸ
δῶρόν σου. ἴσθι εὐνοῶν τῷ ἀντιδίκῳ σου ταχὺ ἕως ὅτου 25
εἶ μετ᾽ αὐτοῦ ἐν τῇ ὁδῷ, μή ποτέ σε παραδῷ ὁ ἀντίδικος
τῷ κριτῇ, καὶ ὁ κριτὴς τῷ ὑπηρέτῃ, καὶ εἰς φυλακὴν βλη-
θήσῃ· ἀμὴν λέγω σοι, οὐ μὴ ἐξέλθῃς ἐκεῖθεν ἕως ἂν 26

trast Mk. xi. 25. For the thought
cf. Barn. xix. 12, οὐ προσήξεις ἐπὶ
προσευχὴν ἐν συνειδήσει πονηρᾷ.

24. πρῶτον διαλλάγηθι κτλ.] The
verb (here only in the N.T.) occurs
in Jud. xix. 3 (A), 1 Regn. xxix. 4,
1 Esd. iv. 31; a 2nd cent. papyr.
(BU. iii. 846) has διαλάγηθί μοι.
In the N.T. καταλλάσσειν, -λαγή
(Rom., 1, 2 Cor.), and ἀποκαταλ-
λάσσειν (Eph., Col.) denote, as here,
the reconciling of the sinner to him
that is sinned against, not vice versa.
For a Rabb. parallel, Midr. Tanch.
iii. 7 a, see Schechter, Some aspects
of Rabb. Theol. 228. The details of
the passage obviously cannot be
pressed. The offended brother, as
Aug. says, might have travelled far,
even beyond the seas. The scenery
is incidental to the main thought.
(Cf. the similar injunction in Tos.
Baba K. x. 18, quoted by Abrahams,
Camb. Bibl. Ess. 189.) Since, however, the scenery is placed in Jerusalem, and Galileans would seldom
be able to bring a gift to the temple
in person (see Schürer, HJP. II. i.
275), it is possible that vv. 23 f.
originally stood in another context,
and were spoken in Judaea. That
they are an altered form of Mk. xi.
25 is improbable.

25. ἴσθι εὐνοῶν κτλ.] On ἴσθι
with a participle see Moulton, i.
226 f. εὐνοεῖν (class.) is rare in bibl.
Gk. : Dan. ii. 43 (LXX.), 3 Mac. vii.
11, and see Field, Hexapla, on Gen.
xxxiv. 15. It is strange, however,

that the offending party should be
exhorted to ' be favourably minded '
towards his opponent. Lk. has δὸς
ἐργασίαν ἀπηλλάχθαι ἀπ᾽ αὐτοῦ
(' to be quit of him '); and since the
cause of complaint, as ' the last
quadrans' (v. 26) shews, is an unpaid
debt, εὐνοῶν may have arisen from a
mistaken rendering of שַׁלֵּם (' pay
back '), as though it meant ' make
peace.' ἀντίδικος is probably the
injured party (so Chrys., Jer.) ; in Ox.
Pap. i. 37 it means ' defendant.' Some
explain it as God (see Allen) ; early
writers understood it of the Law
(Orig., Theoph., Aug.), or the devil
(Clem. Al.). See below. The words
ἕως . . . τῇ ὁδῷ emphasize ταχύ :
' at once, before you and he reach the
presence of the Judge.' ὑπηρέτης
(Lk. πράκτωρ) is an inferior official
in attendance upon a superior (xxvi.
58, Jo. vii. 32, 45 f., xviii. 12, 22,
Ac. v. 22, 26). Each local sanhedrin
had two such, who were Levites in
attendance as police (Jos. Ant. IV.
viii. 14) ; they are called שֹׁטְרִים in
Sanh. 16 b.

26. ἀμὴν λέγω σοι κτλ.] A
picture of inevitable punishment ;
cf. xviii. 30, 34. κοδράντης, quadrans,
is a latinism which passed into late
Heb. as קרדינטס (Jer. Kidd. 12 a). It
was ¼ as (ἀσσάριον, x. 29), c. ⅝
farthing. Plut. has the form κοναδράν-
της. Lk. has λεπτόν (Heb. פרוטה),
which was ½ quadrans (cf. Mk. xii.
42). See HDB. iii. 426 a. On οὐ
μή see Moulton, i. 191.

27 ἀποδῷς τὸν ἔσχατον κοδράντην.   Ἠκούσατε ὅτι
28 ἐρρέθη Οϒ μοιχεϒϲειϲ. Ἐγὼ δὲ λέγω ὑμῖν ὅτι πᾶς ὁ βλέπων γυναῖκα πρὸς τὸ ἐπιθυμῆσαι αὐτὴν ἤδη ἐμοίχευσεν
29 αὐτὴν ἐν τῇ καρδίᾳ αὐτοῦ.   εἰ δὲ ὁ ὀφθαλμός σου ὁ δεξιὸς

It is probable that *vv.* 25 f. are not intended to be, in the main, allegorical. Commentators have varied in their interpretation of the details, and Lk.'s version differs somewhat from Mt.'s in mentioning an ἄρχων (? = ἀρχισυνάγωγος, see Mt. ix. 18 note) as well as a κριτής. The verses can, in the first instance, be understood literally : ' Put matters right while you can with anyone to whom you are in debt, before he hands you over to the synagogue authorities for judgment and punishment.' But the solemn ἀμὴν λέγω σοι indicates that, though the details need not be allegorized, deeper thoughts underlie the words. The day of judgment is close at hand, when the unpaid creditor will be able to claim divine justice. The literal and the metaphorical are inextricably combined. They are more distinctly separated, but with a similar thought, in xviii. 34 f., Lk. xviii. 2–8 a.

27, 28. *Thou shalt not commit Adultery.*

27. On the varieties of order in which the commandments of the Decalogue occur in Jewish and Christian literature see the writer's *Exodus*, 119.

28. ἐγὼ δέ κτλ.] The Lord takes the same attitude as in *v.* 21 f. : the Rabbis had legislated only for actions, not for thoughts. πρὸς τὸ ἐπιθυμ. is not strictly final (Greg. Nyss., Chrys., Isid.), but expresses the result or tendency (Moulton, i. 218 ff.) ; ' whosoever seeth a woman and longeth for her ' (S̃ sin.cur). The unclass. acc. αὐτήν is in accordance

with Ex. xx. 17 ; cf. Sir. i. 26 [33], xl. 22. ἤδη ἐμοίχευσεν : *ipso facto*, before the thought has led to overt action. The teaching is higher than that of the tenth commandment, which deals only with the desire to possess another's property (see the writer's *Exodus, ad loc.*). A nearer approach to the Lord's standard is seen in Job xxxi. 1, 7, 9, Sir. ix. 5, 9, xxiii. 4, xxvi. 9, Jubil. xx. 4, ' Let them not commit fornication with her after their eyes and their heart.' Similar utterances occur in Rabb. writings ; see Lightfoot, *Hor. Heb. ad loc.*

29, 30. *The right eye and hand.*

The passage is similar to xviii. 8 f. (= Mk. ix. 43–47), where hand, *foot*, and eye are spoken of. There it occurs in a collection of sayings about σκάνδαλα, here an appropriate sequence of thought is formed by omitting the ' foot ' : ' rather than yield yourselves to lust, to which eye or hand may tempt you, lose the best member that you have.'

29. εἰ δὲ ὁ ὀφθαλμός κτλ.] The right eye is not more valuable than the left ; it· is an assimilation to ἡ δεξιά (*v.* 30), but it emphasizes the self-sacrifice ; 'quod in nobis optimum est' (Jer.). εἰ with indic. (cf. xviii. 8 f.) assumes an actual fact, ἐὰν σκανδαλίσῃ (Mk.) a possible contingency ; cf. ἐὰν προσφέρῃς (*v.* 23). σκανδαλίζειν (Vg. *scandalizare*, A.V. ' offend ' from Tyndale) seems to be confined to bibl. and eccles. writers, and is always (like σκάνδαλον, see xiii. 41 note) used in an ethical sense ; cf. Dan. xi. 41 (LXX.) = נִכְשְׁל, Sir. ix. 5, xxiii. 8, xxxv. 15 [xxxii.

σκανδαλίζει σε, ἔξελε αὐτὸν καὶ βάλε ἀπὸ σοῦ, συμφέρει
γάρ σοι ἵνα ἀπόληται ἐν τῶν μελῶν σου καὶ μὴ ὅλον τὸ
σῶμά σου βληθῇ εἰς γέενναν· καὶ εἰ ἡ δεξιά σου χεὶρ 30
σκανδαλίζει σε, ἔκκοψον αὐτὴν καὶ βάλε ἀπὸ σοῦ, συμφέρει γάρ σοι ἵνα ἀπόληται ἐν τῶν μελῶν σου καὶ μὴ ὅλον

29 βληθη] απελθη D [om. v. 30] 𝕷 a b c d g¹ h [k om.verb] 𝕾 sin [om. v. 30].
cur me

19] = הֲקִים, Pss. Sol. xvi. 7, and in
Aq., Sym. ἔξελε . . . ἀπὸ σοῦ (so
xviii. 9) expands Mk.'s ἔκβαλε αὐτόν.
Cf. Heliod. ii. 84, τὸν ὀφθαλμὸν
ἐξεῖλε τὸν δεξιόν. The eye is the
very member which should preserve
one from stumbling (cf. the thought
in v. 13, vi. 23), instead of being a
stumbling-block. Several patr. writers
interpret eye and hand as close
friends or relations who must be excommunicated if they cause offence.

συμφέρει γάρ κτλ.] The spiritual
teaching is couched in popular Jewish
language which implies the punishment of the material body in Gehenna
(cf. x. 28). This is expressed even
more vividly in xviii. 8 f., where the
possibility is also pictured of entering
into life maimed or lame. συμφέρει (xviii. 6, xix. 10), and its
equivalent καλόν ἐστιν (xviii. 8 f.,
xxvi. 24), correspond with the Rabb.
נוח ליה. On the use of ἵνα see Blass,
§ 69. 5. For the passive βληθῇ
v. 30 has ἀπέλθῃ (more Aram., cf. viii.
12 note), which may be the true
reading here; the former is used in
xviii. 8 f., where the parallel in Mk.
has both. On 'Gehenna' see v. 22.

30. καὶ εἰ ἡ δεξιά κτλ.] The
omission of the verse in D 𝕾 sin was
probably due to homoeoteleuton, not
to the idea that the hand cannot be
an instrument of lust (Wellh.). Eye
and hand are figurative of all occasions
of sin; cf. xix. 12. The sin itself
comes from the heart (xv. 19). For
a Jewish parallel see Lightfoot, Hor.

Heb. εἰς γέενναν ἀπελθεῖν (cf. xxv.
46) is the opposite of εἰσελθεῖν εἰς
τὴν βασιλείαν (v. 20, vii. 21, xviii.
3, 8 f., xix. 23), τὴν ζωήν (xix. 17),
τὴν χαρὰν τοῦ Κυρίου (xxv. 21, 23).

31, 32. (Lk. xvi. 18.)   Divorce.
Cf. Mt. xix. 9, Mk. x. 11, 12.

These passages contain four statements on the subject : (a) The man
who divorces his wife [except for
fornication (Mt.)], and marries
another, commits adultery (ch. xix.,
Mk., Lk.). (b) The woman who
divorces her husband, and marries
another, commits adultery (Mk.).
(c) The man who marries a divorced
woman commits adultery (here, Lk.).
(d) The man who divorces his wife
[apart from fornication] causes her
to commit adultery (here). Mt.
(xix. 9) adopts (a) from Mk. (who
was possibly influenced by Q); but
he omits (b), probably because the
divorce of a husband by the wife
was a novel and alien custom, permitted by Roman law, but repugnant
to Jewish feeling; see Jos. Ant. xv.
vii. 10 (Salome), XVIII. v. 4 (Herodias).
Since Lk. xvi. 18 follows the saying
about the permanence of the Law
(notice κερέα), which stands at the
head of the section to which Mt. v.
31 f. belongs, it is possible that Lk.
drew (a) not from Mk, but from Q,
which also contained (c) and probably
(d). The Lord may, of course, have
delivered more than one utterance
on divorce.

31 τὸ σῶμά σου εἰς γέενναν ἀπέλθῃ.   Ἐρρέθη δέ
32 Ὃς ἂν ἀπολύσῃ τὴν γυναῖκα αὐτοῦ, δότω αὐτῇ ἀποστάσιον. Ἐγὼ
δὲ λέγω ὑμῖν ὅτι πᾶς ὁ ἀπολύων τὴν γυναῖκα αὐτοῦ
παρεκτὸς λόγου πορνείας ποιεῖ αὐτὴν μοιχευθῆναι, καὶ ὃς

32 πας ο απολυων] אBL *al* minn.*nonn* 𝔏 c f ff¹ g² l m vg 𝕾 pesh. hcl. pal arm
aeth ; os αν απολυση DE *al* minn.*pl* 𝔏 a b g¹ h k 𝕾 sin. cur me | και . . . μοιχαται]
om D 64 𝔏 a b k *codd. Gr. et Lat. ap. Aug.*

31. ἐρρέθη δέ] The change in the
formula suggests that the passage was
not originally part of the sermon.

ὃς ἄν κτλ.] In Dt. xxiv. 1–3 it
is laid down that if a man gives to
his wife a writ of divorcement because
of some ἄσχημον πρᾶγμα, and if
another man marries her and (because he hates her) gives her a writ
of divorcement and [Heb. or] dies,
the former husband may not take
her again to be his wife (see Driver
ad loc.). This, as Aug. recognizes,
is not a law prescribing divorce, but
merely a restriction laid upon a
custom that is taken for granted.
But on the strength of the passage,
divorce was frequently practised on
the most trivial pretexts (see on
xix. 3). ὃς ἄν κτλ. is perhaps a
specimen of the manner in which
the Rabbis paraphrased Deut. ; the
giving of the writ is represented as
explicitly permitted (δότω). In xix.
7 the Pharisees go further, and justify
as a Mosaic *command* the divorce as
well as the writ ; τί οὖν Μωυσῆς
ἐνετείλατο (Mk. ἐπέστρεψεν M.) ;
On ἀπολύσῃ see i. 18 f. ἀποστάσιον
(𝔏 *repudium*) is an abbreviation of
βιβλίον ἀποστασίου (xix. 7, Mk.
x. 4, Is. l. 1, Jer. iii. 8) = סֵפֶר
כְּרִיתֻת ; so Vulg. here, *libellus repudii.*
For its commercial use in papyri see
M.-M. *Vocab. s.v.*

32. ἐγὼ δέ κτλ.] The Lord
declares that, according to the true
spirit of the divine Law, divorce is
sinful ; 'plane Christus vetat divor-
tium, Moyses vero permittit' (Tert.).

The *v.l.* πᾶς ὁ ἀπολύων may be due
to assimilation to Lk. ; ὃς ἂν ἀπολύσῃ
might be due to *v.* 31, xix. 9, and
Mk., but it has strong MS. support.

παρεκτὸς λόγου πορνείας] παρεκτός (= πλήν) is rare : Dt. i. 36
(Aq.), Lev. xxiii. 38 (another translator ; see Field), *Test. Zeb.* i. 4,
Didach. vi. 1. This saving clause
(cf. μὴ ἐπὶ πορνείᾳ, xix. 1) is absent
from Mk. and Lk. ; and S. Paul
(1 Cor. vii. 10 f.) does not appear to
recognize any exception. In Dt.
xxii. 22 the sin is punished, not by
divorce but, by death ; cf. Jos. *Ant.*
iv. viii. 23, *Sanh.* i. 1 (with Hölscher's
note in Fiebig's *Mischnatractate* vi.).
It is probable that it did not come
from the Lord's lips. The Christian
Church, with its authority to bind
and loose (xvi. 19, xviii. 18), early
made the exception to meet a pressing
ethical need ; and since the need
has not ceased, the exception is valid
to-day. Jesus, who declared the near
approach of the divine kingdom, constantly laid down principles without
reference to any limitations which
the complexity of life now demands
(see *vv.* 34, 38, 42, vii. 1). The re-
marriage of either party can claim
the authority neither of Jesus nor
the Church. λόγος πορνείας may
be equivalent to דְּבַר עֶרְוָה, 'a matter
of unchastity' (see Allen), which is
a transposition of עֶרְוַת דָּבָר (ἄσχημον
πρᾶγμα) in Dt. xxiv. 1. For πορνεία
of the sin of a married woman cf.
Hos. ii. 5 [7], Am. viii. 17, Sir.
xxiii. 23.

ἐὰν ἀπολελυμένην γαμήσῃ μοιχᾶται.   Πάλιν ἠκούσατε 33
ὅτι ἐρρέθη τοῖς ἀρχαίοις Ογκ ἐπιορκήсεις, ἀποδώсεις δὲ τῷ
κγρίῳ τογς ὅρκογς сογ.   Ἐγὼ δὲ λέγω ὑμῖν μὴ ὀμόσαι ὅλως· 34

ποιεῖ αὐτ. μοιχευθῆναι κτλ.] For
the pass. cf. Lev. xx. 10, Sir. xxiii.
23. Her re-marriage is assumed as
certain, and her divorce has led her to
it; but since divorce is sinful, and the
first marriage still valid, the second
union is also sinful. In xix. 4-8,
Mk. x. 5-9 the condemnation of
divorce is more fully expressed by
reference to the divine act of creation.
The MS. evidence does not warrant
the omission of καὶ ὃς ἐάν κτλ., nor
can the clause be due to harmonization
with Lk. xvi. 18, which coincides
with it only in a single word. On
ἐάν for ἄν see v. 19.

33-37. *Oaths.*

33. οὐκ ἐπιορκήσεις κτλ.] Not
a quotation, but a summary of the
substance of such passages as Ex. xx.
7, Lev. xix. 12, Num. xxx. 3 [Engl.
2], Dt. xxxiii. 22–24; cf. Eccl. v.
3 f. [Engl. 4 f.]. The words occur
in the *Didache* (ii. 3), and were
probably part of the Jewish teaching
on the 'Two Ways' (see Harnack,
Die Ap.lehre u. d. jüd. beiden Wege [2],
p. 58). ἐπ[ἐφ-]ιορκεῖν occurs in
1 Esd. i. 48, Wisd. xiv. 28, *Ox. Pap.*
i. 255. Cf. ὁ ἐπίορκος (Zach. v. 3).
ἀποδώσεις, rare of fulfilling an oath,
is derived from Dt. *l.c.*; elsewhere
in the N.T. it is used with εὐχή.
The use of oaths and vows by the
Jews, as by other Semites, was
often indiscriminate and frivolous.
Jewish casuistry reached its climax
in the discussions as to their validity; see xv. 5, xxiii. 16–18. The
subject is treated in Mishn. *Shebuoth*, and see Philo, *De spec. leg.*
i.–vi.

34. ἐγὼ δὲ λέγω ὑμῖν κτλ.]

The Lord does not deal with the
observance of oaths; He does not
abrogate the Law, but goes behind
it by forbidding all oaths. 'Evan-
gelica veritas non recipit jura-
mentum, cum omnis sermo fidelis
pro jurejurando sit' (Jer.). Cf. Sir.
xxiii. 9 ff. μὴ ὀμόσαι (aor.) is a
prohibition for the future; S. James
(v. 12) has μὴ ὀμνύετε, attacking
a present evil (Moulton, i. 122–6);
he also paraphrases ὅλως as μήτε
ἄλλον τινὰ ὅρκον. The Lord does
not mention possible limitations to
the general principle (see v. 32 note).
He did not necessarily countenance
the high priest's adjuration, although
He replied to it (see xxvi. 63 f.).
The Anabaptists and Quakers understood the prohibition to be absolute.
On the other hand S. Paul uses
solemn expressions of appeal to God,
and even writes νὴ τὴν ὑμετέραν
καύχησιν (1 Cor. xv. 31) and
ἐνορκίζω ὑμᾶς τὸν Κύριον (1 Thes.
v. 27); and the argument of Heb.
vi. 13–17 would have been impossible had the author thought of
oaths as sinful. The Lord undoubtedly condemns angry or
thoughtless oaths in ordinary conversation, since He could not take
a 'secular' view of anything in
human life; any object by which a
man can swear is so inseparable
from God, that to swear by it is to
swear by Him (vv. 34 b–36; cf xxiii.
21 f.). But this seems, by implication, to allow a reverent oath as a
sacred act. See the 39th Article in
the English Pr. Book. On the
Essene abstinence from oaths, except
at their initiation, see Jos. *BJ.* II
viii. 6 f.

35 μήτε ἐν τῷ ογρανῷ, ὅτι θρόνος ἐcτὶν τοῇ θεοῇ· μήτε ἐν τῇ
γῇ, ὅτι ὙποπόΔιόν ἐcτιν τῶν ποΔῶν αὙτοῇ· μήτε εἰς
36 Ἰεροσόλυμα, ὅτι πόλιc ἐcτὶν τοῇ μεγάλοΥ Βαcιλέωc· μήτε
ἐν τῇ κεφαλῇ σου ὀμόσῃς, ὅτι οὐ δύνασαι μίαν τρίχα
37 λευκὴν ποιῆσαι ἢ μέλαιναν. ἔστω δὲ ὁ λόγος ὑμῶν
ναὶ ναί, οὐ οὔ· τὸ δὲ περισσὸν τούτων ἐκ τοῦ πονηροῦ

μήτε ἐν τῷ οὐρανῷ κτλ.] ἐν =
בְּ (cf. xxiii. 16–22). 'Heaven' is
not here the Jewish periphrasis for
the divine Name, but 'the sky,'
the place where God dwells, as the
next words shew. The 'throne'
implies 'Him that sitteth thereon'
(xxiii. 22), and therefore to swear by
'heaven' is profanation. In Shebuoth
iv. 13 it is said that to swear by the
heavens and by the earth is not an
oath that is binding upon witnesses.

35. ὅτι ὑποπόδιον κτλ.] A reference, with the last clause, to Is. lxvi.
I (quoted in Ac. vii. 49); cf. Lam. ii.
I (Zion is the 'footstool'). R. Gamaliel
II. (A.D. 95) speaks of the temple as
'the footstool of God's glory' (Siphre
43). For ὑποπόδιον cf. also Jam. ii.
3, Ps. cix. [cx.] I (see on Mt. xxii.
44). It occurs in two papyri of the
2nd cent. A.D. (Deissm. BSt. 223),
and in Athenaeus (3rd cent.).

μήτε εἰς Ἰεροσόλυμα κτλ.] The
change of preposition perhaps reflects a Jewish custom alluded to in
Tos. Nedar. i., that an oath 'by Jerusalem' is nothing unless it is sworn
'towards J.' On Ἰεροσόλυμα see ii.
I. ὅτι πόλις κτλ. is a reference
to Ps. xlvii. [xlviii.] 3. If throne
and footstool imply the presence of
God, no less does His own city; it is
that which makes it ἡ ἁγία πόλις
(iv. 5). For μέγας βασιλεύς, a
title assumed by the Assyrian King
(4 Regn. xviii. 19), cf. Ps. xciv.
[xcv.] 3, Tob. xiii. 15.

36. μήτε ἐν τῇ κεφαλῇ κτλ.]
'By the life of thy head' is an oath
in Sanh. iii. 12. The head might

be thought a man's absolute possession; but God alone can so much as
make a hair of it white or black, i.e.
make a man look old, or preserve
the dark hair of his youth; cf. x.
30.

37. ἔστω δέ κτλ.] If the meaning is 'Let your speech be Yea, yea
etc.', the second ναί and οὔ might
be understood as adding emphasis to
the first. But unnecessary emphasis
is what the Lord condemns. In
Sanh. 36 a it is laid down that
הֵן and לֹא, if said twice, are oaths.
A possible rendering is 'But let your
word Yea be [i.e. really mean] yea,
your Nay [mean] nay.' An oath is
quite superfluous or is employed to
give colour to an untruth. The
words are so understood by S. James
(v. 12): ἤτω δὲ ὑμῖν τὸ Ναὶ ναί,
καὶ τὸ Οὒ οὔ, and in references to
Mt. in Just. Apol. i. 16, Clem. Hom.
iii. 55, xix. 2; see also Clem. Strom.
v. 14, vii. 67, Epiph. Haer. xix. 6.
Cf. Ruth Rabba, iii. 18, 'with the
righteous their Yea is yea, and their
Nay nay.'

τὸ δὲ περισσόν κτλ.] For
περισσόν = πλέον see Blass, § 11. 3,
n. 4. ἐκ τ. πονηροῦ ἐστίν: 'results
from the evil' that is in the world
(Aug.). Oaths are the result of
the untruthfulness of men. Or τὸ
πονηρόν is the evil in a man's heart
(cf. xii. 35). Clem. Al., Greg. Nyss.,
al. explain the adj. as masc., referring to the devil (cf. 1 Jo. iii. 12);
but the neuter is more probable, as
in v. 39. S. James (l.c.) paraphrases
ἵνα μὴ ὑπὸ κρίσιν πέσητε. With

ἐστίν. Ἠκούσατε ὅτι ἐρρέθη Ὀφθαλμὸν ἀντὶ 38
ὀφθαλμοῦ καὶ ὀδόντα ἀντὶ ὀδόντος· Ἐγὼ δὲ λέγω ὑμῖν 39
μὴ ἀντιστῆναι τῷ πονηρῷ· ἀλλ' ὅστις σε ῥαπίζει εἰς τὴν
δεξιὰν σιαγόνα σου, στρέψον αὐτῷ καὶ τὴν ἄλλην· καὶ τῷ 40
θέλοντί σοι κριθῆναι καὶ τὸν χιτῶνά σου λαβεῖν, ἄφες αὐτῷ

39 δεξιαν] om D 𝔏 k codd. ap. Aug 𝖘 sin.cur

the whole passage cf. *Secr. Enoch*
xlix. 1 (quoted by Allen), and
Morfill and Charles' note *ad loc.*,
where passages from Philo are quoted.

38–42. (Lk. vi. 29 f.) *Retaliation*.
Lk. has no parallels to *vv.* 38, 39 a,
41.

38. ὀφθαλμόν κτλ.] The quotation is found in Ex. xxi. 24, Dt. xix.
21, Lev. xxiv. 20. The two latter
are elliptical, the accus., as here,
being governed by no verb; Ex. has
δώσει. The law of the *jus talionis*,
like that of divorce (see *v.* 31), was
restrictive rather than permissive;
it limited revenge by fixing an exact
compensation for an injury. Celsus'
question πότερον Μωϋσῆς ἢ Ἰησοῦς
ψεύδεται; is quite unwarranted.
In the Mishna (*Baba K.* viii. 1 ff.)
a money payment is taken for
granted, instead of eye, tooth etc.,
and this had doubtless become the
custom before the time of Jesus.
But the words embody a principle,
born of a sense of justice, which He
did not abrogate, but behind which
He penetrated. His disciples are to
be so free of self that they do not
even desire human justice. He
'fulfils' the ἀκριβεία of the Law by
the ἐπιείκεια of the Gospel (cf. Rom.
xii. 19). As before, He teaches the
principle, without limitations (see *v.*
32 note), by means of concrete instances (see Wendt, *The Teaching of
Jesus*, 130–4); and if modern
Christians took His words *ad literam*,
they would be doing precisely what He
deprecates: they would be exalting

the letter at the expense of the
principle. To decline legal justice
would often involve injustice to
others; S. Paul did not scruple to
appeal to it (Ac. xvi. 37, xxiv.
10–21, xxv. 8–12). For class. injunctions of patience under injuries
see Heinrici, *Beiträge*, iii. 47 f.

39 a. ἐγὼ δὲ λέγω κτλ.] τῷ
πονηρῷ is not 'the wicked man'
('an evil man,' Wicl.), which would
require ἀνθρώπῳ, still less the devil
(contrast Jam. iv. 7) working through
man (Chrys.); the adj., as in *v.* 37,
is neuter. The evil in the world
can shew itself in malice as well as
in untruthfulness.

39 b. ἀλλ' ὅστις κτλ.] The
following injunctions are arranged
in an anticlimax: acts of violence
(*v.* 39 b), legal proceedings (*v.* 40),
official demands (*v.* 41), simple requests (*v.* 42). The *nom. pend.* ὅστις
(cf. *v.* 41) = Aram. יִּמ; Lk. has the
better Gk. τῷ τύπτοντι, as Mt. in
v. 42 (τῷ αἰτοῦντι). For ῥαπίζειν
cf. xxvi. 68, Hos. xi. 4. The Lord
Himself suffered ῥαπίσματα (Mk.
xiv. 65, Jo. xviii. 22, xix. 3; cf.
Is. l. 6), but in Jo. xviii. 22 He is
recorded to have uttered a protest.
δεξιάν (om. in Lk., and see Appar.)
has not the same force as in *v.* 29 f.;
it may be due merely to the natural
tendency to mention the right side
before the left. See, however, a
suggestion in *Expos.*, Jan. 1914, 89.

40. καὶ τῷ θέλοντι κτλ.] After
this dat. the αὐτῷ is superfluous (see
Moulton, i. 69, 225). ὁ θέλων

41 καὶ τὸ ἱμάτιον· καὶ ὅστις σε ἀγγαρεύσει μίλιον ἕν, ὕπαγε
42 μετ' αὐτοῦ δύο. τῷ αἰτοῦντί σε δός, καὶ τὸν θέλοντα ἀπὸ
43 σοῦ δανίσασθαι μὴ ἀποστραφῇς.   Ἠκούσατε ὅτι

41 δυο] pr ετι αλλα D 𝕃 a b c g¹ k 𝕊 sin ; alia duo 𝕃 ff¹ h l vg 𝕊 cur Iren^lat
Aug

(D, as in xvii. 9, 14) followed by αὐτῷ in the Hebraic manner, is possibly the true reading. Lk. hardly improves the grammar : ἀπὸ τοῦ αἴροντος . . . μὴ κωλύσῃς. For the construction σοι κριθῆναι cf. Job ix. 3, xiii. 19, Eur. Med. 609. Lk., omitting the reference to a law-suit, seems to describe an act of violent robbery, mentioning the outer cloak (ἱμάτιον) first because the robber would seize it first. In Mt., when the χιτών is demanded at law, the more valuable ἱμάτιον is to be surrendered also. Cf. Diog. Laert. vi. 6, Διογένει χιτῶνα αἰτοῦντι πτύξας προσέταξε θοἰμάτιον. For the view that the transposition is due to Mt. see Oxf. Stud. 154.

41. κ. ὅστ. σε ἀγγαρεύσει κτλ.] Vg. angariaverit. The word is of Persian origin, ἄγγαροι (perhaps cognate with ἄγγελοι) being the mounted messengers of the Persian King (Herod. viii. 98 ; cf. Xen. Cyr. VIII. vi. 17). But as early as the 3rd cent. B.C. the verb occurs twice in an Egypt. papyrus with reference to a boat for postal service in Egypt (Deissm. BSt. 86 f., M.-M. Vocab. s.v.). It is also found in an Egypt. inscription of A.D. 49, and in Menander, Sic. iv. In Jos. (Ant. XIII. ii. 3) it occurs in the offer made by Demetrius to Jonathan that the animals of the Jews should not be 'impressed' for his service.   Its use in the N.T. (cf. xxvii. 32 = Mk. xv. 21) shews that it had acquired, in the 1st cent., the popular meaning of enforced service of any kind. On the form

ἐνγαρεύειν, a v.l. here and in Mk. l.c., see Deissmann, op. cit. 182. The subst.. -ρεία appears in Jewish writings as אַנְגַּרְיָא (Dalman, Gr. 147). μίλιον, only here in the N.T., is the Lat. milium ; it was adopted by the Jews (in the form מִיל, so 𝕊 vet.pesh here), and by late Gk. writers. The reading ἔτι ἄλλα δύο has strong early support, and is perhaps genuine ; scribes would be less likely to add a mile without reason, than to subtract one for the sake of parallelism with the two cheeks and two garments.

42. τῷ αἰτοῦντί σε κτλ.] The aor. δός and ἀποστραφῇς picture single scenes ; neither beggar nor borrower is to be refused. Lk. gives a general maxim (δίδου and ἀπαίτει) in which the vague τοῦ αἴροντος τὰ σά takes the place of the formal act of borrowing. The alliteration which some have noticed in Lk.'s αἰτοῦντι . . . ἀπαίτει can hardly be other than accidental. For ἀποστρέφεσθαι with acc. cf. Heb. xii. 25, 2 Tim. i. 15, Tit. i. 14. This is one of the clearest instances of the necessity of accepting the spirit and not the letter of the Lord's moral commands (see vv. 32, 34, 38). Not only does indiscriminate almsgiving do little but injury to society, but the words must embrace far more than almsgiving ; 'si de eleemosuna tantum dictum intelligimus, in plerisque pauperibus hoc stare non potest ; sed et divites si semper dederint, semper dare non poterunt' (Jer.).

ἐρρέθη Ἀγαπήςεις τὸν πληςίον ςου καὶ μισήσεις τὸν ἐχθρόν
σου. Ἐγὼ δὲ λέγω ὑμῖν, ἀγαπᾶτε τοὺς ἐχθροὺς ὑμῶν 44
καὶ προσεύχεσθε ὑπὲρ τῶν διωκόντων ὑμᾶς· ὅπως γένησθε 45
υἱοὶ τοῦ πατρὸς ὑμῶν τοῦ ἐν οὐρανοῖς, ὅτι τὸν ἥλιον αὐτοῦ

43–48. (Lk. vi. 27 f., 32–36.)
Thou shalt love thy neighbour. Lk.
has no parallel to v. 43.

43. ἀγαπήσεις κτλ.] The first
four words are quoted from Lev.
xix. 18, where πλησίον means a
'fellow-Israelite,' being parallel with
'the children of thy people,' and in the
preceding verse with 'thy brother.'
Cf. Secr. Enoch l. 4: 'when you
might have vengeance do not repay,
either your neighbour or your enemy.'
The whole clause in Lev., with ὡς
σεαυτόν, is quoted in Mt. xix. 19,
xxii. 39, Rom. xiii. 9, Gal. v. 14,
Jam. ii. 8. On 'love' see x. 37.

The remainder of the verse is an
inference which the Rabbis might
draw from such passages as Dt. xxiii.
4–7 [Engl. 3–6]; cf. Tac. Hist. v. 5,
'apud ipsos fides obstinata, miseri-
cordia in promptu, sed adversus omnes
alios hostile odium.' The Law drew
a distinction between Israelites and
non-Israelites, which, however, was
far from constituting a command to
'hate' enemies; the verb probably
has a comparative sense (see vi. 24
note). But the Lord goes behind it,
and sweeps away all distinctions;
cf. Lk. x. 29–37. The teaching of
the Talmud, as a whole, hardly goes
beyond that of the present verse: it
enjoins patience under injuries,
kind treatment of others in order to
receive an equivalent, love of proselytes and of those who are well
disposed towards the Law; but of
love to enemies it says nothing.
See Bischoff, Jesu u. d. Rabb. 63–6,
and a good article by Kleinert in
ThStKrit., 1913, 1–30.

44. ἐγὼ δὲ λέγω ὑμῖν κτλ.]

Lk. has ἀλλὰ ὑμῖν λέγω τοῖς
ἀκούουσιν, and adds two injunctions:
'do good to them that hate you,'
and 'bless them that curse you';
for διωκόντων he has the more
literary ἐπηριαζόντων, which is
added here in some MSS., with Lk.'s
other injunctions. The form 'Pray
for your enemies, love them which
hate you' was current at an early
date; cf. Just. Apol. i. 15, Dial.
133, Didache i. 3. καὶ προσεύχεσθε
κτλ.: 'Verbum enim Dei . . . ipse
hoc fecit in cruce' (Iren.). Jer.
finely says 'sciendum est ergo
Christum non impossibilia praecipere
sed perfecta.'

45. ὅπως γένησθε κτλ.] Sons are
those who partake of their Father's
character (cf. v. 9 note). On τοῦ ἐν
οὐρανοῖς see v. 16. For τοῦ πατρὸς
κτλ. Lk. has ὑψίστου (not in Mt.;
Mk.¹, Lk. Ac.⁷), perhaps with Ps.
lxxxi. [lxxxii.] 6 in mind (Dalman);
but Sir. iv. 10 is a closer parallel.

ὅτι τὸν ἥλιον κτλ.] The thought
is found in several Gk. and Lat.
writers (see Wetstein, ad loc.). If
God sent earthly gifts to His friends
and withheld them from His enemies
(in the spirit of v. 43), the natural
world would be a chaos; in so far as
His sons fall short of His nature,
the spiritual world is a chaos. Contrast Targ. Eccl. xi. 3, 'If the clouds
are filled with rain, on the earth
they pour their waters on account
of the purity of the righteous; but
if there is none pure in that generation, upon the sea and the wilderness
they come down, that men may not
be gratified by them.' The same
spirit is seen in the Talmud, though

ἀνατέλλει ἐπὶ πονηροὺς καὶ ἀγαθοὺς καὶ βρέχει ἐπὶ δικαίους
46 καὶ ἀδίκους. ἐὰν γὰρ ἀγαπήσητε τοὺς ἀγαπῶντας ὑμᾶς,
τίνα μισθὸν ἔχετε ; οὐχὶ καὶ οἱ τελῶναι τὸ αὐτὸ ποιοῦ-
47 σιν ; καὶ ἐὰν ἀσπάσησθε τοὺς ἀδελφοὺς ὑμῶν μόνον, τί
περισσὸν ποιεῖτε ; οὐχὶ καὶ οἱ ἐθνικοὶ τὸ αὐτὸ ποιοῦσιν ;

there are passages which speak of God sending rain in mercy upon the wicked (sée Bischoff, *op. cit.* 67). ἀνατέλλειν is used elsewhere intransitively of the sun 'rising'; transitively only of the production of plants by the earth (Gen. iii. 18, Dt. xxix. 23 [22]);' and by God (*Pss. Sol.* xi. 7 ; cf. Is. lxi. 11). The Heb. root צמח, which it represents in the LXX., can in Aram. mean also 'to shine'; the Lord may have referred, therefore, not to sunrise but to sunshine generally (ἐπιλάμπει, Clem. Al. ⁴⁄₅, *Excerpt. Theod.* ix. 3). βρέχει is a late word, transitive, as here, in Gen. xix. 24, Ex. ix. 23, Ps. lxxvii. [lxxviii.] 24, *al.*, intrans. in Jam. v. 17, Apoc. xi. 6. The *chiasmus* πονηρούς, ἀγαθούς–δικαίους, ἀδίκους is a Gk. artifice, perhaps an expansion of the original. For the illustration from Nature Lk. has simply ὅτι αὐτὸς χρηστός ἐστιν ἐπὶ τοὺς ἀχαρίστους καὶ πονηρούς.

46. ἐὰν γὰρ ἀγαπήσητε κτλ.] The divine reward which is missed by those who love only their friends is defined in *vv.* 45, 48—the attainment of the Father's character (see *v.* 9 note). Lk. expresses this more clearly : καὶ ἔσται ὁ μισθὸς ὑμῶν πολύς, καὶ ἔσεσθε υἱοὶ ὑψίστου. For τίνα μισθὸν ἔχετε ; he has ποία ὑμῖν χάρις ἐστίν ; (χάρις Lk. Ac.²⁵ ; not in Mt., Mk.). Just. (*Apol.* i. 15): τί καινὸν ποιεῖτε ; is possibly derived from an older text. A confusion between Aram. חדתא ('new') and חסדא (= χάρις) is improbable.

οὐχὶ κ. οἱ τελῶναι κτλ.] Lk. οἱ ἁμαρτωλοί, and in his two following

verses (see Mt. ix. 10 note). The τελῶναι ('customs officers') were not *publicani* (Vulg.; hence Engl. 'publicans') : the latter were mostly Romans of equestrian rank, while the τελῶναι were subordinate officials, mostly Jews, in their pay. The *publicani* leased the τέλη (*i.e.* the customs on exports) of the several districts at a fixed sum, and made what profit they could, which led their underlings to exercise gross oppression. For this reason, and because they took money for an alien power, they were considered by the Jews as outcasts of society. See further Schürer, *HJP.* I. ii. 66–71, and Swete on Mk. ii. 15. τελώνης is coupled with ἐθνικός (xviii. 17), ἁμαρτωλοί (ix. 10 and elsewhere), and πόρναι (xxi. 31 f.).

47. καὶ ἐὰν ἀσπάσησθε κτλ.] A salute is a smaller matter than love ; Lk. has ἀγαθοποιῆτε. The omission of the verse in 𝕃 k 𝕊 sin is probably due to homoeoteleuton. περισσόν (only *v.* 37 in the synn.) : 'more,' *sc.* than the world, and the Scribes and Pharisees (see *v.* 20). ἐθνικός (vi. 7, xviii. 17, 3 Jo. 7 ; -κῶς Gal. ii. 14) is not found again before Iren. (III. xxv. 2), 'ethnicorum quidam.' If it means 'Gentile,' ἀδελφοί means 'fellow-Jews'; but 𝕊 vet.pesh have ܚܢܦܐ, which can mean either 'hypocrites' or 'profane, godless persons' (see the *v.l.* in vi. 7) ; if this was the original word, it refers to the *outcast* Jews, the 'sinners' (so Lk. vi. 34), who are so often coupled with the τελῶναι. (The lesser uncials read τελῶναι here.) ἀδελφοί will in that case mean 'fellow *religious* Jews.'

Ἔσεσθε οὖν ὑμεῖς τέλειοι ὡς ὁ πατὴρ ὑμῶν ὁ οὐράνιος τέλειός 48 ἐστιν.

Προσέχετε δὲ τὴν δικαιοσύνην ὑμῶν μὴ ποιεῖν ἔμ- 1 VI προσθεν τῶν ἀνθρώπων πρὸς τὸ θεαθῆναι αὐτοῖς· εἰ δὲ μήγε, μισθὸν οὐκ ἔχετε παρὰ τῷ πατρὶ ὑμῶν τῷ ἐν τοῖς οὐρανοῖς. Ὅταν οὖν ποιῇς ἐλεημοσύνην, μὴ 2

1 δεῖ¹⁰] אLZ 1 33 209 𝔏 g¹ 𝔖 pesh.hcl me aeth ; om BDE al 𝔏vet [exc. g¹]. vg 𝔖 cur

48. ἔσεσθε οὖν κτλ.] Cf. Dt. xviii. 13. The fut., as in Heb. or Aram., expresses a command (Vulg. *estote*) ; cf. vi. 5 ; see Blass, § 64. 3. οὖν sums up the teaching of *vv.* 17–47 : 'So then, ye are to be perfect' ; cf. vii. 12, 24, x. 32. ὑμεῖς is emphatic, in contrast with the τελῶναι and ἐθνικοί, or with the Scribes and Pharisees (*v.* 20). While ἔσεσθε τέλειοι may be a reference to Dt. *l.c.*, the comparison with the divine character recalls Lev. xi. 44, xix. 2, where, however, the subject is the avoidance of unclean food, and other ritual requirements. For this negative τελειότης there is offered the positive and spiritual 'fulfilment' of the Law taught throughout the chapter. Lk. has the simpler ἔσεσθε οἰκτίρμονες, which is perhaps nearer to the original. τέλειος recurs in the Gospels in xix. 21 only (contrast Mk. x. 21, Lk. xviii. 22). On ὁ οὐράνιος see vi. 9 b. A combination of Mt. and Lk. appears in Just. *Apol.* i. 15, *Dial.* 96 (see Bousset, *Justin*, 80–83).

vi. 1–6, 16–18 (Mt. only). REAL RIGHTEOUSNESS AND PHARISAIC OSTENTATION, with a DIGRESSION ON PRAYER (*vv.* 7–15).

1. προσέχετε κτλ.] A general warning, introductory to the section. The connecting δέ, whether 'and' or 'but,' is out of place, and the MS. evidence is against it. προσέχετε (sc. τὸν νοῦν, which is never expressed in bibl. Gk.) takes inf. without μή in Ac.

xx. 28 ; the negative force is usually expressed by ἀπό in the N.T. The externality of Jewish 'righteousness' is expressed by the verb ποιεῖν, and the high place which almsgiving occupied in it is illustrated by the variants ἐλεημοσύνην and δόσιν. To give alms was beyond the letter of the Law, an *opus supererogatum* to which special merit attached. The thought is characteristic of *Tobit* (see xii. 9, xiv. 11) ; cf. 2 Cor. ix. 9, Dan. iv. 24 (Theod.). The LXX. (including Sir.) has ἐλεημοσύνη 17 times, and ἔλεος thrice, for צְדָקָה or צֶדֶק, and the Aram. צִדְקְתָא often has the same meaning (*e.g.* 𝔖 vet.pesh have it in *v.* 2). Clem. (*Strom.* viii. 69) describes δικαιοσύνη as ἡ ἕξις ἡ μεταδοτική.

To make one's good deeds a θέατρον for an admiring audience (cf. xxiii. 5) is to be a ὑποκριτής (*vv.* 2, 5, 16). For class. parallels see Wetstein, *ad loc.* The thought is in sharp contrast with that in *v.* 16. On the dat. αὐτοῖς see Blass, § 37. 4. For εἰ δὲ μήγε (μή) after a negative cf. ix. 17 (Mk., Lk.), 2 Cor. xi. 16 ; it occurs in the LXX.[5] and in late class. Gk. Wellh. compares Aram. וְאַלָּא. μισθὸν οὐκ ἔχετε anticipates *vv.* 2, 5, 16 ; good deeds cannot merit more than one reward ; to gain it from men is to lose it from God. See on v. 12.

2–4. *Almsgiving.*

2. ὅταν οὖν κτλ.] Almsgiving is not belittled ; it is assumed to be a

σαλπίσῃς ἔμπροσθέν σου, ὥσπερ οἱ ὑποκριταὶ ποιοῦσιν ἐν
ταῖς συναγωγαῖς καὶ ἐν ταῖς ῥύμαις, ὅπως δοξασθῶσιν ὑπὸ
τῶν ἀνθρώπων· ἀμὴν λέγω ὑμῖν, ἀπέχουσιν τὸν μισθὸν
3 αὐτῶν. σοῦ δὲ ποιοῦντος ἐλεημοσύνην μὴ γνώτω ἡ ἀρι-
4 στερά σου τί ποιεῖ ἡ δεξιά σου, ὅπως ᾖ σου ἡ ἐλεημοσύνη
ἐν τῷ κρυπτῷ· καὶ ὁ πατήρ σου ὁ βλέπων ἐν τῷ κρυπτῷ

practice of the disciples. On ποιεῖν
for ποιεῖσθαι see Moulton, i. 159.
The 2nd sing. alternates with the
plur. (ὑμῖν) as in vv. 6, 17 ; contrast
v. 8. ἐλεημοσύνη, a late word, is
not used specifically for 'almsgiving'
earlier than B. Sira. There is perhaps a reference to the practice of
sounding trumpets on the occasions
of public fasting in times of drought.
Services were held in the streets (cf.
v. 5) to pray for rain, fasting was
universal (cf. v. 16), and almsgiving
was understood to be essential for
the divine acceptance of the prayers
(see Büchler, JThS., Jan. 1909,
266 ff.). If this is not the explanation, σαλπίσῃς is metaphorical
(Chrys., al.) like bucinare (k). Cf.
Achilles Tat. viii. 10, on a crime
committed ὑπὸ σάλπιγγι, Cic. ad
Fam. XVI. xxi. 2, Juv. xiv. 152. Cyr.
Al. and others assume that it was a
Jewish custom to summon the poor
by trumpets to receive alms. Leo
(Serm. xv. 2) deprecates fasting without almsgiving, as 'non tam purgatio
animae quam carnis afflictio.'

ὑποκριτής (Mt.¹⁵, Mk.¹, Lk.⁴), an
'interpreter' (of riddles or dreams)
or an 'actor,' had no sinister force
earlier than Polybius (see xxxv. 2).
In the Gospels it represents Aram. and
NH. חנף, which can mean 'hypocriti-
cal,' 'flattering' (see on v. 47), but
in earlier. Heb. means only 'profane,'
'impious'; cf. Job xxxiv. 30, xxxvi.
13 (LXX., Aq., Sym., Th. ὑποκριτής).
In Pss. Sol. iv. 7, 25 ὑπόκρισις is
a charge of profane impiety brought
by the Pharisaic author against the

worldly graecizing Sadducees. In
Mt. the word is used, with stern
irony, of the Pharisees, almost as a
class designation, often with the
force of 'hypocrite'; cf. however
xxiv. 51 with Lk. xii. 46. ποιοῦσιν
is not π. ἐλεημοσύνην, but refers to
σαλπίσῃς; cf. ὥσπερ οἱ ἐθνικοί (v. 7).
For the late word ῥύμη (see Kennedy,
Sources, 16) cf. Lk. xiv. 21, Ac. ix.
11, xii. 10, Is. xv. 3. It occurs in
Paris Pap. 51 (160 B.C.).

ὅπως δοξασθῶσιν κτλ.] Another
contrast with v. 16. On ἀμὴν λέγω
ὑμ. see v. 18. The δόξα received
from men is a full quittance of the
reward due to them (see on v. 1).
For ἀπέχειν cf. Lk. vi. 24, Gen.
xliii. 22 [23]; it occurs in papyri
as a commercial formula of receipt ;
ἀποχή is 'a receipt' (Deissmann,
Bible St. 229). And see Wilcken's
Ostraka, ii. passim. Cf. ἀπολαμβάνειν
(Lk. xvi. 25).

3. μὴ γνώτω κτλ.] For some
curious explanations of this see
Tholuck, Serm. on the Mt. 302.
Lightfoot (Hor. Heb.) refers to certain
ritual acts in which only the right
hand might be used. But the words
are merely figurative of secrecy. R.
Eliasar (beg. of 2nd cent. A.D.) said
'He who giveth alms in secret is
greater than Moses our teacher' (Bab.
Bath. 6 b).

4. καὶ ὁ πατήρ σου κτλ.] ἐν
τῷ κρυπτῷ occurs only in v. 6,
Rom. ii. 29, Sym. Ps. cxxxviii.
[cxxxix.] 15 ; cf. ἐν κρυπτῷ, Jo. vii.
4, 10, xviii. 20, Theod., 2 Regn. xii.
12. It is not found in the LXX.,

ἀποδώσει σοι.   Καὶ ὅταν προσεύχησθε, οὐκ ἔσεσθε 5
ὡς οἱ ὑποκριταί· ὅτι φιλοῦσιν ἐν ταῖς συναγωγαῖς καὶ ἐν
ταῖς γωνίαις τῶν πλατειῶν ἑστῶτες προσεύχεσθαι, ὅπως
φανῶσιν τοῖς ἀνθρώποις· ἀμὴν λέγω ὑμῖν, ἀπέχουσι τὸν
μισθὸν αὐτῶν.   σὺ δὲ ὅταν προσεύχῃ, εἴϲελθε εἰϲ τὸ 6
ταμεῖόν ϲου καὶ κλείϲαϲ τὴν θύραν ϲου πρόϲευξαι τῷ πατρί

4 σοι] *add* εν τω φανερω EK *al* 𝕷 a b c f g¹ h q 𝕾 sin.pesh.hcl.pal arm aeth
[*simil. in v.* 6]

which usually has ἐν κρυφῇ. The
gloss ἐν τῷ φανερῷ (see Appar.)
expresses the true thought of the
passage : the reward will be given
in the coming Kingdom. With ὁ
βλέπων ἐν τ. κρ. cf. *Sotah* 9 a,
'she does it in secret, but He who
sits in the secret place, the most
High, looks upon her.' It is unnatural to take the second ἐν τ.
κρυπτῷ with ἀποδώσει. Wellhausen
refers to the construction ראה ב
(Aram. חמא ב), so that τῷ κρυπτῷ
might be the object of the verb.

5, 6. Prayer.

5. ὅτι φιλοῦσιν κτλ.] For
φιλεῖν c. inf. (a class. constr. only here
in the N.T.) cf. Is. lvi. 10. Standing
was the usual attitude in prayer (see
Swete on Mk. xi. 25). If, therefore,
the emphasis is on ἑστῶτες, it represents עמד, 'continue,' 'persist,'
referring to the length of their
prayers ; if it is on the places
where they pray, Jesus condemns
their enjoyment of publicity. Prayer
in the synagogue was uttered by
one member of the congregation
(the שליח צבור), who 'passed in front
of the chest [containing the rolls of
the Law],' *i.e.* 'led in prayer'
(Schürer, *HJP.* II. ii. 67, 78 f.). It
is perhaps to this public act that
the Lord refers. For the practice
of praying in the streets there is
no Jewish evidence, except on the
occasions of public fasts (see *v.* 2 note,

Schürer, *HJP.* II. ii. 71 f.). πλατεῖα
is here synonymous with ῥύμη (*v.* 2) ;
in Lk. xiv. 21 they are distinguished.
φανῶσιν [*sc.* προσευχόμενοι] does
not imply a pretence (cf. *vv.* 16, 18) ;
it is equivalent to θεαθῆναι (*v.* 1).
On the last sentence see *v.* 2.

6. εἴσελθε κτλ.] Apparently a
reminiscence of Is. xxvi. 20 : βάδιζε,
λαός μου, εἴσελθε εἰς τὰ ταμεῖά
σου, ἀπόκλεισον τὴν θύραν σου,
ἀποκρύβηθι, with the substitution
of 'pray' for 'hide.' For prayer
in a chamber cf. 4 Regn. iv. 33,
Dan. vi. 10, Tob. iii. 11. But the
'chamber' is here figurative, as in
xxiv. 26, Lk. xii. 3 (cf. Mt. x. 27),
Eccl. x. 20. 'The secret of religion
is religion in secret.' 'Omnis rerum
veritas est in abscondito' (Bengel).
ὥσπερ οἱ ὑποκριταὶ μὴ ποιεῖτε μηδέν,
ἀλλὰ μετὰ πάσης ἀληθείας ἀνα-
βλέπετε πρὸς τὸν πατέρα τὸν ἀπο-
κεκρυμμένον ἐν τοῖς οὐρανοῖς (Grenf.
and Hunt, *New Sayings of Jesus,* 18).
On the form ταμεῖον (cf. xxiv. 26)
see Thackeray (*Gramm. O.T.* i. 63 f.).
τῷ ἐν τῷ κρυπτῷ : cf. *v.* 18. Wellh.
notes the 'symmetrical tautology'
of the last two clauses, after the
manner of the Heb. *mashal* or proverb ; cf. *vv.* 19, 24, vii. 3 f., 7 f.,
17 f.

7, 8. *The wrong method of praying.*

The sequel of *v.* 6 is *v.* 16 ;
Mt. here groups sayings on Prayer

σου τῷ ἐν τῷ κρυπτῷ· καὶ ὁ πατήρ σου ὁ βλέπων ἐν
7 τῷ κρυπτῷ ἀποδώσει σοι. Προσευχόμενοι δὲ μὴ βατταλο-
γήσητε ὥσπερ οἱ ἐθνικοί, δοκοῦσιν γὰρ ὅτι ἐν τῇ πολυλογίᾳ
8 αὐτῶν εἰσακουσθήσονται· μὴ οὖν ὁμοιωθῆτε αὐτοῖς, οἶδεν
γὰρ ὁ θεὸς ὁ πατὴρ ὑμῶν ὧν χρείαν ἔχετε πρὸ τοῦ ὑμᾶς

7 εθνικοι] υποκριται B 𝕾 cur   8 ο θεος] ℵ*B sah ; om uncc.caet minn
verss. caet | αιτησαι αυτον] ανοιξαι το στομα D 𝕷 h

from other contexts. These two
verses condemn verbosity in prayer ;
προσευχόμενοι takes the place of
ὅταν προσεύχησθε (προσεύχῃ) in
vv. 5 f., and there is no alternation,
as in vv. 2 ff., 5, 16 ff., of plural
and singular.

7. προσευχόμενοι δέ κτλ.] Except in writers dependent upon Mt.,
βατταλογεῖν is unknown earlier than
Simplicius (Comm. in Epict. Enchir.
xxvii.), c. 530 A.D. Its derivation
is doubtful. Some connect it with
βατταρίζειν 'to stutter,' hence to
utter meaningless sounds ; others
with the Heb. אָטָב (Lev. v. 4, Ps.
cvi. 33), 'to speak thoughtlessly.' A
fanciful derivation is from Βάττος,
a Libyan king who stammered
(Eust.). It perhaps connected with
the Aram. בַּטָּל (baṭṭāl), 'idle, useless.' 𝕾 sin renders 'do not be
saying idle things' (ܠܐ ܬܐܡܪܘܢ) ; and
in xii. 36 𝕾 cur uses the same
word for ἀργόν. Hesych. βατολογία,
ἀργολογία. In that case it is a
contraction of βατταλο-λογεῖν (as
idolatria of idolo-latria). Possibly
it is an onomatopoeic like 'babble'
(Tynd.). D has βλαττολογεῖν : cf.
blatero, blether. 𝕷 multum loqui,
multiloqui esse, and 'speke moche'
(Wycl.), make it equivalent to
πολυλογία, but the Lord speaks, in
this clause, of quality, not of
quantity. The mistaken rendering
'Use not vain repetitions' (A.V.,
R.V.) is sometimes taken to forbid
all repetitions in prayer ; but Jesus

Himself, at least on one occasion,
'prayed the third time, saying the same
thing again' (xxvi. 44). On ἐθνικοί,
and the v.l. ὑποκριταί, see v. 47.

δοκοῦσιν γάρ κτλ.] For the
thought of πολυλογία in prayer see
Is. i. 15, Sir. vii. 14. 'Absit ab
oratione multa locutio, sed non desit
multa precatio' (Aug. Ep. 130).

8. οἶδεν γάρ κτλ.] Cf. v. 32,
Is. lxv. 24. The Father knows, but
because He is the Father His children
must pray. 'Aliud est enim narrare
ignoranti, aliud scientem petere'
(Jer.). ὁ θεός should probably be
omitted (see Appar.) ; the expression
'God your Father' is not found elsewhere in the N.T.

9–13. (Lk. xi. 2–4.) The Lord's
Prayer.

Lk. has a shorter form, omitting
(1) ἡμῶν ὁ ἐν τοῖς οὐρανοῖς, (2)
γενηθήτω . . . ἐπὶ γῆς, (3) καὶ μὴ
εἰσενέγκῃς . . . τοῦ πονηροῦ, and
he differs in the form of the petitions
for bread and for forgiveness. He
also relates that the Prayer was a
response to the disciples' request
that Jesus would teach them to pray
as John also taught his disciples.
As regards the omission of clauses
Lk.'s form is probably nearer to the
original ; he could not have omitted
them had the longer form been
known to him ; and the tendency
of liturgical formulas is towards en-
richment rather than abbreviation.

As would be expected from the
lips of Jesus, the prayer is Jewish

αἰτῆσαι αὐτόν.   Οὕτως οὖν προσεύχεσθε ὑμεῖς   9
Πάτερ ἡμῶν ὁ ἐν τοῖς οὐρανοῖς·

in language and thought. Much of
it is traceable to the O.T., but later
Jewish writings supply some fairly
close parallels. The *Shemoneh-esreh*
('Eighteen [Benedictions]') is a collection of Heb. prayers, which, though
it did not reach its final form till
after 70 A.D., existed in the main
considerably earlier; and Jesus may
have known it. (For a translation
see Schürer, *HJP.* II. ii. 85–7.)
In it occur the words 'Thou art
holy, and *thy Name is holy.*' '*Forgive us, our Father, for we have
sinned.*' The Aram. *Ḳaddīsh* begins
'*Magnified and hallowed be* His great
Name; may His Kingdom reign.'
In the evening service, in the
Authorized Daily Pr. Bk. of the
Jews, occur the petitions '*Our God
who art in heaven,* assert the unity
of *Thy Name,* and establish *Thy
Kingdom* continually'; and in the
morning prayer (cf. *Berak.* 60 b)
'and *cause us not to come . . . into
the hands of temptation.*'

The chief patr. writings on the
Prayer, besides those which deal with
the whole Sermon, are Tert. *De Or.*
i.–ix., Cypr. *De Or. Dom.*, Orig. *De
Or.* xviii.–xxx., Greg. Nyss. *De Or.
Dom.* See also Cyr. *Catech.* xxiii.,
Chromatius, *in Mat. Tract.* xiii. f.,
Chrys. *Hom. in Or. Dom.* Modern
monographs are Bp. Chase, *The
Lord's Prayer in the Early Church,*
Dibelius, *Das Vaterunser,* Loeschcke,
*Die Vaterunser-Erklärung d. Theoph.
v. Ant.* (in Bonnwetsch and Seeberg's
Neue Stud.), Walther, *Gesch. d. gr.
Vaterunser-Exegese.* On the use of the
Prayer in the Liturgy see Scudamore,
Not. Euch.[2] 580 f., 654 ff.

9 a. οὕτως οὖν κτλ.] A short
summary of prayer is provided for
the disciples, as a pattern (οὕτως)

for other prayers, both in the form
and balance of the whole, and in the
subject of each petition. The later
Jews also employed a summary (a
מֵעֵין) in addition to the liturgical
prayers (Lightfoot, *Hor. Heb.*). The
sentence is probably due to Mt., who
inserts the Prayer at this point, the
emphatic ὑμεῖς standing in contrast
with the ἐθνικοί of v. 7. The
Didache (viii.) transforms the sentence
into a liturgical order: τρὶς τῆς
ἡμέρας οὕτω προσεύχεσθε.

9 b. πάτερ ἡμῶν κτλ.] See v. 16
note. Lk. has πάτερ only, which
originates in אַבָּא, 'Abba,' as also ὁ
πατήρ and πάτερ μου (see Burkitt,
Ev. da Meph. ii. 47), and perhaps
even πάτερ ἡμῶν (Dalman, *Words,*
192). In any case the plur. pronoun
does not imply that Jesus stood in
the same relation to God as the
disciples: they are taught the words
which they themselves are to use.
'Abba' was the Lord's own form of
address to God (xi. 25 f., xxvi. 39, 42,
Lk. xxiii. 34, 46), which was adopted
by the early Church (Rom. viii. 15,
Gal. iv. 6). In pre-Christian times
it was seldom, and only in late
writings, that the individual Israelite
spoke of God as his Father: *e.g.*
Sir. xxiii. 1, 4, Wisd. ii. 16, Tob.
xiii. 4, 3 Macc. v. 7, Jubil. i. 24
(see Charles' note). But there was
a growing readiness to apply the
title. In prayers 'Our Father' was
sometimes employed (as early as Tob.
l.c.; it occurs twice in the *Shemoneh-
esreh*; and Aḳiba (*c.* 120 A.D.) began
a prayer with 'Our Father and
King' (*Taan.* 25 b)). But motives
of reverence caused the far more
frequent use of 'Our [your, their]
Father which is in heaven' (see on
v. 16), which would easily find its

'Αγιασθήτω τὸ ὄνομά σου,

10   ἐλθάτω ἡ βασιλεία σου,

γενηθήτω τὸ θέλημά σου,

way into the Lord's Prayer in the synagogue services of Palestinian Christians. The Aram. דבשמיא can be variously rendered ὁ ἐν οὐρανοῖς (xii. 50, xviii. 10, 19), ὁ οὐράνιος (v. 48, vi. 14, 26, 32), as well as ὁ ἐν τοῖς οὐρ.; cf. ὁ ἐξ οὐρανοῦ (Lk. xi. 13); and the occurrence of the Prayer in the *Didache* (viii.) with ὁ ἐν τῷ οὐρανῷ shews that it was some time before the Gk. form was fixed. The frequency with which ὁ ἐν [τοῖς] οὐρανοῖς occurs in Mt. may have been due to the influence of the Prayer in the form that he knew it.

ἁγ. τὸ ὄνομά σου] 'Any benediction in which "the Name" does not occur is no benediction' (*Berak.* 40 b). The intimacy of 'Our Father' is balanced and supplemented by the reverent desire that His Name, *i.e.* His Nature and Being, may be treated as holy. τὸ γὰρ ἁγιασθήτω τοῦτο ἔστιν δοξασθήτω (Chrys.); cf. Jo. xii. 27. This is possible in the present (ἅγιον τὸ ὄνομα αὐτοῦ, Lk. i. 49), and the clause might be regarded merely as a parenthetical expansion of the address to the Father; but in its fulness ἁγιασθήτω is a future consummation, only to be reached when the divine Kingdom comes; cf. Ez. xxxvi. 23. A further meaning was sometimes attached to the words: 'cum dicimus Sanctificetur nomen tuum, id petimus, ut sanctificetur *in nobis*' (Tert. *De Orat.* iii.); similarly Cypr., *al.* Cf. the reading of D in Lk.: ἁγ. ὄν. σου ἐφ' ἡμᾶς, which is perhaps an echo of O.T. passages which speak of the calling of the divine Name upon men (*e.g.* Is. xliii. 1, lxiii. 19), or was derived from the petition for the Holy Spirit; see on *v.* 10.

10. ἐλθάτω ἡ βασ. σου] 'Any benediction in which *malkūth* ('kingdom') does not occur is no benediction' (*Berak.* 40 b). The petition is for the future advent of God to establish His sovereignty on earth. It is 'grandis audaciae, et purae conscientiae, regnum Dei postulari et judicium non timere' (Jer.; similarly Cyr. Jerus.). Other writers express the thought of the advancement of a *present* kingdom. πρὸ τοῦ οὐρανοῦ, τὴν γῆν οὐρανὸν ἐκέλευσε ποιῆσαι (Chrys.).

This clause, like the foregoing, underwent alterations. In Lk. the minusc. 700ᵏⁱᵉᵍ has ἐλθέτω τὸ πνεῦμά σου ἐφ' ἡμᾶς καὶ καθαρισάτω ἡμᾶς, which is found in Greg. Nyss. and Max.; and Tert. (or Marcion, on whom he comments, *Marc.* iv. 26) substitutes a petition for the Holy Spirit for 'hallowed be Thy Name.' The same writer, when he quotes the Prayer from Mt., transposes this and the next petition.

γενηθήτω κτλ.] Absent from Lk. The source of the first four words was probably the prayer in Gethsemane, as Mt. gives it (xxvi. 42); a prayer used by the Lord might safely be added to the prayer which He taught. The words can have a present force; 'non ut Deus faciat quod vult, sed ut nos facere possimus quod Deus vult' (Cypr.). Cf. the Rabb. sayings: 'Be . . . strong as a lion to do the will of thy Father which is in heaven' (*Aboth*, v. 20), 'Do His will as if it were thy will' (*ib.* ii. 4), 'If anyone keeps the Law, and does the will of his Father which is in heaven, etc.' (*Siphri*, Ugol. 872). But, like the two preceding, the petition can refer to the future:

ὡς ἐν οὐρανῷ καὶ ἐπὶ γῆς·
Τὸν ἄρτον ἡμῶν τὸν ἐπιούσιον   11
δὸς ἡμῖν σήμερον·

10 ως] om D* 𝔏 a b c k Tert

'may the time come when Thy will shall be perfectly accomplished,' which cannot be till Thy Name is perfectly hallowed and Thy Kingdom completely established. ﹩ cur has 'Thy wills'; cf. vii. 21 (א), Mk. iii. 35 (B), Ac. xxi. 14, *Gosp. Heb.* (*ap.* Epiph. *Haer.* xxx. 14) ἔφη· οὗτοί εἰσιν οἱ ἀδελφοί μου καὶ ἡ μήτηρ οἱ ποιοῦντες τὰ θελήματα τοῦ πατρός μου.

ὡς ἐν οὐρανῷ κτλ.] Without ὡς (see Appar.) the meaning is the same; cf. Ps. cxxxiv. [cxxxv.] 6. For the correspondence between the earthly and the heavenly cf. xvi. 19, xviii. 18. If the clause was not originally part of the Prayer, its origin cannot be determined. The rhythm allows, if not requires, it to refer to all the foregoing petitions (so Orig. *Op. Imperf.*; see Nestle, *ZNW.* vi. 108); and so taken it brings out more clearly the eschatological force of each. In *Ac. Thos.* there is a stop before 'in earth as in heaven'; and this arrangement is adopted in accurate copies of the Engl. Prayer Book.

11. τὸν ἄρτον κτλ.] Aspirations for God's glory are followed by petitions for human needs. The petition is of extreme value as shewing that material things do not lie outside the region of prayer. Marcion, using Lk.'s form, writes σου for ἡμῶν, applying the words to spiritual food. On the plur. ἡμῶν Cypr. well says, 'Publica est nobis et communis oratio, et quando oramus, non pro uno sed pro populo toto oramus, quia totus populus unum sumus.' The unique ἐπιούσιον is discussed in the Add. note. If it is not a corrupt form, it is probably to be connected with ἡ ἐπιοῦσα [ἡμέρα]. In liturgical use 'bread for the coming day' could denote either 'bread for the day then in progress,' or 'bread for the morrow,' according as the Prayer was used in the morning or in the evening. δὸς ἡμ. σήμερον is a petition for the immediate need; Lk. has a generalized request, δίδου ἡμῖν τὸ καθ' ἡμέραν, which may have been an early variation due to the account of the manna (τὸ καθ' ἡμέραν εἰς ἡμέραν, Ex. xvi. 5); but the expression, which is class., is confined to Lk. in the N.T. (xix. 47, Ac. xvii. 11), and see his καθ' ἡμέραν which he adds in ix. 23.

Additional Note on ἐπιούσιον.

Orig. (*De Orat.* 27) states that the adjective is unique in Gk. literature, and 'seems to have been coined by the evangelists.' It occurs (in three late MSS.) in 2 Mac. i. 8 after τοὺς ἄρτους (the shewbread); on this see Deissm. *Bible St.* 214. It is apparently an endeavour to represent an Aram. expression for which there was no Greek equivalent. The possible Heb. and Aram. expressions are collected by Nestle (*Exp. T.* xxi. 43).

The following explanations have been proposed:
(1) Some patristic writers derived it from ἐπί and οὐσία. Jer. (Mt.

12   καὶ ἄφες ἡμῖν τὰ ὀφειλήματα ἡμῶν,

text and comm., but not in Lk.) renders *supersubstantialem*, explaining it
as 'super omnes substantias.' Orig. refused to apply the words to material
bread, and explains the adj. as εἰς τὴν οὐσίαν συμβαλλόμενον, 'contributing
to existence.' Tert., Cypr., and Aug. were willing to combine a literal and
spiritual meaning. But in view of the forms ἐπουσία, ἐπουσιώδης, and
other words from ἔπειμι, the retention of the ι is doubtful; and a philosophical term is unlikely to have been introduced into a prayer used by
simple Palestinian Christians.

(2) From ἐπί and ὤν (οὖσα). 'Bread which is at hand' might mean
'bread for immediate needs.' But this is open to the same philological
objection.

(3) The generally accepted derivation is from ἐπ' and ἰοῦσα, referring
to ἡ ἐπιοῦσα [ἡμέρα], the form being perhaps suggested or facilitated by
that of the LXX. word περιούσιος (Ex. xix. 5, Dt. vii. 6; cf. Tit. ii. 14).
This has been variously understood :—

(*a*) 𝔏 vet *quotidianum*, which Jer. adopted in Lk. (though adhering to
a spiritual interpretation, in his later writings he wavered : 'panem nostrum
substantivum, sive *supervenluum…quotidianum* sive *super omnes substantias*).
Chrys. ἐφήμερον : cf. Jam. ii. 15 (τῆς ἐφημέρου τροφῆς), where ff¹ Jer. have
victu quotidiano.

(*b*) 𝔖 cur in Mt. [𝔖 sin is wanting] has 'our continual bread of the day';
sin.cur in Lk., 'the continual bread of every day'; *Ac. Thos.* and Jacob of
Serug, 'the continual bread of the day.' These may be paraphrases derived
from לֶחֶם הַתָּמִיד (cf. Num. iv. 7), but they may be double renderings of
ἐπιούσιον (see (*d*)).

(*c*) Memph. Cop. in Mt. have 'the bread of to-morrow' (cf. Prov. xxvii.
1, οὐ γὰρ γινώσκεις τί τέξεται ἡ ἐπιοῦσα). In the *Gosp. Heb.* Jer. found
the word *mahar*—'panem nostrum crastinum, id est futurum'; he explains
it as 'panem quem daturus es nobis in regno tuo,' but the literal meaning
is quite suitable. See P. Schmiedel, *SchweizThZ.*, 1913, 204–20.

(*d*) In Prov. *l.c.* ἡ ἐπιοῦσα (a *hap. leg.* in the LXX.) represents the single
word יוֹם; ἐπιούσιον may, therefore, stand for the Aram. דְּיוֹמָא, 'of the day.'
Ephr. says 'The bread of the day shall suffice thee, as thou hast learnt in
the Prayer.'

This is perhaps a reference to Ex. xvi. 4 : the manna was to be gathered
'a matter *of a day* in its day.' If, then, the original expression was 'the
bread of the day,' it was suitable for a morning prayer, in reference to the
day just begun; but that can also be the meaning of ἡ ἐπιοῦσα [ἡμέρα]
(see Wratislaw, *Churchman*, July, 1888), so that the useful word ἐπιούσιον
could cover both meanings, 'of the day [just begun]' and 'of the morrow.'
When the prayer found its way into writing in Mt. and Lk., or their
respective recensions of Q, a second equivalent for 'of the day' appeared
in each by the side of ἐπιούσιον, *i.e.* σήμερον in Mt. and τὸ καθ' ἡμέραν
in Lk.

12. καὶ ἄφες κτλ.] The thought of   thoroughly Jewish; cf. xxiii. 16
sins (Lk. τὰς ἁμαρτίας) as debts was   (note), Lk. xiii. 4. The Targg. have

ὡς καὶ ἡμεῖς ἀφήκαμεν τοῖς ὀφειλέταις ἡμῶν·
καὶ μὴ εἰσενέγκῃς ἡμᾶς εἰς πειρασμόν,   13
ἀλλὰ ῥῦσαι ἡμᾶς ἀπὸ τοῦ πονηροῦ.

חוּבָא ('debt') for 'sin' (Gen. xx. 9), 'guilt' (xxvi. 10), 'transgression' (xxxi. 36), 'iniquity' (Jer. xvi. 10). But ὀφείλημα elsewhere in the N.T. (Rom. iv. 4 only), and in the LXX. is used only of a literal debt. *Didache* has the sing., τὴν ὀφειλὴν ἡμῶν. ἀφιέναι is 'to let [the debt] go' unpaid (Aram. שְׁבַק); in the sense of 'forgive' it never takes acc. of person in the N.T.; when not expressed, the acc. of the debt or sin is always to be supplied.

ὡς καὶ ἡμεῖς κτλ.] Lk. καὶ γὰρ αὐτοὶ ἀφίομεν. *Didache*, Chrys. ὡς καὶ ἡμεῖς ἀφίεμεν. Cypr. 'sicut et nos remittimus.' Bas. διότι ἀφήκαμεν καὶ ἡμεῖς. Bp. Chase suggests that the Aram. original was וְאַף אֲנַן נִשְׁבּוּק ('and we will also forgive'), as in S cur (Lk.) and Aphr. But there are other variations. S cur (Mt.), 'so that we also may forgive.' Jac. of Serug, 'that we also may forgive.' But Aphr. in his comment paraphrases: 'Forgive me and I forgive' (ܫܒܩ partcp.); and S pal has the plur. partcp. Tert. writes 'remittere nos quoque profitemur debitoribus nostris' (*De Orat.*), but also 'debitoribus denique dimissuros nos in oratione profitemur' (*Adv. Marc.*). The verb, therefore, was handed down variously as past, present, and future; and only a timeless Aram. participle דְּאַף שָׁבְקִין אֲנַן) will account for all: 'because we also forgive' may imply that we have done so, or habitually do so, or intend to do so. (For the last cf. Lk. xix. 8, where S vet.pesh have participles for δίδωμι and ἀποδίδωμι.) For τ. ὀφειλέταις ἡμ. Lk. has παντὶ ὀφείλοντι ἡμῖν.

13. κ. μὴ εἰσενέγκῃς κτλ.] The original was probably וְלָא תַעֵל, 'and cause us not to enter' (S sin.cur (Lk.), pesh (Mt., Lk.), Diat Ar). Cf. S cur (Mt.), Jac. of Serug, 'and cause us not to come.' So in the Jewish prayer quoted above. The causative can have a *permissive* force ('allow us to enter'), which is obscured in the Gk. The words correspond (cf. *Ep. Polyc.* vii. 2) with xxvi. 41, Mk. xiv. 38 (ἔλθητε), Lk. xxii. 40, 46 (εἰσέλθητε). Tert. has 'non sinet nos deduci,' and other glosses are found: 'ne patiaris nos induci' (Cypr., *al.*), 'ne passus fueris induci nos' (k, with slight variations in other lat. MSS.). In the *King's Book* (1543 A.D.) the petition runs 'And lette us not be ledde.'

πειρασμός includes 'trial' (cf. Lk. xxii. 28, 1 Pet. iv. 12) as well as 'temptation,' though trial may be a cause of joy if it must be encountered (Jam. i. 2). To 'enter into' must not be limited to mean 'yield to' (Dion. Al., Orig.); temptation or trial, like hunger, may be for man's good, but the Prayer contains petitions against both. πειρασμός is primarily the fiery trial which is about to usher in the End; cf. 2 Pet. ii. 9, which is possibly an echo of this and the following clause. Some Lat. writers (Hil., Chrom., Jer., Aug., Ps.-Aug.) add a gloss, to limit temptation: 'quem ferre [sufferre] non possumus'; its source is 1 Cor. x. 13.

ἀλλὰ ῥῦσαι κτλ.] Absent from Lk. The gender of τ. πονηροῦ is uncertain (as in xiii. 38, Jo. xvii. 15, 2 Thes. iii. 3, 1 Jo. v. 19); the neuter occurs in Lk. vi. 45, Rom. xii. 9, and probably Mt. v. 37, 39; the

14 Ἐὰν γὰρ ἀφῆτε τοῖς ἀνθρώποις τὰ παραπτώματα αὐτῶν,
15 ἀφήσει καὶ ὑμῖν ὁ πατὴρ ὑμῶν ὁ οὐράνιος· ἐὰν δὲ μὴ
ἀφῆτε τοῖς ἀνθρώποις τὰ παραπτώματα αὐτῶν, οὐδὲ ὁ
16 πατὴρ ὑμῶν ἀφήσει τὰ παραπτώματα ὑμῶν.   Ὅταν
δὲ νηστεύητε, μὴ γίνεσθε ὡς οἱ ὑποκριταὶ σκυθρωποί,

masc. in xiii. 19, Eph. vi. 16, 1 Jo. ii. 13 f., iii. 12, v. 18, and is interpreted here of the devil by Tert., Cypr. and many Gk. writers following Orig. The *Didache*, on the other hand, is probably right in interpreting it ἀπὸ παντὸς πονηροῦ. The use of ἀπό rather than ἐκ is not conclusive for the masc. In either case the words, if genuine, describe a deliverance leading to the bliss of the approaching Kingdom.

[ὅτι σοῦ ἐστιν ἡ βασιλεία καὶ ἡ δύναμις καὶ ἡ δόξα εἰς τοὺς αἰῶνας· ἀμήν] This is a liturgical addition, not found in Gk. or Lat. commentators, except Chrys. and his followers. It occurs in EGKLMSUVΔΠ 𝔏 f g¹ (om. *amen*) q 𝔖 cur (om. 'and the power').pesh.pal aeth arm go. It appears to combine two ancient elements: (1) 'the power and the glory' (added to the Prayer in the *Didache*, and by Greg. Nyss.), (2) 'the kingdom and the glory' (𝔖 cur in Mt.). The former is probably Hellenistic, the latter Hebraic (cf. Ps. cxliv. [cxlv.] 11 f., 1 Ch. xxix. 11). Two unique forms are found: 'quoniam est tibi virtus (= ἡ δύναμις) in saecula saeculorum' (k), and 'because Thine is the strength and the power for ever and ever' (Theb.). The doxology was added in Mt.'s form of the prayer, not in Lk.'s, because being the fuller it was preferred for liturgical purposes. The opening ὅτι appears to contrast σοῦ with τ. πονηροῦ, shewing that the latter was currently understood as masculine. Other liturgical doxologies are given by Bp. Chase. A short form σοῦ

γάρ ἐστιν ἡ δόξα εἰς τοὺς αἰῶνας occurs on a Christian amulet of the sixth cent. (Milligan, *Pap.* no. 55).

14, 15. ἐὰν γάρ κτλ.] Absent from Lk. (cf. Clem. Rom. xiii. 2, ἀφίετε ἵνα ἀφεθῇ ὑμῖν, and see *Ep. Polyc.* ii. 3). The verses were probably added, from another context, as a marginal note on v. 12 b, with which γάρ connects them; they may have been formed on the basis of Mk. xi. 25, which Mt. omits after xxi. 22. As there, sins are not debts but παραπτώματα. On the necessity of forgiveness see xviii. 21–35; and cf. Sir. xxviii. 2, ἄφες ἀδίκημα τῷ πλησίον σου, καὶ τότε δεηθέντος σου αἱ ἁμαρτίαι σου λυθήσονται. On ὁ οὐράνιος see v. 9 b.

16–18. *Fasting.* The sequel of v. 6.

16. ὅταν δὲ νηστεύητε] When public fasts were held in the autumn to pray for rain (see *v.* 2 note), the stricter Jews would fast on Mondays and Thursdays during the drought (*Taan.* i. 4–7). This 'fast of the hypocrites' is referred to in the *Didache* (viii.), and fasting on Wednesdays and Fridays is enjoined. The Lord, as in the case of almsgiving and prayer (*vv.* 2, 5), assumed that His audience practised fasting as an ordinary act of piety, although He defended the omission of it by His personal followers as long as He was with them (ix. 14 ff.).

μὴ γίνεσθε κτλ.] For σκυθρωπός in connexion with fasting see Dan. i. 10 (Theod.); cf. Lk. xxiv. 17, Gen. xl. 7, Sir. xxv. 23. ἀφανίζουσιν:

ἀφανίζουσιν γὰρ τὰ πρόσωπα αὐτῶν ὅπως φανῶσιν τοῖς
ἀνθρώποις νηστεύοντες· ἀμὴν λέγω ὑμῖν, ἀπέχουσιν τὸν
μισθὸν αὐτῶν. σὺ δὲ νηστεύων ἄλειψαί σου τὴν κεφαλὴν 17
καὶ τὸ πρόσωπόν σου νίψαι, ὅπως μὴ φανῇς τοῖς ἀνθρώ- 18
ποις νηστεύων ἀλλὰ τῷ πατρί σου τῷ ἐν τῷ κρυφαίῳ· καὶ
ὁ πατήρ σου ὁ βλέπων ἐν τῷ κρυφαίῳ ἀποδώσει σοι.

Μὴ θησαυρίζετε ὑμῖν θησαυροὺς ἐπὶ τῆς γῆς, ὅπου σὴς 19

lit. 'make invisible,' hence 'disfigure,'
i.e. with ashes, and by leaving the
hair and beard untended, or by
colouring the face to look pale as
though by fasting (Chrys., *al.*); cf.
Nicostr. (Stob. *Serm.* 74. ˙ 62): a
woman should not use χρώματος
... ἀφανίζοντος τὰς ὄψεις. In the
LXX. it means only 'destroy,' as in
v. 19 f. below; cf. Jam. iv. 14. See
M.-M. *Vocab. s.v.* The alliteration
ἀφανίζουσιν ... φανῶσιν is probably
accidental. σκυθρωποί is possibly a
doublet of ἀφανίζουσιν: the corresponding clause in *v.* 5 ends at
ὑποκριταί, and 𝔖 cur omits σκυθρ.,
but renders ἀφαν. by ܪܟܕܒܝܢ
'who make gloomy,' while σκυθρ. is
ܚܕܒܝ‌ܢ in 𝔖 pesh (so Gen. xl. 6 f.,
and 𝔖 vet.pesh Lk. xxiv. 17).

ὅπως φανῶσιν κτλ.] See *v.* 5
note; as there, τ. ἀνθρώποις must
be taken with φανῶσιν, not with
νηστεύοντες, though 'fasting unto
men' may be paralleled by Col. iii.
23, Eph. vi. 7. On ἀμὴν λ. ὑμῖν
and ἀπέχουσιν see *v.* 2 note. Sham
piety is referred to in *Sotah* 19 a,
20 c, and in 22 b King Jannai speaks
of 'dyed' or 'coloured' men, who
pretend to be Pharisees.'

17. σὺ δέ κτλ.] Anointing and
washing suggest feasting (Lk. vii. 44,
46, Ps. ciii. [civ.] 15). In *Ber.*
Rabba 74 Jacob is said so to have
acted, though secretly mourning over
Joseph's death; and God declared
that because he concealed his sorrow,
He would manifest it to the world.

18. ὅπως μή κτλ.] The transposition of τ. ἀνθρώποις and νηστεύοντες in B k was probably to produce
a clearer contrast between 'men' and
'thy Father.' The class. κρυφαῖος is
not found elsewhere in the N.T., but
occurs four times in the LXX. See
on τ. ἐν τ. κρυπτῷ (*v.* 6).

19–34. TRUE RIGHTEOUSNESS IN
ITS ATTITUDE TO WEALTH.

This section was not an original
part of the Sermon. The parallels
in Lk. are as follows: *Treasure, vv.*
19–21 = Lk. xii. 33 f. *The single
eye, vv.* 22 f. = Lk. xi. 34–36. *The
single service, v.* 24 = Lk. xvi. 13.
Earthly anxiety, vv. 25–34 = Lk. xii.
22–31.

19–21. (Lk. xii. 33 f.) *Treasure.*
The thought of the earthly and
heavenly reward in *vv.* 1–6, 16–18,
is here pursued in that of earthly
and heavenly wealth. And the recurrence of ἀφανίζειν (though with a
different meaning) supplies a formal
connexion with *v.* 16.

19. μὴ θησαυρίζετε κτλ.] Lk.
πωλήσατε τὰ ὑπάρχοντα κτλ. is an
echo of Lk. xviii. 22, and βαλλάντιον
is used only by him (x. 4, xxii. 35 f.).
The parallelism and tautology of
Mt. are Hebraic, and probably nearer
to the original. He gives a genuine
picture of Oriental wealth, garments
etc. stored in barbaric abundance,
too numerous for use. S. James (*v.*
3) seems to have had the saying in
mind. For σής cf. Is. li. 8, Pind.

καὶ βρῶσις ἀφανίζει, καὶ ὅπου κλέπται διορύσσουσιν καὶ
20 κλέπτουσιν· θησαυρίζετε δὲ ὑμῖν θησαυροὺς ἐν οὐρανῷ,
ὅπου οὔτε σὴς οὔτε βρῶσις ἀφανίζει, καὶ ὅπου κλέπται οὐ
21 διορύσσουσιν οὐδὲ κλέπτουσιν· ὅπου γάρ ἐστιν ὁ θη-
22 σαυρός σου, ἐκεῖ ἔσται καὶ ἡ καρδία σου. Ὁ λύχνος

Fragm. 22, Διὸς παῖς ὁ χρυσός·
κεῖνον οὐ σὴς οὐδὲ κὶς δάπτει.
The abstr. βρῶσις (𝔏 aerugo) is usually explained as 'rust' (cf. Jam.
l.c. κατίωται); cf. Ep. Jerem. 11,
οὗτοι δὲ (idols) οὐ διασώζονται ἀπὸ
ἰοῦ καὶ βρωμάτων. But βρῶσις
never has this meaning; in the LXX.
it is always the 'act of eating,' or
'food' (exc. Mal. iii. 11 = אֹכֶל,
'locust'). It probably denotes, therefore, the 'devouring,' by mice or
other vermin, of wealth stored in
barns; k Cypr. Aug. comestura. For
ἀφανίζειν 'to cause to disappear' cf.
Cant. ii. 15 (contrast v. 16 above).
For διορύσσειν cf. xxiv. 43, Mk. ii.
4, Ez. xii. 5, Job xxiv. 16, Aristoph.
Plut. 565, κλέπτειν καὶ τοὺς τοίχους
διορύττειν. Lk. has κλέπτης οὐκ
ἐγγίζει, possibly from a confusion of
קבון with יקרבון.

20. θησαυρίζετε κτλ.] Cf. v. 12
note, Test. Levi xiii. 5 (quoted at v.
1), Pss. Sol. ix. 9, ὁ ποιῶν δικαιοσύνην θησαυρίζει ζωὴν ἑαυτῷ παρὰ
κυρίῳ.

21. ὅπου γάρ κτλ.] Lk. has ὑμῶν
for σου, but the alternation of the
sing. and plur. is characteristic of
the Sermon in Mt. The hortatory
language of Deuteronomy exhibits
the same feature. Just. (Apol. i. 15)
writes ὅπου γάρ ὁ θησαυρός ἐστιν,
ἐκεῖ καὶ ὁ νοῦς ἀνθρώπου (similarly
Clem. Strom. VII. xii. 77, Macar. Hom.
xliii. 3); but καρδία is more than
νοῦς: if the heart is in heaven, both
the φρονεῖν and the ζωή of Col. iii.
2 are included. The converse of the
saying is found in Sextus, Prov. 136,

ὅπου σου τὸ φρονεῖν, ἐκεῖ σου τὸ
ἀγαθόν. Tert. quotes it correctly
(Scorp. 3), and also in a converse form
(ad Mart. 2; cf. De Anima 57).

22, 23. (Lk. xi. 34 ff.) The single
eye.

22. ὁ λύχνος κτλ.] The original
context of the saying is not known;
Mt. and Lk. place and understand
it differently. It recalls Prov. xx.
27 [21], φῶς Κυρίου πνοὴ ἀνθρώπων,
ὃς ἐραυνᾷ ταμεῖα κοιλίας: the spirit,
or self-consciousness, of man enables
him to know himself; cf. 1 Cor.
ii. 11. It may have been, in its
true context, the Lord's version of
γνῶθι σεαυτόν. For the purpose of
illustration He adds the mention
of the 'eye,' considered as the means
whereby light reaches the whole
body. (Cf. Philo, De Op. Mund. 17,
ὅπερ νοῦς ἐν ψυχῇ, τοῦτο ὀφθαλμὸς
ἐν σώματι, Arist. Top. i. 14, ὡς
ὄψις ἐν ὀφθαλμῷ, νοῦς ἐν ψυχῇ, and
see ὀφθαλμοὶ τῆς καρδίας, Clem.
Rom. i. 36, Mart. Polyc. ii.) The
application of the simile is confined
to v. 23 b, εἰ οὖν κτλ. 'If the eye,
the lamp which illuminates the body,
is ἁπλοῦς, the body is lit up within;
if it is πονηρός, the body is dark
within. In the same way, if the
inner light be extinguished, how
great is the darkness (or, as Lk., Take
heed that the inner light be not
extinguished).' ἁπλοῦς and πονηρός
probably represent תם and רע. The
former recurs in bibl. Gk. in Prov.
xi. 25 only, but it and its cognates
are used by Aquila for תָּם, תֹּם.
As used of eyes cf. Test. Iss. iii. 4

τοῦ σώματός ἐστιν ὁ ὀφθαλμός. ἐὰν οὖν ᾖ ὁ ὀφθαλμός
σου ἁπλοῦς, ὅλον τὸ σῶμά σου φωτινὸν ἔσται · ἐὰν δὲ ὁ 23
ὀφθαλμός σου πονηρὸς ᾖ, ὅλον τὸ σῶμά σου σκοτινὸν
ἔσται. εἰ οὖν τὸ φῶς τὸ ἐν σοὶ σκότος ἐστίν, τὸ σκότος
πόσον. Οὐδεὶς δύναται δυσὶ κυρίοις δουλεύειν · ἢ γὰρ 24

πορευόμενος ἐν ἁπλότητι ὀφθαλμῶν,
iv. 6 πάντα ὁρᾷ ἐν ἁπλότητι. It
is nowhere found strictly of physical
soundness; but for πονηρός = 'ill'
cf. Just. *Apol.* i. xxii. [τὸν Ἰησοῦν]
ἐκ γενετῆς πονηροὺς ὑγιεῖς πεποιη-
κέναι, and the class. πονηρῶς ἔχειν.
The choice of the adjs., however, was
probably influenced by the spiritual
application which was to follow.
φωτινόν and σκοτινόν probably
represent Aram. substs. 'light' and
'darkness,' as σκότος in the last
clause. For φῶς = λύχνος cf. Xen.
Hell. v. 1. 8 φῶς ἔχων...ἀφηγεῖτο,
'since he had a lamp, he led the
way.' But φῶς was more suitable
than λύχνος to the spiritual application. τὸ σκότος πόσον may mean
'What a terrible kind of darkening
that is!', referring directly to the
preceding σκότος, or, more probably,
'How terrible is the resultant darkness of thy whole being!'

In Lk. the words are attached to
the saying that a lamp is not hidden,
but placed on a lampstand (= Mt.
v. 15), but it has no clear connexion
either with this or with the surrounding context. In Mt. it follows
the sayings on the right and wrong
ways of performing religious duties
(*vv.* 1–18), and the right and wrong
treasure (*vv.* 19–21), and precedes
those on the right and wrong Master
(*v.* 24) and the right and wrong
objects of desire (*vv.* 25–34); he
seems, therefore, to have interpreted
it of a right and wrong spirit with
regard to earthly possessions. An
'evil eye' was a common Jewish
expression for a jealous or grudging

spirit; cf. xx. 15, Deut. xv. 9, Prov.
xxiii. 6, Sir. xiv. 10, *Ab.* ii. 13,
15, v. 19; and its converse ἁπλοῦς
ὀφθαλμός might be taken to connote
liberality; cf. the use of ἁπλῶς,
-ότης, in Jam. i. 5, Rom. xii. 8,
2 Cor. viii. 2, ix. 11, 13. The
passage is discussed by Brandt, *ZNW.*,
1913, 97–116, 177–201, and Bacon,
Expos., March 1914, 275–88.

24. (Lk. xvi. 13.) *The Single Service.*
οὐδείς κτλ.] Lk. οὐδεὶς οἰκέτης.
The right and wrong spirit with regard to earthly possessions is followed
by service to a right and wrong
master—God and Money. δουλεύειν
must have its full force : men can
work for two employers, but no slave
can be the property of two owners.
Lk. attaches the saying to others
concerning 'mammon.'

ἢ γάρ κτλ.] The second ἤ is
not 'or *at least*,' as though the first
pair of verbs were stronger than the
second ; 'love' and 'hate' have a
comparative force, as in v. 43, Lk.
xiv. 26, Jo. xii. 25, Gen. xxix. 33,
Deut. xxi. 15, Mal. i. 2 f. ἀνθέξεται,
'hold fast to,' is hardly a natural contrast with 'despise,' nor is 'endure'
(Ʂ cur), *patietur* (𝔏 vet), *sustinebit*
(k vulg.), 'susteyne' (Wicl.). A
better meaning is that in Jer. viii. 2
('the host of heaven οἷς ἐδούλευσαν
... καὶ ὧν ἀντείχοντο [דְּרָשׁוּם]),
Zeph. i. 6 (τοὺς μὴ ἀντεχομένους
τοῦ κυρίου), *i.e.* 'look to' for support
and help, or in Is. lvii. 13 (οἱ δὲ
ἀντεχόμενοί μου בִּי [הַחוֹסֶה]), *i.e.*
'hope in.' If the original was סבר
(see *e.g.* Targ^{onk} Gen. xlix. 18), it

τὸν ἕνα μισήσει καὶ τὸν ἕτερον ἀγαπήσει, ἢ ἑνὸς ἀνθέξεται
καὶ τοῦ ἑτέρου καταφρονήσει· οὐ δύνασθε θεῷ δουλεύειν
25 καὶ μαμωνᾷ. Διὰ τοῦτο λέγω ὑμῖν, μὴ μεριμνᾶτε τῇ

would produce an assonance with בסר, 'despise.' On the symmetrical tautology of the passage see vi. 6.

οὐ δύνασθε κτλ.] 'Et tamen non dixit qui habet divitias sed qui servit divitias' (Jer.). Either God or wealth must be hated and despised or loved and trusted. The Lord, as before, states the principle without compromise or limitation (see v. 32, note). The masc. μαμωνᾶς occurs in Suidas ii. 679. The spelling -μμ- is confined to a few minuscules, some Lat. MSS. and writers, and Goth. The word is not found in the Heb. O.T., but occurs in Sir. xxxi. 8 (LXX. χρυσίον), and is frequent in the Targg. as the equivalent of various Heb. words, chiefly בֶּצַע, 'gain.' See also Ab. ii. 16, 'Let the mamon of thy neighbour be dear to thee as thine own.' It may be an abbreviation of מַטְמוֹן, 'something hidden or stored up' (see Dalman, Gr. 135 n.), or of מַאֲמוֹן, 'something entrusted.' The latter is the more probable; it is the spelling in a codex of S pal in Lk. xvi. 13, and there seems to be a play on the root אמן in Lk. xvi. 11; cf. also Ps. xxxvi. [xxxvii.] 3, where πλοῦτος represents a misreading of אֱמוּנָה. The change of ṭm into mm or m is unknown, and the Targg. never employ מִמּוֹן to render the Heb. מַטְמוֹן. Aug. speaks of a Punic word mammon, meaning lucrum, which he traces to the Phoenicians. Chrys. renders μ. by χρυσός, but Jer. says 'divitiae . . . non aurum ut quidam putant.' The Aram. word is preserved probably because Wealth is personified; 'injustitiae enim au-

torem et dominatorem totius saeculi nummum scimus omnes' (Tert.); and Orig. (hom. in Jerem.), commenting upon the personified κοιλία in Phil. iii. 19, adds θεοῦ σού ἐστιν ὁ μαμωνᾶς καὶ κύριος: similarly Didasc. III. vii. 3 f. (ed. Funk, 195). This is a point of view from which covetousness is idolatry (Col. iii. 5). The personification led to the mediaeval idea that Mamon was a heathen god or deity; and even Greg. Nyss. took it to be a name of Beelzebul.

25–34. (Lk. xii. 22 31.) Earthly Anxiety. The context in Lk. is different, though it also deals with the hoarding of wealth.

25. διὰ τοῦτο κτλ.] The connexion of thought seems to be 'Therefore give up the service of wealth, which only causes anxiety' (cf. Heb. xiii. 5); this perhaps implies the popular derivation of μέριμνα from μέρος, -ίζω: he who tries to serve God and Wealth μεμέρισται (cf. 1 Cor. vii. 32 f.). Lk. also has διὰ τοῦτο, but introduces the verse with 'And He said to His disciples,' shewing that διὰ τοῦτο was in his source, but referred to an antecedent unknown to us.

μὴ μεριμνᾶτε κτλ.] Vulg. ne solliciti sitis. R.V. 'be not anxious.' Engl. Verss. before A.V. (except Wicl.) 'be not careful' (cf. Phil. iv. 6 A.V.), i.e. full of care. ψυχή stands for the life principle, common to man and beast, which is embodied in the σῶμα (see x. 28 note): the former needs food, the latter clothing. ἢ τί πίητε is perhaps due to v. 31; the evidence is uncertain; C D and S sin are here wanting.

ψυχῇ ὑμῶν τί φάγητε ἢ τί πίητε, μηδὲ τῷ σώματι ὑμῶν
τί ἐνδύσησθε· οὐχὶ ἡ ψυχὴ πλεῖόν ἐστι τῆς τροφῆς καὶ τὸ
σῶμα τοῦ ἐνδύματος ; ἐμβλέψατε εἰς τὰ πετεινὰ τοῦ οὐρα- 26
νοῦ ὅτι οὐ σπείρουσιν οὐδὲ θερίζουσιν οὐδὲ συνάγουσιν
εἰς ἀποθήκας, καὶ ὁ πατὴρ ὑμῶν ὁ οὐράνιος τρέφει αὐτά·
οὐχ ὑμεῖς μᾶλλον διαφέρετε αὐτῶν ; τίς δὲ ἐξ ὑμῶν μερι- 27

25 η τι πιητε] B 𝔏 c f g¹ h m q me sah [om η] arm ; και τι π. E al 𝔖 pesh.hcl
go ; om ℵ 1 4 22 𝔏 a b ff¹ k l vg 𝔖 cur.pal aeth

οὐχὶ ἡ ψυχὴ κτλ.] The argument
is a fortiori : if God has given the
greater things, the life and the body,
He can surely provide the lesser,
food and clothing (so Jer., Aug.).
οὐχί represents either הלא (nonne)
or הא (ecce) ; see Thackeray, GrOT.
126. Lk. has a positive statement,
ἡ γὰρ ψυχή κτλ.
26. ἐμβλέψατε κτλ.] Lk. κατανοήσατε τοὺς κόρακας (κατανοεῖν,
Lk.⁸, Mt.¹, Mk.⁰). That Lk. selected
particular birds as a parallel to the
particular flowers in v. 28 (Harnack)
is unlikely ; he may have been
influenced by Ps. cxlvi. [cxlvii.] 9,
or Job xxxviii. 41. Mt. employs a
frequent O.T. expression.
καὶ ὁ πατήρ κτλ.] For the use
of καί ('and yet') cf. i. 19, x. 29
(Blass, § 77. 6). On ὁ οὐράνιος see
v. 9 b ; Lk., perhaps rightly, has ὁ
θεός (cf. v. 30). For the thought
cf. Ps. ciii. [civ.] 27, Pss. Sol. v. 11,
τὰ πετεινὰ καὶ τοὺς ἰχθύας σὺ
τρέφεις. The birds are an example
not of idleness but of freedom from
anxiety ; 'labor exercendus est, solli-
citudo tollenda' (Jer.).
οὐχ ὑμεῖς κτλ.] μᾶλλον has lost
its comparative force (Blass, § 44. 3)—
'Do ye not greatly differ from them ?'
(cf. Mk. vii. 36); in Lk.'s πόσῳ
μᾶλλον it is pleonastic. διαφέρειν
(perhaps Aram. שׁוי) does not strictly
mean 'to excel,' though that is implied ; see x. 31, xii. 12. In Ox. Pap.
iv. 655 (as restored) the thought is

applied to the lilies (v. 28) : πολλῷ
κρείσσονές ἐστε τῶν κρίνων ἅτινα
αὐξάνει οὐδὲ νήθει.
27. τίς δέ κτλ.] ἡλικία is often
rendered 'age' (so k [Mt.] e [Lk.]),
because the saying is taken, as in Lk.,
to describe something trifling which
man cannot perform (see v. 28 note) ;
and passages can be cited (e.g. Ps.
xxxix. 5) in which measures of space
are used metaphorically of time. But
the arrangement of vv. 25–30 favours
the meaning 'stature' (𝔖 vet.pesh
𝔏 vet.vg., Tert., Hil.). In v. 25
the contents of the section are
summed up, i.e. Be not anxious
about (a) food for the bodily life, (b)
clothing for the bodily frame ; then
(a) the bodily life is dealt with in
v. 26, and (b) the bodily frame in
vv. 27 ff., the latter containing an
a priori argument after the manner
of v. 25 : To add a cubit to one's
stature is not something trifling, but
a portentous miracle ; man cannot
do it, but God can ; why then (v. 28)
be anxious about the lesser thing,
raiment ? This close conjunction of
v. 27 with v. 28 is supported by
𝔖 cur : 'but which of you can add to
his stature one cubit, that about
(ܗ‎ܳ‎) clothing ye are anxious ?'
πῆχυς was the recognized unit of
man's height ; πῆχυν εἶπε διότι
κυρίως μέτρον τῶν ἡλιχιῶν ὁ πῆχύς
ἐστι (Euth.) ; cf. ἄνδρες τετραπήχεις
(Ar. Vesp. 552). For ἡλικία 'height'
cf. Lk. xix. 3, and (= קוֹמָה) Ez. xiii.

μνῶν δύναται προσθεῖναι ἐπὶ τὴν ἡλικίαν αὐτοῦ πῆχυν
28 ἕνα ; καὶ περὶ ἐνδύματος τί μεριμνᾶτε ; καταμάθετε τὰ
κρίνα τοῦ ἀγροῦ πῶς αὐξάνουσιν· οὐ κοπιῶσιν οὐδὲ νήθου-
29 σιν· λέγω δὲ ὑμῖν ὅτι οὐδὲ Σολομὼν ἐν πάσῃ τῇ δόξῃ
30 αὐτοῦ περιεβάλετο ὡς ἓν τούτων. εἰ δὲ τὸν χόρτον τοῦ
ἀγροῦ σήμερον ὄντα καὶ αὔριον εἰς κλίβανον βαλλόμενον
ὁ θεὸς οὕτως ἀμφιέννυσιν, οὐ πολλῷ μᾶλλον ὑμᾶς, ὀλιγό-
31 πιστοι ; μὴ οὖν μεριμνήσητε λέγοντες Τί φάγωμεν ; ἤ
32 Τί πίωμεν ; ἤ Τί περιβαλώμεθα ; πάντα γὰρ ταῦτα τὰ

18 (LXX. Sym.), Cant. vii. 7 (Sym.).
An Oxyr. fragm. (iv. 655. 13 f.) has τίς
ἂν προσθ[εί]η ἐπὶ τὴν ἡλικίαν ὑμῶν,
αὐτὸς δώσει ὑμῖν τὸ ἔνδυμα ὑμῶν.

28. καὶ περί κτλ.] 'Why then
etc.' (Lk. εἰ οὖν κτλ.). For the use
of καί cf. Mk. x. 26 (Blass, § 77. 6).
The position of περὶ ἐνδύματος
heightens the emphasis of the
question. Lk. has εἰ οὖν οὐδὲ
ἐλάχιστον δύνασθε (understanding
ἡλικία, unlike Mt., to mean 'age')
τί περὶ τῶν λοιπῶν μεριμνᾶτε ;
καταμάθετε κτλ.] The verb occurs
in the LXX. and Sym., but not elsewhere in the N.T. Lk. κατανοήσατε
(see v. 26 note). τ. κρίνα τ. ἀγροῦ,
in parallelism with τ. πετεινὰ τ.
οὐρανοῦ, may be wild flowers in
general ; in Ex. xxv. 31 [30] κρίνα =
פְּרָחִים, 'flowers,' 'blossoms.' Besides
lilies they might include anemones,
poppies, gladioli and irises. Post
(HDB. 'Lily') prefers the last two,
because their stems would be the
most useful for fuel (v. 30). In
Lk. τ. ἀγροῦ is omitted, and τ. κρίνα
perhaps denotes a particular flower ;
he also omits πῶς αὐξάνουσιν. The
flowers perform neither men's work
in the field (κοπιῶσιν), nor women's
work at home (νήθουσιν) ; Lk. (D) has
two stages in the making of clothing,
πῶς οὔτε νήθει οὔτε ὑφαίνει.

29. λέγω δέ κτλ.] Lk. omits ὅτι.
The words have the glamour of a
sentence from a child's fairy tale.

On the form Σολομών see i. 6.
On Jewish and other legends about
Solomon see Fabricius, Cod. Pseudepig.
V.T. 1014-70.

30. εἰ δὲ τὸν χόρτον κτλ.] The
common χόρτον instead of κρίνα
heightens the comparison ; Lk.
heightens it further by transposition,
εἰ δὲ ἐν ἀγρῷ τ. χόρτον κτλ. For
ἀμφιέννυσιν Lk. has the later ἀμφιάζει
(see M.-M. Vocab. s.v.). ὀλιγόπιστος
occurs in Lk. (derived from Q), in this
saying only ; elsewhere in the N.T.
it is confined to Mt. viii. 26, xiv. 31,
xvi. 8 (cf. Act. Thom. 28), and is not
found in the LXX. or in non-bibl.
Gk. The Rabb. אֱמוּנָה קְטַנֵּי (see
Lightfoot, Hor. Heb.) was perhaps in
use in the 1st cent.

31. μὴ οὖν κτλ.] The simple
Hebraic style is lost in Lk. ; and
his μὴ μετεωρίζεσθε (cf. 2 Mac. vii.
34), instead of τί περιβαλώμεθα,
generalizes the anxiety (as his τῶν
λοιπῶν for Mt.'s ἐνδύματος, v. 28).
Cf. the rebuke in Epict. I. ix. 19,
ὅταν χορτασθῆτε σήμερον, κάθησθε
κλάοντες περὶ τῆς αὔριον πόθεν
φάγητε.

32. πάντα γάρ κτλ.] The two
clauses give two reasons for not being
anxious, the second γάρ (Lk. δέ) being
parallel with the first. τὰ ἔθνη are
the 'Gentiles' as distinct from 'the
Jews' ; Lk., for his Gentile readers,
adds τοῦ κόσμου, i.e. the heathen
world as distinct from Christians.

ἔθνη ἐπιζητοῦσιν· οἶδεν γὰρ ὁ πατὴρ ὑμῶν ὁ οὐράνιος ὅτι
χρῄζετε τούτων ἁπάντων. ζητεῖτε δὲ πρῶτον τὴν βασι- 33
λείαν καὶ τὴν δικαιοσύνην αὐτοῦ, καὶ ταῦτα πάντα προστεθήσεται ὑμῖν. μὴ οὖν μεριμνήσητε εἰς τὴν αὔριον, ἡ 34
γὰρ αὔριον μεριμνήσει αὐτῆς· ἀρκετὸν τῇ ἡμέρᾳ ἡ κακία
αὐτῆς.

33 τὴν βασιλειαν ... αυτου] tr βασ. et δικ. B ; post βασ. add του θεου EG al 𝕷 vet. plcr.
vg [exc. am.harl *] 𝕾 cur. pesh. hcl. pal ; post βασ. add αυτου 236 440 me aeth |
αυτου] του θεου 𝕷 k ps-Ath   34 αυτης¹°] pr τα περι Δ ; τα εαυτης EKM al

ὁ οὐράνιος (see *v.* 9 note) and ἁπάντων
are absent from Lk.

33. ζητεῖτε δέ κτλ.] Lk. has his
favourite πλήν (¹⁵, Mt. ⁵ ; once in
Mk. as a preposition). The thought
emphasized by πρῶτον (which Lk.
omits) is illustrated in the Lord's
Prayer, where God's Name, Kingdom,
and Will, precede the petition for
bread. Lk. has simply τὴν βασιλείαν αὐτοῦ· Mt.'s καὶ τ. δικαιοσύνην
is an insertion similar to that of
τ. δικαιοσύνην in *v.* 6 (see note);
the disciples are to seek the divine
Kingdom and the vindication which
it will bring to them. In cod. B
βασιλείαν and δικαιοσύνην are
transposed, the latter being wrongly
understood as the present moral
condition which must precede entrance into the Kingdom (see v. 20).
αὐτοῦ must evidently be taken with
both substantives, though Mt. elsewhere uses ἡ βασιλεία with no
further definition (see viii. 12 note);
the *v.ll.* are attempts to remove the
ambiguity.

Another form of the saying gained
currency : αἰτεῖτε τὰ μεγάλα καὶ
τὰ μικρὰ ὑμῖν προστεθήσεται, καὶ
αἰτεῖτε τὰ ἐπουράνια καὶ τὰ ἐπίγεια
ὑμῖν προστεθήσεται. Orig. quotes
it with ὁ σωτήρ . . . φησιν ; Ambr.
similarly with 'scriptum est';
Clem. Al. and Eus. quote the first
half (see Resch, *Agrapha*², 111). It
reapplies the thought of *vv.* 25 b,

27 f.—If God can give the greater
things, He can surely give the lesser.

34. μὴ οὖν κτλ.] Absent from Lk.
Though μὴ μεριμνήσητε forms a
link with the preceding verses, the
thought is different ; the trust in
God, enjoined in *vv.* 25-33, involves
a happy confidence that no day shall
have its κακία, because He will
provide. The present saying, if a
genuine utterance of Jesus, must
have belonged to a different context.
For the personification of ἡ αὔριον
cf. Prov. xxvii. 1. She 'will bear
the anxiety of herself'; but μεριμνᾶν
does not elsewhere take a gen., and
αὐτῇ is suggested by 'ipse cogitabit
sibi' (k Cypr.), 'sollicitus erit *sibi*
ipse' (b c vulg.); μερ. αὐτῆς, however,
may be a lit. rendering of יצף דילה
(so 𝕾 cur with the words transposed),
'is anxious about *its* own,' in which
case the *v.l.* τὰ ἑαυτῆς is a correction
which gives the true sense. For
ἀρκετόν, a rare word, cf. x. 25, 1 Pet.
iv. 3, Jos. *BJ.* iii. 130, *Anth. Pal.*
ix. 749 ; it occurs in Chrysipp. and
in two pap. of the 2nd and 3rd
centt. (see Allen). On the neut.
predicate see Blass, § 31. 2. κακία
(here only in the Gospp.) is frequent
in the LXX. for רָעָה, 'trouble'; elsewhere in the N.T. it is used only
of moral badness. Jer. (*Ep. ad
Amandum*) criticizes the O.L. rendering *malitia*, preferring *afflictio*.

Both parts of the verse have Rabb.

VII. 1   Μὴ κρίνετε, ἵνα μὴ κριθῆτε· ἐν ᾧ γὰρ κρίματι κρίνετε
2 κριθήσεσθε, καὶ ἐν ᾧ μέτρῳ μετρεῖτε μετρηθήσεται ὑμῖν.
3 τί δὲ βλέπεις τὸ κάρφος τὸ ἐν τῷ ὀφθαλμῷ τοῦ ἀδελφοῦ
4 σου, τὴν δὲ ἐν τῷ σῷ ὀφθαλμῷ δοκὸν οὐ κατανοεῖς ; ἢ πῶς

parallels ;—(a) *Sanh.* 100 b : 'Be
not anxious for the morrow, for thou
knowest not what a day may bring
forth [cf. Prov. *l.c.*]; perhaps on
the morrow he is not, and he is
found troubling himself about a
world which is not his' (cf. Jam. iv.
14). (b) *Berak.* 9 a: 'There is
enough trouble in its hour.'

vii. 1–5. (Lk. vi. 37 f., 41 f.)
Against judging.

There is no connexion of thought
with the preceding verses ; the Sermon as it stood in Q is taken up at the
point where Mt. left it, at the end
of ch. v. Lk. couples the verses by
καί with the commands ' Love your
enemies ' and ' Be merciful.'

1. μὴ κρίνετε κτλ.] Not only
false judgment is forbidden, but a
censorious habit of mind ; cf. Jam.
iv. 12. ἵνα μὴ κριθῆτε (Lk. καὶ οὐ
μὴ κρ.) may refer to divine judgment,
whether immediate, or at the Last
Day (cf. 1 Cor. iv. 5, Jas. v. 9), or,
as Mt. interprets it, to human judgment ; those who judge others must
expect similar treatment ; see next
verse. As often, the principle is
laid down without mention of possible
limitations (see v. 32, note). The
words are quoted in *Ep. Polyc.* ii. 3 ;
and cf. Clem. *Cor.* xiii. 2, ὡς κρίνετε
οὕτως κριθήσεσθε.

2. ἐν ᾧ γάρ κτλ.] Mt. understands both halves of the verse to
refer to adverse judgments. But
Lk., though, for the first half, he
gives καὶ μὴ καταδικάζετε κτλ., continues with injunctions of a kindly
attitude towards others—ἀπολύετε
κ. ἀπολ., δίδοτε κ. δοθ. ὑμῖν, μέτρον
καλὸν . . . δώσουσιν εἰς τ. κόλπον

ὑμ., where the impers. δώσουσιν may
mean 'other men,' or possibly God.
Mk. iv. 24 has ἐν ᾧ μέτρῳ μετρεῖτε
μετρηθήσεται ὑμῖν (adding καὶ
προστεθήσεται ὑμῖν, possibly a
reminiscence of the saying drawn
from Q in Mt. vi. 33, Lk. xii. 31),
but referring to the spirit in which
a man attends to teaching which he
receives (see Swete). Clem. Rom.
(xiii. 2) knew the saying : ᾧ μέτρῳ
μετρεῖτε ἐν αὐτῷ μετρηθήσεται ὑμῖν.
Cf. *Ep. Polyc.* ii., Clem. Al. *Strom.*
ii. 18. It was perhaps a current
proverb; cf. *Sotah* i. 7 : 'With the
measure wherewith a man measures
do they (? God) measure to him,' a
saying which probably belongs to
the 1st cent. A.D.

3. τί δὲ βλέπεις κτλ.] An illustration of the warning in *v.* 1. It
was perhaps another current proverb:
R. Tarphon (beg. 2nd cent. A.D.)
lamented that men in his day could
not accept reproof ; if one said to
another ' Cast the mote out of thine
eye,' he would answer ' Cast the beam
out of thine eye' (*Erach.* 16 b ; cf.
B. *Bath.* 15 b) ; but this was possibly
an attack on the N.T. words. For
the thought cf. Rom. ii. 1, *Kidd.*
70 a, ' He who accuses another of a
fault, has it himself.' Plut. *De Cur.*
515 d, τί ἀλλότριον . . . κακὸν ὀξυ-
δερκεῖς τὸ δ' ἴδιον παραβλέπεις ;
Hor. *Sat.* I. iii. 25.

κάρφος (der. κάρφω) is a piece of
dried wood or straw ; *festuca* (Vulg.),
stipula (k). In Gen. viii. 11 it is
used for טָרָף, 'plucked off.' ' Mote '
is the rendering in all Engl. versions.

4. ἢ πῶς κτλ.] Lk. πῶς δύνασαι
λέγειν, and before ἄφες he inserts

ἐρεῖς τῷ ἀδελφῷ σου Ἄφες ἐκβάλω τὸ κάρφος ἐκ τοῦ
ὀφθαλμοῦ σου, καὶ ἰδοὺ ἡ δοκὸς ἐν τῷ ὀφθαλμῷ σου;
ὑποκριτά, ἔκβαλε πρῶτον ἐκ τοῦ ὀφθαλμοῦ σου τὴν δοκόν, 5
καὶ τότε διαβλέψεις ἐκβαλεῖν τὸ κάρφος ἐκ τοῦ ὀφθαλμοῦ
τοῦ ἀδελφοῦ σου. Μὴ δῶτε τὸ ἅγιον τοῖς κυσίν, μηδὲ 6
βάλητε τοὺς μαργαρίτας ὑμῶν ἔμπροσθεν τῶν χοίρων, μή
ποτε καταπατήσουσιν αὐτοὺς ἐν τοῖς ποσὶν αὐτῶν καὶ
στραφέντες ῥήξωσιν ὑμᾶς. Αἰτεῖτε, καὶ δοθήσεται ὑμῖν· 7

ἀδελφέ (voc. frequent in Ac., not
found in Mt., Mk.). For ἄφες cf.
xxvii. 49, *Ox. Pap.* 413 ἄφες ἐγὼ
αὐτὴν θρηνήσω (see Blass, § 64. 2).
On ἐκβάλλειν see viii. 12.

5. ὑποκριτά κτλ.] See vi. 2, note.
He is a hypocrite because his un-
kind criticism takes the outward
form of a kindly act. On πρῶτον
for πρότερον see Blass, § 11. 5. δια-
βλέπειν, apart from this context,
occurs only in Mk. viii. 25, and not
in the LXX. Aq. has διάβλεψις in
Is. lxi. 1.

6. *Dogs and swine.* If the verse
stood in Lk.'s source, he may have
omitted it because it was distasteful
to his Gentile readers, whom Jews
called 'dogs.' Hil., *al.* explain the
'dogs' as the heathen, and the 'swine'
as heretics. But as the original context is unknown, an exact interpretation is impossible. In its
present position the saying seems
intended to supply a necessary
limitation of the command 'Judge
not': the disciple must, after all,
exercise some discrimination (? in
teaching). But the transition is
abrupt. τὸ ἅγιον, both in number
and meaning, is strange in parallelism
with τοὺς μαργαρίτας. It may have
been originally due to a mistaken
rendering of the Aram. קדשא, which
can also mean ear-ring(s); cf. Prov.
xi. 22, where 'an ear-ring (Targ.
קדשא) in a swine's mouth' is a
simile for incongruity. The render-

ing τὸ ἅγιον might arise from the
application of the word to sacrificial
flesh; cf. the converse regulation
in Ex. xxii. 31. The widespread
liturgical formula τὰ ἅγια τοῖς ἁγίοις,
used before the distribution of the
Eucharistic elements (cf. Cyr. Jer.
Myst. v. 19, Chrys. *Hom. in Heb.* 17,
Const. Ap. viii. 12), led to the reading
τὰ ἅγια in min. 157, Chrys., *al.* The
words are quoted in *Didache* ix., in
forbidding the admission of the un-
baptized to the Eucharist, and by
Tert. (*De Praescr.* xli.), who blames
heretics for admitting them. On
the saying τὰ μυστήριά μου ἐμοὶ
καὶ τοῖς ἐμοῖς, which Theod. couples
with this, see Resch, *Agrapha²*, p. 108 f.

μή ποτε κτλ.] If not merely intended to heighten the effect of the
simile, this may describe the violence
of religious enemies who have learnt
enough of Christ's teaching to use it
as a handle for persecution.

7-11. (Lk. xi. 9-13.) *The value
of Prayer.*

In Lk. the passage follows the parable of the friend at midnight, and
the Lord's Prayer. Here it stands in
no apparent relation with the context.

7, 8. αἰτεῖτε κτλ.] With the
symmetrical tautology of the verses
see vi. 6 (note). The emphasis is
on the imperatives (*v.* 7) and participles (*v.* 8); it is only by asking,
etc., that the desired end can be
won. As often, no conditions or
limitations are attached to the state-

8 ζητεῖτε, καὶ εὑρήσετε· κρούετε, καὶ ἀνοιγήσεται ὑμῖν. πᾶς
γὰρ ὁ αἰτῶν λαμβάνει καὶ ὁ ζητῶν εὑρίσκει καὶ τῷ
9 κρούοντι ἀνοιγήσεται. ἢ τίς ἐξ ὑμῶν ἄνθρωπος, ὃν
10 αἰτήσει ὁ υἱὸς αὐτοῦ ἄρτον—μὴ λίθον ἐπιδώσει αὐτῷ ; ἢ
11 καὶ ἰχθὺν αἰτήσει—μὴ ὄφιν ἐπιδώσει αὐτῷ ; εἰ οὖν ὑμεῖς

8 ανοιγησεται] ανοιγεται B 𝕾 cur. pesh. hcl. pal me   9 τις] B* L 𝕃 b
c g¹ h me sah ; *add* εστιν אB²CE *al* 𝕃 a f ff¹ g² k q vg Cyp | ον] *add* εαν אᵇE *al* 𝕃
f ff¹ g² k q vg 𝕾 hcl Cyp

ment; in xviii. 19 success is gained
by corporate prayer, iu xxi. 22 by
believing prayer, but in every case
πλὴν οὐχ ὡς ἐγὼ θέλω ἀλλ᾽ ὡς σύ
(xxvi. 39) is to be understood. ὁ δὲ
κακῶς ζητῶν οὐχ εὑρίσκει (Orig.).
With ζητεῖτε κτλ. cf. Prov. viii. 17,
Ox. Pap. iv. p. 4 f. μὴ παυσάσθω ὁ
ζητῶν... ἕως ἂν εὔρῃ. With κρυύετε
κτλ. cf. *Meg.* 12 b, 'Mordecai knocked
at the doors of mercy, and they were
opened to him'; *Pesikta* 176 a,
R. Benaiah (*c.* A.D. 200) said that a
man should deeply study the Mishna,
'for if he knocks it will be opened
to him.' 'Knock' (whether the
following vb. be fut. or pres.) does
not necessarily mean 'Strive to
enter the Kingdom' (Zahn); the
2nd and 3rd clauses are pictorial
illustrations of the first.

9. ἢ τίς κτλ.] ὃν... ὁ υἱὸς αὐτοῦ
seems to be a reproduction of the
Aram. ברה ...ד, and the insertion of
μή causes an anacoluthon by forming a separate question. Lk. τίνα
δὲ ἐξ ὑμ. τὸν πατέρα αἰτήσει ὁ υἱὸς
ἰχθύν avoids the former but not the
latter. The *v.ll.* do not succeed in
improving the construction.

ἐπιδώσει] *porriget* (Vulg.), 'Will
hand to him'; cf. Lk. iv. 17, xxiv.
30, 42. It needs a higher than
human wisdom and love to test a
son by giving him stones instead of
loaves (iv. 1–4). For 'loaf' and 'stone'
Lk. substitutes 'egg' and 'scorpion'
after 'fish' and 'serpent.'

10. ἢ καὶ ἰχθύν κτλ.] Fish
would be, next to bread, one of the
commonest articles of food near the
Sea of Galilee; the town of Taricheae,
at the S.W. corner of the lake, derived its name from the curing of
fish. Stones on the shore, and
possibly water-snakes, suggested
themselves as substitutes. Lk. adds
ἢ καὶ αἰτήσει ᾠόν, μὴ ἐπιδώσει αὐτῷ
σκορπίον; (see Plummer). The Lord
may have employed all three illustrations, two of which were differently
preserved in the two recensions of
Q; cf. xxiv. 40 f. note.

11. εἰ οὖν κτλ.] With πονηροὶ
ὄντες cf. xii. 34. Lk. ὑπάρχοντες
(not in Mt., Mk.; Lk., Ac.³¹). In
comparison with God, all men—even
kind parents—are 'evil' (cf. xix. 17).
There can be no reference to original
sin (Jer.) ; nor must πονηροί be confined to the meaning 'niggardly.'
Aug. asks 'Quomodo mali dant
bona ?' and replies 'Quisquis ea
malus dat, non de suo dat; domini
est enim terra et plenitudo ejus.'
For οἴδατε cf. xxvii. 65, Jam. iv. 17.
On ὁ ἐν τ. οὐρανοῖς see vi. 9. Lk.
has the unique ὁ ἐξ οὐρανοῦ, 'the
Father who [gives] from heaven';
cf. Jam. i. 17. Lk. defines ἀγαθά
by substituting πνεῦμα ἅγιον, 'an
outpouring of the Holy Spirit';
ἀγαθά is probably nearer to the
original, including material blessings
(cf. vi. 25–33) as well as spiritual
(cf. Rom. viii. 32).

πονηροὶ ὄντες οἴδατε δόματα ἀγαθὰ διδόναι τοῖς τέκνοις
ὑμῶν, πόσῳ μᾶλλον ὁ πατὴρ ὑμῶν ὁ ἐν τοῖς οὐρανοῖς
δώσει ἀγαθὰ τοῖς αἰτοῦσιν αὐτόν. Πάντα οὖν ὅσα ἐὰν 12
θέλητε ἵνα ποιῶσιν ὑμῖν οἱ ἄνθρωποι, οὕτως καὶ ὑμεῖς
ποιεῖτε αὐτοῖς· οὗτος γάρ ἐστιν ὁ νόμος καὶ οἱ προφῆται.

12. (Lk. vi. 31.) *The Golden Rule.*
In Lk. this follows the passage
which is parallel with Mt. v. 42.
Mt. appears to have removed it to
this point to form a general conclusion to the main body of his
Sermon, the rest of it being an
epilogue.

πάντα οὖν κτλ.] οὖν is not in
logical sequence with *v.* 11, but
sums up the Sermon to this point
(cf. *v.* 24, v. 28). Lk. has καθὼς
θέλετε ἵνα κτλ., and for οὕτως he
has ὁμοίως after αὐτοῖς. The
thought is found widely in negative
forms : *e.g.* Tob. iv. 15, ὃ μισεῖς μηδενὶ
ποιήσῃς, Philo (*ap.* Eus. *Praep.* viii.
7), ἃ τις παθεῖν ἐχθαίρει μὴ ποιεῖν
αὐτόν, Hillel, 'What is hateful to
thee, thou shalt not do to thy neighbour ; this word is the whole law, and
all else is commentary' (*Shabb.* 31 a),
Ac. xv. 29 (D), ὅσα μὴ θέλετε ἑαυτοῖς
γείνεσθαι ἑτέρῳ μὴ ποιεῖν (so Iren.,
Cypr.). Other parallels, pagan,
Jewish, and Christian, are collected
by G. Resch, *Das Aposteldekret*,
132-141. The positive form is im-
measurably higher, and appears to be
the Lord's own coinage. It is imitated by Justin (*Dial.* 93), καὶ ὁ τὸν
πλησίον ὡς ἑαυτὸν ἀγαπῶν, ἅπερ
ἑαυτῷ βούλεται ἀγαθά, κἀκείνῳ
βουλήσεται : similarly *Clem. Hom.*
vii. 4.

οὗτος γάρ κτλ.] Absent from
Lk. Cf. xxii. 40, and Hillel's saying
quoted above ; see also *Ber. R.* xxiv.
(Wünsche, 112) on 'This is the
book etc.' (Gen. v. 1). The Golden
Rule is the distilled essence of that
'fulfilment' (v. 17) which is taught

in the Sermon. As in v. 17, xxii.
40, it is possible that καὶ οἱ προφῆται
is a later addition. For οὗτος
(instead of τοῦτο) attracted to the
gender of νόμος see Kühner-Gerth,
§ 369.

13–27. EPILOGUE. Like the
Book of the Covenant (Ex. xx.–xxiii.),
the Deuteronomic code (Dt. xii.–
xxviii.), and the Law of Holiness
(Lev. xvii.–xxvi.), the Lord's commentary on the Law closes with
warnings and exhortations, compiled
from various sources on a basis
which is represented by Lk. xiii. 24,
vi. 43–46, xiii. 26 f., vi. 47–49. It
consists of three contrasts : the *Two
Ways* (*vv.* 13 f.), *Profession and real
Fruit* (*vv.* 15–23), the *Two Foundations* (*vv.* 24–27).

13, 14. (Lk. xiii. 24.) *The Narrow
Gate ; the Two Ways.*

In Lk., where there is no contrast
between 'narrow' and 'broad,' and
the ὁδός is not mentioned, a crowd
is pictured struggling to enter by a
narrow *door*, *i.e.* perhaps to gain
admission, at the Last Day, into the
Kingdom. Lk. gives the words as
a reply to the question εἰ ὀλίγοι οἱ
σωζόμενοι ; and the use of θύρα led
to the appending of words parallel
with Mt. vii. 23. The difference,
however, between πύλη and θύρα
cannot be pressed : each might represent the Aram. תרע (so ﬡ) ;
and the verbs εἰσέρχεσθαι (Mt.,
Lk.), εὑρίσκειν (Mt.), ἰσχύειν (Lk.)
may all point to ממא. For εἰσέρχεσθαι in connexion with the Kingdom
see v. 20 note.

13 Εἰσέλθατε διὰ τῆς στενῆς πύλης· ὅτι πλατεῖα καὶ
εὐρύχωρος ἡ ὁδὸς ἡ ἀπάγουσα εἰς τὴν ἀπώλειαν, καὶ
14 πολλοί εἰσιν οἱ εἰσερχόμενοι δι᾽ αὐτῆς· ὅτι στενὴ ἡ πύλη
καὶ τεθλιμμένη ἡ ὁδὸς ἡ ἀπάγουσα εἰς τὴν ζωήν, καὶ
15 ὀλίγοι εἰσὶν οἱ εὑρίσκοντες αὐτήν.   Προσέχετε

13 πλατεια] ℵ* 𝕷 a b c h k m ; *add* η πυλη ℵᵇBC *al* 𝕷 f ff¹ g ¹·² m q vg 𝕾 cur.
pesh. hcl. pal me sah arm aeth   14 οτι] ℵ*B*ı** 𝕷 m me ; τι ℵᵇᶜB²E *al* 𝕷
vet. vg 𝕾 cur. pesh. hcl. pal aeth Cyp Lcif

Mt.'s picture is based upon Jer.
xxi. 8 ; cf. Dt. xxx. 19. The simile
of the Two Ways had a wide currency
in Jewish and Christian writings :
e.g. Did. i.–vi., *Barn.* xviii.–xx., *Secr.
Enoch* xxx. 15, 4 Esd. vii. 7 f., *Test.
Abr.* (James, 88 ff., 112 ff. ; cf.
51 ff.). See Harnack, *Die Apostel-
lehre u. d. jüd. beiden Wege,* 57.

13. ὅτι πλατεῖα κτλ.] The insertion of ἡ πύλη after πλατεῖα has
strong support, but the presence of
πύλη in the first clause and in the
following verses would lead to its insertion, and the singulars ἡ ἀπάγουσα
and δι᾽ αὐτῆς refer only to ἡ ὁδός.
In the O.T. εὐρύχωρος connotes
freedom and prosperity (Ps. xxx.
[xxxi.] 9, Hos. iv. 16, Is. xxx. 23) ;
πλατύς and εὐρύχ. occur together in
Is. xxxiii. 21. For the road to
destruction cf. Ps. i. 6, Prov. xiii.
15, xiv. 12, Sir. xxi. 10. ἀπώλεια
recurs in the synn. in xxvi. 8 (Mk.
xiv. 4) only, with a different meaning. καὶ πολλοί κτλ. : 'and many
are they who enter [into destruction]
by it.' For διά cf. ii. 12.

14. ὅτι στενή κτλ.] Parallel with
the ὅτι of *v.* 13 ; cf. vi. 32 γὰρ . . .
γάρ. The *v.l.* τί forms an exclamation combining the πύλη of *v.* 13 a
with the ὁδός of *v.* 13 b. The way
that leads to life involves straits
and afflictions; cf. Ac. xiv. 22.
θλίβεσθαι is not elsewhere used of
place in N.T. or LXX., but the metaphorical meaning makes itself felt

in the simile. θλίψις and στενοχωρία
are coupled in Rom. ii. 9, viii. 35,
as in Deut. xxviii. 53 *al.* ζωή has
an eschatological force in the synn.
(see on xviii. 8, and Add. n.) ; cf.
Ber. R. 9, 'Which way is it that
leads to the life of the age to come ?'
For the Jewish use of the word see
Dalman, *Words,* 158 ff., Volz, *Jüd.
Esch.* Index *s.v.* 'Leben.' The fuller
form ζωὴ αἰώνιος occurs in xix. 16,
29 (Mk., Lk.), xxv. 46, Lk. x. 25.
In the 4th Gosp. Christ is the ὁδός
(xiv. 4 f.), the πύλη (x. 7, 9), and
the ζωή (v. 26, xi. 25, xiv. 6), which
men can have *now* (i. 4, iii. 36 *al.*),
but progressively (iv. 14). On the
Gk. and Heb. words for 'life' see
Burkitt, *ZNW.,* 1911, 228 ff.

15–23. (Lk. vi. 43–46, xiii. 26 f.)
Profession and real Fruit.

Throughout the section Mt. shapes
the sayings into condemnations of
false *teachers* ; the shorter passages
in Lk. speak only of unreality in
personal religion.

15. προσέχετε κτλ.] The narrow
road is hard to find ; beware of false
prophets who profess to guide you,
but for their own advantage. The
verse, absent from Lk., is akin to
xxiv. 11, 24, where the coming of
false prophets is predicted ; here
they are a present evil. False
Christian prophets did not appear
till after the Lord's death, when the
struggles with Judaizing Christians

ἀπὸ τῶν ψευδοπροφητῶν, οἵτινες ἔρχονται πρὸς ὑμᾶς ἐν
ἐνδύμασι προβάτων ἔσωθεν δέ εἰσιν λύκοι ἅρπαγες. ἀπὸ 16
τῶν καρπῶν αὐτῶν ἐπιγνώσεσθε αὐτούς· μήτι συλλέγουσιν
ἀπὸ ἀκανθῶν σταφυλὰς ἢ ἀπὸ τριβόλων σῦκα ; οὕτω πᾶν 17
δένδρον ἀγαθὸν καρποὺς καλοὺς ποιεῖ, τὸ δὲ σαπρὸν δένδρον καρποὺς πονηροὺς ποιεῖ· οὐ δύναται δένδρον ἀγαθὸν 18

began ; cf. 1 Jo. iv. 1. False *Jewish*
prophets are mentioned in Ac. xiii.
6, 2 Pet. ii. 1. Their counterparts
in Christianity are also called
ψευδοδιδάσκαλοι (2 Pet. *l.c.*), ψευδ-
απόστολοι (2 Cor. xi. 13). In Zach.
xiii. 2, Jerem.⁹ ψευδοπροφήτης represents נָבִיא, his falseness being
shewn by the context. The pseudo-
prophet of Apoc. xvi. 13, xix. 20, xx.
10 symbolizes a different peril (see
Swete on xiii. 11). For προσέχειν
ἀπό see Blass, § 34. 1 n.

οἵτινες κτλ.] On ὅστις for ὅς
see ii. 6. In outward appearance
they are sheep, *i.e.* Christians.
ἐνδύμ. προβάτων seems to mean no
more than this, but some see in it a
reference to the prophet's mantle of
hair (cf. iii. 4, Zach. xiii. 4). Tert.,
Just., Clem. Al. have δέρμασιν, which
Blass would read here. For λύκοι
in this sense cf. Ez. xxii. 27, Zeph.
iii. 3, Jo. x. 12, Ac. xx. 29. Wolves
call for greater caution than dogs
and swine (*v.* 6), οἱ μὲν γὰρ ὡμο-
λογημένοι καὶ φανεροί, οὗτοι δὲ
συνεσκιασμένοι (Chrys.).

16–20. (Lk. vi. 43 f.) *Good and
bad trees.*

16. ἀπὸ τῶν καρπῶν κτλ.] Mt.
has added the first sentence to connect the simile of the trees with the
prophets ; the plur. ἐπιγινώσεσθε
corresponds with προσέχετε. In
xii. 33 he has ἐκ γὰρ τοῦ καρποῦ
τὸ δένδρον γινώσκεται, which is a
closer parallel with Lk.'s ἕκαστον
γὰρ δένδρον ἐκ τοῦ ἰδίου καρποῦ
γινώσκεται. Cf. Ign. *Eph.* xiv. 2,

φανερὸν τὸ δένδρον ἀπὸ τοῦ καρποῦ
αὐτοῦ. For the thought cf. Sir.
xxvii. 6. On καρπός see iii. 8.

μήτι συλλέγουσιν κτλ.] This
sentence and *v.* 18 appear in Lk. in
the converse order ; and he·has a
positive statement (οὐ γὰρ . . .
συλλέγ.) for the question. For μήτι
('numquid') expecting the answer
No, cf. xii. 23, xxvi. 22. 'Thorns'
and 'thistles' occur together in Heb.
vi. 8, Gen. iii. 18, Hos. x. 8. Lk.
has 'figs from thorns,' and 'a grape-
cluster from a bramble-bush' (βάτος),
adding, with the latter, the correct
verb τρυγῶσιν. S. James (iii. 12)
imitates the saying. [Cf. *Berak.* 48 a
'A gourd a gourd [*i.e.* each gourd]
is known by its branch'; and there
are many class. parallels.

17. οὕτω κτλ.] Absent from
Lk. In quality, as in species, like
produces like. With Semitic redundancy the statement is made
first positively, and then (*v.* 18)
negatively.

18. οὐ δύναται κτλ.] A closer
parallel with Lk. than xii. 33, where
ποιεῖν is used differently. ἀγαθός
alternates with καλός, and σαπρός
with πονηρός, apparently for the
sake of variety (in xii. 33 and Lk.
only καλός and σαπρός are used);
and for the same reason ἐνεγκεῖν
with ποιεῖν ; cf. Ez. xvii. 8. The
saying must be balanced by instances
in which the Lord saw the possibilities of good in bad people. Here,
as in xii. 33 ff., He deals with the
principle that evil *as such* cannot

καρποὺς πονηροὺς ἐνεγκεῖν, οὐδὲ δένδρον σαπρὸν καρποὺς
19 καλοὺς ποιεῖν. πᾶν δένδρον μὴ ποιοῦν καρπὸν καλὸν
20 ἐκκόπτεται καὶ εἰς πῦρ βάλλεται. ἄραγε ἀπὸ τῶν καρπῶν
21 αὐτῶν ἐπιγνώσεσθε αὐτούς. Οὐ πᾶς ὁ λέγων μοι Κύριε
κύριε εἰσελεύσεται εἰς τὴν βασιλείαν τῶν οὐρανῶν, ἀλλ᾿ ὁ
ποιῶν τὸ θέλημα τοῦ πατρός μου τοῦ ἐν τοῖς οὐρανοῖς.
22 πολλοὶ ἐροῦσίν μοι ἐν ἐκείνῃ τῇ ἡμέρᾳ Κύριε κύριε, οὐ

produce good; cf. Job xiv. 4. σαπρός
is not 'rotten,' for a rotten tree
would produce no fruit of any kind,
but 'worthless'; cf. xii. 33, xiii. 48.
At this point Lk. (vi. 45) has a saying
which Mt. inserts at xii. 35.

19. πᾶν δένδρον κτλ.] Absent
from Lk. Repeated *verbatim* from
iii. 10 (see note). For other instances
in which echoes of the Baptist's
teaching are ascribed to Jesus see
iii. 2 note. The saying is further
echoed in Jo. xv. 6.

20. ἄραγε κτλ.] Absent from Lk.
The words resume *v.* 16 b, an inference
being drawn from the intervening
argument: 'so then you see that,
etc.' The strengthened form ἄραγε
occurs only in xvii. 26; cf. Ac.
xvii. 27.

21–23. (Lk. vi. 46, xiii. 26 f.)
Warning against Self-deception.

21. οὐ πᾶς κτλ.] Lk. (vi. 46) has
τί δέ με καλεῖτε κ. κ. καὶ οὐ ποιεῖτε
ἃ λέγω; which is in harmony with
his next verse (= Mt. *v.* 24); in Lk.
the character of disciples in the present is dealt with, in Mt. that of the
false teachers, which will be revealed
at the Last Day. For κύριε κύριε
cf. xxv. 11, Ps. cviii. [cix.] 21, cxl.
[cxli.] 8. τάδε λέγει κύριος κύριος
is frequent in Ezek. κύριε (Aram.
מרי) often occurs as a form of polite
address to Jesus in Mt., Lk., Jo.; in
Mk. only in vii. 28, by a foreigner.
But here it is more than that, since
in *v.* 22 it is addressed to Him in

His supreme power at the Last Day.
During His lifetime not only the
Jews (viii. 19, xii. 38, xxii. 16, 24,
36), but also the disciples (Mk. iv.
38, ix. 38, x. 35, xiii. 1, Lk. xxi. 7;
cf. Mt. xxvi. 18), probably addressed
Him only as διδάσκαλε, *i.e.* Rabbi
(Mk. ix. 5, xi. 21, Jo.⁷; cf. Mt. xxiii.
7 f., xxvi. 25, 49), for which Lk.
usually has ἐπιστάτα (see Dalman,
Words, 324–340); in Mk. x. 51,
Jo. xx. 16 the still more respectful
ῥαββουνί is used. κύριε was the
later title of worship, adopted in
consequence of the Resurrection (cf.
1 Cor. xii. 3). In two passages (viii.
25, xvii. 4) Mt. uses the later title
where Mk. and Lk. have the earlier.
The present verse affords no indication that Q was later in date than
Mk. (Wellh.); see Mackennal, *Inter-*
preter, Oct. 1912. On ποιῶν τὸ
θέλημα [א θελήματα] κτλ. see vi.
10 b note, and cf. xii. 50.

22. πολλοί κτλ.] Lk. (xiii. 26),
beginning τότε ἄρξεσθε λέγειν,
pictures men at the Last Day
claiming to have been *disciples,*
because they had associated with
Jesus on earth; Mt. pictures 'many'
claiming to have been Christian
preachers and *miracle-workers.* 'That
Day' (*dies irae dies illa*) is a common
eschatological expression; cf. Is. x.
20, Hos. i. 5, Am. ix. 11, Mt. xxiv.
36, xxvi. 29 (Mk. xiv. 25), Lk. xvii.
31, xxi. 34, 2 Thes. i. 10, 2 Tim. i.
18, iv. 8; for Apocalyptic reff. see
Volz, *Jüd. Esch.* 188 f.

τῷ σῷ ὀνόματι ἐπροφητεύσαμεν, καὶ τῷ σῷ ὀνόματι δαιμόνια
ἐξεβάλομεν, καὶ τῷ σῷ ὀνόματι δυνάμεις πολλὰς ἐποιήσαμεν ;
καὶ τότε ὁμολογήσω αὐτοῖς ὅτι Οὐδέποτε ἔγνων ὑμᾶς · 23
ἀποχωρεῖτε ἀπ' ἐμοῦ οἱ ἐργαζόμενοι τὴν ἀνομίαν.

οὐ τῷ σῷ ὀνόματι κτλ.] Compare
the false prophets in Israel, Jer. xiv.
14 f., xxvii. 15. The dative is here
instrumental, and has the same force
as ἐν, ἐπί c. dat. (see on xxviii. 19) and
διά, ἀπό which occur in patr. writings.
Attempts to exorcise by the name of
Jesus were both successful (Mk. ix. 38)
and unsuccessful (Ac. xix. 13–16);
unworthy Christians 'preached Christ'
(Phil. i. 17), and miracles of healing
were probably performed by the use
of His name as a magical formula ;
see Heitmüller, *Im Namen Jesu*,
Tambornino, *De Antiquorum Dae-
monismo*, 27–54, and extracts from
a Christian incantation in Milligan,
Pap. No. 47. Miracles are not of
the first importance (Lk. x. 20), and
a faith which can do them is not
necessarily a right faith (1 Cor. xiii.
2). 'Adde : commentarios et observa-
tiones exegeticas ad libros et loca V.
et N.T. scripsimus, homilias insignes
habuimus, etc.' (Beng.).

23. καὶ τότε κτλ.] Lk. (xiii.
27) has καὶ ἐρεῖ, the subject being
ὁ οἰκοδεσπότης. The synn. contain
many references to the Last Judgment, and to judgment by the Son
of Man ; but the latter is not spoken
of in Mk. or Lk. before the prediction
of the Passion which followed S.
Peter's confession, and only in Mt.
does Jesus explicitly claim to be
Himself the Judge.

οὐδέποτε κτλ.] All the time that
ye were prophesying, etc., in My
name, I never recognized you for
what you professed to be. For
ἔγνων cf. 2 Tim. ii. 19, which seems
to be influenced by the present passage ; and see Mt. xxv. 12, where

οἶδα has a somewhat different force.
Lk. here has λέγω ὑμῖν οὐκ οἶδα
ὑμᾶς πόθεν ἐστέ.

ἀποχωρεῖτε κτλ.] A quotation
from Ps. vi. 9, ἀπόστητε ἀπ' ἐμοῦ
πάντες οἱ ἐργαζόμενοι τὴν ἀνομίαν.
Lk. has ἀπόστητε ἀπ' ἐμοῦ πάντες
ἐργάται ἀδικίας : this agrees with
the LXX. in the first half, and Mt. in
the second. For the thought cf.
xxv. 41. ἀποχωρεῖν recurs in the
N.T. in Lk. ix. 39, Ac. xiii. 13 only,
and is rare in the LXX. ; ἀφιστάναι
is frequent in the LXX. and in Lk.,
Ac., but does not occur in Mt., Mk.
ἀνομία and ἀδικία are both frequent
in the LXX., but Mt. uses the former
only, and Lk. the latter only (each
4 times), none of them in parallel
passages except here. The relation,
therefore, of the source or sources of
the evangg. to the LXX. in this
passage remains a problem.

On the apocryphal saying attributed
to the Naz. Gosp., ἐὰν ἦτε ἐν τῷ
κόλπῳ μου καὶ τὸ θέλημα τοῦ πατρός
μου τοῦ ἐν οὐρανοῖς μὴ ποιῆτε, ἐκ
τοῦ κόλπου μου ἀπορρίψω ὑμᾶς (cf.
2 Clem. iv.), see *Texte u. Untersuch.*,
1911, 297 f.

24–27. (Lk. vi. 47–49.) *The Two
Foundations.*

In Mt. the houses are built upon
rock and sand respectively ; in Lk.
the digging is emphasized, which is
deep enough to reach rock (which
Harnack improbably thinks is due
to the writer's reflexion that in this
case the nature of the soil is im-
material), while the second house is
built 'upon the ground without a
foundation.' In Mt. the rain, the
floods (ποταμοί), and the winds cause

24   Πᾶς οὖν ὅστις ἀκούει μου τοὺς λόγους τούτους καὶ
ποιεῖ αὐτούς, ὁμοιωθήσεται ἀνδρὶ φρονίμῳ, ὅστις ᾠκοδό-
25 μησεν αὐτοῦ τὴν οἰκίαν ἐπὶ τὴν πέτραν. καὶ κατέβη ἡ
βροχὴ καὶ ἦλθαν οἱ ποταμοὶ καὶ ἔπνευσαν οἱ ἄνεμοι καὶ
προσέπεσαν τῇ οἰκίᾳ ἐκείνῃ, καὶ οὐκ ἔπεσεν, τεθεμελίωτο
26 γὰρ ἐπὶ τὴν πέτραν. Καὶ πᾶς ὁ ἀκούων μου τοὺς λόγους
τούτους καὶ μὴ ποιῶν αὐτοὺς ὁμοιωθήσεται ἀνδρὶ μωρῷ,
27 ὅστις ᾠκοδόμησεν αὐτοῦ τὴν οἰκίαν ἐπὶ τὴν ἄμμον. καὶ
κατέβη ἡ βροχὴ καὶ ἦλθαν οἱ ποταμοὶ καὶ ἔπνευσαν οἱ
ἄνεμοι καὶ προσέκοψαν τῇ οἰκίᾳ ἐκείνῃ, καὶ ἔπεσεν, καὶ ἦν
ἡ πτῶσις αὐτῆς μεγάλη.

24 τουτους] om B* 𝕷 a g¹ k m 𝕾 pal Cyp

a great 'fall'; in Lk. the flood
(ποταμός) alone breaks against the
house and causes a great 'breaking up.'
24. πᾶς οὖν κτλ.] οὖν introduces
the conclusion of the whole Sermon;
cf. v. 12, v. 48. τούτους refers to
the foregoing sermon; its omission
(see Appar.) is probably a harmonization with Lk. : πᾶς ὁ ἐρχόμενος πρός
με καὶ ἀκούων μου τῶν λόγων κτλ.
See Plummer (St. Mat.) on the greatness of the claim involved in μου.
Cf. Prov. i. 33, and for the contrast
between the two houses, Prov. xiv.
11. The fut. ὁμοιωθήσεται occurs
only in v. 26, xxv. 1, but has parallels
in the LXX.; Mt. also has ὡμοιώθη
(see xiii. 24 note). Lk.: ὑποδείξω ὑμῖν
τίνι ἐστὶν ὅμοιος (ὑποδ. in this sense
in Lk., Ac. only). See xi. 16 note.
φρόνιμος and μωρός are absent from
Lk.; cf. Mt. xxv. 1 ff.; the latter is
confined to Mt.[7] of the synn., the
former occurs in Mt.[7], Lk.[2] On
ὅστις for ὅς see ii. 6. πέτρα is not
the rock of xvi. 18 (Jer.), nor Christ's
teaching (Chrys.); the rock foundation is simply a metaphor for a
condition of safety (cf. Ps. xxvi.
[xxvii.] 5, xxxix. [xl.] 3, lx. [lxi.] 3).
See the similar metaphor in Sir. xxii.
16–18.
25. καὶ κατέβη κτλ.] βροχή is

a rare word; cf. Ps. lxvii. [lxviii.] 10,
civ. [cv.] 32, Sym. Prov. xxv. 23
(all = בְּשֶׁם), Orac. ap. Clem. Prot.
viii. 77. In two papyri of the 1st
and 2nd cent. βροχαί are artificial
inundations (Ox. ii. 280. 5, iii. 593),
and ἄβροχος, 'not inundated,' is
fairly frequent. οἱ ποταμοί are the
rush of waters caused by the torrent
of rain. Lk. πλημμύρης δὲ γενομένης
προσέρηξεν ὁ ποταμός, omitting rain
and winds. προσπίπτειν (usually
'fall down,' 'do obeisance') nowhere
occurs with the exact meaning 'fall
against'; but cf. Prov. xxv. 20,
προσπεσὸν πάθος ἐν σώματι καρδίαν
λυπεῖ. Lachmann, followed by Blass,
conjectures προσέπαισαν; see Field
on Sym. Ps. xc. [xci.] 12 (LXX. προσ-
κόπτειν). With Lk.'s προσέρηξεν cf.
Aq. Ps. ii. 9 (LXX. συντρίψεις). The
original of both, and of προσέκοψεν
27) may have been אתמרא, as in 𝕾.
καὶ οὐκ ἔπεσεν κτλ.] Lk. καὶ οὐχ
ἴσχυσεν σαλεῦσαι αὐτὴν διὰ τὸ καλῶς
οἰκοδομῆσθαι αὐτήν. The complete
difference of wording, with identity
of meaning, points to the free use of
the parable by early preachers. For
a Rabb. parallel see JThS. xiv. 618.
27. καὶ προσέκοψαν κτλ.] προσ-
κόπτειν (usually 'stumble against')
occurs in Is. iii. 5 for רהב, 'to

Καὶ ἐγένετο ὅτε ἐτέλεσεν ὁ Ἰησοῦς τοὺς λόγους τού- 28
τους, ἐξεπλήσσοντο οἱ ὄχλοι ἐπὶ τῇ διδαχῇ αὐτοῦ· ἦν 29
γὰρ διδάσκων αὐτοὺς ὡς ἐξουσίαν ἔχων καὶ οὐχ ὡς οἱ
γραμματεῖς αὐτῶν.

storm' (see note above). καὶ ἦν ἡ
πτῶσις κτλ. 'And [the extent of]
its ruin was great,' *i.e.* 'large portions of the house fell.' πτῶσις is
frequent in the LXX. for מַפָּלָה,
מַפֶּלֶת; in Nah. iii. 3 βαρεῖα
πτῶσις = כֹּבֶד פֶּגֶר, 'a mass of corpses'
(‖ πλῆθος τραυματιῶν). Lk. ἐγένετο
τὸ ῥῆγμα μέγα (cf. Am. vi. 11 [12]).

28, 29. *Editorial Conclusion.*

28. καὶ ἐγένετο κτλ.] A formula
employed by Mt. after each of his
five principal collections of the Lord's
sayings (*i.e.* chs. v.–vii., x., xiii., xviii.,
xxiii.–xxv.), as a transition to the
following narrative.   Since the
Λογίων κυριακῶν ἐξήγησις of Papias
consisted of five books (Eus. *HE.* iii.
38) Nestle suggests (*ZNW.*, 1900,
252 ff.) that the Logia used by Mt.
may have been arranged in five
groups. The phrase is somewhat
similar in Lk. vii. 1 a, and may have
been suggested here by Q. καὶ
ἐγένετο (a LXX. expression, common
in Lk.) is not found in Mt. except in
these formulas.

ἐξεπλήσσοντο κτλ.] The ὄχλοι
were not present at the delivery of
the Sermon (v. 1), but Mt. mechanically follows Mk. i. 22 (= Lk. iv. 32) ;
he now returns to the Marcan
narrative, which he last employed
in iv. 23.   The ἐξουσία of Jesus
was felt, not in the novelty of all
that He said, but in His inborn
knowledge of right and wrong. The
Scribes rested mainly on the authority
of antiquity and precedent. The
Apocalyptic writers claimed to give
out something new, learned by immediate inspiration, but their specula-
tions did not touch the life of the
masses ; the Lord dealt not merely
with the future, but also with the
living present as a preparation for
it. Cf. Jo. vii. 46 ; and see Swete
on Mk. i. 22.

29. ἦν γάρ κτλ.] The construction
is modelled on the Aram. (see Moulton
i. 227). In Mk. the best reading
omits αὐτῶν ; its addition in Mt.
reflects a feeling against the Jews as
a hostile body ; cf. iv. 23, ix. 35, x.
17, xi. 1, xiii. 54.

Additional Note on the Sermon on the Mount.

Mt.'s material may be arranged as follows :

§ 1. Discourse common to Mk. and Lk.—

Mt.	Lk.		Mt.	Lk.
(a) v. 3	vi. 20	(c) vii. 1, 2	vi. 37, 38 b
4, 6*	21 b, 21 a		3–5	41, 42
5, 7–10	—		12*	31
11, 12	22, 23	(d)	16–20	43, 44
(b) 38–42	29, 30		21	46
43–48*	27, 28, 32–ₓ 36		24–27	47–49

§ 2. Scattered passages collected by Mt.—

v. 13	xiv. 34, 35	vi. 19–21	xii. 33, 34
	(Mk. ix. 50)	22, 23	xi. 34–36
15	xi. 33 (viii. 16,	24	xvi. 13
	Mk. iv. 21)	25–33	xii. 22–31
18, 19	xvi. 17	vii. 7–11	xi. 9–13
25, 26	xii. 58, 59	13, 14	xiii. 24
32	xvi. 18	22, 23	xiii. 26, 27
vi. 9–13	xi. 2–4		

§ 3. Passages peculiar to Mt.—

v. 14, 16, 23, 24, 31, vi. 7, 8, 14, 15, vii. 6, 15.

§ 4. Discourse peculiar to Mt.—

Thesis: v. 17 (18 f.), 20.

(1) The Righteousness of the Scribes, v. 21–37, 38–48 : Murder (*vv.* 21, 22), Adultery (*vv.* 27–30), False Oaths (*vv.* 33–37).

(2) The Righteousness of the Pharisees, vi. 1–6, 16–18 : The general Principle (*v.* 1), Alms (*vv.* 2–4), Prayer (*vv.* 5, 6), Fasting (*vv.* 16–18).

Our Lord must frequently have delivered public discourses, which were not collections of disjointed aphorisms, but formal handlings of definite themes. And it need not be supposed that the disciples were so lacking in ability that they could not remember some of these themes, and the main outline of His treatment of them. Two themes which they would be more likely to remember than any others are (1) the moral characteristics that He desired to see in His followers, and (2) the relation of these characteristics to the laws and customs of His nation. The first of these, found in § 1 above, forms the whole content of Lk.'s sermon. With the exception of a few verses (indicated by asterisks) the order is the same in both gospels. The section comprises : (*a*) The condition which Jesus pronounces happy. (*b*) Injunctions of friendliness and love. (*c*) Prohibitions of behaviour which will injure this friendliness. (*d*) Concluding sayings which declare that character is shewn by its results. This discourse doubtless stood in Q, as also the scattered passages in § 2. Whether Q contained any of the sayings in § 3 cannot be determined ; but the notes shew, in each case, that they do not stand in their original context. § 4, which contains the remainder of Mt.'s material, consists of a complete and coherent discourse on the second of the two great themes. Harnack (*Sayings*, 129) thinks that it cannot have stood in Q, because it is too distinctively anti-Jewish. That it was the work of Mt., or of any other early Christian, is utterly improbable. The moral insight which could penetrate to the spiritual 'fulfilment' of the Mosaic laws is that of the Lord Himself, and of none other. But Lk.'s omission of the verses needs to be accounted for. Stanton (*Gosp. as Hist. Doc.* 80–4) suggests that the Logian document in its original Aramaic form contained (*a*) the common material of Mt. and Lk. (§§ 1, 2), and (*b*) the verses in § 4, virtually in the form in which Mt. now has them ; this Aram. original appeared in two Greek translations, one intended for Jews, the other for Gentiles ;

Καταβάντος δὲ αὐτοῦ ἀπὸ τοῦ ὄρους ἠκολούθησαν αὐτῷ 1 VIII.

and the translator of the latter omitted all that he deemed unsuitable for Gentiles, including ἠκούσατε . . . ἐγὼ δὲ λέγω ὑμῖν in the sayings on Retaliation and on Love and Hatred ; and having omitted the condemnations of hypocrisy in alms, prayer, and fasting, he added the Woes (Lk. vi. 24 ff.) as a sort of generalization of them (cf. Lk.'s ἀπέχετε τὴν παράκλησιν ὑμῶν with Mt.'s ἀπέχουσιν τὸν μισθὸν αὐτῶν). It is true that Lk. would hardly have ventured to set aside the passage on the Law, if he had found it ready translated in his document ; but it is scarcely less improbable that a translator would have set it aside if he had found it in his Aram. document. Moreover the explanation does not account for the fact that in Mt. Retaliation (v. 39-42) is *followed* by Love and Hatred (v. 44-48), while Lk. inserts the former in the middle of the latter. Allen (p. 71) thinks that Lk. must have derived his sermon from an unknown source, after it had passed through many alterations and mutilations, and that he, or the writer of his source, omitted the passages about the Law because of their polemical character. Votaw (*HDB*. Extr. vol. p. 1 ff.) allows a large place not only to Aram. oral tradition, but, in the case of Lk., to Greek written records, as well as a Greek form of the Logia, and in the case of both evangelists, to their own selection and presentation of the Gospel material.

While it is clear that Mt. and Lk. employed different recensions of Q, the history of which cannot be traced, the most serious difficulty would be removed if we could suppose that the discourse on the Law (§ 4) was originally circulated as an independent document. Mt. may have found it so, or it may already have been attached, at some point (not necessarily in the Sermon) to the recension of Q which he used. Finding the sayings on Retaliation, and on Love and Hatred, arranged in the form in which Lk. has them, he altered the order, adding vv. 38 and 43, and ἐγὼ δὲ λέγω ὑμῖν, thus making them similar to the preceding sayings in his discourse. Derivation from an independent source would also account for the Greek form Ἱεροσόλυμα (v. 35) in an utterance of Jesus (see on xxiii. 37). Lastly, the command 'Judge not' (vii. 1) affords no sequence with the preceding verses, but is closely connected with v. 44-48 (Love excludes censorious judgment) ; and in Lk. the parallels to v. 48 and vii. 1 are placed together ; Mt. vi., therefore, was interpolated by Mt., and not omitted by Lk. or his source, for polemical or other reasons.

viii. 1-4. (Mk. i. 40-45, Lk. v. 12-16.) A LEPER HEALED.

Having made use (in vii. 29) of Mk. i. 22, Mt. here omits the healing of the demoniac (Mk. i. 23-28, Lk. iv. 33-37). Of the three reasons which Allen suggests for this, perhaps the most cogent is that it was useful to place the incident of the leper immediately after the Sermon, because it illustrates the Lord's attitude to-

wards legal ceremonies. On the disarrangement of Mk. in Mt. viii., ix. see Hawkins, *ExpT.* xii. 471 ff., xiii. 20 ff.

1. καταβάντος δέ κτλ.] On the gen. absol. followed by αὐτῷ (cf. v. 5) see Moulton i. 74. The ὄχλοι πολλοί are those of iv. 25 ; but ὅρα μηδενὶ εἴπῃς (v. 4) implies that no crowds were present. On the position of the incident in Mk. see J. Weiss,

2 ὄχλοι πολλοί. Καὶ ἰδοὺ λεπρὸς προσελθὼν προσεκύνει
3 αὐτῷ λέγων Κύριε, ἐὰν θέλῃς δύνασαί με καθαρίσαι. καὶ
ἐκτείνας τὴν χεῖρα ἥψατο αὐτοῦ λέγων Θέλω, καθαρίσθητι·
4 καὶ εὐθέως ἐκαθερίσθη αὐτοῦ ἡ λέπρα. καὶ λέγει αὐτῷ ὁ
Ἰησοῦς Ὅρα μηδενὶ εἴπῃς, ἀλλὰ ὕπαγε σεαυτὸν ΔεῖΖΟΝ τῷ

Das ält. Ev. 152. Lk. writes 'And
it came to pass when He was
in one of the cities,' in accordance
with the words of Jesus in Lk. iv.
43. The command 'shew thyself to
the priest' suggests that Jerusalem
was near, and that the incident
occurred in Judaea ; which is borne
out by Lk. iv. 44, where Ἰουδαίας is
the true reading. See n. before v. 1.

2. καὶ ἰδού κτλ.] On καὶ ἰδού see
i. 20. For λεπρός (so Mk.) Lk. has
ἀνὴρ πλήρης λέπρας : an extreme
case appealed to him as a physician.
On the impf. προσεκύνει 'besought'
see Blass, § 57. 4. κύριε (so Lk.) is
absent from Mk. ; see vii. 21 note.
The Jewish feeling that leprosy was
pollution shews itself in the fact that
in the Gospels the healing of it is
always καθαρίζειν, not θεραπεύειν or
(except Lk. xvii. 15) ἰᾶσθαι. Cf. x.
8, xi. 5, Lk. iv. 27, xvii. 14. In
the O.T. καθαρίζειν mean 'to pronounce clean' (טִהַר) ; cf. Lev. xiii. 6,
23, 34, 37 ; hence J. Weiss (*l.c.*)
suggests that the man asked Jesus
to pronounce him clean, but that
Jesus, being loyal to the Law, told
him to go to the priest ; a narrative
which originally illustrated His
attitude to the Law was transformed
by tradition into a miracle.

3. καὶ ἐκτείνας κτλ.] Mk.'s σπλαγχνισθείς (D 𝕷 ὀργισθείς) is omitted ;
Mt. and Lk. frequently omit words
which ascribe human emotions to
Jesus; cf. the omission of ἐμβριμησά-
μενος αὐτῷ in the next verse (see
Hawkins, *Hor. Syn.* 96, 99, Allen, p.
xxxi.). Mt., however, uses σπλαγχνίζεσθαι five times, and ἐμβριμᾶσθαι

in ix. 30. By touching the leper,
the Lord allowed the ceremonial law
of uncleanness to give way before
the higher principle of love ; see
xv. 11 note. Patr. writers contrast
Elisha who did not touch Naaman
the leper.

4. ὅρα μηδενὶ εἴπῃς] The man
was to report himself to the priests,
but not publish openly the manner
of his cure. For similar injunctions
of silence see ix. 30, xii. 16 (Mk. iii.
12), xvii. 9 (Mk. ix. 9), Mk. i. 34
(Lk. iv. 41), v. 43 (Lk. viii. 56), vii.
36, viii. 26 ; the Lord's purpose
seems to have been to suppress the
growth of public excitement about
Himself which would make people
flock to Him as a mere wonder-
worker, instead of listening to His
message, and would also impede His
work by fanning the hostility of
the authorities. See Sanday, *JThS.*,
Apr. 1904, Burkitt, *AJTh.*, Apr.
1911. For ὁρᾶν μή cf. xviii. 10, and
βλέπειν μή xxiv. 4 ; neither occurs
in the LXX. ; contrast the imper.
alone (Mt. ix. 30, xxiv. 6), and ὁρᾶτε
καί (xvi. 6, Lk. xii. 15, Ex. xxv. 40).

ἀλλὰ ὕπαγε κτλ.] In accordance
with Lev. xiv. 2. When the ceremonial law did not conflict with
higher principles, the Lord observed
it as a loyal member of His race (cf.
Lk. xvii. 14). τὸ δῶρον : cf. v. 23 f.,
xv. 5, xxiii. 18 f. ; it is the Heb. and
Aram. קָרְבָּן, קֻרְבָּן (*Korban*, cf. Mk. vii.
11), and refers to the offerings specified in Lev. xiv. 10. Mk., Lk. have
προσένεγκε περὶ τοῦ καθαρισμοῦ
σου ἅ [Lk. καθώς] κτλ, explaining
the law more clearly for non-Jewish

ἱερεῖ, καὶ προσένεγκον τὸ δῶρον ὃ προσέταξεν Μωυσῆς εἰς μαρτύριον αὐτοῖς.   Εἰσελθόντος δὲ αὐτοῦ εἰς Καφαρ- 5 ναούμ προσῆλθεν αὐτῷ ἑκατόνταρχος παρακαλῶν αὐτὸν καὶ λέγων Κύριε, ὁ παῖς μου βέβληται ἐν τῇ οἰκίᾳ παρα- 6

readers. Jesus, as Man, speaks from the intellectual standpoint of His day and country in naming Moses as the author of the passage in Lev. The man's offering was to be εἰς μαρτύριον αὐτοῖς (cf. x. 18 (Mk., Lk.), xxiv. 14, Mk. vi. 11 (Lk. ix. 5); elsewhere only Jam. v. 3), i.e. a witness to the priests, not that he had recovered, a fact which they would investigate as the Law enjoined, but either that there was a Power in the world capable of healing leprosy, or, more probably, that Jesus was not hostile to the Law, since He had bidden the man to obey it.

Mt. shuns Mk.'s remaining statements that the man disobeyed Jesus by publishing the matter, thereby forcing Him to remain in deserted places whither the people thronged to Him (see Allen). Lk. tones them down to διήρχετο δὲ μᾶλλον ὁ λόγος περὶ αὐτοῦ, omitting ὥστε μηκέτι αὐτὸ δύνασθαι κτλ., and characteristically adds that Jesus was 'praying' while in retirement. On features of Mk.'s narrative appearing in Mt. ix. 30 f. see Add. note p. 129.

5–13. (Lk. vii. 1–10, xiii. 28 f.; cf. Jo. iv. 46–53.) A CENTURION'S SERVANT HEALED.

Lk. places the incident immediately after the Sermon on the Plain, a position which it probably held in Q; he shews, as often, that he employed a different recension of the source from that known to Mt., but the only reason for doubting that the incident stood in Q is the assumption that the latter contained only sayings of Jesus, with no nar-

rative or with the briefest possible narrative settings. Lk. connects the incident with the Sermon by ἐπειδὴ ἐπλήρωσεν πάντα τὰ ῥήματα αὐτοῦ εἰς τὰς ἀκοὰς τοῦ λαοῦ (see Mt. vii. 28 note).

5. εἰσελθόντος δέ κτλ.] For the gen. absol. followed by αὐτῷ see v. 1. 'After these things' (Ṣ sin 𝕃 k), instead of the first clause, possibly represents the true reading (see Burkitt, Ev. da Meph. ii. 237). On Capharnaum see iv. 13. The form ἑκατόνταρχος occurs in Xen.; א* has the earlier -χης. In Jo. iv. 46 he is a βασιλικός, 'an officer of the king' (i.e. of Herod Antipas); cf. Aphr. 'a king's slave'; and some have thought that he was a Jew (e.g. Ambr.); but Mt. and Lk. almost certainly thought of him as a Gentile. The class. meaning of παρακαλεῖν, 'to call to one's aid,' passes in later Gk. into that of 'beseech,' rare in the LXX., but common in the N.T.; cf. vv. 31, 34.

6. κύριε κτλ.] Lk. has δοῦλος for παῖς. Mt. may have understood παῖς to mean υἱός (so Jo.); contrast τ. δούλῳ μου (v. 9). βέβληται, 'has been laid (on a bed of sickness)' answers to the Aram. רמא; cf. v. 14, ix. 2, Mk. vii. 30, Aesop, Fab. 257, λύκος ὑπὸ κυνῶν δηχθεὶς καὶ κακῶς πάσχων ἐβέβλητο. On βασανιζό-μενος see iv. 24. In Lk. the servant's illness is described by the evang., κακῶς ἔχων ἤμελλεν τελευτᾶν, and the centurion does not come, but sends 'elders of the Jews,' who explain that he is worthy of receiving the favour that he asks, 'for he loveth our nation and himself built our synagogue for us,' i.e. he was a

7 λυτικός, δεινῶς βασανιζόμενος. λέγει αὐτῷ Ἐγὼ ἐλθὼν
8 θεραπεύσω αὐτόν. ἀποκριθεὶς δὲ ὁ ἑκατόνταρχος ἔφη
Κύριε, οὐκ εἰμὶ ἱκανὸς ἵνα μου ὑπὸ τὴν στέγην εἰσέλθῃς·
9 ἀλλὰ μόνον εἰπὲ λόγῳ, καὶ ἰαθήσεται ὁ παῖς μου· καὶ
γὰρ ἐγὼ ἄνθρωπός εἰμι ὑπὸ ἐξουσίαν τασσόμενος, ἔχων
ὑπ' ἐμαυτὸν στρατιώτας, καὶ λέγω τούτῳ Πορεύθητι, καὶ
πορεύεται, καὶ ἄλλῳ Ἔρχου, καὶ ἔρχεται, καὶ τῷ δούλῳ
10 μου Ποίησον τοῦτο, καὶ ποιεῖ. ἀκούσας δὲ ὁ Ἰησοῦς
ἐθαύμασεν καὶ εἶπεν τοῖς ἀκολουθοῦσιν Ἀμὴν λέγω ὑμῖν,
11 παρ' οὐδενὶ τοσαύτην πίστιν ἐν τῷ Ἰσραὴλ εὗρον. λέγω

10 παρ' ουδενι ... Ισραηλ] B 4 22 (1 118* 209 om εν τ. Ισ.) 𝔏 a g¹ k q vg 𝔖 cur
me aah aeth; ουδε εν τ. Ισ, τοσ. II. uncc.*rel* minn.*rel* 𝔏 b c ff¹ g² h l vg 𝔖 sin.
pesh.go (*ut Lc*)

Gentile well disposed to Judaism, and perhaps a proselyte.

7. ἐγὼ ἐλθών κτλ.] The patient's condition made it impossible for him to be brought to Jesus, and the hope is implied, which Lk. makes explicit, that Jesus will come to him. The Lord's answer should probably be printed as a question (see next verse). If the centurion was a Gentile, it was pollution for a Jew to enter his house, and Jesus tries his faith by asking 'Am I to come and heal him? —I a Jew?' ἐγώ is emphatic, and θεραπεύσω is a deliberative subj.

8. οὐκ εἰμὶ ἱκανός κτλ.] Cf. iii. 11. On ἵνα see Moulton, i. 208. ἱκανὸς ἵνα (not in LXX.) occurs only in the parallel, Lk. vii. 6, a sign of dependence upon a written Gk. source. The centurion assents to the question ('Yes, I know I am not worthy'), but only as a preliminary to the further request (see xv. 27 note). If the Lord's words ἐγὼ ἐλθών κτλ. are a direct statement assenting to the request that He would come, the humble answer, with its profound faith, is called forth by no apparent cause. On the position of μου see *JThS.*, Jan. 1909, 263. εἰπὲ λόγῳ: for the dat. of

the instrument cf. *v.* 16, Ac. ii. 40, and for the use of εἰπεῖν cf. iv. 3. Lk. relates that Jesus went with them, and when He was near the house the centurion sent friends saying κύριε μὴ σκύλλου (cf. Mk. v. 35 = Lk. viii. 49), οὐ γὰρ ἱκανός εἰμι κτλ.

9. καὶ γὰρ ἐγώ κτλ.] For καὶ γάρ, *nam etiam*, cf. xv. 27 (Mk. vii. 28), Mk. x. 45 (see Blass, § 78. 6). ὤν would be expected for εἰμί, and ἔχω for ἔχων (Wellh.): 'for even I [in my subordinate position], a man placed under authority, have soldiers, etc.,' so that I know what it is to receive obedience to a word of command. ἄνθρωπός εἰμι does not imply that he thought Jesus was other than man; the implied contrast is not with ἄνθρ. but with ὑπὸ ἐξουσίαν: Jesus was subject to no human authority in His work.

10. ἀκούσας δέ κτλ.] The Lord, as Man, was not above surprise; cf. Mk. vi. 6. Mt. does not often preserve words ascribing to Him human emotions (see *v.* 3 note). On ἀμὴν λέγω ὑμ. see v. 18.

παρ' οὐδενί κτλ.] Jesus often spoke of the faith of those who appealed to Him; see ix. 22, 29, xv. 28, Mk. x. 52, Lk. vii. 50, xvii.

δὲ ὑμῖν ὅτι πολλοὶ ἀπὸ ἀνατολῶν καὶ ΔΥCΜῶΝ ἥξουσιν καὶ
ἀνακλιθήσονται μετὰ Ἀβραὰμ καὶ Ἰσαὰκ καὶ Ἰακὼβ ἐν
τῇ βασιλείᾳ τῶν οὐρανῶν· οἱ δὲ υἱοὶ τῆς βασιλείας ἐκ- 12
βληθήσονται εἰς τὸ σκότος τὸ ἐξώτερον· ἐκεῖ ἔσται ὁ

12 ἐκβληθησονται] אᵃBCE *al* minn 𝕷 f ff¹ g² vg me sah ; ἐξελευσονται א 𝕷 k
𝕾 *omn* Cyp½ [ibunt 𝕷 a b c g¹ h q Iren^lat Aug]

19, and cf. Mt. ix. 2 ; it was as necessary on the side of the recipient as
the exercise of power on His (cf. xiii.
58 = Mk. vi. 6) ; ἡ πίστις δύναμίς
τις τοῦ θεοῦ (Clem. Al.). It was not
belief in Him as divine, but confidence
that He could perform a miracle ;
many Jews shewed such a faith, but
only the Canaanite woman reached
the same height as the centurion, in
believing that the wonder could be
wrought at a distance (see xv. 28).
But in both cases the chief matter
to the evang. (emphasized in the *v.l.*
as in Lk.) is the notable exception in
the mission of Jesus to Jews.

11, 12. (Lk. xiii. 28, 29.) The
original context of these words is
doubtful. Mt., in placing them
here, understands them to refer to
the admission of Gentiles into the
Kingdom ; the centurion's faith is
interpreted as a 'faith unto salvation.'
Lk. places them, more suitably, after
the passage which is parallel with
Mt. vii. 21 f., in a context which
contains no mention of Gentiles.

11. λέγω δὲ ὑμῖν ὅτι κτλ.] The
saying, an allusion to Ps. cvi. [cvii.]
3 (cf. also Mal. i. 11), is thus connected with the incident. Lk. omits
πολλοί, and after δυσμῶν adds καὶ
ἀπὸ βορρᾶ καὶ νότου, either based
on a text of the Ps. which read מִיָּמִין
for מִיָּם, or interpreting for Gentile
readers Mt.'s O.T. expression which
means 'from all quarters of the
world' (cf. xxiv. 27). The joys of the
coming age were frequently depicted
in Jewish writings as a banquet, cf.

xxii. 1–14, xxvi. 29, Lk. xiv. 15,
xxii. 30, Apoc. xix. 9 (see Dalman,
Words, 110–13, Volz, *Jüd. Esch.* 331);
different minds would treat the symbol with varying degrees of material
literalism or of spiritual understanding. Lk. transfers the names of the
patriarchs (adding καὶ πάντας τοὺς
προφήτας) to the next verse, which
he places first. For the bearing of
the passage on xi. 11 see note there.

12. οἱ δὲ υἱοὶ κτλ.] Cf. xiii.
38 (see Deissm. *Bible St.* 162 ff.).
Another Jewish thought: sonship
involves heirship. In virtue of their
birth, Jews thought that they had
a natural right to the privileges of
the Kingdom ; 'a son of the age to
come' occurs frequently in the Talm.,
cf. οἱ υἱοὶ τοῦ αἰῶνος τούτου, Lk.
xvi. 8 (see Dalman, *Words*, 115 f.).
In the Lord's mouth the words can
mean 'all Jews who trust in their
Judaism,' in contrast not necessarily
with Gentiles, as Mt. understands it
by placing the saying here, but with
Jews whose character truly fitted
them for the Kingdom (see iii. 9, v.
3, 10, vii. 21); cf. υἱὸς γεέννης (xxiii.
15). ἡ βασιλεία, with no further
definition, occurs only in Mt., iv. 23,
ix. 35, xiii. 19, 38, xxiv. 14, in the
last three, as here, in words ascribed
to the Lord. Dalman (*Words*, 95 f.)
holds that the expression arose in
the Christian Church later than the
life of Jesus, since in early Jewish
literature 'the Kingdom' meant only
the secular government.

ἐκβληθήσονται κτλ.] The Aram.

13 κλαυθμὸς καὶ ὁ βρυγμὸς τῶν ὀδόντων.   καὶ εἶπεν ὁ Ἰησοῦς
τῷ ἑκατοντάρχῃ Ὕπαγε, ὡς ἐπίστευσας γενηθήτω σοι· καὶ
14 ἰάθη ὁ παῖς ἐν τῇ ὥρᾳ ἐκείνῃ.   Καὶ ἐλθὼν ὁ Ἰησοῦς
εἰς τὴν οἰκίαν Πέτρου εἶδεν τὴν πενθερὰν αὐτοῦ βεβλημένην

יצא, 'to go out' (see the v.l. ἐξελεύσονται), does duty for a passive
corresponding to שלח, 'to send out.'
The latter is sometimes rendered by
βάλλειν, ἐκβάλλειν (cf. v. 29 f., vii.
4 f., ix. 25, 38, xii. 20, 35, xiii. 52,
xviii. 8 f., xxii. 13, xxv. 30, Mk. i.
12, and cf. xv. 17 [ἐκβάλλεται] with
Mk. vii. 19 [ἐκπορεύεται]). Lk. has
ὑμᾶς δὲ ἐκβαλλομένους ἔξω. The
depicting of the state of final punishment as darkness is characteristic of
Jewish apocalypse ; cf. Wisd. xvii.
21, and the reff. in Allen (ad loc.),
Bousset, Rel. d. Jud. 266, Weber, Jüd.
Theol. 393, Volz, Jüd. Esch. 284 f.
τὸ σκότος τὸ ἐξώτ. recurs only in
xxii. 13 (where, as here, the darkness
is contrasted with the banqueting
hall) and xxv. 30. ἐξώτερον does
not differ in meaning from ἔξω (Lk.);
in Jos. BJ. III. ix. 2 ἐξωτέρω is a prep.
with the gen. (cf. τὸ ἐσώτερον, Heb.
vi. 19).

ἐκεῖ ἔσται κτλ.] In Lk., by the
transposition of the verses, this stands
at the beginning, so that ἐκεῖ has
nothing to refer to ; the Engl. idiom
'there shall be weeping' obscures this.
Elsewhere the sentence is found only
in Mt. (xiii. 42, 50, xxii. 13, xxiv.
51, xxv. 30); the Lord may have
used it more than once, but it would
easily become a stereotyped formula
in Christian teaching, and be added
in some cases by the evang. The
'gnashing of teeth' may be derived
from Ps. cxi. [cxii.] 10; cf. xxxvi.
[xxxvii.] 12. For the 'weeping'
Allen cites Enoch cviii. 3, 5, Secr.
Enoch xl. 12. See the kindred
metaphor in Apoc. xvi. 10. Lk.

here adds (v. 30) a sentence similar
to Mt. xix. 30, xx. 16.

13. καὶ εἶπεν κτλ.] With ἐν τ.
ὥρᾳ ἐκ. (so Jo. iv. 53) cf. ἀπὸ τῆς
ὥρας ἐκείνης (ix. 22, xv. 28, xvii. 18).
With the whole verse cf. xv. 28. It
is possible, as there, to hold either
that the authoritative word of Jesus
effected the cure, or—which is not
essentially different—that He knew,
and declared, that God would heal the
sufferer because of the suppliant's faith.

14, 15. (Mk. i. 29–31, Lk. iv. 38 f.)
PETER'S WIFE'S MOTHER HEALED.

14. καὶ ἐλθών κτλ.] In Mk.,
Lk. the Lord came straight from the
synagogue, where the man with the
unclean spirit was healed ; but
Mt. has omitted that incident. For
Πέτρου Lk. has 'of Simon,' Mk. 'of
Simon and Andrew,' adding 'with
James and John,' who, according to
Mk., had just been called at the
lake-side near Capharnaum. Since
Lk. places the call of the four (three)
apostles after this incident (v. 1–11),
Spitta thinks that the Simon here
mentioned was, in the original
tradition, not Peter. In Jo. i. 44
Andrew and Peter belong to Bethsaida, not Capharnaum. Mt. omits
Andrew, James, and John because
his narrative is removed at a distance
from the account of their call.
εἶδεν abbreviates Mk.'s καὶ εὐθὺς
λέγουσιν αὐτῷ περὶ αὐτῆς : Lk. the
physician describes it as a consultation, κ. ἠρώτησαν αὐτὸν π. αὐτ.,
and his συνεχομένη πυρετῷ μεγάλῳ
is more circumstantial than πυρέσ-
σουσα. On βεβλημένην (Mk. κατέ-
κειτο) see v. 6.

καὶ πυρέσσουσαν· καὶ ἥψατο τῆς χειρὸς αὐτῆς, καὶ ἀφῆκεν 15
αὐτὴν ὁ πυρετός, καὶ ἠγέρθη, καὶ διηκόνει αὐτῷ. Ὀψίας 16
δὲ γενομένης προσήνεγκαν αὐτῷ δαιμονιζομένους πολλούς·
καὶ ἐξέβαλεν τὰ πνεύματα λόγῳ, καὶ πάντας τοὺς κακῶς
ἔχοντας ἐθεράπευσεν· ὅπως πληρωθῇ τὸ ῥηθὲν διὰ Ἡσαίου 17

15. καὶ ἥψατο κτλ.] Mt. abbreviates Mk.'s καὶ προσελθὼν ἤγειρεν αὐτὴν κρατήσας τῆς χειρός. For the manual contact Lk. has ἐπιστὰς ἐπάνω αὐτῆς ἐπετίμησεν τῷ πυρετῷ. The restored woman waited at a meal upon Him (αὐτῷ): Mk., Lk. αὐτοῖς; in Mk. this means Jesus and the disciples; in Lk., who has not yet related the call of any disciples, it must mean Jesus and the people in the house, Simon and perhaps his wife. The imperf. διηκόνει (so Mk., Lk.) represents the Aram. narrative idiom, or possibly means 'she began to minister.'

16, 17. (Mk. i. 32–34, Lk. iv. 40 f.) THE SICK HEALED AT EVEN.

16. ὀψίας δέ κτλ.] It was the Sabbath (see Mk. i. 21, 29, 32), and the people, therefore, waited till sunset to be healed. Mk.'s addition ὅτε ἔδυσεν ὁ ἥλιος (Lk. similarly) is omitted by Mt., since he does not mention that it was the Sabbath. προσήνεγκαν (Mt.[15], Mk.[3], Lk.[4]) takes the place of the imperf. ἔφερον (Mk.), which either is an Aramaism or denotes that 'case after case arrived' (Swete). Mk. relates that they brought πάντας, and that the Lord healed πολλούς: Mt. transposes them, avoiding the implication that some were not healed; cf. xii. 15 with Mk. iii. 10. Both Mt. and Lk. omit Mk. v. 33, 'And the whole city was congregated at the door' [i.e. of Simon's house]. For other omissions of Mk.'s (sometimes vague) references to a house see ix. 2, xii. 22, xv. 15, 21, xvii. 19, xviii. 1, xix. 9.

καὶ ἐξέβαλεν κτλ.] πνεύματα, with no definition to shew that evil spirits are meant, is not found elsewhere in the N.T. Mk., Lk. have δαιμόνια. On λόγῳ see v. 8; Mk. does not state the method of cure; Lk. has τὰς χεῖρας ἐπιτιθείς; see the converse in v. 15. Mt. avoids the statement of Mk., Lk. that Jesus suffered not the demons to speak, because they knew Him (to be the Messiah, Lk.): cf. his omission at xii. 15 of Mk. iii. 11. For other general statements of healing see iv. 23 note. Mk., Lk. mention the sick before the demoniacs; Mt. transposes them, connecting the former with the quotation which he adds.

17. ὅπως πληρωθῇ κτλ.] Mt. only. On the formula see i. 22. The quotation is from Is. liii. 4. The LXX. runs οὗτος τὰς ἁμαρτίας [ἀνομίας אAQ] ἡμῶν φέρει καὶ περὶ ἡμῶν ὀδυνᾶται. Mt.'s rendering probably stood in his Gk. version of a collection of Aram. testimonia. The two Heb. verbs נשא and סבל, here used as parallels (ἔλαβεν and ἐβάστασεν), both mean 'to bear,' the former of taking up a load, the latter of supporting its weight. In Is. vv. 11 f. the latter occurs again (v. 11) with עָוֹן ('guilt' or 'punishment'), the former (v. 12) with חֵטְא ('sin' or 'punishment'): the Servant of Yahweh carries the burden of the sicknesses and pains, and of the punishment, of others. But He does so as a substitute or equivalent for others, the verbs thus virtually gaining the meaning 'to take away'; the

τοῦ προφήτου λέγοντος Αγτὸς τὰς ἀσθενείας ἡμῶν ἔλαβεν καὶ
τὰς νόσογς ἐβάστασεν.

18 Ἰδὼν δὲ ὁ Ἰησοῦς ὄχλον περὶ αὐτὸν ἐκέλευσεν ἀπελ-
19 θεῖν εἰς τὸ πέραν.   Καὶ προσελθὼν εἰς γραμματεὺς

sicknesses and pains of the people *are*
their punishment. The LXX. translators seem not to have perceived
this identity, since they render the
verbs by φέρει and ὀδυνᾶται in *v.* 4,
but by ἀναφέρειν in *vv.* 11, 12. Mt.
similarly, or his source, makes no
reference to the propitiatory value of
the Servant's work; he quotes only
v. 4, and quotes the wording of it
mechanically, as in other instances,
to illustrate the immediate incident,
using the Greek verbs in their
collateral force of 'to take away.'
The passage, *as Mt. employs it*, has
no bearing on the doctrine of the
Atonement (see on xx. 28 *fin.*).
Deissmann's suggestion (*Bible St.*
102 f.) that Mt. transposes the Heb.
clauses is unnecessary.

18. (Mk. iv. 35, Lk. viii. 22.)
PROPOSAL TO CROSS THE LAKE.

Mt. here makes a serious departure
from Mk.'s order. According to Mk.
i. 39 Jesus made a tour in Galilee
(so Mt. iv. 23), in the course of
which He healed a leper (Mk. i. 40–
45, Mt. viii. 1–4), and returned to
Capharnaum (Mk. ii. 1), at and near
which various incidents and discourses are related (Mk. ii.–iv. 34),
which Mt. places for the most part
in chs. ix., xii., xiii. Mt. (viii. 18,
23–34) now makes the sequel to the
first stay at Capharnaum what Mk.
(iv. 35–v. 20) makes the sequel to
the second; and he omits Mk. i. 35–
38 (Lk. iv. 42 f.) in which the
disciples express their disappointment that Jesus withdrew Himself
from the crowds in the moment of
success.

ἰδὼν δέ κτλ.] See iv. 23 note.
Mk. gives the lateness of the hour
(ὀψίας γενομένης) as the reason for
the Lord's retirement. ἐκέλευσεν
ἀπελθεῖν, the command of a Master,
takes the place of λέγει (εἶπεν)
διελθῶμεν (Mk., Lk.). On πέραν see
iv. 15; τὸ πέραν is confined to Mt.
and Mk.

19–22. (Lk. ix. 57–60.) TWO
CANDIDATES FOR DISCIPLESHIP.

The section is placed too early;
it belongs, as Lk. has it, to the
period of the last journey to Jerusalem, for (1) Jesus no longer had
'where to lay His head'; Capharnaum had, therefore, ceased to be
'His own city' (ix. 1), and He no
longer had a house of His own (ix.
10, Mk. ii. 15); (2) if He is on His
way to the boat, late in the evening
(*v.* 16), the request 'suffer me first to
go and bury my father' is impossible.
Mt. possibly wished to record early
in the ministry typical instances of
unworthy discipleship. Since his
tendency is to arrange incidents in
groups of three, his recension of Q
probably did not include Lk.'s third
instance (*v.* 61 f.).

19. καὶ προσελθὼν κτλ.] For
εἷς = τις (Lk.) cf. ix. 18, xii. 11, xiii.
46, xix. 16, xxvi. 69 (Blass, § 45. 2,
Moulton, i. 97). The scribe was
already a μαθητής: cf. ἕτερος τῶν
μαθητῶν (*v.* 21). The one speaker
addressed Jesus as διδάσκαλε, the
other as κύριε (see vii. 21 note), both
of which are absent from Lk. With
ἀκολουθήσω κτλ. cf. Lk.'s form (xxii.
33) of S. Peter's impulsive words.
The speaker's motive may have been

εἶπεν αὐτῷ Διδάσκαλε, ἀκολουθήσω σοι ὅπου ἐὰν ἀπέρχῃ.
καὶ λέγει αὐτῷ ὁ Ἰησοῦς Αἱ ἀλώπεκες φωλεοὺς ἔχουσιν 20
καὶ τὰ πετεινὰ τοῦ οὐρανοῦ κατασκηνώσεις, ὁ δὲ υἱὸς τοῦ
ἀνθρώπου οὐκ ἔχει ποῦ τὴν κεφαλὴν κλίνῃ. Ἕτερος δὲ 21
τῶν μαθητῶν εἶπεν αὐτῷ Κύριε, ἐπίτρεψόν μοι πρῶτον
ἀπελθεῖν καὶ θάψαι τὸν πατέρα μου. ὁ δὲ Ἰησοῦς λέγει 22
αὐτῷ Ἀκολούθει μοι, καὶ ἄφες τοὺς νεκροὺς θάψαι τοὺς

sincere ; there is nothing to indicate that it was covetousness (as Jer., Thphlact.). The scribe does not say that he will accompany Jesus wheresoever His wanderings may take Him, but 'whithersoever Thou art [at this moment] departing'; and the Lord's reply is to the effect that He is not on His way home, nor to any definite resting-place, for He has none. For ὅπου = 'whither' cf. Mk. vi. 10, Jo. viii. 21 f.

20. αἱ ἀλώπεκες κτλ.] φωλεός is a late word occurring in Aristot., Plut., Luc. ; φωλεύουσι is used by a translator of Job xxxviii. 40 (Field, *Hexapla*). κατασκηνώσεις are 'roosts,' *i.e.* leafy σκηναί for settling at night (*tabernacula, habitacula*), not nests. The subst. occurs in the LXX. (4 times), only of the tabernacling of God in the sanctuary ; in Sym. Ps. xlviii. [xlix.] 12 of human dwellings (= LXX. σκηνώματα), and in Polyb. of the act of encamping. The verb -νοῦν (very frequent in the LXX.) is used of birds in Ps. ciii. [civ.] 12, Dan. iv. 18 (Theod.), Mt. xiii. 32 (Mk., Lk.).

ὁ δὲ υἱός κτλ.] If the words had been addressed to one of the Twelve, the title Son of Man would have been intelligible after S. Peter's confession (xvi. 16 f.) but not before ; but to anyone else it could have no meaning at all ; see pp. xix. ff., xxv. The explanation is forced and unnatural that, as in Dan. vii. 13, the principal source of the title, 'Son of Man' (*i.e.*

Human being) is contrasted with the symbolic beasts, so here it is contrasted with the literal foxes and birds.

21. ἕτερος δέ κτλ.] Clem. (*Strom.* iii. 4) identifies him with Philip. Both men were μαθηταί : the first had impulsively offered himself for permanent companionship without a call, the second delays to accept a call that has been given (Lk. transposes the ἀκολούθει μοι of v. 22, so as to record the call) ; but the Lord sees that the one will find it hard to sacrifice his house, and the other his relatives, for His sake (cf. xix. 29).

ἐπίτρεψόν μοι κτλ.] On πρῶτον see Blass, § 11. 5. The redundant ἀπελθεῖν, and the simple co-ordination of the verbs (Lk. ἀπελθόντι θάψαι), are both Semitic. On the duty of burying a father cf. Gen. l. 5 f., Tob. iv. 3, vi. 15. The necessity of burying a relative freed a Jew from reading the Shᵉma (*Berak.* iii. 1).

22. ἀκολούθει μοι κτλ.] The Lord's call is more imperative than Elijah's (1 Kings xix. 20) ; cf. Mt. x. 37. δεῖ μὲν γὰρ καὶ τοὺς γονεῖς τιμᾶν, ἀλλὰ τὸν θεὸν προτιμᾶν (Thphlact.). The first νεκρούς is generally explained as 'spiritually dead' (cf. Lk. xv. 24, 32), referring to other members of the man's family. In our ignorance of the circumstances this sounds somewhat harsh, though it may have been the incentive that the waverer needed. The Gk. perhaps obscures an Aram. proverb analogous

23 ἑαυτῶν νεκρούς.   Καὶ ἐμβάντι αὐτῷ εἰς πλοῖον ἠκο-
24 λούθησαν αὐτῷ οἱ μαθηταὶ αὐτοῦ.   καὶ ἰδοὺ σεισμὸς μέγας
   ἐγένετο ἐν τῇ θαλάσσῃ, ὥστε τὸ πλοῖον καλύπτεσθαι ὑπὸ
25 τῶν κυμάτων· αὐτὸς δὲ ἐκάθευδεν. καὶ προσελθόντες
26 ἤγειραν αὐτὸν λέγοντες Κύριε, σῶσον, ἀπολλύμεθα. καὶ

to 'Let the dead past bury its dead.'
Another suggestion is that the infin.
θάψαι (Aram. לְמִקְבַּר) is a misreading
of the participle לְמְקַבֵּר : ' Leave the
dead *to him that buries* their dead
bodies,' *i.e.* 'Leave your father's body
to be buried by anyone that will do
it'; cf. Ez. xxxix. 15, ἕως ὅτου
θάψωσιν αὐτὸ οἱ θάπτοντες. Wendt
(*Lehre Jesu*, 290) thinks that the
man's father may have been still
alive, and that the request was an
excuse for indefinite delay. He cites
an interesting modern parallel. But
nothing is said (as in xix. 22) to
shew that the Lord's appeal to either
of the men was unsuccessful, and
Lk.'s additional words σὺ δὲ ἀπελθὼν
διάγγελλε τὴν βασιλείαν τοῦ θεοῦ
perhaps imply the opposite. ἑαυτῶν
is not emphatic: its force was often
weakened in late Gk.; cf. xviii. 31,
xxi. 8, xxv. 1, 4, 7. Moulton (i.
87 f.) cites instances from papyri.

23–27. (Mk. iv. 36–41, Lk. viii.
23–25.) A STORM ON THE LAKE.
See note on *v.* 18.

23. καὶ ἐμβάντι κτλ.] Mt. and
Lk. abbreviate Mk., who relates that
the disciples 'leaving the crowd take
Him as He was in the boat' (where
He had been preaching, Mk. *v.* 1);
Lk., who does not mention that the
preaching was in a boat (*v.* 4), introduces the incident with ἐγένετο δὲ
ἐν μίᾳ τῶν ἡμερῶν καὶ αὐτὸς ἐνέβη
εἰς πλοῖον. The preaching explains
the Lord's physical weariness. Other
boats, according to Mk., also went
with them, but they play no further
part in the story. Spitta suggests

that 'as He was' means 'by Himself,' and that the subject of 'they
take Him' is the fishermen, not
the disciples, who make use of the
other boats, the subject of παρα-
λαμβάνουσιν having fallen out; ? οἱ
ἁλεεῖς.

24. καὶ ἰδού κτλ.] Mt. draws a
picture of the scene as though by
an onlooker: an upheaval (σεισμός)
of the waters, so that the boat
was concealed (καλύπτεσθαι) in the
trough of the waves. Mk. and Lk.
speak of a λαῖλαψ ἀνέμου, 'and the
waves hurled themselves against the
boat, so that the boat was already
filled' (Mk.).

αὐτ. δὲ ἐκάθευδεν] Omitting Mk.'s
descriptive detail ' in the stern upon
the cushion.' That the narrative is
based on that of Jonah, the dis-
obedient prophet (Jon. i. 5 b, 6, 15 f.),
is inconceivable.

25. καὶ προσελθόντες κτλ.] Mt.,
with his characteristic participle,
loses Mk.'s Semitic simplicity, καὶ
ἐγείρουσιν αὐτὸν καὶ λέγουσιν αὐτῷ.
In Mt. the disciples' cry implores
the unskilled Passenger to do what
the trained boatmen cannot, and yet
astonishment is caused by the result
(*v.* 27); in Mk. and Lk. they awake
Him, not with words which shew any
expectation of a miracle, but because
the boat is in danger. And the
result is not so much astonishment
as terror (Mk.): terrified astonishment (Lk.). Mt. and Lk. (ἐπιστάτα
ἐπιστάτα ἀπολλύμεθα) shun the
touch of reproach in Mk.'s οὐ μέλει
σοι ὅτι ἀπολλύμεθα.

λέγει αὐτοῖς Τί δειλοί ἐστε, ὀλιγόπιστοι; τότε ἐγερθεὶς
ἐπετίμησεν τοῖς ἀνέμοις καὶ τῇ θαλάσσῃ, καὶ ἐγένετο
γαλήνη μεγάλη. Οἱ δὲ ἄνθρωποι ἐθαύμασαν λέγοντες 27
Ποταπός ἐστιν οὗτος ὅτι καὶ οἱ ἄνεμοι καὶ ἡ θάλασσα
αὐτῷ ὑπακούουσιν;   Καὶ ἐλθόντος αὐτοῦ εἰς τὸ πέραν 28

26. τί δειλοί ἐστε; κτλ.] ὀλιγόπιστοι (see vi. 30 note) softens the
severity of Mk.'s πῶς οὐκ ἔχετε
πίστιν; (Lk. ποῦ ἡ πίστις ὑμῶν;).
Mt. often softens or omits statements
derogatory to the disciples; see xiii.
16 (prelim. n.), xiv. 33, xvi. 9, xvii.
4, 9, 23, xviii. 1, xix. 23, xx. 17, 20
(see, however, xxvi. 8).   Mk. and
Lk. place the question, with more
probability, after the stilling of
the storm.   For δειλός cf. Apoc.
xxi. 8.

τότε ἐγερθείς κτλ.] 'roused from
sleep' (cf. i. 24, ii. 13 f., 20 f.),
corresponding with ἤγειραν. R.V. has
'he arose' (Vulg. surgens), but 'awoke'
in Mk., Lk. for διεγερθείς.   The Lord
'rebuked' the winds and the lake,
as though they were conscious beings
possessed with demons (cf. xvii. 18).
Vulg. imperavit loses the thought.
Mk. emphasizes it by adding the
words of rebuke, σιώπα πεφίμωσο
(cf. φιμώθητι, addressed to an unclean
spirit, Mk. i. 25).   This is important.
The incident is related, not primarily
for the sake of recording a miracle,
but as an instance of the subduing
of the powers of evil, which was one
of the signs of the nearness of the
Kingdom; see xii. 28.

καὶ ἐγένετο κτλ.]   Preceded in
Mk. by καὶ ἐκόπασεν ὁ ἄνεμος
(possibly a later assimilation to Mk.
vi. 51).   Jesus performs the action
of God Himself (Ps. lxxxix. 10,
cvii. 23–30).   J. Weiss explains that
by 'an astonishing coincidence' the
storm happened to lull at the moment
that Jesus spoke!

27. οἱ δὲ ἄνθρωποι] These are

not the occupants of the other boats,
which Mt. does not mention, nor
the crowds on the shore (Chrys.);
Jer. says 'non discipuli, sed nautae
et qui in navi erant.' This would
agree with Spitta's suggestion (see
v. 23).   But ἄνθρωποι with the
article elsewhere in Mt. (27 times)
always means 'men,' 'people'; see
e.g. xvi. 13.   Mt. seems to have
understood the subject of the verb
in Mk. to be the disciples, but
shrinks from ascribing to them a
doubt as to the nature of the Lord's
person.   By adding δί ἄνθρωποι he
converts the passage into an editorial
remark on the wonder produced in
men's minds.

28–34. (Mk. v. 1–20, Lk. viii. 26–
39.)   Two Demoniacs of Gadara.

28. καὶ ἐλθόντος κτλ.]   On τὸ
πέραν see v. 18.   Γαδαρηνῶν is the
best reading in Mt., Γερασηνῶν in
Mk., Lk.   Γεργεσηνῶν, resembling
the O.T. Γεργεσαῖοι, is probably
due to Origen, who points out that
neither Gadara nor 'Gerasa of
Arabia' fulfils the requirements of
the narrative.   Gerasa is probably
the modern Kersa or Gersa at the
mouth of the Wady Semak, on the
E. of the lake, a little to the N. of
the middle point (Sanday, Sacr. Sites,
25–29, 92 f.).   If Mt. knew only the
larger Gerasa in Decapolis, 30 m.
S.E. of the lake, he may have substituted Gadara, 6 m. from the lake
in the same direction, μητρόπολις
τῆς Περαίας καρτερά (Jos. BJ. iv.
vii. 3).   But whatever was the name
of the district (Jos. ib. III. x. 10
speaks of 'Gadaritis'), the πόλις of

εἰς τὴν χώραν τῶν Γαδαρηνῶν ὑπήντησαν αὐτῷ δύο δαιμονιζόμενοι ἐκ τῶν μνημείων ἐξερχόμενοι, χαλεποὶ λίαν
29 ὥστε μὴ ἰσχύειν τινὰ παρελθεῖν διὰ τῆς ὁδοῦ ἐκείνης. καὶ
ἰδοὺ ἔκραξαν λέγοντες Τί ἡμῖν καὶ σοί, υἱὲ τοῦ θεοῦ;
30 ἦλθες ὧδε πρὸ καιροῦ βασανίσαι ἡμᾶς; Ἦν δὲ μακρὰν

28 Γαδαρηνων] א* (Γαϛ.) BC*ΜΔ minn.*nonn* S sin.pesh ; Γερασηνων L *omn*
sah ; Γεργεσηνων אᶜCᶜ3*al* minn.*pler* me go arm aeth

v. 33 was not necessarily that which
gave it its name ; it may have been
any village near the eastern shore.

δύο δαιμονιζόμενοι κτλ.] Mk.,
Lk. mention only one ; cf. ix. 27,
xx. 30. That Mt. here compensates
for his previous omission of the cure
of a demoniac (see note before viii. 1)
is not more probable than that Mk.,
Lk. mention only the more important
of the two. Mk. describes the sufferer
as ἄνθρωπος ἐν πνεύματι ἀκαθάρτῳ :
Lk. ἀνήρ τις ἔχων δαιμόνια. Mk.
uses the singular until the swine
have been mentioned, and thereafter
the plural, which is explained in
v. 9, 'he saith unto Him, My name
is Legion, for we are many.' Lk.
has the singular in v. 29 f. only.
This alternation of one demon and
many is avoided by Mt., who uses
the plural throughout because there
were two demoniacs. He did not
think, as some suggest in the case
of Mk., Lk., that many demons were
necessary because there were many
swine. τῶν μνημείων : Sanday (*l.c.*)
states, against Wilson (quoted by
Swete), that there are tombs near
Kersa. By haunting tombs, the
maniacs acted in keeping with their
obsession that they were dominated
by spirits. In two words Mt. summarizes. Mk. vv. 3–5, which Lk.
reproduces briefly in v. 29 ; but Mt.
alone adds ὥστε μὴ ἰσχύειν κτλ.

29. τί ἡμῖν κτλ.] The demoniacs,
or the demons, knew that there
could be no συμφώνησις Χριστοῦ

πρὸς Βελίαρ (2 Cor. vi. 15). The
expression 'What is there in common
to us and thee ?' occurs in the O.T.
(cf. Judg. xi. 12, 2 Regn. xvi. 10,
3 Regn. xvii. 18), and in class. Gk.
(see Wetstein, *ad loc.*) ; cf. xxvii. 19,
Mk. i. 24, Jo. ii. 4.

υἱὲ τοῦ θεοῦ] For the use of the
title by demons cf. Mk. iii. 11, Lk.
iv. 41 ; Lk. there shows that he
understood it to be equivalent to
'the Messiah' ; see also Mt. xvi. 16
(contrast Mk. viii. 29), xxvi. 63 (Lk.
xxii. 70), xxvii. 54 (Mk. xv. 39 ;
contrast Lk. xxiii. 47). Dalman
(*Words*, 268–276) holds that it was
not in common use as a Messianic
title (see iii. 17, note), and that it
was not used of Jesus by any of His
contemporaries, but, in the cases of
demons, was substituted by the
evangg. for a Messianic title. Mk.,
Lk. add τοῦ ὑψίστου (cf. Mt. v. 45
with Lk. vi. 35), which is a marked
feature in Lk., Ac., and probably
'did not really belong to the popular
speech, but characterized the language of religious poets and authors
following a biblical style' (Dalman,
op. cit. 198).

ἦλθες ὧδε κτλ.] Mk. ὁρκίζω σε
τὸν θεὸν μή με βασανίσῃς. Lk.
δέομαί σου μ. μ. βασ. It was a
current belief that the Last Day
would put an end to the power
of demons over mankind ; cf. *Eth.
Enoch* xv. f., *Jubil.* x. 8, 9. The
maniacs, speaking the language of the
demons within them, acknowledge

ἀπ᾽ αὐτῶν ἀγέλη χοίρων πολλῶν βοσκομένη. οἱ δὲ δαίμονες 31
παρεκάλουν αὐτὸν λέγοντες Εἰ ἐκβάλλεις ἡμᾶς, ἀπόστειλον ἡμᾶς εἰς τὴν ἀγέλην τῶν χοίρων. καὶ εἶπεν αὐτοῖς
Ὑπάγετε. οἱ δὲ ἐξελθόντες ἀπῆλθαν εἰς τοὺς χοίρους· καὶ 32
ἰδοὺ ὥρμησεν πᾶσα ἡ ἀγέλη κατὰ τοῦ κρημνοῦ εἰς τὴν
θάλασσαν, καὶ ἀπέθανον ἐν τοῖς ὕδασιν. Οἱ δὲ βόσκοντες 33
ἔφυγον, καὶ ἀπελθόντες εἰς τὴν πόλιν ἀπήγγειλαν πάντα
καὶ τὰ τῶν δαιμονιζομένων. καὶ ἰδοὺ πᾶσα ἡ πόλις 34

the Messiah, and think that His
functions must already have begun.
In Mk. and Lk. the words are a shriek
of despair because the hour of torment
has arrived ; in Mt. this is expressed
more vividly—'Surely Thou hast
come too early !' In Mk. and Lk.
the cry is caused by the fact that
Jesus had already commanded the
demons to depart ; Mt. omits this
(perhaps because ·it implied that the
command was not instantly obeyed),
also the question, 'What is thy
name ?' the answer, and the entreaty
that He would not send them ἔξω
τῆς χώρας (Mk.)—εἰς τὴν ἄβυσσον
(Lk.). Mt. often, though not always,
omits questions asked by Jesus,
sometimes apparently shrinking from
implying ignorance on His part ;
see notes on ix. 22, xiv. 17, xvi. 4,
12, xvii. 11, 14, 18, xviii. 1, xix. 4,
xxvi. 18.

30. ἦν δὲ μακράν κτλ.] S vet.
pesh 'beyond them.' L vet.vulg. non
longe seems to be an intentional correction. Mk., Lk. ἐκεῖ πρὸς [Lk. ἐν]
τῷ ὄρει. Nestle would explain μακράν
and πρὸς τ. ὄρει as due to different
pointings of the Aram. לטורא. The
swine were probably owned by some
rich Gentile. The population of
the district was a mixture of Jews
and Greeks (Jos. BJ. III. iii. 5).

31. οἱ δὲ δαίμονες κτλ.] There
is no other certain use of δαίμων in
N.T. or LXX. ; some MSS. add it in
Mk. xii. 5, and it is a variant for

δαιμόνιον in Lk. viii. 29, Apoc.
xvi. 14, xviii. 2, Is. lxv. 11. The
imperf. παρεκάλουν may represent
the Aram. construction ; it is probably the true reading in Mk. ; on
the word see v. 5. ἀπόστειλον, like
πέμψον (Mk.), is permissive, 'Cause
[i.e. allow] us to go' (cf. vi. 13 note) ;
Lk. ἐπιτρέψῃ. On this verse and
32 a see Add. note.

32. καὶ ἰδοὺ κτλ.] 'Not only
are there [at Kersa] tombs near at
hand, but here alone is there a cliff
that falls sheer almost into the lake'
(Sanday, op. cit.). Mt., Lk. omit
Mk.'s ὡς δισχίλιοι (see Plummer,
St. Luke); cf. xiv. 17, 19, xxvi. 9.
ἀπέθανον : Mk. ἐπνίγοντο, Lk.
ἀπεπνίγη. Mk. has ἐν τῇ θαλάσσῃ
following εἰς τὴν θάλασσαν : Mt.
varies, and Lk. omits, it.

33. οἱ δὲ βόσκοντες κτλ.] So Lk.
The adj. describes a class ; cf. xiii.
3, xxi. 12, xxv. 9, xxvi. 25, 46, 48,
Mk. vi. 14, Jer. xxxviii. [xxxi.] 10.
Mk. adds αὐτούς. After πόλιν Mk.,
Lk. add καὶ εἰς τοὺς ἀγρούς (cf. Mk.
vi. 36, 56), i.e. the country places,
or hamlets, round. πάντα κτλ. is
added by Mt. For the use of τά cf.
τὸ τῆς συκῆς (xxi. 21).

34. καὶ ἰδοὺ κτλ.] A brief
summary of Mk. vv. 15–17, Lk. vv.
35–37 a. Hostility for the loss
of the swine, and gratitude for the
removal of the scourge of the district,
are alike swallowed up by fear of
the Wonder-worker. On εἰς ὑπάν-

ἐξῆλθεν εἰς ὑπάντησιν τῷ Ἰησοῦ, καὶ ἰδόντες αὐτὸν παρ-

τησιν αὐτῷ see xxv. 1 note. παρ- παρακαλεῖν, as often, and μεταβῇ
εκάλεσαν (Lk. ἠρώτησαν) takes the (Mt.⁵, Mk.⁶, Lk.¹) of ἀπελθεῖν (Mk.,
place of Mk.'s characteristic ἤρξαντο Lk.).

Additional Note on viii. 28–34.

That the narrative possesses a historical foundation is often denied.
The suggestion that it was a popular tale originally unconnected with Jesus,
does not help matters. Few scholars now doubt that on several occasions
He restored persons, believed to be dominated by evil spirits, to a normal
state of mind, and consequently of body. The scientific study of Nature
has brought to the scientific study of Theology a priceless boon in the
realization that mind can exert powerful influence over matter, an
influence whose results are evident but its laws still unknown. In
the present instance the sovereign power of the Lord's personality healed
a maniac who was obsessed with the idea that a multitude of demons dwelt
within him. Everyone in the neighbourhood no doubt firmly believed
the same; whether Jesus also thought so, or not, does not affect the
credibility of the cure, though there is plenty of evidence in the Gospels
that, as Man, He shared the contemporary beliefs as to demoniacal possession.
The unique feature of the narrative is the part played by the swine.
Their presence in a semi-pagan district causes no difficulty, nor the fact that
a sudden fright made them start down a steep slope, so that they were
drowned in the lake. The problem is to explain the connexion between
their panic and the healing of the man. If the Lord miraculously caused
the swine to stampede, it was to confirm the man's peace of mind, and so
complete the cure, by giving him an optical demonstration that that which
had troubled him had departed from him for ever. Of the rationalizing
explanations which have been proposed the simplest is that the wildness of
the maniac, as he rushed past the swine, perhaps shrieking, towards Jesus,
frightened them into a panic, which the efforts of their keepers to restrain
them only increased. The cure of the man coincided with their rush over
the cliff, which contributed to his certainty and peace of mind. Not only
he himself would believe that the demons had passed from him into the
swine, but also the disciples, the swineherds, and the inhabitants of the
district; and hence there were added to the narrative the accounts of the
demons' request to enter the swine, and the permission granted to them.
If vv. 31, 32 a are due to 'the reports of chroniclers whose minds were
necessarily coloured by the prevailing beliefs of the age, psychic and cosmic'
(Whitehouse, in HDB. i. 594), the remainder of the narrative does not
essentially differ from those of other cures of demoniacs performed by the
Lord.

Another, more drastic, explanation is that the narrative was derived
from the account which the healed man himself gave of his experiences.
The bestiality into which he had sunk was such that when he was rescued
from it he thought of the demons which left him as being in the form of
swine which perished.

ἐκάλεσαν ὅπως μεταβῇ ἀπὸ τῶν ὁρίων αὐτῶν.   Καὶ 1 IX.
ἐμβὰς εἰς πλοῖον διεπέρασεν, καὶ ἦλθεν εἰς τὴν ἰδίαν
πόλιν. Καὶ ἰδοὺ προσέφερον αὐτῷ παραλυτικὸν ἐπὶ κλίνης 2
βεβλημένον. καὶ ἰδὼν ὁ Ἰησοῦς τὴν πίστιν αὐτῶν εἶπεν
τῷ παραλυτικῷ   Θάρσει, τέκνον· ἀφίενταί σου αἱ ἁμαρτίαι.

The Jewish ideas on possession by demons may be seen in Menzies
Alexander, *Demonic possession in N.T.*, Edersheim, *L. and T.* ii. 770–6,
JQR., July and Oct. 1896, Weber, *Jüd. Theol.* 254 ff., Bousset, *Rel. d. Jud.*
331 ff.

ix.–xvi. 20. Opposition to the
Lord now begins, culminating in a
plot to destroy Him (xii. 14), and
the ascription of His works to
diabolical agency (xii. 24). Throughout this period He forbade those
who were healed to publish the fact
(ix. 30, xii. 16, Mk. v. 43, vii. 36,
viii. 26), He arranged for the carrying on of His work by the apostles
(ch. x.), He taught under the veiled
form of parables (ch. xiii.), He withdrew from His opponents (xii. 15),
and finally left Jewish territory for
a time (xiv. 13).

ix. 1–8. (Mk. ii. 1–12, Lk. v. 17–
26.) A PARALYTIC HEALED AND
FORGIVEN.

Mt. now reverts to Mk.'s order ;
see on viii. 18. He greatly abbreviates
Mk.'s narrative, confining himself to
the essential points.

1. καὶ ἐμβάς κτλ.] The first
clause is an editorial link ; in Mk.,
Lk., Jesus has not crossed the water,
but has been touring in Galilee. ἡ
ἰδία πόλις is Capharnaum (Mk.) ;
see on iv. 13. On ἴδιος see Blass,
§ 48. 8. Mk. adds ἠκούσθη ὅτι
ἐν οἴκῳ ἐστίν, and he speaks of
the πολλοί who filled even the
approaches to the doorway while
Jesus was preaching. Lk. rewrites
the whole : the company consists of
'Pharisees and teachers of the law,
who had come from every village of

Galilee and Judaea and Jerusalem,
καὶ δύναμις Κυρίου ἦν εἰς τὸ ἰᾶσθαι
αὐτόν, which strikingly follows the
statement in the previous verse that
He had been in the desert places
praying. If the healing of the leper
occurred in Judaea (see on viii. 1
and n. before v. 1), Lk., who does
not mention the arrival at Capharnaum, probably represents this
incident also as taking place in
Judaea.

2. καὶ ἰδού κτλ.] On βεβλημένον
see viii. 6. Only Mk. says that he
was αἰρόμενον ὑπὸ τεσσάρων. Mt.
omits the crowds and the house (see
on viii. 16), and hence the breaking
of the roof, and the letting down
of the bed (Mk. κράβαττον). If his
narrative stood alone, there would
be nothing to shew that the bed
was not brought to Jesus in the
open street, which would not require
less faith in His power to heal.

καὶ ἰδών κτλ.] Mt. adds θάρσει
as in *v.* 22. The paralytic himself
may be included in αὐτῶν ; but the
power of faith in obtaining blessings
for another is illustrated in viii. 10,
xv. 28, Jam. v. 15. It rests upon the
real unity of human life. ἀφίενται,
remittuntur. Lk. has the Doric
ἀφέωνται. The pres. means either
' are in a state of remission,' not
different from the perf., or ' are at
this moment remitted,' an aoristic
pres. (Blass, § 23. 7, § 56. 4, n. 1).

3 Καὶ ἰδού τινες τῶν γραμματέων εἶπαν ἐν ἑαυτοῖς Οὗτος
4 βλασφημεῖ. καὶ εἰδὼς ὁ Ἰησοῦς τὰς ἐνθυμήσεις αὐτῶν
εἶπεν "Ινα τί ἐνθυμεῖσθε πονηρὰ ἐν ταῖς καρδίαις ὑμῶν;
5 τί γάρ ἐστιν εὐκοπώτερον, εἰπεῖν Ἀφίενταί σου αἱ
6 ἁμαρτίαι, ἢ εἰπεῖν "Εγειρε καὶ περιπάτει; ἵνα δὲ εἰδῆτε

4 εἰδως] BME²Π¹ minn 𝔖 pesh.hcl sah arm ; ιδων ℵCDE*al 𝕷 omn 𝔖 sin.pal me

3. καὶ ἰδού κτλ.] Mt. abbreviates
Mk. v. 6 f., omitting 'who can forgive sins but One, God?' which is
implied in βλασφημεῖ (see xii. 31).
The first appearance of the scribes
(viii. 19 f. is placed too early) introduces the first note of conflict. εἶπαν
ἐν ἑαυτ.: Mk. διαλογιζόμενοι ἐν ταῖς
καρδίαις αὐτῶν. They did not express their thoughts aloud, as might
be inferred from Lk. ἤρξαντο δια-
λογίζεσθαι. See next verse. For
the contemptuous οὗτος cf. xii. 24,
xiii. 55, xxvi. 61, xxvii. 47.
4. καὶ εἰδώς κτλ.] Mk. ἐπιγνοὺς
τῷ πνεύματι αὐτοῦ, Lk. ἐπιγνούς ;
all record an intuition. If the v.l.
ἰδών is correct, the Lord 'saw' what
was in their minds, either by intuition (cf. xii. 25 note), or possibly,
as He 'saw' the faith of the man's
friends (v. 2), by their actions. Their
looks and gestures might lead Him
to realize that they were thinking,
what such an audience would be
likely to think, that He had claimed
a divine prerogative. His intuition,
like His sympathy, though human,
was profound, because of the per-
fection of His humanity in its union
with the will of God ; it does not
in itself δείκνυσιν ἑαυτὸν θεόν
(Thphlact.). ἐνθύμησις recurs only
in xii. 25, Ac. xvii. 29, Heb. iv. 12,
Sym. Job xxi. 27, Ez. xi. 21. The
LXX. has ἐνθύμημα (freq. in Ezek.).
On the verb see i. 20. On καρδίαις
see Swete on Mk. v. 6. ἵνα τί (sc.
γένηται), freq. in the LXX., occurs in
xxvii. 46 (LXX.), Lk. xiii. 7, Ac. iv.

25 (LXX.), vii. 26, 1 Cor. x. 29
(Blass, § 50. 7).
5. τί γάρ ἐστιν κτλ.] The deeply
rooted Hebrew conviction that suffering was the punishment of sin
is found passim in the O.T. ; it is
seen in the disciples' question in
Jo. ix. 2. In the present case Jesus
knew that the paralytic had sinned,
and His audience would feel sure
that as long as the suffering remained,
the sin was still being punished,
and therefore unforgiven. To say
effectually 'thy sins are forgiven'
appeared to them futile and impossible ; to say effectually 'arise and
walk' was no less difficult. It is
the equal difficulty of both that is
implied in the Lord's question. The
healing of the sufferer would, according to the ideas of the time, be the
only possible proof that his sins
were forgiven. εὐκοπώτερον (so Mk.,
Lk.): cf. xix. 24 (Mk., Lk.), Lk. xvi.
17, εὔκοπος, Sir. xxii. 15, 1 Mac.
iii. 18, εὐκοπία, 2 Mac. ii. 25 ; the
words (der. εὖ κοπιᾶν) belong to the
later Gk. On the position of σου
see JThS., Jan. 1909, 263 f. Lk.,
with Mt., has ἔγειρε κ. περιπάτει,
omitting Mk.'s καὶ ἆρον τὸν κράβατ-
τόν σου, which is repeated two verses
later, unless it is here a gloss in Mk.
6. ἵνα δέ κτλ.] Identical with Mk.
as far as ἁμαρτίας. It is probable
that here, as in xii. 8, 32, the Lord
did not use the personal title 'the
Son of Man,' but an Aram. expression
which meant 'men,' 'mankind' ;
see pp. xix. ff., xxv. Sin separates

ὅτι ἐξουσίαν ἔχει ὁ υἱὸς τοῦ ἀνθρώπου ἐπὶ τῆς γῆς ἀφιέναι
ἁμαρτίας— τότε λέγει τῷ παραλυτικῷ Ἔγειρε ἀρόν σου
τὴν κλίνην καὶ ὕπαγε εἰς τὸν οἶκόν σου. καὶ ἐγερθεὶς 7
ἀπῆλθεν εἰς τὸν οἶκον αὐτοῦ. Ἰδόντες δὲ οἱ ὄχλοι ἐφοβή- 8
θησαν καὶ ἐδόξασαν τὸν θεὸν τὸν δόντα ἐξουσίαν τοιαύτην
τοῖς ἀνθρώποις.

Καὶ παράγων ὁ Ἰησοῦς ἐκεῖθεν εἶδεν ἄνθρωπον καθή- 9
μενον ἐπὶ τὸ τελώνιον, Μαθθαῖον λεγόμενον, καὶ λέγει αὐτῷ

the individual from the one life of
men in God; and not only the Son
of Man, but any man, has authority
to represent mankind as a spokesman,
and to re-admit a sinner into union
with the one life, *i.e.* to forgive sins.
(In the Church, as a corporate body,
while any member has this authority
(see xviii. 15, note), it is officially
delegated to chosen representatives;
cf. Jo. xx. 23.) ἐπὶ τῆς γῆς emphasizes this: 'Man upon earth'
suggests as its complement 'God in
heaven.' The ἐξουσία is not δύναμις:
it is not inherent but delegated, as
Mt. shews in the last words of *v.* 8.

τότε λέγ. τῷ παραλυτικῷ] Mk.
λέγ. τῷ παρ. Lk. εἶπεν τῷ παρα-
λελυμένῳ. The parenthesis is different in each case, but the use of
a parenthesis shews the dependence
of Mt. and Lk. upon Mk. In the
command, which the Lord addresses
without a pause to the paralytic,
τὴν κλίνην takes the place of Mk.'s
τὸν κράβαττον (a dialectal word for
a poor man's pallet): Lk. τὸ κλινί-
διον. 'The command points to his
being an inhabitant of Capernaum,
and not one of the crowd from outside. He would therefore remain as
a standing witness to Jesus' (Swete).

8. ἐφοβήθησαν κτλ.] Mk. ὥστε
ἐξίστασθαι πάντας, Lk. καὶ ἔκστασις
ἔλαβεν ἅπαντας... καὶ ἐπλήσθησαν
φόβου. All the three evangg. relate
that they glorified God; Lk. adds
that the healed man did so first.

τὸν δόντα κτλ., which refers not to
the miracle of healing, but to the
forgiveness of sins guaranteed by it,
is a valuable interpretation of the
significance of the event (see above),
which Mt. substitutes for Mk.'s colloquial exclamation, λέγοντας ὅτι
οὕτως οὐδέποτε εἴδαμεν: Lk. ὅτι
εἴδαμεν παράδοξα σήμερον.

9. (Mk. ii. 13 f., Lk. v. 27 f.) THE
CALL OF MATTHEW.

καὶ παράγων κτλ.] The word is
used rather loosely where ὑπάγων
would be expected (cf. *v.* 27); it is
taken from the next verse in Mk.,
where it is rightly used of passing
along by the lake. Mt., Lk. omit
Mk.'s πάλιν εἰς τὴν θάλασσαν· καὶ
πᾶς ὁ ὄχλος ἤρχετο πρὸς αὐτόν,
καὶ ἐδίδασκεν αὐτούς. The custom-
officers (see v. 46 note) would sit
by the landing-stage to collect custom
dues on exports carried across the
lake to territory outside Herod's rule.
τελώνιον (𝕃 *teloneum*) is both the
'toll' (Strabo XVI. i. 27) and the
'custom-house' as here (so Rheims
vers.). A.V. 'receit of custome'
follows Cranmer's and the Geneva
Bibles. For ἐπί with acc. of place
where see Blass, § 43. 1.

Μαθθαῖον λεγόμενον] Mk. Λευεὶν
(D 13 69 124 𝕃 vet [nonn] Orig.[vid.]
Ἰάκωβον) τὸν τοῦ Ἀλφαίου (see
Swete). Lk. τελώνην ὀνόματι Λευείν.
Mt. identifies the custom-officer as
Matthew the apostle (x. 3), following
a non-Marcan tradition; this has

10 Ἀκολούθει μοι· καὶ ἀναστὰς ἠκολούθησεν αὐτῷ.   Καὶ
ἐγένετο αὐτοῦ ἀνακειμένου ἐν τῇ οἰκίᾳ, καὶ ἰδοὺ πολλοὶ
τελῶναι καὶ ἁμαρτωλοὶ ἐλθόντες συνανέκειντο τῷ Ἰησοῦ
11 καὶ τοῖς μαθηταῖς αὐτοῦ.   καὶ ἰδόντες οἱ Φαρισαῖοι ἔλεγον

been usually, though not universally, accepted. The derivation is uncertain : (1) מתי (similar to מתא on a Palmyr. inscr.), an abbreviation of a late Jewish name מתתיה, מתתיה or מתתיהו ‘the gift of Yah’ (Dalman); (2) an abbreviation of אמתי (Amittai) or אמתי (Nöldeke, al.); either is possible. For a double Semitic name cf. Simeon (Simon) and Kephas. It is probable that previous intimacy with Jesus had prepared the way for the call ἀκολούθει μοι (cf. iv. 20 note). Lk. (καὶ καταλιπὼν πάντα) emphasizes the sacrifice involved ; fishermen could return to their boats (Jo. xxi. 3), but a τελώνης threw up his occupation altogether (see Swete on Mk. ii. 14). It did not, according to Lk., mean forsaking his house and possessions, since he at once invited Jesus to a meal in his house.

10–13. (Mk. ii. 15 ff., Lk. v. 29–32.) A MEAL WITH CUSTOM-OFFICERS AND SINNERS.

10. καὶ ἐγένετο κτλ.] With the following καὶ ἰδού the construction is Semitic ; Mk. also has καὶ ... καί, but with the historic pres. γίνεται. Lk. remodels the sentence. ἀνακεῖσθαι in bibl. Gk. is ‘to recline’ at a meal (1 Esd. iv. 10, Tob. ix. 6 (א), Mk. xiv. 18, xvi. 14, etc.); Mk., Lk. have the class. κατακεῖσθαι (cf. Jdth. xiii. 15, Mk. xiv. 3, 1 Cor. viii. 10), which is used of one sleeping (Prov. vi. 9) or ill (Mk. i. 30 al.).

ἐν τῇ οἰκίᾳ] Mk. adds αὐτοῦ, which is ambiguous, since αὐτόν, and αὐτοῦ may refer respectively to Jesus and Levi (so Lk.), or vice versa, or both may refer to Jesus. But συνανέκειντο τῷ Ἰησοῦ κτλ. (Mt.,

Mk.) suggests rather that Jesus was the host ; Matthew (Levi) might hesitate to ask many custom-officers and sinners to meet him, but Jesus could freely invite them to His own house, and this gives further point to the metaphor καλέσαι in v. 13. If Capharnaum had become ἡ ἰδία πόλις (v. 1), it is improbable that He lodged permanently in ‘the house of Simon’ (so Memph.) ; see v. 28, iv. 13, xvii. 25 (notes).

καὶ ἰδοὺ κτλ.] On the τελῶναι see v. 46. ἁμαρτωλός was a Jewish term of depreciation with a wide variety of usage, applicable alike to the despised condition of a custom-officer (Lk. xix. 7 ; cf. Lk. vi. 32 with Mt. v. 46), Gentile nationality (Gal. ii. 15 ; see Mt. v. 47 note), heresy (Jo. ix. 16, 24 f. 31, 1 Mac. ii. 44, 48), and open immorality (Lk. vii. 37).

11. καὶ ἰδόντες κτλ.] Mk. has ‘Scribes who belonged to the Pharisees’ (cf. Ac. xxiii. 9) ; Lk. ‘the Ph. and their Scribes,’ combines Mt. and Mk. The details needed to explain ἰδόντες are not given by Mt. In Mk. the Scribes followed (καὶ ἠκολούθουν αὐτῷ καὶ γραμματεῖς) with the rest of the company to the house. But if it was mealtime nothing would induce them to enter. They saw the group of despised persons go in, obviously for a meal (cf. Lk. xv. 2), and their question to the disciples would be asked later in the day, respect for the popular Rabbi preventing them from questioning Him personally, as they did later when their hostility increased (xii. 2, 10). The Jewish estimation of eating

τοῖς μαθηταῖς αὐτοῦ Διὰ τί μετὰ τῶν τελωνῶν καὶ ἁμαρτωλῶν ἐσθίει ὁ διδάσκαλος ὑμῶν; ὁ δὲ ἀκούσας εἶπεν 12
Οὐ χρείαν ἔχουσιν οἱ ἰσχύοντες ἰατροῦ ἀλλὰ οἱ κακῶς
ἔχοντες. πορευθέντες δὲ μάθετε τί ἐστιν Ἔλεος θέλω καὶ 13
οΥ θΥϲίΑΝ· οὐ γὰρ ἦλθον καλέσαι δικαίους ἀλλὰ ἁμαρτω-

13 αμαρτωλους] add εις μετανοιαν CE al 𝕷 c g^{1.2} ⸋ sin.hcl^{mg·}pal me sah

with Gentiles is seen in Ac. xi. 3,
Gal. ii. 12. It was not forbidden
in the O.T.; but the necessity
of refraining from meats offered to
idols, from forbidden ¡foods, and from
blood, led the stricter Jews to shun
not only meals, but all intercourse,
with Gentiles. At an early date
the Christian Church broke loose
from these bonds; and the recital
of such incidents as the present
would help in her emancipation.
Mt. and Lk. both have διὰ τί for
Mk.'s ὅτι (see Swete, and Blass, § 50.
5). Mk.'s ἐσθίει καὶ πίνει has a
touch of scorn by the omission of
the subject; Lk. avoids this by
ἐσθίετε καὶ πίνετε, Mt. by the
respectful ἐσθίει ὁ διδάσκαλος ὑμῶν.

12. ὁ δὲ ἀκούσας κτλ.] The
question was either overheard by
Jesus, or at once reported to Him,
and He replied to the Pharisees.
The reply is identical in Mk.; Lk.
has ὑγιαίνοντες for ἰσχύοντες. It
was perhaps a current proverb; for
parallels in pagan Gk. writers see
Swete. Here it involves the thought
that as a Physician the Lord was
bound to come into close contact
with οἱ κακῶς ἔχοντες, regardless of
the contagious pollution which the
Pharisees shunned; cf. Ephr. Ev.
Conc. Expos., 'sed ubi dolores sunt,
ait, illic festinat medicus' (Resch,
Agrapha², 202).

13 a. πορευθέντες κτλ.] This
half verse, peculiar to Mt., opens with
a Rabb. formula צא ולמד (see Wetstein,
ad loc.). A redundant use of πορευ-

θῆναι, frequent in Mt. (cf. xii. 45,
xviii. 12, xxv. 16, xxvii. 66), and
Lk., is not found in Mk.; cf. ἀπελθεῖν
xiii. 28. The quotation is from
Hos. vi. 6, agreeing with the Heb.
(not the LXX. ἔλεος θέλω ἢ θυσίαν),
and is ascribed to Jesus again, by
Mt. only, in xii. 7. The insight
into the deeper meaning implicit in
the words is different from the
verbal literalism which characterizes
many of the citations made by the
evang. The Lord doubtless quoted
the passage on some occasion, but
perhaps not here: the splendid
simplicity of His argument rests
upon the very fact that it is not an
act of 'mercy,' but an obvious duty,
for a physician to visit the sick
rather than the healthy. θυσία is
quoted as denoting any kind of
ritual correctness; here it is the
avoidance of contact with sinners.
It has no bearing on the Lord's
attitude to Jewish sacrifices, as it
was understood by the Ebionites
(ap. Epiph. Haer. xxx. 16), ὅτι ἦλθεν
καταλῦσαι τὰς θυσίας. No instance
is known of the quotation of the
passage before the time of Jesus;
but Johanan b. Zakkai, who was
opposed to resistance to Rome, employed it (A.D. 70) to shew that in
spite of the destruction of Jerusalem,
God wants, and gives, mercy and
not sacrifice.

13 b. οὐ γὰρ ἦλθον κτλ.] Mt.
adds the γάρ: 'study Hosea's words,
for they contain the principle on
which I work.' In Mk., Lk. the

14 λούς.   Τότε προσέρχονται αὐτῷ οἱ μαθηταὶ Ἰωάνου
λέγοντες Διὰ τί ἡμεῖς καὶ οἱ Φαρισαῖοι νηστεύομεν, οἱ
15 δὲ μαθηταὶ σοῦ οὐ νηστεύουσιν; καὶ εἶπεν αὐτοῖς ὁ
Ἰησοῦς Μὴ δύνανται οἱ υἱοὶ τοῦ νυμφῶνος πενθεῖν

14 νηστευομεν] ℵ*B 27 71 ; add πολλα uncc.*caet* 𝔏 *omn* 𝔖 sin ['eagerly'].pesh.
hcl pal me sah

sentence rightly explains the simple
truth of the proverb about the
physician : 'if these ἁμαρτωλοί had
been δίκαιοι, I would not have
come to invite them to be healed.'
There may be, though the words do
not necessitate it, an implied rebuke
of the Pharisees who thought themselves δίκαιοι (Chrys., Thphlact., *al.*).
καλέσαι gains additional point if it
was Jesus who had invited the guests
to His own house (see *v.* 10 note ; and
cf. xxii. 3 f., 8 f.). Lk. interprets it
by adding εἰς μετάνοιαν, 'in order
to explain why the δίκαιοι were not
called' (Allen); but in Mk., and in
the best text of Mt., the verb stands
alone. In the epistles it becomes a
part of the Christian vocabulary ; cf.
Rom. viii. 30, ix. 11, 1 Cor. vii. 15,
17 f., 20 ff. *al.* On ἦλθον see v. 17.

14, 15. (Mk. ii. 18–20. Lk. v.
33–35.) A QUESTION ABOUT FASTING.

14. τότε προσέρχονται κτλ.] The
question follows, not inappropriately,
the narrative of the feast ; but there
is no definite connexion between
them. Mt.'s usual τότε is no evidence
of a chronological sequence (see on
ii. 7). Mk. relates that, at a time
when John's disciples and the
Pharisees were observing a fast,
'*they* come and say etc.' ; the subject
may be the persons just mentioned,
or the verb is impersonal. Mt.,
understanding Mk. to mean that
John's disciples were the questioners,
rewrites his opening verse accordingly ;
Lk. οἱ δὲ εἶπαν refers, on the
contrary, to the Pharisees and scribes.
The Baptist's disciples are mentioned

again in xi. 2 (Lk. vii. 18 f.), xiv.
12 (Mk. vi. 29), Lk. xi. 1, Jo. i.
35, iii. 25, iv. 1. They probably
played a larger part in the early
history of the Church than our
records would suggest. In *Clem.
Hom.* ii. 23 Simon Magus is said
to have been the chief of them. On
a modern sect claiming to be
descended from them see *DCA.* i. 884.

διὰ τί κτλ.] It was perhaps an
occasion of public fasting during the
autumn drought (see vi. 2). The
strict asceticism of the Baptist (xi. 18)
and of the Pharisaic Rabbis (Lk.
xviii. 12) was imitated by their
disciples : the disciples of the Son of
Man, who 'came eating and drinking,' imitated Him. πολλά should
probably be inserted (Lk. πυκνά).
It is adverbial, and equivalent to
the Aram. אדיס (cf. xiii. 3, xvi. 21,
xxvii. 19). 𝔖 sin has 'diligently' ;
but this may be a repetition of its
rendering of πυκνά in Lk., where
the MS. is now wanting. To the
fasting Lk. alone adds καὶ δεήσεις
ποιοῦνται: cf. Lk. xi. 1. For οὐ
νηστεύουσιν, 'are not fasting,' Lk.
has ἐσθίουσιν καὶ πίνουσιν, *i.e.* make
a practice of not fasting ; cf. xi. 18 f.

15. μὴ δύνανται κτλ.] Lk. μὴ
δύνασθε τ. υἱοὺς . . . ποιῆσαι νηστεῦ-
σαι ; In Mk. the thought expressed
by the question is repeated tauto-
logically by a negative statement,
which Mt., Lk. omit ; and Mt. con-
denses Mk.'s ἐν ᾧ and ὅσον χρόνον
into ἐφ' ὅσον [*sc.* χρόνον], which is
used with this meaning in 2 Pet.
i. 13 only, and with a different mean-

ἐφ’ ὅσον μετ’ αὐτῶν ἐστιν ὁ νυμφίος; ἐλεύσονται δὲ
ἡμέραι ὅταν ἀπαρθῇ ἀπ’ αὐτῶν ὁ νυμφίος, καὶ τότε νη-

ing in Mt. xxv. 40, 45 only; it does
not occur in the LXX. 'The sons of
the bridechamber' is a late Heb. expression for the wedding-guests =
בְּנֵי הַחֻפָּה; see *Tos. Berak.* ii. 10 (ed.
Zuckermandel, p. 4): 'the friends
of the bridegroom (cf. Jo. iii. 29) and
all the sons of the bridechamber,'
and instances in Jastrow, *Dict. Targ.*
s.v. חופה. The reading of D οἱ υἱ.
τ. νυμφίου, 𝕃 *filii sponsi*, is due to
a misunderstanding of the expression.
For idiomatic uses of υἱός cf. οἱ δύο
υἱοὶ τῆς πιότητος (Zech. iv. 14), οἱ
υἱοὶ τῆς ἄκρας (1 Mac. iv. 2), Mt.
viii. 12, xiii. 38, xxiii. 15, Mk. iii.
17, Lk. x. 6, xvi. 8, xx. 34, 36 ; see
Deissm. *Bible St.* 162 ff. νυμφών
recurs in bibl. Gk. only in xxii. 10,
Tob. vi. 14, 17 ; cf. *Acta Phil.* c. 29,
Heliod. vii. 8. There is, of course,
no reference here to the Messianic
feast of the future age (cf. xxii.
2); the Bridegroom is Jesus in His
human companionship with His
disciples. πενθεῖν (Mk., Lk. νησ-
τεύειν), which Mt. appears to use for
the sake of variety, though perhaps
influenced by the thought of the
Lord's death, is the mourning of
which fasting is one sign. For
νυμφίος cf. xxv. 1 etc., Jo. ii. 9,
iii. 29, Apoc. xviii. 23.

ἐλεύσονται δέ κτλ.] So Mk., but
with the tautological addition in the
singular ἐν ἐκείνῃ τῇ ἡμέρᾳ (Lk.
ἐν ἐκείναις ταῖς ἡμέραις), on which
see Jülicher (*Gleichnisreden*, ii. 183)
against H. Holtzm. and J. Weiss.
The vb. ἀπαίρειν, used here by the
three synn., is not found elsewhere
in the N.T.; the active intransitively (= נסע), 'to march, journey,'
is frequent in the LXX. and class.
Gk. (cf. μετῆρεν, xiii. 53, xix. 1);
transitively it occurs only in Ps.

lxxvii. [lxxviii.] 26 (MSS.), 52, of God
bringing the east wind, and leading
Israel like a flock (both = הִסִּיעַ),
and 1 Mac. vi. 33 of removing a
camp. The evidence of bibl. Gk.,
therefore, does not support the sense
of a *violent* removal. Some (*e.g.* J.
Weiss) think that the sentence, being
a definite prediction of the Lord's
death, is a later addition ; Wellh.
assigns the whole verse to a date when
the Christian Church wanted an
authoritative basis for her practice
of fasting. But even if the Lord
was thinking of a violent death,
which was not impossible, considering
the Baptist's arrest, and the growing
tension between Himself and the
religious authorities, He did not fore-
tell it to the disciples until xvi. 21, and
his hearers in the present case would
think only of the death which He
would undergo in the ordinary course
of nature, which to all appearance was
improbable for many years to come.
The Baptist, on the other hand, who
was the 'bridegroom' for his friends
and followers, was in prison, and
in imminent peril of death, and the
fasting of his disciples was therefore
natural. The verse perhaps formed
the basis of Jo. iii. 29.

16, 17. (Mk. ii. 21 f., Lk. v. 36–
39.) THE OLD AND THE NEW.

If these verses are in their true
context, they appear to mean, 'The
Baptist's *régime* of life for his disciples
is not to be entirely condemned, but
it is impossible for My disciples to
adhere to it, and at the same time
to live in accordance with their new
and deeper view of things.' But
though Mt. supplies a connecting
link with the preceding verses (δέ),
Mk. has none ; and Lk. separates it

16 στεύσουσιν.   οὐδεὶς δὲ ἐπιβάλλει ἐπίβλημα ῥάκους ἀγνάφου
ἐπὶ ἱματίῳ παλαιῷ· αἴρει γὰρ τὸ πλήρωμα αὐτοῦ ἀπὸ

by a fresh introduction : ἔλεγεν δὲ
καὶ παραβολὴν πρὸς αὐτοὺς ὅτι. The
passage has probably been drawn
from another context, and deals with
the whole Jewish system of religious
thought, as maintained under its
traditional forms.   Possibly it reflects 'arguments that Jesus had
first of all used with Himself' (King,
Ethics of Jesus, 117).   V. 16 (The
New Cloth) teaches that it is foolish
to attach mechanically to the Jewish
system any fragment of the new and
vigorous ethics or practice taught by
Jesus; the Jewish forms, though
threadbare, can still be useful; but
to patch them up is to ruin them.
The truth is illustrated in Rom. xiv.
13–23, 1 Cor. viii. 9–13. It does
not conflict with Mt. v. 17; the
worn-out coat is not the Mosaic
Law, but the system deduced from
it.   V. 17 (The New Wineskins)
goes further.   The new practice is
the outcome of the new spirit; and
it would be even more fatal to
attempt to force the Jewish forms to
receive the new spirit, for it would
immediately burst its bonds, and
thereby ruin itself as well as the
bonds.   Some forms it must have,
as wine must be put into a bottle,
but they must be forms of a new
kind, such as will expand with its
expansion.   'Free' thought, that
recognizes no authoritative control,
is as useless as spilt wine.   'It is
very striking that Jesus shews the
necessity of a new form, while in
actual fact He left everything in
this respect to His Church after His
death' (Wellhausen).   On the Lord's
use of illustrations in pairs see Oxf.
Stud. 195.
    16. ἐπίβλημα κτλ.]   'A patch

[consisting] of an uncarded strip';
commissuram panni rudis (𝔏).   ἐπίβλημα occurs in connexion with
dress in Is. iii. 22, Sym. Jos. ix.
5 [11], τὰ σανδάλια ἐπιβλήματα
ἔχοντες.   For ῥάκη, 'strips' of cloth,
cf. Jer. xlv. [xxxviii.] 11, Artemid.
27, Ox. Pap. i. 117. 14.   ἄγναφος is
'not cleaned' by carding or combing,
hence 'new, undressed'; the similar
ἄγναπτος occurs in Plut.   See M.-M.
Vocab. s.v.   In Lk. a further thought
is introduced ; the patch is not of undressed cloth, but is torn from a new
garment, and the result is 'he will
both tear the new, and the patch
which is [taken] from the new will
not harmonize with the old.'
    αἴρει γὰρ κτλ.]   'For [if he does]
its patch drags away from the
garment.'   The new strip is thought
of as sewn along the frayed edge of
the garment.   Mt. avoids Mk.'s εἰ δὲ
μή, producing an ellipse.   αὐτοῦ probably refers to the following ἱματίον,
but it is possible to treat it as
masculine, 'his patch.'   Mk. has
αἴρει τὸ πλήρωμα ἀπ' αὐτοῦ, adding
loosely as an explanation (perhaps a
late gloss) τὸ καινὸν τοῦ παλαιοῦ
'the new (patch) from the old
(garment).'   πλήρωμα can be rendered
'that which fills'; Lightfoot (Coloss.
255 ff.) is driven to a forced explanation by adhering to the passive sense
of 'completeness,' as the result of
πληροῦν ; see, however, J. Armitage
Robinson, Ephes. 255 ff.   But πλήρωμα may be a rendering of an Aram.
word from the root מלא, 'to fill'
(Wellh.) ; the same root is used in
Syr. for 'to mend,' and ܟܠܒ means
a 'cobbler.'   Thus ἐπίβλημα and
πλήρωμα are virtually the same, a
'patch' put on to fill a gap.

τοῦ ἱματίου, καὶ χεῖρον σχίσμα γίνεται. οὐδὲ βάλλουσιν 17
οἶνον νέον εἰς ἀσκοὺς παλαιούς· εἰ δὲ μήγε, ῥήγνυνται οἱ
ἀσκοί, καὶ ὁ οἶνος ἐκχεῖται καὶ οἱ ἀσκοὶ ἀπόλλυνται·
ἀλλὰ βάλλουσιν οἶνον νέον εἰς ἀσκοὺς καινούς, καὶ ἀμφότεροι συντηροῦνται.

Ταῦτα αὐτοῦ λαλοῦντος αὐτοῖς ἰδοὺ ἄρχων εἰς προσελ- 18

18 εις προσελθων] ℵᵇB 𝔏 a b c ff¹ vg 𝔖 [pesh ελθων αρχ. εις προσελθων] ; om
εις ℵ* 13 157 al ; εις ελθων KSVΔII minn.pl 𝔏 d f 𝔖 sin.hcl arm aeth go ;
εισελθων ℵᶜCDE al minn.pl ; τις [προσ]ελθων vel τις εισελθ. C³GLUΓ al [quidam
princeps veniens h k ; quid. pr. accessit et g¹ 𝔖 pal]

καὶ χεῖρον κτλ.] 'and a worse rent
is the result.' σχίσμα is literal, but
its metaphorical meaning is implied ;
cf. I Cor. xii. 25.

17. οὐδὲ βάλλουσιν κτλ.] Cf.
Anacr. 36, βάλλ' οἶνον ὦ παῖ ; and see
M.-M. Vocab. s.v. For οἶνος νέος, wine
recently made, cf. Is. xlix. 26, Sir. ix.
10 ; contrast καινός in Mt. xxvi. 29,
wine of a new kind, such as has not existed before. The ἀσκοί, on the other
hand, are not νέοι, but καινοί, fresh,
unused ; cf. Heb. viii. 8, xii. 24
(Westcott). The adjs., however, are
not strictly distinguished in late Gk.
παλαιοί and καινοί are both applied
to ἀσκοί in Jos. ix. 10 [4], 19 [13]. Cf.
the proverbial references to worn-out
ἀσκοί in Job xiii. 28 (LXX.), Ps. cxviii.
[cxix.] 83. The meaning of the skins
and the wine is discussed above ; it
introduces confusion to explain the
old skins as the Scribes and Pharisees,
the new as the disciples (Jer.). For
εἰ δὲ μήγε see vi. 1 note. On the
form ἐκχεῖται see Blass, § 17. Mk.'s
καὶ ὁ οἶνος ἀπόλλυται καὶ οἱ ἀσκοί
is expanded in Mt., Lk. with two
verbs ; and to his terse ἀλλ' οἶνον
νέον εἰς ἀσκοὺς καινούς Mt. adds
βάλλουσιν, Lk. βλητέον. In Mt.
the thought is emphasized by the
addition of the last three words. In
Lk. an additional saying (v. 39) from
another context is added in many

MSS., entirely out of harmony with
the rest of the passage.

18–26. (Mk. v. 21–43, Lk. viii.
40–56.) HEALING OF A CHILD, AND
OF A WOMAN IN THE STREET.

After making use of Mk. ii. 1–22,
Mt. now picks up the other Marcan
thread, which he adopted in viii. 18
(see note), 23–34, postponing for later
use (a) conflicts with the Pharisees
(Mk. ii. 23–iii. 6, 20–30), and an
accompanying incident (vv. 31–35),
(b) a series of parables (Mk. iv. 1–34),
(c) the call of the Twelve and their
names (Mk. iii. 13–19), and omitting
Mk. iii. 7–12. For (a), (b), and (c)
see notes on xii. 1, xiii. 1, and x. 1.

18. ταῦτα . . . αὐτοῖς] An
editorial setting for the following
incident. In Mk., Lk. Jesus returned
across the lake, to find a crowd waiting for Him ; Mt. has already related
the return in v. 1.

ἰδοὺ ἄρχων κτλ.] Mk., Lk. give
his name Jairus, and relate that
he fell down at the feet of Jesus.
Mt. greatly abbreviates Mk.'s narrative throughout. The reading εἶς
προσελθών best accounts fcr the v.ll.,
some of which seem to have arisen
from εἶς being misread as εἰς. On
εἶς = τις see viii. 19 ; and on the
impf. προσεκύνει see Blass, § 57. 4.
ἄρχων (Mk. ἀρχισυνάγωγος, Lk.
ἄρχων τῆς συναγωγῆς) = רֹאשׁ הַכְּנֶסֶת,

θὼν προσεκύνει αὐτῷ λέγων ὅτι Ἡ θυγάτηρ μου ἄρτι ἐτε-
λεύτησεν· ἀλλὰ ἐλθὼν ἐπίθες τὴν χεῖρά σου ἐπ᾽ αὐτήν, καὶ
19 ζήσεται. καὶ ἐγερθεὶς ὁ Ἰησοῦς ἠκολούθει αὐτῷ καὶ οἱ
20 μαθηταὶ αὐτοῦ. Καὶ ἰδοὺ γυνὴ αἱμορροοῦσα δώδεκα ἔτη
προσελθοῦσα ὄπισθεν ἥψατο τοῦ κρασπέδου τοῦ ἱματίου
21 αὐτοῦ· ἔλεγεν γὰρ ἐν ἑαυτῇ Ἐὰν μόνον ἅψωμαι τοῦ ἱμα-

the supervisor of the synagogue
worship; cf. Lk. xiii. 14, Ac. xiii.
15 (plur.), xiv. 2 (D), xviii. 8, 17;
see Schürer, HJP. II. ii. 63 ff. It
had a wider meaning, however, than
ἀρχισυνάγωγος: it is used for a
chief Pharisee (Lk. xiv. 1), any
Jewish religious leader (Jo. iii. 1,
vii. 26), or (plur.) for high priests
(Ac. iv. 5); and, like the Rabb.
ארכונטס, ארכונא (Dalman, Gr. 148), it
seems to denote a rich or important
man (Lk. xviii. 18; see Mt. xix. 16
note). And see M.-M. Vocab. s.v.
ἡ θυγάτηρ μου κτλ.] Mk. τὸ
θυγάτριόν μου, giving her age as 12
years (v. 42); Lk. θυγάτηρ μονογενής
(cf. Lk. vii. 12, ix. 38; elsewhere in
the N.T. the adj. is used only of the
Son of God). Mt. omits the message
sent later to the ruler that the child
was dead (Mk. v. 35), but anticipates
it by giving his words as ἄρτι ἐτελεύτησεν (for Mk.'s ἐσχάτως ἔχει, in
extremis est); Lk. has ἀπέθνησκεν,
'was dying.'
ἀλλὰ ἐλθών κτλ.] This avoids
Mk.'s elliptical ἵνα [i.e. αἰτέω ἵνα]
ἐλθ. ἐπιθῇς. The ruler may have
known by report, or had himself
seen, that the Lord was wont to heal
by the imposition of hands. καὶ
ζήσεται takes the place of Mk.'s
redundant ἵνα σωθῇ καὶ ζήσῃ, but
in Mt. the verb means 'come to life,'
in Mk. 'continue to live.' On the
consec. καί see Blass, § 77. 6.
19. καὶ ἐγερθεὶς κτλ.] The participle is added by Mt. only (cf. i. 24
note), and also the mention of the
disciples at this point, instead of (as

in Mk., Lk.) later in the narrative.
Mk., Lk. relate that a crowd accom-
panied Jesus, and pressed round Him
(Mk. συνέθλιβον, Lk. συνέπνιγον).

20. καὶ ἰδοὺ κτλ.] In vv. 20–22
Mt. relates in the briefest language
the cure of the woman, which Mk.,
Lk. record at some length. She was
αἱμορροοῦσα: Mk., Lk. οὖσα ἐν
ῥύσει αἵματος. She had suffered for
12 years, i.e. since Jairus' daughter
was born (Mk. v. 42). Mk., and in
a modified form Lk., speak of the
failure of physicians to cure her.
She could not approach openly, but
came behind (ἐν τῷ ὄχλῳ Mk.),
because she was ceremonially unclean,
and contact with her was pollution.
While Mk. says that she touched
His garment, Mt., Lk. mention the
sacred part of it, τὸ κράσπεδον, which
Mk.'s Roman readers would not have
understood. This was the corner
(Zech. viii. 23), or the tassel (צִיצִת,
Num. xv. 38 f., Dt. xxii. 12) which
hung from it, Vulg. fimbria; see
HDB. art. 'Fringes,' and Swete, ad
loc. Marc.; cf. Mt. xiv. 36, xxiii. 5.
The word passed into Aram. as
כְּרוֹסְפַד (Targ.Onk Num. l.c.).

21. ἔλεγεν γὰρ κτλ.] After her
recovery she would joyfully relate
to many her inward thoughts. Lk.
omits the verse. For μόνον instead
of Mk.'s κἂν cf. xiv. 36 with Mk. vi.
56. Except in this narrative σώζειν
is not used by Mt. in this sense, nor
in the LXX.; but cf. Mk. v. 23, vi.
56, x. 52, Lk. viii. 36, xvii. 19, Jo.
xi. 12, Ac. xiv. 9.

τίου αὐτοῦ σωθήσομαι. ὁ δὲ Ἰησοῦς στραφεὶς καὶ ἰδὼν 22
αὐτὴν εἶπεν Θάρσει, θύγατερ· ἡ πίστις σου σέσωκέν
σε. καὶ ἐσώθη ἡ γυνὴ ἀπὸ τῆς ὥρας ἐκείνης. Καὶ ἐλθὼν ὁ 23
Ἰησοῦς εἰς τὴν οἰκίαν τοῦ ἄρχοντος καὶ ἰδὼν τοὺς αὐλητὰς
καὶ τὸν ὄχλον θορυβούμενον ἔλεγεν Ἀναχωρεῖτε, οὐ γὰρ 24

22 Ιησους om אּ*D 𝔏 a b c k q 𝔖 sin

22. ὁ δὲ Ἰησοῦς κτλ.] Mt. omits
the account in Mk., Lk. of the Lord's
question (see viii. 29 note) τίς μου
ἥψατο τῶν ἱματίων; (Lk. τίς ὁ ἁψά-
μενός μου;) asked because He realized
that δύναμις had gone forth from
Him; also the answer of the disciples
(Lk., Peter), and the woman's confession. θαρσεῖ is added by Mt. only,
as in v. 2. The disease was probably,
like that of the paralytic, due to sin;
but faith rendered the sinner a τέκνον
in the one case, a θυγάτηρ in the
other. The vocative should perhaps
be spelt θυγάτηρ in all three gospels,
as in Jo. xii. 15, Ruth ii. 2, 22;
cf. θυγατῆρος, Sir. xxxvi. 26 (א).
For ἡ πίστις σ. σέσωκ. σε (so Mk., Lk.)
cf. Mk. x. 52, Lk. xvii. 19. On the
operation of faith see viii. 10 note;
it was not the magic of the tassel
which restored her.

καὶ ἐσώθη κτλ.] Mt. alone adds
ἀπὸ τ. ὥρας ἐκ., emphasizing the
immediacy and permanence of the
cure (as in xv. 28, xvii. 18; cf. viii.
13), but they are implied in Mk.:
'go (ὕπαγε, cf. Jas. ii. 16) into peace
and be sound from thy scourge,' and
Lk.: 'go (πορεύου) into peace.' On
the legends connected with the
woman see Swete; her name is said
to have been Βερονίκη or Veronica.

23. καὶ ἐλθὼν κτλ.] Mt. omits
all that is not essential to the main
fact. Mk. relates that a message
came to the ruler that he was not to
trouble the Rabbi further, because
the child was dead; Jesus, dis-
regarding (παρακούσας, cf. Mt. xviii.

17) what was being said, encouraged
the ruler, and then allowed only
Peter, James, and John to accompany
Him to the house. Lk.'s narrative
is similar, but he has ἀκούσας for
παρακούσας, and places the choice
of Peter, James, and John after the
arrival at the house; they only, with
the child's parents (whom Mk.
mentions later), were admitted to
the room.

καὶ ἰδών κτλ.] Mt. alone, from
a knowledge of Jewish customs,
mentions the flute-players, of whom
there were probably several, the
house being that of an important
person; cf. Jos. BJ. III. ix. 5,
Kethub. iv. 4: at the burial of a
wife, 'R. Judah says, Even a poor
man in Israel will not have less than
two flute-players and one waiting-
woman.' Both Mt. and Mk. imply
that the hired mourners were not in
the bedroom; they were probably
congregated in the courtyard, where
Jesus addressed them, and after their
dismissal entered (v. 25) ὅπου ἦν τὸ
παιδίον (Mk. v. 40).

24. ἀναχωρεῖτε κτλ.] On ἀναχωρεῖν see ii. 12. The command of
a Master takes the place of Mk.'s
τί θορυβεῖσθε καὶ κλαίετε (Lk. μὴ
κλαίετε). κοράσιον, a colloquial
term of later Gk., occurs in Arrian
and Lucian, and in the LXX., especially
Ruth and Esther (= נַעֲרָה); elsewhere
in the N.T. it is used only of the
daughter of Herodias (xiv. 11, Mk.
vi. 28). Lk.'s account clearly relates
a real raising from the dead, since

ἀπέθανεν τὸ κοράσιον ἀλλὰ καθεύδει· καὶ κατεγέλων αὐτοῦ.
25 ὅτε δὲ ἐξεβλήθη ὁ ὄχλος, εἰσελθὼν ἐκράτησεν τῆς χειρὸς
26 αὐτῆς, καὶ ἠγέρθη τὸ κοράσιον. Καὶ ἐξῆλθεν ἡ φήμη
27 αὕτη εἰς ὅλην τὴν γῆν ἐκείνην.   Καὶ παράγοντι

he adds 'knowing that she was dead' after 'and they laughed at Him' in *v.* 53, and 'her spirit returned' in *v.* 55 (cf. ·ἀφῆκεν τὸ πνεῦμα Mt. xxvii. 50). But, whatever Mt. and Mk. may themselves have thought of the incident, there is not a word in their narratives to shew that the Lord's statement 'the maiden [Mk. the child] is not dead but sleepeth' was not literally true. καθεύδειν is, indeed, equivalent to τεθνηκέναι in Dan. xii. 2 (LXX., Theod.), 1 Thes. v. 10 (cf. κοιμᾶσθαι Jo. xi. 11 ff.); but here the verbs are not synonymous but contrasted. If it was literally true, those who sent the message to the ruler (Mk. *v.* 35) were mistaken in thinking that the child was dead. Mt. and Mk. would have united in agreeing that the Lord *could* raise one who had died (cf. xi. 5); only Lk. records explicitly that He actually did so in the present instance.

25. ὅτε δὲ ἐξεβλήθη κτλ.] Mk. αὐτὸς δὲ ἐκβαλὼν πάντας. The verb need not imply forcible action (see viii. 12 note); the crowd was 'dismissed' from the courtyard; cf. Ac. ix. 40. All the synn. record the hand-grasp, which was part of the means of restoration; but Mt. omits, probably only for the sake of brevity, the Aram. words of command ταλιθὰ κούμ [or κούμι] given by Mk., with their interpretation τὸ κοράσιον, σοὶ λέγω, ἔγειρε (Lk. ἡ παῖς ἔγειρε).

καὶ ἠγέρθη τὸ κ.] The pass. of ἐγείρειν in Mt. means 13 times 'to rise from a lying or sitting posture,' 12 times 'to rise from the dead.' ἀνέστη (Mk., Lk. here) Mt. uses in the former sense in ix. 9, xxvi. 62,

in the latter it is a *v.l.* in xvii. 9 only. Mk. adds that 'she walked about (περιεπάτει), for she was twelve years old,' and that they (Lk. 'her parents') were amazed; Lk. records here, Mk. in the next verse, that Jesus ordered food to be given her.

26. καὶ ἐξῆλθεν κτλ.] φήμη (class.) recurs in bibl. Gk. only in Lk. iv. 14, Prov. xvi. 2 [xv. 30], 2 Mac. iv. 39, 3 M. iii. 2, 4 M. iv. 22; cf. the verb in *v.* 31 below. The verse takes the place of Mk.'s statement 'and He enjoined them greatly (διεστείλατο αὐτοῖς πολλά) that no one should know this'; Lk. 'but He exhorted (παρήγγειλεν) them to tell no one what had happened.' For similar injunctions of silence, and their purpose, see viii. 4 note. The present miracle obviously could not be permanently concealed, because the restored child would be seen by the inhabitants, and the report would naturally spread. τὴν γῆν ἐκείνην is the district round Capharnaum; for this narrow use of γῆ (= χώρα) cf. *v.* 31, ii. 6, iv. 15, x. 15, xi. 24; it is not found in Mk., Lk.

27–31. Two Blind Men healed.

The passage is peculiar to Mt., and may be a duplicate of the incident in xx. 29–34. See Add. note below.

27. καὶ παράγοντι κτλ.] The next verse suggests that the miracle is placed in Capharnaum. Mt. has δύο τυφλοί in xx. 30 and δύο δαιμονιζόμενοι in viii. 28; in both places Mk., Lk. speak only of one sufferer. υἱὲ Δαυείδ is used by the blind men in xx. 30 (Mk., Lk.); elsewhere the Lord is addressed by the title in Mt.

ἐκεῖθεν τῷ Ἰησοῦ ἠκολούθησαν δύο τυφλοὶ κράζοντες
καὶ λέγοντες Ἐλέησον ἡμᾶς, υἱὲ Δαυείδ. ἐλθόντι δὲ 28
εἰς τὴν οἰκίαν προσῆλθαν αὐτῷ οἱ τυφλοί, καὶ λέγει αὐτοῖς
ὁ Ἰησοῦς Πιστεύετε ὅτι δύναμαι τοῦτο ποιῆσαι; λέγουσιν
αὐτῷ Ναί, κύριε. τότε ἥψατο τῶν ὀφθαλμῶν αὐτῶν λέγων 29
Κατὰ τὴν πίστιν ὑμῶν γενηθήτω ὑμῖν. καὶ ἠνεῴχθησαν 30
αὐτῶν οἱ ὀφθαλμοί. Καὶ ἐνεβριμήθη αὐτοῖς ὁ Ἰησοῦς
λέγων Ὁρᾶτε μηδεὶς γινωσκέτω· οἱ δὲ ἐξελθόντες διεφήμι- 31

30 ενεβριμηθη] ℵ B* 1 22 118 ; ενεβριμησατο B² etc minn.caet

only (xv. 22, xxi. 9, 15; cf. i. 1,
xii. 23, who never misses an opportunity of emphasizing His Messiahship). Popular Messianic hopes
centred on a Davidic king, though
'Son of David' as a title of the
Messiah is not found earlier than
Pss. Sol. xvii. 23. After the 1st
cent. A.D. it became frequent (Dalman,
Words, 316 ff.). Here, as in xx. 30,
it might possibly be only a form of
polite address, though the idea that
Jesus was possibly the Messiah may
have been already in the air, as it
had recently been with regard to the
Baptist (see Lk. iii. 15). For the
spelling Δαυείδ see i. 6.

28. ἐλθόντι δέ κτλ.] By 'the
house' is probably meant the Lord's
own house in Capharnaum; see *v.*
10 note. As in xv. 23 Mt. relates
that He at first disregarded the
request. The question πιστεύετε
κτλ. did not merely seek information,
but was a spur to their faith.

29. τότε ἥψατο κτλ.] So in xx.
34, ἥψ. τ. ὀμμάτων αὐτ. The best
commentary on κατὰ τὴν πίστιν
κτλ. is xiii. 58 (Mk. vi. 5 f.); see viii.
10 note.

30. καὶ ἠνεῴχθησαν κτλ.] A
Hebraic expression for the recovery
of sight; cf. Is. xxxv. 5, xlii. 7 (Ac.
xxvi. 17), 4 Regn. vi. 17; in the
N.T. it recurs only in xx. 33, and
Jo. ix. (7 times), x. 21.

καὶ ἐνεβριμήθη κτλ.] 'vehemently
charged them.' The middle is used
(as in some other verbs expressive of
emotion, Blass, § 20. 1) in Mk. i. 43,
xiv. 5, Jo. xi. 33; and ἐνεβριμήσατο
is possibly the true reading here.
The word βριμᾶσθαι, akin to βρέμω,
fremo, denotes lit. to 'snort with
indignation' (Aristoph. *Eq.* 855, Xen.
Cyr. iv. 5. 9); the compound ἐμβριμ. is
used of the snorting of horses (Aesch.
Theb. 461), and of the raging or
fuming of Brimo (Luc. *Necyom.* 20).
In the O.T. the verb and the subst.
ἐμβρίμημα and -μησις occur in the
LXX. (Dan. xi. 30, Lam. ii. 6), and
other Gk. translations, either for זעם,
'to be indignant' (11 times), or נער,
'to rebuke' (twice). But in none
of the N.T. passages is there any
cause for indignation or rebuke (𝔏
comminatus est, Wicl. 'threatened').
The word describes rather a rush of
deep feeling which in the synoptic
passages shewed itself in a vehement
injunction, and in Jo. xi. 33 in look
and manner. See Warfield, 'On
the emotional life of our Lord,'
Princeton Bibl. and Theol. Stud. On
the Lord's injunctions of silence see
viii. 4. On ὁρᾶτε with another imperative (cf. xxiv. 6) see Blass, § 79. 4.

31. οἱ δὲ ἐξελθόντες κτλ.] The
vehement command in Mk. i. 44 was
met with the same disobedience;
διαφημίζειν (*diffamare*) also is there

32 σαν αὐτὸν ἐν ὅλῃ τῇ γῇ ἐκείνῃ.   Αὐτῶν δὲ ἐξερ-
33 χομένων ἰδοὺ προσήνεγκαν αὐτῷ κωφὸν δαιμονιζόμενον· καὶ
ἐκβληθέντος τοῦ δαιμονίου ἐλάλησεν ὁ κωφός. καὶ ἐθαύμασαν οἱ ὄχλοι λέγοντες Οὐδέποτε ἐφάνη οὕτως ἐν τῷ
34 Ἰσραήλ. οἱ δὲ Φαρισαῖοι ἔλεγον Ἐν τῷ ἄρχοντι τῶν
δαιμονίων ἐκβάλλει τὰ δαιμόνια.

32 κωφον] אB 𝔖 pesh me sah aeth ; pr ανθρωπον CDE al 𝔏 omn 𝔖 sin['mutum
quemdam'].hcl.pal   34 om vers. D 𝔏 a k 𝔖 sin

used (elsewhere Mt. xxviii. 15 only),
a late word, not found in the LXX.
In Mk. the object is τὸν λόγον, here
it is Jesus Himself. On γῆ = χώρα
see v. 26.

32, 33. A DUMB DEMONIAC
HEALED.

The passage is peculiar to Mt.,
and may be a duplicate of the
incident in xii. 22 f.; cf. Lk. xi. 14.
See Add. note below.

32. αὐτῶν δέ κτλ.] Jesus and
His disciples may be meant, but
more probably the two blind men;
as they emerged from the house
another patient.was brought. προσήνεγκαν is impersonal, more Aram.
κωφός, lit. 'blunt,' 'dull,' can be
applied to the faculty either of
speaking (as here, xii. 22, Lk. xi. 14)

or of hearing (xi. 5, Mk. vii. 32, 37,
ix. 25); 'moris est scripturarum
κωφόν indifferenter vel mutum vel
surdum dicere' (Jer.). The insertion
of ἄνθρωπον (see xi. 19 note) before
κωφόν has strong support.

33. καὶ ἐθαύμασαν κτλ.] If the
miracle was performed in the house,
the ὄχλοι did not witness it, but
they would soon hear of it. οὐδέποτε
κτλ. : cf. Mk. ii. 12. For the use
of οὕτως as a quasi-subject cf. Jud.
xix. 30 (A), οὔτε ἐγενήθη οὔτε ὤφθη
οὕτως.

34. οἱ δέ κτλ.] The verse was
probably a scribal insertion due to
xii. 24, Lk. xi. 15, where it follows
the cure of the dumb demoniac;
possibly it was added here to form
an antecedent to x. 25.

Additional Notes on ix. 27–33.

(1) Vv. 27–31. Mk. twice relates the cure of a blind man (viii. 22–26,
x. 46–52); Mt. twice relates the cure of two blind men (here, xx. 29–34).
The second instances in Mt. and Mk. are parallels, but the present passage
is widely different from Mk. viii. 22–26, and cannot be derived from it,
although both of Mt.'s narratives appear to contain a reminiscence of Mk.
viii. 22–26 in the touching of the eyes. Mt. may have derived it from an
unknown source, but more probably it is compiled by a later hand from xx.
29–34 and Mk. x. 46–52, with i. 43–45. Notice the following points of
similarity to ch. xx. : (1) δύο τυφλοί. (2) ἐλέησον ἡμᾶς υἱὲ Δαυείδ. The
title occurs also in Mk. x., where it is not, as in Mt., a characteristic of the
evangelist. (3) The Lord asked them a question as a spur to their faith
(note ποιῆσαι and ποιήσω). (4) He touched their eyes. (5) He spoke of
their faith (Mk.; not Mt. in ch. xx.) (6) 'Their eyes were opened' (see
note on v. 30 above); xx. 33 'that our eyes may be opened.' Thus all the

Καὶ περιῆγεν ὁ Ἰησοῦς τὰς πόλεις πάσας καὶ τὰς κώμας, 35
διδάσκων ἐν ταῖς συναγωγαῖς αὐτῶν καὶ κηρύσσων τὸ εὐαγγέλιον τῆς βασιλείας καὶ θεραπεύων πᾶσαν νόσον καὶ
πᾶσαν μαλακίαν.   Ἰδὼν δὲ τοὺς ὄχλους ἐσπλαγ- 36
χνίσθη περὶ αὐτῶν ὅτι ἦσαν ἐσκυλμένοι καὶ ἐριμμένοι

essential points in the two accounts are the same.   But the remainder of
the narrative seems to be due to Mk. i. 43-45 ; note the uncommon words
ἐμβριμᾶσθαι and διαφημίζειν, and the fact that the Lord's injunction was
disobeyed, which are the very points that Mt. omits in viii. 2-4.

(2) *Vv.* 32, 33 are closely similar to Lk. xi. 14.   Mt. (xii. 22 f.) has
another short narrative of the healing of a demoniac who was blind and dumb,
in which, as in the other two, the astonishment of the crowds is recorded,
and which is inserted, as Lk. *l.c.*, as a substitute for Mk. iii. 20 f. (an
incident which both evangelists probably shrank from recording), to form
a suitable introduction to the discourse on Beelzebul.   For this purpose Lk.
preferred the first of Mt.'s two stories, which were very possibly doublets
from different sources, because it spoke more distinctly of the casting out
of the demon ; and he either adapted it, or assimilated it to some short
narrative known to him from another source.

The reason for Mt.'s insertion of the two miracles after ix. 18-26 was
probably to complete a triplet (the recovery gained secretly by the woman
in the street not being reckoned as a miracle performed by Jesus).   Each of
the three narratives ends with a statement of the growing fame which the
miracles brought to the Lord, by which the way was prepared for the work
of the apostles dealt with in the next section.   Wellhausen and H. J.
Holtzmann suggest that *vv.* 27-33 were added to complete the series of
miracles in xi. 5.   But the paralytic, and the κωφός who recovers *speech* in
ch. ix., scarcely correspond with the χωλοὶ περιπατοῦσιν and κωφοὶ ἀκούουσιν
of xi. 5.

35-x. 4. PRELUDE TO THE MIS-
SION OF THE TWELVE.

Mt. (*v.* 26) left Mk. at v. 43.   He
does not use Mk. vi. 1-6 a till xiii.
53-58, but continues with Mk. vi.
6 b, 7, which he expands in *v.* 35
and x. 1, adding other material in
vv. 36-38, x. 2-4.

35. καὶ περιῆγεν κτλ.]   The expansion of Mk. vi. 6 b takes the
form of a *résumé* of the Lord's work.
As far as κώμας it is based on Mk.'s
καὶ περιῆγεν τὰς κώμας κύκλῳ διδάσκων, after which it is identical
with Mt. iv. 23, except for the
omission of ἐν τῷ λαῷ (see notes
there).

36. ἰδὼν δέ κτλ.]   The wording
is influenced by that of Mk. vi. 34,
of which Mt. uses only a part in the
corresponding place, xiv. 14.

The constr. σπλαγχνίζεσθαι περί
τινος does not occur elsewhere (see
Swete).   In the N.T. the verb is
confined to the synn. ; cf. Prov. xvii.
5 (A), 2 Mac. vi. 8, Sym. 1 Regn.
xxiii. 21 and Ez. xxiv. 21, *Test. Zeb.*
4, 6, 7.

ἐσκυλμένοι καὶ ἐριμμένοι]   Not
in Mk. ; *vexati et jacentes* (Vulg.),
vex. et projecti (𝕷 vet.).   σκύλλειν,
originally to 'flay' or 'mangle'
(Aesch. *Pers.* 577), came to mean
'harass' or 'annoy' (Mk. v. 35, Lk.

37 ὡσεὶ πρόβατα μὴ ἔχοντα ποιμένα. τότε λέγει τοῖς μαθηταῖς
αὐτοῦ Ὁ μὲν θερισμὸς πολύς, οἱ δὲ ἐργάται ὀλίγοι·
38 δεήθητε οὖν τοῦ κυρίου τοῦ θερισμοῦ ὅπως ἐκβάλῃ ἐργά-
X. ι τας εἰς τὸν θερισμὸν αὐτοῦ. Καὶ προσκαλεσάμενος τοὺς

vii. 6, viii. 49); so in *Ox. Pap.* 295
(A.D. 35), *Tebt.* 421. Allen gives
other meanings in the papyri. For
the subst. σκυλμός cf. 3 Mac. iii. 25,
vii. 5; it also has a variety of
meanings in the papyri. ἐριμμένοι
can hardly mean 'scattered abroad'
(Tynd., Cranm., A.V.), nor 'mentally
dejected' (Allen), but 'cast down,'
wounded or dead. Both participles
refer to the people *as sheep*, mis-
handled and lying helpless. They
form a comment on ἀπολωλότα
(x. 6), and describe metaphorically
the grievous state of unreadiness
for the Last Day into which the
Jews had fallen from want of
spiritual guidance.

ὡσεί κτλ.] An echo of such
passages as Num. xxvii. 17, 3 Regn.
xxii. 17, 2 Chron. xviii. 16, Judith
xi. 19.

37, 38. ὁ μὲν θερισμός κτλ.] In
Lk. x. 2 this saying occurs at the
beginning of the Charge to the
Seventy (see note before x. 5 below).
Palestine was like a field of ripe
corn ready for reaping (cf. Jo. iv.
35); the masses were longing so
eagerly for the Messiah that they
were ripe for receiving the tidings
that the Kingdom was at hand, and
could be gathered into the company
of the Lord's disciples if only there
were enough preachers. The simile
is quite different from that in xiii.
39, Mk. iv. 29. For θερισμός,
a rare and somewhat late word
(frequent in LXX.) cf. also Jo. *l.c.*,
Apoc. xiv. 15. It is possible that
the saying belongs to a somewhat
earlier stage in the ministry (J.
Weiss): Mt. does not include it in

the mission Charge, but introduces
it (τότε λέγει τ. μαθ. αὐτ.) as a
separate saying from the preceding,
and the change of metaphor from
sheep to corn is sudden. If the
Lord said it to some of the disciples
soon after their call, the present
mission of the Twelve was an answer
to the prayer which He enjoined.
On ἐκβάλῃ see viii. 12. ἐργάτης
(cf. x. 10), common in the N.T.,
occurs in the LXX. only in Wisd. xvii.
17, Sir. xix. 1, xl. 18, 1 Mac. iii. 6.

x. 1. καὶ προσκαλεσάμενος κτλ.]
The Lord's personal authority, which
expected obedience, made an inefface-
able impression upon the disciples;
cf. xv. 32, xx. 25; He also 'summoned' the multitude (xv. 10), a
child (xviii. 2), and even the Scribes
(Mk. iii. 23). τοὺς δώδεκα as a
definite body are here abruptly
mentioned for the first time; in
basing this verse on Mk. vi. 7 a, Mt.
assumes the previous selection of the
Twelve (Mk. iii. 14), and transfers
their names to this place from Mk.
iii. 16–19. Besides *vv.* 2, 5, xi. 1,
Mt. speaks of them as 'the Twelve'
in xx. 17, xxvi. 14, 20, 47; and in
xix. 28 it is implied that their
number was purposely chosen to
correspond with that of the tribes
of which Israel was still ideally
composed (Ac. xxvi. 7); so Barn.
viii. 3, οἷς ἔδωκεν τοῦ εὐαγγελίου
τὴν ἐξουσίαν, οὖσιν δεκαδύο εἰς
μαρτύριον τῶν φυλῶν. Mt., Lk.
omit Mk.'s καὶ ἤρξατο αὐτοὺς ἀπο-
στέλλειν δύο δύο; but Mt. seems
to imply the fact by placing the
names in pairs, and Lk. found it in
the source from which he drew x. 1.

δώδεκα μαθητὰς αὐτοῦ ἔδωκεν αὐτοῖς ἐξουσίαν πνευμάτων
ἀκαθάρτων ὥστε ἐκβάλλειν αὐτὰ καὶ θεραπεύειν πᾶσαν
νόσον καὶ πᾶσαν μαλακίαν.   Τῶν δὲ δώδεκα ἀποστόλων 2
τὰ ὀνόματά ἐστιν ταῦτα· πρῶτος Σίμων ὁ λεγόμενος
Πέτρος καὶ 'Ανδρέας ὁ ἀδελφὸς αὐτοῦ καὶ 'Ιάκωβος ὁ
τοῦ Ζεβεδαίου καὶ 'Ιωάνης ὁ ἀδελφὸς αὐτοῦ, Φίλιππος 3

ἔδωκεν αὐτοῖς κτλ.] For ἐξουσία
with gen. of the obj. cf. Dan. v. 4
(LXX.), τὸν θεὸν ... τὸν ἔχοντα τὴν
ἐξουσίαν τοῦ πνεύματος αὐτῶν. Lk.
has ἐπί with acc. (see Swete on Mk.
vi. 7). πνεῦμα ἀκάθαρτον (Mk.¹¹,
Lk.⁶, Ac.²) recurs in Mt. in xii. 43
only; and cf. Apoc. xvi. 13, xviii. 2.
It has its origin in O.T. ideas; see
Zech. xiii. 2 (= רוּחַ הַטֻּמְאָה, 'the
spirit of uncleanness'); cf. πν. ψευδές
(3 Regn. xxii. 22 f.), πν. πονηρόν
(Jud. ix. 23, 1 Regn. xvi. 14 ff., 23);
see also *Test. Benj.* 2, καὶ τὰ ἀκάθαρτα
πνεύματα φεύξονται ἀφ' ὑμῶν, and
Test. Iss. vii. 7. Mt. alone explains
the nature of the ἐξουσία by adding
ὥστε ἐκβάλλειν αὐτά: in the remaining words πᾶσαν κτλ. (which
are also part of the ἐξουσία, though
the νόσοι and μαλακίαι are probably
not thought of as due to the unclean
spirits) he imitates iv. 23, ix. 35;
Lk. has καὶ νόσους θεραπεύειν. The
disciples' work was to be that of
their Master, with an authority
delegated, as His own was from the
Father (vii. 29).

2–4. (Mk. iii. 16–19, Lk. vi. 14–
16.) THE NAMES OF THE TWELVE.

2. τῶν δὲ δώδεκα κτλ.] Mk. has
καὶ ἐποίησεν τοὺς δώδεκα, since he
places the list in connexion with
their first appointment. ἀπόστολος,
a title conferred by Jesus Himself
(Mk. iii. 14, Lk. vi. 13), occurs frequently in Lk., Ac., but not again
in Mt.; Mk. has it also in vi. 30,
Jo. only in xiii. 16 (not as a title;
but cf. xvii. 18). In the O.T. it

stands for שָׁלִיַּ, 3 Regn. xiv. 6 (A,
Aq.), and צִירִים, 'ambassadors,' Is.
xviii. 2 (Sym.).

πρῶτος Σίμων κτλ.] As the name
stands first on the list, πρῶτος would
be superfluous if it did not mean
'first and foremost' (cf. Jam. iii. 17),
a position which was confirmed, if
not won, at Caesarea Philippi (Mt.
xvi. 17 ff.). His prominence in Mt.
is natural in a Gospel for Jewish
Christians; cf. xiv. 28–31, xv. 15,
xvi. 17 ff., xvii. 24–27, xviii. 21.
This prominence must have been
recognized earlier than the time of
the evangelist. There is absolutely
no evidence that it implied hostility
towards S. Paul. ὁ λεγ. Πέτρος is
a reference to the fact stated by Mk.,
καὶ ἐπέθηκεν ὄνομα τῷ Σ. Πέτρον
(Lk. ὃν καὶ ὠνόμασεν Π.). Σίμων
is a graecized form of Συμεών
(שִׁמְעוֹן); cf. Ac. xv. 14, 2 Pet. i. 1
(*v.l.*); both occur in 1 Mac. ii. 1, 3.
'Ανδρέας his brother, and Φίλιππος,
had pure Gk. names. Bethsaida, to
which all three are said originally
to have belonged (Jo. i. 44), was a
Hellenistic town. The names being
placed in pairs, Andrew follows his
brother (as in Lk.); it was probably
thought that the Lord was likely
to have sent out brothers together.
In Mk., Andrew comes fourth, after
the sons of Zebedee, the three most
trusted disciples being named first.
Mt., Lk. omit Mk.'s parenthesis
about the sons of Zebedee, 'and He
attached to them a name Boanerges
which is Sons of Thunder' (see
Swete).

καὶ Βαρθολομαῖος, Θωμᾶς καὶ Μαθθαῖος ὁ τελώνης, Ἰάκω-
4 βος ὁ τοῦ Ἀλφαίου καὶ Θαδδαῖος, Σίμων ὁ Καναναῖος καὶ

3 Θαδδαιος] אB 17 124 𝕷 c ff¹ g² l vg me sah ; Λεββαιος D 122 𝕷 k codd.ap.
Aug Or ; Λεβ. ο επικληθεις Θαδ. C² E al 𝕷 f 𝔖 pesh.hcl.pal arm aeth ; Θαδ. ο
επικλ. Λεβ. 13 146 ; Judas Zelotes 𝕷 a b g¹ h q ; Judas son of James 𝔖 sin [post
Simon the C.]

3. Βαρθολομαῖος is 'son of Talmai' or 'Tolomai' (not Ptolemaeus, which would require τ for θ). Θωμᾶς is 'Twin,' cf. Jo. xi. 16, xx. 24, xxi. 2. On Μαθθαῖος see ix. 9. The three names are Aramaic. Mk. transposes the two latter. Mt. adds ὁ τελώνης (see on v. 46), identifying the apostle with the Matthew of ix. 9. ὁ τοῦ Ἀλφαίου (see on xxvii. 56) distinguishes this James from the son of Zebedee. In Mk. ii. 14 Levi is called the son of Alphaeus, but this A. was not necessarily the father of James. On the Aram. form Ḥalphai see Lightfoot, Galat. 267 n. For further notes on these names see Swete. Θαδδαῖος : this is probably the true reading in Mt. and Lk. ; in both occurs a variant Λεββαῖος, which appears to be derived from the Heb. לב, 'heart,' as a gloss on Θαδδαῖος which was thought to be derived from the Aram. תד (גּדּא) = Heb. שַׁד, 'breast.' Dalman (Words, 40) connects Θαδδ. with Θευδᾶς, and Λεββ. with the Nabataean לבאי. Hort (Notes, 11 f.) suggests that Λεββ. 'is apparently due to an early attempt to bring Levi (Λευείς) the publican (Lk. v. 27) within the Twelve' (see Burkitt, Ev. da Meph., ad loc.). But in Lk. vi. 16, Ac. i. 13, and in 𝔖 sin here (in each case after Simon the Zealot) the name Ἰούδας Ἰακώβου takes the place of Thaddaeus (probably the 'Judas not Iscariot' of Jo. xiv. 22) ; and Allen (Enc. Bibl., art. 'Thaddaeus')

suggests that Θαδδ. represents an original יהודה or יהודא = Judah (Judas), and cites instances of θ representing the initial gutturals ח, ה, and א. On the lat. reading Judas Zelotes, and on the conflation Λεββαῖος ὁ ἐπικληθεὶς Θαδδαῖος, see Hort, l.c.

4. Σ. ὁ Καναναῖος (so Mk.) is interpreted by Lk. as Σ. τὸν καλούμενον ζηλωτήν, and (Ac. i. 13) Σ. ὁ ζηλωτής. Καν. is connected with קנא, 'to be zealous' ; see 4 Mac. xviii. 12, where Phinehas is called ὁ ζηλωτής (referring to Num. xxv. 11, 13). The title may have been given him by the Lord, or the other disciples, to describe a feature in his character ; but if the termination -αῖος arises from the plural termination in the Aram. קנאניא, as Φαρισαῖος from פרישיא (Schürer, HJP. I. ii. 80 f., II. ii. 19 ; see, however, Dalman, Words, 2, n. 4), it must denote a member of a sect or party. Dalman (ib. 50) thinks that the original form was Καnnαῖος = קַן, 'a zealot.' It is improbable that he had been a revolutionist, such as those described in Jos. Ant. XVIII. i. 1, 6, BJ. II. viii. 1 ; but he may have been a religious zealot (cf. Ac. xxi. 20, Gal. i. 14), who had learned from the Lord a righteousness exceeding that of the Scribes and Pharisees. Jer. (ad loc.) explains it as 'de vico Chana Galilaeae,' but this would require Κανaῖος. The TR Κανανίτης cannot mean Canaanite (A.V.), which is Χαναναῖος (see xv. 22).

Ἰούδας ὁ Ἰσκαριώτης ὁ καὶ παραδοὺς αὐτόν.   Τούτους 5
τοὺς δώδεκα ἀπέστειλεν ὁ Ἰησοῦς παραγγείλας αὐτοῖς
λέγων

Εἰς ὁδὸν ἐθνῶν μὴ ἀπέλθητε, καὶ εἰς πόλιν Σαμαρειτῶν

Ἰούδας ὁ Ἰσκαριώτης] So Jo. xii.
4 (cf. xiv. 22); Ἰ. Ἰσκαρ. (Mt. xxvi.
14); Ἰ. ὁ καλούμενος Ἰσκαρ. (Lk.
xxii. 3); but Ἰ. Ἰσκαριώθ in Mk. iii.
19, xiv. 10, Lk. vi. 16. In Jo. vi. 71,
xiii. 2, 26 he is Ἰ. Σίμωνος Ἰσκαρι-
ώτου, but ℵ in the former passage,
and D in the two latter, have ἀπὸ
καρυώτου, which probably points to
the Aram. דקריות, in which case
Ἰσκαριώθ (corrupted to Ἰσκαριώτης)
represents איש קריות, 'a man of
Kerioth' (Dalman, Words, 51): cf.
Ἰστοβος (Jos. Ant. VII. vi. 1) =
Εἰστώβ (2 Regn. x. 6, 8)=איש טוב,
'a man [men] of Tob.' On the
identification of Kerioth see Swete.
παραδούς, 'delivered up,' does not in
itself express treachery as προδούς
would have done (see xvii. 22 note).
Judas is once called προδότης (Lk. vi.
16), but the verb is never applied to
his action. This reticence of the
evangelists was due to their knowledge that the παράδοσις was part
of the divine plan; cf. Ac. ii. 23.
On the aor. see Blass, § 58. 4 n.

5–42. CHARGE TO THE TWELVE.

This is the second of the five
principal discourses into which Mt.
has collected sayings of the Lord
(see on vii. 28). It falls into four
sections : (a) vv. 5 b–16, (b) vv. 17–
23, (c) vv. 24–39, (d) vv. 40–42.
The first and last of these contain
material which appears to represent
the original Charge in a form which
combines features of Mk. and Q,
Mk. (vi. 8–11) being closely followed
in Lk. ix. 3–5, and Q being represented in a Lucan form in a Charge
to the Seventy (Lk. x. 3–12, 16), as
follows :

	Mt. x.	Lk. x.
(a) vv.	5 b, 6	—
	7, 8	9
	9, 10 a	4 a
	(Mk. vi. 8 f., Lk. ix. 3)	
	10 b	7 b
	11–14	5–11
	(Mk. vi. 10 f., Lk. ix. 4 f.)	
	15	12
	16	3
(d)	40	16
	41	—
	42	— (cf. Mk. ix. 41)

5 a. τούτους κτλ.] On δώδεκα
see v. 2 ; ἀπέστειλεν continues the
thought of ἀπόστολος in the same
verse. παραγγείλας is due to Mk. vi.
8; the verb is frequent in Lk. (Ev.⁴,
Ac.¹¹), but in Mt., Mk. it recurs only
in xv. 35 = Mk. viii. 6.

5 b. εἰς ὁδὸν κτλ.] 'To the way
leading to the Gentiles'; for the
gen. cf. iv. 15, Jud. xx. 42, εἰς ὁδὸν
τῆς ἐρήμου. Perhaps ἀπελθεῖν is to
be understood strictly, 'depart,' sc.
out of Jewish territory. On the
chief Hellenistic towns of Palestine
see Schürer, HJP. II. i. 57–149.
The apostles, like their Master (xv.
24), were sent to Jews only. There
is nothing in the chapter, or in
Mk.'s account, at variance with this.
Lk.'s omission of the words has
been understood to imply that the
Seventy were to go to Gentiles as
well as Jews. This, however, is not
stated. In a writing intended for
Gentiles, the emphatic words were
probably omitted to avoid misconcep-
tion. Some have thought that the
mission of the Seventy is altogether
unhistorical, but that is only a conjecture from the undoubted fact that

6 μὴ εἰσέλθητε· πορεύεσθε δὲ μᾶλλον πρὸς τὰ πρόβατα τὰ
7 ἀπολωλότα οἴκου Ἰσραήλ. πορευόμενοι δὲ κηρύσσετε λέ-
8 γοντες ὅτι Ἤγγικεν ἡ βασιλεία τῶν οὐρανῶν. ἀσθενοῦντας
θεραπεύετε, νεκροὺς ἐγείρετε, λεπροὺς καθαρίζετε, δαιμόνια
9 ἐκβάλλετε· δωρεὰν ἐλάβετε, δωρεὰν δότε. Μὴ κτήσησθε

Lk. has assigned to it the Charge
which Mt. assigns to the mission of
the Twelve.

καὶ εἰς πόλιν κτλ.] On the
Samaritans, and the Jewish estimate
of them, see Schürer, *HJP*. II. i. 5-
8; cf. Sir. l. 25 f. The Samaritan
district is described in Jos. *BJ*. III.
iii. 4. It was the custom of Jews
who wished to travel from Galilee to
Judaea to avoid the Samaritans by
passing into the Hellenistic districts
on the E. of Jordan; but the Lord's
double prohibition confined the
apostles to Galilee (contrast xxviii.
19). In Lk. ix. 52, Jo. iv. 4 f., He
is related to have passed through
Samaria, but not for the purpose of
preaching; see xix. 1 note.

6. πορεύεσθε δέ κτλ.] If the
Jewish nation could be brought to
repentance, the new age would
dawn; see Ac. iii. 19 f., Jo. iv. 22.
But when they proved obdurate,
τῷ αὐτῶν παραπτώματι ἡ σωτηρία
τοῖς ἔθνεσιν (Rom. xi. 11). τὰ
πρόβατα . . . Ἰσραήλ (repeated in
xv. 24) is an allusion to Jer. l. [xxvii.]
6, πρόβατα ἀπολωλότα ἐγενήθη ὁ
λαός μου. The participle is not
'lost' (A.V., R.V.) in the sense of
'strayed,' but 'perished' (Wicl.;
oves quae perierunt, Vulg.); see ix. 36
note. 'House of Israel' is found
passim in the O.T., but in the N.T.
recurs only in xv. 24, Ac. ii. 36, vii.
42 (LXX.), Heb. viii. 8, 10 (LXX.).
οἴκου without the art. represents the
Heb. construct state.

7. πορευόμενοι δέ κτλ.] Throughout their journey (pres. partcp.) the
content of their message was to be

the same as that of their Master (see
iv. 17 note). Lk. places this, and
the acts of healing, a little later in
the Charge to the Seventy (x. 9).

8. ἀσθενοῦντας κτλ.] Lk. has
the first item only; Mt. expands with
a series similar to that in xi. 5. The
miracles were not mere acts of kindness, but had the far more momentous
meaning (as in the Lord's work) of
signs of the nearness of the Kingdom;
see xii. 28 note. Some have thought
the mention of them here to be
merely a reflexion of apostolic experiences in the early days of the
Church; but it is noteworthy that
lepers are never mentioned in the
N.T. outside the synopt. Gospels.
νεκροὺς ἐγείρετε is omitted in the
later uncials, perhaps owing to the
absence of this sign of power from
v. 1. On καθαρίζετε see viii. 2.

δωρεάν κτλ.] Mt. only. δωρεάν
(frequent in LXX. = חִנָּם)· recurs in
the Gospp. in Jo. xv. 25 (from
LXX.) only; elsewhere Paul. Epp.[4],
Apoc.[2] The object to be supplied
with ἐλάβετε is the power of healing (v. 1), with δότε the healing
itself. The command is directed
against the receiving of payment
for acts of ministry. The Mishna
(*Bechor*. iv. 6, *Ned*. iv. 3) contains
similar injunctions. S. Paul rigidly
abstained from it (2 Cor. xi. 7 ff.; cf.
1 Cor. ix. 18, 2 Cor. xii. 13–18,
1 Thes. ii. 9, Ac. xx. 33–35). See
also Ac. iii. 6 (referred to by Ambr.),
viii. 18–20. The abuse here guarded
against soon grew rife in the Church;
see *Didache*, xi.–xiii., esp. xi. 6,
ἐξερχόμενος δὲ ὁ ἀπόστολος μηδὲν

χρυσὸν μηδὲ ἄργυρον μηδὲ χαλκὸν εἰς τὰς ζώνας ὑμῶν,
μὴ πήραν εἰς ὁδὸν μηδὲ δύο χιτῶνας μηδὲ ὑποδήματα 10

λαμβανέτω εἰ μὴ ἄρτον, ἕως οὗ
αὐλισθῇ· ἐὰν δὲ ἀργύριον αἰτῇ,
ψευδοπροφήτης ἐστί.

9, 10. *No provision for the tour.*
Mk. (*vv.* 8 f.) has the series : staff,
bread, wallet, money (χαλκός),
[sandals], coats. Lk. ix. 3 is based
on this, transposing bread and wallet
(see Swete), writing ἀργύριον for
χαλκόν, and omitting sandals. But
Q (Lk. x. 4; cf. xxii. 35) has a
different series : purse, wallet, shoes ;
and Mt. follows this order, dealing
with money (three items), wallet,
clothing (two items), and adds the
prohibition of a staff.

9. μὴ κτήσησθε κτλ.] 'Do not
procure,' *i.e.* as a provision before
starting ; not *nolite possidere* (Vulg.).
Mk. and Lk. ix. have αἴρετε, Lk. x.
βαστάζετε. It is not a prohibition
against accepting payment for acts of
ministry, since κτήσησθε governs all
the accusatives down to ῥάβδον, and
they can hardly have been thought
of as given in payment ; and if that
were the meaning, the concluding
ἄξιος γάρ κτλ. would be inexplicable.
Mt. takes Mk.'s χαλκόν, alters Lk.'s
ἀργύριον, both of which mean
'money' in general, and by prefixing
χρυσόν forms a climax, 'neither
gold, nor silver, nor (even) bronze.'
The ζώνη was used for carrying
money ; cf. Hor. *Ep.* ii. ii. 40, 'ibit
eo quo vis qui zonam perdidit'; see
HDB., art. 'Bag.'

10. μὴ πήραν κτλ.] Cf. Judith
x. 5, xiii. 10, 15, Sym. 1 Regn. xvii.
40, Martial iii. 53. 2, 'Cum baculo
peraque senex.' The wallet would,
if it were part of their outfit, be used
for carrying food for each day's
journey; but it was forbidden, which

probably means that, though they
might accept hospitality, they were
not to accept food to carry with
them. On πήρα as a beggar's wallet
see *Exp. T.*, Nov. 1906, 62. The
χιτών was the coat worn over the
σινδών (shirt), and under the ἱμάτιον
(cloak); they were not to procure two
of these for the journey. It is not
clear whether this means that a
second coat was not to be carried for
future use, or that two were not to
be worn together ; but Mk. has μὴ
ἐνδύσησθε δύο χ., and this may be
the meaning of μήτε ἀνὰ δύο χιτῶνας
ἔχειν in Lk. ix. (cf. Jos. *Ant.* XVII. v.
7, who speaks of ὁ ἐντὸς χιτών of a
slave, ἐνεδεδύκει γὰρ δύο, and see
Mk. xiv. 63). Coats are not mentioned in Lk. x. On the other hand,
ὑποδήματα are not mentioned in Lk.
ix., but are forbidden in Mt. and Lk.
x. (= Q). This probably means that
there was originally no mention of
them in Mk., where the insertion of
ἀλλὰ ὑποδεδεμένους σανδάλια, which
disturbs the construction, was probably a scribal note, perhaps added
by one who thought that the
ambiguous μὴ κτήσησθε (Lk. βαστάζετε) ὑποδήματα meant that shoes
were not to be *carried*, but that the
apostles were to go simply in those
which they wore at the moment.
Spitta (*ZWTh.*, 1913, 36–45, 116 f.)
conjectures in Lk. ὑπενδύματα or
ὑποδύματα, 'underclothing.' With
regard to the staff there is a direct
contradiction. It is not mentioned
in Lk. x., but while Mt. and Lk. ix.
have μηδὲ [μήτε] ῥάβδον, Mk. has
εἰ μὴ ῥάβδον μόνον. In this case
the increased strictness of the injunction may have been due to
early tradition. In Diat. and 𝔖 sin

11 μηδὲ ῥάβδον· ἄξιος γὰρ ὁ ἐργάτης τῆς τροφῆς αὐτοῦ. εἰς
ἣν δ᾽ ἂν πόλιν ἢ κώμην εἰσέλθητε, ἐξετάσατε τίς ἐν αὐτῇ
12 ἄξιός ἐστιν· κἀκεῖ μείνατε ἕως ἂν ἐξέλθητε. εἰσερχόμενοι

ῥάβδος is rendered 'stick' in Mk.,
but 'staff' in Mt., Lk., as though an
ordinary walking-stick were permitted, but not something more
formidable to serve as a weapon of
defence; but the distinction was
probably Tatian's invention. ℥ pesh
has 'stick' (Vulg. *virga*) in all three
gospels. Aug., *al.* explain the forbidden ῥάβδος as literal, but the
permitted one as metaphorical of
apostolic authority.

The object of all the prohibitions
was probably not a stern asceticism.
The apostles were to exercise the
trust in God's providence enjoined
in vi. 25 f., 28–33. The part which
the prohibitions played in determin-
ing the aims of S. Francis of Assisi
is well known.

ἄξιος γάρ κτλ.] The ἐργάτης
sent into the harvest (ix. 38) would
be right in accepting the supply of
real needs from those to whom he
preached. Cf. *Didache*, xiii. 1. Lk.
(x. 7) places the saying in connexion
with the acceptance of hospitality,
and although it speaks of food, he
has τοῦ μισθοῦ for τῆς τροφῆς. But
τροφή in the case of a labourer or
slave is virtually μισθός; cf. xxiv. 45,
Thuc. vi. 93, viii. 57. The Lucan
form is quoted in 1 Tim. v. 18,
either as Scripture, or (if ἡ γραφή
refers only to the foregoing quotation) as a well-known saying.

Lk. (x. 4) here adds μηδένα κατὰ
τὴν ὁδὸν ἀσπάσησθε (cf. 4 Regn. iv.
29), in contrast with the salutation
to be given when they entered a
house (*v.* 5). The urgency of their
work admitted of no delays.

11–16. *Manner of life during the
tour.* Mk., followed by Lk. (ix.), has

two simple injunctions: (1) in any
house that they enter they are to remain, until they leave the place; (2)
as they depart from any place that
refuses to receive them, they are to
shake off the dust of their feet as a
witness against them. Mt. and Lk.
(x.) give fuller material from Q,
which they found differently treated
in the respective recensions which
they used.

11. εἰς ἣν κτλ.] This command,
given in Mt. only, forms a preparation
for the following κἀκεῖ μείνατε κτλ.
which comes from Mk.: whenever
they enter a city or village they
must inquire in it for a worthy
householder; 'and there,' *i.e.* in his
house, they must lodge all the time
that they are in the place. In Mk.
and Lk. (ix.) there is no ambiguity
in ἐκεῖ, since the preceding sentence
speaks only of entrance into a *house.*
In Lk. (x.) the command takes the
form μὴ μεταβαίνετε ἐξ οἰκίας εἰς
οἰκίαν: they must not appear to be
seeking more comfortable lodgings;
no reason must cause a change when
once their host was known to be
'worthy.' What constituted worthi-
ness is not stated, but it would
naturally be readiness to receive the
preachers and their message; see an
instance in Ac. xvi. 15. For the
absolute use of ἄξιος cf. xxii. 8, Apoc.
iii. 4, xvi. 6, 2 Mac. xv. 21.

12. εἰσερχόμενοι δέ κτλ.] *V.* 11
has described the procedure to be
adopted in any town or village; *vv.*
12, 13 describe the procedure at any
given house. An explanation often
given is that the inquiry for a worthy
householder was to be made among
the inhabitants of the town (so Jer.),

δὲ εἰς τὴν οἰκίαν ἀσπάσασθε αὐτήν· καὶ ἐὰν μὲν ᾖ ἡ οἰκία 13
ἀξία, ἐλθάτω ἡ εἰρήνη ὑμῶν ἐπ᾽ αὐτήν· ἐὰν δὲ μὴ ᾖ ἀξία, ἡ
εἰρήνη ὑμῶν ἐφ᾽ ὑμᾶς ἐπιστραφήτω. καὶ ὃς ἂν μὴ 14
δέξηται ὑμᾶς μηδὲ ἀκούσῃ τοὺς λόγους ὑμῶν, ἐξερχόμενοι

and that having heard of one, on entering his house (εἰς τὴν οἰκίαν) they were to salute it. But *v.* 13 assumes the possibility that after entering a house they may find it to be unworthy. The inquiry, therefore, was probably to be made at a house, *by questioning the householder* whether he would receive them and their message; but before making the inquiry (Lk. πρῶτον), they were to give the house the privilege of a salutation, which, if the owner proved unworthy, would be ineffectual. εἰσερχ. εἰς τ. οἰκίαν means 'On entering the house where you intend to make the inquiry.' Wellhausen's explanation—'the guest may at first be unknown, but he then reveals himself to be a missionary, and thereupon experiences varying treatment' —is less simple. See the writer's note in *JThS.*, July 1910. Mt.'s ἀσπάσασθε and Lk.'s λέγετε· εἰρήνη represent the same Aram. original; ἀσπάζεσθαι = שְׁאַל לְשָׁלוֹם in Ex. xviii. 7, Jud. xviii. 15 (A), and in Sym. 1 Regn. xxv. 5, xxx. 21, 2 Regn. viii. 10, where LXX. has ἐρωτᾶν [τὰ] εἰς εἰρήνην.

13. καὶ ἐάν κτλ.] Lk. has the more Semitic κ. ἐὰν ᾖ ἐκεῖ υἱὸς εἰρή-νης. For ἐλθάτω and ἐπιστραφήτω he has ἐπαναπαήσεται (-παύσεται) and ἀνακάμψει, verbs which are fairly frequent in the LXX.; for the former see espec. Num. xi. 25, 4 Regn. ii. 15. A greeting uttered by apostles was not a mere friendly wish (οὐκ ἀσπασμὸς τοῦτό ἐστι ψιλός, ἀλλ᾽ εὐλογία, Chrys.) but had, so to speak, an objective existence (cf. Is. xlv. 23, lv. 11, Zech. v. 3 f.); it would 'come'

(Mt.) or 'settle' (Lk.) upon the house that was worthy of it; otherwise it would return, undiminished and available for future use, upon the speakers (ἐφ᾽ ὑμᾶς; so Lk.). The preposition may, indeed, imply the further thought that it will be to the benefit of the speakers. The practical benefits that a worthy house would receive are those enumerated in *vv.* 7, 8.

14. καὶ ὃς ἄν κτλ.] Mk., followed by Lk. ix., deals only with the case of a τόπος, *i.e.* a city as a whole, that refused to receive the apostles. The account in Lk. x. is confused: ἐσθίετε τὰ παρατιθέμενα ὑμῖν (*v.* 8), which can only describe entertainment in a *house*, forms part of their reception by a *city* (*vv.* 8, 9), which is placed after their reception and entertainment in a house (*vv.* 5–7). Mt. continues to confine himself to the dealings with a particular house-holder (ὃς ἄν); but a scribe has introduced confusion by inserting ἢ τῆς πόλεως after τῆς οἰκίας (see next verse).

ἐξερχόμενοι κτλ.] 'At the moment that you emerge' is the counterpart of εἰσερχόμενοι (*v.* 12); it forms an abrupt anacoluthon after ὃς ἄν. To shake off dust implies the shaking off of pollution, a strong figure for the disavowal of fellowship. They were to treat the unworthy house-holder as though he were a Gentile. See Edersheim, *LT.* i. 643 f., Wetstein, *ad loc.* Mk. has τὸν χοῦν, which recurs in the N.T. in Apoc. xviii. 19 only, but is more frequent in the LXX. than κονιορτός, which in class. Gk. denotes dust stirred up as a

ἔξω τῆς οἰκίας ἢ τῆς πόλεως ἐκείνης ἐκτινάξατε τὸν κονι-
15 ορτὸν τῶν ποδῶν ὑμῶν. ἀμὴν λέγω ὑμῖν, ἀνεκτότερον
ἔσται γῇ Σοδόμων καὶ Γομόρρων ἐν ἡμέρᾳ κρίσεως ἢ τῇ
16 πόλει ἐκείνῃ.   Ἰδοὺ ἐγὼ ἀποστέλλω ὑμᾶς ὡς πρό-

15 Γομόρρων] Γομορρας CDLMP 1 22 al 𝕷 ff¹ h k

cloud. In Lk. x. the city is to be
addressed, 'the very dust which has
stuck to our feet from your city we
wipe off against you; but know
this, that the Kingdom of God hath
drawn near.' In Mk. and Lk. ix.
the shaking off of the dust is εἰς
μαρτύριον αὐτοῖς (ἐπ' αὐτούς).

15. ἀμήν κτλ.] Lk. λέγω δὲ
ὑμῖν: see v. 18 note. ἀνεκτότερον
ἔχειν describes the condition of a
convalescent in Ox. Pap. 939. 25.
In bibl. Gk., apart from this context, the word does not recur, except
in the similar sayings xi. 22, 24.
The principle involved in 'more
tolerable' is that laid down in Lk.
xii. 47 f. The expression 'land of
Sodom' is elsewhere found only in
xi. 24. On γῆ = χώρα see ix. 26.
Γόμορρα as a neut. plur. occurs 5
times in the LXX.; in accordance with
the Heb. it should be a fem. sing.,
as in the v.l. here Γομόρρας, 2 Pet.
ii. 6, and 9 times in the LXX. Lk.
x. 12, and Mt. xi. 24 omit καὶ Γομ.
For Sodom as typical of sin that
receives divine punishment cf. also
Lk. xvii. 29, Rom. ix. 29, 2 Pet. ii.
6, Jude 7, Jubil. xxxvi. 10. In
Sanh. x. 3 it is said 'the men of
Sodom have no portion in the age
to come.'

ἐν ἡμέρᾳ κρίσεως] So xi. 22,
24, xii. 36, Judith xvi. 17 (20);
εἰς ἡμέραν κρ. 2 Pet. ii. 9, iii. 7;
ἐν τῇ ἡμ. τῆς κρ. 1 Jo. iv. 17.
Lk. has ἐν τῇ ἡμ. ἐκείνῃ (x. 12),
and ἐν τῇ κρίσει (x. 14). All
denote the Judgment Day to come.
See also the apocalyptic passages

cited by Allen, ad loc. On the
omission of the article in a fixed
formula see Blass, § 46. 9. Since the
'Day' marked the advent of the
Kingdom which was already near
(v. 7), the punishment of the city
was soon to fall.

Like the insertion of ἢ τῆς πόλεως
in v. 14, this verse dealing with a
city disturbs Mt.'s account of the
procedure enjoined upon the apostles.
It is a duplicate of xi. 24, added
here by harmonization with Lk. x.
12, where the saying has been
transposed from its true position
after v. 15 in order to form an impressive continuation of the saying
about rejection of a city. It is
probable, therefore, that throughout
the whole section Mt. originally had
no mention of a city, but only of a
house. See the note in JThS. referred to above.

16 a. ἰδοὺ ἐγώ κτλ.] 'Mittit
ergo agnos inter lupos ut com-
plerentur illud: Tunc lupi et agni
simul pascentur' (Ambr.). Lk. (x. 3)
places the saying near the beginning
of the Charge, with which tradition
connected it, doubtless on account of
the word ἀποστέλλω. But there is
no evidence that the apostles during
their short tour were ever in peril;
in Mt. ix. 36, x. 6 their hearers are
πρόβατα; they did not become
wolves till the Lord's death. In
Mt. the saying forms a link between
the Charge and the section on persecution which follows. There is
no emphasis on ἐγώ, which Lk.
omits; the Semitic idiom would

βατα ἐν μέσῳ λύκων· γίνεσθε οὖν φρόνιμοι ὡς οἱ ὄφεις
καὶ ἀκέραιοι ὡς αἱ περιστεραί. προσέχετε δὲ ἀπὸ τῶν ἀν- 17
θρώπων· παραδώσουσιν γὰρ ὑμᾶς εἰς συνέδρια, καὶ ἐν ταῖς
συναγωγαῖς αὐτῶν μαστιγώσουσιν ὑμᾶς· καὶ ἐπὶ ἡγεμόνας 18

17 δε] om D 𝔏 a c g¹ k m 𝔖 sin. pal. diat^{Eph}

require the pronoun and a participle.
It carries encouragement nevertheless, standing at the head of the
predictions of persecution (so Chrys.).
Lk. has ἄρνας for πρόβατα, perhaps
to heighten the contrast with λύκων.
For the metaphor cf. Herod. iv. 149,
καταλείψειν ὄιν ἐν λύκοισιν. On
ἐν μέσῳ (B εἰς μέσον) see Blass,
§ 40. 8.

16 b. γίνεσθε οὖν κτλ.] Since
Lk. omits the saying, Mt. has perhaps
drawn it from another context.
The Lord perhaps used a current
proverbial expression. Ign. ad
Polyc. ii. 2 alludes to it. The
thought, without the metaphors,
occurs in Rom. xvi. 19. In Midr.
Cant. ii. 14, R. Juda (c. A.D. 200)
said 'God saith of the Israelites,
Towards me they are sincere as
doves, but towards the Gentiles they
are prudent as serpents.' Cf. Test.
Naph. viii. 9, γίνεσθε οὖν σοφοὶ ἐν
θεῷ, τέκνα μου, καὶ φρόνιμοι. For
φρόνιμος of the serpent cf. Gen. iii.
1 (= עָרוּם). The thought is confined
to the single characteristic of
prudence; cf. Lk. xvi. 1–8. Naz.
Gosp. seems to have had 'more
prudent than serpents' (φ. ὑπὲρ ὄφ.,
see Texte u. Unters., 1911, p. 39, 90).
ἀκέραιος, 'pure, unmixed' as applied
to wine, metals etc., is used with
'dove' in Sym. Cant. v. 2, vi. 8 [9],
ἡ ἀκεραία μου (= תַּמָּתִי); in bibl.
Gk. it recurs only in Est. xvi. 6,
Rom. xvi. 19, Phil. ii. 15. 'Sim-
plicitas columbarum ex Spiritus
sancti specie demonstratur' (Jer.).
Contrast Philo, Qu. Rer. Div. 25, 48,

where the dove is a picture of wisdom,
of the Nous, and of the Logos. For
the strange patristic exegesis of the
wisdom of the serpent see Zahn, ad
loc.

17–23. (xxiv. 9, 13, Mk. xiii.
9–13, Lk. xxi. 12–19; cf. Lk. xii.
11, 12.) Predictions of persecution.
Mt. here attaches to the Charge a
group of sayings which belong to a
late period of the Lord's life. Mk.
is closely followed. Lk. largely
coincides with him in contents and
order, but in language is quite independent. Having placed the
verses here, Mt. in ch. xxiv. summarizes them as briefly as possible.

17. προσέχετε δέ κτλ.] δέ is
not 'but'; as often in Mt. it merely
links separate sayings; there is some
authority for its omission. On
προσέχειν ἀπό for Mk.'s late and
rare βλέπετε δὲ ὑμᾶς ἑαυτούς see
Blass, § 34. 1. For Mt.'s use of
οἱ ἄνθρωποι see viii. 27 note. On
συνέδρια, the local courts of discipline,
see v. 22. Having been tried by
the elders of the synagogue, who
formed the court, offenders were
scourged in the synagogue buildings;
see Eus. HE. v. xvi. 12. Mt.'s expression takes the place of Mk.'s
pregnant εἰς συναγωγὰς δαρήσεσθε
(lit. 'be flayed,' a LXX. word). On
αὐτῶν see vii. 29.

18. καὶ ἐπὶ ἡγ. δέ κτλ.] 'Nay
more' (καὶ . . . δέ). ἡγεμόνες in
1 Pet. ii. 14 are any governors subordinate to the emperor (βασιλεύς);
but apart from the present context
(except Mt. ii. 6) the word always

δὲ καὶ βασιλεῖς ἀχθήσεσθε ἕνεκεν ἐμοῦ εἰς μαρτύριον αὐ-
19 τοῖς καὶ τοῖς ἔθνεσιν. ὅταν δὲ παραδῶσιν ὑμᾶς, μὴ μεριμνήσητε πῶς ἢ τί λαλήσητε· δοθήσεται γὰρ ὑμῖν ἐν ἐκείνῃ
20 τῇ ὥρᾳ τί λαλήσητε· οὐ γὰρ ὑμεῖς ἐστὲ οἱ λαλοῦντες
ἀλλὰ τὸ πνεῦμα τοῦ πατρὸς ὑμῶν τὸ λαλοῦν ἐν ὑμῖν.
21 παραδώσει δὲ ἀδελφὸς ἀδελφὸν εἰς θάνατον καὶ πατὴρ

stands in the N.T. for the Procurator
of Judaea (Pilate Mt. xxvii. xxviii.,
Lk. xx. 20; Felix Ac. xxiii. 24 etc.;
Festus *ib.* xxvi. 30). βασιλεῖς are
here (contrast xvii. 25) the Herodian
princes, *e.g.* Antipas (xiv. 9, Mk. vi.
14, 22), Agrippa I. (Ac. xii. 1),
Agrippa II. (Ac. xxv. 13). ἕνεκεν
ἐμοῦ (so Mk.) is not different from
Lk.'s ἕνεκ. τοῦ ὀνόματός μου (see *v.*
22 note): in the immediate expectation of His own violent death, in
which the words were spoken, the
Lord could speak of their sufferings
for His sake, or His name's sake, *i.e.*
not, as in later times, merely for
bearing the Christian name, but
because they had been associated
with Him.

εἰς μαρτύριον κτλ.] Cf. viii. 4.
αὐτοῖς refers both to the Jewish 'kings'
and to the Gentile 'governors.' By
the apostles' trial Gentiles would
have an opportunity of hearing their
message; cf. 2 Tim. iv. 16 f. But
the addition of καὶ τοῖς ἔθνεσιν, an
adaptation of Mk.'s καὶ εἰς πάντα
τὰ ἔθνη πρῶτον δεῖ κηρυχθῆναι τὸ
εὐαγγέλιον, implies mission work
beyond the borders of Palestine.
See note on xxiv. 14 and compare
the addition of τῶν ἔθνων in xxiv. 9.

19. ὅταν δέ κτλ.] The substance
of *vv.* 19, 20 must have stood in
Q. Lk. follows Mk. more closely
in xii. 11 f. than in xxi. 14 f.
The command is 'Be not anxious
about the manner or matter of your
defence' (so Lk. xii. 11). On τί see
Moulton i. p. 93. Mk. has μὴ
προμεριμνᾶτε, Lk. xxi. 14 μὴ προ-

μελετᾶν 'prepare, or practise, beforehand.' Self-defence before Jewish
kings and heathen governors would
be a terrible ordeal for humble
Galileans. The injunction applied
to cases when preparation of a speech
would ordinarily be impossible;
'non omnis praeparatio ex eo nobis
prohibetur' (Beng.). The real preparation is to have the heart already
full (xii. 34 b, 35, Ac. iv. 20).

20. τὸ πνεῦμα κτλ.] Mk. τὸ πν.
τὸ ἅγιον, Lk. xii. 12 τὸ ἅγιον πν.,
but xxi. 15 ἐγὼ γὰρ δώσω κτλ.
The last is certainly a later thought
(cf. 2 Tim. iv. 17), and recalls the
promise to Moses, Ex. iv. 11 ff.
Mt. never uses 'the holy Spirit,' and
his expression is unique. But
the Spirit, though it is that of the
transcendent Father, is immanent
in the disciples (Mt. alone adds τὸ
λαλοῦν ἐν ὑμῖν); He speaks in man
as He prays in man (Rom. viii. 26,
Gal. iv. 6), and He annuls human
individuality as little in the one
case as in the other. It is possible
that Jesus had in mind Joel ii. 28 f.
[iii. 1 f.]; the gift of the Spirit was
to be one of the signs of the approach
of the new age, and it would help
the disciples in their persecutions.

21. παραδώσει δέ κτλ.] 'Hoc in
persecutionibus fieri crebro videmus'
(Jer.). Mk. has καὶ παραδ., but is
otherwise identical till the end of
the next verse. The words are an
echo of Mic. vii. 6, which is adapted
in *vv.* 35 f. θανατώσουσιν, 'procure
the death of,' *morte eos afficient* (cf.
1 Regn. xxii. 21, Sus. 28) is

τέκνον, καὶ ἐπαναστήσονται τέκνα ἐπὶ γονεῖς καὶ θανατώσουσιν αὐτούς. καὶ ἔσεσθε μισούμενοι ὑπὸ πάντων διὰ τὸ 22
ὄνομά μου· ὁ δὲ ὑπομείνας εἰς τέλος οὗτος σωθήσεται.

equivalent to παραδώσουσιν εἰς
θάνατον. xxiv. 9 has simply ἀποκτενοῦσιν. Lk. qualifies it, θανατώσουσιν ἐξ ὑμῶν, since the honour of
martyrdom was reserved for few.
Social strife is often spoken of in the
apocalypses as an accompaniment
of the last days; see Allen, ad loc.
It was to be one of Elijah's functions
to reconcile fathers and children
(Mal. iv. 6 [iii. 24], Sir. xlviii. 10).

22. καὶ ἔσεσθε κτλ.] So Mk.,
Lk.; in xxiv. 9 τῶν ἐθνῶν is added
after πάντων. The periphrasis for
μισήσεσθε perhaps implies 'Ye shall
be (continually) in the condition of
being hated' (Blass, § 62. 2). The
'name,' as often in the O.T., and still
more frequently in the Targg. and
Rabb. writings, stood for the 'person';
and such expressions as ὑπὲρ τοῦ
ὀνόματός μου (Ac. ix. 16), ἕνεκεν τ.
ὄν. μου (Mt. xix. 29), ὑπὲρ τ. ὀνόμ.
τοῦ Κυρίου (Ac. xv. 26), and even
ὑπὲρ τ. ὀνόματος (id. v. 41, 3 Jo. 7),
may be only Semitic equivalents for
ὑπὲρ Χριστοῦ (cf. 2 Cor. xii. 10,
Phil. i. 29), ἕνεκεν ἐμοῦ (Mt. v. 11,
x. 18), and the like; cf. the Rabb.
לְשֵׁם, which frequently denotes no
more than 'for the sake of' (see v.
41 note).

ὁ δὲ ὑπομείνας κτλ.] So xxiv. 13
and Mk.; Lk. has ἐν τῇ ὑπομονῇ
ὑμῶν κτήσεσθε ('ye shall win') τὰς
ψυχὰς ὑμῶν, which does not differ
in meaning. ὑπομείνας is absolute
(cf. 2 Tim. ii. 12), and must not be
connected with εἰς, as e.g. ὑπ. εἰς
εἰρήνην (Jer. xiv. 19), εἰς τὸν νόμον
αὐτοῦ (Ps. cxxix. [cxxx.] 5). The
absolute use is not frequent in the
LXX., where it usually has a personal
object. The importance of ὑπομονή,

while the thought is not absent from
Jewish writings (see Volz, Jüd. Esch.
172), became a marked feature in
apostolic teaching, the verb or subst.
occurring 42 times in the Epp. and
Apoc. See further Swete on Mk.
xiii. 13. The meanings of εἰς τέλος
vary in the LXX. and N.T., as in class.
Gk.: 'for ever' = לָנֶצַח (Ps. lxxvi.
[lxxvii.] 9, לָעַד (Ps. ix. 19); 'continually' (Lk. xviii. 5); 'finally'
(2 Mac. viii. 29); 'utterly' = לְכָלָה
(2 Ch. xii. 12), תָּמָם (Jos. viii. 24),
Jo. xiii. 1, 1 Thes. ii. 16. In the
N.T. there occur also ἕως, μέχρι,
ἄχρι τέλους. It is less defined than
εἰς τὸ τέλος 'till the end of the age,'
usque ad finem, Vulg. (contrast xxiv.
13 with 14). Many would have no
opportunity of shewing endurance
till the Last Day, since they would
already have suffered martyrdom
(v. 21). εἰς τέλος is therefore 'continually,' i.e. to the utmost extent or
intensity of the persecutions. This
is simpler than to connect it with
σωθήσεται, with the meaning 'finally.'
The thought of the whole passsage
has its best commentary in Apoc. ii.
10. The conceptions of σωθῆναι
(σωτηρία) in the Jewish apocalypses
varied from a crude materialism to
a lofty spirituality, but they were
always those of deliverance and victory
which would be granted to the
nation (or the righteous members of
it) in the coming Kingdom (see HDB
art. 'Salvation,' Volz, Jüd. Esch.
332); cf. xix. 25 (note), xxiv. 13,
22, Lk. xiii. 23, Ac. ii. 21, xv. 1;
and σωτηρία, Lk. i. 69, 71, 77,
Jo. iv. 22. After the Resurrection
Christians came to perceive more
clearly that 'salvation,' like the

23 ὅταν δὲ διώκωσιν ὑμᾶς ἐν τῇ πόλει ταύτῃ, φεύγετε εἰς τὴν
ἑτέραν· ἀμὴν γὰρ λέγω ὑμῖν, οὐ μὴ τελέσητε τὰς πόλεις

23 ετεραν] add εαν δε [vel καν] εν τη αλλη [vel ετερα, vel εκ ταυτης] διωκωσιν
[-ουσιν D, εκδιωξουσιν L 247] υμεις φευγετε εις την αλλην DL 1 13 247 al
𝕷 a b ff¹ g¹·² h k q 𝕊 sin.diat^Eph [(?) vide Burkitt, Ev. da Meph.]

coming of the Kingdom, was not
merely a future event, but a present
process leading to a consummation.

23. ὅταν δέ κτλ.] A continuation
of the thought προσέχετε ἀπὸ τῶν
ἀνθρώπων (v. 17 a). Regard to this
command would have restrained the
fanatical eagerness for martyrdom of
which the later history of the Church
supplies so many examples. The
injunction to the disciples not to
mind how often they flee (the reason
for which is given in the following
words) is emphasized in some MSS.
by an additional clause (see Appar.).

ἀμὴν γάρ κτλ.] On the formula
see v. 18. Were these words part
of the original charge, they would
imply that the disciples were to
preach in each town to which they
fled, and that before they had fled
to, and preached in, every town in
Israel, the Son of Man would come.
But it is impossible to maintain that
the Lord expected the end of the
age before the disciples had finished
their tour, because (1) vv. 17–22
(with which Mt. closely connects
this verse) belong to the position in
which Mk. xiii. 9–13 stands, as is
shewn by Mt.'s parallel (xxiv. 9, 13);
(2) the thought of fleeing from
persecution differs toto caelo from
that of the imperious action commanded in v. 14; the original Charge
and the present section belong to
different periods and reflect different
conditions; (3) there was nothing in
the message commanded in v. 7 to
call forth persecution.

By combining this verse, as a real
part of the Charge, with Mk. vi.
30 f., Schweitzer allows himself to
reach the conclusion that Jesus was
disappointed at the delay of the
Parousia of the Son of Man, so
that when the disciples returned,
the prediction not having been
verified, His plans, and His attitude
towards the multitude, were altered,
and He started to travel about with
the Twelve only (Quest. of the Hist.
Jesus, 357 63).

οὐ μὴ τελέσητε κτλ.] The opening γάρ connects the words with
φεύγετε — 'Ye will not have exhausted, passed through the whole
number of, the cities in your flight';
cf. the class. ἐκπληροῦν (Eur. Or. 54),
so explere (Virg. Aen. xii. 763, Tibull.
I. iv. 69), complere (Lucr. ii. 323).
It is not the band of missionaries,
but the community of the disciples,
that is to flee; and the cities of Israel,
i.e. the Jewish cities in Palestine,
will afford them enough places of
refuge, because the Son of Man is
coming so soon. 𝕊 sin inserts 'the
house of' before 'Israel' (cf. v. 6);
Diat^Ephr omits 'of Israel,' extending
the expression to all the cities of the
Roman world, interpreting the injunctions as applying to Christian
missionary activity. At the outbreak of the Jewish war in A.D. 66
the Christians fled, not to a Jewish
town, but to Pella (Eus. HE. III. v. 3,
Epiph. Haer. xxix. 7, xxx. 2), a
heathen town of the Decapolis (see
xxiv. 16); this, however, was not a
flight from religious persecution. On
οὐ μή see Moulton, i. 191.

τοῦ Ἰσραὴλ ἕως ἔλθῃ ὁ υἱὸς τοῦ ἀνθρώπου. Οὐκ ἔστιν 24
μαθητὴς ὑπὲρ τὸν διδάσκαλον οὐδὲ δοῦλος ὑπὲρ τὸν κύριον
αὐτοῦ. ἀρκετὸν τῷ μαθητῇ ἵνα γένηται ὡς ὁ διδάσκαλος 25
αὐτοῦ, καὶ ὁ δοῦλος ὡς ὁ κύριος αὐτοῦ. εἰ τὸν οἰκοδεσπότην Βεεζεβοὺλ ἐπεκάλεσαν, πόσῳ μᾶλλον τοὺς οἰκιακοὺς

25 Βεεζεβουλ] אB; Βεελζ. CE al 𝕷 a f ff¹ q 𝕾 hcl arm aeth; Βελζ. DLX 𝕷 b
[Velzebul] g¹ [Beizebul] h k me; Beelzebub 𝕷 c g² vg 𝕾 sin.pesh

ἕως ἔλθῃ κτλ.] Since the words
are unconnected with the mission
Charge, they cannot mean that the
Lord would meet the disciples at some
appointed spot during their tour.
Orig. explains ἔλθῃ as analogous
with the ἐλευσόμεθα of Jo. xiv.
23, a frequent spiritual intercourse
(similarly Chrys., al.); but the evang.
could not have used ἕως with an aor.
to express this. Calvin, and many
modern writers, explain it of the
coming of the Holy Spirit at Pentecost. This was no doubt the beginning of its actual fulfilment. But
the meaning of 'the coming of the
Son of Man' is too distinctive in the
Gospels to allow us to suppose that
this was the thought in the Lord's
mind at the time. (See p. xxvi.)
For other instances of His use of the
title, without explicitly applying it
to Himself, see p. xix., group I.

24–39. *Further collected sayings
on persecution.*

24. οὐκ ἔστιν κτλ.] The disciple
cannot expect to earn less hatred
than his Teacher, etc.; it should be
enough (v. 25) for him that he is as
his Teacher, *i.e.* that he does not
suffer more than He. This would
be unintelligible to the disciples till
after the prediction (in xvi. 21) that
their Master was to suffer. It cannot
have belonged to the original Charge.
Jesus may have been alluding to a
current proverb; cf. *Berak.* 58 b 'It
is enough for the slave that he should
be as his master (כרבו),' and other

passages in Wetstein. Its true force
is probably given in Lk.'s context
(vi. 40). The δοῦλος clause, here
and in v. 25, is absent from Lk.,
but it is used in Jo. xiii. 16 (after a
reference in v. 13 to the διδάσκαλος
and κύριος of the present verse), and
(in connexion with persecution) xv. 20.

25. ἀρκετόν κτλ.] On ἀρκετόν
see vi. 34; for the use of ἵνα see
Moulton, i. 208. ὁ δοῦλος: *sc.* ἔστω
or ἔσται. But Wellh. conjectures
ὁ μαθητής for the dat.

The thought in Lk. is not very
different: 'however well equipped,
he will not be superior to his teacher.'

εἰ τ. οἰκοδεσπότην κτλ.] This
saying, confined to Mt., was perhaps
spoken soon after the scene in xii.
22–32. The term of reproach is
variously spelt, and its meaning is
doubtful. The form *Beelzebub* occurs
in Gk. in Sym. 4 Regn. i. 2 f., 6, 16
(LXX. Βάαλ μυῖαν) = בַּעַל זְבוּב, but
in the N.T. only in two 𝕷 MSS.,
Vulg. and 𝕾; from the Vulg. it is
adopted in all Engl. versions. Riehm
suggests that in the time of Jesus
the word was בַּעַל דְּבָבָא, 'Lord of
enmity,' *i.e.* Satan. If so, Βεελζε-
βούλ, for which the textual evidence
is decisive, may have been a popular
corruption of it. Two derivations
are suggested for the form Βεε(λ)ζε-
βούλ: (1) In bibl. Heb. the root זבל
denotes 'to exalt,' hence *z͏ᵉbūl* 'a
lofty place, or abode' (1 Kings viii.
13, Is. lxiii. 15), either the temple
(so also in later Heb.) or heaven.

26 αὐτοῦ. μὴ οὖν φοβηθῆτε αὐτούς· οὐδὲν γάρ ἐστιν κεκα-
λυμμένον ὃ οὐκ ἀποκαλυφθήσεται, καὶ κρυπτὸν ὃ οὐ γνω-
27 σθήσεται. ὃ λέγω ὑμῖν ἐν τῇ σκοτίᾳ, εἴπατε ἐν τῷ φωτί·

Thus 'Lord of [a lofty] Dwelling' is thought to be the name of an evil spirit or demon. Some even find a word-play in οἰκοδεσπό-της (lord of a house), and a reference to this meaning in xii. 29 (see *JBL.*, 1912, 34 ff.). (2) It is connected with the Aram. and late Heb. זְבֶל = 'dung.' If it was the name of a heathen deity or a demon, as it is treated in xii. 24 (see note), זְבָל may have been substituted for z^ebûb in scorn (as it is for זֶבַח, a heathen 'sacrifice' in Bab. *Ab. Zara* 18 b). But the name of a demon as a term of reproach for a man is strange. The Heb. use of *baal* in expressions denoting personal characteristics was so wide that 'lord (master, owner) of dung' may well have been a vulgar insult with no reference to a demon. The interpretation of it as the name of a demon may have been the cause of the awkward *v.l.* in B* τῷ οἰκο-δεσπότῃ and τοῖς οἰκιακοῖς, 'If they have laid [alliance with] B. to the charge of the master of the house, how much more to his household.'

οἰκιακοί (𝔖 sin 'the sons of his house'): a late word, recurring in bibl. Gk. in *v.* 36 only. It is used in *Ox. Pap.* 294. 17 for a member of the household of a government official. The *v.l.* οἰκειακοί means 'those who are his own.'

26–33. (Lk. xii. 2–9.) A series of sayings from Q connected by the thought 'Fear not' (*vv.* 26, 28, 31). In Lk. they are placed in connexion with the opposition of the Pharisees to the Lord's teaching (xi. 53 f.). Mk. has parallels with *vv.* 26, 33.

26. μὴ οὖν κτλ.] Apart from the first four words, given in Mt. only, the saying occurs, in a different form, in Mk. iv. 22 (Lk. viii. 17), of the coming to light of a truth concealed by a parable ; in Lk. xii. 2 (from Q) it is the coming to light of a man's true nature concealed by hypocrisy. In Mt. the connexion of thought is difficult, and the passage can hardly be in its true position. It may be explained (1) by the preceding or (2) by the following words : (1) 'Face insults fearlessly, for everything that you undergo, however secretly, shall be known,' the thought being somewhat similar to that in vi. 4, 6, 18 ; (2) Preach fearlessly in spite of insults, for everything that I tell you in secret, I wish you to proclaim openly.' In *Ox. Pap.* iv. 654. 27 ff. the words occur : [πᾶν τὸ μὴ ἔμπροσ]θεν τῆς ὄψεώς σου καὶ [τὸ κεκρυμμένον] ἀπὸ σοῦ ἀποκαλυφ[θ]ήσετ[αί σοι· οὐ γάρ ἐσ]τιν κρυπτὸν ὃ οὐ φανε[ρὸν γενήσεται] καὶ τεθαμμένον ὃ ο[ὐκ ἐγερθήσεται].

27. ὃ λέγω κτλ.] In Lk. (xii. 3) the thought passes from the hypocrisy of the Pharisees to the secret words of the disciples. The verse is a good instance of Semitic parallelism, the two halves having exactly the same meaning ; but in Mt. they mean 'What you have heard in secret, speak,' in Lk. 'what you have spoken in secret shall be heard.' εἰς τὸ οὖς ἀκούετε is unique ; λαλεῖν εἰς τὰ ὦτα is frequent in the LXX. (cf. Ex. xi. 2) ; ἀκούειν ἐν [τοῖς] ὠσίν also occurs ; but the sing. οὖς makes clearer the action of whispering. Cf. ἀποκαλύπτειν τὸ ὠτίον (1 Regn. xx. 2, 13), προσέθηκέν μοι ὠτίον ἀκούειν (Is. l. 4 ; cf. *v.* 5).

καὶ ὃ εἰς τὸ οὖς ἀκούετε, κηρύξατε ἐπὶ τῶν δωμάτων. καὶ 28
μὴ φοβηθῆτε ἀπὸ τῶν ἀποκτεινόντων τὸ σῶμα τὴν δὲ
ψυχὴν μὴ δυναμένων ἀποκτεῖναι· φοβεῖσθε δὲ μᾶλλον τὸν
δυνάμενον καὶ ψυχὴν καὶ σῶμα ἀπολέσαι ἐν γεέννῃ. οὐχὶ 29
δύο στρουθία ἀσσαρίου πωλεῖται; καὶ ἓν ἐξ αὐτῶν οὐ

δῶμα means 'roof' nearly always in
the LXX., and always in the N.T.
(xxiv. 17 (Mk., Lk.), Lk. v. 19, Ac.
x. 9). Jer. says it had that meaning
'in orientalibus provinciis.'

28. καὶ μὴ φοβηθῆτε ἀπό κτλ.]
The Hebraic construction (= מִן יָרֵא),
frequent in the LXX., does not occur
in the N.T. apart from this context.
In Lk. it is preceded by λέγω δὲ
ὑμῖν τοῖς φίλοις μου (Jo. xv. 14 f.).
On the varieties in the spelling of
ἀποκτείνειν see Blass, § 17.

τὴν δὲ ψυχήν κτλ.] Lk. καὶ
μετὰ ταῦτα μὴ ἐχόντων περισσότερόν
τι ποιῆσαι. Patristic writers freely
combined Mt. and Lk.; see Resch,
Agrapha², 169. The vagueness of
psychological ideas allowed the use
of ψυχή (נפשא) in three different
senses in the synn.: (1) The life principle common to men and animals,
which requires food (vi. 25), and
which man can kill (Mk. iii. 4; cf.
Mt. ii. 20); (2) The seat of the
thoughts and feelings, parallel with
καρδία and διάνοια (xxii. 37), and
with πνεῦμα (Lk. i. 46 f.); cf. Mt.
xxvi. 38, Jo. xii. 27 with Jo. xiii. 21;
(3) Something higher than either,
comprising all that makes up the real
Self (so here); cf. xvi. 26 with Lk. ix.
25. In the present passage it is
distinct from the body, but can be
destroyed with the body in Gehenna.
In v. 39 (1) and (3) are combined.

φοβεῖσθε δέ κτλ.] The change
of construction to φοβεῖσθαι with
acc. may be intentional: in the O.T.
when God is the object of fear, יָרֵא מִן
is rare in the Heb., and φοβ. ἀπό
never occurs in the LXX., except in

φοβ. ἀπὸ προσώπου (Hag. i. 12,
Eccl. iii. 14, viii. 12 f.); the preposition is liable to suggest the
shunning of that which is to be
feared. In Lk. the sentence is preceded by ὑποδείξω δὲ ὑμῖν τίνα
φοβηθῆτε. That τὸν δυνάμενον
κτλ. is God and not the devil is
clear from Lk., τὸν . . . ἔχοντα
ἐξουσίαν ἐκβαλεῖν εἰς τὴν γέενναν:
the devil has no such ἐξουσία. This
was understood by all the early
interpreters; cf. Jam. iv. 12. The
Christian is never bidden to fear
the devil, but to fight him (ib. v. 7,
1 Pet. v. 9, Eph. vi. 11). On the
meaning of ἀπολέσαι see v. 39, on
the body in Gehenna, v. 29, and on
Gehenna, v. 22. With the whole
verse cf. the striking parallels in
Wisd. xvi. 13, 4 Mac. xiii. 14 f.;
and see Epict. Discourses, i. 1, quoted
by Plummer, St. Mat. ad loc.

29. οὐχὶ δύο κτλ.] Lk. οὐχὶ
πέντε στρ. πωλοῦνται ἀσσαρίων
δύο; On the market-stalls they
might be sold at a halfpenny a brace
or five for a penny. στρουθίον
occurs seven times in the LXX. for
צִפּוֹר, any small bird. Sparrows are
probably meant; the passage implies
that they were eaten, as they are
to-day in Mediterranean countries.
ἀσσάριον is the Gk. diminutive form
of the Roman as, which was 1/16th of
a denarius. The latter, till the time
of Nero, was about 9½d., and the
ἀσσάριον, therefore, slightly more
than a halfpenny. It was hebraized
as אִסָּר. See HDB. iii. 427 b, 429 a.
In τοῦ ἀσσαρίου (D) the article
preserves a Semitic construction.

30 πεσεῖται ἐπὶ τὴν γῆν ἄνευ τοῦ πατρὸς ὑμῶν. ὑμῶν δὲ καὶ
31 αἱ τρίχες τῆς κεφαλῆς πᾶσαι ἠριθμημέναι εἰσίν. μὴ οὖν
32 φοβεῖσθε· πολλῶν στρουθίων διαφέρετε ὑμεῖς. Πᾶς οὖν
ὅστις ὁμολογήσει ἐν ἐμοὶ ἔμπροσθεν τῶν ἀνθρώπων, ὁμολογήσω κἀγὼ ἐν αὐτῷ ἔμπροσθεν τοῦ πατρός μου τοῦ ἐν

29 ανευ] add της βουλης 𝔏 pler [non k l vg] go Iren^lat Or Tert Cyp

καὶ ἕν κτλ.] For the adversative
καί see Blass, § 77. 6. The bird
falls through cold, hunger, or storm,
not in spite of, but with the knowledge of the Father. The inexorable,
and apparently cruel, laws of nature
are not outside the loving care of
God. Lk. has οὐκ ἔστιν ἐπιλελησ-
μένον ἐνώπιον τοῦ θεοῦ. ἐνώπιον
is characteristic of Lk. (²⁰ Ac.¹⁵, Mt.⁰,
Mk.⁰) as τ. πατρὸς ὑμῶν οf Mt. ; cf.
vi. 26 with Lk. xii. 24, another
reference to birds. οὐ πεσεῖται κτλ.
recalls Am. iii. 5, εἰ πεσεῖται ὄρνεον
ἐπὶ τὴν γῆν [Heb. 'into a snare on
the earth'] ἄνευ ἰξευτοῦ; which may
have influenced Mt., and also led to
the εἰς τὴν παγίδα of some Gk.
commentators. Cf. Ber. R. 79 : 'If
a bird is not captured without
Heaven, how much less the life of a
man.' ἄνευ (class.) recurs in the N.T.
in 1 Pet. iii. 1, iv. 9 only ; cf. Gen.
xli. 44, 4 Regn. xviii. 25, Am. l.c.
The gloss τῆς βουλῆς (see Appar.)
rightly expresses the meaning.

30. ὑμῶν δὲ κτλ.] The position
of the pronoun (not so in Lk.)
expresses an emphatic comparison
with the sparrows. In your case
the watchfulness of the Father's
care, to the smallest details, is even
more wonderful. The expression is
different from that in Lk. xxi. 18
(see Mt. xxiv. 9 note).

31. μὴ οὖν κτλ.] Not because
they would escape martyrdom, but
because, like the sparrows, not one of
them would suffer death 'without
their Father.' Wellhausen suggests

that the Aram. אסֹין has been misunderstood, and that the meaning is
'Ye are much (πολλῷ) better than
sparrows'; cf. vi. 26, xii. 12.

32. πᾶς οὖν κτλ.] οὖν ('So
then') sums up the thought of
endurance under persecution which
has been the subject of vv. 17–31
(cf. v. 48, vii. 12, 24). Lk. has λέγω
δὲ ὑμῖν as he has in v. 4. ὁμολογεῖν
ἐν (Lk. xii. 8 only) is an Aram., not
a Heb. construction = ב אורי. The
verb has various shades of meaning
in the N.T. as in the LXX.; with
regard to a fact, to acknowledge or
admit it (vii. 23, Jo. i. 20, Ac. xxiii.
8, Heb. xi. 13), to swear or promise
it (xiv. 7, Ac. vii. 17), to confess
[sins] (1 Jo. i. 9) ; with regard to a
person, to praise him (Heb. xiii. 15),
and, as here, to 'acknowledge him,'
i.e. to endorse his claims, to declare
agreement with, or adherence to, him
(Rom. x. 9, 1 Jo. ii. 23). With the
whole expression cf. Apoc. iii. 5.
'Before men' and 'before my Father'
refer to courts of judgment, human
(cf. 1 Tim. vi. 12) and divine. For
ὁμολογήσω Lk. (probably rightly) has
ὁ υἱὸς τοῦ ἀνθρώπου ὁμολογήσει :
cf. the parallel to v. 33 in Mk. viii.
38 (Lk. ix. 26), where Mt. (xvi. 27)
has a different saying. On 'My
Father which is in heaven' see v.
16, vi. 9. Lk. has τῶν ἀγγέλων τοῦ
θεοῦ, a periphrasis for God, which is,
again, probably the more original
(cf. Lk. xv. 10). In xvi. 27 (Mk.,
Lk.) both the Father and the angels
are spoken of.

τοῖς οὐρανοῖς· ὅστις δὲ ἀρνήσηταί με ἔμπροσθεν τῶν ἀν- 33
θρώπων, ἀρνήσομαι κἀγὼ αὐτὸν ἔμπροσθεν τοῦ πατρός μου
τοῦ ἐν τοῖς οὐρανοῖς.   Μὴ νομίσητε ὅτι ἦλθον βαλεῖν 34
εἰρήνην ἐπὶ τὴν γῆν· οὐκ ἦλθον βαλεῖν εἰρήνην ἀλλὰ
μάχαιραν. ἦλθον γὰρ διχάσαι ἄνθρωπον κατὰ τοῦ πατρὸς 35
ἀυτοῦ καὶ θυγατέρα κατὰ τῆς μητρὸς ἀυτῆς καὶ νύμφην κατὰ τῆς
πενθερᾶς ἀυτῆς, καὶ ἐχθροὶ τοῦ ἀνθρώπου οἱ οἰκιακοὶ ἀυτοῦ. 36
Ὁ φιλῶν πατέρα ἢ μητέρα ὑπὲρ ἐμὲ οὐκ ἔστιν μου ἄξιος· 37

33. ὅστις δέ κτλ.] Lk. ὁ δὲ
ἀρνησάμενός με. 'It is no threat
which he here voices, but a solemn,
sobering, inevitable law' (King,
Ethics of Jesus, 129). 2 Tim. ii. 12 b
seems to be an allusion to the
saying. For ἀρνήσομαι Lk. has
ἀπαρνηθήσεται, sc. by the Son of
Man.

34–36. (Lk. xii. 51–53.) *Family
divisions.* A repetition of the
thought of v. 21.

34. μὴ νομίσητε κτλ.] Cf. v. 17.
βαλεῖν is not a sudden or violent
action ; it does not here differ from
δοῦναι (Lk.); cf. ix. 17, xxv. 27,
xxvi. 12, xxvii. 6. The orig. Aram.
may have meant 'give,' or 'bring,
cause to come'; cf. ἐκβάλλειν, viii.
12 note. The 'sword' is not literal
war, but διαμερισμός (Lk.); cf. Heb.
iv. 12 : as the word of God sifts the
components of man's being, so will
the same word, as proclaimed by
Jesus, do in human society. ἦλθον
βαλεῖν does not strictly express a
purpose, but 'I came to do that
which will inevitably divide society
into camps.' It in no way conflicts
with the result of the Incarnation :
ἐπὶ γῆς εἰρήνη ἐν ἀνθρώποις εὐδοκίας
(Lk. ii. 14). On ἦλθον see v. 17.

35. ἦλθον γάρ κτλ.] διχάζειν,
not elsewhere in bibl. Gk., is used
by Aq. Lev. i. 17, Dt. xiv. 6. The
effect of the Lord's work was the
opposite of that expected from
Elijah (Mal. iv. 6 [iii. 24]); the

saying may definitely have meant
'I am not Elijah.' The following
words are based upon Mic. vii. 6 (cf.
v. 21 above); υἱὸς ἀτιμάζει πατέρα,
θυγάτηρ ἐπαναστήσεται (Heb. קָמָה
partcp.) ἐπὶ τὴν μητέρα αὐτῆς,
νύμφη ἐπὶ τὴν πενθερὰν αὐτῆς,
ἐχθροὶ πάντες ἀνδρὸς οἱ ἐν τῷ οἴκῳ
αὐτοῦ. Micah (vii. 1–6) describes
the rottenness of the social life of his
day ; Jesus uses the words to describe
one of the signs of the fast approaching end of the age. The verse was
similarly applied in Rabb. writings
(*Sanh.* 97 a, *Sota* 49 b). Lk. introduces the O.T. allusion with a verse
(52) which is absent from Mt., and
arranges a series of antitheses, 'father
against son and son against father
etc.,' to which the simpler adaptation
in Mt. is preferable. For νύμφη
'daughter-in-law' cf. Gen. xi. 31,
Lev. xx. 12, Ruth i. 6 ff. *al.*, Jos.
Ant. v. ix. 1 ; for the class. meaning
'bride' common in the LXX., cf. xxv.
1 (*v.l.*), Jo. iii. 29, Apoc.[4]

36. καὶ ἐχθροί κτλ.] Lk. omits
this part of the quotation. Mt. is
nearer to the Heb. than the LXX.
On οἰκιακοί see v. 25. The Lord
here speaks from personal experience;
see Mk. iii. 21.

37, 38. (Lk. xiv. 26 f.) *Conditions
of discipleship.*

37. ὁ φιλῶν κτλ.] In Lk. the
passage probably stands in its true
setting: speaking to the crowds who
accompany Him, Jesus warns them

καὶ ὁ φιλῶν υἱὸν ἢ θυγατέρα ὑπὲρ ἐμὲ οὐκ ἔστιν μου ἄξιος·
38 καὶ ὃς οὐ λαμβάνει τὸν σταυρὸν αὐτοῦ καὶ ἀκολουθεῖ ὀπίσω
39 μου, οὐκ ἔστιν μου ἄξιος. ὁ εὑρὼν τὴν ψυχὴν αὐτοῦ ἀπο-

of what it will cost to become
disciples; it is not enough εἴ τις
ἔρχεται πρός με, he must also *hate*
his father, etc. (cf. Mt. vi. 24 note).
See a good note by Denney, *ExpT.*
xxi. 41. φιλεῖν is to ἀγαπᾶν as
amare to *diligere*; the latter is a
voluntary and deliberate disposition
of mind, springing from admiration,
esteem, or benevolence; the former
is a state of mind compelled naturally
by sense and emotion; cf. Prov. viii.
17, ἐγὼ τοὺς ἐμὲ φιλοῦντας ἀγαπῶ,
Dio Cass. xliv. 48, ἐφιλήσατε αὐτὸν
ὡς πατέρα καὶ ἠγαπήσατε ὡς εὐ-
εργέτην. A true disciple feels an
irresistible personal affection for the
Master, greater than that of a son
for his father. The same affection
can be felt for the Wisdom of God
(Prov. *l.c.*, Wisd. viii. 2), but neither
in LXX. nor N.T. is φιλεῖν ever used
of love to God Himself.

οὐκ ἔστιν κτλ.] Cf. Wisd. iii. 5,
εὗρεν αὐτοὺς ἀξίους ἑαυτοῦ, Heb. xi.
38. On the use in inscriptions see
Deissmann, *Bible St.* 248. Lk. enlarges the list of relationships after
the manner of Mk. x. 29 f. (which
belongs to a different occasion), adding wife, children, brothers, sisters,
ἔτι τε καὶ τὴν ψυχὴν ἑαυτοῦ, and
ends with οὐ δύναται εἶναί μου
μαθητής. In Mt. the hearers were
already disciples.

38. καὶ ὃς κτλ.] The thought
advances a step, as in Lk.'s ἔτι τε κ.
τ. ψυχὴν ἑ. There must be a
readiness not only to sacrifice family
life, but to follow Jesus to the very
death. In Lk. this is a general
warning to the crowds (see above);
in Mt. it is the climax of the passages
on persecution. Lk. has βαστάζει

for λαμβάνει (cf. viii. 17 note), and
ἔρχεται for ἀκολουθεῖ. It was
customary for a condemned criminal
to carry his cross to the place of
execution; cf. Artem. ii. 56, ὁ μέλλων
αὐτῷ [*sc.* σταυρῷ] προσηλοῦσθαι
πρότερον αὐτὸν βαστάζει, Plut. *De
sera Num. vind.* ix., τῶν κολαζομένων
ἕκαστος κακούργων ἐκφέρει τὸν
αὑτοῦ σταυρόν, Cic. *De Div.* i. 26,
'servus . . . furcam ferens ductus
est.' It is open to question whether
the Lord intended this to be a prediction of the exact manner of His
death. If He did, the words must
have been uttered later than the
turning-point at Caesarea Philippi,
when He for the first time παρρησίᾳ
ἐλάλει (Mk. viii. 32) concerning His
death. If spoken before that time
they would be understood metaphorically; crucifixion was so terribly
frequent (see *e.g.* Jos. *Ant.* XVII. x. 10),
that it might well be typical of any
violent death or suffering. In Mk.
viii. 34 (= Mt. xvi. 24, see note, Lk.
ix. 23), perhaps a doublet of the
present saying from Q, a similar injunction, in a positive form, is addressed to 'the crowd with His
disciples' (Mk.), 'to all [*sc.* the dis-
ciples]' (Lk.), 'to His disciples' (Mt.).
Elsewhere the form of the Lord's
death is mentioned, before the Passion
itself, only in Mt. (xx. 19, xxvi. 2).

39. (Lk. xvii. 33. Cf. Mt. xvi.
25 = Mk. viii. 35 = Lk. ix. 24; Jo.
xii. 25.) *Self-sacrifice the only true
life.*

The five forms in which the synn.
preserve this paradox are probably
derived from one Aram. original.
(1) Mt. xvi. 25 and parallels have ὃς
ἐὰν θέλῃ, Lk. xvii. 33 ὃς ἐὰν ζητήσῃ

λέσει αὐτήν, καὶ ὁ ἀπολέσας τὴν ψυχὴν αὐτοῦ ἕνεκεν ἐμοῦ
εὑρήσει αὐτήν. Ὁ δεχόμενος ὑμᾶς ἐμὲ δέχεται, καὶ ὁ 40
ἐμὲ δεχόμενος δέχεται τὸν ἀποστείλαντά με. ὁ δεχόμενος προ- 41

(to be taken with περιποιήσασθαι,
not with τ. ψυχήν): both verbs
can represent בעש. Mt. here omits
this. (2) All have ἀπολέσαι in both
clauses (= אובד). (3) The opposite of
'destroy' is 'save alive,' represented
by σῶσαι (= אחי) in Mt. xvi. 25
(first clause), Mk., Lk. ix. 24 (both
clauses); in Lk. xvii. 33 by περιποιήσασθαι and ζωογονήσει (used
in the LXX. respectively 10 and 11
times for חיה), both of which ܫ sin
renders by ܐܚܝ. But ἀπολέσαι
can also mean 'lose,' the opposite
of 'find'; hence Mt. here has ὁ
εὑρών and εὑρήσει, the latter also
being used in xvi. 25 (second clause).
The placing of this saying to follow that on the taking up of the
cross is due to the Marcan tradition.
Lk. (xvii. 33, from Q) has it in a
different context.

ὁ εὑρών κτλ.] On the three
meanings of ψυχή in the Gospels
see v. 28. He that has kept his
[physical] life from martyrdom, will
lose the higher life of the soul, his
true self; and he that has sacrificed
the former, because of the loyalty of
his discipleship to Me, will hereafter
discover that he has gained the
latter. Cf. Sir. li. 26 (Heb., not
LXX.) 'He that giveth his life findeth
her (Wisdom).' Epictetus (iv. i. 165)
says of Socrates τοῦτον οὐκ ἔστι
σῶσαι αἰσχρῶς, ἀλλὰ ἀποθνήσκων
σώζεται, οὐ φεύγων. S. Paul's words
are as true of the ψυχή as of the
σῶμα (i Cor. xv. 36): οὐ ζωοποιεῖται
ἐὰν μὴ ἀποθάνῃ. On the death of
the ψυχή see the fine passage in Philo,
Alleg. Leg. i. 33. Lk. (xvii. 33) omits
ἕνεκεν ἐμοῦ, forming a proverbial
saying of universal application; but

it is preserved in Mk. and parallels,
Mk., however, adding καὶ τοῦ εὐαγγελίου (see Mt. xvi. 25). For the
formal parallelism of the saying cf.
xxiii. 12.

40–42. (Lk. x. 16; cf. Jo. xiii.
20.) Conclusion of the missionary
Charge.

40. ὁ δεχόμενος κτλ.] Lk. has
ὁ ἀκούων, adding the converse ὁ
ἀθετῶν (cf. Jo. xii. 48). The verse
is parallel with Mk. ix. 37 (Mt. xviii.
5, Lk. ix. 48), ὑμᾶς, which is suitable
to the Charge, taking the place of
ἓν τῶν παιδίων τοιούτων (see on v.
42 below). ὁ δεχόμενος in the first
clause attaches itself to the thought
of vv. 11–14, 'he that receives you
into his house.' ἐμὲ δέχεται finds
an echo in xxv. 35–40; and cf.
xviii. 20. The claim of Jesus to
come from God is as great as that in
Jo. xii. 44, 48 f., xiii. 20, xx. 21, and
is implicit in the ἦλθον, -θεν, of Mt.
v. 17, ix. 13, x. 34 f., xx. 28; cf. Heb.
iii. i (ἀπόστολον). An early recognition of the thought is seen in Clem.
Cor. xlii. 1 f.: οἱ ἀπόστολοι ἡμῖν εὐ-
ηγγελίσθησαν ἀπὸ τοῦ κυρίου Ἰησοῦ
Χριστοῦ, Ἰησοῦς ὁ Χριστὸς ἀπὸ τοῦ
θεοῦ ἐξεπέμφθη. ὁ Χριστὸς οὖν ἀπὸ
τοῦ θεοῦ, καὶ οἱ ἀπόστολοι ἀπὸ τοῦ
Χριστοῦ.

41. ὁ δεχόμενος κτλ.] Mt. only.
As in vii. 15 ff. the words belong to a
time when Christian prophets were a
recognized class, distinct from apostles.
The hospitality extended to such
prophets was at a later date much
abused; see v. 8, vii. 15, notes. εἰς
ὄνομα corresponds to the Rabb. לְשֵׁם,
'for the sake of' (see v. 22); cf.
Berak. xvii. 1, 'Every one who occu-

φήτην εἰς ὄνομα προφήτου μισθὸν προφήτου λήμψεται, καὶ
ὁ δεχόμενος δίκαιον εἰς ὄνομα δικαίου μισθὸν δικαίου λήμ-
42 ψεται. καὶ ὃς ἂν ποτίσῃ ἕνα τῶν μικρῶν τούτων ποτήριον
ψυχροῦ μόνον εἰς ὄνομα μαθητοῦ, ἀμὴν λέγω ὑμῖν, οὐ μὴ
ἀπολέσῃ τὸν μισθὸν αὐτοῦ.

42 απολεση τον μισθον] απολυται ο μισθος D 𝕃 a b c g¹ h k q 𝕾 sin.cur me aeth
Cyp

pies himself with the Law for its
own sake (לשמה, *i.e.* simply because
it is the Law)'; and see Taylor on
Aboth v. 22. In *Ox. Pap.* 37 (A.D.
49) occurs ὀνόματι ἐλευθέρου, 'in
virtue of being free-born.' He that
received a prophet from no ulterior
motive, but simply *qua* prophet ('ut
prophetam,' Jer.), would receive a
reward in the coming age equal to
that of his guest. See Heitmüller,
Im Namen Jesu, 112 ff.

καὶ ὁ δεχόμενος κτλ.] There
were many in the Church who
were neither apostles nor itinerant
prophets, but who exhibited a
righteousness exceeding that of the
Scribes and Pharisees. To give
hospitality and fellowship to a δίκαιος, solely on account of what he
is, will be followed by the same
heavenly reward as his.

42. καὶ ὃς ἂν κτλ.] A fourth
class, neither apostles, prophets, nor
persons eminent for their righteousness, consisted of the obscure and
simple believers (cf. τ. μικρῶν τούτων
τῶν πιστευόντων εἰς ἐμέ, xviii. 6).
They were the μικροί of the Church
who formed the majority, as distinct
from the μεγάλοι; cf. the O.T. expression in Heb. viii. 11, Apoc. xi.
18, xix. 5, xx. 12. The words are
here taken from Mk. ix. 41, which
Mt. omits in his parallel passage
(see xviii. 6 note). The context
in Mk. is concerned with παιδία
(v. 37) and μικροί (v. 42); and it
is possible that an editor of Mk.,

later than Mt., substituted ὑμᾶς,
thereby bringing the saying into
connexion with the incident of the
non-disciple who exorcized in the
name of Jesus, which is interposed
in *vv.* 38–40. If so, neither Mk.'s
ὑμᾶς, nor Mt.'s ὑμᾶς in *v.* 40 above,
can be taken as evidence that the
Lord used παιδία or μικροί as a
designation of the Twelve. (That
He so used it was the view of
many of the older expositors (cf.
Tert. *Marc.* iv. 35), and is maintained
in *DCG.*, art. 'Little Ones,' where it
is explained with reference to Is.
lx. 22, Zech. xiii. 7.) The tender
expression is an abiding encouragement, both to children and also to
S. Paul's ἀδύνατοι (Rom. xv. 1), or
ἀσθενεῖς, ἀσθενοῦντες τῇ πίστει
(Rom. xiv. 1, 1 Cor. viii. 10 ff., ix.
22), and to the mass of obscure and
simple believers. Clem. *Cor.* xlvi.
cites Lk. xvii. 2, substituting ἕνα
τῶν ἐκλεκτῶν for τ. μικρῶν τούτων
ἕνα.

εἰς ὄνομα μαθητοῦ] Apparently
a paraphrase of Mk.'s ἐν ὀνόματι ὅτι
Χριστοῦ ἐστε. But there is a *v.l.*
in Mk. ἐν ὀνόματί μου; if, as is probable, ὅτι Χ. ἐστε was a gloss in Mk.
later than Mt., μου either may have
been an abbreviation of μαθητοῦ, or
was inadvertently read as such by
Mt.

ἀμήν κτλ.] See v. 18 note. B.
Weiss takes αὐτοῦ to refer to μαθητοῦ, carrying on the thought of v.
41. The *v.l.* ἀπόληται ὁ μισθός

Καὶ ἐγένετο ὅτε ἐτέλεσεν ὁ Ἰησοῦς διατάσσων τοῖς δώ- 1 XI.
δεκα μαθηταῖς αὐτοῦ, μετέβη ἐκεῖθεν τοῦ διδάσκειν καὶ
κηρύσσειν ἐν ταῖς πόλεσιν αὐτῶν.

Ὁ δὲ Ἰωάνης ἀκούσας ἐν τῷ δεσμωτηρίῳ τὰ ἔργα τοῦ 2
χριστοῦ πέμψας διὰ τῶν μαθητῶν αὐτοῦ εἶπεν αὐτῷ   Σὺ εἶ 3

which has strong authority, reflects
the Aram. construction, which is
smoothed by the reading in the text.
   xi. 1. καὶ ἐγένετο κτλ.] On the
formula, concluding a collection of
sayings, see vii. 28.   διδάσκειν, 'to
teach,' κηρύσσειν, 'to proclaim'; see
on iv. 23.   On the gen. τοῦ δ. see
Moulton, i. 216 f.   The Twelve
having been sent forth, nothing is
said in Mt. of their return, but they
are found with Jesus at xii. 1; their
return is related in Mk. vi. 30, Lk.
ix. 10 (see on Mt. xiv. 13).   αὐτῶν
is used loosely of the Jewish nation;
see on vii. 29.

   2–6.   (Lk. vii. 18–23.)   THE
BAPTIST'S QUESTION ANSWERED.
   2. ὁ δὲ Ἰωάνης κτλ.]   The Lucan
account is longer, relating that the
Baptist's disciples told him περὶ
πάντων τούτων (i.e. the foregoing
miracles), and that he sent two of
his disciples to ask the question.
His confinement was not so rigorous
that his friends could not gain access
to him (cf. xxv. 36).   Herod, holding a high opinion of him (Mk. vi.
20), treated him well; cf. Ac. xxiv.
23.   He was confined, according to
Jos. Ant. XVIII. v. 2, in the fortress
of Machaerus on the E. of the Dead
Sea.   The causes of his imprisonment and death are not related till
xiv. 3–12 (see n. there, and on iv.
12).   Lk. does not here mention
that he was in prison, and Spitta
(ThStKr., July 1910) maintains, un-
convincingly, that he was still at
liberty.   The statement of his im-

prisonment in Lk. iii. 20 is not
decisive (see on Mt. iv. 12), but the
aorists ἐξήλθατε in v. 7 ff. (Lk. v.
24 ff.) imply that his activity had
ceased.

   τοῦ χριστοῦ] Except in i. 17,
and probably 18, none of the
evangelists elsewhere employs the
title by itself in his own narrative
(contrast i. 16, xvi. 21, Mk. i. 1).
Mt. expresses his own knowledge of
what the Baptist only suspected and
hoped.   The addition of πέμψας is
Hebraistic; cf. Gen. xxvii. 42.   On
the aor. partcp. see Blass, § 74. 3.   It
is possible that Lk. δύο τινὰς τῶν
μαθητῶν has arisen from a misreading of διά.

   3. σὺ εἶ κτλ.]   The force of
ἕτερος ('another kind of person')
cannot be pressed; in Lk. the readings in vv. 19 f. vary between ἕτερον
and ἄλλον, and the same Aram.
word underlies both.   ὁ ἐρχόμενος
was not, so far as is known, a recognized title of the Messiah; it seems
to refer to a heavenly Personality,
not clearly defined, who might be
variously thought of as a Messiah
or some Forerunner of the Kingdom.
See p. 34 f.   Some have seen in
the Baptist's question an evidence
of depression or despair natural to
one in imprisonment.   Others, an
attempt to force the Lord's hand
by extorting an open declaration.
Origen's explanation ἡ τοῦ Ἰωάνου
ἐρώτησις οὐκ αὐτοῦ μόνον ἦν χάριν,
ἀλλὰ καὶ τῶν ἀποσταλέντων is
widely adopted by patristic and later

4 ὁ ἐρχόμενος ἢ ἕτερον προσδοκῶμεν; καὶ ἀποκριθεὶς ὁ
Ἰησοῦς εἶπεν αὐτοῖς Πορευθέντες ἀπαγγείλατε Ἰωάνει ἃ
5 ἀκούετε καὶ βλέπετε· τυφλοὶ ἀναβλέπουσιν καὶ χωλοὶ περιπατοῦσιν, λεπροὶ καθαρίζονται καὶ κωφοὶ ἀκούουσιν, καὶ
6 νεκροὶ ἐγείρονται καὶ πτωχοὶ εὐαγγελίζονται· καὶ μακάριος

writers; *i.e.* he knew the truth (cf.
Jo. i. 29, 36), but wished to convince
his disciples. But if the notes on
iii. 14, and on p. 35 f. are correct,
he did not know it. The wonderful
works of Jesus led him to hope, but
the popular expectations did not
ascribe miracles to the Messiah, and
Jesus had not, on the other hand,
done what the Messiah was expected
to do. Cf. Tert. *c. Marc.* iv. 18.
For patristic passages which connect
the words with Christ's preaching in
Hades see Heinrici, *Beiträge*, v. 118 f.

4. καὶ ἀποκριθεὶς κτλ.] In Lk.
(*v.* 21) the Lord's answer is prepared
for by the statement that 'in that
hour He healed many of diseases
and scourges and evil spirits, and
to many blind He gave sight.' But
this does not embrace the list of
miracles that the messengers were
to report to John. It is impossible
to suppose that the latter were all
performed, including the raising of
the dead, while the messengers were
waiting for their answer. Either
the works enumerated in *v.* 5 are
spiritual and not literal (Keim, *al.*;
see *ExpT.*, 1906, 286), although
Lk.'s insertion in *v.* 21 shews that
he did not so regard them, or, more
probably, the Lord spoke of His
preaching and of some cures just
wrought before the messengers' eyes,
and His words were amplified in
tradition on the basis of the Old
Testament (see next verse).

5. τυφλοί κτλ.] No instances
have occurred, before this point, of
the healing of the lame or the deaf;
see Add. n. on ix. 32, 33 (p. 129).

For ἀναβλέπειν with this meaning
cf. xx. 34, Jo. ix. 11, 15, 18, Ac.
ix. 12, 17 f., xxii. 13, Tob. xi. 8 (א),
xiv. 2, Is. xlii. 18. On πτωχοί see
v. 3. The pass. εὐαγγελίζεσθαι with
a personal subject is found in Heb.
iv. 2, 6; the verb, frequent in Lk.,
Ac. Paul., is elsewhere confined to
1 Pet.[3] and Apoc.[2] On the subst.
εὐαγγέλιον see iv. 23. The passage
recalls Is. lxi. 1, the actions of the
anointed Prophet (cf. Lk. iv. 18),
and Is. xxxv. 5 f., the actions of
God. Some had wondered whether
John himself were the Messiah (Lk.
iii. 15), but finding he was not,
they may have transferred the idea
to Jesus. The Baptist now had the
same hope, but since Jesus shewed
no signs of aiming at earthly power,
he was doubtful. The answer meant,
in effect, 'Ponder My works; they
are not what you expect from the
Messiah, but they shew that the
powers of evil are being undermined,
and that the Messianic age is very
close' (cf. xii. 28, Lk. x. 17 f.). The
Lord would not openly declare the
truth, which was to be revealed in
due time to the Twelve (xvi. 16 f.),
but the Baptist was encouraged to
persevere in his hope. Possibly the
bystanders understood neither question nor answer; they may not even
have heard them. In the subsequent
conversation with the people (*v.* 14)
Jesus gave them a hint of the truth.

6. καὶ μακάριος κτλ.] Not a remark to those present, but part of
the message to John, purposely
vague: in spite of the ambiguity of
the reply, and undisturbed by any

ἐστιν ὃς ἂν μὴ σκανδαλισθῇ ἐν ἐμοί.   Τούτων δὲ 7
πορευομένων ἤρξατο ὁ Ἰησοῦς λέγειν τοῖς ὄχλοις περὶ
Ἰωάνου Τί ἐξήλθατε εἰς τὴν ἔρημον θεάσασθαι; κάλαμον
ὑπὸ ἀνέμου σαλευόμενον; ἀλλὰ τί ἐξήλθατε ἰδεῖν; ἄν- 8
θρωπον ἐν μαλακοῖς ἠμφιεσμένον; ἰδοὺ οἱ τὰ μαλακὰ
φοροῦντες ἐν τοῖς οἴκοις τῶν βασιλέων. ἀλλὰ τί ἐξήλ- 9
θατε; προφήτην ἰδεῖν; ναί, λέγω ὑμῖν, καὶ περισσότερον
προφήτου. οὗτός ἐστιν περὶ οὗ γέγραπται   10

further reports which might reach
him, the Baptist must not relinquish
his brave hope. For σκανδ. ἐν cf.
xiii. 57 (Mk. vi. 3), xxvi. 31, 33,
Sir. ix. 5, xxiii. 8, xxxv. 15 [xxxii.
19] = בְּ וַיִּכְשֵׁל. On the verb, and
the subst. σκάνδαλον, see v. 29,
xiii. 41.

7–11. (Lk. vii. 24–28.) THE
LORD'S ESTIMATE OF THE BAPTIST.
7. τούτων δέ κτλ.] The pres.
partcp. represents the messengers as
still in sight; Lk. has the aor.
ἀπελθόντων. With ἤρξατο Mt.
passes to a new phase in the narrative; see on iv. 17. It is usual to
mark the interrogation, in this and
the two following verses, after θεάσασθαι and ἰδεῖν: but it stands more
naturally and vividly after ἐξήλθατε
—'Why went ye out into the wilderness ?' This is supported in v. 8 by
ἄνθρωπον ἰδεῖν (א* Jer.), and in v. 9
by προφήτην ἰδεῖν (א*BZ f k me
Orig.). The two verbs θεάσασθαι
and ἰδεῖν stood in Q, but the distinction was probably not marked in the
original Aram., and is disregarded in
𝔏 and 𝔖. On the ἔρημος see iii. 1.
κάλαμον κτλ.] The long cane
grass was plentiful in the Arabah,
by the banks of the Jordan and its
tributaries. Did you go out to see
the very ordinary sight of cane grass
shaken by wind ? (cf. 3 Macc. ii. 22).
κάλαμον is probably collective, as in
Job xl. 16 [21], Ps. lxvii. (lxviii.)
30, Is. xix. 6, xxxv. 7. There is

no contrast intended between the
moral strength of the Baptist and
the weak pliability of the reed.
8. ἀλλὰ τί κτλ.] If you did not
go to see cane grass, you went to see a
man ; but what kind of man ? ἀλλά
has the force of the Aram. אֶלָּא 'if
not' (so 𝔖). After μαλακοῖς Lk.
adds ἱματίοις. The hearers could
not but reflect that John was not
a time-serving courtier ; but the
primary object of the words was
probably to form a contrast with
the prophet's hairy mantle (iii. 4).
Cf. Jos. BJ. I. xxiv. 3, where ἐσθῆτες
βασιλικαί are contrasted with ἐκ
τριχῶν πεποιημέναι. Lk. expands
οἱ τὰ μαλακὰ φοροῦντες with more
varied vocabulary, and writes ἐν τοῖς
βασιλείοις for the Hebraistic ἐν τ.
οἴκοις τ. βασιλέων.
9. προφήτην ἰδεῖν; κτλ.] Either
(1) εἴδετε or, less probably, (2) ἰδεῖν
can be understood before περισσότερον : (1) You expected to see a
prophet ? Yes, and you saw more ;
(2) You expected to see a prophet ?
Yes, and to see more—the Messiah
Himself. (See further on v. 11.)
The ellipse in the former case is not
more harsh than in English. It is
unnecessary to make περισσ. προφ.
the predicate of οὗτός ἐστιν (Wellh.).
περισσότερον is neuter, as πλεῖον
(xii. 41 f.), μεῖζον (xii. 6). On the
word see Blass, § 11. 3, n. 4.
10. οὗτός ἐστιν κτλ.] The
quotation is from Mal. iii. 1, and is

Ἰδοὺ ἐγὼ ἀποστέλλω τὸν ἄγγελόν μου πρὸ προσώπου σου,
ὃς κατασκευάσει τὴν ὁδόν σου ἔμπροσθέν σου.

11 ἀμὴν λέγω ὑμῖν, οὐκ ἐγήγερται ἐν γεννητοῖς γυναικῶν μείζων
Ἰωάνου τοῦ βαπτιστοῦ· ὁ δὲ μικρότερος ἐν τῇ βασιλείᾳ

identical in Lk., except for the omission of ἐγώ; in Mk. i. 2 ἐγώ and ἔμπροσθεν are omitted. The LXX., following the Heb., has ἰδοὺ ἐξαποστέλλω τὸν ἄγγελόν μου· καὶ ἐπιβλέψεται [וּפִנָּה; see on Mt. iii. 3] ὁδὸν πρὸ προσώπου μου. The synn. use a form of the words in which they are addressed to the Messiah (σου ter) by God, perhaps derived from an Aram. version current in the synagogues. It is probable that the quotation was not spoken by Jesus, but inserted editorially by Mt. (as it is by Mk. in i. 2), for it anticipates the new and mysterious announcement made in v. 14, and interrupts the connexion of thought in vv. 9, 11 (see below). In Lk. the quotation may be due to a marginal gloss (J. Weiss), since Lk. gives no other saying of Jesus which identifies John and Elijah.

11. ἀμὴν κτλ.] On ἀμήν (om. by Lk.) see v. 18. ἐγήγερται, 'hath been raised up,' sc. on the stage of history; cf. Judg. ii. 16, 18 (Targ. אקים), Mt. xxiv. 11, 24, Jo. vii. 52, Ac. xiii. 22. Lk.'s ἐστιν avoids the Hebraistic metaphor. γεννητὸς γυναικός 'a mortal man' occurs five times in Job; cf. Sir. x. 18 (Heb.). In Lk. there is some authority for προφή-της after γυναικῶν, which, however, sacrifices what appears to be the true meaning of the words. He omits, perhaps rightly, τοῦ βαπτιστοῦ, which the Lord probably never used, and is not recorded to have used except in this and the following verse. μικρότερος may be equivalent either to μικρός or μικρότατος; see on ἐλάχιστος v. 19.

The passage is often explained to mean that the least Christian is greater than the greatest Jew, because the former is in the Kingdom and the latter is not. But the Kingdom of Heaven is *future*; and if the patriarchs were to share in it (viii. 11), why not one who was at least as great as they? The meaning probably is that anyone, however humble and obscure, who shall be admitted into the Kingdom, will be greater then than John is now. Cf. Jer. 'quod omnis sanctus qui jam cum Deo est major sit illo qui adhuc constitit in praelio.' ἐστιν is timeless, and would not be represented in Aram. This is much better than the explanation that John, who is the greatest among men now, will—although admitted to the Kingdom —be the least then, because of his impatient doubt concerning Jesus (J. Weiss). Tert., Orig., *al.* strangely understand ὁ μικρότερος of Jesus Himself; Ambrose, of the angels.

The connexion of thought, then, with v. 9 is this: (1) with an ellipse of εἴδετε in v. 9: 'That which you saw in the wilderness was more than a prophet; indeed no greater man has ever lived; and yet the meanest person, who shall have entered the Kingdom, will be greater than John is now'; (2) with an ellipse of ἰδεῖν the words do not so naturally lead to a climax: 'That which you expected to see in the wilderness was more than a prophet [*i.e.* the Messiah]: he is not the Messiah, it is true, but still no greater man has ever lived; and yet etc.' In either case v. 10 interrupts the thought.

τῶν οὐρανῶν μείζων αὐτοῦ ἐστίν. ἀπὸ δὲ τῶν ἡμερῶν 12
Ἰωάνου τοῦ βαπτιστοῦ ἕως ἄρτι ἡ βασιλεία τῶν οὐρανῶν

12-15. (Lk. xvi. 16.) FURTHER
SAYINGS ABOUT THE BAPTIST.

12. ἀπὸ δέ κτλ.] It is unlikely
that the opening words (to ἕως ἄρτι)
were spoken by Jesus at this period
of His ministry, while the Baptist
was still alive, if at all. But the
remainder of the verse must have
been based, at least, upon a genuine
utterance ; Mt. introduces it with a
remark appropriate to his own date :
'Ever since the days of John the
Baptist (on τ. βαπτιστοῦ see last
note) the words ἡ βασιλεία κτλ.
have proved true.' ἄρτι is characteristic of Mt. (⁷ Mk.°, Lk.°).

ἡ βασιλεία κτλ.] Quae sub-
obscura videtur esse locutio (Ambr.).
The verb can be either passive or
middle. The *passive*, though somewhat less frequent, has classical
authority ; it is so rendered here in
𝕃 k Vulg. ' vim patitur,' a b ' cogitur,'
𝔖 sin.cur ' oppressed,' pesh ' treated
with violence,' and by Hil., Jer., Cyr.
In *Ox. Pap.* 294 (A.D. 22) it is used
of earnest persuasion, ἐγὼ δὲ βιάζομαι
ὑπὸ φίλων γενεσθαι κτλ. The
middle, ' to act violently' or ' press
in, or forwards, violently' is adopted,
though with a different subject, by
Lk. (xvi. 16), and is frequent in
Josephus ; cf. Ex. xix. 24, Clem.
Strom. vi. 149 Χριστιανοὶ εἶναι
βιαζόμεθα, ὅτι μάλιστα βιαστῶν
ἐστιν ἡ βασιλεία, Lucian, *Herm.*
22 ἁρπαζόντων καὶ βιαζομένων καὶ
πλεονεκτούντων. Allen refers to
Ditt. *Syll.* 379, *id.* 893. 5, and *Tebt.
Pap.* 6. 31. But even if the future
Kingdom could be intelligibly said to
press forward violently, the transition
of thought in βιασταὶ ἁρπάζουσιν
αὐτήν would be abrupt and awkward.
If, as is probable, β. is passive, it may

represent מתאנסה (cf. Sir. xxxiv.
[xxxi.] 21, ἐβιάσθης = נאנסה) : and
βιασταί and ἁρπάζουσιν may both
stand for words from the same root.
The Naz. Gosp. seems to have had a
word which a translator rendered
διαρπάζεται (*Texte u. Unters.*, 1911,
pp. 22, 39, 288). Three meanings
are possible : (1) The Kingdom is
violently treated, oppressed, in the
person of its members. In this case
the words must be later than the
Resurrection, for Christians, as such,
were not persecuted before then.
But in no other passage does ' the
K. of Heaven ' stand, like ἐκκλησία,
for the persons who share in it.
(2) The Kingdom is treated as a
ἁρπαγμός, and violently snatched
at, *i.e.* by those who thought of the
Messianic blessings as political, and
tried to reach them by rebellion and
war, as, *e.g.*, in A.D. 6, when the
Romans for the first time subjected
Judaea to taxation. The Lord Himself was tempted (iv. 8 f.) to reach
an earthly sovereignty ; cf. Jo. vi.
15. This was very probably His
meaning. If so, the passage originally
belonged to another context ; but
in placing it here, Mt. apparently
understood the verbs in a good, not
a bad, sense, as follows. (3) The
Kingdom, since the days when the
Baptist heralded its approach, is
violently stormed by enthusiastic
people ; *e.g.* toll-gatherers and harlots,
whom the orthodox considered excluded from it (cf. xxi. 31 f., Lk. vii.
29 f.), and the μικρότερος of *v.* 11
(which perhaps suggested the connexion of thought to the evangelist's
mind). Allen (p. 118) refers to a
Talmudic tradition (Bab. *Eduyoth*,
viii. 7), which illustrates, if it does

13 βιάζεται, καὶ βιασταὶ ἁρπάζουσιν αὐτήν. πάντες γὰρ οἱ
14 προφῆται καὶ ὁ νόμος ἕως Ἰωάνου ἐπροφήτευσαν· καὶ εἰ
15 θέλετε δέξασθαι, αὐτός ἐστιν Ἡλείας ὁ μέλλων ἔρχεσθαι.
16 Ὁ ἔχων ὦτα ἀκουέτω. Τίνι δὲ ὁμοιώσω τὴν γενεὰν ταύτην;

not underlie, Mt.'s use of the words, that Elijah, when he came, would separate from Israel those who had been wrongfully ('by force' בזרע) received into it, and would receive into it those who had been wrongfully separated from it. This explanation gives point to Lk. vii. 29 f., which takes the place of the present passage, and also accounts for the actual parallel in Lk. xvi. 16, where Lk. adopts Mt.'s interpretation, and, transposing this and the following verse, throws the whole into a simple Gk. form. Neither Lk.'s εὐαγγελίζεται nor βιάζεται (middle) can represent an Aram. word (Dalm. *Words*, 140 ff.). For instances of the late and rare βιαστής (= βιατάς Pindar) see Wetstein. (In Philo, *Agr.* 19 Cohn and Wendl. read βίας τῶν for βιαστῶν.)

13. πάντες γάρ κτλ.] A logical connexion implied by γάρ is difficult to discern. But if *v.* 12 originally belonged to another context, γάρ refers to *v.* 11, and the connexion is clear : A greater than John has never been, and yet he is not at present in the Kingdom, *for* he is the hinge upon which history turns. All the prophets, and indeed (καί) the Law before them, pointed forwards to the Kingdom ; that series of prophecies ended with John (for the use of ἕως cf. Ac. xiii. 20), who heralded its actual, imminent arrival ; he was thus the greatest of mortals, since he was entrusted with a message greater than that of the prophets. For the intensive καί cf. *v.* 9, 1 Cor. ii. 2 (Blass, § 77. 7). Possibly underlying the words is the thought that the pre-

diction about Elijah in Malachi forms the closing words of the 'Prophets.' The Law also contained predictions of an ideal future, *e.g.* Gen. xii. 2 f., xxii. 17 f., Deut. xviii. 15, 18 f. With the personification of the Law cf. Gal. iii. 8. On the augment in ἐπροφήτευσαν see Blass, § 15. 7. Lk. gives a less natural turn to the words : ὁ νόμος καὶ οἱ προφῆται μέχρι Ἰωάνου 'the O.T. Canon,' *i.e.* the Jewish dispensation, 'reached to John.'

14. καὶ εἰ θέλετε κτλ.] Cf. xix. 11 f. The people found it hard to accept the saying that one who was in prison was Elijah. But if he were he, all the signs that were expected to usher in the Messiah's advent ought, as they supposed, to have appeared. The mysterious hint that the Lord gave was lost upon them. The disciples were away on their mission, but were taught the truth later (xvii. 11 ff.). ὁ μέλλων ἔρχεσθαι is not a title, but expresses the current expectations. See on *v.* 3 ; and for Rabbinic passages on Elijah see Wetstein, *ad loc.*

15. ὁ ἔχων κτλ.] So xiii. 9, 43. In Lk. viii. 8, xiv. 35 ἀκούειν is added after ὦτα ; so in Mk. iv. 9 with ὃς ἔχει, and iv. 23, vii. 16 (MSS.) with εἴ τις ἔχει. The expression is imitated in Apoc. ii. 7, 11, 17, 29, iii. 6, 13, 22, xiii. 9, ὁ ἔχων [εἴ τις ἔχει] οὓς ἀκουσάτω. Cf. Is. l. 4 προσέθηκέν μοι ὠτίον ἀκούειν. Philo has βοῶν . . . τοῖς ὦτα ἔχουσιν ἐν ψυχῇ. In every N.T. passage the saying is ascribed to the Lord, except in Apoc. xiii. 9, and there only does it refer to the

ὁμοία ἐστὶν παιδίοις καθημένοις ἐν ταῖς ἀγοραῖς ἃ προσφωνοῦντα τοῖς ἑτέροις λέγουσιν

16 ἑτέροις] ἑταίροις G al 𝕃 ff¹ l vg 𝕊 hcl arm aeth

utterance which follows it. Its purpose is to call upon the hearers to take to heart the teaching which has just been given, so far as they have insight to understand it. Tert. (c. Marc. iv. 19) suggests as its origin Isaiah's words: 'Aure audietis et non audietis.' Dibelius (ThStKr., 1910, 461) unnecessarily explains it as a formula of a later age, when the simple words of the Gospel were treated as concealing a deeper esoteric meaning.

16–19. (Lk. vii. 31–35.) PARABLE OF THE CHILDREN'S GAME.

16, 17. τίνι δέ κτλ.] Lk. τ. οὖν ὁμ. τοὺς ἀνθρώπους τῆς γενεᾶς ταύτης; (cf. Lk. xi. 31), adding καὶ τίνι εἰσὶν ὅμοιοι; (cf. Lk. xiii. 18). For the double question cf. Is. xl. 18. The formula has Rabb. parallels, the most frequent being 'A parable (מָשָׁל); to what is the matter like? [It is like] to, etc.' (Bacher, Term. i. 121). γενεά is used by the Lord always in rebuke or condemnation, except in xxiv. 34 (Mk., Lk.), Lk. xvi. 8. It recalls such passages as Deut. xxxii. 5, Ps. xciv. [xcv.] 10; cf. Ac. ii. 40, Phil. ii. 15. The perverseness of Moses' generation repeated itself in that to which the greater than Moses had come. It never means the whole Jewish race but those to whom He is speaking, as representative of their generation. Cf. xii. 39, 41 f., xvi. 4, xvii. 17, xxiii. 36. Lk. places the passage to follow the contrast, drawn in vii. 29 f., between the people and the Pharisees and Lawyers, as though the latter only were 'the men of this generation'; in Lk. xi. 29, on the other hand, they are the people,

but in Mt. xii. 39, xvi. 4, Mk. viii. 12 the Pharisees.

ὁμοία ἐστίν κτλ.] For ὁμοία cf. xiii. 31, 33, 44 f., 47, 52, xx. 1; less frequently ὡμοιώθη (see on xiii. 24). The comparison deals (as in xiii. 24 and elsewhere) with the general situation depicted in the parable; strictly speaking, 'this generation' was similar, not to the children who uttered their complaints but, to those who refused to play; for the προσφωνοῦντα can hardly be the Pharisees, demanding this and that manner of life from the Baptist and Jesus: they made no such demand. ἐν τ. ἀγοραῖς implies that the children's games were a frequent spectacle; ἐν ἀγορᾷ (Lk.) pictures a single scene. Mt. often prefers a plural (see Allen on viii. 26).

ἃ προσφωνοῦντα κτλ.] In Mt. one party of children appears to make the whole complaint to another (ἑτέροις; the v.l. ἑταίροις coaequalibus (vg) does not alter the meaning); in Lk. each party speaks in turn (ἀλλήλοις, Lat. ad invicem), the one crying ηὐλήσαμεν; the other ἐθρηνήσαμεν. This may mean either that each party querulously wants the game of its choice, or that both cries are part of the game (Wellh.). The latter would give point to the rhyming termination in Aram. רקדתון (ye danced) and ספדתון (ye lamented). The children may have sat in two rows facing one another, and chanting rhymed responses. How the game proceeded we cannot imagine. But if the Lord had watched it, with His unfailing sympathy for children, the words of their rhyme afforded Him all the illustration He needed; and

17   Ηὐλήσαμεν ὑμῖν καὶ οὐκ ὠρχήσασθε·
      ἐθρηνήσαμεν καὶ οὐκ ἐκόψασθε·
18 ἦλθεν γὰρ Ἰωάνης μήτε ἐσθίων μήτε πίνων, καὶ λέγουσιν
19 Δαιμόνιον ἔχει· ἦλθεν ὁ υἱὸς τοῦ ἀνθρώπου ἐσθίων καὶ
   πίνων, καὶ λέγουσιν Ἰδοὺ ἄνθρωπος φάγος καὶ οἰνοπότης,
   τελωνῶν φίλος καὶ ἁμαρτωλῶν. καὶ ἐδικαιώθη ἡ σοφία

if He referred, not to a sulky quarrel, but to a game, it adds irony to the application in *v.* 18 : the state of mind of 'this generation' can no more be taken seriously than the words of children at play.

18. ἦλθεν γάρ κτλ.] On ἦλθεν (= ἐλήλυθεν Lk.) see v. 17. μήτε ἐσθίων μ. πίνων is figurative of John's ascetic mode of life. The addition of ἄρτον and οἶνον in Lk. (there is strong evidence for their omission) is possibly due to a scribe's literalism in view of Mt. iii. 4, Lk. i. 15. λέγουσιν (Lk. λέγετε) is impers., referring loosely to 'this generation.' John's fasting was, apparently, not in accordance with Pharisaic custom, so they ascribed it to the instigation of a demon. The Lord is related to have suffered a similar reproach for different reasons (Mk. iii. 30, Jo. x. 20).

19. ἦλθεν κτλ.] For instances of the Lord's intercourse with the social life of men cf. viii. 15, ix. 10, xxvi. 6, Lk. vii. 36, x. 38 ff., xiv. 1, xv. 2 ; the disciples were bidden to act similarly, Lk. x. 7 f. φάγος, late and very rare, is a subst. (= φαγᾶς), ἄνθρωπος being redundant, as in ix. 32 (*v.l.*), xiii. 28, 45, 52, xviii. 23, xx. 1, xxi. 33, xxii. 2. For οἰνοπότης (used by Polyb.) cf. Prov. xxiii. 20; οἰνοποτεῖν Prov. xxiv. 72 [xxxi. 4]. On τελῶναι see v. 46. The contrast between the Lord's manner of life and that of the Baptist is doubtless based on a genuine utterance ; but the hand of the evangelist is probably to be seen

in the title 'Son of Man' (see p. xvii. f.).

καὶ ἐδικαιώθη κτλ.] The verb has the forensic force, 'has been proved right,' which it bears in the O.T. ; cf. Ps. l. [li.] 6, Sir. xviii. 2 ; see *HDB.* iv. 279 b. On the 'timeless aorist' see Moulton, i. 135-40. Σοφία, as in the Jewish Wisdom literature, is the divine Wisdom, God Himself in action ; cf. Lk. xi. 49 (see on Mt. xxiii. 34). Lk. has τ. τέκνων αὐτ. πάντων. The reading in Mt. is doubtful. Jesus almost certainly said 'children,' ἔργων being an interpretation either by Mt. himself or a scribe. The 'children' of Wisdom are those who are, or claim to be, obedient to her words and sharers in her nature ; cf. Prov. viii. 32, Sir. iv. 11 [12], xv. 2, and the analogous use of υἱοί in viii. 12, xiii. 38, xxiii. 15, Lk. xvi. 8, xx. 36. The saying has been variously explained : (1) ἐδικ. ἀπό means 'justified *from*' ; cf. Ac. xiii. 39, Rom. vi. 7, Sir. xxvi. 29, *Test. Sim.* 6, ὅπως δικαιωθῶ ἀπὸ τῆς ἁμαρτίας τῶν ψυχῶν ὑμῶν. The τέκνα are then the charges laid against Wisdom, the false inferences drawn from the behaviour of Jesus and the Baptist. This is far-fetched and improbable. But it may have been this use of ἀπό which led to the much simpler ἔργων, *i.e.* the deeds laid to the charge of Wisdom. 'Justified *as a result of* her works' would require ἐκ (cf. xii. 37, Jas. ii. 21, 24 f., Rom. iii. 20 *al.*), which forbids the conjecture made in

ἀπὸ τῶν ἔργων αὐτῆς.   Τότε ἤρξατο ὀνειδίζειν τὰς 20
πόλεις ἐν αἷς ἐγένοντο αἱ πλεῖσται δυνάμεις αὐτοῦ, ὅτι οὐ
μετενόησαν· Οὐαί σοι, Χοραζείν· οὐαί σοι, Βηθσαιδάν· 21

19 εργων] אB* 124 *codd. ap. Hier* ℥ pesh.hcl^txt me aeth ; τεκνων B²CDE *al*
𝔏 vet [*om* κ. εδικ . . . αυτης b].vg ℥ sin.cur.hcl^mg go

JThS., Apr. 1904, 455. Lagarde
suggested that τέκνα and ἔργα both
represent the Aram. עבדיא; but
παῖδες or δοῦλοι would be the more
natural rendering ; παῖδες, however,
might be altered to τέκνα in the
course of tradition. Cf. 4 Esd. vii.
64 (lat. *operibus*, Eth. 'sons,' Syr.
'servants'). (2) ἀπό = מִן קֳדָם (Heb.
מִפְּנֵי) 'against,' 'in opposition to'
(Wellh.), the τέκνα being the hostile
Jews, who imagine themselves to be
the true sons of Wisdom (cf. viii. 12).
(3) 'Wisdom found her justification
far from all her children,' *i.e.* amongst
quite other people than those who
gave themselves out to be her children
(O. Holtzm.). (4) ἀπό 'from the side
of' virtually has the force of ὑπό ;
cf. xvi. 21 (= Mk. viii. 31 ὑπό), Is.
xlv. 25 ἀπὸ Κυρίου (ביהוה) δικαιωθή-
σονται. Wisdom is shewn to be in
the right, acquitted, by Her children,
i.e. not only by Jesus and the Baptist,
but by all (πάντων Lk.) those who
truly exhibit their parentage. In
contrast with the shallow caprice of
'this generation' who condemned the
actions of the Wisdom by whom both
Himself and John were inspired, the
Lord places those who accepted His
and John's manner of life at its true
worth. This is the best explanation,
and is supported by the position in
which Lk. places the section, to follow
vii. 29 f., ὁ λαὸς . . . καὶ οἱ τελῶναι
ἐδικαίωσαν τὸν θεόν. The saying
quoted by Orig. as occurring 'in the
Gospel,' καὶ ἀποστέλλει ἡ σοφία τὰ
τέκνα αὐτῆς, seems to combine the
present passage with Lk. xi. 49
(Resch, *Agrapha²*, 184).

20–24. (Lk. x. 13–15.) CONDEMNA-
TION OF GALILEAN TOWNS.

In Lk. the section is inserted in
the Charge to the Seventy, following
the sayings with regard to the cities
that will not receive them (see on Mt.
x. 15). That cannot have been its
original position, and here it has no
connexion with the preceding or
following verses : it is an isolated
pair of exclamations the true context
of which is unknown.

20. τότε ἤρξατο κτλ.] Mt.'s
editorial introduction to the sayings ;
see iv. 17 on ἤρξατο. For ὀνειδίζειν
'reproach' cf. 'Mk.' xvi. 14, Wisd.
ii. 12, Sir. viii. 5 ; but Jer. has
deplorat and *plangit*, Eus. (*Onom.*
χοραζείν) ταλανίζει.

ἐγένοντο looks back like a pluperf.
at the Galilean ministry as wholly,
or to a large extent, completed. The
force of αἱ πλεῖσται (cf. xxi. 8) may
be either comparative, 'the majority
of His δυν.,' or elative, 'His very
numerous δυν.,' *plurimae virtutes ejus*
(Moulton, i. 79). As used in the
Gospp. of the Lord's wonderful works
δυνάμεις (never in Jo.) expresses their
nature, σημεῖα (Jo. only) their purpose. The fact that not a single
incident at Chorazin is recorded
illustrates the fragmentariness of our
records.

21. οὐαί σοι κτλ.] οὐαί, apart
from the synn., occurs in 1 Cor. ix.
16, Jude 11, Apoc.⁹ ; a late word
corresponding with Heb. אוֹי, הוֹי,
Aram. וי (cf. Onk. Num. xxi. 29),
Lat. *vae* ; it expresses sorrowful pity
no less than anger.

ὅτι εἰ ἐν Τύρῳ καὶ Σιδῶνι ἐγένοντο αἱ δυνάμεις αἱ γενόμεναι ἐν ὑμῖν, πάλαι ἂν ἐν σάκκῳ καὶ σποδῷ μετενόησαν.
22 πλὴν λέγω ὑμῖν, Τύρῳ καὶ Σιδῶνι ἀνεκτότερον ἔσται ἐν
23 ἡμέρᾳ κρίσεως ἢ ὑμῖν. Καὶ σύ, Καφαρναούμ, μὴ ἕως
ΟΥΡΑΝΟΥ ΥΨΩΘΗΟΗ; ἕως ἅΔΟΥ ΚΑΤΑΒΗΟΗ. ὅτι εἰ ἐν Σοδόμοις

23 μη . . . υψωθηση] אBC [D*L η ante Καφ.] 1** 22 42 𝔏 a b c ff¹.² [g¹ η]
g² k l vg 𝕾 cur me arm aeth; η υψωθης EFGS al; η . . . υψωθεισα KMNΠ*Σ al go
[quae exaltata es 𝔏 f h q 𝕾 sin.pesh.hcl] | καταβηση] BD 𝔏 omn 𝕾 sinᴸᵉʷⁱˢ·cur
aeth ; καταβιβασθηση אCE etc 𝕾 pesh.hcl me arm

Chorazin, a plural word of unknown meaning, mentioned in Menaḥ.
85ᵃ as Ḥᵉrāzîm, is the modern
Ḥerazeh, 2¼ miles NNW. of Tell
Ḥum (probably Capharnaum, cf. iv.
13); see Sanday, Sacred Sites, 24.
It was deserted when Eus. (Onom.)
wrote. The suggestion that XᵒPᵃZᵉ·N
is נצרא (Naẓora, Nazareth) read backwards, is ingenious ; but it is doubtful if צ was ever transliterated as Z
(Burkitt, Syr. Forms of N.T. Proper
Names, from Proc. Brit. Acad. vol. v.).
For a tradition connecting Chorazin
with Anti-Christ see ExpT. xv. 524.
Bethsaida is בית צידא ' House [i.e.
Place] of fishing, or of game.' It is
probable that one Bethsaida only is
mentioned in the Gospp. (Mk. vi.
45, viii. 22, Lk. ix. 10, Jo. i. 44,
xii. 21), the modern el-Tell, to which
' Philip gave the dignity of a city,
by the lake of Gennesaret . . . and
called it Julias after the name of
Caesar's daughter ' (Jos. Ant. XVIII.
ii. 1). It stood on the E. bank of
the Jordan, about a mile NE. of the
point where it runs into the lake.
There may perhaps have been an
old and a new part of the town.
The former, which Jesus would prefer
to the fashionable Greek city, may
have stood on the shore of the lake,
which probably extended further N.
than at present. See on xiv. 22,
and Sanday, op. cit. 41 f., 48.
εἰ ἐν Τύρῳ κτλ.] Two heathen

cities, in O.T. times full of wealth
and wickedness, and denounced by
the prophets (Am. i. 9 f., Is. xxiii.,
Jer. xxv. 22, xlvii. 4, Ez. xxvi. ff.).
σάκκῳ κ. σποδῷ: cf. Is. lviii. 5,
Jon. iii. 6, Est. iv. 3, Dan. ix. 3 ; Lk.
adds καθήμενοι. With the thought
of penitence awakened by divine
kindness cf. Lk. v. 8, Rom. ii. 4.
22. πλὴν κτλ.] They did not
repent, it is true, but they had less
opportunity than you. πλήν with
the force of ἀλλά, frequent in the
LXX., is confined in the N.T. to sayings ascribed to Jesus in Mt.⁵ and
Lk.¹⁵; it is a preposition in Mk. xii.
32, Jo. viii. 10. On ἀνεκτότερον
κτλ. see x. 15.
23. καὶ σύ κτλ.] On the name
Capharnaum, and its site see iv. 13.
Some of the δυναμεῖς performed
there are grouped in chs. viii. f.   μὴ
ἕως κτλ. : an adaptation of the
rebuke to Babylon (Is. xiv. 13, 15),
σὺ δὲ εἶπας τῇ διανοίᾳ σου Εἰς τὸν
οὐρανὸν ἀναβήσομαι . . . νῦν δὲ εἰς
ᾅδην καταβήσῃ, the first clause
being treated negatively — ' Shalt
thou go up as high as heaven ? '
(For μή = num, expecting the answer
No, see Blass, § 75. 2), the second as
a simple statement—'. . . thou shalt
come down.' It is less natural to
make μή govern the second clause
only (Wellh.), '[Take heed] lest,
though thou art exalted . . ., yet to
Hades thou come down.' Like

ἐγενήθησαν αἱ δυνάμεις αἱ γενόμεναι ἐν σοί, ἔμεινεν ἂν μέχρι
τῆς σήμερον. πλὴν λέγω ὑμῖν ὅτι γῇ Σοδόμων ἀνεκτότερον 24
ἔσται ἐν ἡμέρᾳ κρίσεως ἢ σοί.

Ἐν ἐκείνῳ τῷ καιρῷ ἀποκριθεὶς ὁ Ἰησοῦς εἶπεν Ἐξομο- 25
λογοῦμαί σοι, πάτερ κύριε τοῦ οὐρανοῦ καὶ τῆς γῆς, ὅτι
ἔκρυψας ταῦτα ἀπὸ σοφῶν καὶ συνετῶν, καὶ ἀπεκάλυψας

Babylon, Capharnaum was lifted
up with worldly pride, which made
her despise the Lord's miracles.
Hades expresses the lowest shame, as
Heaven the highest renown; cf.
Ps.-Sol. i. 5, ὑψώθησαν ἕως τῶν
ἄστρων (with Ryle and James' note).
The readings ἡ . . . ὑψώθης and ἡ
. . . ὑψωθεῖσα were probably due to
the accidental omission of the μ of μή
after Καφαρναούμ. καταβήσῃ, as
in Is., is probably the true reading
both here and in Lk.; the pass.
καταβιβασθήσῃ was an assimilation to ὑψωθήσῃ, or a scribe was
influenced by the collocation, in
Ez. xxxi. 10-16, of ὑψωθῆναι, κατα-
βαίνειν, and καταβιβάζειν.

ὅτι εἰ κτλ.] The remainder of
the verse is absent from Lk., because
he transposes the next verse to
precede οὐαί σοι, Χοραζείν; see on
x. 15.

**25-27. (Lk. x. 21, 22.) THE
LORD'S THANKSGIVING.**

25. ἐν ἐκείνῳ κτλ.] The same
note of time is used in xii. 1, xiv. 1.
Luke has (ἐν) αὐτῇ τῇ ὥρᾳ seven
times. ἀποκριθεὶς εἶπεν (on the aor.
partcp. see Blass, § 74. 3) does not
imply any question or remark to
which the Lord's words are an answer
(cf. xii. 38, xvii. 4, xxii. 1, xxviii. 5);
this and the like expressions are
probably not genuinely Aram., but
due to O.T. influence (Dalm. *Words*,
24 f.). Lk. has ἠγαλλιάσατο ἐν τῷ
πνεύματι τῷ ἁγίῳ καὶ εἶπεν (the
first verb is confined, in the synn.,
to Lk., except Mt. v. 12, and 'the

Holy Spirit' is a characteristic of
his writings).

ἐξομολογοῦμαι κτλ.] So Lk.,
except ἀπέκρυψας. On πάτερ see v.
16, vi. 9 b. The prayer of Jesus
recalls the 'prayer of Jesus, son of
Sirach': ἐξομολογοῦμαί σοι κύριε
βασιλεῦ (Sir. li. 1; cf. v. 17); cf.
2 Regn. xxii. 50. 'Lord of heaven
and earth' is known, in bibl. Gk.,
only in Tob. vii. 17; Judith ix. 12 has
δέσποτα τῶν οὐρανῶν καὶ τῆς γῆς.

ὅτι ἔκρυψας κτλ.] Equivalent to
ὅτι κρύψας ταῦτα ἀπεκάλυψας. Jesus
was thankful, not that the σοφοί
were ignorant but, that the νήπιοι
knew; cf. Is. xii. 1, Rom. vi. 17 (both
rightly paraphrased in the R.V.).
ταῦτα here seems to refer to the
significance of the miracles which
the Galilean towns had failed to
understand; but Lk. places the
saying at the moment when the
Seventy returned, and ταῦτα refers
—not to their power over evil spirits
(Wendt), but—to the subject of their
preaching. If vv. 20-24 are not
in their original position, ταῦτα may
refer to the methods of the divine
Wisdom, which were understood only
by the true 'children of Wisdom' (vv.
16-19). But Mt. has preserved an
isolated saying, so that the antecedents
of ταῦτα are lost (see below). σοφῶν
κ. συνετῶν is probably a reminiscence
of Is. xxix. 14, which is quoted in
1 Cor. i. 19, where the next two verses
read like a comment on the Lord's
words. On σοφ. and συν. see Lightfoot on Col. i. 9. The meaning of

26 αὐτὰ νηπίοις· ναί, ὁ πατήρ, ὅτι οὕτως εὐδοκία ἐγένετο
27 ἔμπροσθέν σου. Πάντα μοι παρεδόθη ὑπὸ τοῦ πατρός μου,

νήπιοι is seen in Ps. xviii. [xix.] 7,
cxviii. [cxix.] 130 = פְּתָיִים, 'simple,'
' open-minded ' ; contrast Mt. xxi. 16
= Ps. viii. 3, עֹלְלִים 'infants.'

26. ναί κτλ.] Lk. transposes
εὐδοκία and ἐγένετο. The ναί repeats in thought ἐξομολογοῦμαι,
' Yea, I thank Thee, because.' On
ὁ πατήρ for the vocative see Blass,
§ 33. 4 ; and cf. vi. 9 b. εὐδοκία
ἔμπροσθέν σου was a common periphrasis to avoid the anthropomorph-
ism involved in God's volition ; cf.
xviii. 14 ; contrast Lk. xii. 32.
רעוא קדם is frequent in the Targg.
(e.g. Onk. Gen. xxiv. 42), and רצון
מלפניך in Rabb. prayers (Dalm.
Words, 211).

27. πάντα μοι κτλ.] For ἐπιγιν.
τ. υἱόν Lk. has γινώσκει τίς ἐστιν ὁ
υἱός, and for οὐδέ τ. πατ. τις ἐπιγιν.
he has καὶ τίς ἐστιν ὁ πατήρ. These
are not essentially different. ἐπι-
γινώσκειν does not imply fuller knowledge than γινώσκειν. The former
'directs attention to some particular
point in regard to which " knowledge" is affirmed.' ' So that to
perceive a particular thing, or to
perceive who a particular person is,
may fitly be expressed by ἐπιγινώ-
σκειν. There is no such limitation
about the word γινώσκειν, though of
course it may be so limited by its context' (J. A. Robinson, Ephesians, 249).
This limitation Lk.'s context supplies.
For a somewhat different view see
Moulton, i. 113. Several patr.
writers omit βούληται and read
ἀποκαλύψῃ. Ṣ pal has 'and to
whomsoever the Son willeth to reveal,
He reveals ' ; cf. 𝔏 a, 'et cuicumque
voluerit filius revelavit.'

The passage was widely quoted
in the early Church, both by
orthodox and heretics. The many

differences of reading are given in
an elaborate study of the words by
Harnack, Sprüche u. Reden Jesu, 189–
216 (Engl. Sayings of Jesus, 272–
310). His treatment of the evidence
is severely criticized by Dom Chapman
in JThS., July 1909, 552 ff. Two
variations are important, the evidence
for which is given in the Add. n.
(1) For the pres. (ἐπι)γινώσκει is
found the aor. ἔγνω. And οἶδε also
occurs. (2) The clause 'no one
knoweth the Son, etc.' is placed
after 'no one knoweth the Father,
etc.' The former clause is omitted
in 𝔏 a (Lk.). The textual conclusions
that Harnack draws are (1) that Mt.
originally had ἐπιγινώσκει and Lk.
ἔγνω, (2) that in Mt. the original
order of the clauses in question is
uncertain, but in Lk. 'knoweth the
Father' stood first. But Chapman
shows that the patr. evidence
assigns ἔγνω to Mt., and he does not
consider it ' more than an interesting
" Western " variant,' while the placing
of 'knoweth the Son' after ' knoweth
the Father' was due to an occa-
sional carelessness. Harnack further
maintains that the original words
are rightly represented by (1) the
' historic' aor. ἔγνω, (2) the omission
of the clause ' knoweth the Son.'
But (1) ἔγνω is not necessarily an
historic aor. ; like (ἐπι)γινώσκει it
can mean 'he knoweth,' and both
might represent an Aram. perfect.
(2) Having regard to purely external
evidence, the variation in order
may indicate that the words τὸν υἱὸν
[τίς ἐστιν ὁ υἱὸς] εἰ μὴ ὁ πατὴρ οὐδὲ
[καὶ] are of doubtful authenticity ;
but intrinsically they cause no
difficulty in whichever position they
stand, as is shewn below.

The interpretation of the verse

καὶ οὐδεὶς ἐπιγινώσκει τὸν υἱὸν εἰ μὴ ὁ πατήρ, οὐδὲ τὸν

stands on four points : (a) the relation of πάντα to ταῦτα (v. 25); (b) the meaning of παρεδόθη ; (c) of (ἐπι)-γινώσκει (ἔγνω) ; (d) the expressions ὁ πατήρ and ὁ υἱός.

(a) πάντα is not identical with ταῦτα, but includes it as the greater the less. Whether ταῦτα refers to vv. 20–24, or to vv. 16–19, or (more probably) to a context now lost, it stands for truths which the Father has revealed to babes ; and He has revealed them through the Son, because to Him *all things* were delivered. πάντα is not πᾶσα ἐξουσία (xxviii. 18) but a *complete revelation*. To interpret πάντα as including failure as well as success, the hiding of truth from the wise as well as the revealing of it to babes, and to explain οὐδεὶς ἐπιγινώσκει as ' Alas ! no one knoweth,' is contrary to the spirit of thankful joy which pervades the words : they do not give the impression of a *Confiteor* (so Burkitt, *JThS.*, 1911, 296).

(b) παρεδόθη can therefore have the significance ·rightly claimed for it by J. Weiss and others, the ' entrusting' of a teaching or revelation ; cf. the use of the verb in xxv. 14, Ac. vi. 14. The thought of a pre-temporal act must not be pressed ; the Father, of course, determined it before all time, but on the human lips of Jesus the aor., no less than ἀπεκάλυψας, referred to an historical act in time. He knew, when He spoke, that the παράδοσις was a fact.

(c) There is no real difference in meaning between (ἐπι)γινώσκει and ἔγνω, as said above. Iren. (iv. 1)

condemns ἔγνω as due to those ' who want to be cleverer than the apostles,' because they interpret it ' as though the true God has been known to none before the coming of our Lord, and they say that God who was proclaimed by the prophets was not the Father of Christ.' But the meaning of the verb is determined by that of πάντα παρεδόθη : ' no one knoweth the full truth by a complete divine revelation' (cf. 1 Cor. xiii. 12). The 4th Gospel (*e.g.* i. 10, x. 15, xiv. 7, 17, 20, xvi. 3, xvii. 3, 25 ; see also iii. 34 f.) meditates in detail upon this γνῶσις, but contains nothing deeper or vaster than these words of the Lord preserved in Q.

(d) The absolute use of ' the Father' and ' the Son,' found *passim* in the 4th Gospel, is also vouched for by Mk. xiii. 32 (Mt. xxiv. 36). ' The Father' and ' the Son', form the content of the knowledge which Jesus claimed. He alone, by a divine παράδοσις to His human consciousness, knew the Father's nature, and His own Sonship with all that it involved (see p. xxiv. f.).

The passage may therefore be paraphrased as follows : I thank Thee, O Father, that it was Thy good pleasure to reveal these things to babes through My teaching. I alone can do it because the whole truth has been entrusted to Me. None except Thee could know my Sonship, so as to reveal it to Me ; and none except Myself, the Son, could know Thee, the Father. [Or transpose the clauses]. Thus I can reveal both truths to whomsoever I will.

Additional note on xi. 27.

The patristic evidence for the two principal variants is as follows : (1) (ἐπι)γινώσκει Just. *Dial.* (once), Clem. Al. (twice), Eus. (twice), Marcion (*ap.*

πατέρα τις ἐπιγινώσκει εἰ μὴ ὁ υἱὸς καὶ ᾧ ἐὰν βούληται ὁ

Tert.), Iren., Adamant. (once).   ἔγνω Just. *Apol.* (twice).   Marcosians and Valentinians (*ap.* Iren.ˡᵃᵗ), Tert., Clem., Orig., Eus., Did. (once), *Clem. Hom.*, Adamant. (once).   οἶδε Eus., Alexand. Al., Adamant. (once each).

(2) The clauses stand as in the text in Clem. Al., Iren. (sometimes), Athan. (once), Tat.ᵃʳᵃᵇ, Cyr. Al.   The clause 'knoweth the Son' stands after 'knoweth the Father' in Marcion (*ap.* Tert.), Marcosians (*ap.* Iren.ˡᵃᵗ), Just., Tat.ᵉᵖʰʳ, Iren. (sometimes), *Clem. Hom.*, Eus.   To these may be added U 𝔏 b o in Lk.

Much has been written on this verse, as may be seen in the exhaustive review by Schumacher, *Die Selbstoffenbarung Jesu bei Mat. xi. 27* ; but it may be useful to indicate some modern types of interpretation.

HARNACK (*op. cit.*) explains thus.   πάντα μοι παρεδόθη refers not to any divine or Messianic powers granted to Jesus, but simply to His teaching, the knowledge of God, with which the whole section (*vv.* 25–27) deals. This is the παράδοσις entrusted to Him (cf. xv. 2 f., 6, 1 Cor. xv. 3, Jude 3), and to Him first, as Son, who has approached nearer than other men to the Father's mind.   No one in the past knew (ἔγνων not (ἐπι)γινώσκει) the Father as He does, and therefore He can reveal this knowledge to whom He will.   It is to the νήπιοι that He has revealed it ; ἀπεκάλυψας and ἀποκαλύψῃ correspond with one another.   This interpretation necessitates the omission of the clause 'no one knoweth the Son save the Father.'   The clause (Harnack says) is quite unexpected, since the thanksgiving deals at the beginning and the end with the knowledge of *God*.   And the historic aorist suits the knowledge of the Father by the Son, but not that of the Son by the Father.   The clause was probably added by Mt., in the same spirit as that of xxviii. 18, and was carried over by scribes into Lk.

J. WEISS (*Die Schriften d. N.T.*) admits that the difference between ἔγνω and (ἐπι)γινώσκει cannot be pressed.   He understands the 'knowledge' to be a deep sense of personal contact with God (cf. Gal. iv. 9, 1 Cor. xiii. 12).   The πάντα entrusted to Jesus by the Father are not that which has been revealed to babes, since the passage deals with that which has been revealed to none but Himself.   It was a sudden revelation of what the Father is, which no one else had received.   This necessitates the placing of the clause 'knoweth the Son' after 'knoweth the Father.'   It need not be omitted : at the same moment that He rejoiced in the illuminating knowledge of the Father, Jesus felt clearly how little He was Himself understood ; no one knew what He, the Son, really was, except the Father.   It was the secret of His own personality, His Messiahship, which came as a solution of the question which had troubled His soul.   He had thought that His call to the Messiahship involved the huge burden of winning the whole nation; and yet the mass of them, especially the Scribes, remained so dull and unimpressionable !   Was He the Chosen of God after all ?   But the doubts melted away at this supreme moment.   He realized that the secret of His Person was meant only for a few godlike souls, to whom it was specially revealed.   And freed from the greater burden, He now understood that His work was to bring this revelation to the few.—But this explanation is so largely subjective, and presupposes so detailed a knowledge of phases in the Lord's self-consciousness, that it is unconvincing.

DOM CHAPMAN (*op. cit.*) finds a solution in the parallelism of the passage. 'The clause which rightly stands first, οὐδεὶς ἔγνω τίς ἐστιν ὁ υἱὸς εἰ μὴ ὁ πατήρ, would need a converse addition, καὶ ᾧ ἂν βούληται ὁ πατὴρ ἀποκαλύψαι. But a clause to this effect is actually to be found in the preceding verse, ἐξομολογ. σοι, πάτερ . . . ὅτι . . . ἀπεκάλυψας αὐτὰ νηπίοις. What has the Father revealed? Undoubtedly the things concerning the Son.' The thought is therefore as follows: 1 (*a*) The Father reveals 'these things' [*sc.* concerning the Son] to babes, for so it seems good to Him; 1 (*β*) all that I have is from the Father, so that He alone knows the Son, and consequently He alone can reveal Him. In the same way, 2 (*β*) Only the Son knows the Father, 2 (*a*) and can reveal Him to whomsoever He thinks good to do so.—But this explanation takes no real account of 'All things are delivered unto Me by My Father'; the clause forms no part of the parallelism, and is not treated as an essential part of the passage. ταῦτα is assumed to mean the things concerning the nature of the Son, which the previous context does not warrant. And a particular order of the clauses is necessitated—a necessity which was not recognized by Just., Iren., and Euseb.

NORDEN (*Agnostos Theos*, 277–308) treats *vv.* 25–30 as one whole, which falls into three parts: (*a*) *vv.* 25 f. (addressed to God), (*b*) *v.* 27 (speaking of God in the third person), (*c*) *vv.* 28–30 (addressed to men). He sees the same arrangement in Sir. li.: (*a*) *vv.* 1–12, (*b*) *vv.* 13–22, (*c*) *vv.* 23–30. But there is no real affinity with this, in spite of similarities of language, for Sir. (*a*) is merely a thanksgiving for deliverance from danger, and does not form one whole with (*b*) (*c*), which are a separate alphabetical poem.

The παράδοσις is a delivery of knowledge, a communication of a mystery, intended not for the wise but for babes, which is a gift to the Son only, for Him to reveal to whom He will; He therefore calls to the toiling and heavy-laden to learn it. Norden cites passages from Greek mystery-writings in which special knowledge is divinely communicated for delivery to initiated persons, and the language and order of thoughts are in some respects similar; and he concludes that both Mt. and Sir. have derived their ideas from the 'mystical-theosophical literature of the East.' Gnostics thought that it was to the 'wise' that the mysteries were revealed, but in deliberate opposition to their esoteric claims the evangelist writes 'babes,' and 'toiling and heavy-laden.' In *vv.* 25 f. ταῦτα and αὐτά have no antecedent to which they refer. But this was because the Jewish form of the ῥῆσις, both in Mt. and Sir., was influenced by the language of the Psalter, which led to ἐξομολογοῦμαι being placed at the beginning, whereas logically it should (as *e.g.* in a passage in Ps.-Apuleius) have stood after the content of the revelation had been described; that is to say, ταῦτα and αὐτά refer to πάντα in *v.* 27. And Mt. chose the colourless words ταῦτα and αὐτά 'to help himself out of the difficulty' caused by the transposition. The passage, therefore, is not a genuine utterance of Jesus, for He must not be reckoned among the mystical theosophists of the East, but is the work of Q.

This treatment of the passage labours under the presupposition that because the line of thought finds parallels elsewhere (and only differs from the parallels under the influence of the Psalter), it must have been derived.

28 υἱὸς ἀποκαλύψαι.   Δεῦτε πρός με πάντες οἱ κοπιῶντες καὶ
29 πεφορτισμένοι, κἀγὼ ἀναπαύσω ὑμᾶς.   ἄρατε τὸν ζυγόν μου

But all the Hebrew prophets, like other prophets, were convinced that they
had received a special revelation.   It is an inevitable certainty of all mystics,
and requires no literary derivation to explain it.   And the exclusion from
knowledge of 'the wise and prudent,' if derived, is derived from Is. xxix. 14.
The Lord's certainty (displayed, *e.g.*, throughout the Sermon on the Mount)
that He possessed a unique revelation to give to men, and in particular to
the 'poor,' the 'meek,' the 'persecuted,' is quite enough to account for the
words.   As to details : Norden confuses the 'babes' and the 'toiling and
heavy-laden,' quite distinct thoughts.   His explanation of ταῦτα and αὐτά
will commend itself to few.   And since, on his theory, *vv.* 28–30 form 'an
integral part of the scheme of the composition' of the passage, Lk.'s omission
of them is inexplicable, and he confesses himself unable to explain it.

28–30. THE YOKE OF CHRIST.

In *vv.* 25 ff. and 28 ff. are preserved two utterances of Jesus of
central importance, in both of which
He speaks about Himself, and makes
high claims.   Mt. has done well to
place them side by side.   But it is
doubtful if they were originally
connected : Q, as represented in Mt.,
Lk., contained the former, but the
latter is confined to Mt.   The 'babes'
receive the revelation of the nature
of the Father and the Son ; the
'toiling and heavy-laden' are invited
to accept the 'light yoke'; they
belong to quite different spheres of
thought.   *Vv.* 28 ff. form a beautiful
introduction to xii. 1–13, where two
typical instances are given of the
χρηστότης of Christ's yoke as compared with the law of the Sabbath.
As *v.* 25 recalls Sir. li. 1, so several
words and phrases in *vv.* 28 ff. echo
Sir. li. 23–27, which may have been
one cause for the juxtaposition of
the sayings.

28. δεῦτε κτλ.]   Cf. Sir. li. 23
ἐγγίσατε πρός με.   They are summoned who find it hard toil to
observe the Law, and upon whom
their religious leaders 'bind heavy
burdens' (xxiii. 4); cf. Lk. xi. 46,
the only other instance of φορτίζειν

in the N.T.   ἀναπαύειν, often of
temporary rest or refreshment (M.-M.
Vocab. s.v. ἀνάπαυσις, -παύω, Lightft.
on Philem 7) is act, not uncommonly
in the LXX., and in 1 Cor. xvi. 18,
Philem. 20, elsewhere mid. or pass.
in the N.T.   κοπιῶντες : cf. Sir. li.
27, ἐκοπίασα = יִגַעְתִּי, 'I toiled';
Geneva vers. 'are weary' (cf. 2 Regn.
xxiii. 10, Is. xl. 31).

29. ἄρατε κτλ.]   'My yoke' is
the yoke which I lay upon you;
cf. Sir. li. 26 τὸν τράχηλον ὑμῶν
ὑπόθετε ὑπὸ ζυγόν.   It suggests a
contrast with 'the yoke of the law'
(cf. Ac. xv. 10) : this and similar
expressions are common in Jewish
writings ; in *Ab.* iii. 8 (see Taylor)
it is said that if any one takes upon
him the 'yoke of Torah,' the yoke
of civil government and the yoke of
worldly care are removed from him ;
cf. *Apoc. Bar.* xli. 3 'the yoke of
Thy law'; *Berak.* 13 a 'the yoke
of the Kingdom of Heaven,' and
'the yoke of [the] commandment';
see also Ps. Sol. vii. 8, xvii. 32.
Owing to this verse, the commands
of Jesus are called in Did. 6 ὁ ζυγὸς
τοῦ κυρίου.   With καὶ μάθετε ἀπ'
ἐμοῦ cf. Sir. li. 26 καὶ ἐπιδεξάσθω ἡ
ψυχὴ ὑμῶν παιδείαν.   For the ἀπό
cf. xxiv. 32, Col. i. 7.

ἐφ᾽ ὑμᾶς καὶ μάθετε ἀπ᾽ ἐμοῦ, ὅτι πραΰς εἰμι καὶ ταπεινὸς
τῇ καρδίᾳ, καὶ εγρήϲεϲτε ἀνάπαυϲιν τᾶιϲ ψγχαῖϲ ὑμῶν· ὁ γὰρ 30
ζυγός μου χρηστὸς καὶ τὸ φορτίον μου ἐλαφρόν ἐστιν.
ʼΕν ἐκείνῳ τῷ καιρῷ ἐπορεύθη ὁ ʼΙησοῦς τοῖς σάββασιν 1 XII.

ὅτι πραΰς εἰμι κτλ.] ὅτι may
assign the reason ('because'), or
introduce the fact to be learnt ('that
I am, etc.,' Aram. ד as in ܤ sin.cur),
or ד may be the relative ('I who
am, etc.') misunderstood by a translator. On the Lord's claim to be
'gentle' see C. H. Robinson, *Stud.
in the Character of Christ*, ch. i.
S. Paul could appeal to the πραΰτης
τοῦ Χριστοῦ as to a recognized fact
(2 Cor. x. 1); cf. the Christian
addition in *Test. Dan.* vi., the σωτὴρ
τῶν ἐθνῶν is ἀληθὴς καὶ μακρόθυμος,
πρᾶος καὶ ταπεινός. For πραΰς see
v. 5, and for the dat. τῇ καρδίᾳ v. 3,
8; to learn gentleness from Him is
to win a Beatitude. On ταπεινο-
φροσύνη and πραότης see Trench,
Synon. 139–47. The original Aram.
perhaps contained a play on words;
'give rest,' 'gentle,' 'rest,' and
perhaps also 'light' (v. 30), may all
be represented by derivatives of ניח.
The collocation ζυγόν and ταπεινός
is echoed in Clem. *Cor.* xvi. 17.

καὶ εὑρήσετε κτλ.] Cf. Sir. vi.
24 ff., li. 27, Jer. vi. 16 (Heb.) 'and
find ye rest for your soul' (but LXX.
ἁγνισμόν). Christ *gives* rest (ἀναπαύσω), and yet He tells men actively
to find or obtain it (cf. the paradox
in Phil. ii. 12 f.). τ. ψυχαῖς ὑμ. 'for
yourselves'; see on x. 39.

30. ὁ γὰρ ζυγός κτλ.] χρηστός
in the LXX. often = טוב, of persons
'kind,' of things 'valuable.' Here
the χρηστότης of the Lord deter-
mines the character of His yoke.
No English adj. embraces both 'kind'
and 'good.' φορτίον refers to the
πεφορτισμένοι (v. 28). With the

thought of ἐλαφρόν cf. 1 Jo. v. 3.
The 'lightness' of Christ's yoke does
not conflict with such passages as
v. 20, x. 38, xvi. 24, nor with the
struggles which it involved for a
S. Paul against the 'law in his
members' (Rom. vii. 22 f.). The
pressure of the Jewish law was
always a φορτίον κοπιῶντι, but
Christ's yoke, in proportion as it is
accepted, gives the buoyancy and
life which enable men to meet His
much greater demands. *Cui servire
est regnare.*

xii. 1–8. (Mk. ii. 23–28, Lk. vi.
1–5.) THE DISCIPLES IN THE CORN-
FIELD; THE SABBATH.

Mt. returns to the earlier Marcan
narrative at the point at which he
left it at ix. 18 (see note); in the
present chapter he combines it with
other instances of hostility to Jesus,
and His utterances connected with
them.

1. ἐν ἐκείνῳ κτλ.] See on xi.
25; Mk. and Lk. have no note of
time (on the reading δευτεροπρώτῳ
in the latter see Plummer *ad loc.*,
and Burkitt, *Gosp. Hist.* 81 n.). The
plur. σάββασιν (B σαββάτοις) arose
from the form of the Aram. sing.
shabbāthā, which, transliterated, was
misunderstood as plural, σάββατον
being formed as the singular; the
mistake is found in the LXX. and
Josephus. The plur. σπόριμα is
known only in Sym. 1 Regn. viii.
15 (LXX. σπέρματα), where it is
parallel to 'vineyards'; for the
singular (σπέρμα σπόριμον) cf. Gen.
i. 29, Lev. xi. 37.

διὰ τῶν σπορίμων· οἱ δὲ μαθηταὶ αὐτοῦ ἐπείνασαν, καὶ
2 ἤρξαντο τίλλειν στάχυας καὶ ἐσθίειν. οἱ δὲ Φαρισαῖοι
ἰδόντες εἶπαν αὐτῷ Ἰδοὺ οἱ μαθηταί σου ποιοῦσιν ὃ οὐκ
3 ἔξεστιν ποιεῖν ἐν σαββάτῳ. ὁ δὲ εἶπεν αὐτοῖς Οὐκ
ἀνέγνωτε τί ἐποίησεν Δαυεὶδ ὅτε ἐπείνασεν καὶ οἱ μετ’
4 αὐτοῦ; πῶς εἰσῆλθεν εἰς τὸν οἶκον τοῦ θεοῦ καὶ τοὺς

οἱ δὲ μαθηταί κτλ.] Mt. alone
says ἐπείνασαν, in view of v. 3 ; on
the form see Blass, § 16. 1, § 22. 1.
On ἤρξαντο see iv. 17. τίλλειν
κτλ.: Mk. ὁδὸν ποιεῖν τίλλοντες (see
Swete), Lk. ἔτιλλον . . . καὶ ἤσθιον
ψώχοντες ταῖς χερσίν ; Mk. takes
for granted the actions added by
Mt. and Lk. To pluck ears in
another man's field was ordinarily
allowed (Deut. xxiii. 24 [26]), and
is still a common practice (E. Robinson, *Bibl. Res.* i. 493. 9), but was
forbidden on the Sabbath (Bab.
Shabb. 73 b), being considered equivalent to reaping (so Maimon., see
Lightfoot, *Hor. Heb.* on v. 2) ; but
the disciples shewed, by their action,
that they had already grasped their
Master's principle. The ripeness of
the corn places the incident in the
spring, during the few weeks after
the Passover (see p. xiii.).

2. οἱ δὲ Φαρισαῖοι κτλ.] Mt.
alone says ἰδόντες, implying that
they also were walking through the
corn. In Lk. the complaint (τί
ποιεῖτε) is addressed to the disciples.
π. ἐν σαββάτῳ (Lk. π. τοῖς σάββασιν), absent from Mk., is added
for the sake of clearness, since plucking ears was lawful on other days.

3. οὐκ ἀνέγνωτε κτλ.] For the
formula cf. v. 5, xix. 4, xxi. 16, 42,
xxii. 31. With all their biblical
erudition the Pharisees were often
blind to the principles taught in their
Scriptures. Mt. and Lk. avoid Mk.'s
pleonastic χρείαν ἔσχεν καὶ ἐπείνασεν.
In 1 Sam. xxi. 1–6 David is related

to have come alone to the priest,
but to have told him he had
'appointed his young men to such
and such a place' ; on the basis of
this, Jesus assumed that ' they that
were with him' shared the bread
with David. That they hungered
is ' an inference from the facts,
added to bring out the parallel'
(Swete).

4. πῶς εἰσῆλθεν κτλ.] Another
inference from the facts. The 'house
of God' would be understood to mean
the tent which housed the ark ; see
HDB. iv. 654 b. On πῶς (so probably
Mk. ; Lk. ὡς) see Blass, § 70. 2 n.
Mk. adds ἐπὶ Ἀβιαθὰρ ἀρχιερέως
(om. D 𝕷 𝕾 sin) ; the omission in
Mt., Lk. may be a correction, since
the priest was Ahimelech (LXX.
Abimelech), but it was perhaps a
later erroneous gloss in Mk. ἔφαγον
(if the reading is right) abbreviates
Mk.'s ἔφαγεν, καὶ ἔδωκεν καὶ τοῖς
σὺν αὐτῷ οὖσιν, but Mt. adds to the
next clause οὐδὲ τοῖς μετ’ αὐτοῦ.
Lk. follows Mk., but uses Mt.'s preposition. The Gk. expression οἱ
ἄρτοι τῆς προθέσεως (1 Regn. xxi. 6,
1 Chr. ix. 32, xxiii. 29, Neh. x. 33)
denotes that the loaves were *placed
before* God ; Vulg. *panes propositionis*;
the Heb. לֶחֶם הַמַּעֲרֶכֶת that they were
placed in order ; cf. עֶרֶךְ לָחֶם (Ex. xl.
21 [23]), ἡ πρόθεσις τ. ἄρτων (Heb.
ix. 2). Other varieties are found in
2 Chr. ii. 4, xiii. 11, 2 Mac. x. 3,
Ex. xxv. 30, xxxix. 18 [36]. See the
writer's *Exodus* 165 f., and Deissmann
B.St. 157.

ἄρτους τῆς προθέσεως ἔφαγον, ὃ οὐκ ἐξὸν ἦν αὐτῷ φαγεῖν
οὐδὲ τοῖς μετ' αὐτοῦ, εἰ μὴ τοῖς ἱερεῦσιν μόνοις; ἢ οὐκ 5
ἀνέγνωτε ἐν τῷ νόμῳ ὅτι τοῖς σάββασιν οἱ ἱερεῖς ἐν τῷ
ἱερῷ τὸ σάββατον βεβηλοῦσιν καὶ ἀναίτιοί εἰσιν; λέγω 6
δὲ ὑμῖν ὅτι τοῦ ἱεροῦ μεῖζόν ἐστιν ὧδε. εἰ δὲ ἐγνώκειτε 7

4 εφαγον] אB 481 ; εφαγεν CD etc minn verss

ὃ οὐκ ἐξὸν ἦν κτλ.] Mk., Lk.
ἔξεστιν: Mt. expresses more clearly
the assumption, on which the Lord's
argument is based, that what was
true in N.T. times (cf. Jos. *Ant.* III.
x. 7), and in the age when Lev. xxiv.
9 was written, was also true in the
time of David. The incident illustrates xi. 30 ; Christ's yoke consisted
in the observance of principles; and
the greatest of these is charity (cf.
v. 7 below). See *Camb. Bibl. Essays*,
226.

5. ἢ οὐκ ἀνέγνωτε κτλ.] Mt.
alone adds another argument from
O.T. usage, bearing more directly
upon the Sabbath question. Not
only was a concession made to Israel's
hero, but the Law *commanded* the
priests in the temple to break the
letter of the Sabbath law by doing
work ; *e.g.* the shew-bread was
changed (Lev. xxiv. 8), and the
burnt-offering was doubled (Num.
xxviii. 8 f.); cf. Jubil. l. 10 f. : no
work must be done on the Sabbath
'save burning frankincense, and
bringing oblations and sacrifices before the Lord.' Other temple duties
permitted on the Sabbath are given
in *Pesach.* vi. 1 f., *Erub.* x. 11–15 ;
and see Jo. vii. 22 f. τ. σάββατον
βεβηλοῦν: cf. Is. lvi. 2, 6, Ez. xx. 13,
etc., Neh. xiii. 17 f., 1 Mac. i. 43, 45,
ii. 34 ; βεβ. is to make 'common'
(לֹל) that which is sacred : see *HDB*.
art. ' Holy ' ; cf. Ac. xxiv. 6. κοινοῦν
(not in LXX.) has the same force,
Ac. xxi. 28. Nothing could be more
startling than to hear the word

applied to the sacred offices of the
priests ; cf. Zeph. iii. 4. ἀναίτιος
recurs in the N.T. in *v.* 7 only ; in
the LXX. (Deut.⁴ Sus.¹) it is always of
'innocent blood' (see M.-M. *Vocab.*
s.v.), but Sym. uses it of persons.

6. λέγω δὲ κτλ.] This verse, if
spoken by Jesus, probably belonged
to another context. The two references to the O.T. have taught that
need, private or public, must override law, a principle summed up in
v. 7. But this verse introduces a
different thought, irrelevant to the
principle of ἔλεος which the Lord is
inculcating : ' if the temple can demand that its servants shall break
the law, much more can I, who am
more than the temple.' But the
disciples had been engaged in no
service demanded by Jesus. The
verse serves to prepare for *v.* 8, in
which Mt. understands 'the Son of
Man' to mean the Messiah. With
μεῖζόν ἐστιν ὧδε cf. *v.* 41 f., parallels
which forbid Jerome's explanation,
' quod major templo sit locus qui
Dominum templi teneat.'

7. εἰ δὲ ἐγνώκειτε κτλ.] A reference to Hos. vi. 6, which Mt. has
already ascribed to Jesus in ix. 13
(see note). There it suited the context ill, but here it well sums up the
teaching of *vv.* 3–5 ; nevertheless the
verse interrupts the sequence of γάρ
in *v.* 8. It was probably a genuine
utterance spoken on another occasion.
θυσία is figurative of obedience to
the letter of the law at any cost.
The disciples are as ἀναίτιοι as the

τί ἐστιν ˝Ελεος θέλω καὶ ΟΥ θΥϹίΑΝ, οὐκ ἂν κατεδικάσατε
8 τοὺς ἀναιτίους. κύριος γάρ ἐστιν τοῦ σαββάτου ὁ υἱὸς
9 τοῦ ἀνθρώπου. Καὶ μεταβὰς ἐκεῖθεν ἦλθεν εἰς τὴν
10 συναγωγὴν αὐτῶν· καὶ ἰδοὺ ἄνθρωπος χεῖρα ἔχων ξηράν.
καὶ ἐπηρώτησαν αὐτὸν λέγοντες Εἰ ἔξεστι τοῖς σάββασιν
11 θεραπεύειν; ἵνα κατηγορήσωσιν αὐτοῦ. ὁ δὲ εἶπεν αὐτοῖς

priests in the temple (v. 5). Lk. has no parallel to this verse. In Mk. its place is taken by 'And He said unto them, The Sabbath was made (ἐγένετο) on account of man, not man on account of the Sabbath' (for which there are Rabb. parallels); this is the true premiss of the next saying.

8. κύριος γάρ ἐστιν κτλ.] Mk. ὥστε κύριός ἐυτιν ὁ υἱ. τ. ἀνθρ. καὶ τοῦ σαββ. Lk. has the same, but omitting ὥστε and beginning with καὶ ἔλεγεν αὐτοῖς ὅτι, due to Mk.'s καὶ ἔλεγεν αὐτοῖς in the preceding verse. In Mk. 'the Son of Man' (perhaps a wrong translation of the Aram.) clearly means 'man,' not the Messiah : the Sabbath was made on man's account ; it follows therefore (ὥστε) that man is lord even of the Sabbath, and can do work on it if need arise. There can be little doubt that this was the Lord's meaning (cf. v. 31 f., ix. 6). But Mt., Lk. omit Mk.'s premiss. Mt., with γάρ, connects the saying concerning the Messiah with τοῦ ἱεροῦ μεῖζον (v. 6) : God is the 'Lord of the Sabbath,' because He ordained it, and the Messiah is equal to Him. On the non-canonical incident recorded in Lk. (D) see Plummer ad loc.

9–14. (Mk. iii. 1–6, Lk. vi. 6–11.) HEALING OF A WITHERED HAND.

9. καὶ μεταβάς κτλ.] Cf. xi. 1, xv. 29 ; Mk. πάλιν, Lk. ἐγένετο . . . εἰσελθεῖν, both characteristic. Lk. adds καὶ διδάσκειν, and ἐν ἑτέρῳ (D om.) σαββάτῳ, but Mt. implies

that the Lord proceeded at once from the field to the synagogue. On his addition of αὐτῶν see vii. 29.

10. καὶ ἰδού κτλ.] Mk., Lk. καὶ ἦν ἐκεῖ. ξηράν (so Lk.) describes the present condition of the hand (cf. Jo. v. 3), ἐξηραμμένην (Mk.) points to the past, when the affliction began ; cf. 3 Regn. xiii. 4, Zech. xi. 17. Lk. says it was his 'right hand.' In Gosp. Heb. (ap. Jerome) the man implores for help : 'caementarius (a mason) eram, manibus victum quaeritans ; precor te, Jesu, ut mihi restituas sanitatem ne turpiter mendicam cibos.'

καὶ ἐπηρώτησαν κτλ.] The onlookers (Lk. 'the Scribes and Pharisees') speak their thoughts aloud ; their εἰ ἔξεστιν is met by ἔξεστιν (v. 12) ; in Mk., Lk. they only 'watched Him whether He would heal on the Sabbath,' Lk. adding 'But He knew their reasonings.' For εἰ with a direct question cf. xix. 3 (Blass, § 77. 2). In the Mishna it is laid down that 'every case where life is in doubt [i.e. danger] supersedes the Sabbath' (Joma, viii. 6); see Schürer, HJP. II. ii. 104. The withered hand was not such.

11. ὁ δὲ εἶπεν κτλ.] Mk., Lk. relate that Jesus bade the sufferer stand forth in the midst, and that He asked those present 'Is it lawful on the Sabbath to do a kindness or to do an injury, to save life or to kill ?'; Mk. adds that 'they were silent,' and that His glance round at them was 'with anger, being grieved

Τίς ἔσται ἐξ ὑμῶν ἄνθρωπος ὃς ἕξει πρόβατον ἕν, καὶ
ἐὰν ἐμπέσῃ τοῦτο τοῖς σάββασιν εἰς βόθυνον, οὐχὶ κρατήσει
αὐτὸ καὶ ἐγερεῖ; πόσῳ οὖν διαφέρει ἄνθρωπος προβάτου. 12
ὥστε ἔξεστιν τοῖς σάββασιν καλῶς ποιεῖν. Τότε λέγει τῷ 13
ἀνθρώπῳ Ἔκτεινόν σου τὴν χεῖρα· καὶ ἐξέτεινεν, καὶ
ἀπεκατεστάθη ὑγιὴς ὡς ἡ ἄλλη. Ἐξελθόντες δὲ οἱ 14
Φαρισαῖοι συμβούλιον ἔλαβον κατ᾿ αὐτοῦ ὅπως αὐτὸν ἀπολέσωσιν.   Ὁ δὲ Ἰησοῦς γνοὺς ἀνεχώρησεν ἐκεῖθεν. 15

at the hardness of their heart'—an
expression of emotion which Mt. often
avoids; see on viii. 3. He inserts
instead a verse found (in substance,
but differently worded) in Lk. xiv. 5
in connexion with the healing of the
dropsical man.

τίς ἔσται κτλ.] Cf. vii. 9. On
ἕν (om. 𝔖 sin.cur 𝔏 ff¹ k) equivalent
to an indefinite article see viii. 19.
Lk. has υἱὸς [? ὄνος] ἢ βοῦς for
πρόβατον ἕν, φρέαρ for βόθυννον,
and ἀνασπάσει for κρατήσει καὶ
ἐγερεῖ. The rescue of animals on the
Sabbath or festivals is permitted in
Rabb. writings under various conditions; see Wetstein ad loc. and on
Lk. xiv. 5.

12. πόσῳ οὖν κτλ.] Mt. only.
On διαφέρειν see vi. 26. The second
clause summarizes the thought of
Mk. v. 4, and ἔξεστιν answers the
question asked in v. 10, but by the
substitution of καλῶς ποιεῖν (Mk.,
Lk. ἀγαθοποιεῖν) for θεραπεύειν the
Lord raises the whole problem into a
loftier sphere. καλῶς ποιεῖν and
ἀγαθοποιεῖν both stand in the LXX.
for היטיב; cf. Lev. v. 4, Jer. iv. 22,
Zech. viii. 15.

13. τότε λέγει κτλ.] An echo of
ix. 6. The command called forth the
faith which was operative towards the
cure. For ἀπεκατεστάθη cf. Ex. iv.
7, Lev. xiii. 16 = שׁוּב with the same
force; and cf. 3 Regn. xiii. 6. On
the double augment, found also in
papyri, see WH. Notes, 162; Blass,

§ 15. 7, M.-M. Vocab. s.v. ὑγιὴς ὡς
ἡ ἄλλη is added by Mt. alone.

14. ἐξελθόντες κτλ.] The incident marks a crisis in the Lord's life,
being the culminating point of the
opposition of the Jewish religious
authorities. Mk. adds εὐθὺς μετὰ τῶν
Ἡρῳδιανῶν (see on Mt. xvi. 6, xxii.
16); Lk. rewrites the whole verse.
συμβούλιον (class. συμβουλή): a late
word, explained by Plut. (Rom. xiv.)
as synonymous with κωνσίλιον (con-
silium). Deissmann (B.St. 238) cites
Dittenberger Syll. 242 and two
papyri (c. 200 A.D.). But in 4 Mac.
xvii. 17 (v.l. συνέδριον), Theod. Prov.
xv. 22 (LXX. συνέδρια), Prot. Jac.
viii. 2, it means 'a council.' σ.
λαμβάνειν is used by Mt. only:
xxii. 15, xxvii. 1, 7, xxviii. 12.
Mk. here has ἐδίδουν (v.l. ἐποίησαν),
xv. 1 ποιήσαντες (v.l. ἑτοιμάσαντες).

15–21 (cf. Mk. iii. 7–12). THE
LORD'S AVOIDANCE OF PUBLICITY.

In vv. 15 f. Mt. sums up Mk. iii.
7–12. Mk. illustrates the magnitude
and magnetism of the Lord's miracles;
Mt. mainly draws attention to a
trait in His character.

15. ὁ δὲ Ἰησοῦς κτλ.] He had
friends among the people who might
warn Him of the plot. He departed
(on the vb. see ii. 12) because further
strife might lead to His arrest, or at
least hinder His work by dragging it
into publicity. τὸ γὰρ ριψοκίνδυνον
οὐ θεάρεστον (Theoph.). πάντας is
substituted for Mk.'s πολλούς; cf. viii.

Καὶ ἠκολούθησαν αὐτῷ πολλοί, καὶ ἐθεράπευσεν αὐτοὺς
16 πάντας, καὶ ἐπετίμησεν αὐτοῖς ἵνα μὴ φανερὸν αὐτὸν ποιή-
17 σωσιν· ἵνα πληρωθῇ τὸ ῥηθὲν διὰ Ἡσαίου τοῦ προφήτου
λέγοντος

18   Ἰδοὺ ὁ παῖς μοΥ ὃν ἡρέτισα,
       ὁ ἀγαπητός μοΥ ὃν εὐδόκησεν ἡ ψΥχή μοΥ·
       θήσω τὸ πνεῦμά μοΥ ἐπ' αὐτόν,
       καὶ κρίσιν τοῖς ἔθνεσιν ἀπαγγελεῖ.
19   Οὐκ ἐρίσει οὐδὲ κραΥγάσει,

16. For other general statements
of healing see iv. 23 note.

16. καὶ ἐπετίμησεν κτλ.] On the
injunctions of silence see viii. 4. Mk.
καὶ πολλὰ ἐπετίμα αὐτοῖς, sc. the
unclean spirits, who were crying out
'Thou art the Son of God.' Mt.,
who omits this, as he does the incident
in Mk. i. 23 ff., makes the pronoun
refer to all who were healed, so that
ἐπετίμησεν has the force of 'charged
severely'; cf. xvi. 20, Mk. viii. 30.
The word is confined to the Gospels
(Mt.[7], Mk.[9], Lk.[12]), except 2 Tim. iv. 2,
Jude 9.

17–21. ἵνα πληρωθῇ κτλ.] On
the formula see i. 22. The quotation,
from Is. xlii. 1–4, agrees in some
points with the LXX. against the M.T.,
and *vice versa*. The Aram. collection
of *testimonia* from which it was
probably derived was translated from
a Heb. recension differing both from
that used by the LXX. and from the
M.T.

18. ἰδού κτλ.]   ὃν ἡρέτισα =
בְּחַרְתִּי בּוֹ (M.T. אֶתְמָךְ־בּוֹ). LXX.
Ἰακὼβ ὁ παῖς μου, ἀντιλήμψομαι
αὐτοῦ. Theod., like M.T., omits
'Jacob' (Swete, *Intr. O.T. in Gk.* 395).
αἱρετίζειν, not elsewhere in the N.T.,
occurs in the LXX.: cf. 1 Chr. xxviii.
6; and see Pss. Sol. ix. 17, xvii. 5,
Kaibel, *Epigr. Graec.* no. 252.

ὁ ἀγαπητός . . . ψυχή μου] So
M.T.; LXX. ὁ ἐκλεκτός μου, προσ-

εδέξατο αὐτὸν ἡ ψ. μ. Theod. has
ἐκλεκτός with LXX., but εὐδόκησεν
with Mt. On the occurrence of the
words at the Baptism, and the
Messianic titles ἀγαπητός and ἐκλεκτός, see iii. 17.

θήσω κτλ.] M.T. נָתַתִּי, a prophetic perf., LXX. ἔδωκα. καὶ κρίσιν
κτλ. M.T. מִשְׁפָּט לַגּוֹיִם יוֹצִיא. ἀπαγ-
γελεῖ may be a free rendering of
יוֹצִיא, but perhaps represents another
word, *e.g.* יוֹדִיעַ, since יוֹצִיא is rendered
below by ἐκβάλῃ. LXX. [om. καί]
κρίσιν τοῖς ἔθνεσιν ἐξοίσει. The
Lord did not make a practice of
preaching to Gentiles (xv. 24), but
the apostles claimed His authority
for doing so (xxviii. 19). κρίσις in
Mt. has not the wide meaning of
מִשְׁפָּט, almost 'religion'; he understands it of the fast approaching
judgment.

19. οὐκ ἐρίσει οὐδὲ κραυγάσει]
i.e. לֹא יִרִיב וְלֹא יִצְעָק. The verbs
are transposed in M.T. לֹא יִצְעַק וְלֹא
יִשָּׂא, and LXX. οὐδὲ κεκράξεται οὐδὲ
ἀνήσει. Targ. has 'cry nor shout
nor lift up (יְרִים) his voice'; and see
Field, *Hexapla, ad loc.* The text
underlying the translation used by
Mt. seems to have had the Aram.
יְרִיב ('cry') as an equivalent for
יִשָּׂא (so ﺵ pesh in Isaiah, and ﺵ
sin.cur here); but the translator gave
it the Heb. meaning 'strive.' For
Mt. the words are a prediction of

ογΔέ ἀκογϲει τιϲ ἐν ταῖϲ πλατείαιϲ τὴν φωνὴν αγτογ·

κάλαμον ϲγντετριμμένον ογ κατεάΣει   20
καὶ λίνον τγφόμενον ογ ϲβέϲει,
    ἕωϲ ἂν ἐκβάλη εἰϲ νῖκοϲ τὴν κρίϲιν·
    καὶ τῷ ὀνόματι αγτογ ἔθνη ἐλπιογϲιν.   21

Τότε προσήνεγκαν αὐτῷ δαιμονιζόμενον τυφλὸν καὶ 22

the care which the Lord took to
avoid an open quarrel with the
Pharisees, and self-advertisement as
the Messiah ; the former He avoided
by departing (v. 15), the latter by
His prohibition (v. 16). For κραυ-
γάζειν cf. 2 Esd. iii. 13, Jo. xi. 43.
    οὐδὲ ἀκούσει κτλ.] i.e. יַשְׁמִיעַ
impers., M.T. יְשַׁמַּע. LXX. ἀκουσθή-
σεται = יִשָּׁמַע.

20. κάλαμον . . . σβέσει] This
and LXX. correspond with M.T. The
thought here is similar to that in
xi. 30 ; the Messiah will comfort and
help the weak-hearted, in contrast
with the Pharisees who care only
for such as do stand (cf. ix. 13).
The crushed reed and the smoulder-
ing flax (i.e. wick) are those who are
morally all but powerless. He who
'came to send fire on the earth'
would not quench, but would carefully tend, the faintest sign of its
kindling. See Cheyne, Isaiah ad
loc. On the augment in κατεάξει
see Blass, § 24 (s.v. ἀγνύναι), a form
not found in the LXX. Moulton
(Class. Rev., 1901, 36) cites a subst.
κατέαγμα from a papyrus (2nd cent.
A.D.). τύφειν (class.) is unique in
bibl. Gk.
    ἕως ἄν κτλ.] = עַד יוֹצִיא לָנֶצַח מִשְׁפָּט.
M.T. has two clauses, represented in
the LXX. by ἀλλὰ εἰς ἀληθείαν
(לָאֱמֶת) ἐξοίσει κρίσιν and ἕως ἄν
θῇ ἐπὶ τῆς γῆς κρίσιν. The Heb.
underlying Mt. may have been
influenced by Hab. i. 4, לֹא יֵצֵא לָנֶצַח
מִשְׁפָּט. In Heb. נֶצַח means 'permanence,' 'perpetuity,' in Aram.

'victory'; the latter was adopted in
the Gk. translation which Mt. used.
Cf. 1 Cor. xv. 54 = Is. xxv. 8, LXX.
ἰσχύσας, but S. Paul and Aq., Sym.,
Theod. εἰς νῖκος. For the evangelist
the rendering was important : the
Lord's earthly activities were those
which the prophet predicted of the
Messiah, and His final victorious
judgment was certain.

21. καὶ τῷ ὀνόματι κτλ.] LXX.
καὶ ἐπὶ τ. ὀν. Heb. 'And for His
law shall (the) isles hope.' The
announcement to the Gentiles of
future judgment (v. 18) was also a
message of hope. ἐλπίζειν with
dat. (class.) is not found elsewhere
in bibl. Gk. ; καί is, therefore,
perhaps a corruption of κἀν (D καὶ
ἐν). Blass, § 5. 2.

22, 23 (cf. Lk. xi. 14). HEALING
OF A BLIND AND DUMB MAN.

Both Mt. and Lk. substitute this
for Mk. iii. 20 f. (an incident which
they probably shrank from recording),
to form a suitable introduction to
the discourse on Beelzebul. See
further Add. note on ix. 32 f.

22. τότε προσήνεγκαν κτλ.] On
the impers. verb, avoided in the v.l.,
see iv. 24. The man's maniacal
obsession so affected his nerves as to
render him blind and dumb. The
verse has the appearance of being a
greatly abbreviated account from a
longer one which Mt. had before
him (κωφόν in the last clause is for
τυφλὸν καὶ κ.) ; his chief object was
to introduce the charge in v. 24 and
the following discourse.

κωφόν· καὶ ἐθεράπευσεν αὐτόν, ὥστε τὸν κωφὸν λαλεῖν
23 καὶ βλέπειν. Καὶ ἐξίσταντο πάντες οἱ ὄχλοι καὶ ἔλεγον
24 Μήτι οὗτός ἐστιν ὁ υἱὸς Δαυείδ; οἱ δὲ Φαρισαῖοι ἀκούσαντες εἶπον Οὗτος οὐκ ἐκβάλλει τὰ δαιμόνια εἰ μὴ ἐν

23. καὶ ἐξίσταντο κτλ.] They
were beside themselves (with astonishment). In Mk.'s narrative the
relatives of Jesus said of Him ἐξέστη,
and Mt. adapts the word. Lk. has
ἐθαύμασαν. Spitta's conjecture, if
it could be proved correct, would be
welcome, that Mk.'s οἱ παρ' αὐτοῦ
means not His relatives but the
disciples (but cf. e.g. Sus. 33), and
that the subject of ἐξέστη is ὁ ὄχλος,
which has fallen out by the mutila-
tion of the MS., together with an
account of the miracle which roused
their excitement.

καὶ ἔλεγον κτλ.] Mt. only. μήτι
expects the answer No, but the
possibility of the truth lies behind
the question; cf. Jo. iv. 29. οὗτος
is emphatic: 'this man' who, in
spite of His miraculous power,
answers so little to our notions of
the Messiah. The οὗτος in the
Pharisees' retort (v. 24) corresponds
with it. The use of υἱὸς Δαυείδ is
characteristic of Mt., who takes every
opportunity of laying stress on the
Messiahship of Jesus; see ix. 27 note,
and p. xvii. f.

**24. (Mk. iii. 22, Lk. xi. 15.) THE
CHARGE OF DEMONIACAL AGENCY.**

οἱ δὲ Φαρισαῖοι κτλ.] Mk. οἱ
γραμματεῖς οἱ ἀπὸ Ἱεροσολύμων
καταβάντες, officials from the capital;
cf. Mk. vii. 1. Lk. simply τινὲς δὲ
ἐξ αὐτῶν, referring to the ὄχλοι.
The Pharisees reply, with a contemptuous οὗτος (cf. ix. 3), echoing
the οὗτος in v. 23. They speak
authoritatively to the bystanders and
the healed man, to prevent them
from becoming the Lord's followers.
With οὐκ . . . εἰ μή, which has an

Aram. flavour, cf. xiii. 57, xiv. 17,
xv. 24, xvii. 8, xxi. 19. Mk. has
two clauses: (1) He hath Beelzebul,
(2) In the prince of the demons He
casteth out the demons. The former
is interpreted by Mk. (v. 30) as 'He
hath an unclean spirit,' which, according to the ideas of the time, was not
very different from ἐξέστη (Mk. v.
21); cf. Jo. x. 20. But it is possible that Βεελ. ἔχει was corrupted,
under the influence of the O.T. name
Beelzebub, from an expression of mere
vulgar insult connected with the late
Heb. בֶּל 'dung,' with no reference
to a demon; see x. 25 note. In
Mt., Lk. the inference is drawn that
Beelzebul and the prince of the
demons were one and the same,
which the following discourse in Mk.
does not support. The use of the
preposition ἐν τῷ B., corresponding
with ב, is also akin to that found in
papyri (*Expos.* VI. vii. 112)—'armed
with,' i.e. with the help, or instru-
mentality, of; cf. v. 28 (Lk. xi. 20),
xxvi. 52, Lk. xxii. 49. Τὸ ἄρχοντι
Lk. more correctly prefixes the
article; cf. Mt. ix. 34. In Jewish
traditions the prince of demons
had various names, e.g. Asmodaeus
(Targ. Eccl. i. 12; cf. Tob. iii. 17),
Mastema (Jub. x. 8, see Charles),
Azazel (see Bousset, *Rel. d. Jud.*
381–94), Samael (see Edersheim,
LT. ii. 755 ff.). Cf. also Enoch
lxix. 2, 4.

**25–30. (Mk. iii. 23–27, Lk. xi.
17–23.) THE LORD'S REPLY TO
THE CHARGE.**

Mt. and Lk. appear to have used
not only Mk., but also their respective recensions of Q. The synoptic

τῷ Βεεζεβοὺλ ἄρχοντι τῶν δαιμονίων. Εἰδὼς δὲ τὰς ἐν- 25
θυμήσεις αὐτῶν εἶπεν αὐτοῖς Πᾶσα βασιλεία μερισθεῖσα
καθ' ἑαυτῆς ἐρημοῦται, καὶ πᾶσα πόλις ἢ οἰκία μερισθεῖσα
καθ' ἑαυτῆς οὐ σταθήσεται. καὶ εἰ ὁ Σατανᾶς τὸν Σατανᾶν 26
ἐκβάλλει, ἐφ' ἑαυτὸν ἐμερίσθη· πῶς οὖν σταθήσεται ἡ
βασιλεία αὐτοῦ; καὶ εἰ ἐγὼ ἐν Βεεζεβοὺλ ἐκβάλλω τὰ 27
δαιμόνια, οἱ υἱοὶ ὑμῶν ἐν τίνι ἐκβάλλουσιν; διὰ τοῦτο

25 ειδως] ιδων אᵇD 𝕷 ff¹ k 𝕾 sin.cur me

relations are discussed in *JBL.*, 1913, 57–73.

25. εἰδὼς δέ κτλ.] The *v.l.* ἰδών does not alter the sense ; an act of real intuition is described. On this, and on ἐνθυμήσεις (Lk. διανοήματα), see ix. 4. Mk. introduces the discourse differently : 'And having summoned them He spake to them in parables.'

πᾶσα βασιλεία κτλ.] Lk. similarly. Mk. begins ' How can Satan cast out Satan,' which Mt. adapts in *v.* 26. The Lord appeals to a fact of common experience in history to illustrate the truth about the 'kingdom' of the prince of the demons. ἐρημοῦν, common in the LXX., occurs in the N.T., apart from this context, only in Apoc.[3] Mt., Lk. probably found it in their source, and preferred it to Mk.'s repeated οὐ δύναται σταθῆναι (στῆναι).

καὶ πᾶσα πόλις κτλ.] Mk. has a second conditional : καὶ ἐὰν οἰκία κτλ. Lk. καὶ οἶκος ἐπὶ οἶκον πίπτει (either 'a house [divided] against a house falleth,' or possibly 'house falleth against house'). Only Mt. has πόλις, making a triad of illustrations. 'House' here (not, however, in *v.* 29) may, as in Aram., denote a political district (Wellh.) : a whole kingdom, or any district in it, destroys itself by internal divisions. Cf. Soph. *Ant.* 687 f., Cic. *Lael.* 7.

26. καὶ εἰ κτλ.] Mt. adapts Mk. *v.* 23, instead of following his εἰ ὁ Σατ.

ἀνέστη ἐφ' ἑαυτόν (Lk. ἐφ' ἑαυτὸν διεμερίσθη). On Σατανᾶς see iv. 10. For the question πῶς οὖν (similarly Lk.) Mk. has the tautological 'and cannot stand, but hath an end.' Lk. adds ' because ye say that in Beelzebul I cast out the demons,' explaining the identity of Beelzebul and Satan. Mk. 'Because they said, He hath an unclean spirit.'

27, 28. These verses are identical in Lk. (except δακτύλῳ for πνεύματι, and perhaps the omission of ἐγώ in the latter verse), but absent from Mk. They must have stood here in Q, but appear to be isolated sayings from different contexts. They contain a second line of defence. Your own Jewish exorcists—do they work with the help of Beelzebul ? If not, they condemn you for your arbitrary condemnation of me (*v.* 27). The only alternative is that I work by the Spirit of God ; in which case something further follows (*v.* 28).

27. καὶ εἰ κτλ.] οἱ υἱοὶ ὑμῶν stands first in the clause, in emphatic contrast with ἐγώ. The 'sons' are not merely the pupils of the Pharisees, for Lk. does not mention the Pharisees, nor can it refer to the apostles as being Jews by birth (Hil., Chrys., Jer.) ; it denotes 'your fellow-Jews' in general. For magic employed by Jews for exorcizing demons see Tob. viii. 1–3, Jos. *Ant.* VIII. ii. 5, *BJ.* VII. vi. 3, Midr. Num. (Wünsche, 465) ; and cf. Ac. xix.

28 αὐτοὶ κριταὶ ἔσονται ὑμῶν. εἰ δὲ ἐν πνεύματι θεοῦ ἐγὼ
ἐκβάλλω τὰ δαιμόνια, ἄρα ἔφθασεν ἐφ᾽ ὑμᾶς ἡ βασιλεία
29 τοῦ θεοῦ. ἢ πῶς δύναταί τις εἰσελθεῖν εἰς τὴν οἰκίαν τοῦ

13 f., Just. *Dial.* 85 οἱ ἐξ ὑμῶν
ἐπορχισταὶ τῇ τέχνῃ, ὅπερ καὶ τὰ
ἔθνη, χρώμενοι ἐξορκίζουσιν. Iren.
(*Haer.* II. vi. 2) says that Jews in his
day drove out demons by invoking
the name of the Lord. On exorcism
by Christians see vii. 22. Jesus
neither denies the reality of Jewish
exorcisms, nor does He express a
view as to the power by which they
were performed ; He argues from
His opponents' ground. ἔσονται is
an Aram. imperf., not a definite
future.

28. εἰ δέ κτλ.] It is difficult
to think that this verse originally
followed *v.* 27 ; the Lord there
assumes that the Pharisees would
claim divine power for their Jewish
exorcists, but here He treats His own
working by divine power as marking a crisis in history. The sayings
must have been spoken on different
occasions, and from different points
of view. For πνεύματι Lk. has
δακτύλῳ (cf. Ex. viii. 19, xxxi. 18),
which is probably genuine, for Lk.
would hardly have avoided πνεῦμα,
which occurs so frequently in his
writings, and, on the other hand,
Mt. seems to use πνεῦμα to prepare
for the thought of *vv.* 31 f.

ἄρα ἔφθασεν κτλ.] If God's
power is already overcoming Satan's
power, then God's sovereignty has
already begun to exercise an influence, and must be so near as
virtually to have arrived. φθάνειν,
only in this context in the Gospels,
means not 'anticipate' but 'arrive,'
as usually in late Gk. when followed
by a preposition ; cf. Rom. ix. 31,
2 Cor. x. 14, Phil. iii. 16, 1 Thes. ii.
16 (contrast iv. 15). In the LXX.

it sometimes has this meaning without a preposition (Neh. xviii. 1 [vii.
73], Cant. ii. 12). For φθάνειν ἐπί
cf. Theod. Dan. iv. 25 (על מטא).
The aor. ἔφθασεν refers to a moment
in the near past, *i.e.* when Jesus began
to cast out demons (Moulton, i. 135,
140) ; but it does not follow that He
spoke of the Kingdom in a sense
other than eschatological. ἔφθασα
in mod. Gk. can mean 'I am coming
immediately' (Moulton, i.² 247), and
S cur.pesh 'hath drawn near' is
correct. Cf. Dan. iv. 8, Theod.
ἔφθασεν, LXX. ἤγγιζεν. The verb may
represent either קרב (Dalm.) or מטא
(J. Weiss). ἡ βασ. τοῦ θεοῦ (instead
of τῶν οὐρανῶν 32 times) is elsewhere
confined in Mt. to xix. 24, xxi. 31, 43
(see pp. xix., xxiii.). He must have
found it in his source, and left it
unaltered, perhaps in the present case
because it formed a better parallel to
ἐν πνεύματι θεοῦ, and also a sharper
contrast with ἡ β. αὐτοῦ (*v.* 26), the
Divine Personality standing over
against the Satanic. The distinction
which Allen draws between the two
expressions is hardly convincing.

29. ἢ πῶς κτλ.] The immediate
sequel of πῶς κτλ. in *v.* 26. How
can Satan be supposed to ruin himself ? Or, since the answer to that
is obvious, how can he be ruined
without being first defeated ? Mk.
gives the same connexion of thought
by οὐ δύναται . . . ἀλλ᾽ οὐ δύναται.
Mt. follows Mk. fairly closely ; Lk.
has the parable in a different form.
The words recall Is. xlix. 24 f., μὴ
λήμψεταί τις παρὰ γίγαντος σκῦλα ;
. . . ἐάν τις αἰχμαλωτεύσῃ γίγαντα,
λήμψεται σκῦλα, and Ps. Sol. v. 4,
οὐ γὰρ λήψεται σκῦλα ἄνθρωπος

ἰσχυροῦ καὶ τὰ σκεύη αὐτοῦ ἁρπάσαι, ἐὰν μὴ πρῶτον δήσῃ
τὸν ἰσχυρόν; καὶ τότε τὴν οἰκίαν αὐτοῦ διαρπάσει. ὁ μὴ 30
ὢν μετ᾽ ἐμοῦ κατ᾽ ἐμοῦ ἐστίν, καὶ ὁ μὴ συνάγων μετ᾽
ἐμοῦ σκορπίζει. Διὰ τοῦτο λέγω ὑμῖν, πᾶσα ἁμαρτία καὶ 31

παρὰ ἀνδρὸς δυνατοῦ. Cf. also Is. liii. 12. The art. in ὁ ἰσχυρός is generic, but hints at the particular strong man that is meant. His binding began with his defeat in the wilderness (iv. 1–11). In οἰκίαν (Lk. αὐλήν) there is possibly a play on the name Beelzebul, 'Lord of dwelling' (see x. 25). σκεύη (= Aram. מַנִין, Heb. כֵּלִים) is a wide term embracing all the contents of the house; Lk. τὰ ὑπάρχοντα αὐτοῦ. If the details may be pressed allegorically, the σκεύη are not the demons (Holtzm.) but the bodies and souls of men. σκεύη δὲ τοῦ ἰσχυροῦ οἱ ὑπαγόμενοι τοῖς θελήμασιν αὐτοῦ (Orig.); cf. Ac. ix. 15, Rom. ix. 21–23, 2 Tim. ii. 20 f. ὅπλα (cf. Rom. vi. 13) can also represent מַנִין, which is probably the explanation of Lk.'s καθωπλισμένος and πανοπλίαν. Mt. seems to use ἁρπάσει and διαρπάσει (both frequent in LXX. for גֵּזֵל) merely for variety.

30. ὁ μὴ ὢν κτλ.] Identical in Lk., but absent from Mk. A stern warning which Jesus might have spoken on many occasions: 'neutrality towards My work is impossible; indifference means hostility.' But though it stood here in Q, its connexion with the foregoing incident is doubtful, since to lay a charge of demoniacal agency is not neutrality but bitter enmity. Mt. may have seen a connexion with v. 23 f.: the people were half inclined to believe in the Lord's Messiahship, but instead of 'gathering' them into the number of His disciples, the Pharisees had tried to 'scatter' them. The metaphors might refer to sheep (cf. Jo. x.

12, xi. 52, Ez. xiii. 5, Zech. xi. 16), or to corn (cf. iii. 12, xiii. 30); they are different in xxv. 24.

The saying is inverted in Mk. ix. 40 = Lk. ix. 50, and connected, as here, with the casting out of demons. But they are not contradictory, if the one was spoken to the indifferent about themselves, and the other to the disciples about some one else. They correspond with the warnings 'Test yourselves' (2 Cor. xiii. 5), and 'Judge not' (Mt. vii. 1). A parallel to both is seen in Cic. Q. Lig. ix.: 'Te enim dicere audiebamus, nos omnes adversarios putare nisi qui nobiscum esset; te omnes qui contra te non essent tuos.' Ligarius perhaps inverted a current saying; similarly Jesus may here be using a current saying, which He inverts in Mk. l.c. (cf. Mt. vii. 12). That both sayings were current in Palestine, and to be traced to Cicero (Nestle, ZNW., 1912, 84 ff.), is very improbable. Still more so that ὁ μὴ ὢν κτλ. are the words of Beelzebul (von Dobschütz, Th.St.Kr., 1912, 356 f.; Fridrichsen, ZNW., 1912, 273 ff.).

31, 32. (Mk. iii. 28, 29, Lk. xii. 10.) *Blasphemy against the Holy Spirit.*

The two verses are a doublet of the same saying; v. 31 is an abbreviation of Mk.; v. 32 is from Q. Lk. is based on Q, but in τῷ . . . βλασφημήσαντι he is influenced by Mk. Each verse helps to explain difficulties in the other.

31. διὰ τοῦτο κτλ.] Mk. ἀμὴν λ. ὑ. Mt. thus connects the saying more closely with the preceding in-

βλασφημία ἀφεθήσεται τοῖς ἀνθρώποις, ἡ δὲ τοῦ πνεύ-
32 ματος βλασφημία οὐκ ἀφεθήσεται. καὶ ὃς ἐὰν εἴπῃ λόγον
κατὰ τοῦ υἱοῦ τοῦ ἀνθρώπου, ἀφεθήσεται αὐτῷ· ὃς δ᾽ ἂν
εἴπῃ κατὰ τοῦ πνεύματος τοῦ ἁγίου, οὐκ ἀφεθήσεται αὐτῷ
33 οὔτε ἐν τούτῳ τῷ αἰῶνι οὔτε ἐν τῷ μέλλοντι.   *Η

cident. Lk. has it in another, less suitable, context.

πᾶσα ἁμαρτία κτλ.] Mt. abbreviates Mk.'s impressive tautology. He writes τ. ἀνθρώποις for Mk.'s τ. υἱοῖς τῶν ἀνθρώπων, which recurs in the N.T. only in Eph. iii. 5. V. 32 and Lk. have κατὰ τοῦ υἱοῦ [εἰς τὸν υἱὸν] τοῦ ἀνθρώπου, which suggests that the sing. originally stood in Mk. in the sense of 'man' (cf. Mt. ix. 6), but was altered to prevent the words being understood to mean that the Son of Man could need forgiveness. J. Weiss explains that 'the Son of Man' means Jesus as a private person, but the Holy Spirit means the divine power that worked in Him. But 'the Son of Man' is the last expression that He would have chosen for Himself as a private person.

V. 31 and Mk. raise a serious difficulty. 'Every sin and blasphemy' is exhaustive, and Mk. is even more emphatic; it must include sins and blasphemies against God as well as against men; how, then, is blasphemy against the Holy Spirit so much more heinous than against God? The sharp contrast is lacking, which is found in v. 32 and Lk., between 'the Son of Man' and 'the Holy Spirit.' It is probable that the contrast there is between man and the Holy Spirit, and that the same contrast was expressed in the Aram. underlying v. 31 and Mk.; 'man' ('men') was wrongly connected with ἀφεθήσεται.

βλασφημεῖν (-μία) in the LXX. is always blasphemy against God (against Bel in Theod. Bel 9), but

in class. Gk. usually slander against men; for the latter cf. Rom. iii. 8, 1 Cor. x. 30. ἡ δὲ τοῦ πν. βλασφ. is an abbreviation of Mk.'s ὃς δ᾽ ἂν βλασφημήσῃ εἰς τὸ πν. τὸ ἅγιον. Cf. LXX. Dan. iii. 96 [29]. After ἄφεσιν Mk. continues εἰς τὸν αἰῶνα, ἀλλὰ ἔνοχός ἐστιν αἰωνίου ἁμαρτήματος. Mt. places his corresponding words at the end of the next verse.

32. καὶ ὃς ἐάν κτλ.] Lk. καὶ πᾶς ὃς ἐρεῖ λόγον εἰς (cf. Ac. vi. 11). In the second clause Mt. has ὃς δ᾽ ἂν εἴπῃ, Lk. τῷ δὲ βλασφημήσαντι. No distinction, therefore, can be drawn between 'say a word [i.e. anything] against' and 'blaspheme.' Cf. Job ii. 9, εἰπόν τι ῥῆμα = בֵּרֵךְ 'curse.' 'The Son of Man' probably means 'man' (see above). 'How could the Pharisees be supposed to be able to distinguish between the Son of Man (= Christ?) acting as such, and the Son of Man driving out devils by the power of the Spirit?' (Allen). 'Si operatio una est, una est contumelia' (Ambr.).

οὔτε ἐν τούτῳ κτλ.] An expansion of Mk.'s εἰς τὸν αἰῶνα. Lk. has no time reference. Jewish writers after the fall of Jerusalem often contrast 'this age' with 'the coming age,' but such expressions are foreign to pre-Christian Jewish writings, and are rare in the N.T.; cf. Mk. x. 30 (Lk. xviii. 30, not Mt.), Eph. i. 21; ὁ αἰὼν οὗτος and ἐκεῖνος Lk. xx. 34 f., not Mt., (Mk.). Dalman (Words, 148–54) doubts if Jesus ever used the expressions; His thoughts were filled by the 'Kingdom of Heaven'; see Bousset, Rel. d. Jud. 278 ff., Volz, Jüd. Esch. 57.

ποιήσατε τὸ δένδρον καλὸν καὶ τὸν καρπὸν αὐτοῦ καλόν, ἢ

With four forms of the saying before us the Lord's exact words cannot be determined. But it seems fairly certain that He draws a contrast between slandering men and slandering the Spirit of God: the one shall be forgiven, the other not. Lk., though apparently influenced both by Mt. and Mk., is probably the nearest to the original purport of the saying. The words have occasioned many heart-burnings, mostly to sensitive consciences far removed from the sin of blasphemy. This is due to the difficulty felt by the Western mind in grasping the meaning of Jewish phraseology. The unpardonable sin is usually explained as the expression of a hardened state of mind which deliberately denounces as evil that which the sinner knows to be good; he says, with his eyes open, 'Evil be thou my good'; 'fingit enim falsum esse quod scit esse verum' (Ps.-Aug.). And this hardened state is, by its very nature, permanent, and excludes the possibility of repentance. Such a thought possibly underlies 1 Jo. v. 16; but is it possible to read so profound and hopeless a depth of evil into the word 'blaspheme,' not to mention 'speak a word against'? In Jewish phraseology serious sin was often spoken of as unpardonable. See Num. xv. 30 f., He that sinneth deliberately blasphemeth (מְגַדֵּף) Yahweh, and shall be cut off from his people 'with his iniquity upon him,' *i.e.* unforgiven. 1 Sam. iii. 14, 'The iniquity of Eli's house shall not be atoned for by sacrifice or offering for ever.' Is. xxii. 14, 'This your iniquity shall not be atoned for till ye die' (*i.e.* never). Rabbinic parallels 'there is no forgiveness for him,' 'there is no forgiveness for him for ever' are given by

Dalman, *Words*, 147. And cf. Philo De Profugis on Ex. xxi. 17 (Mangey i. 558): '[The lawgiver] wellnigh shouts and cries aloud that no forgiveness is to be given to those who blaspheme the Divine Being. For if those who have spoken evil of mortal parents are carried away on the road to death, of what punishment ought they to be deemed worthy who continue to blaspheme the Father and Maker of all? And what evil-speaking could be more shameful than to say, not concerning us but concerning God, that He is the source of evil?' If the Lord spoke as a Jew to Jews, and used a type of expression current in His day, and derived from the O.T., He meant, and would be understood to mean, no more than that blasphemy against the Holy Spirit, by whose power He worked, was a terrible sin,—more terrible than blasphemy against man.

33-35. (Lk. vi. 43, 44 a, 45.) CHARACTER SHEWN BY DEEDS AND WORDS.

The section, appended loosely to the foregoing, can hardly be in its original context. Mt. perhaps saw a link in the thought that the Lord, being a 'good tree,' could not produce the 'bad fruit' of alliance with Beelzebul. Orig.: δένδρον καλόν, ἢ τὸ ἅγιον πνεῦμα· σαπρόν, τὸ ἀκάθαρτον πνεῦμα.

33. ἢ ποιήσατε κτλ.] The saying appears in another, probably more original, form in vii. 16 a, 17 f., where, as in Lk., δένδρον is the subject, not the object, of ποιεῖν, and the verb, consequently, has a different meaning. The original of καὶ τὸν καρπὸν αὐ. καλόν probably meant 'and then its fruit will be good' (so the 𝔖 can be rendered), the acc.

ποιήσατε τὸ δένδρον σαπρὸν καὶ τὸν καρπὸν αὐτοῦ σαπρόν·
34 ἐκ γὰρ τοῦ καρποῦ τὸ δένδρον γινώσκεται. γεννήματα
ἐχιδνῶν, πῶς δύνασθε ἀγαθὰ λαλεῖν πονηροὶ ὄντες; ἐκ
35 γὰρ τοῦ περισσεύματος τῆς καρδίας τὸ στόμα λαλεῖ. ὁ
ἀγαθὸς ἄνθρωπος ἐκ τοῦ ἀγαθοῦ θησαυροῦ ἐκβάλλει ἀγαθά,
καὶ ὁ πονηρὸς ἄνθρωπος ἐκ τοῦ πονηροῦ θησαυροῦ ἐκ-
36 βάλλει πονηρά. Λέγω δὲ ὑμῖν ὅτι πᾶν ῥῆμα ἀργὸν ὃ
λαλήσουσιν οἱ ἄνθρωποι, ἀποδώσουσιν περὶ αὐτοῦ λόγον ἐν

being due to attraction. For the consec. καί see Blass, § 77. 6. On the clause ἐκ γὰρ τοῦ καρποῦ κτλ. see vii. 16.

34. γεννήματα κτλ.] The first sentence is peculiar to Mt., and possibly was not spoken by Jesus. The Baptist used the same term of reproach (see on iii. 7, cf. xxiii. 33), followed by the same metaphor. But the words are valuable as shewing the degree of sternness which the evangelist felt justified in ascribing to Jesus. There were no doubt grada-tions of evil, and possibilities of good in the hearers, but the words only express the principle that like pro-duces like (cf. Job xiv. 4). They can have no reference to 'original sin,' nor do they imply that there are any who *cannot* be good. Cf. vii. 11.

ἐκ γάρ κτλ.] Lk. has this at the end of the next verse. That which fills the heart flows out of it. In its present position this perhaps implies that blasphemy against the Holy Spirit could not be excused as mere words which the speakers did not mean. But otherwise it expresses a general principle capable of many applications. ἀνδρὸς χαρακτὴρ ἐκ λόγων γνωρίζεται (Menander). S. James (iii. 10 f.) perhaps has it in mind in his metaphor of the fountain coupled with that of the fruit-tree. περίσσευμα occurs only in Mk. viii. 8, 2 Cor. viii. 14, Jam. i. 21 (*v.l.*), Eccl.

ii. 15 (probably a Christian gloss in the LXX.).

35. ὁ ἀγαθός κτλ.] Another metaphor for the same truth; a man can bring out of his treasure (cf. xiii. 52) only what is there. Lk. interprets it by adding τῆς καρδίας after θησαυροῦ (cf. Mt. vi. 21), and for ἐκβάλλει (see on viii. 12) he writes προφέρει, frequent in class. Gk. for the utterance of words. The metaphor and the thought are found in *Test. Asher*, i.

36. λέγω δέ κτλ.] This, and the next, verse are peculiar to Mt., and introduce the new thought of judg-ment; not only good and bad, but even 'idle' words must be accounted for. ῥῆμα is used, in preference to λόγος, because of the following ἀποδώσουσιν λόγον. A ῥῆμα ἀργόν (α-εργον) is one that does not, and is not intended to, effect anything. Vulg. *otiosum*, k Cyp. (less well) *vacuum*. 'Sine utilitate loquentis dicitur et audientis' (Jer.). Cf. 'the voice of a fool in many idle (במילין) words' (Targ. Eccl. v. 2); αἱρετώτερόν σοι ἔστω λίθον εἰκῆ βαλεῖν ἢ λόγον ἀργόν (Pythag.). The adj. is applied to men (xx. 3, 6), a fruit-tree (2 Pet. i. 8), fallow land (Jos. *Ant.* XII. ix. 5), the Sabbath (*BJ.* IV. ii. 3). Aram. idiom is reflected in the *nom. pendens* πᾶν ῥῆμα, and the indefinite fut. λα-λήλουσιν, 'which men [ever] speak.' On ἐν ἡμ. κρίσεως see x. 15.

ἡμέρᾳ κρίσεως· ἐκ γὰρ τῶν λόγων σου δικαιωθήσῃ, καὶ ἐκ 37
τῶν λόγων σου καταδικασθήσῃ.

Τότε ἀπεκρίθησαν αὐτῷ τινὲς τῶν γραμματέων καὶ 38
Φαρισαίων λέγοντες Διδάσκαλε, θέλομεν ἀπὸ σοῦ σημεῖον
ἰδεῖν. ὁ δὲ ἀποκριθεὶς εἶπεν αὐτοῖς Γενεὰ πονηρὰ καὶ μοι- 39
χαλὶς σημεῖον ἐπιζητεῖ, καὶ σημεῖον οὐ δοθήσεται αὐτῇ εἰ
μὴ τὸ σημεῖον Ἰωνᾶ τοῦ προφήτου. ὥσπερ γὰρ ἦν Ἰωνᾶϲ 40

37. ἐκ γάρ κτλ.] The change
from ῥῆμα to λόγοι, and the unexpected use of the 2nd pers. sing.,
suggest that the verse is drawn from
another context. It was possibly a
current proverb. On δικαιωθῆναι ἐκ
see xi. 19.

38–42. (Lk. xi. 29–32.) A SIGN
REFUSED.

The Marcan parallel to this section
from Q is found in Mk. viii. 11 f.
= Mt. xvi. 1, 2 a, 4.

38. τότε κτλ.] On ἀπεκρίθησαν.
see xi. 25. In Lk. the request for a
sign is made earlier (v. 16) by some
of the people, while others were
charging Jesus with alliance with
Beelzebul; he adds here that the
Lord spoke 'while the crowds were
pressing up.' On διδάσκαλε see vii.
21. The σημεῖον which they wanted
was something more than a 'miracle'
of healing, in which sense the word,
though characteristic of the 4th Gosp.
(cf. also 'Mk.' xvi. 17, 20), is not used
by the synoptists. They asked for
something which would substantiate
His unique claims to authority. Lk.,
influenced by Mk. (cf. Mt. xvi. 1),
calls it 'a sign from heaven.' Mt.
may have understood the request as
a further attempt to discredit Jesus
in the eyes of the people; they had
said (v. 23), Can this be the
Messiah? Let Him, then, do something of a higher order than exorcism,
which, on His own admission, was
performed by the Jews themselves.
But in Mk. it follows, though it is

not connected with, the feeding of
the 4000. Rabbinic teachers were
sometimes asked to give signs (Edersheim, L. and T. ii. 68 f.), a request for
which there were O.T. precedents
(Ex. iv. 8 f., Is. vii. 11). See 1 Cor.
i. 22.

39. γενεὰ πονηρά κτλ.] So in
xvi. 4. Mk. simply ἡ γενεὰ αὐτή.
In Lk. γεν. πον. is a predicate of
ἡ γεν. αὐτή. The γενεά appears to
refer to the Scribes and Pharisees, as
in xvi. 4 and Mk.; in Lk. to the
multitudes (see on xi. 16). μοιχαλίς
(cf. Jam. iv. 4) is an echo of O.T.
teaching from Hosea onwards; Israel
is God's unfaithful bride. See the
verdict of Josephus on his generation
(B.J. v. x. 5, xiii. 6).

καὶ σημεῖον . . . αὐτῇ] So xvi.
4 and Lk. Mk. has the Hebraic
εἰ δοθήσεται. The exception εἰ μή
κτλ. occurs (om. τ. προφήτου) in
xvi. 4 and Lk., but is absent from Mk.
It seems to have stood in Q; Mt. (v.
40) interprets it of the Resurrection,
Lk. (v. 30) of the Advent.

40. ὥσπερ γάρ κτλ.] Lk. has 'For
as Jonah became a sign to the
Ninevites, so shall also the Son of
Man be to this generation.' This
does not refer to the Resurrection; nor
is the 'sign of Jonah' the preaching
of Jesus. If we did not possess
Mt., no other explanation would be
thought of than that of the Messiah's
Advent. The Son of Man will come,
as it were from a foreign land, with
a message of doom to this genera-

ἐν τῇ κοιλίᾳ τοῦ κήτους τρεῖς ἡμέρας καὶ τρεῖς νύκτας, οὕτως
ἔσται ὁ υἱὸς τοῦ ἀνθρώπου ἐν τῇ καρδίᾳ τῆς γῆς
41 τρεῖς ἡμέρας καὶ τρεῖς νύκτας. ἄνδρες Νινευεῖται ἀναστήσονται ἐν τῇ κρίσει μετὰ τῆς γενεᾶς ταύτης καὶ κατακρινοῦσιν αὐτήν· ὅτι μετενόησαν εἰς τὸ κήρυγμα Ἰωνᾶ, καὶ
42 ἰδοὺ πλεῖον Ἰωνᾶ ὧδε. βασίλισσα νότου ἐγερθήσεται ἐν

tion as Jonah did to the Ninevites.
Lk.'s verse may well be a genuine
utterance.   Mt.'s substitute is 'a
gloss which formed no part of the
original saying' (Sanday, Inspiration, 433). ἦν Ἰωνᾶς . . . νύκτας is
quoted verbatim from LXX. Jon. ii.
1 [Engl. i. 17]. The verse cannot
be genuine : (1) it differs from Lk.,
(2) the title 'the Son of Man' as
applied by Jesus to Himself occurs
too early (see on xvi. 20), and (3)
as a prediction it is inaccurate, for
the Lord was 'in the heart of the
earth' not three but two nights.
μετὰ τρεῖς ἡμέρας occurs in Mk.
(viii. 31, ix. 31, x. 34 ; so Mt. once,
xxvii. 63), but that does not include
a third night : the parallels in Mt.,
Lk. have τῇ τρίτῃ ἡμέρᾳ. In regarding Jonah as a type, Mt. did not
weigh details. Justin (Tryph. 107)
tacitly corrects him, μετὰ τὸ ἐκβρα-
θῆναι αὐτὸν τῇ τρίτῃ ἡμέρᾳ ἀπὸ
τῆς κοιλίας τοῦ ἀδροῦ ἰχθύος, and
the Naz. Gosp. seems to have omitted
τρεῖς . . . νύκτας (see Texte u. Unters.,
1911, 39, 290). The 'heart of the
earth' probably means not the tomb
but Hades (so Iren. Tert.) ; cf. Eph.
iv. 9, κοιλία ᾅδου Jon. ii. 3, Sir.
li. 5.

41. ἄνδρες κτλ.] This and the
following verse are transposed in
Lk., perhaps to conform to the O.T.
chronology ; but more probably the
transposition is due to Mt., and the
sayings were originally unconnected
with the 'sign of Jonah.' ἄνδρες
is without the article, being determined by the adj. : 'the men of

Nineveh'; cf. βασίλισσα νότου, v.
42 (Blass, § 46. 9). ἐν τῇ κρίσει :
not 'in the judgment' as ἐν ἡμ.
κρίσεως (x. 15, xi. 22, 24, xii. 36) ;
'to rise [stand] up in judgment with'
would, in Aram., mean simply 'accuse.'
The future has the same force as in
αὐτοὶ κριταὶ ἔσονται ὑμῶν (v. 27).
Their condemnation is not in words,
but in the fact introduced by ὅτι.
'Ex ipsorum comparatione isti merito
damnabuntur' (Aug.) ; cf. Rom. ii. 27.
ὅτι μετενόησαν κτλ.] Jonah
preached doom (Jon. iii. 4), Jesus the
good tidings of the nearness of the
Kingdom (iv. 17 note). As a Prophet,
Jesus was 'something more than Jonah.'
For εἰς = πρός or ἐν (ב) cf. Ac. vii.
53 ; Blass, § 39. 5.

42. βασίλισσα κτλ.] In the LXX.
νότος is usually the Negeb or Teman,
the region S. of Judah ; but here it
stands for Sheba (Σαβά 3 Regn. x. 1).
It either represents Yemen ('South'),
the first instance of the name for
S.W. Arabia (Wellh.), or is due to a
confusion of Teman with the Arab.
Têmā (Θαιμάν Is. xxi. 14) (Zahn).
Jos. (Ant. VIII. vi. 5) speaks of the
queen as reigning over Egypt and
Ethiopia, perhaps confusing שׁבא and
סבא (Gen. x. 7) ; and the Ethiopians
are still said to claim her. ἐγερθ.
and ἀναστήσονται (v. 41) are synonymous.   As a Prophet Jesus was more
than Jonah, as a Teacher than
Solomon. 'Salomo erat sapiens ; sed
hic est Sapientia' (Beng.).   The
wisdom of Jesus is described in xi.
27, and those who come to Him
(v. 28 f.) receive more than the queen

τῇ κρίσει μετὰ τῆς γενεᾶς ταύτης καὶ κατακρινεῖ αὐτήν·
ὅτι ἦλθεν ἐκ τῶν περάτων τῆς γῆς ἀκοῦσαι τὴν σοφίαν
Σολομῶνος, καὶ ἰδοὺ πλεῖον Σολομῶνος ὧδε.   Ὅταν 43
δὲ τὸ ἀκάθαρτον πνεῦμα ἐξέλθῃ ἀπὸ τοῦ ἀνθρώπου,
διέρχεται δι' ἀνύδρων τόπων ζητοῦν ἀνάπαυσιν, καὶ οὐχ
εὑρίσκει. τότε λέγει Εἰς τὸν οἶκόν μου ἐπιστρέψω ὅθεν 44
ἐξῆλθον· καὶ ἐλθὸν εὑρίσκει σχολάζοντα καὶ σεσαρωμένον
καὶ κεκοσμημένον. τότε πορεύεται καὶ παραλαμβάνει μεθ' 45

of the South. Like Chorazin, etc.
(xi. 21 ff.) this generation had rejected
greater privileges than were offered
to foreigners of old.

43–45. (Lk. xi. 24–26.) RETURN
OF THE UNCLEAN SPIRIT.

43. ὅταν κτλ.] In Lk. this follows
'He that is not with Me is against
Me' (Mt. v. 30): the mere absence
of the defilement is not enough ; such
a state of neutrality cannot last. In
Mt. there is no connexion with the
preceding verses, except 'this generation' in v. 45 ; he places the passage
here as a fresh denunciation against
them. On ἐξέλθῃ 'is cast out' see
viii. 12. For ἀπό = ἐκ (cf. xvii. 18) see
Blass, § 40. 2. On ἀκάθαρτον πνεῦμα
see x. 1. τοῦ ἀνθρώπου may refer
to a man mentioned in a previous
lost portion of the discourse, or the
art. is generic (cf. xiii. 3). It was a
popular belief that demons dwelt in
the deserts or in ruins (Is. xiii. 21,
xxxiv. 14, Bar. iv. 35, Tob. viii. 3,
Apoc. xviii. 2) ; see the Babyl. in-
cantations quoted by Allen (ad loc.).
But here the demon is unsatisfied
by any other resting - place than a
human being ; cf. Enoch xv., and
see Burkitt, Jewish and Chr. Apoc.
21 f. For ἀνάπαυσις cf. Gen. viii. 9,
Num. x. 33, Is. xi. 10.

44. εἰς τὸν οἶκον κτλ.] ἐξῆλθον
corresponds formally with ἐξέλθῃ in
v. 43, but the demon is ironically
represented as implying that he left
his victim voluntarily, as a man leaves

his house to go for a walk. With
the dramatic monologue cf. Lk.
xii. 19.

καὶ ἐλθόν κτλ.] This can be,
in Semitic idiom, the protasis of
a conditional sentence : 'and if he
come and find it, etc.,' the apodosis
being introduced by τότε (v. 45) ; so
Ṣ sin.cur. σχολάζοντα κτλ. describes
three stages in the restoration of the
house to the condition which it had
enjoyed before the demon's tenancy :
'free [from litter or lumber], swept
[from dirt and cobwebs], and put in
order.' σχολάζειν (trans.) occurs in
Aq. Mal. iii. 1 and Sym. Is. lvii. 14,
2 Chr. xxxi. 11, where the LXX. or
other translators have ἀποσκευάζειν,
ἑτοιμάζειν, or καθαρίζειν : here it has
the corresponding intrans. force. It
is used of an empty place in Plut.
G. Grac. vii., Timol. xxii. For
σαροῦν, a late form of σαίρειν, cf.
Lk. xv. 8, Herm. Sim. IX. x. 2 f.,
αἱ δὲ παρθένοι λαβοῦσαι σάρους
ἐσάρωσαν. κεκοσμημένον may mean
'adorned' (Lk. xxi. 5, Apoc. xxi. 19)
or 'set in order' ; cf. xxv. 7, Ez.
xxiii. 41, Sir. xxix. 26. Oecum.
explains a νεωκόρος as ἱερόδουλος ὁ
τὸν ναὸν κοσμῶν ἢ σαρῶν.

45. τότε πορεύεται κτλ.] Purity
and order being abhorrent to an unclean spirit, he proceeds to destroy
them. τότε, like Heb. ׀, introduces
the apodosis, of which v. 44 b was
the protasis. For the redundant
πορεύεται see ix. 13 a note. With

ἑαυτοῦ ἑπτὰ ἕτερα πνεύματα πονηρότερα ἑαυτοῦ, καὶ εἰσελ-
θόντα κατοικεῖ ἐκεῖ· καὶ γίνεται τὰ ἔσχατα τοῦ ἀνθρώπου
ἐκείνου χείρονα τῶν πρώτων. Οὕτως ἔσται καὶ τῇ γενεᾷ
ταύτῃ τῇ πονηρᾷ.

46   Ἔτι αὐτοῦ λαλοῦντος τοῖς ὄχλοις ἰδοὺ ἡ μήτηρ καὶ
οἱ ἀδελφοὶ αὐτοῦ ἱστήκεισαν ἔξω ζητοῦντες αὐτῷ λαλῆσαι.

47 om vers. ειπεν δε τις αυτω ιδου η μητηρ σου και οι αδελφοι σου εξω εστηκασιν
ζητουντες σοι λαλησαι ℵ*BLΓ 126 225 238 400* 𝕃 ff¹ k 𝕾 sin.cur

the 'seven other spirits' Allen compares the seven spirits of Babyl.
demonology ; Jer. refers to the seven-
fold power of the divine Spirit in
Is. xi. But seven and eight merely
stand for a large number ; cf. Eccl. xi.
2, Mic. v. 5. The demon hoped to
guard against the possibility of being
driven out again. κατοικεῖ ἐκεῖ: cf.
Apoc. ii. 13, *Test. Naph.* viii. 6, ὁ
διάβολος οἰκειοῦται αὐτὸν ὡς ἴδιον
σκεῦος.

καὶ γίνεται . . . πρώτων] Cf.
xxvii. 64, Job viii. 7, Sir. xli. 3,
and the warning in Jo. v. 14. In
2 Peter ii. 20 the words are perhaps
alluded to. For the consecutive καί
('so that') see Blass, § 77. 6 ; on
πρῶτος for πρότερος Blass, § 11. 5.

οὕτως ἔσται κτλ.] Absent from
Lk. the words are perhaps, but not
necessarily, a comment added by Mt.
'This generation' is not the Scribes
and Pharisees (as γενεά v. 39), for
they had undergone no change which
could be likened to the departure of
an evil spirit, but the Jews of the
Lord's time. His preaching, and
that of the Baptist, had produced a
momentary impression, but if they
did not follow up their repentance
by opening their souls to the divine
Spirit they would suffer a worse
relapse. It is a stern warning, but
need not imply that He already
despaired of them.

46–50. (Mk. iii. 31–35, Lk. viii. 19–
21.) THE MOTHER AND BRETHREN
OF JESUS.

The Marcan narrative, left at *v.*
32, is taken up. Lk. has a shorter
account from a different source, placed
to follow, instead of preceding, the
parable of the Sower ; 'who hear the
word of God and do it' (Lk. *v.* 21)
echoes the thought of the good soil
in the parable.

46. ἔτι αὐτοῦ κτλ.] The last note
of place was in *v.* 15, 'He departed
thence,' *i.e.* from the synagogue at
Capharnaum. In Mk., Lk. the
incident is not connected with the
foregoing, but Mk. seems to imply that
Jesus was still in the house (probably
in Capharnaum) mentioned in iii.
19 b. The relatives had come from
Nazareth for a purpose recorded only
in Mk. iii. 21 ; but finding Him
surrounded by a crowd, naturally
waited till they could secure privacy
with Him. For the various views
on the 'brethren of the Lord' see
Lightfoot, *Galat.* 252–91; J. B. Mayor,
St. James, v. ff. ; or *HDB.* i. 320–6,
and *Expos.* July and Aug. 1908.
Though Mt. does not say that Jesus
was in a house (see on xiii. 1),
he preserves Mk.'s ἔξω, which can
hardly mean 'on the outskirts of
the crowd.' ζητοῦντες αὐτῷ λαλῆσαι
abbreviates a verse and a half in Mk.

47. This verse is absent from the
true text, Mt. having already sum-

ὁ δὲ ἀποκριθεὶς εἶπεν τῷ λέγοντι αὐτῷ Τίς ἐστιν 48
ἡ μήτηρ μου, καὶ τίνες εἰσὶν οἱ ἀδελφοί μου; καὶ 49
ἐκτείνας τὴν χεῖρα αὐτοῦ ἐπὶ τοὺς μαθητὰς αὐτοῦ
εἶπεν Ἰδοὺ ἡ μήτηρ μου καὶ οἱ ἀδελφοί μου· ὅστις 50
γὰρ ἂν ποιήσῃ τὸ θέλημα τοῦ πατρός μου τοῦ ἐν οὐρανοῖς,
αὐτός μου ἀδελφὸς καὶ ἀδελφὴ καὶ μήτηρ ἐστίν.

marized Mk.'s equivalent. It was added probably to supply an antecedent to τῷ λέγοντι αὐτῷ (v. 48).

48. ὁ δὲ ἀποκριθεὶς κτλ.] It is not necessary to suppose that the Lord had heard, or knew by intuition, the purpose for which His mother and brethren had come. He uses the opportunity to teach the meaning of spiritual relationship to Himself. The Father was to Him, and must be to His followers, more than mother or brethren; cf. x. 37, xix. 29. Mt. avoids Mk.'s terseness by which ἐστιν serves for both 'mother' and 'brethren.' Lk., for brevity, omits the verse.

49. καὶ ἐκτείνας κτλ.] He points with a gesture to the twelve. In Mk. He does not confine His recognition to them, but spoke 'look-ing round on those who sat about Him.'

50. ὅστις γὰρ ἄν κτλ.] Mk. ὃς ἄν (Blass, § 50. 1, § 65. 7). τοῦ πατρός . . . οὐρανοῖς: Mk., Lk. τοῦ θεοῦ; see on v. 16, vi. 9. On τὸ θέλημα see vi. 10, and Swete on Mk. iii. 35. For the whole phrase cf. vii. 21. αὐτός μου ἀδελφός κτλ., without the article: the person, whoever it be, who does my Father's will, is brother, sister, mother as the case may be. The sisters in the family were not (according to v. 46) present; but the Lord claims 'young men as brothers, old women as mothers, young women as sisters' (1 Tim. v. 2). 'But Christ does not say that any disciple, however loyal, is His Father. In the spiritual sphere His Father is God' (Plummer).

Preliminary Note on Parables.

παραβολή is the LXX. rendering of מָשָׁל some forty-five times; παροιμία occurs in Prov.[4] Sir.[5] only. The word denotes utterances of very various kinds: gnomic and poetical utterances, such as Balaam's (Num. xxiii. f.); cf. Ps. xlviii. [xlix.] 5, lxxvii. [lxxviii.] 2; proverbs (1 Regn. xxiv. 14, 3 Regn. iv. 28 [v. 12], Ez. xii. 23, Eccl. i. 17, xii. 9); taunts (Ps. lxviii. [lxix.] 12, Mic. ii. 4, Jer. xxiv. 9); riddles (Deut. xxviii. 37, Sir. xxxix. 3, xlvii. 15). The oriental genius for picturesque speech found expression in a multitude of such utterances; and among them must be included tales or fables such as those of Jotham (Jud. ix. 8–15) and Nathan (2 Sam. xii. 1–4), which are, to a certain extent, allegories. The 'parable' was no less common in Jewish writings after the time of Jesus. 'Familiare est Syris et maxime Palestinis ad omnem sermonem suam parabolas jungere, ut quod per simplex praeceptum teneri ab auditoribus non potest, per similitudinem exemplaque teneatur' (Jer. on Mt. xviii. 23). Many examples may be seen in Fiebig, *Altjüdische Gleichnisse und die Gleichnisse Jesu*, and Ziegler, *Die Königsgleichnisse des Midrasch*.

In the N.T. the word παραβολή is confined to the synoptists, except

XIII. 1   Ἐν τῇ ἡμέρᾳ ἐκείνῃ ἐξελθὼν ὁ Ἰησοῦς τῆς οἰκίας

1 τῆς οικιας] B 1 124; *pr* εκ אZ 33; *pr απο* CE *etc* [de domo f h q vg]; *om*
D 𝔏 a b c ff¹·² g¹ k 𝔖 sin

Heb. ix. 9 (a 'figure' or 'type'), xi. 19 (ἐν παραβολῇ 'figuratively');
παροιμία occurs only in Jo. x. 6, xvi. 25, 29, 2 Pet. ii. 22.   They denote
three classes of utterances : (1) a proverb, or gnomic saying (*e.g.* Mk. iii.
23–27, Lk. iv. 23, v. 36–39, vi. 39, 2 Pet. *l.c.*); (2) a simple comparison
or analogy, *similitudo* (*e.g.* Mt. xxiv. 32 f. = Mk., Lk.); under this head may
be placed such sayings as those in Mt. v. 13–15 ; (3) pictures drawn from
nature or human life, which illustrate one or more truths.   When more than
one truth is illustrated the picture approaches an allegory, and it is not always
certain which details are intended to illustrate something, and which are
merely part of the scenic framework.   The tendency to allegorize every
detail, seen notably in Philo, but also in Christian writers, *e.g.* Origen and
Hilary, often led to strained, and even grotesque, methods of interpretation,
and was deprecated, *e.g.* by Tertullian (*De Pud.* ix.) and Chrysostom (on
Mt. xx. 1 ff. οὐδὲ χρὴ πάντα τὰ ἐν ταῖς παραβολαῖς κατὰ λέξιν
περιεργάζεσθαι, ἀλλὰ τὸν σκοπὸν μαθόντας δι' ὃν συνετέθη τοῦτον
δρέπεσθαι, καὶ μηδὲν πολυπραγμονεῖν περαιτέρω).   The best modern
exegesis avoids it.   But the opposite extreme must also be guarded against,
i.e. the refusal to admit that more than a single point can be illustrated
in a parable, as *e.g.* by Jülicher, *Die Gleichnisreden Jesu.*   The principal
object in the foreground of a picture is not the only object visible.
Jewish utterances must be judged by Jewish, and not by Greek, rules of
rhetoric (see Abrahams, *Notes on Syn. Gospp.* no. 14).   Parables differ widely
in their nature, and will not come under a single rule.   And although the
admission of this leads to differences of opinion in some cases, the gain exceeds
the loss ; flexibility of treatment is psychologically safer than rigidity in
dealing with language so ζῶν καὶ ἐνεργής as that of the Lord's parables.

---

xiii. 1–52. TEACHING IN PAR-
ABLES.

Mt. follows Mk. in arranging a
collection of parables ; but their
common matter consists only of the
'Sower' (*vv.* 1–9), the reason for parables (*vv.* 10–13), the explanation of
the 'Sower' (*vv.* 18–23), the 'Mustard-
seed' (*v.* 31 f.), and the remark in *v.*
34.   Lk. places the first three together (viii. 4–15); elsewhere (xiii.
18–21) he gives the 'Mustard-seed'
and the 'Leaven,' and (x. 23 f.) the
saying in Mt. *v.* 16 f.   Only Mt.
has the 'Tares,' and its explanation ;
only Mk. has the 'Seed growing of

itself' (iv. 26–29), and this is preceded by some sayings (*vv.* 21–25)
which are scattered elsewhere in Mt.
On the position which the discourse
occupies in the Galilean ministry see
viii. 18.   It is the third of Mt.'s five
principal collections of sayings (see
on vii. 28).

1–9. (Mk. iv. 1–9, Lk. viii. 4–8.)
THE SOWER.

1. ἐν τῇ ἡμέρᾳ κτλ.]   Mk. 'And
again He began to teach by the sea,'
suggesting no sequence with the preceding incident.   Lk. has the parable
in a different context, without mention
of the sea.   τῆς οἰκίας (or ἐκ [ἀπὸ]

ἐκάθητο παρὰ τὴν θάλασσαν· καὶ συνήχθησαν πρὸς αὐτὸν 2
ὄχλοι πολλοί, ὥστε αὐτὸν εἰς πλοῖον ἐμβάντα καθῆσθαι,
καὶ πᾶς ὁ ὄχλος ἐπὶ τὸν αἰγιαλὸν ἱστήκει. καὶ ἐλάλησεν 3
αὐτοῖς πολλὰ ἐν παραβολαῖς λέγων Ἰδοὺ ἐξῆλθεν ὁ σπείρων
τοῦ σπείρειν. καὶ ἐν τῷ σπείρειν αὐτὸν ἃ μὲν ἔπεσεν παρὰ 4
τὴν ὁδόν, καὶ ἐλθόντα τὰ πετεινὰ κατέφαγεν αὐτά. ἄλλα 5
δὲ ἔπεσεν ἐπὶ τὰ πετρώδη ὅπου οὐκ εἶχεν γῆν πολλήν, καὶ

τ. οἱ.) is possibly a gloss ; no house has previously been mentioned, though ἔξω (xii. 46) seems to imply one.

2. καὶ συνήχθησαν κτλ.] The boat would raise the speaker conveniently above the audience, but possibly was also chosen as a safeguard ; the Lord was still popular with many, but His teaching, as the parable implies, was not accepted by all, and since the religious authorities were now hostile, danger was looming. For αἰγιαλός (class.) cf. v. 48, Jo. xxi. 4, Ac.[3] See M.-M. *Vocab. s.v.*

3. καὶ ἐλάλησεν κτλ.] On the adverbial πολλά see ix. 14. Mk. adds καὶ ἔλεγεν αὐτοῖς ἐν τῇ διδαχῇ αὐτοῦ, implying that the discourse which he gives contains only specimens of parables. Lk., giving a single parable, writes εἶπεν διὰ παραβολῆς. ἰδού κτλ.] Mt., Lk. omit Mk.'s opening ἀκούετε (see Swete). ὁ σπείρων : a representative of his class ; see viii. 33 n. It is not explained in v. 18 ff. who he is, but the Lord was doubtless speaking from His own experience, which is that of all who deliver a divine message ; He was not always successful, success being conditioned, in preaching as in healing (Mk. vi. 5), by the receptiveness of those whom He tried to help. The parable is not, as in vv. 24, 31, 33, 44 f., 47, explicitly connected with the Kingdom of Heaven, though the seed is explained in v. 19 as 'the word of the Kingdom.' For an echo of it see Clem. *Cor.* xxiv. 5.

4. καὶ ἐν τῷ σπείρειν κτλ.] Mk.'s Hebraic καὶ ἐγένετο is omitted by Mt., Lk. ἃ μέν are the separate seeds, ὃ μέν (Mk., Lk.) 'one portion of the seed.' They fell, accidentally, upon the path which ran beside, or through (xii. 1), the field. καὶ ἐλθόντα κτλ. is probably a stylistic improvement of the true reading καὶ ἦλθεν . . . καὶ κατ., as in Mk. Lk. adds καὶ κατεπατήθη, which is probably a loosely attached description of the path ; it was trodden hard, so that the birds could take the seed ; it can hardly refer to the seed, which the birds would be less likely to take if it were trodden into the ground. For κατεσθίειν of birds cf. Gen. xl. 17, 3 Regn. xii. 24 m [A xiv. 11], xvi. 4. Cf. 'avidaeque volucres Semina iacta legunt' (Ovid, *Met.* v. 484).

5. ἄλλα δέ κτλ.] Mk. καὶ ἄλλο, Lk. κ. ἕτερον (see v. 4). τὰ πετρώδη (Mk. τὸ πετρῶδες), a class. word, not elsewhere in bibl. Gk. Lk.'s τὴν πέτραν (so 𝕊 in all three Gospels except 𝕊 sin in Mt.) represents the original Aram., rightly interpreted by Mt., Mk. ; it was not a single rock which stood out from the soil, but 'that part of the field which was rock.' For ὅπου κτλ. the simpler Aram. construction is seen in 𝕊 cur, 'and there was not much earth, and in the same hour it sprouted, because' etc. ; 𝕊 sin, 'and because it was a shallow place and not much earth, straightway it sprouted.' In Mk. καί is preserved in a conflate

6 εὐθέως ἐξανέτειλεν διὰ τὸ μὴ ἔχειν βάθος γῆς, ἡλίου δὲ
ἀνατείλαντος ἐκαυματίσθη καὶ διὰ τὸ μὴ ἔχειν ῥίζαν
7 ἐξηράνθη. ἄλλα δὲ ἔπεσεν ἐπὶ τὰς ἀκάνθας, καὶ ἀνέβησαν
8 αἱ ἄκανθαι καὶ ἀπέπνιξαν αὐτά. ἄλλα δὲ ἔπεσεν ἐπὶ τὴν
γῆν τὴν καλὴν καὶ ἐδίδου καρπόν, ὃ μὲν ἑκατὸν ὃ δὲ

7 απεπνιξαν uncc et minn exc. seq. ; επνιξαν אD 13 124 346

καὶ ὅπου (B a^vid), and καὶ ὅτι
(D ff²) followed by καὶ εὐθύς. In
Ps. cxi. [cxii.] 4 ἐξανατέλλειν is used
intransitively of light (זרח); elsewhere trans. (i.e. causatively) Gen. ii. 9,
Ps. ciii. [civ.] 14, cxxxi. [cxxxii.] 17.
Lk. abbreviates vv. 5 b, 6, καὶ φυὲν
ἐξηράνθη διὰ τὸ μὴ ἔχειν ἰκμάδα,
perhaps influenced by Jer. xvii. 8.
6. ἡλίου δέ κτλ.] If the original
verb was צמח (as ܨ sin.cur), the
meaning may be 'when the sun
shone' (see v. 45); a seed of corn
could not spring up in a night, like
a gourd (Jon. iv. 10). The sun
shines 'on the evil and on the good,'
but the effects in each case are
different ; cf. Jam. i. 11, Job viii.
11 ff. 'Segetes . . . modo sol nimius
. . . corripit' (Ovid, Met. v. 482).
For καυματίζειν, a late word (Plut.
Epict.), cf. Apoc. xvi. 8 f.
7. ἄλλα δέ κτλ.] Cf. Theophr.
De Causis Plant. II. xvii. 3 τὸ τῇ
ἀκάνθῃ ἐπισπειρόμενον σπέρμα. On
the abundance of plants in Palestine
which have thorns or prickles see
art. 'Thistles,' HDB. iv. When the
thorns 'mounted up' (ἀναβαίνειν,
cf. Is. v. 6, xxxii. 13, Hos. x. 8 ;
Lk. συμφυεῖσαι) they would keep
light and air from the corn, and
perhaps entwine its roots under-
ground. Cf. Xen. Oec. xvii. 14, τί
γάρ, ἔφη, ἢν ὕλη πνίγῃ συνεξορμῶσα
τῷ σίτῳ; The right reading here is
possibly ἔπνιξαν (cf. xviii. 28) ; Mk.
συνέπ., Lk. ἀπέπ.; in the explanation
(v. 22) συμπνίγειν is used in all
three Gospels. The addition in Mk.
καὶ καρπὸν οὐκ ἔδωκεν, anticipating

καὶ ἄκαρπος γίνεται in the explanation, was perhaps a gloss later than
Mt., Lk. The metaphor in Jer.
iv. 3 'sow not among thorns' is
different.
8. ἄλλα δέ κτλ.] καλήν (Mt.,
Mk.) describes the appearance, ἀγα-
θήν (Lk.) the quality, of the soil ;
but in the explanation Lk. has
καλήν. Τὸ ἐδίδου καρπόν Mk. adds
ἀναβαίνοντα καὶ αὐξανόμενα, καὶ
ἔφερεν, describing the process, from
the earliest stage, of the formation
of the fruit (Swete) ; Lk., ἐποίησεν,
states the finished result. For διδόναι
καρπόν, less common than ποιεῖν,
cf. Lev. xxvi. 20, Ps. i. 3.
ὃ μὲν . . ὃ δὲ . . ὃ δέ] So in v.
23. In Mk. the readings vary
between εις (ter), εν (ter), and εις . .
εν . . εν. The last (BL) is impossible,
and must have arisen from conflation ;
Moulton's suggestion (Expos. VI. vii.
112) 'at all rates up to thirty'
scarcely helps. εἰς and ἐν may be
either εἶς, ἔν, or εἰς, ἐν. Both the
former (אחד בעל) and the latter (ב)
accord with Aram. idiom. The latter
is found in papyri ; Mt. appears
to adopt the former. ἑκατόν (Lk.
ἑκατονταπλασίονα) is probably not
an exaggeration ; cf. Gen. xxvi. 12.
See G. A. Smith, HG. 83, 439 ff.,
612. Wetstein gives instances in
Greece, Italy, and Africa ; Theophr.
Hist. Plant. VIII. vii. 4, in Babylon.
In Mk. the figures rise to a natural
climax ; their reversal in Mt. is
perhaps to indicate more clearly that
even in the fruit-bearing hearers of
the word there are gradations ; the

ἑξήκοντα ὃ δὲ τριάκοντα. Ὁ ἔχων ὦτα ἀκουέτω. Καὶ 9
προσελθόντες οἱ μαθηταὶ εἶπαν αὐτῷ Διὰ τί ἐν παραβολαῖς 10
λαλεῖς αὐτοῖς; ὁ δὲ ἀποκριθεὶς εἶπεν ὅτι Ὑμῖν δέδοται 11

repetition of the numbers in the explanation (v. 23) implies the same. τὸ τέταρτον μέρος ἐσώθη καὶ οὐδὲ τοῦτο ἐξ ἴσης, ἀλλὰ καὶ ἐνταῦθα πολλὴ ἡ διαφορά (Orig.).

9. ὁ ἔχων κτλ.] This does not necessarily imply that the parable is unusually obscure or mysterious; sympathy with the Preacher was needed to grasp its teaching fully. On the expression see xi. 15.

10–15. (Mk. iv. 10–12, Lk. viii. 9 f.) THE REASON FOR PARABLES.

10. καὶ προσελθόντες κτλ.] Mk. describes them as οἱ περὶ αὐτὸν σὺν τοῖς δώδεκα. The Lord was no longer in the boat, but alone (Mk. κατὰ μόνας) with such followers as still clung to Him. Mk. says ἠρώτων αὐτὸν τὰς παραβολάς, apparently 'they asked Him [the meaning of] the parables' (cf. Mt. v. 18 ἀκούσατε τὴν παραβολήν), the plur. shewing that the question was asked at the end of a *series* of parables; but He then gives (1) the reason for parables (v. 11 f.), (2) a rebuke to the disciples for not knowing the meaning of '*this* parable' (v. 13), followed by the explanation of the parable. Since neither is an answer to the question, this cannot have been the original sequence of the sayings. Lk.'s question τίς αὕτη εἴη ἡ παραβολή; leads more directly to the explanation of the parable. But Mt. prepares explicitly for the reason for parables by transforming the question.

11. ὅτι ὑμῖν κτλ.] ὅτι introduces the *orat. rect.* (Blass, § 79. 12); it is not 'because,' in answer to the question διὰ τί; that is given in διὰ τοῦτο (v. 13). μυστήριον, not

found in the Gospels apart from this context, means, as in the LXX. and Apocalypses, a 'secret,' something disclosed to certain persons, which they can reveal to others. It is used in the Pauline Epp.[21] and Apoc.[4] On the development of its meaning in the N.T. see J. A. Robinson, *Ephesians*, 234 ff. Many facts and conceptions of the coming Kingdom were 'secrets,' hidden from all but the disciples. δέδοται γνῶναι τὰ μυστήρια (so Lk.) is a slight expansion of Mk.'s τὸ μυστήριον δέδοται, for the sake of clearness. No other explanation of the difference of wording is needed. Montefiore (*Syn. Gospp.* i. 123) rightly explains Mk.: 'you are permitted to understand its laws and constitutions, the conditions of entering and so on.' If μυστήριον means all this, the plur. in Mt., Lk. is not unnatural. Montef. and others think that the words cannot be genuine, because Jesus cannot have adopted this esoteric attitude. It is possible that Mk.'s semi-technical τοῖς ἔξω (cf. 1 Cor. v. 12, Ecclus. Prol. τοῖς ἐκτός, and the Rabb. הַחִיצוֹנִים), for which Mt. has ἐκείνοις (cf. αὐτοῖς, v. 10), Lk. τοῖς λοιποῖς (cf. 1 Thes. iv. 13, v. 6, Eph. ii. 3); is a later touch. But it is difficult to see why the thought that more could be revealed to the disciples than to others, which recurs in a saying from Q (v. 16 f., Lk. x. 23 f.), should be condemned as 'unworthy of Jesus.' At least He acted upon it during the last months of His earthly life by taking the Twelve into privacy and devoting His time to teaching them alone. And, as Burkitt (*Gosp. Hist.* 86 ff.) points out, the present

γνῶναι τὰ μυστήρια τῆς βασιλείας τῶν οὐρανῶν, ἐκείνοις
12 δὲ οὐ δέδοται. ὅστις γὰρ ἔχει, δοθήσεται αὐτῷ καὶ περισ-
σευθήσεται· ὅστις δὲ οὐκ ἔχει, καὶ ὃ ἔχει ἀρθήσεται ἀπ᾽
13 αὐτοῦ. διὰ τοῦτο ἐν παραβολαῖς αὐτοῖς λαλῶ, ὅτι βλέποντες
οὐ βλέπουσιν καὶ ἀκούοντες οὐκ ἀκούουσιν οὐδὲ συνίουσιν·
14 καὶ ἀναπληροῦται αὐτοῖς ἡ προφητεία Ἡσαίου ἡ λέγουσα

saying appropriately occurs directly after a definite breach had been made with the religious authorities (xii. 22–32). ὑμῖν, as contrasted with τοῖς ἔξω (ἐκείνοις, τ. λοιποῖς), meant primarily the Twelve, because Jesus was speaking to them by themselves. But it would not really be confined to them, but would include all His true followers, and all who were ready to learn from Him. In the last clause Mt. writes οὐ δέδοται for Mk.'s ἐν παραβολαῖς πάντα γίνεται, but makes the point clear, after the intervening v. 12, by the opening words of v. 13.

12. ὅστις γάρ κτλ.] The saying is drawn from common life : the capital of the rich man begets interest, but the poor man, who cannot invest, becomes still poorer. Mk. has it at a later point (iv. 25 = Lk. viii. 18), and it recurs in Mt. xxv. 29 = Lk. xix. 26 (Q). In Mk. both halves of the saying refer to disciples, who have been privileged to receive instruction ; here the two halves refer to disciples and non-disciples respectively. But this cannot be its true context, since parables spoken to those who have *not been given* a knowledge of the mysteries cannot be said to take away that which they have. And its insertion breaks the connexion between *vv.* 11 and 13. καὶ περισσευθήσεται, absent from Mk., Lk., is perhaps due to the preceding καὶ προστεθήσεται ὑμῖν in Mk. iv. 24, omitted by Mt. in his parallel verse (vii. 2). It occurs also in xxv. 29, perhaps

added by Mt. or a scribe to harmonize with the present passage. The passive is not found elsewhere in bibl. or class. Gk.; for the act. cf. 1 Thes. iii. 12. On the consec. καί, 'and so,' see Blass, § 77. 6. In Lk. viii. 18 (not xix. 26) the saying is softened by ὃ δοκεῖ ἔχειν ; but paradox was a feature of the Lord's utterances ; cf. x. 39, xix. 30, xx. 16.

13. διὰ τοῦτο κτλ.] διὰ τοῦτο refers not to what precedes but to the following ὅτι : 'on this account . . . namely because' (cf. xxiv. 44, Jo. v. 16, 1 Jo. iii. 1); it is the answer to διὰ τί (v. 10), corresponding exactly with the question. 'I speak in parables because all except My disciples have rendered themselves morally incapable of grasping the truth ; their own action has produced their punishment.' This avoids the ἵνα of Mk., Lk.; see Add. note. βλέποντες κτλ. is an adaptation of Is. vi. 9 f., which is quoted in full in v. 14 f. βλέπ. οὐ βλέπουσιν (Lk. ἵνα βλέπ. μὴ βλέπωσιν), departing from the Heb. idiom, which is preserved in v. 14 and in Mk., produces a striking paradox, ' though they see, they do not (really) see ' ; cf. Jo. ix. 41.

14. καὶ ἀναπληροῦται κτλ.] Mt., consistent in avoiding Mk.'s ἵνα, does not use his own formula for passages from his Messianic *testimonia,* ἵνα (ὅπως) πληρωθῇ τὸ ῥηθέν (see i. 22). ἀναπληροῦν occurs in the Pauline Epp.[5], but not with the late meaning of the fulfilment of prophecy, which seems to be confined

Ἀκοῇ ἀκούϲετε καὶ οὐ μὴ ϲυνῆτε,
καὶ βλέποντεϲ βλέψετε καὶ οὐ μὴ ἴδητε.
ἐπαχύνθη γὰρ ἡ καρδία τοῦ λαοῦ τούτου,　　　15
καὶ τοῖϲ ὠϲὶν βαρέωϲ ἤκουϲαν,
καὶ τοὺϲ ὀφθαλμοὺϲ αὐτῶν ἐκάμμυϲαν·
μή ποτε ἴδωϲιν τοῖϲ ὀφθαλμοῖϲ
καὶ τοῖϲ ὠϲὶν ἀκούϲωϲιν
καὶ τῇ καρδίᾳ ϲυνῶϲιν καὶ ἐπιϲτρέψωϲιν,
καὶ ἰάϲομαι αὐτούϲ.

to bibl. Gk.; in the LXX. mostly of the completion of a period of time; but cf. 1 Esd. i. 54, εἰς ἀναπλήρωσιν τοῦ ῥήματος τοῦ κυρίου. προφητεία of an O.T. passage occurs only in 2 Pet. i. 20 f.; in Apoc. it is used of predictions in the book itself, in the Pauline Epp. of the utterances of Christian 'prophets.'

ἀκοῇ κτλ.] Verbatim from the LXX. of Is. vi. 9 f.; cf. Jo. xii. 40, Ac. xxviii. 26 f. The sense of the Heb. verbs in v. 9 is imperative; the future lent itself to the thought that the words were to receive fulfilment at a later time. Since οὐ μὴ ἴδητε =וְאַל תֵּֽרְעוּ, ἴδητε is for εἴδητε (LXX. ℵ); see Thackeray, Gr. O.T. in Gk. i. 278; but ἴδωσιν (v. 15)=יִרְאֶה; hence ἰδεῖν and εἶδαν in v. 17.

15. ἐπαχύνθη κτλ.] The LXX., which describes the state of the people as the result of their own acts, not of the prophet's preaching, is more suitable for Mt.'s purpose than the Heb. imperatives. With καὶ τοῖς ὠσίν κτλ. cf. Zech. vii. 11. ~ καμμύειν (= καταμύειν) represents הָשַׁע ('smear over') here, and עצם ('shut') in Is. xxix. 10 (piel), xxxiii. 15 (ḳal). Cf. Philo, De Somn., Mangey i. p. 645. 31, καμμύσαντες τὸ τῆς ψυχῆς ὄμμα. It occurs in the 4th cent. B.C. (see Meineke, Com. Frag. iii. 525); elsewhere only in late Gk. καὶ ἰάσομαι αὐτούς is for the impers. וְרָפָא לֹו; cf. Mk. καὶ ἀφεθῇ αὐτοῖς, which may have been derived from an Aram. synagogue paraphrase.

Additional Note on the Reason for Parables.

In Mk. the reason is given in the form ἵνα βλέποντες βλέπωσι καὶ μὴ ἴδωσιν, καὶ ἀκούοντες ἀκούωσι καὶ μὴ συνίωσιν, μή ποτε ἐπιστρέψωσιν καὶ ἀφεθῇ αὐτοῖς. The ἵνα plays a large part in Wrede's drastic theory (*Das Messiasgeheimnis in d. Evang.*) regarding the Lord's concealment of His Messiahship during His lifetime. See J. Weiss, *Das älteste Evang.* 52–9, Schweitzer, *Quest*, 336–48. Three explanations are possible. (1) Jesus declared that He spoke in parables *in order* to prevent His teaching from being intelligible to any but those who sympathized with Him. In view of the growing opposition to His work, He felt that to utter plain truths would only further alienate men's minds; those who sympathized would learn more, by searching for the veiled meaning, and in proportion to their sympathy and insight (cf. Mk. iv. 33, καθὼς ἠδύναντο ἀκούειν). His main work now was not so much to win recruits as to train the few who had joined Him. (2) But it is unsafe to insist on this as the only possible

16 ὑμῶν δὲ μακάριοι οἱ ὀφθαλμοὶ ὅτι βλέπουσιν, καὶ τὰ ὦτα
17 ὑμῶν ὅτι ἀκούουσιν. ἀμὴν γὰρ λέγω ὑμῖν ὅτι πολλοὶ

explanation. Though parables of the kind collected in Mt. xiii. may belong
to the period of nascent opposition, many others had been employed at an
earlier stage (e.g. v. 13–15, vi. 22–24, vii. 13 f., 24–27, ix. 16 f.), and their
primary object had probably been to illuminate, not to obscure, the truth.
ἵνα may therefore be virtually equivalent to ὥστε : in accordance with a
well-known Hebraic idiom, the *result* is ironically described as a *purpose* (cf.
the use of לְמַעַן in Deut. xxix. 18 [19], Is. xxx. 1, xliv. 9, Jer. vii. 18 f., xxvii.
10, 15, xxxii. 29, Hos. viii. 4, Am. ii. 7, Mic. vi. 16) : 'you have been
granted the spiritual ability to grasp the secret of the Kingdom of God, but to
those outside all my teaching takes the form of parables, *with the only result
that*, though they actually see, they do not perceive, etc.' (3) Mk.'s verse is
possibly, like Mt. *v.* 14 f., an editorial comment : 'in order that Isaiah's
words might be fulfilled, βλέποντες βλέψετε κτλ.,' the grammar of the
sentence being dominated by ἵνα, as in Mt. xviii. 16. Cf. Rom. xv. 21,
1 Cor. i. 31, where S. Paul escapes the same construction only by a
harsh ellipse. This is perhaps supported by the fact that Mk. has μήποτε
ἐπιστρέψωσιν καὶ ἀφεθῇ αὐτοῖς (which Lk. omits, though following Mk.'s
construction), adapting more of the quotation than was strictly relevant.
In this case Mk., Lk. simply express (as Mt. does) the thought of the early
Church, that the obtuseness of many towards the Lord's teaching was a
'fulfilment' of prophecy.

16–23. (Lk. x. 23 f. ; Mk. iv.
13–20, Lk. viii. 11–15.) EXPLANA-
TION OF THE PARABLE OF THE
SOWER.

Mk. introduces this with a rebuke
to the disciples for not understanding
the parable. Mt., concerned with
the privilege of those to whom
'it has been given to know the
mysteries,' substitutes for the rebuke
a beatitude (*v.* 16 f.), drawn from
another context in Q : 'Your eyes
are privileged to see ; hear therefore
(οὖν *v.* 18) the explanation of the
parable.' See on viii. 26 for Mt.'s
tendency to soften or avoid words
derogatory to the disciples.

16. ὑμῶν δὲ κτλ.] ὑμῶν is in emphatic contrast with those described
in *v.* 14 f., the αὐτοῖς and ἐκείνοις of
vv. 10 f., 13. βλέπουσιν (absol.) has
the deeper meaning which it bears
in *v.* 13 (οὐ βλέπ.) ; Lk., more

simply, μακ. οἱ ὀφθ. οἱ βλέποντες ἃ
βλέπετε, and he places the beatitude
in a different context. καὶ τὰ ὦτα
κτλ. is absent from Lk., but he has
καὶ ἀκοῦσαι κτλ. in the next verse,
unless that is a scribal harmonization
with Mt. (Blass).

17. ἀμὴν γὰρ κτλ.] See on v.
18. Lk. omits ἀμήν. For δίκαιοι
Lk. has βασιλεῖς : the former may
be Mt.'s alteration, 'righteousness'
being a feature of his Gospel ; but it
is more suitable to the context, and
there may have been a confusion in
the Aram. between ישרין and שרין (βασιλεύς is a rendering of שׂר in 3
Regn. xxii. 26). With the thought
of the words cf. 1 Pet. i. 10–12, and
Ps. Sol. xvii. 50, xviii. 7, μακάριοι οἱ
γενόμενοι ἐν ταῖς ἡμέραις ἐκείναις,
ἰδεῖν τὰ ἀγαθὰ Ἰσραὴλ [Κυρίου].
ἰδεῖν and βλέπειν cannot be distinguished in meaning ; cf. ὁρᾶν and

προφῆται καὶ δίκαιοι ἐπεθύμησαν ἰδεῖν ἃ βλέπετε καὶ οὐκ
εἶδαν, καὶ ἀκοῦσαι ἃ ἀκούετε καὶ οὐκ ἤκουσαν. Ὑμεῖς 18
οὖν ἀκούσατε τὴν παραβολὴν τοῦ σπείραντος. Παντὸς 19
ἀκούοντος τὸν λόγον τῆς βασιλείας καὶ μὴ συνιέντος,
ἔρχεται ὁ πονηρὸς καὶ ἁρπάζει τὸ ἐσπαρμένον ἐν τῇ καρδίᾳ
αὐτοῦ· οὗτός ἐστιν ὁ παρὰ τὴν ὁδὸν σπαρείς. ὁ δὲ ἐπὶ τὰ 20
πετρώδη σπαρείς, οὗτός ἐστιν ὁ τὸν λόγον ἀκούων καὶ εὐθὺς
μετὰ χαρᾶς λαμβάνων αὐτόν· οὐκ ἔχει δὲ ῥίζαν ἐν ἑαυτῷ 21

βλέπειν (both = ראה) in Job x. 4.
On the form εἶδαν (ἴδαν) see Blass,
§ 21. 1. Iren. and Epiph. appear
to refer to the words in the form
πολλάκις ἐπεθύμησα[ν] ἀκοῦσαι ἕνα
τῶν λόγων τούτων, καὶ οὐκ ἔσχον
τὸν ἐροῦντα (Resch, Agrapha, 179).

18. ὑμεῖς οὖν κτλ.] The words
are from Mt.'s pen, carrying on the
emphatic ὑμῶν δέ of v. 16; see n.
before v. 16. τὴν παραβολήν is
elliptical ('the meaning of the parable'), as τὰς παραβολάς (Mk. iv.
10); similarly Lk., ἔστιν δὲ αὕτη ἡ
παραβολή. The aor. τ. σπείραντος
is 'the man who was described in the
parable as sowing'; cf. ὁ σπαρείς
(vv. 19 f., 22 f.).

19. παντός κτλ.] Since the rest
of his collection consists in parables
of the Kingdom, Mt. writes 'the
word of the Kingdom' for 'the
Sower soweth the word' (Mk.), 'the
seed is the word of God' (Lk.). On
the gen. absol. followed by αὐτοῦ see
Blass, § 74. 5. In ἀκούοντος . . . μὴ
συνιέντος Mt. is again influenced by
the quotation from Isaiah (v. 15);
and cf. v. 23. τ. βασιλείας is an
obj. gen. 'the message about the
Kingdom'; cf. iv. 23. On 'the
Kingdom' without definition see viii.
12. It is striking that in all the
synoptists the single evil spirit (ὁ
πονηρός, Mk. ὁ σατανᾶς, Lk. ὁ
διάβολος: see iv. 1, note) is given as
the interpretation of the plur. τὰ

πετεινά. Orig. wrongly, ὑπὸ τῶν
τῆς πονηρίας πνευμάτων.

οὗτος κτλ.] Mt. has the sing.
throughout; Mk., Lk. the plur. All
identify the seed sown with the
hearers who receive it; in no case
are they the soil into which it falls.
οὗτος here stands for a person, not
the seed (τὸ ἐσπαρμένον): since that
which grows from the seed is the
human character, the seed represents
the germ of it, and the soil the
previous state of the heart (ἐν τῇ
καρδίᾳ). The evil one does not
snatch away the teaching (which may
remain in the memory, and even
convince the intellect), but the living
results of it. Lk. adds ἵνα μὴ πισ-
τεύσαντες σωθῶσιν: the wording
recalls Pauline teaching, but the
thought is not foreign to the context;
πιστεύειν is equivalent to δέχεσθαι
in the next verse.

20. ὁ δέ κτλ.] ἀκούων corresponds with the falling of the
seed upon the soil; λαμβάνων (Lk.
δέχονται) is the appropriation of the
teaching, so that it becomes a living
element in the personality.

21. οὐκ ἔχει κτλ.] ῥίζα is frequently metaphorical in the LXX. (e.g.
4 Regn. xix. 30, Is. xl. 24, Wisd. iii.
15, iv. 3), but nowhere denotes moral
steadfastness; cf., however, ἐρριζω-
μένοι, Eph. iii. 17, Col. ii. 7. Lk.
omits the redundant ἐν ἑαυτῷ (Mk.
-οῖς). πρόσκαιρος, temporalis, 'tem-

ἀλλὰ πρόσκαιρός ἐστιν, γενομένης δὲ ᾿θλίψεως ἢ διωγμοῦ
22 διὰ τὸν λόγον εὐθὺς σκανδαλίζεται. ὁ δὲ εἰς τὰς ἀκάνθας
σπαρείς, οὗτός ἐστιν ὁ τὸν λόγον ἀκούων καὶ ἡ μέριμνα
τοῦ αἰῶνος καὶ ἡ ἀπάτη τοῦ πλούτου συνπνίγει τὸν λόγον,
23 καὶ ἄκαρπος γίνεται. ὁ δὲ ἐπὶ τὴν καλὴν γῆν σπαρείς,

22 αιωνος] א*BD 𝕃 a ff² g¹ h k᾿ arm ; *add* τουτου אᵇCE *etc* 𝕃 b c f ff¹ q vg
𝕊 *omn* me

porary,' 'short-lived,' is a word of
later Gk. ; cf. 2 Cor. iv. 18, Heb. xi.
25, Jos. *BJ.* vi. i. 4. Lk. explains
it, πρὸς καιρὸν πιστεύουσιν.

γενομένης δέ κτλ.] θλίψις, 'affliction' in general, includes διωγμός
'persecution,' a particular form of it.
On the words see Swete. They are
the καῦμα (*v.* 6) which withers the
plants. Strictly speaking, διὰ τὸν
λόγον confuses the metaphor, since
the λόγος is the seed. It may be an
addition, referring to later persecutions on account of the Christian
Gospel. But, if original, it shews
that adherence to the preaching of
Jesus and His disciples had already
begun to provoke hostility ; cf. ἕνεκεν
ἐμοῦ v. 11, ἕνεκεν [ἐμοῦ καὶ] τοῦ
εὐαγγελίου, Mk. viii. 35, x. 29 (see
on Mt. xvi. 25, xix. 29). Lk., by
employing the wider term πειρασμός,
and omitting διὰ τὸν λόγον, perhaps
thinks of daily spiritual temptations ;
cf. his addition of καθ᾿ ἡμέραν in ix.
23 (Mt. xvi. 24). On σκανδαλίζεται
see v. 29 ; Lk. ἀφίσταται (not in
Mt., Mk. ; but Lk.⁴, Ac.⁶).

22. καὶ ἡ μέριμνα κτλ.] After
πλούτου Mk. alone adds καὶ περὶ
τὰ λοιπὰ ἐπιθυμίαι (cf. Lk. xii. 26).
τὸν λόγον (so Mk.) again confuses
the metaphor ; it is not the 'word'
(*i.e.* the seed) which is choked, but
the developed character which should
result from it. Lk. offers a correction, οὗτοι . . . ὑπὸ μεριμνῶν συμ-
πνίγονται : so 𝕊 sin.cur here, 'they
choke him.' On μερ. τοῦ αἰῶνος,

'anxiety belonging to the transitory
life,' see Dalman, *Words*, 154 f. The
addition of τούτου (see Appar.)
introduces an irrelevant contrast
with 'the coming age' (see on xii.
32).

καὶ ἡ ἀπάτη κτλ.] Cf. ἀπ. ἀδικίας
(2 Thes. ii. 10), ἀπ. τῆς ἁμαρτίας
(Heb. iii. 13). 𝕃 f ff¹ g² vg have
fallacia, but the late meaning
'pleasure' is represented in *oblecta-
mentum* (k), *voluptas* (b c ff² g¹ h q) ;
cf. Polyb. ii. lvi. 12, and see Deissm.,
Hellenisierung, 165, n. 5, M.-M. *Vocab.*
s.v. ἀπάτη· ἡ πλάνη παρ᾿ ᾿Αττικοῖς
. . . ἡ τέρψις παρ᾿ ῞Ελλησιν
(Moeris). Hence Lk.'s ἡδονῶν τοῦ
βίου. For the thought cf. 1 Tim.
vi. 10. καὶ ἄκαρπος γίνεται, 'so
that it proves unfruitful' ; for the
καί see Blass, § 77. 6. ἄκαρπος
(class. active, 'making barren,' 'blast-
ing') is metaphorical in Wisd. xv. 4,
1 Cor. xiv. 14, Eph. v. 11, Tit. iii.
14, 2 Pet. i. 8.   *Vv.* 19–22 describe
temptations from within (19), from
the influence of others (20 f.), from
material conditions (22)—'the devil,
the world, and the flesh.'

23. ὁ δέ κτλ.] In ἀκούων καὶ
συνιείς Mt. is again influenced by
Is. vi. 9 f. (see *v.* 14 f.). Mk. ἀκ. καὶ
παραδέχονται, a voluntary appropriation, Lk. ἀκ. κατέχουσιν, a persistent
holding fast, emphasized by his
closing ἐν ὑπομονῇ. For a less
probable explanation of the latter
see *Expos.*, 1891, 379 f. ὃς δή, 'who
is just the man who,' a class. usage ;

οὗτός ἐστιν ὁ τὸν λόγον ἀκούων καὶ συνιείς, ὃς δὴ καρπο-
φορεῖ καὶ ποιεῖ ὃ μὲν ἑκατὸν ὃ δὲ ἐξήκοντα ὃ δὲ τριάκοντα.

Mk., Lk. have the more original καί, whence the *v.ll.* here, τότε D 𝕷 vet.*nonn.*𝕾 sin, *et* 𝕷 vet.*nonn.*vg. 𝕾 cur.pesh. δή, frequent in the LXX., is rare in the N.T.; see Blass,	§ 78. 5. For καρποφορεῖν (Xen., Theophr., Sym., Theod.) cf. Hab. iii. 17, Wisd. x. 7, Mk. iv. 28, and (metaph.) Rom. vii. 4 f., Col. i. 6, 10. On ὃ μέν κτλ. see *v.* 8.

Additional Note on xiii. 18–23.

The genuineness of the explanation of the parable has been questioned
on the grounds that (1) it is allegorical, whereas Jesus confined Himself to
parables and illustrations that bore their meaning plainly on the surface; (2)
this parable is so transparently plain that no explanation was necessary; (3)
the explanation reflects the thought of a later period.   But (1) an allegory
is the expansion of a metaphor; if Jesus employs metaphors, which no one
doubts, it is arbitrary to deny that He could expand them.   His utterances
were often, no doubt, freely spontaneous, but it cannot be assumed that He
never prepared any of them beforehand by prayerful thought.   To Him, as
to any other preacher, this is not derogatory but the reverse.   That few of
His allegories have been preserved may indicate that His use of them
was infrequent, but not that it was unknown.   An artificial explanation at
a later time would be unlikely to leave important details unexplained,
notably the 'Sower' Himself (contrast *v.* 37), the 'wayside,' the 'depth of
earth,' the 'thirty, sixty, and hundred.'   Jesus, with a simplicity markedly
different from patristic subtlety, had a meaning for some details, and the
rest were scenery.   The explanation of the Tares (*vv.* 36–43), the genuineness of which is much more doubtful, offers in style and atmosphere a strong
contrast.   The fact that Jesus gave an explanation of the 'Sower' would
lead to less successful imitations.

(2) If the parable transparently teaches a single truth, modern writers
ought to be agreed upon what it is.   But they are not.   According to some
it is that the Lord's teaching was far from meeting with uniform success.
According to others, the parable contains 'the mystery of the Kingdom
of God' (Mk. iv. 11), *i.e.* it teaches that the Kingdom, owing to the
preaching of the Baptist and Jesus, had already begun its secret growth
in the world.   God was ripening it, so that without human intervention it
would reach its consummation as surely as seed sown in a field—although
some of it may be wasted—will develop into fruit.   The former is the more
natural explanation; but if Jülicher and Schweitzer cannot agree, how can
it be said that the meaning is transparently clear?

(3) That the reports of the synoptists are coloured by their own conditions
and characteristics is not more or less true than in most of the utterances
which they ascribe to Jesus.   Lk. may shew Pauline influence, Mt., Mk.
perhaps hint at the persecutions of Christians in their own day, the whole
passage may breathe the atmosphere of the early Church, and be affected
in its literary form by early Christian preaching, to a greater extent than we

24 Ἄλλην παραβολὴν παρέθηκεν αὐτοῖς λέγων Ὡμοιώθη
ἡ βασιλεία τῶν οὐρανῶν ἀνθρώπῳ σπείραντι καλὸν σπέρμα
25 ἐν τῷ ἀγρῷ αὐτοῦ. ἐν δὲ τῷ καθεύδειν τοὺς ἀνθρώπους
ἦλθεν αὐτοῦ ὁ ἐχθρὸς καὶ ἐπέσπειρεν ζιζάνια ἀνὰ μέσον
26 τοῦ σίτου καὶ ἀπῆλθεν. ὅτε δὲ ἐβλάστησεν ὁ χόρτος καὶ

know. But proof is still wanting that Jesus gave to the disciples no explanation of the parable.

24-30. THE TARES. (Mt. only.) This takes the place of Mk. iv. 26-29 (the Seed growing of itself), Mt. having given the five sayings of Mk. vv. 21-25 elsewhere (i.e. v. 15, x. 26, xi. 15 and xiii. 9, vii. 2, xiii. 12). Mt. probably found his parable in a non-Marcan source, and preferred it, but its similarity to Mk.'s was close enough to lead him to place it at this point; he then adopted the Mustard-seed from Mk. But finding also, in his other source, the Leaven (absent from Mk.), the meaning of which appeared closely allied to that of the Mustard-seed, he inserted it before adopting (v. 34) Mk.'s conclusion (Mk. v. 33 f.). Instead of Mk.'s final words, 'and privately to His disciples He used to explain everything,' Mt. gave the explanation of the Tares, which is thus postponed to some distance from the parable. Then, after three additional parables, he appends his own conclusion at the end of the whole collection. Allen suggests that he found all six parables in his source, arranged in two groups of three, separated by the explanation of the Tares. On the genuineness of the 'Tares' and its explanation see note after v. 43.

24. ἄλλην παραβολήν κτλ.] Cf. vv. 31, 33. παρατιθέναι is 'to lay out, set in order, a repast' (Mk. vi. 41, viii. 6 f., Lk. x. 8, xi. 6, Ac. xvi. 34); the parable is placed before the hearers to appropriate if they choose.

Cf. Ac. xvii. 3, Ex. xix. 7, xxi. 1 (Rashi, 'as a man sets out a table for food'). In the middle it usually means 'to entrust' (Lk. xii. 48, xxiii. 46).

ὡμοιώθη κτλ.] The Kingdom is not, strictly speaking, like the man; but his experiences illustrate an aspect of it. It is important to notice this mode of expression in several parables; cf. vv. 31, 33, 44, 45, 47, xviii. 23, xx. 1, xxii. 2, xxiv. 37, xxv. 1; and see xi. 16. For the aor. ὡμοιώθη cf. xviii. 23, xxii. 2; in the LXX. (e.g. Ps. xlviii. [xlix.] 13, 21) it represents the perf. of דמה. ὁμοία is more frequent in Mt.; see xi. 16. σπέρμα elsewhere in the N.T., except vv. 32 (Mk. iv. 31), 37 f., means 'offspring.' The man's field represents that part of the world in which the message of the Kingdom was preached; see vv. 31, 38.

25. ἐν δὲ τῷ καθεύδειν κτλ.] τ. ἀνθρώπους are not the servants but 'men' in general; see on viii. 27. ζιζάνια, one of four species of tares in Palestine, are perhaps the lolium temulentum, which grows as tall as wheat, and is not usually pulled up till close to the harvest. The word seems to have been taken over from the late Heb. זונין (Kil. i. Ber. Rabb. xxviii. 8). See art. 'Tares' in HDB. iv. For ἀνὰ μέσον (late Gk., LXX.) cf. Mk. vii. 31, 1 Cor. vi. 5, Apoc. vii. 17. See Blass, § 39. 2.

26. ὅτε δέ κτλ.] ὅτε... καὶ... τότε makes the production of the fruit

καρπὸν ἐποίησεν, τότε ἐφάνη καὶ τὰ ζιζάνια. προσελ- 27
θόντες δὲ οἱ δοῦλοι τοῦ οἰκοδεσπότου εἶπον αὐτῷ Κύριε,
οὐχὶ καλὸν σπέρμα ἔσπειρας ἐν τῷ σῷ ἀγρῷ ; πόθεν οὖν
ἔχει ζιζάνια ; ὁ δὲ ἔφη αὐτοῖς Ἐχθρὸς ἄνθρωπος τοῦτο 28
ἐποίησεν. οἱ δὲ αὐτῷ λέγουσιν Θέλεις οὖν ἀπελθόντες
συλλέξωμεν αὐτά ; ὁ δέ φησιν Οὔ, μή ποτε συλλέγοντες 29
τὰ ζιζάνια ἐκριζώσητε ἅμα αὐτοῖς τὸν σῖτον· ἄφετε 30

to precede the appearance of the
tares, which were really coincident
with the green blade (χόρτος, cf.
Mk. iv. 28). The Aram. probably
had, more loosely, *and ... and ... and.*
For βλαστάνειν (LXX. trans. and
intrans.) cf. Mk. iv. 27, Heb. ix. 4.

27. προσελθόντες κτλ.] The
slaves do not appear in the explanation (*vv.* 37 ff.); they are not the
reapers, and their two questions
merely lead up to the Master's words.
τοῦ οἰκοδεσπότου appears rather
abruptly ; he is the same person as
ἀνθρώπῳ (*v.* 24), since the field is
his. οἰκοδεσπότῃ possibly stood
after ἀνθρώπῳ (cf. *v.* 52, xx. 1, xxi.
33), and fell out in a primitive MS.
It is inserted by Epiph. (see Tisch.[8]
ad loc.). The question πόθεν κτλ.
perhaps reflects the idea, found in
the Talmud and still said to be held
by peasants in Palestine, that tares
are wheat that has degenerated
(Buxt. *Lex. s.v.* זונין, Tristram, *Nat.
Hist.* 487); the slaves could not
understand how this had occurred,
since they knew that the seed sown
had been good.

28. ὁ δὲ ἔφη κτλ.] ἐχθρὸς ἄνθρωπος, 'a hostile man,' is probably
a transposition of ἄνθρωπος ἐχθρός
(so 𝔖), 'one that is an enemy';
cf. *vv.* 45, 52, and xi. 19 note. The
Tübingen 'tendency' theory still
finds supporters who see here an
anti-Pauline polemic ! For the redundant ἀπελθόντες cf. *v.* 46, xviii.
30, xxv. 18, 25, xxvii. 5 ; see on

ix. 13 a (πορευθέντες); cf. ὑπάγει
(*v.* 44). For θέλεις with deliberative
subjunctive cf. xx. 32, xxvi. 17, xxvii.
17, 21 (Blass, § 64. 6).

29. ὁ δέ φησιν κτλ.] Some
who think that the parable deals
with the Christian Church, and
therefore deny its genuineness, take
this prohibition to be the central
point in the story : the wicked in
the Church (or heretics, Jer., *al.*)
must not be excommunicated or
destroyed, because men may err in
their judgments ; the separation must
be left to God. But this important
principle of Church politics did not,
at least, suggest itself to the writer
who was responsible for *vv.* 36–43.
See Add. note there. For ἐκριζοῦν
(a late word, LXX., Aq. Sym. Theod.)
cf. xv. 13, Lk. xvii. 6, Jude 12.
The class. ἅμα with dat. occurs here
only (cf., however, xx. 1); with
the reading ἅμα καὶ τὸν σῖτον σὺν
αὐτοῖς (D k) cf. 1 Thes. iv. 17, v. 10.

30. ἄφετε κτλ.] 'Datur locus
poenitentiae' (Jer.). συναυξάνεσθαι
(class.) : not elsewhere in bibl. Gk.
δέσμην : cf. Ex. xii. 22 (= אֲגֻדָּה, a
'tied bunch' of hyssop) ; it represents
the same word with other meanings
in Aq. Sym. Theod. The reading
δ. αὐτὰ δέσμας, 'bind them (so that
they are) bundles,' is possibly right ;
for the double acc. see Blass, § 34. 3.
Epiph. has the distributive δήσατε
δέσμας δέσμας. The Baptist's words
(see on iii. 12) are echoed in πρὸς τὸ
κατακαῦσαι . . . μου.

συναυξάνεσθαι ἀμφότερα ἕως τοῦ θερισμοῦ· καὶ ἐν καιρῷ τοῦ
θερισμοῦ ἐρῶ τοῖς θερισταῖς Συλλέξατε πρῶτον τὰ ζιζάνια καὶ δήσατε αὐτὰ εἰς δέσμας πρὸς τὸ κατακαῦσαι αὐτά,
31 τὸν δὲ σῖτον συνάγετε εἰς τὴν ἀποθήκην μου.   Ἄλλην
παραβολὴν παρέθηκεν αὐτοῖς λέγων Ὁμοία ἐστὶν ἡ
βασιλεία τῶν οὐρανῶν κόκκῳ σινάπεως, ὃν λαβὼν ἄνθρωπος
32 ἔσπειρεν ἐν τῷ ἀγρῷ αὐτοῦ· ὃ μικρότερον μέν ἐστιν πάντων
τῶν σπερμάτων, ὅταν δὲ αὐξηθῇ μεῖζον τῶν λαχάνων ἐστὶν

30 αυτα εις δεσμας] om εις LXΔ 1 al 𝕃 a b c g¹·² ff² q vg 𝔖 sin.cur.pesh ; om αυτα
εις D 𝕃 e f h k Iren^lat Or

31, 32, (Mk. iv. 30–32, Lk. xiii.
18, 19.) THE MUSTARD-SEED.

If the juxtaposition of the
Mustard - seed and the Leaven in
Mt., Lk. is due to Q, the former
parable stood in Q as well as in
Mk. This is supported by the
points in which Mt. and Lk. agree
against Mk. : λαβὼν ἄνθρωπος (Mk.
om.). ἀγρῷ (Mt.) = κῆπον (Lk.), Mk.
τῆς γῆς. δένδρον (Mk. om.). ἐν
τοῖς κλάδοις (Mk. ὑπὸ τὴν σκιάν).

31. ἄλλην κτλ.] See on v. 24.
Mk., Lk. have a double question
introducing the comparison ; see on
xi. 16. Mt. might equally well have
written, as in v. 24 (see note), ὁμοία
ἐστὶν ἀνθρώπῳ κτλ. : the Kingdom
is not, strictly speaking, like a
mustard-seed, but an aspect of it is
illustrated by the growth of the
seed. Rabb. writers use the mustard-
seed as an instance of a very small
quantity (Lightf. Hor. Heb. ad loc.).
For κόκκος, 'a single grain,' distinct
from the collective σπέρμα, cf. xvii.
20, Jo. xii. 24, 1 Cor. xv. 37. A
'grain of mustard-seed' (A.V., R.V.) is
tautologous, and derived from Tyndale
and Cranmer. σίναπι = Attic νᾶπυ,
νῆπυ. 'Athenienses napy appella-
verunt' (Pliny). Lk.'s κῆπος (Jo.
xviii. 1, 26, xix. 41 only) may be
due to the reflexion that the immense
growth was more likely to occur in

a cultivated orchard. The field, or
orchard, or ground (Mk.), is that
part of the world in which the
message of the Kingdom was preached
(cf. vv. 24, 38). λαβών is a Hebraic
redundance ; cf. v. 33, xvii. 27,
xxi. 35, 39, xxvii. 24, 2 Regn.
x. 4.

32. ὃ μικρότερον κτλ.] Mk.'s
broken construction is avoided. The
smallness of the seed with reference
to the size of the plant is proverbial
in the Talmud (Wetstein ad loc.) ;
and cf. xvii. 20. It is not actually
the smallest known. δένδρον probably had a wider use than the
Engl. 'tree' (see art. 'Mustard,' HDB.
iii.) ; cf. δενδρολάχανον (Theophr.
Hist. Plant. I. iii. 4) of a tall herb.
ὥστε ἐλθεῖν κτλ. recalls Dan. iv. 18
[21] Theod., καὶ ἐν τοῖς κλάδοις αὐτοῦ
κατεσκήνουν τὰ ὄρνεα (LXX. πετεινὰ)
τοῦ οὐρανοῦ ; cf. id. 9 [12], Ps. ciii.
[civ.] 12, Ez. xvii. 23. On the form
κατασκηνοῖν see Blass, § 22. 3. On
the subst. -νωσις see viii. 20.

The central thought of the parable
seems to be that the consummation
of the divine Kingdom will be out
of all proportion to the germinal
development now at work (through
the preaching of the Baptist and of
Jesus and His disciples). Details
which go beyond this were probably
intended to be only scenery.

καὶ γίνεται δένδρον, ὥστε ἐλθεῖν τὰ πετεινὰ τοῦ οὐρανοῦ
καὶ κατασκηνοῖν ἐν τοῖς κλάδοις αὐτοῦ· Ἄλλην παρα- 33
βολὴν ἐλάλησεν αὐτοῖς· Ὁμοία ἐστὶν ἡ βασιλεία τῶν
οὐρανῶν ζύμῃ, ἣν λαβοῦσα γυνὴ ἐνέκρυψεν εἰς ἀλεύρου
σάτα τρία ἕως οὗ ἐζυμώθη ὅλον. Ταῦτα πάντα 34
ἐλάλησεν ὁ Ἰησοῦς ἐν παραβολαῖς τοῖς ὄχλοις, καὶ χωρὶς
παραβολῆς οὐδὲν ἐλάλει αὐτοῖς· ὅπως πληρωθῇ τὸ ῥηθὲν 35
διὰ τοῦ προφήτου λέγοντος

35 του προφητου] pr Ησαιου ℵ* 1 13 33 124 153 codd. ap. Eus. et Hier.

33. (Lk. xiii. 20 f.) THE LEAVEN.
ἄλλην κτλ.] Lk.'s formula is similar to that in the 'Mustard-seed,' but his parable is almost verbally identical with Mt.'s. On ὁμοία ἐστὶν ζύμῃ the same is to be said as on ὁμ. ἐ. κόκκῳ (v. 31), and the two parables do not differ in meaning. Cf. the man and the woman in Lk. xv. 4, 8. Leaven in the O.T. occurs only in ritual prohibitions, hence its evil connotation in the N.T. apart from this parable (cf. xvi. 6, 11 f. [Mk., Lk.], 1 Cor. v. 6–8, Gal. v. 9). It cannot here be a picture of the spreading capacity of evil, as though it were a worse picture than that of the tares, for the leaven—contrary to the Lord's teaching about evil in the world — is completely victorious (ἐζυμώθη ὅλον).

ἣν λαβοῦσα κτλ.] ἄλευρον (class. usually plur.) is 'wheaten meal'; in LXX. = קֶמַח. σάτον (cf. Hag. ii. 17 [16]) is the Aram. סָאתָא, Heb. סְאָה. According to Jos. (Ant. IX. iv. 5) and Jer. (in Mat.) it = 1½ Roman modius, i.e. about 1½ peck. Three sata (= one ephah) were used by Sarah (Gen. xviii. 6), Gideon (Jud. vi. 19), and Hannah (1 Sam. i. 24); it was a usual quantity, and can hardly have been intended to bear an allegorical meaning, as e.g. Greeks, Jews, and Samaritans (Th. Mops.),

heart, soul, and spirit (Aug.). In 𝔖 cur σάτα τρία is omitted, and the woman is 'a wise woman.'

34, 35. (Mk. iv. 33, 34.) EDITORIAL CONCLUSION. See note before v. 24.

34. ταῦτα πάντα κτλ.] The aor. ἐλάλησεν is repeated from v. 3, and refers to vv. 4–33 as a single discourse ; the impf. ἐλάλει in the next clause describes the Lord's usual practice. Mk. has the impf. in both cases. By τοιαύταις παραβολαῖς πολλαῖς Mk. implies that he has given only specimens from a large number, and he adds καθὼς ἠδύναντο ἀκούειν—the Lord used to employ parables to suit His hearers' want of spiritual comprehension (see note after v. 15).

καὶ χωρίς κτλ.] This was not the case throughout the whole of the ministry, but must refer to that period of it to which the foregoing parables belong ; in Mk. the meaning must be the same.

35. ὅπως κτλ.] On the formula see i. 22. The reading Ἡσαΐου τοῦ προφ. (see Appar.) is noteworthy. The quotation, which is intended to shew (as in v. 14) that the use of parables was a fulfilment of prophecy, is from Ps. lxxvii. [lxxviii.] 2, the title of which is 'A Maschil for Asaph' (συνέσεως τῷ 'Α.). Jerome (Brev. in Ps. lxxvii.) is represented as saying that 'in Asaph propheta

ʼΑνοίξω ἐν παραβολαῖς τὸ στόμα μου,
ἐρεύξομαι κεκρυμμένα ἀπὸ καταβολῆς.

36 Τότε ἀφεὶς τοὺς ὄχλους ἦλθεν εἰς τὴν οἰκίαν. Καὶ
προσῆλθαν αὐτῷ οἱ μαθηταὶ αὐτοῦ λέγοντες Διασάφησον
37 ἡμῖν τὴν παραβολὴν τῶν ζιζανίων τοῦ ἀγροῦ. ὁ δὲ ἀποκριθεὶς εἶπεν Ὁ σπείρων τὸ καλὸν σπέρμα ἐστὶν ὁ υἱὸς
38 τοῦ ἀνθρώπου· ὁ δὲ ἀγρός ἐστιν ὁ κόσμος· τὸ δὲ καλὸν

35 καταβολης] אᵇB 1 22 𝔏 e k 𝔖 sin.cur; add κοσμου א*ᵉᵗ ᶜ CDE al 𝔏
vet.*pler*.vg 𝔖 pesh.hcl me

invenitur in omnibus veteribus
codicibus.' He thought that an
ignorant scribe, knowing nothing of a
prophet Asaph (cf. 2 Chr. xxix. 30,
LXX.), inserted 'Isaiah' as a better
known name ; and 'arbitror postea a
prudentibus viris esse sublatum' (*in
Mat.*). Porphyry is said to have
jibed at Mt.'s ignorance in writing
Isaiah for Asaph. Not a trace,
however, of MS. evidence for ʼΑσάφ
remains, and Jerome omits it in the
Vulg. Hort (*App.* p. 13 *q.v.*) thinks
that ʼΗσαίου is genuine.

ἀνοίξω κτλ.] The translator of the
testimonia used by Mt. may have been
influenced by the LXX. (ἐν παραβολαῖς), or had a plur. in his text (M.T.
has the sing. יָשָׁל); in the second
clause his text did not differ from the
M.T. ἐρεύξομαι (אַבִּיעָה) 'to pour, or
belch, forth'; cf. Ps. xviii. [xix.] 3 ;
elsewhere in the LXX. mostly of the
roaring of lions. καταβολή in the
sense of 'foundation,' 'beginning,'
occurs in Pind. and late Gk. The
addition of κόσμου in most uncials
is due to the frequency of κατ. κοσμ.
in the N.T. (see on xxv. 34).

**36–43. EXPLANATION OF THE
PARABLE OF THE TARES.**

36. τότε κτλ.] According to
Mt.'s arrangement *vv.* 3–9 were
spoken in the boat, *vv.* 10–23 imply
an interval of privacy with the
disciples, *vv.* 24–33 were spoken in
public, place and occasion not being

recorded, and the present passage,
again, was in privacy in 'the house'
(see *v.* 1). The explanation of the
'Tares' takes the place of Mk.'s words
'and privately to His disciples He
used to explain everything'; see note
before *v.* 24. Mt. seems to imply
that the remaining parables (*vv.* 44–
50) were spoken in privacy.

On ἀφιέναι (cf. Mk. iv. 36, viii. 13)
as distinct from ἀπολύειν (xiv. 15,
22 f., xv. 32, 39) see Field, *Notes*, 9.
διασαφεῖν occurs in xviii. 31, Deut.
i. 5, Dan. ii. 6 (LXX.), 1, 2, 3 Mac.,
and in a Brit. Mus. papyrus (42. 8)
of the 2nd cent. B.C. With the *v.l.*
φράσον in most uncials cf. xv. 15.

37. ὁ σπείρων κτλ.] ὁ σπείρων
is used as a subst., 'the sower of the
good seed,' without reference to
time; cf. ὁ καταλύων (xxvii. 40).
ὁ υἱὸς τ. ἀνθρώπου has no Messianic
reference (contrast *v.* 41). If the
words were spoken by Jesus, they
would point to a time after S.
Peter's confession (xvi. 16) ; but the
genuineness of the explanation of
the parable is doubtful; see note
after *v.* 43.

38. ὁ δὲ ἀγρός κτλ.] By the
'field' the Lord had probably meant
not the world but Palestine (see *vv.*
24, 31) ; 'the world' here points to
a time when missionary activities had
spread much further ; cf. xxvi. 13.
There is no suggestion that the field is
the Church. By the same transfer-

σπέρμα, οὗτοί εἰσιν οἱ υἱοὶ τῆς βασιλείας· τὰ δὲ ζιζάνιά
εἰσιν οἱ υἱοὶ τοῦ πονηροῦ, ὁ δὲ ἐχθρὸς ὁ σπείρας αὐτά 39
ἐστιν ὁ διάβολος· ὁ δὲ θερισμὸς συντέλεια αἰῶνός ἐστιν,
οἱ δὲ θερισταὶ ἄγγελοί εἰσιν. ὥσπερ οὖν συλλέγεται τὰ 40
ζιζάνια καὶ πυρὶ κατακαίεται, οὕτως ἔσται ἐν τῇ συντελείᾳ τοῦ αἰῶνος· ἀποστελεῖ ὁ υἱὸς τοῦ ἀνθρώπου τοὺς 41
ἀγγέλους αὐτοῦ, καὶ συλλέξουσιν ἐκ τῆς βασιλείας αὐτοῦ

ence of thought as in vv. 19 ff., the 'seed' is interpreted as men. On οἱ υἱοὶ τῆς βασιλείας, 'those who are fitted, and therefore destined, for the Kingdom,' see viii. 12. οἱ υἱοὶ τοῦ πονηροῦ, 'those whose character is evil'; the adj. (see on vi. 13) may be either masc. or neut.; the Lat. versions vary. With the former cf. Ac. xiii. 10, 1 Jo. iii. 10; with the latter Eph. ii. 2, Col. iii. 6, Ps. lxxxviii. [lxxxix.] 23. The latter is preferable in view of the personal ὁ διάβολος which follows, and because an abstract τὸ πονηρόν forms a better counterpart to βασιλεία. The expression corresponds with 'those who do iniquity' (v. 41).

39. ὁ δὲ ἐχθρός κτλ.] The action of the devil (on διάβολος see iv. 1), which instils what is evil, is analogous to the preaching of the Son of Man, which instils what is good. And the evil, like the good, becomes an element in men's person-ality, so that the plants which spring up are persons.

ὁ δὲ θερισμός κτλ.] On θερισμός see ix. 37, where, however, it has a different force. Harvest, as an eschatological metaphor, is derived from the O.T. (e.g. Joel iii. 13, Jer. li. 33, Hos. vi. 11). (ἡ) συντέλεια (τοῦ) αἰῶνος, 'the completion of the transitory course of the world,' is confined, in the N.T., to Mt. (vv. 40, 49, xxiv. 3, xxviii. 20); cf. Heb. ix. 26. It is thoroughly Jewish, occurring in different forms in the

Apocalypses (frequent in Apoc. Baruch) and Targums; see Volz, Jüd. Esch. 166. It corresponds with the O.T. בְּאַחֲרִית הַיָּמִים ('at the end of the days'). For the angels as reapers cf. xxiv. 31, Apoc. xiv. 15–19. θεριστής (class.) Bel 33 only.

40. ὥσπερ κτλ.] The formula οὕτως ἔσται κτλ. is repeated in v. 49, and was probably common in Chris-tian preaching. For οὕτως intro-ducing the explanation of a parable cf. xviii. 14, 35, Lk. xii. 21, xiv. 33, xv. 10, xvii. 10.

41. ἀποστελεῖ κτλ.] Cf. xxiv. 31, where 'His angels' (referring to the Son of Man—elsewhere only xvi. 27) are sent to gather the elect. Similarly 'His Kingdom,' xvi. 28; cf. 'My Kingdom,' Lk. xxii. 30. It is the Kingdom of the Son of Man because He inaugurates it by His advent and judgment; it is also 'the Kingdom of their Father' (v. 43). In the Apocalypses, especially parts of Enoch, angels have functions at the day of Judgment; see Volz, Jüd. Esch. 261. The σκάνδαλα will be found in the Kingdom, because it will have come into the world where the tares have been sown. With 'them that do iniquity' they are a duplicate interpretation of the tares, and are perhaps due to Zeph. i. 3 (Heb.), 'I will bring to an end . . . the stumbling-blocks with the wicked' (perhaps אאסף = συλ-λέξω was read). σκάνδαλον, in the synn. xvi. 23, xviii. 7 = Lk. xvii. 1

42 πάντα τὰ ϲκάνδαλα καὶ τοὺϲ ποιοῦνταϲ τὴν ἀνομίαν, καὶ
βαλοῦσιν αὐτοὺς εἰς τὴν κάμινον τοῦ πυρός· ἐκεῖ ἔσται
43 ὁ κλαυθμὸς καὶ ὁ βρυγμὸς τῶν ὀδόντων. Τότε οἱ δίκαιοι

only, is a late form of σκανδάληθρον
(cf. Ar. *Ach.* 687), the 'bait-stick' of
a trap ; cf. σκανδαλίζεσθαι = הֻקַל,
Sir. ix. 5, xxxv. [xxxii.] 15. On
the vb. see v. 29. τοὺς ποιοῦντας
τὴν ἀνομίαν : see vii. 23.

42. καὶ βαλοῦσιν κτλ.] An
allusion to Gehenna (see v. 22, xviii.
9); cf. 4 Esd. vii. 36 'furnace of
Gehenna'; and see Apoc. ix. 2. In
Apoc. xix. 20, xx. 10 the symbolism
is that of a 'lake of fire.' On 'fire'
see iii. 10. On the formula ἐκεῖ ἔσται
κτλ. see viii. 12.

43. τότε οἱ δίκαιοι κτλ.] Perhaps
an allusion to Dan. xii. 3. The
thought corresponds with 'gather

the wheat into my barn' (*v.* 30),
but the symbolism is changed. The
transportation of the righteous out
of this world is not taught in the
Gospels (see on xxiv. 31); when the
wicked are removed the righteous
will shine, like the sun when the
clouds have passed, in the Kingdom
which has been consummated on the
earth, or on a new earth. ἕως ἂν
καταντήσωμεν οἱ πάντες εἰς ἄνδρα
τέλειον, καὶ γένωνται πάντες εἰς
ἥλιος (Orig.). Cf. Apoc. i. 16. For
δίκαιοι, of those who will partake
in the future bliss, cf. *v.* 49, xxv. 37,
46, Lk. xiv. 14. On the formula
ὁ ἔχων κτλ. see xi. 15.

Additional Note on the Parable of the Tares.

Many writers deny the genuineness, not only of the explanation, but
of the parable itself. It is thought to be a later form of the 'Seed growing
of itself' (Mk. iv. 26–29), mainly because it is held that by the 'Kingdom
of Heaven' Mt. here means the Christian Church, containing both bad and
good men. But there is nothing in the parable which necessarily suggests
this ; and in the explanation the field is not the Church but the world.
αὐτοῦ after ἀγρῷ (*v.* 24) is a scenic detail, as in *v.* 31, and need not be
pressed—it is not pressed in the explanation—to mean that the 'field' has
become the possession of the Son of Man. The parables are similar enough
to lead Mt. to place his at this point, to the exclusion of Mk.'s. Both
picture a man who sows seed, which matures, and is reaped at the harvest.
And both contain the thought of the non-interference of men—Mk. in
general, Mt. in a particular respect which appealed to him. Denney (*Expos.*
Aug. 1911) rejects the 'Tares' on the latter ground. But they are not so
similar as to render it improbable that Jesus spoke both at different times.
Mk. describes the secret development due to God alone, which results in
the consummation of the Kingdom ; Mt. the state of human society which
will continue till that consummation, when the good and the bad will be
separated. Only the divine Judgment at the Last Day can decide who are
good and who are bad.

The explanation stands on a different footing. Its genuineness must
not be denied merely on the ground that it allegorizes (see note at the
beginning of the chapter). But the style of *vv.* 37–43 is certainly stilted
compared with that of the explanation of the 'Sower' (*vv.* 18–23); the

ἐκλάμψογcιν ὡς ὁ ἥλιος ἐν τῇ βασιλείᾳ τοῦ πατρὸς
αὐτῶν. Ὁ ἔχων ὦτα ἀκουέτω. Ὁμοία ἐστὶν ἡ 44
βασιλεία τῶν οὐρανῶν θησαυρῷ κεκρυμμένῳ ἐν τῷ ἀγρῷ,
ὃν εὑρὼν ἄνθρωπος ἔκρυψεν, καὶ ἀπὸ τῆς χαρᾶς αὐτοῦ ὑπάγει καὶ πωλεῖ ὅσα ἔχει καὶ ἀγοράζει τὸν
ἀγρὸν ἐκεῖνον. Πάλιν ὁμοία ἐστὶν ἡ βασιλεία τῶν 45
οὐρανῶν ἐμπόρῳ ζητοῦντι καλοὺς μαργαρίτας· εὑρὼν δὲ 46
ἕνα πολύτιμον μαργαρίτην ἀπελθὼν πέπρακεν πάντα ὅσα

interpretation of the successive details is mechanical ; the apocalyptic expectations are of a popular and conventional character, and are expressed, to a large
extent, in stereotyped formulas ; and the use of the title 'the Son of Man'
for Jesus, first in His human life (v. 37), and then in His Messianic glory (v.
41), must be due to Christian tradition. If Jesus Himself gave an explanation of the parable, it is probable that very little of it has been preserved.

44. THE TREASURE. See on v. 36.

ὁμοία κτλ.] The parable, as a
whole, illustrates an aspect of the
Kingdom (see on v. 24), i.e. its
enormous worth, for which any
sacrifice should be made. If the
man bought the field for its market
price, he virtually stole the treasure ;
but the morality of the transaction,
as in the case of the steward (Lk.
xvi. 1–9), and the judge (Lk. xviii.
1–8), is not the point at issue, but
his eagerness to obtain the treasure.
Money was hidden in the earth (cf.
xxv. 25) when there was special need
for its safeguarding, e.g. in time of
war, Jos. BJ. VII. v. 2 ; see Wetstein,
ad loc. For the use of ἀπό cf. xiv.
26, Lk. xxiv. 41, Ac. xii. 14 (Blass,
§ 40. 3). The article in ἐν τῷ
ἀγρῷ must be generic (Blass, § 46. 7) ;
but D Chrys. omit it, perhaps rightly
because the mention of a definite
field is required by the following
τὸν ἀγρὸν ἐκεῖνον. αὐτοῦ is probably
subj. gen., 'his joy' (R.V.), not obj.,
'for joy thereof' (A.V.), although
the latter is a possible construction. With the redundant ὑπάγει
cf. πορευθέντες (ix. 13 a note). The

hist. presents after the aor. ἔκρυψεν
add verve to the narrative.

45, 46. THE PEARL.

45. ὁμοία κτλ.] The Kingdom
is not like the merchant, but his
eagerness illustrates an aspect of it
(see on v. 24)—its enormous worth.
This and the last parable illustrate
the variety of religious experience :
the treasure was discovered accidentally, the pearl after strenuous search.
The comparison of spiritual gain
with pearls (cf. vii. 6) recalls Job
xxviii. 15–19, Prov. iii. 15, viii. 11 ;
it also underlies Apoc. xxi. 19–21 ; cf.
the Syr. Hymn of the soul, translated in ZNW., 1903, 283. ἀνθρώπῳ
ἐμπόρῳ, 'a certain merchant,' is perhaps the true reading ; cf. v. 28.

46. εὑρὼν δὲ κτλ.] For ἕνα =
τινα see viii. 19 ; D 𝔏 𝖘 cur Cypr.
omit it. For πολύτιμος, a rare and
late word (not in LXX.), cf. xxvi. 7
(v.l.), Jo. xii. 3, 1 Pet. i. 7. On
ἀπελθών cf. v. 28. On the aoristic
perf. πέπρακεν see Moulton, i. 142,
145, who quotes ἀπεγραψάμην καὶ
πέπρακα from a papyrus. πάντα
ὅσα, 'all his possessions,' not πάντας
ὅσους, 'all the pearls that he had' ;

47 εἶχεν καὶ ἠγόρασεν αὐτόν. Πάλιν ὁμοία ἐστὶν ἡ
βασιλεία τῶν οὐρανῶν σαγήνῃ βληθείσῃ εἰς τὴν θάλασσαν
48 καὶ ἐκ παντὸς γένους συναγαγούσῃ· ἣν ὅτε ἐπληρώθη
ἀναβιβάσαντες ἐπὶ τὸν αἰγιαλὸν καὶ καθίσαντες συνέλεξαν
49 τὰ καλὰ εἰς ἄγγη, τὰ δὲ σαπρὰ ἔξω ἔβαλον. οὕτως
ἔσται ἐν τῇ συντελείᾳ τοῦ αἰῶνος· ἐξελεύσονται οἱ ἄγγελοι
καὶ ἀφοριοῦσιν τοὺς πονηροὺς ἐκ μέσου τῶν δικαίων
50 καὶ βαλοῦσιν αὐτοὺς εἰς τὴν κάμινον τοῦ πυρός· ἐκεῖ
51 ἔσται ὁ κλαυθμὸς καὶ ὁ βρυγμὸς τῶν ὀδόντων.   Συν-
52 ήκατε ταῦτα πάντα; λέγουσιν αὐτῷ Ναί. ὁ δὲ εἶπεν

'all that he had' (E.VV.) is ambiguous.

47–50. THE NET.

47. ὁμοία κτλ.] The Kingdom
is not, strictly speaking, like a net,
but the parable illustrates an aspect
of it (see on v. 24), i.e. that when it
comes, not all who have heard the
message of it will be found worthy.
The meaning is similar to that of
the 'Tares' and the 'Wedding
garment' (xxii. 11–13). The catch-
ing of fish recalls iv. 19 (ἁλεεῖς
ἀνθρώπων); but it does not follow
that the net represents the Christian
Church and ἐκ παντὸς γένους men
of different nationalities, and that
the parable is therefore not genuine.

σαγήνη, sagena (Vulg.), is a seine,
a large drag-net, 'a great net'
(𐤔 sin.cur); not a retiaculum (k).
Hesych.: πλέγμα τι ἐκ καλάμων.

48. ἣν ὅτε κτλ.] ἀναβιβάζειν
(class.): here only in the N.T.;
frequent in the LXX. αἰγιαλός: cf.
v. 2. ἄγγη: here only; cf. xxv. 4,
ἀγγεῖα, which some MSS. have here.
See M.-M. Vocab. s.v. The σαπρά
were not 'rotten,' for they were caught
alive, but 'worthless' for eating, 'inferior' (𐤔 sin); cf. vii. 18, xii. 33.

49, 50. οὕτως κτλ.] Except v. 49 b
this explanation is a verbatim repetition of vv. 40 b–42 (see notes), which
has been added somewhat mechanically

by the evangelist. 'The angels shall
come forth' (cf. ἀποστελεῖ v. 41) is
suitable to the reapers who were sent
forth into the field, but not to the
fishermen who were sitting on the
beach; and those who caught and
separated the fish were the same
persons, a detail which does not
admit of allegorizing. 'The furnace
of fire' is suitable to the tares but
not to the fish. With ἀφοριοῦσιν
cf. xxv. 32.

The six parables in the chapter
appear to belong to the period after
the Lord's first preaching of the near
approach of the Kingdom, and the
beginning of the hostility of the
religious authorities (viii. 1–8, xii.),
and before the final rupture with
them (xv. 1–20). He seems to be
describing His own experiences. He
and the disciples had preached with
varying success (Sower and Drag-net);
the failures had been due to the
opposing influence of the devil (Tares);
but nevertheless the preaching had
brought to earth the beginnings of
a development which would end in
the splendid consummation (Mustard-
seed and Leaven), to share in which
is a prize worth any sacrifice (Treasure
and Pearl).

51, 52. CONCLUSION. THE GOOD
HOUSEHOLDER.

51. συνήκατε κτλ.] Origen re-

αὐτοῖς Διὰ τοῦτο πᾶς γραμματεὺς μαθητευθεὶς τῇ βασιλείᾳ
τῶν οὐρανῶν ὅμοιός ἐστιν ἀνθρώπῳ οἰκοδεσπότῃ ὅστις
ἐκβάλλει ἐκ τοῦ θησαυροῦ αὐτοῦ καινὰ καὶ παλαιά.

52 τῃ βασιλεια] אBCKΠ 1 13 33 124 346 𝕃 e k me arm aeth ; *pr* εν DM 42 𝕃
vet.*pler*.vg ; εις την βασιλειαν EFGL *etc* minn.*pler*

marks οὐκ ἀγνοῶν ἐρωτᾷ, but the
conditions of the Lord's humanity
did not exclude a real need to ask
for information. Mt. often, but not
always, avoids recording such questions ; see on viii. 29 (*fin.*).

52. διὰ τοῦτο κτλ.] In its present
position this refers to the fact that
the disciples have understood the
parables ; but see below. μαθητεύειν
can be intrans., 'to be, or become,
a disciple' ; cf. xxvii. 57 *v.l.*, Clem.
Protr. xi. 113, μαθητεύσωμεν τῷ
κυρίῳ. The transitive, used here in
the pass., can mean either (*a*) 'to make
some one a disciple' (cf. xxviii. 19,
Ac. xiv. 21) or (*b*) 'to instruct [a
disciple'] (cf. Ign. *Rom.* iii. 1, ἃ
μαθεύοντες [when you give instruc-
tion] ἐντέλλεσθε), Iren. iv. 38. 2,
τὴν . . . παρουσίαν τοῦ κυρίου ἐμα-
θητεύθητε. With (*a*) 'the Kingdom
of Heaven' may be personified,
'made a disciple of the Kingdom
of Heaven,' the expression being
similar to ἐμαθητεύθη τῷ Ἰησοῦ
(xxvii. 57) ; or μαθ. is absolute, as
in xxviii. 19, and the dative means
'with respect to [*i.e.* having accepted
my teaching about] the Kingdom of
Heaven.' But (*b*) is simpler : instructed either 'with a view to (in
order to be ripe for),' or better 'in
[the truths of] the Kingdom of
Heaven.' The last is the meaning
of both the *v.ll.* (see Appar.), and
cf. Orig. (*ad loc.*) μεμαθητευμένος τῇ
κατὰ τὸ γράμμα τοῦ νόμου διδασ-
καλίᾳ, Eus. (on Ps. xli. 7) ὁ τούτοις
μαθητευθείς.

On ἀνθρώπῳ οἰκ. see xi. 19. On
ὅστις for ὅς see ii. 6. ἐκβάλλει :

cf. viii. 12 (note), and xii. 35 which
also illustrates the meaning of θησαυρός. As the well-supplied householder can make good provision for
household or guests, so the heart of
the scribe can produce either new or
old truths according to the needs of
his hearers.

καινὰ καὶ παλαιά] In the present
position of the saying, παλαιά are
the facts of nature and human life
employed as parables, καινά the
new spiritual meanings which the
Christian scribe can draw from them.
But this is a strange use of παλαιά.
The verse has probably been drawn
from a different context, for (1) διὰ
τοῦτο forms no real link, since the
saying is a general statement which
would remain true even if the disciples had answered 'No' instead of
'Yes.' (2) The use of 'scribe' for
a disciple of Christ and a teacher
of Christians ('scribae et notarii
Salvatoris,' Jer.) is usually supported
by reference to xxiii. 34 ; but see
note there. There is nothing to
prepare the reader for so unusual a
meaning of a well-known word. (3)
If by 'things new and old' the
Lord meant that the Christian scribe
develops in knowledge and can continually produce new truths in
addition to his stock of old ones,
the emphasis on καὶ παλαιά is lost ;
we should expect the order 'old and
new.' The saying may have been
spoken when Jesus was maintaining
(as in v. 17) the true relation of His
teaching to the Jewish law : the
former does not annul the latter.
Therefore any scribe, learned in the

53 Καὶ ἐγένετο ὅτε ἐτέλεσεν ὁ Ἰησοῦς τὰς παραβολὰς
54 ταύτας, μετῆρεν ἐκεῖθεν. καὶ ἐλθὼν εἰς τὴν πατρίδα αὐτοῦ
ἐδίδασκεν αὐτοὺς ἐν τῇ συναγωγῇ αὐτῶν, ὥστε ἐκπλήσ-
σεσθαι αὐτοὺς καὶ λέγειν Πόθεν τούτῳ ἡ σοφία αὕτη καὶ
55 αἱ δυνάμεις ; οὐχ οὗτός ἐστιν ὁ τοῦ τέκτονος υἱός ; οὐχ ἡ

law, who accepts instruction as a disciple in the truths taught by Jesus, is enriched; he can teach 'new truths *as well as* old.' γραμματεύς thus has its ordinary meaning, and διὰ τοῦτο has full force. The words, in this case, though Mt. adapted them to the Christian disciple, balance the stern denunciations against the Scribes, of which Mt. preserves so many. The Lord could sometimes speak hopefully of them (cf. Mk. xii. 34), and perhaps did so more often than our scanty records represent.

53–58. (Mk. vi. 1–6, Lk. iv. 16–30.) THE LORD AT NAZARETH.

Mt. returns to his Marcan source, having left it (*v.* 34) at Mk. iv. 34. The intervening material (Mk. iv. 35–v. 43) he has already used (see on viii. 18 and ix. 18). From this point he follows Mk.'s order to the end.

53. καὶ ἐγένετο κτλ.] On the formula see vii. 28. Mk. has simply καὶ ἐξῆλθεν ἐκεῖθεν. For μεταίρειν intrans. cf. xix. 1 (Mk. ἔρχεται); in class. Gk. and LXX.[4] it is trans., but the acc. could be omitted, as in Aq. Gen. xii. 8 (*sc.* σκηνήν) = וַיַּעְתֵּק ; cf. ἀναλύειν, Lk. xii. 36. ἐκεῖθεν here refers to Capharnaum, or to the 'house' (*v.* 36), in Mk. to the house of Jairus.

54. καὶ ἐλθών κτλ.] His πατρίς was Nazareth; cf. Lk. iv. 23. Lk. places the visit at an earlier point, to form a suitable opening to the Ministry, but perhaps based on an account of a visit to Nazareth in Q;

see iv. 13 note. A suggestion regarding Lk.'s account is made in *JThS.*, July 1910, 552–7. For πατρίς of a town Swete cites Philo, *Leg. ad Cai.* 36. Mk. adds 'and His disciples follow Him,' which Mt. takes for granted; they are with Jesus at xiv. 15. ἐδίδασκεν is for Mk.'s ἤρξατο διδάσκειν, an Aramaism (Dalman, *Words*, 26 f.) which Mt. often avoids; see xiii. 1, xiv. 35, xix. 27, xx. 17, 24, 30, xxi. 12, 33, xxiv. 4, xxvi. 67, 71, xxvii. 29. On αὐτῶν, absent from Mk., see vii. 29.

ὥστε κτλ.] Mk. says οἱ πολλοί, 'the majority.' By ἡ σοφία αὕτη Mt. makes the hearers refer to the discourse which they had just heard, while αἱ δυνάμεις must mean 'the miracles reported of Him.' And Mk. somewhat similarly. But this is a little awkward. Some confusion possibly underlies the accounts. Lk. produces a smoother narrative, which, however, presents other difficulties of its own.

55. οὐχ οὗτος κτλ.] This may mean 'he whom we used to know as the carpenter's son'; Joseph need not have been still alive. Jo. vi. 42 is also ambiguous. He was probably dead; he plays no part in the Gospel narratives after Lk. ii. 41–51, and *Prot. Jac.* ix. represents him as an old man before the Lord's birth. Mk. has οὐχ οὗτ. ἐ. ὁ τέκτων, Lk. οὐχὶ υἱός ἐστιν Ἰωσήφ οὗτος; This being the only N.T. evidence, it is uncertain whether Joseph was a carpenter or not. Allen suggests

μήτηρ αὐτοῦ λέγεται Μαριὰμ καὶ οἱ ἀδελφοὶ αὐτοῦ Ἰάκωβος
καὶ Ἰωσὴφ καὶ Σίμων καὶ Ἰούδας ; καὶ αἱ ἀδελφαὶ αὐτοῦ 56
οὐχὶ πᾶσαι πρὸς ἡμᾶς εἰσίν ; πόθεν οὖν τούτῳ ταῦτα
πάντα ; καὶ ἐσκανδαλίζοντο ἐν αὐτῷ. ὁ δὲ Ἰησοῦς εἶπεν 57
αὐτοῖς Οὐκ ἔστιν προφήτης ἄτιμος εἰ μὴ ἐν τῇ πατρίδι
καὶ ἐν τῇ οἰκίᾳ αὐτοῦ. Καὶ οὐκ ἐποίησεν ἐκεῖ δυνάμεις 58
πολλὰς διὰ τὴν ἀπιστίαν αὐτῶν.

Ἐν ἐκείνῳ τῷ καιρῷ ἤκουσεν Ἡρῴδης ὁ τετραάρχης 1 XIV.

that Mt. altered Mk. from motives
of reverence; but Mt. does not shrink
from recording far more insulting
taunts (cf. xi. 19, xii. 24). Mk.'s text
may have been revised at a later
date to avoid a misunderstanding of
υἱός (Stanton). Or possibly 'the carpenter's son' may represent בַּר נַגָּרָא,
which can mean simply 'the carpenter';
cf. *Ab. Zara*, 50 b, *B. Bathra*, 73 b,
Jer. *Kidd.* iv. 66 a. On patristic
and apocryphal passages see Swete.

οὐχ ἡ μήτηρ κτλ.] That they
could name them shewed how in-
timately they knew them.   Allen
thinks that Mt. shrank from the close
juxtaposition of 'the son of the
carpenter' (the legal sonship) and
'the son of Mary' (the physical sonship). But this is perhaps over-
subtle. On the 'brothers' see xii.
46; and on their names see Swete.

56. καὶ αἱ ἀδελφαί κτλ.] πᾶσαι
is absent from Mk.; Mt. may have
known a tradition that there were
more than two. Epiph. (*Haer.* lxxviii.
9) speaks of two, as known in Scripture, Salome and Mary. For apocr.
traditions see Thilo, *Cod. Apochr.*
363 n. They are not mentioned elsewhere in the N.T.; see on xii. 50.
On πρός = παρά see Blass, § 43. 7,
and on the acc. Moulton, i. 106.

57. καὶ ἐσκανδαλίζοντο κτλ.] On
the verb see v. 29. Lk. records only
the subsequent stage, 'they were all

filled with wrath.' οὐκ ἔστιν κτλ.: Jo.
applies the saying on another occasion
(iv. 44). Cf. 'vile habetur quod domi
est' (Seneca), and other parallels in
Wetstein.   The *Logia Jesu* (Oxyr. i.
3) has οὐκ ἔστιν δεκτὸς προφητὴς ἐν
τῇ πατρίδι αὐτοῦ, οὐδὲ ἰατρὸς ποιεῖ
θεραπείας εἰς τοὺς γινώσκοντας
αὐτόν. Mt. omits Mk.'s καὶ ἐν τοῖς
συγγενεῦσιν αὐτοῦ, a reference to
the incident in Mk. iii. 21 which
Mt. avoids recording.   The Lord
accepts His popular reputation as a
Prophet (cf. xvi. 14, xxi. 11, 46,
Mk. vi. 15).

58. καὶ οὐκ ἐποίησεν κτλ.] Mk.
'And He was not able there to do
any mighty work, except that He
laid His hands upon a few sick people
and healed them.'   Mt. is much
briefer, and he tones down 'was not
able'; οὐκ ἐποίησεν might mean either
inability or refusal. See Orig. quoted
by Swete. Mt. preserves the Lord's
wonder at the centurion's faith (viii.
10), yet he here avoids Mk.'s addition
'and He marvelled because of their
unbelief'; see on xii. 11.

xiv. 1, 2. (Mk. vi. 14–16, Lk. ix.
7–9.) HEROD'S IDEA OF JESUS.

1. ἐν ἐκείνῳ κτλ.] The incident
is loosely connected with the Galilean
ministry. Mk., Lk., though with
no note of time, connect it with
the mission of the Twelve, by which
the fame of Jesus was widely spread.

2 τὴν ἀκοὴν Ἰησοῦ, καὶ εἶπεν τοῖς παισὶν αὐτοῦ Οὗτός ἐστιν
Ἰωάνης ὁ βαπτιστής· αὐτὸς ἠγέρθη ἀπὸ τῶν νεκρῶν, καὶ
3 διὰ τοῦτο αἱ δυνάμεις ἐνεργοῦσιν ἐν αὐτῷ. Ὁ γὰρ Ἡρῴδης κρατήσας τὸν Ἰωάνην ἔδησεν καὶ ἐν φυλακῇ ἀπέθετο
διὰ Ἡρῳδιάδα τὴν γυναῖκα Φιλίππου τοῦ ἀδελφοῦ αὐτοῦ,

3 Φιλίππου] om D 𝔏 a c e ff[1] g[1] k vg Aug

Herod had only recently heard of
Him, perhaps because he had been
too fully occupied by his war with
Aretas (see on v. 4). For τετραάρχης
(Mt., Lk.) Mk. has the less accurate
βασιλεύς (see on ii. 22), which Mt.
himself uses in v. 9. Antipas may
have been styled 'king' by courtesy
(Swete), or the title had not dropped
out of the popular speech between
the death of Herod the Great and the
conferring of it again on Agrippa I.
(Zahn). On ἀκοή see iv. 24.

2. καὶ εἶπεν κτλ.] Mt. ascribes
to Herod words which in Mk. form
part of the popular guesses (ἔλεγον;
the v.l. ἔλεγεν was due to Mt.'s εἶπεν).
Mk. adds other guesses (ἄλλοι δὲ
ἔλεγον), Elijah, or a prophet like one
of the prophets (cf. Mk. viii. 28 =
Mt. xvi. 14); but when Herod heard
it he said, 'John whom I beheaded,
he is risen.' Lk. is different: Herod
was perplexed at the popular guesses,
one of which was that John had
risen; but Herod repudiated the
idea : 'John I beheaded, but who
is this, of whom I hear such things?'
Accordingly he 'sought to see Him'
(cf. Lk. xxiii. 8), which was the
last thing he would have sought
had he supposed it was John. For
παῖδες of court attendants cf. Gen.
xli. 10, 37 f., 1 Regn. xvi. 17.

ἀπὸ τῶν νεκρῶν] Only xxvii. 64,
xxviii. 7; ἀπὸ νεκ. Lk. xvi. 30.
The usual ἐκ occurs, in Mt., in xvii.
9 only. διὰ τοῦτο (so Mk.): John
did no miracles (Jo. x. 41), but he
had risen, and was therefore invested

with the powers (αἱ δ.) of which
report told. These powers operate
(ἐνεργοῦσιν, so Mk.) so as to produce
miracles; cf. 1 Cor. xii. 10. On
ἐνεργεῖν, elsewhere only in S. Paul's
Epp., see J. A. Robinson, Ephes.
241–7. Dalman (Words, 201) suggests
that the Aram. was misunderstood,
גבורתא מתעבדן בה, 'mighty deeds
are done by him'; cf. xi. 21, 23.

3–12. (Mk. vi. 17–29; cf. Lk. iii.
19 f.) THE BAPTIST'S DEATH.

3. ὁ γὰρ Ἡρῴδης κτλ.] A parenthetical retrospect, as in Mk. Lk.
omits the narrative, having already
recorded (l.c.) John's imprisonment
and its cause; see on iv. 12. For
ἀπέθετο (not in Mk.) cf. Lev. xxiv.
12, Num. xv. 34, 2 Chr. xviii. 26,
Polyb. xxiv. 8. Herodias was the
sister of Agrippa and daughter (by
Bernice) of Aristobulus the son of
Herod the Great by Mariamne I.
She was married to Herod (Jos. Ant.
XVIII. v. 4), son of Herod the Great
by Mariamne II., and had a daughter
Salome who was married to Philip
the tetrarch. Since Mk., followed
by Mt., says that Herodias, not her
daughter, was married to Philip (so
Just. Dial. 49, ὀρχουμένης τῆς
ἐξαδελφῆς αὐτοῦ τοῦ Ἡρώδου), it
is often assumed that there were two
Philips, half brothers. While this
is not impossible, seeing that two
were named Antipas and Antipater,
error was easy, owing to the complicated intermarriages of Herod's
large family. For κρατεῖν 'to arrest'
cf. xxvi. 48, Jud. xvi. 21.

ἔλεγεν γὰρ ὁ Ἰωάνης αὐτῷ Οὐκ ἔξεστίν σοι ἔχειν αὐτήν· 4
καὶ θέλων αὐτὸν ἀποκτεῖναι ἐφοβήθη τὸν ὄχλον, ὅτι ὡς προ- 5
φήτην αὐτὸν εἶχον. γενεσίοις δὲ γενομένοις τοῦ Ἡρῴδου 6
ὠρχήσατο ἡ θυγάτηρ τῆς Ἡρῳδιάδος ἐν τῷ μέσῳ καὶ

4. ἔλεγεν γάρ κτλ.] The imperf.
perhaps implies a repeated rebuke.
The marriage was legally impossible,
because both Herodias was married
and Antipas, the latter to the
daughter of Aretas, king of Petraea.
When the daughter of Aretas reported
the matter to her father, he made
war upon Antipas and severely
defeated him (Jos. *Ant.* XVIII. v. 1).
See Add. note.

5. καὶ θέλων κτλ.] This is
at variance with Mk.'s account :
'Herodias set herself against him,
and wanted to kill him, and could
not ; for Herod feared John, knowing
him to be a righteous and holy man,
and protected him, and when he
heard him was much perplexed, and
used to enjoy hearing him.' Swete
compares the attitude of Ahab and
Jezebel towards Elijah. If Herod
wanted to kill John, λυπηθείς (*v.* 9)
is inexplicable. But Mk., on the
other hand, is at variance with
Jos. *Ant.* XVIII. v. 2 : Antipas 'fearing lest the extent to which he had
gained the confidence of the people
might lead him to some rebellion
. . . thought it much better to
anticipate any mischief he might
cause, by putting him to death. . . .
So owing to Herod's suspicion, he
was sent as a prisoner to Machaerus
. . . and there killed.' If Herod
did not wish to kill him for rebuking
his immorality, he would hardly
fear political danger from his preaching repentance to the people ; danger
would rather arise from executing a
popular prophet, as Mt. suggests ;
and cf. xxi. 26.

6. γενεσίοις κτλ.] 'When the

birthday celebrations took place,' a
combination of Mk.'s temporal dat.
τ. γενεσίοις and γενομένης ἡμέρας,
producing the appearance of a Lat.
ablat. absol. (Wellh.). For the adj.
cf. Jos. *Ant.* XII. iv. 7, ἑορτάζοντες
τὴν γενέσιον ἡμέραν ; it occurs in
Alciphr., Dio Cass. and Fayûm
papyri. In class. Gk. τὰ γενέσια is
used of a day of memorial for the
dead (cf. Herod. iv. 26), birthday
celebrations being τ. γενέθλια (see
Wetstein). In *Ab. Zara* 10 a the
word is hebraized, and the meaning
'anniversary of the king's accession'
adopted ; but this has no Gk. support.
See Schürer, *HJP.* I. ii. 26 n. Mk.
describes the celebrations as including
'a feast to his dignitaries, chiliarchs,
and chief men of Galilee.'

ὠρχήσατο κτλ.] Mk. has αὐτῆς
(AC minn. 𝔏 vet.vg.) or αὐτοῦ
(אBDLΔ) τῆς Ἡρ. If αὐτοῦ is
the true reading, either Herod's daughter
was named Herodias, or two traditions
gave rise to a conflation 'his —
Herodias' — daughter.' Following
Mt. and αὐτῆς in Mk., many writers
assume that the dancer was Salome,
Herodias' daughter by her first
marriage. (A daughter of Herod by
Herodias could not have been more
than two years old.) But it is at
least surprising that, considering the
status of dancing women in those
days, a princess who was herself
married, if not a widow (Philip died
in A.D. 32, see Add. note), would have
danced at court, even if she were
young enough to be described (*v.* 11)
as a κοράσιον (see Schürer, *HJP.* I.
ii. 28 n.). Lake (*Expos.*, Nov. 1912)
suggests that the confusion may have

7 ἤρεσεν τῷ Ἡρῴδῃ, ὅθεν μετὰ ὅρκου ὡμολόγησεν αὐτῇ
8 δοῦναι ὃ ἐὰν αἰτήσηται. ἡ δὲ προβιβασθεῖσα ὑπὸ τῆς
μητρὸς αὐτῆς Δός μοι, φησίν, ὧδε ἐπὶ πίνακι τὴν κεφαλὴν
9 Ἰωάνου τοῦ βαπτιστοῦ. καὶ λυπηθεὶς ὁ βασιλεὺς διὰ

arisen through an ambiguous use of
the word παῖς, and that the original
tradition spoke of a slave - girl of
either Herod or Herodias.   καὶ
ἤρεσεν τῷ Ἡρ. Herod could enjoy
in one mood the sort of dancing
which found favour in his day (see
Wetstein), and in another the preaching of the Baptist.

7. ὅθεν κτλ.] Mk. adds 'to the
half of my kingdom'; cf. Est. v. 3,
vii. 2. For ὁμολογεῖν 'promise' cf.
Ac. vii. 17, Jer. li. [xliv.] 25.

8. ἡ δέ κτλ.] Mk. relates that
the girl went out, consulted with her
mother, and returned to the banqueting hall. Mt., by adding ὧδε, similarly
implies that the prison was close by;
and the dishes on the table probably
suggested the coarse irony of ἐπὶ
πίνακι. Herod had chosen the site for
the town of Machaerus 'because it lay
so near to Arabia,' and had built a
fortress and palace on the top of a
neighbouring hill (Jos. BJ. VII. vi. 2).
Lake (op. cit.) thinks that Herod
would be unlikely to hold 'great
festivities in a frontier town partly
tributary to his outraged father-in-
law'; and Wieseler places the
banquet at Julias, Fritzsche at
Tiberias; but if Herod was at war
with Aretas, it is not unnatural that
he should have occupied the strong
border town with troops, and held
the banquet there because it was
close to the scene of operations.
Mk.'s tradition contains nothing
which suggests Machaerus; the
πρῶτοι τῆς Γαλειλαίας rather suggests some place in Galilee.   But
Lk., who locates John's activity in
πᾶσα ἡ περίχωρος τοῦ Ἰορδάνου

(iii. 3), and relates his imprisonment
in connexion with it (iii. 19 f.), seems
to imply that both were in Peraea,
so that Machaerus could be the place
of imprisonment.   προβιβάζειν, in
class. Gk. 'lead forward,' hence
metaph. 'bring to the point,' 'induce'; in the LXX. 'give instructions'
Ex. xxxv. 34 (הוֹרֹת), 'repeat [for
instruction]' Dt. vi. 7 (שִׁנַּן). It is
a v.l. for συνεβίβασαν (Ac. xix. 33).
The meaning here is clearly 'instructed,' not 'being put forward'
(R.V.), nor 'being before instructed'
(A.V. and earlier Engl. verss.).   πίναξ
(Vg. discus), originally a wooden board;
hence a writing tablet (cf. πινακίδιον,
Lk. i. 63, Sym. Ez. ix. 2), or any
flat plate; A.V., R.V. 'charger' (as
in Num. vii. 13 etc., Ezr. i. 9); see
HDB. s.v.

9. καὶ λυπηθείς κτλ.] 'Although
grieved.' Mk. περίλυπος γενόμενος.
See on v. 5. For the plur. ὅρκους
of the words of an oath cf. Num. v.
21 (AF), 2 Mac. iv. 34, vii. 24.   To
keep a rash oath may be worse than
to break it (Orig., see ZNW., 1911,
288).   The keeping of oaths would
not be a strong point in one whom
the Lord called 'that fox' (Lk. xiii.
32); he kept this one only from
fear of men.   On another occasion
his weak compliance with Herodias'
wishes led to his ruin (Jos. Ant. XVIII.
vii. 2).   That he feared his guests
suggests that they, as well as Herodias,
were hostile to the Baptist (cf. xvii.
12), fearing that his influence with
Herod might be injurious to their
national hopes, since many Jews hated
the Herodian rule. See JThS., 1900,
520-7. On κελεύειν with the pass.

τοὺς ὅρκους καὶ τοὺς συνανακειμένους ἐκέλευσεν δοθῆναι,
καὶ πέμψας ἀπεκεφάλισεν Ἰωάνην ἐν τῇ φυλακῇ· καὶ 10
ἠνέχθη ἡ κεφαλὴ αὐτοῦ ἐπὶ πίνακι καὶ ἐδόθη τῷ κορασίῳ, 11
καὶ ἤνεγκεν τῇ μητρὶ αὐτῆς. Καὶ προσελθόντες οἱ μαθη- 12

see Blass, § 69. 8. The vb. is confined to Mt. (?) and Lk. (Ev.¹, Ac.¹⁸).

10. καὶ πέμψας κτλ.] An abbreviation of Mk.'s account of the
sending of the executioner who
beheaded John. Mt.'s ἀπεκεφάλισεν
means 'caused to be beheaded.' The
execution without trial was, like the
marriage of Herodias, a violation of
Jewish law, which, moreover, did not
sanction the practice of beheading,
though it was a Roman and Greek
custom. On legends regarding the
Baptist's head, and the festivals of
the *Decollatio* and *Inventio capitis*, see
Swete, and art. 'John the Baptist'
in *DCAnt.*

11. καὶ ἠνέχθη κτλ.] Mk. has
ἤνεγκεν and ἔδωκεν of the executioner.
For κοράσιον of a young marriageable
woman cf. Est. ii. 2 etc., Tob. vi. 12
etc. ; it is a late word ; Lob. *Phryn.*
74 f. Schürer (*HJP.* I. ii. 28 n.),

who assumes that she was Salome,
accepts a calculation by which she
was 18 years old, and still un-
married.

12. καὶ προσελθόντες κτλ.] John's
disciples (see on ix. 14) may have
been waiting in the neighbourhood
to hear his fate. Access to the
prison was not difficult (cf. xi. 2), and
the news no doubt reached them immediately (Mk. ἀκούσαντες). Special
permission, as in the case of Jesus,
was probably given for the burial.
πτῶμα, *cadaver*, is used of a human
body after a violent death, tortured
(Mk. xv. 45), or wounded in battle
(Apoc. xi. 8 f., Ps. cix. [cx.] 6, Ez. vi.
5 (Α)), or lying exposed (Mt. xxiv.
28). αὐτόν, as in Mk. *l.c.* and vi.
29 (ℵ), reverently draws the attention
from the corpse to the person. The
last clause καὶ ἐλθόντες is added by
Mt. ; see next verse.

Additional Note on the Chronology of the Baptist's Death.

Prof. Kirsopp Lake (*Expos.*, Nov. 1912) makes some interesting suggestions on this subject. According to Lk. iii. 1 the Baptist began his work in
the 15th year of Tiberius, *i.e.* A.D. 28–9. If the Lord's baptism and ministry
followed very soon afterwards, and if 'about thirty' (Lk. iii. 23) means
'thirty-two,' the data in Lk. iii. can nearly be stretched to agree with Mt.
ii. 19, 22, in which the flight into Egypt, and therefore the Lord's birth,
is dated just before the death of Herod the Great, *i.e.* 4 B.C. But they do
not agree with Lk. ii. 1 f. ; and Prof. Ramsay, justifying S. Luke regarding
the census in the time of Quirinius, insists that the birth of Jesus must
have been in 9–8 B.C. (see *Expos.*, Nov., Dec. 1912). But Prof. Lake is led
to place the whole chronology much later. The following are his main
points : (a) Jos. (*Ant.* XVIII. iv. 6) relates the death of Herod the tetrarch
of Trachonitis in the 20th year of Tiberius, *i.e.* A.D. 33 or 35, and says
(v. 1) that 'at this time' hostilities began between Aretas and Antipas, in
consequence of the latter's intrigue with Herodias. Aretas severely defeated
him. Herod complained to Tiberius, who sent Vitellius to punish Aretas,
but while the expedition was on its way Tiberius died. This was in 37,

ταὶ αὐτοῦ ἦραν τὸ πτῶμα καὶ ἔθαψαν αὐτόν, καὶ ἐλθόντες

and Aretas' war was therefore in 36. Prof. Lake argues, perhaps with over-confidence, that it is contrary both to political and psychological probability that there should be a delay of eight years, as Schürer supposes, between the insult to Aretas' daughter and the war. Herod, therefore, married Herodias in 34–5, and the Baptist's death was at the same time. If, then, Jesus died later than John, *the Crucifixion cannot have been earlier than 35*. (*b*) Pilate severely crushed a rising in Samaria. The Samaritans appealed to Vitellius, who, having held an inquiry, sent Pilate to Rome to answer to the Emperor. But before he reached Rome he heard of the death of Tiberius. Since Gaius was proclaimed emperor in succession to Tiberius on March 18, A.D. 37, Pilate's rule in Palestine ceased between the Passovers of 36 and 37. Therefore *the Crucifixion cannot have been later than 36*. (*c*) Mt. and Jo. mention Caiaphas as the high-priest at the time of the Crucifixion. He was removed by Vitellius in favour of Jonathan, who, in turn, was removed in favour of Theophilus—the latter just after the Passover of 37. Jonathan was, therefore, high-priest of the year 36, and cannot have been appointed before the Passover of that year. Therefore *the last Passover of Caiaphas as high-priest was in 36*. (*d*) The chronology of S. Paul's life causes difficulty. If, as is probable, S. Paul was in Corinth in 50, the shortest possible chronology places the Council of Jerusalem in 48. And even if that is to be identified with the conference related in Gal. ii., and parts of years are reckoned as whole years, the 'fourteen years' of Gal. ii. 1 puts back S. Paul's conversion at least to 35, if not to 33. The Crucifixion could not, then, have been later than 32. But if ΔΙΑΙΔΕΤΩΝ (διὰ δεκατεσσάρων ἐτῶν) be read ΔΙΑΔΕΤΩΝ (διὰ τεσσάρων ἐτῶν), with the omission of a single ι, the fourteen years, whose history is a complete blank, are reduced to four, and *the Crucifixion can in that case be dated 36*.

Wellhausen altogether rejects Mk.'s account of the connexion of the Baptist with Herod, and his death at the request of the dancing-girl, and thinks that his death took place long before Herod's marriage with Herodias. But though Mk.'s account presents some difficulties in details, as the notes have shewn, they do not justify its complete rejection, especially as Josephus so far supports the Marcan account that he says that the people thought Herod's defeat by Aretas to be a divine punishment for his treatment of John, which implies that John died just before the war.

Prof. Lake thinks, though he leaves the matter to experts, that the astronomical conditions affecting the 14th of Nisan as the date of the Crucifixion hold good for A.D. 36 at least as well as for A.D. 29.

This theory has certain advantages: *e.g.* Lk. ii. 1 f. need not be explained by a probable, or improbable, census in 9–8 B.C., but refers to the well-known census (cf. Ac. v. 37) in A.D. 6, and Ramsay's elaborate justification of Lk. is unnecessary. Herod's στρατεύματα in Lk. xxiii. 11 receive an explanation; he had his troops all ready in arms in view of the war which he was waging with Aretas. Above all, if the Lord's ministry was not at an end before the Baptist's death, the accuracy of the Gospels in the light

ἀπήγγειλαν τῷ Ἰησοῦ. Ἀκούσας δὲ ὁ Ἰησοῦς ἀνε- 13
χώρησεν ἐκεῖθεν ἐν πλοίῳ εἰς ἔρημον τόπον κατ᾽ ἰδίαν· καὶ
ἀκούσαντες οἱ ὄχλοι ἠκολούθησαν αὐτῷ πεζῇ ἀπὸ τῶν
πόλεων. Καὶ ἐξελθὼν εἶδεν πολὺν ὄχλον, καὶ ἐσπλαγ- 14

of Josephus is, in that respect, vindicated, and the genuineness of the
important words in Mk. ix. 13 (Mt. xvii. 12) is unimpaired.

On the other hand it necessitates the rejection of the dates in Lk. iii. 1,
excepts as regards Herod and Philip; also of the date, in Mt. ii. 19–23, of
the return from Egypt, apart from which passage 'Herod,' both in Mt. i., ii.,
and in Lk. i. 5, might refer to Herod Antipas, whom Mt. and Mk. both
call βασιλεύς (see on v. 1 above).

The chronology of the Gospels is a complicated, perhaps insoluble,
problem. But the above considerations, which both solve and raise difficulties,
ought to be weighed in all future discussions.

13–21. (Mk. vi. 30–44, Lk. ix.
10–17, Jo. vi. 1–14.) THE FEEDING
OF THE FIVE THOUSAND.

13. ἀκούσας δέ κτλ.] The Lord
departed when the Baptist's disciples
had told (ἀπήγγειλαν) Him of their
master's fate (v. 12). In Mk., Lk.
the occasion is the return of the
Twelve (which Mt. nowhere records;
see xi. 1) from their mission, when
they told (ἀπήγγειλαν) Him all that
they had done and taught. His
subsequent movements were for the
purpose of avoiding the territory of
Antipas (see on v. 22, xv. 21, 29),
and Mt. may have known a tradition
that that motive influenced Him
now, and combined it with Mk. by
using his ἀπήγγειλαν as a link.
There was, in that case, a double
motive for retirement, and the events
of vv. 3–12 are supposed by Mt. to
have occurred only a few days
before those of vv. 1, 2, 13 ff. But
his use of Mk.'s ἀπήγγειλαν has the
appearance of a merely artificial link
between the Lord's retirement and
the narrative just related. Lk. perhaps connected the Lord's retirement
with his statement (v. 9) that Herod
'sought to see Him'; cf. Lk. xiii. 31.

ἀνεχώρησεν κτλ.] Not by Him-

self, for the disciples are present in
v. 15 (cf. xv. 39, xvi. 13). Mk.
ἀπῆλθον. Lk. παραλαβὼν αὐτοὺς
ὑπεχώρησεν. Since His visit to
Nazareth (xiii. 54) He must have
returned to the lake. For 'to a
deserted place' (Mt., Mk.). Lk. has
'to a city called Bethsaida' with no
mention of the boat, as though
relating a walk round the shore. See
on v. 22. On ἀναχωρεῖν see ii. 12.

καὶ ἀκούσαντες κτλ.] Lk. οἱ δὲ
ὄχλοι γνόντες. Mk. has a double
statement, καὶ εἶδον . . . καὶ ἐπέγνωσαν αὐτούς, which looks like a
later conflation. Mk. alone adds
that the people arrived at the landing-
place first. πεζῇ (Mt., Mk.) occurs
in 2 Regn. xv. 17 = בְּרַגְלָיו, where, as
here, there is a v.l. πεζοί (Vg.
pedestres), the plur. adj. frequent
in the LXX. and class. Gk. for 'foot-
soldiers.' πεζῇ 'on foot' occurs in
Homer, but both πεζοί and πεζῇ
(sc. ὁδῷ) in class. Gk. can denote 'on
land' as distinct from 'on sea'; so
S sin in Mk.; cf. πεζεύειν (Ac. xx.
13).

14. καὶ ἐξελθών κτλ.] For ἐξελθεῖν 'disembark' (= ἐκβαίνειν) cf.
Mk. v. 2; it need not be considered
'an impossible reference to the

χνίσθη ἐπ᾽ αὐτοῖς καὶ ἐθεράπευσεν τοὺς ἀρρώστους αὐτῶν.
15 Ὀψίας δὲ γενομένης προσῆλθαν αὐτῷ οἱ μαθηταὶ λέγοντες
Ἔρημός ἐστιν ὁ τόπος καὶ ἡ ὥρα ἤδη παρῆλθεν·
ἀπόλυσον τοὺς ὄχλους, ἵνα ἀπελθόντες εἰς τὰς κώμας
16 ἀγοράσωσιν ἑαυτοῖς βρώματα. ὁ δὲ Ἰησοῦς εἶπεν αὐτοῖς
Οὐ χρείαν ἔχουσιν ἀπελθεῖν· δότε αὐτοῖς ὑμεῖς φαγεῖν.
17 οἱ δὲ λέγουσιν αὐτῷ Οὐκ ἔχομεν ὧδε εἰ μὴ πέντε
18 ἄρτους καὶ δύο ἰχθύας. ὁ δὲ εἶπεν Φέρετέ μοι ὧδε αὐτούς.
19 καὶ κελεύσας τοὺς ὄχλους ἀνακλιθῆναι ἐπὶ τοῦ χόρτου,

ἔρημος τόπος᾽ (Holtzm.), as though it
meant 'emerge (from privacy).' After
αὐτοῖς Mt. omits ' because they were
as sheep not having a shepherd'
(Mk.) which he inserts in ix. 36;
and he relates healing instead of
'and He began to teach them many
things' (Lk. ' He spoke to them concerning the kingdom of God'); cf.
xix. 2, xxi. 14 f. For other general
statements of healing cf. iv. 23.

15. ὀψίας κτλ.] For Mk.'s uncommon ὥρας πολλῆς γενομένης.
Lk. ἡ δὲ ἡμέρα ἤρξατο κλίνειν (cf.
Lk. xxiv. 29). Sunset at the Passover
season (see v. 19; cf. Jo. vi. 4) would be
at about 6 P.M. ἡ ὥρα παρῆλθεν,
'the hour (usual for the evening
meal) has passed.' Mk.'s ὥρα πολλή
is again avoided. Mk.'s ἀγρούς
'hamlets' (cf. Mk. vi. 56) is omitted,
as in viii. 33. βρώματα: Mk. τί
φάγωσιν, Lk. ἐπισιτισμόν. The
plur. perhaps expresses the different
kinds of food which the several
members of the crowd would procure;
cf. Lk. v. 13, Mk. vii. 19. Lk. adds
καταλύσωσιν: many of them were
several miles from home.

16. ὁ δὲ Ἰησοῦς κτλ.] Mt. alone
gives the first clause of the reply;
it corresponds with ἀπελθόντες, v.
15. Lk. shews the emphasis on
ὑμεῖς more clearly by placing it
after φαγεῖν. With the command
cf. 2 Kings iv. 42; other similar
details are the surprised question of

Elisha's servant, and the multiplying
of the food so that some of it was
left. Jesus may well have had the
O.T. story in mind.

17. οὐκ ἔχομεν κτλ.] In Mk.
'five and two fishes' is the answer
to 'how many loaves have ye? Go
see.' Mt., Lk. omit the Lord's
question (see on viii. 29); but Mt.
records it in xv. 34. He also omits,
as derogatory to the disciples, their
question, not untinged with sarcasm,
'are we to go and buy 200 denarii
of bread and give to them to eat?'
For the omission of the 200 cf. v. 19,
viii. 32, xxvi. 9. On οὐκ . . . εἰ
μή cf. xii. 24. The disciples needed
the advice ἐὰν ὀλίγον σοι ὑπάρχῃ,
κατὰ τὸ ὀλίγον μὴ φοβοῦ ποιεῖν
ἐλεημοσύνην (Tob. iv. 8, and cf. 2
Cor. viii. 12). Bread, with fish as a
relish, was the ordinary food of the
poor of the district; cf. vii. 9 f.,
Jo. xxi. 9 f., 13.

18. φέρετε κτλ.] Cf. xvii. 17.
The verse, which is peculiar to Mt.,
adds the note of authority. Like
the woman of Zarephath (1 Kings
xvii. 15), the disciples gave their
small supply.

19. καὶ κελεύσας κτλ.] The mention of grass shews that the ἔρημος
τόπος was not sandy desert (see iii.
1), and perhaps 'green grass' (Mk.)
that the season was spring (cf. Jo.
vi. 4); see p. xiii. Mt. omits Mk.'s
vivid description of the separate

λαβὼν τοὺς πέντε ἄρτους καὶ τοὺς δύο ἰχθύας, ἀναβλέψας εἰς
τὸν οὐρανὸν εὐλόγησεν καὶ κλάσας ἔδωκεν τοῖς μαθηταῖς τοὺς
ἄρτους οἱ δὲ μαθηταὶ τοῖς ὄχλοις. καὶ ἔφαγον πάντες καὶ 20
ἐχορτάσθησαν, καὶ ἦραν τὸ περισσεῦον τῶν κλασμάτων
δώδεκα κοφίνους πλήρεις. οἱ δὲ ἐσθίοντες ἦσαν ἄνδρες 21

parties of diners (συμπόσια συμπόσια), in fixed numbers (κατὰ ἑκατὸν
καὶ κατὰ πεντήκοντα), arranged like
vegetable beds (πρασιαὶ πρασιαί).
λαβών κτλ.] Identical with Mk.
to εὐλόγησεν. See Swete, who
refers to the use of the words in
ancient liturgies. The Lord looked
up to Heaven (cf. Mk. vii. 34) to
speak to His Father; when He
'blessed,' He blessed His Father.
The Jewish form of thanksgiving
was itself a εὐλογία; see on xxvi.
26. Abbreviating Mk.'s account, Mt.
omits τοὺς ἄρτους after κλάσας,
making the fraction (as in Lk.)
refer to both loaves and fishes. The
loaves could easily be broken; they
were thin flat cakes; see E. Robinson,
Bibl. Res. ii. 82, 117 f., 210.

20. καὶ ἦραν κτλ.] The κλάσματα are probably the pieces into
which the Lord broke the food, not
pieces left on the ground by the
crowd. The subject of ἦραν (Mt.,
Mk.) should grammatically be πάντες,
but it is rather the Twelve; cf. xvi.
9, Jo. vi. 12 f. δ. κοφίνους πλήρεις,
'to the amount of 12 full baskets,'
in apposition with τὸ περισσεῦον
(similarly Lk.); cf. Num. xxii. 18,
Jud. vi. 38. Mk., κλάσματα δ.
κοφίνων πληρώματα (cf. Eccl. iv. 6).

The synn. do not state that baskets
were actually employed; a κόφινος
was a stout wicker basket used mostly
for agricultural purposes which the
Twelve would hardly carry with
them; but the word was employed
to denote a measure, containing three
χόες (Hesych.), and, though not
universally known as such, could at
least indicate roughly the amount of
the κλάσματα. That it was probably
not equivalent to πήρα ('wallet') is
shewn by Jud. vi. 19, Ps. lxxx.
[lxxxi.] 7, Aq. Gen. xl. 16 (LXX.
κανοῦν), Lk. xiii. 8 (D 𝕷) κόφινον
κοπρίων, and the passages in non-
bibl. Gk. cited by Hort (see *JThS.*,
July 1909); and cf. *cophinus*, Juv.
iii. 14, vi. 542. Hort thinks it is
rather equivalent to the κάρταλ(λ)ος
in which Jews carried first-fruits to
Jerusalem.

21. οἱ δὲ ἐσθίοντες κτλ.] 'The
eaters'; see on iv. 3. Mk. οἱ φα-
γόντες τοὺς ἄρτους. Mt. heightens,
if possible, the wonder, by adding
the women and children; χωρίς does
not, of course, mean that they were
not present (cf. Orig. *in Mt.* tom.
xi. 3). The arrangement of the
people by hundreds and fifties
(Mk.) would facilitate the numbering.
Lk. omits the verse.

Additional Note on the Feeding of the Five Thousand.

1. It is the only miracle related in all the four gospels. The 4th
Evangelist no doubt recorded it because of the spiritual meaning which it
contained. But it is noteworthy that of the details in which he differs from
the others, there is not one that would surprise us if it stood in the synoptic
accounts. 'This He said testing him, for He himself knew what He would
do' is due to his reflexion, but the fact obviously underlies the command in

the synoptists 'Give ye them to eat.' There is nothing in his narrative that appears to be 'written up' to yield spiritual or mystical meaning. If the writer was not the apostle John, the tradition may well have been handed down from S. Philip or S. Andrew.

2. In the feeding of the 5000, and of the 4000 (Mt. xv. 36, Mk. viii. 6), and in the meal at Emmaus (Lk. xxiv. 30), the central act is described in words which recall the Eucharistic act at the Last Supper (Mt. xxvi. 26, Mk. xiv. 22, Lk. xxii. 19, 1 Cor. xi. 24) :—

5000.	4000.	Emmaus.	Eucharist.
λαβών [Jo. ἔλαβεν].	ἔλαβεν [Mk. λαβών].	λαβών.	λαβών [1 Cor. ἔλαβεν].
εὐλόγησεν [Jo. εὐχαριστήσας].	εὐχαριστήσας.	εὐλόγησεν.	εὐλογήσας [Lk., 1 Cor. εὐχαριστήσας].
κλάσας [Mk., Lk. κατέκλασεν. Jo. om.]	ἔκλασεν.	κλάσας.	ἔκλασεν.
ἔδωκεν [Mk., Lk. ἐδίδου. Jo. διέδωκεν].	ἐδίδου.	ἐπεδίδου.	δούς [Mk., Lk. ἔδωκεν. 1 Cor. om.].

The conclusion can hardly be avoided that in all the meals the evangelists realized that there had been a Eucharistic act, and expressed it in their wording. To the multitudes by the lake, to the Twelve on the night before His death, and to disciples at every Eucharistic feast from then till now, He gives a foretaste of the Feast in the Messianic Kingdom (cf. Mt. xxvi. 29). And the truth implied in the wording of the narratives is drawn out explicitly in Jo. vi. 26–58. The fundamental importance of the incident from this point of view is unaffected by the problem of 'miracle.'

3. Various suggestions have been made which eliminate the 'miraculous': —e.g. Jesus having hospitably given the small supply of food which He and the disciples had with them, those in the crowd who had brought food followed His example and shared it with others (Paulus, *Exeg. Handb.* ii. 205 ff.). The crowd really ate food provided by the forethought of Jesus; but the spiritual food offered in His discourses, which He compared with the physical food afforded by the manna, was converted in tradition into a miraculous feeding of a multitude (Schenkel, *Sketch of Character of Jesus,* 375 f.). Keim (*Jesus of Naz.* iv. 197 ff.) assents, if a historical kernel is needed, to the explanation of Paulus, but thinks that the story is rather legendary, built on such stories as those of the manna and of Elisha's miracle. Strauss (*Leben Jesu,* ii. 215 ff.) holds that it arose from a metaphorical utterance of Jesus, analogous to those in Mk. viii. 15 (Mt. xvi. 6), Lk. xii. 1, together with legendary elements, and reminiscences of the O.T. Olshausen (*Comm. ad loc.*) explains the multiplying of the bread as a natural, but accelerated, process of growth. Wellhausen (*Das Ev. Marci, ad loc.*) echoes Paulus: the number 5000 has been greatly exaggerated in tradition, and Jesus and the disciples shared their food with the people, shewing that He cared for their bodies as well as for their souls. J. Weiss (*Schriften d. N.T.* on Mk.) thinks that the story is the evangelists' method of relating that Jesus gave, in a hidden, parabolic form, a prediction of His own death. Schweitzer (*Quest* 374) believes that in administering an 'eschatological sacrament' Jesus gave a minute portion of food to every one. 'The whole is historical except the closing remark that they were all filled.' With this sentence Sanday (*Bishop Gore's Challenge to Criticism,* 25) agrees, thinking that the

ὡσεὶ πεντακισχίλιοι χωρὶς γυναικῶν καὶ παιδίων.   Καὶ 22
εὐθέως ἠνάγκασεν τοὺς μαθητὰς ἐμβῆναι εἰς πλοῖον καὶ

closing remark comes from the stories of Elijah and Elisha, especially
2 Kings iv. 42 ff.

But none of these explanations accounts for the enthusiasm implied in
v. 22 (Mk. *v.* 45), and related in Jo. vi. 14 f.   It *may* have been due only to
the Lord's preaching, and a 'natural' occurrence *may* have become 'miraculous'
in Christian tradition.   But modern thought is learning not to reject records
of miracles simply because they are miracles; their possibility must, in each
several case, be judged in relation to the paradox of a transcendent God
working immanently, and to the mystery of the Incarnation.   See p. xiv. f.

22–33.   (Mk. vi. 45–52, Jo. vi.
15–21.)   THE WALKING ON THE
WATER.

22. *καὶ ἠνάγκασεν κτλ.*]   Neither
Mt. nor Mk. explains the reason for
this.   Mk.'s favourite *εὐθύς* probably
has no special force, and *ἠνάγκασεν*
(so Mk.; elsewhere in the Gospels
Lk. xiv. 23 only) may be stronger
than the original word; cf. Ϩ vet
'commanded them,' and in Lk. *l.c.*
'make, *or* cause them.'   But at any
rate Jesus found it necessary to make
the disciples leave Him; without
them, for some reason, He could
more easily persuade the crowds to
disperse.   The only reason that
suggests itself is that their enthusiasm
had been raised, and the presence of
the disciples would increase rather
than allay it.   In Jo. it is related
that the crowds wanted to make Him
King; so He departed alone into the
hills, and the disciples embarked.

καὶ προάγειν κτλ.]   The geography
in Mt. is vague: the Lord departed
by boat to a deserted place (*v.* 13);
the disciples were now told to sail
'to the other side,' which sounds like
a return to the western shore; they
were hindered by a contrary wind
(*v.* 24); but when it ceased, they
crossed to the land of Gennesaret,
which was on the western shore
(*v.* 34).   But since they had that very
day left the dominion of Antipas,

Jesus would hardly bid them return
to it.   According to Lk. ix. 10 they
first 'withdrew (not 'sailed') to a
city called Bethsaida.'   The following
narrative requires this to be explained, very improbably, as 'a
desert place near Bethsaida.'   But in
Mk. the Lord bids them precede Him
'to the other side' (as in Mt.), but
with the addition 'to Bethsaida.'
In spite of Jo. xii. 21, it is improbable that there were two
Bethsaidas (see on xi. 21).   If Lk.
is correct, and if Bethsaida is B.
Julias on the N.E. of the lake, the
accounts must be harmonized by
supposing that the 'desert place'
was close to B., but separated from
it by a bay, across which (*εἰς τὸ
πέραν*) the disciples were to sail,
and they would think that He intended to walk round the shore;
but the contrary wind drove them
back to Gennesaret (Capharnaum,
Jo.).   Otherwise the mention of
Bethsaida is incorrect in either Mk.
or Lk.   Stanton (*Gospels*, ii. 157)
suggests that a reviser of Mk. transferred *πρὸς Βηθσ.* from the preceding
narrative, where, according to Lk., it
should stand.   But this does not
explain why Jesus should have sent
the disciples straight back to the
dominion of Antipas.   If Lk. is
incorrect, the 'desert place' may
have been any spot on the eastern

προάγειν αὐτὸν εἰς τὸ πέραν, ἕως οὗ ἀπολύσῃ τοὺς ὄχλους.
23 καὶ ἀπολύσας τοὺς ὄχλους ἀνέβη εἰς τὸ ὄρος κατ᾿ ἰδίαν
24 προσεύξασθαι. ὀψίας δὲ γενομένης μόνος ἦν ἐκεῖ. Τὸ δὲ
πλοῖον ἤδη σταδίους πολλοὺς ἀπὸ τῆς γῆς ἀπεῖχεν,
βασανιζόμενον ὑπὸ τῶν κυμάτων, ἦν γὰρ ἐναντίος ὁ ἄνεμος.
25 Τετάρτῃ δὲ φυλακῇ τῆς νυκτὸς ἦλθεν πρὸς αὐτοὺς περι-

24 σταδιους...απειχεν] B 13 124 238 346 ℥ cur.pesh.pal me arm ; ην εις μεσον της
θαλασσης D ; μεσον τ. θαλ. ην אCE etc 𝕃 omn ℥ hcl aeth

shore from which a sail to B. Julias
could be described as a 'crossing.'

ἕως οὗ κτλ.] This, like the
Aram. דְּ עַד, is virtually 'while'
(Blass, § 65. 10); cf. xxvi. 36. Else-
where in Mt. it is strictly 'until.'

23. καὶ ἀπολύσας κτλ.] The
'mountain' was probably not a
single height, but the high wolds
overlooking the lake. The Lord
had had more than one conflict with
the religious authorities (xii. 1–14,
22 ff.), and had now been obliged to
avoid both the civil authorities and
danger from the enthusiasm of the
crowds. He needed prayer for
strength and guidance. Only at
this crisis and in Gethsemane do Mt.,
Mk. record that He prayed; but if
He did it twice, He did it often, as
Lk. relates (iii. 21, v. 16, vi. 12, ix.
18, 28 f., xi. 1, xxii. 41, 44). See
also Mt. xi. 25 f., xiv. 19, xv. 36, xix.
13, xxvi. 27, xxvii. 46, Mk. ix. 29,
Lk. xxii. 32, xxiii. 34, 46, Heb. v. 7.

ὀψίας κτλ.] The early hours of
the night; cf. Judith xiii. 1. Jo.
σκοτία ἤδη ἐγεγόνει. Mt. adopts
Mk.'s expression, though he has
already used it of an earlier hour in
v. 15. But he can hardly have
thought of the Heb. term 'the two
evenings,' which some Jews explained
(Pesach. 61 a) as the time when the
sun's heat begins to decrease, and
sunset. On the Jewish and Christian
hours of prayer see ZNW, 1911,
90 ff.

24. τὸ δὲ πλοῖον κτλ.] The v.ll.
(see Appar.) correspond with Mk. ἦν
. . . ἐν μέσῳ τ. θ. (see Blass, § 40. 8).
Jo. vi. 19 says 'about 25 or 30 stades.'
The στάδιον (plur. usually στάδιοι)
was about 194 yards, less than a 'fur-
long' (all Engl. verss.). According to
Jos. B.J. III. x. 7, the lake was 40
stades in breadth, nearly 4½ miles.
Mk.'s statement, omitted by Mt., that
Jesus saw them in their distress, is
not necessarily a legendary detail
(Montef.); if a bright moon was
shining, the tossing boat might be
visible from a hill at a distance of 2
to 3 miles. In Mk. βασανιζομένους
refers to the disciples; here it is
picturesquely used of the boat.

25. τετάρτῃ κτλ.] Between 3
and 6 A.M.; more precise than Mk.'s
'about the 4th watch.' The Romans
reckoned four watches (described in
Mk. xiii. 35; cf. Ac. xii. 4), the Jews
three (Lk. xii. 38, Jud. vii. 19). For
φυλακή in this sense cf. also 1 Regn.
xi. 11, Ps. lxxxix. [xc.] 4, cxxix.
[cxxx.] 6, Lam. ii. 19.

περιπατῶν κτλ.] 'Walking over
the lake' (acc.); but in the next
verse they saw Him 'walking on
the lake' (gen.). The acc. expresses
motion (cf. v. 28 f.), a construction
found in Hom. and Hesiod, but also
in Eur. Mk., Jo. have only the
gen., which can also mean 'by, on
the edge of, the sea,' as in Jo. xxi. 1;
cf. Ex. xiv. 2, στρατοπεδεύσεις ἐπὶ
τῆς θαλάσσης (= παρὰ τὴν θάλασ-

πατῶν ἐπὶ τὴν θάλασσαν. οἱ δὲ μαθηταὶ ἰδόντες αὐτὸν 26
ἐπὶ τῆς θαλάσσης περιπατοῦντα ἐταράχθησαν λέγοντες ὅτι
Φάντασμά ἐστιν, καὶ ἀπὸ τοῦ φόβου ἔκραξαν. εὐθὺς δὲ 27
ἐλάλησεν ὁ Ἰησοῦς αὐτοῖς λέγων Θαρσεῖτε, ἐγώ εἰμι· μὴ

σαν, v. 9) ; and περιπατεῖν is strictly
'walk about,' not 'walk forward'
(Abbot, *Joh. Gr.* 2342) ; cf., however,
v. 29. It has been suggested that
Mk., Jo. relate only that Jesus was
on the beach, and that Mt., who
received the tradition in a different
form, expressed this by the change
of preposition. The Johannine
account can, without reference to
the others, be so interpreted. But
in Mk., if Jesus was 'walking about
by the lake,' it is difficult to give a
meaning to ἔρχεται πρὸς αὐτούς, and
to the amazement (v. 51) of the
disciples, unless that refers only to
the cessation of the wind. Mk. adds
καὶ ἤθελεν παρελθεῖν αὐτούς. Mt.
perhaps avoided the implication that
Jesus tried, but was unable (cf. xv. 21).

26. ἰδόντες δέ κτλ.] For φάν-
τασμα cf. Job xx. 8 (A), Wisd. xvii.

15, and with another meaning Is.
xxviii. 7 (A). φαντασίαι, Wisd. xviii.
17. See also πνεῦμα, Lk. xxiv. 37,
Job iv. 15 f. Perhaps the original
word was שֵׁדִין (so 𝔖 vet), 'a demon.'
Cf. the saying ascribed to Jesus after
the Resurrection by Ign. (*Smyrn.* iii.
2): λάβετε, ψηλαφίσατέ με, καὶ
ἴδετε ὅτι οὐκ εἰμὶ δαιμόνιον ἀσώμα-
τον. On ἀπὸ τ. φόβου see xiii. 44.

27. εὐθύς κτλ.] Mk.'s μετ' αὐτοῖς
does not imply mutual conversation ;
·cf. Apoc. i. 12, iv. 1, etc. ἐγώ εἰμι
(cf. xxvi. 22, 25, Mk. xiii. 6, xiv.
62), 'I am—the object which you
see,' or, in other passages, ' the person
of whom you are speaking or thinking' ; cf. αὐτός ἐστιν (xxvi. 48). It
is the converse of the Engl. idiom 'It
is I,' which makes ' I ' the predicate.
The expression is peculiar to the
Gospels.

Additional Note on the Walking on the Water.

The evident purpose of Mt. and Mk., and probably of Jo., is to relate something which indicated superhuman powers on the part of the Lord, powers
ascribed to God (Job xxxviii. 16) and to Wisdom (Sir. xxiv. 5, ἐν βάθει
ἀβύσσων περιεπάτησα). And the closing remarks in the previous Add.
note apply to this, as to all miracles. Lk. possibly omitted the incident
because it might seem to his readers analogous to pagan stories, *e.g.* Hom.
Od. v. 54, Virg. *Aen.* i. 147. Some see in the story merely a symbolical
expression of spiritual truth ; *e.g.* that the early Christians used to say, in
the metaphorical language of the Heb. scriptures, that Christ could save
them even amid the stormy waters of trouble ; or that the departure and
reappearance of Christ symbolized His departure by death and return by
Resurrection. It has also been suggested that an actual post-Resurrection
appearance was transferred to an earlier point. Rationalizing explanations
have been widely adopted : *e.g.* Jesus walked by the shore of the lake, and
hoped to pass the disciples unobserved (Mk.), in order that they might find
Him waiting for them on their arrival. But they caught sight of Him,
though He was too far off for recognition, and, not realizing in the early
twilight how near they were to the shore, were startled at seeing a

28 φοβεῖσθε. ἀποκριθεὶς δὲ ὁ Πέτρος εἶπεν αὐτῷ Κύριε, εἰ
σὺ εἶ, κέλευσόν με ἐλθεῖν πρὸς σὲ ἐπὶ τὰ ὕδατα· ὁ δὲ
29 εἶπεν Ἐλθέ. καὶ καταβὰς ἀπὸ τοῦ πλοίου Πέτρος περιε-
πάτησεν ἐπὶ τὰ ὕδατα καὶ ἦλθεν πρὸς τὸν Ἰησοῦν.
30 βλέπων δὲ τὸν ἄνεμον ἐφοβήθη, καὶ ἀρξάμενος καταποντί-
31 ζεσθαι ἔκραξεν λέγων Κύριε, σῶσόν με. εὐθέως δὲ ὁ
Ἰησοῦς ἐκτείνας τὴν χεῖρα ἐπελάβετο αὐτοῦ καὶ λέγει
32 αὐτῷ Ὀλιγόπιστε, εἰς τί ἐδίστασας; καὶ ἀναβάντων
33 αὐτῶν εἰς τὸ πλοῖον ἐκόπασεν ὁ ἄνεμος. οἱ δὲ ἐν τῷ
πλοίῳ προσεκύνησαν αὐτῷ λέγοντες Ἀληθῶς θεοῦ υἱὸς
34 εἶ.   Καὶ διαπεράσαντες ἦλθαν ἐπὶ τὴν γῆν εἰς Γεν-

---

30 ανεμον] אB* 33 me; add ισχυρον B²CDE etc minn.caet 𝕃 omn 𝕾 omn

---

human form. Reassured by His voice, they came to land and took Him
into the boat for the short distance of the passage that remained. Paulus
suggests that Jesus walked through shallow water to the boat [an action to
which fishermen are daily accustomed], and was thought by the disciples to
have walked on the surface ! See Salmon, *Human Element*, 322–4.

28–31. (Mt. only.) S. PETER ON
THE WATER.

28. ἀποκριθείς κτλ.] On the
prominence given to S. Peter in Mt.
see x. 2. A strong point in favour
of the story is its faithful reflexion
of the apostle's character. But to
those who doubt its historicity, it
can be freely admitted that the facts
related are of much less importance
than their spiritual significance. They
are an acted parable of his proud
impulsiveness (xxvi. 33, 35), his fall
and repentance (*id.* 69–75), and his
restoration (Lk. xxii. 31 f., xxiv. 34, Jo.
xxi. 15 ff.). Two details are echoes
of the earlier story of the storm :
κύριε, σῶσόν με (cf. viii. 25), and
ὀλιγόπιστε, εἰς τί ἐδίστασας ; (26).

30. βλέπων κτλ.] Cf. Ex. xx.
18 ἑώρα . . . τὴν φωνήν, Apoc. i. 12
βλέπειν τὴν φωνήν. The addition of
ἰσχυρόν (see Appar.) was an obvious
correction. καταποντίζεσθαι: cf.
xviii. 6, Ex. xv. 4 (A); elsewhere it
is metaph., 'swallow up,' 'destroy.'

31. εὐθέως κτλ.] On ὀλιγόπιστε
see vi. 30. For ἐδίστασας (class.)
cf. xxviii. 17.

32. καὶ ἀναβάντων κτλ.] Mt.
adapts Mk.'s ἀνέβη (sc. Jesus) to include S. Peter.

33. οἱ δέ κτλ.] Mk. says that
they were greatly amazed, and himself adds a censure on the apostles,
' for they did not understand about
the loaves, but their heart was
hardened.' Mt. spares them (see on
viii. 26) by relating that they uttered
a profession of faith far in advance
of the ποταπός ἐστιν οὗτος of viii.
27, and one which anticipates xvi. 16.
Mk.'s censure, however, is possibly a
later addition. On the aor. προσεκύνησαν see Blass, § 57. 4.

34–36. (Mk. vi. 53–56.) HEALING
IN GENNESARET.

34. καὶ διαπεράσαντες κτλ.] ἦλθ.
ἐπὶ τὴν γῆν, 'they arrived at *terra
firma*' (𝕾 vet, 'they went up to the
dry land'), in contrast with their
stormy passage. The form Gennesar

νησαρέτ.   καὶ ἐπιγνόντες αὐτὸν οἱ ἄνδρες τοῦ τόπου ἐκείνου 35
ἀπέστειλαν εἰς ὅλην τὴν περίχωρον ἐκείνην, καὶ προσήνεγκαν
αὐτῷ πάντας τοὺς κακῶς ἔχοντας, καὶ παρεκάλουν αὐτὸν 36
ἵνα μόνον ἄψωνται τοῦ κρασπέδου τοῦ ἱματίου αὐτοῦ· καὶ
ὅσοι ἥψαντο διεσώθησαν.

Τότε προσέρχονται τῷ Ἰησοῦ ἀπὸ Ἱεροσολύμων Φαρι- 1   XV.
σαῖοι καὶ γραμματεῖς λέγοντες   Διὰ τί οἱ μαθηταί σου 2

(D* [see Chase, *Syr. Lat. Text*, 105]604
[Greg. 700], 𝔏 𝔖) is probably more
correct ; cf. 1 Mac. xi. 67, Jos. *BJ.* II.
xx. 6, III. x. 1, 7. See on Mt. ii. 23.
גניסר occurs in the Targums, גינוסר
chiefly in the Talmud. But it is not
necessarily the true Gk. reading in the
gospels ; see Burkitt, *Syr. Forms of
N.T. Proper Names*, 15. It was a
small triangular plain of great fer-
tility, lying between Capharnaum and
Tiberias, and sometimes gave its name
to the lake (cf. Lk. v. 1, Jos. *ll.c.*).

35. καὶ ἐπιγνόντες κτλ.] The
Lord is not recorded to have visited
the place before, but some of the
inhabitants must have seen Him in
Capharnaum. For ἀπέστειλαν Mk.
has περιέδραμον : they did not expect Him to stay long. προσήνεγκαν
is for Mk.'s ἤρξαντο περιφέρειν : see
on xiii. 54. Mk.'s addition ὅπου
ἤκουον ὅτι ἐστιν, and his next verse,
imply that Jesus visited several
villages, cities, and hamlets in the
neighbourhood. Mt. abbreviates this,
as though He stayed in the same
place all the time.

36. καὶ παρεκάλουν κτλ.] On
the verb see viii. 5, and on κράσπεδον
ix. 20. For διασώζειν of healing
(Mk. ἐσώζοντο) cf. Lk. vii. 3.

xv. 1–20. (Mk. vii. 1–23.) Discourse on Clean and Unclean.

It is possible that this was not
the original position of the discourse ;
Mt., Mk. have no note of place or
time, while *vv.* 21 ff. form a natural
sequel to ch. xiv. : Jesus had wished

to avoid Herod's dominion, and would
leave it as soon as possible. The
discourse was perhaps delivered in
Judaea (cf. ch. xxiii.), where the
points at issue between the Rabbinic
schools would be more likely to be
brought up for discussion than in
the north. It falls into three parts,
addressed in turn to the Scribes and
Pharisees (*vv.* 1–9), the people (*v.*
10 f.), and the disciples (*vv.* 12–20).

1–9. *Teaching given to the Scribes
and Pharisees.*

1. τότε κτλ.] The unusual order
Pharisees and Scribes is due to Mk.,
who writes καὶ συνάγονται πρὸς
αὐτὸν οἱ Φαρισαῖοι καί τινες τῶν
γραμματέων ἐλθόντες ἀπὸ Ἰ. which
seems to mean 'the Pharisees (of the
place), and certain of the Scribes
from Jerusalem who happened to
have come thither.' But Mt. understands ἐλθόντες to refer to both.
On Ἱεροσόλυμα see ii. 1.

2. διὰ τί κτλ.] In Mk. the
question is prepared for by the statement that they had seen some of
the disciples eating κοιναῖς χερσίν,
τοῦτ᾽ ἔστιν ἀνίπτοις, followed by a
note (*v.* 3 f.) on Jewish customs,
which was either a later addition
in Mk. for Gentiles, or omitted
by Mt. as unnecessary for Jewish
readers. The question is asked as
though Jesus were the leader of a
Rabbinic 'school,' who might have a
right to His own opinion on a detail
in the 'tradition.' This academical
attitude is clearer in Mk.'s οὐ

παραβαίνουσιν τὴν παράδοσιν τῶν πρεσβυτέρων; οὐ γὰρ
3 νίπτονται τὰς χεῖρας ὅταν ἄρτον ἐσθίωσιν. ὁ δὲ ἀποκριθεὶς εἶπεν αὐτοῖς Διὰ τί καὶ ὑμεῖς παραβαίνετε τὴν

περιπατοῦσιν κατά, which need not
imply blame, than in Mt.'s παραβαίνουσιν. The 'elders' were the
great teachers of the past and present
(cf. Heb. xi. 2); the 'tradition' was
the oral law, handed down by them,
not yet complete, and codified later
in the Mishna. See Taylor on
Aboth iii. 20, and his add. n. 2. It
was the accurate performance of it
which made the Pharisees 'separated'
persons. The common people did
not know, much less observe, its
details. Its rules of conduct by
which men must 'walk' were called
halaka (cf. περιπατοῦσιν, Mk.).

οὐ γὰρ νίπτονται κτλ.] A paraphrase of Mk.'s ἀλλὰ κοιναῖς χερσὶν
ἐσθίουσιν τὸν ἄρτον. On the disputes between the schools of Hillel
and Shammai on the subject see
Berach. viii. 2–4 (Schürer, *HJP.* II.
ii. 111, and the literature cited).
Handwashing before meals was not
an O.T. requirement. Hart (*JQR.*
xix. 626–30) suggests possible reasons
for the rise of the practice. Büchler
(*Exp. T.* xxi. 34–40) holds that
rigorous rules of purification, as
applying to laymen, were a development later than the time of Jesus,
and that Mk.'s τοῦτ' ἔστιν ἀνίπτοις
was a later gloss. 'The Pharisees
in the report of Mk. must have
meant priests who had recently
joined the ranks of the Pharisees,
and had adopted the strict rules of
purification instituted by the rabbis
for the priests in order to safeguard
the levitical purity of the priestly
dues. The rabbis were the authors
and expounders of these laws, but
they had no occasion to observe
them themselves.' If this is correct,

the incident must have occurred in
the house of such a Pharisee (cf. Lk.
xi. 37 f.), who expected guests at his
table to observe the same rules as
he did. But Margoliouth (*Exp. T.*
xxii. 261 ff.) suggests that the later
codification of rules for the laity
was the result of a practice already
growing up, and rightly maintains
Mk.'s authority as a witness for the
1st century, only admitting that his
καὶ πάντες οἱ Ἰουδαῖοι must not be
unduly pressed.

3–6. In Mk. the Lord's reply
(*vv.* 9–13) follows the reference to
Isaiah (*vv.* 6 ff.), in Mt. (*vv.* 3–6) it
more logically precedes it (*vv.* 7 ff. ;
see note). In Mt. the two form a
continuous denunciation, in Mk.
they are distinct, and introduced
respectively by ὁ δὲ εἶπεν αὐτοῖς
and καὶ ἔλεγεν αὐτοῖς.

3. διὰ τί κτλ.] The Scribes'
question was academic, and Jesus
sweeps it away by attacking, as a
general principle, the position which
the 'tradition' had come to occupy
in relation to the divine law of
Moses. καὶ ὑμεῖς παραβαίνετε corresponding with παραβαίνουσιν (*v.* 2)
takes the place of Mk.'s καλῶς
ἀθετεῖτε, which is either interrogative
(Wellh.) or sharply ironical. ἐντολήν
is identical with λόγον (*v.* 6). In
the LXX. it is used, as here, of the
Law as a whole, in 4 Regn. xxi. 8
(= תּוֹרָה), Ps. xviii. [xix.] 9, cxviii.
[cxix.] 96 (= מִצְוָה). When the
ἐντολή and the παράδοσις clashed,
the former was sacrificed to the
latter. 𝔖 sin.cur have 'commandments' for both, which Merx thinks
original, because there was at that
time no 'tradition' about hand-

ἐντολὴν τοῦ θεοῦ διὰ τὴν παράδοσιν ὑμῶν; ὁ γὰρ θεὸς 4
εἶπεν Τίμα τὸν πατέρα καὶ τὴν μητέρα, καί Ὁ κακολογῶν
πατέρα ἢ μητέρα θανάτῳ τελευτάτω· ὑμεῖς δὲ λέγετε Ὃς ἂν 5
εἴπῃ τῷ πατρὶ ἢ τῇ μητρί Δῶρον ὃ ἐὰν ἐξ ἐμοῦ ὠφεληθῇς,

4 ειπεν] אᵃBDTᶜ 1 124 𝕃 vet[exc. f].vg 𝕊 sin.cur.pesh me arm aeth ;
ενετειλατο λεγων א* ᵉᵗ ᵇ CE etc 𝕃 f 𝕊 hcl

washing; the practice 'was only
instituted by Hillel and Shammai'
(Montef.).

4. ὁ γὰρ θεός κτλ.] Mk. Μωυσῆς
γὰρ εἶπεν. Mt. makes a sharper
antithesis between divine and human
ordinances (ὁ γὰρ θεὸς . . . ὑμεῖς
δέ). The law of filial piety is selected
as a signal instance, and cited in its
positive and negative form, from
Ex. xx. 12 (Deut. v. 16) and xxi.
16 [17]; cf. Lev. xx. 9, Deut. xxvii.
16. The v.l. ἐνετείλατο λέγων may
have been due to Deut. v. 16 ὃν
τρόπον ἐνετείλατο Κύριος ὁ θεός σου.
The omission, after πατέρα and
μητέρα, of σου in the first quotation
(cf. xix. 19) and of αὐτοῦ in the
second, which are retained in M.T.,
LXX., Targᴼⁿᵏ, perhaps represents the
emphatic state of the nouns in the
Palestinian Aram. of the time; see
on vi. 9. κακολογεῖν, 'to curse,'
'speak evil of' (R.V.), is not strictly
the converse of 'to honour,' but has
the general force of ἀτιμάζειν; cf.
Deut. xxvii. 16 (מְקַלֶּה) with Driver's
note. θανάτῳ τελευτάτω (Mt., Mk.)
= מוֹת יָמוּת: so Ex. xxi. 16 [17]
AF, where B has τελευτήσει θ., one
of three different renderings of the
same Heb. in successive verses. In
Sanh. vii. 8 the punishment is
stoning.

5. ὑμεῖς δέ κτλ.] Cf. ἐγὼ δὲ λέγω
ὑμῖν (v. 22 etc.). Like the Scribes
Jesus dealt independently with the
Law, but He claimed to 'fulfil' it,
while they emptied it of its force.

δῶρον] Mk. κορβάν, ὅ ἐστιν δῶρον.

Korbān (קָרְבָּן), 'that which is brought
near' as an offering, an exilic and
post-exilic term (Lev.⁴⁰, Num.³⁸, Ez.²,
Neh.² [קָרְבָּן], and frequently in the
Targums), is not transliterated in
the LXX., but rendered δῶρον. So
Theod. Ez. xx. 28; elsewhere, in
the few extant passages, the later
translators have προσφορά or other
renderings. In Mt. xxvii. 6, Jos.
B.J. II. ix. 4, it is the money in the
temple treasury; in Jos. Ant. IV.
iv. 4 it is used of persons who
dedicate themselves for a fixed period.

(1) According to the text the
words are a vow: 'that by which
you might have received advantage
from me is hereby dedicated as an
offering.' So 𝕃 a g¹ Ephr.(see Burkitt,
Ev. da Meph. ad loc.), 𝕊 sin (Mk.):
'[It is] Corban what thou shalt be
profited from me'; Vulg. (Mk.):
'Corban quodcunque ex me tibi
profuerit.' Cf. Nedar. i. 2, 4, ix. 2,
7, xi. 4, 11, B. Kama, ix. 10. Its
actual dedication is not really contemplated; it was dedicated (i.e.
unavailable) only as regards the
parent, or other person, who hoped
to receive it. On the binding effect
of a mere verbal promise of dedication see Philo, ap. Eus. Praep. viii.
7. If this is the true explanation,
the sanction which the Scribes gave
to the act was not motived by
collusion with the temple priests (as
Theophlct. αὐτοὶ δὲ τὰ ἀφιερωθέντα
κατήσθιον); the δῶρον not being
really offered, they received no
advantage from it. The passage

6 οὐ μὴ τιμήσει τὸν πατέρα αὐτοῦ· καὶ ἠκυρώσατε τὸν λόγον

6 τον λογον] אᵃBD 𝕷 a b ff¹·² e 𝔖 sin.cur.pesh.hcl^mg me arm aeth ; τ. νομον
א*ᵉᵗ ᵇCTᶜ 13 124 346 ; την εντολην E etc 𝕷 c f g¹ q vg 𝔖 hcl^txt

merely speaks of their attitude
towards the vexed question of vows.

(2) But 'Corban!' could be
merely an oath : 'By the offering
[on the altar]!' cf. xxiii. 18. See
Jos. c. Ap. i. 22, where Theophrastus
is quoted as mentioning τὸν καλούμενον ὅρκον κορβάν as current
among Jews, but forbidden by the
laws of the Tyrians. 𝔖 sin here has
'Corban! if thou shalt [i.e. thou
shalt not] be profited from me.' This
is possibly original. The angry oath
of refusal to help the parents is
binding. Corruptions appear such
as 'My Corban, thou shalt be profited from me' (𝔖 cur); 'donum meum
proficiet tibi' (e); 'munus quodcunque
est ex me tibi proderit' (Vulg.); these
perhaps point to an interrogative
form, i.e. a refusal.

οὐ μὴ τιμήσει κτλ.] This avoids
Mk.'s anacoluthon, ἐὰν εἴπῃ ἄνθρωπος . . . οὐκέτι ἀφίετε αὐτόν κτλ.
But it is doubtful if Mt. intended it to be the words of the
Scribes; 'he shall not honour' is
merely the equivalent in the Lord's
mouth of 'ye no longer permit him
to do aught, etc.' Honour to parents
includes the duty of supporting
them; cf. 1 Tim. v. 3. In Gosp.
Naz. the Scribes themselves are represented as saying to their parents
κορβάν ὃ ὑμεῖς ὠφεληθήσεσθε ἐξ
ἡμῶν (Texte u. Unters., 1911, 40,

289 f., where parallels are cited).
And see Orig. quoted by Swete.

6. καὶ ἠκυρώσατε κτλ.] Mk.
ἀκυροῦντες. A late word occurring in
Gal. iii. 17, 1 Esd. vi. 31, 4 Mac.⁶,
Aq.⁶, Sym.; Allen cites three Oxyr.
papyri of the 2nd cent. A.D. and
other passages. In Aq. it always
represents הָפֵר 'to break,' 'annul';
e.g. in Ps. cxviii. [cxix.] 126 ἠκύ-
ρωσαν τὸν νόμον σου. On the aor.
with a perf. force see Moulton, i. 140.
The reading λόγον (as in Mk.) has
the best early support; it refers to
the divinely inspired Pentateuch,
and does not differ in meaning from
νόμον. But the latter may have
arisen as a more exact parallel to
ἐντολήν (v. 3). The other v.l. (τὴ)ν)
ἐντολήν in the lesser uncials has
the same object. διὰ τ. παράδοσιν
ὑ. Mk. τῇ παραδόσει ὑμῶν ᾗ
παρεδώκατε. The διά need not
mean 'for the purpose of substituting
the tradition'; but that was in
practice the result of annulling God's
law. Mk. adds καὶ παρόμοια τοιαῦτα
πολλὰ ποιεῖτε, which may be due
to the hand that added καὶ ἄλλα
πολλά κτλ. in Mk. v. 4. Instances
in the Mishna which may be called
παρόμοια are seen in the system of
Erubin, whereby the law of the
Sabbath could be formally kept but
virtually annulled (see Schürer, HJP.
II. ii. 120 ff.).

Additional Note on xv. 1-6.

The passage is severely criticized by Montefiore (Syn. Gosp. i. 164 ff.).
He points out that the fulfilment of vows is laid down in the Pentateuch
(Deut. xxiii. 21 ff., Num. xxx. 2 ff.), and maintains that 'the annulling, not
the maintenance, of vows was the work of tradition,' so that while the
5th commandment in the Decalogue might clash with another Mosaic

τοῦ θεοῦ διὰ τὴν παράδοσιν ὑμῶν. ὑποκριταί, καλῶς 7
ἐπροφήτευσεν περὶ ὑμῶν Ἡσαίας λέγων

command, it could not be said to be abrogated by the scribal tradition. Further, he shews that 'according to the Rabbinic law as codified in the Mishna, and commented on in the Talmud, the Rabbis are on the side of Jesus, and take his very line.' *Nedar.* viii. 1 deals with two sorts of vows —a rash vow from which a man's father would not materially suffer, and a vow which definitely concerns his parents. In the former case the majority of the Rabbis, against R. Eliezer, declared the vow binding; in the latter they agreed with him that 'the door is opened to him (*i.e.* the vow may be annulled) on account of the honour of father and mother.'

But does not such a discussion imply that before the time of R. Eliezer the matter was very much an open question? To a large extent, no doubt, the Mishna was a codification of ancient material. But when the Rabbis differed, the Mishnic rule represented, as often as not, a compromise between the stricter and laxer view. It is precarious to argue that, because the majority of the Mishnic Rabbis had agreed to adopt a certain view, that must have been the prevailing one in the time of Jesus. The principle of making religion easier for the masses was, indeed, embraced by the school of Hillel and by its descendants after the fall of Jerusalem, and the annulling of vows was one of its results. But it is too much to say, with respect to the period of the Lord's life and earlier, that 'the annulling of vows was the work of tradition.' Even in the Mishna (*Chag.* i. 8) it is admitted that 'the rules concerning the dissolving of vows fly about in the air, and there is nothing upon which they can rest,' though some early teachers contrived to find biblical support for them (see Hart, *JQR.* xix. 643). The school of Shammai were opposed to laxity, and it is probable that the priestly, Sadducean, party were largely opposed to novelties in the scribal tradition. And before the destruction of the temple the priests, though their influence was on the wane, were naturally more powerful than afterwards. If, therefore, the Gospel narrative is substantially accurate, and it is the only approach to contemporary evidence that we possess, we must conclude that the annulling of vows was still a new movement advocated by only a small minority, who would agree with Jesus, while the tendency of the tradition was to place 'sacrifice' above 'mercy.' The Lord's reply to the complaint about 'unwashen hands' condemns, with a particular illustration, the effects produced by this tendency. It does not say that 'the horrid Rabbis taught that by a convenient vow a man might easily find a way of disobeying the fifth commandment' (Montefiore).

7–9. Mt. closes the denunciation with a reference to Isaiah ; in Mk. (*vv.* 6–8) this forms a separate and introductory section, in which *v.* 8 (om. in 𐤔 sin and by Mt.) is a doublet of *v.* 9. The section in Mk. is probably editorial, and Mt., by his transposition, uses it to the best advantage.

7. ὑποκριταί κτλ.] See on vi. 2. Mt. makes a vocative from Mk.'s ὑμῶν τ. ὑποκριτῶν. For καλῶς cf. the similar rebuke in Ac. xxviii. 25.

8   Ὁ λαὸς οὗτος τοῖς χείλεσίν με τιμᾷ,
       ἡ δὲ καρδία αὐτῶν πόρρω ἀπέχει ἀπ᾽ ἐμοῦ·
9   μάτην δὲ σέβονταί με,
       διδάσκοντες διδασκαλίας ἐντάλματα ἀνθρώπων.

10 Καὶ προσκαλεσάμενος τὸν ὄχλον εἶπεν αὐτοῖς Ἀκούετε καὶ
11 συνίετε· οὐ τὸ εἰσερχόμενον εἰς τὸ στόμα κοινοῖ τὸν ἄν-

8, 9. ὁ λαὸς οὗτος κτλ.] Mk. (perhaps) has οὗτος ὁ λ., but is otherwise identical. The quotation is from Is. xxix. 13. It shews no trace of the M.T. where it differs from the LXX.; the first clause of the LXX. is compressed, and the last (διδάσκοντες ἐντάλματα ἀνθρώπων καὶ διδασκαλίας) is rearranged. Cf. Col. ii. 22. διδασκαλίας κτλ., 'teaching [as their] teachings commandments of men.'

10, 11. (Mk. vii. 14 f.) *Teaching given to the people.*

10. καὶ προσκαλεσάμενος κτλ.] See on x. 1. The people have not been mentioned since the previous chapter. But Mk. adds πάλιν (which Mt. nearly always omits, Allen, p. xx.), connecting the discourse with the healings at Gennesaret. He seems to picture the people as retreating to the background when the Scribes appeared; but on the departure of the latter, Jesus summons them to approach again. But, as said above, the discourse probably belongs to Judaea, not to Galilee. ἀκούετε κ. συνίετε is an echo of xiii. 13 ff.

11. οὐ τὸ εἰσερχόμενον κτλ.] The great truth is stated first negatively and then positively. In Mk. the saying is gnomic and somewhat epigrammatic in form: 'there is nothing from outside a man entering into him which can defile him; but the things which come out of a man are they which defile a man.' Mt. makes it shorter, but more explicit. By inserting εἰς τὸ στόμα he defin-

itely refers to food, an aspect of the teaching which is not explicit in Mk. except in *v.* 19 (Mt. *v.* 17), εἰς τὴν κοιλίαν. He thus *interprets* the saying, so that it ceases to be a παραβολή (*v.* 15) needing explanation. The original utterance perhaps did not refer particularly to food, but was general in scope. Mk.'s εἰσπορευόμενον εἰς αὐτόν would easily be inserted under the influence of the following exposition.

As the passage stands, a concrete instance, that of *foods*, is employed to point the argument, and hence the evangelists have placed the passage in connexion with the question in *v.* 2. But it is important to notice that the Lord does not here oppose the scribal tradition, but the Mosaic law itself. The Jewish dietary laws were elaborated by the Rabbis, but were laid down in Lev. xi., and other laws on uncleanness in Lev. xiii.–xv.; cf. Hag. ii. 12 f. Jesus could rebuke the Scribes for annulling the Mosaic law, and yet, on this fundamental point, annulled it Himself. He felt free to commit Himself to this formal inconsistency, because the kernel of His teaching was that the spirit transcends the letter. The scribal tradition had the effect of exalting the external. His ethics subordinated it to the spiritual; and He made no exception in the case of Mosaic commands. The principle involved is well stated by Montefiore: 'Things cannot be religiously either clean or unclean; only persons. And persons cannot be defiled by things,

θρωπον, ἀλλὰ τὸ ἐκπορευόμενον ἐκ τοῦ στόματος τοῦτο
κοινοῖ τὸν ἄνθρωπον.   Τότε προσελθόντες οἱ μαθηταὶ 12
λέγουσιν αὐτῷ Οἶδας ὅτι οἱ Φαρισαῖοι ἀκούσαντες τὸν λόγον
ἐσκανδαλίσθησαν; ὁ δὲ ἀποκριθεὶς εἶπεν Πᾶσα φυτεία 13
ἣν οὐκ ἐφύτευσεν ὁ πατήρ μου ὁ οὐράνιος ἐκριζωθήσεται.
ἄφετε αὐτούς· τυφλοί εἰσιν ὁδηγοί· τυφλὸς δὲ τυφλὸν ἐὰν 14

14 τυφλοι εισιν οδηγοι] BD [Ⴝ cur]; add τυφλων אᵃLZ 1 13 33 124 346
𝕷 vet.*pler.*vg Ⴝ pesh. hcl me arm aeth ; οδ. εισ. τυφλοι א*ᵉᵗ ᵇ 209 ; οδ. εισ. τυφλων
K Ⴝ sin.[cur *vide* Burkitt] ; οδ. εισ. τυφλοι τυφλων CE *etc* 𝕷 q

they can only be defiled by them-
selves, by acting irreligiously' (*Syn.
Gosp.* i. 169; see the whole note).
'In Nature there's no blemish but
the mind' (Shakesp.); cf. Rom. xiv. 14.
Allen (p. 167) cites an interesting
Buddhist parallel.

κοινοῖ τὸν ἄνθρωπον] *i.e.* render
a man religiously ' common,' the reverse of sacred, and so unclean, incapable of performing religious acts. So
Heb. ix. 13 ; cf. Ac. xxi. 28 ; in the
LXX. only 4 Mac. vii. 6 (א), οὐδὲ τὴν
. . . γαστέρα ἐκοίνωσας μιαροφαγίᾳ.
'Verbum proprie scripturarum est,
et publico sermone non teritur' (Jer.).
For κοινός (cf. Mk. vii. 2) in this sense
cf. 1 Mac. i. 47, 62 ; elsewhere in the
LXX. usually ἀκάθαρτος; cf. Ac. x. 14,
28, xi. 8. τὸ ἐκπορευόμενον is the
spiritual counterpart of the material
τὸ εἰσερχόμενον ; and ἐκ τοῦ στόματος must not be confined to sinful
words ; it merely completes the verbal
parallelism, and is rightly interpreted
in *v.* 18 f.

12–20. *Teaching given to the
disciples.* 12–14 a are peculiar to
Mt.; 14 b has a parallel in Lk. vi.
39.

12. οἶδας κτλ.] *v.* 11 contains
probably no more than the crucial
point in a whole discourse delivered
to people ; not till that was ended
could the disciples, according to Mt.'s
grouping of the sayings, ask their
question, in which τὸν λόγον seems

to refer to *vv.* 3–6, which had sent
the Pharisees away ' scandalized,'
because the Lord had dealt with a
Rabbinic question ' with authority,
and not as the Scribes.' But *vv.* 12–
14 break the immediate connexion
of *v.* 15 with *v.* 11. Though the
Pharisees were doubtless scandalized
by the teaching contained in the latter
verse, *v.* 12 seems to be Mt.'s editorial
introduction to the sayings which he
here draws from other contexts. On
σκανδαλίζειν see v. 29.

13. πᾶσα φυτεία κτλ.] This
seems to refer to the Pharisees themselves, not to their tradition ; as in
the parable of the Sower and the
Tares, the plants are persons ; and
the time of their rooting out will be
the same as that when the tares are
gathered and burnt. φυτεία : only
here in the N.T. ; LXX., 4 Regn. xix.
29, Mic. i. 6, Ez. xvii. 7. Lit. the
'act of planting' (Plato, Xen.), it is
here equivalent to φύτευμα or φυτόν.
Ign. (*Trall.* xi., *Phil.* iii.) applies the
passage to heretics. *Asc. Is.* iv. 3 perhaps alludes to it, but with reference
to the Church, τὴν φ. ἣν φυτεύουσιν
οἱ δώδεκα ἀπόστολοι τοῦ ἀγαπητοῦ.
The metaphor recalls that of iii. 10 ;
cf. Lk. xiii. 6–9, Jo. xv. 1–8. Allen
cites a parallel in *Chag.* 15 a. For
' My heavenly Father' Ⴝ sin has
' the Father which is in Heaven ' ; see
on vi. 9.

14. ἄφετε κτλ.] ' Be not disturbed

15 ὁδηγῇ, ἀμφότεροι εἰς βόθυνον πεσοῦνται. Ἀποκριθεὶς δὲ
16 ὁ Πέτρος εἶπεν αὐτῷ Φράσον ἡμῖν τὴν παραβολήν. ὁ
17 δὲ εἶπεν Ἀκμὴν καὶ ὑμεῖς ἀσύνετοί ἐστε; οὐ νοεῖτε ὅτι

at their disapproval; it is worthless, because they are blind leaders.' The reading is doubtful (see Appar.). The text, or ὁδ. εἰ. τυφλοί, accords with xxiii. 24. On the other hand S. Paul (Rom. ii. 19) refers to the boast of the Jewish teacher ὁδηγὸν εἶναι τυφλῶν, which may have been proverbial (Sanday and Headlam). Possibly, therefore, the true reading is ὁδηγοί εἰσιν τυφλων or τυφλῶν εἰ ὁδ. They are 'leaders of the blind; you can therefore disregard them, because you are not blind.' The common reading ὁδηγοί εἰσι τυφλοὶ τυφλῶν is either a conflation, or perhaps due to τυφλὸς τυφλόν in the following proverb. Classical parallels are given by Wetstein.

τυφλὸς δέ κτλ.] Lk. vi. 39 has 'And He spake a parable unto them: Can a blind (man) lead a blind (man)? Will they not both fall into a ditch?' This occurs in Lk.'s Sermon on the Plain, but the introductory formula suggests that that was not the original context. Perhaps neither evangelist has it in its true position; but Lk.'s interrogative form is characteristic of the Lord's utterances. 'To fall into a pit' is a proverbial expression in the O.T.; cf. Is. xxiv. 18, Jer. xxxi. [xlviii.] 44, Ps. vii. 15, Prov. xxvi. 27.

15. ἀποκριθείς κτλ.] Mk. here begins the teaching to the disciples; he places the words in their mouth 'when He had gone into the house from the crowd.' On Mt.'s omission of 'the house' see viii. 16; and on the prominence given to S. Peter see x. 2. τὴν παραβολήν is the saying in v. 11, which Mt., however, has already interpreted (see above). On παραβολή see n. before ch. xiii.

16. ἀκμήν κτλ.] An adv. acc. (Blass, § 34. 7), 'at the acme, the prime, the critical moment,' and so 'at the present moment,' 'yet,' = ἔτι (Lob. Phryn. 123); 𝕷 adhuc. It is frequent in Polyb. and later Gk. See M.-M. Vocab. s.v. Mk. οὕτως, 'even so,' in spite of all My teaching. καὶ ὑμεῖς 'ye also' as well as the people (cf. Jo. vi. 67). ἀσύνετοί 'lacking in intelligence' (see Lightfoot on σύνεσις Col. 1. 9) looks back to συνίετε (v. 10) and recalls οὐδὲ συνίουσιν (xiii. 13). Contrast συνετοί (xi. 25).

17. οὐ νοεῖτε κτλ.] The explanation now given adds nothing essentially new to the παραβολή in v. 11 as Mt. has it (see note). Of the problems raised for the first Christians by the Jewish laws concerning clean and unclean none were more pressing than those dealing with foods; and the Lord's great saying would soon be quoted and expounded especially in that connexion; vv. 17–20, therefore, are probably not a genuine utterance of Jesus, but a popular exposition. Mt. omits Mk.'s v. 18 b (which repeats the saying uttered to the people), and abbreviates v. 19, but with the addition εἰς τὸ στόμα as before.

εἰς τ. κοιλίαν χωρεῖ] 'it goeth (merely) into the belly,' i.e. 'not into the heart,' as Mk. says. ἀφεδρών (see M.-M. Vocab. s.v.), connected with ἄφεδρος (Lev. xii. 5), is generally taken to be equivalent to ἄφοδος or ἀπόπατος, secessus (Vulg.). Wellh. holds that εἰς ἀφ. ἐκβάλλεται (Mk. ἐκπορεύεται) misrepresents the Aram. ל נפק 'goes out of' (see viii. 12 note), and explains ἀφ. as the 'intestine,' its physiological function being referred to in Mk.'s καθαρίζων πάντα τὰ

πᾶν τὸ εἰσπορευόμενον εἰς τὸ στόμα εἰς τὴν κοιλίαν χωρεῖ
καὶ εἰς ἀφεδρῶνα ἐκβάλλεται; τὰ δὲ ἐκπορευόμενα ἐκ τοῦ 18
στόματος ἐκ τῆς καρδίας ἐξέρχεται, κἀκεῖνα κοινοῖ τὸν
ἄνθρωπον. ἐκ γὰρ τῆς καρδίας ἐξέρχονται διαλογισμοὶ 19
πονηροί, φόνοι, μοιχεῖαι, πορνεῖαι, κλοπαί, ψευδομαρτυρίαι,
βλασφημίαι. ταῦτά ἐστιν τὰ κοινοῦντα τὸν ἄνθρωπον, τὸ 20
δὲ ἀνίπτοις χερσὶν φαγεῖν οὐ κοινοῖ τὸν ἄνθρωπον.

βρώματα. But Mk. would surely have written καθαρίζοντα. If, as most writers think, Mk.'s clause is a comment referring to Jesus Himself, it may have been a late addition, 'shewing how the author viewed the Antioch controversy in the apostolic church' (Moffatt), or Mt. may have wished to avoid the admission that Jesus was opposed to the Mosaic law; see on v. 20. The point of the passage is that the belly is not the real man, so that food which enters the former cannot affect the latter. On the unwise use made of the principle by 'liberal' Christians in S. Paul's day see Lake, *Earlier Epp. of S. Paul*, 177, 381.

18. τὰ δέ κτλ.] Mt. mentions 'the mouth' for the fourth time; Mk. ἐκ τ. ἀνθρώπου. But *words* are far from exhausting the contents of the heart, as the following verse, and still more Mk.'s list, shew.

19. ἐκ γὰρ κτλ.] Evil thoughts 'come forth from the heart' only when they issue in action; Mt. therefore, after διαλ. πον., selects external actions, in the form of six plurals. Mk. has οἱ διαλ. οἱ κακοί, *i.e.* all those contents of the heart which are evil, and then specifies, without the article, twelve details, six plur. and six sing. Except for βλασφημίαι Mt. follows the order of the Decalogue in M.T. and LXX.[A] (see on v. 27). Swete compares the catalogues of sin in Wisd. xiv. 25 f., Rom. i. 29 ff., Gal. v. 20 f., Eph. iv.

31, v. 3 ff., Col. iii. 5 ff., *Did.* v., Herm. *Mand.* viii. 5. The first of these has in common with Mt., Mk. murder, theft, adultery, and, with Mk., lasciviousness.

20. ταῦτα κτλ.] The first half of the verse abbreviates Mk.; the second, absent from Mk., is added by Mt. to recall the circumstance in connexion with which the discourse is placed. The effect is to represent *vv.* 10–20 as aimed not against the Mosaic law, but against the scribal tradition.

21–28. (Mk. vii. 24–30.) THE CANAANITE WOMAN.

The literary history of the narrative is disputed; *e.g.* it is held that Mt. derived it, except v. 21, from Q (B. Weiss), or, possibly, that Mt. and Mk. derived it independently from different recensions of Q (Loisy); most writers, however, agree that Mt. wrote it on the basis of Mk. Its absence from Lk. is due either to its absence from the form of Mk. which Lk. employed (Wendling), or, more probably, to intentional omission by Lk. because it would not be acceptable to his Gentile readers (Hawkins, Stanton). If Mt. had no other source than Mk., he contributes an unusual amount from his own pen, and that of a highly artistic and dramatic character. The incident must have possessed a profound interest for him. The style and vocabulary are full of his characteristic features.

21   Καὶ ἐξελθὼν ἐκεῖθεν ὁ Ἰησοῦς ἀνεχώρησεν εἰς τὰ μέρη
22Τύρου καὶ Σιδῶνος. Καὶ ἰδοὺ γυνὴ Χαναναία ἀπὸ τῶν
ὁρίων ἐκείνων ἐξελθοῦσα ἔκραζεν λέγουσα Ἐλέησόν με,
κύριε υἱὸς Δαυείδ· ἡ θυγάτηρ μου κακῶς δαιμονίζεται.
23ὁ δὲ οὐκ ἀπεκρίθη αὐτῇ λόγον.   καὶ προσελθόντες οἱ

22 εκραζεν] ℵᵃBD 1 𝕷 c ff¹ k q 𝕾 cur.diatᴱᵖʰ·[pesh. pal 'came out crying'];
εκραξεν ℵ*Z 13 124 ; εκραυγασεν CE al [(ex)clamavit 𝕷 a e f ff² g¹·² vg 𝕾 sin.hcl]

21. καὶ ἐξελθών κτλ.] ἐκεῖθεν
refers to Gennesaret. τ. μέρη Τ. κ.
Σ. is Mt.'s general expression for
Phoenicia, which bounded Galilee
on the north (Jos. BJ. III. iii. 1);
but Mk. distinguishes τὰ ὅρια Τύρου
from Sidon (cf. Mk. v. 31). ἀνεχώρησεν εἰς and Mk.'s ἀπῆλθεν εἰς
mean different things; in Mt. Jesus
went only in the direction of the
foreign country, in Mk. He (apparently) entered it: 'and having
entered into a house, He wished no
one to know, and could not be hid.'
Mt. avoids not only the mention of
a house (see on viii. 16), but especially
of a house in a foreign country, and
also the statement that Jesus was
unable to do something that He
wished (cf. xiv. 24).
22. καὶ ἰδού κτλ.] The Canaanites,
including the Phoenicians, were the
ancient pre-Israelite occupiers of
Palestine; hence Mt. shews his biblical
and archaeological interest by writing
Χαναναία for Mk.'s accurate Ἑλληνίς,
Συροφοινίκισσα (see Swete). Jos.
(c. Ap. i. 13) says: 'Of the Phoenicians
the Tyrians have had the most ill-
feeling towards us.' Mt. omits as
self-evident Mk.'s ἀκούσασα περὶ
αὐτοῦ, but characteristically represents her as knowing of Jesus as
'Son of David' (see on xii. 23).
ἀπὸ τῶν ὁρίων κτλ.] Jesus did
not, as in Mk., enter a house in
Phoenicia where the woman 'entered
and fell at His feet'; on the contrary,
she came out from Phoenicia to Jesus

who was still in Galilee; at first she
kept on crying (if ἔκραζεν is the right
reading) from a distance, but at
last approached and did obeisance.
On κύριε (so Mk. here only) see vii.
21. Mt. avoids Mk.'s diminutive
θυγάτριον (cf. ix. 18), and πνεῦμα
ἀκάθαρτον (see on x. 1).
23. ὁ δέ κτλ.] This and the
next verse are peculiar to Mt., and
have led some to think that Mt.
was dependent upon a source other
than Mk.; they stand or fall with
Mt.'s statements which represent
the woman as crying after Jesus in
the road. Mt. seems to have been
strongly impressed with the limitation of the Lord's ministry to Jews;
and he pictures, with artistic skill, a
scene which emphasizes it, heighten-
ing, by the series of delays on His
part, the woman's final success.
Jesus was silent, trying her faith.
J. Weiss thinks that He was engaged
in internal debate whether to allow
His compassion to override the
limits of His mission.
καὶ προσελθόντες κτλ.] ἐρωτᾶν
(usually 'to ask a question') means 'to
ask for, beseech' in xvi. 1, Mk. vii. 26,
Lk.⁹, Jo.¹²; in the LXX., Ps. cxxxvi.
(cxxxvii.) 3, and in the expression
ἐρ. τὰ εἰς εἰρήνην. Cf. Jos. Ant.
VII. viii. 1. Allen cites a Fayûm
papyrus, and passages from inscriptions. On the form ἠρώτουν see
Blass, § 22. 1. ἀπόλυσον αὐτήν:
'Do what she asks, so that she
may go away'; cf. Lk. xiv. 4.

μαθηταὶ αὐτοῦ ἠρώτουν αὐτὸν λέγοντες Ἀπόλυσον αὐτήν,
ὅτι κράζει ὄπισθεν ἡμῶν. ὁ δὲ ἀποκριθεὶς εἶπεν Οὐκ 24
ἀπεστάλην εἰ μὴ εἰς τὰ πρόβατα τὰ ἀπολωλότα οἴκου
Ἰσραήλ. ἡ δὲ ἐλθοῦσα προσεκύνει αὐτῷ λέγουσα Κύριε, 25
βοήθει μοι. ὁ δὲ ἀποκριθεὶς εἶπεν Οὐκ ἔστιν καλὸν 26
λαβεῖν τὸν ἄρτον τῶν τέκνων καὶ βαλεῖν τοῖς κυναρίοις.
ἡ δὲ εἶπεν Ναί, κύριε, καὶ γὰρ τὰ κυνάρια ἐσθίει ἀπὸ 27

27 γαρ] om B 𝕷 e 𝕊 sin.pesh.pal.diat^Eph

'Sic solebat Jesus dimittere' (Beng.).
Their request may have arisen from
mere annoyance or from their
knowledge that He always repressed
public excitement about Himself.

24. οὐκ ἀπεστάλην κτλ.] See
the corresponding injunction to the
apostles (x. 6). If this was uttered
for the woman to overhear, it was
for the further trying of her faith.
On the view that the Lord was
debating in His mind what to do
(see above), His answer expresses a
continuance of the struggle. On
οὐκ ... εἰ μή see xii. 24.

25. ἡ δὲ ἐλθοῦσα κτλ.] The
woman has hitherto been at a distance, but at last approaches, the
dramatic cry of v. 22 giving place
to the simple appeal 'Sir, help me.'
On the force of the impf. προσεκύνει
see Blass, § 57. 4. Mk. εἰσελθοῦσα
(sc. into the house) προσέπεσεν πρὸς
τοὺς πόδας αὐτοῦ.

26. οὐκ ἔστιν καλόν κτλ.] The
Lord's power of healing was not a
fixed quantity, such that He would
rob Jews if He expended it upon a
Gentile; He simply uses, as so often,
a homely metaphor; it would not
be right to give the household food
to dogs. This may express a continuation either of His own mental
struggle, or, more probably, of the
woman's trial. But if the words
were audible to her, we may be sure
that a half-humorous tenderness of
manner would deprive them of all

their sting. Mk. prefixes 'Let the
children first be fed.' It must
remain doubtful whether this was a
later addition, made at a time when
Gentiles had begun to be 'fed,' or
whether Mt., with his Judaic leanings,
omitted it. But the former is the
more probable, because the πρῶτον,
though full of meaning for the Christian reader, would have little for the
woman. The dimin. κυνάριον need
not express contempt; it would
denote a household pet; τὰ κυνίδια
τῆς οἰκίας (Orig.); cf. τραπεζῆες
κύνες (Hom.). But the Aram. would
have no diminutive; Jesus may have
meant dogs in general, and the
woman first introduced the thought
of pet dogs—'the dogs under the
table' (Mk.).

27. ναί, κύριε κτλ.] ναί denies
οὐκ ἔστιν καλόν: 'Yes, it is! for
the very dogs eat, etc.' On καὶ
γάρ see viii. 9. If γάρ is omitted,
as in Mk., ναί acquiesces: 'Yes, that
is true! and yet the dogs, etc.'
Similarly with the v.l. in Mk.
ἀλλὰ καί (D 𝕷). Swete explains
differently, holding that Jesus, with
the word κυνάριον, purposely gave
the woman a door of hope, through
which she was not slow to enter.
κυρίων emphasizes, even more than
Mk.'s παιδίων, the superiority of
Jew to Gentile. The Hebraic ἐσθίειν
ἀπό (אכל מן), frequent in the LXX., is
not found elsewhere in the N.T.;
cf. ἐσθ. ἐκ (1 Cor. ix. 7, xi. 28).

τῶν ψιχίων τῶν πιπτόντων ἀπὸ τῆς τραπέζης τῶν κυρίων
28 αὐτῶν. τότε ἀποκριθεὶς ὁ Ἰησοῦς εἶπεν αὐτῇ Ὦ γύναι,
μεγάλη σου ἡ πίστις· γενηθήτω σοι ὡς θέλεις. καὶ ἰάθη
ἡ θυγάτηρ αὐτῆς ἀπὸ τῆς ὥρας ἐκείνης.

29 Καὶ μεταβὰς ἐκεῖθεν ὁ Ἰησοῦς ἦλθεν παρὰ τὴν θάλασσαν
30 τῆς Γαλιλαίας, καὶ ἀναβὰς εἰς τὸ ὄρος ἐκάθητο ἐκεῖ. καὶ
προσῆλθον αὐτῷ ὄχλοι πολλοὶ ἔχοντες μεθ' ἑαυτῶν χωλούς,
κυλλούς, τυφλούς, κωφούς, καὶ ἑτέρους πολλούς, καὶ ἔριψαν
αὐτοὺς παρὰ τοὺς πόδας αὐτοῦ, καὶ ἐθεράπευσεν αὐτούς·
31 ὥστε τὸν ὄχλον θαυμάσαι βλέποντας κωφοὺς λαλοῦντας

With τ. πιπτ. ἀπὸ τ. τραπέζης cf.
Lk. xvi. 21. After αὐτῶν, Ϭ vet.pesh
add 'and live' (not in Mk.).

28. τότε κτλ.] Mt. and Mk.
describe the close of the incident
independently, Mt. echoing the
language used in other accounts of
cures, and emphasizing the woman's
'faith' (see on viii. 10). Mk. has
'On account of this saying go, the
demon hath gone out from thy
daughter. And departing to her
house she found the child laid upon
the bed and the demon gone out.'
As in the only other instance of the
cure of a Gentile (viii. 13), the
authoritative word is spoken at a
distance from the sufferer; and the
remark made there with regard to
the miracle applies here.

29–31. HEALINGS BY THE LAKE.
This takes the place of Mk. vii.
31–37, the healing of a deaf and
dumb man, which Mt. avoids,
probably for three reasons: (1) Jesus
used material means, saliva, in
connexion with the cure (see on xvi.
12); (2) He groaned; (3) He gave
repeated commands which were not
obeyed. For similar summaries of
miracles see on iv. 23.

29. καὶ μεταβάς κτλ.] Mk. has
two geographical notices, διὰ Σιδῶνος
and ἀνὰ μέσον τῶν ὁρίων Δεκαπόλεως.
See Swete on the route. Well-

hausen's suggestion that an original
בציד meant not 'via Sidon' but 'to
Bethsaida' is unnecessary. The
Lord made a long detour to avoid
the dominion of Antipas (see Burkitt,
Gosp. Hist. 92 f.). Mt. omits this
northern route, because he avoided
relating that Jesus entered the
Tyrian district (see v. 21). He thus
has nothing to shew that τὸ ὄρος
was on the E. of the lake, except
that v. 31 implies that the crowd
was Gentile. The journey must
have lasted some months; at the
feeding of the 5000 the grass was
green, and the arrival at the lake
was soon followed by the journey to
Jerusalem at the time of the Passover.
Having left the crowds, and His
enemies, Jesus at last had an
opportunity of teaching His disciples.

30. χωλούς κτλ.] The order
differs in groups of uncials, and
cannot be determined with certainty.
The reading ὑπὸ τ. πόδ. (D 𝕷 b) is
accepted by some writers, and understood literally, reference being made
to the custom among modern
dervishes (Merx ad loc.; Weinrich,
Antike Heilungswunder, 67–73). But
it need only refer to the position
which Jesus occupied on the slope
of the hill. Cf. Jam. ii. 3.

31. ὥστε κτλ.] Apart from the
last clause, the verse echoes Mk. vii. 37.
'The God of Israel' implies that

καὶ χωλοὺς περιπατοῦντας καὶ τυφλοὺς βλέποντας· καὶ
ἐδόξασαν τὸν θεὸν Ἰσραήλ.　Ὁ δὲ Ἰησοῦς προσ- 32
καλεσάμενος τοὺς μαθητὰς αὐτοῦ εἶπεν Σπλαγχνίζομαι ἐπὶ
τὸν ὄχλον, ὅτι ἤδη ἡμέραι τρεῖς προσμένουσίν μοι καὶ
οὐκ ἔχουσιν τί φάγωσιν· καὶ ἀπολῦσαι αὐτοὺς νήστεις οὐ
θέλω, μή ποτε ἐκλυθῶσιν ἐν τῇ ὁδῷ. καὶ λέγουσιν αὐτῷ 33
οἱ μαθηταί Πόθεν ἡμῖν ἐν ἐρημίᾳ ἄρτοι τοσοῦτοι ὥστε
χορτάσαι ὄχλον τοσοῦτον; καὶ λέγει αὐτοῖς ὁ Ἰησοῦς 34
Πόσους ἄρτους ἔχετε; οἱ δὲ εἶπαν Ἑπτά, καὶ ὀλίγα
ἰχθύδια. καὶ παραγγείλας τῷ ὄχλῳ ἀναπεσεῖν ἐπὶ τὴν γῆν 35
ἔλαβεν τοὺς ἑπτὰ ἄρτους καὶ τοὺς ἰχθύας καὶ εὐχαριστήσας 36
ἔκλασεν καὶ ἐδίδου τοῖς μαθηταῖς οἱ δὲ μαθηταὶ τοῖς ὄχλοις.

the crowd was mainly Gentile, such
as would be found in the hellenized
cities of Gaulonitis on the E. of the
lake. It is an O.T. expression, cf.
Ps. xl. [xli.] 14, echoed in Lk. i. 68 ;
cf. Ac. xiii. 17.

32–38. (Mk. viii. 1–9.) FEEDING OF THE FOUR THOUSAND.

The marked similarity to the
account of the 5000 (xiv. 13–21)
suggests that they are duplicates
of the same story. See Add. note
after xvi. 12 on the series of narratives
in xv. 32–xvi. 12 in their relation
to those in xiv. 13–xv. 31. It is
often supposed, from the locality,
that the 4000 were Gentiles ; but the
locality in the former story was
practically the same ; the 5000
were Galileans who had followed
Jesus into the foreign territory.
The notes on this section should be
supplemented throughout by those
on xiv. 13–21.

32. ὁ δὲ Ἰησοῦς κτλ.] Jesus here
takes the initiative, in xiv. 15 the
disciples. ἤδη ἡμ. τρεῖς is grammatically a parenthesis (Blass, § 33. 2) ;
this is simpler than to supply εἰσίν,
making προσμέν. and ἔχ. dat. plur.
D has ἤ. ἡμ. τρ. εἰσὶν καὶ προσμέν.

The account in ch. xiv. does not
mention the three days. προσμέν.
μοι, 'they cling, attach themselves,
to me' ; Vulg. perseverant mecum ;
cf. Ac. xi. 23, xiii. 43. οὐκ ἔχουσιν
κτλ. : they had not fasted for three
days, but had finished all the food
that they had with them, and now
had nothing. ἀπολῦσαι . . . οὐ θέλω
for Mk.'s ἐὰν ἀπολύσω 'heightens
the note of mastery and dignity of
Christ's words' (Allen). Mk.'s
addition 'and some of them have
come from far' is in keeping with
the other account, in which
Galileans followed the Lord from
the west of the lake.

33. πόθεν κτλ.] In the other
account the touch of sarcasm in Mk.,
Lk. is suppressed by Mt., but here, and
in Mk. viii. 4, it is still discernible.
ἡμῖν cannot mean ' We cannot do it,
but [because of the previous miracle]
we know that Thou canst' (Plummer).
Mk. has simply τις.

34. πόσους κτλ.] Mk. has the
same question in the other account
also, where Mt. omits it. In the
answer, Mt. abbreviates Mk. by
adding καὶ ὀλ. ἰχθ., which Mk.
mentions separately, and with a
separate εὐλογία.

37 καὶ ἔφαγον πάντες καὶ ἐχορτάσθησαν, καὶ τὸ περισσεῦον
38 τῶν κλασμάτων ἦραν ἑπτὰ σφυρίδας πλήρεις. οἱ δὲ ἐσθίοντες
ἦσαν τετρακισχίλιοι ἄνδρες χωρὶς γυναικῶν καὶ παιδίων.
39 Καὶ ἀπολύσας τοὺς ὄχλους ἐνέβη εἰς τὸ πλοῖον, καὶ ἦλθεν
εἰς τὰ ὅρια Μαγαδάν.
XVI. 1 Καὶ προσελθόντες οἱ Φαρισαῖοι καὶ Σαδδουκαῖοι πειρά-

37. καὶ ἔφαγον κτλ.] Identical
with xiv. 20, except ἑπτὰ σφυρίδας
for δώδεκα κοφίνους, and the transposition of ἦραν. The σφυρίς (cf.
Ac. ix. 25) did not differ from the
κόφινος in size, but in material, and
to a certain extent in use. It was a
flexible mat basket (*sporta, sportula*;
the former always in 𝔏 in N.T.),
employed for carrying fish or fruit;
it was often part of a fisherman's
equipment. κόφινοι also, however,
are mentioned as receptacles for
fragments of food after a meal (*e.g.*
Pollux, vi. 94, vii. 173). On the
late form (for σπυρίς) see WH. *Notes*,
148. It occurs in papyri (Deissm.
Bible St. 158, 185).

38. οἱ δέ κτλ.] Mt. alone mentions the women and children, as in
xiv. 21.

39. (Mk. viii. 10.) RETURN TO
THE WEST OF THE LAKE.

καὶ ἀπολύσας κτλ.] Mk.'s μετὰ
τῶν μαθητῶν αὐτοῦ is omitted as
self-evident; cf. xiv. 13. τὸ πλοῖον
has the generic article; no boat
has been mentioned; cf. Mk. vi. 32.
In such cases B generally omits the
article.

εἰς τὰ ὅρια Μαγαδάν] Mk. εἰς
τὰ μέρη Δαλμανουθά (contrast *v.* 21,
where Mt. has μέρη, Mk. ὅρια).
Neither place has been identified.
Aug., finding *Magedan* in some MSS.
of Mk., assumed 'eundem locum esse
sub utroque nomine.' Eus. *Onom.*,
Μάρκος δὲ τῆς Μεγαιδὰν μνημονεύει·
καί ἐστι νῦν ἡ Μαγαιδανὴ περὶ τὴν
Γερᾶσαν, would locate it on the east

of the lake; but the authorities
would be unlikely to seek Jesus (xvi.
1 ff.) in what was practically pagan
territory. The reading Μαγδαλά in
the lesser uncials (Mt.) and in 1 13 etc.
(Mk.) substitutes a well-known for
an unknown name; it was within a
Sabbath day's journey of Tiberias
(*Enc. Bibl. s.v.* 'Magdala'). Swete
refers to Jos. xv. 37, where
מִגְדַּל־ is represented by Μαγαδά (B)
and Μαγδάλ (A). Various suggestions have been made with regard to
'Dalmanutha': it is a doublet of
εἰς τὰ μέρη, ܠܕܠܡܢܘܬܐ (R. Harris,
Cod. Bez. 178; see Nestle, *Phil. Sacr.*
17), or a corruption of Μαγδαλουθά
(Dalm. *Gram.* 133 n.; see *Words*, 66),
or of Migdal-nunya, 'Fish-tower,' a
place near Tiberias (Cheyne, *Enc.
Bibl.* 1635), or that τὰ μέρη Δ. is a
corruption of Τιβεριάδα Ἀμαθοῦς or
something similar (Burkitt, *AJTh.*,
1911, 174). Whatever the name
was, the place probably lay on the
western shore.

xvi. 1, 2 a, 4. (Mk. viii. 11–13;
cf. Mt. xii. 38–42, Lk. xi. 29–32.)
A SIGN REFUSED. Lk. omits the
Marcan version, having already given
that from Q.

1. καὶ προσελθόντες κτλ.] Mk.
κ. ἐξῆλθον (cf. Mk. iii. 6) οἱ Φαρ.
Mt.'s addition of the Sadducees is in
keeping with *vv.* 6, 11 f. On the
sect see Add. n. after xxii. 33. The
religious and ecclesiastical authorities
combined against Jesus, as against
the Baptist (see on iii. 7). Mk., on the
other hand (*v.* 15, as in iii. 6), couples

ζοντες ἐπηρώτησαν αὐτὸν σημεῖον ἐκ τοῦ οὐρανοῦ ἐπιδεῖξαι αὐτοῖς. ὁ δὲ ἀποκριθεὶς εἶπεν αὐτοῖς ['Οψίας γενομένης 2 λέγετε Εὐδία, πυρράζει γὰρ ὁ οὐρανός· καὶ πρωί Σήμερον 3 χειμών, πυρράζει γὰρ στυγνάζων ὁ οὐρανός. τὸ μὲν πρόσωπον τοῦ οὐρανοῦ γινώσκετε διακρίνειν, τὰ δὲ σημεῖα τῶν καιρῶν οὐ δύνασθε.] Γενεὰ πονηρὰ καὶ μοιχαλὶς σημεῖον 4 ἐπιζητεῖ, καὶ σημεῖον οὐ δοθήσεται αὐτῇ εἰ μὴ τὸ σημεῖον Ἰωνᾶ. καὶ καταλιπὼν αὐτοὺς ἀπῆλθεν. Καὶ ἐλθόντες 5 οἱ μαθηταὶ εἰς τὸ πέραν ἐπελάθοντο ἄρτους λαβεῖν. ὁ δὲ 6 Ἰησοῦς εἶπεν αὐτοῖς Ὁρᾶτε καὶ προσέχετε ἀπὸ τῆς ζύμης

2, 3 οψιας...δυνασθε] om אBVXΓ 13* 124* al codd.pler. ap. Hier 𐤔 sin.cur arm

---

the Pharisees with Herod, *i.e.* the religious and civil authorities. In Mt. xii. 38 (see note) it is the Scribes and Pharisees who ask for a sign. On ἐρωτᾷν 'beseech' see xv. 23.

2 a. ὁ δὲ . . . εἶπεν] Mk.'s expression of emotion καὶ ἀναστενάξας τῷ πνεύματι αὐτοῦ is avoided ; see on viii. 3. The reply is given in *v.* 4.

2 b, 3. (Lk. xii. 54–56.) The MS. authority is decisive against the genuineness of the passage. It appears to be an imitation of Lk., but refers to the *colour* of the clouds, not to the direction in which the wind blows them. Zahn suggests that it, together with Mk. xvi. 9–20 and Jo. viii. 1–11,' was due to Papias. πυρράζειν appears to be Byzantine (LXX. πυρρίζειν, Lev. xiii. 19, 42 f.). στυγνάζειν is used of human emotion (Ez. xxvii. 35, xxxii. 10 = שׁמם, Mk. x. 22), and so στυγνότης in Polyb. IV. xxi. 1 ; but στυγνός is an epithet of the night in Wisd. xvii. 5. γινώσκειν with inf. 'to understand how to' (cf. Is. vii. 15, viii. 4) is unique in the N.T. For τὰ σημ. τ. καιρῶν Lk. has τὸν καιρὸν τοῦτον, which points more distinctly to the imminence of the new age.

4. γενεά κτλ.] See xi. 16, and for the whole answer see on xii. 38 f. It avoids Mk.'s question, 'Why doth this generation seek a sign ?' (see on viii. 29), and it adds 'except the sign of Jonah.' ἀπῆλθεν abbreviates Mk.'s ἐμβὰς ἀπῆλθεν εἰς τὸ πέραν, but places εἰς τὸ πέραν in the next verse.

5–12. (Mk. viii. 14–21, Lk. xii. 1.) CONVERSATION ABOUT LEAVEN.

5. καὶ ἐλθόντες κτλ.] Mt. adds οἱ μαθηταί, perhaps 'to make it clear that the subject of ἐπελάθοντο did not include Christ' (Allen). The transference of εἰς τὸ πέραν makes the conversation to be held not in the boat (Mk.), which Mt. does not mention, but after the arrival at the other side of the lake ; but if they had already reached Bethsaida (Mk. *v.* 22) they could at once buy bread. Mk. adds, 'and they had not save one loaf (ἕνα ἄρτον) with them in the boat,' which J. Weiss fancifully suggests was a mystical addition of a Johannine type, referring to Christ as the Bread of Life.

6. ὁρᾶτε κτλ.] See on viii. 4. On προσέχετε ἀπό (Mk. βλέπετε ἀπό) see x. 17. Mk. has 'the leaven of the Pharisees and the leaven of Herod,' which is obscure. It is not even certain

7 τῶν Φαρισαίων καὶ Σαδδουκαίων. οἱ δὲ διελογίζοντο ἐν
8 ἑαυτοῖς λέγοντες ὅτι Ἄρτους οὐκ ἐλάβομεν. γνοὺς δὲ ὁ
Ἰησοῦς εἶπεν Τί διαλογίζεσθε ἐν ἑαυτοῖς, ὀλιγόπιστοι, ὅτι
9 ἄρτους οὐκ ἔχετε; οὔπω νοεῖτε, οὐδὲ μνημονεύετε τοὺς
πέντε ἄρτους τῶν πεντακισχιλίων καὶ πόσους κοφίνους
10 ἐλάβετε; οὐδὲ τοὺς ἑπτὰ ἄρτους τῶν τετρακισχιλίων καὶ
11 πόσας σφυρίδας ἐλάβετε; πῶς οὐ νοεῖτε ὅτι οὐ περὶ ἄρτων
εἶπον ὑμῖν; προσέχετε δὲ ἀπὸ τῆς ζύμης τῶν Φαρισαίων
12 καὶ Σαδδουκαίων. τότε συνῆκαν ὅτι οὐκ εἶπεν προσέχειν

whether two different kinds of leaven
are meant. If it is one kind only,
it may refer to their striving after
political power (Wendt), or, more
probably, to their hostility to Jesus,
which had caused so hurried a departure that bread had been forgotten (see
note after v. 12). Mt., substituting
'Sadducees' for 'Herod,' interprets
'leaven' as 'teaching' (v. 12). In
Lk., where the warning, delivered
in the presence of the people, has no
connexion with lack of bread, but
follows a statement (xi. 53 f.) that
the Scribes and Pharisees tried to
catch Jesus in His talk, 'the leaven
of the Pharisees' is explained by
'which is hypocrisy.'

7. οἱ δέ κτλ.] ἐν ἑαυτοῖς, Mk.
πρὸς ἀλλήλους; see on xxi. 25 b.
This verse is probably the continuation of v. 5, and means simply 'they
were [anxiously] discussing among
themselves, saying (ὅτι recit.), We
did not bring any bread.' This
being due to the hurried departure
from the hostility of the authorities,
and the warning about leaven referring to the same, they were
wrongly combined in the Marcan
tradition, so that the disciples are
represented as thinking, with extraordinary obtuseness, that Jesus meant
'leaven' literally. As it stands, ὅτι
ἄρτ. οὐκ ἐλάβομεν (Mk. ἔχομεν) may
express surprise at the warning, when
they had no bread of any kind with

them (ὅτι recit.), or it may be
elliptical: '[He said that] because we
have taken, etc.' (see Kühner-Gerth,
ii. 371 n. 4).

8. γνοὺς δέ κτλ.] The Lord
rebukes them for want of trust, in
being anxious about bread in spite
of the miracles which they had seen.
On ὀλιγόπιστοι see vi. 30.

9. οὔπω κτλ.] In Mk. the rebuke
is more severe; it speaks of their
heart as 'hardened' (πεπωρωμένην),
and echoes the rebuke in Mk. iv. 12
(Mt. xiii. 13 ff.). On Mt.'s avoidance
of this severity see viii. 26. By
doing so he makes μνημονεύετε
govern the following acc. (cf. 1 Thes.
ii. 9, Apoc. xviii. 5). ἐλάβετε (and
in v. 10) is chosen as a parallel with
λαβεῖν (v. 5) and ἐλάβομεν (v. 7).
Mk.'s ἤρατε is the verb employed in
all the synoptic accounts of the two
miracles. Mt. omits (and in v. 10)
the disciples' reply: Mk. λέγουσιν
αὐτῷ δώδεκα and καὶ λέγουσιν
ἑπτά.

10. οὐδέ κτλ.] The evangelists
frame the words to refer to the two
miracles as separate events.

11, 12. πῶς κτλ.] Mk. closes the
incident with καὶ ἔλεγεν αὐτοῖς·
πῶς οὐ νοεῖτε; Mt. adds two verses
to explain the occurrence of the
warning of v. 6 in the context in
which he found it placed by Mk.
τῶν ἄρτων (v. 12) is probably a gloss,
to make it clear that literal leaven

ἀπὸ τῆς ζύμης τῶν ἄρτων ἀλλὰ ἀπὸ τῆς διδαχῆς τῶν
Φαρισαίων καὶ Σαδδουκαίων.

12 των αρτων] אᶜBL 157 48 ᵉᵛ 𝕃 g ¹·² l vg me aeth ; *om* D 124* 𝕃 a b ff² 𝕊 sin arm
Lcif ; των Φαρισαιων και Σαδδουκαιων א* 33 (*om. κ. Σαδδ.*) 𝕃 ff¹ 𝕊 cur ; του αρτου
uncc.*rel* minn.*pler* 𝕃 c f q 𝕊 pesh

is meant ; so τοῦ ἄρτου in the
lesser uncials. The addition τῶν
Φαρισαίων καὶ Σαδδουκαίων is a
mechanical repetition from *v.* 6.

Mt. here omits Mk. viii. 22–26,
the arrival at Bethsaida, and the

healing of a blind man, probably for
three reasons : Jesus uses material
means, saliva, for the cure (cf. note
on xv. 29–31) ; He asks the man a
question (see on viii. 29) ; and the
cure is not immediate but gradual.

Additional Note on xiv. 13–xvi. 12.

The events in this section marked a crisis in the Lord's life. The
preaching of the Twelve was followed by danger, for His fame reached the
ears of Herod. The hostility of the religious authorities and the popular
enthusiasm obliged Him to seek privacy with the disciples.

The section consists of two parts, xiv. 13–xv. 31 and xv. 32–xvi. 12,
which are probably not consecutive, but parallel, and serve to supplement
each other. This can be seen more clearly in Mk., though Mt., for the most
part, follows him closely. (On Lk.'s omission of Mk. vi. 45–viii. 26 see
Oxf. Stud. 61–74.) The events may be sketched as follows :—

	Mt.	Mk.		Mt.	Mk.
(a)	xiv. 13-21.	vi. 31-44.	Miraculous feeding of a multitude somewhere on the east of the lake.	xv. 32-38.	viii. 1-9.
(b)	22-33.	45-52.	Crossing the lake.	39 a.	10 a.
(c)	34-36.	53-56.	Arrival at the west of the lake.	39 b.	10 b.
(d)	xv. 1-20.	vii. 1-23.	Conflict with the authorities.	xvi. 1-4 a.	11, 12.
(e)	21-28.	24-31.	Avoidance of the dominion of Antipas.	4 b-12.	13-21.
(f)	29-31.	32-37.	Healing on the east of the lake.	*vacat.*	22-26.

Either this is an extraordinary instance of history repeating itself, or, as
Wellhausen suggests, an extended duplication has taken place in the
tradition.

(a) The similarities in the accounts of the two miracles are so close that,
if they occurred in the Old Testament, few students would hesitate to
pronounce them duplicates from different sources. The differences are such
as 'would be likely to arise in the oral transmission of what was originally
the same narrative' (Stanton, *Gospels as Hist. Doc.* ii. 159).

(b) In xv. 39 a (Mk. viii. 10 a) the bare fact is recorded of the crossing
to the western shore. In xiv. 22–33 (Mk. vi. 45–52) occurrences are related
in connexion with it.

(c) In xv. 39 b (Mk. viii. 10 b) 'the regions of Magadan' (Mt.), 'the
parts of Dalmanutha' (Mk.) probably represent approximately the same

13   Ἐλθὼν δὲ ὁ Ἰησοῦς εἰς τὰ μέρη Καισαρίας τῆς

district as that named Gennesaret in xiv. 34 (Mk. vi. 53). But in the latter, as in (b), occurrences are related in connexion with it.

(d) Jesus was attacked by the religious authorities. In xvi. 1–4 a (Mk. viii. 11, 12) they asked for a sign, which Jesus refused. But in xv. 1–20 (Mk. vii. 1–23) their complaint leads to a discourse on Clean and Unclean. The former, in this case, probably stands rightly in this position, while xv. 1–20 seems to describe a different occasion; and if the landing at Gennesaret is the same as that at Magadan (Dalmanutha), the request for a sign forms a good sequel to the healings recorded in xiv. 35 f. (Mk. vi. 54 ff.); the Pharisees asked for a marvel more convincing than healings.

(e) The conflict with the authorities led to a departure so hurried that the disciples forgot to provide themselves with food. Mk. makes the situation at this point clearer than Mt. It was necessary at once to leave the dominion of Antipas, because Herodian officials had made common cause with the Pharisees (Mk. viii. 15; see on Mt. xvi. 6 f.). The retirement from his territory is recorded in both forms of the tradition: in the former a long journey is made via the Tyrian district (where the daughter of the Canaanite woman was healed) and the Decapolis to the lake; in the latter this is not recorded, but the end of it appears in Mk. viii. 22 (not in Mt.), 'and they come to Bethsaida.' If this is not the end of the same journey, Jesus, in going to Magadan (Dalmanutha), had returned, with no stated reason, to Herod's dominion, which He wished to avoid. The only detail in the itinerary of the second tradition which conflicts with that in the first lies in the words 'having embarked' and 'in the boat' (Mk. viii. 13 f.; not Mt.). The compiler of Mk.'s second tradition knew that Jesus had left Herod's dominion, and that He arrived at Bethsaida; but not being possessed of the Tyrian narrative he would, very naturally, assume that He crossed the lake in the ordinary way. Apart from this, the conversation about leaven could be explained as held on the road, as they started for Phoenicia.

(f) The two traditions in Mk. differ as to the act of healing performed on the east of the lake. But it is noteworthy that only in these two cases is the Lord recorded to have used saliva. Both can, of course, be historical, in which case one or other of them belonged to a different occasion; but the striking point of similarity caused them to occupy the same position in the two traditions. (Mt. substitutes a general statement of healing for the one, and omits the other.)

13–20. (Mk. viii. 27–30, Lk. ix. 18–21.) S. Peter's Confession of Faith.

13. ἐλθών κτλ.] Mk. has ἐξῆλθεν, i.e. out of Bethsaida, which Mt. has not mentioned, and adds καὶ μαθηταὶ αὐτοῦ, omitted by Mt. as unnecessary (cf. xiv. 13). Lk. has no note of place;

Jesus was praying κατὰ μόνας (see on xiv. 23). The moment was critical. The public ministry in Galilee was at an end, the journey towards the Cross was soon to begin; and He wished to draw the disciples into closer sympathy with Himself than ever before. So He led them northwards again,

Φιλίππου ἠρώτα τοὺς μαθητὰς αὐτοῦ λέγων Τίνα λέγουσιν
οἱ ἄνθρωποι εἶναι τὸν υἱὸν τοῦ ἀνθρώπου; οἱ δὲ εἶπαν 14
Οἱ μὲν Ἰωάνην τὸν βαπτιστήν, ἄλλοι δὲ Ἡλείαν, ἕτεροι
δὲ Ἰερεμίαν ἢ ἕνα τῶν προφητῶν. λέγει αὐτοῖς Ὑμεῖς δὲ 15
τίνα με λέγετε εἶναι; ἀποκριθεὶς δὲ Σίμων Πέτρος εἶπεν 16
Σὺ εἶ ὁ χριστὸς ὁ υἱὸς τοῦ θεοῦ τοῦ ζῶντος. ἀποκριθεὶς 17

13 τινα] ℵ B 𝔏 c vg⳽ pal me aeth ; *add* με uncc.*rel* minn 𝔏 vet ⳽ sin.cur.pesh.
diat ^{Eph}

into the ' parts' (Mk. the ' villages ') of
Caesarea Philippi. Formerly Paneas,
it was named after Philip the tetrarch,
who had rebuilt it, and was thus distinguished from the Caesarea on the
Mediterranean. It lay πρὸς ταῖς
πηγαῖς τοῦ Ἰορδάνου (Jos. *Ant.* XVIII.
ii. 1), at the foot of Hermon, about
23 miles from Bethsaida. Mt. places
the incident after the arrival at
Caesarea, Mk. ἐν τῇ ὁδῷ.

τίνα λέγουσιν κτλ.] By employing the Messianic title, so well known
to himself, Mt. anticipates the revelation to S. Peter (*v.* 16). Mk. τ. με
λέγ. οἱ ἄνθρ. εἶν.; Lk. τ. με οἱ
ὄχλοι λέγ. εἶν.; The addition of
με in Mt. (see Appar.) is probably
due to Mk., Lk., but if it is correct,
τ. υἱὸν τ. ἀνθρώπου may be a scribe's
gloss. It is impossible to explain it,
with Iren., *al.*, as a double question :
' . . . say that I am? The Son of
Man ? '

14. οἱ δὲ εἶπαν κτλ.] They had
not liked to tell Him the guesses
that they had heard from time to
time. The first guess had been
made by Antipas (xiv. 2), the second
expressed a wide-spread expectation
(xvii. 10 f., xxvii. 47, Jo. i. 21 ; see
p. 34 f.). Mt. alone has 'Jeremiah'
(cf. ii. 17, xxvii. 9), to whom the
other evangelists never refer. For
popular traditions about him see 2
Mac. ii. 1–12, xv. 14 f., and 4 Esd. ii.
18, 'mittam tibi adiutorium pueros
meos Isaiam et Hieremiam,' which

illustrates the expectation of other
prophets also (and see xvii. 3).

15. ὑμεῖς δέ κτλ.] The question,
with its emphatic ὑμεῖς, is identical
in the three synoptists. The tone
of the disciples' answer may have
indicated their attitude to the popular
guesses, but not their own convictions.
The joy with which the Lord received
S. Peter's answer shews the eagerness
with which He must have asked the
question. Spitta is led by his preference for Lk. to explain the question
as meaning ' What have you been
saying about Me in your preaching ? '
Peter answered, 'We have been saying
that Thou art "the Messiah of God"';
and in the next verse Jesus rebukes
them for doing so, and bids them in
future to say nothing about it.

16. ἀποκριθεὶς κτλ.] The double
name Simon Peter (Mk. ὁ Πέτρος,
Lk. Πέτρος), frequent in Jo., recurs
in the synoptists in Lk. v. 8 only
(but see Mt. iv. 18, x. 2). It looks
forward to *v.* 17 f. S. Peter was the
first to realize the truth, but when is
not stated ; *v.* 20 does not make it
clear whether the others had learnt
it before this moment.

σὺ εἶ κτλ.] Mk. σὺ εἶ ὁ χριστός,
Lk. τὸν χ. τοῦ θεοῦ, neither of
which is found in the O.T. ; see,
however, 2 Regn. xxiii. 1, χριστὸς
θεοῦ Ἰακώβ. But (ὁ) χρ. Κυρίου is
frequent, and χρ. μου, αὐτοῦ, also
occur. Mt.'s addition, 'the Son of
the living God,' is based on the O.T.

δὲ ὁ Ἰησοῦς εἶπεν αὐτῷ   Μακάριος εἶ, Σίμων Βαριωνᾶ, ὅτι
σὰρξ καὶ αἷμα οὐκ ἀπεκάλυψέν σοι ἀλλ' ὁ πατήρ μου ὁ
18 ἐν τοῖς οὐρανοῖς· κἀγὼ δέ σοι λέγω ὅτι σὺ εἶ Πέτρος,

On the 'Son of God' see viii. 29.
ὁ θεὸς ὁ ζῶν occurs only in xxvi.
63, Ps. xli. [xlii.] 3, but θεὸς ζῶν
is frequent in the Epp. and the LXX.
The Sonship which Jesus claimed
was the present fact of which the
Messiahship was to be the future, and
immediate, outcome (see p. xxiv. f.).
The Resurrection first gave to the
disciples the realization of the double
truth (cf. Rom. i. 4) which Mt. here expresses.   S. Peter's inspired certainty
of that for which the Baptist had
dimly hoped (xi. 3) was in advance
of the popular guesses (v. 14, ix. 27,
see n.), but on the other hand lacked
elements which had still to be learnt
(v. 21).   In Mk., Lk. the disciples
had never before confessed the Lord's
Messiahship; and the two following
verses imply that it was a conviction
expressed for the first time.   The
previous confession in xiv. 33 is
condemned on literary grounds; and
the present scene is deprived of all
significance if the disciples knew the
truth from the first, as in Jo. i. 41
(see p. 35, n. 3).

17-19. Absent from Mk., Lk. On
the prominence of S. Peter in Mt.
see x. 2.   Wellhausen says that it
is impossible that the passage can
have been written during his lifetime, so that he could read it.   Why
it is impossible is not clear.   But
in any case the facts might be true,
though not committed to writing
before his death.   Palestinian traditions reached Mt. which were unknown to Mk. and Lk.   Various
explanations are suggested by those
who deny its genuineness: e.g. it is
an elaborated version of the apostle's
call, or of the Lord's first meeting

with him, or of His appearance to
him after the Resurrection; or it
is an offset of his fall; or, more
generally, a story which grew up
to account for the position accorded
to him as head of the Church in
Apostolic times.   The last is probably
true of v. 19.   But vv. 17, 18 stand
on a different footing; they deal
with the Lord's Messiahship and
Resurrection, and assign no official
position to S. Peter.

17. μακάριος κτλ.]   On the exclamation see v. 3.   On the form
Σίμων, the name by which the Lord
always (except Lk. xxii. 34) addressed
S. Peter, see x. 2.   'Bar-jona' is
probably 'son of Jonah' (not 'John'
as in Jo. i. 42, xxi. 15 ff., and Gosp.
Heb.).   יוֹנָא (Heb. יוֹנָה) is not found
as an abbreviation of יוֹחָנָן, although
Ἰωνάν -νάς -νά (= John) occur in
some LXX. MSS. (Hatch-Redp. iii.
s.v.).   'Flesh and blood' is frequent
in Rabb. writings for humanity in
contrast with God; cf. Gal. i. 16,
Eph. vi. 12, Heb. ii. 14.   Human
lips had not taught him the truth.
Jesus, therefore, throughout His
human life till this point had never
revealed it to the disciples; hence
He cannot, before this point, have
applied to Himself the Messianic
title 'the Son of Man' (see p. xxiv. f.).
He had spoken of His Sonship (xi.
27), but not of the further truth
which it involved.

18. κἀγὼ δέ κτλ.]   The emphasis
is not on 'Thou art Peter' over
against 'Thou art the Christ,' but
on κἀγώ: 'The Father hath revealed
to thee one truth, and I also tell
you another.'   On καὶ . . . δέ see
Blass, § 77. 12 (fin.).   The name

καὶ ἐπὶ ταύτῃ τῇ πέτρᾳ οἰκοδομήσω μου τὴν ἐκκλησίαν,

Peter had been conferred long before (Mk. iii. 16, Lk. vi. 14). It is here introduced as affording a word-play : ' Thou art *Kêphā*, and on this *Kêphā* I will' etc. (cf. Gen. xxvii. 36). The Aram. word is fem., and rightly represented by πέτρα 'rock'; Πέτρος 'stone' is not intended to differ in meaning, but was chosen because the masc. was more suitable for a man's name. As a subst. (= λίθος) it occurs in bibl. Gk. in 2 Mac. i. 16, iv. 41 only. Thus the word-play need not necessarily have originated only in the Gk. (as Dell, *ZNW.*, 1914, 1 ff.).

καὶ ἐπὶ ταύτῃ κτλ.] It does not follow from the word-play that 'this rock' must be Peter. It *can*, indeed, be he ; cf. the similar metaphors applied to apostles in Gal. ii. 9, Eph. ii. 20, Apoc. xxi. 14, and the Rabb. legend quoted by Taylor, *Jewish Fathers*[2], 160 : 'When the Holy One . . . saw Abraham who was going to arise, He said, Lo I have discovered a *petra* (פטרא) to build and to found the world upon. Therefore He called Abraham *rock* (צור), as it is said, Look unto the rock whence ye were hewn.' In this case the words are addressed to Peter as an individual, not as bishop of Rome. But if he is the 'rock,' ταύτῃ is strange after the direct σὺ εἶ Π. It would be more natural if the Lord were speaking of him in the third person to the other disciples. Nor is it more natural if the 'rock' is Jesus Himself (Aug. *in Jo. tract.* cxxiv. *al.*). The reference is probably to the truth which the apostle had proclaimed ; the fact of the Lord's Messiahship was to be the immovable bed-rock on which His ' ecclesia ' would stand secure. Cf. 1 Cor. iii. 10 f. (S. Paul's *teaching* is a

'foundation,' at the same time that Jesus Christ is the ' foundation '), Ps. cxviii. [cxix.] 152, εἰς τὸν αἰῶνα ἐθεμελίωσας αὐτά [*sc.* τὰ μαρτύριά σου]. This is almost necessitated by the next clause, 'and the gates of Hades, *etc.*'

οἰκοδομήσω κτλ.] ἐκκλησία recurs only in xviii. 17 in the Gospels. In the LXX. it usually represents קָהָל, *i.e.* Israel, either as a body or assembled as a congregation. Cf. Ac. vii. 38 (an O.T. reference), Heb. ii. 12 (LXX.). Occasionally = עֵדָה, the ecclesiastical term employed in P, which is mostly rendered by συναγωγή, the latter being also the rendering of several other words. In later Aram. עדתא and כנישתא are related as ἐκκλησία and συναγωγή. Eus. (*Theoph.* iv. 11) uses the former for Christian, the latter (ܟܢܘܫܬܐ) for Jewish, assemblies. Epiph. (*Haer.* xxx. 18) says of the Ebionites on the E. of Jordan συναγωγὴν δὲ οὗτοι καλοῦσι τὴν ἑαυτῶν ἐκκλησίαν, καὶ οὐχὶ ἐκκλησίαν. But עדתא does not seem to have been an early Palest. word. $ cur. pesh have it here and in xviii. 17, while the Pal. lect. has ܟܢܘܫܬܐ in both places. $ sin has the latter in xviii. 17, but is not extant here. It is probable, therefore, that the original word here was כנישתא, the Lord employing, as a native of Palestine, the Palest. word to describe His body of followers. That body would be built up upon the foundation fact of His Messiahship ; it did, in fact, grow into the Catholic Church. For Mt.'s Greek readers ἐκκλησία was the only possible word to express the Christian body as distinct from Jews. J. Weiss objects that ' my Church ' "assumes an emancipa-

19 καὶ πύλαι ᾅδου οὐ κατισχύσουσιν αὐτῆς· δώσω σοι τὰς

tion from the Church of the Jewish people, 'the congregation of Jahwe,' which Jesus can scarcely have expected or striven for in this manner." But He had just ended His public ministry in Galilee, had taken the disciples a long journey alone, and was about to go to Jerusalem with the avowed intention of being killed ; no moment was more suitable for preparing His followers to become a new body, isolated both from the masses and from the civil and religious authorities.

καὶ πύλαι κτλ.] Hades, like the *ecclesia*, is spoken of as a building. But the meaning can hardly be 'not even the gates of Hades shall surpass it in strength' (Plummer); the gates of one building cannot strictly be compared with another building considered as a whole. The usual explanation is that there will be warfare between Hades and the *ecclesia*, and that the former will not be victorious. This might refer to persecutions (Wellh.) or to temptations. It is assumed that 'the gates of H.' are equivalent to 'Hades,' and that again to the powers of evil which dwell there : 'the organized powers of evil shall not prevail against the organized society which represents My teaching' (Allen). But apart from this awkward metonymy, it is doubtful if Hades was ever thought of as the *abode* of the powers of evil, from which they emerge to injure men. In xi. 23 (Lk. x. 15) it symbolizes punitive destruction, in Lk. xvi. 23 an intermediate state of punishment, and in Ac. ii. 27 [LXX.], 31 it is the state of the departed generally, *i.e.* death ; in Apoc. (i. 18, vi. 8, xx. 13 f.) it is always coupled with θάνατος. In the O.T. the 'gates of Hades (Sheol)'

never bears any other meaning (Is. xxxviii. 10, Wisd. xvi. 13, 3 Mac. v. 51 ; cf. Ps. Sol. xvi. 2) ; so 'the bars of Sheol' (Job xvii. 16, not LXX.). It is synon. with 'gates of death' (Ps. ix. 14 [13], cvi. [cvii.] 18, Job xxxviii. 17). (For the 𐤔 rendering 'the gate-bars of Sheol' in Ephr., *al.* see Burkitt, *Ev. da Meph.* ii. 119, 156, 170.) And that is probably the Lord's meaning. The *ecclesia* is built upon the Messiahship of her Master, and death, the gates of Hades, will not prevail against her by keeping Him imprisoned. It was a mysterious truth, which He was soon to tell them in plain words (*v.* 21) ; it is echoed in Ac. ii. 24, 31. The meaning is not altered if αὐτῆς refers to πέτρα, but the pron. more naturally refers to the nearer subst. Loisy's explanation (death prevails against all men, but it shall not prevail against the Church) is allied to this, but he does not point out the allusion to the Resurrection. Tatian seems to have read 'And He said, Blessed art thou, Simon ; and the gates of Hades shall not prevail against thee ; thou art Peter' (Harnack, *Z. f. Kircheng.* IV. iv. 484), which Wernle (*Die Syn. Frage*, 135) explains as a promise to S. Peter that he should not die before the Parousia. For κατισχύειν c. gen. cf. Wisd. vii. 30 (אA) σοφίας δὲ οὐ κατισχύει κακία.

19 a. δώσω σοι κτλ.] Roman, and many Protestant, writers explain the 'keys' as the authority to admit to, or exclude from, the Church ; the former claiming the authority for all bishops of Rome, the latter confining it to the apostle, and pointing, for instance, to his admission of the Gentiles. This, however, is not the meaning naturally sug-

κλεῖδας τῆς βασιλείας τῶν οὐρανῶν, καὶ ὃ ἐὰν δήσῃς ἐπὶ
τῆς γῆς ἔσται δεδεμένον ἐν τοῖς οὐρανοῖς, καὶ ὃ ἐὰν λύσῃς
ἐπὶ τῆς γῆς ἔσται λελυμένον ἐν τοῖς οὐρανοῖς.   Τότε 20

gested by the metaphor. S. Peter is not to be the 'coelestis regni janitorem' (Hil.), but the chief steward, the *major domus*, in the Kingdom ; the 'keys' are the symbol of rule and authority, entrusted by the real Holder, the οἰκοδεσπότης ; cf. Apoc. iii. 7 (based on Is. xxii. 22).

The genuineness of the words δώσω . . . οὐρανῶν is very doubtful. The conception of the 'Kingdom of Heaven' is utterly different from that expressed elsewhere in the Lord's teaching. It is here the Christian Church in which the apostle is given the chief authority. And if Jesus really gave him this authority in the hearing of the disciples, the subsequent dispute (xviii. 1) as to which of them was the greatest is inexplicable, and scarcely less so the question asked by the apostle himself in xix. 27.

19 b. καὶ ὃ ἐάν κτλ.] The apostle is to hold not only administrative, but also legislative, authority. 'Bind' and 'loose' appear to represent the Aram. אסר and שרא, which were technical terms for the verdict of a teacher of the Law who, on the strength of his expert knowledge of the oral tradition, declared some action or thing 'bound' *i.e.* forbidden, or 'loosed' *i.e.* permitted. Many things, *e.g.*, which the school of Shammai 'bound,' that of Hillel 'loosed.' The apostle would, in the coming Kingdom, be like a great scribe or Rabbi, who would deliver decisions on the basis, not of the Jewish law, but of the teaching of Jesus, which 'fulfilled' it. His decisions on earth would be endorsed 'in Heaven,' *i.e.* by God. (On the periphrasis for the divine name see Dalm. *Words*, 213 f., 218 f.)

That the words describe an authority to absolve from sin, and to refuse to absolve, is improbable in view of the Jewish parallels. λύειν is, indeed, used of forgiving in the O.T. (Is. xl. 2, Sir. xxviii. 2), and similarly שרא in the Talm. and Midrashim (Dalm. *op. cit.*) ; but there is no evidence that the converse could be expressed by δέειν. It was natural that patr. writers should connect the saying with Jo. xx. 23, but there is no necessary connexion ; nor can it be shewn that the latter passage was due to a misunderstanding of the present one. But even if it was, the authority of the Church to forgive the sins of its members does not stand or fall with either passage ; it rests ultimately upon the truth underlying Mt. ix. 6 (see note). The two halves of the present verse contain different metaphors and meanings. In xviii. 18 the same authority to bind and loose is given to all the disciples, and that passage has probably been applied by the evangelist to S. Peter.

20. τότε κτλ.] S. Peter now knew the fact of the Messiahship, but was still ignorant (*v.* 21 f.) of all that it involved ; the masses, therefore, would certainly misinterpret it of an earthly sovereignty, and be roused to excitement or even rebellion. ἐπετίμησεν (see on xii. 16) has good support, but may be due to Mk., Lk. ; for the *v.l.* διεστείλατο with the late meaning 'enjoined' cf. Ac. xv. 24, Heb. xii. 20, and Mk.[5] The explicit ὅτι αὐτός ἐ. ὁ χριστός for Mk.'s περὶ αὐτοῦ (Lk. τοῦτο) was rendered necessary by the interposition of *vv.* 17–19.

ἐπετίμησεν τοῖς μαθηταῖς ἵνα μηδενὶ εἴπωσιν ὅτι αὐτός
ἐστιν ὁ χριστός.

21   ΑΠΟ ΤΟΤΕ ἤρξατο Ἰησοῦς Χριστὸς δεικνύειν τοῖς μαθηταῖς αὐτοῦ ὅτι δεῖ αὐτὸν εἰς Ἱεροσόλυμα ἀπελθεῖν καὶ
πολλὰ παθεῖν ἀπὸ τῶν πρεσβυτέρων καὶ ἀρχιερέων καὶ
γραμματέων καὶ ἀποκτανθῆναι καὶ τῇ τρίτῃ ἡμέρᾳ ἐγερθῆ-

20 επετιμησεν] B*D codd. ap. Or 𝕷 e 𝕾 cur; διεστειλατο אB**CE etc 𝕷 vet.pler. vg
𝕾 pesh. hcl me aeth   21 Ιησους Χριστος] א*B* me; om אa; o [om B²D]
Ιησους אbB²CDE etc verss. [exc. me]

21–23. (Mk. viii. 31–33, Lk. ix.
22.) First Prediction of the
Passion. Rebuke to S. Peter.
(For subsequent predictions see xvii.
22 f., xx. 17 ff. ; cf. xvii. 12, xxvi. 2.)
21. ἀπὸ τότε κτλ.] Mt. here
marks the opening of the second
division of the Lord's teaching (see
on iv. 17): from this time onwards
He taught that Messiahship involved
suffering and death. It was ordered
in the divine providence (δεῖ; cf.
xvii. 10, xxiv. 6, xxvi. 35, 54, Mk.
viii. 31, xiii. 10, and more frequently
in Lk.). The idea of a suffering
Messiah was probably alien to the
Jewish thought of the time (Dalman,
Der leidende u. d. sterbende Messias),
and proved an insoluble enigma to
the disciples (cf. xvii. 23). For a
good study of the thoughts of Jesus
on the subject see E. F. Scott, The
Kingdom and the Messiah, ch. viii.
Ἰησοῦς Χριστός is probably the true
reading; the title may have been
an early scribal addition (Allen), but
Mt. probably added it as being suitable at the present juncture; and
having named the Messiah he writes
αὐτόν for τὸν υἱὸν τοῦ ἀνθρώπου
(Mk., Lk.).
εἰς Ἱεροσόλυμα κτλ.] Mt. adds
the mention of Jerusalem, and omits
καὶ ἀποδοκιμασθῆναι (Mk., Lk.). On

Ἱεροσόλυμα see ii. 1. On ἀπό (Mt.,
Lk.) for ὑπό (Mk.) see Moulton, i.
102. At what period the Lord first
knew that He would suffer a violent
death cannot be determined; the
probability must often have suggested
itself when He set His face against
the current ideas and practices, and
when He avoided the dominion of
Antipas, after the Baptist's death;
cf. also ix. 15, Lk. xiii. 32 f. The
several predictions of His Passion
may not represent His actual words,
but they rightly express the fact that
He spoke, from now onwards, freely
on the subject.
'Elders, high-priests, and Scribes'
includes the whole Sanhedrin (see on
ii. 4). All who did not belong to
the last two classes were called 'elders,'
laymen as well as less important
priests; cf. γερουσία (1 Mac. xii.
6, 3 Mac. i. 8) and the early זִקְנֵי
יִשְׂרָאֵל (Exod. xvii. 5). For the late
form ἀποκτανθῆναι (so Mk., Lk.) cf.
Mk. ix. 31, 1 Mac. ii. 9.
καὶ τῇ τρίτῃ κτλ.] So Lk. Mk.
κ. μετὰ τρεῖς ἡμέρας ἀναστῆναι. If
the Messiah was to come from Heaven,
He must first depart thither, and the
Resurrection was therefore 'necessary.' The argument is the converse
of that in Eph. iv. 9. 'On the third
day' and 'after three days' were

ναι. καὶ προσλαβόμενος αὐτὸν ὁ Πέτρος ἤρξατο ἐπι- 22
τιμᾶν αὐτῷ λέγων "Ἴλεώς σοι, κύριε· οὐ μὴ ἔσται σοι
τοῦτο. ὁ δὲ στραφεὶς εἶπεν τῷ Πέτρῳ "Ὕπαγε ὀπίσω μου, 23
Σατανᾶ· σκάνδαλον εἶ ἐμοῦ, ὅτι οὐ φρονεῖς τὰ τοῦ θεοῦ

understood to mean the same. The former occurs almost universally in patr. citations from the Gospels, and was adopted in the Creeds, varied only by διὰ τριῶν ἡμέρων or τριή-μερον. See on xii. 40, and Swete on Mk. viii. 31. Cf. Jer. xxxiv. 14, 'at the end of seven years,' corresponding with Deut. xv. 12, 'in the seventh year.' ἐγερθῆναι and ἀνα-στῆναι are both used by Mk., Lk. (only the former by Mt.) of the Resurrection; cf. Is. xxvi. 19 (both verbs), Dan. xii. 2 (Theod. and LXX. respectively). ἀναστῆναι ἐπὶ τὸ ἔργον, ἐγερθῆναι ἐξ ὕπνου (Ammon.). Mk. adds καὶ παρρησίᾳ τὸν λόγον ἐλάλει. The disciples had now learnt enough to be in a position to hear the truth in plain language. (On an interesting variant in Mk. see Burkitt, *JThS.*, Oct. 1900, 110 ff.)

22. καὶ προσλαβόμενος κτλ.] Lk. spares the apostle by omitting the passage. προσλαβόμενος (so Mk.) does not recur in the Gospels. It may be merely redundant, like λαβών (xiii. 31 note); cf. the frequent וַיִּקַּח in the O.T. But it may mean literally that Peter 'drew Him to him,' with a gesture implying protection if not superiority (cf. Ac. xviii. 26, Rom. xiv. 1, xv. 7, Philem. 17). It need not mean that he took Him aside. Ṣ cur (Mt.) has 'drew near and said,' sin (Mk.) 'as though pitying Him said to Him.'

ἴλεώς σοι κτλ.] Mt. alone supplies the words of the remonstrance. The first three are a mere exclamation, '[May God be] gracious to thee, Lord !' (Aram. חָס, Heb. חָלִילָה); cf.

2 Regn. xx. 20, 1 Chr. xi. 19, 1 Mac. ii. 21. ἴλεως ἡμῖν Πλάτων καὶ ἐνταῦθα (Letronne, *Recueil des Inscr. gr. et lat. de l'Égypte*, ii. 286; and see 524). μὴ γένοιτο is equivalent; cf. Lk. xx. 16, where Ṣ cur has ܐܡܝܢ as here, adding 'and it shall not be.' On οὐ μή see Moulton, i. 188 ff.

23. ὁ δέ κτλ.] Mk. ἐπιστραφείς. Jesus turned, not away from, but towards him, thus facing the disciples (ἰδὼν τ. μαθητὰς αὐτοῦ Mk.) who were behind. Mk. seems to suggest that He spoke because He saw them, *i.e.* saw in their looks that they were of the same mind as S. Peter, whose remonstrance had been persuasive enough to constitute a real temptation.

ὕπαγε κτλ.] The words have been explained metaphorically as a command to the Satan that spoke in the apostle to move behind Jesus, instead of standing in His way to the Cross. But μου is possibly an early mistake for σου, which would be a lit. rendering of an Aram. idiom, equivalent to ὕπ. ὀπίσω or simply ὕπαγε. On this, and on the name 'Satan,' see iv. 10. It was a critical instance of the temptation there depicted, to work out His victorious career according to human promptings and not after the divine way of suffering.

σκάνδαλον κτλ.] The first three words are in Mt. only. As a man who harboured demons identified himself with them (Mk. v. 9), so the Lord treated Peter as possessed, addressing him and Satan in the same sentence. He rebuked not his impulsiveness but his 'bent of mind' (φρόνημα), which,

24 ἀλλὰ τὰ τῶν ἀνθρώπων.   Τότε ὁ Ἰησοῦς εἶπεν
τοῖς μαθηταῖς αὐτοῦ Εἴ τις θέλει ὀπίσω μου ἐλθεῖν,
ἀπαρνησάσθω ἑαυτὸν καὶ ἀράτω τὸν σταυρὸν αὐτοῦ καὶ
25 ἀκολουθείτω μοι.   ὃς γὰρ ἐὰν θέλῃ τὴν ψυχὴν αὐτοῦ
σῶσαι ἀπολέσει αὐτήν· ὃς δ᾽ ἂν ἀπολέσῃ τὴν ψυχὴν
26 αὐτοῦ ἕνεκεν ἐμοῦ εὑρήσει αὐτήν.   τί γὰρ ὠφεληθήσεται

on the subject of the Messiah, had not yet fully reached to τὰ τοῦ θεοῦ, but still clung to the current notions and hopes ; to him 'Christ crucified' was a stumbling-block (1 Cor. i. 23), and he thereby became himself a stumbling-block. On σκάνδαλον see xiii. 41. For φρονεῖν τά τινος cf. Est. xvi. 1, 1 Mac. x. 20, and non-bibl. reff. in Swete. S. Paul widens its range to include the spiritual state of the whole man (Rom. viii. 5 ff., Phil. iii. 19, Col. iii. 2).

24–28. (Mk. viii. 34–ix. 1, Lk. ix. 23–27 ; cf. Mt. x. 38 f., Lk. xiv. 27, xvii. 33.) SELF-SACRIFICE.

24. τότε κτλ.] Mk. καὶ προσ-καλεσάμενος τὸν ὄχλον᾽ σὺν τοῖς μαθηταῖς αὐτοῦ. Lk. εἶπεν δὲ πρὸς πάντας. Mt., Lk. follow Mk. in placing the section here, as cognate to the Lord's predictions of His sufferings. But the mention of the ὄχλος is unexpected, and suggests that the passage belongs to a different context. Mt. avoids the difficulty by making it addressed only to the disciples. Spitta, who thinks that all the events in Mk. vi. 35–viii. 27 a (Mt. xiv. 15–xvi. 13 a) are a later addition to the Grundschrift, as also the feeding of the 5000 in Lk. ix. 12–17, reads too much into Lk.'s εἶπεν δὲ πρὸς πάντας, explaining it as a return to the multitudes after the Lord had retired κατὰ μόνας for prayer (v. 18), the multitudes being those who had followed Him to Bethsaida (v. 10 f.).

εἴ τις κτλ.] So Mk. to ἕνεκεν ἐμοῦ. A follower of Jesus must be prepared for self-surrender even to the death. The same sequence, attached to another saying on the condition of discipleship, occurs in Q (x. 38, Lk. xiv. 27, omitting ἀπαρ-νησάσθω ἑαυτ.). The disciple must be prepared not only for private self-mortification, but for public humiliation, 'crucifixion.' This was what S. Peter had just deprecated for his Master. ἀράτω represents the same Aram. as λαμβάνει (Lk. βαστάζει) in x. 38, where, as here, the words do not necessarily predict the exact manner of the Lord's death. Lk.'s addition καθ᾽ ἡμέραν is a spiritual comment of abiding value. ὀπίσω μ. ἐλθεῖν (Lk. ἔρχεσθαι) represents the same Aram. as ἀκολουθείτω μου and ἀκολούθει (Lk. ἔρχεται) ὀπίσω μου in x. 38. The meaning may therefore be (imitating an Aram. construction), 'If any wishes to be My follower, let him . . . take up his cross, and (so) let him—i.e. and then he may—be My follower,' a positive form of the negative warning in Lk. xiv. 27 (Wellh.). In any case 'deny himself and take up his cross' defines the true meaning of 'following.'

25. ὃς γάρ κτλ.] See on x. 39. After ἕνεκεν ἐμοῦ (so Lk.) Mk. has καὶ τοῦ εὐαγγελίου, which is probably due to later editing ; see on iv. 17, xix. 29.

26. τί γάρ κτλ.] A similar thought, emphasizing the former half of the paradox in v. 25. Cf. Apoc. Bar. li. 15, 'For what then have

ἄνθρωπος ἐὰν τὸν κόσμον ὅλον κερδήσῃ τὴν ·δὲ ψυχὴν
αὐτοῦ ζημιωθῇ; ἢ τί δώσει ἄνθρωπος ἀντάλλαγμα τῆς
ψυχῆς αὐτοῦ; μέλλει γὰρ ὁ υἱὸς τοῦ ἀνθρώπου ἔρχεσθαι 27
ἐν τῇ δόξῃ τοῦ πατρὸς αὐτοῦ μετὰ τῶν ἀγγέλων αὐτοῦ,
καὶ τότε ἀποδώςει ἑκάςτῳ κατὰ τὴν πρᾶξιν ἀγτογ·   ἀμὴν 28

men lost their life, and for what
have those who were on earth ex-
changed their souls?' A supple-
mentary thought is contained in
1 Cor. xiii. 3. The κόσμος is 'the
external considered as a counter
attraction to the spiritual and
eternal' (Swete); see 1 Cor. vii. 33 f.,
Gal. vi. 14, Jam. iv. 4. It is frequent in the Johannine writings;
see especially 1 Jo. ii. 15 ff.

τὴν δὲ ψυχήν κτλ.] 'Be forced
to lose his (higher) self as the price
or fine' (so Lk., ἑαυτὸν δὲ ἀπολέσας
ἢ ζημιωθείς), not only at the final
Judgment, however close that may
be, but now by an inherent necessity.
It is either God or mammon. For
ζημιοῦν c. acc. of price cf. Deut. xxii.
19, Prov. xix. 16 [19] (AC), Philo,
Ebr. 3 (quoted by Swete). κέρδος and
ζημία are contrasted in Phil. iii. 7;
cf. two sayings of Menander, quoted
by Lightfoot, Hor. Heb. ad loc.

ἢ τί δώσει κτλ.] Mk. τί γὰρ
δοῖ. A man must give, surrender, his
life, and nothing less, to God; no
ἀντάλλαγμα is possible (cf. Ps. xlviii.
[xlix.]8). This emphasizes the thought
of v. 25 b, while v. 26 a emphasizes that
of v. 25 a. Lk. misses the parallelism
by omitting this sentence. In Mk.
γάρ is parallel, not consecutive, with
the former γάρ, and Mt. so understands it. The metaphor of price
continues. ἀντάλλαγμα (not elsewhere in N.T.; ἄλλαγμα also in
LXX.) is an equivalent for exchange:
purchase-money (3 Regn. xx. [xxi.]
2 (A), Job xxviii. 15), a bribe (Am.
v. 12), an equivalent for a ψυχή
or person (Sir. vi. 15, xxvi. 14, xliv.

17). The only real equivalent for
human life is the Perfect Life (xx.
28). The saying cannot mean that
a lost soul can never be redeemed:
'or els what shall a man geve to
redeme his soule agayne with all?'
(Tynd.).

27. μέλλει γάρ κτλ.] Nothing
is more valuable than the higher
self, for there is a Judgment to
come. Mt. forms this sentence out
of a saying in Mk. (Lk.) similar to
that in Mt. x. 33 (Lk. xii. 9). For
the thought of the Messiah in glory
cf. Enoch xlv. 3, lxi. 8, lxii. 2, 5,
lxix. 27 (cited by Allen); but His
glory is the glory of the Father.
Lk. distinguishes them: ἐν τῇ
δόξῃ αὐτοῦ καὶ τοῦ πατρὸς καὶ
τῶν ἁγίων ἀγγέλων. The Parousia
with the angels is based on Zech.
xiv. 5, καὶ ἥξει κύριος ὁ θεός μου,
καὶ πάντες οἱ ἅγιοι μετ' αὐτοῦ.
For 'the holy ones' of the angels
(Mk., Lk. 'the holy angels,' cf. Job
v. 1 (LXX.), Ac. x. 22, Apoc. xiv. 10)
see Job l.c. (Heb.), Dan. iv. 10 [13]
(LXX. ἄγγελος, Theod. ἅγιος), viii.
13, Jude 14 (= Enoch i. 9), and
probably 1 Thes. iii. 13 (see Milligan); cf. also Bousset, Rel. d. Jud.²
369. Only Mt. adds αὐτοῦ after
ἀγγέλων, emphasizing the divine
authority of the glorified Christ;
cf. xiii. 41, xxiv. 31.

καὶ τότε κτλ.] The words recall
Ps. lxi. [lxii.] 13; cf. Prov. xxiv. 12,
Ps.-Sol. xvii. 10, Apoc. xxii. 12.
For πρᾶξιν cf. Sir. xxxii. [xxxv.] 24,
ἕως ἀνταποδῷ ἀνθρώπῳ κατὰ τὰς
πράξεις αὐτοῦ. The expectation
that the Judgment would take place

λέγω ὑμῖν ὅτι εἰσίν τινες τῶν ὧδε ἑστώτων οἵτινες οὐ μὴ
γεύσωνται θανάτου ἕως ἂν ἴδωσιν τὸν υἱὸν τοῦ ἀνθρώπου
ἐρχόμενον ἐν τῇ βασιλείᾳ αὐτοῦ.

XVII. 1   Καὶ μεθ᾽ ἡμέρας ἓξ παραλαμβάνει ὁ Ἰησοῦς τὸν·Πέτρον

at the *beginning* of the Messianic Kingdom, found in the earlier apocalypses, prevails in the N.T. except in the Apoc., where, as in the later apocalypses, it is postponed till the end of the temporary Messianic rule. The Judgment is spoken of in Mt. indifferently as the act of the Son (vii. 22 f., xiii. 41, xxv. 31–46), or of the Father (vi. 4, 6, 18, x. 28, 32 f., xviii. 35). Mk., Lk. ('the Son of Man shall be ashamed of him') probably imply the former; Mt. states it explicitly.

28. ἀμήν κτλ.] Connected with the foregoing in Mt., Lk.: the arrival of the Son of Man for judgment will take place in the near future. But Mk. begins with καὶ ἔλεγεν αὐτοῖς as though it were an isolated saying from another context. On ἀμήν κτλ. see v. 18. τ. ὧδε ἑστώτων (Lk. τ. αὐτοῦ ἑστηκότων); cf. xxvi. 73, Dan. vii. 16; this transposes Mk.'s order τινες ὧδε τῶν ἑστηκότων, his participle probably representing the Aram. קָיְמִין 'living,' 'alive' (freq. in Targ.); see Burkitt, *Ev. da Meph.* on Mk. ix. 1. οἵτινες 'who [for all that]'; see Moulton, i. 92. 'Taste death' is found in N. Heb. and Aram., but not in the O.T.; cf. Jo. viii. 52, Heb. ii. 9; 'see death,' Ps. lxxxviii. [lxxxix.] 49, Lk. ii. 26. They will not taste death because the great consummation will prevent it; cf. 1 Thes. iv. 15.

For the Hebraic ἐν τῇ β. αὐτ. 'in,' or *with*, His sovereignty' cf. Lk. xxiii. 42 (ℵAC). Mk. has τ. βασιλείαν τοῦ θεοῦ ἐληλυθυῖαν ἐν δυνάμει. Lk. τ. βασ. τοῦ θεοῦ. Mt.'s form of the words continues the foregoing

thought of the divine prerogatives of the Messiah (on which he dwells more than Mk. and Lk.), but that need not involve a different conception. of the 'kingdom'; nor need 'arrived in power' (Mk.) imply a contrast with a present kingdom which is not in power. The saying, in all three forms, is in accord with x. 23, xxiv. 34 (Mk. xiii. 30, Lk. xxi. 32); and some definite utterances of Jesus on the immediacy of His return are presupposed by the expectations of it in apostolic times. It is false exegesis to blur the strong Jewish colouring of His words. But Christians can recognize that they received, or rather began to receive, their fulfilment at Pentecost, and that every subsequent catastrophe, or crisis, or demonstration of divine power, has been a gateway to a new era, a step in the age-long process of their complete fulfilment, the culmination of which is beyond our sight. It is even less permissible to explain them literally as referring to the Transfiguration (*Exc. Theod.* ap. Clem. Al. § 4; this Valentinian explanation was followed by Hil., Ephr., Chrys., Jer., and others); in no sense can the Kingdom of God, or the Son of Man, be said to 'come' in that vision.

xvii. 1–8. (Mk. ix. 2–8, Lk. ix. 28–36; cf. 2 Pet. i. 16 b–18.) THE TRANSFIGURATION.

1. καὶ μεθ᾽ ἡμέρας κτλ.] So Mk. This means 'on the sixth day,' on the analogy of 'after three days' (Mk. viii. 31). Lk., less precisely, 'about eight days after these words.' Like

καὶ Ἰάκωβον καὶ Ἰωάνην τὸν ἀδελφὸν αὐτοῦ, καὶ ἀναφέρει
αὐτοὺς εἰς ὄρος ὑψηλὸν κατ᾽ ἰδίαν. καὶ μετεμορφώθη 2
ἔμπροσθεν αὐτῶν, καὶ ἔλαμψεν τὸ πρόσωπον αὐτοῦ ὡς
ὁ ἥλιος, τὰ δὲ ἱμάτια αὐτοῦ ἐγένετο λευκὰ ὡς τὸ φῶς.
καὶ ἰδοὺ ὤφθη αὐτοῖς Μωυσῆς καὶ Ἠλείας συνλαλοῦντες 3

2 φως] χιων D 𝔏 vet [exc. q]. vg ⳝ cur aeth

David (2 Sam. xxiii. 8 ff.), the Son
of David had his picked body of
three; they were allowed to accompany Him in the house of Jairus
(Mk. v. 37), and in Gethsemane (Mt.
xxvi. 37); and see Mk. i. 29, xiii.
3. Πέτρον alone has the article:
'the Peter who has just been
mentioned' (Blass, § 46. 10). ἀναφέρειν 'to cause to go up' is rare;
Lk. xxiv. 51, Neh. xii. 31, Dan. vi.
23 (Theod.) only; elsewhere in the
N.T. (Heb., Jam., 1 Pet.) it is 'to
offer (sacrifice).' If the high mountain (ὄρος ἅγιον 2 Pet.) was near
Caesarea, it was probably Mt.
Hermon, some 14 miles to the north.
The other disciples were left either
at the foot, or probably at Caesarea
(see v. 14). On the tradition that
it was Mt. Tabor in the S. of Galilee
see iv. 8. Lk. says, 'He went up
into the mountain to pray' (see on
xiv. 23) which, with ὕπνῳ (v. 32),
implies that it was night.

2. καὶ μετεμορφώθη κτλ.] So
Mk. Lk. ἐγένετο ... τὸ εἶδος τοῦ προσώπου αὐτοῦ ἕτερον, perhaps because
'metamorphosis' might suggest to
Gentile readers stories of pagan
mythology. For the word cf. Sym.
Ps. xxxiii. [xxxiv.], title (LXX. ἠλ-
λοίωσεν); with Lk.'s wording cf. Dan.
iii. 19, and (Theod.) v. 6, 9, vii. 28.
The deeper force of μεταμορφοῦσθαι
is seen in 2 Cor. iii. 18 (with reference
to the shining on Moses' face), Rom.
xii. 2. The rendering 'transfigured'
(all Engl. versions) is due to the
Vulg. transfiguratus est; in Rom.,

2 Cor., A. and R.V. 'transformed,'
Vulg. reformamini and transfor-
mamur.

καὶ ἔλαμψεν ... ἥλιος] Mt. only;
cf. Apoc. i. 16. Allen quotes Secr.
Enoch i. 5, xix. 1, 2 (4) Esd. vii.
97, and Enoch xiv. 20, 'His raiment
did shine more brightly than the
sun.' ἐγένετο λευκά: Mk. στίλ-
βοντα λευκὰ λίαν. Mk. (ἱματισμός)
λευκὸς ἐξαστράπτων. Each evang.
selects his words independently.
Mt., Lk. omit Mk.'s homely comparison, 'such as a fuller on earth
cannot so whiten'; Mt. substitutes
ὡς τὸ φῶς, carrying on the preceding
thought. χιών (also a v.l. in Mk.)
was a natural gloss; cf. xxviii. 3,
Apoc. i. 14, Dan. vii. 9. Lk.'s description is somewhat more prosaic
throughout, but he describes no less
than the others a super-earthly
phenomenon.

3. καὶ ἰδού κτλ.] The sing.
ὤφθη (so Mk.) is almost impers., 'an
appearance occurred of M. and E.' Except in Ac. vii. 26 the pass. is always
used in the N.T. of a supernatural
appearance. Elijah's expected reappearance held a large place in the
popular expectations (see p. 34 f.),
and Mk. names him first, Ἠλείας σὺν
M.; so in LXX. (against the Heb.) of
Mal. iv. 4, 6 [iii. 22 f.]. Ass. Mos.
(probably 1st cent. A.D.) shews that
Moses also played a part in the
current hopes. In Lk., Moses and
Elijah, like Jesus, were seen by the
disciples 'in glory,' and he continues,
'they were speaking of His exodus

4 μετ᾿ αὐτοῦ. ἀποκριθεὶς δὲ ὁ Πέτρος εἶπεν τῷ Ἰησοῦ
Κύριε, καλόν ἐστιν ἡμᾶς ὧδε εἶναι· εἰ θέλεις, ποιήσω ὧδε
τρεῖς σκηνάς, σοὶ μίαν καὶ Μωυσεῖ μίαν καὶ Ἠλείᾳ μίαν.
5 ἔτι αὐτοῦ λαλοῦντος ἰδοὺ νεφέλη φωτινὴ ἐπεσκίασεν
αὐτούς, καὶ ἰδοὺ φωνὴ ἐκ τῆς νεφέλης λέγουσα Οὗτός
ἐστιν ὁ υἱός μου ὁ ἀγαπητός, ἐν ᾧ εὐδόκησα· ἀκούετε
6 αὐτοῦ. καὶ ἀκούσαντες οἱ μαθηταὶ ἔπεσαν ἐπὶ πρόσωπον

which He was about to accomplish
in Jerusalem,' which lays stress on a
single aspect in the thought of the
vision (see Add. n.).

4. ἀποκριθεὶς κτλ.] See on xi.
25. Lk. 'And Peter and they that
were with him were weighed down
with sleep, but when they awoke
they saw His glory and the two men
standing with Him. And it came
to pass that as they were departing
from Him Peter said, etc.' κύριε :
Mk. ῥαββεί, Lk. ἐπιστάτα ; see on
vii. 21. Peter says ἡμᾶς and εἶναι,
not ἡμῖν and μένειν : 'bonum est
nos hic esse' (𝕃), 'it is a good
thing that we are here' (so 𝕊 sin
Mk.), sc. 'so that we can take means
to keep Moses and Elijah a little
longer.' The ordinary rend. 'it is
good for us to be here' is found in
𝕊 cur.pesh. The Mount of Transfiguration is always more enjoyable
than either the daily ministry or
the way of the Cross ; the apostle
looked back to the former, and forward to the latter, and the moment
of respite was luxury. Wendling's
suggestion, however, is possible,
that the words are an awe-struck
question, 'Is it right for us to be
here ? And are we to make (καὶ
ποιήσωμεν Mk., Lk.) etc.,' in keeping
with Mk.'s statement 'for he knew
not what to answer, for they were
terrified' (Lk. 'not knowing what
he was saying'), which Mt. omits,
perhaps to spare S. Peter. εἰ θέλεις
κτλ. : with the comma this means

'If Thou wishest, let me make';
without it, εἰ introduces a direct
question (cf. xii. 10), 'Dost Thou
wish me to make' (cf. xiii. 28).

5. ἔτι αὐτοῦ κτλ.] The acc. αὐτούς pictures the motion of the cloud
as it enveloped them (Mk. αὐτοῖς).
The pron. in Mt., Mk. refers to the
Three (𝕊 sin in Mk. has the sing.,
which Wellh. prefers) ; and the true
meaning of the cloud is indicated in
Mt.'s φωτινή : it was the Shekinah
(see Add. n.) resting upon them,
from which the divine Voice proceeded. Lk. retains the latter point,
but represents the cloud as covering
the disciples also, 'and they feared
as they entered into the cloud' (see
patr. reff. in Swete). For ἐπισκιάζειν
cf. Ex. xl. 29 [35], Lk. i. 35. The
same thought with a different metaphor is expressed by (ἐπι)σκηνοῦν, Jo.
i. 14, 2 Cor. xii. 9, Apoc. vii. 15.

οὗτός ἐστιν κτλ.] Mt. alone
adds ἐν ᾧ εὐδόκησα, probably from
the Voice at the Baptism. Lk. has
ἐκλελεγμένος for ἀγαπητός. On the
various forms of the sentence, and
on the Voice, see iii. 17. ἀκούετε
αὐτοῦ (Lk. αὐτ. ἀκ.) is added only
here (see Add. n.), the point of which
is seen by reference to Deut. xviii.
15, 'a prophet from your brethren
like unto me shall the Lord thy God
raise up unto thee, him ye shall hear.'

6, 7. καὶ ἀκούσαντες κτλ.] These
verses occur in Mt. only, expanding
Mk.'s ἔκφοβοι ἐγένοντο ; the voice
was the climax of the vision, and

αὐτῶν καὶ ἐφοβήθησαν σφόδρα.   καὶ προσῆλθεν ὁ Ἰησοῦς 7
καὶ ἁψάμενος αὐτῶν εἶπεν Ἐγέρθητε καὶ μὴ φοβεῖσθε.
ἐπάραντες δὲ τοὺς ὀφθαλμοὺς αὐτῶν οὐδένα εἶδον εἰ μὴ 8

prostrated them with terror ; cf. Ac.
xxii. 7, Apoc. i. 17, Ez. i. 28, Dan.
x. 8 f.

8. ἐπάραντες κτλ.] The vision
vanished, and they found only
'Jesus Himself,' *i.e.* as they ordinarily

knew Him, unless αὐτὸν Ἰ. represents
the Aram. constr. לֵיהּ לִישׁוּע (Wellh.)
for the simple acc. Ἰησοῦν. The
position of αὐτόν varies in the MSS.,
and the lesser uncc. omit it. On
οὐκ . . . εἰ μή see xii. 24.

Additional Note on the Transfiguration.

1. The spiritual significance to be found in the narrative is great.
Almost every detail lends itself to allegorical treatment ; but three main
points are to be noticed : the metamorphosis (*v.* 2), the converse with Moses
and Elijah (*v.* 3), and the divine endorsement (*v.* 5). (1) The true μορφή
(cf. Phil. ii. 6, and Orig. quoted by Swete) of the Son of God is momentarily
revealed under the symbol of a more than earthly brightness ; it is 'the
glory of His Father' (xvi. 27). The shining of Moses' face with a borrowed
glory (Ex. xxxiv. 29 ff.) had symbolized the divine origin of the Law ; but
that was 'being done away,' whereas the glory of Christ will be permanent
(2 Cor. iii. 7–11). (2) The abiding validity of the Law and the Prophets as
'fulfilled' by Christ (Mt. v. 17) is symbolized by the harmonious converse
which He holds with their representatives, Moses and Elijah. Both had
held converse with God on the high mountain (Exod. xxxi. 18, 1 Kings xix.
9 ff.), which is now repeated with the Son of God. (3) The Three are
enveloped in the 'cloud,' the ancient symbol of the divine Presence (Exod.
xl. 29 [35] : ἐπεσκίαζεν (שָׁכַן) ἐπ' αὐτὴν [sc. τὴν σκηνὴν] ἡ νεφέλη : 1 Kings
viii. 10 f.). The Sonship of Christ is divinely attested ; to 'hear Him' is to
hear the eternal Truth, of which the Law and the Prophets were but partial
expressions. (It narrows the meaning to refer 'hear Him' to the prediction
of suffering in *v.* 21.) To attempt, therefore, to provide for the continuous
presence of Moses and Elijah was a grave mistake ; all that Christians need
is to have that of 'Jesus Himself.'

The vision thus represents the quintessence of Christian teaching on the
relation of the Old Covenant to the New. The glory of the former lies in
the fact that it is contained in, and transcended by, the latter. A particular
thought is suggested in Lk. : 'they were speaking of His exodus which He
was about to accomplish in Jerusalem.' Many expositors have brought this
into such prominence that the main teaching is apt to fall into the background. It symbolizes the truth that His death is foreshadowed in the Law
and the Prophets, πληροῦν referring to this fulfilment of the O.T. The
object of the whole vision is sometimes taken to be the encouragement of the
disciples to a firm faith in their Master in spite of the Crucifixion (*e.g.* Chrys.,
Hil.). J. Weiss, laying stress on *v.* 9 (Mk. ix. 9), finds in the scene
principally an anticipation of the Resurrection. But the teaching in Mt.,

9 αὐτὸν Ἰησοῦν μόνον. Καὶ καταβαινόντων αὐτῶν ἐκ τοῦ
ὄρους ἐνετείλατο αὐτοῖς ὁ Ἰησοῦς λέγων Μηδενὶ εἴπητε τὸ
ὅραμα ἕως οὗ ὁ υἱὸς τοῦ ἀνθρώπου ἐκ νεκρῶν ἐγερθῇ.
10 Καὶ ἐπηρώτησαν αὐτὸν οἱ μαθηταὶ λέγοντες Τί οὖν οἱ

Mk., with a wider range, deals with the entire fulfilment of the Jewish religion in Christianity.

2. Criticism of the historical value of the narrative must be subjective. The early attempts (e.g. of Paulus, Hase, and Schleiermacher) to rationalize it have been abandoned. Some dismiss it as a legend. Wellhausen suggests that it was a post-Resurrection appearance to the three disciples (cf. Apoc. Pet. ii., iii.); but others admit the possibility of a real mystic vision, or psychic experience, enjoyed by the three disciples, or (J. Weiss) by S. Peter alone. The modern study of so-called 'sub-conscious' and mystic states supplies analogous instances. The disciples, and perhaps especially the chief disciple, must have pondered much on the relation of the Lord's person and teaching to the Jewish religion. Jesus had spoken before of Moses and Elijah as representative of the Law and the Prophets, and they shared the current expectations of their reappearance. They had just been for months under the profound influence of His personality. And it is entirely in accordance with probability that they had 'sub-consciously' grasped the truths He had taught them with far greater vividness than their normal consciousness realized. Intense light and heavenly voices are the symbols by which mystics have most frequently attempted to describe their deepest intuitions (e.g. Ac. xxii. 6–8).

9–13. (Mk. ix. 9–13.) CONVERSA-
TION DURING THE DESCENT.

9. καὶ καταβαινόντων κτλ.] For the construction see Blass, § 74. 5. To relate the vision during the Lord's earthly life would only rouse excited curiosity (see on viii. 4). After He had risen, His Messiahship was the principal subject of Christian teaching. Mk.'s ἃ εἶδον is interpreted by Mt. as ὅραμα (Vulg. visionem, more accurate than O.L. visum), which recurs only in Ac. (11), always of mystic visions (unless vii. 31 = Exod. iii. 3 is an exception); freq. in LXX. of dreams and prophetic visions. On ἐγερθῇ (Mk. ἀναστῇ) see xvi. 21. Lk. omits the conversation, but says 'and they were silent and declared to no one in those days any of the things that they had seen.' Mk. adds here 'and they kept the saying

(ἐκράτησαν, i.e. probably in their memory), discussing among themselves what the rising from the dead meant' (see Swete, and J. Weiss, Das ält. Ev. 55). Mt. avoids recording their want of comprehension in spite of the prediction already made to them (xvi. 21); see on viii. 26.

10. τί οὖν κτλ.] τί = διὰ τί. Mk. ὅτι (see Swete). οὖν connects the question with the subject of the Resurrection, which, little as they could understand its meaning, was at least seen to involve the Messiah's presence on earth, whereas the Scribes (Mk., Pharisees and Scribes) said that Elijah must precede Him. Mk., following the same line of thought, places the saying here, but with no connecting particle, and the words may originally have belonged to another context, in which the

γραμματεῖς λέγουσιν ὅτι Ἠλείαν δεῖ ἐλθεῖν πρῶτον; ὁ δὲ 11
ἀποκριθεὶς εἶπεν Ἠλείας μὲν ἔρχεται καὶ ἀποκαταϲτήϲει
πάντα· λέγω δὲ ὑμῖν ὅτι Ἠλείας ἤδη ἦλθεν, καὶ οὐκ ἐπ- 12

Messiah's advent had just been mentioned, *e.g.* after xvi. 28 (Mk. ix. 1). On δεῖ see xvi. 21, and on πρῶτον for πρότερον Blass, § 11. 5.

11. Ἠλείας κτλ.] The *orat. recta* of the Scribes' teaching ; cf. γεννᾶται (ii. 4). In contrast with their teaching, Jesus says (*v.* 12, λέγω δέ) that Elijah had already come in the person of the Baptist. But it cannot be said of the Baptist that he 'set right, restored, all things'; Mt.'s μέν . . . δέ implies, 'It is true that the scribes teach that Elijah cometh, etc., but I say he has already come ; but so far from restoring all things, they did unto him whatever they wished.' If this is the meaning in Mt., Jesus *corrects* the scribal tradition. Mt. abbreviates Mk., which is no less obscure. Mk.'s μέν should perhaps be omitted (with DL 𝔏 𝔖), but in any case καὶ πῶς γέγραπται is difficult unless the first sentence is interrogative : ' Elijah having come first restoreth (prophetic pres.) all things ? Then how is it that Scripture foretells the passion of the Messiah ?' *i.e.* Why is the Passion necessary if Elijah's work is to put everything right first ? Then Mk.'s following verse (ἀλλὰ λέγω κτλ.) solves the difficulty by shewing that Elijah has indeed come, but did not restore all things because he (*i.e.* the Baptist) was killed, and therefore the prophecies of the Passion find room for fulfilment. Other less likely explanations are mentioned by Allen, to which may be added the suggestion to transpose Mk. *vv.* 12 a and 12 b.

The scribal teaching is based on Mal. iii. 24 [iv. 5], but 'restoreth

all things' covers much more than Malachi's description of Elijah's functions. They are already amplified in Sir. xlviii. 10, 'to turn the heart of father to son, and to establish (καταστῆσαι) the tribes of Jacob.' This is further explained in *Eduyoth* viii. 7, perhaps contemporary with Jesus.

12. λέγω δέ κτλ.] On ἦλθεν = ἐλήλυθεν (Mk.) see Moulton, i. 135 f. Mt. alone has κ. οὐκ ἐπέγνωσαν αὐτ., 'they did not recognize him (as Elijah).' On the verb see xi. 27. The masses had been stirred by his call to repentance, but no one had realized his true significance. ἐπέγνωσαν and ἐποίησαν may be impersonal (cf. καλέσουσιν, i. 23, παραδώσουσιν xxiv. 9) ; but possibly the subject is the Scribes, some of whom may have been in alliance with 'the chief men of Galilee' (Mk. vi. 21), and have fanned the flame of Herodias' hostility, fearing that the Baptist's influence with Herod would be injurious to their national hopes (see *JThS.*, July 1900, 520–7). The reference is clearly to his execution. For ἐν αὐτῷ (Mk. αὐτῷ) cf. ἐν ἐμοί, Mk. xiv. 6 (= εἰς ἐμέ, Mt. xxvi. 10) ; see Blass, § 34. 4. ἐποίησαν ὅσα ἠθ. imitates O.T. descriptions of human tyranny, Eccl. viii. 3, Dan. viii. 4, xi. 16, 36, 2 Mac. vii. 16, Sir. viii. 15. Mk.'s καθὼς γέγραπται ἐπ' αὐτόν is omitted ; it is probably a reference to one or more apocalyptic passages, which may also have been the basis of Apoc. xi. 7 ; or possibly it arose out of a scribe's note on Mk.'s preceding verse, recording καθώς as a *v.l.* for καὶ πῶς.

ἔγνωσαν αὐτὸν ἀλλὰ ἐποίησαν ἐν αὐτῷ ὅσα ἠθέλησαν· οὕτως
13 καὶ ὁ υἱὸς τοῦ ἀνθρώπου μέλλει πάσχειν ὑπ᾽ αὐτῶν. τότε
συνῆκαν οἱ μαθηταὶ ὅτι περὶ Ἰωάνου τοῦ βαπτιστοῦ εἶπεν
αὐτοῖς.

14 Καὶ ἐλθόντων πρὸς τὸν ὄχλον προσῆλθεν αὐτῷ ἄνθρωπος
15 γονυπετῶν αὐτὸν καὶ λέγων Κύριε, ἐλέησόν μου τὸν
υἱόν, ὅτι σεληνιάζεται καὶ κακῶς ἔχει, πολλάκις γὰρ
16 πίπτει εἰς τὸ πῦρ καὶ πολλάκις εἰς τὸ ὕδωρ· καὶ προσήνεγκα αὐτὸν τοῖς μαθηταῖς σου, καὶ οὐκ ἠδυνήθησαν

15 εχει] ℵBLZ^vid 𐄂 sin.pesh sah Chr ; πασχει uncc.rel minn.omn 𐄂 omn 𐄂
cur me

οὕτως κτλ.] The equivalent of
Mk.'s καὶ πῶς γέγραπται . . . ἐξου-
δενηθῇ.

13. τότε κτλ.] A comment added
by Mt. Their knowledge of the
Lord's Messiahship made plain to
them what had been to the people
an enigma (xi. 14). The truth
received permanent expression in the
Church in the words of Lk. i. 76 f.

14-21. (Mk. ix. 14-29, Lk. ix.
37-43 a.) A LUNATIC BOY HEALED.
Mt., Lk. greatly abbreviate Mk.;
possibly they also made use of an
earlier form of the story.

14. καὶ ἐλθόντων κτλ.] For the
omission of the pron. (class. and
frequent in papyri) cf. v. 26 (Blass,
§ 74. 5). A crowd, including Scribes,
had gathered round the disciples
(Mk.), to which Mt. refers, without
explanation. It would hardly be
found as far north as the Hermon ;
if that was the scene of the Transfiguration, Jesus and the three
disciples walked thither and returned
by themselves. Lk. says 'on the
next day,' which, if the incident
occurred at night (see on v. 1), means
the next astronomical day, not the
next Jewish day, i.e. later in the
same evening (as 𐄂 sin.cur sah 'on
that day,' D 𐄂 vet.nonn 'in the course

of the day'). In Mk., the Scribes
were disputing with the other disciples ; when the crowd saw Jesus
they were amazed, and ran to Him
and saluted Him ; and it was when
He asked the subject of the dispute
that the father of the boy answered.
Mt. alone says that he approached
the Lord and knelt to Him (γονυπετῶν
αὐτόν, cf. Mk. x. 17), leaving the
boy, apparently, in the crowd (v. 17).

15. κύριε κτλ.] Mt., Lk. reproduce the substance of Mk. independently. σεληνιάζεται (iv. 24 only)
takes the place of ἔχοντα πνεῦμα
ἄλαλον, four details (ῥήσσει, ἀφρίζει,
τρίζει τοὺς ὀδόντας, ξηραίνεται) are
summarized as κακῶς ἔχει (cf. iv. 24,
viii. 16), or possibly κ. πάσχει (see
Appar.) which is class. but unique in
the N.T.. The remainder of the verse
is taken from Mk., but from a later
point in the conversation. Lk. alone
adds that the son was μονογενής. The
symptoms seem to point to epilepsy.

16. καὶ προσήνεγκα κτλ.] Mt.
himself (v. 18) ascribes the affliction
to a demon, but not (as in Mk.,
Lk.) the boy's father, who here says
θεραπεῦσαι for ἐκβαλῶσιν (Mk.,
Lk.). The dispute with the Scribes
had apparently been due to the
disciples' failure to uphold their
Master's prestige in His absence.

αὐτὸν θεραπεῦσαι. ἀποκριθεὶς δὲ ὁ Ἰησοῦς εἶπεν Ὦ 17
γενεὰ ἄπιστος καὶ διεστραμμένη, ἕως πότε μεθ᾽ ὑμῶν
ἔσομαι ; ἕως πότε ἀνέξομαι ὑμῶν ; φέρετέ μοι αὐτὸν ὧδε.
καὶ ἐπετίμησεν αὐτῷ ὁ Ἰησοῦς, καὶ ἐξῆλθεν ἀπ᾽ αὐτοῦ 18
τὸ δαιμόνιον· καὶ ἐθεραπεύθη ὁ παῖς ἀπὸ τῆς ὥρας
ἐκείνης. Τότε προσελθόντες οἱ μαθηταὶ τῷ Ἰησοῦ κατ᾽ 19
ἰδίαν εἶπαν Διὰ τί ἡμεῖς οὐκ ἠδυνήθημεν ἐκβαλεῖν αὐτό ;
ὁ δὲ λέγει αὐτοῖς Διὰ τὴν ὀλιγοπιστίαν ὑμῶν· ἀμὴν γὰρ 20

20 ολιγοπιστιαν] אB 1 13 22 33 124 346 𐤔 cur.pal me sah arm aeth ; απιστιαν
CDE *etc* 𝔏 *omn* 𐤔 pesh.hcl

17. ὦ γενεά κτλ.] Mt., Lk. add
καὶ διεστραμμένη, a reminiscence of
Deut. xxxii. 5 (adopted in Phil. ii.
15 ; cf. Ac. ii. 40). On γενεά see
xi. 16. The people, the boy's
father (Mk. *v.* 23), and the disciples,
were all in their own way ἄπιστοι.
Lk., who omits the conversation in
v. 19 f., understands γενεά to refer
only to the people, whose want of
faith rendered the disciples unable to
perform the cure (cf. Mk. vi. 5 f.).
J. Weiss strangely argues (*Das ält.
Ev.* 249) that the 'disciples' to whom
the father appealed (Mk. *v.* 18) were
identical with the ὄχλος, and that
therefore the Lord had only three
chosen followers, not twelve. There
is no 'contradiction' between the
failure from want of faith and the
ἐξουσία conferred in Mk. vi. 7 (Mt. x.
8). οὐδὲ γὰρ ἀεὶ οἱ αὐτοὶ ἦσαν
(Chrys.), a bitter experience with
which all workers for God can
sympathize.

ἕως πότε κτλ.] How long must
I live and work among you before
you will understand the power of
God ? Cf. Jo. xiv. 9. It is 'the
Lord's *quousque tandem*' (Swete).
φέρετέ μοι κτλ. Cf. xiv. 18, where
the problem was different, but the
solution, as in all hard cases, the
same. The boy had been left in the
care of the crowd, who now ἤνεγκαν
αὐτὸν πρὸς αὐτόν (Mk.).

18. καὶ ἐπετίμησεν κτλ.] The
boy and the demon are identified
(αὐτῷ). That he was not a man
but a παῖς (so Lk. ; Mk. παιδίον) is
not mentioned till this point. Mt.
probably avoided purposely two
features in Mk.'s much longer
account ; Jesus asked the father a
question (see on viii. 29), and the
cure was not instantaneous, for the
spirit rent the boy after the command
'Come out of him' (cf. Mk. i. 26,
viii. 22–26, omitted by Mt.). For
ἀπ᾽ αὐτοῦ (Mk. ἐξ αὐ.) cf. xii. 43 ;
Blass, § 40. 2. Mt. alone says ἀπὸ
τ. ὥρας ἐκ. ; see on ix. 22. Lk.
adds, 'And all were astonished at
the majesty (μεγαλειότητι) of God.'

19. τότε κτλ.] Mk. καὶ εἰσελθόντος αὐτοῦ εἰς οἶκον. See on
viii. 16.

20. διὰ τήν κτλ.] Mk. τοῦτο τὸ
γένος ἐν οὐδενὶ δύναται ἐξελθεῖν εἰ
μὴ ἐν προσευχῇ : the power of
personality that can drive out demons
can be maintained only by prayer.
Mt., carrying on the thought of ὦ
γενεὰ ἄπιστος (*v.* 17), leads up, by
the word of rebuke, to a saying on
the πίστις which can work miracles.
There is some support for the *v.l.*
ἀπιστίαν, which, however, may have
been due to γενεὰ ἄπιστος ; if it is
genuine, ὀλιγοπ. must have been
an early substitute, coined on the
analogy of ὀλιγόπιστος (see on vi.

λέγω ὑμῖν, ἐὰν ἔχητε πίστιν ὡς κόκκον σινάπεως, ἐρεῖτε
τῷ ὄρει τούτῳ Μετάβα ἔνθεν ἐκεῖ, καὶ μεταβήσεται, καὶ
οὐδὲν ἀδυνατήσει ὑμῖν.

22   Συστρεφομένων δὲ αὐτῶν ἐν τῇ Γαλιλαίᾳ εἶπεν αὐτοῖς

21 *om vers.* τουτο δε το γενος ουκ εκπορευεται [εκβαλλεται ℵᵇ] ει μη εν προσευχη
και νηστεια ℵ*B 33 𝕷 e ff¹ 𝕾 cur.pal sah aeth ; *add* ℵᵇCDE *etc* 𝕷 vet.*pler*.vg
𝕾 pesh.hcl me arm   22 συστρεφομενων] ℵB 1 𝕷 a b f ff² n q vg 𝕾 sin.cur.
pesh 'while they were abiding,' sahᶜᵒᵈ 'while they were going'; αναστρεφο-
μενων uncc.*rel* minn.*rel* 𝕷 c ff¹ ; στρεφ. me sah Or

30) in order to lessen the severity.
The result is paradoxical, for the
following words teach that faith,
however ὀλίγη, can do marvels.

ἀμὴν γάρ κτλ.] See on v. 18.
In xxi. 21 (Mk. xi. 23) a similar
saying, but without mention of the
mustard-seed, follows the withering
of the fig-tree ; in Lk. xvii. 6 (probably Q) it is the answer to the prayer
of the apostles πρόσθες ἡμῖν πίστιν.
Lk. there has the 'mustard-seed,' but
'sycamine-tree' instead of mountain.
Mt. here combines Mk. and Q. For
κόκκον σινάπεως see xiii. 31.

ἐρεῖτε κτλ.] In placing the saying here, Mt. may have thought of
the mountain of the Transfiguration ;
in xxi. 21 it is the M. of Olives.
In the latter, the command is 'be
thou taken up and cast into the
sea' ; in Lk. the command to the
tree is 'be thou rooted out and
planted in the sea.' For ἐκεῖ = ἐκεῖσε
cf. ii. 22 (Blass, § 25. 2). To remove
mountains may have been a current
proverbial expression ; 'an uprooter
of mountains' occurs in the Talm.
of rabbis who removed difficulties
of exegesis in the Law (Lightft. *Hor.
Heb.* on xxi. 21). S. Paul, who
combines it with πίστις (1 Cor. xiii.
2), probably knew the present saying. On the Lord's use of 'extreme
expressions' see Sanday, *Life of Chr.
in Recent Research*, 26 f.

καὶ οὐδέν κτλ.] Faith in God
places man in possession of the power
of God ; cf. Gen. xviii. 14, Job. xlii.
2, Lk. i. 37 ; cf. Phil. iv. 13.

[21.] τοῦτο δὲ τὸ γένος οὐκ ἐκπορεύεται 'εἰ μὴ ἐν προσευχῇ καὶ
νηστείᾳ. The verse was a gloss
derived from Mk. when καὶ νηστείᾳ
had already been added to it.

22, 23.   (Mk. ix. 30 ff., Lk. ix.
43 b–45.) SECOND PREDICTION OF
THE PASSION (see on xvi. 21 ff.).

22. συστρεφομένων κτλ.] Mk.
κἀκεῖθεν ἐξελθόντες παρεπορεύοντο
διὰ τῆς Γ. Lk. has no note of
place ; he relates that Jesus said
θέσθε ὑμεῖς εἰς τὰ ὦτα ὑμῶν τοὺς
λόγους τούτους, *i.e.* what the people
were saying in astonishment at His
works, contrasting it with His future
treatment at the hands of men. The
Lord now returned to the territory
of Antipas, but secretly (Mk. οὐκ
ἤθελεν ἵνα τις γνοῖ). The journey
to Capharnaum was the first stage
in the movement towards Jerusalem.
For συστρέφειν cf. Ac. xi. 28 D
(συνεστραμμένων δὲ ἡμῶν), xxviii. 3 ;
συστροφή Ac. xix. 40, xxiii. 12. In
the LXX. the verb means to conspire,
or to collect for battle. If the partcp.
here were aor. or perf. it could mean
'when they had collected'—at a fixed
rendez-vous. But the pres. tense is
difficult. Swete suggests that, for

ὁ Ἰησοῦς Μέλλει ὁ υἱὸς τοῦ ἀνθρώπου παραδίδοσθαι εἰς
χεῖρας ἀνθρώπων, καὶ ἀποκτενοῦσιν αὐτόν, καὶ τῇ τρίτῃ 23
ἡμέρᾳ ἐγερθήσεται. καὶ ἐλυπήθησαν σφόδρα.

Ἐλθόντων δὲ αὐτῶν εἰς Καφαρναοὺμ προσῆλθον οἱ τὰ 24

the sake of secrecy, 'they broke up into small parties which mustered at certain points in the route.' But even if the one word could mean as much as this, the aor. εἶπεν αὐτοῖς is against it. This takes the place of Mk.'s ἐδίδασκεν γὰρ τοὺς μαθητὰς αὐτοῦ, which gives a reason for the privacy. Zahn thinks that they 'kept together,' closer to Jesus than usual. But more probably Mt. avoids all reference to the wish for privacy, and συστρ. αὐτ. means 'while they were moving about together.' The v.l. ἀναστρεφομένων has nearly the same meaning : 𝕃 vet. vulg. *conversantibus eis* [*ipsis*] ; 𝕾 'and when they were abiding.'

μέλλει κτλ.] The coming events are the Betrayal, Death, and Resurrection. παραδίδοσθαι need not be an exact prediction of the action of Judas, as though the Lord added a fresh detail to His former prediction. παραδιδόναι is used quite generally of 'handing over' some one to the authorities (iv. 12, v. 25, x. 17, 19, 21, xx. 19, xxiv. 9). It is presupposed in xvi. 21, 'suffer many things from the elders, etc.' It is very improbable that it refers, as in Rom. viii. 32, to the action of God (Orig. ; see Abbott, *Paradosis*, 31, 57, and *Son of Man*, xi.).

καὶ ἀποκτενοῦσιν] The sentence is omitted in Lk. On τ. τρίτῃ ἡμ. (Mk. μετὰ τρεῖς ἡμέρας) see xvi. 21. Their sorrow was for His betrayal and death, regardless of His promised Resurrection. καὶ ἐλυπ. σφ. takes the place of Mk.'s οἱ δὲ ἠγνόουν τὸ ῥῆμα, καὶ ἐφοβοῦντο αὐτὸν ἐπερωτῆσαι, to avoid recording their

continued inability to grasp the truth (see on viii. 26). But Mt. follows Mk. in giving yet a third prediction of the Passion (xx. 17 ff.). A suffering Messiah remained an insoluble enigma until after the Resurrection.

24–27. (Mt. only.) THE COIN IN THE MOUTH OF THE FISH.

24. ἐλθόντων κτλ.] On the narratives in Mt. in which S. Peter is prominent see x. 2. Mk. also (v. 33) relates the arrival at Capharnaum. Jesus probably no longer had a house there (cf. iv. 13, ix. 10, 28), but friends would give Him hospitality. If He lodged with Simon (see v. 25), it would account for the question being addressed to the latter.

The δραχμή (Lk. xv. 8), N.Heb. זוז, was ¼ shekel (cf. 1 Sam. ix. 8). The δίδραχμον or double-drachm (cf. Jos. *Ant*. XVIII. ix. 1), ½ shekel, about 1s. 4½d., was the amount of the annual contribution (originally ⅓ shekel, Neh. x. 32) made for the maintenance of the temple services by every male Jew above the age of 19 (Philo, *De Mon.* ii. 3), a practice based on Exod. xxx. 11–16. Since the didrachm was seldom coined in the time of Jesus, two persons must usually have combined to pay a tetradrachm or στατήρ (v. 27) = a shekel, or in late Heb. סֶלַע. After the destruction of Jerusalem, when the contribution was demanded by the Romans for the temple of Jupiter Capitolinus (Jos. *BJ*. VII. vi. 6, Suet. *Domit.* 12), many Christians would naturally wish to claim exemption, as not being Jews. But this narrative

δίδραχμα λαμβάνοντες τῷ Πέτρῳ καὶ εἶπαν Ὁ διδάσκαλος
25 ὑμῶν οὐ τελεῖ τὰ δίδραχμα ; λέγει Ναί. καὶ ἐλθόντα
εἰς τὴν οἰκίαν προέφθασεν αὐτὸν ὁ Ἰησοῦς λέγων Τί σοι
δοκεῖ, Σίμων ; οἱ βασιλεῖς τῆς γῆς ἀπὸ τίνων λαμβάνουσιν
τέλη ἢ κῆνσον ; ἀπὸ τῶν υἱῶν αὐτῶν ἢ ἀπὸ τῶν ἀλλοτρίων ;
26 εἰπόντος δέ Ἀπὸ τῶν ἀλλοτρίων, ἔφη αὐτῷ ὁ Ἰησοῦς
27 Ἄραγε ἐλεύθεροί εἰσιν οἱ υἱοί· ἵνα δὲ μὴ σκανδαλίσωμεν

would be useful in indicating the attitude that they ought to take.

οἱ τὰ δίδραχμα κτλ.] For the pres. partcp. see on iv. 3. The plur. τὰ δ. means the several didrachms which they collected. If the plur. at the end of the verse is not repeated by an oversight, it may mean 'the (successive) didrachms' which He should pay year by year. There is nothing to suggest that the question was asked in malice (Chrys.). The tax was collected in the month Adar (*Shek.* i. 1, 3), *i.e.* about March ; the chronological position of the incident is in keeping with this.

25. λέγει ναί κτλ.] He knew that Jesus had consistently observed the principle involved in v. 17–20. Jesus knew, before he spoke, that he was going to ask Him about it ; possibly He was with him and overheard the demand, and on entering the house spoke before the apostle had time to broach the subject (B. Weiss). S sin has 'his house,' *i.e.* Simon's.

τί σοι δοκεῖ κτλ.] An expression characteristic of Mt. (xviii. 12, xxi. 28, xxii. 17, 42, xxvi. 66 ; cf. Lk. x. 36, Jo. xi. 56). On the name Σίμων see xvi. 17. τέλη were the local taxes or customs collected by the τελῶναι ; κῆνσος was the capitation tax (see on xxii. 17, where Lk. has φόρος). They are mentioned together in Rom. xiii. 7. The plur. βασιλεῖς is a general reference to the Roman power, υἱοί being not merely members of the royal family but, in Hebraic metaphor, all Roman citizens.

26. εἰπόντος κτλ.] For the omission of the pron. cf. *v.* 14. On ἄραγε see vii. 20. The argument is that if earthly kings do not tax their own families or people, the same is true of God ; the Jews, as ἀλλότριοι, pay taxes to 'the Great King' (v. 35), who dwelleth in the temple (xxiii. 21), but the Son of God and His followers, as υἱοί, have the right of exemption (ἐλεύθ. εἰσιν). This reflects so strong an anti-Jewish feeling that its genuineness must be considered extremely doubtful. Christian reflexion of a different kind is seen in an apocryphal addition in min. 561 (Cod. Algerinae Peckover): ἔφη Σίμων, ναί. λέγει ὁ Ἰησοῦς, δὸς οὖν καὶ σὺ ὡς ἀλλότριος αὐτῶν (similarly Arab. Diat. trans. Hamlyn Hill, 142). In this case Jesus is the only υἱός, and is exempt ; Simon is one of the ἀλλότριοι, and must therefore pay ; and the next verse means 'But lest we should offend them, we will both pay.' See Rendel Harris, *JBL.*, Dec. 1889, 79–89.

27. ἵνα δέ κτλ.] On σκανδαλίζειν see v. 29. The avoidance of offence, vehemently enjoined in xviii. 6 f., is a principle echoed by S. Paul (1 Cor. x. 23–xi. 1) and S. Peter (1 Pet. ii. 16). βάλε ἄγκιστρον : cf. Is. xix. 8. ἀναβάντα, as in Aram., takes the place of a passive verb. On στατήρ see *v.* 24 ; it is a *v.l.* for ἀργύρια in xxvi. 15. ἀντί, 'an

αὐτούς, πορευθεὶς εἰς ·θάλασσαν βάλε ἄγκιστρον καὶ τὸν
ἀναβάντα πρῶτον ἰχθὺν ἆρον, καὶ ἀνοίξας τὸ στόμα αὐτοῦ
εὑρήσεις στατῆρα· ἐκεῖνον λαβὼν δὸς αὐτοῖς ἀντὶ ἐμοῦ καὶ
σοῦ.

Ἐν ἐκείνῃ τῇ ὥρᾳ προσῆλθον οἱ μαθηταὶ τῷ Ἰησοῦ λέ- 1   XVIII.
γοντες Τίς ἄρα μείζων ἐστὶν ἐν τῇ βασιλείᾳ τῶν οὐρανῶν ;
καὶ προσκαλεσάμενος παιδίον ἔστησεν αὐτὸ ἐν μέσῳ αὐτῶν 2

equivalent for,' expresses the fact
that the money was a capitation
tax ; cf. xx. 28.

In its present form the narrative
cannot be rationalized. It relates
a miracle of foreknowledge. It is
unnatural to make the words mean
'as soon as you have opened its
mouth, *i.e.* extracted the hook, you
will be able to [sell the fish and
thereby] obtain a stater.' Blass
omits ἀνοίξας τὸ στ. αὐτ. and conjectures εὑρήσει (for -σεις), 'it [the
fish] will fetch a stater.' It has
even been suggested that Jesus
humorously referred to His poverty :
'If a stater is required, you will
have to get it from a fish,' perhaps
with an allusion to a legend or
current proverb. It is quite improbable that the story itself is a legend,
like that of the ring of Polycrates
(Herod. iii. 42) ; but it cannot be
denied that the miracle is different
in character from others performed
by the Lord. Its effect was simply
to provide Himself with money.
Moreover the actual occurrence of
the miracle is not recorded. The
possibility must be recognized that
some words uttered by Him were
altered in the course of tradition.

xviii. A discourse on the right
behaviour of Christ's followers to
one another ; the fourth of Mt.'s
five principal collections of sayings ;
see on vii. 28. It begins with a
short collection in Mk. ix. 33–48,
attached, as in Mk., to the disciples'

dispute about precedence. The sayings in Mk., most of which Mt. adopts
nearly as they stand, are linked by
verbal connexions with little real
unity, though Mt. perhaps saw in
them the underlying thought that
as Jesus was about to perform His
supreme act of service as a prelude to
His Messianic glory, so His followers
must be prepared for humility and
service if they were to gain the
Kingdom.

1–5. (Mk. ix. 33–37, Lk. ix. 46 ff.)
THE QUESTION OF PRECEDENCE.
HUMILITY.

1. ἐν ἐκείνῃ κτλ.] Mk.'s 'in the
house' is omitted (see viii. 16) ; also
the Lord's question (see viii. 29),
'What were you disputing on the
road ?' and to spare the disciples
(see viii. 26) Mt. alters 'but they
were silent, for they had disputed
among themselves on the road which
was the greatest' into the simple
question which he relates that they
asked.

τίς ἄρα κτλ.] The particle is not
a connexion with the preceding incident ; it is a colloquialism, 'who
now' ; Vulg. *quis putas* ; cf. xxiv.
45. Mk.'s τίς μείζων (Lk. τὸ τίς ἂν
εἴη μ., cf. Lk. xxii. 24), 'who is the
greatest,' *sc.* at the present time, is
interpreted by Mt. of precedence in
the coming Kingdom. And he frames
the answer to correspond with it (see
on xx. 25).

2. καὶ προσκαλεσάμενος κτλ.] See
x. 1. Mk. λαβών. To this incident

3 καὶ εἶπεν Ἀμὴν λέγω ὑμῖν, ἐὰν μὴ στραφῆτε καὶ γένησθε
ὡς τὰ παιδία, οὐ μὴ εἰσέλθητε εἰς τὴν βασιλείαν τῶν
4 οὐρανῶν. ὅστις οὖν ταπεινώσει ἑαυτὸν ὡς τὸ παιδίον τοῦτο,
5 οὗτός ἐστιν ὁ μείζων ἐν τῇ βασιλείᾳ τῶν οὐρανῶν· καὶ ὃς

Mk. prefixes a verse, which has the effect of separating it from the disciples' dispute : 'and .sitting down He called (ἐφώνησεν) the Twelve [though in the previous verses they were already present], and saith unto them, If any wishes to be first, he shall be last of all and servant (διάκονος) of all.' Mk., therefore, did not interpret this as a warning of the penalty of striving for precedence (J. Weiss), but as a command as to the way in which to be truly 'first.' In Lk. a saying with the latter meaning follows the incident, 'he that is least among you, he is great' (cf. Mt. xx. 26, xxiii. 11, Mk. x. 43 f., Lk. xxii. 26).

ἐν μέσῳ αὐτῶν (so Mk.) : Lk.'s παρ' ἑαυτῷ perhaps means in the place of honour (Spitta). Mt., Lk. omit Mk.'s tender touch, 'having embraced him.' On the tradition that the child was Ignatius see Lightft. *Ign.* i. 27. Swete suggests that it was S. Peter's child ; cf. viii. 14, 1 Cor. ix. 5, which shew that the apostle was married.

3. ἀμήν κτλ.] See on v. 18. *Vv.* 3, 4 are in Mt. only, but the present verse is perhaps an echo of Mk. x. 15, which Mt. omits in his parallel passage (xix. 14 f.). Without a childlike spirit, the disciples, so far from being the greatest in the Kingdom, will not enter it at all. 'De individuo, de quo quaerebant, non respondet' (Beng.). For στραφῆτε cf. Jo. xii. 40 (= שׁוּב) ; more usually ἐπιστρέφειν (xiii. 15 = Ac. xxviii. 27, Lk. xxii. 32, Ac. iii. 19) ; the corresponding subst. is μετάνοια. The first step towards γένεσθαι ὡς τὰ παιδία is γεννηθῆναι ἄνωθεν (Jo. iii. 3–6).

4. ὅστις κτλ.] 'He will be the greatest who has the least idea that he is great.' A positive statement, the complement of the negative in *v.* 3 (cf. the parallelism in xvi. 25). The double aspect is seen also in xxiii. 12. The child in their midst (τοῦτο) represented the class which symbolizes the ideal. This reversal of the world's valuation is strikingly expressed in *Acts of Phil.* xxxiv.: ἐὰν μὴ ποιήσητε ὑμῶν τὰ κάτω εἰς τὰ ἄνω (καὶ τὰ ἄνω εἰς τὰ κάτω καὶ τὰ δεξιὰ εἰς τὰ ἀριστερὰ) καὶ τὰ ἀριστερὰ εἰς τὰ δεξιά, οὐ μὴ εἰσ-έλθητε εἰς τὴν βασιλείαν μου [τῶν οὐρανῶν].

5. καὶ ὃς κτλ.] Expositors (*e.g.* Chrys.) have explained the connexion thus : You must not only shew a childlike spirit, but you must honour for My sake those who do so. But the emphasis is rather on ἐμὲ δέχεται. The thought is that in xxv. 40, and the sole connexion with the preceding verses is the word παιδίον. In Mk., Lk. there is no καί, as in Mt., to lead up to it. Mt. omits Mk.'s remaining words, 'and whosoever receiveth Me, receiveth not Me but Him that sent Me' (Lk. similarly), but he uses them in x. 40, interpreting 'one of these children' as referring to the disciples (ὑμᾶς). See also on x. 42. The true solution of the difficulties is doubtful. Some take the incident of the child to be an altered form of that in xix. 13 ff. (Mk. x. 13 ff.), and possibly, as said above, *v.* 3 is derived from Mk. x. 15. But in any case this verse must originally have been unconnected with the incident. δέξηται :

ἐὰν δέξηται ἐν παιδίον τοιοῦτο ἐπὶ τῷ ὀνόματί μου, ἐμὲ δέχεται· ὃς δ᾽ ἂν σκανδαλίσῃ ἕνα τῶν μικρῶν τούτων τῶν 6 πιστευόντων εἰς ἐμέ, συμφέρει αὐτῷ ἵνα κρεμασθῇ μύλος ὀνικὸς περὶ τὸν τράχηλον αὐτοῦ καὶ καταποντισθῇ ἐν τῷ πελάγει τῆς θαλάσσης. Οὐαὶ τῷ κόσμῳ ἀπὸ τῶν σκανδάλων· 7

the 'reception' of another for the Lord's sake might take a particular form, as in x. 40 ff. (cf. Ac. xxi. 17, Gal. iv. 14, Col. iv. 10), or, more generally, that of acceptance into fellowship, like προσλαμβάνεσθαι (Rom. xiv. 1, xv. 7). ἐπὶ τ. ὀνόμ. μ. (so Mk., Lk.), 'on the ground of My name,' seems to be equivalent to εἰς τ. ὄν. μ. (= לְשֵׁם), 'for My sake'; see on x. 41. But possibly its usual force, 'with an invocation of My name' (invoking the blessing and co-operation of Jesus in performing the act), underlies the words. See Heitmüller, Im Namen Jesu, 113.

6-9. (Mk. ix. 42-48, Lk. xvii. 1 f.) ON STUMBLING-BLOCKS.

Mt. omits Mk. ix. 38-40 (on the non-disciple who exorcized in the Lord's name), and v. 41, which he has used in x. 42.

6. ὃς δ᾽ ἂν κτλ.] On σκανδαλίζειν see v. 29. ἕνα τ. μικρῶν τ. has the same force as ἐν παιδίον τοιοῦτο; the μικροί are the obscure and simple believers (τοὺς πτωχούς, τοὺς εὐκαταφρονήτους, τοὺς ἀγνῶτας, Chrys.), in contrast with the μεγάλοι (see on x. 42). If τ. πιστευόντων εἰς ἐμέ is a gloss (J. Weiss), it is not because of the faith ascribed to them, but because the construction, frequent in Jo., is unique in the synn. πιστ. ἐπί occurs in xxvii. 42.

συμφέρει κτλ.] Mk. καλόν ἐστιν, Lk. λυσιτελεῖ; see on v. 29. For the pass. κρεμασθῇ Mk., Lk. have the intrans. περίκειται, following the Aram. idiom. μύλος ὀνικός (so Mk.; Lk., less precisely, λίθος μυλικός)

denotes a large mill driven by an ass (𝕷 'mola asinaria'; cf. Ov. Fasti, vi. 318, 'pumiceas versat asella molas' and Rabb. רֵחַיִם שֶׁל חֲמוֹר), as distinct from a hand-mill (χειρομύλη), which is called simply μύλος in xxiv. 41, Apoc. xviii. 22, and LXX. In late Heb. חֲמוֹר is used, in various connexions, of a piece of wood which supports a weight, and in Xen., al. ὄνος is the upper of two mill-stones; but with that meaning μυλικὸς ὄνος would rather have been used here.

καταποντισθῇ (Mk. βέβληται, Lk. ἔρριπται) appears in the (?)quotation in Clem. Cor. xlvi. 8. ἐν τ. πελάγει τ. θαλ., 'far out in the open sea,' a vivid substitute for εἰς τὴν θάλασσαν (Mk., Lk.). For the class. πέλαγος cf. Ac. xxvii. 5, 2 Mac. v. 21. The force of the words is heightened by the fact that drowning was not a Jewish punishment. In Jos. Ant. XIV. xv. 10 it is an act of vengeance; in Aboda Zara, iii. 3, 9, 'to cast into the Salt Sea' is an expression for the destruction of heathen objects.

7. οὐαί κτλ.] Mk. omits the verse; Lk., omitting the first clause, transposes this and the preceding verse. Some think that this points to an abbreviation of Q by Mk. (Oxf. Stud. 175) οὐαί (see on xi. 21) here expresses not anger, but sympathetic sorrow. θρηνεῖ ὡς φιλάνθρωπος τὸν κόσμον (Thphlact.); cf. xxiv. 19, Apoc. xii. 12. οὐαὶ ἀπό occurs only here in bibl. Gk., οὐ. ἐκ in Apoc. viii. 13. Cf. Ber. R. x. 11, 'Woe to the world because of His judgment' (מְדִינוֹ). For ἀπό 'because of' cf. xiii. 44. On σκάνδαλον see xiii. 41.

ἀνάγκη γὰρ ἐλθεῖν τὰ σκάνδαλα, πλὴν οὐαὶ τῷ ἀνθρώπῳ
8 δι' οὗ τὸ σκάνδαλον ἔρχεται. Εἰ δὲ ἡ χείρ σου ἢ
ὁ πούς σου σκανδαλίζει σε, ἔκκοψον αὐτὸν καὶ βάλε
ἀπὸ σοῦ· καλόν σοί ἐστιν εἰσελθεῖν εἰς τὴν ζωὴν κυλλὸν
ἢ χωλόν, ἢ δύο χεῖρας ἢ δύο πόδας ἔχοντα βληθῆναι
9 εἰς τὸ πῦρ τὸ αἰώνιον. καὶ εἰ ὁ ὀφθαλμός σου σκανδαλίζει

ἀνάγκη κτλ.] Lk. ἀνένδεκτόν
ἐστιν τοῦ τὰ σκ. μὴ ἐλθ. Cf. 1 Cor.
xi. 19. ἀνάγκη does not exclude
man's responsibility, which is presupposed in the next clause. The
same problem is involved in xx. 23,
xxi. 37, xxii. 14, xxv. 34, xxvi. 24.
On πλήν see xi. 22. In Clem. Hom.
xii. 29 the saying is ascribed to Jesus
τὰ ἀγαθὰ ἐλθεῖν δεῖ, μακάριος δὲ
δι' οὗ ἔρχεται· ὁμοίως καὶ τὰ κακὰ
ἀνάγκη ἐλθεῖν, οὐαὶ δὲ δι' οὗ ἔρχεται
(similarly Aphr. Hom. v.); see Resch,
Agrapha², 106, who compares 1 Cor.
ix. 16.

8. εἰ δέ κτλ.] The causing of
σκάνδαλα to others is now followed
by the causes of σκάνδαλα to oneself:
inevitable in the world, they can be
avoided by the individual when they
proceed from himself. κ. βάλε ἀπὸ
σοῦ, added by Mt., completes the
picture of renunciation. This is the
meaning of the same sayings in v.
29 f. But their present position was
perhaps due to an early application
of them to the excommunication of
unworthy 'members' of the Christian
body. Mt. here compresses into one
Mk.'s two sayings about hand and foot.
καλόν κτλ.] εἰς τὴν ζωήν (see
vii. 14) is equivalent to εἰς τ.
βασιλείαν τ. θεοῦ (Mk. v. 47); in
contrast with ἡ ζωὴ αὕτη (1 Cor.
xv. 19) it is the ζωὴ αἰώνιος (Mt.
xix. 16, 29, xxv. 46), ἡ ζ. ἡ

μέλλουσα (1 Tim. iv. 8), ἡ ὄντως ζ.
(id. vi. 19), which will be enjoyed by
those who 'enter' (see v. 20) the
Kingdom. βληθῆναι (see on v. 29,
viii. 12) εἰς τ. πῦρ τ. αἰώνιον
corresponds with Mk.'s ἀπελθεῖν εἰς
τὴν γέενναν, εἰς τ. πῦρ τ. ἄσβεστον
(cf. Mt. iii. 12), and in v. 9 βλ. εἰς
τ. γέενναν τ. πυρός with Mk.'s βλ.
εἰς τ. γέενναν. In v. 29 f. it is εἰς
γέενναν. The expression which Jesus
actually employed cannot be determined, but 'into Gehenna' has the
largest support. They are all Jewish
in phraseology, and must be interpreted as such. τὸ πῦρ τὸ αἰώνιον,
no less than τ. π. τ. ἄσβεστον, would
suggest to a Jew of that day 'unending fire,' but with the underlying
thought that its beginning would
coincide with that of ἡ ζωὴ ἡ
αἰώνιος. See Add. n. Thphlact.'s
comment, αἰσθητὴν τιμωρίαν εἶπεν,
ἐκφοβῶν ἡμᾶς διὰ τούτου τοῦ
αἰσθητοῦ ὑποδείγματος, would express the attitude of many of the
apocalyptic writers.

9. καὶ εἰ κτλ.] ἔξελε . . . καὶ
βάλε expands Mk.'s ἔκβαλε. The
word μονόφθαλμος (Attic ἑτερόφθ.)
was used by Herod. and revived in
later Gk. τοῦ πυρός, found also in
v. 22, here takes the place of Mk.'s
quotation from Is. lxvi. 24, 'where
"their worm dieth and the fire
is not quenched."'

Additional Note on αἰώνιος.

1. αἰώνιος in the LXX. corresponds with the word עוֹלָם (Aram. עָלַם)
following another subst. in the constr. state. It could be used of things that

σε, ἔξελε αὐτὸν καὶ βάλε ἀπὸ σοῦ· καλόν σοί ἐστιν
μονόφθαλμον εἰς τὴν ζωὴν εἰσελθεῖν, ἢ δύο ὀφθαλμοὺς
ἔχοντα βληθῆναι εἰς τὴν γέενναν τοῦ πυρός.   Ὁρᾶτε 10

had existed for a long time in the *past*: boundaries (Prov. xxii. 28),
mountains (Mic. ii. 9), hills (Hab. iii. 6), deserted places (Is. lviii. 12), days
(Is. lxiii. 11), times (in the N.T., Rom. xvi. 25, 2 Tim. i. 9, Tit. i. 2). When
used of the *future* it seldom attained to the full content of 'everlasting,'
because few of the O.T. writers had any clear idea of the future life. עוֹלָם
meant a futurity of indefinite, because unknown, duration; the plur. was
sometimes employed intensively.   Hence αἰώνιος connoted perpetuity,
permanence, inviolability: God's covenant (Gen. ix. 16 and freq.) or
ordinance (Ex. xii. 14 and freq.), the gates of Zion (Ps. xxiii. [xxiv.] 7, 9),
and her foundations (Is. lviii. 12), the boundaries of the sea (Jer. v. 22).
For this meaning cf. Philem. 15.   It is the meaning which it bears both in
class. Gk. and in the later vernacular; see M.-M. *Vocab. s.v.*

2. It was when suffering Israel began to hope for a future life that עוֹלָם
first gained an added significance, and this although the distinct conceptions
(due to the influence of the Gk. αἰών) of 'this age' and 'the age to come'
were probably not formed in pre-Christian Heb. thought (Dalman, *Words*,
147–51).   In Dan. xii. 2 the righteous and the wicked are said to rise εἰς
ζωὴν αἰώνιον and εἰς αἰσχύνην αἰ. respectively. Cf. Ps. Sol. iii. 16, Enoch
xxxvii. 4, xl. 9, 2 Mac. vii. 9 (αἰ. ἀναβίωσις ζωῆς), 4 Mac. xv. 3.   And for
future punishment αἰώνιος is attached to βάσανος (4 Mac. ix. 9, xiii. 15),
ὄλεθρος (id. x. 15; cf. 2 Thes. i. 9), πῦρ (id. xii. 12; cf. Mt. xviii. 8, xxv.
41), ἀπώλεια (Ps. Sol. ii. 35 *v.l.*), κόλασις (Mt. xxv. 46, *Test. Rub.* v. 5, *Gad.* vii.
5).   The word thus gained an eschatological character, and meant virtually
'everlasting,' regardless of its derivation from αἰών.   Thus αἰώνιον ἁμάρτημα
(Mk. iii. 29) would in Heb. be חַטָּאת עוֹלָם, a sin that deserves κόλασις
αἰώνιος.   The adj., in Hebraic writings, never loses the thought of the lapse
of time.   Combining past and future, it is applied to God: Is. xxvi. 4 (not
Heb.), xl. 28, Bar. iv. 8, 20, 22, 35, Sus. 35 (Theod. 42), 2 Mac. i. 25,
Rom. xvi. 26.

3. After Christ's Resurrection, Christians gradually realized that, though
the final judgment did not come, the Messianic age had already begun; and
αἰώνιος once more gained an added significance under the influence of Gk.
thought.   It still retained its eschatological force when the writers
looked forward to the Advent, but it could also apply *now*, to the life lived by
Christians 'with Christ in God'; so that it was virtually equivalent to
'spiritual,' denoting a condition apart from the limitations of time.   In the
Epp. of S. Paul and Ep. Heb. the meaning oscillates between the two, but in
S. John's Gosp. and 1st Ep. the latter is the dominating thought.

10–14. (Lk. xv. 3–7.) THE
' LITTLE ONES' AS GOD VIEWS THEM.

In the remainder of the chap.
Mt. includes in his collection some

sayings found in Lk. (Q) but none
in Mk.

10. ὁρᾶτε κτλ.] The verse is
peculiar to Mt. Its position shews

μὴ καταφρονήσητε ἑνὸς τῶν μικρῶν τούτων, λέγω γὰρ
ὑμῖν ὅτι οἱ ἄγγελοι αὐτῶν ἐν οὐρανοῖς διὰ παντὸς βλέπουσι
12 τὸ πρόσωπον τοῦ πατρός μου τοῦ ἐν οὐρανοῖς. τί ὑμῖν
δοκεῖ ; ἐὰν γένηταί τινι ἀνθρώπῳ ἑκατὸν πρόβατα καὶ

11 *om vers.* ηλθε γαρ ο υιος του ανθρωπου [ζητησαι και] σωσαι το απολωλος
אBL* ı* 13 33 𝕷 e ff¹ 𝕾 sin.pal me sah ; *add* DE *etc* 𝕷 vet.*pler*.vg 𝕾 cur.pesh.
hcl arm aeth

that he understood μικροί in the
same sense as in *vv.* 6, 14 ; hence D
al. add here τῶν πιστευόντων εἰς
ἐμέ from *v.* 6. But in its original
context it *may* have been spoken of
children only. To despise the simple
and obscure believer was characteristic of many of the Pharisees of
that day (cf. Lk. xviii. 9); rabbis
spoke of the masses as עַם הָאָרֶץ
(ὁ λαὸς τῆς γῆς). Hillel used to
say ' the *'am hā'āreᶎ* is not pious '
(Aboth ii. 6); cf. Jo. vii. 49. On
ὁρᾶν μή see viii. 4.

οἱ ἄγγελοι κτλ.] It was a Jewish
belief that a nation could have a
guardian angel, *e.g.* Israel, Persia,
and Greece (Dan. x. 13, 20 f., xii. 1);
cf. *Test. Dan* v., vi., *Levi* v. (see
Volz, *Jüd. Esch.* 194 f., Driver on
Deut. xxxii. 8). A development of
this is seen in the 'angels' of the
Churches (Apoc. i. 20), who, as
representatives rather than guardians,
are so closely identified with the
Churches that they receive the
praise or blame due in each case.
The angels of the ' little ones ' may
also be explained as, in some sense,
their counterparts, represented by
whom they never fail to behold the
Presence of God, βλέπουσι τὸ πρόσωπον, as the high court officials
who have access to a human king ;
cf. 4 Regn. xxv. 19, Est. i. 14 (Heb.) ;
and see Tob. xii. 15. If the μικροί
are children only, the passage implies
that their innocence gives to their
angels this access to the divine

Presence, an access which must be increasingly denied them as the earthly
child falls increasingly into sin, so that
διὰ παντός holds good only as long
as their innocence is preserved. But
if the μικροί include all who are
' little,' whether in age, worldly
importance, or religious development,
including (as *vv.* 12 ff. imply) sinners,
the access of their angels to God's
presence is a beautiful expression
of His unceasing knowledge and
care, which is extended to all believers
alike (cf. v. 8). The 'angel,' therefore, symbolizes the believer's relation
to God. See Moulton, *JThS.*, July
1909, 514 ff., who traces the belief
to a Magian origin ; Sanday, *Life of
Chr. in Rec. Research,* 315-24.

[11.] ἦλθεν γὰρ ὁ υἱὸς τοῦ ἀνθρώπου σῶσαι τὸ ἀπολωλός] A gloss,
taken from Lk. xix. 10, to form a link
between *v.* 10 and the following
saying.

12. τί ὑμῖν δοκεῖ ; κτλ.] See
on xvii. 25. Lk. τίς ἄνθρωπος ἐξ
ὑμῶν. Mt. gives the parable (which
appears in Lk. xv. 3-7) as another
saying on the ' little ones ' (*v.* 14),
who include not only the innocent
but also the erring. If *vv.* 8 f. refer
to excommunication, that thought
may also be present to the evang.
here : God will not lose one of the
' little ones ' till all efforts at rescue
have been exhausted. See also *v.* 15.
The sheep has wandered (πλανηθῇ)
by its own fault, a thought which
is lacking in Lk.'s ἀπολέσας. τὰ ὄρη

πλανηθῇ ἓν ἐξ αὐτῶν, οὐχὶ ἀφήσει τὰ ἐνενήκοντα ἐννέα ἐπὶ
τὰ ὄρη καὶ πορευθεὶς ζητεῖ τὸ πλανώμενον ; καὶ ἐὰν 13
γένηται εὑρεῖν αὐτό, ἀμὴν λέγω ὑμῖν ὅτι χαίρει ἐπ᾽ αὐτῷ
μᾶλλον ἢ ἐπὶ τοῖς ἐνενήκοντα ἐννέα τοῖς μὴ πεπλανημένοις.
οὕτως οὐκ ἔστιν θέλημα ἔμπροσθεν τοῦ πατρός μου τοῦ ἐν 14
οὐρανοῖς ἵνα ἀπόληται ἓν τῶν μικρῶν τούτων.   Ἐὰν 15

12 αφησει et και] BD[αφιησιν]L 124 157 346 𝕃 vet [exc m q]. vg arm aeth ;
αφεις et om και ℵE etc 𝕃 m q   14 μου] BFHIΓ minn.pauc 𝕊 sin me sah arm
aeth ; υμων ℵDE al minn.pl 𝕃 omn 𝕊 cur.pesh ; om Aphr

(Lk. ἐν τῇ ἐρήμῳ) are the high pastures
where the sheep graze at will ;
one of them has wandered too far.

οὐχὶ ἀφήσει κτλ.] For the acc.
after ἐπί cf. ix. 9. With the v.l.
ἀφεὶς . . . ἐπὶ τὰ ὄρη πορευθείς,
it has the same meaning 'on the
mountains,' and must not be connected with πορευθείς (Chrys.).
ἀφήσει is part of the picture ; the
ninety-nine are in safety, and are
not sacrificed for the sake of the one.
τὸ πλανώμενον pictures the act of
wandering, τὸ ἀπολωλός (Lk.) the
lost condition. Lk. adds the triumph-
ant ἕως εὕρῃ αὐτό.

13. καὶ ἐὰν γένηται κτλ.] Sc.
αὐτῷ (cf. v. 19) or αὐτόν. It is not
the Heb. constr. ל היה with inf.
(Jülicher) ; see Ges. Kautzsch, § 114 h.
Lk. here enlarges : the man 'lays it
on his shoulders rejoicing,' and
invites his friends and neighbours to
share his joy. The thought is that
of ix. 13 ; there is no suggestion
that the ninety-nine are self-righteous
and impenitent. The verse in Lk.
corresponding with the present one
is not part of the parable but its
explanation, which in Mt. follows in
a different form.

14. οὕτως κτλ.] See on xiii. 40.
On the Jewish periphrasis θέλημα
ἔμπροσθεν see xi. 26. The authorities
for μου and ὑμῶν are divided ; see
on vi. 9. ἐν is the true reading, the

neut. being carried over by the
evang. from v. 12 ; it is corrected to
εἷς in a few later uncc., some 𝕃
MSS. and Vg. ; there could be no
difference in Aram. It is assumed,
but not stated, that it is God who
seeks the sheep ; His means of rescue
may be a man, as in v. 15. The
parable only expresses the principle
that a wandering sheep must be
rescued. The question whether Mt.
or Lk. is nearer to its original form
cannot be answered. Mt., as always,
is more Jewish in phraseology. He
can hardly have added v. 14 from
his own pen ; it must have been the
occurrence of τ. μικρῶν τ. in his
source that led him to place the
passage here. If the evangg. used
a common source, it was in very
different recensions.

15–20 (cf. Lk. xvii. 3). DUTIES
OF DISCIPLES TO THEIR FELLOW
BELIEVERS.

These sayings, peculiar to Mt.
except v. 15, are arranged with the
following line of thought ; the duty
of 'gaining' a brother is enjoined,
privately if possible (v. 15), if not,
by appeal to one or two other brethren
(v. 16) ; then to the whole body of
believers (v. 17) ; if that fails, excommunication must follow (id.),
since the Church possesses official
authority to bind and loose (v. 18),
and the smallest number of its

δὲ ἁμαρτήσῃ ὁ ἀδελφός σου, ὕπαγε ἔλεγξον αὐτὸν μεταξὺ
σοῦ καὶ αὐτοῦ μόνου. ἐάν σου ἀκούσῃ, ἐκέρδησας τὸν
16 ἀδελφόν σου· ἐὰν δὲ μὴ ἀκούσῃ, παράλαβε μετὰ σοῦ
ἔτι ἕνα ἢ δύο, ἵνα ἐπὶ cτόΜΑΤΟC Δʏ́Ο ΜΑΡΤʏ́ΡΩΝ Η̅ ΤΡΙῶΝ CΤΑΘΗ̅
17 ΠᾶΝ Ρ̇Η̅ΜΑ· ἐὰν δὲ παρακούσῃ αὐτῶν, εἰπὸν τῇ ἐκκλησίᾳ·
ἐὰν δὲ καὶ τῆς ἐκκλησίας παρακούσῃ, ἔστω σοι ὥσπερ ὁ

15 αμαρτηση] אB 1 22 234* sah; add εις σε uncc.*rel* minn.*pl* 𝕴 omn 𝕾
sin.cur.pesh me

members can obtain answers to prayer (*v.* 19), and can be sure of the presence of the Master (*v.* 20). It is probable that behind the section lie some genuine sayings; but in its present form it belongs to a date when the Church was already an organized Body. It is the most distinctly ecclesiastical passage in Mt.'s Gospel.

15.●ἐὰν δέ κτλ.] A wandering sheep must be rescued, and a fellow man may be the means. The addition εἰς σέ is perhaps correct, but may be due to Lk. xvii. 4; or it arose from the reflexion that private rebuke presupposes a private wrong, which, however, is far from being the case. Lk. (xvii. 3) has 'if thy brother sin, rebuke him, and if he repent, forgive him,' continuing with a saying similar to Mt. *v.* 21, and preceded by a parallel to Mt. *vv.* 6, 7. In Lk. ἀδελφός means a fellow man, in Mt. a fellow disciple. ἔλεγξον is either 'convince' him of his fault (cf. Jo. viii. 9, 46, 1 Cor. xiv. 24), or better 'reprove' (Lk. ἐπιτίμησον). The Aram. idiom is followed in μεταξὺ σοῦ κ. αὐτοῦ, which 𝕾 vet uses for κατ' ἰδίαν in xvii. 19, xx. 17, Mk. ix. 28. μόνου emphasizes the thought of privacy; cf. Mk. ix. 2, κατ' ἰδίαν μόνους. Forgiveness (Lk. ἀφές) is involved in ἐκέρδησας. For the verb cf. 1 Cor. ix. 19 ff., 1 Pet. iii. 1.

16. ἐὰν δέ κτλ.] One or two

other brethren would make two or three in all, whose united efforts at reconciliation may be successful. Or they are witnesses who would be prepared to give evidence before the Church, if necessary, that they had tried to convince the sinner. Neither of these is the sense of μάρτυρες in Deut. xix. 15 which is here quoted (cf. 2 Cor. xiii. 1), and σταθῇ πᾶν ῥῆμα is strictly irrelevant; but a merely verbal appeal, probably by the evangelist, is made to the words δύο ἢ τριῶν. His ἵνα, an abbreviation of ἵνα πληρωθῇ τὸ ῥηθέν or the like, makes the verb (LXX. στήσεται) conjunctive; see Add. n. p. 192 on the force of ἵνα in Mk. iv. 12.

17. ἐὰν δέ κτλ.] For παρακούειν 'disregard,' a meaning found in later Gk. (Polyb., Plut.), cf. Mk. v. 36, Is. lxv. 12, Est. iii. 3, 8, Tob. iii. 4, *Test. Dan* ii. 3. On ἐκκλησία see xvi. 18, where it denotes the small body of the Lord's followers as distinct from the Jewish Church. It has the same meaning here, if the words are a genuine utterance. But if they are not, as the following sentence suggests, ἐκκλησία probably means the local body of Christians in a town or district.

ἔστω κτλ.] 'Treat him as an outcast.' The words are surprising if spoken by Jesus. ἐθνικοί and τελῶναι are mentioned in v. 46 f., and the former in vi. 7, their standard of kindness and of prayer respectively

ἐθνικὸς καὶ ὁ τελώνης. Ἀμὴν λέγω ὑμῖν, ὅσα ἐὰν 18
δήσητε ἐπὶ τῆς γῆς ἔσται δεδεμένα ἐν οὐρανῷ καὶ ὅσα
ἐὰν λύσητε ἐπὶ τῆς γῆς ἔσται λελυμένα ἐν οὐρανῷ. Πάλιν 19
ἀμὴν λέγω ὑμῖν ὅτι ἐὰν δύο συμφωνήσωσιν ἐξ ὑμῶν ἐπὶ
τῆς γῆς περὶ παντὸς πράγματος οὗ ἐὰν αἰτήσωνται,
γενήσεται αὐτοῖς παρὰ τοῦ πατρός μου τοῦ ἐν οὐρανοῖς.
οὗ γάρ εἰσιν δύο ἢ τρεῖς συνηγμένοι εἰς τὸ ἐμὸν ὄνομα, 20
ἐκεῖ εἰμὶ ἐν μέσῳ αὐτῶν.

being contrasted with that demanded
from disciples, but in neither case
are they synonymous with outcasts.
Elsewhere the Lord's attitude to
τελῶναι is one of tender sympathy :
ix. 10 f., x. 3, xi. 19, Lk. xviii. 10 ff.,
and espec. Mt. xxi. 31 f. The passage
seems to belong to a period of Jewish
hostility, which was met in a spirit
unlike the Master's.

18. ἀμήν κτλ.] See on v. 18.
'Bind' and 'loose' must have the
same meaning as in xvi. 19, q.v.
They need not refer to excommunication and forgiveness, but in the
present context of the verse that
appears to be what the evang. had
in mind. The authority is given
to all the disciples considered as
an *ecclesia*. It seems to be applied
to the retaining and remitting of
sins as early as the account of the
martyrs at Lyons (Eus. *H.E.* v. 2):
ἔλυον μὲν ἅπαντας, ἐδέσμευον δὲ
οὐδένα. On Cyprian's use of the
verse (*De Unit.* iv.) see Archbp.
Benson's *Cypr.* 181. It is not impossible that the verse is based on a
genuine saying, of the same nature
as xix. 28.

19. πάλιν κτλ.] A link with the
context is supplied by the contrast
between 'on earth' and 'in Heaven,'
and by the words 'two or three' (v.
20). For συμφωνεῖν cf. xx. 2, 13,
Lk. v. 36, and see 1 Cor. vii. 5,
2 Cor. vi. 15. On ἐάν with fut.
ind. see Blass, § 65. 5. παρά (like

מְנָת) describes the performance of
the request as a *quasi* concrete thing
proceeding from God ; cf. xxi. 42
(lxx.).

20. οὗ γάρ κτλ.] The agreement
of two is not a magic which forces
God to answer, but implies that they
have met *as disciples* (on εἰς τ. ἐμ.
ὄνομα see xxviii. 19), which involves
the making only of such requests
as the Master will endorse. The
thought of the saying finds Jewish
and Christian parallels : *Aboth*, iii.
3 (see Taylor), 'Two that are sitting
and occupied with the words of
Torah, the Shekinah is among them,'
and iii. 9 ; Grenf.-Hunt, *Oxyr. Pap.*
i. 9 (as restored) ὅπου ἐὰν ὦσιν δύο
οὐκ εἰσὶν ἄθεοι, καὶ ὅπου εἷς ἐστὶν
μόνος, λέγω ἐγώ εἰμι μετ' αὐτοῦ.
Ephr [Diat] 'Where one is there I also
am, and where two are, there will I
also be.' A negative form appears
in D, οὐκ εἰσὶν γὰρ δύο . . . ὄνομα,
παρ' οἷς οὐκ εἰμὶ ἐν μ. αὐτ. The
separatists denounced by Cyprian
(*De Unit.* x.–xii.) relied on this verse,
'as if the Lord meant to commend
not unity but paucity.'

If a genuine saying underlies vv.
19, 20, it could not mean to the
Lord's hearers all that it could to
Christians of a later date — the
universal presence of the Divine
Humanity expressing itself in the
Church ; cf. xxviii. 20. But Jesus
may have said something of the
same nature as x. 40, xxv. 35 f,

21   Τότε προσελθὼν ὁ Πέτρος εἶπεν αὐτῷ Κύριε, ποσάκις
ἁμαρτήσει εἰς ἐμὲ ὁ ἀδελφός μου καὶ ἀφήσω αὐτῷ; ἕως
22 ἑπτάκις; λέγει αὐτῷ ὁ Ἰησοῦς Οὐ λέγω σοι ἕως ἑπτάκις
23 ἀλλὰ ἕως ἑβδομηκοντάκις ἑπτά. Διὰ τοῦτο ὡμοιώθη ἡ

42 f. : you can pray with My full
endorsement because you are Mine,
especially when two of you are united
as Mine ; the Father will hear you,
because when you pray, I pray.

21, 22. (Lk. xvii. 4.) ON FOR-
GIVENESS.

21. τότε κτλ.] On the prominence
of S. Peter in Mt. see x. 2. Lk. does
not mention him here. The construction ἁμαρτήσει . . . καὶ ἀφήσω
is Hebraic ; Wellh. compares Is. v. 4.

22. οὐ λέγω κτλ.] In Lk. unlimited forgiveness is differently expressed : 'and if seven times a day
he sins against thee, and seven times
turn to thee saying, I repent, thou
shalt forgive him.' οὐ can be taken
with λέγω (cf. Jo. xvi. 26) : 'I decline to say seven times (as you
propose)'; some, less naturally, make
λέγω σοι a parenthesis.

ἑβδ. ἑπτά] If this is a cardinal
number ('seventy times seven'), it
does not strictly answer the question
ποσάκις; D corrects it to ἑβδ.
ἑπτάκις, and the verss. so render it,
'seventy-times seven-times'; 'quad-
ringentis nonaginta vicibus' (Jer.) ;
and see Aphr. in Burkitt (Ev. da
Meph. ad loc.). But Orig., Aug. have
'seventy-seven times.' The same
ambiguity is seen in Gen. iv. 24,
ὅτι ἑπτάκις ἐκδεδίκηται ἐκ Κάιν,
ἐκ δὲ Λάμεχ ἑβδομηκοντάκις ἑπτά,
a parallel noted as early as Tert. (Orat.
vii.). The Heb. וְשִׁבְעָה שִׁבְעִים = 77,
but the LXX. by omitting the 'and'
leaves it doubtful whether 70 + 7 or
70 × 7 is meant. (In Hom. Il. xxii.
349, quoted by Moulton, καί makes
the meaning clear.) The saying in

Mt., and the apostle's question leading to it, have possibly been framed
under the influence of this passage
in Gen. : the unlimited revenge of
primitive man has given place to the
unlimited forgiveness of Christians.

Jer. (c. Pelag. iii. 2) cites from the
Gosp. Heb. (see Texte u. Unters., 1911,
39, 69) : 'si peccaverit, inquit, frater
tuus in verbo et satis tibi fecerit,
septies in die suscipe eum. Dixit
illi Simon discipulus eius, Septies in
die ? Respondit dominus et dixit ei,
Etiam ego dico tibi, usque septuagies
septies.' It continues with a reference
to the universality of guilt, which is
foreign to the context : 'etenim in
prophetis quoque postquam uncti
sunt spiritu sancto inventus est sermo
peccati.' With the Christian standard
compare that in Joma 86 b, 87 a
(quoted by Allen), in which, on
the strength of O.T. sentences, three
times is laid down as a fixed limit
for forgiveness.

23–35. (Mt. only.) PARABLE OF
THE UNFORGIVING DEBTOR.

23. διὰ τοῦτο κτλ.] 'Because
unlimited forgiveness is the duty of
a disciple, therefore when the Kingdom of Heaven comes those who
have not followed the divine example
will be punished, as this parable represents.' The Kingdom is not like
the King, but his actions illustrate
an aspect of it ; see xiii. 24. On
ἀνθρώπῳ β. 'a certain king' see xi.
19. A king, as the subject of a
parable, appears also in xxii. 1–13,
Lk. xiv. 31. It was a very common
feature in Jewish parables (e.g. those
in Mechilta, Fiebig, Altjüd. Gleichn.,

βασιλεία τῶν οὐρανῶν ἀνθρώπῳ βασιλεῖ ὃς ἠθέλησεν συνᾶραι
λόγον μετὰ τῶν δούλων αὐτοῦ· ἀρξαμένου δὲ αὐτοῦ συναίρειν 24
προσήχθη εἷς αὐτῷ ὀφειλέτης μυρίων ταλάντων. μὴ 25
ἔχοντος δὲ αὐτοῦ ἀποδοῦναι ἐκέλευσεν αὐτὸν ὁ κύριος
πραθῆναι καὶ τὴν γυναῖκα καὶ τὰ τέκνα καὶ πάντα ὅσα ἔχει
καὶ ἀποδοθῆναι. πεσὼν οὖν ὁ δοῦλος προσεκύνει αὐτῷ 26
λέγων Μακροθύμησον ἐπ᾽ ἐμοί, καὶ πάντα ἀποδώσω σοι.
σπλαγχνισθεὶς δὲ ὁ κύριος τοῦ δούλου ἐκείνου ἀπέλυσεν 27
αὐτόν, καὶ τὸ δάνιον ἀφῆκεν αὐτῷ. ἐξελθὼν δὲ ὁ δοῦλος 28
ἐκεῖνος εὗρεν ἕνα τῶν συνδούλων αὐτοῦ ὃς ὤφειλεν αὐτῷ
ἑκατὸν δηνάρια, καὶ κρατήσας αὐτὸν ἔπνιγεν λέγων Ἀπόδος

and Ziegler, *Die Königsgleichn. d. Midrasch*), but Jesus more often spoke of the 'master' or 'owner' of slaves, field, vineyard, etc. ; and since the βασιλεύς is called κύριος in *vv.* 25, 27, 31 f., 34, and δοῦλος (*v.* 32) and συνδοῦλος (*vv.* 31, 33) are mentioned, it is possible that the single word βασιλεῖ has here been added, or substituted for οἰκοδεσπότῃ, which is found in Chrys. *ad loc.* For συνᾶραι λόγον 'to cast up accounts,' perhaps a Latinism, *rationes conferre*, cf. xxv. 19. It occurs in a 2nd cent. papyrus (BU. 775), and with συναίρεσθαι in Hogarth's *Fayum Towns*, 261 (1st cent.), *Ox.* i. 113 (2nd cent.); also λόγου σύναρσις (Deissm. *Light from Anc. East*, 118).

24. ἀρξαμένου κτλ.] On εἷς = τις see viii. 19. A talent was 6,000 denarii, or £240. The immense sum owed cannot be explained as imperial taxes passing through the hands of a high official. Judaea, Idumaea, and Samaria paid in one year only 600 talents, and Galilee and Peraea 200 (Jos. *Ant.* XVII. xi. 4). The amount expresses limitless forgiveness. For the Jewish thought of sin as a debt see vi. 12.

25. μὴ ἔχοντος κτλ.] He and his family and belongings are to be sold (cf. 2 Kings iv. 1), though their price would cover but a fraction of the debt. For the class. ἔχειν 'be able,' 'have (the means)' cf. Lk. vii. 42, xiv. 14, Heb. vi. 13. On the gen. absol. followed by acc. see Blass, § 74. 5, on the construction with ἐκέλευσεν § 69. 8, and on the *orat. rect.* ἔχει § 56. 9.

26. πεσών κτλ.] On the impf. προσεκύνει 'besought,' distinct from the aor. 'did obeisance,' see Blass, § 57. 4.

27. σπλαγχνισθείς κτλ.] Release from slavery is the answer to μακροθύμησον, but remission from the debt goes far beyond it. δάνιον (here only in the N.T., cf. Deut. xv. 8, 10, xxiv. 11) is a 'loan'; the master has lent money, and the interest has enormously accumulated. This heavy oriental usury is of the scenery of the parable; its teaching is concerned only with forgiveness. On ἀφῆκεν see M.-M. *Vocab.* 97 a.

28. ἐξελθών κτλ.] 'A hundred denaria,' about £4, was a 600,000th part of his own remitted debt. κράτησας is illustrated by the Roman *manus iniectio* ; the creditor was allowed to take the debtor forcibly before the authorities (Plaut. *Poen.* III. v. 45 ; cf. Lk. xii. 58). ἔπνιγεν 'throttled' was an additional act of violence. ἀπόδ. εἴ τι ὀφείλεις

29 εἴ τι ὀφείλεις. πεσὼν οὖν ὁ σύνδουλος αὐτοῦ παρεκάλει
αὐτὸν λέγων Μακροθύμησον ἐπ᾽ ἐμοί, καὶ ἀποδώσω
30 σοι. ὁ δὲ οὐκ ἤθελεν, ἀλλὰ ἀπελθὼν ἔβαλεν αὐτὸν εἰς
31 φυλακὴν ἕως ἀποδῷ τὸ ὀφειλόμενον. ἰδόντες οὖν οἱ
σύνδουλοι αὐτοῦ τὰ γενόμενα ἐλυπήθησαν σφόδρα, καὶ
ἐλθόντες διεσάφησαν τῷ κυρίῳ ἑαυτῶν πάντα τὰ γενόμενα.
32 τότε προσκαλεσάμενος αὐτὸν ὁ κύριος αὐτοῦ λέγει αὐτῷ
Δοῦλε πονηρέ, πᾶσαν τὴν ὀφειλὴν ἐκείνην ἀφῆκά σοι, ἐπεὶ
33 παρεκάλεσάς με· οὐκ ἔδει καὶ σὲ ἐλεῆσαι τὸν σύνδουλόν
34 σου, ὡς κἀγὼ σὲ ἠλέησα; καὶ ὀργισθεὶς ὁ κύριος αὐτοῦ
παρέδωκεν αὐτὸν τοῖς βασανισταῖς ἕως οὗ ἀποδῷ πᾶν τὸ
35 ὀφειλόμενον. Οὕτως καὶ ὁ πατήρ μου ὁ οὐράνιος ποιήσει
ὑμῖν ἐὰν μὴ ἀφῆτε ἕκαστος τῷ ἀδελφῷ αὐτοῦ ἀπὸ τῶν
καρδιῶν ὑμῶν.

35 υμων] add τα παραπτωματα αυτων uncc (exc ℵBDL) minn.*pler* 𝔏 f h 𝔖 pesh arm

is 'an expression of pitiless logic'
(B. Weiss): 'if you owe anything,
pay!' εἴ τι is not equivalent to
ὅ,τι.

29. πεσών κτλ.] The repetition,
almost *verbatim*, of *v.* 26, heightens
the cruelty of the refusal. On
παρεκαλεῖ see viii. 5.

30. ὁ δέ κτλ.] On the redundant
ἀπελθών see xiii. 28; cf. ἐλθόντες
v. 31. For βάλλειν εἰς φυλακήν
cf. *v.* 25. On imprisonment for
debt among Greeks and Romans see
Deissm. *Light from Anc. East,* 267.

31. ἰδόντες κτλ.] ἐλυπήθησαν
expresses sorrowful indignation (cf.
Mk. iii. 5) at the creditor combined
with pity for the debtor. On διεσάφησαν see xiii. 36. For the un-
emphatic ἑαυτῶν see viii. 22.

32. τότε κτλ.] He who will not
forgive another is a δοῦλος πονηρός
no less than he who is unfaithful to
his Master's trust (xxv. 26, Lk.
xix. 22). For ὀφειλή, a late word
(not in LXX.), cf. Rom. xiii. 7, 1 Cor.
vii. 3. It occurs in the Lord's
Prayer in the *Didache* (see on vi. 12),
and in papyri of the 1st and 2nd

cent.: *Ox.* ii. 286. 18, 272. 16, and
others in Deissm. *Bible St.* 221.
Moulton, *Expos.*, July 1910, 92.

34. καὶ ὀργισθείς κτλ.] βασανισταῖς (here only in bibl. Gk.) must
not be weakened to 'gaolers';
tortures were employed both in
Maccabean and Herodian times.
But the word reaches out beyond
the parable, and expresses in Jewish
symbolism the thought of punishment, not purgatorial but punitive,
in Gehenna: cf. viii. 29, Apoc. xiv.
10 f., xviii. 7, 10, 15, xx. 10. ἕως
οὗ ἀποδῷ: *i.e.* perpetually, for the
debt could never be paid; cf. *v.* 26.

35. οὕτως κτλ.] The parable is
an echo of *v.* 7, vi. 12, 14 f.; cf. Mk.
xi. 25, Jam. ii. 13. The important
addition ἀπὸ τ. καρδιῶν ὑμ. is not
found elsewhere; forgiveness is to
be granted 'not grudgingly or of
necessity.' Cf. ἐκ καρδίας Rom. vi.
17, 1 Pet. i. 22. The addition in
the T.R. τὰ παραπτώματα αὐτῶν
(see Appar.) is probably due to vi.
15. ὀφειλήματα would have been
more in keeping with the parable.
See on vi. 12.

Καὶ ἐγένετο ὅτε ἐτέλεσεν ὁ Ἰησοῦς τοὺς λόγους τούτους, ι XIX.
μετῆρεν ἀπὸ τῆς Γαλιλαίας καὶ ἦλθεν εἰς τὰ ὅρια τῆς
Ἰουδαίας πέραν τοῦ Ἰορδάνου. καὶ ἠκολούθησαν αὐτῷ 2
ὄχλοι πολλοί, καὶ ἐθεράπευσεν αὐτοὺς ἐκεῖ.

XIX.–XXV. JOURNEY TO THE SOUTH, AND MINISTRY IN JUDAEA.

xix. 1, 2. (Mk. x. 1.) THE JOURNEY.
1. καὶ ἐγένετο κτλ.] On the
formula at the end of a discourse see
vii. 28. On μεταίρειν see xiii. 53 ;
Mk. ἐκεῖθεν ἀναστάς, the last place
mentioned being Capharnaum (Mk.
ix. 33). The course of the journey
is doubtful, owing to the obscurity
of εἰς τ. ὅρια τ. Ἰουδαίας πέραν τ.
Ἰορδάνου, the uncertainty of the
reading in Mk., εἰς τ. ὅρια τ.
Ἰουδ. [?καὶ] πέραν τ. Ἰορδ, and
Lk.'s statement (xvii. 11) that Jesus
'passed through the midst of Samaria
and Galilee.' If Lk. is correct, Mt.
must not be understood to describe
a route to Judaea via Peraea, for
though this was frequently taken
by Jews in order to avoid Samaritan
territory (see x. 5), Peraea was part
of the dominion of Antipas, which
Jesus wished to shun. The Peraean
route is, indeed, assumed in A and
later MSS. in Mk. (διὰ τοῦ πέραν
τ. Ἰορδ.), regardless of Lk. The reading καὶ πέραν in Mk. (אBCL) implies
a route to Peraea via Judaea. Swete
(ad loc.) and Bp. West Watson
(JThS., 1910, 269 ff.) explain this as
a summary of movements partly in
Judaea, and partly on the E. of the
Jordan, including the events related
in Jo. vii. 14, x. 22, 40, xi. 1–44, 54.
But Mk.'s whole verse, taken by
itself, suggests nothing but two
successive stages in a single journey,
in which Jesus may have crossed the
Jordan at Jericho or elsewhere, and
recrossed it, arriving at Jericho (Mk.
v. 46). But Mk. without καί (= Mt.)
is still obscure. Wellh. takes τ.

Ἰουδ. πέραν τ. Ἰορδ. to be an un-
grammatical equivalent for τ. Ἰ.
τῆς πέραν τ. Ἰ., 'trans-Jordanic
Judaea,' i.e. that part of the country
E. of the Jordan which belonged to
the Jews. Cf. Strabo XVI. ii. 21,
Tac. Hist. v. 6. Burkitt (Gosp. Hist.
96 f., JThS., 1910, 412 ff.) conjectures
that while Jesus went through
Samaria, as Lk. relates, Peter and
most of the disciples went via Peraea,
meeting Him at the spot where the
pilgrim route crossed the Jordan
into Judaea ; from Peter's, and therefore the narrator's, point of view,
the route on the west of Jordan
which Jesus took with at least James
and John (Lk. ix. 51–56) was πέραν
τ. Ἰορδάνου (cf. εἰς τὸ πέραν, of the
W. of the lake, Mk. v. 21). The
Lord could thus avoid the territory
of Antipas, and travel without
attracting attention. On this supposition, τ. ὅρια may mean either
the boundary (τὰ ἄκρα Orig.), or the
region as a whole ; but the latter is
probably always the meaning in the
N.T. Till xx. 17 Jesus is not far
from the northern boundary, which
ran from Antipatris to the Jordan,
about 17 m. north of Jericho ; then
He is on the road ; and in xx. 29
He leaves Jericho.

2. καὶ ἠκολούθησαν κτλ.] Mk.
'And crowds came together again
unto Him, and as He was accustomed
He was teaching them again.' Mt.
speaks of healings, not of teaching
(see xiv. 14). On general statements
of healing see iv. 23.

3 Καὶ προσῆλθαν αὐτῷ Φαρισαῖοι πειράζοντες αὐτὸν καὶ
λέγοντες Εἰ ἔξεστιν ἀπολῦσαι τὴν γυναῖκα αὐτοῦ κατὰ
4 πᾶσαν αἰτίαν ; ὁ δὲ ἀποκριθεὶς εἶπεν Οὐκ ἀνέγνωτε ὅτι
5 ὁ κτίσας ἀπ᾽ ἀρχῆς ἄρϲεν καὶ θῆλγ ἐποίηϲεν αγτογϲ καὶ εἶπεν

3 εξεστιν] אBLΓ 125* 301 475 ; add ανθρωπω אᵉCDE etc 𝔏 omn 𝔖 omn me
sah 4 κτισας] B 1 22 33 124 [𝔏 e constituit] arm ; ποιησας אCDE etc 𝔏 vet
[exc e].vg [fecit]

3–9. (Mk. x. 2–12 ; cf. Mt. v.
31 f., Lk. xvi. 18.) TEACHING ON
DIVORCE.

▸ 3. καὶ προσῆλθαν κτλ.] If the
omission in Mk. (D a b k 𝔖 sin) of
προσελθόντες οἱ Φαρισαῖοι is correct,
and not an early scribal slip, the
question was asked by the people.
It was a test question (πειράζοντες,
cf. xvi. 1, xxii. 18, 35), the answer
to which might be expected to give
them a further handle against Jesus ;
and a special edge was given to it by
the recent divorce of Antipas, from
whose territory He had just arrived.
For εἰ in a direct question cf. xii. 10
(Blass, § 77. 2). The subj. of αὐτοῦ
is omitted, the addition of ἀνθρώπῳ
being clearly a correction ; cf. ἑαυτόν,
Jam. i. 27. Mk. has ἀνδρί.

κατὰ πᾶσαν αἰτίαν] The school
of Hillel allowed divorce for the
most trifling causes ; see Philo, Leg.
Spic. v., Jos. Ant. IV. viii. 23, Vita,
76, Gittin ix. 10 ('even if she has
burnt his food in cooking it') ; that
of Shammai, on the other hand,
said 'A man shall not divorce his
wife unless he has found in her a
matter of shame' (ibid.). See on v.
32. By the addition of κατὰ πᾶσ.
αἰτ. in Mt. the gloss μὴ ἐπὶ πορνείᾳ
in v. 9 is prepared for. The effect
is that the questioners appear to be
trying to inveigle Jesus into taking
a side in the Rabbinic dispute. But
see on v. 9. In Mk. their purpose
is different, their question turning
not on the scribal interpretation, but
on the validity of the law itself.

4. ὁ δέ κτλ.] In Mk., Jesus at
once refers to the Mosaic law, as
they expected that He would ; He
asked τί ὑμῖν ἐνετείλατο Μωυσῆς ;
and when they referred to Deut.
xxiv. 1, He carried them back to
the still earlier ordinance at the
Creation. In Mt., the latter reference
is placed first, and when they appeal
to Moses (the Lord's τί ἐνετείλατο
M. ; being placed in their mouth, v.
7), He meets them, and refers to the
Creation a second time. This formed
the culminating breach with the
Pharisees ; Jesus criticizes not the
scribal tradition but the Law. On
οὐκ ἀνέγνωτε see xii. 3.

ὁ κτίσας κτλ.] ἀπ᾽ ἀρχῆς is to
be taken with ἐποίησεν : 'the Creator
"made them male and female" from
the beginning.' For the absol. ὁ
κτίσας cf. Rom. i. 25. Mt. alters
Mk.'s ἀπὸ δὲ τῆς ἀρχῆς κτίσεως (for
which Allen cites Jewish parallels
from Ass. Mos. i. 17, xii. 4, Pes. Rab.
K. 21). The v.l. ὁ ποιήσας was
probably due to ἐποίησεν in the
quotation (Gen. i. 27, v. 2) ; the
LXX. uses it both for ברא and עשה in
the narrative of the Creation. The
same argument against divorce is
found in the Fragm. of a Zadokite
Work, vii. 2 (see Charles).

5. καὶ εἶπεν κτλ.] Sc. ὁ κτίσας.
But since in Gen. ii. 24 the words are
not spoken by God, and in Mk. both
quotations are statements made by
Jesus, the nota interr. should perhaps follow αὐτούς, Jesus being the
subject of εἶπεν. The LXX. has

Ἕνεκα τούτου καταλείψει ἄνθρωπος τὸν πατέρα καὶ τὴν μητέρα καὶ κολληθήσεται τῇ γυναικὶ αὐτοῦ, καὶ ἔσονται οἱ δύο εἰς σάρκα μίαν; ὥστε οὐκέτι εἰσὶν δύο ἀλλὰ σὰρξ μία· ὃ οὖν ὁ θεὸς 6 συνέζευξεν ἄνθρωπος μὴ χωριζέτω. λέγουσιν αὐτῷ Τί οὖν 7 Μωυσῆς ἐνετείλατο δοῦναι βιβλίον ἀποστασίου καὶ ἀπολῦσαι; λέγει αὐτοῖς ὅτι Μωυσῆς πρὸς τὴν σκληροκαρδίαν ὑμῶν 8

αὐτοῦ after πατέρα and μητέρα, and προσκολληθήσεται. Mk. has αὐτοῦ (with LXX.^{Luc.}) after πατέρα only, and he omits 'and shall cleave unto his wife.' S. Paul quotes the passage, with variations of reading, as a type in Eph. v. 31, and part of it as a warning in 1 Cor. vi. 16 f.

6. ὥστε κτλ.] . So Mk., except μία σάρξ. The teaching contained in the quotations is driven home. The first human male and female were intended solely for each other; the principle involved in their creation was that their union was complete and indissoluble. And they were the norm for each succeeding pair. Each married couple is a reproduction of Adam and Eve, and their union is therefore no less indissoluble. The Mosaic precept (v. 8) was a concession to Nature as it actually is, which if unregulated would tend to promiscuity; but the Lord appeals from it to ideal Nature as pictured in Eden.

ὃ οὖν κτλ.] The words were 'introduced into the English Form of Matrimony in 1548, but had previously stood in the Gospel of the Ordo sponsalium' (Swete). συνζευγνύναι is not used of marriage elsewhere in Scripture (contrast Ez. i. 11, and 23 (A)); Aq. has συνζυγία and -γος in Ez. xxiii. 17, 21; cf. Aesch. Choëph. 589. The verb occurs in Jos. Ant. I. xix. 10, and διαζευγνύναι, of the dissolution of marriage, id. IV. viii. 23. For χωρίζειν of nuptial separation (used in Polyb.) cf. 1 Cor.

vii. 10 f., 15; and the use perhaps underlies Rom. viii. 35, 39.

7. λέγουσιν κτλ.] The questioners appeal to Deuteronomy against Genesis; in Mk., Jesus appeals to Gen. against Deut. (see on v. 4). The reason for Mt.'s transposition is not clear, but it can hardly have been merely because Gen. stands before Deut. (Wernle). In Mk. (v. 3). τί = 'What'; Mt., placing the words in the questioners' mouths, makes τί = 'Why.' In Mk. the Lord says ἐνετείλατο, and they reply with ἐπέτρεψεν; Mt. transposes the verbs, assigning to Him the more accurate expression; Moses did not command, he only permitted, divorce. On βιβλ. ἀποστασίου see v. 31.

8. λέγει κτλ.] Moses regulated, but thereby conceded, the practice of divorce; both were with a view to (πρός) the nation's (ὑμῶν) hardness of heart: since they persist in falling short of the ideal of Eden, let it at least be within limits. Cf. S. Paul's attitude to the Law (Gal. iii. 17 ff.). σκληροκαρδία (confined to bibl. Gk.) recurs in the N.T. in 'Mk.' xvi. 14 only. In the LXX. it corresponds with 'uncircumcision of heart' (Deut. x. 16, Jer. iv. 4; cf. Ac. vii. 51), and 'rage, or pride, of heart' (Sir. xvi. 10); the adj. -διος to 'crooked' (Prov. xvii. 20) and 'stubborn' (Ez. iii. 7). The last (קְשִׁי) is the ordinary meaning of σκληρός in the LXX. (cf. -ρύνειν Heb. iii. 8, iv. 7); and cf. Jude 15; but in the N.T. it also denotes 'stern' (Mt. xxv. 24), 'fierce'

ἐπέτρεψεν ὑμῖν ἀπολῦσαι τὰς γυναῖκας ὑμῶν, ἀπ᾽ ἀρχῆς δὲ
9 οὐ γέγονεν οὕτως. λέγω δὲ ὑμῖν ὅτι ὃς ἂν ἀπολύσῃ τὴν
γυναῖκα αὐτοῦ μὴ ἐπὶ πορνείᾳ καὶ γαμήσῃ ἄλλην μοιχᾶται.

9 μη επι πορνεια] אCINZ *al* minn.*pler* 𝕃 g² vg 𝕾 pesh.hcl arm aeth ;
παρεκτος λογου πορνειας BD 1 33 𝕃 vet. [*exc* g²] 𝕾 sin[*om* λογου].cur.pal me sah |
και γαμηση αλλην] אCDIZ *al* minn.*pler* 𝕃 vet [*exc* ff¹m].vg 𝕾 sin.cur.pesh.hcl sah
arm aeth ; ποιει αυτην μοιχευθηναι BC*N 1 4 𝕃 ff¹ m me [𝕾 pal *confl* κ. γαμ. αλλ. *et*
ποι. αυτ. μοιχ.] | μοιχαται] אC³DLS 69 *al* 𝕃 a b e ff¹·² g¹ h l m 𝕾 sin.cur me ; *add*
και ο απολελυμενην γαμησας [*vel* γαμων] μοιχαται BC¹INZ *al* minn.*pler* 𝕃 c f g² q vg
𝕾 pesh.hcl.pal arm aeth

(Jam. iii. 4), or 'difficult' (Jo. vi. 60).
The last clause ἀπ᾽ ἀρχῆς κτλ. is added
by Mt., reinforcing the teaching of *v.* 4.

9. λέγω δὲ ὑμῖν κτλ.] Not quite
like the ἐγὼ δὲ λέγω ὑμῖν of v. 22,
28, etc. ; the Mosaic concession has
already been contrasted with the
divine principle, and Jesus now
endorses the latter. Mk. has 'And
in the house (see on viii. 16) again
the disciples asked Him concerning
this.' In Mt. the words are a
continuation of the reply to the
Pharisees, but a conversation with the
disciples (absent from Mk.) is added
in *vv.* 10–12. For the various statements on divorce see on v. 31 f. Mt.
here follows Mk. *v.* 11, but omitting
ἐπ᾽ αὐτήν after μοιχᾶται, perhaps
thinking it ambiguous, since it might
grammatically refer to either woman.

μὴ ἐπὶ πορνείᾳ] Cf. v. 32,
παρεκτὸς λόγου πορνείας (read here
in some MSS.). In both cases the
saving clause is added in Mt. only.
It cannot be supposed that Mt.
wished to represent Jesus as siding
with the school of Shammai (see on
v. 3); the close connexion of *v.* 9
with *v.* 8 shews that he understood
Him to be further emphasizing the
ideal of creation, and any reference
to Rabbinic disputes is beside the
mark. The addition of the saving
clause is, in fact, opposed to the spirit
of the whole context, and must have
been made at a time when the practice

of divorce for adultery had already
grown up. (In Herm. *Mand.* iv. 1,
a reference to this passage, it is
definitely enjoined.) Whether the
writer of the gloss thought that the
divorcer was free in such a case to
marry again is not clear, though it
seems to be implied. But that either
Jesus thought so in spite of His
clear teaching on the first man and
woman, or Mt. who coupled *v.* 9
with *v.* 8, is inconceivable (μοιχείαν
δὲ ἡγεῖται τὸ ἐπιγῆμαι ζῶντος θατέ-
ρου τῶν κεχωρισμένων, Clem. *Strom.*
ii. 145). 𝕾 cur here, and 𝕾 sin in v.
31, Mk. x. 2, 11 f., render ἀπολύειν by
'leave' ; but in both Gospp., and in
all the variant readings, the verb must
bear the same meaning ; it cannot be
confined to a separation *a mensa et
toro* as distinct from divorce.

Mk. further says (*v.* 12), 'and if
she, having put away her husband,
marry another, she committeth
adultery.' The divorce of a man
by his wife was a Greek and Roman,
but not a Jewish, custom (Jos. *Ant.*
xv. vii. 10); hence, probably, Mt.'s
omission of the words. Under the
influence of Gk. habits and thought
Herodias could leave her husband
Philip and be married to Antipas
(Mt. xiv. 3 f.), and Salome, her great-
aunt, divorced Costobarus (Jos. *l.c.* ;
see also XVIII. ix. 6). S. Paul
assumed (1 Cor. vii. 10 f., 13) that
it was legal at Corinth, though he

λέγουσιν αὐτῷ οἱ μαθηταί Εἰ οὕτως ἐστὶν ἡ αἰτία τοῦ 10
ἀνθρώπου μετὰ τῆς γυναικός, οὐ συμφέρει γαμῆσαι. ὁ δὲ 11
εἶπεν αὐτοῖς Οὐ πάντες χωροῦσι τὸν λόγον, ἀλλ' οἷς
δέδοται. εἰσὶν γὰρ εὐνοῦχοι οἵτινες ἐκ κοιλίας μητρὸς 12

opposed the practice. If the words are genuine in Mk., the question put to Jesus was appropriate at the moment of His first reappearance in public after avoiding Herod's territory, and the answer may have contained an implied reference to Herodias (Burkitt, *Gosp. Hist.* 98 ff.).

10–12. (Mt. only.) On Celibacy.

10. εἰ οὕτως κτλ.] If αἰτία refers to the αἰτία of *v.* 3, the meaning is, ' If the cause (for divorce) that a man has against his wife stands thus,' *i.e.* if adultery is the only cause. The disciples, in this case, are represented as shrinking from the strict rule of the school of Shammai, and the verse must be due to the hand that added κατὰ πᾶσαν αἰτίαν (*v.* 3), and μὴ ἐπὶ πορνείᾳ (*v.* 9). But the meaning is obscurely expressed, both αἰτία and μετά needing mental explanation. αἰτία is probably a Latinism (cf. Mk. v. 33 D): ' If the *case* of a man with his wife stands thus.' Cf. the *v.l.* of some minn. in Mk. v. 33, εἶπεν αὐτῷ πᾶσαν τὴν αἰτίαν αὐτῆς. M.-M. (*Vocab. s.v.*) quote two passages from papyri in which this meaning is approached. For οὕτως as a predicate see i. 18.

11. ὁ δὲ εἶπεν κτλ.] If οὕτως in *v.* 10 refers to the indissolubility of marriage, the Lord's reply is difficult. He cannot be supposed to agree with the disciples that ' it is not advantageous to marry,' after His solemn statement that marriage was a divine ordinance ; and it is awkward to make τ. λόγον [τοῦτον] refer to the quotation in *v.* 4 f. :

' all cannot make room in their lives for the divine ordinance of indissoluble marriage, because some for physical reasons cannot marry, and some for spiritual reasons will not.' It is probable that *vv.* 10–12 originally stood in another context, following some utterance on self-denial for the sake of the Kingdom of Heaven, which might include the renunciation of marriage (cf. Lk. xiv. 26, xviii. 29); and both οὕτως ἐ. ἡ αἰτία and τ. λόγον [τοῦτον] refer to this. For χωρεῖν ' to find room for,' ' be capable of containing ' (class.) cf. Jo. ii. 6, xxi. 25 ; in late Gk. it is metaph., as here and *v.* 12 ; cf. 2 Cor. vii. 2. For the thought of ἀλλ' οἷς δέδοται cf. 1 Cor. vii. 7. Neither Jesus nor S. Paul lays down any particular form of self-denial as obligatory in all cases ; in *v.* 21 a different form is recommended to one who needed it, and in *v.* 29 (to which Lk. adds ἢ γυναῖκα) the general principle is stated. Jesus is far removed from an asceticism which shuns marriage as wrong in itself. Contrast the tone of the *Gosp. Egypt.* (Clem. *Strom.* III. iii. 92), ' On Salome inquiring when should be known the things of which He spoke, the Lord said, When ye shall have trampled on the vesture of shame, and when the two become one, and the male with the female, neither male nor female.' For ἀλλά = εἰ μή (cf. Aram. '*illâ*) see Mk. iv. 22, ix. 8 (AC).

12. εἰσὶν γὰρ κτλ.] The verse illustrates οἷς δέδοται : ' *for* while some are eunuchs involuntarily, others have deliberately embraced the life of self-renunciation.' Or

ἐγεννήθησαν οὕτως, καὶ εἰσὶν εὐνοῦχοι οἵτινες εὐνουχίσθησαν
ὑπὸ τῶν ἀνθρώπων, καὶ εἰσὶν εὐνοῦχοι οἵτινες εὐνούχισαν
ἑαυτοὺς διὰ τὴν βασιλείαν τῶν οὐρανῶν. ὁ δυνάμενος χωρεῖν
χωρείτω.

13 Τότε προσηνέχθησαν αὐτῷ παιδία, ἵνα τὰς χεῖρας
ἐπιθῇ αὐτοῖς καὶ προσεύξηται· οἱ δὲ μαθηταὶ ἐπετίμησαν
14 αὐτοῖς. ὁ δὲ Ἰησοῦς εἶπεν Ἄφετε τὰ παιδία καὶ μὴ

possibly all three classes are instances
of οἷς δέδοται, the divine 'gift'
taking, in the case of the first two,
the form of outward circumstances.
The description of these can hardly be
metaphorical, as some have thought.
The condition of the first two is
dealt with in *Yebam.* viii. 4–6 ; cf.
vi. 6. The description of the third
is, of course, metaphorical, as many
patr. writers realized, and describes
spiritual self-renunciation, as complete as though the physical act had
been performed. Cf. the Agraphon
in Clem. *Strom.* III. xv. 97, ὁ κατὰ
πρόθεσιν εὐνουχίας ὁμολογήσας μὴ
γῆμαι ἄγαμος διαμενέτω. *Paed.* III.
iv. 26, εὐνοῦχος ἀληθὴς οὐχ ὁ μὴ
δυνάμενος ἀλλ' ὁ μὴ βουλόμενος
φιληδεῖν. Origen, in his youth, as
is well known, is said by Eus. (*H.E.*
VI. viii. 1 f.) to have understood it
literally, and performed the act upon
himself, and was not without imita-
tors, though in later life he explained
the words in a spiritual sense. On
the patr. treatment of the passage see
Bauer, *NT Stud.* for Heinrici, 235 ff.
The aor. εὐνούχισαν points to a time
before the words were spoken. If
they are genuine, the Lord may be
referring to the fact that some of
the disciples had given up thoughts
of marriage in order to follow Him.
S. Peter probably left his wife during
the period in which he followed
Jesus (Lk. xviii. 28 f.), though she
accompanied him afterwards (1 Cor.
ix. 5); tradition held the apostle
John to be a celibate (*eunuchus*, Jer.

on Is. lvi. 3 f., *Christi spado*, Tert.
Monog. xvii.); and for Jesus Himself
also self-dedication to His Father's
business may possibly have involved
a conscious act of abnegation.

ὁ δυνάμενος κτλ.] The warning
of *v.* 11 is repeated, τὸν λόγον
[τοῦτον] being understood as the obj.
of the verb : 'let him only who is
able (by divine gift) to make room
in his life for the call to renunciation, make room for it.' Justin
(*Apol.* i. 15) so understood it, πλὴν
οὐ πάντες τοῦτο χωροῦσι. But it
may originally have been a distinct
saying, equivalent to 'he that hath
ears to hear, let him hear,' which Mt.
placed here owing to the recurrence
of the verb. It is so used in Ign.
Smyrn. vi. 1, ὁ χωρῶν χωρείτω.

13–15. (Mk. x. 13–16, Lk. xviii.
15–17.) JESUS BLESSES CHILDREN.

13. τότε κτλ.] If marriage is
hallowed, so are children. In Mk.,
the aim of those who brought them
was 'that He might touch them,' a
magical power being expected to flow
from the great Rabbi (see Orig.
quoted by Swete); by adding καὶ
προσεύξηται (see on xiv. 23) Mt.
anticipates Mk.'s κατευλόγει, making
them desire what the Lord actually
gave. Lk. has καὶ τὰ βρέφη, 'even
infants,' but in the next verse he
adopts Mk.'s παιδία.

14. ὁ δὲ Ἰησοῦς κτλ.] Mt., Lk.
omit Mk.'s ἠγανάκτησεν (see on viii.
3). The Lord was indignant because
they ought by this time to have real-

κωλύετε αὐτὰ ἐλθεῖν πρός με, τῶν γὰρ τοιούτων ἐστὶν ἡ
βασιλεία τῶν οὐρανῶν. καὶ ἐπιθεὶς τὰς χεῖρας αὐτοῖς 15
ἐπορεύθη ἐκεῖθεν.

Καὶ ἰδοὺ εἷς προσελθὼν αὐτῷ εἶπεν Διδάσκαλε, τί 16
ἀγαθὸν ποιήσω ἵνα σχῶ ζωὴν αἰώνιον; ὁ δὲ εἶπεν αὐτῷ 17
Τί με ἐρωτᾷς περὶ τοῦ ἀγαθοῦ; εἷς ἐστὶν ὁ ἀγαθός· εἰ

ized how high a place 'little ones' of all kinds held in the Father's sight (cf. xviii. 1–6, 10–14). ἐλθεῖν is the act of the children then present; ἔρχεσθαι (Mk., Lk.) is applicable to all. τῶν γὰρ τοιούτων κτλ., 'for the Kingdom of Heaven belongs to such'; its possessors are to be children and all others who have the child-like spirit; 'talium, non istorum, ut ostenderet non aetatem regnare sed mores' (Jer.). The thought is put in other words in v. 3, 5, 8. In Mk. (v. 15), Lk. (v. 17) a saying is added enlarging upon it, the equivalent of which Mt. has already given in xviii. 3. When the K. of Heaven was understood to be the Church, the words were naturally applied to Christian Baptism. Mt.'s passage was read in the Gospel of the Sarum Ordo ad faciendum Catechumenum; in the Engl. Prayerbooks Mk.'s was substituted.

15. καὶ ἐπιθείς κτλ.] Mk.'s tender ἐναγκαλισάμενος is omitted (cf. xviii. 2 with Mk. ix. 36). Lk. omits the act of blessing altogether. ἐπορεύθη ἐκ. is taken from the opening of Mk.'s next narrative, ἐκπορευομένου δὲ αὐτοῦ (sc. ἐκ τῆς οἰκίας) εἰς ὁδόν.

16–22. (Mk. x. 17–22, Lk. xviii. 18–23.) THE RICH YOUNG MAN.

16. καὶ ἰδού κτλ.] 'The children . . . were nearer the Kingdom than they could suppose themselves to be. The rich man . . . was farther from it than he supposed himself to be' (Plummer). For εἷς (so Mk. ; τις Lk.) see viii. 19. Mk.'s vivid 'ran and knelt to Him' is omitted. Lk. calls

him an ἄρχων; of the meanings given in ix. 18 the last, 'a rich, or important, man' suits the context best.

διδάσκαλε κτλ.] On the title see vii. 21. Mk., Lk. διδ. ἀγαθέ, τί ποιήσω ἵνα (Lk. ποιήσας). Mt. prepares for the alteration which he makes in the Lord's reply, by transferring the adj. to the question. For σχῶ 'get' (Mk., Lk. κληρονομήσω) cf. xxi. 38. εἰς τὴν ζωὴν εἰσελθεῖν (v. 17) is synonymous; see vii. 14, xviii. 8, and Add. n.

17. τί με ἐρωτᾷς κτλ.] Mk., Lk. τί με λέγεις ἀγαθόν ; οὐδεὶς ἀγαθὸς εἰ μὴ εἷς ὁ θεός. Mt.'s alteration avoids words which might seem derogatory to Jesus; but rightly understood they are not. The questioner employed the adj. neither in irony nor in flattery. It may have been merely an expression of politeness. But his question shewed that his conception of goodness was inadequate, since he treated it as quantitative, and attainable by a definite act or series of acts. Jesus therefore gave to the adjective its deepest meaning. The reply, in Mk., Lk. did not answer his question, but shewed him that goodness lay in being rather than doing, that it meant living the life of God. Jesus did not imply that He Himself was not good; He started from the questioner's word, and from his moral standpoint. In Mt. the meaning is essentially the same, though the simplicity of the question and answer is lost, and εἷς ἐστὶν ὁ ἀγαθός does not logically correspond with the neut. ἀγαθόν.

18 δὲ θέλεις εἰς τὴν ζωὴν εἰσελθεῖν, τήρει τὰς ἐντολάς. λέγει
αὐτῷ   Ποίας;   ὁ δὲ Ἰησοῦς ἔφη   Τό   Ογ φονεγceic, Ογ
19 μοιχεγceic, Ογ κλέψεις, Ογ ψεγΔομαρτγρήceic, Τίμα τὸν πατέρα
καὶ τὴν μητέρα, καί Ἀγαπήceic τὸν πληcίον coγ ὡc ceαγτόν.
20 λέγει αὐτῷ ὁ νεανίσκος Ταῦτα πάντα ἐφύλαξα· τί ἔτι
21 ὑστερῶ; ἔφη αὐτῷ ὁ Ἰησοῦς Εἰ θέλεις τέλειος εἶναι,

εἰ δὲ θέλεις κτλ.] This half verse,
with the following question Ποίας;
interprets the simple τὰς ἐντολὰς
οἶδας of Mk., Lk. Any other commandments would, of course, have
served, but those in the second table
of the Decalogue were the most
suitable specimens for shewing, in
a practical form, what it meant to
live the life of God.

18. λέγει κτλ.] The strict sense
of ποίας 'what kind of commandments' (cf. Rom. iii. 27) would be
irrelevant; it is equivalent to τίνας,
and carries on the τί of v. 16 (cf.
xxii. 36, xxiv. 42 f., Blass, § 50. 6).
Only Mt. prefixes the art. to the
commandments. οὐ follows the LXX.;
Mk., Lk. have μή with conj. throughout. The order of the first four
of the commandments here and in
Mk. is that in Exod. xx. (M.T. and
LXX. ᴬ𝐅ᴸ), and Deut. v. (M.T. and
LXX. ᴬ𝐅), Jos. Ant. III. v. 5, and
Didache ii. 1.   The first two are
transposed in Lk., Mk. (ANX al 𝕃),
Rom. xiii. 9, Jam. ii. 11; in some
Heb. MSS. of Exod. and Deut., including the Nash papyrus, and in
Deut. LXX. ᴮᴸ; Philo (De Decal. xxiv.,
xxxii., Mangey ii. 300) and Tert. (De
Pud. v.) base an argument on this
order; and it is found in Theoph.,
Clem. Al., and other Christian
writers. Before τίμα Mk. alone adds
μὴ ἀποστερήσῃς (perhaps a later
addition; B*KΔP 𝔖 sin omit), either
with μισθὸν πένητος understood,
a reference to Deut. xxiv. 14 (AF),
or with a more general meaning
akin to that of the tenth command-

ment. Mt.'s addition ἀγαπήσεις κτλ.
is to the same effect, but goes deeper.
Cf. Herm. Mand. viii. 5, Simil. VI.
v. 5. 'It is the reverse of suum
cuique' (Wohlenberg).

19. τίμα κτλ.] Cf. xv. 4, Eph.
vi. 2. This commandment receives
emphasis in all the three accounts by
being placed out of its order. Perhaps
the rich young man was of humble
origin, and in need of the reminder.
On the omission of σου see xv. 4.

ἀγαπήσεις κτλ.] From Lev. xix.
18; see Mt. xxii. 39. It can hardly
be genuine here, as Orig. saw. The
commandments from the Decalogue
were such as to draw from the rich
man his confident ἐφύλαξα, but this
is of a higher order, and anticipates
the teaching which he still needed,
and received in v. 21. See Gosp.
Heb. quoted at v. 22.

20. λέγει κτλ.] Mt. alone describes
him as νεανίσκος, apparently formed
from Mk.'s ἐκ νεότητός μου. The
word, however, need not imply one
too young to say 'from my youth'
or to be an ἄρχων; in the LXX. it is
applied to warriors (e.g. Gen. xiv. 24,
2 Chr. xi. 1, Is. xiii. 18). ἐφύλαξα
(so Lk.) interprets Mk.'s ἐφυλαξάμην
in the sense in which the mid. is
frequent in the Pentateuch. But the
latter is not used actively elsewhere
in the N.T., and may mean 'from all
these things I have guarded myself'
(cf. Ac. xxi. 25, 2 Tim. iv. 15).

τί ἔτι ὑστερῶ;] Taken from Mk.'s
ἕν σε ὑστερεῖ in the Lord's answer.
Some think that Mt. purposely draws
an unfavourable picture of the rich

ὕπαγε πώλησόν σου τὰ ὑπάρχοντα καὶ δὸς τοῖς πτωχοῖς,
καὶ ἕξεις θησαυρὸν ἐν οὐρανοῖς, καὶ δεῦρο ἀκολούθει μοι.
ἀκούσας δὲ ὁ νεανίσκος τὸν λόγον τοῦτον ἀπῆλθεν λυπού- 22

man (cf. xxii. 35–40 where he omits Mk. xii. 32 ff.), and that the question is intended to reveal a proud complacency. But it might equally express a pathetic despair. Mk. pictures a genuine earnestness (προσδραμὼν κ. γονυπετήσας αὐτόν) which called forth the Lord's affection (ἠγάπησεν αὐτόν). Mt., Lk. omit this expression of emotion (see on viii. 3), but not necessarily because they thought the man unworthy of it.

21. εἰ θέλεις κτλ.] 'If you desire to be really fitted to get eternal life.' The thought corresponds exactly with that of εἰ θέλεις κτλ. in v. 17. It is Mt.'s substitute for Mk.'s ἕν σε ὑστερεῖ (Lk. ἔτι ἕν σοι λείπει). To give his possessions to the poor would not in itself constitute τελειότης (cf. 1 Cor. xiii. 3), but it might be, in the case of the rich man, a supreme expression of love, the one thing that he lacked, in other words of the ἀγαθόν that he asked about, the divine life lived now, which is the sole preparation for eternal life. Once in possession of this, he would have eternal life as a treasure stored in heaven (cf. vi. 20 f.), and he would take unfettered the next step—to follow Jesus as one of His band of disciples. The words are not a universal command of voluntary poverty, but a concrete instance which applied to the given case, and no doubt can apply to many another. 'Of the form embodied in this precept it is probably safe to say Ὁ δυνάμενος χωρεῖν χωρείτω' (Swete); see Clem. Quis Dives 13 ff. Another method of expressing the Love which is τελειότης is given in v. 44–48. Cf. Martha's χρεία ἑνός (Lk. x. 41), and the many

ways in which Love can shew itself (1 Cor. xiii. 4–7).

22. ἀκούσας κτλ.] So Lk., avoiding Mk.'s στυγνάσας ἐπὶ τῷ λόγῳ. On ἦν ἔχων (so Mk.) as shewing Aramaic influence see Blass, § 62. 2 ; for the opposite view, Moulton, i. 227. κτήματα: probably 'landed property,' more definite than possessiones (Vulg.); cf. Ac. ii. 45 (distinguished from ὑπάρξεις, v. 1. It stands for 'vineyard,' Prov. xxix. 34 [xxxi. 16], Hos. ii. 15 (17), and 'field,' Prov. xxiii. 10. He was a κτήτωρ χωρίων ἢ οἰκιῶν (Ac. iv. 34) who could not rise to the demand made upon him.

In Gosp. Heb. (Orig.lat Comm. in Mat. xv. 14) the Gospel story is compressed, but 'give to the poor' is expanded : 'Another rich man said unto Him, "Master, by doing what good thing shall I live ? " He said unto him, "Man, do the law(s) and the prophets." He answered Him, "I have done them." He said unto him, "Go, sell all that thou possessest and distribute to the poor, and come, follow Me." But the rich man began to scratch his head, and it pleased him not. And the Lord said unto him, "How sayest thou, I have done the law and the prophets ? Whereas it is written in the law Thou shalt love thy neighbour as thyself; and lo, many of thy brethren, sons of Abraham, are clothed in filth, dying from hunger, and thy house is full of many good things, and nothing at all goeth forth from it to them." And He turned and said to Simon His disciple sitting by Him, "Simon, son of John, it is easier for a camel to go through the eye of a needle, than a rich man into the Kingdom of Heaven."

23 μενος, ἦν γὰρ ἔχων κτήματα πολλά.   Ὁ δὲ Ἰησοῦς
εἶπεν τοῖς μαθηταῖς αὐτοῦ   Ἀμὴν λέγω ὑμῖν ὅτι πλούσιος
δυσκόλως εἰσελεύσεται εἰς τὴν βασιλείαν τῶν οὐρανῶν·
24 πάλιν δὲ λέγω ὑμῖν, εὐκοπώτερόν ἐστιν κάμηλον διὰ τρήματος ῥαφίδος εἰσελθεῖν ἢ πλούσιον εἰς τὴν βασιλείαν τοῦ
25 θεοῦ.   ἀκούσαντες δὲ οἱ μαθηταὶ ἐξεπλήσσοντο σφόδρα
26 λέγοντες Τίς ἄρα δύναται σωθῆναι;   ἐμβλέψας δὲ ὁ Ἰησοῦς

23–26. (Mk. x. 23–27, Lk. xviii. 24–27.) CONCERNING RICHES.

23. ὁ δὲ Ἰησοῦς κτλ.] Mk. καὶ περιβλεψάμενος (Mk.⁶, Lk. vi. 10 only) ὁ 'l. λέγει. On ἀμὴν λ. ὑ. see v. 18. For the thought cf. Sir. xxxiv. [xxxi.] 8 f., Lk. vi. 24, 1 Tim. vi. 9. 'Aurum enervatio virtutum' (Aug.). The adj. δύσκολος is used (class.) of persons, 'hard to please,' 'discontented'; cf. Theod. Ez. ii. 6; of things, 'unpleasant'; cf. Jer. xxix. 9 [xlix. 8], Ditt. Syll. 213. 33 (cited by Allen). The meaning 'difficult' is found in the marg. of a single MS. in 4 Regn. ii. 10, δύσκολον ᾐτήσω (see Field, Hexapla). Mt., Lk. omit Mk. v. 24, 'And the disciples were amazed (ἐθαμβοῦντο) at His words. And Jesus again answering saith unto them, Children, how hard it is to enter into the Kingdom of God' (cf. xx. 17 with Mk. x. 32). In D 235 b ff² Mk.'s v. 24 is placed after v. 25, forming a climax in the series of sayings, and adding point to the disciples' question.

24. πάλιν κτλ.] πάλιν comes from Mk.'s omitted verse. On εὐκοπώτερον see ix. 5. τρήματος ῥαφίδος: Mk. τρυμαλιᾶς ῥ., using a LXX. word for a hole or fissure in a rock, Lk. τρήματος βελόνης, the latter a more literary word. τρῆμα and the v.l. τρύπημα are class.; for ῥαφίς Allen cites Ox. Pap. iv. 736. 75 (A.D. 1). The camel was the largest beast of burden known in Palestine; cf. xxiii. 24. Such sayings were no doubt pro-

verbial. The words in the Koran, Sur. vii. 38, 'They shall not enter Paradise until a camel pass through the eye of a needle,' is possibly derived from the Gospels; but cf. the similar sayings about an elephant in Berak. 55 b, Bab. Mez. 38 b (Lightfoot, Hor. Heb. ad loc.). An Indian parallel is given by H. M. Elliot, Hist. of India, iii. 553. The popular hyperbole must not be explained away, by understanding κάμηλος as a ship's cable (hence in some late MSS. the spelling κάμιλος, which Suid. and a Schol. on Ar. Vesp. 1030 state to mean a 'rope'), or ῥαφίς as a narrow gorge or gate (see Swete). ἡ βασ. τοῦ θεοῦ (for τῶν οὐρανῶν) is elsewhere confined in Mt. to xii. 28, xxi. 31, 43. Its retention here from Mk. may have been an oversight on Mt.'s part, but much more probably a harmonization with Mk. which has been rightly corrected in the earliest versions. Gosp. Heb. has 'regnum coelorum' (see above).

25. ἀκούσαντες κτλ.] Lk. spares the disciples by omitting, a second time, their astonishment, and ascribing their exclamation to οἱ ἀκούσαντες. τίς ἄρα: Mk., Lk. καὶ τίς (see Blass, § 77. 6). σωθῆναι is equivalent to 'get eternal life' (v. 16), and 'enter into life' (v. 17) or 'into the Kingdom' (v. 24).' See on x. 22. The question does not mean 'Who can be saved if even the rich man finds it hard?'; it was generally the poor, not the rich, who were thought of as the 'pious.' Nor is it a

εἶπεν αὐτοῖς Παρὰ ἀνθρώποις τοῦτο ἀδύνατόν ἐστιν, παρὰ
δὲ θεῷ πάντα ΔΥΝΑΤΑ. Τότε ἀποκριθεὶς ὁ Πέτρος εἶπεν 27
αὐτῷ Ἰδοὺ ἡμεῖς ἀφήκαμεν πάντα καὶ ἠκολουθήσαμέν σοι·
τί ἄρα ἔσται ἡμῖν; ὁ δὲ Ἰησοῦς εἶπεν αὐτοῖς Ἀμὴν λέγω 28
ὑμῖν ὅτι ὑμεῖς οἱ ἀκολουθήσαντές μοι, ἐν τῇ παλινγενεσίᾳ
ὅταν καθίσῃ ὁ υἱὸς τοῦ ἀνθρώπου ἐπὶ θρόνου δόξης αὐτοῦ,

confession of the disciples that they, like all men, would be rich if they could, and therefore came under the same condemnation. But τίς stands for τίς πλούσιος; Quis dives salvus?

26. παρὰ ἀνθρώποις κτλ.] Even rich men, Matthew (ix. 9), Joseph (xxvii. 57), Zacchaeus (Lk. xix. 9), and many others (Ac. iv. 34–37), could be moved by God 'who wishes all men to be saved' (1 Tim. ii. 4). Compare with this saying Lk. i. 37 (Gen. xviii. 14), Mk. ix. 23, 2 Cor. ix. 8, Job xlii. 2, Zech. viii. 6.

27–30. (Mk. x. 28–31, Lk. xviii. 28 ff.; cf. Lk. xxii. 28 ff., xiii. 30.) THE REWARD OF SELF-SACRIFICE.

27. τότε κτλ.] Mk. ἤρξατο λέγειν ὁ Π. (see on xiii. 54). Another mistake of the chief apostle, a self-complacency which the Petrine tradition in Mk. faithfully records: 'we at any rate have thrown off the fetters of wealth.' Mt.'s addition, τί ἄρα ἔσται ἡμῖν; 'what then will happen to us?' or 'what then shall we get when we enter the Kingdom?' heightens the self-centredness, and leads more directly to the reply as Mt. gives it.

28. ἀμήν κτλ.] See on v. 18. Mk. has the opening formula; but not the remainder of the verse, which occurs in a different form in Lk. xxii. 28 ff., beginning 'Ye are they who have persevered with Me in My temptations (or trials, πειρασ-μοῖς),' an expression which Mt. may purposely have avoided. Lk. continues 'and I have appointed for

you, as My Father appointed for Me, a kingdom, that ye may eat and drink at My table in My kingdom.' These high *personal* claims to divine authority (ἐγώ ... μοι ... μου ... μου) do not appear in Mt., who is unlikely to have omitted them had they stood in his source.

ἐν τῇ παλινγενεσίᾳ] The expectation of the 'new birth' of the world (cf. ὠδῖνες xxiv. 8) rests on such passages as Is. lxv. 17, lxvi. 22, and is widely found in Jewish apocalyptic (cf. Apoc. xxi. 1, 5, 2 Pet. iii. 13). It was to be either a transformation of the world, or a new world after the destruction of the old one. The Aram. חֲדָתָא עָלְמָא 'a new world' (cf. ⳨ pesh here) in the *Kaddish* prayer is the nearest equivalent. See Volz, *Jüd. Esch.* 296 f., Dalm. *Words*, 177–9. For παλινγεν. Allen cites Philo, *V. Mos.* ii. 12 (the world's renewal after the flood), *De Mund.* xv. (after being burnt). For the former see Clem. 1 Cor. ix. 4, and for the latter the Stoic ideas (Zeller, *Stoics, Epic., and Scept.* 166 f.). Jos. (*Ant.* XI. iii. 9) uses it of the restoration of Judah. The words began to find their true fulfilment at Pentecost; hence the use of παλινγεν. in Tit. iii. 5; cf. Jo. iii. 3, 1 Pet. i. 3, and καινὴ κτίσις, 2 Cor. v. 17, Gal. vi. 15.

ὅταν καθίσῃ κτλ.] Cf. xxv. 31, and the passages in Enoch cited on xvi. 27. 'Throne of glory' with reference to God is frequent in the O.T.

καθήσεσθε καὶ ὑμεῖς ἐπὶ δώδεκα θρόνους κρίνοντες τὰς
29 δώδεκα φυλὰς τοῦ Ἰσραήλ. καὶ πᾶς ὅστις ἀφῆκεν οἰκίας
ἢ ἀδελφοὺς ἢ ἀδελφὰς ἢ πατέρα ἢ μητέρα ἢ τέκνα ἢ
ἀγροὺς ἕνεκεν τοῦ ἐμοῦ ὀνόματος, πολλαπλασίονα λήμψεται
30 καὶ ζωὴν αἰώνιον κληρονομήσει. Πολλοὶ δὲ ἔσονται πρῶτοι

καθήσεσθε κτλ.] When sin has
ceased, 'judgment' will mean government of an ideal Israel ; cf. Ps. Sol.
xvii. 26, συνάξει λαὸν ἅγιον, οὗ ἀφ-
ηγήσεται ἐν δικαιοσύνῃ, καὶ κρινεῖ
φυλὰς λαοῦ ἡγιασμένου.   In the
O.T. κρίνειν often means 'govern'
(e.g. Ps. ix. 4, 8). For the association
with Christ in 'judgment' cf. Apoc.
xx. 4, and the request in Mt. xx. 21.
The thought is based on Dan. vii.
22. 'The twelve tribes of Israel'
(cf. 'the whole house of Isr.' Ez.
xxxvii. 11, 19–22) are Israel restored
to its ideal state, which is one aspect
of the παλινγενεσία ; and they are
governed by the ideal body of twelve
Apostles ; cf. Apoc. xxi. 12, 14.

The position of this verse in Mt.
and in Lk. is equally surprising ; here
it follows Peter's self - complacent
question, and obscures the force of
the following reply ; in Lk. it stands
between a rebuke to the disciples
for their strife as to which was the
greatest, and a warning to Peter.
It must have been spoken at a
moment not of rebuke, but of grateful
appreciation of their service. The
present form of the verse, with its
symbolic 'Twelve,' may be due to
later thought ; but it is not impossible that the Apostles, who had
followed Jesus, and preached the
coming of the Kingdom, were
promised an authoritative position
in it.

29. καὶ πᾶς κτλ.]   To Peter's
question in v. 27 the Lord replies 'It
is indeed true that self-sacrifice will
receive its reward (v. 29), but in the
coming Kingdom many expectations,

ambitious and humble alike, will
be contradicted' (v. 30). To leave
'home' (οἰκίαν Mk., Lk.) involves the
renunciation of kindred ; Mt.'s plur.
οἰκίας refers, like ἀγρούς, merely to
property. Lk. adds 'or wife' (see on
v. 11 above), combines 'mother' and
'father' under γονεῖς, and omits
ἀγρούς.   Mk. continues ἕνεκεν ἐμοῦ
(= τοῦ ἐμοῦ ὀνόματος Mt., see x. 22).
καὶ ἕνεκεν τοῦ εὐαγγελίου (see on iv.
17, xvi. 25), which Lk. interprets as
εἵνεκεν τῆς βασιλείας τοῦ θεοῦ.

πολλαπλασίονα κτλ.]   Cf. Test.
Zeb. vi., ὁ γὰρ μεταδιδοὺς τῷ πλησίον λαμβάνει πολλαπλασίονα παρὰ
Κυρίου.   Mk., with an unusual
construction, οὐδεὶς ἔστιν ὃς ἀφῆκεν
. . . ἐὰν μὴ λάβῃ ἑκατονταπλασίονα,
Lk. οὐδεὶς . . . ὃς οὐχὶ μὴ [ἀπο]λάβῃ
πολλαπλασίονα. Mt., Lk. omit
Mk.'s repetition of οἰκίας κτλ., but
Lk. retains his distinction between
'in this time' and 'in the coming
age' (see on Mt. xii. 32). Mt., by
omitting the notes of time, makes
the compensation coincident with
'everlasting life,' an alteration which
is more consonant with the Lord's
usual teaching on the immediate
imminence of the Kingdom. Mk.'s
μετὰ διωγμῶν is probably a later
addition. The multiplied reward
is obviously metaphorical, since it
includes fathers and mothers, and
(Lk.) wives, which evoked Julian's
derision. On ζωὴ αἰώνιος see xviii.
8, and Add. n., and on κληρονομήσει
v. 5.

30. πολλοὶ δέ κτλ.]   'But there
will be many instances of (such as
are) first being last, and last first.'

ἔσχατοι καὶ ἔσχατοι πρῶτοι. Ὁμοία γάρ ἐστιν ἡ βασιλεία 1 XX.
τῶν οὐρανῶν ἀνθρώπῳ οἰκοδεσπότῃ ὅστις ἐξῆλθεν ἅμα πρωὶ
μισθώσασθαι ἐργάτας εἰς τὸν ἀμπελῶνα αὐτοῦ· συμφωνήσας 2
δὲ μετὰ τῶν ἐργατῶν ἐκ δηναρίου τὴν ἡμέραν ἀπέστειλεν
αὐτοὺς εἰς τὸν ἀμπελῶνα αὐτοῦ. καὶ ἐξελθὼν περὶ τρίτην 3
ὥραν εἶδεν ἄλλους ἑστῶτας ἐν τῇ ἀγορᾷ ἀργούς· καὶ 4
ἐκείνοις εἶπεν Ὑπάγετε καὶ ὑμεῖς εἰς τὸν ἀμπελῶνα, καὶ
ὃ ἐὰν ᾖ δίκαιον δώσω ὑμῖν· οἱ δὲ ἀπῆλθον. πάλιν δὲ 5

πολλοί refers to both, and the predicate stands second in each case, as
Mk.'s οἱ ἔσχ. πρῶτοι and Mt. xx. 16,
shew. Lk. omits the verse here,
but has it in a different form in
xiii. 20. In Barn. vi. 13 occurs the
saying ἰδοὺ ποιῶ τὰ ἔσχατα ὡς τὰ
πρῶτα (see Resch, *Agrapha*², p. 167).
Cf. *Ox. Pap.* iv. 654. 25 ff. Some
explain the verse as the continuation
of the promise in *v.* 29, 'and (δέ)
the great ones of the world (*e.g.* the
rich man above) and My humble
followers who have forsaken all for
Me, will find their positions reversed,
receiving condemnation and bliss
respectively.' But it is more probably
a rebuke to Peter, and refers to *ranks*
in the Kingdom. The following
parable has no bearing on the
meaning; the words 'first' and
'last,' which led Mt. to place it
here, have a different force.

1–16. (Mt. only.) PARABLE OF
THE LABOURERS IN THE VINEYARD.

1. ὁμοία κτλ.] The Kingdom
is not like the man, but his actions
illustrate an aspect of it; see on
xiii. 24. For ὁμοία see xi. 16, the
redundant ἄνθρωπος xi. 19, and
ὅστις = ὅς ii. 6. ἅμα may be adverbial (see M.-M. *Vocab. s.v.*), or
πρωί is used as a subst. in the dat.,
'with the early morning'; cf. ἀπὸ
πρωί (Ac. xxviii. 23); Moulton, i. 99.
For ἅμα as a preposition cf. xiii. 29.
The vineyard in Scripture supplies

a variety of teaching; see xxi. 28 ff.,
33 ff., Lk. xiii. 6 ff., 1 Cor. ix. 7, Prov.
xxiv. 45 [30], Cant. i. 6, viii. 11 f.,
Is. i. 8, v. 1 ff., Jer. xii. 10.

2. συμφώνησας κτλ.] For συμφ.
cf. xviii. 19. 'At the rate of a
penny a day' (Vulg. *ex denario
diurno*) may be the meaning, although
a single day is contemplated ; or τ.
ἡμ. may be loosely added, 'for the
day in question.' On the use of ἐκ
(om. in *v.* 13) see Blass, § 36. 8.
The δηνάριον, a word which passed
into rabb. Heb., was worth about
9½d. ; Tobit (v. 15) received nearly
the same, δραχμὴν τῆς ἡμέρας; in
Ber. R. lxi. the silver and gold of
which the Israelites spoiled the Egyp-
tians is reckoned as their pay for
past labour at a denarius a day.

3–7. καὶ ἐξελθών κτλ.] The
labourers were free men, but out of
work (ἀργοί, *i.e.* α-εργοι, Vulg. *otiosos*).
The conversation with each group
is summarized as briefly as possible :
hence the abrupt use of the art.
with ἀμπελῶνα, the vineyard having already been the subject, and the
omission in the last instance (*v.* 7)
of the promise of payment. ὃ ἐὰν
ᾖ δίκαιον would not mean, to the
labourers, anything that he thought
fit to give them, but the right
proportion of the ordinary denarius
wage. That the late workers trusted
him without bargaining is an irrelevant thought.

6 ἐξελθὼν περὶ ἕκτην καὶ ἐνάτην ὥραν ἐποίησεν ὡσαύτως.
περὶ δὲ τὴν ἑνδεκάτην ἐξελθὼν εὗρεν ἄλλους ἑστῶτας, καὶ
λέγει αὐτοῖς Τί ὧδε ἑστήκατε ὅλην τὴν ἡμέραν ἀργοί;
7 λέγουσιν αὐτῷ Ὅτι οὐδεὶς ἡμᾶς ἐμισθώσατο· λέγει αὐτοῖς
8 Ὑπάγετε καὶ ὑμεῖς εἰς τὸν ἀμπελῶνα. ὀψίας δὲ γενομένης
λέγει ὁ κύριος τοῦ ἀμπελῶνος τῷ ἐπιτρόπῳ αὐτοῦ Κάλεσον
τοὺς ἐργάτας καὶ ἀπόδος τὸν μισθὸν ἀρξάμενος ἀπὸ τῶν
9 ἐσχάτων ἕως τῶν πρώτων. ἐλθόντες δὲ οἱ περὶ τὴν ἑνδε-
10 κάτην ὥραν ἔλαβον ἀνὰ δηνάριον. καὶ ἐλθόντες οἱ πρῶτοι
ἐνόμισαν ὅτι πλεῖον λήμψονται· καὶ ἔλαβον τὸ ἀνὰ
11 δηνάριον καὶ αὐτοί. λαβόντες δὲ ἐγόγγυζον κατὰ τοῦ
12 οἰκοδεσπότου λέγοντες Οὗτοι οἱ ἔσχατοι μίαν ὥραν ἐποίησαν, καὶ ἴσους αὐτοὺς ἡμῖν ἐποίησας τοῖς βαστάσασι τὸ
13 βάρος τῆς ἡμέρας καὶ τὸν καύσωνα. ὁ δὲ ἀποκριθεὶς ἑνὶ
αὐτῶν εἶπεν Ἑταῖρε, οὐκ ἀδικῶ σε· οὐχὶ δηναρίου συν-

8. ὀψίας κτλ.] This was the
12th hour (see *v.* 9, 12), *i.e.* 6 P.M.
ἐπίτροπος (Vulg. *procurator*) is here
equivalent to οἰκονόμος, 'steward'
or 'bailiff,' as in Lk. viii. 3 (contrast
Gal. iv. 2, Jos. *BJ.* II. viii. 5 f.).
His presence is part of the scenery
of the parable; he must not be
allegorically explained as the Messiah;
elsewhere in the Gospels the Messiah
at the last day is never *commanded*
by God; He and God are represented,
in different passages, as supreme.

For the ellipse ἀρξ. ἀπὸ . . .
ἕως cf. Lk. xxiii. 5. ἀρξ. ἀπό occurs
also in Lk. xxiv. 27, 47, 'Jo.' viii.
9, Ac. i. 22, viii. 35, x. 37, almost
equivalent to the simple ἀπό; cf. Plato
(*e.g.* vi. 771 C, μεχρὶ τῶν δώδεκα ἀπὸ
μιᾶς ἀρξάμενος), and see M.-M. *Vocab.*
s.v. The prevailing patr. explanations
of the successive groups of labourers
are (1) the righteous in successive
ages from Adam till Christian times,
(2) those who give themselves to God's
service at successive ages in human
life from childhood till old age (*e.g.*
Jer. *ad loc.*, Aug. *Serm.* lxxxvii. 7);
see B. Weiss, *Matth.*, *ad loc.*

10. ἐλθόντες κτλ.] τὸ ἀνὰ δην.,
'the denarius apiece (which the
others received)'; for ἀνά cf. Lk.
ix. 3, 14, Apoc. iv. 8. Vulg. *singulos
denarios*. For καί 'and yet' see
Blass, § 77. 6.

λαβόντες κτλ.] The murmuring
will not take place at the last day;
it is part of the scenery of the parable.
γογγύζειν occurs in *Ox. Pap.* i. 33,
iii. 14 (2nd. cent. A.D.); it is found
in old Ionic (Lob. *Phryn.* 358), and
in bibl. and late Gk.

12. οὗτοι κτλ.] ἐποίησαν
'laboured' (Aram. עבד; cf. עשׂה
Ruth ii. 19) does not govern μίαν
ὥραν (as in Ac. xv. 33); Vulg.
rightly *una hora fecerunt*; the
emendation ἐπόνησαν is unnecessary.
For καύσων (a late word) 'heat' cf.
Gen. xxxi. 40, Is. xlix. 10; in the
LXX. it is usually the hot east wind,
sirocco (קָדִים).

13. ὁ δέ κτλ.] The householder
replied to a ringleader who had voiced
their complaint. For the kindly
ἑταῖρε 'comrade' cf. xxii. 12, xxvi.
50, in each case to one who had
wronged the speaker.

ἐφώνησάς μοι; ἆρον τὸ σὸν καὶ ὕπαγε· θέλω δὲ τούτῳ 14
τῷ ἐσχάτῳ δοῦναι ὡς καὶ σοί· οὐκ ἔξεστίν μοι ὃ θέλω 15
ποιῆσαι ἐν τοῖς ἐμοῖς; ἢ ὁ ὀφθαλμός σου πονηρός ἐστιν
ὅτι ἐγὼ ἀγαθός εἰμι; Οὕτως ἔσονται οἱ ἔσχατοι πρῶτοι 16
καὶ οἱ πρῶτοι ἔσχατοι.

Μέλλων δὲ ἀναβαίνειν Ἰησοῦς εἰς Ἱεροσόλυμα παρ- 17

16 εσχατοι²⁰] אBLZ 36 me sah ; add πολλοι γαρ εισι κλητοι ολιγοι δε εκλεκτοι
CD al minn.pler 𝔏 omn 𝔖 omn arm aeth

14. θέλω δέ κτλ.] 'And (in
spite of your complaints) my will is,'
or, as in 𝔖 sin.cur, 'And if my
will is,' v. 15 being treated as the
apodosis.

15. οὐκ ἔξεστιν κτλ.] For the
disjunctive ἤ in an interrogative
cf. xxvi. 53 (Blass, § 77. 2, 11): 'if
I may do what I will with my own
property, the only explanation of
your conduct is that you are envious
because I am liberal.' On ὀφθ.
πονηρός and ἀγαθός see vi. 23.
For the extension of the instrum. ἐν
cf. xxv. 16 (Moulton, i. 61).

16. οὕτως κτλ.] A repetition of
xix. 30 in a different form, as though
that saying were illustrated by the
parable, which, however, obviously
does not teach that the position of
'first' and 'last' will be reversed,
but that the human standards of
payment for work done (see Rom. iv.
4) will be transcended by a reward
which is sheer χάρις; it is not
quantitative, and therefore cannot
differ in amounts. See Add. n. on
v. 12. 1 Cor. iii. 12–15, cited by
Zahn, belongs to a different circle of
ideas.

It is instructive to compare with
the Lord's parable that in Jer. Berak.
ii. 5 c: 'When Rabbi Bun bar Chija
was asleep, Rabbi Sera went up to
him and spake: Sweet is the sleep

of the labourer, whether he have
eaten much or little. Like a king
who had hired many labourers, one
of whom so distinguished himself by
industry and skill that the king
took him by the hand and walked
up and down with him. In the
evening the labourers came, and
the skilful one among them, to receive their pay. The king gave
them all the same pay. Wherefore
those who had worked the whole
day murmured, and spake: We have
worked the whole day, and this man
only two hours, and yet he also has
received his whole pay. The king
answered: This man hath wrought
more in two hours than you in the
whole day. Even so hath Rabbi
Bun bar Chija in twenty-eight years
wrought more in the Law than
many studious scholars in a hundred
years.'

17–19. (Mk. x. 32–34, Lk. xviii.
31–34.) THIRD PREDICTION OF THE
PASSION (see xvi. 21).

17. μέλλων κτλ.] The Lord
was now on the road between the
northern boundary of Judaea and
Jericho (see on xix. 1). A final
decision, involving an intense
struggle, must be made, to go to the
capital and die. Mk. says 'and
Jesus was going before them, and
they were amazed (ἐθαμβοῦντο), and

ἔλαβεν τοὺς δώδεκα μαθητὰς κατ᾽ ἰδίαν, καὶ ἐν τῇ ὁδῷ
18 εἶπεν αὐτοῖς Ἰδοὺ ἀναβαίνομεν εἰς Ἱεροσόλυμα, καὶ ὁ υἱὸς
τοῦ ἀνθρώπου παραδοθήσεται τοῖς ἀρχιερεῦσιν καὶ γραμ-
19 ματεῦσιν, καὶ κατακρινοῦσιν αὐτὸν θανάτῳ, καὶ παραδώσουσιν αὐτὸν τοῖς ἔθνεσιν εἰς τὸ ἐμπαῖξαι καὶ μαστιγῶσαι
καὶ σταυρῶσαι, καὶ τῇ τρίτῃ ἡμέρᾳ ἐγερθήσεται.
20 Τότε προσῆλθεν αὐτῷ ἡ μήτηρ τῶν υἱῶν Ζεβεδαίου

they that followed were afraid' (the last clause being possibly a doublet of the preceding). Engaged in His inward struggle (cf. Lk. ix. 51) He walked alone, but His resolve taken He 'again (Mk.) took the disciples into His company' (παρέλαβεν, cf. xvii. 1, xxvi. 37), by allowing them to overtake Him. Mt.'s κατ᾽ ἰδίαν implies the presence of other followers (see xxvii. 55).

If this is the right explanation of Mk.'s account, the Lord did not, as some have supposed, merely intend to make in Jerusalem another attempt to convince the Jews of His Messiahship, an attempt which failed. εἶπεν: Mk. ἤρξατο λέγειν; see on xiii. 54.

18. ἰδού κτλ.] The opening clause (so Mk., Lk.) expresses the resolve that He had made; they knew already that they were going to the capital for the Passover, but they could not know the struggle that it had caused Him. Lk. continues 'and all the things that have been written through the prophets shall be accomplished unto the Son of Man.' In Mt., Mk. the three principal events foretold in xvi. 21, xvii. 23 are repeated, i.e. παραδο-θήσεται (see on xvii. 23), σταυρῶσαι (Mk. ἀποκτενοῦσιν), ἐγερθήσεται (Mk. ἀναστήσεται). The first of these is amplified with details perhaps added to the tradition after the events, the handing over to the Gentiles, i.e. the Roman soldiers, the

mockery, the spitting (Mk.), and the scourging; and in Mt. the form of death is specified for the first time (see on x. 38, xxvi. 2), but in Mk., Lk. the Crucifixion is not mentioned before the Passion itself. For κατα-κρίνειν with dat. of the punishment (= ψήφῳ θανάτου), a late constr., cf. 2 Pet. ii. 6, Dan. (LXX.) iv. 34 a (so κρίνειν Ez. xxxviii. 22, καταδικάζειν Wisd. ii. 20; see Lob. Phryn. 475); class. κατακρ. τινος θάνατον.

19. καὶ παραδώσουσιν κτλ.] It is not clear why Mt. omits Mk.'s ἐμπτύσουσιν, since he records it in xxvii. 30. On the last four words (Mk. μετὰ τρεῖς ἡμ. ἀναστήσεται) see xvi. 21. Lk. adds a statement of the disciples' inability to understand the saying, similar to that in Lk. ix. 45 (see on Mt. xvii. 23).

20–28. (Mk. x. 35–45; cf. Lk. xxii. 24–27.) THE SONS OF ZEBE-DEE. TEACHING ON HUMILITY.

20. τότε κτλ.] The mother's name was probably Salome (see on xxvii. 56), and possibly a sister of the Lord's mother (Jo. xix. 25), in which case family relationship may have been thought to justify the desire for precedence. Why Mt. substitutes 'the sons of Zebedee' for their names (also xxvi. 37, xxvii. 56 ; cf. Jo. xxi. 2) is not clear. In Mk. it is James and John themselves who approach with the request. That Mt. altered the account to spare the disciples (see on viii. 26) is more probable than that an editor of

μετὰ τῶν υἱῶν αὐτῆς προσκυνοῦσα καὶ . αἰτοῦσά τι ἀπ᾽
αὐτοῦ. ὁ δὲ εἶπεν αὐτῇ Τί θέλεις; λέγει αὐτῷ Εἰπὲ 21
ἵνα καθίσωσιν οὗτοι οἱ δύο υἱοί μου εἷς ἐκ δεξιῶν καὶ εἷς
ἐξ εὐωνύμων σου ἐν τῇ βασιλείᾳ σου. ἀποκριθεὶς δὲ ὁ 22
Ἰησοῦς εἶπεν Οὐκ οἴδατε τί αἰτεῖσθε· δύνασθε πιεῖν τὸ

Mk. did so to spare the mother. That she incited them is not impossible ; she was among the company (xxvii. 55 f.). In *v.* 22 the Lord addresses the sons, as in Mk. In Mk. there is no parallel to προσκυνοῦσα, and the request is introduced by the confident words 'we want thee to do for us whatever we ask Thee.' On αἰτεῖν and αἰτεῖσθαι (*v.* 22) see Moulton, i. 160.

21. ὁ δὲ εἶπεν κτλ.] τί θέλεις; avoids Mk.'s mixed construction τί θέλετέ με ποιήσω ὑμῖν; Mt. does not always omit questions asked by Jesus (see on viii. 29). Jerome overconfidently says 'non venit de ignorantia.'

εἰπέ κτλ.] A word of royal command ; Mk. δὸς ἡμῖν. δεξιῶν (for Mk.'s ἀριστερῶν) in conjunction with καθίσωσιν may be due to the well known καθοῦ ἐκ δεξιῶν μου (Ps. cix. [cx.] 1). For 'right' and 'left' as places of honour see Jos. *Ant.* VI. xi. 9. βασιλείᾳ (for Mk.'s δόξῃ) emphasizes the thought of enthronement next to the King (cf. xix. 28) ; there is no reference to a banquet, for which καθίζειν (-ῆσθαι) are not used in the N.T. The request of the two, and the indignation of the others, follow the prediction of suffering in *v.* 18 f., as the dispute in xviii. 1 (Mk. ix. 33) follows the similar prediction in xvii. 22 f. (Mk. ix. 31 f.), and in both cases the scene is ἐν τῇ ὁδῷ (Mk.). The possibility must be recognized that they are doublets of the same account. Lk. omits the present narrative, but

places the following discourse on humility in connexion with the disciples' φιλονεικία after the account of the Last Supper (xxii. 24 ff.). See *v.* 25 below.

22. ἀποκριθείς κτλ.] They were under a double misapprehension : 1st that they could obtain exaltation without suffering, and 2nd that it was in the power of Jesus to promise this exaltation. They must learn the condition εἴπερ συνπάσχομεν ἵνα καὶ συνδοξασθῶμεν (Rom. viii. 17) ; cf. 2 Tim. ii. 12. There is, again, no thought· of a banquet ; the Cup, closely connected in Mk. with the Baptism (which Mt. omits), is a metaphor for sorrow or suffering, frequent in the O.T. (Ps. lxxiv. [lxxv.] 9, Is. li. 17, Jer. xxxii. 1 ff., 13 f. [xxv. 15 ff., 27 f.], Lam. ii. 13, Ez. xxiii. 31 f., Mart. Is. v. 13, 'For me alone hath God mingled the cup'). Cf. Polycarp's thanksgiving (*Mart.* xiv., Eus. *HE.* IV. xv. 33) that he was counted worthy τοῦ λαβεῖν [με] μέρος ἐν ἀριθμῷ τῶν μαρτύρων ἐν τῷ ποτηρίῳ τοῦ Χριστοῦ σου. Mk.'s πίνω (representing an Aram. partcp.) is rightly interpreted by μέλλω πίνειν. The drinking destined for the two disciples was to be a single act (πιεῖν).

Mk.'s next clause, ἢ τὸ βάπτισμα ὃ ἐγὼ βαπτίζομαι βαπτισθῆναι (cf. Lk. xii. 50), is omitted, probably for brevity, since the two metaphors had for Mt. the same meaning. If there is any difference, the Baptism may express the suffering as ordained by God, the Cup as its voluntary acceptance.

ποτήριον ὃ ἐγὼ μέλλω πίνειν; λέγουσιν αὐτῷ Δυνάμεθα.
23 λέγει αὐτοῖς Τὸ μὲν ποτήριόν μου πίεσθε, τὸ δὲ καθίσαι

λέγουσιν κτλ.] It was not the
first time that they had shewn a
zeal 'not according to knowledge';
see Mk. ix. 38, Lk. ix. 54. Like Peter
(xxvi. 33, 35), they answered pre-
cipitately, perhaps also προσδοκοῦντες
ἀκούσεσθαι ὅπερ ᾔτησαν (Chrys.);
but the δύναμις which they so lightly
claimed was afterwards theirs in the
power of the Resurrection.

23. τὸ μὲν ποτήριον κτλ.] Mk.'s
καὶ τὸ βάπτισμα ὃ ἐγὼ βαπτίζομαι
βαπτισθήσεσθε is omitted. James
soon won the honour (Ac. xii. 2.
That 'brother of John' there means
'brother of J. Mark' or of any other
John than the apostle is very improbable). John's martyrdom would seem
to be vouched for by the Lord's prediction; but a widespread tradition from
the time of Irenaeus (see quotations in
Eus. HE. III. xxiii., IV. xiv., v. viii.
20, 24) represented John as residing
at Ephesus, held in great honour
throughout Asia Minor, till he died
a natural death at an advanced age,
in the reign of Trajan. See also
Jer. on Gal. vi. 10. This perhaps
receives support from Jo. xxi. 22.
The evidence for his martyrdom, on
the other hand, is much slighter;
see J. A. Robinson, Hist. Character
of St. John's Gosp. 64–80, Enc. Bibl.
2509. If the Ephesine tradition is
genuine, the Lord's prediction perhaps finds a partial fulfilment in his
exile at Patmos διὰ τὸν λόγον τοῦ
θεοῦ καὶ τὴν μαρτυρίαν Ἰησοῦ (Apoc.
i. 9); Tert. De Praescr. 36, Clem.
Quis Dives, 42, Orig. in Mat. t. xvi.
6, Eus. HE. III. xviii., Jer. in Mat. ad
loc. and De Vir. Ill. 10. But his
exile is uncertain, since Apoc. l.c.,
the sole evidence for it, is not explicit. And it is strange that the

meaning of the Cup and Baptism
should have been so different in the
cases of the two brothers. The effect,
as Swete says, is that 'the Lord's
words are thus seen to assign to these
two no more than He assigns to all
disciples (Mk. viii. 34, Rom. viii. 17,
2 Tim. ii. 11 ff.).' The question
is complicated by the uncertainty as
to the authorship of the Apoc., and
the persons named John. Attempts
were apparently made to harmonize
the tradition of John's late death
with the present passage: he was
compelled, it is said, by Domitian to
drink a cup of poison (Tisch. Acta
Ap. Apocr. 269; cf. 'Mk.' xvi. 18),
and he was plunged into a bath of
boiling oil (Tert. l.c., Jer. in Mat.),
without injury. Another attempt,
avoidance of the definite prediction,
is perhaps to be seen in 𝔖 cur (Mt.),
'ye are able that ye should drink,'
and 𝔖 sin (Mk.), 'ye are able that ye
should drink . . . ye are able that
ye should be baptized.'

τὸ δὲ καθίσαι κτλ.] Not yet
invested with Messianic authority,
Jesus could not assign ranks in the
future Kingdom. ἀλλά is, therefore,
not equivalent to εἰ μή (as e.g. in xix.
11), as though it was His to give,
but only to those for whom it was
prepared. There is an ellipse requiring δοθήσεται to be supplied.
(𝕷 d renders ἀλλ' οἷς as aliis (ἄλλοις),
so in Mk. 𝕷 k al. 𝔖 sin (see Burkitt),
which are perhaps attempts to avoid
the difficulty.) But the words do not
deny that when the Son is in His
glory He will dispense rewards according to the Father's will expressed in
ἡτοίμασται (Mt. alone adds ὑπὸ τοῦ
πατρός μου). How little the verb,
though implying foreknowledge and

ἐκ δεξιῶν μου καὶ ἐξ εὐωνύμων οὐκ ἔστιν ἐμὸν δοῦναι,
ἀλλ' οἷς ἡτοίμασται ὑπὸ τοῦ πατρός μου. καὶ ἀκούσαντες 24
οἱ δέκα ἠγανάκτησαν περὶ τῶν δύο ἀδελφῶν. ὁ δὲ Ἰησοῦς 25
προσκαλεσάμενος αὐτοὺς εἶπεν Οἴδατε ὅτι οἱ ἄρχοντες
τῶν ἐθνῶν κατακυριεύουσιν αὐτῶν καὶ οἱ μεγάλοι κατεξουσιάζουσιν αὐτῶν. οὐχ οὕτως ἐστὶν ἐν ὑμῖν· ἀλλ' ὃς 26
ἂν θέλῃ ἐν ὑμῖν μέγας γενέσθαι ἔσται ὑμῶν διάκονος,
καὶ ὃς ἂν θέλῃ ἐν ὑμῖν εἶναι πρῶτος ἔσται ὑμῶν δοῦλος· 27

26 εστιν] BDZ 𝕷 m sah ;   εσται ℵCE etc 𝕷 vet [exc m].vg 𝕊 cur.pesh.hcl me
aeth arm

election, annuls human responsibility
is seen in xxv. 34, 1 Cor. ii. 9,
2 Tim. ii. 21 ; and see on xviii. 7.
The paradox is not solved by Jerome's
note 'Regnum coelorum non est
dantis sed accipientis, non enim est
acceptio personarum apud Deum.'

24. ἀκούσαντες κτλ.] Their indignation caused so sharp a division
that they receive the quasi-title 'the
Ten.' If περί (so Mk.) is to be
pressed, they did not openly attack
the two brothers, but expressed their
resentment among themselves.   τ.
δύο ἀδελφῶν avoids (as in v. 20)
Mk.'s mention of their names.
ἠγανάκτησαν : Mk. ἤρξαντο ἀγαν. ;
see on xiii. 54.

25. ὁ δὲ Ἰησοῦς κτλ.] On προσ-
καλεσ. (so Mk.) see x. 1. In Lk.
xxii. 24–27 the following sayings
are occasioned by a dispute about
precedence, not (as Mt., Mk.) in the
coming Kingdom but now (τὸ τίς
αὐτῶν δοκεῖ εἶναι μείζων) ; see on
Mt. xviii. 1, where a similar diver-
gence occurs.

οἴδατε κτλ.] Worldly rulers are
used as an object lesson ; in xviii.
1 f. it was a little child. οἱ ἄρχοντες
simplifies Mk.'s οἱ δοκοῦντες ἄρχειν
(see Swete). The Lord does not
condemn civil authority ; His attitude to it is shewn in xvii. 27, xxii.
21 ; but He teaches that the secular
principle, that it is the great who

rule, is to be reversed in the life of
His followers. It is another application of οἱ ἔσχατοι πρῶτοι. The
ἔθνη are primarily the Romans (cf.
v. 19) ; their rulers (Lk. βασιλεῖς)
lord it over them, and their great
ones, subordinate officials (cf. μεγισ-
τᾶνες Mk. vi. 21), exercise a delegated
ἐξουσία. Lk. οἱ ἐξουσιαζόντων αὐτῶν
εὐεργέται καλοῦνται, a practice found
especially in Syria and Egypt. The
advice μηδ' ὡς κατακυριεύοντες τῶν
κλήρων (1 Pet. v. 3) is perhaps an
allusion to the saying. The unique
κατεξουσιάζουσιν was possibly coined
as a parallel to κατακυριεύουσιν.
Clem. Al. has κατεξουσιαστικὸς
ῥάβδος.

26. οὐχ οὕτως κτλ.] A statement
of a present spiritual principle to
which they already conform if they
are true disciples ; so Mk. (Lk. ὑμεῖς
δὲ οὐχ οὕτ.). ἔσται, a command,
is perhaps the true reading in Mt.
ἀλλ' ὃς ἂν κτλ., 'anyone who wishes
to prove (γενέσθαι) truly great.'
Lk. ἀλλ' ὁ μείζων ἐν ὑμ. γινέσθω ὡς
ὁ νεώτερος shews that ἔσται ὑμῶν
διάκονος (Mt., Mk.) is not a penalty,
but the only method of being great.
Cf. Lk. ix. 48, Test. Jos. xvii. 8, ἤμην
ἐν αὐτοῖς ὡς εἷς τῶν ἐλαχίστων.
The saying appears in a shorter form
in xxiii. 11.

• 27. καὶ ὃς ἂν κτλ.] The truth is
emphasized by repetition, but also

28 ὥσπερ ὁ υἱὸς τοῦ ἀνθρώπου οὐκ ἦλθεν διακονηθῆναι ἀλλὰ
διακονῆσαι καὶ δοῦναι τὴν ψυχὴν αὐτοῦ λύτρον ἀντὶ πολλῶν.

by the choice of words : as πρῶτος
is higher than μέγας, so is δοῦλος
lower than διάκονος.

28. ὥσπερ κτλ.] Identical in
Mk., except καὶ γάρ for ὥσπερ. On
the claim involved in ἦλθεν see v.
17, x. 40. For the first half (to
διακονῆσαι) Lk. has 'for who is
greater, he that sitteth (at table)
or he that serveth ? Is not he that
sitteth (at table) ? But I am in
your midst as he that serveth.' In
private, as in political, life, the great
are masters ; but the reversal of the
principle is ideally exemplified by the
fact that the Master serves. Whichever is the original form, the substance is allowed on all hands to be
genuine. 'Servire est regnare' is
the essence of Christian ethics ; cf.
I Cor. ix. 19, 2 Cor. iv. 5, Gal. v. 13,
Rom. xii. 10, Phil. ii. 3.

καὶ δοῦναι κτλ.] His crowning act
of service (cf. Rom. xvi. 4, I Thes.
ii. 8). Wellh. and Loisy strangely
criticize the transition from 'service'
to 'self-sacrifice' as a μετάβασις εἰς
ἄλλο γένος. Except in this saying
λύτρον (Vulg. redemptio) is not found
in the N.T. In the LXX., both sing.
and more frequently plur., it stands
for כֹּפֶר, פִּדְיוֹן, גְּאֻלָּה, and (Is. xlv. 13)
for מְחִיר, as a legal term, in one case
of the Levites whom God takes as
an equivalent for the first - born
(Num. iii. 12), elsewhere always of
money given as an equivalent for a
person or thing ; each of the following contains a different instance :
Exod. xxi. 30, xxx. 12, Lev. xix. 20,
xxv. 24, 51 f., xxvii. 31, Num. iii.
46, xviii. 15. Similar words are
λύτρωσις and ἀντίλυτρον (see Field,
Hex. on Ps. xlviii. [xlix.] 9 ; cf.
I Tim. ii. 6) ; cf. also ἀντάλλαγμα
τῆς ψυχῆς (Mt. xvi. 26 note). The

Lord says that He came to give
His own ψυχή as an equivalent for
many ; cf. the use of ἀντίψυχος :
4 Macc. vi. 29, ἀντίψυχον αὐτῶν
λάβε τὴν ἐμὴν ψυχήν, xvii. 22
martyrs ὥσπερ ἀντίψυχον γεγονότας
τῆς τοῦ ἔθνους ἁμαρτίας, and it
continues, 'and through the blood
of those pious men and their propitiatory death, the divine providence
saved Israel which before had been
afflicted.' And see 2 Macc. vii. 37 f.,
4 Macc. i. 11. Addressed by Jewish
lips to Jewish ears the words would
not be startling or obscure. Jesus
was going deliberately to death,
knowing that since His own Person
was unique, in that He was the Son
of the Father, and destined to be
revealed as the Son of Man, His
surrendered life would be an equivalent for many lives. (ἀντὶ πολλῶν
must not be taken with δοῦναι, as
though He said that He came to do
what others had failed in doing.)

πολλῶν (cf. xxvi. 28) is contrasted
with His single self ; they would be
primarily 'the lost sheep of the
house of Israel,' but the word in no
way defines the extent of the efficacy
of His self-surrender. Jerome's comment 'non dixit . . . "pro omnibus"
sed "pro multis," id est pro his qui
credere voluerint' is, as Swete says,
quite unwarranted. The Lord's
words do not state, but neither do
they exclude, the truth to which
Christians attained when the Resurrection had revealed the mystery of
His Person, and enabled them to
translate λύτρον ἀντὶ πολλῶν into
ἀντίλυτρον ὑπὲρ πάντων (I Tim. ii.
6), and ἱλασμὸς . . . περὶ ὅλου τοῦ
κόσμου (I Jo. ii. 2).

Further, as πολλῶν does not
define the extent, so λύτρον does

Καὶ ἐκπορευομένων αὐτῶν ἀπὸ Ἰερειχὼ ἠκολούθησεν 29

not define the method; ἀντί (cf.
xvii. 27) forms part of the metaphor,
and cannot be pressed to support
any particular theory of the Atonement. All such theories must take
account of what Christ *is*, not merely
of what He said as a Jew to Jews.
Nevertheless the universal acceptance
by Christian writers of the 'redeem-
ing' value of His death must owe
its origin to some words from Him.
See the various expressions used:
λυτροῦν, 1 Pet. i. 18, Tit. ii. 14
(see Westcott, *Hebrews*, p. 295 f.);
λύτρωσις, Heb. ix. 12; ἀπολύτρωσις,
Rom. iii. 24, Eph. i. 7, Col. i. 14,
Heb. ix. 15; ἀγοράζειν, 1 Cor. vi.
20, vii. 23, 2 Pet. ii. 1; ἐξαγοράζειν,
Gal. iii. 13.

It is just possible that Jesus had
in mind Is. liii. 12, παρεδόθη εἰς
θάνατον ἡ ψυχὴ αὐτοῦ . . . καὶ
αὐτὸς ἁμαρτίας πολλῶν ἀνήνεγκεν,
where πολλῶν illustrates the meaning here. If Jewish writers did not
interpret the prophecy as referring
to a suffering Messiah before the 3rd
cent. A.D. (Dalman, *Der leidende und
sterbende Messias*, and *Iesaja 53 das
Prophetenwort von Sühnleiden des
Heilmittlers*), that is no reason for
denying that Jesus could have
applied it to Himself. Lk. xxii. 37
is the only record of His having
actually quoted it, but see Mt. xxi.
38, xxv. 40, xxvi. 54. In viii. 17,
and perhaps xxvi. 28, the reference
is due to the evangelist.

An interesting addition occurs here
in DΦ Ϟ cur (not sin) pesh cod.mg
𝕃 *plur.* vulg (6 mss.): ὑμεῖς δὲ ζητεῖτε ἐκ μικροῦ αὐξῆσαι καὶ (+ μὴ
Ϟ cur) ἐκ μείζονος ἔλαττον εἶναι.

εἰσερχόμενοι δὲ καὶ παρακληθέντος
δειπνῆσαι, μὴ ἀνακλίνεσθε εἰς τοὺς
ἐξέχοντας τόπους μήποτε ἐνδοξό-

τερός σου ἐπέλθῃ, καὶ προσελθὼν ὁ
δειπνοκλήτωρ εἴπῃ σοι· ἔτι κάτω
χώρει, καὶ καταισχυνθήσῃ. ἐὰν δὲ
ἀναπέσῃς εἰς τὸν ἥττονα τόπον καὶ
ἐπέλθῃ σοι ἥττων, ἐρεῖ σοι ὁ δειπνο-
κλήτωρ· σύναγε ἔτι ἄνω, καὶ ἔσται
σοι τοῦτο χρήσιμον.

The latter portion is a paraphrase
of, or an independent parallel with,
Lk. xiv. 8–10. The former, without μή, carries on the thought of
v. 26, the secret of true greatness.
It may have been current at one
time by itself. With the negative,
Ϟ cur connects it with the second
portion, forming a saying similar
to xxiii. 11, Lk. xiv. 11, xviii. 14.

29–34. (Mk. x 46–52, Lk. xviii.
35–43.) DEPARTURE FROM JERICHO.
TWO BLIND MEN RESTORED TO SIGHT.
See Add. n. after ix. 34.

29. καὶ ἐκπορευομένων κτλ.]
Jericho is about 15 m. distant from
Jerusalem. For an account of the
town see Swete. The last stage in
the momentous journey now begins.
Mk. records the arrival thither as
an event in itself; καὶ ἔρχονται εἰς
Ἰερειχώ. Mt. omits this, but Lk. is
led by it to place the incident ἐν
τῷ ἐγγίζειν αὐτὸν εἰς Ἰερ., a diver-
gence of no importance, but which
does not admit of harmonization,
and Lk. relates the narrative of
Zacchaeus in the town (xix. 1–11).
'They that followed' (Mk. x. 32, see
v. 17 above) had now become a
great multitude; pilgrims for the
feast had probably joined them.
The secrecy previously observed (see
on xvii. 22) had already been abandoned, and by performing a miracle
in public the Lord shewed that He
had no wish to preserve it. Lk.,
who omits Mk. x. 32, has nothing
to explain the presence of an ὄχλος,

30 αὐτῷ ὄχλος πολύς. καὶ ἰδοὺ δύο τυφλοὶ καθήμενοι παρὰ
τὴν ὁδόν, ἀκούσαντες ὅτι Ἰησοῦς παράγει, ἔκραξαν λέγοντες
31 Κύριε, ἐλέησον ἡμᾶς, υἱὸς Δαυείδ. ὁ δὲ ὄχλος ἐπετίμησεν
αὐτοῖς ἵνα σιωπήσωσιν· οἱ δὲ μεῖζον ἔκραξαν λέγοντες
32 Κύριε, ἐλέησον ἡμᾶς, υἱὸς Δαυείδ· καὶ στὰς ὁ Ἰησοῦς
ἐφώνησεν αὐτοὺς καὶ εἶπεν Τί θέλετε ποιήσω ὑμῖν;
33 λέγουσιν αὐτῷ Κύριε, ἵνα ἀνοιγῶσιν οἱ ὀφθαλμοὶ ἡμῶν.
34 σπλαγχνισθεὶς δὲ ὁ Ἰησοῦς ἥψατο τῶν ὀμμάτων αὐτῶν,
καὶ εὐθέως ἀνέβλεψαν καὶ ἠκολούθησαν αὐτῷ.

30. καὶ ἰδού κτλ.] In Mk., Lk.
there is only one blind man, a
beggar, named ὁ υἱὸς Τιμαίου Βαρτί-
μαιος (Mk.). The knowledge of his
name may imply that he was known
in apostolic times; perhaps he became
a follower of the Lord. But Mk. is
not likely to have omitted all mention of the second, because he was
less important (Aug.). Cf. Mt.'s
mention of two demoniacs (viii. 28),
two blind men (ix. 27). Ἰησοῦς·
Mt. omits ὁ Ναζαρηνός (Mk.), ὁ
Ναζωραῖος (Lk.), as in xxviii. 5,
perhaps because it was, during the
Lord's lifetime, a popular nickname,
sometimes used in contempt; cf.
xxvi. 71, Mk. i. 24, Jo. xviii. 5–7,
xix. 19, Ac. vi. 14, xxiv. 5. Afterwards it was adopted by Christians;
see Mt. ii. 23 (note), Mk. xvi. 6,
Lk. xxiv. 19, and in Ac. ἔκραξαν:
Mk. ἤρξατο κράζειν; see on xiii. 54.
κύριε κτλ.] κύριε (not in Mk.,
Lk.) is doubtful here (but not in v.
31). Only on this occasion in Mk.,
Lk. is Jesus addressed as 'Son of
David,' a title frequent in Mt.; see
on ix. 27. The crowd apparently
took no notice of it, and it may have
been only a form of polite address.
In v. 33 only κύριε (Mk. ῥαββουνί)
is used. On the liturgical use of the
petition 'O Son of David, etc.' and
of the Kyrie eleison see Swete.
31. ὁ δὲ ὄχλος κτλ.] Mk. πολλοί,
Lk. οἱ προάγοντες. The rebuke was

in the same spirit as that in xix. 13;
the great Prophet must not be
bothered. μεῖζον (Mk., Lk. πολλῷ
μᾶλλον): this class. adverbial use
is unique in bibl. Gk.; cf. μέγα, Jer.
iv. 5, Prov. xviii. 11, 3 Macc. vi. 17.
32. καὶ στάς κτλ.] Mt., Lk.
abbreviate Mk.'s account: 'And
Jesus stood and said, Call him; and
they call the blind man, saying to
him, Be of good cheer, rise, He
calleth thee. And he casting away
his cloak leapt up and came to
Jesus.' The question τί θέλετε
κτλ. was asked although the need
was evident to all; but a blind
beggar might merely have asked for
alms; the question drew forth the
confident prayer for healing. Cf.
ix. 28. For the delib. conj. with
θέλετε cf. xiii. 28.
33. ἵνα ἀνοιγῶσιν κτλ.] See on
ix. 30. For the 2nd aor. see Blass,
§ 19. 3. Ꞩ cur (Mt., Lk.) and Tatian
(Hill, p. 167 n.) add 'that we [I]
may see Thee.'
34. σπλαγχνισθείς κτλ.] See on
ix. 36. An expression of emotion
in Mt., absent from Mk., is unusual.
ὄμμα recurs only in Mk. viii. 23,
where the Lord lays His hands on
the eyes of a blind man (a narrative
omitted by Mt.); this clause may
be a reminiscence of it. Mk., Lk.
have, 'And Jesus said to him, Go
(om. Lk.), thy faith hath saved thee.'
καὶ εὐθέως κτλ.] On ἀναβλέπειν

Καὶ ὅτε ἤγγισαν εἰς Ἱεροσόλυμα καὶ ἦλθον εἰς Βηθφαγὴ 1 XXI.
εἰς τὸ Ὄρος τῶν Ἐλαιῶν, τότε Ἰησοῦς ἀπέστειλεν δύο
μαθητὰς λέγων αὐτοῖς Πορεύεσθε εἰς τὴν κώμην τὴν 2

see xi. 5. Mt., Lk. omit Mk.'s ἐν τῇ ὁδῷ, but Lk. characteristically adds 'glorifying God, and all the people when they saw gave praise to God.'

xxi. 1–11. (Mk. xi. 1–11, Lk. xix. 29–38, Jo. xii. 12–19.) THE ENTRY INTO JERUSALEM.

1. καὶ ὅτε κτλ.] On Ἱεροσόλυμα see ii. 1. Jo. dates the arrival at Bethany 6 days before Passover, *i.e.* Saturday Nisan 8th, and the Entry on the following day. Mk. probably has εἰς Βηθφ. καὶ Βηθανίαν without ἦλθον. The site of Bethphage, no mention of which is known earlier than the Gospels, has not yet been determined, but it apparently lay on the Eastern slope, or at the foot, of Olivet, a little further from Jerusalem than Bethany. In Mt.'s time it may have been as well known as Bethany, or better (Plummer); or he simply omits the latter name as redundant (Allen). For accounts of the place see Ganneau, *PEFQ.*, 1878, 51–61, Neubauer, *Géogr. du Talm.* 147–9. According to Orig. (*in Mat.*) and Jer. (*in Mat.*) it was a village of the priests. The name appears to mean 'House [*i.e.* place] of young figs,' Talm. בית פאגי (Neubauer) or פגי (Dalman, *Gram.* 152); see Burkitt, *Ev. da Meph.* i., on Lk. xix. 4.

Bethany, the modern *el-'Azariyeh* (*Lazarium* in *Peregr. Silviae*) lay on a SE. spur of Olivet, 15 stades from Jerusalem (Jo. xi. 18); the main road to the city through Bethany crosses the southern shoulder of the range. The name is sometimes explained as 'House of unripe fruits' or 'of dates.'

τὸ Ὄρος τῶν Ἐλαιῶν] So xxiv. 3, xxvi. 30, Mk. (xi. 1, xiii. 3, xiv. 26),

Lk. xxii. 39, 'Jo.' viii. 1, Zech. xiv. 4; cf. 2 Regn. xv. 30, 2 Esd. xviii. 15. But in Ac. i. 12 the proper name Ἐλαιῶν is used; cf. Mk. xi. 1 (B) τὸ Ἐλαιῶν, K *ad montem Eleon*, Jos. *Ant.* VII. ix. 2 τὸ Ἐλαιῶνος ὄρος. The accent is doubtful in Lk. xix. 29, xxi. 37. See Deissmann, *Bible St.* 208–12, and *Expos.*, Dec. 1903, 429, where Moulton notes the frequency of the term. -ών = 'a place of,' especially in connexion with trees. The form Olivet in the synopt. account in Wicl., Tynd., Cranm., and in 2 Sam. xv. 30 (A.V.), is derived from the Vulg. *ad montem Oliveti* (Mt., Jo.), *qui vocatur O.* (Lk., Ac.). 'Ascenditur mons Oliveti id est in Eleona' (*Peregr. Silv.* 70). On the range of hills, now called *Jebel-et-Ṭur*, running N. and S. about ¾ mile from Jerusalem, see *HDB.* iii. 617, *DCG.* ii. 106.

ἀπέστειλεν κτλ.] Probably in the afternoon, since it was already evening when the Lord reached the city and 'looked round at everything' in the temple (Mk. xi. 11). Jo. xii. 12 places it 'on the morrow,' after the incident in Bethany which is parallel with Mt. xxvi. 6–13.

2. πορεύεσθε κτλ.] If the words were spoken at Bethphage, Bethany was probably within sight. The Lord was well known to one family there (xxvi. 6), and probably to others, from one of which the ass could be borrowed. His knowledge that it would be tied close to the entrance of the village may have been miraculous, or as some would say an instance of 'second sight' (see on xxvi. 18), but not necessarily; if He was acquainted with the

κατέναντι ὑμῶν, καὶ εὐθὺς εὑρήσετε ὄνον δεδεμένην καὶ
3 πῶλον μετ᾽ αὐτῆς· λύσαντες ἀγάγετέ μοι. καὶ ἐάν τις
ὑμῖν εἴπῃ τι, ἐρεῖτε ὅτι Ὁ κύριος αὐτῶν χρείαν ἔχει·
4 εὐθὺς δὲ ἀποστελεῖ αὐτούς. Τοῦτο δὲ γέγονεν ἵνα πληρωθῇ
τὸ ῥηθὲν διὰ τοῦ προφήτου λέγοντος

5 Εἴπατε τῇ θυγατρὶ Σιών
Ἰδοὺ ὁ βασιλεύς coy ἔρχεταί coι
πραΰc καὶ ἐπιβεβηκὼc ἐπὶ ὄνον
καὶ ἐπὶ πῶλον υἱὸν ὑποζυγίου.

village and with the owner of the
colt, He might know that he usually
kept his ass, or asses, at a given spot.
Mk., Lk. emphasize the sacredness
of the purpose for which it was
required by adding 'upon which no
man had yet sat' (cf. Num. xix. 2,
Deut. xxi. 3, 1 Sam. vi. 7; Swete
compares Lk. i. 34, xxiii. 53). Mt.
does so by a reference to prophecy,
which, however, leads him to speak
mistakenly of two animals (see v. 5).
πῶλος (class.) is the young of any
animal, mostly the horse, but in
bibl. Gk. always of the ass. It was
not, therefore, substituted for ὄνος to
avoid derision from Western readers
(Keim). ἀγάγετε (so Lk.) is chosen
as more suitable than Mk.'s φέρετε.

3. καὶ ἐάν κτλ.] An abbreviation
of Mk.'s καὶ . . . εἴπῃ· τί ποιεῖτε
τοῦτο; his τί being used in a different sense. ὅτι (so Lk.) is recit.
Mk. εἴπατε· ὁ κύριος κτλ. The title
used, absolutely, of Jesus, is frequent
in Lk. but does not occur elsewhere
in Mt., Mk. (cf. 'Mk.' xvi. 19). If
genuine it means 'the Master,' but
it may be due to later Christian
thought, emphasizing His divine
authority. αὐτῶν (Mk., Lk. αὐτοῦ)
is taken with ὁ κύριος in ๕ cur (Mt.),
sin (Mk.), sin.cur (Lk.), and Ephr.,
as though Jesus claimed to be the
real master of the animal (see
Burkitt, Ev. da Meph. ii. 121 ff., or
JThS., 1900, 569 ff.).

εὐθὺς δέ κτλ.] The subj. of the
verb in Mt. is τις; but in Mk. it is
Jesus : 'hath need of it, and is
sending (will send) it back here at
once.' Mt. lays stress on the obedience that the demand will receive.

4. τοῦτο δέ κτλ.] On the formula
see i. 22. By placing the quotation
at this point instead of later in connexion with the ride, Mt. seems to
suggest that the Lord Himself had
the words in mind.

5. εἴπατε κτλ.] The first four
words are from Is. lxii. 11, the remainder from Zech. ix. 9 which
begins χαῖρε σφόδρα, θύγατερ Σιών·
κήρυσσε, θύγατερ Ἰερουσαλήμ. The
words δίκαιος καὶ σώζων αὐτός are
omitted, the passage being made to
refer to the single fact of the riding
on the ass. In Zech. it is the
animal of peace, in contrast with
the chariot, the horse, and the battle
bow, and the 'meekness' of the king
is shewn in his use of it. Mt. employs
a rendering of וְעַל עַיִר בֶּן אֲתֹנוֹת independent of the LXX. καὶ πῶλον
νέον (Aq., Sym., Th. and Quinta all
have υἱός for בֶּן). The parallelism
of the Heb. 'on an ass, even (!) on a
colt' (καὶ ἐπὶ πῶλον) led to the
mistaken tradition followed by Mt.
that two animals were brought; see
v. 7. ὑποζύγιον (class. any beast of
burden) always stands for 'he-ass'
in LXX., Sym., Th., except Jud. v.
10 (A); cf. 2 Pet. ii. 16 (LXX. ἡ

Πορευθέντες δὲ οἱ μαθηταὶ καὶ ποιήσαντες καθὼς συνέταξεν 6
αὐτοῖς ὁ Ἰησοῦς ἤγαγον τὴν ὄνον καὶ τὸν πῶλον, καὶ 7
ἐπέθηκαν ἐπ᾽ αὐτῶν τὰ ἱμάτια, καὶ ἐπεκάθισεν ἐπάνω
αὐτῶν. ὁ δὲ πλεῖστος ὄχλος ἔστρωσαν ἑαυτῶν τὰ ἱμάτια 8
ἐν τῇ ὁδῷ, ἄλλοι δὲ ἔκοπτον κλάδους ἀπὸ τῶν δένδρων καὶ

7 επ᾽ αυτων] επ᾽ αυτον D 𝔏 a b e f ff¹·² g²h q ; 'on the colt' 𝕾 pesh.pal ; *om*
𝕾 cur | επανω αυτων] επ᾽ αυτου D 𝔏 b c e f ff¹·² h q 𝕾 pesh.pal ; desuper [*om pron*]
𝔏 g¹·² l vg Opt

ὄνος). It is used for an ass in
papyri (Deissm. *Bible St.* 160 f.).
In Jo. xii. 15 the quotation is in
a still shorter form : 'Fear not (cf.
Is. xliv. 2), daughter of Sion, behold
thy King cometh, sitting upon the
foal of an ass.'

6. *πορευθέντες κτλ.*] Mt. summarizes Mk.'s detailed account of the
finding of the colt tied by the door
outside ἐπὶ τοῦ ἀμφόδου, 'in the
street' (see Swete, and Dalm. *Words*,
68). Justin (*Apol.* i. 32) speaks of
it as πρὸς ἄμπελον δεδεμένος, and
refers to Gen. xlix. 11. Did he read
ἐπὶ τὸν ἄμπελον in Mk. ? ἤγαγον
(so Lk.): Mk. φέρουσιν, as in *v.* 2.

7. *καὶ ἐπέθηκαν κτλ.*] Mk. 'they
throw their cloaks upon it'; Lk.
'having cast their cloaks upon the
colt.' But in Mt. 'they placed their
cloaks upon *them*' (the two animals!).
'Their cloaks' are, as in Mk., Lk.,
the disciples' cloaks, not the saddle-
cloths of the animals, for which the
word is quite unsuitable. B. Weiss
is reduced to the supposition that
they prepared both animals, being
uncertain which Jesus would choose.
But if the incongruity is to be avoided,
it is more likely that ἐπ᾽ αὐτῶν is a
primitive corruption of ἐπ᾽ αὐτόν or
ἐπ᾽ αὐτὸν αὐτῶν [or ἑαυτῶν, cf. *v.* 8].
In any case ἐπάνω αὐτῶν in the next
clause can mean 'upon the cloaks'
(Orig., *al.*), though it might grammatically mean 'upon the animals'
(cf. Jud. i. 14 (A) ἐπάνω τοῦ ὑποζυγίου).

8. *ὁ δὲ πλεῖστος κτλ.*] Either
with a comparative force, contrasted
with ἄλλοι δέ, or elative, corresponding with Mk.'s πολλοὶ . . . ἄλλοι δέ.
See on xi. 20. Lk. does not mention
the ὄχλος ; the disciples themselves
spread their garments on the road,
and ἅπαν τὸ πλῆθος τῶν μαθητῶν
praised God. But the crowd does
not 'suddenly appear, as though
sprung out of the ground' (J. Weiss);
see on xx. 17, 29. With the act
of homage cf. 4 Regn. ix. 13 ; and
see E. Robinson, *Bibl. Res.* i. 473,
ii. 162. For ἑαυτῶν = αὐτῶν cf.
viii. 22.

ἄλλοι δέ κτλ.] Mk. ἄ. δ. στιβάδας,
κόψαντες ἐκ τῶν ἀγρῶν. Lk. omits
the sentence. στιβάς is a 'litter'
of leaves, grass, straw, or the like
(see Swete) ; it was taken from the
cultivated spots bordering on the
road, and would include 'branches
from the trees,' and among them
doubtless the date-palms (τὰ βαΐα
τῶν φοινίκων Jo.). Cf. the triumphal
entry of Judas Macc. (1 Macc. xiii.
51). Jo. alone relates the *carrying*
of branches by the crowd, as was
done at the F. of Tabernacles. Mt.
uses his tenses with care : part of
the crowd spread their cloaks once
(ἔστρωσαν) when the ride began,
and when the colt had passed over
them they would pick them up
and follow, and part continued to
pluck (ἔκοπτον) branches and to
spread them (ἐστρώννυον) as they
moved in front.

9 ἐστρώννυον ἐν τῇ ὁδῷ. οἱ δὲ ὄχλοι οἱ προάγοντες αὐτὸν
καὶ οἱ ἀκολουθοῦντες ἔκραζον λέγοντες

Ὡσαννὰ τῷ υἱῷ Δαυείδ·
Εὐλογημένος ὁ ἐρχόμενος ἐν ὀνόματι Κυρίου·
Ὡσαννὰ ἐν τοῖς ὑψίστοις.

10 καὶ εἰσελθόντος αὐτοῦ εἰς Ἱεροσόλυμα ἐσείσθη πᾶσα ἡ

9. οἱ δὲ ὄχλοι κτλ.] Mk.'s intrans.
προάγοντες is made trans., as always
in Mt. (see xiv. 22). Jo. speaks only
of a crowd that came out from the
city to meet Jesus.

ὡσαννά κτλ.] Lk. says that the
shouts began 'when He was now
approaching the descent of the Mt.
of Olives,' in which case the holy
city had just come into view. See
HDB. iii. 619. 'Hosanna' is from
Ps. cxviii. 25, the last of the Hallel
psalms which would soon be sung at
the Passover. It is the Heb. הוֹשַׁע
נָא (for הוֹשִׁיעַ) 'save we pray Thee,'
not the Aram. אוֹשַׁענא 'save us.' The
Heb. form was used liturgically at
the F. of Tabernacles (Sukk. iv. 14)
and later as the name given to the
7th day of the festival (Vay. R. 37),
and even to the branches used at it
(Sukk. 30 b); see Dalman, Gr. 198,
Words 220-3. In the psalm it is
a prayer to God for help (LXX. ὦ
Κύριε, σῶσον δή), but in the time
of the evangelists it had become
possible to employ it as a mere
shout of praise, so that Mt. adds
'to the Son of David,' and in the
last clause Mt., Mk. have 'H. in the
Highest,' which Lk. interprets as
'Peace in Heaven and glory in the
Highest.' Weymouth's paraphrase,
'God save the Son of David,' does
violence to the dative; הוֹשִׁיעַ is
followed by לְ in Ps. lxxi. [lxxii.] 4,
cxiv. [cxvi.] 6, but the construction
is impossible in Gk. In Did. x., in
the post-Communion thanksgiving
the refrain appears as ὡσ. τῷ θεῷ

Δαυείδ. On 'Son of David' in Mt.
see xii. 23. In Lk. also Jesus is
greeted as the Messianic king,
βασιλεύς being inserted in the next
clause. It is difficult to determine
whether Mt., Lk. are independent of
Mk., or whether their insertions are
derived from his clause 'Blessed be the
coming kingdom of our father David.'

εὐλογημένος κτλ.] From Ps.
cxvii. [cxviii.] 26 LXX. The words
were addressed to pilgrims as they
approached the temple: 'Blessed in
the name of Yahweh is he that
cometh,' and the crowd must probably have used them in that sense
(cf. the v.l. in Lk. εὐλ. ὁ βασ. ἐν
ὀνόμ. Κυρ.). 'Hosanna in the
Highest' (Gosp. Naz. ap. Jer. 'osanna
barrama' = ברמא in excelsis) does not
mean 'Let the Messiah be praised
in Heaven'; as in 'praise Him in
the Highest' (Ps. cxlviii. 1), the
angels are invoked to shout Hosanna
to God, which is clearly the meaning
of Lk.'s 'glory in the Highest' (cf.
Lk. ii. 14, and Apoc. vii. 10, 'Salvation to our God'). But the expression is not derived from Ps. cxviii.;
if it was added by the evangelists,
the shouts of the people were confined to the words of the Psalm, and
they used הוֹשַׁע נָא in its true sense.

Ṣ cur and Diatⁿʳ here add different
combinations of Jo. xii. 13 and Lk. xix.
37; see Burkitt, Ev. da Meph. ad loc.

10-11. καὶ εἰσελθόντος κτλ.]
Vv. 10, 11 are peculiar to Mt., and
are possibly a later addition. The
upheaval of the 'whole city' is a

πόλις λέγουσα Τίς ἐστιν οὗτος; οἱ δὲ ὄχλοι ἔλεγον Οὗτός 11
ἐστιν ὁ προφήτης Ἰησοῦς ὁ ἀπὸ Ναζαρὲθ τῆς Γαλιλαίας.

hyperbolical statement as in ii. 3 (probably a scribal addition). The Galilean pilgrims give the information to the Jews in the city. ὁ προφήτης is 'the well-known prophet.' He had been treated as such in the North (xiii. 57), and this estimation of Him delayed His arrest (xxi. 46). On Ναζαρέθ see ii. 23. For 'N. of Galilee' cf. Mk. i. 9; the village was so little known that it was necessary to define its locality.

Additional Note on the Entry into Jerusalem.

The synoptists clearly convey the impression that Jesus deliberately rode into the city as the Messiah, and that He was acclaimed as such by the crowds that accompanied Him. But His Messiahship, whatever mistaken guesses may have been made by the people early in His ministry, had been a secret from every one until S. Peter received the revelation at Caesarea Philippi, and the disciples were then forbidden to tell anyone what they had learnt, nor is there any record that the prohibition was afterwards withdrawn. Bartimaeus, indeed, addressed Him as 'Son of David,' and he may have thought of the political Messiah of popular expectation, but no notice of it was taken by the crowd. When Jesus mounted the ass, the action was very ordinary, and could not by itself suggest that He was the Messiah, though He knew the truth, and may possibly have had in mind the words from Zech. which Mt. quotes. And yet the very fact of a wonder-working prophet approaching the capital with an enthusiastic following could not but suggest to some that He was aiming at becoming a popular hero who might use His power to incite the thousands of Passover pilgrims to rebellion. The thoughts of those who shouted Hosanna are reflected in Mk. xi. 10, 'Blessed is the coming kingdom of our father David.' J. Weiss and others lay unnecessary stress on the fact that the triumphal entry was not brought up against Jesus at His trial. (May it not have been referred to by some of the witnesses who could not agree?) The crowd need not be thought of as a vast mass of people, large enough to create at once an upheaval in the city. When the Lord, on arrival, took no such steps as were expected of Him, the enthusiasm of the rustics waned at once. Nevertheless the Messianic idea filtered through the city, and the authorities soon heard rumours. This is suggested by the question about the capitation tax, and by the Lord's problem about the Son of David. And the Messianic claim was finally the ground, or the partial ground (see on xxvi. 63), for His delivery to Pilate for sentence. Thus the shouts at the Entry, though they probably did not claim Him explicitly as the Messiah, were the expression of a momentary outburst of mistaken enthusiasm. The Lord, who was going to Jerusalem on purpose to die, did not prevent it, since there was no need to do so. It was genuine as far as it went, and would afterwards serve to teach the crowd how different were His claims from their idea of them, and also to bring Him into prominence in the city, and so to lead to His death.

12   Καὶ εἰσῆλθεν Ἰησοῦς εἰς τὸ ἱερόν, καὶ ἐξέβαλεν πάντας
τοὺς πωλοῦντας καὶ ἀγοράζοντας ἐν τῷ ἱερῷ καὶ τὰς
τραπέζας τῶν κολλυβιστῶν κατέστρεψεν καὶ τὰς καθέδρας

12 ιερον אBL 𝔏 b me sah arm aeth ; add του θεου uncc.rel 𝔏 vet (exc b). vg
𝔖 cur.pesh [sin vac]

Dalman (Words, 222), J. Weiss (Die Schriften d. NT. 177), and others,
think that all the Messianic colouring of the narrative is a later addition,
and that Jesus was greeted simply as a prophet.   Wellhausen, on the other
hand, says 'It seems very likely that the people were inclined to regard
Him as the Messiah, and to interpret His journey to Jerusalem Messianically.
The step from Prophet to Messiah was easily taken; "false prophet"
(ψευδοπροφήτης) and "false Messiah" (ψευδόχριστος) in Josephus and the
Gospels mean much the same thing.'   Schweitzer (Quest. 391–5) holds
that the Entry was to Jesus Himself Messianic, but the crowd greeted Him
as Elijah (see Add. n. 2, p. 34 f.), and that His Messianic secret was not
divulged till Judas betrayed it to the authorities (see on xxvi. 63).

12, 13.   (Mk. xi. 15–18, Jo. ii. 14–
17.)   CLEANSING OF THE TEMPLE.

12. καὶ εἰσῆλθεν κτλ.]   On the
order of events see Add. n. below.
There is some authority for the reading τὸ ἱερ. τοῦ θεοῦ (see Appar.), which
is otherwise found only in 1 Esd. v. 54.
But it may be an early gloss.   It
looks forward to ὁ οἶκός μου (v. 13),
and heightens the horror of the
abuses practised there.   ἐξέβαλεν :
Mk., Lk. ἤρξατο ἐκβάλλειν ; see on
xiii. 54.   Jo. says 'having made a
whip of cords.'   τοὺς πωλοῦντας (so
Mk., Lk.) describes a class (cf. viii.
33), indicating an acquaintance with
the custom on the part of the framer
of the narrative.   See Lightfoot,
Hor. Heb., ad loc., Edersheim, L. and
T. i. 369 ff., Abrahams, Note 21.
Lk. omits all the remaining details.
Jo. speaks of 'oxen and sheep and
doves,' but other requisites such as
wine, oil, and salt, would also be
sold.   τὸ ἱερόν here is the Court of
the Gentiles, called in the Talm.
'the Mountain of the House,' where
traffic was authorized at all times in
what was afterwards known as 'the

shops of the sons of Hanan (Annas).'
The traffic was not confined to the
Passover week.

καὶ τὰς τραπέζας κτλ.]   The Jews
of the Dispersion were obliged to
exchange their Greek and Roman
coins for Jewish money, by which
the κολλυβισταί made great gain.
κόλλυβος, 'a small coin' (Ar. Pax,
1200), came to mean the 'rate, or
premium, of exchange' (Cic. Verr.
ii. 3. 78, Att. xii. 6. 1).   It is said
to be a Phoenician word, cognate
with חלק, 'to exchange.'   In Rabb.
times anyone who even wanted small
change for a shekel had to pay an
additional sum, or κόλλυβος, which
passed into late Heb. as קולבון
(Shek. i.).   τὰς περιστεράς are 'the
doves required for sacrifice,' which
would include the 'turtle-doves and
young pigeons' for the purification
of poor women (Lev. xii. 8 ; cf. Lk.
ii. 22 f.), and poor lepers (Lev. xiv.
22), and certain other purifications
(Lev. xv. 14, 29).

Mk. adds 'and did not allow that
anyone should carry a vessel through
the temple' (see Swete, and Abrahams,

τῶν πωλούντων τὰς περιστεράς, καὶ λέγει αὐτοῖς Γέγραπται 13
Ὁ οἶκός μογ οἶκος προσεγχῆς κληθήσεται, ὑμεῖς δὲ αὐτὸν ποιεῖτε

l.c.). Mt.'s omission of this is surprising; possibly it was a later
addition in Mk.

The narrative does not suggest that
the buyers and sellers submitted to
expulsion because Jesus was supported
by a crowd of followers. It was
the power of character that did the
deed. 'Mihi inter omnia signa quae
fecit hoc videtur mirabilius esse' (Jer.).
Orig. thought that unless a miracle
was to be postulated, the incident
must be interpreted symbolically.

13. *καὶ λέγει κτλ.*] The quotation is from Is. lvi. 7 (LXX.). Lk.
has ἔσται for κληθήσεται (see on
Mt. v. 9). In Mt., Lk. the Lord
draws a contrast between prayer and
robbery. Mk. adds the remaining
words from Is., πᾶσιν τοῖς ἔθνεσιν :
Gentiles could not pray in the court
to which alone they were admitted,
because of the noise of the traffic.
But the Lord does not speak of
noise and distraction, but wickedness. The words are probably a
scribal addition in Mk. to complete
the quotation. Wellhausen suggests
that Jesus took πᾶσιν τ. ἔθν. with

κληθήσεται, 'shall be called *by* all
nations.' J. Weiss, even less probably, explains that 'when the later
evangelists wrote, this prophecy was
given up as impossible of fulfilment ;
the Temple has been destroyed, and
the nations have found another
temple in the Church.'

ὑμεῖς δὲ κτλ.] An allusion to
Jer. vii. 11 (LXX.), where the prophet
refers to the social and religious
corruption of the Jews who trusted
to the inviolateness of the temple.
The Lord rebukes the exorbitant
prices charged by the sellers. These
are illustrated by the story of Rabban
Simon ben Gamaliel, who caused
doves to be sold for silver coins
instead of for gold (Lightfoot, *Hor.
Heb.*). Worshippers could, of course,
bring their animals or birds with
them, but if they lived at a distance
it was necessary to buy them on the
spot, and the sellers could ask any price
they chose. Jo. has 'take these things
hence, make not My Father's house
a house of merchandise,' possibly an
allusion to Zech. xiv. 21, with a play
on the word 'Canaanite,' a 'trafficker.'

Additional Note on the Cleansing of the Temple.

1. *The order of events.* In Mk., the Lord having entered the temple
and looked round at everything (*i.e.* on Sunday), departed to Bethany for
the night, since it was already late (xi. 11). The next morning (Monday)
He cursed the fig-tree on the way to the city (22–14), and on His arrival
cleansed the temple (15–19). He again departed for the night, and next
morning (Tuesday) on his way to the city found the fig-tree withered
(20 f.), and on His arrival was questioned as to His authority (27–33). As
compared with this, Mt. loses record of Monday night, and brings together
the cursing and the withering of the tree. The former was perhaps for the
sake of brevity, and the latter in order to heighten the marvel. But the
disarrangement was possibly the work of a later hand in Mk. (see on *v.* 23) ;
J. Weiss suggests that it was due to Jo. xii. 1. It is quite improbable that

14 cπΗλΔιοΝ λΗcτῶΝ. Καὶ προσῆλθον αὐτῷ τυφλοὶ καὶ χωλοὶ

Mt. passed accidentally from Mk. v. 11 ('and He entered into Jerusalem into the temple') to v. 15 ('and they come into Jerusalem, and when He had entered into the temple'), and then, finding that he had omitted the cursing of the fig-tree, inserted it immediately before the account of its withering.

Lk. relates only the cleansing of the temple (xix. 45–48), with no note of time to shew that it did not occur on the day of the entry. He also records, before the arrival at the city, (1) the request of some Pharisees in the shouting crowd that Jesus would rebuke His disciples, and His reply (39, 40), which perhaps has some connexion with Mt. xxi. 14–17 (see note), (2) His lament over the city (41–44).

2. *The position of the incident.* Jo. places it at the beginning of the Ministry (ii. 13–17), the only instance of so fundamental a departure from the synoptic order. That the event happened twice is hardly conceivable. The modern tendency to condemn the fourth Gospel when it differs from the synoptists has exceptions. J. Weiss (*e.g.*) argues for the Johannine position of the narrative: (1) that after all His preaching about the inwardness of worship, the Lord's zeal for the outward, ceremonial purity of the temple is surprising; (2) that His action would be possible only at a time when the attention of the authorities had not yet been directed against Him. But (1) apart from the subjectiveness of the argument, few would admit that He had a deeper conception of the inwardness of worship at the end of His ministry than at the beginning. (2) The authorities would be as ready to take cognisance of the act at the beginning as at the end. That the Lord was unknown to them when He appeared in the temple would not increase His chances of success; on the contrary, His popularity with the people at the end of the ministry, though it was not the reason for the submission of the buyers and sellers, would be a protection, as related in Mk. xi. 18 = Lk. xix. 47 f.

Weiss is on safer ground when he says that the only discernible reason for the Johannine position is that the fourth evangelist possessed a tradition to that effect. It has been thought that he displaced it in order to illustrate the Lord's Messianic authority at the outset. But, as Brooke says (*Camb. Bibl. Essays* 308), 'there is nothing definitely Messianic about the act. "The zeal of my Father's house hath consumed me" will adequately explain the action.' Moreover Mk. since he relates only one visit to Jerusalem would be compelled to place it in that visit; and he implies (xi. 18) that it was the immediate cause of the plans for the Lord's arrest; but Lk. (xix. 47) does not follow him, and Mt. omits the verse. Suggestions of a subjective character are made by J. A. Robinson in favour of the Johannine position (*Hist. Character of St. John's Gosp.* 25). There is not enough evidence to determine the question, but there is enough to forbid an off-hand decision in favour of the synoptists.

14–16. (Mt. only.) CHILDREN IN THE TEMPLE. REBUKE TO THE CHIEF PRIESTS AND PHARISEES.

14. καὶ προσῆλθον κτλ.] The Lord stayed in the temple for some time, teaching (Mk., Lk.), healing (Mt.). For general statements of healing see on iv. 23; and for Mt.'s records of healing instead of preaching cf. xiv. 14, xix. 2.

ἐν τῷ ἱερῷ, καὶ ἐθεράπευσεν αὐτούς. Ἰδόντες δὲ οἱ ἀρχιερεῖς 15
καὶ οἱ γραμματεῖς τὰ θαυμάσια ἃ ἐποίησεν καὶ τοὺς παῖδας
τοὺς κράζοντας ἐν τῷ ἱερῷ καὶ λέγοντας Ὡσαννὰ τῷ υἱῷ
Δαυείδ ἠγανάκτησαν καὶ εἶπαν αὐτῷ Ἀκούεις τί οὗτοι 16
λέγουσιν; ὁ δὲ Ἰησοῦς λέγει αὐτοῖς Ναί· οὐδέποτε
ἀνέγνωτε ὅτι Ἐκ ϲτόματοϲ νηπίων καὶ θηλαζόντων κατηρτίϲω
αἶνον; Καὶ καταλιπὼν αὐτοὺς ἐξῆλθεν ἔξω τῆς 17
πόλεως εἰς Βηθανίαν, καὶ ηὐλίσθη ἐκεῖ.

15. ἰδόντες κτλ.] The section
appears to be composite. Since the
question asked of Jesus in v. 16
refers solely to the shouts of the
children, the words τὰ θαυμάσια ἃ
ἐποίησεν καί seem to be inserted
only to link v. 14 with what follows.
θαυμάσιος, though frequent in the
LXX., is not found elsewhere in the
N.T., the thought of thaumaturgy
in connexion with Jesus being carefully avoided. It suggests the hand
of an editor.

καὶ τοὺς παῖδας κτλ.] The
quotation in v. 16 shews that παῖδες
is used in the sense of παιδία, not
'youths' but 'children.' It is extremely improbable that children
shouted in the temple courts; if they
had done so, it would be instantly
stopped by the temple police. A
band of them collected there is itself
an improbability. The shouts are
an echo of the shouts on the Mt. of
Olives. Lk. xix. 39 f. contains a
more probable account, that some
Pharisees (שׂ sin 'people') on the
road with the crowd (perhaps over-
taken on their way to the city) said
to Jesus 'Teacher, rebuke Thy
disciples'; and He replied 'I say
unto you that if these are silent, the
stones will shout.' Does an Aram.
original lie behind both narratives,
'stones' (Lk.) and 'children' (Mt.)
representing אבניא and בניא ? (cf. iii.
9). If so, the tradition which
reached Mt., and helped to give rise

to his narrative, may have contained
the words 'the *children* will shout.'
But he seems also to have been influenced by Mk. xi. 18, 'and the
high priests and Scribes heard, and
sought how they might destroy
Him.' This combination of enemies
occurs for the first time. Except in
ii. 4, and the predictions in xvi. 21,
xx. 18, Mt. has not mentioned the
high priests till this point. But
they now take the lead, the temple
being under their official supervision,
and are mentioned by Mt. 17 times
as a class in the remainder of the
Gospel.

16. οὐδέποτε κτλ.] See on xii. 3.
The quotation is from Ps. viii. 3
(LXX.), αἶνον being suitable to the
occasion, but not the Heb. עֹז
('strength'). κατηρτίσω (see on iv.
21), 'Thou hast provided Thyself
with'; Vulg. less well *perfecisti*;
Engl. Vv. 'perfected.' The Psalm
was one which Christians early learnt
to interpret Messianically; cf. 1 Cor.
xv. 27, Heb. ii. 6–9.

17–22. (Mk. xi. 11 b–14, 20–26.)
A FIG-TREE CURSED AND WITHERED.
SUBSEQUENT SAYINGS.

17. καὶ καταλιπών κτλ.] The
previous section is linked with the
Marcan narrative, which is now continued. The class. αὐλίζεσθαι (cf.
Lk. xxi. 37) is frequent in the LXX.
for לִין, לוּן, not necessarily of passing
the night in the open air. The

18 Πρωὶ δὲ ἐπαναγαγὼν εἰς τὴν πόλιν ἐπείνασεν. καὶ
19 ἰδὼν συκῆν μίαν ἐπὶ τῆς ὁδοῦ ἦλθεν ἐπ᾿ αὐτήν, καὶ
οὐδὲν εὗρεν ἐν αὐτῇ εἰ μὴ φύλλα μόνον, καὶ λέγει αὐτῇ
Οὐ μηκέτι ἐκ σοῦ καρπὸς γένηται εἰς τὸν αἰῶνα· καὶ

Lord might have lodged with the owner of the borrowed colt, and the disciples elsewhere in the village. But Mk. (xi. 19) merely says that 'they [or He] went outside the city,' with no mention of Bethany. Lk. has three characteristic generalizations (xix. 47 f., xxi. 37 f., xxii. 39), the two latter of which relate that the Lord spent the night habitually on the Mt. of Olives, 'according to (His) custom,' *sc.* on previous occasions when He visited Jerusalem (xxii. 39). This would explain not only His hunger in the morning, but also how it was that Judas knew where He was to be found when He spent the night of the betrayal in Gethsemane on the western slope (cf. Jo. xviii. 2). Lk.'s summary statements produce the appearance, contrary to Mt., Mk., of a longer period than four days spent at Jerusalem before the Passover (and cf. Lk. xx. 1, 'in one of those days').

18. πρωὶ δέ κτλ.] For ἐπανάγειν 'to return' cf. Sir. xvii. 26, xxvi. 28, 2 Macc. ix. 21. In Lk. v. 3 f., 2 Macc. xii. 4 (*v.l.*) it means 'to move out to sea' in a boat.

19. καὶ ἰδών κτλ.] For μία = τις cf. xxvi. 69; see on viii. 19. On οὐδὲν . . . εἰ μή see xii. 24. Both physically by His hunger, and mentally by His disappointed expectation (Mk. 'came if perchance He might find anything on it'), the Lord's real Humanity is indicated. The fruit-buds of the fig begin to appear before the leaves, but the latter are fully developed before the fruit. The tree bears what might be called two crops: the real fruit is not ripe till August

or September in Palestine, but fruit of a sort ripens in small quantities much earlier, and even if not fully matured in April, unless in an early season, would be quite eatable. The natives to-day prefer it, in many cases, to the real fruit. It was this early fruit that the sight of leaves led Jesus to expect; but He found none. Cf. Lk. xiii. 7. Mk.'s addition 'for it was not fig-time' is difficult. If the leaves were out, it *was* the time for the early crop, so that καιρὸς συκῶν can refer only to the autumn. Mt. may have omitted the clause because he saw its difficulty, and shrank from the appearance of unreasonableness on the part of Jesus; but it may have been an unskilful gloss by a later hand.

οὐ μηκέτι κτλ.] Mk. μηκέτι εἰς τὸν αἰῶνα ἐκ σοῦ μηδεὶς καρπὸν φάγοι. Mt. alters the wish to a prediction, which is virtually a prohibition. οὐ μηκέτι occurs elsewhere in the Gk. bible only in Tob. vi. 8.

καὶ ἐξηράνθη κτλ.] Mk. καὶ ἤκουον οἱ μαθηταὶ αὐτοῦ. Mk. relates that on the next morning they saw the tree in a withered state, and that Peter remembered the curse. If Mt. has altered Mk.'s order (see Add. n. 1 after *v.* 13) it was in order to heighten the marvel. παραχρῆμα is elsewhere used only by Lk. (Ev.[10], Ac.[7]), always in connexion with a miraculous or striking event.

The Lord's action must have had for its purpose to teach some truth to the disciples. If the narrative is historical, the tree fulfilled a more important function by dying than

ἐξηράνθη παραχρῆμα ἡ συκῆ. καὶ ἰδόντες οἱ μαθηταὶ 20
ἐθαύμασαν λέγοντες Πῶς παραχρῆμα ἐξηράνθη ἡ συκῆ ;
ἀποκριθεὶς δὲ ὁ Ἰησοῦς εἶπεν αὐτοῖς Ἀμὴν λέγω ὑμῖν, 21
ἐὰν ἔχητε πίστιν καὶ μὴ διακριθῆτε, οὐ μόνον τὸ τῆς
συκῆς ποιήσετε, ἀλλὰ κἂν τῷ ὄρει τούτῳ εἴπητε Ἄρθητι
καὶ βλήθητι εἰς τὴν θάλασσαν, γενήσεται· καὶ πάντα 22
ὅσα ἂν αἰτήσητε ἐν τῇ προσευχῇ πιστεύοντες λήμψεσθε.

by living, and it is false sentiment to think of it as badly treated. It is playing with the narrative to rationalize it, and it is something worse to suggest that Jesus was venting upon the tree His disappointment at finding no fruit. But if it was an acted lesson, what was the lesson ? In the two sayings which follow (see below), it is simply the power of faith. But it is difficult to avoid the doubt whether the Lord would have employed an act of destruction to teach this; only as a warning of punishment could it have its full force. And in any case the sayings seem to be collected from other contexts. If they were originally unconnected with the incident, the Lord may have given an explanation of it which is now lost. But the possibility cannot be denied that the acted parable is really the parable in Lk. xiii. 6–9, or some other parable or metaphorical saying about a withered tree, which was transformed into an act in the course of tradition. Whether an act or a parable, it is probably, as most commentators are agreed, a symbolic denunciation of Jerusalem or the Jewish nation. Cf. Lk. xxiii. 31. Wellhausen (on Mk. xiii. 28 f.) gives a different, but improbable, explanation, restated by Schwartz in ZNW., 1904, 80–4.

20. καὶ ἰδόντες κτλ.] Mk. καὶ ἀναμνησθεὶς ὁ Πέτρος λέγει αὐτῷ. Peter is more prominent in Mt. than

in Mk. (see on x. 2), but cf. xxiv. 3 with Mk. xiii. 3, and xxviii. 7 with Mk. xvi. 7. The question 'How is it that the fig-tree has suddenly withered ?' so Vulg. (not an exclamation, as in A.V. and most earlier Engl. versions), takes the place of Mk.'s exclamation, 'Rabbi, behold the fig-tree which Thou didst curse is withered !'

21. ἀμήν κτλ.] See on v. 18. ἐάν κτλ. : Mk. ἔχετε πίστιν θεοῦ. For the force of πίστις see xvii. 20. κ. μὴ διακριθῆτε abbreviates Mk.'s 'and doubts not in his heart, but believes that what he speaketh cometh to pass,' and is placed earlier in the saying. Jam. i. 6 seems to have been influenced by the words.

οὐ μόνον κτλ.] The sentence (to ἀλλά) is added by Mt. It implies that to remove a mountain is a greater act than to wither a tree by a word (cf. Jo. xiv. 12). But the contrast would be clearer between removing a mountain and removing a tree ; possibly, therefore, τὸ τῆς συκῆς ('the action concerning the fig-tree,' cf. τὰ τῶν δαιμονιζομένων viii. 33) is related to the form of the saying in Lk. xvii. 6, which speaks of the removing of a sycamine. Mt. has already shewn in xvii. 20 acquaintance with Lk.'s source.

22. καὶ πάντα κτλ.] The substance of Mk. is condensed. The power of prayer is taught in vii. 7–11, xviii. 19, and the power of faith frequently; here they are combined. But the

23 Καὶ ἐλθόντος αὐτοῦ εἰς τὸ ἱερὸν προσῆλθαν αὐτῷ
διδάσκοντι οἱ ἀρχιερεῖς καὶ οἱ πρεσβύτεροι τοῦ λαοῦ
λέγοντες Ἐν ποίᾳ ἐξουσίᾳ ταῦτα ποιεῖς ; καὶ τίς σοι ἔδωκεν
24 τὴν ἐξουσίαν ταύτην ; ἀποκριθεὶς δὲ ὁ Ἰησοῦς εἶπεν
αὐτοῖς Ἐρωτήσω ὑμᾶς κἀγὼ λόγον ἕνα, ὃν ἐὰν εἴπητέ μοι
25 κἀγὼ ὑμῖν ἐρῶ ἐν ποίᾳ ἐξουσίᾳ ταῦτα ποιῶ· τὸ βάπτισμα

saying must have been spoken in another context. Mk. connects it with the preceding by διὰ τοῦτο ; but the command to the mountain is not a prayer, nor the sentence pronounced on the fig-tree even in Mk.'s μηκέτι . . . φάγοι, much less in Mt.

Mk., or possibly a scribe, adds (v. 25) a third saying, given in a different form in Mt. vi. 14, on the necessity of forgiveness when praying. It is noteworthy for the expression 'your Father which is in Heaven,' otherwise confined to Mt. Yet another saying is added in the T.R. in Mk. (v. 26), from Mt. vi. 15.

23–27. (Mk. xi. 27–33, Lk. xx. 1–8.) THE AUTHORITY OF JESUS CHALLENGED.

23. προσῆλθαν κτλ.] διδάσκοντι interprets Mk.'s περιπατοῦντος αὐτοῦ (cf. Jo. x. 23), as though comparing Jesus with Gk. peripatetic teachers. With those who approached Him Mk., Lk. include 'the Scribes,' completing the classes which composed the Sanhedrin (see on ii. 4).

ἐν ποίᾳ ἐξουσίᾳ κτλ.] For ποῖος =τίς see xix. 18. ταῦτα ποιεῖς speaks not of teaching but of actions, and seems to refer to the cleansing of the temple, of which the authorities had full right to demand an explanation. But ταῦτα is strange after a night's interval, and the incident may originally have occurred on the same day as the cleansing. In any case they are closely connected, and possibly belong together

to the beginning of the ministry (see Add. n. 2 after v. 31); in Jo. ii. 18 the Jews ask, with a different question, for the Lord's credentials. In that case the peremptory request for information followed not long after the similar request made to the Baptist (Jo. i. 19, 21 f.), and the counter question asked by Jesus about him, and the fear evinced by the questioners owing to his fame as a prophet, are entirely in place. It is noteworthy that in Lk. the Scribes ask their question when Jesus was teaching in the temple καὶ εὐαγ-γελιζομένου : the preaching of good tidings points to the beginning rather than to the end of the ministry.

καὶ τίς κτλ.] The second question goes behind the first : Whatever claim to authority you make, who gave you the right to make it ? Is it God or man ? Mt., Lk. omit Mk.'s redundant addition ἵνα ταῦτα ποίῃς.

24. ἀποκριθείς κτλ.] Lk. omits ἕνα as though it were equivalent to τινα (see viii. 19), but its strict meaning is quite suitable : 'you have asked two questions, but I will ask only one.' λόγον is a 'thing,' a 'point'; cf. Jer. xlv. [xxxviii.] 14 ἐρωτήσω σε λόγον.

25. τὸ βάπτισμα κτλ.] The vivid πόθεν ἦν is inserted by Mt. only. John's baptism was the outward expression of his life work, the call to repentance, so that to 'believe him' (vv. 25, 32) and to 'be baptized by him' (Lk. vii. 29 f.) were one and the same. ἐξ οὐρανοῦ in contrast with

τὸ Ἰωάνου πόθεν ἦν ; ἐξ οὐρανοῦ ἢ ἐξ ἀνθρώπων ; οἱ
δὲ διελογίζοντο ἐν ἑαυτοῖς λέγοντες Ἐὰν εἴπωμεν Ἐξ
οὐρανοῦ, ἐρεῖ ἡμῖν Διὰ τί οὖν οὐκ ἐπιστεύσατε αὐτῷ ;
ἐὰν δὲ εἴπωμεν Ἐξ ἀνθρώπων, φοβούμεθα τὸν ὄχλον, 26
πάντες γὰρ ὡς προφήτην ἔχουσιν τὸν Ἰωάνην· καὶ 27

25 εν] BLM^{mg}Z al.pauc ; παρ' ℵCDE etc   26 εχουσιν] ειχον 1 al.pauc
𝕃 a c f ff¹ g² h q 𝕊 sin.cur.pesh.pal^{clim}

ἐξ ἀνθρώπων is a Jewish periphrasis
for 'from God' (cf. xvi. 19 b). The
same alternative was discussed with
reference to the apostles (Ac. v. 38 f.).
The question corresponded with the
second put by the Lord's opponents,
since an answer to that would include an answer to the first. He
did not set them a mere trap.
His work and John's were, up to a
certain point, very similar, and both
were recognized as prophets such as
had not appeared since the close of
the canon. Any decision that the
authorities had come to about John
answered of itself the question about
Jesus. Thus the reply was, on the surface, quite unambiguous. But more
lay behind it. The authority of the
two 'prophets' was that of the
destined Messiah and of His forerunner 'Elijah' respectively. The
Twelve, who had understood the
statement about the Baptist in xvii.
11, could realize this, but if the
authorities could not make up their
minds about John, they could still less
understand the truth about Jesus.

οἱ δέ κτλ.] ἐν (v.l. παρ') ἑαυτοῖς
and πρὸς ἑαυτούς (Mk., Lk.) have
the same meaning ; cf. xvi. 7 with
Mk., and xxi. 38 with Mk., Lk. It
was impossible for them to discuss the
question with each other ; their
hesitation shewed that the same
hurried thoughts had passed through
the minds of all. The prepositions
admit of either a reflexive or a
mutual sense for the pronoun ; but

the former alone is possible here.
𝕊 sin (Mk., Lk.) makes the meaning
clear by omitting the preposition and
pronoun. παρ' ἑαυτοῖς recurs only
in Rom. xi. 25, xii. 16.

26. ἐὰν εἴπωμεν κτλ.] So Lk.
Mk. ἀλλὰ εἴπωμεν, a delib. conjunct.
forming the protasis ; and Mk.
suppresses their apodosis but supplies
it himself, ἐφοβοῦντο τ. λαόν, as
though they shrank from expressing
even to themselves their fear of the
people.   In Lk. their fear is explicit,
ὁ λαὸς ἅπας καταλιθάσει ἡμᾶς.
That such a thing was possible in
the temple court is shewn by Jo.
viii. 59, x. 30.   Mt. substitutes
ὄχλος for λαός, since he never uses
the latter without the thought of
the Jewish nation as such (see iv.
23, xxvi. 5).

πάντες γὰρ κτλ. avoids Mk.'s
loose constr. ἅπαντες γὰρ εἶχον τὸν
Ἰ. ὄντως ὅτι προφήτης ἦν. The
words, in all three accounts, can express an opinion held after John's
death ; but the fear of the people's
anger is more easily understood if
his work were still in progress and
the country thrilled with the first
enthusiasm about him. Cf. Herod's
fear from the same cause, xiv. 5.
The v.l. εἶχον makes the clause a
remark of the evang. as in Mk.
𝕊 sin.cur. 'as to a prophet they
were holding to him' is a mis-
rendering of ἔχειν ὡς, 'to regard as.'
For the constructions with ἔχειν see
Blass, § 34. 5, § 70. 2 ; cf. v. 46.

ἀποκριθέντες τῷ Ἰησοῦ εἶπαν Οὐκ οἴδαμεν. ἔφη αὐτοῖς καὶ
αὐτός Οὐδὲ ἐγὼ λέγω ὑμῖν ἐν ποίᾳ ἐξουσίᾳ ταῦτα ποιῶ.
28 Τί δὲ ὑμῖν δοκεῖ ; ἄνθρωπος εἶχεν τέκνα δύο. προσελθὼν
τῷ πρώτῳ εἶπεν Τέκνον, ὕπαγε σήμερον ἐργάζου ἐν
29 τῷ ἀμπελῶνι· ὁ δὲ ἀποκριθεὶς εἶπεν Ἐγώ, κύριε· καὶ
30 οὐκ ἀπῆλθεν. προσελθὼν δὲ τῷ δευτέρῳ εἶπεν ὡσαύτως·
ὁ δὲ ἀποκριθεὶς εἶπεν Οὐ θέλω· ὕστερον μεταμεληθεὶς
31 ἀπῆλθεν. τίς ἐκ τῶν δύο ἐποίησεν τὸ θέλημα τοῦ πατρός ;

27. οὐκ οἴδαμεν κτλ.] It was
their duty to the nation to have
formed an authoritative opinion
about the Baptist ; but they preferred
an admission of ignorance to being
stoned on the one hand and to telling
the truth on the other, and this pre-
cluded any statement on the part of
Jesus.

28-32. (Mt. only.) PARABLE OF
THE TWO SONS.

The parable is the first of a trilogy,
all teaching that the leaders of the
nation being unworthy, those whom
they despise will take their place (v.
31, v. 43, xxii. 10).

28. τί δέ κτλ.] See on xvii. 25.
The characters of the two τέκνα are
akin to those of the two υἱοί in Lk.
xv. 11 ff. 'Work in the vineyard' is
only of the scenery of the parable ;
obedience alone is the point at issue.
When the owner speaks to his son,
'the vineyard' is enough ; the
addition of μου is unnecessary. For
πρῶτος = πρότερος see Blass, § 11. 5.

29. ἐγώ, κύριε] He answers
with polite deference ; cf. Gen. xxxi.
35. Even if this son should be
placed second (see below), ἐγώ is not
emphatic, in contrast with the other
son, but is equivalent to ἰδοὺ ἐγώ
= הִנֵּנִי (Ac. ix. 10, and frequently
in the LXX.).

30. οὐ θέλω κτλ.] A blank refusal with no title of respect. The
absence of a connecting particle with

ὕστερον adds vivacity (cf. λέγουσιν,
λέγει v. 31) ; it is a marked feature of
the Johannine style, but rare in the
synn., and the more noticeable because
a contrast is implied. Many MSS.
and versions naturally add δέ. On
ὕστερον see iv. 2.

31. τίς κτλ.] Cf. Lk. x. 36. On
ἀμὴν λ. ὑ. see v. 18. The customs-
officers (see on v. 46) and harlots
were, of all classes, the furthest
removed, in the estimation of the
religious authorities, from the hope
of entering the Kingdom, while the
authorities themselves were universally considered the most certain of
reaching it. The Lord reverses this
estimate (cf. Lk. xviii. 10–14). They
'are ahead of you' (προάγουσιν ὑμᾶς,
see on xiv. 22). The pres. tense
represents a timeless Aram. partcp.,
which has not necessarily a future
meaning. Like the Scribe who
answered discreetly, they were 'not
far from the Kingdom of God'
(Mk. xii. 34) ; they were walking
in front of their religious leaders on
'the road that leads to life' (Mt.
vii. 14). The words neither imply
nor deny that those addressed would
finally reach the Kingdom. ἡ βασ.
τοῦ θεοῦ (instead of τῶν οὐρανῶν)
is elsewhere confined in Mt. to xii.
28, xix. 24, xxi. 43 (see notes). Mt.'s
reason for retaining it here from his
source cannot be determined ; it
may have been an oversight, or,
more probably, an early scribal slip.

λέγουσιν Ὁ ὕστερος. λέγει αὐτοῖς ὁ Ἰησοῦς Ἀμὴν λέγω
ὑμῖν ὅτι οἱ τελῶναι καὶ αἱ πόρναι προάγουσιν ὑμᾶς εἰς
τὴν βασιλείαν τοῦ θεοῦ. ἦλθεν γὰρ Ἰωάνης πρὸς ὑμᾶς 32

In אCLXΔΡΣΦ al minn.*pler* 𝕃
c f q vg 𝔖 cur.pesh.hcl the order of
the two sons is reversed, and πρῶτος
is read for ὕστερος in v. 31. This
is supported by D 𝕃 *pler*.vg^codd
𝔖 sin, but with ἔσχατος (*novissimus*,
ܐ̈ܚܪܝܐ Ephr. 'second') in v. 31.
If the text (B 4 13 69 *al* vg^codd 𝔖 pal
me arm aeth^vid) is not original, it may
have resulted from a wish to bring
the parable into closer conformity
with its interpretation in v. 31 b.
The first son addressed would be
the more important (Hil. has ' filius
senior' and 'junior'), and would correspond with the religious authorities,
so that the son who said ἐγώ, κύριε
was placed first. Or if the sons were
allegorized as Jew and Gentile, the
same order would result. Wellhausen
and Merx accept the reading of D,
and explain that the authorities, in
their dilemma, defiantly answered
'the last,' and that Jesus, prevented
from employing their own answer
against them, replied indignantly
in v. 31 b, which is not, therefore,
an interpretation of the parable.
Jerome, though he rejects the reading, explains similarly: 'dicamus
. . . Judaeos tergiversari, et nolle
dicere quod sentiunt.' Allen, more
probably, suggests that the reading
ἔσχατος was due to anti-Pharisaic
feeling, to make them formally
approve of the conduct of the dis-
obedient son; 'they say and do
not' (xxiii. 3). And ἔσχατος may
then have led to the transposition
in B, by which they were again
made to give the right and obvious
answer; or the two motives, anti-
pharisaic and allegorizing, may have

led to ἔσχατος and ὕστερος respectively.

32. ἦλθεν κτλ.] A further application of the parable, added as an
explanation (γάρ) of v. 31 b. But
the application is obscure. Some explain it thus: the customs-officers and
harlots had disobeyed God (οὐ θέλω),
but owing to John's preaching they
repented (μεταμεληθεὶς ἀπῆλθεν);
the religious authorities had professed
righteousness (ἐγώ, κύριε), but when
John preached to them they refused
to believe him (οὐκ ἀπῆλθεν). Allen's
suggestion is not less improbable, that
the son who said οὐ θέλω illustrates
the authorities, in their refusal to
believe John, and that the repentance of the same son illustrates that
of the customs-officers and harlots—
the other son being disregarded. The
difficulty arises from the fact that
while the parable speaks of relations
with God, this verse deals with
attitudes towards the Baptist. The
father's command to his sons to *work*
can hardly represent John's call to
repent. The 'repentance' of the son
in the parable is not equivalent to
the 'belief' of those who listened
to John, and the behaviour of the
authorities towards John is not
really like anything in the parable.
The verse seems to be composed of
elements drawn partly from the
parable and v. 31, and partly from
v. 25 f., the latter leading to the
mention of John and to πιστεῦσαι
αὐτῷ. It may be based, however, on a
genuine utterance, unconnected with
the parable; and the same possibly
underlies Lk.'s words in vii. 29 f.
See Harnack, *Sayings*, 118.

ἐν ὁδῷ δικαιοσύνης, καὶ οὐκ ἐπιστεύσατε αὐτῷ· οἱ δὲ
τελῶναι καὶ αἱ πόρναι ἐπίστευσαν αὐτῷ· ὑμεῖς δὲ ἰδόντες
33 οὐδὲ μετεμελήθητε ὕστερον τοῦ πιστεῦσαι αὐτῷ.   Ἄλλην
παραβολὴν ἀκούσατε. Ἄνθρωπος ἦν οἰκοδεσπότης ὅστις
ἐφύτευσεν ἀμπελῶνα καὶ φραγμὸν αὐτῷ περιέθηκεν καὶ ὤρυξεν

32 οὐδε] B 1 13 22 33 *al* 𝕃 vet [*exc* c e].vg 𝔖 cur.pesh.hcl me aeth ; ου אCL *al*
minn.*pler* 𝔖 pal ; *om* D 𝕃 c e

ἐν ὁδῷ κτλ.] John *came with*
(*i.e.* brought) the path of righteousness as the subject of his preaching ;
cf. Ps. lxx. [lxxi.] 16, εἰσελεύσομαι
ἐν δυναστίᾳ (בִּגְבֻרוֹת) τοῦ Κυρίου,
lxv. [lxvi.] 13. For ὁδός as a subject of preaching cf. xxii. 16, Ac.
xvi. 17, xviii. 25. It describes a
manner of life ; cf. vii. 13 f., Lk. i.
79, Ac. ii. 28, and frequently in the
O.T. = דֶּרֶךְ.

ὑμεῖς δὲ κτλ.] 'Having seen
(it),' *i.e.* that they believed him.
οὐδέ is to be connected with ὕστερον :
they did not arrive even at a late
repentance. The reading οὐ is probably a correction for smoothness.
Without the negative, as in D, the
words are a question : 'did ye repent
afterwards, so as to believe him ?'
They might be rendered 'ye repented
afterwards of believing him' ; but the
religious authorities never believed
John and then changed their minds.
τοῦ πιστεῦσαι is epexegetic, giving
'the content rather than the purpose
of μετεμελήθητε' (Moulton, i. 216 f.).

33–46. (Mk. xii. 1–12, Lk. xx.
9–18.) PARABLE OF THE HUSBAND-
MEN AND THE HEIR.

33. ἄλλην κτλ.] Mk. καὶ ἤρξατο
(see on xiii. 54) αὐτοῖς ἐν παραβολαῖς
λαλεῖν, which is equivalent to παραβολικῶς, since only one parable is
given (unless the 'Corner-stone' was
reckoned as another) ; cf. Mt. xxii.
1. In Lk. it is addressed πρὸς τὸν
λαόν, the Lord turning from the

authorities to them ; but the former
were still present. The 'Sower' and
the 'Mustard-seed' are the only
other parables given by all the synn.,
and 'all three are taken from agri-
culture' (Plummer).

ἄνθρωπος κτλ.] On ἄνθρωπος =
τις see xiii. 28, and on ὅστις = ὅς
ii. 6. Mt. alone adds οἰκοδεσπότης :
cf. xiii. 52, xx. 1. Lk., by omitting
the fence, the vat, and the tower,
obscures the clear allusion to Is. v.
1 f. Israel is often, in the O.T.,
compared with a vineyard or a vine,
so that the audience could not
mistake the meaning. The fence
(φραγμός, cf. Lk. xiv. 23) was a
protection against wild beasts ; cf.
Ps. lxxix. [lxxx.] 13. The wine-
press usually consisted of two parts,
the ληνός (Vulg. *torcular*), where the
grapes were crushed (Is. lxiii. 2, Joel
iii. [iv.] 13), and the ὑπολήνιον
(Mk. Vulg. *lacus*, but *torcular* in the
O.T.) into which the juice fell (Is.
xvi. 10, Joel *l.c.*). The latter always
represents יֶקֶב, the former various
words, chiefly גַּת and less correctly
יֶקֶב. προλήνιον (Is. v. 2) is perhaps
a trough for grapes placed higher
than the ληνός, or a second pit to
receive the juice ; see *Enc. Bibl.*
5311 ff. The tower (πύργος) was
for the use of vine-dressers and
watchers (2 Chr. xxvi. 10) ; a mere
hut sometimes sufficed (Is. i. 8).
Often a fence was not made, but the
owner of this vineyard provided for
its well-being with the utmost care.

ἐν αὐτῷ ληνὸν καὶ ᾠκοδόμησεν πύργον, καὶ ἐξέδετο αὐτὸν
γεωργοῖς, καὶ ἀπεδήμησεν. ὅτε δὲ ἤγγισεν ὁ καιρὸς τῶν 34
καρπῶν, ἀπέστειλεν τοὺς δούλους αὐτοῦ πρὸς τοὺς γεωργοὺς
λαβεῖν τοὺς καρποὺς αὐτοῦ. καὶ λαβόντες οἱ γεωργοὶ τοὺς 35
δούλους αὐτοῦ ὃν μὲν ἔδειραν, ὃν δὲ ἀπέκτειναν, ὃν δὲ
ἐλιθοβόλησαν. πάλιν ἀπέστειλεν ἄλλους δούλους πλείονας 36
τῶν πρώτων, καὶ ἐποίησαν αὐτοῖς ὡσαύτως. ὕστερον δὲ 37

For allegorical explanations in patr. writings see Swete.

καὶ ἐξέδετο κτλ.] In the parable in Isaiah good fruit is expected, here loyalty on the part of the workers. The γεωργοί were not slaves (like ἀμπελουργός in Lk. xiii. 7), but tenants, their annual rent being a fixed quantity, or proportion, of fruit—a common custom in Palestine (Edersheim, L. and T. ii. 423; see Plato, Legg. 806 D, quoted by Swete). For γεωργός of a worker in a vine-yard cf. Gen. ix. 20. ἀπεδήμησεν, as in xxv. 14 f., reflects the conception of God's separateness from the world; as a transcendent King or Lord He is frequently pictured in the O.T. as sending messengers, angelic or human. It is His absence, rather than His departure, that is illustrated in the parable. Christianity, while retaining this Hebrew conception, has learnt the complementary truth of the divine Immanence.

34. ὅτε δέ κτλ.] Mt. expresses more clearly than Mk.'s τῷ καιρῷ (Lk. καιρῷ) the shortness of the time required by the scenery of the parable, which, however, corresponds with the whole of Israel's history, in every age of which God sent His messengers. δούλους refers more distinctly to these than δοῦλον (Mk., Lk.). τ. καρποὺς αὐτοῦ (Mk., Lk. ἀπὸ τῶν καρπῶν [Lk. τοῦ καρποῦ] τοῦ ἀμπελῶνος) are a fixed amount, or percentage, a detail which cannot be allegorized. What God asks (τὰ τοῦ θεοῦ xxii. 21) is described in iii. 8.

35, 36. καὶ λαβόντες κτλ.] For the redundant λαβόντες see xiii. 31. The treatment of the servants differs in each of the accounts. Mt., speaking of them in the plur., places together 'beat,' 'killed,' and 'stoned,' and when a larger number is sent, emphasizing the earnestness of the demand, writes, 'they did to them likewise.' Mk., Lk. describe the different treatment of each, Mk. arranging a climax, ἔδειραν, ἐκεφαλίωσαν, ἠτίμασαν, ἀπέκτειναν. (On ἐκεφαλίωσαν see Swete, and Allen's suggestion in JThS., 1909, 298 ff., that the translator followed by Mk. misread אבאישו ('ill-treated') as אראישו which he took to be a verb connected with ראיש 'a head'). Lk. has 'beat' (twice), 'dishonoured,' 'wounded,' reserving 'killed' for the Son. All have δέρειν, lit. 'to flay,' its only meaning in the LXX. (Lev. i. 6, 2 Chr. xxix. 34, xxxv. 11; v.l. in each case ἐκδέρειν), but in the N.T. always 'to beat,' first found in the slang of Aristophanes.

The audience could not fail to see the allusion to the treatment of prophets in the past; cf. v. 12, xvii. 12, xxiii. 31, 37.

37. ὕστερον κτλ.] Mk. ἔσχατον; see on iv. 2. τὸν υἱὸν αὐτοῦ for Mk.'s ἕνα υἱὸν ἀγαπητόν treats 'one' and 'beloved' as identical; cf. Jud. xi. 34 (A) καὶ ἦν αὕτη μονογενὴς

ἀπέστειλεν πρὸς αὐτοὺς τὸν υἱὸν αὐτοῦ λέγων Ἐντραπήσονται
38 τὸν υἱόν μου. οἱ δὲ γεωργοὶ ἰδόντες τὸν υἱὸν εἶπον ἐν
ἑαυτοῖς Οὗτός ἐστιν ὁ κληρονόμος· δεῦτε ἀποκτείνωμεν
39 αὐτὸν καὶ σχῶμεν τὴν κληρονομίαν αὐτοῦ· καὶ λαβόντες
40 αὐτὸν ἐξέβαλον ἔξω τοῦ ἀμπελῶνος καὶ ἀπέκτειναν. ὅταν
οὖν ἔλθῃ ὁ κύριος τοῦ ἀμπελῶνος, τί ποιήσει τοῖς γεωργοῖς
41 ἐκείνοις ; λέγουσιν αὐτῷ Κακοὺς κακῶς ἀπολέσει αὐτούς,

αὐτῷ ἀγαπητή. But for Mk.'s readers, as for us, they could express both the uniqueness of the Son and His Messiahship (see iii. 17). ἀπέστειλεν (so Mk.): like the prophets the Son was an ἀπόστολος (Heb. iii. 1) ; cf. Mt. x. 40, xv. 24, Lk. iv. 18, 43, and frequently in Jo.ev.ep. For ἐντρέπεσθαί τινος 'turn towards,' 'pay respect to' cf. Lk. xviii. 2, 4, Heb. xii. ꞅ ; in class. Gk. it takes the acc. (cf. Wisd. vi. 7). The Owner's confidence in the mission of the Son gives the measure of the crime which disappointed it. Lk.'s ἴσως detracts from the confidence, and softens the irony. The thought of God's 'disappointment' involves the paradox of divine knowledge and man's freedom of choice ; see on xviii. 7.

38. οἱ δὲ γεωργοί κτλ.] The scene recalls the narrative of Joseph (Gen. xxxvii. 18 ff.), whose brothers said δεῦτε ἀποκτείνωμεν αὐτόν. The futility of the husbandmen's idea that the murder of the Heir would give them the inheritance, contributes to the picture of their insensate hostility ; it need not imply that the Jewish leaders themselves thought of Jesus as the Heir. Behind His words possibly lay the thought of Is. liii. 12, κληρονομήσει πολλοὺς . . . ἀνθ' ὧν παρεδόθη εἰς θάνατον ἡ ψυχὴ αὐτοῦ (see on xx. 28 fin.). Christians afterwards worked out the thought that all God's sons can be united in the heirship as συνκληρονόμοι (Rom. viii. 17), an extension of the Jewish

use of 'inherit' seen in Mt. v. 5, xix. 29, xxv. 34 ; see Westcott on Heb. i. 2. δεῦτε (xxviii. 6, Jo. iv. 29, xxi. 12), like δεῦρο (xix. 21), is frequent in the LXX. for לְךְ, לְכוּ (Targ. איתא, איתו).

39. καὶ λαβόντες κτλ.] Mk. 'And they took and killed him, and cast him outside the vineyard,' i.e. his body was cast out unburied, as the final insult. Mt., Lk. place the casting outside before the murder, perhaps reading more into the allegory, i.e. either that Jesus was rejected, and treated as cast out from the community (cf. ἐκβάλλειν in Lk. vi. 22, Jo. ix. 34), or that He was killed outside Jerusalem (Heb. xiii. 12). In a Christian allegory something would probably have been added to represent the Resurrection of the Son ; its absence favours the genuineness of the parable.

40. ὅταν οὖν κτλ.] The question is rhetorical ; in Mk., Lk. the Lord answers it Himself, but Mt. represents the audience as answering, and thus pronouncing their own condemnation.

41. κακούς κτλ.] Lit. 'because they are bad, he will badly destroy them.' The assonance (not in Mk., Lk.) is an expedient of literary Gk. ; cf. Wisd. vi. 6 δυνατοὶ δὲ δυνατῶς ἐτασθήσονται, Dem. De Cor. 267, Soph. Phil. 1369 ; but it was perpetuated in popular language (Moulton, Expos., May 1909, 477). Wellhausen thinks that the original was ביש ביש, 'very

καὶ τὸν ἀμπελῶνα ἐκδώσεται ἄλλοις γεωργοῖς, οἵτινες
ἀποδώσουσιν αὐτῷ τοὺς καρποὺς ἐν τοῖς καιροῖς αὐτῶν.
λέγει αὐτοῖς ὁ Ἰησοῦς Οὐδέποτε ἀνέγνωτε ἐν ταῖς γραφαῖς 42

Λίθον ὃν ἀπεδοκίμασαν οἱ οἰκοδομοῦντες
οὗτος ἐγενήθη εἰς κεφαλὴν γωνίας·

badly'; this occurs in the 𝔖, where, however, it may be only an attempt to reproduce the sound of the Gk. (Burkitt, *Ev. da Meph.* ii. 123). ἀπολέσει need not be an *ex eventu* reference to the fall of Jerusalem; the destruction of the sinful nation was the constant burden of the prophets. ἐκδώσεται (for δώσεται Mk., Lk.) continues the ἐξέδετο of *v.* 33. The last sentence, οἵτινες κτλ., is added by Mt. only (cf. Ps. i. 3); Mk., Lk., stopping at ἄλλοις, imply that others will be given the *opportunity* forfeited by the first tenants; Mt., with the Christian Church in his mind, goes further in stating that they will prove worthy of it. The audience might recall such passages as Jer. iii. 15, xxiii. 1–4, which speak of the rejection of Israel's religious leaders in favour of others. This is the main point to which the parable has led; cf. *v.* 31, xxii. 8–10. But it was natural for patr. writers to apply it to the apostles; it can further illustrate the duties of the Church's leaders in all times, and also the succession by Gentiles to the privileges forfeited by the Jews; see Swete.

42. οὐδέποτε κτλ.] See on xii. 3. αἱ γραφαί, always plur. in Mt., are the contents of the O.T. canon. Mk.: οὐδὲ τὴν γραφὴν ταύτην ἀνέγνωτε, 'have ye not read even this (well-known) passage of Scripture?' The quotation is from Ps. cxvii. [cxviii.] 22 f.; the Hosanna verse (*v.* 9 above) follows almost immediately, and the whole passage must have been well known. The γεωργοί now become

οἰκοδομοῦντες; cf. the change of metaphor in 1 Cor. iii. 9. In the Psalm it is Zion, *i.e.* Israel, that was despised and well-nigh destroyed by the world powers; but its glories had been restored by the Maccabean victories; see Briggs *ad loc.* If the quotation is by Jesus Himself, it is an explanation of *v.* 41, and leads directly to *v.* 43: the pious members of the Jewish race oppressed and misused by their religious leaders will be advanced to honour. If it was added by Christian teachers, the 'Stone' is Jesus the Messiah. The words are applied to the Messiah in the Targ., and the use of 'Stone' as referring to the Messiah is found among the Jews as early as Justin (*Dial.* xxxiv., xxxvi.); see Rend. Harris, *Expos.,* Nov. 1906, 407 f.; cf. also Targ. Is. xxviii. 16, *Sanh.* 38 a (quoted by Sanday and Headl. on Rom. ix. 33). In the N.T. the passage from the Ps. is referred to in Ac. iv. 11, the similar metaph. in Is. xxviii. 16 in Eph. ii. 20, and the latter is combined with Is. viii. 14 in Rom. ix. 33; all the three O.T. passages are combined in 1 Pet. ii. 6 ff. (see Hort).

λίθον ὅν κτλ.] The LXX. is a literal rendering of the MT. For the acc. by attraction λίθον ὅν see Blass, § 50. 3. ἀποδοκιμάζειν (for מאס) is 'to reject *after trial*,' a thought absent from the Heb. verb, but appropriate in the present case; Ac. iv. 11 has ἐξουθενημένος, more usual in the LXX. for מאס. κεφαλὴν γωνίας (= ראשׁ פִּנָּה, not elsewhere in the O.T.) is probably 'the furthest

παρὰ Κυρίου ἐγένετο αὕτη,
καὶ ἔστιν θαυμαστὴ ἐν ὀφθαλμοῖς ἡμῶν;

43 διὰ τοῦτο λέγω ὑμῖν ὅτι ἀρθήσεται ἀφ' ὑμῶν ἡ βασιλεία
τοῦ θεοῦ καὶ δοθήσεται ἔθνει ποιοῦντι τοὺς καρποὺς αὐτῆς.
44 Καὶ ὁ πεσὼν ἐπὶ τὸν λίθον τοῦτον συνθλασθήσεται· ἐφ'

extremity (not 'the top') of the
corner,' a poetical equivalent for פִּנָּה.
In Zech. iv. 7 הָאֶבֶן הָרֹאשָׁה perhaps
has the same meaning, as also ἀκρο-
γωνιαῖος (= פִּנָּה Is. xxviii. 16, and
Sym. in Ps. *l.c.*). A corner stone is
more important than any other stone
in the foundation, since it bears a
greater weight.

παρὰ Κυρίου κτλ.] The remainder
is omitted by Lk., probably for
brevity, as being less essential for
the illustration of the parable. On
παρά see xviii. 19. αὕτη (= זֹאת,
which does the work of a neut., cf.
Jud. xix. 30) is the fact that the
rejected stone is restored to honour.

43. διὰ τοῦτο κτλ.] Because the
husbandmen must be punished—a
truth supported by Scripture—*therefore*, etc. The vineyard, which is
the community of Israel, is the
'Kingdom of God.' τοῦ θεοῦ and
not τῶν οὐρανῶν is used (see on *v.*
31, xii. 28, xix. 24) because the
meaning is different from that of
'Kingdom of Heaven.' The verse,
added by Mt. only, gives a correct
explanation of the parable. The
ἔθνος is the Israel of the future,
advanced to honour by the death of
the Son. They are the new body of
husbandmen, and at the same time
the vineyard which yields fruit.
For τ. καρποὺς αὐτοῦ of *v.* 34 is
substituted τ. κ. αὐτῆς, referring to
the βασιλεία.

The genuineness of the parable is
often denied, on the ground that it
reflects developed Christian thought.
But, as the notes have shewn, it con-

tains nothing distinctively Christian.
That it is to some extent an allegory
causes no difficulty (see Prelim. n. on
ch. xiii.). The Lord knew that He
was the Son, sent to die for His
nation ; not for all its members,
since some refused to repent, but
' for many ' (Mk. x. 45). He was
confident that His death, at the
hands of the Jewish leaders, would
bring about the consummation that
was soon to come, when there would
emerge an ideal Israel, a purified
nation, such as the prophets of old
had longed for. In the parable,
accordingly, the murder of the Son
results in the downfall of the
husbandmen, and the advancement
of others who will duly render the
fruits of the vineyard. In point of
fact, the ' nation ' who were advanced
to honour proved to be the Christian
Church. That was the divine translation in history of the Lord's expectations expressed in Jewish form. But
it is noteworthy that the evangelists
did not allow their knowledge of this
to colour their record of the parable.
(See Burkitt, *Third Internat. Congr.
for Hist. Rel.* ii. 321–8.)

44. καὶ ὁ πεσών κτλ.] Lk. πᾶς
ὁ π. and ἐκεῖνον for τοῦτον. His
to stumble at the stone (cf. Is. viii. 14
= Rom. ix. 32 f.) would involve
spiritual injury, but to be punished
by it would be something far more
terrible. For συνθλᾶν of divine
punishment cf. Ps. lxvii. [lxviii.] 22,
cix. [cx.] 5 f. λικμᾶν in its lit.
meaning 'to winnow' (Is. xvii. 13,
Ruth iii. 2) is unsuitable to the

ὃν δ᾽ ἂν πέσῃ λικμήσει αὐτόν. Καὶ ἀκούσαντες 45
οἱ ἀρχιερεῖς καὶ οἱ Φαρισαῖοι τὰς παραβολὰς αὐτοῦ
ἔγνωσαν ὅτι περὶ αὐτῶν λέγει· καὶ ζητοῦντες αὐτὸν 46
κρατῆσαι ἐφοβήθησαν τοὺς ὄχλους, ἐπεὶ εἰς προφήτην

metaphor; but it seems to have the more general force of 'break into small pieces,' Vulg. *conteret, comminuet* (Lk.); cf. ἐξελίκμησεν Judith ii. 27. Deissmann, *Bible St.* 225 f., gives an instance from a papyrus. It is used of divine punishment in Jer. xxx. 10 [xlix.] 32, Ez. xxx. 23, 26. The verse is probably a gloss. Allen thinks it was inserted in Mt. and transferred to Lk., or inserted in both by the glossator. But its omission in Mt. by D 33 𝔏 *nonn* 𝕾 sin, but by no MSS. in Lk., suggests rather its transference from Lk. to some early MSS. of Mt. Allen also suggests that a copyist, led by ἔθνει (*v.* 43) to think of Dan. ii. 44 (Theod.), καὶ ἡ βασιλεία αὐτοῦ λαῷ ἑτέρῳ οὐχ ὑπολειφθήσεται, built up the gloss from the following clause, λεπτυνεῖ καὶ λικμήσει πάσας τὰς βασιλείας, together with the thought of Is. viii. 14 f.

45. ἀκούσαντες κτλ.] Mk. does not name the Lord's opponents; Mt., Lk. remind the reader who they were (see *v.* 23, Lk. xx. 1), but Mt. writes 'the Pharisees' for 'the elders of the people,' and Lk. omits 'the elders.' The plur. τ. παραβολάς (Mk., Lk. τὴν παραβολήν) refers to the series of three which Mt. places together. ἔγνωσαν κτλ.: Mk. 'and they sought to arrest Him, and feared the people, for they knew, etc.' (similarly Lk.), where ἔγνωσαν γάρ probably gives the reason, not for their fear, but for ἐζητοῦν αὐτὸν κρατῆσαι. Mt. rearranges the clauses, and supplies a reason for their fear.

ἐπεί κτλ.] The enthusiasm kindled both by Jesus and the Baptist (*v.* 26,

xiv. 5) as prophets was a new element in Jewish life, from which the conservatism of the religious leaders shrank, because it endangered their vested interests. The people were well able to distinguish a real prophet both from the apocalyptists and from the Scribes. For the Hebraic εἰς προφ. cf. 1 Regn. i. 13, Job xli. 23 [24]; see *v.* 26 above.

Mk. adds καὶ ἀφέντες αὐτὸν ἀπῆλθον, which Lk. omits, and Mt. postpones to xxii. 22, because he here adds another parable conveying the same lesson.

xxii. 1–10. (Cf. Lk. xiv. 16–24.) PARABLE OF THE WEDDING FEAST.

In spite of the differences between this parable and that in Lk. *l.c.*, there is a close similarity of thought and purpose. In each case the guests having rejected the invitation, others of a lower grade of society are invited instead of them. The Lucan parable is recorded to have been uttered when the Lord was at a meal in a Pharisee's house. He had said (*v.* 13 f.) that to invite the poor, maimed, blind, and lame, who could not offer an invitation in return, would be rewarded in the resurrection of the righteous. One of His fellow-guests understood Him to refer to the feast in the Kingdom of God (*v.* 15); and the parable is given as His reply. These two thoughts—the feast, and the invitation of the poor—seem to have led Lk. to place it at this point. But the summons to the poor, because the first invited guests were not worthy, is a thought entirely different from that of the advice in

XXII. 1 αὐτὸν εἶχον.   Καὶ ἀποκριθεὶς ὁ Ἰησοῦς πάλιν εἶπεν
2 ἐν παραβολαῖς αὐτοῖς λέγων Ὡμοιώθη ἡ βασιλεία τῶν
οὐρανῶν ἀνθρώπῳ βασιλεῖ, ὅστις ἐποίησεν γάμους τῷ υἱῷ
3 αὐτοῦ. καὶ ἀπέστειλεν τοὺς δούλους αὐτοῦ καλέσαι τοὺς
4 κεκλημένους εἰς τοὺς γάμους, καὶ οὐκ ἤθελον ἐλθεῖν. πάλιν

v. 13. If, as is probable, the two
parables are a doublet from one
original, Mt. has placed his in the
more appropriate position, the teaching being similar to that in xxi. 31
and 41, but Lk. has preserved the
more original form. Mt. has changed
'a certain man' into 'a certain king,'
'a great supper' into 'a wedding
feast for his son,' 'a slave' into
'slaves'; he omits the excuses, and
a later hand has added the acts of
violence to the slaves, the destruction
of the murderers and the burning of
their city. (See notes.)

1. καὶ ἀποκριθείς κτλ.] See xi.
25. ἐν παραβολαῖς is equivalent to
παραβολικῶς (see on xxi. 33), since
Mt. gives what purports to be only
one parable.

2. ὡμοιώθη κτλ.] On the formula,
and the comparison of the Kingdom
with a man, see xiii. 24 ; on ἀνθρώπῳ
βασιλεῖ see xi. 19, xiii. 28. Lk.
has ἄνθρωπός τις ; Mt. makes more
explicit the reference to God. See on
xviii. 23. For ὅστις = ὅς cf. ii. 6. In
Lk. the δεῖπνον μέγα is the Messianic
banquet in the coming Kingdom
(cf. Mt. viii. 11) ; in Mt. the wedding-
feast of the King's son is a Christian
symbol of the joy of the union of
Christ and His Church (Apoc. xix.
7, 9 ; cf. Eph. v. 25 ff., Apoc. xxi.
2, 9), but it is doubtful if Jewish
writers ever thought of the Messianic
banquet as a *wedding*-feast ; see
Volz, *Jüd. Esch.* 331. The plur.
γάμοι, *nuptiae* (*v.* 9, xxv. 10, Lk.
xii. 36, xiv. 8), which alternates with
the sing. in *vv.* 8, 11 f., belongs to
later Gk. ; both occur in the LXX.

3. καὶ ἀπέστειλεν κτλ.] καλ. τ.
κεκλημένους seems to imply (as Lk.
also) that the guests had been invited previously, the announcement
now being that the feast was ready.
It is idle to discuss whether this
was a Jewish custom. It is required
by the parable, as also that the feast
remained ready and untouched during the mission of the other servants,
the continued refusal, and the gathering of guests from the roads. The
nation had received their summons
from the prophets of old, and they
now learnt from the Baptist, the
disciples, and Jesus Himself, that the
great moment had arrived. Their
preaching is represented in Lk. as
the work of a single servant ; Mt.
expresses the parable's meaning
more clearly by the plural, perhaps
influenced by Prov. ix. 1–6 (*v.* 3
ἀπέστειλεν τοὺς ἑαυτῆς δούλους),
which may have suggested to Jesus
the symbolism of the parable.

4. πάλιν κτλ.] The second mission
recalls xxi. 36 ; Lk. has no parallel
to it. It expresses only the urgency
of the call. τὸ ἄριστον κτλ.: cf. *Aboth*
iii. 25 'Everything is prepared for
the banquet' (see Taylor). The rare
word σιτιστός is used by Sym. in
Ps. xxi. [xxii.] 13, Jer. xxvi. [xlvi.]
21, Jos. *Ant.* VIII. ii. 4 ; σιτευτός
(cf. Lk. xv. 23, 27, 30) is commoner.
ἄριστον passed into late Heb. ; in
the parable it is an early meal, since
the remaining events belong to the
same day ; that Mt. preferred it for
this reason to Lk.'s δεῖπνον (Zahn)
is doubtful. With the call δεῦτε
κτλ. cf Apoc. xix. 17.

ἀπέστειλεν ἄλλους δούλους λέγων Εἴπατε τοῖς κεκλημένοις
Ἰδοὺ τὸ ἄριστόν μου ἡτοίμακα, οἱ ταῦροί μου καὶ τὰ
σιτιστὰ τεθυμένα, καὶ πάντα ἕτοιμα· δεῦτε εἰς τοὺς
γάμους. οἱ δὲ ἀμελήσαντες ἀπῆλθον, ὃς μὲν εἰς τὸν 5
ἴδιον ἀγρόν, ὃς δὲ ἐπὶ τὴν ἐμπορίαν αὐτοῦ· οἱ δὲ λοιποὶ 6
κρατήσαντες τοὺς δούλους αὐτοῦ ὕβρισαν καὶ ἀπέκτειναν.
ὁ δὲ βασιλεὺς ὠργίσθη, καὶ πέμψας τὰ στρατεύματα 7
αὐτοῦ ἀπώλεσεν τοὺς φονεῖς ἐκείνους καὶ τὴν πόλιν αὐτῶν
ἐνέπρησεν. τότε λέγει τοῖς δούλοις αὐτοῦ Ὁ μὲν γάμος 8
ἕτοιμός ἐστιν, οἱ δὲ κεκλημένοι οὐκ ἦσαν ἄξιοι· πορεύεσθε 9

5. οἱ δέ κτλ.] For ἀμελεῖν, elsewhere always c. gen., cf. Heb. ii. 3, Jer.
iv. 17. ἀγρός and ἐμπορία (ἅπαξ
λεγ. in the N.T.) correspond with the
purchase of a field and of live stock
in Lk., but his γυναῖκα ἔγημα has
no parallel in Mt. ἴδιον has lost its
strict force, and is equivalent to the
following αὐτοῦ; see Blass, § 48. 8,
Deissmann, Bibl. St. 123.

6,7. οἱ δὲ λοιποί κτλ.] These verses
refer to the persecution of Christian
apostles and preachers, and the sack
of Jerusalem by the Roman armies,
who, as God's instrument of punishment, are 'His armies.' But with
the exception of the Baptist no one
who proclaimed that the Kingdom
was at hand had been put to death
when the Lord spoke, and Jerusalem
had not yet been burnt. Even if
these could be regarded as predictions,
the verses fit awkwardly with the
rest of the parable, and must be a
later addition, for ὃς μὲν . . . ὃς δέ
(v. 5) embrace all the invited guests,
so that οἱ δὲ λοιποί is unexpected;
οὐκ ἦσαν ἄξιοι seems a very inadequate description of the murderers
of the servants; and the δοῦλοι of
v. 8 ff. are evidently the same as
those of v. 3 f., not Christians who
preached to Gentiles after the fall
of Jerusalem (Zahn). The violence
to the servants, and the punishment,

are an echo of xxi. 35 f., 41, but
with the addition of the explicit
reference to the burning of the city.
Harnack (Sayings, 121 ff.) suggests
that the verses are the remnant of a
complete parable, which Lk. has
combined in another form with that
of the Pounds (i.e. Lk. xix. 12, 14,
15 a, 27); but except that a king
executed punishment, Mt. and Lk.
have not a single detail in common;
see on xxv. 14–30.

9. πορεύεσθε κτλ.] Mt. has related a double mission to the invited
guests; Lk. now relates a double
mission, (1) in the squares and
streets of the city to the poor, the
maimed etc., whom the wealthier
citizens, who were first invited,
despised and avoided; these would
correspond with the τελῶναι and
πόρναι of Mt. xxi. 31; (2) out
among the country roads and hedges;
'to the Jew first, and also to the
Gentile.' If this is Lk.'s meaning,
Mt. is truer to the original; the
διέξοδοι τ. ὁδῶν (Vulg. exitus viarum)
are the 'ends of the roads,' i.e.
central spots whence the high roads
or streets diverge, where the poor
might be found collected. In v. 10
the servants go simply εἰς τ. ὁδούς.
διέξοδοι (Herod., al.) is frequent in
Num., Josh. for תוֹצְאוֹת. And see
Moulton, Expos., Dec. 1908, 565.

οὖν ἐπὶ τὰς διεξόδους τῶν ὁδῶν, καὶ ὅσους ἐὰν εὕρητε
10 καλέσατε εἰς τοὺς γάμους. καὶ ἐξελθόντες οἱ δοῦλοι ἐκεῖνοι
εἰς τὰς ὁδοὺς συνήγαγον πάντας οὓς εὗρον, πονηρούς
τε καὶ ἀγαθούς· καὶ ἐπλήσθη ὁ νυμφὼν ἀνακειμένων.
11 εἰσελθὼν δὲ ὁ βασιλεὺς θεάσασθαι τοὺς ἀνακειμένους εἶδεν
12 ἐκεῖ ἄνθρωπον οὐκ ἐνδεδυμένον ἔνδυμα γάμου· καὶ λέγει
αὐτῷ Ἑταῖρε, πῶς εἰσῆλθες ὧδε μὴ ἔχων ἔνδυμα γάμου ;
13 ὁ δὲ ἐφιμώθη. τότε ὁ βασιλεὺς εἶπεν τοῖς διακόνοις

10. συνήγαγον κτλ.] Allen suggests that the verb represents the
Aram. כנס, Pael 'to gather,' Aphel
'to bring in,' 'invite.' Since the
parable teaches simply that unworthy
guests are rejected in favour of others,
πονηρούς τε καὶ ἀγαθούς introduces
a different thought (cf. xiii. 47 f.), and
is probably a gloss introduced in view
of vv. 11–13 ; this use of τε καί is
unique in Mt. On νυμφών see ix. 15.

11–14. (Mt. only.) PARABLE OF
THE WEDDING GARMENT.

This appears to be a portion of a
parable of which the opening is lost.
The people collected indiscriminately
from the roads, without previous
notice, could not come in festal array.
The conjecture that it was a Jewish
custom in the time of Jesus for a
host to supply his guests with
garments is based solely on the
parable. The lost opening must
have related that a king issued
invitations to a feast; it need not
have occupied more than a single
verse (as e.g. Lk. xiv. 16). The
teaching is similar to that of the
'Tares' (xiii. 24–30 ; see n. after
v. 43) and the 'Net' (xiii. 47–50).
At the Advent of the King it will
be found that men of different kinds
have received the invitation, and
some will be found unworthy. There
is nothing which necessitates the
thought of good and bad men within
the *Christian* community.

11. εἰσελθών κτλ.] θεάσασθαι

strikes the keynote at once ; at God's
Advent He will inspect those to
whom the message of the Kingdom
has been preached, to determine who
are worthy. The one defaulter
represents all who are unworthy.
ἔνδυμα γάμου (cf. γαμικὴ χλανίς
Aristoph. *Av.* 1693) symbolizes everything that renders men fitted for
a share in the joys of the Kingdom
(cf. iii. 8, v. 20). It naturally lends
itself to the Christian thought
Χριστὸν ἐνεδύσασθε ; 'vestem super-
coelestis hominis' (Jer.) ; see Tert.
Scorp. 6, Hil. *in Mat. ad loc.*, who
refer to Baptism. ἔνδυμα is confined
to Mt. (7) in the N.T. except Lk. xii.
23.

12. ἑταῖρε κτλ.] Cf. xx. 13, xxvi.
50. The condescension, which seems
to assume that the man probably has
a good excuse, heightens the sternness
which follows. μὴ ἔχων regards
the fact οὐκ ἐνδεδυμένον from the
king's point of view ; see Moulton,
i. 231 f. φιμοῦν, lit. 'to muzzle,'
or 'gag' (cf. 1 Cor. ix. 9 = 1 Tim.
v. 18 [LXX.]), is used metaph. in late
writers ; cf. *v.* 34, Mk. i. 25, iv. 39,
1 Pet. ii. 15, Prov. xxvi. 10 (Theod.),
φιμῶν ἄφρονα φιμοῖ χόλους.

13. τότε κτλ.] The διάκονοι are
a necessary feature of the parable, as
the means of the offender's ejection,
but perhaps they symbolize the angels
in their functions at the last day
(cf. xiii. 39, 41, 49, xxiv. 31). The
parable passes into the reality ; the

Δήσαντες αὐτοῦ πόδας καὶ χεῖρας ἐκβάλετε αὐτὸν εἰς τὸ
σκότος τὸ ἐξώτερον· ἐκεῖ ἔσται ὁ κλαυθμὸς καὶ ὁ βρυγμὸς
τῶν ὀδόντων. πολλοὶ γάρ εἰσιν κλητοὶ ὀλίγοι δὲ ἐκλεκτοί. 14
Τότε πορευθέντες οἱ Φαρισαῖοι συμβούλιον ἔλαβον 15

speaker being now the divine King.
It cannot be maintained that Jesus
Himself could not so have spoken;
but since the punishment, apart from
the binding of the feet and hands,
is described in the same terms as in
viii. 12, xxv. 30, the verse, in its
present form, is probably due to the
evangelist. It may be influenced
by Enoch x. 4, δῆσον τὸν Ἀζαὴλ
ποσὶν καὶ χερσίν, καὶ βάλε αὐτὸν εἰς
τὸ σκότος. Wellhausen refers to an
Arab custom of binding the feet of
a guest rejected from the court. For
'feet and hands' cf. Jo. xi. 44, Ac.
xxi. 11. The reading of D 𝕷
ἄρατε is apparently followed by
𝕾 sin.cur 'take hold of him'; but
see Burkitt, Ev. da Meph. ii. 124 f.

A Rabb. parable is attributed
(Shabb. 153 a) to Johanan b. Zakkai
(c. A.D. 100), and another version
(Midr. Ḳoh. ix. 8) to R. Judah ha-
Nasi (c. A.D. 170), which are similar
in thought to the parable of the
Wedding Garment. See Wünsche,
Neue Beitr. 252 f. Mt.'s parable,
in its original form, was current in
Jewish-Christian circles, and was
possibly employed by Jews without
knowledge of its origin.

14. πολλοί κτλ.] In the O.T.
ἐκλεκτός (בָּחִיר; see on iii. 17) is used,
in the sing. or plur., of the nation
of Israel; but the failure of the
nation to fulfil its destiny led to the
use of the term, in later Jewish
writings, for the 'righteous,' in contrast with the rest of the nation;
cf. Wisd. iii. 9 (‖ οἱ πεποιθότες
and οἱ πιστοί), iv. 15 (‖ ὅσιοι),
Enoch i. 1, v. 7 f., xxv. 5. In
Apoc. Abr. 29 a definite number of

them is given; cf. Apoc. Bar. xxx.
2, lxxv. 5. See Volz, Jüd. Esch.
315 f., and the passages quoted by
Allen. If then, in Jewish thought,
the 'elect' are the righteous or pious,
the word involves not only divine
predetermination but also human
responsibility (see on xviii. 7); they
are κλητοὶ καὶ ἐκλεκτοὶ καὶ πιστοί
(Apoc. xvii. 14). ἐκλεκτοί occurs in
Lk. xviii. 7, and in the eschatological
discourse (Mt. xxiv. 22, 24, 31, and
Mk.). There is no reason to think
that Jesus employed it in any other
than the Jewish sense. Many Jews
had received the call, but few had
become 'elect' by accepting it. If
it was a current saying, γάρ may
mean 'for the saying is true, Many
etc.' In Ep. Barn. iv. 14 it is introduced by ὡς γέγραπται, according
to J. Weiss not a reference to the
Gospel, but to the same source from
which the Lord drew it: cf. 4 Esd.
viii. 3 'Many were created, but few
shall be saved,' ix. 15 'More are
they that perish than those who
shall be saved.' S. Paul, treating
of the Church as an ideal, identifies
the 'called' and the 'elect,' but
Jesus speaks of facts as they were.
The saying, however, though doubtless genuine, may not be in its
original position; neither of the
foregoing parables contains the
thought that the 'elect' are a small
minority. It is inserted, still less
appropriately, in several authorities
after xx. 16.

15–22. (Mk. xii. 13–17, Lk. xx.
20–26.) THE QUESTION ABOUT THE
CAPITATION TAX.

15. τότε κτλ.] In Mk., Lk. the

16 ὅπως αὐτὸν παγιδεύσωσιν ἐν λόγῳ. καὶ ἀποστέλλουσιν
αὐτῷ τοὺς μαθητὰς αὐτῶν μετὰ τῶν Ἡρῳδιανῶν λέγοντας
Διδάσκαλε, οἴδαμεν ὅτι ἀληθὴς εἶ καὶ τὴν ὁδὸν τοῦ θεοῦ
ἐν ἀληθείᾳ διδάσκεις, καὶ οὐ μέλει σοι περὶ οὐδενός, οὐ γὰρ

emissaries are sent by all the members of the Sanhedrin to whom the parable had been addressed, in Mt. by the Pharisees only, the priestly party appearing later, as the Sadducees (v. 23). Their consultation is expanded from Mk.'s ἵνα αὐτὸν ἀγρεύσωσιν λόγῳ. On πορευθέντες see ix. 13 a, and on συμβ. ἔλαβον xii. 14. For παγιδεύειν, 'to catch in a trap' (παγίς), used metaph. see 1 Regn. xxviii. 9, Eccl. ix. 12, Test. Joseph vii. 1, περιεβλέπετο ποίῳ τρόπῳ με παγιδεῦσαι. Cf. παγίδευμα Aq. Eccl. vii. 27 [26], LXX. θήρευμα (cf. Lk. xi. 54). ἐν λόγῳ (Mk. λόγῳ) is either 'conversation,' or better 'by a remark (of His).' The cleansing of the temple had been a revolutionary act against the religious authorities; they now hoped to extort a revolutionary pronouncement against the civil authorities. Lk. expresses this : ὥστε παραδοῦναι αὐτὸν τῇ ἀρχῇ καὶ τῇ ἐξουσίᾳ τοῦ ἡγεμόνος.

16. καὶ ἀποστέλλουσιν κτλ.] For 'disciples of the Pharisees' cf. Mk. ii. 18. In Mk. the Sanhedrin send 'certain of the Pharisees.' The 'Herodians' associated with them are probably not Herod's soldiers but his political partisans. The termination -ιανός, of Lat. origin (cf. Caesariani), came to be employed to form names of sects, and the word, like Χριστιανοί or Χρηστ- (Ac. xi. 26), may have been a nickname used by opponents; 'quos illudentes Pharisaei . . . Herodianos vocabant' (Jer.). Jos. BJ. I. xvi. 6 has Ἡρωδεῖος. They are mentioned elsewhere in Mk. iii. 6 only, as com-

bining with the Pharisees against Jesus in Galilee; and see on Mt. xvi. 6. The same party had probably come up for the feast, perhaps in company with Herod. Since he was appointed by Rome, and superintended, among other things, the payment of taxes, the Herodians would support the payment, while the patriotic Pharisees hated it. They now asked Jesus His opinion on the burning question which divided them. If He pronounced in favour of the tax, He would make Himself unpopular with the people; if against it, which was what they desired, they would have a ground of accusation against Him.

διδάσκαλε κτλ.] See on vii. 21. Mt., placing in pairs the positives and the negatives, brings together the two statements about truth, which Mk. places first and last : the Lord's character and teaching were alike true, and they no doubt knew it though they spoke ironically. ἀληθής (so Mk.) is characteristic of the 4th Gosp., but is not found elsewhere in the synn. Lk. ὀρθῶς λέγεις καὶ διδάσκεις. The ὁδὸς τ. θεοῦ is 'the manner of life required by God'; see on xxi. 32. Smith, JThS., Jan. 1915, 242.

καὶ οὐ μέλει κτλ.] Cf. Mk. iv. 38, Lk. x. 40, Job xxii. 3. They knew also, though still speaking ironically, that He was fearlessly impartial, and would shew it in replying to their question. βλέπ. εἰς πρόσωπον, 'to pay regard to appearance,' to be biassed by a man's wealth or position, is not found elsewhere; but cf. 1 Regn. xvi. 7, ἄνθρωπος

βλέπεις εἰς πρόσωπον ἀνθρώπων· εἰπὸν οὖν ἡμῖν τί σοι 17
δοκεῖ· ἔξεστιν δοῦναι κῆνσον Καίσαρι ἢ οὔ; γνοὺς δὲ 18
ὁ Ἰησοῦς τὴν πονηρίαν αὐτῶν εἶπεν Τί με πειράζετε,
ὑποκριταί; ἐπιδείξατέ μοι τὸ νόμισμα τοῦ κήνσου. οἱ 19
δὲ προσήνεγκαν αὐτῷ δηνάριον. καὶ λέγει αὐτοῖς Τίνος 20
ἡ εἰκὼν αὕτη καὶ ἡ ἐπιγραφή; λέγουσιν Καίσαρος. τότε 21
λέγει αὐτοῖς Ἀπόδοτε οὖν τὰ Καίσαρος Καίσαρι καὶ τὰ

ὄψεται εἰς πρ. (יְרָאֶה לְעֵינָיִם). The
usual expressions for partiality are
הִכִּיר פָּנִים (LXX. ἐπιγνῶναι, αἰδεῖσθαι,
αἰσχύνεσθαι πρ.), and " נָשָׂא פ (LXX.
θαυμάζειν [cf. Jude 16], λαμβάνειν,
ὑποστέλλεσθαι πρ.). Lk. here has
οὐ λαμβάνεις πρ., and in the N.T.
(not LXX.) occur προσωπολημπτεῖν
(Jam. ii. 9), -πτης (Ac. x. 34), -ψία
(Jam. ii. 1, Rom. ii. 11).

17. εἰπόν κτλ.] The first clause
is added by Mt.; on τί σοι δοκεῖ
see xvii. 25. Their question reflects
their usual plane of thought: ἔξεστιν,
is it warranted by anything in the
Law or the Scribal tradition? (cf. xii.
2, 4, 10, 12, xiv. 4, xix. 3, xxvii. 6).
It was because the Lord spoke from
a different plane that His answer, as
on other occasions, was so impreg-
nable. κῆνσος (so Mk.; Lk. φόρος),
a latinism, = census, which passed
also into Aram. as קֶנְסָא, was a
capitation-tax; D (Mk.) ἐπικεφά-
λαιον, k capitularium, ܫ (Mt.,
Mk.) 'head-money.' Besides the
indirect taxation involved in the
customs (τέλη, cf. xvii. 25), two
direct taxes were levied in the pro-
vinces (of which Judaea was now
one), the tributum soli or agri, and
the tributum capitis, the former
assessed by valuation, the latter equal
for all males over 14 and females
over 12, up to the age of 65. For
the latter tax, which was paid direct
into the imperial exchequer, silver
denaria were struck, with the figure
of Caesar and a superscription, e.g.

ΤΙΒΕΡΙΟΥ ΚΑΙΣΑΡΟΣ. Apart
from their hatred of the foreign
domination, the figure was deeply
offensive to the Jews as savouring of
idolatry. See Schürer, HJP. I. ii.
77, 109 ff., HDB. 'Money' iii. 428,
and photograph no. 13 before p. 425.

18. γνοὺς δέ κτλ.] Mk. ὁ δὲ
εἰδὼς (? ἰδὼν) αὐτῶν τὴν ὑπόκρισιν,
Lk. κατανοήσας δὲ αὐτῶν τὴν παν-
ουργίαν describe the penetration with
which He perceived their cunning at
the moment. Mt. reflects on their
character as a body: 'recognizing
their (habitual) wickedness,' i.e. recognizing that this was an instance
of it. ὑποκριταί (see on vi. 2) is
added after Mk.'s τί με πειράζετε;

19. τὸ νόμισμα κτλ.] Mk., Lk.
δηνάριον. The 'coin of the tax'
being required only at the periods
when the tax was due, neither the Lord,
nor perhaps any of the audience, had
one at hand. If so, the delay would
heighten the interest and increase
the number of the bystanders. For
νόμισμα (a ἅπαξ λεγ. in the N.T.),
cf. 1 Mac. xv. 6 and a v.l. Neh.
vii. 71. Sym. uses it for a small
coin, gerah (Num. iii. 47), keṣiṭah
(Job xlii. 11). In 2 Esd. viii. 36
it means 'a decree.'

20. τίνος κτλ.] The fourth
question that the Lord put to His
opponents (see xxi. 25, 31, 40); in
every case, according to Mt., their
answer was turned against them.

21. ἀπόδοτε κτλ.] The questioners
had said δοῦναι (v. 17), as though of

22 τοῦ θεοῦ τῷ θεῷ. καὶ ἀκούσαντες ἐθαύμασαν, καὶ ἀφέντες
αὐτὸν ἀπῆλθαν.

23 Ἐν ἐκείνῃ τῇ ἡμέρᾳ προσῆλθον αὐτῷ Σαδδουκαῖοι,
24 λέγοντες μὴ εἶναι ἀνάστασιν, καὶ ἐπηρώτησαν αὐτὸν
λέγοντες Διδάσκαλε, Μωυσῆς εἶπεν Ἐὰν τιϲ ἀποθάνη μη

23 λέγοντες] אBD al 𝔏 ff¹ [negantes] 𝔖 sin.cur.pesh ['and they say to him'] ;
pr οι אCE al 𝔏 vet.vg 𝔖 hcl.pal me sah arm

a gift which might be withheld; the
Lord replies with ἀπόδοτε, the payment of a rightful due. With their
nationalist notions of a political
theocracy they thought that Caesar's
government and God's were incompatible; see the words of Judas the
Gaulonite (Jos. *Ant.* XVIII. i. 1), and
Eleazar (*BJ.* VII. viii. 6). The answer
of Jesus shewed that it was not so.
That which is stamped with a man's
image is his property; Caesar's coins
were therefore his, and must obviously
be rendered to him; but that did
not prevent God's property from
being rendered to Him. τὰ τοῦ
θεοῦ would suggest to the audience
sacrifices (cf. Heb. v. 1, τὰ πρὸς τὸν
θεόν) and other dues. But it is
possible that the thought of εἰκών
also underlay the words: man was
made κατ' εἰκόνα θεοῦ (Gen. i. 27),
so that τὰ τοῦ θεοῦ embrace a man's
whole being and life, including his
civil duties. Though the spiritual
was of greater importance than the
temporal, which was so soon to come
to an end, yet the two cannot clash
in so far as the greater includes the
less. If this reads more into the
words than was intended, yet they
formed the basis of the attitude of
S. Paul and S. Peter: submission to
civil government must be rendered
'for conscience' sake,' and 'for the
Lord's sake' (Rom. xiii. 1-7, 1 Pet.
ii. 13-17); see Sand. Headl. *Romans*,
369-72.

22. καὶ ἀκούσαντες κτλ.] They

must have been astonished (Mk.
ἐξεθαύμαζον) not only at His alert-
ness, but also, like the common
people (v. 33, vii. 28 f.), at His aloofness from their plane of thought.
Lk. adds ἐσίγησαν. In Mt. their
departure (see on xxi. 46) makes
way for the Sadducees who now
approach.

23-33. (Mk. xii. 18-27, Lk. xx.
27-40.) THE QUESTION ABOUT THE
RESURRECTION.

23. ἐν ἐκείνῃ κτλ.] The note of
time is given by Mt. only; but
though the conversation, unlike the
foregoing, is 'a theological debate of
the most objective kind' (J. Weiss),
there is no reason why it should not
have been held on the same day.
The Sadducees (see Add. n. after v.
33) already mentioned five times in
Mt. (iii. 7, xvi. 1, 6, 11 f.), appear
for the first time in Mk., Lk. The
reading λέγοντες, in the best MSS.,
represents the denial of the Resurrection as forming the beginning of
their conversation with Jesus; but
Mk. οἵτινες λέγουσιν, and Lk. οἱ
λέγοντες, shew that οἱ, omitted
accidentally after Σαδδουκαῖοι, is
rightly restored in the lesser uncials.
On the growth of the doctrine of a
general Resurrection see Volz, *Jüd.
Esch.* 127 ff.

24. διδάσκαλε κτλ.] See vii. 21.
They employ a paraphrase, differing
in each of the synn., of Dt. xxv. 5,
where the provision of the Levirate

ἔχων τέκνα, ἐπιγαμβρεύσει ὁ ἀδελφὸς αὐτοῦ τὴν γυναῖκα αὐτοῦ
καὶ ἀναστήσει σπέρμα τῷ ἀδελφῷ αὐτοῦ. ἦσαν δὲ παρ᾽ ἡμῖν 25
ἑπτὰ ἀδελφοί· καὶ ὁ πρῶτος γήμας ἐτελεύτησεν, καὶ μὴ
ἔχων σπέρμα ἀφῆκεν τὴν γυναῖκα αὐτοῦ τῷ ἀδελφῷ αὐτοῦ·
ὁμοίως καὶ ὁ δεύτερος καὶ ὁ τρίτος, ἕως τῶν ἑπτά· ὕστερον 26
δὲ πάντων ἀπέθανεν ἡ γυνή. ἐν τῇ ἀναστάσει οὖν τίνος 28
τῶν ἑπτὰ ἔσται γυνή ; πάντες γὰρ ἔσχον αὐτήν. ἀποκριθεὶς 29
δὲ ὁ Ἰησοῦς εἶπεν αὐτοῖς Πλανᾶσθε μὴ εἰδότες τὰς γραφὰς
μηδὲ τὴν δύναμιν τοῦ θεοῦ· ἐν γὰρ τῇ ἀναστάσει οὔτε 30

marriage is only for two brothers living on the same estate; and in the Heb. it is valid when the deceased brother leaves no *male* issue (בֵּן), but the LXX. has σπέρμα; cf. Jos. *Ant.* IV. viii. 23 (ἄτεκνος). See Driver, *Deut. ad loc.* The clause ἀναστήσει κτλ. is drawn from Gen. xxxviii. 8, which relates an instance of the practice; and Mt.'s ἐπιγαμβρεύσει, a technical term (=יִבֵּם) for which Mk., Lk. have λάβῃ (as in LXX. Deut. *l.c.* λήμψεται), is derived from the same passage. Aq. uses the verb in Deut. *l.c.*; in the LXX. it stands elsewhere for הִתְחַתֵּן, without the Levirate meaning.

25. ἦσαν δέ κτλ.] In Mk., Lk. a hypothetical case is put; Mt.'s addition παρ᾽ ἡμῖν represents it as an actual recent occurrence. It is probable that the Levirate custom was exceptional in the time of Jesus, though it was theoretically upheld in late Rabbinic law. The ceremony of חֲלִיצָה ('shoe-loosing,' Deut. xxv. 9) practically replaced it. For the Attic γήμας cf. Lk. xiv. 20, 1 Cor. vii. 28 ; D *al* have the later γαμήσας.

καὶ μὴ ἔχων κτλ.] An expansion of Mk.'s καὶ ἀποθνήσκων οὐκ ἀφῆκεν σπέρμα, transferring the verb so as to give it a more ordinary meaning.

26. ὁμοίως κτλ.] Mt. avoids Mk.'s redundant repetition of the points in the case.

28. ἐν τῇ ἀναστάσει κτλ.] The question ridicules the idea of a future life, as materialistically understood by many of the Jews ; 'the second life only the first renewed' ; see Enoch x. 17, and a passage from *Sohar* quoted by Swete. The official doctrine of later Rabbis, however, was more spiritual ; see *Berak.* 17 a, quoted by Montefiore on Mk. xii. 18. As before, the questioners' thoughts were on a different plane from the Lord's, and He evaded the dilemma by rising above it. ἀνάστασις is the state of existence consequent upon rising; cf. ἐν τῇ παλινγενεσίᾳ (xix. 28).

29. πλανᾶσθε κτλ.] Mk. οὐ διὰ τοῦτο πλ., explaining more distinctly that ignorance was the cause of their mistake. In this, the priestly *élites* were like the priests of old (Hos. iv. 6, Jer. xiv. 18, Mal. ii. 1–8). They were ignorant not only of the true meaning of God's word (*v.* 31), but also of the true nature of His power over human destiny (*v.* 30). Cf. 1 Cor. xv. 33 f., μὴ πλανᾶσθε . . . ἀγνωσίαν γὰρ θεοῦ τινὲς ἔχουσιν. 'The Power of God' is a periphrasis for the divine name in Lk. xxii. 69 ('the Power' Mt. xxvi. 64, Mk.), and 'Power' is sometimes an effluence or emanation from God (Ac. viii. 10; cf. Lk. i. 35, v. 17, xxiv. 49); but here it is simply 'what God can do'; cf. τὸ δυνατὸν αὐτοῦ (Rom. ix. 22).

30. ἐν γάρ κτλ.] Though rejecting the materialistic conception of

γαμοῦσιν οὔτε γαμίζονται, ἀλλ' ὡς ἄγγελοι ἐν τῷ οὐρανῷ
31 εἰσίν· περὶ δὲ τῆς ἀναστάσεως τῶν νεκρῶν οὐκ ἀνέγνωτε
32 τὸ ῥηθὲν ὑμῖν ὑπὸ τοῦ θεοῦ λέγοντος Ἐγώ εἰμι ὁ θεὸς Ἀβραὰμ

the Resurrection, they knew no
other ; Jesus puts before them something more spiritual. S. Paul, confronted by the same materialism,
summed up his answer in the far-
reaching paradox 'it is raised a
spiritual body' (1 Cor. xv. 35–44).
For the late γαμίζειν cf. xxiv. 38,
Lk. xvii. 27, xx. 35, 1 Cor. vii. 38,
ἐκγαμίζειν or γαμίσκειν being a
variant in every case. The addition
of θεοῦ after ἄγγελοι in אL was
probably due to the LXX. (cf. Lk. xii.
8 f., xv. 10, Jo. i. 51 [LXX.], Heb. i.
6 [LXX.]).

Lk. words the reply of Jesus very
differently : ' the sons of this age
marry and are given in marriage
(or ? beget and are begotten ; see
Burkitt, *Ev. da Meph.* ii. 299) ; but
they that are counted worthy to
obtain that age and the resurrection
from the dead neither marry nor
are given in marriage ; nor can they
die any more, for they are angelic
(ἰσάγγελοι), and are sons of God,
being sons of the resurrection.' Lk.,
or some source which he employs,
may have adopted an explanatory
paraphrase heard from the lips of a
Jewish-Christian preacher. It introduces the new thought that when
there is no death, marriage for the
propagation of the race will be unnecessary.

31. περὶ δέ κτλ.] On οὐκ ἀνέγνωτε see xii. 3. The nature of
resurrection has been declared ; the
fact is now proved from Scripture.
S. Paul treats these in the converse
order (1 Cor. xv. 1–34 and 35–57).
For τὸ ῥηθέν see i. 22. That which
was said (to Moses) was said to you
(cf. xix. 8). Blass unnecessarily omits
ὑμῖν, with very slight authority. In

Mk., the Lord refers to the section
in Exodus, ἐν τῇ βίβλῳ Μωυσέως
ἐπὶ τοῦ βάτου (see Swete) ; in Lk.,
Moses is made the speaker of the
words, καὶ Μ. ἐμήνυσεν ἐπὶ τῆς
βάτου, ὡς λέγει κτλ.

32. ἐγώ εἰμι κτλ.] From Exod.
iii. 6. The repetition of θεός in
Exod. gives a sonorous solemnity ;
but religious reflexion can find in
it an emphasis on 'the distinct
relation in which God stands to
each individual saint' (Swete). The
argument is this : God cannot be a
God of those who are dead ; but
God said He was the God of the
patriarchs ; therefore, though they
died long before, they were not
dead. This presents two difficulties :
(1) It is an *argumentum ad literam*,
which, though it would appeal to
His hearers, is unlike the Lord's
usual methods of reference to the
O.T. In Exod. the words mean
that Yahweh is the God whom
Moses' father and the patriarchs
used to worship. The doctrine of
the resurrection is made to stand
on the use of the genitives with
θεός. A profound truth, however,
is involved, and the possibility must
be allowed that Jesus condescended
to a rabbinic style of argument.
(2) An existence of the personality
after the death of the body, which
the words support, is not equivalent
to the resurrection of the body ; the
latter does not follow from the
argument, unless the patriarchs were
already 'raised' in the body when
God spoke, for which there is no
evidence elsewhere, Jewish or Christian. The utmost that the argument
yields is that they, and therefore
other dead persons, not being really

καὶ ὁ θεὸc Ἰcαὰκ καὶ ὁ θεὸc Ἰακώβ; οὐκ ἔστιν ὁ θεὸς νεκρῶν
ἀλλὰ ζώντων. Καὶ ἀκούσαντες οἱ ὄχλοι ἐξεπλήσσοντο 33
ἐπὶ τῇ διδαχῇ αὐτοῦ.

32 ο θεος⁴°] BLΔ 1 33 157* 209 238 me sah ; *om* ο אD 28 67 *al* ; *add* θεος EF *etc*
minn.*pler* 𝔖 hcl arm [(ο) θεος *solum* 𝕷 *omn* 𝔖 sin.cur.pesh.pal]

dead are *capable* of resurrection. It
is true that 'the resurrection of the
body follows, when it is understood
that the body is a true part of
human nature' (Swete); but this
corollary is not attributed to Jesus.
It is not impossible that the mention
of 'the Scriptures' (*v.* 29) led early
preachers to supply a proof from
the O.T.

οὐκ ἔστιν κτλ.] In Mk., and
perhaps here, the true reading is
οὐκ ἔστιν θεός, 'He is not a God
of dead persons,' or, less probably,
'there does not exist a God of dead
persons.' The former seems to be
supported by 𝔖 sin.cur, 'and lo the
God not of the dead but of the
living.' Lk. places θεός with emphasis
at the beginning : 'but *God* [*i.e.* One
who can bear that title] is not (a God)
of the dead.' Copyists seemed to

have assumed a similar ellipse of
θεός before νεκρῶν in Mt., Mk., ὁ θεός
becoming the subject of ἔστιν ; later
uncials went further and supplied
the ellipse by a second θεός before
νεκρῶν. Lk. adds the reflexion
πάντες γὰρ αὐτῷ ζῶσιν, life is not
life except in relation to Him ; cf.
4 Macc. vii. 19, xvi. 25. Mk. adds
πολὺ πλανᾶσθε.

33. καὶ ἀκούσαντες κτλ.] Doubtless a constant effect of the Lord's
teaching ; cf. vii. 28, Mk. xi. 18.
Mk. gives no conclusion to the
incident ; Lk. frames one by adapting Mk.'s beginning and ending
of the following incident (which
he gives elsewhere, x. 25–28), *i.e.*
the approval of certain of the
Scribes, and 'for they no longer
dared to ask him anything' (see
v. 46 below).

Additional Note on the Sadducees.

The Sadducees were the 'modernists' of their day, and comparatively
few in number. Connected with the best priestly families (Ac. v. 17, Jos.
Ant. xx. ix. 1), their aims were rather political than religious. They were
aristocrats, who 'persuaded only the well-to-do, and had no following among
the masses' (*Ant.* XIII. x. 6). Sympathizing with the *Aufklärung* brought
about by contact with Greek thought and customs, they despised, as a class,
the legalism of the patriotic Pharisees, and their ardent hopes of deliverance
from foreign rule and of the glories of a future age, and hence lent no
countenance to the scribal tradition, nor to the apocalyptic literature, which
taught for the most part the continued life of the soul and future rewards
and punishments. Though there is no contemporary evidence that they
rejected any part of the O.T. canon (as stated, *e.g.*, by Origen on *vv.* 29, 31 f.
of this chapter), yet they adhered mainly to the Pentateuchal law and to
the early stages of Israelite thought. To the Jewish religious thought of
their day, their attitude was one of contemptuous aloofness. Their denial,
therefore, of a resurrection (see the dispute between Gamliel II. and some

34   Οἱ δὲ Φαρισαῖοι ἀκούσαντες ὅτι ἐφίμωσεν τοὺς Σαδ-
35 δουκαίους συνήχθησαν ἐπὶ τὸ αὐτό. καὶ ἐπηρώτησεν εἷς
36 ἐξ αὐτῶν νομικὸς πειράζων αὐτόν Διδάσκαλε, ποία ἐντολὴ

34 επι το αυτο] uncc [exc D] 𝕷 ff¹ g¹·² q vg 𝕾 pesh.hcl.pal me arm ; επ' αυτον D
𝕷 b c e f ff² h 𝕾 sin.cur aeth   35 νομικος] om 1 118 209 𝕷 e 𝕾 sin

Sadducees in *Sanh.* 90 b, 91 a), and of the existence of angels and spirits
(Ac. xxiii. 8 ; cf. Jos. *Ant.* XVIII. i. 4, *BJ.* II. viii. 14), were not the only, or
perhaps even the principal, features of their 'advanced' views. See, *e.g.*,
their assertion of man's freedom of will, and denial of Fate and Providence
(Jos. *Ant.* XIII. v. 9, *BJ. l.c.*).

Their name Σαδδουκαῖοι is derived from Zadok (צָדוֹק), the double δ
being due to the (perhaps more original) form Σαδδούκ, which occurs eleven
times in LXX^B and occasionally in Lucan MSS. Who this Zadok was supposed to be is uncertain, but he was probably the priest appointed by
Solomon (1 Kings ii. 35), from whom the more important priests of the
second temple traced their descent (Ez. xl. 46 etc., 1 Chr. vi. 53 [38], ix. 11).
Schürer (*HJP.* II. ii. 1–43) gives a useful account of both the Sadducees
and the Pharisees. On a party of reformed Sadducees see Charles, *Fragments
of a Zadokite Work,* Introd.

34–40. (Mk. xii. 28–34, Lk. x.
25–28.) THE QUESTION ABOUT THE
GREAT COMMANDMENT.

34. οἱ δὲ Φαρισαῖοι κτλ.] Mt.
alone relates, as in *v.* 15, an action
of the Pharisees as a party. Their
delight at the discomfiture of the
Sadducees draws them together (ἐπὶ
τὸ αὐτό, cf. Lk. xvii. 35) in the
crowd. The expression was possibly
suggested by Ps. ii. 2, a point which
is missed in the *v.l.* ἐπ' αὐτόν, though
the thought of hostility is retained ;
cf. Ac. iv. 26 f., where the words from
the Ps. are followed by συνήχθησαν
. . . ἐπὶ τὸν ἅγιον παῖδά σου Ἰησοῦν.
On φιμοῦν see *v.* 12 ; Mt. perhaps
uses it here contemptuously. Mk.
καλῶς ἀπεκρίθη αὐτοῖς.

35. καὶ ἐπηρώτησεν κτλ.] On εἷς
=τις see viii. 19. νομικός, as a
subst., is elsewhere confined to Lk.[6],
except Tit. iii. 13. Mk. has its
equivalent γραμματεύς (so 𝕾 cur
here); cf. νομοδιδάσκαλος (Lk. v. 17,
Ac. v. 34). It should perhaps be
omitted. If it is genuine, Mt. must

have retained it from Q, but in
xxiii. 2, 13 he prefers γραμματεῖς
where Lk. (xi. 46, 52) has νομικοί.
On the Scribes see v. 20. The
question propounded did not, like
those in *vv.* 17, 28, offer a dilemma
or a snare ; in πειράζων αὐτόν Mt.'s
anti-Pharisaic feeling shews itself. In
Mk. the Scribe evinced no hostility ;
he spoke with admiration, and was
earnestly commended. Aug.: 'tentans
accesserit, domini tamen responsione
correctus est' (*De Cons. Ev.* ii. 141)
does not meet the difficulty. Lk. has
ἐκπειράζων αὐτὸν λέγων, but the two
participles are awkward, and in
several MSS. the correction καὶ λέγων
was made. ἐκπ. αὐτόν was probably
a scribal addition to Lk. from Mt.

36. διδάσκαλε κτλ.] See on vii.
21. Mk. ποία ἐστὶν ἐντ. πρώτη
πάντων; he never uses the word
νόμος. The Scribes recognized that
commandments in the Law were of
varying degrees of importance (see
on v. 19), and the questioner asked.
which of them (ποία = τίς, see on

μεγάλη ἐν τῷ νόμῳ; ὁ δὲ ἔφη αὐτῷ Ἀγαπήσεις Κύριον 37 τὸν θεόν coy ἐν ὅλη καρδίᾳ coy καὶ ἐν ὅλη τῇ ψυχῇ coy καὶ ἐν ὅλη τῇ διανοίᾳ coy· αὕτη ἐστὶν ἡ μεγάλη καὶ πρώτη ἐντολή. 38 δευτέρα ὁμοία αὕτη Ἀγαπήσεις τὸν πλησίον coy ὡς ceαγτόν. 39 ἐν ταύταις ταῖς δυσὶν ἐντολαῖς ὅλος ὁ νόμος κρέμαται καὶ 40

xix. 18), or, less probably, what class of commandment, in the estimation of Jesus, stood first. For μεγάλη = μεγίστη see v. 19 ; the superl. occurs only in 2 Pet. i. 4, and is rare in the LXX. except in 2, 3, 4 Macc.

37. ἀγαπήσεις κτλ.] From Deut. vi. 5. Mt., Lk. omit the preceding verse of Deut. which Mk. gives, ἄκουε Ἰσραήλ, κύριος ὁ θεὸς ἡμῶν κύριος εἷς ἐστιν. Deut. vi. 4–9, containing the central article of Israel's creed, together with xi. 13–21, Num. xv. 37–41, was called the *Shᵉmaʿ* ('Hear') from its opening word, and as a recognized formula 'undoubtedly belongs to the time of Christ' (Schürer, *HJP.* II. ii. 77, 84). Deut. has ἐξ ὅλης τῆς διανοίας σου (לְבָבֶךָ), καὶ ἐξ ὅλ. τ. ψυχῆς σ., κ. ἐξ ὅλ. τ. δυνάμεως σ. (מְאֹדֶךָ), ἐξ being a loose rendering of בְּ. All the synn. agree in writing 'with all thy heart' as the beginning of the series, which is probably due to 4 Regn. xxiii. 25, where Josiah is said to have 'turned to the Lord with all his heart (καρδία, לְבָבוֹ), and with all his strength (ἰσχύι, מְאֹדוֹ), and with all his soul' (A with M.T. transposes ἰσχύι and ψυχῇ as in Lk.). Thus καρδία and διάνοια in the synn. have the effect of a double rendering of the same Heb. word : they are sometimes interchanged in LXX. text and MSS. (Hatch, *Essays,* 104). The same passage probably accounts for the ἰσχύς clause in Mk., Lk., which Mt. omits, and for the use of ἐν instead of ἐξ in Mt., Lk., *i.e.* in Q. See *Oxf. Stud.* 41–5, and Add. n. below.

On the distinction between ἀγαπᾶν and φιλεῖν see x. 37.

38. αὕτη κτλ.] This takes the place of Mk.'s πρώτη ἐστιν, which precedes the quotation.

39. δευτέρα κτλ.] 'A second similar (one) is this.' The difficulty of the text, supported by the lesser uncials (א is without accents or breathings) entitles it to consideration ; but it may be a mechanical repetition of the preceding αὕτη, under the influence of Mk.'s δευτέρα αὕτη. The minn. and versions support αὐτῇ (D ταύτῃ), and B has δευτέρα ὁμοίως without the pronoun. Lk. adds the following quotation without intervening words in the form καὶ τὸν πλησίον κτλ. It is taken from Lev. xix. 18, already quoted in Mt. v. 43, xix. 19. The Lord's comment upon its meaning as Mt. gives it consists in coupling it with the previous commandment as similar to it in content and importance. Love to God and neighbour is the highest application of τὰ τοῦ θεοῦ and τὰ Καίσαρος. See also 1 Jo. iv. 21. R. Aḳiba is said to have described the second of these commandments as the greatest in the Law (*Siphra* on Lev. xix. 18, *Ber. R.* xxiv.). The double injunction was perhaps known as a summary of duties before the time of Jesus ; cf. *Test.* Issach. 5 ἀγαπᾶτε Κύριον καὶ τὸν πλησίον, *id.* 7 τὸν Κύριον ἠγάπησα ἐν πάσῃ ἰσχύι μου· ὁμοίως καὶ πάντα ἄνθρωπον ἠγάπησα. See also *Test. Dan* 5.

40. ἐν ταύταις κτλ.] Mk. μείζων τούτων ἄλλη ἐντολὴ οὐκ ἔστιν. All

41 οἱ προφῆται.   Συνηγμένων δὲ τῶν Φαρισαίων ἐπηρώ-

the religious and moral demands in Scripture are valid because they can be ultimately traced to these two. For the metaphor cf. Is. xxii. 24; and see Gen. xliv. 30 (LXX.), Judith viii. 24, *Berak.* 63 a 'Which is a small sentence, and yet one on which all essentials of the Law hang?' (The answer is Prov. iii. 6.) Class. exx. are given by B. Weiss.. The verse should be studied in connexion with v. 17, vii. 12; as there, it is probable that 'and the prophets' is a later addition: it seems to be attached as an afterthought to the sing. verb, and in *v.* 36 the lawyer does not mention the prophets.

Mt. omits Mk.'s conclusion, that the Scribe approved of the answer, adding that the keeping of these two commandments 'is more than all the whole burnt-offerings and sacrifices (*sc.* enjoined in the Law). And Jesus, seeing that he answered with understanding (νουνεχῶς), said to him, Thou art not far from the Kingdom of God.' And he postpones till *v.* 46 Mk.'s last sentence, 'and no one any longer dared to question Him.' This is unexpected in Mk., after the friendly conversation with the Scribe. J. Weiss (*Das ält. Ev.* 282) suggests that it originally belonged to the incident of the capitation-tax, and that the two intervening sections are not in their true position.

Additional Note on xxii. 34–40.

The section is instructive from the point of view of synoptic study. Lk. (x. 25–28) gives it in a different context from Mt., Mk. The question asked is different: 'Teacher, by doing what shall I inherit eternal life?' Cf. Lk. xviii. 18. Jesus does not adduce Scripture in reply, but makes the lawyer do so by asking him 'What is written in the Law? How readest thou?' and his answer omits the opening words of the Sh^ema', which Mk. gives. In the quotation from Deut. Lk. has ἐξ once and ἐν thrice, while Mk. has ἐξ and Mt. ἐν throughout, and the second quotation follows immediately. And he omits Mk.'s conclusion. These differences are such that Lk.'s section can hardly be considered a reproduction of Mk.'s. He agrees with Mk. (*a*) in recording that the Lord commended the lawyer (ὀρθῶς ἀπεκρίθη), (*b*) in the addition of the ἰσχύς clause, though he places it before, Mk. after, the διάνοια clause, (*c*) in the use of ἐξ in the καρδία clause. But (*a*) Q as well as Mk. probably contained a commendation which Mt.'s anti-Pharisaic feeling led him to omit; (*b*) the explanation of the ἰσχύς clause is disputed: Hawkins thinks that Mk. and Lk. derived it independently from 4 Regn. xxiii. 25, others that it is a Marcan reminiscence of Q; (*c*) the use of ἐξ is due to the LXX. of Deut. Lk.'s account, therefore, is probably quite independent of Mk.'s, and is derived from Q, while Mt.'s combines features from both Mk. and Q.

41–46. (Mk. xii. 35–37 a, Lk. xx. 41–44.) THE LORD'S QUESTION ABOUT THE SON OF DAVID.

41. συνηγμένων κτλ.] As before, Mt. alone represents the Pharisees as combining in a distinct group, συνηγμένων carrying on the συνήχ-θησαν of v. 34. Allen is perhaps right in seeing in the frequent mention of the Pharisees (xxi. 45,

τησεν αὐτοὺς ὁ Ἰησοῦς λέγων Τί ὑμῖν δοκεῖ περὶ τοῦ 42
χριστοῦ; τίνος υἱός ἐστιν; λέγουσιν αὐτῷ Τοῦ Δαυείδ.
λέγει αὐτοῖς Πῶς οὖν Δαυεὶδ ἐν πνεύματι καλεῖ αὐτὸν 43
κύριον λέγων

ΕἶπΕΝ ΚΎΡΙΟϹ τῷ κΥρίῳ ΜΟΥ   ΚΆΘΟΥ ἐκ ΔΕΞΙῶΝ ΜΟΥ   44
ἔωϲ ἄΝ θῶ τοΫϹ ἐχθροΫϹ ϹοΥ ὙποκΆτω τῶΝ ποΔῶΝ ϹοΥ.

xxii. 15, 34, 41) a preparation for the following chapter of denunciations against them. Mk.'s καὶ ἀποκριθεὶς (see on Mt. xi. 25) ὁ Ἰησοῦς ἔλεγεν διδάσκων ἐν τῷ ἱερῷ gives no time connexion with the last incident. Lk.'s εἶπεν δὲ πρὸς αὐτούς probably refers to the people in general, not to the Sadducees in his foregoing section. Spitta adopts the latter, and sees the true connexion of thought in Lk.'s sequence : as human marriages, so the Messiah's human sonship will count for nothing in the coming age (*Streitfragen*, 152 ff.) ; on the Sadducees' theory that there is no resurrection, how can David speak of his son as his Lord ? He is his son in this age, but his 'Lord in the age to come (*Synopt. Grund- schrift*, 325 f.).

42. τί ὑμῖν δοκεῖ κτλ.] With this characteristic phrase (see on xvii. 25) Mt. alters Mk.'s πῶς λέγουσιν οἱ γραμματεῖς into a question addressed to them. Lk. has the impers. πῶς λέγουσιν. The use of the title ὁ χριστός 'the Messiah' is seldom attributed to Jesus : xxiii. 10, xxiv. 5, 23 (Mk. xiii. 21), Lk. xxiv. 26, 46. On the Jewish use see Dalman, *Words*, 289– 94. In Mk., Lk. Jesus assumes, as a current opinion, that the Messiah is Son of David (see Dalm. *op. cit.* 316 ff.), in Mt. the Pharisees are made to reply in such a way that their answer is turned against them, as in xxi. 31, 41, xxii. 21.

43. πῶς οὖν κτλ.] David was inspired ; cf. Ae. i. 16, ii. 30, 2

Sam. xxiii. 2. He spoke 'in a state of spirit ' ; cf. Ez. xi. 24, xxxvii. 1, Lk. ii. 27, Apoc. i. 10. Mk. ἐν τῷ πν. τῷ ἁγίῳ. Allen cites ' David said in the Holy Spirit ' as a rabb. formula ; see Wünsche, *Neue Beitr.* 270, Bacher, *Exeg. Term.* ii. 202 ff. In καλεῖ αὐτ. κύριον Mt. (not Mk., Lk.) anticipates the point of the following quotation.

On the Jewish opinions with regard to the Davidic authorship and editorship of the Psalms see Briggs, *Psalms*, i. p. liv. : Jesus was 'arguing with the Pharisees in the *Halacha* method on the basis of received opinion. There were no good reasons why Jesus and the Apostles should depart from these opinions, even if they did not share them. There was no reason why Jesus as a teacher should have come to any other opinion on this subject than his contemporaries held.' The mystery of ' the One Christ' will remain a mystery, but the fact that there were limits to His human knowledge in intellectual matters is an axiom of modern study. The point of His words, however, lies not in the fact that He thought David to be the author of Ps. cx., but that His opponents did.

44. εἶπεν κτλ.] נְאֻם יְהוָה לַאדֹנִי 'an utterance of Yahweh to my lord.' From Ps. cix. [cx.] 1, quoted also in Ac. ii. 34 f., and (from κάθου) Heb. i. 13, and alluded to in 1 Cor. xv. 25, Eph. i. 20, 22, Heb. x. 13 ; references to the Session occur in Ac. vii. 55 f., Rom. viii. 34, Col. iii.

45 εἰ οὖν Δαυεὶδ καλεῖ αὐτὸν κύριον, πῶς υἱὸς αὐτοῦ ἐστίν;
46 καὶ οὐδεὶς ἐδύνατο ἀποκριθῆναι αὐτῷ λόγον, οὐδὲ ἐτόλμησέν
τις ἀπ᾽ ἐκείνης τῆς ἡμέρας ἐπερωτῆσαι αὐτὸν οὐκέτι.

1, Heb. i. 3, viii. 1, xii. 2, 1 Pet.
iii. 22. All the synn. and Ac. have
the proper name Κύριος for LXX. ὁ
κύριος. The substitution of ὑποκάτω
(Mt., Mk.) for ὑποπόδιον (LXX., Lk.,
Ac., Heb.) may have been due to
Ps. viii. 7 (cf. 1 Cor., Eph. ll.c.). ἕως
does not place a limit to the duration
of the Session, but marks an epoch
or turning-point in the future ; cf.
Hos. x. 12 (see BDB. עַד, II. 1 b).

The Lord assumed that Ps. cx.
referred to the Messiah, but not, as
in the case of the Davidic sonship,
that this was a current opinion ; to
His hearers the interpretation was
probably new. Though the Simil.
Enoch (xlv. 3, li. 3, lv. 4, lxi. 8,
lxii. 2) speak of the Messiah as
sitting upon the throne of God, and
in Test. Levi viii., xviii. a Priest-King
is ideally described, no direct reference to this Ps. as referring to the
personal Messiah is known in Jewish
writings until c. A.D. 260, in words
ascribed to Hamma bar Hanina, ' God
will place the Son of David on His
right hand and Abraham on His
left'; see Bacher, Ag. d. pal. Am. i.
457, and Midr. Ps. cx. 1 (Wünsche).
In Justin's day Jewish teachers
applied it to Hezekiah (Dial. 33,
83 ; cf. 56).

45. εἰ οὖν κτλ.] If David addressed the Messiah as ' Lord,'
' Master,' He must be more than
merely his son ; πλεῖον Δαυεὶδ ὧδε.
The better minds before the time of
Jesus had been feeling after the
truth that the Messiah was of divine
origin, but it did not till later take
a prominent place in Jewish thought.
To the common people, to whom,
according to Mk., Lk., He appears

to have been speaking (cf. Mk. v.
37 b), it was a new idea, put before
them with a convincing scriptural
proof. It was far from being a mere
dialectic victory, shewing that their
religious leaders misunderstood the
scriptures ; nor was He simply disclaiming for Himself an earthly
sovereignty, still less denying the
Davidic descent of the Messiah, and
therefore of Himself, an idea which,
though treated as obvious by some
modern writers, did not occur to the
early Christians ; cf. Rom. i. 3 f.
The disciples alone, who had learnt
the truth of His Messiahship, could
realize that He spoke of Himself.
Ep. Barn. xii. 10 refers to the passage
in the Psalm as proving that Jesus
was οὐχὶ υἱὸς ἀνθρώπου ἀλλὰ υἱὸς
τοῦ θεοῦ.

46. καὶ οὐδείς κτλ.] Mk., Lk.
with dramatic effectiveness close the
incident abruptly at this point. ' He
had answered all their questions ; a
single instance was enough to shew
that they could not answer His'
(Swete). οὐδὲ ἐτόλμησεν κτλ. : a
second addition by Mt., taken from
Mk. xii. 34 b, and postponed to
form a conclusion to the series of
discussions. He strengthens it by
ἀπ᾽ ἐκ. τῆς ἡμερᾶς, but since the
Lord's death was so soon to follow,
ἡμερᾶς is virtually ὥρας (the reading
of DE* 𝔏 a q 𝔖 sin.cur) ; cf. viii. 13,
ix. 22, xv. 28, xvii. 18.

xxiii. 1–36. (Mk. xii. 37 b–40 ;
on Lk. see below.) DENUNCIATIONS
AGAINST THE PHARISEES.

Mk. having preserved at this
point a warning against the Scribes,
Mt. places the discourse here, leading

Τότε ὁ Ἰησοῦς ἐλάλησεν τοῖς ὄχλοις καὶ τοῖς μαθη- 1 XXIII.
ταῖς αὐτοῦ λέγων Ἐπὶ τῆς Μωυσέως καθέδρας ἐκάθισαν 2
οἱ γραμματεῖς καὶ οἱ Φαρισαῖοι. πάντα οὖν ὅσα ἐὰν 3

to the Apostrophe to Jerusalem (*vv.*
37 ff.), and that to the eschatological
discourse (xxiv.) and parables (xxv.).
Thus chs. xxiii.–xxv. form virtually
one collection of sayings, the last of
the five principal collections in Mt.
(see on vii. 28). Many of the sayings
in the present chapter occur, in
various positions, in Lk., chiefly in
ch. xi. Mt. and Lk. seem to have
used different recensions of Q, and
Lk. or his source omits much that
would be uninteresting if not unintelligible to Gentile Christians.
The synoptic relations are as follows :

Mt.	Mk.	Lk.
v. 1	xii. 37 b, 38 a.	xx. 45
2, 3		
4		xi. 46
5		
6	39	xx. 46 c, xi. 43 a.
	38 b.	46 a.
7 a.	38 c.	46 b, xi. 43 b.
7 b–10		
11 (=xx. 26 f.)	(cf. ix. 35, x. 43 f.)	(cf. ix. 48 b, xxii. 26)
12		(cf. xiv. 11, xviii. 14)
	40	xx. 47
13		xi. 52
15–22		
23		42
24		
25, 26		39–41
27, 28		44
29–31		47, 48
32, 33		
34–36		49–51

The discourse in Mt. is arranged
in three parts : *vv.* 1–12, Warning
to the people and the disciples not
to imitate the Scribes and Pharisees
in their pride of place and power ;
vv. 13–32, Seven Woes addressed to
the Scribes and Pharisees ; *vv.* 33–36,
Warning of punishment.

1–12. (Mk., Lk. see above.) *Warning against the Scribes and Pharisees.*

1. τότε κτλ.] Mk. 'And the
multitude listened to Him with
pleasure ; and in His teaching He
said.'

2. ἐπὶ τῆς Μωυσέως κτλ.] The
heirs of Moses' authority by an
unbroken tradition can deliver *ex
cathedra* pronouncements on his
teaching. Cf. Aboth i. 1 on the
traditio legis, and Rosh ha-shanah
25 a, 'every council of three in Israel
is like the council of Moses' (cited
by Allen). The expression 'Moses'
seat' is not known again till the
4th cent. : in Pesikta 7 a Aha uses
it of a seat of a special shape (like
Solomon's throne, 1 Kings x. 19)
reserved for the president of the
Sanhedrin. See *Rev. des Études juives*,
xxxiv. 299, and Levi or Jastrow
s.v. קתדרא. Only the Scribes were
strictly the successors of Moses ;
many of them were Pharisees, but
not all Pharisees were Scribes (see on
v. 20). ἐκάθισαν (aor.) may have a
pres. force, like a Semitic perf. ; or
it may look back over the period
during which, by common consent,
the Scribes had constituted themselves Moses' successors : 'they have
occupied (Vg. *sederunt*) the seat of
M.' Less probably, 'the editor
writes from his own standpoint, and
looks back upon the period when
the Scribes and Pharisees were in
power' (Allen).

3. πάντα οὖν κτλ.] This echoes
v. 18 f., and need not be considered
'too conservatively Jewish' to be
genuine (J. Weiss) ; it is so Jewish
that it could hardly have originated
in later tradition even in Jewish-

εἴπωσιν ὑμῖν ποιήσατε καὶ τηρεῖτε, κατὰ δὲ τὰ ἔργα αὐτῶν
4 μὴ ποιεῖτε, λέγουσιν γὰρ καὶ οὐ ποιοῦσιν. δεσμεύουσιν δὲ
φορτία βαρέα καὶ ἐπιτιθέασιν ἐπὶ τοὺς ὤμους τῶν ἀνθρώπων,
αὐτοὶ δὲ τῷ δακτύλῳ αὐτῶν οὐ θέλουσιν κινῆσαι αὐτά.
5 πάντα δὲ τὰ ἔργα αὐτῶν ποιοῦσιν πρὸς τὸ θεαθῆναι τοῖς
ἀνθρώποις· πλατύνουσι γὰρ τὰ φυλακτήρια αὐτῶν καὶ

4 δε¹°] אBLMΔΠ 1 33 *al* 𝔏 a b c ff¹·² g¹·² 1 q vg 𝔖 *omn* me sah ; γαρ D*E *al* 𝔏 e f h

Christian circles. κατὰ δέ κτλ. :
but since their actions, in fact, fall
short of the ideal at which their
teaching aims, do not imitate them.
This echoes v. 20 (cf. *v.* 23 b below).
λέγουσιν κ. οὐ ποιοῦσιν : literally,
this would mean that they did not
observe the rules which they professed. But this is contrary to fact,
and is not borne out by *v.* 4 f. The
clause need not be due to Mt.'s anti-
Pharisaic feeling. It expresses para-
doxically the fact that they did not
(in God's sight) do what they appeared to do. Though they scrupulously observed their own rules, their
motive and manner deprived their
actions of all value. See vi. 1 f., 5,
16, xii. 7, xv. 7–9, Lk. xviii. 9–14.
    4. δεσμεύουσιν δέ κτλ.] δέ is
merely 'and'; the *v.l.* γάρ seems to
be due to a mistaken idea that δεσμ.
and οὐ θέλ. κινῆσαι are instances of
λέγουσιν and οὐ ποιοῦσιν respectively. Lk. xi. 46 has the 2nd pers.,
'ye burden men with grievous (δυσβάστακτα) burdens, etc.' Divine
commands are in themselves a rightful φορτίον which every man must
bear (see Lightft. on φορτίον and
βάρος, Gal. vi. 2, 5), but the Scribes
made them oppressive (βαρέα), while
the Lord's higher interpretation of
them made even τὰ βαρύτερα τοῦ
νόμου (*v.* 23) 'light'; see on xi. 30.
καὶ δυσβάστακτα (cf. Prov. xxvii. 3)
was an early addition from Lk.
    αὐτοὶ δέ κτλ.] The driver of a
beast of burden could ease it by re-

moving some of the weight that it
carried. The Scribes would not move a
finger to ease the burdens which their
rules imposed. The school of Hillel,
indeed, tended to laxity, but in the
time of Jesus they were probably in
a minority; see Add. II. on xv. 1–6.
That the Scribes would not themselves *bear* the burdens that they
imposed is contrary to fact (see
above); their observance of their
own rules is implied in τὰ ἔργα (*v.* 5).
For κινεῖν 'to move' or 'remove'
cf. Apoc. ii. 5, vi. 14, Num. xiv. 44,
Prov. xvii. 13. Lk. οὐ προσψαύετε.
    5. πάντα δέ κτλ.] They will not
ease the burdens of others, and the
manner in which they bear them
themselves is bad. The verse, peculiar
to Mt., is a commentary on *v.* 3 b :
the motive which inspired the works
annulled their value. πρὸς τὸ θεαθ.
is an echo of vi. 1.

    πλατύνουσι κτλ.] φυλακτήρια
(Vulg. *phylacteria*), class. ' fortifica-
tion' or 'outpost,' is not found in
the LXX. or elsewhere in the N.T. A
translator of Ez. xiii. 18 uses it for
כְּסָתוֹת ? 'fillets' (see Field, *Hexapla*).
Lit. 'protecting charms,' 'amulets,' it
here stands for the late Heb. *tᵉphillin*
(lit. 'prayers'), a word applied to
the small leathern cases (still worn
at the present day on the forehead
and left arm by Jews at the daily
Morning Prayer) containing four
strips of parchment inscribed with
the words of Exod. xiii. 1–10, 11–
16, Deut. vi. 4–9, xi. 13–21, which

μεγαλύνουσι τὰ κράσπεδα, φιλοῦσι δὲ τὴν πρωτοκλισίαν 6
ἐν τοῖς δείπνοις καὶ τὰς πρωτοκαθεδρίας ἐν ταῖς συναγωγαῖς καὶ τοὺς ἀσπασμοὺς ἐν ταῖς ἀγοραῖς καὶ καλεῖσθαι 7
ὑπὸ τῶν ἀνθρώπων 'Ραββεί. ὑμεῖς δὲ μὴ κληθῆτε 8
'Ραββεί, εἷς γάρ ἐστιν ὑμῶν ὁ διδάσκαλος, πάντες δὲ
ὑμεῖς ἀδελφοί ἐστε· καὶ πατέρα μὴ καλέσητε ὑμῶν ἐπὶ 9

are claimed as the scriptural authority for the practice. The first passage speaks figuratively of 'a *sign* upon thy hand' and 'a *memorial* between thine eyes,' the other three of a *sign* and *frontlets* (טוֹטָפֹת), which came to be interpreted of objects to be worn. See *HDB.*, art. 'Phylacteries.' Ϩ sin.cur render it 'the straps of their frontlets.' On κράσπεδα see ix. 20. The verse is perhaps the equivalent of περιπατεῖν ἐν στολαῖς (Mk., Lk.) interpreted with more technical Jewish knowledge.

6. φιλοῦσι κτλ.] Lk. xi. 43 (from Q) speaks of πρωτοκαθεδρία followed by ἀσπασμοί, while Mk. xii. 38 b, 39 (Lk. xx. 46) has ἐν στολαῖς περιπατεῖν—ἀσπασμοί—πρωτοκαθ-εδρίαι—πρωτοκλισίαι. Mt. adopts the last, and perhaps the first, from Mk., but places ἀσπασμοί at the end, adding further sayings about titles of respect. For πρωτοκλισία cf. Lk. xiv. 7 f., where it is contrasted with ὁ ἔσχατος τόπος ; and see Jos. *Ant.* xv. ii. 4, παρὰ τὰς ἑστιάσεις προκατακλίνων ἐξηπάτα, πατέρα καλῶν. πρωτοκαθεδρίαι : according to Tos. Megill. iv. 21 (Zuckermandel) the chief seats were on the platform facing the congregation, with their backs to the chest in which the rolls of Scripture were kept (see Edersheim, *L. and T.* i. 436). The different arrangement referred to by Schürer (*HJP.* II. ii. 75) was that of the Essenes. Neither word is known apart from the Gospels and writers who quote them.

7. καὶ καλεῖσθαι κτλ.] 'Ραββεί,

רַבִּי 'my master' (xxvi. 25, 49), from its use as a term of respect by scholars to their teachers, acquired the meaning διδάσκαλε (see on vii. 21). The reading 'Rabbi, Rabbi' (D Ϩ sin.cur Just., cf. *v.l.* Mk. xiv. 45) may be due to later Jewish usage. After N.T. times the pron. suffix lost its force, and the word became a title like *Monsieur* (see Schürer, *HJP.* II. i. 315 f.).

8. ὑμεῖς δέ κτλ.] This and *v.* 10 appear to be later additions to the Lord's words. The crowd might understand ἀδελφοί to mean 'fellow-men' or 'fellow-Jews,' but the words 'one is your Teacher,' which refer to Jesus Himself, would have no meaning for them. It is an injunction by Christian preachers to Christian 'brethren.' Blass unnecessarily adopts μαθηταί from Clem. Al.

9. καὶ πατέρα κτλ.] This saying, to which *vv.* 8, 10 were attached, is doubtless genuine, but may have been spoken in a different context. The section is a warning against imitating the Scribes in their desire for honour from men ; but this verse warns against giving to men a title due to God alone. *Abba* was not commonly a mode of address to a living person, but a title of honour for Rabbis and great men of the past ; see instances in Schürer, *HJP.* II. i. 316, Dalman, *Words*, 339 ; and cf. πατέρων ὕμνος (Sir. xliv. title) and the Mishn. *Pirke Aboth*. S. Paul (1 Cor. iv. 15) and the monks to whom Jer. refers, claimed a very different fatherhood. The awkward ὑμῶν, 'call [no one] a

10 τῆς γῆς, εἷς γάρ ἐστιν ὑμῶν ὁ πατὴρ ὁ οὐράνιος· μηδὲ
11 κληθῆτε καθηγηταί, ὅτι καθηγητὴς ὑμῶν ἐστιν εἷς ὁ χρι-
12 στός· ὁ δὲ μείζων ὑμῶν ἔσται ὑμῶν διάκονος. Ὅστις δὲ
   ὑψώσει ἑαυτὸν ταπεινωθήσεται, καὶ ὅστις ταπεινώσει ἑαυτὸν
14 ὑψωθήσεται.   Οὐαὶ δὲ ὑμῖν, γραμματεῖς καὶ Φαρισαῖοι

13 add. vers. ουαι υμιν γραμματεις και φαρισαιοι υποκριται οτι κατεσθιετε τας οικιας
των χηρων και προφασει μακρα προσευχομενοι· δια τουτο ληψεσθε περισσοτερον κριμα
EF al. mu minn.pler 𝔏 f 𝔖 pesh.hcl aeth ; eadem post v. 14 minn.nonn 𝔏 b c ff² h r
𝔖 cur.palᴬ

father of yours,' is perhaps an alteration of the Hebraic ὑμῖν (D 𝔖 sin ;
Aphr. ' for ourselves '). εἷς γάρ κτλ. :
'For one is your Father — the
heavenly (one).' On ὁ οὐράνιος see
vi. 9 b.

10. μηδέ κτλ.] καθηγητής, unique
in the Bible, is similar to ὁδηγός
(v. 24, xv. 14, Rom. ii. 19) in
describing the authority of a teacher ;
contrast ἡγούμενος (Sir. xxx. 27
[xxxiii. 19], xliv. 4, Lk. xxii. 26, Heb.
xiii. 7, 17, 24), an administrative
official. The original was probably
מוֹרֶה (Móreh) or perhaps רַב (Rab) ;
there is no reason for thinking that
while διδάσκαλος represents Rab,
καθηγητής stands for the more
honourable Rabbān, -bōn (Zahn).
It is very improbable that Jesus
described Himself, the Teacher, as
' the Messiah,' which meant something quite different both to Him
and to the Jews. The verse, with v.
8, the meaning of which is identical,
belongs to later Christian thought.
They may be a double version of one
saying.

11. ὁ δὲ μείζων κτλ.] A shorter
form of the saying in xx. 26 (Mk. x.
43 f., Lk. xxii. 26) ; a similar saying
is added in Mk. ix. 35 (Lk. ix. 48 b) ;
see on Mt. xviii. 1. μείζων ὑμ.
(= μέγιστος ὑμ. ; see on v. 19) is
equivalent to μέγας ἐν ὑμῖν (xx. 26,
Mk., where Lk. has ὁ μείζων ἐν ὑμῖν).
As in those passages, the words de-

scribe not the future penalty for
trying to be the greatest, but the
true method of becoming so. μείζων
still plays on the word Rab in the
preceding verses.

12. ὅστις δέ κτλ.] Lk. has the
saying in two other contexts, xiv.
11, xviii. 14. Cf. Erub. 13 b 'Everyone that humbleth himself the Holy
One, blessed be He, exalteth, and
everyone that exalteth himself the
Holy One . . . humbleth.' These
complementary truths find an echo
in xviii. 3 f., Lk. i. 52.

14-32. Seven Woes. Three Woes
(vv. 14-22) deal with the teaching of
the Scribes, three (vv. 23-28) with
the life of the Pharisees (cf. v.
20 n.), and the last (vv. 29-32) is
directed against the nation as a
whole. An arrangement of seven
perhaps stood in Q ; Lk. xi. 39-52
contains seven denunciations, with
six Woes. Cf. the (originally seven)
Woes in Is. v. 8-24.

14. οὐαί κτλ.] The First Woe.
On οὐαί see xi. 21, and on ὑποκριταί
vi. 2. κλείετε κτλ. : you prevent
men from knowing how to gain
entrance into the Kingdom ; you
lock the narrow gate that leads to
life. Lk. gives an interpretation
of this : ἤρατε τὴν κλεῖδα τῆς
γνώσεως, ' the key which admits
to knowledge,' i.e. ' the knowledge
of salvation' (Lk. i. 77). κλείετε

ὑποκριταί, ὅτι κλείετε τὴν βασιλείαν τῶν οὐρανῶν ἔμπροσθεν τῶν ἀνθρώπων· ὑμεῖς γὰρ οὐκ εἰσέρχεσθε, οὐδὲ τοὺς
εἰσερχομένους ἀφίετε εἰσελθεῖν. Οὐαὶ ὑμῖν, γραμματεῖς καὶ 15
Φαρισαῖοι ὑποκριταί, ὅτι περιάγετε τὴν θάλασσαν καὶ τὴν
ξηρὰν ποιῆσαι ἕνα προσήλυτον, καὶ ὅταν γένηται ποιεῖτε

and ἤρατε are perhaps both to be
traced to the Aram. אחד, which can
mean either 'to shut' or 'to seize.'

ὑμεῖς γάρ κτλ.] The Kingdom is
near at hand, and you are not living
the manner of life required for entrance into it. For the force of the
pres. cf. προάγουσιν xxi. 31, and for
the verb see on v. 20. Lk.'s aor. εἰσ-
ήλθατε describes an entrance not into
the Kingdom but into the knowledge
which can finally bring men into it.
οὐδὲ ἀφίετε: Lk. καὶ ἐκωλύσατε.
On the conative ptcp. τ. εἰσερχομένους, 'those who are in process of
entering—trying to enter,' see Blass,
§ 58. 4. Wellhausen unnecessarily
denies the genuineness of the saying,
explaining the Kingdom as the
Christian Church, which the Rabbis
tried to prevent men from joining.
Lk. places this denunciation, the
most severe in the whole series, at
the end as a climax. In Mt. its
position produces a sharp contrast
between the deterrent effect of the
Scribes' teaching and their efforts at
proselytizing (v. 15), and also between 'the Kingdom of Heaven'
and 'Gehenna.'

15. ὅτι περιάγετε κτλ.] The Second
Woe. The words seem to imply
that the number of converts due to
Pharisaic efforts was not large; and
the zeal of Palestinian Jews probably
declined after the fall of Jerusalem.
But Hellenistic Judaism met with
much greater success, reasons for
which are suggested by Schürer,
HJP. II. ii. 297–311; and in II. iii.
270–320 he describes 'Jewish works
under a heathen mask,' written for

the purpose of propaganda. An
instance of the difference between
Hellenistic and Pharisaic Judaism
may be seen in Jos. Ant. xx. ii. 4.
Wetstein gives references to Jewish
missionary efforts, and Roman opposition. Loisy gratuitously suggests
that the verse is a late addition
containing a hidden attack on S.
Paul. προσήλυτος (Ac. ii. 10, vi. 5,
xiii. 43) is the regular LXX. rendering
of גר. In the O.T. this meant a
foreigner living in Palestine under
Israelite protection, a meaning expressed in the Mishna by gêr tôshāb,
and in later Rabb. writings by gêr
hasha'ar ('proselyte of the gate').
Later it was used in a religious sense
of one who adopted Judaism by
circumcision and observance of the
Law; νομίμοις προσεληλυθυῖα τοῖς
Ἰουδαικοῖς (Jos. Ant. XVIII. iii. 5);
frequent in the Mishna, it was expressed more fully in later rabb.
writings as gêr hazedek ('proselyte
of righteousness'). This is to be distinguished from a σεβόμενος [τὸν
θεόν] (Ac. xiii. 50, xvi. 14, Jos. Ant.
XIV. vii. 2) or φοβούμενος τὸν θεόν
(Ac. x. 2, 22, xiii. 16, 26), a Gentile
favourably disposed to Judaism; see
Lake, Earlier Epp. of S. Paul, 37 ff.

καὶ ὅταν κτλ.] A 'son of
Gehenna,' one fitted, and therefore
destined, for Gehenna (see v. 22),
is the converse of 'sons of the
Kingdom' (xiii. 38), which the Jews
claimed to be (viii. 12). 'The more
converted the more perverted.' 'Sons
of Gehinnom' occurs in Rosh Hash.
17 b. For other idiomatic uses of
υἱός see ix. 15. On the late form

16 αὐτὸν υἱὸν γεέννης διπλότερον ὑμῶν. Οὐαὶ ὑμῖν, ὁδηγοὶ
τυφλοὶ οἱ λέγοντες Ὃς ἂν ὁμόσῃ ἐν τῷ ναῷ, οὐδέν ἐστιν,
17 ὃς δ᾽ ἂν ὁμόσῃ ἐν τῷ χρυσῷ τοῦ ναοῦ ὀφείλει· μωροὶ καὶ
τυφλοί, τίς γὰρ μείζων ἐστίν, ὁ χρυσὸς ἢ ὁ ναὸς ὁ ἁγιάσας
18 τὸν χρυσόν; καί Ὃς ἂν ὁμόσῃ ἐν τῷ θυσιαστηρίῳ, οὐδέν
ἐστιν, ὃς δ᾽ ἂν ὁμόσῃ ἐν τῷ δώρῳ τῷ ἐπάνω αὐτοῦ ὀφείλει·
19 τυφλοί, τί γὰρ μεῖζον, τὸ δῶρον ἢ τὸ θυσιαστήριον τὸ
20 ἁγιάζον τὸ δῶρον; ὁ οὖν ὁμόσας ἐν τῷ θυσιαστηρίῳ ὀμνύει
21 ἐν αὐτῷ καὶ ἐν πᾶσι τοῖς ἐπάνω αὐτοῦ· καὶ ὁ ὁμόσας ἐν

διπλότερον (= διπλάσιον) see Blass,
§ 11. 5. Justin's reference (*Dial.*
122) to the words without ὑμῶν
hardly makes it probable that the
pron. was originally absent : ' two-
fold more a son of G. [*sc.* than
he was before]' (Wellh.). J. Weiss
thinks this less stern.

16. ὁδηγοί κτλ.] *The Third Woe.*
The omission of 'Scribes and Pharisees,
hypocrites' in this Woe only, suggests
that *vv.* 16–22 were an independent
group of sayings. On 'blind leaders'
see xv. 14.

ὃς ἄν κτλ.] The 'gold of the
temple' would include various
ornaments and utensils among the
ἀναθήματα (Lk. xxi. 5); they, as
well as the gift on the altar, may
have been included in thought when
the oath 'by Corban!' (see xv. 5)
was uttered. If the casuistries in
these verses find no exact parallels
in later Heb. writings, it does not
follow that they were unknown in
the time of Jesus; possibly, however,
they are rhetorical instances, caricatur-
ing to some extent other well known
hair-splittings. That it was Rabbinic
avarice that gave importance to the
'gold' and the 'gift' (Holtzmann)
is scarcely probable. For ὁμόσαι
ἐν cf. v. 34, 36 and *Kidd.* 71 a 'By
the temple!' *Taanith* 24 a 'By the
temple service!' ὀφείλει is the
rabb. חַיָּב, '*debitor*' or '*reus*': the
oath binds as by a debt, which so

long as it is unpaid is guilt (see on
vi. 12). The converse οὐδέν ἐστιν
is expressed in the Mishna by פָּטוּר,
'freed,' 'absolved.'

17–19. μωροί κτλ.] That the
word μωροί is attributed to Jesus, in
spite of v. 22, is striking; it shews
that not the word but the spirit in
which it is uttered is what matters.
The principle that sacredness is a
quality imparted by contact was
well recognized in Heb. thought
(see *HDB.* ii. 'Holiness [in the
O.T.]'), and ought to have made
the casuistry on this point impossible;
the dedication of gold and gift by
the offerers could not impart to them
more sacredness than that which
they acquired by their presence in
the temple. The aor. ἁγιάσας expresses the sacredness which the gold
had acquired in the past, when it was
placed in the temple; the pres. ἁγιάζον
(v. 19), that which the gift on the
altar at the moment was acquiring.

20–22. ὁ οὖν κτλ.] The argument in *v.* 20, from the greater to
the less, leads to the larger thought
in *vv.* 21 f., an argument from the
less to the greater. The latter treats
not of casuistical oaths, as in *vv.* 16–
19, but of the careless use of oaths
in general. An oath by temple or
heaven is intensely solemn and
binding, because it involves an oath
by Him who dwells in them; cf.
v. 34 f.

τῷ ναῷ ὀμνύει ἐν αὐτῷ καὶ ἐν τῷ κατοικοῦντι αὐτόν· καὶ 22
ὁ ὀμόσας ἐν τῷ οὐρανῷ ὀμνύει ἐν τῷ θρόνῳ τοῦ θεοῦ καὶ
ἐν τῷ καθημένῳ ἐπάνω αὐτοῦ. Οὐαὶ ὑμῖν, γραμματεῖς 23
καὶ Φαρισαῖοι ὑποκριταί, ὅτι ἀποδεκατοῦτε τὸ ἡδύοσμον καὶ
τὸ ἄνηθον καὶ τὸ κύμινον, καὶ ἀφήκατε τὰ βαρύτερα τοῦ
νόμου, τὴν κρίσιν καὶ τὸ ἔλεος καὶ τὴν πίστιν· ταῦτα δὲ

23 δε εδει] BCL *al* 𝔏 a d g² h rᵛⁱᵈ 𝔖 pesh.hcl me aeth ; *om* δε אDΓ 𝔏 c e f ff¹·² g¹ l
vg 𝔖 pal arm ; *om* εδει 𝔖 sin.cur

23. ὅτι ἀποδεκατοῦτε κτλ.] *The
Fourth Woe. Vv.* 23–28, dealing
with legalism in daily life, correspond
with Lk. xi. 39–44 addressed to
the Pharisees as distinct from the
lawyers ; cf. Φαρισαῖε τυφλέ (*v.* 26
below). In Lev. xxvii. 30, all 'the
seed of the land' and 'the fruit of
the tree' is commanded to be tithed,
in Deut. xiv. 22 f. 'all the increase
of thy seed which cometh forth from
the field year by year,' which is defined as 'corn, wine, and oil'; but the
Scribal tradition extended it to include every sort of herb. ἡδύοσμον
(so Lk.) was a popular name for
μίνθη (Vulg. *menta*), 'mint.' ἄνηθον
is probably not 'anise' but 'dill'
(R.V. marg.), the Rabb. שבתא ; Nestle
(*ExpT.* Aug. 1904) suggests that
Lk.'s πήγανον (Vulg. *ruta*), 'rue,'
may be due to a misreading of this
as שברא. κύμινον, for which Lk.
has πᾶν λάχανον, is a loan-word
from Heb. כמון (Is. xxviii. 25, 27).

καὶ ἀφήκατε κτλ.] 'Ye have
left alone,' not very different from
Lk.'s παρέρχεσθε. On the 'heavy'
and 'light' precepts in the Law see
v. 19 ; for Jesus the former are
moral and social requirements.
βαρύτερα perhaps represents יקיר (so
𝔖) ; cf. Dan. ii. 11 (LXX. Theod.
βαρύς). Lk. omits τ. βαρ. τ. νόμον,
possibly because Gentile Christians
would not understand the allusion ;
not because it was difficult to

reconcile with the 'heavy burdens'
of *v.* 4, Lk. xi. 46 (Klost.-Gressm.).
κρίσις is 'justice' (מִשְׁפָּט), care that
the rights of others are respected ; cf.
Ps. c. [ci.] 1, where it is coupled with
ἔλεος (חֶסֶד), and similarly κρίμα,
Mic. vi. 8, Zech. vii. 9. πίστις
is not 'belief' but 'fidelity' (אֱמוּנָה or
אֱמֶת), a social virtue like the others ;
it is coupled with ἔλεος (Prov. xiv.
22) and κρίμα (Jer. v. 1). Lk.'s
τὴν κρίσιν καὶ τὴν ἀγαπὴν τοῦ θεοῦ
(om. πίστιν) might mean '(human)
justice, and love towards God' ; but
since ἀγαπή is evidently an equivalent
of ἔλεος, both probably representing
רחם (cf. Hos. ii. 23, where ἠλεημένην
is a variant for ἠγαπημένην), the
meaning must be 'God's judgment
and love' (cf. Rom. ii. 3 f.) ; hence
Marcion could read κλῆσιν for
κρίσιν. Mt. seems the more original.

ταῦτα δὲ ἔδει κτλ.] ταῦτα are
the βαρύτερα, and ἐκεῖνα the Scribal
minutiae ; the Lord admitted the
validity of the latter when they did
not conflict with principles. The
positive and negative injunctions
perhaps further indicate the relative
importance of the two. The second
half, which is in the spirit of *v.* 3 a,
need not be considered a Judaistic
addition, although D (Lk.) omits it.
Lk.'s παρεῖναι repeats the prep. in
παρέρχεσθε. Burkitt (*Ev. da Meph.*
ii. 252 f.) suggests that δὲ ἔδει is a
conflation of the true reading δέ with

24 ἔδει ποιῆσαι κἀκεῖνα μὴ ἀφεῖναι. ὁδηγοὶ τυφλοί, διυλίζοντες
τὸν κώνωπα τὴν δὲ κάμηλον καταπίνοντες. Οὐαὶ ὑμῖν, γραμ-
25 ματεῖς καὶ Φαρισαῖοι ὑποκριταί, ὅτι καθαρίζετε τὸ ἔξωθεν
τοῦ ποτηρίου καὶ τῆς παροψίδος, ἔσωθεν δὲ γέμουσιν
26 ἐξ ἁρπαγῆς καὶ ἀκρασίας. Φαρισαῖε τυφλέ, καθάρισον

the *v.l.* ἔδει, the former supported by
‎רּ in 𝕾 sin.cur (Mt., Lk.); ποιῆσαι
and μὴ ἀφεῖναι would in that case be
a lit. rendering of the Heb. and Aram.
idiom. ‎ל with inf., requiring ἔδει to be
added in thought ; cf. ‎לְהַכּוֹת 'thou
oughtest to have smitten' 2 Kings
xiii. 19, and see Lk. iv. 8 (𝕾 sin).

24. ὁδηγοί κτλ.] Mt. only. In-
sects and camels being unclean
were forbidden as food (Lev. xi. 4,
42 f.), but the point of the proverb
lies in their size (cf. Mt. xix. 24);
they illustrate the observance of the
lesser, and the disregard of the
weightier, matters. Cf. Jer. *Shabb.*
107. 'He that kills a flea on the
Sabbath is as guilty as if he
killed a camel.' Klost. - Gressm.
suggest a word-play, *gamlā* ('camel'),
and *ḳamlā* for ‎קלמא, ‎קלמתא (the
Targ. equivalent for the 'mosquitoes'
of Exod. viii. 12 [16] ff.). διυλίζειν,
to 'strain' wine (Am. vi. 6, Theod.
Is. xxv. 6), is not known elsewhere *c.
acc.* of that which is 'strained out';
cf. the use of καθαρίζειν, Deut. xix. 13.

25. ὅτι καθαρίζετε κτλ.] *The Fifth
Woe.* Another form of the same
rebuke: externals are valueless if
important internal matters are disregarded. Since in *v.* 27 a similar
rebuke is expressed not in metaphor
but by a simple comparison, the cup
and dish are probably intended to
be as literal as the whited sepulchres.
The vessels are cleansed externally,
i.e. ceremonially (not outside, as
distinct from inside), but they are
still defiled because their contents are
the result of (ἐξ) robbery and greed.

Contrast the constr. γέμουσιν ὀστέων
(*v.* 27); the prep., however, is sometimes used with the contents themselves ; cf. Jo. xii. 3, and ἀπό in
the LXX. (= ‎מִן). (For the washing
of vessels cf. Mk. vii. 3 f., and the
note at Mt. xv. 2, on Jewish rules of
purification.) Lk. adds difficulty to
the words by interpreting the cup
and dish (πίναξ) as metaphors for
the Pharisees (τὸ δὲ ἔσωθεν ὑμῶν
γέμει, cf. Sir. xix. 26); but it is
difficult, in this case, to see why the
dish is mentioned separately. Wellhausen understands τ. ποτηρίου and
τ. παροψίδος as explanatory genitives:
they represent 'the external' (τὸ
ἔξωθεν), but from an inward point
of view (ἔσωθεν) they are metaphors
of the Pharisaic heart. But this is
cumbrous. παροψίς, 'a side dish,'
'a dainty' (ὄψον), was used in late
Gk. for the plate itself. ἀκρασία
(cf. ἀκρατεῖς, 2 Tim. iii. 3) is 'want
of self-control,' which can shew itself
in incontinence (1 Cor. vii. 5), or, as
here, in an unrestrained desire for
gain. Lk. πονηρία.

26. Φαρισαῖε κτλ.] The unexpected sing. is probably a mistaken
rendering of ‎פרישא, which can be
either plur. or sing. Lk. has ἄφρονες.
The cup must have the same meaning, whether literal or metaphorical,
as in *v.* 25. The literal yields the
same good sense: cleanse first the
contents of your vessels (*i.e.* cease to
enrich yourselves by wrongful
methods), and their external uncleanness will count for nothing.
Since αὐτοῦ is certainly the true
reading, the mechanical addition of

πρῶτον τὸ ἐντὸς τοῦ ποτηρίου καὶ τῆς παροψίδος, ἵνα
γένηται καὶ τὸ ἐκτὸς αὐτοῦ καθαρόν. Οὐαὶ ὑμῖν, γραμ- 27
ματεῖς καὶ Φαρισαῖοι ὑποκριταί, ὅτι παρομοιάζετε τάφοις
κεκονιαμένοις, οἵτινες ἔξωθεν μὲν φαίνονται ὡραῖοι ἔσωθεν
δὲ γέμουσιν ὀστέων νεκρῶν καὶ πάσης ἀκαθαρσίας· οὕτως 28

26 και της παροψιδος] om D 1 209 21ᵉᵛ 𝕃 a ê ff² | αυτου] B*DE* 1 13 28 69 124
157 al 𝕃 a e aeth ; αυτων אB²CE² al minn.pler ℘ pesh.hcl.pal arm ; om 53 2ᵉᵛ
𝕃 c f ff¹·² g¹·² h l r vg ℘ sin

καὶ τ. παροψίδος in the mass of
authorities (including some that have
αὐτοῦ) must be wrong.

Lk. has πλὴν τὰ ἔνοντα δότε ἐλεημοσύνην, καὶ ἰδοὺ πάντα καθαρὰ ὑμῖν
ἐστιν, which Wellhausen explains as
due to a misreading of דכי ('cleanse')
as זכי ('give alms'). Lk. will then
have expressed the same teaching as
Mt., and the original underlying
both may have been simply 'Cleanse
the inside, and the outside is clean.'
This is preceded in Lk. by οὐχ ὁ
ποιήσας τὸ ἔξωθεν καὶ τὸ ἔσωθεν
ἐποίησεν; 'Did not He (God) who
made outward things also make
inward, spiritual, things?'; or,
transposing ἔξωθεν and ἔσωθεν (as
in C D Γ 𝕃 a c e Cyp), 'has not he
(anyone) who has prepared (set in
order, cleansed) the inside also
prepared the outside?' In the
latter case Lk.'s two sentences express
the same thought.

27. ὅτι παρομοιάζετε κτλ.] The
Sixth Woe. Against external pro-
priety which conceals internal
wickedness. Lk. has a different
simile : ἔστε ὡς τὰ μνημεῖα τὰ ἄδηλα,
καὶ οἱ ἄνθρωποι οἱ περιπατοῦντες
ἐπάνω οὐκ οἴδασιν. To walk over
a grave caused pollution, which must
be avoided by anyone who wished
to enter the temple (cf. Num. xix.
16); hence the custom (Shek. i. 1,
Moed Ḳat. 1 a, 5 a) of chalking
graves with white marks on the
15th Adar before the Passover

(cf. the precautions in Jo. xi. 55,
xviii. 28). This illustrates Lk.'s
words. Mt.'s also are generally supposed to refer to it; and it is pointed
out that the white marks would
be recent when the words were
spoken. But white-chalked graves
do not afford a good simile of
hypocrisy, since they proclaim to
all, instead of concealing, their
inward pollution. The difficulty is
not lessened if οἵτινες . . φαίνονται
ὡραῖοι is omitted as a gloss. The
contrast must lie between the outward appearance and the bones and
uncleanness concealed within. Cf.
S. Paul's τοῖχε κεκονιαμένε (Ac.
xxiii. 3), ἐν κεκονιαμένοις, apparently
'ornamented rooms' (Prov. xxi. 9),
and κονίαμα, the 'plaster' (גִּירָא) of
the wall in the king's chamber
(Dan. v. 5). If the words refer not
to white-washing but to the orna-
mental plastering of the walls of
sepulchres, ὡραῖοι can refer to their
clean, white appearance in the sunshine. 'Our metaphor of "white-
washing" moral evil is more in
harmony with Mt. than with Lk.'
(Plummer). And this gives point
to the juxtaposition of v. 29, 'build
the tombs . . . and adorn the
sepulchres.' παρομοιάζετε (from the
class. παρόμοιος, cf. Mk. vii. 13), 'be
somewhat similar to,' occurs in Eccl.
writers, but not elsewhere in bibl. Gk.

28. οὕτως κτλ.] Perhaps an
addition by Mt.; the meaning of

καὶ ὑμεῖς ἔξωθεν μὲν φαίνεσθε τοῖς ἀνθρώποις δίκαιοι,
29 ἔσωθεν δέ ἐστε μεστοὶ ὑποκρίσεως καὶ ἀνομίας. Οὐαὶ
ὑμῖν, γραμματεῖς καὶ Φαρισαῖοι ὑποκριταί, ὅτι οἰκοδομεῖτε
τοὺς τάφους τῶν προφητῶν καὶ κοσμεῖτε τὰ μνημεῖα τῶν
30 δικαίων, καὶ λέγετε Εἰ ἤμεθα ἐν ταῖς ἡμέραις τῶν πατέρων
ἡμῶν, οὐκ ἂν ἤμεθα αὐτῶν κοινωνοὶ ἐν τῷ αἵματι τῶν
31 προφητῶν· ὥστε μαρτυρεῖτε ἑαυτοῖς ὅτι υἱοί ἐστε τῶν
32 φονευσάντων τοὺς προφήτας. καὶ ὑμεῖς πληρώσατε τὸ
33 μέτρον τῶν πατέρων ὑμῶν. ὄφεις γεννήματα ἐχιδνῶν, πῶς

32 πληρωσατε] אB²CL *al* minn.*pler* 𝕷 vet.*pler*.vg 𝕾 pesh.hcl.pal me ; πληρω-
σετε B* 60 𝕷 e [f impletis] 𝕾 sin ; επληρωσατε DH

the simile must have been clear to
the hearers without explanation. It
is an echo of vi. 1 f., 5, 16. ἀνομία
(see on vii. 23) with stern irony is
ascribed to those who scrupulously
observed the Law.

29. ὅτι οἰκοδομεῖτε κτλ.] *The
Seventh Woe.* This may have been
placed with the others in Q to
complete the number seven, and the
mention of tombs supplied a link ;
but *vv.* 29–35 are addressed not to
the Scribes and Pharisees but to the
nation as a whole. For 'prophets
and righteous men' cf. xiii. 17. The
building and adorning of their
sepulchres was by way of reparation
for their murder. Lk., more tersely,
'Ye build the sepulchres of the
prophets and your fathers killed
them.' For the reverent care of the
reputed tombs of ancient heroes see
Ac. ii. 29, Jos. *Ant.* XVI. vii. 1, *BJ.*
IV. ix. 7. The 'tombs of the
prophets' on the slope of the Mt. of
Olives (E. Robinson, *Res.* iii. 254,
Baedeker⁷ 73 f.) are probably of
Christian origin.

31. ὥστε κτλ.] 'If your fathers
had not made martyrs you could
not honour them,' so that you
proclaim yourselves the sons, at any
rate, of the murderers. Montefiore
(*ad loc.*) pronounces this 'ironical,

but also rather absurd.' But it
contains the thought, which is not
at all absurd, that 'sons' are those
who inherit their fathers' character
(cf. v. 9, 45). You bear witness to
the murder-taint in your blood'
(Allen) ; and it was soon to shew
itself when the mob cried 'Crucify
Him !' Lk. : 'so then ye are wit
nesses and consent to the works of
your fathers, because they killed them
and ye build.'

32. καὶ ὑμεῖς κτλ.] The Lord's
irony is at its height in πληρώσατε,
which the *v.ll.* πληρώσετε and
ἐπληρώσατε were probably attempts
to soften. 'Complete then on your
part (καὶ ὑμεῖς) the measure of your
fathers,' *i.e.* Go on to the measure of
guilt that they reached. For the
thought of πληρώσατε cf. 1 Thes.
ii. 16, Gen. xv. 16, Dan. viii. 23,
2 Macc. vi. 14. καὶ ὑμεῖς can
hardly belong to the end of *v.* 31
(Zahn) ; it would probably have
come after υἱοί ἐστε.

33. ὄφεις κτλ.] *Vv.* 33–36 are
a *Concluding Warning.* The verse,
peculiar to Mt., is an echo of the
Baptist's words (see on iii. 7, xii.
34). πῶς φύγητε; delib. conj.
(Blass, § 64. 6) ; 'how are you to
escape ?' *sc.* so long as you continue
to act as the offspring of your fathers.

φύγητε ἀπὸ τῆς κρίσεως τῆς γεέννης; διὰ τοῦτο ἰδοὺ ἐγὼ 34
ἀποστέλλω πρὸς ὑμᾶς προφήτας καὶ σοφοὺς καὶ γραμ-
ματεῖς· ἐξ αὐτῶν ἀποκτενεῖτε καὶ σταυρώσετε, καὶ ἐξ αὐτῶν
μαστιγώσετε ἐν ταῖς συναγωγαῖς ὑμῶν καὶ διώξετε ἀπὸ
πόλεως εἰς πόλιν· ὅπως ἔλθῃ ἐφ' ὑμᾶς πᾶν αἷμα δίκαιον 35
ἐκχυννόμενον ἐπὶ τῆς γῆς ἀπὸ τοῦ αἵματος Ἄβελ τοῦ
δικαίου ἕως τοῦ αἵματος Ζαχαρίου υἱοῦ Βαραχίου, ὃν

Their escape is not judicially pronounced impossible. They were 'sons of Gehenna' (v. 15) and fit for the 'sentence of (being cast into) G.' κρίσις is virtually κρῖμα (cf. δικαίωσις Rom. v. 18). On Gehenna see v. 22.

34. διὰ τοῦτο] Therefore—that you may have an opportunity of completing the measure of your fathers. Lk. also has διὰ τοῦτο: therefore—that you may have an opportunity of shewing your consent to the work of your fathers.

ἰδοὺ ἐγώ κτλ.] Lk. 'the Wisdom of God said, I will send unto them.' Mt. interprets this as referring to Christ Himself, and writes ὑμᾶς for αὐτούς. It is often assumed that Jesus was quoting an apocryphal passage known to His hearers ; Spitta (*Th. Stud. u. Kr.*, 1909, 355, *Synopt. Grundschrift*, 333 f.) suggests that it came from the 'Midrash of the book of the kings' mentioned in 2 Chr. xxiv. 27. He may have done so, but the words do not require it. If the Wisdom of God is God Himself in action (cf. xi. 19), Lk.'s expression is equivalent to 'Thus saith the Lord' ; and Jesus echoes the language of 2 Chr. xxiv. 19 (the story of Zachariah's murder), cf. *id.* xxv. 15 f., xxxvi. 15 f. (ἄγγελοι and προφῆται). On the other hand Lk.'s ἀποστόλους is distinctively Christian, while Mt.'s 'wise men and Scribes' can be strictly Jewish ; thus Lk. also interprets the Wisdom of God to mean Christ. But both probably preserve features of the original

utterance, which spoke simply of God's dealings with the Jewish nation : 'Therefore the Wisdom of God (hath) said, Behold I am sending to them prophets, and wise men, and Scribes.'

ἐξ αὐτῶν κτλ.] For the partitive ἐξ (= מֵ‍) cf. Lk. xxi. 16. Mt. expands Lk.'s two verbs ἀποκτενοῦσιν καὶ ἐκδιώξουσιν : (1) 'and crucify' (the order 'crucify and kill' would be more natural) seems to be a reference to the Lord's death ; and perhaps the tradition of S. Peter's death was known to him ; (2) 'scourge . . . from city to city' may have been derived from x. 17, 23.

35. ὅπως ἔλθῃ κτλ.] ὑμᾶς, as before, is for Lk.'s 3rd pers. (τῆς γενεᾶς ταύτης). Lk. has τὸ αἷμα πάντων τῶν προφητῶν for the Hebraic πᾶν αἷμα δίκαιον (cf. Joel iii. [iv.] 19, Lam. iv. 13), and ἀπὸ καταβολῆς κόσμου (see on Mt. xiii. 35) for the equally Hebraic ἐπὶ τῆς γῆς, which probably refers to the sacred 'land' of Palestine to which bloodshed is a defilement (cf. Num. xxxv. 33 f.). αἷμα ἐκχυννόμενον (on the form see Blass, § 17) is best represented by the single word 'bloodshed,' the pres. ptcp. being timeless. The expression is echoed in Apoc. xviii. 24.

ἀπὸ τοῦ αἵματος κτλ.] Mt.'s addition τοῦ δικαίου (which may agree with αἵματος or Ἄβελ, cf. xxvii. 24) may have been due to some tradition or apocr. writing ; cf. Heb. xi. 4, 1 Jo. iii. 12. υἱοῦ Βαραχίου is absent from Lk. The

36 ἐφονεύσατε μεταξὺ τοῦ ναοῦ καὶ τοῦ θυσιαστηρίου. ἀμὴν λέγω ὑμῖν, ἥξει ταῦτα πάντα ἐπὶ τὴν γενεὰν ταύτην.

name, whether written by Mt. or a scribe, was probably accidental, and due to familiarity with that of Zachariah son of Barachiah the prophet (Zach. i. 1), or of the Zach. named in Is. viii. 2 (LXX.). The usual explanation is almost certainly right (see Add. n.) that the reference is to Z. son of Jehoiada the priest, who was slain ' in the court of the house of Yahweh' (2 Chr. xxiv. 20 ff.; see above on ἰδοὺ ἐγὼ ἀποστέλλω κτλ.), and that the expression means all the martyrdoms related in the Heb. O.T. from Genesis to the last book 2 Chron. The fact that Urijah's

murder (Jer. xxvi. 23) was chronologically later does not affect the force of the words. In ὃν ἐφονεύσατε (Lk. τοῦ ἀπολομένου) Mt. continues his use of the 2nd pers., which refers to the nation as a whole.

36. ἀμήν κτλ.] Lk. ναί; see on v. 18. ταῦτα πάντα are all the acts of bloodshed; they will 'come,' i.e. be visited upon (Lk. 'be required from') the generation of Jews then living (see on xi. 16). The words express the nearness of the Judgment, and lead on to the lament in vv. 37 ff., and the eschatological discourse and parables which follow.

Additional Note on Zachariah son of Barachiah.

Origen accepts a tradition, mentioned also by Chrys., that the Z. referred to was the Baptist's father (cf. Prot. Jac. 23). Many explain it as the Z. son of Baruch or Barischaeus, who, after being acquitted of planning to betray Jerusalem to Vespasian, was murdered in A.D. 68-9, by two Zealots in the midst of the temple (Jos. BJ. IV. v. 4). Βαραχίου may have been a scribal gloss later than 69; but if not, and if this is the Zachariah referred to, the whole passage, used by Mt., Lk., must have been interpolated in Q later than that date. And there are other difficulties. (1) The Scribes and Pharisees, who are rebuked as responsible for the murder, themselves belonged to the classes of whom the Zealots murdered 12,000 at about the same time as Zachariah's death. (2) Not being a priest, he was unlikely to have been 'between the temple and the altar.' (3) Jesus says in effect, ' you will kill prophets who will be sent to you, in order that all the past guilt of your fathers may be visited on you'; this is deprived of all point if the guilt of the generation whom He addressed is included in 'all the bloodshed from Abel to Zachariah.'

On the other hand, if Βαραχίου is a mere slip, Z. son of Jehoiada answers all requirements. Jerome (in Mat.) says that in the Naz. Gosp. 'filium Joiadae reperimus scriptum'; and an old scholion on Mt. runs Ζαχαρίαν δὲ τὸν Ἰωδαὲ λέγει· διώνυμος γὰρ ἦν. Chrys. mentions the latter as a current explanation. Since Jehoiada was a priest, his son probably was also, so that he could be 'between the temple and the altar.' This may have been a traditional explanation of 'the court of the house of Yahweh' (2 Chr.); in the Talm. and Midr. it is discussed in which court Zachariah was killed, and it is decided that it was in the court of the priests, i.e. near the altar (see Zahn, ad loc.). And this is borne out by Lk.'s ἐκζητήθῃ

Ἰερουσαλήμ Ἰερουσαλήμ, ἡ ἀποκτείνουσα τοὺς προφήτας 37
καὶ λιθοβολοῦσα τοὺς ἀπεσταλμένους πρὸς αὐτήν,—ποσάκις
ἠθέλησα ἐπισυναγαγεῖν τὰ τέκνα σου ὃν τρόπον ὄρνις

τὸ αἷμα. As Abel's blood cried for vengeance, so Zachariah, when he was
being murdered, cried 'May Yahweh look upon it and require it'
(וְיִדְרֹשׁ). LXX. has καὶ κρινάτω, but αἷμα ἐκζητεῖν is a common LXX.
equivalent for 'require blood' (e.g. Gen. xlii. 22, 2 Regn. iv. 11). Lk. may
have consciously imitated O.T. language, but on the other hand Mt.'s ἔλθῃ
ἐφ᾿ ὑμᾶς may be based on 'His blood be on us and on our children'
(xxvii. 25). See the discussion of the whole passage by Dom Chapman,
JThS., Apr. 1912, 398–412. Zachariah's story played a considerable part
in rabb. traditions, some of which go back to an early date; see Allen,
DCG. i. 171, Nestle, ExpT. xiii. 562, ZNW., 1905, 198–200.

37–39. (Lk. xiii. 34 f.) APO-
STROPHE TO JERUSALEM.

The variations between Mt. and
Lk. are slight; the passage must
have stood in Q very much in its
present form. But its original
position cannot be determined.
Stanton (Gospp. as Hist. Doc. ii. 96)
suggests that it preceded Lk. xvii.
22–37, which Mt. includes in ch.
xxiv. Harnack, following Schmiedel,
attaches v. 37 f. to vv. 34–36 as
part of the quotation from the con-
jectured apocryphal writing, which
was given in Q, but (it is supposed)
clearly indicated as a quotation;
and he finds in it a difference of
style from that of the words of
Jesus in Q, in the fact that Q uses
ὡς, not ὃν τρόπον. If Mt. preserves
its true position, v. 37 possibly formed
part of the words that Jesus ascribed
to the Wisdom of God. But there
is nothing which forbids the whole
passage to be understood as an
exclamation by Jesus Himself.

37. Ἰερουσαλήμ κτλ.] Mt. adopts
the form of the name from Q, where
it represented the Aram. form used
by Jesus; elsewhere he always has
the Gk. form (see on ii. 1), including
two sayings of Jesus (v. 35, xx. 18),
the latter from Mk., the former from

a source the nature of which is uncertain (see p. 101). The participles
with the art., representing the Semitic
idiom for the vocative, are almost
substantives, 'the killer of . . . the
stoner of . . .' (Moulton, i. 127);
hence the use of αὐτήν for σε (cf.
Lk. i. 45).

ποσάκις κτλ.] If these are the
words of the Wisdom of God, they
may refer to the many occasions in
the national history on which God
gave to Jerusalem opportunities of
submitting trustfully to Him. But
Jesus Himself is probably the subj.
of ἠθέλησα. Wellhausen explains
that He had often tried, through
the apostles, to draw (ἐπισυναγαγεῖν,
כנש) the Jews into His συναγωγή
(כנשתא) or Church. But the simile
of the bird suggests something more
personal and immediate. The words
need not imply many previous visits
to Jerusalem, though our records are
so fragmentary that this is not impossible; even those recorded in the
4th Gosp. were hardly numerous
enough to account for ποσάκις. Jesus
may have meant 'How often (when
I was away in Galilee) did I long
to come to Jerusalem and gather
you all into My discipleship and
protect you in the coming Judg-

38 ἐπισυνάγει τὰ νοσσία αὐτῆς ὑπὸ τὰς πτέρυγας, καὶ οὐκ
ἠθελήσατε; ἰδοὺ ἀφίεται ὑμῖν ὁ οἶκος ὑμῶν.   λέγω γὰρ
39 ὑμῖν, οὐ μή με ἴδητε ἀπ᾿ ἄρτι ἕως ἂν εἴπητε

Εὐλογημένος ὁ ἐρχόμενος ἐν ὀνόματι Κυρίου.

XXIV. 1   Καὶ ἐξελθὼν ὁ Ἰησοῦς ἀπὸ τοῦ ἱεροῦ ἐπορεύετο, καὶ
προσῆλθον οἱ μαθηταὶ αὐτοῦ ἐπιδεῖξαι αὐτῷ τὰς οἰκοδομὰς

38 υμων] BL 𝕷 ff² 𝕾 sin ; add ερημος ℵCD al minn.omn 𝕷 vet [exc ff²].vg
𝕾 pesh.hcl.pal me sah arm aeth

ment ; and now that I have come,
you have refused to be gathered.'
ἐπισυναγαγεῖν is for the late and
colloquial -άξαι which Lk. may have
found in Q (M.-M. *Vocab. s.v.* ἄγω).
ὃν τρόπον (Ac. i. 11, 2 Tim. iii. 8)
is frequent in the LXX. for כַּאֲשֶׁר,
etc.   For the simile cf. Deut. xxxii,
11, Is. xxxi. 5, Ps. xxxvi. 7.   νοσσίον,
usually νεοσσίον, is the dimin. of the
commoner νοσσός, νεοσσός. Lk. has
the collective νοσσιά, 'brood' (R.V.).
For both cf. Ps. lxxxiii. [lxxxiv.] 4.
'Hen' and 'chickens' (Engl. versions)
wrongly suggest a particular bird.
The *mother* bird is more suitable to
the simile than the masc., and need
not point to Wisdom (σοφία, הָכְמָה)
as the speaker.

38. *ἰδού κτλ.*] The presence of
God, which would have saved you
in the coming Judgment through
Me, His Representative and Prophet,
is now finally deserting you. οἶκος
is not the temple only, but the city
with the temple as its centre, which
is virtually the nation ; cf. Jer. xii. 7,
'I have forsaken My house, I have
cast off My heritage,' Enoch lxxxix.
56, 'He forsook their house and
tower' (*i.e.* city and temple); and
other passages quoted by Allen.
ὑμῖν is a dat. *incomm.*, 'to your
sorrow.'   The addition of ἔρημος,
perhaps due to Jer. xxii. 5, expresses
a different thought, the destruction
of the city by the Romans.

39. *λέγω γάρ κτλ.*] Lk. omits
γάρ (by which Mt. explains more
carefully that the Lord's absence
from the city involves its desertion
by God) and ἀπ᾿ ἄρτι. The quotation from Ps. cxvii. [cxviii.] 26,
εὐλογημένος κτλ., was shouted by
the crowd at the Entry into Jerusalem
(see on xxi. 9), and was not in itself
Messianic. Lk. places the present
passage *before* the Entry, so that the
words are a prediction of it, and, like
Mt., understands them as Messianic ;
but as Mt. places them they gain
their full force : 'God is deserting
you, because I am about to depart
by death ; and you will not see Me
till I return as the heavenly Messiah.'
For ἀπ᾿ ἄρτι cf. xxvi. 29, 64, in
each case referring to the immediate
coming of the End (elsewhere only
Jo. xiv. 7, Apoc. xiv. 13).

xxiv. 1, 2.   (Mk. xiii. 1 f., Lk. xxi.
5 f.)   THE DESTRUCTION OF THE
TEMPLE FORETOLD.

1. *καὶ ἐξελθών κτλ.*] All the
discourses since xxi. 23 have been
placed in the temple. Mk., Lk.
prefix to these verses the incident
of the widow's mite, which in Mk.
follows the saying about 'devouring
widows' houses.' Mt.'s omission of
the incident was probably to bring the
verses into conjunction with 'your
house is left unto you' (xxiii. 38).
καὶ προσῆλθον κτλ.] In Mk. the

τοῦ ἱεροῦ· ὁ δὲ ἀποκριθεὶς εἶπεν αὐτοῖς Οὐ βλέπετε 2
ταῦτα πάντα; ἀμὴν λέγω ὑμῖν, οὐ μὴ ἀφεθῇ ὧδε λίθος

speaker is 'one of the disciples'; Lk. has τινων λεγόντων, both with an expression of admiration, in Mk. for the size of the stones and the building, in Lk. for the beauty of the stones and the dedicated objects (cf. 2 Macc. ix. 16). Herod's temple is described in Jos. *B.J.* v. v., and its stones are stated (*Ant.* xv. xi. 3) to have measured *c.* 25 × 8 × 12 cubits.

2. ἀμήν κτλ.] Mt. alone gives the formula; see on v. 18. The destruction is pictured in general terms. The actual destruction was by fire. For λίθος ἐπὶ λίθον cf. Hag. ii. 15; and for καταλύειν of the destruction of a building cf. 4 Regn. xxv. 10 (A), 2 Esd. v. 12 (A).

3–36. (Mk. xiii. 3–32, Lk. xxi. 7–33.) DISCOURSE ON THE LAST THINGS.

Some predictions of Jesus concerning the nearness of the End probably formed the basis upon which a Jewish-Christian writer compiled a series of sayings, many of them couched in the conventional language of Jewish eschatology. This theory of a Small Apocalypse is widely accepted, in various forms, by modern writers. See the works cited by Moffatt, *LNT.²* 209. Those who reject it offer different explanations, *e.g.* B. Weiss, *Quellen des Lucasev.* 105–14, J. Weiss, *ThStKr.*, 1892, 246–70, and *Das ält. Ev.* 273–83, Zahn, *IntrNT.* i. 224, ii. 500, 571 f., and Comm. on Mt., Bacon, *IntrNT.* 211, and *Beg. of Gosp. Hist.*, Clemen, *ThLZ.*, 1902, 523 ff., Spitta, *ThStKr.*, 1909, 348–401. The last stands almost alone in maintaining the superiority of Lk.'s account dealing with the fall of Jerusalem, which

he thinks Mt. and Mk. have transformed into a prediction of a cosmic catastrophe. The contents of the little document are grouped round three main predictions (cf. Apoc. ix. 12, xi. 14), which are found in Mk. xiii. *v.* 8, *vv.* 14, 17–20, *vv.* 24–27. There is some difference of opinion as to its whole extent, various writers assigning to it (in addition to the three main predictions) more or less of Mk. *vv.* 5–7, 12, 15, 16, 21, 22, 28–30. The compiler of it gave some doubtless genuine sayings of Jesus, and also some that reflect a later date when Christians had begun to realize that some delay must be expected before the Parousia. The delay would not, indeed, be long, because Jesus had declared that the End would come within that generation (Mk. *v.* 30, Mt. *v.* 34); but certain events must precede it. This document reflects distinctively Christian conditions. That it was Jewish-Christian, and not purely Jewish, is clear also from the fact that Mk. was willing to incorporate it and ascribe it to Jesus. Mt. and Lk., on the basis of Mk., compiled their discourses each in his own way. Mt. adds a few verses to Mk., including three sayings from Q (*vv.* 26–28, which Lk. gives in an eschatological passage xvii. 22–37), and summarizes briefly in *v.* 9 the sayings on the persecution of Christ's disciples (Mk. *vv.* 9, 11, 12) which he has already added to the discourse at the Mission of the Twelve (x. 17–21). Lk. frames his discourse to bear mainly on the destruction of Jerusalem. Mt. and Mk. seem to assume that this will be one of the events preceding the Parousia, since they, like Luke, place the discourse in conjunction with the incident in

3 ἐπὶ λίθον ὃς οὐ καταλυθήσεται. Καθημένου δὲ αὐτοῦ ἐπὶ
τοῦ Ὄρους τῶν Ἐλαιῶν προσῆλθον αὐτῷ οἱ μαθηταὶ κατ᾽
ἰδίαν λέγοντες Εἰπὸν ἡμῖν πότε ταῦτα ἔσται, καὶ τί τὸ

vv. 1, 2 ; but the discourse, as they record it, speaks neither of temple nor city being destroyed. The date of the Small Apocalypse was probably a little after A.D. 60, 'when it was felt that "the birth-throes" were beginning, while trials of greater intensity, though of the same general character, might well be anticipated' (Stanton).

The discourse in Mt., Mk. is as follows :—

1. (*a*) *Warning*. False Messiahs, and wars, must precede the End (Mk. 5–7, Mt. 4–6).

(*b*) *The Beginning of the Pangs* (Mk. 8, Mt. 7, 8).

2. (*a*) *Warning*. You will suffer persecutions (Mk. 9–13, Mt. 9–14).

[Mt. 10–12 adds a prediction of false prophets, and apostasy.]

(*b*) *The Climax of the Pangs* (Mk. 14–20, Mt. 15–22).

3. (*a*) *Warning*. False Messiahs and false prophets will deceive (Mk. 21–23, Mt. 23–25).

[Mt. 26–28 adds (from Q = Lk. xvii. 23 f., 37) a warning that the Parousia will be sudden.]

(*b*) *Cosmic Catastrophe at the Parousia* (Mk. 24–27, Mt. 29–31).

4. *The End is near*. (*a*) A parable (Mk. 28, 29, Mt. 32, 33).

(*b*) A statement (Mk. 30–32, Mt. 34–36).

Epilogue teaching the necessity of watchfulness :—

Mk. 33–37. Parable of slaves watching for their master.

Mt. 37–xxv. 46. Warning from the example of the Flood, followed by a series of parables.

(Lk. 34–36 gives a warning, without a parable.)

3. καθημένου κτλ.] The Lord has now moved to the Mt. of Olives, the discourse being thus separated from the incident in *vv*. 1, 2, though the first of the questions asked (πότε ταῦτα ἔσται) refers to the destruction of the temple. Lk. makes this reference still clearer by omitting to relate the change of scene. The discourse in Mt., Mk. supplies no answer to this question. But if Mk., as is probable, wrote just before A.D. 70, he must have realized that the fall of the city and temple was imminent, but understood the discourse to mean that the troubles now threatening were not the immediate sign of the End. Mt., who wrote after 70, could use the same discourse to encourage readers who were disappointed that although the city had fallen the Parousia was still delayed. And Lk., dealing more freely with his material, offers the same encouragement with an explicit reference to the fall of the city.

κατ᾽ ἰδίαν] The discourse is a secret revelation to a chosen few— a standing feature of Jewish apocalypse. Mk. confines it to Peter, James, John, and Andrew.

καὶ τί κτλ.] συντελ. τ. αἰῶνος (see xiii. 39) is a technical phrase formed out of Mk.'s ὅταν μέλλῃ ταῦτα συντελεῖσθαι πάντα (Lk. ταῦτα γίνεσθαι). τῆς σῆς παρουσίας is added by Mt. ; the subst. is confined in the synn. to this chapter of Mt. (*vv*. 27, 37, 39) but in the Epistles is frequently used of Christ's Advent. In the LXX. it occurs in the late books Neh., Judith, 2, 3 Macc., but never with an eschatological force. In class. Gk. it tends

σημεῖον τῆς σῆς παρουσίας καὶ συντελείας τοῦ αἰῶνος.
καὶ ἀποκριθεὶς ὁ Ἰησοῦς εἶπεν αὐτοῖς Βλέπετε μή τις 4
ὑμᾶς πλανήσῃ· πολλοὶ γὰρ ἐλεύσονται ἐπὶ τῷ ὀνόματί μου 5
λέγοντες Ἐγώ εἰμι ὁ χριστός, καὶ πολλοὺς πλανήσουσιν.
μελλήσετε δὲ ἀκούειν πολέμους καὶ ἀκοὰς πολέμων· ὁρᾶτε, 6
μὴ θροεῖσθε· δεῖ γὰρ γενέσθαι, ἀλλ᾽ οὔπω ἐστὶν τὸ τέλος.
ἐγερθήσεται γὰρ ἔθνος ἐπὶ ἔθνος καὶ Βασιλεία ἐπὶ Βασιλείαν, 7

rather to the meaning 'presence' than 'arrival'; but the latter is illustrated by its use in papyri (2nd and 3rd cent. A.D.) for the visit of a king or other official. See Milligan, *Thess.* 145 f., who suggests that the Apost. writers derived its use from Mt. But perhaps the organization of the empire was already leading to its use for an official visit, and Christians adopted it for the visit of their King. Such expressions as δευτέρα παρουσία (Chrys.), *secundus adventus* (Jer.), 'my second coming' (Secr. Enoch xxxii. 1), 'the last coming' (*id.* xlii. 5) were natural from the Christian point of view, but since Christ was not yet invested with Messianic glory, 'arrival' could be used as correctly in the case of the Christian as of the Jewish Messiah.

4–6. (Mk. *vv.* 5–7, Lk. *vv.* 8 f.) *Warning. False Messiahs, and Wars, must precede the End.*

4. καὶ ἀποκριθεὶς κτλ.] Mk. ἤρξατο λέγειν (see on xiii. 54). βλέπετε μή (so Mk., Lk.) elsewhere in bibl. Gk. occurs only in Paul. Epp.³ and Heb.²; cf. ὅρα μή (viii. 4).

5. πολλοὶ γάρ κτλ.] False claimants will arrogate to themselves My powers, 'making use of My name' (see Heitmüller, *Im Namen Jesu,* 63), *i.e.* the name of Messiah which I bear. Mt. for clearness adds ὁ χριστός to the vague boast ἐγώ εἰμι (Mk., Lk.). No such definite claim to Messiahship is known till that of Barkokba in the reign of Hadrian;

but other claims were made which deceived many (cf. Ac. v. 36 f., viii. 9, xxi. 38), and such are frequently mentioned by Josephus in the course of the Jewish war. The masses welcomed each hero as he appeared (see Volz, *Jüd. Esch.* 209), since the popular mind still thought not of a. heavenly but a purely human Messiah. Cf. Trypho in Just. *Dial.* xlix., ἄνθρωπος ἐξ ἀνθρώπων γενήσεται.

6. μελλήσετε κτλ.] Wars then being waged, and wars 'commonly expected and on all men's tongues' (Swete). The plur. ἀκοαί elsewhere in the N.T. means 'ears'; but cf. 1 Regn. ii. 24 b, Dan. xi. 44 (Theod.), ἀκοαὶ . . . ταράξουσιν αὐτούς. For ἀκ. πολέμων Lk. has ἀκαταστασίας, restless revolts against Roman authority. On ὁρᾶτε see ix. 30. θροεῖν act. 'to cry aloud,' pass. (in late Gk.) 'to be frightened' (at a cry or rumour); cf. Cant. v. 4, 2 Thes. ii. 2 (a similar warning against a too immediate expectation of the End).

δεῖ γάρ κτλ.] These occurrences are divinely decreed (see on xvi. 21). For τέλος in this technical sense the LXX. has πέρας (Am. viii. 2, Ez. vii. 2 f., etc., Theod. Dan.⁷).

7, 8. (Mk. *v.* 8, Lk. *v.* 10 f.) *The Beginning of 'Pangs.'*

7. ἐγερθήσεται κτλ.] γάρ (Mt., Mk.) which links the verse with the preceding, is absent from Lk., who introduces the saying with τότε ἔλεγεν αὐτοῖς, suggesting that he

8 καὶ ἔσονται λιμοὶ καὶ σεισμοὶ κατὰ τόπους· πάντα δὲ
9 ταῦτα ἀρχὴ ὠδίνων.   τότε παραδώσουσιν ὑμᾶς εἰς θλίψιν καὶ
ἀποκτενοῦσιν ὑμᾶς, καὶ ἔσεσθε μισούμενοι ὑπὸ πάντων τῶν
10 ἐθνῶν διὰ τὸ ὄνομά μου.   καὶ τότε ϲκανδαλιϲθήϲονται πολλοὶ

knew the saying independently of
Mk., and unconnected with the foregoing warning.

The horrors described are not
local disturbances, but are spread
over the known world; nations and
kingdoms are in hostility with one
another (not each divided against
itself, as in xii. 25, Is. xix. 2). It
was a commonplace of Apocalyptic
that universal war would be a sign of
the End; cf. *Ber.R.* xlii. (Wünsche p.
194) 'When thou seest the kingdoms
fighting against one another, look
and expect the foot of the Messiah';
and see Sib. iii. 538, 635 ff., 660 f.,
v. 361, 4 Esd. xiii. 29–31, *Sanh.*
97 a (Volz, *Jüd. Esch.* 182).

καὶ ἔσονται κτλ.] Famine and
earthquake as instruments of divine
punishment are frequent in O.T.
prophecy. The former is constantly
coupled with 'the sword' in Jerem.,
and is connected in late apocalypses
with the age of Antichrist (see
Bousset, *Antichr. Legend,* 195 ff.);
the latter is a marked eschatological
feature (cf. Ez. xxxviii. 19 f., Hag.
ii. 6 f., Zach. xiv. 4 f., Enoch i. 6;
and see Apoc. vi. 12 ff., xi. 13,
xvi. 18). Mk. confines κατὰ τόπους
to σεισμοί, which is perhaps Mt.'s
intention also, Lk. to λοιμοὶ καὶ
λιμοί. Lk. alone adds φόβητρά τε
καὶ σημεῖα ἀπ᾽ οὐρανοῦ μεγάλα
ἔσται, of which his *v.* 25 (= Mt. *v.*
29) is the immediate sequel.

8. πάντα κτλ.] They are only the
'beginning of pangs'; the Birth is
not yet. Lk. omits the verse. The
thought of the birth-pangs which
issue in the Messianic age (cf. παλιν-

γενεσία xix. 28) is expressed in rabb.
writings collectively as 'the pang
(חֶבְל) of the Messiah'; cf. *Sanh.* 98 b
(ascribed to Elieser ben Hyrkanos, *c.*
A.D. 100), *Mechilta,* 50 b, *Shabb.*118 a,
Keth. 111 a.

9–14. (Mk. *vv.* 9–13, Lk. *vv.*
12–19.) *Warnings of Persecution;
false prophets and apostasy.*

9. τότε κτλ.] The verse summarizes in a word or two the predictions
which Mt. has already inserted in
x. 17–21 (see notes there). This
brevity causes παραδώσουσιν to be
impers.; in x. 17 the subj. is
ἄνθρωποι. And θλίψις sums up the
trials in the courts and scourgings
in the synagogues. In x. 22 a τῶν
ἐθνῶν is absent (as in Mk.); its
addition here, like that of καὶ τοῖς
ἔθνεσιν in x. 18, implies a later
development of Christianity, and a
longer interval before the End. Lk.'s
addition καὶ θρὶξ ἐκ τῆς κεφαλῆς
ὑμῶν οὐ μὴ ἀπόληται, which, if
literal, contradicts θανατώσουσιν ἐξ
ὑμῶν, must be understood spiritually, as equivalent to κτήσεσθε τὰς
ψυχὰς ὑμῶν. It is quite different
from the saying in Mt. x. 30, Lk.
xii. 7.

10. καὶ τότε κτλ.] *Vv.* 10–12
are peculiar to Mt. The thought of
family divisions (x. 21) is here transformed into that of the apostasy of
Christians: many will stumble at
persecution, and will deliver up their
fellow Christians. On σκανδαλίζειν
see v. 29; the same word is used
of Jews καθ᾽ ὥραν τῆς συντελείας
(Dan. xi. 40 f.); and see Volz, *Jüd.
Esch.* 179.

καὶ ἀλλήλους παραδώσουσιν καὶ μισήσουσιν ἀλλήλους·
καὶ πυλλοὶ ψευδοπροφῆται ἐγερθήσονται καὶ πλανήσουσιν 11
πολλούς· καὶ διὰ τὸ πληθυνθῆναι τὴν ἀνομίαν ψυγήσεται 12
ἡ ἀγάπη τῶν πολλῶν. ὁ δὲ ὑπομείνας εἰς τέλος οὗτος 13
σωθήσεται. καὶ κηρυχθήσεται τοῦτο τὸ εὐαγγέλιον τῆς 14
βασιλείας ἐν ὅλῃ τῇ οἰκουμένῃ εἰς μαρτύριον πᾶσιν τοῖς
ἔθνεσιν, καὶ τότε ἥξει τὸ τέλος. Ὅταν οὖν ἴδητε τὸ Βδέλγμα 15

11. καὶ πολλοί κτλ.] On ψευδοπροφῆται see vii. 15. They are not
false claimants to Messiahship (v. 5),
from whom they are distinguished
in v. 24, but false Christian teachers.
For ἐγερθήσονται, 'raised up on the
stage of history,' see xi. 11 ; it implies that their appearance was by
divine ordinance, to test the faithfulness of Christians.

12. καὶ διά κτλ.] πληθύνειν in
connexion with sins is frequent in
the LXX. Mt. possibly alludes to
Dan. xii. 4 (with רָעָה for דְּעַת) in a
translation known to him ; cf. LXX.
with Theod. On ἀνομία see vii. 23.
The increasing wickedness, one of
the signs preceding the End (4 Esd.
v. 2, 10, Enoch xci. 7), will prove
too much for the majority (τ. πολλῶν)
of Christians ; the example, and the
fear, of men will cool the ardour
of their love ; cf. Apoc. iii. 15 f.
ἀγάπη, elsewhere in the synn. Lk.
xi. 42 only, but occurring in every
other book of the N.T. except Ac.,
Jam., is used of 'love to God' in
Wisd. iii. 9, vi. 18, Sir. xlviii. 11 ;
apart from the LXX. the only pre-
Christian passage in which it is
known in this sense is Philo, Quod
Deus Immut. § 14 (Mangey, i. 283).

13. ὁ δέ κτλ.] See on x. 22 b.
Lk. has ἐν τῇ ὑπομονῇ ὑμῶν κτήσεσθε τὰς ψυχὰς ὑμῶν.

14. καὶ κηρυχθήσεται κτλ.] Mk.
v. 10, which Mt. represents by καὶ
τοῖς ἔθνεσιν in x. 18 (see note), is
now reproduced at a later point in

the discourse. τοῦτο is added to
Mk.'s τὸ εὐαγγέλιον (cf. xxvi. 13).
'This Gospel of the Kingdom' (see
on iv. 23, ix. 35) means 'the good
tidings in this discourse that the
Kingdom is near.' Mk.'s πάντα τὰ
ἔθνη are the nations of the Roman
empire, the civilized world, as Mt.
(τῇ οἰκουμένῃ) understood. Mission
preaching throughout that area would
not seem to the writer to require
more than a few years to accomplish.
It was the ambition of S. Paul.
But had the words been a genuine
utterance of Jesus Himself, it is
difficult to think that S. Peter and
the other apostles could have acted
as they did ; see Gal. ii. 7 ff., Ac.
x.–xi. 18.

15–22. (Mk. vv. 14–20, Lk. vv.
20–24.) The Climax of the ' Pangs.'

15. ὅταν οὖν κτλ.] οὖν connects
the section with the preceding τὸ
τέλος. Mk. ὅταν δέ introduces a
new stage in the progress of events.
' The abomination of desolation,'
an allusion to Daniel, as Mt. notes,
is the LXX. equivalent for הַשִּׁקּוּץ
מְשֹׁמֵם (Dan. xi. 31) and שִׁקּוּץ שֹׁמֵם
(xii. 11), 'an abominable thing that
layeth waste,' referring to ix. 27.
The writer of Dan. refers to the
heathen altar, and probably an
image of Zeus Olympios (see BDB.
s.v. שִׁקּוּץ), which Antiochus Epiph.
erected in the temple (1 Macc. i. 54,
59, vi. 7, 2 Macc. vi. 1–5), and
which ' laid waste' the Jewish worship and the sanctity of the temple.

τῆc ἐρημώcεωc τὸ ῥηθὲν διὰ Δανιὴλ τοῦ προφήτου ἑστὸς
16 ἐν τόπῳ ἁγίῳ, ὁ ἀναγινώσκων νοείτω, τότε οἱ ἐν τῇ Ἰουδαίᾳ
17 φευγέτωσαν εἰς τὰ ὄρη, ὁ ἐπὶ τοῦ δώματος μὴ καταβάτω

In Mk. the reference is vague and cryptic, the masc. ἑστηκότα implying a person or personification, who will stand ὅπου οὐ δεῖ. Mt. notes the fulfilment of prophecy (τὸ ῥηθέν κτλ., see on i. 22); he makes the grammatical correction ἑστός, and writes ἐν τόπῳ ἁγίῳ, which may mean Jerusalem (2 Macc. iii. 1 f.), or even the Holy Land generally, but probably the temple (Ac. vi. 13, xxi. 28). Lk. interprets the βδέλυγμα as κυκλουμένην ὑπὸ στρατοπέδων Ἰερουσαλήμ, but echoing Dan. by adding τότε γνῶτε ὅτι ἤγγικεν ἡ ἐρήμωσις αὐτῆς. Some expositors think of the desecration of the temple by Zealots just before Titus besieged the city (Jos. BJ. IV. iii. 6–8, vi. 3); others of some action by the Romans similar to that of Antiochus : e.g. Pilate's introduction into the city of the standards bearing the image of Caesar (BJ. II. ix. 2), Caligula's attempt to set up his own statue in the temple (Ant. XVIII. viii. 8), the erection of Vespasian's equestrian statue in the Holy of Holies (Jer.), or of the statue of Titus on the site of the ruined temple (Chrys.). But the mysterious vagueness of Mk.'s masc. ἑστηκότα, with no reference to city or temple, is probably an allusion to the dread figure of Antichrist, analogous to the ' Man of Lawlessness' in 2 Thes. ii. 4, whose appearance is preceded by a 'revolt' from God ; cf. Matt. v. 12, Did. xvi. 4, αὐξανούσης γὰρ ἀνομίας . . . καὶ τότε φανήσεται ὁ κοσμοπλάνος. This cryptic language is unlike anything attributed to Jesus elsewhere. The author of the passage shared the widespread Jewish expecta-

tion of the coming of Anti-Christ (see Bousset, Anti-Chr. Legend).

ὁ ἀναγινώσκων νοείτω] So Mk. This can hardly be a call by the writer of the Apocalypse to his readers to note carefully what it says. The compiler of Mk. who assigned the whole discourse to Jesus could not have been so careless as to betray the extraneous origin of the passage by leaving the expression untouched. It may quite well be a remark added by himself or the apocalyptist : ' Let the reader note the new and terrible meaning which is given to the words in Daniel.' For the use of νοεῖν cf. 2 Tim. ii. 7, Jer. ii. 10.

16. τότε κτλ.] The hills of Judaea abounded in caves and safe hiding-places ; cf. 1 Macc. ii. 28, Ez. vii. 16. In Lk. the flight is from the besieging armies, in Mt., Mk. from the persecutions to be waged by Antichrist. It cannot be an ex eventu reference to the flight of Christians to Pella (see on x. 23), for Pella was not in the mountains, but at the foot of the eastern range, in the Jordan valley, about 17 m. south of the Lake of Galilee, and would be reached by travelling up the valley.

17. ὁ ἐπὶ τοῦ δώματος κτλ.] The warning not to come down is difficult after the command to flee. In Mt. the emphasis might be on ἆραι— not that he is not to come down at all, but that he is not to attempt to save his property; but in Mk., μὴ καταβάτω μηδὲ εἰσελθάτω, the coming down itself is expressly forbidden. Holtzmann supposes that the flight is to be across the roofs of the neighbouring houses ! Vv.

ἆραι τὰ ἐκ τῆς οἰκίας αὐτοῦ, καὶ ὁ ἐν τῷ ἀγρῷ μὴ ἐπι- 18
στρεψάτω ὀπίσω ἆραι τὸ ἱμάτιον αὐτοῦ. οὐαὶ δὲ ταῖς ἐν 19
γαστρὶ ἐχούσαις καὶ ταῖς θηλαζούσαις ἐν ἐκείναις ταῖς
ἡμέραις. προσεύχεσθε δὲ ἵνα μὴ γένηται ἡ φυγὴ ὑμῶν 20
χειμῶνος μηδὲ σαββάτῳ· ἔσται γὰρ τότε θλίψις μεγάλη 21

17, 18 (Mk. 15, 16) can hardly have stood in the Apocalypse (see next verse). They find a parallel in Lk. xvii. 31, which speaks of the suddenness of 'the day when the Son of Man is revealed,' and the warning 'let him not turn back' is illustrated by reference to Lot's wife, following the description of the sudden overthrow of Sodom. In the present passage Lk. employs the insertion in Mk., but alters it by a reference to Jerusalem, 'and let those who are in the midst of it (αὐτῆς) depart, and those who are in the country parts not enter into it (αὐτήν),' where the pronouns, which refer to the city, occur very abruptly after 'Judaea.' But his first clause, 'Then let them that are in Judaea flee to the mountains,' has perhaps been added by copyists by harmonization with Mt., Mk., so that the pronouns are the continuation of ἡ ἐρήμωσις αὐτῆς (Wellh., Spitta).

18. καὶ ὁ ἐν κτλ.] Mk. εἰς τὸν ἀγρόν; see Moulton, i. 63, 234 f. ἆραι τὸ ἱμάτιον αὐτοῦ (so Mk.) is absent from Lk. xvii. 31; it supplies an object for which the labourer would turn back. Vv. 17, 18 in their original context meant that neither the leisured man on the roof, nor the field labourer, must attempt to save their property; they must be ready to meet the Son of Man bereft of everything.

19. οὐαὶ δὲ κτλ.] The continuation of v. 16. Alas for those who cannot flee; it were better to be childless (cf. Lk. xxiii. 29). οὐαί (see on xviii. 7) and ἐν ἐκείν. τ. ἡμ.

are echoes of many O.T. warnings. In Mt., Mk. it means 'in the days of Antichrist,' in Lk. 'in the days of the siege.' With the whole verse cf. Apoc. Bar. x. 13–16, referring to the fall of Jerusalem.

20. προσεύχεσθε κτλ.] In Mk. the subj. of γένηται is not expressed; it refers to the catastrophe in general. Wintry or stormy weather would add a last horror to the situation. χειμών is either 'winter' (Jo. x. 22, 2 Tim. iv. 21) or 'storm' (xvi. 3, Ac. xxvii. 20). Wetstein and Lightfoot quote a rabb. tradition that at the destruction of the first temple God lengthened the days, so that it occurred in the summer and not in the winter. μηδὲ σαββάτῳ (Mt. only) has a strongly Jewish ring. In Maccabean days the pious had sacrificed themselves to slaughter for Sabbatarian scruples (1 Macc. ii. 31–38); and Jesus, though opposed to this (xii. 7, 12, Mk. ii. 27), could possibly have spoken the words knowing to what length the scruples might lead. But they have more probably been added by Mt. himself. If they were by the apocalyptist, Mk. must have omitted them for Gentile readers.

21. ἔσται κτλ.] An echo of Dan. xii. 1; cf. 1 Macc. ix. 27 and Ass. Mos. viii. (a reference to Antichrist contemporary with the evangelists): 'veniet in eos ultio et ira, quae talis non fuit in illis a saeculo usque ad illum tempus.' Mk.'s ἔσονται γὰρ αἱ ἡμέραι ἐκεῖναι θλίψις, a Semitic idiom (Ges. K. § 145 c.d.), possibly points to a reading הָעֵת for עֵת in

οἷα οὗ γέγονεν ἀπ᾽ ἀρχῆς κόσμου ἔως τοῦ νῦν οὐδ᾽ οὐ μὴ
22 γένηται. καὶ εἰ μὴ ἐκολοβώθησαν αἱ ἡμέραι ἐκεῖναι, οὐκ
ἂν ἐσώθη πᾶσα σάρξ· διὰ δὲ τοὺς ἐκλεκτοὺς κολοβωθή-
23 σονται αἱ ἡμέραι ἐκεῖναι. Τότε ἐάν τις ὑμῖν εἴπῃ Ἰδοὺ
24 ὧδε ὁ χριστός ἤ ῟Ωδε, μὴ πιστεύσητε· ἐγερθήσονται γὰρ
ψευδόχριστοι καὶ ψευδοπροφῆται, καὶ δώσουσιν σημεῖα μεγάλα
καὶ τέρατα ὥστε πλανᾶσθαι εἰ δυνατὸν καὶ τοὺς ἐκλεκτούς·
25 ἰδοὺ προείρηκα ὑμῖν. ἐὰν οὖν εἴπωσιν ὑμῖν Ἰδοὺ ἐν τῇ
26

Dan. *l.c.* οἷα is for Mk.'s οἷα τοιαύτη
= אֲשֶׁר כָּמֹהָ (cf. 'quae talis,' Ass.
Mos.), and κόσμου for Mk.'s κτίσεως
ἣν ἔκτισεν ὁ θεός. Lk. transforms
the θλίψις of the days of Antichrist
into 'great distress (ἀνάγκη) upon
the land, and wrath unto this people,'
and in the next verse gives a prediction of the sack of Jerusalem,
not in detail, but in general terms
suggested by the O.T. (for πατουμένη
cf. Zach. xii. 3, Dan. viii. 13, 1 Macc.
iii. 45, 51, iv. 60; and see Ps. Sol.
ii. 20, xvii. 25, Apoc. xi. 2).

22. καὶ εἰ μή κτλ.] Mk. ἐκο-
λόβωσεν Κύριος (יהוה) τὰς ἡμέρας.
For the vb. (lit. 'amputate') cf.
2 Regn. iv. 12. The meaning is either
that the period of Antichrist's sway
is limited (cf. the fixed periods in
Dan. viii. 14, ix. 24–27, xii. 7, 11 f.),
or that the days themselves were
made shorter than 24 hours; cf.
v. 20, Ep. Barn. iv. 3 (according to
J. Weiss not a reference to Mt., but
to some Jewish work): 'To this end
the Master hath cut short (συντέ-
τμηκεν) the seasons and the days,
that His Beloved might hasten, and
come to his inheritance.' And see
Volz, *Jüd. Esch.* 164 f., Bousset,
Antichr. Legend, 218 f. ἐκλεκτούς
(see on xxii. 14) is for Mk.'s redundant
ἐκλ. οὓς ἐξελέξατο, and the fut.
κολοβωθήσονται for his proph. aor.
Lk. omits the verse since it does
not deal with the destruction of
Jerusalem.

23–25. (Mk. *vv.* 21–23.) *Warning against false Messiahs and false
prophets.*

23. τότε κτλ.] The words are
represented by Mt., Mk. as spoken
after the tribulation of Antichrist,
as though yet further delay must be
expected before the Parousia; but
this conflicts with εὐθέως κτλ. in
v. 29, which forms the true sequel
of *v.* 22. ἰδοὺ ὧδε κτλ. is spoken
not by the deceivers but, as in *v.* 26,
by those who are excited and misled
by their claims. For ὧδε . . . ὧδε
(Mk. ὧδε . . . ἐκεῖ) cf. Exod. ii. 12,
3 Regn. xviii. 45, xxi. 40.

24. ἐγερθήσονται κτλ.] On the
verb see *v.* 11. The false Messiahs
(cf. *v.* 5) and the false prophets (cf.
v. 11, vii. 15) are allied, but not
identical. The false claimants of
the Messiah's office are to be distinguished from ἀντίχριστοι (1 Jo. ii.
18) whose opposition is focused in
the ἀντίχριστος. The latter originates in Jewish thought; the former
is probably of Christian coinage. In
καὶ δώσουσιν (Mk. ποιήσουσιν) Mt. is
influenced by Deut. xiii. 1 [2], ἐὰν . . .
προφήτης δῷ σοι σημεῖον ἢ τέρας.
'Sign' and 'portent' (אות and מופת,
see Driver, *Deut.* 75) are often combined in the O.T., especially in Deut.

25. ἰδού κτλ.] Mk. ὑμεῖς δὲ
βλέπετε· πρ. ὑμ. πάντα. If some
of the elect could be deceived, the
apostles, being forewarned, should be
safe. In Mk. this forms the close

ἐρήμῳ ἐστίν, μὴ ἐξέλθητε· Ἰδοὺ ἐν τοῖς ταμείοις, μὴ 27
πιστεύσητε· ὥσπερ γὰρ ἡ ἀστραπὴ ἐξέρχεται ἀπὸ ἀνατολῶν καὶ φαίνεται ἕως δυσμῶν, οὕτως ἔσται ἡ παρουσία
τοῦ υἱοῦ τοῦ ἀνθρώπου· ὅπου ἐὰν ᾖ τὸ πτῶμα, ἐκεῖ 28
συναχθήσονται οἱ ἀετοί. Εὐθέως δὲ μετὰ τὴν θλίψιν τῶν 29

of the warning; Mt. adds to it, and
therefore omits πάντα.

26–28. (Lk. xvii. 23 f., 37.)
*Warning of the suddenness of the
Parousia.*

26. ἐὰν οὖν κτλ.] Mt., with a
connecting οὖν (Lk. καὶ ἐροῦσιν),
enriches the discourse with a passage
from another context in Q. V. 26
is possibly a doublet of v. 23; in Lk.
ἰδοὺ ἐκεῖ ἰδοὺ ὧδε the similarity is
closer; this is interpreted in Mt.,
or in his recension of Q, as 'out
yonder in the wilderness' and 'here
in our midst but concealed' (cf. Deut.
xxxii. 25, ἔξωθεν ... καὶ ἐκ τῶν τα-
μείων). Some might expect a Messiah
who, like other revolutionary leaders,
proclaimed Himself openly; others a
Messiah who was preparing for His
revolution in secret, and known only
to a few (cf. Jo. vii. 27); but no one
who could be pointed out at a given
place would be the real Messiah.
On the form ταμεῖον see vi. 6. For
πιστεύσητε (cf. v. 23) Lk. has διώ-
ξητε, a class. use unique in bibl. Gk.
The Pauline use to which Harnack
refers is never with a personal object.

27. ὥσπερ κτλ.] Cf. Apoc. Bar.
liii. (with Charles' notes) where the
Messiah is symbolized by lightning
on a cloud which illuminates the
whole earth. The lightning is not
only sudden (as in Lk. x. 18) but
visible over a vast area; 'no one
will foresee it, and all will see it at
once' (Plummer). Cf. *Ep. Jer.* 60,
Lucan x. 34 f., 'fulmenque quod
omnes Percuteret pariter populos.'
The O.T. expression 'from East to

West' (cf. viii. 11), *i.e.* in all quarters
of the world, is interpreted by Lk.
for Gentile readers as ἐκ τῆς ὑπὸ τὸν
οὐρανὸν εἰς τὴν ὑπ' οὐρανόν (an
ellipse which occurs in the LXX., and
is characteristic of Job). On the *term.
techn.* παρουσία see v. 3; Lk. has
the simpler ὁ υἱ. τ. ἀνθρ. [ἐν τῇ
ἡμέρᾳ αὐτοῦ]; cf. v. 37.

28. ὅπου ἐάν κτλ.] A proverbial
saying, perhaps current at the time.
Cf. Job xxxix. 30. In Lk. xvii.
37 it answers, or rather refuses
to answer, the disciples' question,
'Where Lord?' But in Mt. it
expresses inevitableness. Had Amos
written it he might have said, 'Shall
a corpse lie on the ground and the
vultures not be gathered there?'
(cf. Am. iii. 3–8). It does not
describe the Messiah descending from
heaven upon the nation dead in sins,
nor the false Messiahs and prophets
making the people their prey, nor
the eagles on the Roman standards
in the attack on Jerusalem; the last
is not the subject dealt with either
in Mt. or Lk. *l.c.* For πτῶμα Lk.
prefers σῶμα, perhaps applying it in
thought to the nation. ἀετός, like
נֶשֶׁר, stands for various kinds of eagles
and vultures; see *HDB.* 'Eagle.'

29–31. (Mk. vv. 24–27, Lk. vv.
25–28.) *The Moment of the Parousia.*

29. εὐθέως κτλ.] This is the true
sequel of vv. 15 f., 19–22; the
θλίψις is that of v. 21, the climax
of the 'Pangs' being followed immediately by the End. In Mk.
(ἀλλὰ ἐν ἐκείναις ταῖς ἡμέραις μετὰ
τ. θλ. ἐκείνην) both the tribulation

ἡμερῶν ἐκείνων ὁ ἥλιος ϲκοτιϲθήϲεται, καὶ ἡ ϲελήνη οὐ δώϲει τὸ
φέγγοϲ αὐτῆϲ, καὶ οἱ ἀϲτέρεϲ πεϲοῦνται ἀπὸ τοῦ οὐρανοῦ, καὶ
30 αἱ δυνάμειϲ τῶν οὐρανῶν ϲαλευθήϲονται· καὶ τότε· φανήσεται
τὸ σημεῖον τοῦ υἱοῦ τοῦ ἀνθρώπου ἐν οὐρανῷ, καὶ τότε
κόψονται πᾶϲαι αἱ φυλαὶ τῆϲ γῆϲ καὶ ὄψονται τὸν υἱὸν τοῦ

(see Mk. *vv.* 17, 19) and the Parousia are in 'those days,' *i.e.* they are successive events in the same period (see Burkitt, *JThS.*, Apr. 1911, 460); and ἀλλά adds a note of encouragement: the tribulation will be terrible (*vv.* 14–20), *but* the Parousia will follow it at once. Mt. is probably not more original, but only more circumstantial. Mk. was unlikely to avoid his favourite εὐθέως, had it stood in his source.

ὁ ἥλιος κτλ.] Convulsions of the heavenly bodies, normally so unerring in obedience to God's laws, were a standing feature of Hebrew eschatology; see Is. xiii. 10, xxiv. 21, 23, xxxiv. 4, Jer. iv. 23, Ez. xxxii. 7 f., Joel ii. 10, iii. 3 f. [Engl. ii. 30 f.], Am. v. 20, Zeph. i. 15, Hag. ii. 6, 21, Enoch lxxx. 4, Test. Levi iv. 1, 4 Esd. v. 4, Ass. Mos. x. 5; cf. 2 Pet. iii. 12, Apoc. vi. 12 f. πεϲοῦνται: Mk. ἔϲονται πίπτοντεϲ, which, if not an Aramaism for the fut. verb, describes the scene in progress, star after star falling (Blass, § 62. 2). Lk. has 'There shall be signs in the sun and moon and stars,' followed by troubles on earth, 'distress of nations, in perplexity at the sound of the sea and brine . . . fear and expectation.' The 'powers of the heavens' are the צְבָא הַשָּׁמַיִם; cf. Is. xxxiv. 4, Targ. Ps. xcvi. 11 חֵילֵי דִשְׁמַיָּא. They include the sun, moon, and stars, to which they are added as a summary, as in Deut. iv. 19, xvii. 3, 4 Regn. xxiii. 5, Jer. viii. 2. ϲαλευθήϲονται, generally of an earthquake, is extended to the firmament; cf. Hag. ii. 6.

30. καὶ τότε κτλ.] The great moment at last arrives. The first two clauses (to τῆϲ γῆϲ) are peculiar to Mt. The 'sign of the Son of Man' is connected with His Person, and is different from the 'signs in the sun, moon, and stars.' It may have been an eschatological feature known to Mt.'s Jewish readers but not to us. Patr. writers thought of the sign of the Cross (see Swete on Mk. xiii. 26). It is possibly an allusion to the ensign (נֵס, LXX. σημεῖον, σύσσημον) which would be set up by Yahweh as a rallying-point for His dispersed people (Is. xi. 12, xviii. 3, xlix. 22), and by the offspring of the root of Jesse (Is. xi. 10 Heb.), a thought continued in the 'trumpet' (*v.* 31) sounded for the gathering of the elect. σημεῖον in this case is something in the sky visible to all (see Bousset, *Antichr. Legend*, 232 f.), *e.g.* a shining light surrounding the Son of Man, the δόξα πολλή of *v.* 31. Or, less probably, it may be the sign *consisting of* the Son of Man.

καὶ τότε κόψονται κτλ.] Mt. has a double description of the same event: *v.* 30 a the Parousia and the mourning of the tribes, *v.* 30 b, 31 the Parousia and the gathering of the elect. The words appear to be based on Zach. xii. 10 ff., κόψονται ἐπ' αὐτόν . . . κόψεται ἡ γῆ κατὰ φυλὰς φυλάς, but with a wider meaning, the prophet speaking only of the tribes of Israel, and the land of Palestine. Mt. differs both from the Heb. and LXX., but agrees with Apoc. i. 7, where the quotation is

ἀνθρώπογ ἐρχόμενον ἐπὶ τῶν νεφελῶν τοŷ οὐρανοŷ μετὰ δυνάμεως
καὶ δόξης πολλῆς· καὶ ἀποστελεῖ τοὺς ἀγγέλους αὐτοῦ 31
μετὰ cάλπιγγοc μεγάληc, καὶ ἐπιcγνάζογcιν τοὺς ἐκλεκτοὺς αὐτοῦ
ἐκ τῶν τεccάρων ἀνέμων ὀπ᾽ ἄκρων ογρανῶν ἕως τῶν ἄκρων

31 μεγαλης] אLΔ 1 118 209 *al* 𝔏 e 𝔖 sin.pesh me arm ; *pr* φωνης ΒΧΓΠ *al*
minn.*pler* ; *idem ante* σαλπιγγος 𝔖 hcl.*pal aeth ; *pr και* φωνης D 𝔏 vet.*pler*.vg

combined with another from Zach.,
which is also found in Jo. xix. 37,
differing from Heb. and LXX. Both
in Mt. and Apoc. it is in conjunction
with the passage from Dan. which
follows. All these quotations were
probably drawn from a collection of
testimonia, in which stood a group
of quotations bearing on the Parousia.
καὶ ὄψονται κτλ.] An allusion
to the crucial passage, Dan. vii. 13 f.:
ἰδοὺ ἐπὶ (Aram. עַל, Theod. μετά, so
Mk. xiv. 62, Apoc. i. 7) τῶν νεφελῶν
τοῦ οὐρανοῦ ὡς υἱὸς ἀνθρώπου
ἤρχετο (Theod. ἐρχόμενος). Mk. has
ἐν νεφέλαις, Lk. ἐν νεφέλῃ. The
τὸν υἱ. τοῦ ἀνθρ. of the synn. is due
to the Lord's use of the Messianic
title, which would naturally cause
the inclusion of the passage among
the *testimonia*. In xxvi. 64 the
same form of the quotation is used.
μετὰ δυνάμεως κτλ.] So Lk. ;
Mk. μ. δυν. πολλῆς καὶ δόξ., which
probably means 'with a great host
and (with) glory,' *i.e.* the host of
angels who are mentioned in the
next verse ; see xvi. 27. In Mt., Lk.
the meaning may be the same, if
πολλῆς agrees with both substs. (for
δυν. πολλή in this sense cf. 2 Chr.
xxiv. 24, Ez. xxxviii. 15) ; if with
δόξης only, μετὰ δυνάμεως is 'with
(a display of) power,' or perhaps
'armed with (divine) power.'
31. καὶ ἀποστελεῖ κτλ.] In xiii.
41 it is said that the Son of Man
will send *His* angels (αὐτοῦ being
added by Mt. as here ; cf. xvi. 27),
their task being to collect and destroy

all that is bad ; here it is to gather
all that is good. In iii. 12 both
actions are ascribed to the Messiah
Himself. The 'great trumpet' (sing.)
is not sounded by the angels ; it is
a well-known eschatological feature,
which recalls Is. xxvii. 13, the
gathering of the exiles τῇ σάλπιγγι
τῇ μεγάλῃ. Cf. Zach. ix. 14, Ps.
Sol. xi. 1, 4 Esd. vi. 23, 1 Thes. iv.
16, 1 Cor. xv. 52, *Shemoneh Esreh* 10
(quoted by Allen). Behind the symbolism may lie the account of the
Theophany in Exod. xix. 16, to which
may be due the addition of φωνῆς (see
Appar.) ; cf. Blass, § 35. 6.
καὶ ἐπισυνάξουσιν κτλ.] Mk.
ἐπισυνάξει, omitting αὐτοῦ as before.
ἐπί is 'to the Son of Man' in the
clouds. Heaven and earth are destroyed, and nothing is said as to
any place to which the elect will be
finally gathered. See Milligan, and
von Dobschütz, on 1 Thes. iv. 17,
which S. Paul utters ἐν λόγῳ Κυρίου,
possibly a reference to the saying in this
passage. Nor is a resurrection mentioned, nor a physical transformation,
as in 1 Cor. xv. For ἐκ τ. τεσσ. ἀν.
cf. Ezek. xxxvii. 9, Dan. viii. 8, xi. 4,
and especially Zach. ii. 6 [10]. ἀπ᾽
ἄκρων κτλ. strengthens the thought.
The sky being a vault resting on the
earth, the ἄκρα (the plur. being due to
the plur. οὐρανοί) are the extreme edge
where they are in contact. Cf. Deut.
xxx. 4. The same idiom, but with
γῆς for οὐρανῶν, occurs in Deut. xiii.
7 [8], Jer. xii. 12. Mk. combines
them : ἀπ᾽ ἄκρου γῆς ἕως ἄκρ.

32 ἀῦτῶν.   Ἀπὸ δὲ τῆς συκῆς μάθετε τὴν παραβολήν·
ὅταν ἤδη ὁ κλάδος αὐτῆς γένηται ἁπαλὸς καὶ τὰ φύλλα
33 ἐκφύῃ, γινώσκετε ὅτι ἐγγὺς τὸ θέρος· οὕτως καὶ ὑμεῖς,
ὅταν ἴδητε πάντα ταῦτα, γινώσκετε ὅτι ἐγγύς ἐστιν ἐπὶ θύραις.
34 ἀμὴν λέγω ὑμῖν ὅτι οὐ μὴ παρέλθῃ ἡ γενεὰ αὕτη ἕως ἂν

οὐρανῶν. Lk. omits the verse, but
adds (v. 28), 'And when these things
begin to come to pass, lift up yourselves and raise your heads, because
your redemption draweth nigh.'
But since τούτων refers to the signs
in vv. 10 f., 25 f., not to the Parousia
(v. 27), either vv. 27, 28 have been
transposed, or the former was a
later addition in Lk.

32, 33. (Mk. xiii. 28 f., Lk. xxi.
29 ff.) PARABLE OF THE FIG-TREE.
This was doubtless a genuine
utterance of Jesus; but it cannot be
in its original position, since in vv.
29–31 the End has come, but in v.
33 'all these things' are only signs
that it is near. Mk., or the apocalyptist, must have found it somewhere
in conjunction with other predictions
of signs preceding the End, and
placed it in the discourse at an unsuitable point.

32. ἀπὸ δέ κτλ.]   τὴν παραβολήν
is 'its parable,' the analogy which it
offers.. Lk.'s καὶ εἶπεν παραβολὴν
αὐτοῖς shews a knowledge that it was
not originally a continuation of the
discourse. Any tree would have served
as an illustration, but the Lord must
be thought of as pointing to some
fig-trees near by. Lk., who places
the discourse in the temple, writes
'behold the fig-tree and all the trees.'
ὅταν κτλ.] The branch grows
soft with fresh spring sap. ἁπαλός,
usually of the human body, is used
of a plant in Lev. ii. 14 (B*, Aq.),
Cratin. Chir. ii., and of fresh fruit in
Herod.; cf. ἁπαλότης Ez. xvii. 4, 9.
For the trans. ἐκφύῃ cf. Sym. Ps.

ciii. [civ.] 14. But ἐκφυῇ, with
τὰ φύλλα as the subj., 'the leaves
sprout,' makes good sense, and is supported by 𝕃 vet.pler.vulg. 𝕾 sin.cur
in Mt. and Mk., and by Ephr[diat].
τὸ θέρος covers broadly the period
from soon after the Passover till the
fruit harvest. It is not, as sometimes, equivalent to θερισμός, though
the harvest is a frequent symbol of
the End, since the leaves sprout long
before. θέρος, in this context only
in the N.T., never has the art. in
the LXX.; it may represent the emphatic state קַיִץ.

33. οὕτως κτλ.] The γινώσκετε
(ind.) of v. 32 implies that 'all
men know'; here it is imper. (Vulg.
scitote). The subj. of ἐγγύς ἐστιν is
not expressed, but must have been
clear in the original context of the
parable.   It may have been τὸ
τέλος (קֵץ), perhaps with an allusion
to the word-play in Am. viii. 2.
Mt., Mk., in placing it in its present
position, seem to have understood
the subj. to be 'the Son of Man' (v.
30); hence the addition of ἐπὶ θύραις,
which suggests a personal subj.; cf.
Jam. v. 9 (perhaps a reminiscence of
the passage), Apoc. iii. 20.   Lk.,
omitting ἐπὶ θύραις, supplies ἡ
βασιλεία τοῦ θεοῦ as the subj.

34–36. (Mk. xiii. 30–32, Lk. xxi.
32 f.) THE NEARNESS OF THE END.
34. ἀμήν κτλ.] See on v. 18.
The truth illustrated by the parable
is now stated plainly. 'This generation' cannot mean the Jews as a
people, or mentioned in general (Jer.),
or believers in Christ (Orig., Chrys.,

πάντα ταῦτα γένηται. ὁ οὐρανὸς καὶ ἡ γῆ παρελεύσεται, 35
οἱ δὲ λόγοι μου οὐ μὴ παρέλθωσιν. Περὶ δὲ τῆς ἡμέρας 36

Thphlact.), or the (future) generation that will experience these things (Klosterm.); as in xi. 16 and elsewhere it must be the particular generation of Jews to whom, or of whom, the words were spoken. In the O.T. a 'generation' is reckoned at 40 years, by Herod. (ii. 142) and Heracl. (Plut. *Def. Orac.* 11) about 30 years. H. Holtzmann thinks that in Lk. it represents about a century, since the verse refers to the fall of Jerusalem. But the original reference is not to that event, either literally, or 'regarded as the type of the end of the world' (Plummer), but to the passing away of heaven and earth (*v.* 31). It is impossible to escape the conclusion that Jesus, as Man, expected the End within the lifetime of His contemporaries; cf. x. 23, xvi. 28. πάντα ταῦτα refers to all the events described in *vv.* 9 f., 15–22, 29–31. For παρέρχεσθαι in this sense cf. Ps. lxxxix. [xc.] 6 f., Wisd. ii. 4.

35. ὁ οὐρανός κτλ.] The dissolution of heaven and earth would constitute the end of the present age (see Targ. Jer. Exod. xii. 30, transl. by Wetstein), throughout which the Law was expected to abide (see on v. 18). Christians can see in the saying the truth that the Lord's words, which are the ὄντως νόμος, will abide even after the dissolution, but the immediate force is 'the world shall pass away, and My prediction of it will not fail'; cf. Is. xl. 8. For παρέρχεσθαι of words cf. Ps. cxlviii. 6, Dan. vi. 12 (Theod.). Mk., Lk. have οὐ μὴ παρελεύσονται; see Moulton, i. 190–2.

36. περὶ δέ κτλ.] The genuineness of the verse is doubted by few; no Christian would have ascribed

the words to the Lord if He had not said them. It remains a standing wonder that those who believed in Him as God Incarnate, so faithfully recorded His human ignorance; see Scott Holland's essay in *Jesus or Christ?* On the problem of His limitations of knowledge see Gore, *The Incarnation*, 162 ff., 267, *Dissertations*, 111 ff., Mason, *Conditions*, 120 ff., Sanday, *Christologies*, 71–8, and the works on the *Kenosis* which he cites. The words are usually taken to mean that God alone knows at what day and hour the End will come; and that Jesus, though He declared throughout His ministry that the End would be immediate, did not know its exact date. This is possible. For men's ignorance of the time of the End see parallels in Volz, *Jüd. Esch.* 171. If, as some think, the verse conflicts with the Lord's certainty that it was to be immediate, the same must be the case with the Epilogue which each evang. appends to the discourse; for the disciples knew of its imminence from His lips, and yet they are exhorted to watch, because they know not the day and hour. But another explanation is also possible. εἰδέναι περί τινος is not found elsewhere in bibl. Gk., and γινώσκειν π. τ. only in 2 Esd. v. 17, Tob. i. 19 (א), Jo. vii. 17 (contrast the acc. in Jud. iv. 8, Mt. xxv. 13, and Gen. xxvii. 2, Eccl. ix. 12, Mt. xxiv. 50). God alone possesses knowledge *concerning* the day and hour, *i.e.* what it will be like—the terror and glory of it, all that it will mean to the bad and the good. Jesus does not say 'that day *or even* hour'; and to express a knowledge of the exact time 'that hour or even day' would have been

ἐκείνης καὶ ὥρας οὐδεὶς οἶδεν, οὐδὲ οἱ ἄγγελοι τῶν οὐρανῶν
37 οὐδὲ ὁ υἱός, εἰ μὴ ὁ πατὴρ μόνος. ὥσπερ γὰρ αἱ ἡμέραι
τοῦ Νῶε, οὕτως ἔσται ἡ παρουσία τοῦ υἱοῦ τοῦ ἀνθρώπου·
38 ὡς γὰρ ἦσαν ἐν ταῖς ἡμέραις ἐκείναις ταῖς πρὸ τοῦ κατα-
κλυσμοῦ τρώγοντες καὶ πίνοντες, γαμοῦντες καὶ γαμίζοντες,

36 ουδε ο υιος] א*ᵉᵗᵇBD 13 28 86 124 𝕃 vet.*pler codd.pler ap. Hier* ℥ pal aeth
arm ; *om* אᵃE *etc* 𝕃 g¹·² vg ℥ sin.pesh.hcl me *codd.Gr.Adam. et Pier. et codd.Gr.
ap. Amb.*

more natural. The addition of καὶ
(Mk. ἢ τῆς) ὥρας is rhetorical, the
'day' and the 'hour' having the
same meaning; cf. *v.* 42 ff. (ἡμέρα
... φυλακῇ ... ὥρᾳ) with Lk. xii.
39 f. (ὥρᾳ ... ὥρᾳ) and see Dan. xii.
13 (LXX.) ἔτι γάρ εἰσιν ἡμέραι καὶ
ὧραι εἰς ἀναπλήρωσιν συντελείας,
where Theod. (B*) omits καὶ ὧραι.
For ἢ in a neg. sentence equivalent
to καί see on v. 17. On ἡ ἡμέρα
ἐκείνη see vii. 22.

οὐδὲ ὁ υἱός] The words are
certain in Mk., but in Mt., though
the evidence for them is strong, they
may be a scribal addition ; he often
avoids words which imply limitation
of the Lord's knowledge (see on viii.
29) and would be the more likely
to avoid a plain statement of it.
On the other hand scribes might
equally shun the words, Mt. and not
Mk. suffering from the omission
because the former gospel was the
more popular and widely used. If
Mt. himself omitted the words, his
addition of μόνος after Mk.'s εἰ μὴ
ὁ πατήρ may have been intentional,
suggesting the truth without stating
it explicitly ; δοκεῖ τῷ Μάρκῳ
συμφέρεσθαι κατὰ τὴν ἔννοιαν (Bas.).
The absolute use of 'the Son' in
contrast with 'the Father,' unique
in Mk., is found in Mt. xi. 27 = Lk.
x. 22 (Q) (cf. also Mt. xxi. 37 f.) as
well as in Jo.ᵉᵛ· ᵉᵖ·. Its rarity in
the synn. may suggest that Jesus did
not use it often, but there can be
little doubt of its genuineness.

εἰ μή κτλ.] Connected with
οὐδεὶς οἶδεν, the intervening words
being a parenthesis; see Blass, § 65.
6. On ὁ πατήρ see vi. 9. For the
Father's knowledge of the time of
the End cf. Zach. xiv. 7, Ps. Sol.
xvii. 23, Apoc. Bar. xxi. 8, and
see Volz, *Jüd. Esch.* 115 f., 165 f.

37–xxv. 46. EPILOGUE. Mk.'s
Epilogue is in xiii. 33–37, Lk.'s
in xxi. 34–36.

37–39. (Lk. xvii. 26 f.) WARN-
ING FROM THE EXAMPLE OF THE
FLOOD. Lk. abbreviates, but adds a
warning from the overthrow of
Sodom.

37. ὥσπερ κτλ.] The Parousia
is like the days of Noah, *i.e.* they
illustrate an aspect of it (see on xiii.
24)—men's unpreparedness. On
παρουσία see *v.* 3 ; Lk. ἐν τ. ἡμέραις
τοῦ υἱ. τ. ἀνθρ. (cf. *v.* 27 above)
affords a closer comparison with ἐν
τ. ἡμ. Νῶε.

38. ὡς γάρ κτλ.] The behaviour
in the days before the Flood is like
the Parousia, *i.e.* is like the behaviour
of men when the P. will occur.
τρώγειν, lit. to chew raw fruit or
vegetables, recurs only in Jo. vi. 54,
56 ff., xiii. 18 (= Ps. xl. [xli.] 10,
ἐσθίων). On γαμεῖν and γαμίζειν
see xxii. 30. Lk.'s pass. ἐγαμίζοντο
seems the more natural, but for
that reason Mt. may be the more
original. ἄχρι, here only in Mt.,
frequent in Lk., Ac., must be due
to Q.

ἄχρι ἧς ἡμέρας εἰϲᾷλθεν Νῶε εἰϲ τὴν κιβωτόν, καὶ οὐκ 39
ἔγνωσαν ἕως ἦλθεν ὁ κατακλυσμὸς καὶ ἦρεν ἅπαντας, οὕτως
ἔσται ἡ παρουσία τοῦ υἱοῦ τοῦ ἀνθρώπου. τότε ἔσονται δύο 40
ἐν τῷ ἀγρῷ, εἷς παραλαμβάνεται καὶ εἷς ἀφίεται· δύο 41
ἀλήθουσαι ἐν τῷ μύλῳ, μία παραλαμβάνεται καὶ μία ἀφίεται.
γρηγορεῖτε οὖν, ὅτι οὐκ οἴδατε ποίᾳ ἡμέρᾳ ὁ κύριος ὑμῶν 42
ἔρχεται. ἐκεῖνο δὲ γινώσκετε ὅτι εἰ ᾔδει ὁ οἰκοδεσπότης ποίᾳ 43
φυλακῇ ὁ κλέπτης ἔρχεται, ἐγρηγόρησεν ἂν καὶ οὐκ ἂν εἴασεν

39. καὶ οὐκ κτλ.] Lk. omits
οὐκ ἔγν. ἕως. The Flood is a frequent type in apocal. literature of
the final destruction of the world;
e.g. Enoch x. 2, liv. 7 ff., lxv., lxxxiii.
f., cvi., Jos. Ant. I. ii. 3 (flood and fire);
cf. Nah. i. 8, Dan. ix. 26.

40, 41. (Lk. xvii. 34 f.) Two
ILLUSTRATIONS.

40. τότε ἔσονται κτλ.] The
illustrations teach that the Parousia
will be without warning, and that
there will be, as in the days of
Noah, a sharp severance between
the good and the wicked. Mt. gives
two men and two women at work;
Lk. two men sleeping together (ἐπὶ
κλίνης μιᾶς), and two women working together (ἐπὶ τὸ αὐτό). The
latter may be due to the reflexion
that the End might come either by
night or by day. But Jesus perhaps
gave three illustrations; cf. vii. 9 f.
παραλαμβάνεται and ἀφίεται are
prophetic pres. (Lk. has fut.): the
good man will be 'received' (cf. Jo.
xiv. 3) by the angels (v. 31), the
bad man will be 'left' to his fate
(xxiii. 38). The converse — taken
for punishment, and left in safety—
is possible but less probable.

41. δύο κτλ.] On ἀλήθειν (Attic
ἀλέειν) see Lob. Phryn. 151. ἐν = בְּ,
'at the mill'; the reading μυλῶνι
(D), pistrino, 'mill-house,' is a mistaken correction. On μύλος see
xviii. 6. For grinding as the work

of a slave girl cf. Exod. xi. 5. See
E. Robinson, Researches, i. 485.

42–44. (Mk. xiii. 33, Lk. xii. 39 f.)
THE HOUSEHOLDER AND THE THIEF.

42. γρηγορεῖτε κτλ.] This warning leads up to, and underlies, all
the parables which follow. 'Your
Lord' is a Christian title for Christ,
and can hardly have been used by
Jesus of the Son of Man. Mk.'s
πότε ὁ καιρός ἐστιν is more
probable. On ποίᾳ = τίνι see xix.
18. Mk. vv. 34–37 contain an
illustration of a householder, which
recalls the parable of the Talents
(Mt. xxv. 14 ff.), and further injunctions to 'watch' (γρηγορεῖτε,
not ἀγρυπνεῖτε as in v. 33). The
first of these runs, γρ. οὖν· οὐκ οἴδατε
γὰρ πότε ὁ κύριος τῆς οἰκίας ἔρχεται,
in which the 2nd pers. is strangely
combined with the parabolic 'master
of the house.' These verses therefore
may have been added to Mk. v. 33
on the basis of Mt., Lk.

43. ἐκεῖνο δέ κτλ.] 'That other
thing ye know,' in contrast with
the preceding thing, which the
hearers did not know (see Blass,
§ 49. 3). In Lk., where there is no
contrast, τοῦτο is used. For φυλακῇ
(see xiv. 25) Lk. has ὥρᾳ, probably
for variety, having used φυλ. twice
in the preceding verse. ἐγρήγ. ἂν
καί, absent from Lk., emphasizes the
thought that fills Mt.'s epilogue.
On διορύσσειν see vi. 19. The

44 διορυχθῆναι τὴν οἰκίαν αὐτοῦ. διὰ τοῦτο καὶ ὑμεῖς γίνεσθε
ἕτοιμοι, ὅτι ᾗ οὐ δοκεῖτε ὥρᾳ ὁ υἱὸς τοῦ ἀνθρώπου
45 ἔρχεται. Τίς ἄρα ἐστὶν ὁ πιστὸς δοῦλος καὶ φρόνιμος ὃν
κατέστησεν ὁ κύριος ἐπὶ τῆς οἰκετείας αὐτοῦ τοῦ δοῦναι
46 αὐτοῖς τὴν τροφὴν ἐν καιρῷ ; μακάριος ὁ δοῦλος ἐκεῖνος
47 ὃν ἐλθὼν ὁ κύριος αὐτοῦ εὑρήσει οὕτως ποιοῦντα· ἀμὴν
λέγω ὑμῖν ὅτι ἐπὶ πᾶσιν τοῖς ὑπάρχουσιν αὐτοῦ καταστήσει

comparison of the Parousia with the breaking in by a thief is not found in Jewish apocalypses, and may have originated with Jesus ; cf. 1 Thess. v. 2, 2 Pet. iii. 10, Apoc. iii. 3, xvi. 15. For its occurrence at night cf. Mt. xxv. 6, where Jer. says 'traditio Judaeorum est Christum media nocte venturum, in similitudinem Aegypti temporis quando Pascha celebratum est.' But the point of the simile is the unexpectedness of the occurrence.

44. διὰ τοῦτο κτλ.] διὰ τ. (Lk. καί) looks back to the parable, not forward to ὅτι. The verse need not be a harmonizing addition in Lk. (Harnack) ; Mt. places the warning at the beginning and the end of the parable, from Mk. and Q respectively.

45–51. (Lk. xii. 42–46.) THE GOOD AND BAD SERVANT.

Lk. opens with 'And Peter said, Lord, speakest Thou this parable to us or also to all ?' Cf. Mk. xiii. 37, 'What I say to you I say to all, Watch,' which is perhaps based on Lk. (see on v. 42). The answer in Lk. has not been preserved.

45. τίς ἄρα κτλ.] τίς is not emphatic, as though it implied that few faithful servants can be found. ἄρα may be inferential : 'since such a state of readiness is requisite, who then etc.' (Holtzmann) ; or it is 'who now ?' (Vulg. quis putas), adding vivacity (cf. xviii. 1). In the former case the answer is supplied by v. 46 as an exclamation ; in the latter the

meaning is 'any faithful and prudent servant' (the adjectives being proleptic) appointed for a certain duty (45), if he performs that duty (46), will be rewarded (47), τίς being virtually 'whoever' (= מִי), v. 47 a quasi apodosis, and v. 46 parenthetical. Cf. the broken construction in Lk. xi. 5–8. Lk. has οἰκονόμος for δοῦλος (in keeping with his responsible duty), θεραπεία (so D in Mt.) for the rare and late οἰκετεία (for which cf. Sym. Job i. 3, Jos. Ant. VIII. vi. 3, XII. ii. 3), the more technical σιτομέτριον (cf. the verb, Gen. xlvii. 12, 14) for τροφή (cf. x. 10), and the more accurate διδόναι, a repeated action, for δοῦναι.

Some see in the δοῦλοι only a detail in the scenery of the parable ; Wellhausen explains them of Church leaders, some of whom had begun to abuse their office ; in this case the parable was not spoken by Jesus. But they may refer to the apostles and the Jewish religious leaders : the former are to prepare for the Parousia by being good stewards, the latter, who abuse their office (cf. xxiii. 4 f., 14 f., Lk. xx. 47) will be punished 'with the hypocrites.'

47. ἀμήν κτλ.] See on v. 18 ; Lk. ἀληθῶς. The reward of faithfulness is to be trusted with higher responsibilities ; cf. xxv. 21, 23, Lk. xvi. 10 a. Since the parable deals with the Parousia, the words apply to higher activities in the age to come.

αὐτόν. ἐὰν δὲ εἴπῃ ὁ κακὸς δοῦλος ἐκεῖνος ἐν τῇ καρδίᾳ 48
αὐτοῦ Χρονίζει μου ὁ κύριος, καὶ ἄρξηται τύπτειν 49
τοὺς συνδούλους αὐτοῦ, ἐσθίῃ δὲ καὶ πίνῃ μετὰ τῶν
μεθυόντων, ἥξει ὁ κύριος τοῦ δούλου ἐκείνου ἐν ἡμέρᾳ ᾗ 50
οὐ προσδοκᾷ καὶ ἐν ὥρᾳ ᾗ οὐ γινώσκει, καὶ διχοτομήσει 51
αὐτὸν καὶ τὸ μέρος αὐτοῦ μετὰ τῶν ὑποκριτῶν θήσει· ἐκεῖ

48. ἐὰν δέ κτλ.] κακός is proleptic, as πιστός and φρόνιμος in
v. 45 ; Lk. ὁ δ. ἐκεῖνος. Lk. adopts
an O.T. style in adding ἔρχεσθαι to
χρονίζει ὁ κύρ. μ. (cf. Exod. xxxii. 1).
For the thought cf. xxv. 5, 2 Pet.
iii. 4 ; and there are O.T. counterparts : Ez. xi. 3, xii. 22, 27, Am.
vi. 3.

49. καὶ ἄρξηται κτλ.] He employs his authority for tyranny over
those who will not support him in
his evil ways, and for self-indulgence
with those who will. For class.
parallels see Wetstein *ad loc.* Lk.
partly loses the latter point by καὶ
μεθύσκεσθαι for μετὰ τῶν μεθυόντων.

50. ἥξει κτλ.] In both cases
ᾗ = ἥν, attracted to the previous
dat. : 'in a day that he does not
look out for (cf. Lam. ii. 16), and in
an hour that he knows not (cf. xxv.
13)'—and therefore ought to have
looked out for. For προσδοκᾷν cf.
xi. 3 (spoken by a servant who was
on the look-out) ; elsewhere only Lk.[6],
Ac.[5], 2 Pet.[3]

51. καὶ διχοτομήσει κτλ.] A
punishment literally inflicted in
ancient times; cf. 1 Chr. xx. 3,
Am. i. 3 (LXX.), Sus. 59, Heb. xi.
37, Herod. ii. 139. 2, vii. 39. 5 (δια-
τέμνειν), Suet. *Calig.* 27 'multos
. . . medios serra dissecuit.' In
Exod. xxix. 17, the verb is used of
dividing a sacrificial victim into
pieces (διχοτομήματα). καὶ τὸ μέρος
κτλ. is a parallel description of
the fate of the same person. The
expression is Hebraic. μερίς in the

LXX. (חֵלֶק) has various meanings :
'landed property' (Num. xviii. 20),
'fellowship' (2 Regn. xx. 1), 'lot, or
punishment' (Job xxvii. 13, Is. xvii.
14). μέρος less often loses its literal
spatial force. It is natural to make ὁ
κύριος the subj. of θήσει, but it is possibly ὁ δοῦλος ; cf. Ps. xlix. [l.] 18,
μετὰ μοιχῶν τὴν μερίδα σου ἐτίθεις.
There is deeper irony if the slave is
pictured as bringing *himself* to the
same lot as the hypocrites. For
ὑποκριτῶν (see on vi. 2) Lk. has
ἀπίστων. On the formula ἐκεῖ κτλ.
added by Mt. see viii. 12.

xxv. 1–13. (Mt. only.) PARABLE
OF THE TEN VIRGINS.

In xxiv. 45 the slave was
'faithful and prudent'; the present
parable gives an instance of φρόνιμοι,
the following of πιστοί. Almost
every detail lends itself to allegorical
treatment, useful for the preacher.
Some of its analogies are well drawn
out by Plummer. But from a
historical point of view it must be
determined how much the Lord
probably intended to convey to His
hearers. And the remarks in the
opening note on ch. xiii. apply here.
The central thought is 'Be in
readiness for the Parousia,' but the
story is too much elaborated to
admit of all the details being
dismissed as merely scenery.

Its genuineness is often doubted
on the ground that it pictures the
long delay of the Parousia, and
points to a date when the immediate
Advent had ceased to be expected.

XXV. 1 ἔσται ὁ κλαυθμὸς καὶ ὁ βρυγμὸς τῶν ὀδόντων. Τότε
ὁμοιωθήσεται ἡ βασιλεία τῶν οὐρανῶν δέκα παρθένοις,
αἵτινες λαβοῦσαι τὰς λαμπάδας ἑαυτῶν ἐξῆλθον εἰς

The virgins are explained as the
Christian Church, and their slumber
while waiting is the sleep of death
which comes to wise and foolish
alike ; the bride is not mentioned,
because the virgins are not the
Church as a single ideal body, but
the several members of it. But
though some details may have been
added or altered from this point of
view (see v. 11 f.), the bulk of the
parable may well have been spoken
by Jesus. The delay of the Bridegroom is sufficiently explained by
the fact that the Son of Man had
not yet come (cf. xxiv. 48), and no
one knew when He would. That
the bride, the well-known Christian
symbol of the Church, is not
mentioned in the ordinary text is
noteworthy (see below) ; and the
virgins need no more point to
Christians than the men in the field
or the women at the mill (xxiv. 40 f.) ;
it is related only that five of them
were 'taken' and five were 'left.'
The parable in Lk. xii. 35 ff. similarly
illustrates a state of readiness ; men-
servants waiting for their master's
return (sc. with his bride) from the
wedding. But there is no good
reason for regarding the present
parable as an elaboration of it.

1. τότε κτλ.] 'The next parable
which illustrates an aspect of the
Kingdom shall be the following.'
On τότε see ii. 7 ; to refer it to
xxiv. 50 f., 'at the time when the
wicked servant is punished, then, etc.,'
is awkward and improbable. For
the verb see vii. 24. The Kingdom
is not like the virgins, but their
story illustrates an aspect of it ;
see xiii. 24. 'Ten' probably denotes

no more than a large group, making
a good display with their lanterns.
The virgins cannot be uninvited
guests, nor bridesmaids, for they
would be with the bride and Bridegroom (see below) ; they are maid-
servants at the house of the bride's
father. παρθένοι does not symbolize
purity of heart, for that is a state
of readiness, which was not the case
with all. On αἵτινες for αἱ see ii. 6.
λαμπάς, like לַפִּיד, is usually a 'torch,'
as in class. Gk. (cf. Juv. vii. 16, xv.
4 f., Jo. xviii. 3, Apoc. viii. 10), not
a lamp (λύχνος), though it may
have the latter meaning in Ac. xx.
8. Here it may be a lamp attached
to a pole ; see Lightfoot, Hor. Heb.
ad loc. On ἑαυτῶν = αὐτῶν (so vv. 4,
7) see viii. 22.

ἐξῆλθον κτλ.] From whence is
not stated. Their own houses, the
Bridegroom's house, and (Jülicher)
the new house made ready for the
bridal pair, have all been suggested.
But Jewish custom requires the
house of the bride's father, where
the festivities took place (cf. Jud.
xiv. 10–18, Tob. vi. 13, viii. 19),
when the bride was conducted thither
by the bridegroom after the marriage
ceremony. ἐξῆλθον anticipates ἐξέρχεσθε in v. 6, vv. 2–5 containing
a retrospect explaining why the
foolish ones, though they started,
did not meet the Bridegroom with
the others. εἰς ὑπάντησιν (ἀπάντ.,
συνάντ.) c. gen. or dat. is mostly
the LXX. equivalent of לִקְרַאת. 'It
seems that the special idea of the
word was the official welcome of a
newly arrived dignitary' (Moulton,
i. 14 n.), so that it here corresponds
with the thought of the Parousia

ὑπάντησιν τοῦ νυμφίου.   πέντε δὲ ἐξ αὐτῶν ἦσαν μωραὶ καὶ 2
πέντε φρόνιμοι· αἱ γὰρ μωραὶ λαβοῦσαι τὰς λαμπάδας 3
αὐτῶν οὐκ ἔλαβον μεθ᾿ ἑαυτῶν ἔλαιον· αἱ δὲ φρόνιμοι 4
ἔλαβον ἔλαιον ἐν τοῖς ἀγγείοις μετὰ τῶν λαμπάδων
ἑαυτῶν.   χρονίζοντος δὲ τοῦ νυμφίου ἐνύσταξαν πᾶσαι 5

1 νυμφιου] add και της νυμφης DX* 1* 124* 209 262* 𝕃 omn 𝕊 sin.pesh.hcl*
arm Or^lat Hil

(see on xxiv. 3). Moulton's instances from the papyri do not remove the impression that its N.T. use is Hebraistic.

τοῦ νυμφίου] Contrast the parabolic use in ix. 15. The addition καὶ τῆς νύμφης (see Appar.) is probably genuine; its intrinsic difficulty is in its favour, and the MS. evidence is strong. The idea widely entertained by early Christians was that the Bridegroom, Christ, would come at the last day to fetch His Bride, the Church. καὶ τ. νύμφης, being incompatible with this, was omitted. But this allegorical conception is absent from the parable, which teaches only the necessity of readiness for the Messiah's arrival, which will be soon and sudden. The virgins, therefore, are to be ready for the bridegroom and bride, i.e. for the marriage procession. This variance from the idea of the Bride current in the early Church favours the genuineness of the parable.

2. πέντε κτλ.] This represents a distinction between the ready and the unready at the Parousia, but not that they will be equal in number; see vii. 14, xxii. 14. Two Jewish parables of 'wise' and 'foolish' people are given by Allen from Shabb. 152 b, 153 a. And see vii. 24.

3. αἱ γὰρ μωραί κτλ.] Some were clearly foolish, for they acted as follows. They did not take no oil at all; that would be foolish

beyond the requirement of the parable. They had oil in their lanterns, but not expecting delay had taken no extra oil. The next verse makes this clear.

4. αἱ δὲ φρόνιμοι κτλ.] The ἀγγεῖα (cf. ἄγγη xiii. 48) are not the lanterns themselves, but vessels containing extra oil (cf. Num. iv. 9, where they are distinct from the λύχνοι); this is rendered certain by the prep. μετά; and if the λαμπάδες were torches it is obvious.

5. χρονίζοντος κτλ.] This recalls xxiv. 48. It is not to the purpose of the parable to explain why the Bridegroom delayed; the point is that the foolish virgins were not prepared for his coming whenever it might be. 'They fell asleep (ἐνύσταξαν) and were sleeping (ἐκάθευδον)'; see 2 Regn. iv. 6 (LXX.). No blame is attached to this, since all slept. Plummer's explanation that 'this seems to be a merciful concession to human weakness' is surely improbable. If the verse is the work of the evangelist it may represent the sleep of death which all undergo before the Advent. But if it is a genuine part of the parable it may be merely a scenic detail, enhancing the suddenness of the midnight cry. The wise could afford to sleep, but the foolish wasted the time in which they could have rectified their mistake. It is clear that vv. 2–5 do not follow in time the action of v. 1, otherwise the strange explanation is

6 καὶ ἐκάθευδον. μέσης δὲ νυκτὸς κραυγὴ γέγονεν Ἰδοὺ ὁ
7 νυμφίος, ἐξέρχεσθε εἰς ἀπάντησιν. τότε ἠγέρθησαν πᾶσαι
αἱ παρθένοι ἐκεῖναι καὶ ἐκόσμησαν τὰς λαμπάδας ἑαυτῶν.
8 αἱ δὲ μωραὶ ταῖς φρονίμοις εἶπαν Δότε ἡμῖν ἐκ τοῦ ἐλαίου
9 ὑμῶν, ὅτι αἱ λαμπάδες ἡμῶν σβέννυνται. ἀπεκρίθησαν δὲ
αἱ φρόνιμοι λέγουσαι Μήποτε οὐ μὴ ἀρκέσῃ ἡμῖν καὶ
ὑμῖν· πορεύεσθε μᾶλλον πρὸς τοὺς πωλοῦντας καὶ ἀγοράσατε
10 ἑαυταῖς. ἀπερχομένων δὲ αὐτῶν ἀγοράσαι ἦλθεν ὁ νυμφίος,

9 ου μη] ουκ ℵALZ 33 126 al

necessary that the virgins slept at some other house, or in the open air, near the city gate.

6. μέσης κτλ.] Cf. Exod. xii. 29 f., and see on xxiv. 43 above. It is needless to enquire who raised the cry; it only depicts the startling suddenness of the event. On γέγονεν for ἐγένετο (B) see Blass, § 59. 4, and for a different view Moulton, i. 146. For the absolute εἰς ἀπάντησιν cf. 1 Regn. xiii. 15 (so ὑπάντ. Jud. xi. 34, συνάντ. Num. xxii. 34); see on v. 1.

7. τότε κτλ.] The lanterns would be lit at first when the Bridegroom was momentarily expected, but extinguished when the virgins lay down to sleep. κοσμεῖν includes the trimming and lighting of the wick, and in the case of the wise the replenishing of the oil in the lanterns from the vessels. In Ez. xxiii. 41 it stands for עָרַךְ, which is used in Ps. cxxxii. 17 of preparing a lamp. Here it probably represents the Aram. תְּקַן (so סִין) 'make straight,' 'arrange'; cf. Eccl. i. 15, vii. 13. This is the point of time anticipated by ἐξῆλθον in v. 1; the next stage is during the walk from the house.

8. αἱ δὲ μωραί κτλ.] The oil has been variously interpreted; but it seems to represent, as broadly as possible, everything necessary for preparedness. It will be futile, at the supreme moment, to appeal to the preparedness of others.

9. ἀπεκρίθησαν κτλ.] The reply is not selfish but quite inevitable, because a sharing of the oil would result in none of the lanterns having enough to last. Preparedness is a quality, not a something which can be shared quantitively. The negative is usually explained as μήποτε [τοῦτο γενέσθω], οὐ μή, 'certainly not, it is impossible that there should be enough, etc.' (for the ellipse cf. xxvi. 5, Exod. x. 11). But μήποτε may be virtually a deprecating 'perhaps' (cf. Tob. x. 2), which can be followed by οὐ μή or, as in the v.l., οὐκ (see Moulton, i. 192 f., and 188 ff.). The reply is thus gentler, but not the less decisive.

πορεύεσθε κτλ.] It is irrelevant to object that shops would be shut at midnight; oil might still be obtainable; there would probably, for that matter, be a supply at the house. And the words are not ironical (Aug.). The sole point illustrated is that self-preparation at the last moment is impossible. ἑαυταῖς (= ὑμῖν) is a dat. commodi, the emphasis lying on ἀγοράσατε. For τοὺς πωλοῦντας, describing a class, cf. xxi. 12.

10. ἀπερχομένων κτλ.] While they were hurrying away the Bridegroom arrived, and αἱ ἔτοιμοι (which

καὶ αἱ ἕτοιμοι εἰσῆλθον μετ᾽ αὐτοῦ εἰς τοὺς γάμους, καὶ
ἐκλείσθη ἡ θύρα. ὕστερον δὲ ἔρχονται καὶ αἱ λοιπαὶ 11
παρθένοι λέγουσαι Κύριε κύριε, ἄνοιξον ἡμῖν· ὁ δὲ ἀποκριθεὶς 12
εἶπεν Ἀμὴν λέγω ὑμῖν, οὐκ οἶδα ὑμᾶς. Γρηγορεῖτε 13

sums up the significance of the
parable) turned back with him in
procession to the house where the
wedding-feast (γάμους, see on xxii.
2) was to be held. καὶ ἐκλείσθη
κτλ. : cf. Gen. vii. 16, of those who
were 'ready' in the days of Noah.
The Lord probably ended the parable,
with dramatic skill, at this point.

11, 12. ὕστερον κτλ.] Vv. 11,
12 appear to be an addition. An
earthly bridegroom would hardly act
or speak thus ; he is here the divine
judge. A partial parallel is seen in
Lk. xiii. 25 (Q), which Mt. has already
used in vii. 21ff. On ὕστερον see
iv. 2. ἔρχονται is, in the narrative, a
historic pres. ; but this is the only
instance in the parable, and it conveys
the impression of a *prophetic* pres.,
spoken from the evangelist's point of
view. On ἀμὴν λ. ὑ. see v. 18.
οὐκ οἶδα ὑμᾶς (cf. vii. 23), 'I am
not acquainted with you'; Lk. adds
πόθεν ἐστέ.

13. γρηγορεῖτε κτλ.] Probably
a further addition by Mt. The
verb is not strictly suited to the
parable; it has no reference to the
slumbering of the virgins, but
signifies, as in xxiv. 42 (cf. 44), 'be
ready'; cf. Ac. xx. 31, 1 Cor. xvi.
13. ὅτι κτλ. echoes xxiv. 36, 42,
44, 50.

14–30 (cf. Lk. xix. 11–27). PAR-
ABLE OF THE TALENTS.

The genuineness of the parable,
as of the preceding, is denied by
some. Wellhausen unnecessarily assumes that 'the servants in all the
parables are the Christians,' and the
Kingdom of Heaven the early Church,

so that the long absence of the
ἄνθρωπος ἀποδημῶν is the long interval between the Ascension and
the Parousia. But though Mt., by
placing the parable here, interpreted
it of Christ, it may really refer to
God ; and the 'absence' of God from
the world is an O.T. thought ; cf. xxi.
33. The servants are not Christians
but Jews ; and those who are faithful,
and ready for the day of reckoning,
are those who prove diligent in the
fulfilment of life's duties.

In Lk. xix. 11–27 the parable of
the Pounds is in many respects
closely similar. The Lord could,
of course, have uttered two similar
parables on the same subject ; but
there are features in Lk. which
appear due to later Christian thought,
such as are conspicuously absent from
Mt. Lk. states that it was spoken
'because He was near to Jerusalem,
and they thought that the Kingdom
of God was about to appear immediately.' It teaches that the Lord
(ἄνθρωπός τις εὐγενής) must first go
to a far country (*i.e.* Heaven) to
receive a kingdom (as some of the
Herodian princes were obliged to
travel to Rome) and to *return* ; that
His citizens (*i.e.* the Jews) hated
Him, and sent a message after Him
that they would not have Him for
their King ; and that on His return,
having received the Kingdom, He
rewarded His servants (*i.e.* the
Christians) by placing them in command over cities, which being now
King He was able to do, and slew
His enemies. (On Harnack's view
of this see xxii. 6 f. note.) In *Gosp.
Naz.* Mt.'s parable is combined with

14 οὖν, ὅτι οὐκ οἴδατε τὴν ἡμέραν οὐδὲ τὴν ὥραν.   Ὥσπερ
γὰρ ἄνθρωπος ἀποδημῶν ἐκάλεσεν τοὺς ἰδίους δούλους καὶ
15 παρέδωκεν αὐτοῖς τὰ ὑπάρχοντα αὐτοῦ, καὶ ᾧ μὲν ἔδωκεν
πέντε τάλαντα ᾧ δὲ δύο ᾧ δὲ ἕν, ἑκάστῳ κατὰ τὴν ἰδίαν
16 δύναμιν, καὶ ἀπεδήμησεν. εὐθέως πορευθεὶς ὁ τὰ πέντε
τάλαντα λαβὼν ἠργάσατο ἐν αὐτοῖς καὶ ἐκέρδησεν ἄλλα
17 πέντε· ὡσαύτως ὁ τὰ δύο ἐκέρδησεν ἄλλα δύο· ὁ δὲ τὸ
18

16 ευθεως πορευθεις] ℵ*B 𝔏 b g¹ [ευθ. δε πορ. 1 118 124 243 26ᵉᵛ 𝔏 c f ff¹·² h qr
Opt ; ευθ. ευθ. δε πορ. 𝔖 pal]; ευθ πορευθεις δε ℵᶜADL etc minn.pler 𝔏 vg 𝔖 sin.
pesh.hcl | εκερδησεν] εποιησεν ℵ*A*ΧΓΔII minn.pler 𝔏 q 𝔖 pesh

that of the Prodigal Son and of the
slave in xxiv. 49. See *Texte u.
Unters.*, 1911, 34, 59 ff., 293 f.

14. ὥσπερ κτλ.] The ellipse
must be supplied by οὕτως ἡ βασιλεία τῶν οὐρανῶν or the like ; cf.
Mk. xiii. 34. γάρ connects the
parable with the preceding warning.
παρέδωκεν supplements the following ἔδωκεν : talents are gifts, but
primarily a trust ; they are *Gaben*
which involve *Aufgaben*. On ἀπεδήμησεν see xxi. 33, and the note above.

15. καὶ ᾧ μέν κτλ.] The household of so rich a man would not
be confined to three servants ; they
are selected instances. In Lk. ten
servants are given one mina each,
and three selected instances are dealt
with. Whether this is the more
original is difficult to determine.
The mina (= £4) may have been substituted in Lk. for the talents (one
talent was 6,000 denarii, or £240)
in view of *v.* 21, ἐπὶ ὀλίγα (Lk. ἐν
ἐλαχίστῳ) ; the large sum (cf. xviii.
24) suggests the greatness of the privileges entrusted by God to the Jews.

ἑκάστῳ κτλ.] Cf. Mk. xiii. 34,
where ὡς ἄνθρωπος ἀποδημῶν and
ἕκαστον τὸ ἔργον αὐτοῦ may be
echoes of this passage (see on xxiv.
42). The privileges entrusted to
a nation are unequally shared by its
members. (The thought in xx. 2–6
is analogous.) This is not unjust,

but a divine ordinance. And the
requirements from each are graduated
(cf. Lk. xii. 48, 2 Cor. viii. 12).
In Lk. the same amount was assigned
to each, to test their capacity of
being entrusted with larger amounts
hereafter. Both are spiritually true.
In Mt. both servants double their
money, shewing the same zeal, and
their reward is the same, in Lk.
they multiply it by 10 and 5 respectively, and their reward is
graduated (see Add. n. after v. 12).
The parable does not deal with the
possibility that those who received
most might have failed in their trust,
but it exhorts those who have received
little to be diligent with that little.

16. εὐθέως κτλ.] He at once set
to work. The reading πορευθεὶς δέ
connects εὐθέως with ἀπεδήμησεν ;
but εὐθέως and εὐθύς, in the best
readings, always precede the verb in
the N.T. (except Mk. i. 28). He
employed the money as capital with
which (instrum. ἐν, cf. xx. 15) he did
business. For the vb. cf. Apoc. xviii.
17, Prov. xxix. 36 [xxxi. 18] (סָחַר),
ἐργασία Ac. xvi. 16, 19, xix. 24 ;
Zahn cites *CIG.* 3920 for ἐργαστής,
a sea-faring merchant. Lk. has
πραγματεύσασθαι. In *vv.* 17, 20,
22 ἐκέρδησεν, -σα recurs, but here
ἐποίησεν (cf. Lk. v. 18, ἔπραξα *v.*
23) has some support.

18. ὁ δέ κτλ.] ἀπελθών (as in

ἐν λαβὼν ἀπελθὼν ὤρυξεν γῆν καὶ ἔκρυψεν τὸ ἀργύριον
τοῦ κυρίου αὐτοῦ. μετὰ δὲ πολὺν χρόνον ἔρχεται ὁ κύριος 19
τῶν δούλων ἐκείνων καὶ συναίρει λόγον μετ᾽ αὐτῶν. καὶ 20
προσελθὼν ὁ τὰ πέντε τάλαντα λαβὼν προσήνεγκεν ἄλλα
πέντε τάλαντα λέγων Κύριε, πέντε τάλαντά μοι παρέδωκας·
ἴδε ἄλλα πέντε τάλαντα ἐκέρδησα. ἔφη αὐτῷ ὁ κύριος 21
αὐτοῦ Εὖ, δοῦλε ἀγαθὲ καὶ πιστέ, ἐπὶ ὀλίγα ἦς πιστός,
ἐπὶ πολλῶν σε καταστήσω· εἴσελθε εἰς τὴν χαρὰν τοῦ
κυρίου σου. προσελθὼν καὶ ὁ τὰ δύο τάλαντα εἶπεν 22
Κύριε, δύο τάλαντά μοι παρέδωκας· ἴδε ἄλλα δύο τάλαντα
ἐκέρδησα. ἔφη αὐτῷ ὁ κύριος αὐτοῦ Εὖ, δοῦλε ἀγαθὲ καὶ 23
πιστέ, ἐπὶ ὀλίγα ἦς πιστός, ἐπὶ πολλῶν σε καταστήσω·
εἴσελθε εἰς τὴν χαρὰν τοῦ κυρίου σου. προσελθὼν δὲ καὶ 24
ὁ τὸ ἓν τάλαντον εἰληφὼς εἶπεν Κύριε, ἔγνων σε ὅτι

v. 25) is redundant; see xiii. 28.
On the hiding of money or valuables
in the earth see xiii. 44. In Lk. the
man laid up his mina in a napkin
(σουδαρίῳ), which could indeed be
hidden in the earth. Which is the
more original cannot be determined.
That Lk.'s word is a latinism is no
evidence against its genuineness.

19. μετὰ δέ κτλ.] Cf. v. 5, xxiv.
48. On συναίρει λόγον see xviii.
23.

20. καὶ προσελθών κτλ.] The
redundance and repetitions in vv.
20–23, which Lk. reduces to the
briefest limits, are characteristic of
popular Semitic narrative. In Mt.
the servants say ἐκέρδησα, in Lk.
they say that the money προσ-
ηργάσατο, ἐποίησεν.

21. ἔφη κτλ.] εὖ is not an interjection elsewhere in the N.T. or
LXX.; Lk. εὖγε 'Bravo!' (so lat.
vulg. here euge) is probably right;
in the LXX. it stands for הֶאָח or הֶאָח,
Alas! or Aha! ἐπί, 'in authority
over' (cf. Heb. iii. 6) takes acc. and
gen. as well as the class. dat. (cf. xxiv.
47); see Blass, § 43. 1. πολλῶν corresponding with ὀλίγα seems to mean

'many talents': responsibilities in the
coming Kingdom will be analogous
to, but greater than, those entrusted
now. 'The joy of your Lord,' i.e. the
joy that your Lord gives, and shares
with you, is a unique expression for
the bliss of the divine Kingdom. It is
echoed in Rom. xiv. 17. Wellhausen
notes that χαρά stands for מִשְׁתֶּה,
'feast,' in Est. ix. 17, and εὐφραίνε-
σθαι (Lk. xii. 19, xv. 23 f.) is epulari
in 𝕃; but the introduction, by a
single word, of the thought of the
Messianic banquet, would be rather
abrupt. The verse, however, which
is absent from Lk., may be added by
Mt., and the speaker is the divine
Master, not the householder of the
parable. On εἰσέρχεσθαι in connexion with the Kingdom see v.
20.

24. προσελθών κτλ.] He approached as the others had done,
but defiantly. εἰληφώς for λαβών
(v. 20) is for the sake of variety.
For σκληρός in this sense cf. Is. xix.
4, 1 Esd. ii. 23, and see on σκληροκαρδία (xix. 8). Lk.'s αὐστηρός (cf.
2 Macc. xiv. 30) possibly sounded
less insolent to Greek ears.

σκληρὸς εἶ ἄνθρωπος, θερίζων ὅπου οὐκ ἔσπειρας καὶ
25 συνάγων ὅθεν οὐ διεσκόρπισας· καὶ φοβηθεὶς ἀπελθὼν
ἔκρυψα τὸ τάλαντόν σου ἐν τῇ γῇ· ἴδε ἔχεις τὸ σόν.
26 ἀποκριθεὶς δὲ ὁ κύριος αὐτοῦ εἶπεν αὐτῷ Πονηρὲ δοῦλε καὶ
ὀκνηρέ, ᾔδεις ὅτι θερίζω ὅπου οὐκ ἔσπειρα καὶ συνάγω ὅθεν
27 οὐ διεσκόρπισα; ἔδει σε οὖν βαλεῖν τὰ ἀργύριά μου τοῖς
τραπεζείταις, καὶ ἐλθὼν ἐγὼ ἐκομισάμην ἂν τὸ ἐμὸν σὺν

27 τα αργυρια] 𝕭*B ; το αργυριον 𝕭ᶜACD etc minn verss

θερίζων κτλ.] You enrich your-
self at the cost of others. The first
metaphor is clear. The second
might refer to sowing seed (for
συνάγειν cf. vi. 26, xiii. 30), or
threshing (scattering) corn (for συνάγειν cf. iii. 12), or even to gathering
sheep scattered over the moorlands
(cf. Jo. xi. 52); see Mt. xii. 30.
But more probably it refers to
money, 'you gather gain (cf. Job xx.
15, Hag. i. 6) where you have not
spent' (cf. Ps. cxi. [cxii.] 9 = 2 Cor.
ix. 9), which seems to be the meaning of Lk.'s αἴρεις ὃ οὐκ ἔθηκας.
The words can hardly mean 'If I
had gained anything you would have
taken it,' or 'If I had lost it you
would have held me responsible'
(Plummer); a slave, as his master's
chattel, would expect nothing else.
He sums up the master's character
as that of a hard money-making
Jew; and it is not a mere insult; the
master seems to accept the character.
Cf. the use of undesirable characters
in other parables (Lk. xvi. 1–8, xviii.
1–8).

25. καὶ φοβηθείς κτλ.] I feared
the possibility of losing instead of
gaining in trade. ἴδε ἔχεις τὸ σόν:
you cannot blame me for restoring
your own property safe and sound.
The master's use of τὸ ἐμόν makes it
improbable that the further thought
is implied, 'Your own, and not
something extra, gained dishonestly
from others.'

26. ἀποκριθείς κτλ.] 'Wicked'
and 'slothful' are the counterpart of
'good' and 'faithful.' His want of
faithfulness was shewn by sheer
laziness. ᾔδεις κτλ.: the master
'smites him with his own weapon'
(B. Weiss) without disclaiming the
character ascribed to him.

27. ἔδει σε κτλ.] If you were
too lazy to trade, you might at least
have deposited the money with the
bankers instead of in the earth, so
that I should have received some, if
only a little, interest. βαλεῖν (Vulg.
mittere) with the dat. is equivalent
to Lk.'s ἔδωκας; for the verb cf. x.
34, Mk. xii. 41 f. The plur. τὰ
ἀργύρια may refer to the separate
shekels of which the talent was composed (cf. xxvi. 15, xxvii. 3, 5 f., 9,
xxviii. 12, 15); but the true reading
may be τὸ ἀργύριον, as in Lk. On
the consec. καί (= ὥστε) see Blass,
§ 77. 6. τραπεζεῖται, argentarii,
nummularii (Vulg.), did business at
a money-table (Lk. ἐπὶ τράπεζαν);
cf. xxi. 12. For ἐκομισάμην, 'received as my due,' Lk. has the more
commercial ἔπραξα (cf. Lk. iii. 13).
τόκος (τεκεῖν) is the interest which
money 'breeds'—'the breed of barren
metal'; Heb. law, as also the better
minds in Greece and Rome, condemned the practice of usury. The
saying ascribed to the Lord (ap.
Clem. Strom. i. 28. 177) γίνεσθε δὲ
δόκιμοι τραπεζῖται, τὰ μὲν ἀποδο-
κιμάζοντες τὸ δὲ καλὸν κατέχοντες

τόκῳ. ἄρατε οὖν ἀπ᾽ αὐτοῦ τὸ τάλαντον καὶ δότε τῷ 28
ἔχοντι τὰ δέκα τάλαντα· τῷ γὰρ ἔχοντι παντὶ δοθήσεται 29
καὶ περισσευθήσεται· τοῦ δὲ μὴ ἔχοντος καὶ ὃ ἔχει ἀρθήσεται ἀπ᾽ αὐτοῦ. καὶ τὸν ἀχρεῖον δοῦλον ἐκβάλετε εἰς τὸ 30
σκότος τὸ ἐξώτερον· ἐκεῖ ἔσται ὁ κλαυθμὸς καὶ ὁ βρυγμὸς

(see Resch, *Agrapha*[2], 112–5 for other passages) has a meaning quite foreign to the parable, and can hardly have been derived from it.

28. ἄρατε οὖν κτλ.] The faithful servants were entrusted with larger capital; the lazy one is deprived of the privilege of responsibility. If the words formed part of the original parable, the imper. is addressed to other servants in the room; Lk. καὶ τοῖς παρεστῶσιν εἶπεν. The evangelist, in adding *v.* 30, may have thought of the angels, the instruments of judgment at the Parousia.

καὶ δότε κτλ.] This half verse, and *v.* 29, have their parallel in Lk., and must have stood in Q; but they are difficult. Whether he that had the 10 talents was to receive the extra one as a gift, or as a further increase of capital, is not clear; nor why he is preferred to the other equally faithful servant. But a greater difficulty is caused by ἔχοντι, which must have the same meaning in *v.* 29. The clause (perhaps the whole verse) seems to have been introduced at an early date to supply a particular instance of the general principle which follows. Lk. (*v.* 25) adds ' and they said unto Him, Lord, he hath ten minas,' which some take to be an exclamation addressed to Jesus by His audience.

29. τῷ γὰρ ἔχοντι κτλ.] The paradox occurs, with differences of wording, in xiii. 12 and Mk. iv. 25 (Lk. viii. 18). It was doubtless a genuine utterance of the Lord, and

can be spiritually applied in many ways. But it cannot be applied to the five talents given to the first servant and the five which he gained; they are a trust, while ἔχειν describes a real possession, a real condition of heart and life. The true ἔχειν in the present case is the character shewn in faithful diligence, and the increase which could be 'given' would be the higher degrees of faithful diligence to which he could advance. But this would be as true of the second servant as of the first. In the following parable the sheep are οἱ ἔχοντες and the goats οἱ μὴ ἔχοντες (Jülicher). For the absol. τῷ ἔχοντι (to which παντί is added for emphasis; Lk. παντὶ τ. ἔχ.) cf. Soph. *Aj.* 157; οἱ οὐχ ἔχοντες, Eur. *Suppl.* 240. On Mt.'s addition καὶ περισσευθήσεται see xiii. 12. τοῦ δὲ μὴ ἔχοντος cannot strictly depend upon ἀρθήσεται, which would make ἀπ᾽ αὐτοῦ superfluous; it is of the nature of a *casus pendens.* Cf. the Semitic construction . . . לְמִי אַיִן מִמֶּנּוּ וג'; see Blass, § 74. 5, Wellh. *Einl.* 19 f.

30. καὶ τὸν ἀχρεῖον κτλ.] The counterpart of 'enter into the joy of thy Lord.' The speaker is not the master in the parable, but the divine Judge. Lk. omits the verse, which is probably an addition by Mt. The same description of punishment occurs in viii. 12, xxii. 13 (see notes). The servant who fails in his duty is ἀχρεῖος, but even when we have done our duty we must say δοῦλοι ἀχρεῖοί ἐσμεν (Lk. xvii. 10).

31 τῶν ὀδόντων.   Ὅταν δὲ ἔλθῃ ὁ υἱὸς τοῦ ἀνθρώπου
ἐν τῇ δόξῃ αὐτοῦ καὶ πάντες οἱ ἄγγελοι μετ᾽ αὐτοῦ, τότε
32 καθίσει ἐπὶ θρόνου δόξης αὐτοῦ, καὶ συναχθήσονται
ἔμπροσθεν αὐτοῦ πάντα τὰ ἔθνη, καὶ ἀφορίσει αὐτοὺς

31–46. (Mt. only.) THE SHEEP
AND THE GOATS.

This is not a parable, but a prophetic picture of the Judgment, the
only parabolic features being the
simile of the sheep and the goats in
v. 32, and its metaphorical use in *v.*
33. It has much of the rhythmic
parallelism of Heb. poetry; see
Burney's Heb. translation in *JThS.*,
Apr. 1913. The thought of Judgment by the Son of Man must have
been familiar to many; see *e.g.* the
picture in Enoch lxii. of 'the Son of
Man seated on the throne of His
glory'; the 'righteous' are rewarded,
and their oppressors descend 'into
the flame of the pain of Sheol' (lxiii.
10). This may have formed an
actual background of the present
passage. See Burkitt, *Jewish and
Chr. Apoc.* 23–5. Its genuineness is
doubted by some on the grounds that
the Son of Man is Judge and King,
whereas in x. 32 f. 'He appears only
as the most important witness at
God's Judgment' (J. Weiss), and
that 'My brethren' (*v.* 40) means
Christians, while no Christians had,
by the time of Jesus, been in prison.
It is thought to deal solely with the
treatment of Christians by Christians.
Some even suppose that the gathering of 'all the nations' (*v.* 32) implies
that by the time of the Judgment
all nations will be Christian. Others
explain that only the judgment of
non-Christians (cf. xxiv. 14, 30, xxviii.
19) is described, based on their
treatment of one another, while the
Christians already stand by the King,
safe from judgment. Another explanation is that Gentiles are judged

for their treatment of the brethren
of the Son of Man, or non-Christians
for their treatment of Christians.
This places the passage on a level
with that in Enoch, emptying it
of moral value for Christians, and
merely leading them to gloat over
the condemnation of their enemies.
In defending the genuineness of this,
or of any other utterance, ascribed to
the Lord, it is unsafe to lay too much
stress on its originality and sublimity
(see *e.g.* Sanday, *Life of Chr. in Recent
Research,* 128), since this tends to
set arbitrary limits to the effects of
divine inspiration upon the evangelist. The principal defence must be
that, rightly understood, it contains
nothing essential which makes its
genuineness impossible, as the following notes will shew. Whether, or
to what extent, the familiar features
of Jewish Apocalyptic have been
added or heightened by the evangelist cannot be known.

31. ὅταν δέ κτλ.] The Lord speaks
of the Son of Man in the 3rd person,
and only the Twelve would know
that He spoke of Himself as He was
to be. The Messianic King (*vv.* 34,
40) appears invested, at last, with His
royal functions. On the 'glory' of
the Son of Man see xvi. 27, and on the
angels attending Him xiii. 41, xvi. 27,
xxiv. 31. ἄγγελοι is an interpretation of ἅγιοι (קְדֹשִׁים) in Zach. xiv. 5.

32. καὶ συναχθήσονται κτλ.] The
expectation of a resurrection of all
men for judgment is implied; cf.
Dan. xii. 2, Enoch li. 1, Test.
Benj. x., Sib. iv. 178–190, 4 Esd.
vii. 32, xiv. 35; see Volz, *Jüd. Esch.*
243–8. πάντα τὰ ἔθνη do not

ἀπ᾽ ἀλλήλων, ὥσπερ ὁ ποιμὴν ἀφορίζει τὰ πρόβατα ἀπὸ
τῶν ἐρίφων, καὶ στήσει τὰ μὲν πρόβατα ἐκ δεξιῶν 33
αὐτοῦ τὰ δὲ ἐρίφια ἐξ εὐωνύμων. τότε ἐρεῖ ὁ βασιλεὺς 34
τοῖς ἐκ δεξιῶν αὐτοῦ Δεῦτε, οἱ εὐλογημένοι τοῦ πατρός
μου, κληρονομήσατε τὴν ἡτοιμασμένην ὑμῖν βασιλείαν
ἀπὸ καταβολῆς κόσμου· ἐπείνασα γὰρ καὶ ἐδώκατέ μοι 35

merely form part of the 'grand background' (Wellh.) of the picture, and
then fall out of sight; αὐτούς refers
to them, and therefore the whole
passage; they are the individuals
comprising the ἔθνη (cf. Ac. xxvi. 17),
and include all human beings, those
placed on the right hand as well as
those on the left. ἀφορίζειν in this
connexion recurs only in xiii. 49,
but the thought plays a large part
in the teaching ascribed to Jesus; cf.
vii. 19–23, 24–27, viii. 11 f., x. 32 f.,
xii. 36 f., xiii. 30, 40 ff., xxii. 12 f.,
xxiv. 40 f., 46–51, xxv. 10–12.

ὥσπερ ὁ ποιμήν κτλ.] A striking
instance of a homely illustration
conveying a tremendous truth. With
a lightning touch the whole drama
is described, and the ease and certainty
of the irrevocable separation. Sheep
in Palestine may have been mainly
white, and goats black (cf. Cant. iv.
1, vi. 5), or the former were more
valuable, or more gentle (cf. Ez. xxxiv.
17, 20 ff.); or, more simply, two
classes are thought of within the
flock, with no symbolic meaning in
the colours.

33. καὶ στήσει κτλ.] The right
side and the left being, according to
ancient thought, lucky and unlucky,
the former was the place of honour;
cf. Test. Benj. x. 4, τότε ὄψεσθε
Ἐνὼχ . . . καὶ Ἰακὼβ ἀνισταμένους
ἐκ δεξιῶν ἐν ἀγαλλιάσει, and class.
instances in Wetstein.

34. τότε ἐρεῖ κτλ.] The thought
of the Son of Man as King has
been prepared for by the 'throne of
His glory' (v. 32). As the Messiah

was εὐλογημένος (xxi. 9, xxiii. 39),
so are those whom He accepts.
'Ye blessed ones' is absolute,
followed by 'who belong to My
Father'; cf. the genitives in 1 Cor.
iii. 23. The E.V. 'ye blessed of My
Father' obscures this. On κληρονομήσατε see v. 5. For the thought
of ἡτοιμασμένην cf. xx. 23 (note),
Heb. xi. 16; it is frequent in Apoc.
writings (Volz, Jüd. Esch. 124). It
implies foreknowledge and election,
and yet the following verses assume
real human responsibility (see on
xviii. 7). καταβολὴ κόσμου (xiii.
35 καταβολή), apparently unknown
outside the N.T., occurs in Lk. xi.
50, Jo. xvii. 24, Epp.[5], Apoc.[2]; cf. Ass.
Mos. i. 14 'ab initio orbis terrarum,'
4 Esd. vi. 1 'initio terreni orbis,'
Plut. Aq. an Ign. ii., ἅμα τῇ πρώτῃ
καταβολῇ τῶν ἀνθρώπων.

35, 36. ἐπείνασα κτλ.] Vv. 35–
40 while reflecting Jewish thought
express a new and unique truth.
Kindness to the poor and suffering
finds wide recognition in Jewish
writings: cf. Is. lviii. 7 (hungry,
homeless, naked), Job xxii. 7, Prov.
xxv. 21 (hungry, thirsty), Ez. xviii.
7, Tob. iv. 16 (hungry, naked), Sir.
vii. 35 (sick); cf. Ned. 40 a, 'he
who visits the sick will be saved
from the judgment of Gehinnom.'
For a verbal parallel cf. Test. Jos. 1,
ἐν ἀσθενείᾳ ἤμην καὶ ὁ ὕψιστος ἐπ-
εσκέψατό με· ἐν φυλακῇ ἤμην καὶ
ὁ σωτὴρ ἐχαρίτωσέ με. And see
Wetstein. The best rabb. thought
placed 'performance of kindnesses'
on a higher level than mere alms-

φαγεῖν, ἐδίψησα καὶ ἐποτίσατέ με, ξένος ἤμην καὶ συνηγάγετέ
36 με, γυμνὸς καὶ περιεβάλετέ με, ἠσθένησα καὶ ἐπεσκέψασθέ
37 με, ἐν φυλακῇ ἤμην καὶ ἤλθατε πρός με. τότε ἀποκριθήσονται αὐτῷ οἱ δίκαιοι λέγοντες Κύριε, πότε σε
εἴδαμεν πεινῶντα καὶ ἐθρέψαμεν, ἢ διψῶντα καὶ ἐποτίσαμεν ;
38 πότε δέ σε εἴδαμεν ξένον καὶ συνηγάγομεν, ἢ γυμνὸν
39 καὶ περιεβάλομεν ;   πότε δέ σε εἴδομεν ἀσθενοῦντα ἢ ἐν
40 φυλακῇ καὶ ἤλθομεν πρός σε ;   καὶ ἀποκριθεὶς ὁ βασιλεὺς

giving; cf. *Sukk.* 49 b, *Ab.* i. 2
(Taylor), ' On three things the world
standeth, on the Torah, the Worship,
and the performance of kindnesses.'
In inculcating kindness, the Lord
speaks of it as a criterion by which
all mankind will be judged ; but the
non-mention of other criteria does
not exclude them. The uniqueness
of the verses lies not in their ethical
teaching but in the new conception
of the Son of Man ; see *v.* 40. For
συνηγάγετε cf. Deut. xxii. 2 (אסף
Targ[onk] כנש), Jud. xix. 18. Allen
compares the late Heb. כנסת ארחים,
' reception of travellers,' hospitality.

37–39. τότε ἀποκριθήσονται κτλ.]
The δίκαιοι (cf. xiii. 43, 49) are
those who are shewn to be such by
being placed at the King's right
hand ; ' hoc ipso judicio declarati '
(Beng.). They are the ἐκλεκτοί (xxii.
14, xxiv. 31), the υἱοὶ τῆς βασιλείας
(xiii. 38). Their question shews
that their kindnesses had been
wrought with no reference to, or
thought of, Christ, they did them
not as Christians or to Christians.
The large heart of the Lord transcends all limits : kindness is kindness the world over. The same wide
truth is taught negatively in Am.
i.–ii. 3.

40. καὶ ἀποκριθεὶς κτλ.] The
verse recalls x. 40, 42, xviii. 5, but
the claim of the human Jesus in
those passages is here the claim of
the exalted Son of Man ; cf. Ac. ix.

5. In the whole range of Jewish
Apocalyptic the awful and transcendent Messiah is never pictured
as a Being of human love and sympathy. The Lord seems to carry on
the thought of Is. liii. (which He
interpreted Messianically, see on xx.
28 *fin.*) from His passion and death
to His glory ; He will not only
suffer as the Representative of His
nation, but when invested with His
cosmic functions will identify Himself
with all sufferers. This does not
mean that the title 'Son of Man'
denotes the Ideal or Representative
Man ; but He could sympathize, as
it was felt that God could sympathize ;
cf. Is. lxiii. 9 (K[e]ri, E.V.), Prov. xix.
14 [17], *Ab.* ii. 13 'One that
borroweth from Man is as he that
borroweth from God.' And see
Edmunds, *Buddh. and Chr. Gosp.* 105,
' Whoever, O monks, would wait
upon me, let him wait upon the sick.'
More than this would have been
unintelligible to the disciples at the
time. After the Resurrection, and
helped by the influence of Greek
thought, Christians were divinely
led to the conception of the mystical
oneness of an immanent Christ with
humanity. εἶδες γάρ, φησίν, τὸν
ἀδελφόν σου, εἶδες τὸν θεόν σου
(Clem. *Strom.* I. xix. 94, II. xv. 71).
' Vidisti, inquit, fratrem, vidisti
dominum tuum' (Tert. *De Orat.* xxvi.).
The value of the conception cannot
be better shewn than in the words

ἐρεῖ αὐτοῖς Ἀμὴν λέγω ὑμῖν, ἐφ' ὅσον ἐποιήσατε ἑνὶ
τούτων τῶν ἀδελφῶν μου τῶν ἐλαχίστων, ἐμοὶ ἐποιήσατε.
τότε ἐρεῖ καὶ τοῖς ἐξ εὐωνύμων Πορεύεσθε ἀπ' ἐμοῦ 41
κατηραμένοι εἰς τὸ πῦρ τὸ αἰώνιον τὸ ἡτοιμασμένον τῷ
διαβόλῳ καὶ τοῖς ἀγγέλοις αὐτοῦ· ἐπείνασα γὰρ καὶ οὐκ 42
ἐδώκατέ μοι φαγεῖν, καὶ ἐδίψησα καὶ οὐκ ἐποτίσατέ με,
ξένος ἤμην καὶ οὐ συνηγάγετέ με, γυμνὸς καὶ οὐ περι- 43
εβάλετέ με, ἀσθενὴς καὶ ἐν φυλακῇ καὶ οὐκ ἐπεσκέψασθέ

41 κατηραμενοι] אBL 33 102 ; pr οι AD al minn.pler

of one who is unable to share it : 'Judaism also has taught and still teaches the worth of every human soul. But the particular motive— for *his* sake—is necessarily wanting to its adherents. They have to say for God's sake instead of Jesus's sake, and doubtless the peculiar combination in Jesus, as simple Christian believers hold—of the man and the God—has given an immense power to this special motive, "for his sake." It would be foolish not to recognize the force and grandeur of ethical motive in a religion, because, as the religion is not one's own, one cannot share, or be stimulated by, that motive' (Montefiore, *The Syn. Gosp.* ii. 754).

ἐφ' ὅσον κτλ.] For ἐφ' ὅσον (not in LXX.) cf. Rom. xi. 13 ; elsewhere in the N.T. it means 'as long as.' τούτων refers to the classes of sufferers just mentioned, not, as some explain, to a group standing by the Son of Man in the picture. ἑνὶ τ. ἐλαχίστων corresponds with ἕνα τ. μικρῶν (x. 42) and παιδίον τοιοῦτον ἕν (xviii. 5). The love and sympathy of the Son of Man for all sufferers is profoundly expressed in τ. ἀδελφῶν μου, and the truth remains even if the expression is not genuine. It is omitted in *v.* 45, perhaps by accident or for brevity ; but it is possibly a gloss added by one who thought that the ἐλάχιστοι must be Christians. Its

omission here in B* ff¹,² and in some quotations in Clem., Orig., Hil., Amb., al. was probably due to v. 45.

41. τότε ἐρεῖ κτλ.] Those on the right are οἱ δίκαιοι, but a terrible reticence suppresses the epithet for those on the left (cf. *v.* 41, αὐτοί *v.* 44, οὗτοι *v.* 46). The latter are 'accursed' (*sc.* by My Father), but they do not 'belong to My Father'; cf. *v.* 34. κατηραμένοι might mean 'accursed now by My judgment'; but the addition of the article (see Appar.) is probably a right correction. Jewish language is again employed. For fire as a symbol of punishment see iii. 10, and for αἰώνιον see Add. n. after xviii. 9.

τὸ ἡτοιμασμένον κτλ.] The devil and his angels take the place of the ὑμῖν of *v.* 34 ; the fire is already prepared for them because they are already condemned, but meet their final doom at the Judgment. For Jewish parallels see Volz, *Jüd. Esch.* 273 f. If the ἀπὸ καταβολῆς κόσμου of *v.* 34 is intentionally omitted, there may be a reference to the thought that while the Kingdom was prepared for the righteous from the beginning, the fall of the wicked angels and their condemnation occurred later in time. Rabb. writers differ as to whether Gehenna was prepared before or after the creation. On διάβολος see iv. 1, and for his angels cf. Apoc. xii. 7, 9.

44 με. τότε ἀποκριθήσονται καὶ αὐτοὶ λέγοντες Κύριε, πότε
σε εἴδομεν πεινῶντα ἢ διψῶντα ἢ ξένον ἢ γυμνὸν ἢ ἀσθενῆ
45 ἢ ἐν φυλακῇ καὶ οὐ διηκονήσαμέν σοι; τότε ἀποκριθήσεται
αὐτοῖς λέγων Ἀμὴν λέγω ὑμῖν, ἐφ᾽ ὅσον οὐκ ἐποιήσατε
46 ἑνὶ τούτων τῶν ἐλαχίστων, οὐδὲ ἐμοὶ ἐποιήσατε. καὶ
ἀπελεύσονται οῠτοι εἰc κόλαcιν αἰώνιον, οἱ δὲ δίκαιοι εἰc ζωΗν
αἰώνιον·

XXVI. 1   ΚΑΙ ΕΓΕΝΕΤΟ ὅτε ἐτέλεσεν ὁ Ἰησοῦς πάντας τοὺς
       2 λόγους τούτους, εἶπεν τοῖς μαθηταῖς αὐτοῦ Οἴδατε ὅτι

44. τότε ἀποκριθήσονται κτλ.]
Their self-defence, like the disclaimer
of the righteous, is that they have
had no opportunities of ministering
to the Son of Man.

46. καὶ ἀπελεύσονται κτλ.] On
ἀπέρχεσθαι and its equivalent βληθῆναι see v. 29 f., xviii. 8 f. The
latter would here be impossible
because the verb is required also for
the second clause. On ζωή see vii.
14, xviii. 8.

xxvi., xxvii. THE LAST DAYS OF
THE LORD'S EARTHLY LIFE.

xxvi. 1–5. (Mk. xiv. 1 f., Lk.
xxii. 1 f.) THE DATE. PLANS OF
THE SANHEDRIN FOR THE ARREST.

1. καὶ ἐγένετο κτλ.] See on vii.
28.

2. οἴδατε κτλ.] Mt. alone relates that the Lord reminded the
disciples of the date, introducing a
reference to His death, already thrice
predicted (xvi. 21 ff., xvii. 22 f., xx.
17 ff.). Mk. simply states the date,
ἦν δὲ τὸ πάσχα καὶ τὰ ἄζυμα μετὰ
δύο ἡμέρας, where 'after two days'
can be understood literally, not, as
some explain it, as equivalent to
'on the next day.' It is true that
'after three days' (Mk. viii. 31)
is interpreted by Mt. (see xvi. 21)
and Lk. as 'on the third day'; but
in both Gk. and Aram. 'on the

morrow' can be expressed by a single
word, though not 'on the day after
to-morrow.' Cf. Hos. vi. 2, where
'after two days' seems to be synonymous with 'on the third day.' If,
then, the Crucifixion was on Friday,
this verse deals with Wednesday.
Mt. follows Mk. in this, but omits
καὶ τὰ ἄζυμα, either as superfluous
or, more probably, as incorrect, since
in Lev. xxiii. 5 f., Num. xxviii. 16 f.
the Passover is commanded for the
14th and Mazzoth (ἄζυμα) for the
15th of the first month. The same
looseness of expression, however, is
found in Jos. Ant. XVII. ix. 3.
Allen's conjecture is unnecessary,
that 'after two days' is due to a
misreading of an Aram. expression
meaning 'after some days.' Lk.,
with Mk., identifies the festivals but
avoids numbering the days: ἤγγιζεν
δὲ ἡ ἑορτὴ τῶν ἀζύμων ἡ λεγομένη
πάσχα. For other notes on the
chronology see vv. 6, 17.

πάσχα, invariable in the N.T.
(Evv.[26], Ac. xii. 4, 1 Cor. v. 7, Heb.
xi. 28), is the usual LXX. transliteration of פסח (Aram. פסחא, פיסחא);
φάσεκ (-χ) is confined to Jer.
xxxviii. [xxxi.] 8 and 2 Chr. (xxx.[6],
xxxv.[12]), but is used by Aq. Sym.;
Philo and Josephus have πάσχα, the
latter also φάσχα. On the α for the
Heb. Aram. e or i see Nestle, ExpT.
xxi. 521, Dalman, Gr.[2] 138.

μετὰ δύο ἡμέρας τὸ πάσχα γίνεται, καὶ ὁ υἱὸς τοῦ
ἀνθρώπου παραδίδοται εἰς τὸ σταυρωθῆναι. Τότε 3
συνήχθησαν οἱ ἀρχιερεῖς καὶ οἱ πρεσβύτεροι τοῦ λαοῦ εἰς
τὴν αὐλὴν τοῦ ἀρχιερέως τοῦ λεγομένου Καιάφα, καὶ 4
συνεβουλεύσαντο ἵνα τὸν Ἰησοῦν δόλῳ κρατήσωσιν καὶ
ἀποκτείνωσιν· ἔλεγον δέ Μὴ ἐν τῇ ἑορτῇ, ἵνα μὴ θόρυβος 5
γένηται ἐν τῷ λαῷ.

καὶ ὁ υἱός κτλ.] 'The Passover, *when* the Son of Man etc.' For καί instead of a subordinate clause cf. *v.* 45 (Blass, §77. 6). The words are not so much a prediction as a reference to that in xx. 17 ff. (see note). On παραδίδοται see xvii. 22, and on the prophetic pres. Blass, § 56. 9.

3. τότε κτλ.] The aorists describe a meeting of the Sanhedrin on a definite occasion ; Mk., followed by Lk., has the imperf. ἐζήτουν, a general statement that they were searching for an opportunity, but Mt. interprets it as meaning that they were consulting at the time that the words of *v.* 2 were uttered. In *v.* 5, however, he adopts Mk.'s imperf. ἔλεγον. The event from which Mk. (*v.* 1 a) reckons 'after two days' is probably the action of Judas (*v.* 10), separated by the parenthesis in *vv.* 1 b, 2, and by the account of the anointing at Bethany. The αὐλή (*atrium*), not strictly the 'palace' (A.V.) but its 'court' (R.V.), whither the Lord was taken from Gethsemane (*v.* 58), was suitable for an informal meeting. In the LXX. it mostly stands for the court of the tabernacle or the temple, but occasionally for that of a palace or mansion (*e.g.* 2 Regn. xvii. 18, Tob. ii. 9, and freq. in Est.). Joseph Caiaphas (so Jos. *Ant.* XVIII. ii. 2) was high priest c. A.D. 18–36. In Jo. xviii. 13 he is stated to be son-in-law of Hannas (or Ananos, son of Seth, high priest

A.D. 6–15). On the numerous appointments to the office see Schürer, *HJP.* II. i. 197–206. The surname is strictly a subst., ? 'the Soothsayer,' קַיְפָא (Dalm. *Wörterb.* קיף).

5. ἔλεγον δέ κτλ.] Jesus on the contrary had said (*v.* 2) that it would be on the festival, and He was right. Mt. can hardly, however, have intended to express this contrast by δέ (Spitta). Mk. has ἔλ. γάρ, explaining their continued unsuccess (ἐζήτουν) or the necessity of craft. μὴ ἐν τῇ ἑορτῇ : they spoke of avoiding disturbance only, not a violation of Jewish law. Possibly there was no law at that time forbidding an arrest on a feast day. But to the high-priestly rulers, who took the lead in the plots, the letter of the law may have been less important than fear of the Romans and the desire to do away with Jesus. ἐν τ. ἑορτῇ may, however, mean 'in the period of the (seven day) festival' ; cf. Neh. viii. 14. They could hardly have wished to postpone the arrest till after the pilgrims had dispersed, since Jesus also would naturally be expected to depart when the festival was over, and their opportunity would be lost. Nor was there any reason, such as Herod had in S. Peter's case (Ac. xii. 3 f.) for keeping Him in prison. They had been scheming for some time, but found no opportunity till the last moment, when Judas betrayed Him. They

6 Τοῦ δὲ Ἰησοῦ γενομένου ἐν Βηθανίᾳ ἐν οἰκίᾳ Σίμωνος
7 τοῦ λεπροῦ, προσῆλθεν αὐτῷ γυνὴ ἔχουσα ἀλάβαστρον
μύρου βαρυτίμου καὶ κατέχεεν ἐπὶ τῆς κεφαλῆς αὐτοῦ
8 ἀνακειμένου. ἰδόντες δὲ οἱ μαθηταὶ ἠγανάκτησαν λέγοντες

7 βαρυτιμου] ΒΓΔΘᵉ al minn.*pler* ℵ sin.hclᵗˣᵗ.pal ; πολυτιμου ℵADLMΠ 33 157
al ℵ pesh.hclᵐᵍ

acted as secretly as they could on
Thursday night, and if the Crucifixion took place on Friday afternoon,
the arrest probably did not break
the law, because the festival began
at 6 p.m. on Friday. The tumult
that they feared might arise between
the Jews of the city and the pilgrims
from the north, the latter holding
Jesus to be a prophet, if not the
Messiah. It is strange, however,
that they should fear an uproar only
during the festival; since the city
was already crowded with pilgrims
who flocked to Jesus in the temple
(Lk. v. 37 f.), the uproar would take
place if He were arrested before the
festival began. Lk. has simply
ἐφοβοῦντο γὰρ τὸν λαόν. Mk.,
Lk. use λαός in sense of ὄχλος, but
Mt. thinks of them as a nation (see
on iv. 23, xxi. 26) distinct from the
Romans to whom the Sanhedrin
would be answerable.

6–13. (Mk. xiv. 3–9, Jo. xii.
1–8.) THE ANOINTING AT BETHANY.

6. τοῦ δὲ Ἰησοῦ κτλ.] The incident is unconnected in time with
the events of *vv.* 1–5 (see on *v.* 3);
Mt. and Mk. assign no date, and
Mk. does not record that the Lord
returned to Bethany after the walk
to the city and the cursing of the
fig-tree (Mk. xi. 12 ff.), while Lk.
xxi. 37 suggests that He passed each
night in the open air (see on Mt.
xxi. 17). Jo. xii. 1 gives the date as
six days before the Passover, the day
before the Entry (see on Mt. xxi. 1),
and this is accepted by a consensus of

opinion. Jo. does not name Simon ;
he relates that 'they made Him a
supper there,' at which Martha
waited, Lazarus was one of the diners,
and Mary performed the act of loving
reverence. When the Petrine narrative took shape, Mary was probably
still living, and the omission of her
name in Mk. was natural. If Martha's
house (cf. Lk. x. 38) was Simon's,
the latter may have been the father
of the family (Thphlact.), or Martha's
husband, either now dead or separated from her by his leprosy, or still
called ὁ λεπρός, though his leprosy
had been cured, to distinguish him
from the many others of the name ;
Jer. compares Μαθθαῖος ὁ τελώνης.

7. προσῆλθεν κτλ.] Alabaster
phials were used for precious oint-
ments ; cf. Theocr. xv. 114, Pliny,
HN. xxxvi. 12, and passages in Swete.
Possibly it was used for any phial
employed for the purpose, as a child's
'marbles' are often made of glass.
The true form is ἀλάβαστος, sometimes neut. plur. in Gk. writers, but
masc. or fem. in the sing. τὸ ἀλάβαστρον occurs in 4 Regn. xxi. 13 (A).
Jo. relates that the woman brought a
λίτρα (Vulg. *libra*), c. 12 oz. βαρυτίμου, *v.l.* πολυτίμου (both late
words), takes the place of Mk.'s class.
πολυτελοῦς. βαρύτ. occurs in Strabo
xvii. 13 ; cf. 'grave pretium' (Sall.).
The ointment was estimated at over
300 *denarii* (Mk., Jo.), the practical
value of which can be gathered from
xx. 2, Mk. vi. 37, Lk. x. 35.

8. ἰδόντες κτλ.] Contrary to his

Εἰς τί ἡ ἀπώλεια αὕτη; ἐδύνατο γὰρ τοῦτο πραθῆναι 9
πολλοῦ καὶ δοθῆναι πτωχοῖς. γνοὺς δὲ ὁ Ἰησοῦς εἶπεν 10
αὐτοῖς Τί κόπους παρέχετε τῇ γυναικί; ἔργον γὰρ καλὸν
ἠργάσατο εἰς ἐμέ· πάντοτε γὰρ τοὺς πτωχοὺς ἔχετε μεθ' 11
ἑαυτῶν, ἐμὲ δὲ οὐ πάντοτε ἔχετε· βαλοῦσα γὰρ αὕτη τὸ 12
μύρον τοῦτο ἐπὶ τοῦ σώματός μου πρὸς τὸ ἐνταφιάσαι με
ἐποίησεν. ἀμὴν λέγω ὑμῖν, ὅπου ἐὰν κηρυχθῇ τὸ εὐαγγέλιον 13

custom (see on viii. 26) Mt. relates
something derogatory to the disciples,
while Mk. says only τινες, and Jo.
speaks of Judas only. They did
not express their indignation openly,
but πρὸς ἑαυτούς (Mk.), in their
minds, or by whispers to each other;
γνοὺς δὲ ὁ Ἰ. (v. 10) shews that
Mt. understood it so. For ἀπώλεια
'waste' cf. Polyb. vi. 59. 5 (contrasted
with τήρησις), and M.-M. Vocab.
s.v.; and see Prov. xxix. 3, ἀπολεῖ
πλοῦτον.

9. ἐδύνατο κτλ.] πολλοῦ is for
Mk.'s ἐπάνω δηναρίων τριακοσίων: cf.
the omission of numbers in viii. 32,
xiv. 17, 19. Almsgiving was probably expected from the Passover
pilgrims (cf. Jo. xiii. 29) as an accompaniment of their worship. There
were many poor in and near Jerusalem;
cf. Mk. x. 46, xii. 42, Lk. xix. 8, Jo.
ix. 8, Ac. iii. 2, vi. 1, Rom. xv. 26,
Gal. ii. 10; and see Gosp. Heb. quoted
at xix. 22.

10. γνοὺς δέ κτλ.] For κόπους
[-ον] παρέχειν (Vulg. molestus esse)
cf. Lk. xi. 7, xviii. 5, Gal. vi. 17.
τῇ γυναικί gives the impression that
she was a stranger, but Mk. has
only αὐτῇ, which is more suitable if
she was Mary. To give to the poor
is to give to the Lord (xxv. 40), but
personal devotion to Him is also a
'good work' (see on v. 16). To the
few who to-day spend themselves
mainly on worship and meditation
(whom Mary again exemplifies in
Lk. x. 39–42) active 'workers' are

warned not to say 'To what purpose
is this waste?' εἰς ἐμέ: Mk. ἐν
ἐμοί; see on xvii. 12.

11. πάντοτε κτλ.] Cf. Deut. xv.
11. Mt., Jo. omit Mk.'s addition
'and whenever ye will ye can
[always] do them good.' For the
thought 'Me ye have not always'
cf. ix. 15, Jo. xvii. 11; a different
truth is expressed in Mt. xviii. 20,
xxviii. 20.

12. βαλοῦσα κτλ.] On βάλλειν
see x. 34. 'With a view to my laying out for burial hath she done it,'
with the implied thought 'though
she does not know it.' Mk. has ὃ ἔσχεν
ἐποίησεν· προέλαβεν μυρίσαι τὸ
σῶμά μου εἰς τὸν ἐνταφιασμόν, which
Preuschen (ZNW., 1902, 252 f.) criticizes on the ground that the anointing
of the body at burial, as distinct from
placing spices in the grave-clothes,
was unknown in Israel; and he
refers to an obscure Roman parallel.
On the difficult form of the words
in Jo. see Westcott. For the late
ἐνταφιάζειν cf. Jo. xix. 40, Gen. l.
2 (חנט 'embalm'), Test. Judah
26, μηδείς με ἐνταφιάσῃ πολυ-
τελεῖ ἐσθῆτι. Gen. l.c. also has
-αστής which occurs in papyri (Deissmann, Bible St. 120).

13. ἀμήν κτλ.] See on v. 18.
Those present condemn her, but she
is to receive honour for all time. It
is difficult to believe that the words
came from the lips of Jesus. Not
only does Jo. omit them, and Lk.
(probably) the whole incident (see

τοῦτο ἐν ὅλῳ τῷ κόσμῳ, λαληθήσεται καὶ ὃ ἐποίησεν
14 αὕτη εἰς μνημόσυνον αὐτῆς.   Τότε πορευθεὶς εἰς τῶν

Add. n.), but the Lord's expectation
of the immediate advent of the
Kingdom, which in iv. 23 *is* the
Gospel, forbids us to think that He
would speak of a world-wide preaching of the Gospel, even if κόσμος
means οἰκουμένη, the Roman world
(see xxiv. 14, note; cf. 'Mk.' xvi.
15). As in xxiv. 14, Mt. adds τοῦτο
to Mk.'s εὐαγγέλιον; there it refers

to the contents of the foregoing discourse; here it seems to be an obscure
reference to Christ's atoning death,
implied in the mention of His em-
balming. εἰς μνημόσ. αὐτῆς : 'for a
reminder of her ' (*sc.* to men). There
is no exact parallel to this; but a
μνημόσυννον of men before God (Ac.
x. 4) is an O.T. thought : Ex. xxviii.
12, xxx. 16, Num. xxxi. 54.

Additional Note on the Anointing at Bethany.

Lk. vii. 36–50 contains a narrative which is parallel in the following
points : Jesus was at a meal in the house of a man named Simon, and a
woman entered and anointed Him with a valuable ointment which she
brought in an alabaster phial ; and objection was raised to the action.   But
all else is different.   The incident is related after the discourse to the
people about the Baptist ; the place is not named ; the host was a Pharisee ;
the woman was a 'sinner '; the objection raised was that, if Jesus were a
prophet (a reputation attached to Him chiefly in Galilee), He would know
what sort of woman she was; and the answer dealt with the greatness of
a penitent's love in proportion to the sins forgiven.   Mt., Mk. say that the
woman was anointing the Lord's head (as a devoted friend might honour a
guest), Lk. that, standing behind at His feet weeping (as a penitent), she
began to bedew His feet with her tears, and was wiping them with her
hair, and kissing them and anointing them.   Jo. (xii. 3) seems to introduce
two details from this account : 'she anointed the feet of Jesus, and wiped
them with the hairs of her head.'   The relation of Lk.'s narrative to Mk.'s
is doubtful ; but it is hardly conceivable that either could simply have grown
out of the other.   It is possible, however, that in Lk.'s source a narrative
of an entirely distinct incident was coloured from the Marcan story by the
addition of the three references to ointment, κομίσασα ἀλάβαστρον μύρου
and καὶ ἤλειφε τῷ μύρῳ (v. 38), and v. 46, apart from which the only real
point of similarity in the two narratives is the very common name Simon ;
and that too may have been taken over from Mk.

14–16. (Mk. xiv. 10 f., Lk. xxii. 3–
6.) THE BARGAIN MADE BY JUDAS.

14. τότε κτλ.] τότε is Mt.'s form
of transition to his next incident
(see on ii. 7), which probably occurred
on the day indicated in *v.* 2 (see on
v. 3). εἷς (Mk. ὁ εἷς, see Swete)
τῶν δώδεκα, Lk. ὄντα ἐκ τοῦ ἀριθμοῦ

τ. δ., expresses a sorrowful indignation which the Church never ceased
to feel; cf. *v.* 47 (Mk., Lk.), Jo. vi.
71 ; and see Mk. xiv. 20.   On
Ἰσκαριώτης see x. 4.   The chief
priests, as the official rulers, were
those with whom the bargain must
be made.   Lk. adds καὶ στρατηγούς

δώδεκα, ὁ λεγόμενος Ἰούδας Ἰσκαριώτης, πρὸς τοὺς ἀρχιερεῖς
εἶπεν Τί θέλετέ μοι δοῦναι κἀγὼ ὑμῖν παραδώσω αὐτόν ; 15
οἱ Δὲ ἔστησαν αὐτῷ τριάκοντα ἀργύρια. καὶ ἀπὸ τότε ἐζήτει 16
εὐκαιρίαν ἵνα αὐτὸν παραδῷ.

Τῇ δὲ πρώτῃ τῶν ἀζύμων προσῆλθον οἱ μαθηταὶ τῷ 17

(sc. τοῦ ἱεροῦ), the Levitical temple
guard, who are mentioned in the
N.T. in Lk., Ac. only.

15. τί θέλετε κτλ.] Virtually
a protasis—' If you give me enough '
—the apodosis being introduced by
a consec. καί (Blass, § 77. 6). The
deliberateness with which Judas
took the initiative is expressed in
Mk.'s ἵνα αὐτὸν παραδοῖ αὐτοῖς,
which Mt. and Lk. expand differently.
There seems to be some emphasis on
ἐγώ—' I, though one of His disciples.'
On παραδώσω see x. 4.

οἱ δὲ ἔστησαν κτλ.] Mk.'s οἱ δὲ
ἀκούσαντες ἐχάρησαν (Lk. καὶ ἐχ.)
is omitted. The arrest could have
been arranged without expense at
some future time, but they were glad
of the offer because it enabled them
to effect it before the festival. Mk.
says that they 'promised' (ἐπηγ-
γείλαντο), Lk. 'made a compact'
(συνέθεντο) to give him money, the
payment of which is assumed in Ac.
i. 18 ; but Mt. relates that they paid
him on the spot. Both ἔστησαν and
the sum named are due to Zach. xi.
12, καὶ ἔστησαν τὸν μισθόν μου
τριάκοντα ἀργυροῦς (sc. σίκλους) ;
see on xxvii. 3–10. For ἱστάναι,
'to place in the scale, weigh' (שׁקל),
cf. also 2 Regn. xviii. 12, Job xxviii.
15, and metaph. Ac. vii. 60. The 30
pieces of silver were shekels = tetra-
drachms = στατῆρας (D a b q), and
equivalent to 120 denarii = £4 : 16s. ;
see on xvii. 24. The plur. ἀργύρια
(see xxv. 27) is confined to Mt.

16. καὶ ἀπὸ τότε κτλ.] Lk. adds
ἄτερ ὄχλου, explaining the 'oppor-

tune moment' as one in which the
arrest could be effected without
disturbance. Mk.'s εὐκαίρως (cf. 2
Tim. iv. 2) may have the same force,
or may mean 'in good time' before
the festival (see on v. 5 above). For
εὐκαιρία, opportunitas, cf. Ps. ix. 10,
cxliv. [cxlv.] 15.

17–20. (Mk. xiv. 12–17, Lk.
xxii. 7–14.) PREPARATIONS FOR
THE PASCHAL MEAL.

17. τῇ δὲ πρώτῃ κτλ.] Mk. καὶ
τ. πρ. ἡμέρα τ. ἀζ., ὅτε τὸ πάσχα
ἔθυον, Lk. ἦλθεν δὲ ἡ ἡμέρα τ. ἀζ.
ἐν ᾗ ἔδει θύεσθαι τὸ πάσχα. Here
is the crux of the chronology. All
the synn. identify (as Mk. v. 1)
the Passover and the first day of
Unleavened Bread ; and Mt. further
identifies the day of the killing of
the lambs with that of the eating of
them, the astronomical but not the
Jewish reckoning. Mt., from his
knowledge of Jewish customs, omits
'when they were killing the Passover
victim,' but, like Lk., follows Mk. in
placing the incident on the day on
which, at 6 p.m., Nisan 14 began, so
that the Last Supper coincides with
the eating of the Passover. But the
chronology of the 4th Gosp. is to
be preferred, according to which the
Lord died at the time that the lambs
were being killed. For (1) the two
disciples would hardly have had
time to make the preparations on
the 14th. (2) Apart from this verse
there is nothing in the present
section which demands that date.
(3) Details of the Last Supper make
its identity with the Passover very

’Ιησοῦ λέγοντες   Ποῦ θέλεις ἑτοιμάσωμέν σοι φαγεῖν τὸ
18 πάσχα ;   ὁ δὲ εἶπεν   Ὑπάγετε εἰς τὴν πόλιν πρὸς τὸν δεῖνα

doubtful. (4) The Sanhedrin had
determined to arrest Jesus before the
festival, yet according to the synoptic
chronology they arrested Him *on* the
festival. (5) No Jew would carry
arms on the festival (*v.* 51 Mk., Lk.),
nor would Joseph have bought linen
(Mk. xv. 46). And if ἀπ’ ἀγροῦ
(Mk. xv. 21, Lk.) means that Simon
was returning from *work*, though
that is not necessarily the meaning,
it must have been before the festival
began. (6) Mk. xv. 42 can only
mean that Joseph buried the Body
at once, because it was Friday afternoon, and the hour when the
Sabbath would begin (6 p.m.) was
near. Hence (Lk. xxiii. 56) the
women could not embalm it at once,
but were obliged to wait till the
Sabbath was over.

The discrepancy between the synn.
and the 4th Gosp. mainly lies in
the present verse. Attempts at
harmonization have been made.
Chwolson, *Das letzte Passahmahl
Christi*, holds that when Nisan 14
fell on a Friday, the lambs were
killed on the previous day, because
there was not time to roast them
before 6 p.m. ; and in such a case
some Jews ate the Passover at the
correct time on Friday night (*i.e.* the
beginning of the Sabbath), while
others, among whom were Jesus and
the Twelve, ate it on the previous
evening. Some have even held that
Jesus, as ‘ Lord of the Sabbath,’ ante-
dated the feast on His own authority.
Spitta, *Urchristentum*, i. 226 ff.,
thinks that the Last Supper, in
Mk.’s original narrative, was on
Thursday, but that the Lucan-Pauline
tradition that it was the Paschal
meal led to the interpolation of Mk.

xiv. 12–16. Allen, on the basis of
a suggestion by Chwolson (*Monatsschr.
f. Gesch. u. Wiss. d. Jud.* lxxiii. 537 ff.),
conjectures that the Aram. קַמְאָה,
‘ first ’ and קַמָּא or קַמֵּי, ‘ before,’
have been confused in Mk., and that
the Aram. underlying his traditions
may have meant ‘ on the day *before*
the Azuma,’ which loosely denoted
‘ on the day before the Passover.’
This would dispose of the principal
difficulty ; but there are other
passages in which the synn. seem to
have been influenced by the conflict-
ing tradition that the Last Supper
was the Paschal meal.

ἄζυμα is the LXX. equivalent of
מַצּוֹת, ‘ unleavened cakes.’ The
festival is called ἡ ἑορτὴ τῶν ἀζ.
(Exod. xxiii. 15, Lk. xxii. 1) or the
whole week αἱ ἡμέραι τ. ἀζ. (Ac. xii.
3, xx. 6). The simple τὰ ἄζ. (only
here, and Mk. xiv. 1, 12) is a class.
use ; cf. τὰ Διονύσια, τὰ Παναθήναια,
and γενέσια (xiv. 6), τ. ἐγκαίνια (Jo.
x. 22).

προσῆλθον κτλ.] Lk. prefixes
to their question a command to Peter
and John to go and prepare the
Passover. For the delib. conj. with
θέλεις see xiii. 28.

18. ὑπάγετε κτλ.] It is not
stated, as in Mk., Lk., that only two
of the disciples received the command.
πρὸς τὸν δεῖνα : a class. use, found
in Aq. Ruth iv. 1, 1 Regn. xxi. 2
[3], 4 Regn. vi. 8 for פְּלֹנִי אַלְמֹנִי.
Mt. thus sums up the description in
Mk., Lk., of the means whereby the
right householder was to be found,
i.e. that they were to follow a man
(probably a slave) whom they would
see carrying a pitcher of water. Mt.
apparently did not attach importance
to the details, which suggests that

καὶ εἴπατε αὐτῷ Ὁ διδάσκαλος λέγει Ὁ καιρός μου
ἐγγύς ἐστιν · πρὸς σὲ ποιῶ τὸ πάσχα μετὰ τῶν μαθητῶν
μου. καὶ ἐποίησαν οἱ μαθηταὶ ὡς συνέταξεν αὐτοῖς ὁ 19
Ἰησοῦς, καὶ ἡτοίμασαν τὸ πάσχα. Ὀψίας δὲ 20

he did not think of them as
miraculous. And they do not
necessitate that explanation ; the Lord
had friends in the city, and had
made His plans.

καὶ εἴπατε κτλ.] The note of
authority is preserved in all the
synn. The householder was an
adherent of Jesus, who would accede
to the request as the owner of the
colt had done (xxi. 2 f.). Only Mt.
has 'My time is at hand,' a markedly
Johannine feature ; it does not mean
'the time of my Passover feast,' but
refers to the approaching Passion
(cf. *v.* 2). Mt. avoids the question
(see on viii. 29) ποῦ ἐστιν τὸ
κατάλυμά μου; The pron. suggests
that an arrangement had already
been made with the owner of the
house ; perhaps τὸ κατάλυμα (Lk.)
has the same force, 'the chamber
that we agreed upon.' The prophetic
pres. πρὸς σὲ ποιῶ has the tone of
a sovereign command. On πρός see
xiii. 56. ποιεῖν, *agere*, 'celebrate'
(cf. Heb. xi. 28, Ac. xviii. 21 D) is
frequent in the LXX. (= עשׂה) in
connexion with the Passover and
other festivals. The conjectures that
the room was the 'upper room' of
Ac. i. 13, and that it was in the
house of the mother of Mark (Ac. xii.
12), so that the owner was Mark's
father (Sanday, *Sacr. Sites* 77), are
possible, but without evidence. In
the latter case, however, the father
not the mother would more likely
have been named in Ac. *l.c.*

19. καὶ ἐποίησαν κτλ.] Mt. omits
the description in Mk. of the room
which the householder would shew
them, and instead of 'they found as

He had said unto them' he relates that
they obeyed the Master's command.
ἡτοίμασαν (so Mk., Lk.) cannot
include the provision of a lamb,
since all the members of a family
who were to partake of it were required to be present at the ceremony
of its slaughter at the temple.
There is not a hint that a lamb
formed part of the Last Supper.
The verb must have the same force
as ἑτοιμάσωμεν (*v.* 17): they arranged
the necessary preliminaries for the
Passover on the next day but one.

20. ὀψίας κτλ.] The sending of
the two disciples perhaps suggests
that secrecy was necessary. Jesus
did not enter the city until dark.
ἀνέκειτο : Mk. ἔρχεται . . . καὶ
ἀνακειμένων αὐτῶν. Some think
that 'the Twelve' in Mk. is a formal
title used by the Church for the
disciples as a body, since Jesus came
to the city with ten only (cf. 1
Cor. xv. 5 ; Holtzm. compares the
'Thirty' at Sparta). But the two
may have returned to report that
the preparations had been made, or
ἔρχεται may mean 'cometh to the
room,' the two having joined the
others somewhere in the city. Lk.
has οἱ ἀπόστολοι.

21-25. (Mk. xiv. 18-21, Lk.
xxii. 21-23, Jo. xiii. 21-30.) THE
PREDICTION OF THE BETRAYAL.

Lk. places this after the Eucharistic
Act. Jo. (xiii. 30) relates that after
the prediction Judas 'went out
immediately,' but this affords no
evidence as to the order, since he
does not record the Eucharistic Act.
If Judas was present at it, he was
the first terrible example of those

21 γενομένης ἀνέκειτο μετὰ τῶν δώδεκα μαθητῶν. καὶ
ἐσθιόντων αὐτῶν εἶπεν ᾿Αμὴν λέγω ὑμῖν ὅτι εἷς ἐξ ὑμῶν
22 παραδώσει με. καὶ λυπούμενοι σφόδρα ἤρξαντο λέγειν
23 αὐτῷ εἷς ἕκαστος Μήτι ἐγώ εἰμι, κύριε ; ὁ δὲ ἀποκριθεὶς
εἶπεν ῾Ο ἐμβάψας μετ᾽ ἐμοῦ τὴν χεῖρα ἐν τῷ τρυβλίῳ
24 οὗτός με παραδώσει· ὁ μὲν υἱὸς τοῦ ἀνθρώπου ὑπάγει

whom S. Paul describes in 1 Cor. xi.
27 ; if he went out before it, it is
another indication that the meal was
not the Passover, in the middle of
which it is extremely improbable
that any Jew would leave the table.

21. καὶ ἐσθιόντων κτλ.] The
meal was in progress (cf. v. 26).
This makes its identity with the
Passover feast improbable, since
every detail of the latter, both word
and act, was prescribed by law and
custom which Jesus was unlikely to
disregard. On παραδώσει see x. 4.
Mk. adds ὁ ἐσθίων μετ᾽ ἐμοῦ, which
anticipates v. 20 (Mt. 23), and has
the appearance of a later addition
due to Ps. xl. [xli.] 10, which is quoted
in Jo. xiii. 18.

22. καὶ λυπούμενοι κτλ.] Mk.
ἤρξαντο λυπεῖσθαι καὶ λέγειν.
They had been warned that He must
suffer, but this was a new horror ;
small wonder that Mt. adds his
characteristic σφόδρα (cf. xvii. 23).
He transposes ἤρξαντο, marking the
beginning of a continuous action (see
on iv. 17), one disciple after another
taking up the accusation ; and he
writes the class. εἷς ἕκαστος for Mk.'s
εἷς κατὰ εἷς (Blass, § 51. 5). For
μήτι see on xii. 23.

23. ὁ ἐμβάψας κτλ.] 'He that
hath dipped.' Mk. εἷς τῶν δώδεκα
(probably a later addition ; see on v.
14 above) ὁ ἐμβαπτόμενος μετ᾽ ἐμοῦ
εἰς τὸ [ἕν] τρύβλιον, which need not
mean that the one who next dipped
was the betrayer, but quite generally,
like Mt.'s aor. (֍ sin partcp. 'he that
putteth forth his hand '), 'one who

has been sharing the meal with me.'
This was purposely ambiguous ; the
betrayer was not revealed, for they had
all dipped ; had he been, the others
would doubtless have tried to prevent
the crime, which the Lord knew was
according to His Father's plan (v.
24). It echoes the thought of Ps.
xl. [xli.] 10 ; see on v. 21. Lk.
expresses it differently : 'behold the
hand of him that betrayeth me (is)
with me on the table.' Those who
identify the meal with the Passover
feast refer to the ḥarōseth, a sauce
composed of fruits, spices, and vinegar,
into which food was dipped. But
sauces were similarly used at other
meals ; cf. Ruth ii. 14 ; and see Pes.
ii. 8, where it is forbidden to put
flour into the Passover ḥarōseth, implying that sauces thickened with
flour were used on other occasions.
ἐμβάπτειν is unique in bibl. Gk.,
except as a v.l. for βάπτειν, Jo. xiii.
26. τρύβλιον, apparently not a
dimin., occurs in Aristoph. and later,
and in the LXX. = קְעָרָה, 'a (deep)
bowl' (Num. vii. 13 etc.), Vulg.
acetabulum. It is not a 'dish' (A.V.,
R.V.) or 'platter' (Wicl., Tynd.), as in
Vulg. parapsis (Mt.), catinus (Mk.).

24. ὁ μὲν υἱός κτλ.] ὑπάγει,
'goeth his way,' sc. to Him from
whom He came, corresponds with the
ἐλθεῖν of v. 17 (see note), and implies
the same high claim. In the 4th
Gosp. (viii. 14, 21, xiii. 3, 33, 36,
xiv. 4 f., 28, xvi. 5, 10, 16 f.) the
thought is brought into prominence.
καθὼς γέγραπται (Lk. κατὰ τὸ
ὡρισμένον) points to such passages

καθὼς γέγραπται περὶ αὐτοῦ, οὐαὶ δὲ τῷ ἀνθρώπῳ ἐκείνῳ
δι' οὗ ὁ υἱὸς τοῦ ἀνθρώπου παραδίδοται· καλὸν ἦν αὐτῷ
εἰ οὐκ ἐγεννήθη ὁ ἄνθρωπος ἐκεῖνος. ἀποκριθεὶς δὲ Ἰούδας 25
ὁ παραδιδοὺς αὐτὸν εἶπεν Μήτι ἐγώ εἰμι, ῥαββεί; λέγει
αὐτῷ Σὺ εἶπας. Ἐσθιόντων δὲ αὐτῶν λαβὼν ὁ 26

as Ps. xxii., Is. liii., and to the
O.T. sacrifices as types; cf. Mk. ix.
12, Lk. xviii. 31, xxiv. 46, 1 Cor.
xv. 3.

οὐαὶ δέ κτλ.] Not a curse (see xi.
21) but an exclamation of anguish.
The paradox of divine determination
and human responsibility here finds
its most tragic expression; see on
xviii. 7. Origen emphasizes the
διά: 'non dixit . . . a quo traditur,
sed per quem traditur.' Judas was
but an instrument, yet he acted
voluntarily, and need not so have
acted. οὐ διότι προώριστο, διὰ τοῦτο
παρέδωκεν· ἀλλὰ διότι παρέδωκεν,
διὰ τοῦτο προώριστο, τοῦ θεοῦ
προειδότος τὸ πάντως ἀποβησόμενον
(Euth. Zig.).

καλὸν ἦν κτλ.] On καλόν see v.
29. A maimed life, or no life at all,
is better than final death. Allen
quotes parallels from Chag. 11 b,
Enoch xxxviii. 2. On εἰ οὐκ, where
the indic. denotes something contrary
to fact, see Blass, § 75. 3, Moulton,
i. 200.

25. ἀποκριθείς κτλ.] The verse
is absent from Mk., Lk. If the
question and answer were really
uttered at the table, it must have
been in whispers. Jo. xiii. 21–30
fills in the story. Brooke (Camb.
Bibl. Ess. 309 f.) suggests that the
Lord dipped food in the bowl for
each disciple in turn, so that 'he it
is for whom I shall dip the sop and
give it to him' (Jo. v. 26) was as
enigmatical as the words in Mt. v.
23; but if He gave it first to Judas,
or at that moment said to him
'what thou doest do quickly,' and

then Judas went out at once, it
would afterwards be realized that He
had, in fact, pointed out the betrayer,
though only Judas knew it at the
time. Mt. here expresses this later
realization. The synn. imply that
the disciples themselves dipped in
the bowl, which they probably did,
as an ordinary custom more than
once during the meal; the dipping
by Jesus was a special act. ὁ παραδιδούς 'the betrayer' describes Judas
as he was afterwards known in the
Church; cf. vv. 46, 48, xxvii. 3 v.l.
On the pres. ptcp. see viii. 33.

σὺ εἶπας] Clearly an affirmative,
probably with the force of an admission. Dalm. Words 309 f., quotes
Tos. Kelim, Bab. k. i. 6, where
אָמַרְתָּ means 'thou art right.'
Here it may mean 'Yes, but it is
thou that hast forced the answer
from me.' And see Thayer, JBL.
xiii. 40–49. See on σὺ εἶπας (v. 64)
and σὺ λέγεις (xxvii. 11).

26–29. (Mk. xiv. 22–25, Lk.
xxii. 15–20, 1 Cor. xi. 23–25.)
THE EUCHARIST.

The following notes deal only with
Mt., Mk. The subject is treated
more fully in the Add. n.

26. ἐσθιόντων κτλ.] The incident
occurred, like the last (v. 21), while
the meal was in progress, which does
not support its identification with
the Passover feast. εὐλογήσας (v.
27 εὐχαριστήσας): He blessed, or
thanked, God; cf. xiv. 19. Ṣ sin
paraphrases rightly 'and blessed
[sc. God] over it.' It was probably
an ordinary Grace, but extraordinary
in being uttered in the middle of the

Ἰησοῦς ἄρτον καὶ εὐλογήσας ἔκλασεν καὶ δοὺς τοῖς
μαθηταῖς εἶπεν Λάβετε φάγετε, τοῦτό ἐστιν τὸ σῶμά
27 μου. καὶ λαβὼν ποτήριον καὶ εὐχαριστήσας ἔδωκεν
28 αὐτοῖς λέγων Πίετε ἐξ αὐτοῦ πάντες, τοῦτο γάρ ἐστιν
τὸ αἷμά μου τῆς Διαθήκης τὸ περὶ πολλῶν ἐκχυννόμενον εἰς

meal. Cf. the Grace in the Jewish
Daily Pr. Bk.: 'Blessed art thou,
Jehovah our God, King of the
Universe, who bringest forth bread
from the earth'; and before partak-
ing of wine: 'Blessed . . . Universe,
Creator of the fruit of the vine.'

ἔκλασεν κτλ.] The breaking is
essential to the full meaning of τοῦτό
ἐστιν: 'this [broken bread] is My
Body,' which thus contains a reference
to the Passion, and virtually includes
the τὸ ὑπὲρ ὑμῶν of S. Paul. The
fraction may have succeeded or accompanied the Benediction; for the aor.
ptcp. in the latter case see Blass, § 58.
4. φάγετε is absent from Mk.; the
act of eating is assumed to be included
in that of taking. No 'explanation'
of 'This is My Body' can be offered
in a commentary; its meaning varies
for Christians with their varieties of
spiritual experience.

27. καὶ λαβών κτλ.] The absence
of the art. with ποτήριον in Mt.,
Mk. suggests that they did not think
of any of the prescribed cups at the
Passover feast. 'Drink ye all of it'
corresponds with 'Eat,' which Mt.
added in the previous verse; Mk.
has καὶ ἔπιον ἐξ αὐτοῦ πάντες.
The emphasis on πάντες, not found
in connexion with the Bread, may
be due to the thought of the New
Covenant (see next verse), from which
none of the Church's first representatives excluded himself, and
which therefore embraced the whole
Church. The words have been used
in support of the Roman practice of
withholding the Cup from the laity,
since those who drank were all

priests. But the same consideration
would serve to prove that the
Sacrament was not intended for the
laity at all.

28. τοῦτο γάρ κτλ.] γάρ is Mt.'s
connexion with the previous command. The words were spoken
during the distribution of the Cup:
Mk. probably means the same, though
he records them after the disciples
had drunk. The reference is to
Exod. xxiv. 4–8, ἰδοὺ τὸ αἷμα τῆς
διαθήκης, the inauguration of God's
covenant with Israel at Sinai. Jesus
inaugurates a covenant for those
whom He had drawn from the old
Israel. μου is attached to the compound subst. 'Blood-of-the-Covenant,'
Bundesblut: 'this is my counterpart
of τὸ αἷμα τῆς διαθήκης at Sinai.'
This unmistakably includes the
thought of sacrifice, i.e. the application of the victim's blood, which is
its life, poured out, set free from its
body, and available for the use of
others. This reference to the Sinai
covenant, though it was not the
cause of the liturgical use of the
Decalogue in the English Communion
Office (see Scudamore, Not. Euchar.²
629 f.), gives additional point to it.
On the Gk. terms for 'covenant' see
Westcott, Hebr. 298 ff., DCL. i. 274.

τὸ περὶ πολλῶν κτλ.] Mk. τὸ
ἐκχ. ὑπὲρ πολλ. For περί cf. Rom.
viii. 3, Gal. i. 4 v.l., Heb. v. 3,
x. 18, 1 Pet. iii. 18, 1 Jo. ii. 2,
iv. 10; its use is connected with the
LXX. περὶ ἁμαρτίας, an equivalent
for the subst. חַטָּאת, 'sin-offering' (cf.
Heb. x. 8). It thus expresses the
sacrificial thought more technically

ἄφεσιν ἁμαρτιῶν· λέγω δὲ ὑμῖν, οὐ μὴ πίω ἀπ᾽ ἄρτι ἐκ 29

than Mk.'s ὑπέρ. The πολλῶν echoes xx. 28 (see note). Mt. alone adds εἰς ἄφεσιν ἁμαρτιῶν (which he avoided in his account of John's baptism, iii. 2), emphasizing still further the sacrificial thought, and perhaps influenced by Is. liii. 12, ἁμαρτίας πολλῶν ἀνήνεγκεν. Mt. thus combines the thoughts of the 'peace-offering,' i.e. communion, and the 'sin-offering,' i.e. reconciliation. But the latter is presupposed in the former, even if Jesus did not say 'for the remission of sins.' Possibly also He did not say 'which is poured out for many'; it is absent from 1 Cor.; but it is fully implied in 'my Covenant-Blood.' The partcp. ἐκχυννόμενον is a prophetic pres., referring to the approaching Passion. The necessary sequel is implied, though not expressed, that the Blood must be sprinkled upon men and presented before God, as Moses sprinkled it upon the people and upon the altar.

29. λέγω δέ κτλ.] The Cup points back to the Israel of old; but it also points forward to the perfected Israel in the days of the Messiah. It is a sacrificial means of communion with God; but it is also a foretaste of the feast of consummated communion. Cf. Did. ix., 'We give thanks . . . for the holy Vine of David thy servant, which Thou didst make known to us through Jesus thy servant.' The Messiah is the true Vine of which His people will partake. For the eschatological aspect of διαθήκη cf. the use of

διατίθεμαι in Lk. xxii. 29. On the Messianic banquet see viii. 11. This consummation would come in the immediate future; the Lord's death, its necessary precursor, was to occur so soon that He would never again join in a meal on earth. For λέγω δέ (Lk. λ. γάρ) Mk.'s ἀμὴν λέγω (see on v. 18) is perhaps a later insertion. ἀπ᾽ ἄρτι (Mk. οὐκέτι, Lk. ἀπὸ τοῦ νῦν): see on v. 64, xxiii. 39. For the γένημα of the vine cf. Is. xxxii. 12, Hab. iii. 17; and see Num. vi. 4. It is used in Polyb. of the produce of the earth; Deissmann (Bible St. 109 f.) gives an instance from a papyrus of 230 B.C. It may be an echo of the Grace for the wine which Jesus had just said (see v. 26). On ἡ ἡμέρα ἐκείνη see vii. 22. Mt. adds μεθ᾽ ὑμῶν, emphasizing further the thought of Christ's communion with His followers. The wine that He would then drink would be 'of a new kind,' καινόν (see ix. 17), the 'fulfilment' (cf. Lk. xxii. 16) of the wine that He now gave them. τοῦ πατρός μου is for Mk.'s τοῦ θεοῦ. Lk. has ἕως ὅτου ἡ β. τ. θεοῦ ἔλθῃ.

None of the synn. makes it clear whether Jesus Himself partook of the Bread and the Cup. For patr. and liturgical passages which assert that He did see Scudamore, op. cit. 612 f., 629. A papyrus fragm. of an Egyptian liturgy has καὶ πιὼν ἔδωκεν αὐτοῖς εἰπών, λάβετε πίετε κτλ. (Schermann, Liturg. Pap. v. Dér-Balyzeh, and Cabrol's art. 'Canon' in Dict. d'arch. chrét. et de liturg.).

Additional Note on the Eucharist.

1. S. Paul states in 1 Cor. xi. 23–25 that he received from the Lord that which he also handed on to the Corinthians, that the Lord Jesus in the night in which He was being betrayed took bread, etc. The

τούτου τοῦ γενήματος τῆς ἀμπέλου ἕως τῆς ἡμέρας ἐκείνης

principal variations from Mk. are : the *omission* of ἔδωκεν αὐτοῖς in the case of both Bread and Cup, of τὸ ὑπὲρ πολλῶν ἐκχυννόμενον, and of the whole verse containing the prediction οὐκέτι οὐ μὴ πίω κτλ. ; the *addition* of τὸ ὑπὲρ ὑμῶν . . . ἀνάμνησιν (v. 24), of μετὰ τὸ δειπνῆσαι, and of τοῦτο ποιεῖτε . . . ἀνάμνησιν (v. 25) ; the *alteration* in the words at the giving of the Cup.

The apostle's claim to have 'received from (ἀπό) the Lord' his account of the Eucharist is similar to the claim made by the prophets of Israel; and in neither their case nor his does it imply a verbal accuracy imparted by divine dictation.   If it did, the synoptic account would be excluded from consideration.   The words in no way deny that Church tradition was a source of his knowledge.   Some hold that his account is dominated by his thought of Christ as the Paschal Lamb (cf. 1 Cor. v. 8); but he writes nothing that necessarily points to a Paschal view of the Eucharist.   'The Cup of Blessing' (1 Cor. x. 16) can hardly refer to the cup which bore that name in the Passover feast ; the latter was the third cup, preceded by part of the Hallel, and followed by a fourth cup and the remainder of the Hallel (Pesach. x. 5–7), while S. Paul places it at the end of the meal.   In Mk. τὸ ἐκχυννόμενον ὑπὲρ πολλῶν expresses the sacrificial value of the Blood ; S. Paul transfers the thought to the Body, in the words τὸ ὑπὲρ ὑμῶν. This, though in keeping with the Paschal thought, does not necessarily identify the Eucharist with the Passover, for the Sinai sacrifice, no less than the Passover, involved the giving of the bodies of the victims on behalf of the nation.   The word καινή added to διαθήκη (cf. 2 Cor. iii. 6) may have been due to reflexion on Jer. xxxi. 31–34, a thought worked out by the writer of Heb. viii. 6–13, ix. 15.   The detail μετὰ τὸ δειπνῆσαι is not one which could be acquired by spiritual reflexion ; it is probably a genuine tradition.   The genuineness of the command τοῦτο ποιεῖτε . . . ἀνάμνησιν is more open to question.   (It cannot have been due to the apostle's supposed view of the Paschal character of the act ; ποιεῖτε has not the same force as in Mt. xxvi. 18 ; it refers simply to the acts of eating and drinking.   Nor can it bear the sacrificial sense of 'offer,' which is not found in connexion with the Eucharist till Just. *Dial.* 41 ; and that is the only known instance in the 2nd cent.)   The Lord expected that He would return in the near future, but the act might still be performed for a memorial of Him until He came.   If the Church's custom of repeating the act led S. Paul to ascribe its origin to a definite command, which the Marcan tradition did not contain, still that custom needs to be accounted for.   It cannot be accounted for if the words 'This is My Body—My Blood' were (as *e.g.* Jülicher thinks) a mere acted parable devoid of all mystery, a bare intimation by Jesus that He was soon to die, and that His death would be a source of blessing to them ; there would have been nothing in this to lead the disciples, or other Christians, to perpetuate the act.   The ascription to Jesus of the command, even if not genuine, would not introduce any radically new feature ; it only interpreted the significance of the Lord's words and actions as summing up and perpetuating the fellowship of the disciples with Himself—a fellowship which they had hitherto enjoyed at every meal which they had shared with Him, and still felt to be an abiding fact, owing to their experiences of

ὅταν αὐτὸ πίνω μεθ᾽ ὑμῶν καινὸν ἐν τῇ βασιλείᾳ τοῦ

His presence after the Resurrection. S. Paul's comment (*v.* 26) 'For as often as . . . till He come' affords a point of contact with the Lord's prediction in the synn. that He would not drink wine again till He drank it in the divine Kingdom (Lk. 'till the kingdom of God come').

2. S. Luke's account (xxii. 15–20) offers difficult problems. *Vv.* 19 b (τὸ ὑπὲρ ὑμῶν διδόμενον)—*v.* 20 (ἐκχυννόμενον), bracketed by W.H., are omitted in D 𝕷 a b e ff²i l; b e also place *v.* 19 a after *v.* 16. ⑊ sin.cur omit *v.* 20, and place the whole of *v.* 19 after *v.* 16; cur omits γάρ (*v.* 18) and διδόμενον (*v.* 19); sin omits τῆς ἀμπέλου (*v.* 18), and inserts in *v.* 17, from *v.* 20, 'after they had supped' and 'this is My Blood, the [*or* a] new covenant.' Sanday (*HDB.* ii. 636) writes of the two texts, in D and in the mass of MSS., 'Either may be original. And this is just one of those cases in which internal evidence is strongly in favour of the text which we call Western. The temptation to expand was much stronger than to contract; and the double mention of the Cup raises real difficulties of the kind which suggest interpolation.' And he holds that the texts of (1) b e (2) ⑊ cur, (3) ⑊ sin represent three steps in a harmonizing process.

The D Text. If *v.* 17 is Lk.'s equivalent for the account of the Cup in Mt., Mk., the Cup precedes the Bread. This seems to find support in *Did.* ix.: 'First as regards the Cup, "We give thee thanks, etc." Then as regards the broken Bread, "We give thee thanks, etc.,"' and it was the order common in Jewish meals. No weight can be attached to S. Paul's mention of the Cup before the Bread in 1 Cor. x. 16, in view of his explicit μετὰ τὸ δειπνῆσαι in xi. 25. But not only is it surprising that Lk. should have omitted the words about the Cup which are given in Mt., Mk., but the parallelism οὐκέτι οὐ μὴ φάγω (*v.* 17), οὐ μὴ πίω ἀπὸ τοῦ νῦν (*v.* 18) suggests that *vv.* 15–18 form a complete whole. In that case *v.* 19 a is an isolated fragment. If it is an interpolation from 1 Cor. (Blass, *Philol. Gosp.* 179 f.), Lk. has no account of the Eucharistic act; but there is no MS. evidence for its omission. If *vv.* 15–18 are one version of what occurred, and *vv.* 19, 20 another (Batiffol, *Études,* 2nd ser. 32, Blakiston, *JThS.* iv. 548–55), the D text forms an impossible transition between them.

The ordinary text. Some hold (*e.g.* Resch, H. Holtzmann, Schweitzer) that Lk. understood *vv.* 15–18 to refer to the Passover meal, and *vv.* 19, 20 to the subsequent Eucharist. Goguel (*L'Eucharistie* 64) thinks that Lk. arranged the order, with a Cup at the beginning and at the end, with a view to the Passover ritual. Burkitt and Brooke, on the other hand (*JThS.* ix. 569–72) suggest that ἐπιθυμίᾳ ἐπεθύμησα κτλ. (*v.* 15) does not shew that the meal was the Passover, but expresses the desire which the Lord had felt to join with the disciples in 'this Passover' (*i.e.* the Passover of this year, which will fall on the morrow), but which was not to be fulfilled. This would be in keeping with the absence of all Paschal features in the meal as described in Mt., Mk., and in 1 Cor.

There seem to be only two alternatives : (*a*) Lk. originally gave no account of the Eucharist, but confined himself to *vv.* 15–18, the whole of *vv.* 19, 20 being an addition made up for the most part of material from 1 Cor., but with the last clause based on Mk. (*b*) *Vv.* 15–17 contain

30 πατρός   μου.   Καὶ   ὑμνήσαντες   ἐξῆλθον   εἰς   τὸ

words spoken at the *beginning* of the meal (which may be paraphrased thus :
'I earnestly longed to eat this year's Passover with you before my death, for
I shall not celebrate another until I feast with you in the kingdom of God.
But let us at least join in a last act of fellowship ; divide this Cup among
you') ; *vv.* 19, 20 (omitting τὸ ὑπὲρ ὑμῶν διδόμενον) describe the Eucharistic
act at the *end* of the meal ; and in *v.* 18 the Lord closed, as He began, with
a prediction that His next feast would be in the kingdom of God, but a
scribe, in order to produce an immediate parallelism, transferred it to its
present position with a connecting γάρ. The last clause of *v.* 20 was
probably a scribe's harmonistic touch, due to the similar words in Mk.

The second alternative provides an explanation of the two Cups, and
also for the fact that ποτήριον is without the article in *v.* 17, but with it
(*the* well known Eucharistic Cup) in *v.* 20. And it also avoids the difficulty,
caused by the D text, of thinking that Lk., who must have been acquainted
both with the Pauline and the Marcan tradition, preferred another, in which
the important Eucharistic words about the Cup were omitted. (The omission
of the whole narrative in Jo. is not to the point ; he preferred to give in
ch. vi. the teaching which it presupposed.) Lk. preserves from a distinct
source, as in other parts of his Passion narrative, the material in *vv.* 15–17,
which, in the main stream of the Church's tradition, had been forgotten as
unessential in comparison with the Eucharistic act ; but in his account of
the latter, he is dependent upon the Pauline tradition. The textual confusion is due to the strange action of scribes who, finding two Cups, retained
the first to the exclusion of the second.

3. In the above notes it has been maintained that the Pauline and Lucan
accounts contain nothing really essential which is not at least implied in
Mt., Mk. Whatever effects the pagan mysteries may have had in colouring
S. Paul's religious vocabulary he did not transform an evening meal for twelve
friends into an abiding sacrament for the Christian Church ; he only brought
certain implicit truths into clearer relief. The Eucharistic words contain two
main elements, the *eschatological* and the *sacrificial*. Some modern writers
give to the one or the other exclusive prominence ; and the same tendency
is seen in early days. The *Didache, e.g.*, reflects the Jewish eschatological
hopes, with no reference to Christ's death, while in Justin's Gentile circles
the Eucharist is a memorial sacrifice ; similarly the former is more explicit
in Mt., Mk., the latter in 1 Cor. But in the mind of Jesus they were complementary aspects of the truth which governed His life work : He was
the destined Messiah ; and to attain to His glory He must suffer for those
to whom He came ; 'as a ransom for many' He must die, that they may
have a share in the Kingdom. Therefore to exclude either element from
His words is to produce the falsity of a half truth.

For bibliographies see *DCL.* 'Covenant' and 'Lord's Supper,' Srawley,
The Early History of the Liturgy, and 'Eucharist' in *EncRelEth.*

30–35. (Mk. xiv. 26–31, Lk.   OLIVES. PREDICTION OF DESERTION
xxii. 31–34, 39 ; cf. Jo. xiii. 37 f.)   AND DENIAL.
DEPARTURE TO THE MOUNT OF   30. καὶ ὑμνήσαντες κτλ.] This

Ὄρος τῶν Ἐλαιῶν. Τότε λέγει αὐτοῖς ὁ Ἰησοῦς 31
Πάντες ὑμεῖς σκανδαλισθήσεσθε ἐν ἐμοὶ ἐν τῇ νυκτὶ
ταύτῃ, γέγραπται γάρ Πατάξω τὸν ποιμένα, καὶ Διασκορπι-
cθήcονται τὰ πρόβατα τῆc ποίμνηc· μετὰ δὲ τὸ ἐγερθῆναί 32

need not have been a ceremonial chanting of the Hallel, *i.e.* Pss. cxiii.–cxviii., of which (according to *Pesach.* x. 5–7) the first two followed the second cup, and the remaining psalms the fourth cup. They doubtless sang one or more of the psalms in use in the Temple. If Zahn's reconstruction [*Kanon* ii. 785] of the Fayûm fragm. of Mk. xiv. 27–30 is right, [ὑμνησάντων δὲ αὐτῶν μετὰ τὸ φ]αγεῖν ὡς ἐξ ἔθους, it can refer, not to the Passover ritual but, to their usual custom after a meal. But Preuschen (*Antilegomena*) and others conjecture [πρὸ δὲ τοῦ μεταλλ-] αγεῖν ὡσαύτως (or ὡς ἐξ ἔθους). For ὑμνεῖν absol. cf. Dan. iii. 91 [24], 1 Mac. xiii. 47; τὸν θεόν or τῷ θεῷ is understood. On the Mount of Olives see xxi. 1.

31. τότε κτλ.] In Mt., Mk. the conversation is apparently placed on the road; Lk. relates the departure to the Mt. of Olives after it. The disciples had remained with the Lord in his πειρασμοί (Lk.), but He knew them well enough to be certain that in the last and greatest they would desert Him. Loisy unnecessarily denies the genuineness of the whole conversation. ἐν ἐμοὶ . . . ταύτῃ is added by Mt. for the sake of explicitness. For ἐν with σκανδ. cf. xi. 6, and on the verb see v. 29.

γέγραπται γάρ κτλ.] Mk. ὅτι γέγ., Fay. Pap. [κατὰ] τὸ γραφέν. The quotation is from Zach. xiii. 7, which in אB runs πατάξατε τοὺς ποιμένας καὶ ἐκσπάσατε τὰ πρόβατα (Tert. *De Fuga* 11, 'evellite oves'). A, vulg., adhere to the Heb.; so Just. (*Dial.* 53), except that he has

τὰ πρόβ. αὐτοῦ for τ. πρ. τῆς ποίμνης. All have an imper. in the first clause. Mk. (followed by Mt., but with assimilations to LXX.[A]) probably took the passage from a collection of *testimonia*, in which futures stood in both clauses, and 'the shepherd' (as Heb. LXX.[A]) instead of the plur. (LXX.[B]). The original does not speak of the sheep as *deserting* the shepherd; they are innocent sufferers; but the wording lent itself to the compiler of the *testimonia*. For a different use of the quotation see Ep. Barn. v. 12.

32. μετὰ δέ κτλ.] So Mk. Any reference to the Resurrection must have been an enigma at the time; it had been foretold (xvi. 21, xvii. 9, 23), but the disciples persistently failed to grasp the truth till the event took place. The genuineness of the verse, however, is very doubtful. If anything can be gathered as to the expectations of Jesus concerning Himself, they were not those of a return to the old relations with His disciples, but of an advent as the super-human Messiah from heaven. All the evidence is against supposing that He intended to establish, or to await, the Kingdom of God in Galilee (J. Weiss). And the same objection forbids the rendering 'I will be your leader in Galilee,' though εἰς and ἐν are often interchanged. When appearances took place in Galilee the inference was drawn that He must have predicted the fact. Possibly this was not the original position of the verse, since it breaks the immediate connexion between *vv.* 31 and 33. It is omitted

33 με προάξω ὑμᾶς εἰς τὴν Γαλιλαίαν. ἀποκριθεὶς δὲ ὁ
Πέτρος εἶπεν αὐτῷ Εἰ πάντες σκανδαλισθήσονται ἐν σοί,
34 ἐγὼ οὐδέποτε σκανδαλισθήσομαι. ἔφη αὐτῷ ὁ Ἰησοῦς
Ἀμὴν λέγω σοι ὅτι ἐν ταύτῃ τῇ νυκτὶ πρὶν ἀλέκτορα
35 φωνῆσαι τρὶς ἀπαρνήσῃ με. λέγει αὐτῷ ὁ Πέτρος Κἂν
δέῃ με σὺν σοὶ ἀποθανεῖν, οὐ μή σε ἀπαρνήσομαι. ὁμοίως
καὶ πάντες οἱ μαθηταὶ εἶπαν.

in the Fay. fragm. of Mk. Lk. omits
it, because he relates appearances in
or near Jerusalem only. προάγειν
can mean 'to walk in front' as
leader (cf. xxi. 9, Mk. x. 32), but
also 'to precede,' i.e. arrive first (cf.
xiv. 22, xxi. 31); the latter meaning
is clearly understood in xxviii. 7,
10.

33. ἀποκριθείς κτλ.] Lk. gives
the Lord's words to Peter : 'Simon,
Simon, behold Satan, etc.', and the
apostle's reply is 'Lord, with Thee I
am ready to go even to prison and
to death.'

34. ἔφη κτλ.] After ὅτι Mk.
has σύ, answering to Peter's ἐγώ,
and an emphatic but redundant
σήμερον. The cock-crowing (cf. Mk.
xiii. 35) marked the third Roman
watch (see on xiv. 25), i.e. 12–3 A.M.
Peter would deny Him thrice before
dawn. It is unnecessary to suppose
that no cock actually crowed, and
that the account has arisen from the
mere reference to cock-crowing as
a note of time. Still less need the
genuineness of the words be doubted
because of a single passage in Bab.
Kam. 82 b, which gives an ideal and
fanciful regulation, supposed to have
prevailed while the temple was in
existence, that cocks were not to be
reared in Jerusalem 'because of the
holy things,' i.e. for fear of pollution.
The Fay. fragm. has ἀλεκτρυών for
the old poet. ἀλέκτωρ, and κοκκύζειν
for φωνῆσαι, and inserts δίς. The last
has considerable support in Mk. (v. 30),

and similarly ἐκ δευτέρου (v. 72),
but καὶ ἀλέκτωρ ἐφώνησεν (v. 68)
and δίς (v. 72) are more doubtful (see
Swete). The second cock-crowing
seems to denote a definite point of
time in Ar. Eccl. 390, Juv. III. ix.
107. Mk. may have wished to
divide the night into four parts :
evening (the Last Supper), midnight
(the arrest), first cock-crowing (the
first denial), second cock-crowing (the
third denial); cf. Mk. xiii. 35, and
the four-fold division of the day of
the Crucifixion (Mk. xv. 1, 25, 33,
42). The other evangelists may
purposely have avoided this exact-
ness, since it deepened the apostle's
guilt, in that the first warning from
the cock fell unheeded on his ears.
But possibly δίς arose from a scribal
corruption, and the other passages
were afterwards altered accordingly.

ἀπαρνήσῃ με] The form of the
denial is not stated ; the other disciples
also 'denied' the Lord by deserting
Him. Lk. interprets it ἀπ. μὴ εἰδέναι
με in accordance with the event. In
x. 33 is declared the final result of
denial, but it can be averted by
penitence.

35. λέγει αὐτῷ κτλ.] Mk.'s ὁ
δὲ ἐκπερισσῶς ἐλάλει is softened by
Mt., and omitted by Lk. κἂν (Mk.
ἐὰν) δέῃ : see on δεῖ (xvi. 21). The
high honour of death for Christ was
after all reserved for him ; see HDB.
iii. 769. On οὐ μή see Moulton, i.
188 ff. Lk. here inserts vv. 35–38
from an unknown source.

Τότε ἔρχεται μετ᾽ αὐτῶν ὁ Ἰησοῦς εἰς χωρίον λεγόμενον 36
Γεθσημανεί, καὶ λέγει τοῖς μαθηταῖς Καθίσατε αὐτοῦ ἕως
οὗ ἀπελθὼν ἐκεῖ προσεύξωμαι. καὶ παραλαβὼν τὸν 37
Πέτρον καὶ τοὺς δύο υἱοὺς Ζεβεδαίου ἤρξατο λυπεῖσθαι

36–46. (Mk. xiv. 32–42, Lk. xxii. 39–46; cf. Jo. xviii. 1 f.) GETHSEMANE.

36. τότε κτλ.] The Mt. of Olives had been the direction of the walk (v. 30); Lk. states it here, omitting the name Gethsemane, and adding κατὰ τὸ ἔθος. The Lord intended, as usual during the last days, to spend the night in the open air; see on xxi. 17. 'Gethsemane' is probably נַּת שְׁמָנִי (= נַּת שְׁמָנִין), 'olive-vat or press' (Dalm. *Gr.* 152); cf. the LXX. Γέθ = Gath, Γεθ[ε]ρεμμών = Gath - Rimmon (Josh. xix. 45), Γεθχόβερ [Γεθόφρα] = Gath-Hepher (4 Regn. xiv. 25). A corrupt popular form is given in 𝔖 sin *Gusmani* (Mk. Gedsemani), 𝔖 pal *Gismanin*, D (Mk.) Γησαμανεί. The name implies that the place was, or had been, a well-known olive orchard (Jo. κῆπος). It was probably fenced in as a private plot, χωρίον, Vulg. *villam* (Mt.), *praedium* (Mk.), which always seems to have this meaning in the N.T. (Jo. iv. 5, Ac. i. 18 f., iv. 34, v. 3, 8, xxviii. 7; cf. 1 Chr. xxvii. 27), though it and χώρα tended to supplant ἀγρός in late Gk. (see M.-M. *Vocab. s.v.* ἀγρός). It lay πέραν τοῦ χειμάρρου τῶν Κέδρων (Jo.). On the site see Swete, and Baedeker, *Palest.* 69 f.

καὶ λέγει κτλ.] There is no reason for supposing that more than the Eleven are included in τ. μαθηταῖς (see on v. 51). They were to remain seated, perhaps near the entrance, while the Lord went apart for prayer. This was probably His habit; cf. xiv. 23, Mk. i. 35, Lk. ix. 18, xi. 1. αὐτοῦ, rare in the N.T. (see Blass,

§ 25. 2 n.²), is substituted for Mk.'s ὧδε (although in v. 38 Mk.'s ὧδε is adopted), possibly under the influence of Gen. xxii. 5, in which Mt. may well have seen a parallel in thought. ἕως οὗ προσεύξ. (Blass, § 65. 10) 'until I shall have prayed,' *donec orem*, is virtually 'while I pray,' *dum adoro* (𝕃 k Mk.); cf. xiv. 22. Mt. adds ἀπελθὼν ἐκεῖ (= ἐκεῖσε, cf. ii. 22, xvii. 20), as though the Lord pointed out the direction.

37. καὶ παραλαβών κτλ.] On the Three see xvii. 1. Loisy finds here a 'Pauline' feature, the motive being to shew that even the chief apostles were dull and apathetic to the last. He supports this by the absence of any statement that when Jesus rejoined the Three, He also rejoined, or summoned, the others. But see on v. 46. The mention of Peter's name alone is perhaps intended to bring him into prominence, as elsewhere in Mt. (see on x. 2). Mk. gives simply the three names.

ἤρξατο κτλ.] See on iv. 17. At this point the Passion, in its full sense, began. λυπεῖσθαι veils its intensity; Mt. shrank from Mk.'s ἐκθαμβεῖσθαι (see Swete), which describes a feeling of 'terrified surprise.' ἀδημονεῖν, if connected with ἀδέω 'to be sated,' and so 'to loathe,' implies a restless, distracted, shrinking from some trouble, or thought of trouble, which nevertheless cannot be escaped. But see M.-M. *Vocab. s.v.* In Plato (see *Phaedr.* 251 D) it is used with ἀπορεῖν 'to be at a loss' where to turn, or what to do. It followed naturally upon the first shock of horror. It occurs in Phil. ii. 26 (see

38 καὶ ἀδημονεῖν. τότε λέγει αὐτοῖς Περίλυπός ἐστιν ἡ ψυχή
μου ἕως θανάτου· μείνατε ὧδε καὶ γρηγορεῖτε μετ᾽ ἐμοῦ.
39 καὶ προελθὼν μικρὸν ἔπεσεν ἐπὶ πρόσωπον αὐτοῦ προσ-
ευχόμενος καὶ λέγων Πάτερ μου, εἰ δυνατόν ἐστιν,

39 προελθων] ΒΜΠ* minn.*nonn* 𝔏 *omn* 𝕊 sin['he removed from them'].pesh
['he departed'].hcl ; προσελθων ℵACD *etc* 1 33 69 *al* 𝕊 pal

Lightft.), and in Aq. Sym. for שׁמם
'be astonied,' עמף 'be faint,' יפח 'be
alarmed,' but not in the LXX. Allen
cites *Ox. Pap.* ii. 298. 45 (1st cent.
A.D.). Orig. *ad loc.* strangely explains
that Jesus only *began* to be sorrowful,
and His Godhead restrained Him
from the fulness of human emotion.

38. τότε λέγει κτλ.] After the
first moment of shock and distress,
the Lord sought human sympathy.
περίλυπος κτλ. recalls Ps. xli. [xlii.]
6, 12 ἵνα τί περίλυπος εἶ, ἡ ψυχή
μου; The remaining words of the
same refrain, ἵνα τί συνταράσσεις με,
seem to colour the utterance in Jo. xii.
27, when the shadow of 'this hour'
fell upon His soul. Only in these
two references to the Psalm is Jesus
recorded to have spoken of His ψυχή,
as the seat of thought and feeling ;
see on x. 28, and Swete on Mk.
v. 34. ἕως θανάτου reveals a deeper
depth, an anguish—not 'which makes
me wish for death,' but—which is as
great as that of death ; cf. Jon. iv. 9,
Sir. xxxvii. 2. γρηγορεῖτε means
'keep awake' physically, as Mt.
understood, adding μετ᾽ ἐμοῦ; and
in *v.* 40. See on *v.* 41.

39. καὶ προελθών κτλ.] Lk.
ἀπεσπάσθη ; see Plummer. Though
needing their company and sympathy,
He could not fight the battle in their
immediate presence. προσελθών
has large uncial support, but is
meaningless. The frequency of its
occurrence in Mt. probably led to
the scribal error, and it was inserted
for harmonization in ACD etc. in

Mk. μικρόν (Lk. ὡσεὶ λίθον βολήν)
is used of space in Xen., but not in
bibl. Gk. apart from this context.
ἐπὶ πρόσωπον αὐτ. : Mk. ἐπὶ τῆς
γῆς, Lk. θεὶς τὰ γόνατα. The
attitude was perhaps that of Elijah,
1 Kings xviii. 42.

πάτερ μου κτλ.] Mt. passes at
once to the *orat. recta*, omitting Mk.'s
summary of the contents of the
prayer, 'that if it were possible the
hour might pass from Him.' Mk.
has Ἀββά, ὁ πατήρ (see Swete) ; Lk.
πάτερ; see on vi. 9. The inspired
insight of the makers of the evangelic
tradition is nowhere more conspicuous
than here. The Lord's words were
not heard by the disciples, since they
were asleep. His prayer was an
agonized struggle, probably, for the
most part, far beyond the possibility
of articulate utterance, and lasting
for a considerable time. But the
records convey a living picture of
what must have been His attitude
of mind.

εἰ δυνατόν κτλ.] 'If Thy plans
render it possible'; cf. Mk.'s summary
above ; Lk. has the same thought in
εἰ βούλει. The human shrinking
from terrors which He had only just
realized in their fulness, made Him
cling to the possibility that the
Father might, after all, raise Him
to His glory by a miracle, without
the suffering. Mk.'s πάντα δυνατά
σοι expresses the certainty that God
could do so, if He willed. παρελθάτω
'pass by,' without coming to Me
(Mk., Lk. παρένεγκε) ; cf. Exod. xii.

παρελθάτω ἀπ᾿ ἐμοῦ τὸ ποτήριον τοῦτο· πλὴν οὐχ ὡς ἐγὼ
θέλω ἀλλ᾿ ὡς σύ. καὶ ἔρχεται πρὸς τοὺς μαθητὰς καὶ 40
εὑρίσκει αὐτοὺς καθεύδοντας, καὶ λέγει τῷ Πέτρῳ Οὕτως
οὐκ ἰσχύσατε μίαν ὥραν γρηγορῆσαι μετ᾿ ἐμοῦ; γρηγορεῖτε 41
καὶ προσεύχεσθε, ἵνα μὴ εἰσέλθητε εἰς πειρασμόν· τὸ μὲν

23, παρελεύσεται κύριος τὴν θύραν, Am. vii. 8, viii. 2. On ποτήριον see xx. 22. In Jo. xviii. 11 it is referred to later in the narrative.

πλήν κτλ.] On πλήν see xi. 22. Mk. ἀλλ᾿ οὐ τί ἐγὼ θέλω ἀλλὰ τί σύ [sc. γενήσεται]. Lk. πλὴν μὴ τὸ θέλημά μου ἀλλὰ τὸ σὸν γινέσθω. On Mk.'s colloquial τί see Swete, and Blass, § 50. 5. The utterance has an important bearing on Christology, as evidence for a human Will, which must be kept by self-denial in unison with the Father's Will. Cf. John Damasc. *De Fide Orth.* iii. 18, quoted by Swete.

In many MSS. of Lk. two verses (43 f.) are inserted, relating the appearance of an angel, and the sweat like drops of blood. Since Lk. records only one of the three acts of prayer, the position assigned to the incident cannot be determined.

40. καὶ ἔρχεται κτλ.] The first struggle was over, and before it re-curred He returned to His friends for the solace of company. Lk. lessens the completeness of their failure : they were κοιμωμένους ἀπὸ τῆς λύπης. The sad rebuke, though addressed to Peter, included the other two ; hence ἰσχύσατε for Mk.'s ἴσχυσας ; in the next verse Mk. also has the plur. Mk.'s Σίμων καθεύδεις ; is omitted. οὕτως (Mk. om.) οὐκ κτλ.: 'Were ye so lacking in the strength to watch with Me for a single hour ?' For οὕτως cf. 1 Cor. vi. 5.

41. γρηγορεῖτε κτλ.] Christians can use the words as a warning, giving to γρηγ. the metaphorical force which it has in xxiv. 42, xxv.

13, 1 Pet. v. 8. But their immediate reference was to the circumstances of the moment, as Lk. under-stood : τί καθεύδετε ; ἀναστάντες προσεύχεσθε ἵνα μή κτλ. If the disciples did not keep awake and pray, as He did, they would not escape trial ; He had prayed to be spared His 'Cup,' and they must pray to be spared the trial of moral strength which their association with Him would involve (ἵνα expressing the content of their prayer). As events proved it was not the Father's will to spare either Him or them, but want of prayer deprived them of the spiritual victory which He won, εἰσακουσθεὶς ἀπὸ τῆς εὐλαβείας (Heb. v. 7). The clause is an echo of the Lord's Prayer (vi. 13), but the force of πειρασμός is different.

τὸ μὲν πνεῦμα κτλ.] The spirit was eager, 'but its προθυμία was not a match for the *vis inertiae* of its colleague, the frail flesh' (Swete). The eagerness had been evinced more than once (*vv.* 33, 35, xiv. 28 ff., Mk. x. 39, Jo. xi. 16). Man's resurrection alone can finally transform weak flesh into a perfect instrument of the spirit (1 Cor. xv. 44, Phil. iii. 21), but spiritual progress in this life is an approxima-tion to it. πνεῦμα is here, as in the best Hebrew thought, the moral life, including will and emotions, distinct from the flesh ; see esp. Is. xxxi. 3 (Heb.) 'their horses are flesh and not spirit'; and cf. Num. xvi. 22, xxvii. 16. A similar contrast is expressed by 'heart' and 'flesh' (Ps. lxxii. [lxxiii.] 26), νοῦς and σάρξ (Rom. vii. 25),

42 πνεῦμα πρόθυμον ἡ δὲ σὰρξ ἀσθενής. πάλιν ἐκ δευτέρου
ἀπελθὼν προσηύξατο λέγων Πάτερ μου, εἰ οὐ δύναται
τοῦτο παρελθεῖν ἐὰν μὴ αὐτὸ πίω, γενηθήτω τὸ θέλημά
43 σου. καὶ ἐλθὼν πάλιν εὗρεν αὐτοὺς καθεύδοντας, ἦσαν
44 γὰρ αὐτῶν οἱ ὀφθαλμοὶ βεβαρημένοι. καὶ ἀφεὶς αὐτοὺς
πάλιν ἀπελθὼν προσηύξατο ἐκ τρίτου τὸν αὐτὸν λόγον
45 εἰπὼν πάλιν. τότε ἔρχεται πρὸς τοὺς μαθητὰς καὶ λέγει
αὐτοῖς Καθεύδετε λοιπὸν καὶ ἀναπαύεσθε· ἰδοὺ ἤγγικεν
ἡ ὥρα καὶ ὁ υἱὸς τοῦ ἀνθρώπου παραδίδοται εἰς χεῖρας

44 παλιν²°] אBL 124 𝔏 a 𝕾 sin me ; om ACD etc minn.*pler* 𝔏 vet.*pler*.vg
𝕾 pesh.hcl.pal sah

ὁ ἔσω ἄνθρωπος and τὰ μέλη (*id.*
22 f.). S. Paul's whole passage (*vv.*
14–25) is a confession of the truth
of the Lord's saying.

42. πάλιν κτλ.] The second
prayer, as given by Mt., shews an
advance upon the first, as though the
Lord had steeled Himself to realize
that the Cup could not pass from
Him. Mk. has simply τὸν αὐτὸν
λόγον εἰπών (not λόγους) : the substance of the prayer was the same
(cf. Exod. xxxiii. 17, Deut. iii. 26) ;
cf. *v.* 44 below. On εἰ οὐ see Blass,
§ 75. 3. γενηθήτω κτλ. was probably
the source of the petition in Mt.'s
form of the Lord's Prayer (vi. 10).

43. ἦσαν γάρ κτλ.] Their eyes
were weighed down (Mk. κατα-
βαρυνόμενοι) as at the Transfiguration
(Lk. ix. 32 βεβαρημένοι ὕπνῳ), and,
as Mk. adds, 'they knew not what to
answer Him ' (cf. Mk. ix. 6).

44. καὶ ἀφεὶς κτλ.] The Lord
left them to their sleep, which was
worse than a rebuke. The substance
of His prayer was again the same,
τὸν αὐτὸν λόγον (see *v.* 42). It
was on a higher plane than S. Paul's
thrice uttered petition (2 Cor. xii. 8).
The use of πάλιν four times in *vv.*
42–44 adds a mournful force. There
is, however, considerable authority
for its omission at the end of the
verse. Mt.'s use of τότε (see on

ii. 7) forbids πάλιν to be placed at
the beginning of *v.* 45, as in W.H.
marg.

45. καθεύδετε κτλ.] The exact
force is doubtful. Wellh. explains
the first clause as an exclamatory
question, ' So then ! are you sleeping
and resting ! ' (cf. *DwTh*, 1895, 978
ff.), and Mk.'s ἀπέχει after λοιπόν
('Enough of sleeping !') as leading
directly to ἐγείρεσθε κτλ., the intervening words being a later insertion.
(On ἀπέχει see Swete, and a suggestion
in *Expos.*, 1905, ii. 459–72.) But
more probably, with the usual meaning of τὸ λοιπόν 'henceforth' (1 Cor.
vii. 29, Heb. x. 13), the words are
one of the rare instances of the Lord's
irony : 'Sleep on, uninterrupted by
further calls to prayer !'   In Mt.,
without ἀπέχει, the irony continues ;
' the hour of the πειρασμός which
you might have gained strength to
meet, has now come !'

ἰδού κτλ.] The ὥρα (cf. Mk. xiv.
35) is the appointed time, when the
divine δεῖ (*v.* 54 ; xvi. 21) is fulfilled.
The thought is a marked feature in
the 4th Gosp. (ii. 4, vii. 30, viii.
20, xii. 23, 27, xiii. 1, xvi. 4,
xvii. 1).   On the temporal force of
καί ('when ') see Blass, § 77. 6.   The
words ὁ υἱός κτλ. are an echo of
former predictions (xvii. 22, xx. 18 f.),
the prophetic pres. taking the place

ἁμαρτωλῶν. ἐγείρεσθε ἄγωμεν· ἰδοὺ ἤγγικεν ὁ παραδιδούς 46
με. Καὶ ἔτι αὐτοῦ λαλοῦντος ἰδοὺ Ἰούδας εἷς 47
τῶν δώδεκα ἦλθεν καὶ μετ᾽ αὐτοῦ ὄχλος πολὺς μετὰ
μαχαιρῶν καὶ ξύλων ἀπὸ τῶν ἀρχιερέων καὶ πρεσβυτέρων
τοῦ λαοῦ. ὁ δὲ παραδιδοὺς αὐτὸν ἔδωκεν αὐτοῖς σημεῖον 48

of μέλλει and of the fut., because
the fulfilment is so close at hand.
ἁμαρτωλῶν perhaps describes the
character of those to whom the Son of
Man will be handed over ; but it may
have the same force as Mk.'s τῶν ἁμ.,
the Gentiles as a class (see on ix. 10).

46. ἐγείρεσθε κτλ.] They were
still lying down, probably with their
backs to the entrance, while Jesus
stood facing it and could therefore
see His enemies approaching in the
light of the Paschal moon ; or, with
tensely strung nerves, could hear
the distant tramp of feet, which the
drowsy disciples had not yet caught.
ἄγωμεν is not a proposal to flee ; it
does not occur in the LXX., but in
the N.T. (Mk. i. 38, Jo. xi. 7, 15 f.,
xiv. 31) it always expresses the
purpose of going to some place or
person ; here it is to meet Judas (cf.
Jo. xviii. 4). There is nothing to
warrant the sneer of Celsus that
Jesus went to the garden in order to
hide (Orig. c. Cels. ii. 10). On ὁ
παραδιδούς see v. 25. It is not stated
that Jesus rejoined or summoned the
other eight disciples, but it is implied
in the πάντες of v. 56. They may
have entered the garden behind
Judas and his band, or Jesus may
have stepped outside the entrance,
where they were awaiting Him, in
His movement to meet Judas.

47–56. (Mk. xiv. 43–50, Lk.
xxii. 47–53, Jo. xviii. 3–11.) THE
ARREST.

47. καὶ ἔτι κτλ.] On εἷς τ.
δώδεκα (see Mk., Lk.) see v. 14. Jo.
(v. 2) explains that Judas knew the

place, because Jesus frequented it
with the disciples. The authorities
had taken precautions, lest His
followers might offer opposition. The
ὄχλος, who seem to have been a
mere hired rabble, were armed with
μάχαιραι, swords or knives (cf.
Gen. xxii. 6, 10), such as private
persons might carry (see v. 51, Lk.
xxii. 36, 38), and some merely with
sticks or clubs. Since no criminal
charge could be alleged, and the
arrest was to be as secret as possible,
the Sanhedrin could not ask for the
services of soldiers. The ὄχλος may
possibly have included, as Lk. states,
some members of the high-priestly
families, captains of the temple, and
elders. But Jo.'s account is, so to
speak, symbolic; he describes an
official arrest by Jews and Gentiles
combined, relating that Judas brought
τὴν σπεῖραν (the garrison in Antonia)
under command of a χιλίαρχος
(tribune), together with ὑπηρέται
(the servants of the Sanhedrin). On
the last see v. 58. τῶν ἀρχιερέων
κτλ. : Mk. adds καὶ τ. γραμματέων ;
see on ii. 4.

48. ὁ δὲ παραδιδοὺς κτλ.] See
on v. 25. ἔδωκεν : Mk. δεδώκει (cf.
xxvii. 18); Mt. never uses the pluperf.
except in ᾔδειν and ἱστήκειν. Lk.
does not mention this prearrange-
ment of a sign. σημεῖον is for Mk.'s
rarer σύσσημον, in the LXX. a signal
or standard, but here with its strict
meaning, a token mutually agreed
upon. The sign was needed evidently
because Jesus was unknown to the
rabble ; they were not among those

λέγων ῝Ον ἂν φιλήσω αὐτός ἐστιν· κρατήσατε αὐτόν.
49 καὶ εὐθέως προσελθὼν τῷ Ἰησοῦ εἶπεν Χαῖρε, ῥαββεί·
50 καὶ κατεφίλησεν αὐτόν. ὁ δὲ Ἰησοῦς εἶπεν αὐτῷ Ἑταῖρε,
ἐφ᾿ ὃ πάρει. τότε προσελθόντες ἐπέβαλον τὰς χεῖρας
51 ἐπὶ τὸν Ἰησοῦν καὶ ἐκράτησαν αὐτόν. καὶ ἰδοὺ εἷς τῶν

50 εταιρε] post παρει D 𝔏 a c f 𝔖 sin.pesh Ephr^diat Diat^ar

who thronged the temple courts when
He was preaching. φιλεῖν 'to kiss'
(LXX. and class.) occurs only in this
context in the N.T. ; cf. φίλημα, Lk.
vii. 45 ; in the Epp. it is the Christian
kiss of brotherhood. On καταφιλεῖν
see next verse. It was an ordinary
mode of salutation to a guest (Lk. l.c.)
or a Rabbi (Wünsche, *Neue Beitr.*
339) ; in this case the lowest depth
of insincerity. αὐτός ἐστιν : 'he is
(the man whom you seek)'; cf. ἐγώ
εἰμι, xiv. 27. For κρατεῖν ' to arrest'
cf. xiv. 3.

49. καὶ εὐθέως κτλ.] Mt. omits
Mk.'s ἐλθών, which resumes the narrative, after the parenthesis. He adds
χαῖρε, an anticipation of the coming
mockery (xxvii. 29). κατεφίλησεν
following φιλήσω perhaps implies
a show of specially warm affection :
cf. Xen. *Mem.* II. vi. 33, ὡς τοὺς μὲν
καλοὺς φιλήσαντος, τοὺς δ᾿ ἀγαθοὺς
καταφιλήσαντος, Lk. vii. 38, 45,
xv. 20, Ac. xx. 37. It is the most
terrible instance of the ἑκούσια
φιλήματα ἐχθροῦ (Prov. xxvii. 6).
Lk. 'as if he shrank from realizing
the scene' (Swete) says only 'drew
near to Jesus to kiss Him' (see next
n.). Jo. does not mention the kiss.

50. ὁ δὲ Ἰησοῦς κτλ.] In Mk.
the Lord is silent ; Lk., who seems
to shrink from recording the act,
appears to represent Him as forestall-
ing and preventing the kiss : 'Judas,
with a kiss dost thou betray the Son
of Man?' ἐφ᾿ ὃ πάρει is variously
explained : 𝔏 *ad quod venisti* is a
literal rendering ; so 𝔖 pesh. But

Vulg^edd (*ad quid*), Ephr. and probably
𝔖 sin (Burkitt) 'Wherefore hast thou
come,' an unexampled use of the
relative. 'For what [a deed] art thou
come !' is open to the same objection.
Blass conjectures αἶρε, or ἑταῖρε αἶρε,
ἐφ᾿ ὃ π., van der Valk ἔπαιρε, 'Comrade take what thou art come to fetch';
but the true position of ἑταῖρε is uncertain (see Appar.), and the pretence
of not knowing what Judas had come
to take is impossible. Diat^ar assumes an ellipse, '*Is it this* for which
thou hast come?' Most writers
supply some such word as ποίησον,
'*Do that* for which, etc.' Possibly ἐφ᾿
ὅ,τι (= δι᾿ ὅ,τι) 'wherefore' should be
read, τι having fallen out before π.
The class. use of ἐπί ' for the purpose
of' recurs in the N.T. in Lk. iv. 43,
2 Tim. ii. 14 only.

τότε κτλ.] Lk. does not state the
fact of the arrest till *v.* 54 (συλλα-
βόντες). ἐπέβαλον κτλ.: cf. Jo. vii.
30, 44, Ac. v. 18, xxi. 27 ; Gen.
xxii. 12 and elsewhere, = שָׁלַח יָד אֶל.
Mk. has the dat. as in Ac. iv. 3,
Est. vi. 2.

51. καὶ ἰδού κτλ.] In Lk. also
(οἱ περὶ αὐτόν . . . εἷς τις ἐξ αὐτῶν)
the assailant is one of the disciples.
Mk.'s εἷς δέ τις τῶν παρεστηκότων
possibly implies that unauthorized
persons had followed with the rabble,
one of which was in sympathy with
Jesus. But in Jo. xviii. 10 (cf. 26)
it is Peter. If this is the true tradition, Peter, hurt by the warning in
v. 34, and shamed by the rebukes
in *vv.* 40, 45, characteristically tried

μετὰ Ἰησοῦ ἐκτείνας τὴν χεῖρα ἀπέσπασεν τὴν μάχαιραν
αὐτοῦ καὶ πατάξας τὸν δοῦλον τοῦ ἀρχιερέως ἀφεῖλεν αὐτοῦ
τὸ ὠτίον. τότε λέγει αὐτῷ ὁ Ἰησοῦς Ἀπόστρεψον τὴν 52
μάχαιράν σου εἰς τὸν τόπον αὐτῆς, πάντες γὰρ οἱ λαβόντες
μάχαιραν ἐν μαχαίρῃ ἀπολοῦνται· ἢ δοκεῖς ὅτι οὐ δύναμαι 53
παρακαλέσαι τὸν πατέρα μου, καὶ παραστήσει μοι ἄρτι
πλείω δώδεκα λεγιῶνας ἀγγέλων ; πῶς οὖν πληρωθῶσιν αἱ 54

to prove his zeal, only to receive
another rebuke. Swete, al. suggest
that in the early years of the tradition the name was concealed for
prudential reasons. Lk. records that
the disciples, having with them two
knives, asked Κύριε, πατάξομεν ἐν
μαχαίρᾳ; and adds the account of
the healing of the slave's ear. He
was probably the leader of the rabble ;
and his name (Jo.) was Malchus.

ἀπέσπασεν with this meaning is
less usual than Mk.'s σπασάμενος,
and is infrequent c. acc. rei ; cf.
Gosp. Pet. vi. 1, ἀπέσπασαν τοὺς
ἥλους. See M.-M. Vocab. s.v. The
redundant ἐκτείνας τὴν χεῖρα (Mt.
only) is an O.T. idiom ; cf. e.g. Gen.
xxii. 10. The partcp. πατάξας (Mk.
ἔπαισεν) describes the same action
as ἀφεῖλεν (see Blass, § 58. 4). For
ὠτίον (Mk., Jo. ὠτάριον), the ear as
a part of the body, Lk. has the Attic
οὖς (Blass, § 27. 4).

52. τότε κτλ.] Vv. 52–54 are
found only in Mt., except the first
clause, given in Jo. as βάλε τ. μάχ. εἰς
τὴν θήκην. Lk. has ἐᾶτε ἕως τούτου
(see Plummer), and the act of healing.
The use of weapons was contrary to
the spirit and aims of Jesus (cf. v. 39,
Jo. xviii. 36), and of the early
Church. The rebuke seems to be
echoed in Apoc. xiii. 10. For λαβεῖν
cf. Gen. xxii. 10. On ἐν μαχ. see
xii. 24.

53. ἢ δοκεῖς κτλ.] On ἤ see xx.
15, and on παρακαλεῖν viii. 5. For
the consecutive καί see Blass, § 77.

6. In the case of Elisha (2 Kings
vi. 17) the heavenly host appeared
for his encouragement ; and every
Christian can spiritually apply the
Lord's words with that meaning.
But in His case, if they appeared it
would be to sweep away the enemy.
He would not ask for them, because
that was not the true path to victory.
But the question arises whether He
could, knowing that, have said that
the Father would send them if He
asked for them. The genuineness of
the words, which are confined to Mt.,
must be considered doubtful. παραστήσει 'present,' 'conduct to My
presence,' marks the authority and
lordship of the Speaker. λεγιών
(on the spelling see Blass, § 6. 3) is
a latinism, legio, employed in late
Gk., and in rabb. Heb. (Dalm. Gr.²
186). The Roman legions did not
come into contact with Judaea till
the outbreak of the war in A.D. 66 ;
but since they were employed in
Syria in the time of Augustus, it
was not impossible for a Palestinian
Jew in the time of Jesus to use
the word. It connoted numerical
greatness ; cf. Mk. v. 9, and see
HDB. s.v. Twelve represents the
perfect completeness of the heavenly
host. The constructions πλείω δ.
λεγιῶνας, and, as in some MSS.,
λεγιώνων, are both class. (L. & S. s.v.
πλείων, Blass, § 36. 12).

54. πῶς οὖν κτλ.] But the
Scriptures have foretold that I must
suffer ; 'how then (if I fight, or

55 γραφαὶ ὅτι οὕτως δεῖ γενέσθαι ; Ἐν ἐκείνῃ τῇ ὥρᾳ εἶπεν
ὁ Ἰησοῦς τοῖς ὄχλοις Ὡς ἐπὶ λῃστὴν ἐξήλθατε μετὰ
μαχαιρῶν καὶ ξύλων συλλαβεῖν με. καθ᾽ ἡμέραν ἐν τῷ
56 ἱερῷ ἐκαθεζόμην διδάσκων καὶ οὐκ ἐκρατήσατέ με. Τοῦτο
δὲ ὅλον γέγονεν ἵνα πληρωθῶσιν αἱ γραφαὶ τῶν προφητῶν.
Τότε οἱ μαθηταὶ πάντες ἀφέντες αὐτὸν ἔφυγον.

pray for angelic help) are the Scriptures to be fulfilled, etc.' The source
of the words appears to be Mk. v. 49 b,
for which Mt., in v. 56, substitutes
a comment of his own. ὅτι οὕτως
κτλ. is the substance of the teaching
of the Scriptures. On δεῖ see xvi.
21, and on οὕτως as predicate i. 18.
A suffering Messiah was foretold in
the O.T., though the Jews had never-
realized it ; see on xx. 28 *fin.*

55. ἐν ἐκείνῃ κτλ.] 'At the same
time' or 'moment.' There was no
word to express a shorter period than
an hour; cf. x. 19, xviii. 1, Jo. iv.
53, Apoc. xi. 13. Lk.[Ev.Ac.] prefers
ἐν αὐτῇ τ. ὡ.

ὡς ἐπὶ λῃστήν κτλ.] So Mk.,
Lk. A half-ironical exclamation ;
sc. θαυμαστόν ἐστιν. 'What a
robber-hunting sally !' This use of
ὡς, occurring in class. Gk., though
more frequently with adjectives (cf.
Rom. x. 15, xi. 33, Gen. xxviii. 17)
and adverbs, is more vivid and
colloquial than the meaning 'as.'
With the latter meaning, the sentence
may be either a question (W.H. here
and in Mk., Lk., Vulg.[edd] in Lk.) or
an indignant statement (𝕃 𝕊).

καθ᾽ ἡμέραν κτλ.] If the note
on v. 48 is correct, the irony continues. The Lord had preached,
but this common rabble had not
been among His hearers. Five days,
Sunday evening to Thursday, had
been available ; and though the
Gospp. relate no public appearance
on the last two days, the words
imply it, unless καθ᾽ ἡμέραν means

(as *e.g.* in Aesch. *Choë.* 818) 'by
day,' *i.e.* in open daylight. Lk. has
καθ᾽ ἡμ. here, but τὸ καθ᾽ ἡμ.
'daily' in xix. 47. ἐκαθεζόμην (Mk.
ἤμην πρὸς ὑμᾶς, Lk. ὄντος μου μεθ᾽
ὑμῶν) pictures Jesus seated authoritatively as a Rabbi ; cf. v. 1. Lk.
adds ἀλλ᾽ αὕτη ἐστὶν ὑμῶν ἡ ὥρα
καὶ ἡ ἐξουσία τοῦ σκότους, an
anticipation of Johannine language.

56. τοῦτο δέ κτλ.] Mt. adapts
his favourite formula (see i. 22),
to expand Mk.'s elliptical ἀλλ᾽ ἵνα
πληρωθῶσιν αἱ γραφαί. This reference by Jesus to the 'fulfilment' of
Scripture is unique in Mk., which
favours its genuineness. Mt. puts it
back to v. 54, and here substitutes
his own comment.

τότε κτλ.] πάντες evidently includes all the Eleven ; see on v. 46.
Holtzmann, *al.* assume that the flight
was into Galilee (see on xxviii. 7),
and that Lk. omits the verse because
he relates appearances of the risen
Christ in and near Jerusalem only.
But it need only mean that they
fled from the spot ; Lk. probably
omitted it to spare ·the disciples.
Peter, at least, did not flee to Galilee,
for he followed afar off. The rabble
had arrested the One whom they
wanted, and had no wish, or authority,
to pursue the fugitives.

Mk. here inserts an account of a
youth who followed Jesus till he
also was arrested, when he left his
linen wrap in their hands and fled
'naked.' See suggestions as to the
story in Swete. If Gethsemane was

Οἱ δὲ κρατήσαντες τὸν Ἰησοῦν ἀπήγαγον πρὸς Καιάφαν 57
τὸν ἀρχιερέα, ὅπου οἱ γραμματεῖς καὶ οἱ πρεσβύτεροι
συνήχθησαν. ὁ δὲ Πέτρος ἠκολούθει αὐτῷ ἀπὸ μακρόθεν 58

a private olive-yard (see on *v.* 36),
the youth may have been a keeper
sleeping in a hut close by, and
awakened by the noise. Mk. writes
τὸν Ἰησοῦν in the next verse, because
the incident has intervened. Mt.
repeats it from Mk., though αὐτόν
(as in Lk.) would have been enough,
which perhaps suggests that the
story stood in Mk. as Mt. knew it,
and was not a later insertion.

57–75. (Mk. xiv. 53–72, Lk. xxii.
54–71, Jo. xviii. 12–27.) JESUS
BEFORE THE SANHEDRIN. PETER'S
DENIAL.

On several points Lk. and Jo.
seem to have obtained more trust-
worthy information than Mk. and
Mt. In Lk. the trial was not held
till morning, the Lord being kept in
the courtyard of the high priest's
house and brutally handled ; within
His sight and hearing Peter denied
Him thrice at intervals. Jo., in the
present order of the text, describes
an informal questioning by Annas
immediately on the arrival of the
Prisoner, who would then be left, as
in Lk., in charge of the gang until
morning ; Annas then sent Him
bound to Caiaphas, of whose action
nothing is said. But the verses
seem to be dislocated, so that Peter's
denial is represented as occurring in
the house of Annas, which has led
some to conjecture that Annas and
Caiaphas occupied apartments in the
same house, or adjacent houses with
a common courtyard. On the order
in ℵ sin see Burkitt, *Ev. da Meph.* ii.
316, and proposals for rearrangement
in Moffatt, *Hist. NT.* 528 f., 693 f.,
or *LNT.* 557 f., and see *Expos.*, July
1907, 55–69.

But in Mt., Mk. the trial, which
Lk. places in the morning, is held
at dead of night, during which the
denial took place, and at the close
of the trial, apparently in the court
where the Sanhedrin met (which is
very improbable), the Lord was
subjected to abuse ; and a brief
reference to a council meeting in
the morning is added (xxvii. 1, Mk.
xv. 1). The placing of the trial at
night is possibly due to a corruption
of the tradition, preserved more
accurately in Jo., of the hasty, informal questioning in the house of
Annas ; the description of the proceedings, on the other hand, was
derived from the tradition of the
morning trial, preserved by Lk., of
which the mention of the morning
meeting (*ll.c.*) was a further reminiscence.

57. οἱ δὲ κρατήσαντες κτλ.] On
Caiaphas see *v.* 3 ; Mk. never names
him, Lk. only in iii. 2, Ac. iv. 6.
In Mk. the whole Sanhedrin, 'high
priests, elders and Scribes' (see on ii.
22), collect after the Prisoner's arrival.
Mt.'s ὅπου συνήχθησαν probably
means the same, not that they had
already assembled. For ὅπου =
'whither' cf. viii. 19.

58. ὁ δὲ Πέτρος κτλ.] For ἀπὸ
μακρόθεν, more usually μακρόθεν in
LXX. (as Lk.), cf. 2 Esd. iii. 13, xxii.
[Neh. xii.] 43, Ps. cxxxviii. [cxxxix.]
2. ἕως . . . ἔσω expands Mk.'s ἕως
ἔσω εἰς, both of which seem to
imply that Peter contrived to do
something rather difficult, which Jo.
explains was due to the good offices of
'another disciple,' who was known
to the high priest. The ὑπηρέται
can hardly have been the men who

ἕως τῆς αὐλῆς τοῦ ἀρχιερέως, καὶ εἰσελθὼν ἔσω ἐκάθητο
59 μετὰ τῶν ὑπηρετῶν ἰδεῖν τὸ τέλος. οἱ δὲ ἀρχιερεῖς καὶ τὸ

arrested Jesus, or they must have
recognized Peter (see on v. 47); they
were in attendance at the high priest's
house, and were sitting about in the
courtyard (αὐλή, see v. 3). Only Mt.
suggests Peter's motive; it was not
to die with his Master, as he had
boasted, but 'to see how the matter
would end.' This takes the place of
Mk.'s καὶ θερμαινόμενος πρὸς τὸ
φῶς. Mk. assumes that a fire has
been lighted (for φῶς cf. 1 Macc. xii.
29, Xen. Cyr. VII. v. 10), which Lk.
and Jo. state explicitly.

59–66. *The Trial.* This is interposed in Mt., Mk. (see above); Lk.
continues the account of the denial,
and then relates the mocking.

Sanh. iv. 1 contains the following
rules : (1) 'Criminal cases must be
tried in the daytime and finished
in the daytime.' (2) 'Criminal cases
may be finished on the same day if
the verdict is Not Guilty, but on the
next day if the verdict is Guilty.'
Both of these were transgressed,
according to the account in Mt.,
Mk., for xxvii. 1 (Mk. xv. 1) does not
relate the pronouncement of a sentence, but only the handing over to
Pilate. It is not certain, however,
whether these rules, drawn up by R.
Meir in the 2nd cent., obtained in
practice in the 1st cent. The proceedings were obviously unfair to the
Prisoner, but the letter of the law
then in force may have been adhered
to. If it was transgressed, it is possible that the Sadducean rulers (who
were 'very rigid in judging offenders,
above all the rest of the Jews,' Jos.
Ant. xx. ix. 1), rather than the Pharisees, were mainly responsible, being
more anxious to condemn one who,
as they thought, threatened their

political privileges, than to observe
traditional rules. Lk. avoids both
difficulties, since he places the trial
in the morning, and records no sentence of death by the Sanhedrin. Jo.
omits the Jewish trial altogether;
Jesus is sent to Caiaphas, and by him
to Pilate.

The Sanhedrin met to find cause
for delivering the Prisoner to the
procurator. That the Jews were
allowed to condemn, though not to
execute, is stated in Jo. xviii. 31, xix.
7, and is presupposed in Mt., Mk.;
see also Mt. v. 22 (where even a local
council is thought of as dealing with
a capital charge), and Jos. *l.c.* which
deals with the procuratorship of
Albinus (A.D. 62). Against this is
adduced a single statement in Jer.
Sanh. i. 1, vii. 2, that 'the right to
pronounce capital sentences was taken
away from the Jews forty years before
the destruction of Jerusalem.' The
origin of this tradition cannot be
traced, but it is valueless as evidence.

The historical value of the accounts
of the trial is denied by some, since
none of the Twelve was present. But
Joseph of Arimathaea (a βουλευτής,
Mk. xv. 43) may have been present,
as Lk. xxiii. 51 implies; the 'other
disciple' (Jo. xviii. 15) cannot be
left entirely out of account; and in
any case, as J. Weiss points out, the
circumstances must have been eagerly
discussed, after the Resurrection,
between Jews and Christians, and
the main points would soon become
common property.

59. οἱ δὲ ἀρχιερεῖς κτλ.] The
whole Sanhedrin took part. Mishnic
law required only 23 members for
a criminal case (*Sanh.* iv. 1). The
conditions of criminal procedure

συνέδριον ὅλον ἐζήτουν ψευδομαρτυρίαν κατὰ τοῦ Ἰησοῦ
ὅπως αὐτὸν θανατώσωσιν, καὶ οὐχ εὖρον πολλῶν προσ- 60
ελθόντων ψευδομαρτύρων. ὕστερον δὲ προσελθόντες δύο
εἶπαν Οὗτος ἔφη Δύναμαι καταλῦσαι τὸν ναὸν τοῦ θεοῦ 61

60 και ουχ . . . ψευδομαρτυρων] אBC*LN 1 118 124 209 𝔏 b ff¹ g¹·²ˡ n vg 𝕊 pesh.
hcl.pal sah arm ; κ. ουχ ευρ. και πολλ. προσελθ. ψευδ. [vel ψευδ. προσελθ.] ουχ
ευρον AC²E al minn.pler 𝔏 a [add exitum rei] f [add culpam] q 𝕊 sin[add ᴸᵉʷⁱˢ 'to
speak the truth'] aeth ; κ. ουχ ευρον το εξης· και πολλοι προσηλθον ψευδομαρτυρες
και ουχ ευρον το εξης D 𝔏 ff² [quicquam in eo] h [in eum quicquam] | δυο] אBL
1 102 118 124 209 𝕊 pesh.pal me sah aeth ; add ψευδομαρτυρες A²CD etc minn.
pler 𝔏 omn 𝕊 sin.hcl arm

tended, in Mishnic times, to become increasingly favourable to the accused : the witnesses were solemnly warned that a false witness must himself suffer death (*id.* 5); they were examined separately; and if the evidence of two of them agreed, the trial began with proofs for the *innocence* of the accused (*id.* v. 4). How much of this was in force in the time of Jesus is not known. His judges demanded the evidence of two witnesses, but disgraced themselves by seeking it to support a predetermined verdict. Hence for Mk.'s μαρτυρίαν Mt. indignantly substitutes ψευδομαρτυρίαν, 'what purported to be witness.' Lk. gives no account of the witnesses, but in *v.* 71 ('why have we further need of witness?') shews that he knew of them. θανατοῦν (cf. x. 21) is 'to procure the death of,' by persuading the procurator to execute.

60. καὶ οὐχ εὖρον κτλ.] All the evidence was false, and no two witnesses agreed. Mk. has καὶ ἴσαι αἱ μαρτυρίαι οὐκ ἦσαν 'the depositions did not tally' (not 'were not adequate,' for the witnesses would take good care of that). For Mt.'s readers, conversant with Jewish practice, οὐχ εὖρον was enough (see Appar.).

ὕστερον κτλ.] Of all the various charges, only this one found its way into the Christian tradition. Mt. makes it a turning-point in the trial ; a charge was 'at last' forthcoming in which two witnesses agreed. Their evidence might, of course, still be false ; whether ψευδομάρτυρες is to be inserted or not, it is clearly Mt.'s meaning. Mk.'s account is different : certain persons (τινες) bare false witness, καὶ οὐδὲ οὕτως ἴση ἦν ἡ μαρτυρία αὐτῶν. See on *v.* 63.

61. οὗτος κτλ.] For the contemptuous οὗτος cf. ix. 3. A mere 'I am able' could not constitute a crime ; Mt. is more concerned with the Lord's power than with the legal aspect of the words ; he may even have wished to soften Mk.'s *I will* destroy this temple made with hands, and διὰ τριῶν ἡμέρων I will build [D 𝔏 ἀναστήσω] another not made with hands.' The Lord must have said something which could be thus represented, though the synn. nowhere record it, but what He said, or meant, is difficult to determine, because His words are obscured by the construction put upon them, not only by His enemies, but also by Christians who naturally saw in them a prediction of His Resurrection. He foretold the destruction of the temple (xxiv. 2, Mk., Lk.), and in Mk. xiii. 2 D 𝔏 Cyp add καὶ διὰ τριῶν ἡμέρων ἄλλος ἀναστήσεται ἄνευ χειρῶν (cf. Dan. ii. 34); but that *He* would

62 καὶ διὰ τριῶν ἡμερῶν οἰκοδομῆσαι. καὶ ἀναστὰς ὁ ἀρχιερεὺς
εἶπεν αὐτῷ Οὐδὲν ἀποκρίνῃ ; τί οὗτοί σου καταμαρτυ-
63 ροῦσιν ; ὁ δὲ Ἰησοῦς ἐσιώπα. καὶ ὁ ἀρχιερεὺς εἶπεν

destroy it may be a perversion by
the witnesses. Similarly Ac. vi. 14
may be S. Stephen's reference to His
actual words, or a perversion of
it. In Jo. ii. 19 He is reported to
have said λύσατε τὸν ναὸν τοῦτον.
Further, διὰ τριῶν ἡμερῶν, *post
triduum* (a class. use, cf. Mk. ii. 1,
Ac. xxiv. 17, Gal. ii. 1), rendered '*in
three days*' in ܣ sin.pesh (and pesh
Mk., Ac. *ll.c.*) appears as ἐν τρισὶν
ἡμέραις in the taunt in xxvii. 40 (and
Mk.), and in Jo. *l.c.* It may have
the same force as μετὰ τρ. ἡμ. (xxvii.
63, Mk. ix. 31, x. 34), referring to
the Resurrection, or merely denote
'after a very short time' (cf. Hos.
vi. 2).

The original utterance, whatever
it was, probably contained a veiled
reference to His future action as the
Messiah. Some explain it to mean
that though the temple would be
destroyed, He would raise up a community of His followers, a true Israel,
as a spiritual temple. More probably
He appropriated the eschatological
belief that in the Messianic age a
new temple and a new Jerusalem
would take the place of the old (see
Volz, *Jüd. Esch.* 334–41). He, as
Messiah, would be the Agent of its
erection. In the light of the Resurrection, Christians soon found an
abiding truth in the words : the new
temple was His risen Body, in which
the Church, His Body, had its
life. τὸν χειροποίητον and ἄλλον
ἀχειροποίητον are perhaps later
additions in Mk. ; cf. Ac. vii. 48,
xvii. 24, 2 Cor. v. 1.

62. καὶ ἀναστάς κτλ.] Mk. adds
εἰς μέσον. According to *Sanh.* iv. 3
the members of the court sat on a

dais or platform in a semi-circle, so
that all could see one another ; and
the high priest would naturally
occupy the central seat. The charge,
in the form that the witnesses
brought it, was as palpably false as
the previous charges, and the Lord's
continued silence was a condemnation
in itself. The high priest went
through the form of inviting the
Accused to defend Himself, which is
permitted in *Sanh.* iv. 4. οὐδὲν
ἀποκρίνῃ is probably a separate
question (as in ܣ), and τί = τί
(ἐστιν) ὅ,τι. The Vulg. 'nihil re-
pondes *ad* ea quae etc.' has class.
support, but ἀποκρ. πρός (cf. xxvii.
14) would be more likely, especially
since the verb already has the acc.
οὐδέν.

63. ὁ δὲ Ἰησοῦς κτλ.] Mk. re-
dundantly 'But He was silent and
answered nothing.' The high priest
was so obviously bent on condemn-
ing the Accused that self-defence
would have implied self-incrimina-
tion. His silence condemned judge
and witnesses alike (cf. xxvii. 12).
There is no reason for thinking that
the narrative is influenced by Is. liii.
7, though the Lord may well have
had the passage in mind.

καὶ ὁ ἀρχιερεύς κτλ.] Since two
witnesses had agreed, and the Accused
offered no defence, the verdict might
have been expected to follow at once.
But something moved the high
priest to ask a further question on
oath. Perhaps there were signs in
the court of sympathy with the
Prisoner. His silence, and no doubt
His bearing and look, were so accus-
ing that the high priest was stung
into forcing from Him a damaging

αὐτῷ Ἐξορκίζω σε κατὰ τοῦ θεοῦ τοῦ ζῶντος ἵνα ἡμῖν
εἴπῃς εἰ σὺ εἶ ὁ χριστὸς ὁ υἱὸς τοῦ θεοῦ. λέγει αὐτῷ 64

admission, though it was not legally requisite. Wellhausen unnecessarily condemns both the question and the reply as later additions. Mk.'s statement (v. 59), that the evidence regarding the alleged utterance about the temple did not tally, would hardly have been omitted by Mt. if he had known it; it was probably a later addition, to avoid the idea that a real charge had been found and proven. Possibly for the same reason Lk. omits the whole account of the trial up to the question 'Art Thou the Christ, tell us,' which he attributes to the court as a whole. This is more probable than that he considered the destruction of the city a divine judgment brought about by Jesus Himself, and therefore omitted the account of the witnesses to avoid recording that the charge was false (*Enc. Bibl.* 1772).

ἐξορκίζω κτλ.] Mk. σὺ εἶ ὁ χριστὸς ὁ υἱὸς τοῦ εὐλογητοῦ; Mt. appears to interpret the true force of the words. See Burkitt, *JThS.* v. 451. Jesus would no longer be silent when the divine Name was invoked. That He thereby countenanced for all time an oath in a law court cannot be deduced. The Christian use of forensic oaths rests rather on broad principles (see on v. 34). Shebuoth iv. 3 speaks of the administering of an oath, to which the response is 'Amen'; *id.* 13 gives instances of divine names and titles which render such an oath binding. For ἐξορκίζειν cf. Gen. xxiv. 3, 3 Regn. xxii. 16; ὁρκίζειν is commoner. For κατά cf. Gen. xxii. 16, Am. iv. 2, Heb. vi. 13, 16. On ὁ θεὸς ὁ ζῶν see xvi. 16; it is akin to the very frequent formula in an oath 'as Yahweh [*or* God] liveth.'

ὁ χριστός κτλ.] Mk. ὁ χ. ὁ υἱ. τ. εὐλογητοῦ, Lk. ὁ χριστός. Mk.'s εὐλογητοῦ has a more Jewish ring than θεοῦ; though it is rare as a title (cf. *Ber.* vii. 3, and 'the Everblessed' Enoch lxxvii. 1), a standing formula is 'The Holy One, blessed be He.' The juxtaposition of ὁ χριστὸς and ὁ υἱός was probably not due to words attributed to Jesus; the high priest was understood by Mt., Mk. to be identifying Messiahship and divine Sonship. It is open to question, however, whether this was done by Jews as early as the time of Jesus (see Dalm. *Words*, 268–73); Apoc. Esd. vii. 28 f. is probably the earliest known instance (see Box p. lvi.). Lk.'s ὁ χριστός may be more correct. He afterwards gives as a separate question (v. 70) 'Art Thou then the Son of God?'

How the high priest knew that Jesus claimed Messiahship cannot be determined, but probably the council rightly understood as Messianic the utterance about the destruction of the temple (v. 61); and the earlier witnesses, though they did not agree, would adduce other things that He had said and done in opposition to Jewish ideas and institutions (*e.g.* ix. 1–8, xii. 1–14, xv. 1–12; and see the threefold charge in Lk. xxiii. 2). Also some in the council may have known that the Messianic idea was in the minds of the populace at the Entry into the city. The Lord's own admission (v. 64) only served to settle them in their determination to condemn Him as a revolutionary Pretender. Schweitzer's conjecture (*Quest.* 394) that the Messianic secret had been betrayed to the authorities by Judas, can be neither proved nor disproved, and is unnecessary.

ὁ Ἰησοῦς Σὺ εἶπας· πλὴν λέγω ὑμῖν, ἀπ᾽ ἄρτι ὄψεσθε
τὸν υἱὸν τοῦ ἀνθρώπου καθήμενον ἐκ δεξιῶν τῆς δυνάμεως
65 καὶ ἐρχόμενον ἐπὶ τῶν νεφελῶν τοῦ οὐρανοῦ. τότε ὁ ἀρχιερεὺς

64. σὺ εἶπας] Mk. ἐγώ εἰμι.
See on v. 25, xxvii. 11. Whether
or not the expression means more
than Mk.'s simple affirmative, the
following words shew that underlying it is the thought ' Thy words,
though verbally correct, mean more
than thou knowest.' In Lk. a direct
reply is avoided : ' If I tell you, ye
will not believe ; and if I ask, ye
will not answer,' but in reply to the
separate question about the Sonship
he has ὑμεῖς λέγετε ὅτι ἐγώ εἰμι.

πλήν κτλ.] See xi. 22. Mk. καί,
Lk. δέ. You have an inadequate
idea of Messiahship, but you will
soon learn the truth. For ἀπ᾽ ἄρτι
(Lk. ἀπὸ τοῦ νῦν, Mk. om.) cf. v. 29,
xxiii. 39 ; it does not occur elsewhere
in the synn., or in the LXX. In the
passages cited it can be rendered
' henceforth,' ' from now onwards,'
but here it refers to a single moment
in the future (ὄψεσθε). It can
hardly be taken with λέγω (Blass).
Lk.'s ἀπὸ τοῦ νῦν has LXX. parallels,
Gen. xlvi. 30, and Tob. xi. 9, ἀπὸ
τοῦ νῦν (הָעַתָּה) ἀποθανοῦμαι, Dan.
x. 17 (Theod.), ἀπὸ τ. ν. οὐ στήσεται
ἐν ἐμοὶ ἰσχύς (LXX. οὐκ ἔστιν), where
it means ' now,' ' the time has come
when.' The Lord's open assertion
of His Messiahship was the beginning of the end, because it would
lead to His condemnation and death,
and therefore to His Resurrection
and Parousia. In v. 29, xxiii. 39,
both referring to the End, the same
thought of immediacy underlies the
expression. Cf. Lobeck, Phryn. 18 ff.,
Abbott, Joh. Gr., 1915, vi.

ὄψεσθε κτλ.] The Lord's assent,
or semi-assent, made it clear that
He was now speaking of Himself,

otherwise the words would be merely
a statement with which every religious Jew would agree. If He did
not identify Himself with the Son
of Man, and only said in effect ' Do
what you will with Me, God's cause
cannot fail, the Son of Man will
surely come ' (J. Weiss, Carpenter),
the climax is lost, and ' ye have
heard the blasphemy ' refers only to
σὺ εἶπας (ἐγώ εἰμι).

The thoughts of Dan. vii. 13 and
Ps. cix. [cx.] 1 are here combined ;
He alluded to the former in xxiv.
30, and whenever He spoke of ' the
Son of Man ' in an eschatological sense
(see p. xxv.) ; the latter He quoted
in xxii. 44. Lk.'s ἔσται... καθήμενος
does not mean ' shall be continually
seated ' ; like ὄψεσθε it pictures the
scene which men would behold at
the moment of the Parousia. ἡ
δύναμις, גבורתא, is a genuine Jewish
periphrasis for the divine Name
(Dalman, Words, 201) ; for Gentile
readers Lk. adds the explanatory τοῦ
θεοῦ. καὶ ἐρχόμενον . . . οὐρανοῦ
(omitted by Lk.) shews that Dan.
was understood to be the source of
the title ' the Son of Man.' Lk.'s
form of the words is echoed in Ac.
vii. 56.

65. τότε κτλ.] Tearing the
garments was a common sign of
sorrow. Commentators refer to 2
Kings xviii. 37 as an instance in
the case of blasphemy, and Jer. compares Ac. xiv. 14. The action may
have been a spontaneous expression
of real horror. A high priest was
not allowed to tear his clothes in
mourning for the dead (Lev. x. 6,
xxi. 10), but the custom which required it on hearing a blasphemy

διέρηξεν τὰ ἱμάτια αὐτοῦ λέγων Ἐβλασφήμησεν· τί ἔτι
χρείαν ἔχομεν μαρτύρων; ἴδε νῦν ἠκούσατε τὴν βλασφη-
μίαν· τί ὑμῖν δοκεῖ; οἱ δὲ ἀποκριθέντες εἶπαν Ἔνοχος 66
θανάτου ἐστίν. Τότε ἐνέπτυσαν εἰς τὸ πρόσωπον αὐτοῦ 67
καὶ ἐκολάφισαν αὐτόν, οἱ δὲ ἐράπισαν λέγοντες Προφήτευσον 68

may have grown up by the 1st cent. In *Sanh.* vii. 5 it is required of all who try the case, and Maimonides later gives exact rules on the subject ; see Buxt. *Lex.* s.v. קְרַע.

ἐβλασφήμησεν κτλ.] The exclamation is given only by Mt. In spite of the agreement of two witnesses (*v.* 60 f.), the high priest had been uneasy ; but if there were any in the council who had sympathized with the Prisoner, they were now silenced, having heard His admission ἀπὸ τοῦ στόματος αὐτοῦ (Lk.), and the high priest clearly expressed his relief at being freed from an awkward situation. Cf. Plato, *Rep.* I. xiii. 340 A, quoted by Plummer. Technically speaking, it was not blasphemy, in the strict sense of saying something against God. But, with their determination to condemn, the court not unnaturally treated as blasphemy words from a young Galilean prisoner which implied ' I shall be seated at God's right hand.'

66. τί ὑμῖν δοκεῖ; κτλ.] See on xvii. 25 ; Mk. τί ὑ. φαίνεται ; On ἔνοχος see v. 21. A Mishnic equivalent is מִתְחַיֵּב בְּנַפְשׁוֹ (*Ab.* iii. 11 f.). And see Edersheim, *LT.* ii. 561. If a formal capital sentence was passed, the rules in *Sanh.* iv. 1 (if then in force) were transgressed (see n. before *v.* 59). Lk., in omitting the verdict, may be nearer to the facts. Or the proceedings may have been rather analogous to those in a magistrate's court to-day, a prisoner on a serious charge being condemned only to the extent of committal to the assizes.

67, 68. (Mk. xiv. 65, Lk. xxii. 63 ff.) INSULTS ENDURED BY JESUS.

67. τότε κτλ.] The subject of the verb is that of εἶπον in the preceding verse, *i.e.* the members of the Sanhedrin. In Mk. it is only τινες, who are distinguished from οἱ ὑπηρέται. The latter seem to be referred to in Mt.'s οἱ δέ, ' and others'; cf. xxviii. 17 (Blass, § 46. 2). Lk., with greater probability, ascribes the brutality only to the gang who had arrested Jesus, the trial not taking place till the next morning ; see n. before *v.* 57. Mt. alone has εἰς τὸ πρόσωπον αὐτοῦ, perhaps influenced by Is. l. 6. Mk. says that they began to spit upon Him, and to cover His face. Lk. omits the spitting,and connects περικαλύψαντες αὐτόν with the following προφήτευ- σον,but in Mk.the meaning is perhaps different (see below). κολαφίζειν is to hit with the fist (κόλαφος ; Att. κόνδυλος).

68. οἱ δέ κτλ.] Mk.'s difficult ῥαπίσμασιν ἔλαβον (see Swete) is avoided. ῥαπίζειν, to hit with a stick (ῥαπίς), came to be used of striking with the hand, esp. of a blow on the head or face ; cf. Is. l. 6, τὰς δὲ σιαγόνας μου [ἔδωκα] εἰς ῥαπίσματα. It is not clear which is meant here, but the evv. probably had Is. in mind. By adding χριστέ, Mt. brings the scene into connexion with the trial : it is as Messiah that Jesus is told to prophecy. τίς ἐστιν ὁ παίσας σε; (Mt., Lk.) is absent from

69 ἡμῖν, χριστέ, τίς ἐστιν ὁ παίσας σε;   Ὁ δὲ Πέτρος
ἐκάθητο ἔξω ἐν τῇ αὐλῇ· καὶ προσῆλθεν αὐτῷ μία
70 παιδίσκη λέγουσα Καὶ σὺ ἦσθα μετὰ Ἰησοῦ τοῦ Γαλιλαίου·

Mk., who perhaps understood the insult differently : the Lord had prophesied to the council of the coming of the Son of Man, and they now jeeringly bade Him prophesy again (𝔖 sin 'Prophesy to us *now*'). The covering of the face may, in this case, have been understood by Mk. as an indication that Jesus was a condemned criminal (cf. Est. vii. 8 (Heb.)), or a mere item in the brutality, with no special purpose. Mt. agrees with Lk., but the last clause may have been added later from Lk.

69 75. (Mk xiv, 66–72, Lk. xxii. 56–62, Jo. xviii. 17 f., 25–27.) PETER'S DENIAL.

Mt. mainly follows Mk.; Lk. is largely, and Jo. entirely, independent. (*a*) Those who accost Peter are different in each Gospel : Mt. two maids, and the bystanders; Mk. the same maid twice, and the bystanders ; Lk. a maid, a second person (ἕτερος), and another man (ἄλλος τις); Jo. the maid who was portress, the bystanders (εἶπον), and one of the slaves, a kinsman of him whose ear Peter cut off. (*b*) In Peter's movements Mt. follows Mk.: he sits in the courtyard, and then retires to the gateway (Mk. porch), and the place of the third denial 'a little afterwards' is not stated; Lk. mentions no change of place; the second denial is 'shortly after' the first, and the third is 'after about an hour's interval'; Jo. gives no movements or intervals of time. (*c*) In the words spoken to, or about, Peter, Mt. follows Mk.: in the first and third case Peter is directly accosted, in the second the words are spoken

to those present ; Lk. exactly reverses this ; and in Jo., Peter is accosted in each case. (*d*) In Peter's replies, Mt. follows Mk. in the first and third, Lk. reverses them, and in the second case, where Mk. has no reply, Mt., Lk. supply it independently.

69. ὁ δὲ Πέτρος κτλ.] This is the sequel of *v.* 58. The αὐλή (see on *v.* 3) was outside the palace, and below (Mk.) the council-chamber. For μία = τις (Lk.) cf. xxi. 19 ; see on viii. 19. παιδίσκη, in class. Gk. = νεᾶνις (Phryn. 216), came to be used specially of a slave girl (Kennedy, *Sources* 41), corresponding with παῖς. Mt. abbreviates Mk.'s account of the girl looking at Peter as he warmed himself (see on *v.* 58), the firelight leading to his recognition.

καὶ σὺ ἦσθα κτλ.] If 'thou *also*' points to another disciple whom she had already recognized in the court, the Johannine tradition of the 'other disciple' who brought in Peter possibly underlies the words. (καὶ occurs also in Mk. *v.* 67, in all three instances in Lk., and in the first two in Jo.) But perhaps καί only adds force to the pronoun : You were actually a follower of Jesus, and yet you venture to come here ! For ἦσθα μετά cf. Mk. iii. 14, Ac. iv. 13. She may have seen him with Jesus in the streets at any time during the preceding five days. τ. Γαλ. anticipates the reference to Peter's northern accent by the third speaker (*v.* 73; Mk., Lk. Γαλιλαῖος εἶ [ἐστιν]) ; Mk. has 'thou wast with the Nazarene, Jesus' (cf. *v.* 71 below), as though the populace of Jerusalem already knew Him by that designation.

ὁ δὲ ἠρνήσατο ἔμπροσθεν πάντων λέγων Οὐκ οἶδα τί λέγεις.
ἐξελθόντα δὲ εἰς τὸν πυλῶνα εἶδεν αὐτὸν ἄλλη καὶ λέγει 71
τοῖς ἐκεῖ Οὗτος ἦν μετὰ Ἰησοῦ τοῦ Ναζωραίου· καὶ πάλιν 72
ἠρνήσατο μετὰ ὅρκου ὅτι Οὐκ οἶδα τὸν ἄνθρωπον. μετὰ 73
μικρὸν δὲ προσελθόντες οἱ ἑστῶτες εἶπον τῷ Πέτρῳ Ἀληθῶς
καὶ σὺ ἐξ αὐτῶν εἶ, καὶ γὰρ ἡ λαλιά σου δῆλόν σε ποιεῖ·
τότε ἤρξατο καταθεματίζειν καὶ ὀμνύειν ὅτι Οὐκ οἶδα τὸν 74

73 δηλον σε ποιει] ομοιαζει D 𝕷 a b c ff² h q 𝕾 sin

70. ὁ δέ κτλ.] Had he not afterwards repented, the consequence
described in x. 33 must have followed.
ἔμπροσθεν πάντων, added by Mt.,
may be due to that passage. 'Non
magna erat tentatio si interrogantem
spectes: major si praesentes' (Beng.).
Mt. omits Mk.'s οὔτε ἐπίσταμαι and
σύ (see Swete). Dalman (Words,
80 f.) suggests that οἶδα represents
the Galilean הכם, not the Judaean
ידע, so that Peter's vocabulary at once
betrayed his origin. Lk.: οὐκ οἶδα
αὐτόν, γύναι (cf. v. 72 below).

71. ἐξελθόντα κτλ.] He retired
into the dimmer light of the vestibule
(προαύλιον Mk.), close to the gateway.
πυλών is the gateway of a private
house (Lk. xvi. 20, Ac. x. 17, xii. 13),
a city (Apoc. xxi. 12 f., xxii. 14), or
a temple (3 Regn. vi. 13 [8]).
On Mk.'s statement at this point,
'and a cock crew,' see on v. 34.
ἄλλη : Mt. seems to have understood
Mk.'s ἡ παιδίσκη to mean 'the maid
who would naturally be on duty at
the gate,' different from the first
speaker. If so, Mk.'s doubtful πάλιν
should probably be omitted. On
Ναζωραῖος see ii. 23.

72. καὶ πάλιν κτλ.] μετὰ ὅρκου,
added by Mt. only, is likely enough;
Peter had been taught not to use
oaths (v. 34); but the old habit, ·in
which Galilean fishermen would not
differ from the rest of the populace,
reasserted itself in a moment of moral

fear and laxity. Mk. does not give
the words of denial; Lk.: ἄνθρωπε
οὐκ εἰμί, in answer to καὶ σὺ ἐξ αὐτῶν
εἶ. In v. 70 οἶδα = scio, but here novi,
γνωρίζω (cf. Exod. v. 2, 4 Regn. ix.
11); הכם has both meanings.

73. μετὰ μικρόν κτλ.] His dialect
(λαλιά) is implied in Mk., Lk., καὶ
γὰρ Γαλειλαῖος εἶ [ἐστιν]. TR in
Mk. adds καὶ ἡ λαλιά σου ὁμοιάζει;
the verb has strong 'Western' support
in Mt. Reference to the 'inaccuracy'
of the Galilean dialect is made in
Erub. 53a; cf. Ac. iv. 13. Its
peculiarities are known chiefly from
the Palest. Talmud; cf. Neubauer,
Géogr. du Talm. 184 f., Dalman, Gr.
4 f., 31 ff., 43–51, Buxt. Lex. s.v. בלל.

74. τότε ἤρξατο κτλ.] He now
began (see on iv. 17), after single
sentences of denial, to invoke a series
of curses on himself, and to utter a
string of oaths. Always impulsive
and highly strung, he now lost his
self-control. But the next moment
(εὐθύς) he was recalled to himself.
Τὸ ἀλέκτωρ ἐφώνησεν Mk. adds ἐκ
δευτέρου; see on v. 34 above. Lk.
states also that the Lord turned and
looked at him; this He could do,
because He was Himself in the courtyard, undergoing insults (see n. bef.
v. 57). καταθεματίζειν (for κατανα-
θεμ.) is used by Iren.; cf. κατάθεμα
Apoc. xxii. 3, Did. xvi. 5. Mk.'s
ἀναθεματίζειν is frequent in the
LXX. All are confined to bibl.
and patr. Gk.

75 ἄνθρωπον. καὶ εὐθὺς ἀλέκτωρ ἐφώνησεν· καὶ ἐμνήσθη ὁ
Πέτρος τοῦ ῥήματος Ἰησοῦ εἰρηκότος ὅτι Πρὶν ἀλέκτορα
φωνῆσαι τρὶς ἀπαρνήσῃ με, καὶ ἐξελθὼν ἔξω ἔκλαυσεν
πικρῶς.

XXVII. 1 Πρωίας δὲ γενομένης συμβούλιον ἔλαβον πάντες οἱ
ἀρχιερεῖς καὶ οἱ πρεσβύτεροι τοῦ λαοῦ κατὰ τοῦ Ἰησοῦ
2 ὥστε θανατῶσαι αὐτόν· καὶ δήσαντες αὐτὸν ἀπήγαγον καὶ
3 παρέδωκαν Πειλάτῳ τῷ ἡγεμόνι. Τότε ἰδὼν Ἰούδας
ὁ παραδοὺς αὐτὸν ὅτι κατεκρίθη μεταμεληθεὶς ἔστρεψεν
τὰ τριάκοντα ἀργύρια τοῖς ἀρχιερεῦσιν καὶ πρεσβυτέροις

75. καὶ ἐμνήσθη κτλ.] Mk. ἀν-
εμνήσθη (cf. Mk. xi. 21) τὸ ῥῆμα,
Lk. ὑπεμνήσθη τοῦ λόγου. The
simple verb is usual in the LXX.
καὶ ἐξελθών κτλ. : Peter left the
courtyard by the gate. In Lk. the
clause is identical, and is substituted for Mk.'s difficult ἐπιβαλὼν
ἔκλαιεν (on which see Swete, and
Moulton, i. 131). In Lk., however,
it is omitted, perhaps rightly, in all
O.L. MSS.

xxvii. 1, 2. (Mk. xv. 1, Lk. xxiii.
1, Jo. xviii. 28.) THE LORD IS
HANDED OVER TO PILATE.

1. πρωίας κτλ.] In Mk. the
entire Sanhedrin (described with
emphatic fulness) meet, only to bind
Jesus and take Him to Pilate. Mt.
inserts ὥστε θανατῶσαι, a repetition
of the object stated in xxvi. 59.
There was no reason whatever for a
second trial; see n. bef. xxvi. 57.
On συμβ. ἔλαβον see xii. 14, and
on ὥστε of purpose (D ἵνα), Blass,
§ 69. 3.

2. καὶ δήσαντες κτλ.] Lk. omits
the binding. He contemptuously
describes the Sanhedrin as ἅπαν τὸ
πλῆθος αὐτῶν. Pilatus ('armed
with a javelin') was the cognomen,
the last of the three names borne by
every free Roman; Pontius (Lk. iii.
1, Ac. iv. 27, 1 Tim. vi. 13) was the

nomen, an ancient Samnite, afterwards Roman, gens. His praenomen,
or personal name, is unknown. He
was appointed procurator (ἡγεμών) of
the province of Judaea (i.e. from
Samaria to the Dead Sea) by Tiberius
in A.D. 26. His record was bad; see
Jos. Ant. XVIII. iii f, B.J, II. ix. 2 ff.,
Philo, Ad Gai. 38. These Jewish
accounts may be prejudiced; but
that he was not of the best type of
Roman governors seems certain; cf.
also Lk. xiii. 1. He was summoned
to Rome in A.D. 36, and succeeded
by Marcellus (see Add. n. after xiv.
12).

3–10. (Mt. only.) THE END OF
JUDAS.

3. τότε ἰδών κτλ.] The incident
was probably added by a later hand.
The Sanhedrin are pictured as still
sitting, after the Lord was led away,
and Judas entered before·they broke
up. The writer, therefore, understood the condemnation to have
taken place at the morning meeting.
ἰδών implies, not that Judas was
present at the meeting, but that he
concluded the result of it by seeing
Jesus led away in bonds. On παραδούς see x. 4, and on the v.l. παραδιδούς xxvi. 25. For στρέφειν
'bring back' cf. Is. xxxviii. 8. On
τὰ τριάκ. ἀργύρια see xxvi. 15.

λέγων "Ημαρτον παραδοὺς αἷμα δίκαιον. οἱ δὲ εἶπαν 4
Τί πρὸς ἡμᾶς ; σὺ ὄψῃ. καὶ ῥίψας τὰ ἀργύρια εἰς τὸν 5
ναὸν ἀνεχώρησεν, καὶ ἀπελθὼν ἀπήγξατο. Οἱ δὲ ἀρχιερεῖς 6
λαβόντες τὰ ἀργύρια εἶπαν Οὐκ ἔξεστιν βαλεῖν αὐτὰ
εἰς τὸν κορβανᾶν, ἐπεὶ τιμὴ αἵματός ἐστιν· συμβούλιον 7
δὲ λαβόντες ἠγόρασαν ἐξ αὐτῶν τὸν 'Αγρὸν τοῦ Κεραμέως
εἰς ταφὴν τοῖς ξένοις. διὸ ἐκλήθη ὁ ἀγρὸς ἐκεῖνος 'Αγρὸς 8
Αἵματος ἕως τῆς σήμερον. Τότε ἐπληρώθη τὸ ῥηθὲν διὰ 9

4 δικαιον] B²ᵐᵍL 𝕃 omn 𝕊 sin [δικαιου].pal.diatᴱᵖʰ me sah arm Cyp ; αθωον
אAB*C etc minn 𝕊 pesh.hcl go

4. ἥμαρτον κτλ.] To 'deliver up
blood' (*i.e.* a living person) finds
analogies in Deut. xxvii. 25 (πατάξαι
ψυχὴν αἵματος ἀθῴου), 1 Regn. xix.
5 (ἁμαρτάνεις εἰς αἷ. ἀθ.), Ps. xciii.
[xciv.] 21 (αἷ. ἀθ. καταδικάσονται).
αἷμα δίκαιον is rare (Joel iii. [iv.]
19, Jon. i. 14, Prov. vi. 17 *v.l.*);
hence the more ordinary αἷ. ἀθῷον
(*v.l.*). See *v.* 24. For τί πρὸς ἡμᾶς ;
cf. Jo. xxi. 22 f. The idiom σὺ
ὄψῃ is commoner in Latin, 'tu
videris'; but cf. *v.* 24 (in another
extraneous passage), Ac. xviii. 15.
Deissmann, *Bibl. St.*, cites a papyrus;
and it occurs in Epict. *Diss.* II. v.
30, IV. vi. 11. ἰδεῖν (1 Regn. xxv.
17) and βλέπειν (2 Chr. x. 16) are
analogous to it.

5. καὶ ῥίψας κτλ.] Not a violent
action; Judas did not throw the
money on the ground, but placed it
in the Treasury (see next verse), as
the prophet did, according to the
original text of Zach. xi. 13 (see
Add. n.). Since this stood in the
court, where even women could
approach it (Lk. xxi. 2), ναός is not
the inner shrine, but the temple
(ἱερόν) in general. Ahitophel the
treacherous friend of David, and
Judas the treacherous friend of the
Son of David, meet a similar end
(2 Sam. xvii. 23 וַיֵּחָנַק). ἀπάγξασθαι
occurs in Tob. iii. 10, and חנק in
Nah. ii. 13 [Engl. 12], the latter shew-

ing that strangling, not necessarily
hanging, is denoted. 𝕊 sin has
the gloss 'hanged himself and was
strangled.' A different tradition,
more gruesome in detail, is preserved
in Ac. i. 18; see Bp. Chase in *JThS.*
Jan. 1912, who quotes a still more
horrible account in Papias. Rendell
Harris (*AJTh.* iv. 490 ff.) thinks that
the tradition, for which Mt.'s account
is a milder substitute, was derived
from the legend of Nadan, son of
Ahikar; and see *id.* xviii. 127–31.

6. οὐκ ἔξεστιν κτλ.] βαλεῖν (see
on x. 34) corresponds with ῥίψας,
and κορβανᾶν with ναόν: they declared that the action of Judas was
wrong (οὐκ ἔξεστιν), because the
price of blood was pollution to the
treasury (cf. Deut. xxiii. 18 [19]).
They therefore took the money out
and employed it for a secular
purpose. On κορβάν, of which Mt.
uses the graecized form, see xv. 5 ;
it is not strictly the γαζοφυλάκιον,
but its contents.

7, 8. See Add. n.

9, 10. τότε κτλ.] On the formula
see i. 22. The omission of 'Ιερεμίου
in 33 157 𝕃 a b 𝕊 sin.pesh was an
obvious correction, since the quotation
is from Zach. xi. 12 f. Of Origen's
alternatives, either that Jeremiah
was written by mistake for Zachariah,
or that the words occurred in an
apocryphal writing of Jeremiah (see

'Ιερεμίου τοῦ προφήτου λέγοντος Καὶ ἔλαβον τὰ τριάκοντα ἀργύρια,
10 τὴν τιμὴν τοῦ τετιμημένου ὃν ἐτιμήσαντο ἀπὸ υἱῶν 'Ισραήλ, καὶ
ἔδωκαν αὐτὸ εἰς τὸν ἀγρὸν τοῦ κεραμέως, καθὰ συνέταξέν μοι

9 Ιερεμιου] Ζαχαριου 22 𝔖 hcl^mg ; Esaiam 𝔏 l ; om 33 157 𝔏 a b codd. ap. Aug
𝔖 pesh   10 εδωκαν] εδωκα ℵ 122 24^ev 31^ev 𝔖 sin.pesh.hcl.pal^A

also Jerome *ad loc.*), the former is probably right. The latter is adopted by Resch (*Texte u. Unt.*, 1896, 7. Teil ii. 336 f.). But the tradition preserved in the verses is exceedingly confused, and such a mistake in the names was easily made : Jeremiah's purchase of a field (xxxii. 6 ff.), and his visit to the potter's house (xviii. 2 f.), may have contributed to it. A purely clerical slip, due to a misreading of an abbreviation, is also possible. Origen's second alternative was adopted by the Nazarenes ; Jerome found it stated in their Gospel that the passage occurred *ad verbum* in an apocryphal book of Jeremiah. Some writers, *e.g.* Cyr., Epiph., Thphlact (quoted by Tischendorf) carefully avoided the difficulty.

Additional Note on xxvii. 3–10.

Four causes seem to have contributed to the formation of the passage : (1) The existence of a cemetery near Jerusalem, in which strangers who died in the city were buried. If it had no existence, the mention of it in *v.* 7 is unaccountable. A tradition grew up as to its origin. (2) The existence of a piece of ground known as the Field of Blood (Aram. דמא חקל ; Ac. i. 19 'Ακελδαμάχ). Klostermann (*Probleme in Aposteltexte* 6 ff.) suggests that this arose from an original Ḥ^aḳél d^amak, 'Field of Sleeping,' *i.e.* a cemetery, which may have been the name of that in which strangers were buried. Since, in the LXX., χ transliterates not only כ but occasionally א, the Greek letters were thought to represent Field of Blood. (3) However this may be, tradition explained Field of Blood in two different ways : in Ac. i. 18 it refers to the blood of Judas, shed in the field which he bought, in Mt. to the blood-money which he received. (4) An O.T. passage was adduced as being 'fulfilled' in the narrative : the 30 pieces of silver received by the prophet as his hire (Zach. xi. 12) underlie the account in Mt. *v.* 3. But the next verse in Zach. was then applied, in two ways : (*a*) it coloured the narrative that it was to illustrate, (*b*) it was added as a definite quotation.

(*a*) Having received his wage, the prophet rejected it, and put it into 'the treasury' (הָאוֹצָר). There is little doubt that this was the original reading (preserved in 𝔖 and implied in Targ.) ; but considering it derogatory to the temple, scribes altered the word to 'the potter' (הַיּוֹצֵר). The writer of Mt.'s tradition knew, and applied, both readings : Judas, having received his wage, rejected it, and put it into the treasury (ναός, κορβανᾶς) ; but considering this derogatory to the temple, the high priests paid it to the potter (for his field). At this point the tradition about the Field of Blood blends with the narrative, producing the complex which now stands in *vv.* 6–8.

Κύριος.   Ὁ δὲ Ἰησοῦς ἐστάθη ἔμπροσθεν τοῦ ἡγεμόνος· 11
καὶ ἐπηρώτησεν αὐτὸν ὁ ἡγεμὼν λέγων Σὺ εἶ ὁ βασιλεὺς
τῶν Ἰουδαίων ; ὁ δὲ Ἰησοῦς ἔφη Σὺ λέγεις.   καὶ ἐν 12
τῷ κατηγορεῖσθαι αὐτὸν ὑπὸ τῶν ἀρχιερέων καὶ πρεσ-

(b) Zach. xi. 13 runs as follows : 'And Yahweh said unto me, Cast it
unto the "potter," the splendid price (lit. the splendour of the price) at
which I was priced by them ; and I took the thirty pieces of silver and cast
it into the house of Yahweh unto the "potter."' (The LXX. has χωνευτήριον
('smelting-furnace') for 'potter,' and departs in other respects from the Heb.
text. It has no bearing on Mt.) The passage is applied thus : 'And Yahweh
said unto me' appears as καθὰ συνέταξέν μοι ὁ Κύριος (cf. Exod. ix. 12).
The command 'Cast it unto the potter' is omitted.   'The splendour of the
price (הַיְקָר) . . . by them' becomes τὴν τιμὴν τοῦ τετιμημένου (הַיְקָר) . . .
Ἰσραήλ. Jesus was 'priced by some of the children of Israel' (for the
partit. ἀπό = מִן cf. Blass, § 40. 2), but 'valued as precious' in the mind of
Christians. The remainder more or less follows the Heb., except that τὸν ἀγρόν
is introduced from the tradition about the Field of Blood. If ἔδωκα is the
true reading, as κ. συνέταξέν μοι ὁ Κ. suggests, ἔλαβον is also 1st pers. sing., as
in the Heb. The reading ἔδωκαν, with ἔλαβον interpreted as 3rd pers.
plur., whether due to Mt. or to a scribe, was a confusion owing to the action
of the high priests recorded in vv. 6 f.

11–14. (Mk. xv. 2–5, Lk. xxiii. 2–
5, Jo. xviii. 29–37.) THE SANHE-
DRIN ACCUSE JESUS BEFORE PILATE.

11. ὁ δὲ Ἰησοῦς κτλ.] The first
clause is added in Mt., the compiler
resuming the narrative of vv. 1, 2
after the foregoing insertion. As to
the place where the scene occurred
see v. 27. Pilate's question, and the
reply σὺ λέγεις, are given identically
by the synn., and the question also
by Jo. But except in Lk. the
question is unexpected, since there
is nothing to shew that Pilate has
received the information which could
lead him to ask it, unless it is to be
assumed that a written charge was
handed to him. In Lk. (v. 2) the
Sanhedrin lay a threefold charge :
(1) 'perverting our nation,' (2) 'forbidding to give taxes to Caesar,' (3)
'saying that He Himself is King
Messiah.' The last expression is
thoroughly Jewish, and favours the
genuineness of Lk.'s account. In

Mt. κατηγορεῖσθαι, Mk. κατηγόρουν
πολλά, follow in the next verse.

σὺ εἶ κτλ.] 'The King of the
Jews' is confined (except ii. 2) to
the accounts of the Passion. Ἰουδαῖος
(in the synn. xxviii. 15, Mk. vii. 3,
Lk. vii. 3, xxiii. 51 only) was employed either by foreigners, or by
the evangelists as Christians distinct
from Jews. (Contrast v. 42, βασιλεὺς
Ἰσραήλ, when the members of the
Sanhedrin are the speakers.) In
Jo. it occurs 71 times (see Westcott,
p. lx.). σὺ λέγεις seems to imply
'Thou art verbally correct, but the
truth is beyond thy comprehension'
(Jo. σὺ λέγεις ὅτι βασιλεύς εἰμι);
see on xxvi. 25, 64.

12. καὶ ἐν τῷ κτλ.] The silence,
which met the accusations and
Pilate's next question, is of the same
kind as in xxvi. 62 f. ; legally it
might be taken as a confession of
guilt, but actually it produced an
uncomfortable effect upon the judge:

13 βυτέρων οὐδὲν ἀπεκρίνατο. τότε λέγει αὐτῷ ὁ Πειλᾶτος
14 Οὐκ ἀκούεις πόσα σου καταμαρτυροῦσιν; καὶ οὐκ
ἀπεκρίθη αὐτῷ πρὸς οὐδὲ ἓν ῥῆμα, ὥστε θαυμάζειν τὸν
15 ἡγεμόνα λίαν. Κατὰ δὲ ἑορτὴν εἰώθει ὁ ἡγεμὼν ἀπολύειν
16 ἕνα τῷ ὄχλῳ δέσμιον ὃν ἤθελον. εἶχον δὲ τότε δέσμιον

Caiaphas was led by it to extort a confession, Pilate to a series of attempts to extricate the Prisoner and himself. Lk. omits mention of the silence, as before; Mk. implies it by Pilate's question οὐκ ἀποκρίνῃ οὐδέν; The class. aor. mid. ἀπεκρίνατο is used in the N.T. either of a solemn utterance (Lk. iii. 16, Jo. v. 17, 19, Ac. iii. 12) as in the LXX., or of a reply in a court of law (Mk. xiv. 61, Lk. xxiii. 9; cf. Jo. v. 11 א), as in papyri (M.-M. *Vocab. s.v.*).

13. τότε κτλ.] On πόσα for ὅσα see Blass, § 51. 4. καταμαρτυροῦσιν for Mk.'s κατηγοροῦσιν is for variety.

14. καὶ οὐκ κτλ.] Mk. ὁ δὲ Ἰ. οὐκέτι οὐδὲν ἀπεκρ. Mt. expresses the emphasis differently: Jesus 'did not reply to a single word,' a class. use of ἀποκρίνεσθαι πρός not found elsewhere in bibl. Gk.; it cannot mean ' to the extent of (uttering) one word.' Pilate's wonder, which Mt. emphasizes (λίαν), was doubtless evoked, not only by the silence, but also by the bearing of the Accused, which repudiated the accusations more completely than words would have done.

Lk. here records Pilate's verdict of Not Guilty, declared to the chief priests and the populace, which called forth more vehement accusations. But the ὄχλος (see on *v.* 17) have not yet appeared; and the verdict is placed too early, since Pilate afterwards sends the Prisoner to be tried by Herod. It should follow that episode, and is, in fact, repeated

in its right place in Lk. *v.* 14 f. Mt., Mk. do not give the verdict; they only imply (*vv.* 17 f., 23) that Pilate judged the Prisoner to be innocent. (For an ingenious treatment of Lk.'s Herod narrative see Verrall, *JThS.* x. 321–53.)

15–26. (Mk. xv. 6–15, Lk. xxiii. 13–25, Jo. xviii. 38–40.) THE POPULACE DEMAND BARABBAS. PILATE SENTENCES JESUS.

15. κατὰ δὲ ἑορτήν κτλ.] εἰώθει ἀπολύειν expands Mk.'s impf. ἀπέλυεν; Jo. also speaks of the custom (συνήθεια), but Lk. does not mention it (*v.* 17 T.R., placed after *v.* 19 in ℵ sin.cur aeth., is a gloss). The release of prisoners, from various causes, was not unknown (cf. Jos. *Ant.* xx. ix. 3), and it occurred at the Lectisternium (Livy v. 13); see also Deissmann, *Light from Anc. East,* 266 f.; but no parallel to the present case can be adduced. ἤθελον: Mk. παρῃτοῦντο 'they begged off.'

16. εἶχον δέ κτλ.] The subject is probably not the Jews but the Romans, who had arrested him in the act of insurrection. ἐπίσημον may mean 'notorious' (περιβόητον ἐν κακίᾳ Chrys.), but seems rather to describe the high reputation in which he was held by the more rebellious section of the Jews, who therefore wished for his release. (The adj. is used of a person in Rom. xvi. 7, 3 Mac. vi. 1 (cf. Cant. v. 11 [Theod., Quinta]), always in a good sense; in Est. v. 4, xvi. 22, 2 Mac. xv. 36 it describes a red-letter day.) The word thus hints at the recent

ἐπίσημον λεγόμενον Βαραββᾶν. συνηγμένων οὖν αὐτῶν 17
εἶπεν αὐτοῖς ὁ Πειλᾶτος Τίνα θέλετε ἀπολύσω ὑμῖν, τὸν
Βαραββᾶν ἢ Ἰησοῦν τὸν λεγόμενον Χριστόν; ᾔδει γὰρ 18
ὅτι διὰ φθόνον παρέδωκαν αὐτόν. Καθημένου δὲ αὐτοῦ 19

17 Βαραββαν] pr Ιησουν τον 1* 118 209* 241** 299** 𝕾 sin.pal arm ; pr τον
[absque Ιησουν] B Or[1,316]

insurrection, though Mt. omits Mk.'s
mention of it.

Βαραββᾶν] בַּר אַבָּא was a common
name in later times. 'Filius magistri
eorum' in Gosp. Heb. (ap. Jer. in
Mt.), and διδασκάλου υἱός mentioned
in scholia in S, and some cursives,
do not necessarily imply a reading
Bar Rabban ; Abba might be understood as the title of a teacher (cf.
xxiii. 9). The name Jesus Barabbas
(see Appar.) which Orig. found in
'quite ancient MSS.' may perhaps
have occurred in Gosp. Heb. ; see
W.H. Notes, 19 f., where the reading
is rejected. But W.H. did not know
𝕾 sin, which contains it. Scribes
would naturally omit it, for the same
reason that made Orig. think the
omission was probably right—'ut ne
nomen Jesu conveniat alicui ini-
quorum.' Ἰησοῦν is almost certainly
genuine, and also Ἰησοῦν τὸν (of
which τόν is preserved in B Orig.) before Βαραββᾶν in v. 17, where Pilate's
Ἰησ. τὸν λεγόμενον Χριστόν implies a previous mention of another
Jesus. The absence of the name in vv.
20 f., 26 does not affect the question.
Burkitt (Ev. da Meph. ii. 277 f.)
suggests that Mt. derived the name
from some tradition known to him,
perhaps that which yielded the story
of Pilate's wife. But Mk.'s unusual
phrase ἦν δὲ ὁ λεγόμενος Βαρ. may
point also to an original ἦν δὲ Ἰησοῦς
ὁ λεγ. B.

17. συνηγμένων κτλ.] The popu-
lace now appeared for the first time.
The Lord had been handed over to
Pilate after a secret arrest and trial,

so that the people as a whole would
know nothing of it. They menacingly
approached (Mk. ἀναβὰς ὁ ὄχλος)
to demand the release of Barabbas.
In Mk. Pilate asked them whether
they would like the King of the Jews
released (a sneer which Mt. represents
by τὸν λεγόμενον Χριστόν, as in v.
22), since he knew that the high
priests had handed Him over because
they envied His popularity. The
people thus learnt that Jesus was a
prisoner, and the high priests had to
persuade them to insist on their
original demand. In Mt., Pilate
gives them their choice between two
prisoners, both named Jesus. Lk.
with less probability makes Pilate
at this point express his intention of
scourging and releasing Jesus, and
the people, who have been present
since the beginning of the trial (see
on v. 14 above), cry out for Barabbas.
Perhaps, however, πανπληθεί refers
only to the Sanhedrin ; cf. ἅπαν τὸ
πλῆθος αὐτῶν (Lk. v. 1). On θέλετε
with conj. see xiii. 28.

18. ᾔδει γάρ κτλ.] Mt., with
anti-Jewish feeling, ascribes the
envy to the whole people, Mk. to the
high priests ; the latter must be
right, since the people had had no
hand in the arrest or condemnation.
παρέδωκαν is for Mk.'s plup. παρα-
δεδώκεισαν ; cf. xxvi. 48.

19. καθημένου κτλ.] 'While he
was sitting.' This incident, found
in Mt. only, is placed in the interval
in which the people were being incited to ask for Barabbas. It probably belonged to the same circle of

ἐπὶ τοῦ βήματος ἀπέστειλεν πρὸς αὐτὸν ἡ γυνὴ αὐτοῦ
λέγουσα Μηδὲν σοὶ καὶ τῷ δικαίῳ ἐκείνῳ, πολλὰ γὰρ
20 ἔπαθον σήμερον κατ᾿ ὄναρ δι᾿ αὐτόν. Οἱ δὲ ἀρχιερεῖς καὶ
οἱ πρεσβύτεροι ἔπεισαν τοὺς ὄχλους ἵνα αἰτήσωνται τὸν
21 Βαραββᾶν τὸν δὲ Ἰησοῦν ἀπολέσωσιν. ἀποκριθεὶς δὲ ὁ
ἡγεμὼν εἶπεν αὐτοῖς Τίνα θέλετε ἀπὸ τῶν δύο ἀπολύσω
22 ὑμῖν; οἱ δὲ εἶπαν Τὸν Βαραββᾶν. λέγει αὐτοῖς ὁ

traditions connected with Pilate as
vv. 24 f., 62–66, xxviii. 11–15. It
is not stated, though perhaps implied,
that his wife learnt the Prisoner's
innocence in her dream (κατ᾿ ὄναρ, cf.
i. 20, ii. 12 f., 19, 22); Pilate could not
have known on the previous night of
the secret arrest, nor have discussed the
case with her. For βῆμα, *tribunal*,
a raised seat or platform, cf. Ac. xii.
21, xviii. 12, 16 f., xxv. 6, 10, 17.
It must have been erected outside
the praetorium, owing to the scruples
of the Jews (cf. Jo. xviii. 28). It
was not necessarily the same as that
mentioned in Jo. xix. 13, which was
placed on the 'pavement,' the locality
of which is doubtful (see *Enc. Bibl.
s.v.*). Tradition named Pilate's wife
Procla, or Claudia Procula (Gosp.
Nicod. 2, in Thilo, *Cod. Apocr.* 522
ff.). Tac. *Ann.* iii. 33 f. relates the
decision that governors in the pro-
vinces might be accompanied by
their wives. On the ellipse of the
verb in μηδὲν σοί κτλ. see Moulton,
i. 183. For the expression cf. xviii.
29.

20. οἱ δὲ ἀρχιερεῖς κτλ.] The
means which they employed are not
stated. To tell the people that Jesus
claimed Messiahship (Schweitzer)
would hardly rouse the fury of a
mob that was clamouring for the
release of an insurrectionary leader;
such a claim would rather recommend
Him to them. More probably they
fanned their fury at the arrest of
Barabbas, their popular hero, and

perhaps also inflamed them against
Jesus by repeating the words about
the destruction of the temple which
the witnesses had brought against
Him. Mt. adds τὸν δὲ Ἰ. ἀπολέσωσιν, as a preparation for their answer
in v. 22.

21. ἀποκριθεὶς κτλ.] Pilate's
question in v. 17 (with ἀπὸ τ. δύο
instead of the names of the prisoners)
is repeated after the interval required
by v. 19. In Mk., Lk. there is no
interval; in the turbulent shouting,
increasingly roused by the inflam-
matory words of the priests, Pilate
could still hear the name Barabbas on
many lips, which led him to ask the
next question.

22. λέγει κτλ.] The class. construction τί ποιήσω Ἰησοῦν (similarly
Mk.) has no exact parallel in the N.T.
(see Blass, § 34. 4), but is found in
the LXX. σταυροῦν = תלה ('to hang')
is found in Est. vii. 9, xvi. 18, and
of 'crucifying' in Polyb. In class.
Gk. it is to 'fence in with stakes,'
while ἀνασταυρ. is to 'impale.'
Montefiore dismisses the famous cry
as unhistorical, because crucifixion
was a Roman, not a Jewish, method
of punishment. But if they wanted
a Roman execution of a Jew, it was
not unnatural to ask for the usual
form of it. Mk. says πάλιν ἔκραξαν
Σταύρωσον αὐτόν, though he has not
previously recorded the cry. Wellhausen explains the πάλιν by the
Aram. תוב, which can mean 'moreover,' 'thereupon.' But perhaps Mk.

Πειλᾶτος Τί οὖν ποιήσω Ἰησοῦν τὸν λεγόμενον Χριστόν ; λέγουσιν πάντες Σταυρωθήτω. ὁ δὲ ἔφη Τί γὰρ κακὸν 23 ἐποίησεν ; οἱ δὲ περισσῶς ἔκραζον λέγοντες Σταυρωθήτω. ἰδὼν δὲ ὁ Πειλᾶτος ὅτι οὐδὲν ὠφελεῖ ἀλλὰ μᾶλλον θόρυβος 24 γίνεται λαβὼν ὕδωρ ἀπενίψατο τὰς χεῖρας κατέναντι τοῦ ὄχλου λέγων Ἀθῷός εἰμι ἀπὸ τοῦ αἵματος τούτου· ὑμεῖς ὄψεσθε. καὶ ἀποκριθεὶς πᾶς ὁ λαὸς εἶπεν Τὸ αἷμα αὐτοῦ 25

24 τουτου] BD 102 𝕷 a b ff² r 𝕾 sin ; *add* του δικαιον ΑΔ 𝕷 f h me sah arm aeth ; *pr* του δικαιον אL *al* minn.*pler* 𝕷 c ff¹ g¹.² q vg 𝕾 pesh. hcl. pal

assumes that it formed part of the shouting in reply to Pilate's first question.

23. τί γάρ κτλ.] 'What crime has he committed ? *for* your shouts imply that he is a criminal.' By descending to argument Pilate shewed that he was giving way, which produced wilder cries.

24. ἰδών κτλ.] Each of the synn. leads up to the fatal sentence in his own way. Lk. says καὶ κατίσχυον αἱ φωναὶ αὐτῶν : he had not the courage to withstand the shouts. Mk. catches the political situation, βουλόμενος ποιῆσαι τὸ ἱκανὸν τῷ ὄχλῳ : he wanted to regain popularity, which his misrule had forfeited (cf. Ac. xii. 3, xxiv. 27). Mt.'s incident probably belongs to the same circle of traditions as *v.* 19 (see note). It increases the guilt of the Jews by lessening that of Pilate (cf. Just. *Trypho*, cviii. ὃν σταυρωσάντων ἡμῶν), a tendency more strongly marked in Gosp. Pet. : 'But of the Jews none washed his hands, neither Herod, nor any of His judges. And when they wished [? did not wish] to wash them, Pilate stood up. And then Herod the king commandeth the Lord to be taken (παραλημφθῆναι, cf. *v.* 27 below) etc.'; here, and in the sentences which follow, Herod is made wholly responsible. In *Acta Pil.* the exoneration of Pilate is carried to extremes (see *ZNW.*, 1902, 92). The

guilt of the Jews is also emphasized in other passages ; see Stanton, *Gospels as Hist. Doc.* i. 51 n.¹, 98.

ὅτι οὐδέν κτλ.] ὠφελεῖ may be impersonal, 'it was of no use' (to try and release Him), or the subj. may be Pilate (cf. Jo. xii. 19). μᾶλλον θόρ. γίν. seems to mean 'the tumult was growing worse' (𝕾 sin 'how much the tumult was increasing') ; cf. Thuc. vii. 25. Origen points out that Pilate's action was a Jewish, not a Roman, custom ; cf. Deut. xxi. 6 f. (referred to in Jos. *Ant.* IV. viii. 16, Sotah ix. 6), Ps. xxv. [xxvi.] 6, lxxii. [lxxiii.] 13. Some explain that Pilate did it to make the people understand his meaning. But it is doubtful if the passage can be regarded as historical. ἀθῷος ἀπό (see Blass, § 40. 3) is modelled on מִדָּם נָקִי ; cf. Num. v. 31, 2 Regn. iii. 28, Ac. xx. 26. τ. αἷμ. τούτου may mean 'this blood' (as 𝕾 sin), or 'the blood of this man,' and the first of the *v.ll.* (see Appar.) 'this righteous blood (cf. *v.* 3, xxiii. 35). On ὑμ. ὄψεσθε see *v.* 4.

25. καὶ ἀποκριθείς κτλ.] The Jewish *nation* invokes the guilt upon itself ; λαός is purposely substituted for ὄχλος. Cf. *v.* 64, from the same circle of traditions. αἷμα 'the guilt of bloodshed' is Hebraic. For similar curses cf. 2 Regn. i. 16, Jer. xxviii. [li.] 35, Ac. xviii. 6 ; and see 2 Regn. xiv. 9.

26 ἐφ᾽ ἡμᾶς καὶ ἐπὶ τὰ τέκνα ἡμῶν. τότε ἀπέλυσεν αὐτοῖς
τὸν Βαραββᾶν, τὸν δὲ Ἰησοῦν φραγελλώσας παρέδωκεν
ἵνα σταυρωθῇ.

27   Τότε οἱ στρατιῶται τοῦ ἡγεμόνος παραλαβόντες τὸν
Ἰησοῦν εἰς τὸ πραιτώριον συνήγαγον ἐπ᾽ αὐτὸν ὅλην τὴν

26. τότε κτλ.] Barabbas was
released to the populace (αὐτοῖς),
Jesus was handed over to the soldiers.
Lk. obscures this, by writing 'and
Jesus he delivered to their will,'
omitting the mockery by the soldiers.
The crowd now probably divided;
the more turbulent section would be
more interested in Barabbas than in
Jesus, and would move away to greet
the former on his exit from prison.
The remainder stayed with the
religious leaders, who went to see
the execution.   φραγελλοῦν is a
latinism (*flagellare*) known only in
Christian writings, except *Test. Benj.*
2.   φραγέλλιον (Jo. ii. 15), -έλλη
are used in late Gk.   Lk. mentions
the scourging only in Pilate's proposed compromise, παιδεύσας αὐτὸν
ἀπολύσω (vv. 16, 22), which the
people rejected.   In Roman practice
it usually occurred, as Mt., Mk. place
it, immediately before execution (Jos.
BJ. II. xiv. 9, v. xi. 1, Livy xxii. 13,
Cic. *Verr.* v. 62. 162).   Jo., much
less probably, places it, together with
the soldiers' mockery, at an earlier
point (xix. 1–3).   It would probably
not be performed in public, but the
effects would be only too visible when
the Lord was led out for execution.

27–31.   (Mk. xv. 16–20, Jo.
xix. 2 f.)   THE MOCKERY BY THE
SOLDIERS.

27. τότε κτλ.] It is gratuitous
to suppose that the scene is only an
expansion of the fact of the scourging (J. Weiss); nor does Lk.'s omission of it suggest that it is a doublet
of the mockery by the servants of
Caiaphas (xxvi. 67 f.).

The soldiers were the troops which
accompanied the Procurator from
Caesarea, his official residence (' Caes.
Judaeae caput,' Tac.), when he came
to Jerusalem to keep order during
the festival.   They were not Jews,
since the latter were exempted from
conscription, but Roman citizens
of various nationalities living in
Palestine.   A centurion and a few
men attended the trial and performed the scourging, but they then
collected the whole σπεῖρα.   This
was strictly a *cohors* of 500–600
men, named according to the district
from which it was recruited (Schurer,
HJP. I. ii. 49 ff.), but here it evidently represents a smaller number.

εἰς τὸ πραιτώριον] Mk. ἔσω τῆς
αὐλῆς, ὅ ἐστιν πρ.   On πραιτώριον
see Lightft. *Philippians*, p. 97.   In
the Gospp. and Ac. xxiii. 35 it means
the official residence of a governor;
in the latter passage it is Herod's
palace at Caesarea, where Felix the
Procurator lived.   Similarly Florus
occupied, as Pilate in the present
instance, the palace at Jerusalem, in
front of which he set his tribunal (Jos.
BJ. II. xiv. 8; cf. *id.* xv. 5, where
it is described as the βασιλικὴ αὐλή).
Mk. here explains, for his Roman
readers, that the Procurator occupied
the palace.   It was a fortified building on the Western hill, capable of
housing troops.   Some place the
scene of the trial at the Castle of
Antonia (cf. Ac. xxi. 35), close to the
temple.   But the synn. say nothing
to suggest that the trial took place
near the temple, and the meaning of
Gabbatha, 'the pavement,' in Jo. xix.

σπεῖραν. καὶ ἐκδύσαντες αὐτὸν χλαμύδα κοκκίνην περιέ- 28
θηκαν αὐτῷ, καὶ πλέξαντες στέφανον ἐξ ἀκανθῶν ἐπέθηκαν 29
ἐπὶ τῆς κεφαλῆς αὐτοῦ καὶ κάλαμον ἐν τῇ δεξιᾷ αὐτοῦ, καὶ
γονυπετήσαντες ἔμπροσθεν αὐτοῦ ἐνέπαιξαν αὐτῷ λέγοντες

28 εκδυσαντες] א*et b AL al minn 𝕃 f ff¹ g¹·² h l vg 𝖲 pesh. hcl^txt·pal sah arm
[add τα ιματια αυτου 33 238 𝖲 hcl^mg] ; ενδυσαντες א^aBD 157 𝕃 a b c ff² q 𝖲 sin[om
περιεθηκαν]. pal^clim

13 is too uncertain to be used as
evidence. In Jo. xviii. 28 the Jews
refuse to enter the praetorium ; but
if it had been the Castle, the resident
troops would not, in any case, have
allowed them to enter. Moreover,
the troops in the ˙Castle were a
standing cohort, distinct from those
which accompanied the Procurator.
See *ZNW.*, 1902, 15–22.

28. καὶ ἐκδύσαντες κτλ.] The
v.l. ἐνδύσαντες, which has good MS.
support, is perhaps right ; it is the
more difficult reading, the partcp.
being identical in meaning with
περιέθηκαν. (𝖲 sin reads ἐνδύσ.,
but avoids the difficulty by omitting
περιέθ. αὐτῷ). If the text be right,
the Lord must have been clothed
again with His own garments after
being stripped for the scourging ;
with ἐνδύσαντες this does not take
place till *v.* 31 (ἐνέδυσαν). χλαμύδα
κοκκίνην is a soldier's scarlet cloak,
a *sagum*, employed in mock imitation
of royal purple (Mk., Gosp. Pet.
πορφύραν). This detail, perhaps
derived from an oral source, is intrinsically probable. For χλαμύς
cf. 2 Mac. xii. 35, 1 Regn. xxiv. 5
(Sym.) ; and see L. & S. *s.v.*

29. καὶ πλέξαντες κτλ.] Cf. Is.
xxviii. 5, ὁ στέφανος . . . ὁ πλεκείς.
It was not a royal διάδημα, but a
garland, such as could be won in
battle or the games (1 Cor. ix. 25,
2 Tim. ii. 5). The King of the Jews
was greeted as a victorious Hero.
On ἄκανθαι see xiii. 7. Thorn

bushes might be growing near by, in
the palace grounds, but would be
less likely in, or near, the Antonia.
Cf. the treatment of an imbecile by
a mob of Alexandrian Jews in order
to insult Agrippa ; 'they spread a
strip of *byblus* and placed it on his
head instead of a diadem . . . and
for a sceptre they handed up to him
a small piece of native *papyrus*, which
they found thrown by the roadside.
And because he was adorned as king
. . . some approached as though to
greet him, others as though to plead
a cause' (Philo, *In Flacc.* Mangey ii.
522). See also Plut. *Pomp.* xxiv.

καὶ κάλαμον κτλ.] A stalk of
cane grass does duty for a sceptre.
This detail, added by Mt., may be
from the same source as the chlamys.
Gosp. Pet. does not mention it. If
it is genuine, the Lord's hands must
have been unbound after the scourging. J. Weiss is over-subtle in
rejecting it on the ground that if
Jesus had retained the reed in His
hand ' He would of His own accord
have been taking part in the comedy.'

καὶ γονυπετήσαντες κτλ.] Mk.'s
equivalent is placed at the end of
the next verse ; Mt. makes all the
details of the mockery to precede
the violence. γονυπετ. avoids Mk.'s
Latinism τιθέντες τὰ γόνατα (*ponere
genua*). Gosp. Pet. gives a different
picture : ' And they that took the
Lord pushed Him as they ran, and
said, Let us carry off the Son of God,
having got power over Him. And

30 Χαῖρε, βασιλεῦ τῶν Ἰουδαίων, καὶ ἐμπτύσαντες εἰς αὐτὸν
ἔλαβον τὸν κάλαμον καὶ ἔτυπτον εἰς τὴν κεφαλὴν αὐτοῦ.
31 καὶ ὅτε ἐνέπαιξαν αὐτῷ, ἐξέδυσαν αὐτὸν τὴν χλαμύδα καὶ
ἐνέδυσαν αὐτὸν τὰ ἱμάτια αὐτοῦ, καὶ ἀπήγαγον αὐτὸν
32 εἰς τὸ σταυρῶσαι.   Ἐξερχόμενοι δὲ εὗρον ἄνθρωπον

they clothed Him in purple, and set
Him upon a seat of judgment, saying,
Judge righteously, O King of Israel.
(Cf. Just. Apol. i. 35, ἐκάθισαν ἐπὶ
τοῦ βήματος καὶ εἶπον Κρῖνον ἡμῖν ;
see Stanton, Gosp. Hist. Doc. 97 ff.)
And one of them brought a thorn
crown and placed it upon the head
of the Lord, and others stood and
spat upon His face, and others struck
His cheeks (cf. Mt. xxvi. 68 note),
others pricked Him with a reed, and
some scourged Him, saying, With
this honour let us honour the Son
of God.'

30. καὶ ἐμπτύσαντες κτλ.] τὸν
κάλαμον : the reed previously placed
in His hand.   J. Weiss speaks of the
'coarse, but fairly good-humoured
soldiers' joke'! and thinks that the
spitting is more suitable to the
malice of the Jews, and was added
from the account of the earlier
mockery.   ὁ βασιλεύς 'you King'
is for Mk.'s βασιλεῦ which would
strictly admit the right to the title
(Moulton, i. 76 f., Blass, § 33. 4).

31. καὶ ὅτε κτλ.] The mockery
was probably quite short, lasting
until the cross and the necessary
instruments for execution were
brought.   A handful of soldiers (four
according to Jo. xix. 23) then did
their work with military precision
under command of a centurion ; and
no further insults from them are
recorded in Mt., Mk., Jo.   Some think
that the whole account is fabricated
on the basis of some pagan custom,
such as the mock coronation which
preceded the Saturnalia of the Baby-

lonian festival of Sacaea (Frazer,
Golden Bough ², ii. 24 f., 253 f., iii.
150 f.), or the buffoonery which
accompanied the mimes, e.g. at
Alexandria (Reich, Der König mit
der Dornenkrone).   That the mock
homage may have been 'determined
by some hazy notion of imitating a
pagan bit of ritual' is possible.   But
'it did not require any coarse pagan
rite to stimulate military horseplay
among soldiers' (Moffatt, 'Trial of
Jesus,' DCG.).

32.   (Mk. xv. 21, Lk. xxiii. 26–32,
Jo. xix. 17.)   THE VIA DOLOROSA.

ἐξερχόμενοι κτλ.] They met
Simon as they came out of the city
(cf. Heb. xiii. 12), so that the Lord
had carried the Cross Himself for a
short distance.   This was customary
(see x. 38), and Jo. rightly says
βαστάζων αὐτῷ τὸν σταυρόν, but
does not mention Simon.   The only
reason for his impressment must have
been that Jesus was physically unable
to carry it further.   A soldier's jest
was very unlikely when they were
performing military duty.   Cyrene,
a Libyan town, received its first
Jewish colonists from Alexandria
(Jos. Ap. ii. 4 ; cf. Ant. xiv. vii. 2).
If Ac. vi. 9 speaks of a synagogue of
Cyrenaeans at Jerusalem (see, however, Blass and Preuschen, ad loc.),
Simon may have been a member of
it.   The name is too common to
allow of his identification with
'Symeon called Niger' who was at
Antioch with Lucius the Cyrenaean,
and others (Ac. xiii. 1).   Mk. alone
adds that he was the father of

Κυρηναῖον ὀνόματι Σίμωνα· τοῦτον ἠγγάρευσαν ἵνα ἄρῃ
τὸν σταυρὸν αὐτοῦ. Καὶ ἐλθόντες εἰς τόπον λεγόμενον 33
Γολγοθά, ὅ ἐστιν Κρανίου Τόπος λεγόμενος, ἔδωκαν αὐτῷ 34
πιεῖν οἶνον μετὰ χολῆς μεμιγμένον· καὶ γευσάμενος οὐκ

34 οινον] אBDKLΠ* minn.*pauc* 𝔏 a b ff¹ g¹·² l r vg 𝔖 sin.hcl^{mg}·pal me sah arm
aeth ; οξος ΑΝΠ² *al* minn.*pler* 𝔏 c f h q 𝔖 pesh.hcl^{txt}·diat^{Eph}

Alexander and Rufus (cf. Rom. xvi.
13), who probably became well
known Christians in Rome, but of
whom Mt., Lk. may have known
nothing, and therefore omitted the
words. Their father's account of
the Crucifixion may well have played
a part in their conversion, and in
the Marcan tradition. Mt. omits
ἐρχόμενον ἀπ' ἀγροῦ (Mk., Lk.),
which need not imply that he was
coming in from work, but only that
he lived, or was lodging in a neighbouring village (cf. 'Mk.' xvi. 12),
and was coming into the city,
perhaps for purposes connected with
the festival.

τοῦτον κτλ.] On ἀγγαρεύειν see
v. 41. Lk.'s φέρειν ὄπισθεν τοῦ
'Ιησοῦ can hardly mean that Simon
was to help Jesus in carrying the
Cross, by supporting the hinder end.
It was possibly added as a reminiscence
of Lk. ix. 23, xiv. 27. A condemned person did not usually carry
the whole cross, but only the cross
beam (*patibulum*); the upright beam
was generally standing ready to receive
it. Lk. gives here the Lord's words
to the women who bewailed Him.

33–50. (Mk. xv. 22–37, Lk.
xxiii. 33–46, Jo. xix. 17–30.) THE
CRUCIFIXION.

33. καὶ ἐλθόντες κτλ.] Mk. κ.
φέρουσιν αὐτόν, 'escort,' 'help, or
drag, along' (cf. Gosp. Pet. ἤνεγκον
δύο κακούργους, Mk. vii. 32, Jo.
xxi. 18). The place was a skull-
shaped mound, known as 'the Skull'
(גָּלְגָּלְתָּא, Heb. גֻּלְגֹּלֶת, Vulg. *quod
est Calvariae locus*; cf. Jud. ix. 53,

4 Regn. ix. 35). Mt. corrects Mk.'s
Gk. form -θάν (cf. ὁ Γολγοθᾶς Cyr.
Cat. xiii.). On the omission of the
second ⅃ see Dalm. *Gr.* 166. 𝔖 sin
omits the first ⅃, and in Mt. the
explanation of the name. The
superfluous λεγόμενος was probably
added accidentally by an early scribe.
The name does not imply that the
skulls of criminals lay there, buried
or unburied, for the whole skeletons
would be there. On the legend that
Adam was buried there see the
writer's art. 'Adam' in *DCG.* On
the site see Swete.

34. ἔδωκαν κτλ.] Mk.'s ἐδιδοῦν
is probably a narrative imperf.,
which Mt. usually avoids, but possibly
it is conative. A narcotic, said to
have been provided by women in
Jerusalem, was commonly given to
those about to be executed. Mk.
has ἐσμυρνισμένον οἶνον. Mt.'s
χολή can hardly be a mere equivalent, although myrrh and gall were
both bitter; it seems to be a reference to Ps. lxviii. [lxix.] 22 (cf. Lam.
iii. 15), perhaps aided by the similarity of Aram. מורה (myrrh) to Heb.
מררה (gall; cf. Job xvi. 14, xx. 14).
The reading ὄξος for οἶνον is also
due to the Psalm, cf. Barn. vii. 3,
σταυρωθεὶς ἐποτίζετο ὄξει καὶ χολῇ,
Gosp. Pet. 'And one of them said,
Give Him to drink gall with vinegar;
and they mixed it and gave Him to
drink, and fulfilled all things, and
accomplished their sins upon their
head.'

καὶ γευσάμενος κτλ.] Mk. ὃς δὲ
οὐκ ἔλαβεν. Mt.'s alteration may

35 ἠθέλησεν πιεῖν. σταυρώσαντες δὲ αὐτὸν Διεμερίϲαντο τὰ
36 ἱμάτια αὐτοῦ Βάλλοντεϲ κλῆρον, καὶ καθήμενοι ἐτήρουν αὐτὸν
37 ἐκεῖ. καὶ ἐπέθηκαν ἐπάνω τῆς κεφαλῆς αὐτοῦ τὴν αἰτίαν

have been derived from an independent tradition; it implies that the
Lord did not know what the bever-
age contained until. He tasted it,
which is in marked contrast with
the passages in which Mt. avoids
implications of ignorance on the
part of Jesus (see on viii. 29). The
refusal of the narcotic cannot have
been for the sake of bearing additional physical pain, but because
a voluntary death for others required
full exercise of will and consciousness to the last.

35. σταυρώσαντες κτλ.] The
single verb suffices in all the Gospels;
the details were well known to all
readers, and the external value of
the Cross does not lie in its physical
tortures. The synn. do not even
mention the nails, a detail which is
supplied in Jo. xx. 25, Gosp. Pet.
(see on *v.* 59 below); but in Lk. xxiv.
39 the scars in the hands and feet, and
Jo. xx. 20, 25 in the hands, are referred to. Hands and feet, in accordance with Lk., are mentioned by
Just. (*Dial.* xcvii.) and subsequent
writers. Possibly, but not necessarily,
Lk. was influenced by Ps. xxi. [xxii.]
17. The Lord's words, in the first
moments of agony, recorded in early
tradition, are given by Lk.: 'Father
forgive them etc.' The docetism of
Gosp. Pet., 'But He was silent as
having no pain' rings the falser by
contrast.

διεμερίσαντο κτλ.] Not a gratuitous insult, as Gosp. Pet. perhaps
implies; 'having placed His garments in front of Him they divided
them and cast the lot upon them';
the clothes were usually the perquis-
ites of the executioners. The same

treatment is described in Ps. xxi.
[xxii.] 19, quoted in Jo., and added
here in some MSS. Since it was a
common practice, the narrative need
not be regarded as a mere product
of the Psalm, though the wording
(cf. *v.* 39) has probably been coloured
by it, including the omission of Mk.'s
τίς τί ἄρῃ. The tradition of the
seamless coat is given only in Jo.

36. καὶ καθήμενοι κτλ.] Mt.
only. It does not mean that they
gloated over the Sufferer; they sat
and guarded Him, as was customary,
to prevent the possibility of rescue.
Lk. says καὶ εἰστήκει ὁ λαὸς θεωρῶν,
adding not only the sneers of the
rulers but mockery by the soldiers
(see on *v.* 43).

Mk. here states ἦν δὲ ὥρα τρίτη
[*i.e.* 9 a.m.] καὶ ἐσταύρωσαν αὐτόν.
If this was not a later addition, Mt.,
Lk. may have omitted it because
they received more accurate information. Jo. is probably correct in
placing the close of the Roman trial
about noon (ὥρα ἦν ὡς ἕκτη), and in
relating that the bodies were removed before the Sabbath began, *i.e.*
before 6 p.m. There was enough
time for the latter if the Lord died
at about 3 o'clock. Mk. seems to
divide the day somewhat artificially
into periods of three hours (Mk. xv.
1, 25, 33, 42; see on Mt. xxvi. 34).

37. καὶ ἐπέθηκαν κτλ.] ἡ ἐπι-
γραφὴ τῆς αἰτίας (Mk.) was the
titulus (Jo. τίτλος), the placard
stating the victim's crime, which
was carried before him, or hung
round his neck, as he walked to execution. Swete cites two examples.
Mt. interprets Mk.'s ἐπιγεγραμμένη.
'Over His head' indicates that the

αὐτοῦ γεγραμμένην ΟΥΤΟΣ ΕΣΤΙΝ ΙΗΣΟΥΣ Ο ΒΑΣΙΛΕΥΣ
ΤΩΝ ΙΟΥΔΑΙΩΝ. Τότε σταυροῦνται σὺν αὐτῷ δύο λῃσταί, 38
εἷς ἐκ δεξιῶν καὶ εἷς ἐξ εὐωνύμων. Οἱ δὲ παραπορευόμενοι 39
ἐβλασφήμουν αὐτὸν ΚΙΝΟΥΝΤΕϹ ΤᾺϹ ΚΕΦΑΛᾺϹ ΑΥΤῶΝ καὶ λέγοντες
Ὁ καταλύων τὸν ναὸν καὶ ἐν τρισὶν ἡμέραις οἰκοδομῶν, 40
σῶσον σεαυτόν· εἰ υἱὸς εἶ τοῦ θεοῦ, κατάβηθι ἀπὸ τοῦ

40 καταβηθι] BLΓΔΠ minn.*pler* 𝔏 f ff1,2 g1,2 l q vg me sah ; *pr* και אAD 𝔏 a b c h
𝔖 sin['save thyself' *post* 'son of God'].pesh.pal

Cross was of the traditional shape, a
crux immissa, not in the form of T
or X. The verse looks back at an
action of the soldiers before they sat
down on guard. Lk. mentions the
titulus still later, in connexion with
the mockery by the soldiers. Jo.
states that the *titulus* was written
in Hebrew (Aramaic), Latin and
Greek, so that Pilate's sneer at the
Jews would reach as many as possible
of the pilgrims in the city.

οὗτός ἐστιν κτλ.] Pilate's sneer
is most acute in Mk.'s terse ὁ βασιλεὺς τῶν Ἰουδαίων. The other
evangg. expand it differently : Lk.
ὁ βασ. τῶν Ἰουδ. οὗτος. Jo. Ἰησοῦς
ὁ Ναζωραῖος ὁ βασ. τ. Ἰουδ. Gosp.
Pet., which ascribes the mockery and
crucifixion to οἱ λαβόντες τὸν
Κύριον (see *v.* 29), *i.e.* probably the
Jews, has οὗτός ἐστιν ὁ βασ. τοῦ
Ἰσραήλ. Whatever was the original
form, the charge on which the Lord
was executed was a claim to King-
ship (see Jo. xix. 12–16). That He
said He would destroy the temple
would have been nothing to Pilate,
even if it had reached his ears ; and
having sacrificed Jesus to save himself from the mob, he was obliged to
put forward an adequate charge.

38. τότε κτλ.] A good instance
of Mt.'s use of τότε (see on ii. 7) ; the
crucifying of the robbers, as well as
the affixing of the *titulus*, must have
preceded the sitting on guard (*v.* 36).
The robbers may have been tools of

Barabbas. Lk. calls them only
κακοῦργοι, relating, at an earlier
point (*v.* 32), that they were led
with Jesus to be destroyed ; he does
not state that they were placed on
either side of Him. On the reference to Is. liii. 12 in the lesser
uncials in Mk. see *Camb. Bibl. Essays,*
240. Reflexion on the words of
Isaiah may have led the early
Christians to attach importance to
the crucifixion of the robbers, but
that it led them to invent the
account is not suggested by anything
in the records.

39. οἱ δὲ κτλ.] Jews again appear
on the scene, with a malice like that
shewn in the trial before the Sanhedrin. The wording is coloured by
Ps. xxi. [xxii.] 8, πάντες οἱ θεωροῦντές
με ἐξεμυκτήρισάν με, ἐλάλησαν ἐν
χείλεσιν, ἐκίνησαν κεφαλήν. Lk.
καὶ εἱστήκει ὁ λαὸς θεωρῶν· ἐξεμυκ-
τήριζον δὲ οἱ ἄρχοντες echoes the
first clause, Mt., Mk. the last ; cf. also
Lam. ii. 15. Shaking the head was
in mock commiseration. The next
verse in the Psalm colours *vv.* 40–42,
and is quoted in *v.* 43.

40. ὁ καταλύων κτλ.] Mk. οὐὰ
ὁ κ. On the pres. partcp. see xiii.
37. σῶσον σεαυτόν is an echo of
Ps. *l.c.* σωσάτω αὐτόν, as is probably
the taunt in Wisd. ii. 18 (see Good-
rick). The two halves of the verse
in Mt. are based upon two claims of
Jesus ; καί (see Appar.) does not disturb
this if it is rendered consecutively,

41 σταυροῦ. ὁμοίως καὶ οἱ ἀρχιερεῖς ἐμπαίζοντες μετὰ τῶν
42 γραμματέων καὶ πρεσβυτέρων ἔλεγον Ἄλλους ἔσωσεν,
ἑαυτὸν οὐ δύναται σῶσαι· βασιλεὺς Ἰσραήλ ἐστιν, καταβάτω νῦν ἀπὸ τοῦ σταυροῦ καὶ πιστεύσομεν ἐπ᾽ αὐτόν.
43 πέποιθεν ἐπὶ τὸν θεόν, ῥυσάσθω νῦν εἰ θέλει αὐτόν· εἶπεν γὰρ
44 ὅτι Θεοῦ εἰμὶ υἱός. τὸ δ᾽ αὐτὸ καὶ οἱ λῃσταὶ οἱ συν-
45 σταυρωθέντες σὺν αὐτῷ ὠνείδιζον αὐτόν.   Ἀπὸ δὲ
ἕκτης ὥρας σκότος ἐγένετο ἐπὶ πᾶσαν τὴν γῆν ἕως ὥρας

'then come down.' On the former
claim see xxvi. 61. εἰ υἱὸς εἶ τοῦ
θεοῦ (which Mk. omits) refers to the
question of Caiaphas (xxvi. 63) and
echoes Satan's temptations (iv. 3, 6).

42. ἄλλους κτλ.] ἔσωσεν, which
must have the same force as σῶσαι,
does not refer to His miracles of
healing, but to His claim to be
King. The virulent sarcasm implies
that He had not, as Messiah, man-
aged to bring 'salvation' (cf. i. 21,
Lk. i. 77, ii. 30) to anyone, but since
He claimed to, let Him save Himself. As Jews they say 'King of
Israel' instead of 'King of the
Jews' which was on the titulus.
Mk. has a double title, ὁ χριστός and
ὁ βασ. Ἰσρ., and Lk. ὁ χριστὸς τοῦ
θεοῦ and ὁ ἐκλεκτός. Mt.'s πιστ. ἐπ᾽
αὐτόν (Ac.⁴, Rom. iv. 24, Wisd. xii.
2) is more than Mk.'s πιστεύωμεν.

43. πέποιθεν κτλ.] A quotation
from Ps. xxi. [xxii.] 9, given by Mt.
only. As in the LXX. (ἤλπισεν),
בּוֹ is read for בְּ, but the rendering
is independent, and probably stood
in Mt.'s collection of testimonia.
νῦν, which heightens the taunt, and
is not represented in Heb. or LXX.,
may have been added by the evang.
He also adds εἶπεν γάρ κτλ., explaining vv. 40–43 and referring again to
xxvi. 63.

Lk. here states that the soldiers
uttered similar taunts, 'offering Him
vinegar.' But the latter would be
an act of kindness, unless the words

mean that the vinegar was offered,
but at the same time withheld. Such
a departure from discipline, however,
by soldiers on official duty is scarcely
probable. It seems to be a confused
variation (omitted in ⅏ sin.cur) of the
account in Mt. v. 48 (Mk. v. 36).

44. τὸ δ᾽ αὐτό κτλ.] Mk. simply
ὠνείδιζον αὐτόν. For τὸ αὐτό, 'in
the same way,' cf. xviii. 9 (D for
καί¹°), Phil. ii. 18. Lk. relates that
one of the malefactors that were
hanged blasphemed Him, and gives
the words of the taunt; that the
other rebuked him, and then spoke
to Jesus and received His reply.

45. ἀπὸ δὲ ἕκτης κτλ.] On the
hour of the Crucifixion see v. 36.
If it took place about noon, the
darkness must be thought of, as
lasting the whole time that the Lord
was on the Cross. τὴν γῆν means
vaguely 'the country,' or Judaea;
Gosp. Pet. 'And it was midday,
and darkness κάτεσχε πᾶσαν τὴν
Ἰουδαίαν,' as the darkness prevailed ἐπὶ πᾶσαν γῆν Αἰγύπτου.
Lk. (אBC*L) adds τοῦ ἡλίου ἐκ-
λείποντος, but AC^bD ⅃ ⅏ (καὶ)
ἐσκοτίσθη (δὲ) ὁ ἥλιος. In Acta
Pil. the Jews explain away the
darkness as due to an ordinary
eclipse; but this could not occur at
the time of a full moon. It is
possible to explain it as 'an extraordinary gloom due to natural
causes' (Swete); but the probability
must be recognized that the account

ἐνάτης. περὶ δὲ τὴν ἐνάτην ὥραν ἐβόησεν ὁ Ἰησοῦς φωνῇ 46
μεγάλῃ λέγων Ἐλωΐ ἐλωΐ λεμὰ cαβαχθανεί; τοῦτ' ἔστιν
Θεέ μου Θεέ μου, ἵνα τί με ἐγκατέλιπες; τινὲς δὲ τῶν ἐκεῖ

46 ελωι ελωι] ℵB [ελωει -ει] 33 *al.pauc* me ; ηλει ηλει DE *etc* minn.*pler* 𝔏 *omn*
𝔖 sin.hcl.pal.[pesh *el el*] | σαβαχθανει] ϛαφθανει D 𝔏 a b h

is influenced by O.T. predictions of
cosmic catastrophes : Joel ii. 10, 31
[iii. 4], iii. [iv.] 15, Is. xiii. 10, l.
3, Jer. xiii. 16, xv. 9. In Am. viii.
9, καὶ δύσεται ὁ ἥλιος μεσημβρίας,
the phenomenon accompanies a
mourning ὡς πένθος ἀγαπητοῦ.

46. περὶ δέ κτλ.] Of the seven
utterances from the Cross (cf. Lk.
xxiii. 34, 43, 46, Jo. xix. 26, 28,
30) this (Mt., Mk.) is the least likely
to be due to Christian imagination
—a very human cry, quoted from
Ps. xxi. [xxii.] 1. It was probably
the Lord's application of it to Himself which led to the large use of the
Psalm in *vv.* 35, 39–43. That it
was a cry of despair from a consciousness of failure is inconceivable from
One who had expected (xx. 22) and
accepted (xxvi. 39, 42) the Cup of
suffering, and who knew that His
death was necessary to make Him a
λύτρον ἀντὶ πολλῶν (xx. 28) and as
a means of reaching His Messianic
glory. The cry was an expression
of His agony of soul and body, but
in that agony is involved the
mystery of the Atonement. The
loud cry would be audible to His
followers afar off (*v.* 55).

θεέ μου κτλ.] The Lord used an
Aram. version, probably current in
the synagogues, which, like the M.T.,
did not contain a word corresponding
with the LXX. πρόσχες μοι. The
translations added by Mt., Mk. are
independent renderings of it. The
reading ϛαφθανεί seems to be a mis-
placed attempt to represent the Heb.
עֲזַבְתָּנִי. D (Mk.) ὠνείδισάς με (as

though interpreting the Aram. עֲזַפְתָּנִי,
'art thou angry with me') avoids the
thought of abandonment by God.
It is improbable that Jesus quoted
the Heb., not only because He
habitually spoke Aramaic, but because
there could have been no reason for
the alteration into Aram. for Greek-
speaking Christians who understood
neither language. ἐλω(ε)ί (Mt., Mk.)
might seem to point to the Heb.
אֱלֹהִי, but the ω may represent the
duller sound of the Aram. ā (Dalm.
Words, 54) ; ἐλωαί would be nearer
to the sound of the Heb. If the
reading ἠλ(ε)ί in Mt. were correct, it
would not prove that the sentence
was Heb., for אֵל was familiar to
Aramaic-speaking Jews, and is used
in Targ.*onk* (Dalm.), and in Targ. Ps.
(*ad loc.*). It is supported by the
docetic account in Gosp. Pet., ἡ
δύναμίς μου, ἡ δύναμίς μου, κατέ-
λειψάς με (see Robinson and James,
p. 21). Ēlī would better suggest
Elījah, but either Mt. or a scribe
might choose it on that account.
λαμά, the Heb. form, is probably
the true reading in Mk. ; Mt. corrects
it to the Aram. λεμά.

47. τινὲς δέ κτλ.] Mk. καὶ τ. τῶν
παρεστώτων (a word characteristic of
his narrative of the Passion, xiv. 47,
69, 70, xv. 39). These may have
been Jewish onlookers, whose reference to Elijah was a mere jibe;
hence, perhaps, Mt.'s scornful οὗτος
(cf. ix. 3) after Ἠλ. φωνεῖ; or
Hellenists who really mistook the
Aram. words. Mk., however, who
uses ὁ παρεστηκώς of the centurion

47 ἑστηκότων ἀκούσαντες ἔλεγον ὅτι   Ἠλείαν φωνεῖ οὗτος.
48 καὶ εὐθέως δραμὼν εἷς ἐξ αὐτῶν καὶ λαβὼν σπόγγον
49 πλήσας τε ὄξογς καὶ περιθεὶς καλάμῳ ἐπότιζεν αὐτόν.   οἱ
δὲ λοιποὶ εἶπαν Ἄφες ἴδωμεν εἰ ἔρχεται Ἠλείας σώσων
αὐτόν. [ἄλλος δὲ λαβὼν λόγχην ἔνυξεν αὐτοῦ τὴν πλευράν,
50 καὶ ἐξῆλθεν ὕδωρ καὶ αἷμα.]   ὁ δὲ Ἰησοῦς πάλιν κράξας

49 αλλος...αιμα] אBCLΓ 5 48 67 115 127* 𝔖 pal aeth ; om ADE etc minn.pler
𝔏 omn 𝔖 sin.pesh.hcl me arm go

(xv. 39), may have meant the soldiers,
unless ἄφετε ἴδωμεν κτλ. in his next
verse was originally the sequel of
this one (see v. 49 below). The
soldiers had brought a jar (Jo. xix.
29) of posca, their usual drink, no
doubt for their own refreshment, and
would probably be unwilling to allow
onlookers to touch it. They may
well have heard of Elijah, the chief
hero of popular expectation.

48. καὶ εὐθέως κτλ.] Mk. δραμὼν
δέ τις καὶ γεμίσας (D καὶ δραμὼν
εἷς καὶ πλήσας). For κάλαμος Jo.
has ὕσσωπος, by which he probably
meant the stalk of some wild plant
which was long enough for the
purpose.

49. οἱ δὲ λοιποί κτλ.] Mk.
λέγων· ἄφετε κτλ., as though the
soldier wished to keep up the strength
of the Crucified a little longer, on
the chance that Elijah would come
and rescue Him before He died.
But this is improbable, since the
soldier, though he might have heard
the popular ideas about Elijah, would
not share them. In Mt. the act
of kindness is met by a jeering protest from others, i.e. Jews (similarly
𝔖 sin.pesh in Mk.). Perhaps the
incident of the vinegar (to λέγων)
was added later to Mk. from Mt.
(which might account for the
omission in Mk. of his favourite
εὐθέως), and ἄφετε κτλ. in Mk. was
originally the sequel of ἴδε Ἠλ.
φωνεῖ. Orig.ˡᵃᵗ transposes vv. 48, 49.

The taunt was perhaps intentionally
heightened by the use of the same
Aram. שבק (ἄφες) as the Lord had
used in His cry. For the construction ἄφες ἴδωμεν cf. vii. 4. σώσων
(cf. vv. 40, 42) is for Mt.'s καθελεῖν.
On the infrequent fut. partcp. see
Blass, § 14, Moulton, i. 230.

The bracketed passage is probably
an adaptation of Jo. xix. 34 in an
early marginal note, the order ' water
and blood ' being due to 1 Jo. v. 6.
Its position before ' Jesus again cried
with a loud voice ' must have been
due to the carelessness of a scribe,
who carried it into his text from
the margin, mechanically making
ἄλλος to follow immediately upon
εἷς (v. 48). The passage is rightly
omitted in ' Western ' authorities
(see Appar.).

50. ὁ δὲ Ἰησοῦς κτλ.] Mk. : ὁ δὲ
Ἰ. ἀφεὶς φωνὴν μεγάλην ἐξέπνευσεν.
Lk. gives the words of the cry, from
Ps. xxx. [xxxi.] 6. Jo. gives τετέλε-
σται as the Lord's last word. Unlike
most victims of crucifixion Jesus did
not die from slow exhaustion ; with
strength enough for a loud cry, He
expired immediately, which roused
the wonder of the centurion (Mk.
v. 39). Mt. perhaps interprets this
with a thought analogous to that in
Jo. x. 17 f., transferring Mk.'s ἀφείς
from the Lord's cry to His spirit,
which He voluntarily let go (Jo.
παρέδωκεν τὸ πνεῦμα, an echo of the
words of the cry given by Lk.) ; but

φωνῇ μεγάλῃ ἀφῆκεν τὸ πνεῦμα.   Καὶ ἰδοὺ τὸ καταπέτασμα 51
τοῦ ναοῦ ἐσχίσθη ἀπ᾿ ἄνωθεν ἕως κάτω εἰς δύο, καὶ ἡ
γῆ ἐσείσθη, καὶ αἱ πέτραι ἐσχίσθησαν, καὶ τὰ μνημεῖα 52

perhaps he merely prefers a LXX.
expression ; cf. Gen. xxxv. 18, and
see Sir. xxxviii. 23, Wisd. xvi. 14.
Gosp. Pet. has a different thought :
καὶ εἰπὼν ἀνελήμφθη. Spitta thinks
that the cry, in conjunction with the
following portents, was thought of as
superhuman, the utterance of a
divine voice, as in Joel iii. 15 f., and
that this explains the centurion's
words in v. 54. But in Mk. the
only portent is the rending of the
veil, of which the centurion could
not have known when he spoke.

51–56. (Mk. xv. 38–41, Lk. xxiii.
47–49.) CIRCUMSTANCES ACCOMPANY-
ING THE LORD'S DEATH.

51. καὶ ἰδού κτλ.] The first
portent is related by Lk. earlier (v.
45) in connexion with the darkness.
Both the tabernacle (Exod. xxvi. 31,
36) and Herod's temple (Jos. BJ. v.
v. 4 f.) had two veils, which hung at
the entrance of the Holy Place and
the Holy of Holies (τὸ δεύτερον καταπέτασμα Heb. ix. 3). Many assume
that the latter is meant, and
interpret the rending mystically, on
the basis of Heb. ix. 8, x. 19 f. But
the evangg. almost certainly picture
a portent visible to all, not only to
the priests who happened to be in
the Holy Place at the moment. The
narrative seems to be similar in
character to Jewish traditions which
were current in connexion with the
approaching fall of Jerusalem : Jos.
BJ. VI. v. 3 f. At Passover time the
great bronze gate of the inner court
opened of its own accord ; and at
Pentecost there was a quaking and a
noise, and the sound of a multitude
saying ' Let us remove hence.' Jer.
Yoma 43 c, Forty years before the

temple was destroyed, the doors, shut
at evening, were found open in the
morning. The Lord's Death, the
fall of Jerusalem, and the End of
the Age, were closely connected in
Christian thought, and the rending
of the veil was a warning sign (cf.
Clem. Recogn. i. 41, ' lamentants ex-
cidium loco imminens '). The very
temple rent its veil in mourning, as
the earth had clothed itself in darkness. That it was rent from top to
bottom (Lk. simply μέσον) shewed
that it was not done by human
hands.

Jer. (in Mt. and Ep. 120. 8) found
it stated in Gosp. Heb. ' non velum
templi scissum, sed superliminare
templi mirae magnitudinis corruisse.'
Nestle's conjecture (ZNW., 1902,
167) that superliminare = כַּפְתֹּר,
which was misunderstood as פָּרֹכֶת
(' veil ') is rightly criticized by Dalm.
(Words, 56) and J. A. Robinson
(Expos. v. 198).

καὶ ἡ γῆ κτλ.] The remaining
portents are given only by Mt. For
a parallel to the earthquake see Jos.
l.c. ; and the rending of the rocks in
conjunction with it recalls 1 Kings
xix. 11. Possibly the earthquake
was assumed as the necessary cause
of the rending of the veil ; but it is
probably analogous to legendary
earthquakes connected with great
crises ; cf. Virg. Georg. i. 475 (at the
death of Caesar), Edmunds, Buddh.
and Christ. Gosp. 189 ('at the entrance
of the Lord into Nirvana ').

52, 53. καὶ τὰ μνημεῖα κτλ.] The
earthquake opened the tombs, and
yet it was not till after the Lord's
resurrection that the saints emerged,
and entered the city. Some think

ἀνεῴχθησαν καὶ πολλὰ σώματα τῶν κεκοιμημένων ἁγίων
53 ἠγέρθησαν, καὶ ἐξελθόντες ἐκ τῶν μνημείων μετὰ τὴν
ἔγερσιν αὐτοῦ εἰσῆλθον εἰς τὴν ἁγίαν πόλιν καὶ ἐνεφανί-
54 σθησαν πολλοῖς. Ὁ δὲ ἑκατόνταρχος καὶ οἱ μετ᾽ αὐτοῦ
τηροῦντες τὸν Ἰησοῦν ἰδόντες τὸν σεισμὸν καὶ τὰ γινόμενα
ἐφοβήθησαν σφόδρα, λέγοντες Ἀληθῶς θεοῦ υἱὸς ἦν οὗτος.
55 Ἦσαν δὲ ἐκεῖ γυναῖκες πολλαὶ ἀπὸ μακρόθεν θεωροῦσαι,

that, in order to preserve the truth that Christ was the Firstfruits of them that slept (1 Cor. xv. 20), αὐτοῦ was substituted for an original αὐτῶν, or that μετὰ τ. ἔγερσιν αὐτοῦ was inserted later. Possibly the rising of the saints was, in an early tradition, the sequel of the earthquake at Christ's resurrection (xxviii. 2), and was mistakenly recorded at this point. There may be a reference to the belief that Jesus, on His descent into Hades, released those imprisoned there (Loofs, *Third Congress for Hist. Rel.* ii. 299), but μετὰ τ. ἔγερσιν αὐτ. cannot mean 'after He had raised them.' ἔγερσις is not used elsewhere of resurrection ; contrast Ps. cxxxviii. [cxxxix.] 2.

The ἅγιοι are the pious Israelites whose resurrection had for some time formed part of the popular eschatology ; especially was this expected of the patriarchs and martyrs (Volz, *Jüd. Esch.* 238 ff.). In *Acta Pil.* (Thilo 810 f.) the passage is referred to the former ; in Ign. *Magn.* ix. to the prophets. Ṣ sin Tat. have 'the righteous,' a more usual designation of O.T. saints ; but ἅγιοι means saints of special note. Pagan parallels to the narrative occur in Ovid, *Met.* vii. 205, Tibul. I. ii. 45. On ἡ ἁγία πόλις see iv. 5.

54. ὁ δὲ ἑκατόνταρχος κτλ.] A reference to *v.* 36. Mk. : ὁ κεντυρίων (so Mk. *v.* 44 f. ; not elsewhere in the N.T.) ὁ παρεστηκὼς ἐξ ἐναντίας αὐτοῦ. Mt. refers to

the foregoing portents (τὰ γινόμενα), Mk. (ὅτι οὕτως ἐξέπνευσεν), and apparently Lk. (τὸ γενόμενον) to the Lord's sudden death. But this in itself would hardly account for the centurion's words. Most MSS. in Mk. add κράξας after οὕτως (D d οὕτως αὐτὸν κράξαντα καὶ ἐξέπν.), as though referring to the loudness of the cry from one at the verge of death. But this is scarcely less difficult. Lk.'s τὸ γενόμενον can hardly refer to the trustful submission of the words 'Father, into Thy hands I commend My spirit' (so Spitta). The narrative of Mk., Lk. remains an unsolved difficulty.

ἀληθῶς κτλ.] υἱὸς θεοῦ without the article could, as a predicate, mean 'the Son of God' (as Ṣ sin), in which case the passage relates the centurion's conversion. That his name, Petronius, was known to tradition (Gosp. Pet.) perhaps implies this. But in the mouth of a pagan the words probably mean 'a superhuman person,' a hero ; cf. Dan. iii. 92 [25] Theod. Lk. substitutes the Jewish term δίκαιος, avoiding the idea of 'demigod' with its heathen associations. In Lk. (*v.* 48) is added, probably by a later hand, that 'all the crowds who came together to that spectacle when they beheld τὰ γενόμενα, returned smiting their breasts,' *i.e.* in remorse, as stated more clearly in Ṣ sin.cur 𝔏 g Gosp. Pet.

55. ἦσαν δέ κτλ.] These were eyewitnesses from whom the Church

αἵτινες ἠκολούθησαν τῷ Ἰησοῦ ἀπὸ τῆς Γαλιλαίας διακονοῦσαι αὐτῷ· ἐν αἷς ἦν Μαρία ἡ Μαγδαληνὴ καὶ Μαρία 56
ἡ τοῦ Ἰακώβου καὶ Ἰωσὴφ μήτηρ καὶ ἡ μήτηρ τῶν υἱῶν
Ζεβεδαίου.

Ὀψίας δὲ γενομένης ἦλθεν ἄνθρωπος πλούσιος ἀπὸ 57

received accounts of the Crucifixion.
Lk. says πάντες οἱ γνωστοὶ αὐτῷ, καὶ
γυναῖκες, of which the former may
have included some of the Twelve.
At least some of the male acquaint-
ances of Jesus in Jerusalem, and
probably Simon the Cyrenaean and
Joseph of Arimathaea, would be
present. All the synn. relate that
they stood 'afar off' (cf. Ps. lxxxvii.
[lxxxviii.] 9. 19); but the prominence
given to three women may possibly
have been due to the fact that they
ventured nearer to the Cross. In
any case the words from the Cross
cannot be rejected merely because
those who stood afar off could not
have heard them. Apart from the
account in Jo. that the Lord's
mother, other women, and the beloved disciple, stood by the Cross,
the centurion, and one at least of the
soldiers, were sympathetic, and might
have spoken afterwards of what they
had heard.

αἵτινες κτλ.] Mk. gives the three
names first, adding 'who when He
was in Galilee used to follow Him
and minister to Him; and [also
beholding were] many others who
came up with Him to Jerusalem.'
Mt., by connecting ἠκολούθησαν and
διακονοῦσαι with the journey to
Jerusalem, loses the distinction between the three and the others. Lk.
relates the διακονία in viii. 3, but
does not mention it here.

56. ἐν αἷς ἦν κτλ.] Mary of
Magdala 'from whom seven demons
had gone out' (Lk. viii. 2; cf. 'Mk.'
xvi. 9) is related by Jo. to have
stood by the Cross. On Magdala

see xv. 39. Mary the mother of
James (Mk. Ἰακ. τοῦ μικροῦ 'the
little') and Joseph (Mk. Ἰωσῆτος):
one of the Twelve was James, son
of Alphaeus (חלפי, so שׂ sin), and in
Jo. a woman who stood by the Cross
was Mary the wife of Clopas; it is
reasonable to explain Clopas as a Gk.
form of Ḥalphai, and to identify the
mother of James with the wife of
Clopas. Of Joseph (Joses) nothing
is known; there is no evidence that
James and Joseph were the Lord's
brothers named in xiii. 55. The
mother of the sons of Zebedee (see
xx. 20): Mk. has Salome. Since
Jo. mentions a third woman at the
Cross, 'His mother's sister,' her
identification with Salome is possible.

57-61. (Mk. xv. 42-47, Lk. xxiii.
50-56, Jo. xix. 38-42.) THE
DESCENT FROM THE CROSS. THE
BURIAL.

57. ὀψίας κτλ.] Just before 6
P.M., at which time the Sabbath
would begin. Mt. omits Mk.'s ἐπεὶ ἦν
παρασκευή, ὅ ἐστιν προσάββατον as
unnecessary for Jewish readers. Lk.
inserts at a later point (v. 54) καὶ
ἡμέρα ἦν παρασκευῆς, καὶ σάββατον
ἐπέφωσκεν (on the verb see xxviii. 1).
The Jewish authorities would not
have wished the bodies to remain
on the Cross on the Sabbath, and
Pilate knew their scruples. Jo.
(xix. 31-34) describes the preparations already made with a view to
their removal. Cf. Gosp. Pet. 'And
Herod said, Brother Pilate, even if
none had asked for Him we should
bury Him, since the Sabbath is

'Αριμαθαίας, τοὔνομα Ἰωσήφ, ὃς καὶ αὐτὸς ἐμαθητεύθη τῷ
58 Ἰησοῦ· οὗτος προσελθὼν τῷ Πειλάτῳ ᾐτήσατο τὸ σῶμα
59 τοῦ Ἰησοῦ. τότε ὁ Πειλᾶτος ἐκέλευσεν ἀποδοθῆναι. καὶ
λαβὼν τὸ σῶμα ὁ Ἰωσὴφ ἐνετύλιξεν αὐτὸ ἐν σινδόνι

57 εμαθητευθη] אCD 1 33 17ᵉᵛ ; εμαθητευσεν ABL etc minn.pler

drawing on (ἐπιφώσκει); for it is
written in the Law that the sun
must not set on one that is slain';
see Jos. *BJ.* IV. v. 2.

πλούσιος κτλ.] Mk. εὐσχήμων
βουλευτής, Lk. βουλευτὴς ὑπάρχων,
καὶ ἀνὴρ ἀγαθὸς καὶ δίκαιος. Mt.
expresses the aspect in which a person
of good social rank (cf. Ac. xiii. 50,
xvii. 12) appeared to the popular
mind ; or possibly he was influenced
by Is. liii. 9. In omitting βουλευτής
he may have shrunk from recording
that a disciple was a member of the
Sanhedrin (if that is the meaning).
Arimathaea is identified in the *Ono-
mast.* with the city of Elkanah in
Ephraim (1 Regn. i. 1, Ἀρμαθάιμ
Σειφά [Σωφίμ]); but Eus. places it
near Diospolis (Lydda) ; cf. 1 Macc.
xi. 34. It was Joseph's native town,
but he now owned land, and probably lived, at Jerusalem.

ὃς καὶ αὐτός κτλ.] He, as well
as the women, had become a disciple. The *v.l.* ἐμαθήτευσεν means
' he was a disciple ' (see on xiii. 52);
cf. Jo. xix. 38, where is added 'but
in secret for fear of the Jews.'
According to Lk. he had already
dissented from their action ; but
now he boldly (Mk. τολμήσας)
avowed himself. He had been pre-
disposed to the preaching of the
Kingdom : Mk., Lk. ὃς κ. αὐτ. ἦν
προσδεχόμενος [προσεδέχετο] τὴν
βασιλείαν τοῦ θεοῦ.

58. οὗτος κτλ.] Mk. τολμήσας
εἰσῆλθεν. The bodies of criminals
were sometimes given to their friends
for burial ; and to approach Pilate

would not be difficult for a Jew in
a high position ; Gosp. Pet. even
calls him 'the friend of Pilate and
of the Lord.' But it needed real
bravery to disregard the scorn of his
fellow Jews. Mt., Lk., either for
brevity or avoiding it for some reason,
omit Mk.'s account of Pilate's wonder
that Jesus was already dead and of
his enquiry of the fact from the
centurion. Possibly it was a later
addition in Mk., but it is difficult
to see any reason for the interpolation.

τότε κτλ.] Mk. ἐδωρήσατο τὸ
πτῶμα τῷ Ἰωσήφ, ' he (graciously)
made a present of the corpse to J.'
Mt. avoids both the verb and the
subst. (see Swete) ; Lk. omits the
clause. In Gosp. Pet. Joseph makes
his request at the time of the trial,
' realizing that they were about to
crucify Him'; and, to throw the
responsibility on the Jews, Pilate is
made to ask Herod for the body.

59. καὶ λαβών κτλ.] Mk., Lk.
καθελών, the usual word in this
connexion (see Swete). Gosp. Pet.
' And then they drew out the nails
from the hands of the Lord, and
laid Him upon the earth ; and the
whole earth was shaken, and there
was great fear. Then the sun shone
out, and the ninth hour was reached
(εὑρέθη).' ἐνετύλιξεν αὐτό : so Lk.
Mk. ἀγοράσας (see on xxvi. 17)
σινδόνα καθελὼν αὐτὸν ἐνείλησεν
τῇ σινδόνι, correcting, by the masc.
pronoun, the impression produced by
πτῶμα (cf. Mt. xiv. 12). Gosp. Pet.,
' And he took the Lord, and bathed

καθαρᾷ, καὶ ἔθηκεν αὐτὸ ἐν τῷ καινῷ αὐτοῦ μνημείῳ ὃ 60
ἐλατόμησεν ἐν τῇ πέτρᾳ, καὶ προσκυλίσας λίθον μέγαν τῇ
θύρᾳ τοῦ μνημείου ἀπῆλθεν. Ἦν δὲ ἐκεῖ Μαριὰμ ἡ 61
Μαγδαληνὴ καὶ ἡ ἄλλη Μαρία καθήμεναι ἀπέναντι τοῦ

and wrapped [Him] in linen.' Mt. alone reverentially adds καθαρᾷ. Jo. adds that Nicodemus brought 'a roll (ἕλιγμα, v.l. μίγμα 'a mixture') of 100 litres of myrrh and aloe,' and that the two men 'bound the body with napkins together with the spices.' Mk., Lk. relate that the women brought spices after the Sabbath was over. If both narratives are accurate, the women either desired to add more spices externally (Swete), or did not know of the action of Nicodemus. But Mk., Lk. seem rather to imply that the women wished to rectify an omission, Joseph having used no spices in the hurried and temporary disposal of the sacred body.

60. καὶ ἔθηκεν αὐτό κτλ.] Mk., Lk. αὐτόν. The tomb is spoken of as well known in Christian tradition (τῷ ... μνημ.); Mk., Lk. ἐν μνήματι. In Mt., Jo. καινῷ emphasizes the fitness of the tomb for its high purpose; Lk. οὗ οὐκ ἦν οὐδεὶς οὐδέπω κείμενος (cf. Mk. xi. 2, Lk. xix. 30). It was, as often in Jerusalem, cut out of the rock. Lk. λαξευτῷ (cf. Deut. iv. 49) means that it was made of hewn stone, which is much less probable. For the late word λατομεῖν cf. Is. xxii. 16.

καὶ προσκυλίσας κτλ.] μέγαν is derived from Mk. xvi. 4, ἦν γὰρ μέγας σφόδρα. Lk. does not mention the stone till the women found it rolled away (xxiv. 2). D 𝕷 c sah in Lk. give here the Homer-like addition, 'and when he had laid Him (c posito eo), he placed at the tomb a stone which twenty (men) could scarce roll.' In Gosp. Pet. the stone

is placed by all who were there (i.e. Elders and Scribes) with the centurion and soldiers. The probable appearance of the stone is shewn by a picture in Latham's The Risen Master. Since the burial had to be hurriedly carried out because the Sabbath had almost begun, this was probably intended only as a temporary resting-place. Lk. adds, 'And it was Preparation day, and Sabbath drew on (ἐπέφωσκεν)'; and Jo. states that the tomb was in a garden 'in the place (i.e. close to) where He was crucified'; 'there, then, they laid Jesus on account of the Preparation of the Jews, because the tomb was near.'

61. ἦν δὲ ἐκεῖ κτλ.] 'The other Mary' (as in xxviii. 1): Mk. 'Mary the [mother] of Joses' (Mk. xvi. 1 'of James,' xv. 40 'of James the Little and Joses'); Lk. 'women who had come with Him from Galilee' (as in v. 49, Mt. 55), their names not being given till xxiv. 10. Lake suggests the complicated explanation that Mk. originally had no names of women, that Mt. represents a second edition of Mk., and the present text of Mk. is a third.

They sat watching till the last offices were ended; Mk.: ἐθεώρουν ποῦ τέθειται, and Lk. similarly. Gosp. Pet. relates that Peter and his companions 'fasted and sat mourning and weeping night and day until the Sabbath' (see xxviii. 7). On ἀπέναντι see M.-M. Vocab. s.v. The use of τάφος here and in xxviii. 1 is probably due to the influence of the inserted section, vv. 62–66; elsewhere in the Gospp. the Lord's tomb is always μνημεῖον or μνῆμα.

62 τάφου.   Τῇ δὲ ἐπαύριον, ἥτις ἐστὶν μετὰ τὴν παρα-
σκευήν, συνήχθησαν οἱ ἀρχιερεῖς καὶ οἱ Φαρισαῖοι πρὸς
63 Πειλᾶτον λέγοντες Κύριε, ἐμνήσθημεν ὅτι ἐκεῖνος ὁ πλάνος
64 εἶπεν ἔτι ζῶν Μετὰ τρεῖς ἡμέρας ἐγείρομαι· κέλευσον οὖν
ἀσφαλισθῆναι τὸν τάφον ἕως τῆς τρίτης ἡμέρας, μή ποτε
ἐλθόντες οἱ μαθηταὶ κλέψωσιν αὐτὸν καὶ εἴπωσιν τῷ λαῷ
Ἠγέρθη ἀπὸ τῶν νεκρῶν, καὶ ἔσται ἡ ἐσχάτη πλάνη
65 χείρων τῆς πρώτης. ἔφη αὐτοῖς ὁ Πειλᾶτος Ἔχετε

**62–66. (Mt. only.) THE GUARD-
ING OF THE GRAVE.**

The verses probably belong to the
same circle of traditions connected
with Pilate as *vv.* 19, 24 f., xxviii.
11–15, which throw additional discredit on the Jews. The following
words are not found elsewhere in
the Gospp. ; πλάνος, πλάνη, ἀσφαλίζειν, κουστωδία, σφραγίζειν ; on
τάφος see above. ἡ ἐπαύριον is
confined to Jo., Ac. (except Mk. xi.
12).

62. τῇ δὲ ἐπαύριον κτλ.] παρασκευή came to be used as the name
of the day Friday, or, more strictly, of
the period from 3 to 6 P.M. on Friday;
cf. Jos. *Ant.* XVI. vi. 2, *Did.* 8
(quoted by Swete). Later Jews
called it עֲרֻבְתָּא ‘the Eve.’ ‘The
day after Friday’ sounds as though the
writer of the section was repudiating
the Jewish Sabbath. συνήχθησαν
κτλ. : the historicity of the verses
is very questionable ; the high priests
and Pharisees would not, on a Sabbath
and a high festival, take any such
action, especially if it brought them
into contact with a pagan.

63. κύριε κτλ.] πλάνος : cf. Jo.
vii. 12, 47, Just. *Dial.* 108, αἵρεσίς
τις ἄθεος καὶ ἄνομος ἐγήγερται ἀπὸ
Ἰησοῦ τινος Γαλιλαίου πλάνου.
Instead of Mt.'s usual ‘on the third
day’ (xvi. 21, xvii. 23, xx. 19), the
writer of the section says ‘after the
third day.’ Nothing is recorded in
the synn. by which the predictions

of the Lord's resurrection could have
reached the ears of the Jewish
authorities, except the words in xii.
40 (see note). They did not interpret
symbolically the saying in xxvi. 61.

64. κέλευσον κτλ.] By the third
day (on which, according to popular
belief, dissolution began, and the
soul finally departed from proximity
to the body) not only would the
Deceiver's prediction have proved
false, but the Jews in general would
know that it had, so that the disciples could not then practise their
fraud. The whole sentence assumes
that the prediction about the third
day was widely known. The passage
arose as an attempt of Christians to
silence the report that the disciples
had stolen the body (xxviii. 15), by
shewing that the religious authorities
had deliberately, and falsely, set it
in motion. But the report, long-
lived in Jewish circles, is valuable
evidence that Jews, no less than
Christians, were convinced that the
Resurrection involved an empty grave.
‘The last error’ would be the belief
in the resurrection of Jesus, ‘the
first’ the belief in His Messiahship.
On κελεύειν with the pass. see Blass,
§ 69. 8, and on ἔσχατος and πρῶτος
for comparatives *id.* § 11. 5. For
ἀπὸ τ. νεκρῶν see xiv. 2.

65. ἔφη κτλ.] Since the guard
was of Roman soldiers, not temple
police, as is shewn by the necessity
of asking Pilate for it, and by xxviii.

κουστωδίαν· ὑπάγετε ἀσφαλίσασθε ὡς οἴδατε. οἱ δὲ 66
πορευθέντες ἠσφαλίσαντο τὸν τάφον σφραγίσαντες τὸν
λίθον μετὰ τῆς κουστωδίας.

Ὀψὲ δὲ σαββάτων, τῇ ἐπιφωσκούσῃ εἰς μίαν σαββάτων, 1 XXVIII.

11–15, ἔχετε is not indic. (Engl.
versions (except Tyndale) 'ye have,'
Vulg. *habetis*) but imper. Tynd.
'take watche men'; cf. 2 Tim. i. 13.
κουστωδία, a latinism, occurs in a
papyrus of A.D. 22 (*Ox.* ii. 294. 20),
and was adopted by later Jews
(Krauss, *Lehnwörter*, ii. 515). The
curt permission to Jews whom he
despised is suitable in the mouth of
the Roman official. For οἴδατε cf.
vii. 11.

66. οἱ δέ κτλ.] The sealing
recalls Dan. vi. 17. A cord, with
its ends fastened by seals to the
stone and the rock, would answer
the purpose. μετὰ τ. κουστ. is not
to be taken closely with ἠσφαλίσαντο; it describes, somewhat loosely,
the second means for making the
grave sure. Gosp. Pet. expresses the
extremest caution by 'seven seals';
it treats of the incident at some
length: the Scribes and Pharisees,
being afraid because all the people
(ὁ λαός) were mourning, and saying
that if such signs accompanied the
death of Jesus how righteous He
must have been, asked Pilate for
soldiers to guard the tomb for three
days (ἐπὶ τρεῖς ἡμέρας), 'lest His
disciples come and steal Him, and
the people suppose that He is risen
from the dead, and they do us harm.'
So Pilate gave them Petronius the
centurion with soldiers. And Elders
and Scribes went with them to the
grave (τάφος); and with the centurion
and soldiers and all who were there
rolled a great stone and set it at the
door of the tomb (μνήματος). And
they sealed it (ἐπέχρισαν) with seven
seals, and pitched a tent there, and

watched. And when the morning
of the Sabbath dawned, a multitude
from Jerusalem and the surrounding
country came to see the tomb with
its seals (ἐσφραγισμένον).'

xxviii. 1–8. (Mk. xvi. 1–8, Lk.
xxiv. 1–11; cf. Jo. xx. 1.) THE
WOMEN AT THE TOMB.

1. ὀψὲ δὲ σαββάτων κτλ.] The
meaning is probably 'late on the
Sabbath,' which finds parallels in
papyri (Moulton, i. 72). 𝕾 sin has
'On the evening of the Sabbath,'
𝕷 *vespere Sabbati*. Blass (§ 35. 4)
explains it as equivalent to 'after
the Sabbath.' Whichever is correct,
Mt. cannot intend to denote Sunday morning, but refers loosely to
Saturday evening. And the next
expression must have the same force :
ἐπιφώσκειν does not imply that sun-
light was beginning; in Lk. xxiii.
54 it is used in connexion with the
time of the Burial on Friday evening
(similarly Gosp. Pet., quoted at *v.*
57), and before the women returned
to prepare spices. It corresponds
with the Aram. נגה, and means the
'drawing on,' the 'beginning,' of
the next (Jewish) day. In Gosp.
Pet. ix. 34 it occurs again, in-
accurately, with reference to Saturday
morning : πρωίας δὲ ἐπιφώσκοντος
τοῦ σαββάτου. See Turner, *JThS.*
xv. 188 ff., and Burkitt, *id.* xv. 538–
46, xvi. 79.

Mk. relates that the women bought
spices διαγενομένου τοῦ σαββάτου,
i.e. after 6 P.M. on Saturday. It
was then too dark for the anointing,
so they waited till the early morning ;
'very early (λίαν πρωί) on the first

ἦλθεν Μαρία ἡ Μαγδαληνὴ καὶ ἡ ἄλλη Μαρία θεωρῆσαι
2 τὸν τάφον. καὶ ἰδοὺ σεισμὸς ἐγένετο μέγας· ἄγγελος γὰρ
Κυρίου καταβὰς ἐξ οὐρανοῦ καὶ προσελθὼν ἀπεκύλισε τὸν
3 λίθον καὶ ἐκάθητο ἐπάνω αὐτοῦ. ἦν δὲ ἡ εἰδέα αὐτοῦ ὡς
4 ἀστραπὴ καὶ τὸ ἔνδυμα αὐτοῦ λευκὸν ὡς χιών. ἀπὸ δὲ τοῦ
φόβου αὐτοῦ ἐσείσθησαν οἱ τηροῦντες καὶ ἐγενήθησαν ὡς

day of the week they come to the
tomb at sunrise' (ἀνατείλαντος τοῦ
ἡλίου, a timeless partcp.), where the
aor., if strictly temporal, would be
inconsistent with λίαν πρωί ; hence
the correction in D, ἀνατέλλοντος.
Lk. has spoken (xxiii. 56) of the
women preparing, not buying, spices
on *Friday* evening, and resting on
the Sabbath ; he now relates that
they arrived on the first day of
the week ὄρθρου βαθέως. At what
hour he reckoned the day to begin
is uncertain, but his note of time is
clearly equivalent to Mk.'s λίαν
πρωί. Jo. has πρωὶ σκοτίας ἔτι
οὔσης.

Mt.'s note of time corresponds
formally with Mk.'s διαγενομένου τοῦ
σαββάτου, but actually with his λίαν
πρωί, since he substitutes θεωρῆσαι
τὸν τάφον for the anointing, because
the latter, according to his account,
would be impossible owing to the
guard and the seal. He apparently
reckons the days according to the
Roman not the Jewish method, and
thus in wording though not in intention represents the arrival of the
women, and therefore the Resurrection, as occurring on Saturday
evening. ἡ ἄλλη Μαρία : see xxvii.
61. Mk. here adds καὶ Σαλώμη.

2–4. καὶ ἰδού κτλ.] This tradition is similar in character to that
in xxvii. 51 b ; but three details
shew a dependence on Mk. : the
presence of an angel, his white vesture,
and the rolling away of the stone.
Mk. relates that the women asked

one another who should roll away
the stone for them, but found it
already rolled away. 'And entering
into the tomb (εἰσελθοῦσαι, B 127
ἐλθοῦσαι) they saw a young man
sitting on the right hand clothed in
a white robe, and they were utterly
amazed.' (The reading of B is
probably a harmonization with Mt.,
where the women could not enter
the tomb because of the guard.)
Their amazement, before he spoke,
shews that the young man was not
an ordinary mortal. Mt. describes
him as 'angel of the Lord,' an O.T.
expression elsewhere in the synn.
confined to the narratives of the
Nativity (Mt., Lk.). In Lk., the
women found the stone rolled away,
'and entering they found not the
body of the Lord Jesus.' And while
they were perplexed at this, *two* men
came upon them (ἐπέστησαν αὐτοῖς,
cf. Lk. ii. 9) in flashing vesture. (On
the angels see Lake, *The Resurrection
of Jesus Christ*, 280 ff.)

If the rolling away of the stone
is an historical fact, the explanation
that 'it was not to let the Lord out
but to let the women in' is the only
possible ; it was divinely permitted
in order gradually to prepare the
minds of those who were to see the
Lord. But, like the appearance of
the angel, or angels, and the earthquake, it is in no way necessary for
a full belief in the Resurrection, the
truth of which does not depend upon
the form which the narratives took
in the growth of Christian tradition.

νεκροί. ἀποκριθεὶς δὲ ὁ ἄγγελος εἶπεν ταῖς γυναιξίν Μὴ 5
φοβεῖσθε ὑμεῖς, οἶδα γὰρ ὅτι Ἰησοῦν τὸν ἐσταυρωμένον
ζητεῖτε· οὐκ ἔστιν ὧδε, ἠγέρθη γὰρ καθὼς εἶπεν· δεῦτε 6
ἴδετε τὸν τόπον ὅπου ἔκειτο· καὶ ταχὺ πορευθεῖσαι εἴπατε 7
τοῖς μαθηταῖς αὐτοῦ ὅτι Ἠγέρθη ἀπὸ τῶν νεκρῶν, καὶ
ἰδοὺ προάγει ὑμᾶς εἰς τὴν Γαλιλαίαν, ἐκεῖ αὐτὸν ὄψεσθε·

5, 6. ἀποκριθείς κτλ.] On the partcp. see xi. 25. ὑμεῖς is emphatic: the soldiers have shewn fear, but you need not. Mk.'s τὸν Ναζαρηνόν is omitted after Ἰησοῦν; see on xx. 30. καθὼς εἶπεν, added by Mt., refers to the predictions recorded in xii. 40, xvi. 21, xvii. 9, 23, xxvi. 32, which are assumed to have been known to all the Lord's followers. Lk. gives the words of the prediction adding 'and they remembered His words.' δεῦτε is added by Mt. because the women were standing at a distance owing to the presence of the guard. ἔκειτο rightly interprets Mk.'s impersonal ἔθηκαν (Mk. xv. 46 has related that Joseph alone ἔθηκεν αὐτόν). Lk.'s 'why seek ye the living with the dead?' is perhaps an allusion to Is. viii. 19.

Only a ludicrous disregard of the intense conviction of the evangg. can explain 'He is not here; see the place where they laid Him' as meaning that the women had come by mistake to the wrong tomb, and that though Jesus had 'risen,' His body was still where it was laid.

7. καὶ ταχύ κτλ.] The command shews that, according to both Mt. and Mk., the disciples had not yet left Jerusalem, for they cannot have represented the angel as enjoining something which he knew to be impossible; and the women could not recount the words ἰδοὺ προάγει κτλ. to the disciples if the latter were already in Galilee. They were to tell them that they would find Him in Galilee

when they arrived. This had been predicted in xxvi. 32 (see note), to which Mk. here refers by καθὼς εἶπεν ὑμῖν; but Mt. having already written καθὼς εἶπεν in v. 6 here makes the angel say ἰδοὺ εἶπον ὑμῖν (unless εἶπον, as is very probable, was an early mistake for εἶπεν). The supposition, therefore, of some modern writers that the disciples had already fled to Galilee (see on xxvi. 56) has no foundation. Beyschlag rightly points out the improbability of the men going home leaving the women (one of whom was the mother of an apostle) to undertake the journey by themselves. If the prediction to which the angel refers is not genuine, and no message respecting Galilee reached the disciples, they must still have returned to their homes in the ordinary course at the end of the festival (as Gosp. Pet. relates); and before they did so, there was time for some appearances of Christ in Jerusalem. The synoptic dating of the Resurrection, not only in prediction but in fact, on the third day, assumes at least one appearance in Jerusalem, for the date must be that of an appearance, and the disciples could not have reached Galilee, a journey of some 60 miles, by Sunday morning. Lk., who relates no Galilean appearances, alters the message to words which ἐλάλησεν ὑμῖν ἔτι ὢν ἐν τῇ Γαλιλαίᾳ (see Add. n.). To the command to tell the disciples Mk. adds, as though by an afterthought, καὶ τῷ Πέτρῳ. If he

8 ἰδοὺ εἶπον ὑμῖν. καὶ ἀπελθοῦσαι ταχὺ ἀπὸ τοῦ μνημείου
. μετὰ φόβου καὶ χαρᾶς μεγάλης ἔδραμον ἀπαγγεῖλαι τοῖς
9 μαθηταῖς αὐτοῦ. καὶ ἰδοὺ Ἰησοῦς ὑπήντησεν αὐταῖς λέγων

was 'leading up either to an appearance to him [Peter] separately, or to
one in which he played an important
part' (Lake), it is strange that Mt.,
who often gives prominence to Peter,
should have omitted the words. It
is difficult, in any case, to see his
reason for omitting them. They
were perhaps a later addition in Mk.,
by one who knew of an appearance to
Peter (cf. 1 Cor. xv. 5, and perhaps
Lk. xxiv. 34).

8. καὶ ἀπελθοῦσαι κτλ.] They
obeyed the injunction ταχὺ πορευ-
θοῦσαι. Mk.'s ἐξελθοῦσαι corresponds with εἰσελθοῦσαι above (see
v. 2 ff.). Mt. substitutes 'fear and
great joy' for Mk.'s τρόμος καὶ
ἔκστασις. Lk. omits all expression
of their feelings.

ἔδραμον κτλ.] Lk. states as a
fact that they declared all these
things to the Eleven and to all the
rest. Mk. ends with the mutilated
sentence καὶ οὐδενὶ οὐδὲν εἶπαν,
ἐφοβοῦντο γὰρ——. Lake supplies
the gap with 'for they were afraid
of the Jews,' or something similar.
But he explains (1) that they did
not tell the disciples, (2) that they
could not tell them because they
could not find them. But if the
latter is true, it was not fear of the
Jews that kept them silent, and
ἐφοβοῦντο γάρ becomes meaningless.
If the former is true, the words
clearly imply that they could have
told them had they not been afraid,
and therefore the disciples were still
in Jerusalem. But to tell them in
secret the wonderful news was not
an action that fear of the Jews would
have prevented. It is quite as likely
that the sentence ran ἐφοβοῦντο γὰρ

φόβον μέγαν (cf. Mk. iv. 41), which
Mt. alters to μετὰ φόβου καὶ χαρᾶς
μεγάλης. Nothing but the improbable supposition that the disciples
had fled, or at least hidden, leaving
their women far from home, unpro-
tected and in danger, requires οὐδενὶ
οὐδὲν εἶπον to mean that they did
not do what Mt. and Lk. relate that
they did. It is perfectly reasonable
to suppose that it means that they
said nothing to anyone on the road
because they were in a condition of
terror, and that Mk. originally went
on to relate that on reaching the
city they told the disciples. Cf.
Mk. i. 44, where the leper is enjoined ὅρα μηδενὶ μηδὲν εἴπῃς, but
to shew himself to the priest 'for a
witness unto them' (see on Mt. viii.
4). Their silence on the road was
omitted by Mt. and Lk. as unessential.
Mk.'s account of 'a young man
clothed in a white robe' who caused
the women a terrified amazement, is
clearly that of an angel; and it is
difficult to think that he related a
flat disobedience to the angelic
command on the part of the holy
women.

9, 10. (Mt. only.) AN APPEARANCE
OF CHRIST TO THE WOMEN.

9. καὶ ἰδού κτλ.] This incident
is probably a late addition. The
Lord's encouragement to the women
(related only by Mt.) cannot have
been due to their silence from fear
(related only by Mk.). He enjoins
them not to be afraid, though they
shew no sign of fear when they see
Him, and to go and tell His disciples,
though they are already on the way
to do so. His words repeat μὴ
φοβεῖσθε (v. 5), and the angel's

Χαίρετε· αἱ δὲ προσελθοῦσαι ἐκράτησαν αὐτοῦ τοὺς πόδας
καὶ προσεκύνησαν αὐτῷ. τότε λέγει αὐταῖς ὁ Ἰησοῦς 10
Μὴ φοβεῖσθε· ὑπάγετε ἀπαγγείλατε τοῖς ἀδελφοῖς μου
ἵνα ἀπέλθωσιν εἰς τὴν Γαλιλαίαν, κἀκεῖ με ὄψονται.
Πορευομένων δὲ αὐτῶν ἰδού τινες τῆς κουστωδίας ἐλθόντες 11
εἰς τὴν πόλιν ἀπήγγειλαν τοῖς ἀρχιερεῦσιν ἅπαντα τὰ
γενόμενα. καὶ συναχθέντες μετὰ τῶν πρεσβυτέρων συμ- 12
βούλιόν τε λαβόντες ἀργύρια ἱκανὰ ἔδωκαν τοῖς στρατιώταις 13
λέγοντες Εἴπατε ὅτι Οἱ μαθηταὶ αὐτοῦ νυκτὸς ἐλθόντες
ἔκλεψαν αὐτὸν ἡμῶν κοιμωμένων· καὶ ἐὰν ἀκουσθῇ τοῦτο 14

injunction (v. 7). The narrative appears to be a doublet of vv. 5–7, containing a later tradition in which the 'young man' (Mk.) was thought of as the Lord Himself. Allen thinks that Mk.'s lost ending, which was known to Mt., contained an account parallel to these verses : that Jesus met and encouraged the women, dispelling their fear which made them tell no one; that Mt. has altered οὐδενὶ οὐδὲν εἶπαν, "and then has continued with the appearance of Christ without noticing that the clause 'they told no one etc.' is necessary to explain the appearance." But, even if Mt. could have made such a slip, the clause does not explain the appearance, for the women, while still on the road, had had no opportunity of telling the disciples. To explain the appearance, Mk. should have related that Jesus knew that their fear *would prevent* them when they reached the city from telling the disciples. The explanation that Mt., with no assignable reason, transposed the words 'ran to tell His disciples' from their true place at the end of *v.* 10 (Sparrow Simpson) is a counsel of despair.

ἐκράτησαν κτλ.] In Lk. xxiv. 39, 40], Jo. xx. 20, 27 contact with the Lord's bodily frame is a help to faith, a thought which does not

seem to be present here ; the women accept the truth instantly, and cling with reverent love. Nor are they forbidden to do so ; contrast Jo. xx. 17, where, moreover, the charge to tell 'My brethren' is given to Mary Magdalene alone. τ. ἀδελφοῖς μου (cf. xxv. 40) implies the continued humanity of the risen Christ. ἵνα ἀπελθῶσιν κτλ. shews how Christian tradition interpreted προάξω ὑμᾶς εἰς τὴν Γαλιλαίαν.

11–15. (Mt. only.) THE BRIBING OF THE SOLDIERS.

11. πορευομένων κτλ.] A continuation of the tradition in xxvii. 62–66, xxviii. 4. The guard had been placed at the disposal of the Sanhedrin, and therefore reported the events to the chief priests. Gosp. Pet. has 'they hastened by night to Pilate.'

12. καὶ συναχθέντες κτλ.] On συμβ. λαμβάνειν see xii. 14. The plur. ἀργύρια is found elsewhere (except xxv. 27, where the reading is doubtful) only in Mt.'s account of the compact made with Judas (xxvi. 15, xxvii. 3, 5 f., 9) ; the Sanhedrin now make an equally cowardly compact with the soldiers. The plur. of ἱκανός in this sense is elsewhere confined to Lk., Ac. and 1 Cor. xi. 30.

14. καὶ ἐάν κτλ.] ἐπί (corrected in some MSS. to ὑπό) implies an accusation against the soldiers 'before

ἐπὶ τοῦ ἡγεμόνος, ἡμεῖς πείσομεν καὶ ὑμᾶς ἀμερίμνους ποιή-
15 σομεν.   οἱ δὲ λαβόντες ἀργύρια ἐποίησαν ὡς ἐδιδάχθησαν.
Καὶ διεφημίσθη ὁ λόγος οὗτος παρὰ Ἰουδαίοις μέχρι τῆς
16 σήμερον ἡμέρας.   Οἱ δὲ ἔνδεκα μαθηταὶ ἐπορεύθησαν

14 επι] NCL etc minn S pesh.hcl.pal ; υπο BD 59 L vet.pler [si hoc audierit
praesis h] vg

the court of ' Pilate ; cf. Mk. xiii. 9,
Ac. xxiv. 19 f., xxv. 9, 26. That
Pilate could have been persuaded to
overlook such a breach of discipline
is very unlikely. Still more so the
statement in Gosp. Pet. : 'Pilate
therefore commanded the centurion
and soldiers to say nothing.' ἀμερίμνους: cf. 1 Cor. vii. 32. It is
perhaps hardly as strong as 'free
from anxiety.' 'We will relieve you
from further trouble in the matter.'
See M.-M. *Vocab. s.v.*

15. καὶ διεφημίσθη κτλ.] This
fact gave rise to the narrative (see
on xxvii. 63). Just. *Dial.* 108
accuses the Jews of charging the
disciples with the theft ; and cf.
Tert. *De Spect.* 30 (quoted by Allen).
Ιουδαίοις (D alone has τοῖς) is not
'some Jews,' but Jews as a class,
distinct from Christians; cf. Jo. iv.
9, Ac. xi. 19. In the synn. this
use of the word is found only in
Mk. vii. 3 (an editorial note). For
the class. τ. σήμερον ἡμέρας cf. Ac.
xx. 26, Rom. xi. 8.

16, 17. AN APPEARANCE OF
CHRIST IN GALILEE.

16, 17. οἱ δὲ ἔνδεκα κτλ.] Here
are two noticeable points : (1) The
sudden mention of 'the mountain'
is independent of *vv.* 7, 10, xxvi. 32,
and the departure to Galilee is therefore not a mere inference from those
passages.   (2) οἱ δὲ ἐδίστασαν.
This does not mean 'some of the
Eleven,' which would have been expressed differently. All the Eleven
worshipped, while 'others' (see on xxvi.
67) doubted. Some facts evidently

underlie the narrative, and they may
have stood in Mk.'s lost ending.
Lk. relates that the women were
bidden to report everything ' to the
Eleven and to all the rest,' and that
they disbelieved them. Mt., as he
has done elsewhere, would avoid
this as derogatory to the disciples ;
and he is very unlikely to have recorded the disbelief of some of the
Eleven at the last moment. That
he recorded it of any of the Lord's
followers is in favour of the genuineness of the tradition. Allen may
be right in conjecturing that Mk.
related the disbelief of the Eleven
(as Lk.), that the Lord appeared to
them in Jerusalem so that their disbelief vanished, and that He then
appointed a mountain in Galilee
where He would meet them. With
them went others of His followers ;
the Eleven, already convinced, worshipped, while the others, who had
not yet seen Him, doubted. While
the evidence of language is indecisive,
there is, as Allen shews, nothing which
forbids the passage to be based on
Mk. οὗ ἐτάξατο : *ubi constituerat ;*
not 'where He had given them
commands,' *i.e.* in the Sermon on
the Mount (B. Weiss). For the verb
cf. 2 Regn. xx. 5. For διστάζειν
cf. xiv. 31.

18–20. THE LAST COMMAND.

It cannot be determined whether
these verses have a Marcan basis ;
they contain, like *vv.* 9 f., 16 f.,
Matthean, but no Marcan, traits of
language ; but that alone is not
decisive. As to their genuineness,

εἰς τὴν Γαλιλαίαν εἰς τὸ ὄρος οὗ ἐτάξατο αὐτοῖς ὁ
Ἰησοῦς, καὶ ἰδόντες αὐτὸν προσεκύνησαν, οἱ δὲ ἐδίστασαν. 17
καὶ προσελθὼν ὁ Ἰησοῦς ἐλάλησεν αὐτοῖς λέγων Ἐδόθη 18
μοι πᾶσα ἐξουσία ἐν οὐρανῷ καὶ ἐπὶ τῆς γῆς· πορευθέντες 19
οὖν μαθητεύσατε πάντα τὰ ἔθνη, βαπτίζοντες αὐτοὺς εἰς τὸ

19 ουν] ΒΔΠ 1 33 al.pauc 𝕃 c e f ff¹·² g¹ q vg 𝕊 pesh.hcl.pal arm aeth ; νυν D
𝕃 a b h m n ; om אAE etc minn. mu Tert Cyp Or al mu | βαπτιζοντες] אA al minn ;
βαπτισαντες BD

the divine claims made by Christ in
v. 18 b, 20 b cause no difficulty, but
they are closely connected with v.
19 which presents considerable difficulty ; and the section must probably
be regarded as the expression by
the evang. of truths which the
Church learnt as a result of the
Resurrection, and on which it still
rests its faith.

18. ἐδόθη κτλ.] His ἐξουσία
during His earthly life had been
great (vii. 29, xxi. 23 f. ; cf. xi.
27), but now it is limitless—the
fulfilment of the vision in Dan. vii.
14 (LXX., καὶ ἐδόθη αὐτῷ ἐξουσία
... καὶ πάντα τὰ ἔθνη τῆς γῆς κατὰ
γένη καὶ πᾶσα δόξα αὐτῷ λατρεύ-
ουσα). For the thought cf. Phil. ii.
9 ff. With ἐν οὐρανῷ κ. ἐπὶ γῆς cf.
vi. 10 ; the consummation for which
the disciples had been taught to pray
was potentially reached by the
Resurrection. ἐδόθη may be a timeless aor., or may refer to the immediate past, i.e. to the Resurrection
(see Moulton, i. 134 ff.).

19. πορευθέντες οὖν κτλ.] Even
if οὖν be omitted the command is
based upon the preceding words.
The omission was probably due to
the frequent use of the verse as an
isolated text. The Lord is no longer
'sent to the lost sheep of the house
of Israel ;' His authority being now
limitless, all nations are to become
His disciples. On μαθητεύειν see
xiii. 52 ; it is not 'instruct' (Vulg.
docete), but describes a comprehensive

duty of which βαπτίζειν and διδάσκειν each form a part. The
evangelizing of all nations was spoken
of in xxiv. 14. But the difficulty
there caused by the words is greater,
if possible, in the present passage.
If the risen Lord commanded it in
one of His latest utterances, the
action of the apostles with reference
to the Gentiles (see e.g. Gal. ii. 9,
Ac. x. xi. 1–18) is inexplicable. The
admission of Gentiles to the Jewish
religion is an expectation found, of
course, in the O.T. But that their
admission into the Jewish-Christian
Church was something quite different
is shewn by the glad surprise expressed that God had 'given to the
Gentiles also repentance unto life'
(Ac. xi. 18). Nor is there a hint in
Acts or Epistles that when the first
apostles confined themselves to
Jews, while recognizing S. Paul as
the apostle of the Gentiles, it was
because of their 'reluctance to
undertake spiritual responsibilities'
(Sparrow Simpson, Resurr. and Mod.
Thought, 260). The universality of
the Christian message was soon learnt,
largely by the spiritual experiences
of S. Paul, which were authoritative
for the Church. And once learnt,
they were early assigned to a direct
command of Christ. It is impossible
to maintain that everything which
goes to constitute even the essence
of Christianity must necessarily be
traceable to explicit words of Jesus.

βαπτίζοντες αὐτούς] The pres.

ὄνομα τοῦ πατρὸς καὶ τοῦ υἱοῦ καὶ τοῦ ἁγίου πνεύματος,

partcp. expresses, like διδάσκοντες, a continuous activity ; each forms part of a continuous μαθητεύειν. The *v.l.* βαπτίσαντες refers to the several acts of administering the rite to individuals (αὐτούς) ; 'make them disciples by baptizing them, and continue the process by teaching them.'

εἰς τὸ ὄνομα κτλ.] In 𝕃 (*in nomine*) this is identified with ἐν (and ἐπὶ) τῷ ὀνόματι ; so Blass. It is true that ἐν and εἰς are often interchanged in late Gk., but Heitmüller (*Im Namen Jesu*) is probably right in distinguishing the expressions. εἰς τὸ ὄνομά τινος (not in LXX., except with a different force in 2 Mac. viii. 4 ; cf. however 3 Mac. ii. 9) is frequent in hellen. inscriptions and papyri, with a financial meaning : a sum of money is paid 'to the account of some one,' in one case ἐξ ὀνόματος of one woman, εἰς ὄνομα of another. Soldiers are said ὀμνῦναι εἰς τὸ ὄνομα Διὸς ὑψίστου (Herodian) : they swore themselves 'into the possession of' the God. In Epiph. xxxviii. 8 pseudonymous writings are said to be written εἰς ὄνομα of biblical characters. Similarly here : 'baptizing them so that they are entered as the possession of the Father,' etc. Cf. Ac. viii. 16, xix. 5, 1 Cor. i. 13, 15. An extension of this is seen in Rom. vi. 3, 1 Cor. x. 2, xii. 13, Gal. iii. 27, where βαπτίζειν εἰς expresses the act whereby a mystical union is produced.

Quite different is the meaning of ἐν (ἐπὶ) τῷ ὀνόματι, ἐξ (ἐκ τοῦ) ὀνόματος, ἐπ' ὀνόματος, and τῷ ὀνόματι. Class. Gk. has a few instances of ἐπὶ τ. ὀν., but ἐν τ. ὀν. with the name of a person has not been discovered outside bibl. Gk. The simple dat. is instrumental, and the others express 'the title, category, ground, under—or with respect to — which something happens.' Heitmüller thus explains all the instances as ultimately involving an appeal to, or invocation of, a name. ἐν or ἐπί *c. dat.* occurs 47 times in the N.T., of which 37 are with the name of Jesus, and 7 of God. In connexion with Baptism cf. Ac. ii. 38, x. 48.

Mt.'s expression occurs in Doctr. of Addai (Burkitt, *Ev. da Meph.* i. 173), Iren.[lat] III. xvii. 1, Tert. *De Bapt.* xiii., *De Praescr.* VIII. xx., *Did.* vii. 1 (in ix. 4 οἱ βαπτισθέντες εἰς ὄνομα κυρίου), and thrice in Eus. : *Ep. Caes.* (*ap.* Socr. *H.E.* I. viii. 38), *c. Marc. Anc.* i. 1, *Theol. Eccl.* iii. 5 (the last two being in his latest works, and the first perhaps due to Socr.). But Eus. very frequently in his earlier works writes as though he knew a text πορευθέντες μαθητεύσατε πάντα τὰ ἔθνη ἐν τῷ ὀνόματί μου, διδάσκοντες κτλ. The passages are cited by Conybeare, *ZNW.*, 1901, 275 ff.; and see *Hibbert Journ.*, Oct. 1902. This, together with the fact that the threefold Name does not occur in connexion with baptism elsewhere in the N.T., leads Conybeare and others to conjecture that Eus. preserves the original reading. (Just. *Apol.* i. 61 has ἐπ' ὀνόματος of baptism in the threefold Name, but in *Tryph.* 39 τινὰς μαθητευομένους εἰς τὸ ὄνομα τοῦ Χριστοῦ αὐτοῦ).

But the threefold Name does not in itself point to a late date for the passage. Jesus spoke of 'the Father' and 'the Son' (xi. 27, Mk. xiii. 32), and 'the Holy Spirit' was an O.T. expression. S. Paul frequently brings the Three into juxtaposition ; *e.g.* 1 Cor. xii. 4 ff., 2 Cor. xiii. 14, Gal. iv. 6 ; and cf. 1 Pet. i. 2. The

διδάσκοντες αὐτοὺς τηρεῖν πάντα ὅσα ἐνετειλάμην ὑμῖν· 20
καὶ ἰδοὺ ἐγὼ μεθ' ὑμῶν εἰμὶ πάσας τὰς ἡμέρας ἕως τῆς
συντελείας τοῦ αἰῶνος.

ἐν τ. ὀνόματί μου of Eus. is also based upon early usage. If, then, the conceptions implied in both expressions are early, there is no reason for supposing that a liturgical expansion was introduced into the text later than Mt., and for preferring the evidence of Eus. to that of all the MSS. and versions (𐎓.sin.cur are wanting). Eus., in quoting Mt., may have been influenced by Lk. xxiv. 47, where baptism is not mentioned. Conybeare suggests that the latter 'has the air of being a *remaniement* of the Eusebian text of Mt.'; but it is quite as probable that Mt., in the ordinary text, gives an interpretation of a traditional saying preserved differently in Lk. The thought of baptism, suggested by the words 'repentance for remission of sins' in Lk.'s passage (cf. Mk. i. 4, Lk. iii. 3), was more likely to have been added by Mt. than omitted by Lk. It is probable, not that Mt.'s text is unsound, but that the whole clause is due to him, and that the Lord did not *at this point* command the rite of baptism. Jo. iv. 1, 2 may preserve a genuine tradition that the Twelve baptized during His lifetime. But that He commanded it before His death is in any case extremely probable, since it best accounts for the early and universal use of the rite in the Church, in spite of two considerations which might otherwise have led to its

avoidance : (1) it was a Jewish custom (see Add. n. p. 33), which the Church might have shunned, together with circumcision, when Gentiles were admitted ; (2) John the Baptist had explicitly drawn a contrast between his water-baptism and the higher Spirit - baptism. The validity of the rite is far from being annulled if the present passage was not an utterance of the risen Christ.

20. διδάσκοντες κτλ.] πάντα are all the moral commands given to the disciples, *i.e.* Christ's 'fulfilment' of the ἐντολαί of Moses (ἐντειλάμενος, Ac. i. 2, is different). The words seem to reflect the conflict with Judaism. ὅσα ἐνετειλάμην ὑμῖν (σοι) is very frequent in the O.T. For τηρεῖν (LXX. usually φυλάσσειν) cf. xix. 17, xxiii. 3, Ac. xv. 5, Jo[ev.ep.]

καὶ ἰδού κτλ.] A world - wide mission, imperative because of Christ's limitless ἐξουσία, is also possible because of His perpetual presence. The expectation that the Parousia of Christ would occur soon had hardly died out even in the 2nd century, but it was not felt to be incompatible with the evangelization of the whole of the known world. Whether spoken by the risen Christ or not, the words express the abiding experience of Christians. καὶ ἰδού is characteristic of Mt., also ἡ συντ. τ. αἰῶνος (see on xiii. 39). πάσας τ. ἡμέρας only here in the N.T., is very frequent in the LXX. (= כָּל־הַיָּמִים).

Additional Note on the Resurrection.

S. Paul (Rom. i. 4) speaks of Jesus Christ 'who was marked out (ὁρισθέντος) as Son of God . . . by the Resurrection of the dead.' It

marked but did not make Him such.   If He was Son of God, the narratives
of His appearances do not comprise the whole basis of the Christian faith.
No one can approach the study of any alleged fact with his mind a *tabula
rasa.*   The Christian presupposition is that the Son of God must of necessity
be alive, with a Humanity in true continuity with that manifested in His
earthly life, and must therefore have risen from the dead.   As in the case
of the Virgin birth, the Resurrection is congruous with all that Christians
believe concerning the Son of God, and is more imperatively required by
the phenomena of the birth and permanence of the Christian Church,
and by the theological and philosophical significance of the Incarnation in
human history.   See Emmet, *Cont. Rev.,* Nov. 1909, 588–99.

But a commentary on a Gospel can deal only with the literary problems
raised by the Gospel narratives.   The following note, therefore, does not
deal with S. Paul's list of appearances (1 Cor. xv. 4–8), nor with the nature
of the Resurrection Body as taught by him in comparison with that implied
in the Gospels, nor with many another problem.   It is probable, almost to
certainty, that he, no less than the evangelists, believed not only that Jesus
rose on the third day, but also that the tomb was empty because He rose.

The above notes have maintained that both Mt. and Mk. imply an
appearance in Jerusalem on Easter day.   The uniform tradition of the
'third day' requires an appearance on that day to account for it.   And
even if the disciples, leaving their women behind, could be supposed to
have transgressed the law by travelling during the whole Sabbath, they
could hardly have covered the 60 miles to Galilee in time to see Jesus there
on Easter day.   That the third day was an inference from one or more
passages of the O.T., and an inference drawn early enough for S. Paul to
have received it in the apostolic tradition before he taught at Corinth, is
barely conceivable.   It requires us to suppose that though no appearance
took place till Galilee was reached, yet some O.T. passages led to the belief
that Jesus had risen some days before He first appeared, and that narratives
were then constructed accordingly.

A difficult problem is raised by the fact that the Third gospel and the
Fourth (apart from Jo. xxi.) relate no appearances except those in or near
Jerusalem.   S. Luke must have known S. Paul's teaching on the Resurrection,
and the tradition which the apostle had received respecting the appearances,
even if he had not read 1 Cor. xv.   He relates (Ac. i. 3) that Jesus was seen
from time to time (ὀπτανόμενος) throughout 40 days.   And yet in his
Gospel he compresses the narrative in such a way that all the events seem
to occur on one day.   He compresses and selects.   He knew of Galilean
appearances, but omits them purposely ; hence his alteration of the Lord's
prediction that He would go to Galilee (Mk. xvi. 7) into a prediction of the
Resurrection uttered 'while He was yet in Galilee' (Lk. xxiv. 6).   The
commands, therefore, 'tarry ye in the city until ye be clothed with power
from on high' (xxiv. 49), and 'not to depart from Jerusalem, but to await
the promise of the Father' (Ac. i. 4), if they were not deliberately written
by Lk. to support his omission of the Galilean appearances, must belong to
a time after the disciples had returned to the city from Galilee—an obvious
conjecture suggested by the evidence, though the reason for their return
is not clear.   Lk.'s notes of time (ch. xxiv.) are explicit as far as *v.* 43 : ' on

the first day of the week' (*v.* 1), ' on that very day ' (*v.* 13), ' that very hour '
(*v.* 33), ' while they were speaking of these things ' (*v.* 36).   But *v.* 44 (' and
He said unto them ') and *v.* 50 (' and He led them out ') are loosely
appended with no temporal connexion : the narrative need no more be
continuous than, *e.g.*, in Lk. v. 33, ix. 59, 61, xi. 5, xii. 13, xvii. 1, 5,
20, 22, xviii. 9.   Thus, while Mt. (Mk.) requires at least one appearance in
Jerusalem on the third day, Lk. leaves open the possibility of the journey
to Galilee.   Various conjectures have been made as to his reason for
omitting the Galilean appearances.   The simplest is that he was not
possessed of Mk.'s lost ending, but was dependent upon a source or sources
ultimately derived from residents in Jerusalem who related only the
appearances which took place in their midst.   On the suggestion that
' Galilee ' is here not the province but a place near Jerusalem see Moffatt,
*LNT.*² 254 f., and the literature there cited.

In the Fourth gospel the narratives are doubtless selected, as always, for
their didactic and doctrinal import, part of which consists in the fact that
the triumph of the Son of God over death is manifested at the capital
of ' the Jews ' who are His foes throughout the gospel.   Those who added
ch. xxi. wished to supply a Galilean appearance, perhaps in particular
an appearance to Simon Peter.   Spitta (*Das Joh. Evang.* 1 ff.) thinks that
the chapter is composite, and that its earlier form originally followed ch. iv.,
as an account of ' the third time (xxi. 14 ; cf. ii. 11, iv. 54) that Jesus
was manifested to His disciples,' which was altered at a later date to
an appearance after the Resurrection.   On the other hand the conjecture is
not without plausibility that Lk. v. 1–11 (see note, p. 48 f.) contains a
narrative based on the same occurrence as that in Jo. xxi., an appearance
in Galilee after the Resurrection.   Both relate a wonderful and unexpected
haul of fish, and in both the Lord speaks to Simon Peter words referring to
his future work in the Church.

INDEX OF GREEK WORDS

*(Those marked with * do not occur in Swete's text of the LXX.)*

A. WORDS NOT FOUND ELSEWHERE IN THE NEW TESTAMENT

441

B. Words not found elsewhere in the Synoptic Gospels

(Those marked with § occur in the Fourth Gospel)

ἀκαθαρσία, xxiii. 27
ἀκέραιος, x. 16
*ἀκρασία, xxiii. 35
ἅμα, xiii. 29, xx. 1
ἀμελεῖν, xxii. 5
ἀμέριμνος, xxviii. 14
ἄμμος, vii. 26
ἀναπληροῦν, xiii. 14
ἄνευ, x. 29
§ἀνιστάναι(trans.), xxii. 24
ἀνομία, vii. 23, xiii. 41,
    xxiii. 28, xxiv. 12
ἀπάντησις, xxv. 6
ἀπέναντι, xxvii. 61
ἀργός, xii. 36, xx. 3, 6
ἄργυρος, x. 9
*ἀρκετός, vi. 34, x. 25
§ἁρπάζειν, xi. 12, xiii. 19
§ἄρτι (ἀπ' ἄρτι), iii. 5, ix.
    18, xi. 12, xxiii. 39,
    xxvi. 29, 53, 64
ἀσφαλίζειν, xxvii. 64 ff.
αὐλητής, ix. 23
αὐτοῦ (adv.), xxvi. 36
ἀφανίζειν, vi. 16, 19 f.
βαρέως, xiii. 15
βάρος, xx. 12
βαρύς, xxiii. 4, 23
βεβηλοῦν, xii. 5
§βῆμα, xxvii. 19
§βρῶσις, vi. 19 f.
*δειγματίζειν, i. 19
δεκατέσσαρες, i. 17
δεσμεύειν, xxiii. 4
δεσμωτήριον, xi. 2
δῆλος, xxvi. 73
διπλοῦς, xxiii. 15
§δωρεάν (adv.), x. 8
*ἐθνικός,   v.   47,   vi.   7,
    xviii. 17
ἐκκλησία, xvi. 18, xviii. 17
ἐκτός, xxiii. 26
ἐλαφρός, xi. 30
ἐλεήμων, v. 7
§ἐλεύθερος, xvii. 26
ἔμπορος, xiii. 45
§ἐμφανίζειν, xxvii. 53
ἐνδέκατος, xx. 6, 9
*ἐνθύμησις, ix. 4, xii. 25
§ἐνταφιάζειν, xxvi. 12

ἐξαίρειν, v. 29, xviii. 9
§ἐξετάζειν, ii. 8, x. 11
ἐπιβαίνειν, xxi. 5
ἐπίσημος, xxvii. 16
εὐνοῦχος, xix. 12
ζυγός, xi. 29 f.
θεμελιοῦν, vii. 25
ἵλεως, xvi. 22
κακία, vi. 34
κάμινος, xiii. 42, 50
καμμύειν, xiii. 15
§καταγνύναι, xii. 20
κατανίνειν, xxiii. 24
κεραμεύς, xxvii. 7, 10
κλητός, xxii. 14
κόκκινος, xxvii. 28
κόλασις, xxv. 46
κονιᾶν, xxiii. 27
κραυγή, xxv. 6
§λάμπας, xxv. 1, 3 f., 7 f.
ληνός, xxi. 23
λίβανος, ii. 11
λίνον, xii. 20
μάγος, ii. 1, 7, 16
*μαθητεύειν, xiii. 52, xxvii.
    57, xxviii. 19
*μαργαρίτης, vii. 6, xiii.
    45 f.
§μεθύειν, xxiv. 49
μέλας, v. 36
μέλος, v. 29 f.
§μεστός, xxiii. 28
μεταμέλεσθαι, xxi. 29, 32,
    xxvii. 3
μύριοι, xviii. 24
μωρός, v. 22, vii. 26
νῖκος, xii. 20
νυστάζειν, xxv. 5
ξένος, xxv. 35, 38, 43 f.,
    xxvii. 7
ὁδηγός, xv. 14, xxiii. 16, 24
ὀδυρμός, ii. 18
ὀκνηρός, xxv. 26
*ὅλως, v. 24
ὅραμα, xvii. 9
*ὀφειλή, xviii. 32
ὀφείλημα, vi. 12
*παλινγενεσία, xix. 28
παραβαίνειν, xv. 2 f.
*παρεκτός, v. 32

παρουσία, xxiv. 3, 27,
    37, 39
παχύνεσθαι, xiii. 15
πέλαγος, xviii. 6
πλάνη, xxvii. 64
πλάνος, xxvii. 63
πλατύνειν, xxiii. 5
πλεῖστος, xi. 20, xxi. 8
πληθύνειν, xxiv. 12
*πολύτιμος, xiii. 46
πραΰς, v. 5, xi. 29, xxi. 5
πρέπον (ἐστί), iii. 15
προσήλυτος, xxiii. 15
προφητεία, xiii. 14
§πρωΐα, xxi. 18, xxvii. 1
σάλπιγξ, xxiv. 31
σαλπίζειν, vi. 2
σείειν, xxi. 10, xxvii. 51,
    xxviii. 4
§σκληρός, xxv. 24
§σμύρνα, ii. 11
§συμβουλεύειν, xxvi. 4
§συμφέρει, v. 29 f., xviii.
    6, xix. 10
σύνδουλος, xviii. 28 f.,
    31, 33, xxiv. 49
συντέλεια, xiii. 39 f., 49,
    xxiv. 3, xxviii. 20
συστρέφειν, xvii. 22
§σφραγίζειν, xxvii. 66
ταῦρος, xxii. 4
τάφος, xxiii. 27, 29,
    xxvii. 61, 64, 66,
    xxviii. 1
τέλειος, v. 48, xix. 21
§τιμή, xxvii. 6, 9
τρίβολος, vii. 16
*τρώγειν, xxiv. 38
§ὑπάντησις, viii. 34, xxv. 1
ὑποζύγιον, xxi. 5
φονεύς, xxii. 7
§φορεῖν, xi. 8
χάλεπος, viii. 28
χολή, xxvii. 34
χρυσός, ii. 11, x. 9,
    xxiii. 16 f.
ψεύδεσθαι, v. 11
ψευδομάρτυς, xxvi. 60
ψυχρός, x. 42
ὡραῖος, xxiii. 27

INDEX OF SUBJECTS

(Figures in brackets refer to the Greek text, not to the notes.)

faith, want of faith, xv, 104–6, 111, 115,
125, 127, 207, 220, 232, 255, 292, 303
fasting, 38, 74, 82, 83, 120, 121, 158
'Father,' God the : of Jesus Christ,
xxiv, [96], 146, 161–5, 185, 227, 240,
247, [264], 267, [270], 288, 356, 369,
383, 390, [392], 395, 436 ; of men,
57, 71, [73–5], 76, 77, [82, 83], 87,
[89], [93], 140, 146, [203], [265], 332
'Field of blood,' 408, 409
Flood, the, 357
flute-players, 125
'fool,' 62, 334
forgiveness by God, 9, 81, 82, 115, 116,
178, 179, 269 ; by men, 81, 82, 116,
117, 243, 266–70
formulas used by Mt., 47, 99, 106, 151,
202 (reff. there), 206, 271, 372
fringe, 124

Gadara, Gerasa, 111, 112
Galilee, xii, xiv, 20, 30, 42, 44, 46–9, 108,
115, 134, 210, 230, [256], 271, 341,
387, 396, 425, 431, 433, 434, 438, 439
Galilee, Sea, Lake of, 43, 45, 92, 111,
113, 117, 213, 217–19, 232, 234, 237,
238
Gehenna, see eschatology
Gennesaret, 21, 217, 220, 221, 226, 230,
238
Gentiles, 11, 12, 14, 22, 28, 33, 34, 47,
72, 88, 91, 100–5, 113, 118, 119, 133,
137, 140, 172, 173, 231–3, 242, 286,
311, 333, 347, 435
geographical notes, 13, 20, 21, 24, 43,
44, 47, 48, 92, 111, 112, 160, 210,
217, 218, 221, 230, 234, 239, 249, 271,
291, 293
Gethsemane, 78, 218, 249, 302, 389–97
golden rule, the, 93
Golgotha, 417
Gomorra, 138

Hades, 182, 242, 424
Hallel, 384
handwashing, 222, 225
harlots, 306, 307
harōseth, 380
harvest, 130 ; see eschatology
Hermon, Mt., 249, 254
Herod Antipas, see Antipas
Herod the Great, 13, 15–17,19, 20, 211,
213
Herodians, 171, 238, 318
Herodias, 208–12, 253, 274
high priest(s), see priests
Hillel, 93, 222, 223, 225, 243, 264, 272,
330
Hosanna, 296
Human nature of Jesus : Emotions :
affection, 279 ; anger, 171 ; compassion,

102, [129], [213], [233], 292 ; disappointment, 302 ; surprise, 104, 207 ;
vehement feeling, 127, 159, 235, 389,
390, 421. Will, united to God's
Will, 116, 391 ; need of prayer, 218
(reff. there) ; temptation, 30, 37–42,
245, 420. Knowledge limited, 355,
356, 418 ; growth in knowledge, xxiv ;
asking questions, 113 (reff. there),
205, 239 ; use of current phraseology
and ideas, xxvi, 41, 103, 114, 179, 327 ;
and see eschatology. Powers limited,
207, 219, 230. Physical weakness,
[38], 110, 302. Continuity of, after the
Resurrection, 433, 438
humility, 51, 167, 259, 260, 289, 290,
332
hypocrisy, 'hypocrite,' 72, 74, 83, 91, 225,
337, 359

'idle words,' 180
Immanuel, 11
impressions produced by life and person
of Jesus, xv–xvii
injunctions of silence, 102 (reff. there),
126
Iscariot, 133

Jairus, 123, 249
James the brother of Jesus, 40, [207]
James the son of Zebedee, 45, 46, 106,
125, 271, 286, 287
Jeremiah, 19, 239, 407, 408
Jericho, 271, 291
Jews, Mt.'s hostile feeling towards, xviii,
99 (reff. there)
John the Baptist, see Baptist
John the son of Zebedee, 45, 46, 106, 125,
271, 276, 286, 287, 378
Jonah, 181, 182, 235
Joseph the husband of Mary, 4–10, 206
Joseph of Arimathaea, 281, 378, 398, 425,
426
'jot' and 'tittle,' 59
Judaea, ministry in, before the last
journey, xiii, 47–49, 63, 102, 115, 221,
226
Judaea, wilderness of, 24
Judas Iscariot, 56, 133, 298, 302, 376,
377, 379, 381, 393, 394, 401, 406–8
judgment, see eschatology

Kaddish, 77
keys, power of the, 242, 243
'King of the Jews,' xvii, 14, 409, 415,
419, 420
'Kingdom of Heaven,' xix (reff. there),
xxiii

latinisms, 56, 63, 70, 145, 269, 275, 319,
395, 414, 429

THE END